R. Gupta

Popular Master Guide

IBPS Specialist Officer

Institute of Banking Personnel Selection

Marketing Officer

(Scale-I)

Preliminary & Main Exams

- Specialised Study & Practice Material Prepared by Experts
- Solved Multiple Choice Questions • Solved Previous Year Paper

by

RPH Editorial Board

2020
EDITION

RAMESH PUBLISHING HOUSE, New Delhi

Published by
O.P. Gupta *for* Ramesh Publishing House

Admin. Office
12-H, New Daryaganj Road, Opp. Officers' Mess,
New Delhi-110002 ✆ 23261567, 23275224, 23275124

E-mail: info@rameshpublishinghouse.com
Website: www.rameshpublishinghouse.com

Showroom
- Balaji Market, Nai Sarak, Delhi-6 ✆ 23253720, 23282525
- 4457, Nai Sarak, Delhi-6, ✆ 23918938

Book Code: R-1795

ISBN: 978-93-86845-78-8

HSN Code: 49011010

SCHEME OF ONLINE EXAMINATIONS

The structure of the Examinations which will be conducted online are as follows:

A. PRELIMINARY EXAMINATION

Sr. No.	Name of Tests	No. of Questions	Maximum Marks	Medium of Exam	Duration
1.	English Language	50	25	English	40 minutes
2.	Reasoning	50	50	English & Hindi	40 minutes
3.	Quantitative Aptitude	50	50	English & Hindi	40 minutes
	Total	**150**	**125**		

Candidates have to qualify in each of the three tests by securing minimum cut-off marks to be decided by IBPS. Adequate number of candidates in each category as decided by IBPS depending upon requirements will be shortlisted for Online Main Examination.

B. MAIN EXAMINATION

Name of Tests	No. of Questions	Maximum Marks	Medium of Exam	Duration
Professional Knowledge (Marketing)	60	60	English & Hindi	45 minutes

Note:

- **Penalty for Wrong Answers (Applicable to both – Preliminary and Main Examinations):** There will be penalty for wrong answers marked in the Objective Tests. For each question for which a wrong answer has been given by the candidate one fourth or 0.25 of the marks assigned to that question will be deducted as penalty to arrive at corrected score. If a question is left blank, i.e. no answer is marked by the candidate, there will be no penalty for that question.
- **Interview:** Candidates who have been shortlisted in the Main examination will be called for an Interview to be conducted by the Participating Organisations and coordinated by the Nodal Banks in each State/UT with the help of IBPS.
- The total marks allotted for Interview are 100. The weightage (ratio) of Online (Main Exam) and interview will be 80:20 respectively.

❑❑❑

Contents

Previous Paper (Solved)

Institute of Banking Personnel Selection [IBPS] Specialist (Marketing) Officer Scale-I Preliminary Exam 2018*

REASONING

Directions (Qs. No. 1-5): *Read the following information carefully to answer the following questions.*

Twelve friends P, Q, R, S, T, U, A, B, C, D, E and F are sitting in a straight line facing north but not necessarily in the same order. F sits third to the right of S. B sits fourth to the right of P, who is not the immediate neighbour of U. C and D are not immediate neighbours of F, who sits second to the right of E. There are two persons between U and A. There are two persons between D and Q. S is not an immediate neighbour of A. E sits at the fifth position from the right end. F is sixth to the right of T. C is not an immediate neighbour of D and Q.

1. Who among the following sit at the extreme ends of the line?
A. B, C
B. P, D
C. T, C
D. R, F
E. None of these

2. Who among the following sits third to the right of the fourth to the left of Q?
A. R
B. C
C. A
D. E
E. None of these

3. How many persons are there between C and the one who sits on the immediate left of S?
A. Two
B. Three
C. Four
D. One
E. None of these

4. Who among the following are immediate neighbours of R?
A. F and D
B. E and T
C. A and C
D. F and Q
E. None of these

5. Which of the following statements is/are true?
A. There are three friends between F and R
B. T and B are immediate neighbours
C. C sits at one of the ends of the line
D. P is on the immediate left of D
E. None of these

Directions (Qs. No. 6-10): *Study the following information carefully and answer the given questions:*

Twelve persons are sitting in two parallel rows containing six persons each, in such a way that there is an equal distance between adjacent persons. In row-1, J, K, L, M, N and O are seated (but not necessarily in the same order) and all of them are facing south. In row-2, C, D, E, F, G and H are seated (but not necessarily in the same order) and all of them are facing north. Therefore, in the given seating arrangement each person seated in a row faces another person of the other row.

M sits third to the left of J. The person facing M sits second to the left of H. Two persons are sitting between H and E. L and K are immediate neighbours. L and K do not sit at any of the extreme ends of the line. Only one person sits between N and L. The person facing K is an immediate neighbour of C. G is not an immediate neighbour of E. D does not face M.

* Based on Memory.

6. Who amongst the following sits seconds to the right of the person who faces F?
A. L B. K
C. N D. J
E. Cannot be determined

7. Which of the following statements regarding N is true?
A. N sits second to the left of L
B. M sits to immediate left of N
C. H faces N
D. K is an immediate neighbour of N
E. The person who faces N is an immediate neighbour of D

8. Who amongst the following faces E?
A. M B. K
C. L D. J
E. Cannot he determined

9. Who amongst the following sits exactly between H and F?
A. G B. C
C. D D. E
E. Cannot be determined

10. Four of the following live are alike in a certain way based on the given seating arrangement and thus form a group. Which is the one that does not belong to the group?
A. O B. C
C. H D. L
E. J

Directions (Qs. No. 11-15): *Study the information given below and answer the questions based on it.*

Some persons were born in the same year but in different months *i.e.* from January to December. Only two persons were born before A. R is the youngest person. The number of person born before Q is same as after R. Two months gap between R and C. P is the 2nd eldest person. S was born in May. M is elder to C but younger to S. K was born in a month which was having 31 days. The number of persons born before A is same as after C. The number of month gap between Q and S is same as M and R. P was not born in March and C was not born in July. R was not born in December. The number of month gap between A and M is same as M and K.

11. Who among the following was born in October?
A. No one B. R
C. K D. S
E. M

12. What is the total number of person?
A. 6 B. 7
C. 8 D. 9
E. 5

13. Who among the following is the eldest?
A. Q B. A
C. C D. R
E. K

14. Which of the following is TRUE?
A. Q was born in February
B. Only one person was born after R
C. M was born in March
D. A was born in a month which was having 30 days
E. C was born in October

15. Who among the following is the youngest?
A. Q B. A
C. C D. R
E. K

Directions (Qs. No. 16-20): *Study the information given below and answer the questions based on it.*

A, B, C, D, E, F, G and H are eight students of a school. They study in standards VI, VII, and VIII with not more than three in any standard. Each of them has a favorite subject from Physics, Geography, English, Marathi, Mathematics, Chemistry, Biology and Economics but not necessarily in the same order.

D likes Chemistry and studies in standard VIII with only H. B does not study in standard VII. E and A study in the same standard but not with B. C and F study in the same standard. Those who study in standard VI do not like Mathematics or Biology. F likes Physics. The one who studies in standard VIII likes English. C does not like Geography. A's favorite subject is Marathi and G does not like Biology.

16. Which of the following groups of students studied in VII standard?
A. DHA B. EAG
C. BCF D. ABC
E. Cannot be determined

17. Which of the following combinations of student-standard-subject is correct?
A. D-VIII-Biology B. A-VI-Marathi
C. G-VII-Math D. F-VIII-Economics
E. None of these

18. What is C's favorite subject?
A. Chemistry B. English
C. Biology D. Economics
E. Geography

19. In which standard does C study?
A. VI B. VII
C. VIII D. Either VI or VIII
E. None of these

20. Which subject does H like?
A. Marathi B. Physics
C. English D. Geography
E. None of these

Directions (Qs. No. 21-25): *Study the information given below and answer the questions based on it.*

Nine boys Vikash, Kamal, Sunil, Saurabh, Rohit, Sanjay, Amit, Anit and Sushil stays in a nine floor building and all of them stays on different floors. Each of them likes different girls namely—Sanjana, Surabhi, Amita, Anita, Komal, Suhana, Kumkum, Saroj and Susheela. Each boys belongs to different cities *i.e.* Patna, Lucknow, Chennai, Varanasi, Mirzapur, Allahabad, Mathura, Noida and Agra but necessarily in the same order. The topmost floor is numbered 9, the floor below it is numbered 8 and so on, and the ground floor is numbered 1.

The one who likes Surabhi stays on an even numbered floor. Sanjay does not belong to Allahabad. The one who belongs to Lucknow stays on the topmost floor. The one who likes Sanjana stays immediately below the one who likes Amita. Sanjay likes Anita and does not stay on the ground floor. Vikash belongs to Chennai and stays on an even numbered floor and he likes Sanjana. Saurabh stays on the second floor and belongs to Mirzapur. There are three boys between the one who likes Suhana and the one who likes Komal. The one who likes Suhana stays below the boy who likes Komal. The one who belongs to Allahabad stays on the third floor. The one who likes Saroj does not stay on sixth floor. There is one floor between the floors in which the one who likes Susheela and the one who likes Kumkum stay. Kamal stays on an even numbered floor below the floor on which Vikash stays. There are two floors between the floors on which the boys who are from Mathura and Chennai. The boy who likes Komal is from Mathura. Sushil belongs to Patna. The one who belongs to Noida stays on the fourth floor. Kamal does not belong to Varanasi and does not like Anita and Komal. There are three floors between the floors on which Sushil and Amit stay. Sunil stays on a floor immediately above the Anit's floor. The one who likes Kumkum stays immediately above Sushil. There is one floor between the floors on which Sanjay and Amit stay.

21. Which among the following boys likes Anita?
A. Sanjay B. Amit
C. Anit D. Rohit
E. Vikash

22. Who among the following stays between the floor of Sunil and Saurabh?
A. Anit B. Amit
C. Kamal D. Vikash
E. Rohit

23. Which of the following combinations is true?
A. Sanjay – Suhana – Varanasi
B. Amit – Amita – Allahabad
C. Rohit – Saroj – Varanasi
D. Sunil – Susheela – Noida
E. Kamal – Surabhi – Chennai

24. If 'Sanjay' is related to 'Mathura', 'Vikash' is related to 'Agra', in the same way 'Kamal' is related to?
A. Allahabad B. Patna
C. Chennai D. Noida
E. Varanasi

25. How many boys stay between the one who likes Amita and the one who likes Kumkum?
A. Five B. Two
C. One D. Six
E. Four

Directions (Qs. No. 26-30): *In these questions, a relationship between different elements is shown in the statements. The statements are followed by two conclusions.*

26. Statements : $A \geq P = S > T, V < B = T > X$

Conclusions : I. $A > X$ II. $P < B$

A. only conclusion I is true
B. only conclusion II is true
C. either conclusion I or II is true
D. neither conclusion I nor II is true
E. both conclusions I and II are true

27. Statements : $S > U > V, Y < U < Z, Z < X > W$

Conclusions : I. $S < Z$ II. $X > Y$

A. only conclusion I is true
B. only conclusion II is true
C. either conclusion I or II is true
D. neither conclusion I nor II is true
E. both conclusions I and II are true

28. Statements : $P < X < Y < Q, S > Y < T, P = V > R$

Conclusions : I. $V < S$ II. $T > R$

A. only conclusion I is true
B. only conclusion II is true
C. either conclusion I or II is true
D. neither conclusion I nor II is true
E. both conclusions I and II are true

29. Statements : $A \geq B > C, D \geq E = F \geq G, H \geq I = E$

Conclusions : I. $H < C$ II. $H > D$

A. only conclusion I is true
B. only conclusion II is true
C. either conclusion I or II is true
D. neither conclusion I nor II is true
E. both conclusions I and II are true

30. Statements : $A \geq B > C, D \geq E \geq F > B, P \geq Q > E = S$

Conclusions : I. $P < B$ II. $S > A$

A. only conclusion I is true
B. only conclusion II is true
C. either conclusion I or II is true
D. neither conclusion I nor II is true
E. both conclusions I and II are true

Directions (Qs. No. 31-35): *In each of the questions below are given four statements followed by four conclusions numbered I, II, III and IV. You have to take the given statements to be true even if they seem to be at variance from commonly known facts. Read all the conclusions and then decide which of the given conclusions logically follows from the given statements disregarding commonly known facts.*

31. Statements : All lotus are beautiful.
All beautiful are Rose.
No Rose are stinky.
All sky are Rose.

Conclusions : I. All stinky are beautiful is a possibility.
II. Some stinky are lotus.
III. Some Rose are Stinky is a possibility.
IV. All beautiful can never be Sky.

A. None follows
B. Only I and IV follow
C. Only II follows
D. Only II and III follow
E. None of these

32. Statements : Some planes are waters.
Some waters are doors.
All doors are guitars.
No guitar is a flat.

Conclusion : I. At least some guitars are Planes.
II. All doors are flat is a possibility.
III. Some planes are both waters and doors.
IV. At least some flat is a door.

A. Only IV follows
B. Only either II or III follow
C. Only III follows
D. Only I follows
E. None follows

33. Statements : Some red are blue.
Some blue are grey.
All grey are white.
No white is black.

Conclusion : I. No black is grey.
II. Some blue are white.
III. Some black are red.
IV. No black is red.

A. Only I and II follow
B. Only either III or IV follows
C. Only I and either III or IV follow
D. Only I, II and either III or IV follow
E. None of these

34. Statements : All red are white.
Some white are pink.
Some pink are yellow.
No yellow is blue.

Conclusion : I. No blue is pink.
II. Some pink are red.
III. Some blue are red.
IV. Some blue are pink.

A. None follows
B. Only either I or IV follows
C. Only I follows
D. Only III & IV follow
E. All follow

35. Statements : All green are pink.
Some pink are black.
Some black are blue.
All blue are white.

Conclusions : I. Some black are white.
II. Some blue are pink.
III. Some pink are green.
IV. No green is white.

A. None follows
B. Only I and III follows
C. Only III follows
D. Only either I or II follows
E. None of these

Directions (Qs. No. 36-40): *In each question below is given a statement followed by two courses of action numbered I and II. You have to assume everything in the statement to be true and on the basis of the information given in the statement. Decide which of the suggested courses of action logically follow(s) for pursuing. Give answer:*

36. Statement : The government of India has launched a new scheme known as "Digital India" to help promote Digital Banking.

Course of action:
I. Traditional Banks should embrace the new scheme as it relates to the modern trend of digitalized banking.
II. Traditional Banks should do nothing as a bunch of money transaction apps cannot replace the traditional banking system, and hail it as a useless scheme.

A. If only course of action I follows
B. If only course of action II follows
C. If both I and II follow
D. If neither I nor II follows
E. If either I or II follows

37. Statement : A student was caught cheating in a class-test.

Course of action:
I. The teacher should report him to the principal.
II. Teacher should accept his test answer sheet and leave him with a final warning.

A. Only course of action I follows
B. Only course of action II follows
C. Both I and II follow
D. Neither I nor II follows
E. Either I or II follows

38. Statement : IT companies have stated that a large number of Engineers employed in their firms are not suitable for employment as they lack basic programming skills.

Course of action:
I. They should fire all unskilled and unproductive employees.
II. They should not fire the employees.

A. Only course of action I follows
B. Only course of action II follows
C. Both I and II follow
D. Neither I nor II follows
E. Either I or II follows

39. Statement : State police of Bihar came under the cloud with recent news that 9 lakh liters of liquor has been missing from the police station after the declaration of Bihar a dry state. The police department claimed that the whole of the liquor had been drunk by rats.

Course of Actions:

I. A thorough investigation should be ordered and those who are liable if any then they must have to be punished.

II. Suspension of those police officers who claim that rats drunk the liquor.

A. If only course of action I follow
B. If only course of action II follows
C. If both the course of action follows
D. If neither course of action fallows
E. Data inadequate

40. Statement : There has been an allegation on some of army officers that they had been involved in illegal arms trade with a few arms smuggler.

Course of Actions:

I. An investigation should be ordered by the Indian government to reveal the actual culprits.

II. They should be punished with court marshal.

A. Only course of action I follows
B. Only course of action II follows
C. Both I and II follow
D. Neither I nor II follows
E. Either I or II follows

Directions (Qs. No. 41-45): *The question below, there is a statement followed by two conclusions/ assumptions numbered I and II. You have to assume everything in the statement to be true. Then consider the two conclusion/assumption together and decide which of them follows/implicit beyond a reasonable doubt from the information given in the statement.*

41. Statement : High pressure boilers are hazardous pieces of equipment, which are strictly regulated with special laws.

Conclusions:

I. If not regulated, high pressure boilers will be easily available in the market

II. High pressure boilers are rare.

A. Only conclusion I follows
B. Only conclusion II follows
C. Both conclusion I and II follows
D. Neither conclusion I nor II follows
E. Either conclusion I or II follows

42. Statement : The principal announced that students who score more than 95% will get special prize and medal. Kevin scored 96% but was found to have cheated in some of the exams.

Conclusions:

I. Kevin is going to get special prize and medal.

II. Kevin might not get any prize.

A. Only conclusion I follows
B. Only conclusion II follows
C. Both conclusion I and II follows
D. Neither conclusion I nor II follows
E. Either conclusion I or II follows.

43. Statement : Using calculator for simpler calculations adversely affects mathematical abilities of children.

Assumptions:

I. Using calculator for complex calculations may not affect mathematical abilities adversely.

II. Complex calculations cannot be done manually without the help of a calculator.

A. Only I is implicit
B. Only II is implicit
C. Either I or II is implicit
D. Neither I or II is implicit
E. Both I and II are implicit

44. Statement : An advertisement by Easy Air, a private airliner reads: 'Travel to Meerut by our airlines and get a chance to win an all-expenses-paid holiday to Bangkok'.

Assumptions:

I. Easy Air flights are available for Bangkok.

II. The city of Meerut has an airport.

A. Only I is implicit
B. Only II is implicit
C. Either I or II is implicit

D. Neither I or II is implicit
E. Both I and II are implicit

45. Statement : Ms. Suu Kyi, a recipient of the Nobel Peace Prize, has found it pragmatic not to challenge the official rhetoric in Myanmar, which suggests the military's actions were aimed at tackling "terror" in Rakhine.

Conclusions:
I. Ms. Suu Kyi does not want to upset the fragile balance of power.
II. Ms. Suu Kyi's action shows lack of empathy for the Rohingya in a country.
A. only conclusion I follows
B. only conclusion II follows
C. both conclusion I and II follow
D. neither conclusion I nor II follows
E. either conclusion I or II follows

Directions (Qs. No. 46-50): *Each of the question below consists of a question and three statements numbered I, II and III given below it. You have to decide whether the data provided in three statement are sufficient to answer the question.*

46. How many daughters does W have?
I. B and D are the sister of M.
II. M's father T is the husband of W.
III. Out of the three children which T has, only one is a boy.
A. I and III are sufficient to answer the question
B. All I, II and III are required to answer the question
C. I and II are sufficient to answer the question
D. Question cannot be answered even with all I, II and III
E. II and III are sufficient to answer the question

47. Among A, B, C, D, E, F and G, is B greater than F?
I. A is either greater or equal to B which is lesser than C which is equal to D which is greater than E which is either greater or equal to F which is equal to G.
II. A is lesser or equal to B which is equal to C which is greater to D which is greater to E which is lesser to F which is lesser to G.
III. A is greater to B which is greater to C which is equal to D which is greater or equal to E which is greater to F which is lesser to G.
A. I and II
B. II and III
C. III
D. Any Two
E. All of the above

48. In which direction is M with respect to N?
I. M is to the south of G, which is to the west of H. G is to the east of T.
II. N is between G and H.
III. N is to the north-west of T.
A. Only I and II
B. Only I
C. Only II and III
D. Only I and III
E. Only I and either II or III

49. Are writers not words?
I. Some writers are covers. No cover is a page.
II. All writers are books. Some books are covers.
III. No book is a word. Some words are pens.
A. Only I
B. Only II and III
C. Only I and III
D. I, II and III together are not sufficient
E. Only I and II

50. Who among Nitesh, Mahi, Rita, Priya, Neha and Rahul, each having different heights, is the tallest?
I. Mahi is taller than Nitesh but shorter than Neha.
II. Only two of them are shorter than Rita.
III. Priya is taller than only Rahul.
A. Only I and III
B. Only I and II
C. Only II and III
D. All I, II and III together
E. None of these

GENERAL ENGLISH

Directions (Qs. No. 51-55): *Read the following passage carefully and answer the questions that follow. Certain words/phrases are printed in bold to help you locate them while answering some of the questions.*

The Cabinet decision to allow spectrum trading will give a huge **impetus** to the on-going efforts for making broadband available in even the remotest parts of the country under the Digital India campaign. There are many compelling reasons why the time is ripe for the introduction of spectrum trading. One of the objectives of the new National Telecom Policy is to achieve a base of 600 million broadband users, with a minimum access speed of 2 Mbps by 2020. The Centre wants to create digital infrastructure to provide utility services like banking, education and healthcare to every Indian citizen. These ambitious targets can be achieved only if every operator in the country has access to adequate spectrum. The more spectrums an operator holds, the more data traffic it can carry over its network. Despite several rounds of auctions in the last two years, the quantum of airwaves with Indian telecom companies is less than that of their global counterparts. Mobile companies in the US and Japan, for instance, are able to offer high speed video services because they have 30-40 MHz of spectrum. In contrast, a 3G operator in India has only 5 MHz. Spectrum trading will allow the operators to get access to a larger pool of air waves, in turn ensuring that spectrum does not lie fallow. The option to trade spectrum also introduces an element of liquidity to its value. Interest in future auctions will increase because operators can bid with the knowledge that they can get returns by further leasing the airwaves. For smaller operators who are looking for an exit, trading gives them the opportunity to monetize their key asset without going through complex merger or acquisition deals.

However, the guidelines approved by the Cabinet have some concern areas which, if not addressed, could make it difficult for operators to trade spectrum. For example, the spectrum seller will have to pay 11 to 13 per cent of the proceeds to the government in the form of licence fee and spectrum usage charge. This could be a major **deterrent** if the operator is debt-laden or in an exit mode. The other big concern is the rule asking operators who bought spectrum in the 800 MHz band in the 2013 auctions, to first pay the price arrived at in the 2015 auction if they want to enter into a trading deal. Though the prices arrived at in the 2013 auctions were significantly lower than in 2015, both were market-driven processes. Thus the Centre's view that it did not receive the full price then is misplaced.

The benefits of sharing resources can be seen in the telecom tower business where operators were able to drive down costs and improve efficiencies by sharing space on towers. Similar sharing is now happening in the optical fibre cable infrastructure. Spectrum trading will benefit consumers, since at least those operators with adequate spectrum will be able to offer better quality of service. That said, quality improvement across the board will be achieved only when more spectrum is made available.

51. According to the given passage, which among the following is TRUE?

A. Mobile companies in the US and Japan are able to offer high speed video services.
B. Mobile companies in US and Japan have 30-40 MHz of spectrum.
C. A 3G operator in India has only 5 MHz Spectrum trading.
D. All are true
E. Only A and B are true.

52. According to the passage, how will Spectrum trading benefit the consumers in India?

A. Quality of services will improve.
B. Broad spectrum will be made available.
C. The cost of telecom companies will rise.
D. All the above
E. Only A and B

53. Which of the following concerns in the guidelines approved by the Cabinet needs to be addressed by the Government?

A. The spectrum seller will have to pay license fee and spectrum usage charge to the government.

B. The cost was higher for the bidders in the auction of 2013.

C. The rule asking operators who bought spectrum in the 2013 auctions, to first pay the price arrived at in the 2015 auction if they want to enter into a trading deal.

D. All of the above

E. Only A and C

54. Which of the following is the MOST SIMILAR in meaning to "impetus"?

A. Momentum B. Block

C. Check D. Hindrance

E. Incentive

55. Which of the following is the MOST OPPOSITE in meaning to "deterrent"?

A. Disincentive B. Encouragement

C. Damper D. Curb

E. Restraint

Directions (Qs. No. 56-65): *Read the following passage carefully and answer the questions that follow. Certain words are printed in bold to help you locate them while answering some of these.*

With half the fiscal year nearly complete, it is not surprising that the government is beginning to **fret** over the slow progress of the disinvestment programme. Of the budgeted ₹ 69,500 crore from PSU stake sales, only ₹ 12,700 crore has been raised so far. Reports that the Centre wants the EPFO to park part of the money that it has been allowed to invest in equity market in the CPSE ETF, highlights this desperation. Almost half the stocks in this ETF are companies that have been hard hit by the crash in commodity prices. This is not an asset the EPFO should be investing in now. The Centre, staring at yet another failure to meet its divestment target, appears ready to use any means to inch towards the target set for this year.

The urgency stems from the tight fiscal condition that the country is currently in. The fiscal deficit for the April to June period has already covered 69.3 per cent of the current year's target. This is despite a 36 per cent increase in indirect tax collection in the first five months of the current fiscal, thanks to the steep hike in excise duty on petrol and diesel, and the higher rate of service tax. A slowdown in income tax collection, along with a wide shortfall in the money raised through selling stakes in public sector companies, can make it a challenge for the Centre to meet this fiscal year's targeted deficit of 3.9 per cent of GDP. The increase in pension pay-outs for defence personnel is expected to add pressure on this goal. Inability to raise sufficient revenue can result in the government cutting back on investments, **pegging** back growth.

But the Centre has only itself to blame for this **predicament.** That the divestment department has gone about its task in a very **lackadaisical** manner in recent times is borne out by the fact that the gap between proceeds from stake sales and the budgeted target has been between 20 and 65 per cent since 2011-12. Given the decision to almost double its target for this fiscal, the Centre could have shown more **alacrity** in front-loading the sales this fiscal year, when the equity market was buoyant. The success of the REC's offer for sale in April highlights investor willingness to subscribe when the outlook for stocks is rosy. The divestment department needs to employ professionals to advise it on the timing of the sales better. Anyone who was tuned in to the stock market would have known that the second half of the year was expected to be rocky for stocks, given the impending monetary policy normalisation by the Fed. The offer for sale mechanism being employed for these stake sales also needs a rethink. With a retail discount of 5 per cent and the almost immediate availability of allotted shares, many investors have taken to short-term speculation through these offers.

56. What is the author of the above passage trying to suggest through it?

A. The tardiness in PSU stake sales will pressure the fiscal deficit.

B. The offer for sale mechanism for stake sales of companies must be remodelled.
C. The disinvestment programme is not furthering with a desired pace.
D. Only A and C
E. All of the above

57. Why the author believes that it is a challenge for the Centre to meet this fiscal year's targeted deficit of 3.9 per cent of GDP?
A. The fiscal deficit for the April to June period has already covered 69.3 per cent of the current year's target.
B. Slowdown in income tax collection.
C. Wide shortfall in the money collected through selling stakes in public sector companies.
D. All of the above
E. None of the above

58. Which among the following statements is **TRUE** according to the passage given above?
A. ₹ 12,500 crore has been raised so far through PSU stake sales.
B. In the first five months of the current fiscal there has been a 36 per cent increase in indirect tax collection.
C. The difference in proceeds from stake sales and the budgeted target is around 20 and 55 per cent since 2011-12.
D. Only A and C
E. Only B and C

59. What could be the results of the Centre's inability to raise sufficient revenues?
A. Government might cut back its investments.
B. The growth of the country could be pegged back.
C. Steep hike in excise duty on petrol and diesel may take place.
D. Only A and B
E. All A, B and C

60. Which among the following is **NOT TRUE** according to the passage given above?
A. A person who knows about stock market would have known that the second half of the year would be unhealthy for stock sales.
B. Many investors have bought the shares of the disinvestment portfolio just because of the 5% retail discount and immediate availability of stocks.
C. The targeted deficit of fiscal year 2011-12 is 3.9% of the GDP.
D. Only B and C
E. All are correct

61. Which among the following express the opposite meaning of the word "Fret" as given in the passage?
A. Affront B. Calm
C. Anguish D. Brood
E. Chafe

62. Which among the following express the opposite meaning of the word "Pegging" as given in the passage?
A. Clinch B. Fasten
C. Remove D. Tighten
E. Pin

63. Which among the following express the similar meaning of the word "Predicament" as given in the passage?
A. Fix B. Fortune
C. Solution D. Quandary
E. Ease

64. Which among the following express the SIMILAR meaning of the word "Lackadaisical" as given in the passage?
A. Abstracted B. Careful
C. Active D. Hard-working
E. Caring

65. Which among the following express the similar meaning of the word "Alacrity" as given in the passage?
A. Avidity B. Cessation
C. Idleness D. Repose
E. Inaction

Directions (Qs. No. 66-71): *In the following passage there are blanks each of which has been numbered. These numbers are printed below the passage and against each, five words/phrases are suggested, one of which fits the blank appropriately.*

Citing intensifying regulatory uncertainty, Wells Fargo is ___66___ roughly 200 agreements with builders, brokers and other real estate firms that the bank uses to bolster its mortgage business. One of the nation's largest mortgage lenders, Wells Fargo ___67___ that it was ending all mortgage marketing services and desk rental agreements with builders and real estate brokers. These arrangements are widespread throughout the highly competitive mortgage industry, where lenders scrap to find ___68___ borrowers. Such arrangements involve, for example, Wells renting desk space from a home builder in an effort to more easily sell mortgages to the home buyers passing through the sales office. "The decision was made as a result of increasing ___69___ surrounding regulatory oversight of these types of arrangements," the bank said in a statement. A bank spokesman said the move was not related to a specific regulatory problem or investigation. Rather, he said, the bank was responding to broader regulatory scrutiny of such arrangements, which are ___70___ by the Real Estate Settlement Procedures Act. The federal law is meant to ___71___ mortgage lenders, real estate brokers, builders and any other party involved in the home buying process from handing out or receiving kickbacks in exchange for referrals.

66. Find out the appropriate word in each case.
A. serving B. giving
C. signed D. having
E. proclaiming

67. Find out the appropriate word in each case.
A. noticed B. say
C. announced D. given
E. established

68. Find out the appropriate word in each case.
A. good B. eligible
C. sustainable D. amiable
E. passable

69. Find out the appropriate word in each case.
A. confusion B. burden
C. pressures D. uncertainty
E. curiosity

70. Find out the appropriate word in each case.
A. held B. told
C. acclaimed D. given
E. governed

71. Find out the appropriate word in each case.
A. provide B. prevent
C. allow D. accept
E. pause

Directions (Qs. No. 72-77): *In the given question, select the sentence which should follow the given statement in a grammatically and conceptually appropriate manner.*

72. Even though the school premises had a lot of space _____________.
A. there were plenty of play areas for the children
B. there was no playground for the children
C. yet it remain underutilized
D. there was no shortage of classrooms
E. none of the above

73. Political power is just as permanent as today's newspaper. Ten years down the line, _______ the most powerful man in any state today.
A. Political power shall have shifted weight into the hands of
B. New political parties shall have emerged
C. Few shall know, or care about
D. A new party may have absorbed into its ranks
E. None of these

74. Evolving in the mid-eighteenth century, from the pleasure houses of Japan where courtesans who would entertain the samurai, _____________
A. would discuss the state matters secretly.
B. would hold plays which would entertain the crowd.
C. the first geisha was actually men.
D. the first geisha were actually men, who entertained the guests with drums and music.
E. the first geisha will be actually men, who entertained the guests with drums and music and were all warriors.

75. The media's relationship with democracy has allowed people ______.

A. As well as the conviction that media should be democratic itself and media ownership concentration is not democratic
B. The right to participate in media and share the information they found and want to contribute to the people through the media.
C. To be seen as a theater in modern societies in which political participation is enacted through a medium of talk and a realm of social life which public opinion can be formed
D. To communicate with one another through digital media and share the information they want to
E. None of the above

76. The influences in our lives—family, school, church, work environment, friends _______

A. all have made their silent unconscious impact on us and help shape our frame of reference, our paradigms, our maps.
B. try to change outward attitudes and behaviours which does very little good in the long run
C. shows how powerfully our paradigms affect the way we interact with other people.
D. begin to realize that others see them differently from their own apparently equally clear and objective point of view
E. None of the above

77. To enjoy good health, to bring true happiness to one's family, to bring peace to all, one must first discipline _______.

A. to clear a good place for man's dwelling
B. and control one's own mind
C. to create a hindrance in the music that is in nature
D. to know the vast world outside
E. None of the above

Directions (Qs. No. 78-82): *Select the phrase/connector from the given three options which can be used to form a single sentence from the two sentences given below, implying the same meaning as expressed in the statement sentences. Pick out the option which when used to start a sentence combines both the above sentences in one.*

78. Flagging off partnerships in a host of economic and development projects through a Memorandum of Understanding has been done. The two Prime Ministers have set the stage for long-term collaboration in spheres ranging from energy and infrastructure to special economic zones.

I. Since
II. While
III. The reason behind the

A. Only I B. Only II
C. Only III D. All of the above
E. None of these

79. New Delhi's anxiety over Chinese presence might be justified. It should avoid using the China lens to view Sri Lanka, respecting the country's autonomy to engage with any willing partner.

I. While II. Awhile
III. Among

A. Only I B. Only II
C. Only III D. Both I and III
E. None of these

80. The Modi government's fiscal deficit bumped to 3.5% of GDP in 2017-18, a slippage from the figure targeted in the budget. 3% of the GDP was envisaged in the fiscal consolidation unveiled earlier.

I. In the first place II. Although
III. As a result

A. Only I B. Only III
C. Only II D. Both II and III
E. All of these

81. The partition was enforced by the ruling government. People started rushing towards their side of the town before the riots began.

I. Nevertheless II. As soon as
III. In place of

A. Only I B. Only III
C. Only I and III D. Only II and III
E. None of these

82. The U.S. Administration announced its intent to withdraw from the Paris Agreement on climate change against a backdrop of rising carbon emissions, extreme weather events that devastated homes; and one of the top three hottest years on record. The momentum continued as other countries held firm in their determination to honour national and international commitments under Paris, in the face of the U.S. announcement.

I. Additionally
II. By comparison
III. Yet

A. Only I
B. Only II
C. Both I and III
D. Only III
E. All of these

Directions (Qs. No. 83-87): *In the given question, there are five sentences numbered 1,2,3,4 and 5. Read the sentences and find out which of the combinations is correct and mark the respective option.*

83. 1. Goa has so much for the fun-loving tourists.
2. Goa is always ready to welcome its guests.
3. No place can beat Goa in India.
4. Thus tourists receive a very warm treatment in Goa.
5. Whenever we think of a beach holiday,

A. 12453 B. 15324
C. 15432 D. 12543
E. 12345

84. 1. Safdar, Ajay and I dashed out of the classroom as the bell rang.
2. He was our leader.
3. It was the lunch break and we had a whole hour to play.
4. Safdar was the tallest, also the strongest amongst us.
5. Ajay and I followed him meekly like lambs.

A. 14523 B. 15423
C. 12345 D. 13524
E. 13425

85. 1. When you infuse creativity into your writing, you try to
2. You can paint it with your words thus selection of words is important
3. Stoke the emotions of your readers by narrating a story
4. In this way you can make a story that they can relate to easily
5. Thus creative writing classes are getting popular these days

A. 13425 B. 13245
C. 14523 D. 13254
E. 12543

86. 1. Online bingo or Internet bingo sites are virtual in nature.
2. It includes online blackjack, slots, roulette and poker.
3. The odds are undoubtedly better online.
4. These sites allow users to place bets on bingo games.
5. There are several benefits of playing online.

A. 14253 B. 12345
C. 12435 D. 14325
E. 15432

87. 1. Hospitals require one centralized software
2. Since all the functions and working of the hospital will depend on it
3. System which smartly manages a lot of functions
4. It should be able to manage a huge crowd and Should not crash easily
5. The entire hospital can then be easily managed by one software solution

A. 12345 B. 13245
C. 12354 D. 13425
E. 14325

Directions (Qs. No. 88-92): *In the following question, a part of the sentence is printed in bold. Below the sentence alternatives to the bold part are given at (A), (B), (C) and (D) which may help improve the sentence. Choose the correct alternative. In case the given sentence is correct, your answer is (E) i.e. No correction required.*

88. Many subsequent attempts at human **self-definition has faced similar problems** in relation to exceptionality.

A. self-defining has faced similar problems
B. self-definition have faced similar problems
C. self-definition has faced similar problem
D. self-definition has faced similarity problems
E. No correction required

89. They wanted to show how desire interacts with the material world, and to **examine how it were entwined with politics.**

A. examination how it were entwined with politics
B. examine how it were entwine with politically
C. examine how it was entwined with politics
D. examine why it were entwined at politics
E. No correction required

90. That all meaningful experience **requires tapping in to a divine realm** will trigger a severe frown in any non-believer.

A. required tapping in to a divine realm
B. requires tapping into a divine realm
C. requires tapping in to at divine realm
D. required tapped in to a divine realms
E. No correction required

91. Although China has recognized India's sovereignty over Sikkim and had initiated the trade at Nathu La pass, the Doklam fiasco **could mean trouble at all** ends.

A. could mean trouble by all
B. could mean trouble for all
C. could meant trouble at all
D. can mean trouble by all
E. No correction required

92. For centuries, caste dictated almost every aspect of Hindu religious and social life, **with every group occupying** a specific place in this complex hierarchy.

A. by every group occupying
B. with each group occupying
C. by each group occupying
D. through every group occupying
E. No correction required

Directions (Qs. No. 93-97): *Rearrange the following six sentences (a), (b), (c), (d), (e) and (f) in the proper sequence to form a meaningful paragraph: then answer the questions given below them.*

(*a*) Having a bank account for the purpose of savings and remittances has always been the central objective behind banking.

(*b*) Keeping in mind the goal of financial inclusion and extending finance to small businesses and low-income households, under-serviced by traditional commercial banks.

(*c*) The Reserve Bank of India's decision to allow 10 players to set up small finance banks out of the 72 applicants may seem conservative.

(*d*) The need for institutions with greater penetration and wide distribution models has, to some extent, been met with the issue of payments banks licences.

(*e*) With more than half the population in India still unable to access such basic services,

(*f*) But by permitting eight microfinance institutions (MFIs) to set up small banks, the RBI has chosen wisely.

93. Which of the following will be the **Fourth** sentence?

A. (*a*) B. (*b*)
C. (*f*) D. (*d*)
E. (*c*)

94. Which of the following will be the **First** sentence?

A. (*a*) B. (*f*)
C. (*c*) D. (*d*)
E. (*e*)

95. Which of the following will be the **Last** sentence?

A. (*f*) B. (*d*)
C. (*c*) D. (*e*)
E. (*a*)

96. Which of the following will be the **Third** sentence?

A. (*a*) B. (*b*)

C. (*c*) D. (*d*)
E. (*e*)

97. Which of the following will be the **Fifth** sentence?
A. (*a*) B. (*f*)
C. (*c*) D. (*d*)
E. (*e*)

Directions (Qs. No. 98-100): *In each question below, a sentence is broken into four parts which are marked as (A), (B), (C) and (D). One of them may be grammatically or structurally wrong in the context of the sentence. The letter of that word is the answer. If there is no wrong word or group of words, your answer will be (E), i.e., 'No error'. (Ignore the errors of punctuation, if any).*

98. (A) There is just not enough/(B) timing in my job to sit around/(C) talking about how we feel/(D) about each other./(E) No error.

99. (A) Reasonable ambition, if supported/(B) at persistent efforts,/(C) is likely to yield/(D) the desired results./(E) No error.

100. (A) Even after worked in the office/(B) for as many as fifteen years,/(C) he still does not understand/(D) the basic objectives of the work./(E) No error.

QUANTITATIVE APTITUDE

Directions (Qs. No. 101-105): *What will come in place of the question mark (?) in the following number series?*

101. 51, 60, 42, 78, ?, 150
A. 96 B. 108
C. 6 D. 144
E. None of these

102. 82, ?, 286, 373, 436, 451
A. 155 B. 175
C. 139 D. 145
E. 187

103. 20, 32, 30, ?, 105, 360, 577.5
A. 85 B. 90
C. 80 D. 75
E. 70

104. 49, 193, 766, 3055, 12208, ?
A. 47062 B. 49643
C. 48105 D. 48817
E. 46611

105. 21, 27, 64, 204, ?, 4150
A. 828 B. 700
C. 510 D. 705
E. 599

Directions (Qs. No. 106-110): *Given below is the table shows five types of mobile phones sold by two sellers (X and Y). Table shows cost price, profit percentage and market price of the phones.*

Table

Brand	X			Y		
	C.P.	Profit%	M.P.	C.P.	Profit%	M.P.
MI	-	-	-	-	25%	-
Lenovo	-	20%	25000	-	12%	-
Vivo	-	-	-	-	-	28000
Apple	-	20%	-	-	-	-
Oppo	-	35%	-	-	30%	-

106. How much percentage C.P. of Lenovo phones sold by seller X is less than M.P. of Oppo sold by seller Y. If X gave 10% discount on Lenovo phone while seller Y gave 20% discount on Oppo phone on M.P.?
A. 23.33% B. 24.43%
C. 27.88% D. 25.59%
E. 29%

107. What is the ratio between C.P. of Apple phone sold by seller X to C.P. of MI phone sold by seller Y, if M.P. of Lenovo sold by X and M.P. of MI sold by Y is 56.25% more than the M.P. of Oppo sold by Y. (take S.P. equals to M.P.)
A. 15/13 B. 12/11
C. 13/12 D. 10/13
E. 18/7

108. If seller Y sells Vivo phone at 20% discount, he got ₹ 2400 as profit and if he give 30% discount, he losses ₹ 400. Then what will be the profit percentage if a total 8 phones sold by seller Y, 2 phones at 20% discount and 6 phones at 30% discount.

A. 1.4% B. 1.2%
C. 1.7% D. 1.5%
E. 1.9%

109. If the ratio between S.P. of lenovo and M.P. of Vivo sold by Y is 3 : 4 then what is the average of cost price of 2 phones of lenovo bought by X and 6 phones of Lenovo bought by Y if X gave 10% discount of M.P.

A. 10000 B. 18750
C. 18710 D. 14750
E. 15000

110. If the average C.P. of Apple and Oppo bought by 'X' is 14000 and average S.P. of Apple and Oppo by 'X' is 18000 then what will be the difference between the C.P. of Apple and Oppo laptop bought by seller 'X'?

A. 4000 B. 5000
C. 6000 D. 7000
E. 9000

Directions (Qs. No. 111-115): *In the following questions two equations are given. You have to solve both the equations and give answers:*

111. $2x^2 - 31x + 84 = 0$
$3y^2 + y - 2 = 0$

A. If $x > y$ B. If $x \geq y$
C. If $x < y$ D. If $x \leq y$
E. If $x = y$ or no relation can be established between x and y.

112. $6x^2 + 14x - 12 = 0$
$6y^2 + 11y + 4 = 0$

A. If $x > y$ B. If $x \geq y$
C. If $x < y$ D. If $x \leq y$
E. If $x = y$ or no relation can be established between x and y.

113. $x^2 - 30x + 216 = 0$
$y^2 - 21x + 108 = 0$

A. If $x > y$ B. If $x \geq y$
C. If $x < y$ D. If $x \leq y$
E. If $x = y$ or no relation can be established between x and y.

114. $8x^2 + 21x - 9 = 0$
$3y^2 + 28y + 25 = 0$

A. If $x > y$ B. If $x \geq y$
C. If $x < y$ D. If $x \leq y$
E. If $x = y$ or no relation can be established between x and y.

115. $4x^2 - 15x + 14 = 0$
$3x^2 - 6x + 3 = 0$

A. If $x > y$ B. If $x \geq y$
C. If $x < y$ D. If $x \leq y$
E. If $x = y$ or no relation can be established between x and y.

116. A man invested certain sum on money of ₹ 10000 in three different schemes P, Q and R in such a way that he will get simple interest as 20%, 39% and 13%. If amount invested in scheme Q is 30% of amount invested in scheme R, he earned an interest of ₹ 4000 in 2 years. Find the amount invested in scheme P.

A. ₹ 5000 B. ₹ 4000
C. ₹ 3000 D. ₹ 1000
E. ₹ 6000

117. According to a new plan rolled out by bank, the rate of simple interest on a sum of money is 10% p.a. for the first 2 years, 12% p.a. for the next three years, and 4% p.a. for the period beyond the first five years. The simple interest accrued on a sum for a period of 9 years is ₹ 11,520. A person invested P amount of sum in this new plan and also invested same P amount of sum for 2 years on the other scheme which offers 10% compound interest. Find the compound interest he got on the sum after 2 years?

A. ₹ 3360 B. ₹ 3450
C. ₹ 3120 D. ₹ 3250
E. None of these

118. Three cooks have to make 80 cakes, they are known to make 20 cakes every minute working together. The first cook began working alone and made 20 cakes having worked for sometime more than 2 minutes. The remaining part of the work was done by the second and the third cook working together. It took a total of 8 minutes to complete 80 cakes. How many minutes would it take the first cook alone to bake 160 cakes for birthday party next day?

A. 30 minutes B. 32 minutes
C. 40 minutes D. 45 minutes
E. None of these

119. Two trains of lengths 200 m and 300 m pass each other with constant and same speeds on parallel tracks in opposite directions. The drivers and guards are at the extremities of the trains. The time gap between the drivers passing each other and first driver-guard pair passing each other is 30 s. How much later will the other driver-guard pair pass by?

A. 20 sec B. 30 sec
C. 15 sec D. 15 sec
E. Can't be determined

120. In a school, there are 76 students. In an examination, the difference between the highest and the least marks is 33. When the average of their marks was taken without considering the highest marks then the average was reduced by 2% but when the average of their marks was taken without considering the least marks then the average of the marks was increased by 3%. Find the original average of the marks of all the candidates?

A. 8.8 B. 9.8
C. 11 D. 19
E. Can't be determined

Directions (Qs. No. 121-125): *What approximate value will come in place of the question mark (?) in the following questions? (You are not expected to calculate the exact value).*

121. 62.5% of 18920 + ? % of 5325 = 16827

A. 86 B. 102
C. 77 D. 82
E. 94

122. $(14.989)^2 + (121.012)^3 + 2090 = ?$

A. 1239219
B. 1119391
C. 1669319
D. 1773876
E. None of these

123. 61.99% of 2004.85+ 69.99% of 1706.03 = ?

A. 2445 B. 2497
C. 2437 D. 2520
E. 2350

124. $(9000)^{1/3} * (10/9) / (40\% \text{ of } 120) = ? / 8\% \text{ of } 600 * (100/81)^{1/2}$

A. 28 B. 21
C. 44 D. 57
E. 69

125. $(15.98)^2 + (19.09)^2 - 29.92\% \text{ of } 799.87 = ?$

A. 354 B. 377
C. 254 D. 294
E. 315

Directions (Qs. No. 126-130): *Study the following information carefully and answer the questions given below:*

The given information briefs about the percentage of work done by five sanitation workers in Municipal Corporation of Delhi and also the number of hours taken by sanitation workers to complete the respective percentage of same work.

Five workers Mahendra, Rampal, Vijay, Ramesh and Suresh do the sanitation work together. Mahendra did 37.5% of the work in 9 hours while Rampal does 20% of the work in 3.2 hours. Vijay took 35 hours to finish 125% of the work while Ramesh took 9 hours to complete 25% of the work. Suresh takes 27 hours to finish 150% of the work.

126. Out of the given five sanitation workers, who has the highest efficiency?

A. Mahendra B. Rampal
C. Vijay D. Ramesh
E. Suresh

127. Out of the given pairs, who will complete the work in the minimum time if they are working together?

A. Mahendra and Ramesh
B. Ramesh and Suresh

C. Rampal and Mahendra
D. Suresh and Mahendra
E. Rampal and Vijay

128. Find the number of hours taken by Mahendra, Ramesh and Suresh for the completion of work if they work together.
A. 6 hours B. 8 hours
C. 12 hours D. 16 hours
E. None of these

129. Mahendra, Rampal and some other sanitation worker named Ajay can complete the work in 8 hours. They are paid ₹ 12000 and the amount is divided between them on the basis of their work done. What is the share of Ajay?
A. ₹ 2000 B. ₹ 3000
C. ₹ 4000 D. ₹ 5000
E. ₹ 6000

130. If Rampal is x% more efficient than Vijay, then find the value of x.
A. 20 B. 25
C. 40 D. 50
E. 75

131. The distance between two stations A and B is 180 km. From a station C, which is between A and B, two cars x and y started simultaneously with speeds of 11 kmph and 13 kmph towards A and B respectively. After reaching their respective destinations, they reverse their direction and continue travelling. When X crosses C and travels an additional 5 km, it crosses y. What is the distance AC?
A. 120 km B. 150 km
C. 80 km D. 70 km
E. None of these

132. Menka, Nishu and Ojasvi entered into a partnership in a partnership company. Ojasvi got retired and her sons Dev and Eshan are taken as partners in the firm. The ratio of share in the profit of Dev and Eshan is 3: 5. Menka's share is double than Eshan's share and Nishu receives ₹ 10500 out of the total profit of ₹ 37500. In what ratio the profit will be shared among Menka, Nishu, Dev and Eshan?
A. 7 : 10 : 3 : 5
B. 10 : 3 : 7 : 5
C. 10 : 7 : 3 : 5
D. 5 : 3 : 7 : 10
E. None of the above

133. Pipes A, B and C are attached to a cuboidal pool which empty it at the rate of 12 litres/hour, 15 litres/hour and 25 litres/hour, respectively. The length, breadth and height of the pool are in the ratio of 7 : 2 : 1 respectively. The sum of the length, breadth and height is 40 m. If pipe A and B are open in the 1st hour and pipe B and C are open in the 2nd hour and this pattern continues, then how long will it take to completely empty (1/500)th of the pool? [Round off to the nearest decimal]
A. 55 hours B. 54 hours
C. 56 hours D. 50 hours
E. 53 hours

134. Three vessels contain alcoholic solutions with the concentrations of alcohol as 0.25, 0.5 and 0.75 respectively. 4 litres from the first, 6 litres from the second and 8 litres from the third are mixed. What is the ratio of alcohol and water in the resultant mixture?
A. 1 : 2 B. 1 : 3
C. 1 : 1 D. 5 : 9
E. 5 : 4

135. The speed of boat A in still water and speed of stream B are 40 km/hr and 20 km/hr respectively. The speed of boat B in still water and speed of stream A are 'x' km/hr and 'y' km/hr respectively. The sum of time taken by boat A to cover 450 km upstream and the same distance downstream in stream A is 24 hours and the sum of the time taken by boat B to cover 320 km upstream and 320 km downstream in stream B is 12 hours. Find $x + y$.
A. 90 km/hr
B. 70 km/hr
C. 20 km/hr
D. 15 km/hr
E. None of these

Directions (Qs. No. 136-140): *The question given is followed by the information in statements. You have to decide the information in which of the statements is necessary and sufficient to answer the question and mark answer accordingly.*

136. Every man in a certain class either belongs to group A, belongs to group B, or belongs to both groups. 20% of group A consists of men and 65% of group B consists of men. What percentage of the two groups together is made up of men?

(1) Group A contains 50 people.
(2) Group B contains 100 people.

A. Statement (1) ALONE is sufficient, but statement (2) alone is not sufficient to answer the question asked
B. Statement (2) ALONE is sufficient, but statement (1) alone is not sufficient to answer the question asked
C. BOTH statements (1) and (2) TOGETHER are sufficient to answer the question asked, but NEITHER statement ALONE is sufficient
D. EACH statement ALONE is sufficient to answer the question asked
E. Statements (1) and (2) TOGETHER are NOT sufficient to answer the question asked, and additional data are needed

137. A 40 m long wire is cut into three pieces. What is the length of the largest piece?

I. Two pieces are each 2 m shorter than the longest piece.
II. Two pieces of the wire are of the same length.

A. I alone
B. II alone
C. Either I alone or II alone
D. Both I and II
E. Both I and II are not sufficient

138. What is the weighted average of marks obtained by Ankur?

I. History, English and Hindi have weights 7, 10, 13 respectively
II. Simple arithmetic mean of History and English is 150, which is twice the average of English and Hindi

A. I alone
B. II alone
C. Either I alone or II alone
D. Both I and II
E. Both I and II are not sufficient

139. If each of the 20 bolts of fabric on a shelf is either 100 per cent cotton, 100 per cent wool, or a mixture of cotton and wool, how many bolts contain both cotton and wool?

(1) Of the 20 bolts, 18 contain some wool and 14 contain some cotton.
(2) Of the 20 bolts, 6 are 100 per cent wool

A. Statement (1) ALONE is sufficient, but statement (2) alone is not sufficient to answer the question asked
B. Statement (2) ALONE is sufficient, but statement (1) alone is not sufficient to answer the question asked
C. BOTH statements (1) and (2) TOGETHER are sufficient to answer the question asked, but NEITHER statement ALONE is sufficient
D. EACH statement ALONE is sufficient to answer the question asked
E. Statements (1) and (2) TOGETHER are NOT sufficient to answer the question asked, and additional data are needed

140. A farmer has a total of 60 pigs, cows, and horses on his farm. How many pigs does he have?

(1) The ratio of horses to cows is 2 : 9.
(2) He has more than 36 cows.

A. Statement (1) ALONE is sufficient, but statement (2) alone is not sufficient to answer the question asked
B. Statement (2) ALONE is sufficient, but statement (1) alone is not sufficient to answer the question asked
C. BOTH statements (1) and (2) TOGETHER are sufficient to answer the question asked, but NEITHER statement ALONE is sufficient
D. EACH statement ALONE is sufficient to answer the question asked
E. Statements (1) and (2) TOGETHER are NOT sufficient to answer the question asked, and additional data are needed

141. Piyush went to buy an article. The shopkeeper sold the article at the marked price but told him to pay 20% tax on the marked price if he asked for the bill. Piyush manages to get the discount of 5% on the actual marked price of the article. Besides he manages to avoid paying 20% tax on the already discounted price. He paid the shopkeeper ₹ 2280 without tax after the discount. What is the amount of discount he got?

A. 500 B. 550
C. 600 D. 650
E. 700

142. One container contains a mixture of spirit and water in the ratio 2 : 3 and another contains the mixture of spirit and water in the ratio 3 : 2. How much quantity from the second should be mixed with 10 litres of the first so that the resultant mixture has ratio of 4 : 5?

A. 2.86 litres B. 3.45 litres
C. 4.31 litres D. 5.67 litres
E. 8.94 litres

143. The average age of a class of 30 students and a teacher reduced by 0.5 years if we exclude the teacher. If the initial average age is 14 years and then the age of the teacher is

A. 29 years B. 30 years
C. 35 years D. 32 years
E. 33 years

144. 3 bell ring at an interval of 48, 72, 108 second. If they ring at 6 : 00 am then after this at what time they will ring together?

A. 6 : 07 : 12
B. 6 : 08
C. 6 : 05 : 13
D. 6 : 10
E. 6 : 12

145. When one-fifth of a number x, is added to 118, it becomes equal to y^2. If one-eighth of y is equal to 2.5, what is the value of x?

A. 1420 B. 1310
C. 1410 D. 1460
E. 1470

Directions (Qs. No. 146-148): *Study the following data carefully and answer the questions:*

Percentage of women opted different specialization

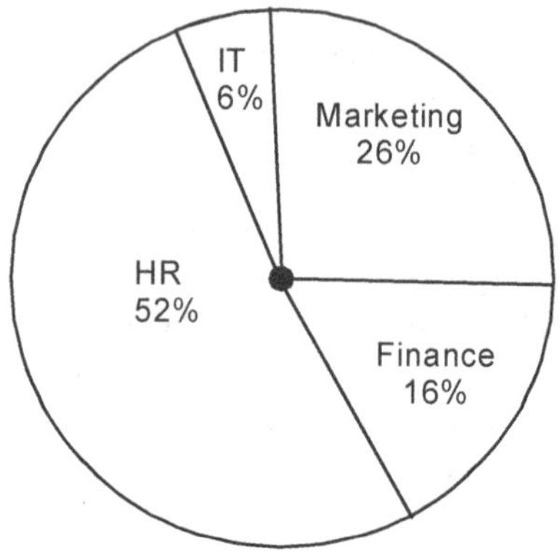

Number of men opted different specialization

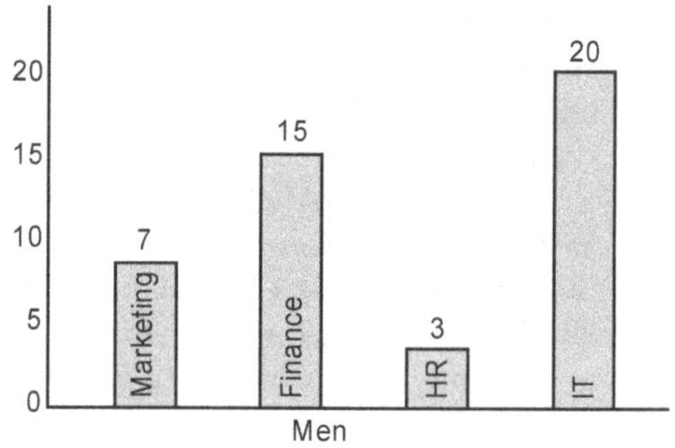

The pie charts shows the distribution of no. women preferring different specialization where the total number of women = 50.

146. If an audit is being conducted by a 10 member finance team, what is the probability that it can accommodate maximum of women?

A. 0.6 B. 0.8
C. 0.7 D. 0.9
E. 0.5

147. A prefectural board is selected comprising of 8 men or 8 women. What is the probability that equal number of men or women is selected from each department?

A. 0.001 B. 0.003
C. 0.005 D. 0.007
E. 0.009

148. What is the probability that number of women in a 20 member dancing club will have no women taking part from HR department?
A. 0.133 B. 0.833
C. 0.633 D. 0.338
E. None of these

Directions (Qs. No. 149-150): *In the following number series, only one number is incorrect. Find out the wrong number in the series.*

149. 25, 21, 30, 14, 139, 3
A. 103 B. 30
C. 25 D. 20
E. 139

150. 1000, 500, 271, 153.5, 97.75, 72.875
A. 271 B. 500
C. 153.5 D. 97.75
E. 72.875

ANSWERS

1	**2**	**3**	**4**	**5**	**6**	**7**	**8**	**9**	**10**
B	D	B	A	B	B	A	C	A	D
11	**12**	**13**	**14**	**15**	**16**	**17**	**18**	**19**	**20**
C	C	A	D	D	B	C	D	A	C
21	**22**	**23**	**24**	**25**	**26**	**27**	**28**	**29**	**30**
A	A	D	D	D	A	B	E	D	D
31	**32**	**33**	**34**	**35**	**36**	**37**	**38**	**39**	**40**
A	E	D	B	B	A	B	B	A	A
41	**42**	**43**	**44**	**45**	**46**	**47**	**48**	**49**	**50**
D	B	D	E	C	E	C	E	B	B
51	**52**	**53**	**54**	**55**	**56**	**57**	**58**	**59**	**60**
D	E	E	A	B	E	D	B	D	E
61	**62**	**63**	**64**	**65**	**66**	**67**	**68**	**69**	**70**
B	C	D	A	A	A	C	B	D	E
71	**72**	**73**	**74**	**75**	**76**	**77**	**78**	**79**	**80**
B	B	C	D	B	A	B	C	A	C
81	**82**	**83**	**84**	**85**	**86**	**87**	**88**	**89**	**90**
A	D	B	E	B	A	D	B	C	B
91	**92**	**93**	**94**	**95**	**96**	**97**	**98**	**99**	**100**
A	B	A	C	B	B	E	B	B	A
101	**102**	**103**	**104**	**105**	**106**	**107**	**108**	**109**	**110**
C	E	C	D	A	C	A	D	B	A
111	**112**	**113**	**114**	**115**	**116**	**117**	**118**	**119**	**120**
A	E	B	E	A	A	A	B	B	A
121	**122**	**123**	**124**	**125**	**126**	**127**	**128**	**129**	**130**
E	D	C	B	B	B	C	B	A	E
131	**132**	**133**	**134**	**135**	**136**	**137**	**138**	**139**	**140**
C	C	B	E	B	E	A	E	A	C
141	**142**	**143**	**144**	**145**	**146**	**147**	**148**	**149**	**150**
C	A	A	A	C	B	D	B	E	B

EXPLANATORY ANSWERS

For Qs. 1-5:

- F sits third to the right of S.
- F is sixth to the right of T.
- C and D are not immediate neighbours of F, who sits second to the right of E.
- E sits at the fifth position from the right end.
- B sits fourth to the right of P, who is not the immediate neighbour of U.
- There are two persons between U and A.
- There are two persons between D and Q.
- S is not an immediate neighbour of A.
- C is not an immediate neighbour of D and Q.

From the above statement, we conclude:

Facing North:

P	C	A	T	B	U	S	E	Q	F	R	D

For Qs. 6-10:

In row-1, J, K, L, M, N and O are seated and all of them are facing south. In row-2, C, D, E, F, G and H are seated and all of them are facing north

- M sits third to the left of J.
- The person facing M sits second to the left of H.
- Two persons are sitting between H and E.
- G is not an immediate neighbour of E.
- D does not face M.
- L and K are immediate neighbours.
- L and K do not sit at any of the extreme ends of the line.
- Only one person sits between N and L.
- The person facing K is an immediate neighbour of C.

According to above statement, we conclude:

J	K	L	M	N	O	Row 1 (Facing South)
C	D	E	F	G	H	Row 2 (Facing North)

For Qs. 11-15:

Month	Person
January (31)	Q
February (28/29)	P
March (31)	-
April (30)	A
May (31)	S
June (30)	-
July (31)	M
August (31)	C
September (30)	-
October (31)	K
November (30)	R
December (31)	-

For Qs. 16-20:

Students	Subjects	Standard
D	Chemistry	VIII
H	English	VIII
E	Biology	VII
A	Marathi	VII
G	Math	VII
C	Economics	VI
F	Physics	VI
B	Geography	VI

For Qs. 21-25:

Floor	Boy	Girl	City
9	Rohit	Amita	Lucknow
8	Vikash	Sanjana	Chennai
7	Sanjay	Anita	Varanasi
6	Kamal	Surabhi	Agra
5	Amit	Komal	Mathura
4	Sunil	Susheela	Noida
3	Anit	Saroj	Allahabad
2	Saurabh	Kumkum	Mirzapur
1	Sushil	Suhana	Patna

26. I. $A > X \rightarrow$ True (as $A \geq P = S > T > X$)

II. $P < B \rightarrow$ False

Hence, only conclusion I follows.

27. I. $S < Z \rightarrow$ False (as $S > U < Z$)

II. $X > Y \rightarrow$ True (as $Y < U < Z < X$)

Hence, only conclusion II follows.

28. I. $V < S \rightarrow$ True (as $V = P < X < Y < S$)

II. $T > R \rightarrow$ True (as $T > Y > X > P = V > R$)

Hence, both conclusions follow.

29. I. $H < C \rightarrow$ False (as there is no relation between H and C)

II. $H > D \rightarrow$ False (as $H \geq I = E \leq D$)

Hence, no conclusion follows.

30. I. $P < B \rightarrow$ False (as $P \geq Q > E \geq F > B$)

II. $S > A \rightarrow$ False (as $P \geq Q > E = S \geq F > B \leq A$)

Hence, no conclusion follows.

31.

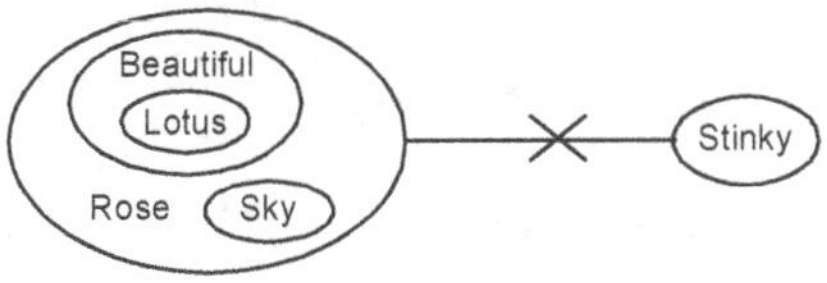

32.

33.

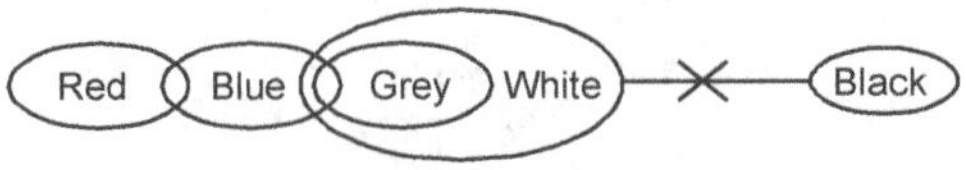

34.

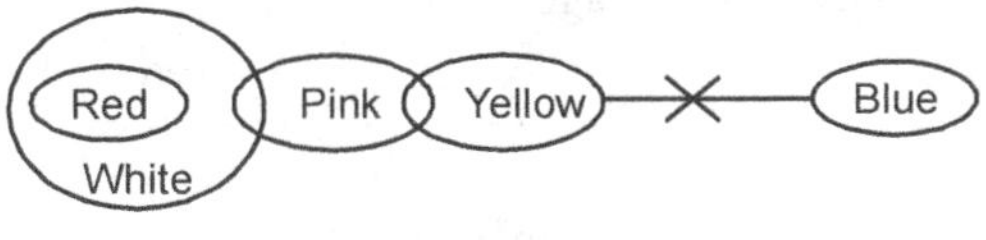

35.

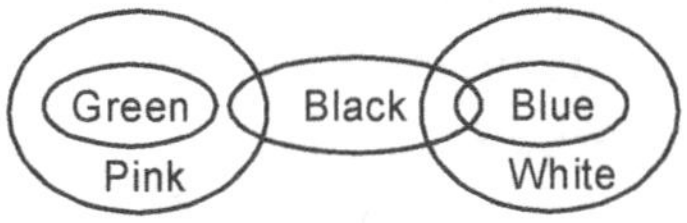

47. From I, $A \geq B < C = D > E \geq F = G$

We can't compare B and F.

From II, $A \leq B = C > D > E < F < G$

We can't compare B and F.

From III, $A > B > C = D \geq E > F < G$

Clearly B is greater to F.

So, Only III is sufficient. Hence, option C.

48. From I,

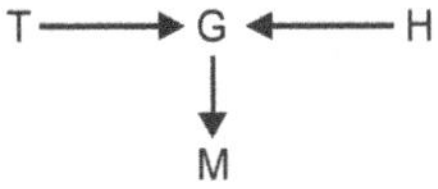

From II, N is between G and H.

From III,

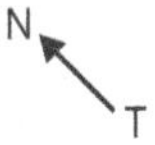

From I and II,

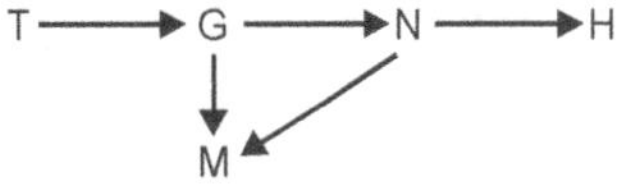

Hence, M is to the south-west of N.

From I and III,

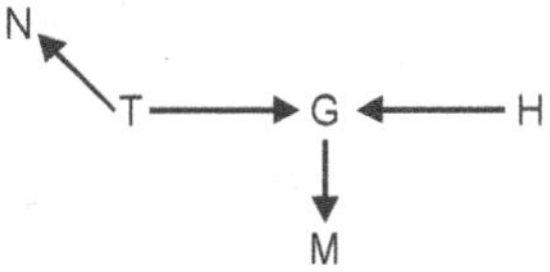

Thus, M is to the south-east of N.

So answer can be found by using I and either II or III.

49. From I,

In this only 'writer' is given nothing information about 'word'.

From II,

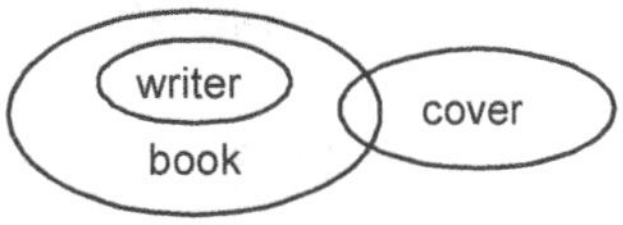

In this only 'writer' is given nothing information about 'word'.

From III,

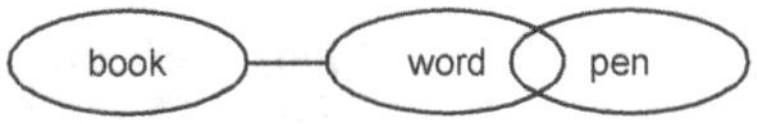

No information about 'writer'

From II and III,

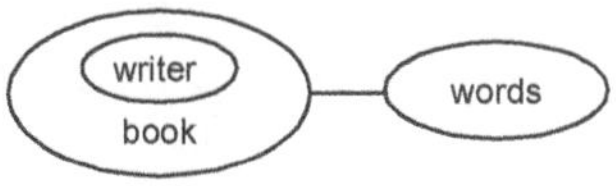

If we combine both II and III we can get that 'no writer is word'.

So, both II and III will be answer.

50. From I. Neha > Mahi > Nitesh

From II. – > – > – > Rita > – > –

Now combining all the statements, we have Neha > Mahi > Nitesh > Rita > – > –

Thus, Neha is the tallest.

101. 51 60 42 78 [6] 150

+9, −18, +36, −72, +144

102. 82 [187] 286 373 436 451

+105, +99, +87, +63, +15

−6, −12, −24, −48

103. 20 32 30 [80] 105 360 577.5

×1.5, ×3.5, ×5.5

×2.5, ×4.5

104. 49 193 766 3055 12208 [48817]

× 4 − 3, × 4 − 6, × 4 − 9, × 4 − 12, × 4 − 15

105. 21 27 64 204 [828] 4150

× 1 + (1 × 6), × 2 + (2 × 5), × 3 + (3 × 4), × 4 + (4 × 3), × 5 + (5 × 2)

106. S.P. of Lenovo sold by X

$$= 25000\left(1-\frac{10}{100}\right) = 22500$$

$$\text{S.P.} = 22500 = \left(1+\frac{20}{100}\right) \times (\text{CP})_{\text{Lenovo}}$$

$\Rightarrow$ C.P. of Lenovo = 18750

S.P. of Oppo sold by Y

$$= 16000\left(1+\frac{30}{100}\right) = 20800$$

$$\text{M.P. (Oppo)} \times \left(1-\frac{20}{100}\right) = 28000$$

$$\text{M.P. (Oppo)} = 26000$$

$$\text{Desired \%} = \frac{(26000-18750)}{26000} \times 100$$

$$= 27.88\%.$$

107. $$\text{Desired ratio} = \frac{\text{C.P. of Apple phone by X}}{\text{C.P. of MI by Y}}$$

$$\text{M.P. of Apple phone} = \left(1+\frac{44}{100}\right) \times 25000$$

$$= 36000$$

$$\text{C.P. of Apple phone} = 36000 \times \frac{100}{120}$$

$$= 30000$$

M.P. of MI phone

$$= 16000\left(1+\frac{30}{100}\right) \times \left(1+\frac{56.25}{100}\right)$$

$$= 16000 \times \frac{130}{100} \times \frac{156.35}{100} = 32500$$

$$\text{C.P. of MI} = 32500 \times \frac{100}{125} = 26000$$

$$\text{Desired ratio} = \frac{30000}{26000} = \frac{15}{13}.$$

108. M.P. after 20% discount

$$= 28000\left(1-\frac{20}{100}\right) = 22400$$

C.P. = 22400 − 2400 = 20000

or, M.P. after 30% discount

$$= 28000\left(1-\frac{30}{100}\right) = 19600$$

C.P. = 19600 + 400 = 20000

Net profit = 2 × 2400 − 6 × 400 = 2400

$$\text{Profit \%} = \frac{2400}{(8 \times 20000)} \times 100 = 1.5\%.$$

109. $$\text{S.P. of Lenovo by Y} = 28000 \times \frac{3}{4} = 21000$$

C.P. of Lenovo bought by X

$$= 25000 \times \frac{90}{100} \times \frac{100}{120} = 18750$$

C.P. of Lenovo bought by

$$= 21000 \times \frac{100}{112} = 18750$$

Desired average

$$= \frac{(2 \times 18750 + 6 \times 18750)}{8} = 18750.$$

110. Let, C.P. of Apple phone = x

C.P. of Oppo = y

According to question,

$$\frac{(x+y)}{2} = 14000$$

$$x + y = 28000 \quad ...(i)$$

$$\frac{x*1.2 + y*1.35}{2} = 18000$$

$$1.2x + 1.35y = 36000 \quad ...(ii)$$

On solving (*i*) and (*ii*) $y = 16000$; $x = 12000$

$$\text{Desired difference} = 16000 - 12000 = 4000.$$

111. (*i*)
$$2x^2 - 31x + 84 = 0$$
$$2x^2 - 24x - 7x + 84 = 0$$
$$2x(x - 12) - 7(x - 12) = 0$$
$$(x - 12)(2x - 7) = 0$$
$$x = 12, \frac{7}{2}$$

(*ii*)
$$3y^2 + y - 2 = 0$$
$$3y^2 + 3y - 2y - 2 = 0$$
$$3y(y + 1) - 2(y + 1) = 0$$
$$(y + 1)(3y - 2) = 0$$
$$y = -1, \frac{2}{3}$$
$$x > y.$$

112. (*i*)
$$6x^2 + 14x - 12 = 0$$
$$6x^2 + 18x - 4x - 12 = 0$$
$$6x(x + 3) - 4(x + 3) = 0$$
$$(x + 3)(6x - 4) = 0$$
$$x = -3, \frac{2}{3}$$

(*ii*)
$$6y^2 + 11y + 4 = 0$$
$$6y^2 + 8y + 3y + 4 = 0$$
$$2y(3y + 4) + 1(3y + 4) = 0$$
$$y = -\frac{4}{3}, -\frac{1}{2}$$

No relation.

113. (*i*)
$$x^2 - 30x + 216 = 0$$
$$x(x - 12) - 18(x - 12) = 0$$
$$(x - 18)(x - 12) = 0$$
$$x = 18, 12$$

(*ii*)
$$y^2 - 21y + 108 = 0$$
$$y^2 - 12y - 9y + 108 = 0$$
$$y(y - 12) - 9(y - 12) = 0$$
$$(y - 9)(y - 12) = 0$$
$$y = 9, 12$$
$$x \geq y.$$

114. (*i*)
$$8x^2 + 21x - 9 = 0$$
$$8x^2 + 24x - 3x - 9 = 0$$
$$8x(x + 3) - 3(x + 3) = 0$$
$$x = 3/8, -3$$

(*ii*)
$$3y^2 + 28y + 25 = 0$$
$$3y^2 + 3y + 25y + 25 = 0$$
$$3y(y + 1) + 25(y + 1) = 0$$
$$y = -1, -\frac{25}{3} \Rightarrow \text{No relation.}$$

115. (*i*)
$$4x^2 - 15x + 14 = 0$$
$$4x^2 - 8x - 7x + 14 = 0$$
$$4x(x - 2) - 7(x - 2) = 0$$
$$(x - 2)(4x - 7) = 0$$
$$x = 2, 7/4$$

(*ii*)
$$3y^2 - 6y + 3 = 0$$
$$3y^2 - 3y - 3y + 3 = 0$$
$$3y(y - 1) - 3(y - 1) = 0$$
$$(y - 1)(3y - 3) = 0$$
$$y = 1, 1 \Rightarrow x > y.$$

116. Amount invested in scheme Q is 30% of Amount invested in scheme R.

$$Q = \left(\frac{30}{100}\right) \times R \Rightarrow \frac{Q}{R} = \frac{3}{10}$$

Let the amount invested in scheme P = P

Ratio = P : Q : R = P : 3 : 10

Let, P = Px, Q = $3x$, R = $10x$

Rate in scheme P = 21%

Rate in scheme Q = 39%

Rate in scheme R = 13%

Rate in scheme Q and R

$$= \left(\frac{3}{13}\right) \times 39\% + \left(\frac{10}{13}\right) \times 13\% = 19\%$$

Time = 2 years

Simple interest in 2 years = 4000

Simple interest in 1 year = 2000

Principal = 10000

$$\text{Rate in 3 schemes} = 2000 \times \frac{100}{10000}$$

Now, By allegation method:

P		Q + R
21%		19%
	20%	
1		1

$$\text{Amount invested by } P = \frac{(10000 \times 1)}{2}$$
$$= ₹\ 5000.$$

117. Rate of interest for a period of 9 years
$= (10 \times 2 + 12 \times 3 + 4 \times 4)\% = 72\%$
Hence, the amount is returning 72% in the form of S.I. according to the new plan of bank.
Now, 72% of P = 11520
$\Rightarrow$ P = ₹ 16000
Now the person invested same amount in 2nd scheme which offers C.I.,

$$\text{Effective rate} = 10 + 10 + 10 \times \frac{10}{100} = 21\%$$
$$\text{C.I.} = 21\% \text{ of } 16000 = ₹\ 3360.$$

118. Let three cooks are x, y and z. And they bake number of cakes in 1 minute $\frac{1}{x}, \frac{1}{y}, \frac{1}{z}$ respectively.
Now, it is given that they can bake 20 cakes in a minute when they work together.

$$\left(\frac{1}{x} + \frac{1}{y} + \frac{1}{z}\right) = 20 \quad ...(i)$$

Now let cook x works for K minutes and K > 2

$$\text{So,} \quad K\left(\frac{1}{x}\right) = 20 \quad ...(ii)$$

And y and z complete remaining work.
They complete the whole work in 8 minutes.

$$(8 - K)\left(\frac{1}{y} + \frac{1}{z}\right) = 60 \quad ...(iii)$$

By equation (i), (ii) and (iii),

$$x = \frac{1}{5}, \frac{1}{10}$$

If we take $x = \frac{1}{10}$ then K = 2 and is equal to 2

So, we will take $x = \frac{1}{5}$

Now x bakes 1 cake in $= \frac{1}{5}$ minute.

$$160 \text{ cake in} = \frac{1}{5} \times 160$$
$$= 32 \text{ minutes.}$$

119.

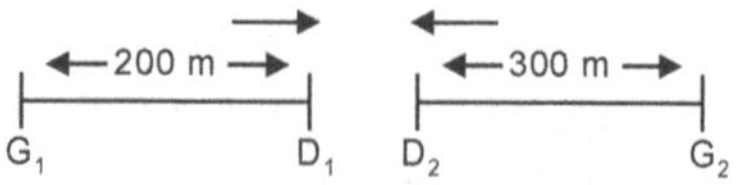

Time gap passing D_1D_2 and D_2G_1 = 30 sec

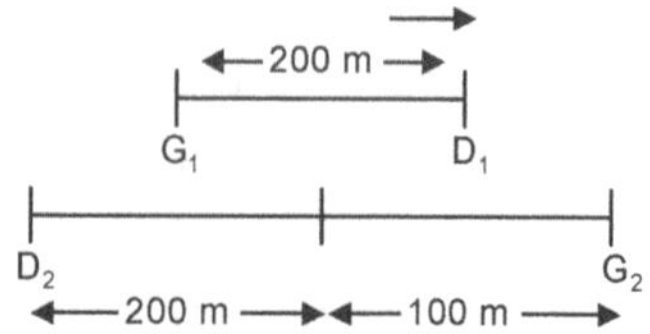

Let Speed of train is x m/s

$$T_{D_1D_2} = \frac{200 + 200}{x + x} = \frac{400}{2x}$$
$$T_{D_2G_1} = \frac{500}{2x}$$
$$\therefore \quad T_{D_2G_1} - T_{D_1G_2} = 30 \text{ sec}$$
$$\frac{500}{2x} - \frac{400}{2x} = 30$$
$$\frac{100}{2x} = 30 \Rightarrow x = \frac{100}{60}$$
$$2x = \frac{10}{3} \text{ m/s}$$

$\because$ Speed of both the train is same

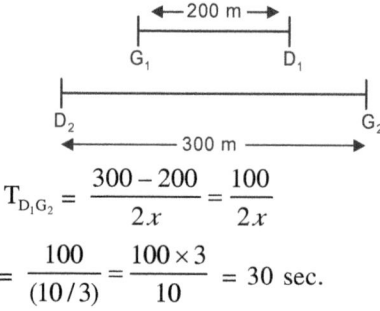

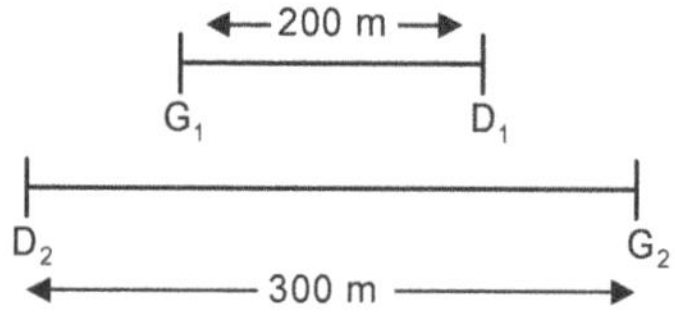

$$T_{D_1G_2} = \frac{300 - 200}{2x} = \frac{100}{2x}$$
$$= \frac{100}{(10/3)} = \frac{100 \times 3}{10} = 30 \text{ sec.}$$

120. Let the original average of the marks of all the candidates = x
The highest marks = a
The least marks = b
Then, according to the question,

$$98\% \text{ of } x = \frac{76x - a}{75}$$
$$98\% \text{ of } 75x + a = 76x \quad ...(i)$$
$$\text{And } 103\% \text{ of } x = \frac{76x - b}{75}$$
$$103\% \text{ of } 75x + b = 76x \quad ...(ii)$$

From equation (i) and equation (ii),

$$98\% \text{ of } 75x + a = 103\% \text{ of } 75x + b$$

$$5\% \text{ of } 75x = a - b$$

According to the question,

$$a - b = 33$$

So, $5\% \text{ of } 75x = 33$

$$5 \times \frac{75x}{100} = 33$$

By solving, $x = 8.8$

121. 62.5% of 18920 + ?% of 5325 = 16827

$\Rightarrow$ 11825 + ?% of 5325 = 16827

$$\Rightarrow \quad ? \times \frac{5325}{100} = 5002$$

$\Rightarrow$? = 94%.

122. $(14.989)^2 + (121.012)^3 + 2090 = ?$

225 + 1771561 + 2090 = 1773876.

123. 61.99% of 2004.85+ 69.99% of 1706.03 = ?

$$\frac{(2005 \times 62)}{100} + \frac{(1706 \times 70)}{100} = ?$$

1243 + 1194 (Approx) = 2437.

124. $$\frac{(9000)^{1/3} \times (10/9)}{(40\% \text{ of } 120)} = \frac{?}{8\% \text{ of } 600} \times \left(\frac{100}{81}\right)^{1/2}$$

? = 20.80 = 21.

125. $16^2 + 19^2 - \frac{29}{100} \times 800$

$$= 256 + 361 - \frac{30}{100} \times 800 = 617 - 240 = 377.$$

For Qs. No. 126-130:

Workers	Percentage of Word Done	Time taken (hours)
Mahendra	37.5%	9
Rampal	20%	3.2
Vijay	125%	35
Ramesh	25%	9
Suresh	150%	27

Time taken by Mahendra to complete 37.5% of the work = 9 hours

Time taken by Mahendra to complete the whole work $= \frac{9}{37.5} \times 100 = 24$ hours

Time taken by Rampal to complete 20% of the work = 3.2 hours

Time taken by Rampal to complete the whole work $= \frac{3.2}{20} \times 100 = 16$ hours

Time taken by Vijay to complete 125% of the work = 35 hours

Time taken by Vijay to complete the whole work $= \frac{35}{125} \times 100 = 28$ hours

Time taken by Ramesh to complete 25% of the work = 9 hours

Time taken by Ramesh to complete the whole work $= \frac{9}{25} \times 100 = 36$ hours

Time taken by Suresh to complete 150% of the work = 27 hours

Time taken by Suresh to complete the whole work $= \frac{27}{150} \times 100 = 18$ hours.

126. As, Rampal takes the minimum number of hours to complete the work, therefore, he has the highest efficiency.

127. So, time taken by Mahendra and Ramesh to complete the work if they are working together

$$= \frac{24 \times 36}{24 + 36} = \frac{72}{5} \text{ hours}$$

So, time taken by Ramesh and Suresh to complete the work if they are working together

$$= \frac{18 \times 36}{18 + 36} = 12 \text{ hours}$$

So, time taken by Mahendra and Rampal to complete the work if they are working together

$$= \frac{24 \times 16}{24 + 16} = \frac{48}{5} \text{ hours}$$

So, time taken by Mahendra and Suresh to complete the work if they are working together

$$= \frac{24 \times 18}{24 + 18} = \frac{72}{7} \text{ hours}$$

So, time taken by Vijay and Rampal to complete the work if they are working together

$$= \frac{28 \times 16}{28 + 16} = \frac{112}{11} \text{ hours.}$$

128. So, one hour work done by Mahendra, Ramesh and Suresh if working together

$$= \frac{1}{24}+\frac{1}{36}+\frac{1}{18}=\frac{1}{8}$$

Therefore, number of hours taken by Mahendra, Ramesh and Suresh if working together = 8 hours.

129. Let the time taken by Ajay to complete the work = x days

Therefore, $\frac{1}{24}+\frac{1}{16}+\frac{1}{x} = \frac{1}{8}$

On solving, we get, $x = 48$ hours

Therefore, ratio of their efficiency

$$= \frac{1}{24}:\frac{1}{16}:\frac{2}{48} = 2 : 3 : 1$$

Therefore, share of Ajay

$$= \frac{1}{2+3+1}\times 12000 = ₹\ 2000.$$

130. So, $\frac{16\times(100+x)}{100} = 28$

On solving, we get, $x = 75$.

131.

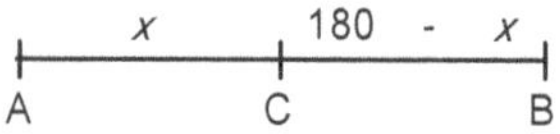

$$\frac{2x+5}{11} = \frac{2(180-x)-5}{13}$$

$$26x + 65 = 22\ (180) - 22x - 55$$

$$48x = 3840$$

$$\therefore \quad x = \frac{3840}{48} = 80 \text{ km}$$

Distance between A and C = 80 km.

132. The ratio of share in the profit of Dev and Eshan is 3 : 5

Menka's share is double than Eshan's share and Nishu receives ₹ 10500 out of the total profit of ₹ 37500

Let Eshan's share be x,

So Menka's would be $2x$ and Dev's share would be $\frac{3x}{5}$

$$\text{Nishu's share} = \frac{10500}{37500} = \frac{7}{25}$$

So, the share of Menka, Dev and Eshan would be

$$= 1-\frac{7}{25} = \frac{18}{25}$$

So, $x+2x+\frac{3x}{5} = \frac{18}{25}$

On solving, we get, $x = \frac{1}{5}$

So, Eshan's share $= \frac{1}{5}$

Menka's share $= \frac{2}{5}$

Dev's share $= \frac{3}{25}$

So the required ratio $= \frac{2}{5}:\frac{7}{25}:\frac{3}{25}:\frac{1}{5}$

So, the ratio in which the profit will be shared among Menka, Nishu, Dev and Eshan

= 10 : 7 : 3 : 5.

133. Length of the pool $= \frac{7}{10}\times 40 = 28$ m

Breadth of the pool $= \frac{2}{10}\times 40 = 8$ m

Height of the pool $= \frac{1}{10}\times 40 = 4$ m

Volume of the pool $= l \times b \times h$

$= 28 \times 8 \times 4 = 896000$ litres

Quantity needed to be emptied

$$= \left(\frac{1}{500}\right)\times 896000 = 1792 \text{ litres}$$

Portion emptied in the 1st 2 hours

= (12 + 15) + (15 + 25)

= 27 + 40 = 67 litres

So, portion emptied in the 1st 53 hours

= 26 × 67 + (12 + 15)

= 1742 + 27 = 1769 litres

Remaining quantity to be emptied

= 1792 − 1769 = 23 litres

This can be emptied by A and B in (23/40) hours = 0.575 hours

So, total time taken = 53.575 hours = 54 hours.

134. The concentration of alcohol in the resulting mixture

$$= \frac{4\times 0.25+6\times 0.5+8\times 0.75}{4+6+8} = \frac{10}{18} = \frac{5}{9}$$

Ratio of Alcohol : Water = 5 : 4.

135. According to the question,

$$\frac{450}{40+y}+\frac{450}{40-y} = 24$$

$$\frac{80}{1600-y^2} = \frac{24}{450}$$

$$1600 - y^2 = 1500$$

$$100 = y^2$$

$$y = 10 \text{ km/hr}$$

$$\frac{320}{x+20}+\frac{320}{x-20} = 12$$

$$\frac{2x}{x^2-400} = \frac{12}{320}$$

$$3x^2 - 160x - 1200 = 0$$

On solving, we get x = 60 km/hr

So, $x + y = 60 + 10 = 70$ km/hr.

137. Let the length of the largest piece be x

From statement I:

$$x + x - 2 + x - 2 = 40$$

$$3x - 4 = 40$$

$$3x = 44$$

$$x = \frac{44}{3} \text{ m}$$

From statement II:

Let the length of shorter piece be y m

$$y + y + x = 40$$

Here the value of y is unknown. Hence, statement I alone is sufficient to answer this question.

138. From statement I:

Only weights are given, H = 7 (history)
E = 10 (english)
Hn = 13 (hindi)

From statement II: $\frac{(H+E)}{2} = 150$

$$H + E = 300$$

$$\frac{(E+Hn)}{2} = \frac{150}{2}$$

$$E + Hn = 150$$

$$\text{Weighted average} = \frac{(7H+10E+13Hn)}{(7+10+13)}$$

Here the individual marks are unknown.

Hence, Both the statements together are not sufficient.

141. Let the marked price of an article be 100

Then, selling price with tax

= 100 + 20% of 100 = 120

New selling price = 100 − 5 = 95

Effective discount = 120 − 95 = 25

At selling price of ₹ 95, he get discount of ₹ 25

At selling price of ₹ 1, he get discount of

$$\left(\frac{25}{95}\right)$$

At selling price of ₹ 2280, he get discount of

$$\left(\frac{25}{95}\right)\times 2280 = 600.$$

142. Ratio of mixture of spirit and water in Container 1 = 2 : 3

Amount of mixture taken = 10 litres

$$\text{Amount of spirit} = \frac{2}{5}\times 10 = 4 \text{ litres}$$

$$\text{Amount of water} = \frac{3}{5}\times 10 = 6 \text{ litres}$$

Ratio of mixture of spirit and water in Container 2 = 3 : 2

Amount of mixture taken = x litres

$$\text{Amount of spirit} = \frac{3}{5}\times x = \frac{3x}{5} \text{ litres}$$

$$\text{Amount of water} = \frac{2}{5}\times x = \frac{2x}{5} \text{ litres}$$

Ratio of mixture of spirit and water in resultant mixture = 4 : 5

$$\text{Therefore, } \frac{\left(4+\frac{3x}{5}\right)}{\left(6+\frac{2x}{5}\right)} = \frac{4}{5}$$

$$\frac{\left(\frac{20}{5}+\frac{3x}{5}\right)}{\left(\frac{30}{5}+\frac{2x}{5}\right)} = \frac{4}{5}$$

$$\frac{(20+3x)}{(30+2x)} = \frac{4}{5}$$

$$100 + 15x = 120 + 8x$$

$$7x = 20$$

$$x = 2.86 \text{ litres.}$$

143. Age of teacher = Total age of (students + teacher) – Total age of students

$= 31 \times 14 - 30 \times 13.5$

$= 434 - 405 = 29$ years.

144. If they all have to ring together then the number must be multiple of 48, 72, 108.

So, in this case just take the LCM of these numbers and add those seconds in 6:00 am.

145. First condition: $\frac{x}{5}+118 = y^2$ ...(*i*)

Second condition: $\frac{y}{8} = 2.5$

$y = 2.5 \times 8$

$y = 20$

Put value of y in equation (*i*)

$\frac{x}{5}+118 = (20)^2 = 400$

$\frac{x}{5} = 400 - 118$

$\frac{x}{5} = 282$

$x = 282 \times 5 = 1410.$

For Qs. No. 146-148.

Gender	Specialization			
	Marketing	Finance	HR	IT
Women (50)	13	8	26	3
Men (45)	7	15	3	20

146. Probability of getting maximum women from finance department $= \frac{8}{10}$

So, the total probability $= \frac{8}{10} = 0.8.$

147. If the 8 members selected are women then each department can accommodate maximum of 2 women

Probability of getting 2 women from each department

$= \frac{2}{13}\times\frac{2}{8}\times\frac{2}{26}\times\frac{2}{3} = 0.0019$

If the 8 members selected are men then each department can accommodate maximum of 2 men

Probability of getting 2 men from each department

$= \frac{2}{7}\times\frac{2}{15}\times\frac{2}{3}\times\frac{2}{20} = 0.0050$

So, the total probability of getting equal number of men or women from each department

$= 0.0019 + 0.0050 = 0.0069 = 0.007.$

148. Total women = 50

Number of women from HR department = 26

Number of women other than HR department = 24

So, 20 women is to be selected from 24 women non – HR department

Probability of getting 20 women from department other than HR

$= \frac{20}{24} = \frac{10}{12} = \frac{5}{6} = 0.8333.$

149. The pattern is:

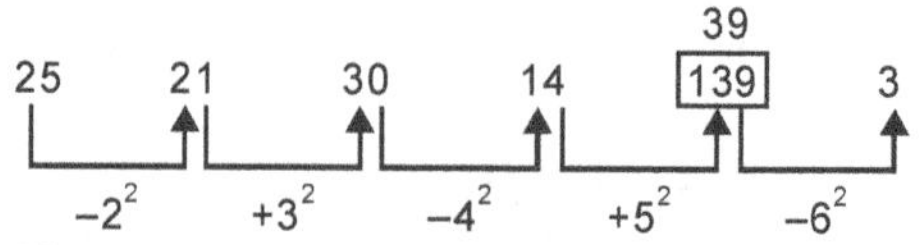

Thus, the incorrect number is 139.

150. The pattern is:

Thus, the incorrect number is 500.

Previous Paper (Solved)

Institute of Banking Personnel Selection [IBPS] Specialist (Marketing) Officer Scale-I Online Main Exam 2018*

PROFESSIONAL KNOWLEDGE

1. An appropriate pricing strategy for a new product to be introduced in the market will be:
A. Average/Marginal cost-plus pricing
B. Skimming/Penetrating pricing
C. Product-line pricing
D. Differential pricing
E. Marginal Pricing

2. Which one of the following practices is not sought to be regulated under the Consumer Protection Act, 1986?
A. Sales of defective goods
B. Supply of services having some deficiency
C. Misleading advertisements
D. Goods supplied free of charge
E. None of these

3. Which is not a centralised communication network system?
A. Wheel Network B. Y-shaped Network
C. Circle Network D. Chain Network
E. Star Network

4. Which of the following is direct marketing?
A. Face-to-face marketing
B. Catalogue marketing
C. Direct mailing
D. Test marketing
E. Indirect marketing

5. Holistic marketing does not include:
A. Internal Marketing
B. Integrated Marketing
C. Performance Marketing
D. Financial Marketing
E. Non-performance Marketing

6. Which of the following is not a distinctive characteristics of services?
A. Transparency B. Intangibility
C. Inseparability D. Perishability
E. None of these

7. To remain dominant, a market leader looks for:
A. ways to expand total market demand
B. attempting to protect its current share
C. increasing its market share
D. all of the above
E. None of these

8. Match the items given in List–I and List–II:

List–I	**List–II**
(*a*) Market Research	1. Sales promotion
(*b*) Financial Plan	2. Form of business
(*c*) Ownership	3. Budgeting
(*d*) Marketing Plan	4. Exploring market opportunity

Codes:

	(*a*)	(*b*)	(*c*)	(*d*)
A.	1	2	3	4
B.	4	3	1	2
C.	4	3	2	1
D.	1	2	4	3
E.	3	2	1	4

9. TePP stands for:
A. Technology for Promotion and Production
B. Trade for Profitability and Productivity
C. Technopreneur Promotion Programme
D. Test and Evaluation Program Plan
E. None of these

* Based on Memory.

10. Cost-plus pricing is not suitable for:
A. Monopoly Pricing
B. Product Tailoring
C. Refusal Pricing
D. Monopsony Pricing
E. None of these

11. The study of gestures and body postures for their impact on communication is known as:
A. Kinesics
B. Proximics
C. Semantics
D. Informal channels
E. None of these

12. Which of the following are most *closely* interconnected?
A. Leadership and organisation structure
B. Leadership and motivation
C. Leadership and planning
D. Leadership and performance appraisal
E. Motivational and Planning

13. _______ is defined as disputes between parties submitted and decided by a neutral third party.
A. Collective Bargaining
B. Affirmation Action
C. Arbitration
D. Negotiation
E. None of these

14. Consider the following statements:
1. Usually people from the same culture, social class and occupation have the same life style.
2. The consumer buying decision will involve the same stages regardless of whether the goods involved are low or high involvement.
3. "Salesmen are born, not made."
4. The ultimate goal of a customer-oriented organisation is to maximise its customer's satisfaction.

Indicate the correct answer through the codes.
Codes:
A. All the statements are true.
B. Statements 1 and 2 are false, others are true.
C. Statement 3 is true, others are false.
D. All are false.
E. All of these

15. Consider the following statements :
(*i*) Brand equity is a function of brand awareness and brand preference.
(*ii*) Product lines tend to shorten over time.
(*iii*) The Standards of Weights and Measures (Packaged Commodities) Rules, 1977 provide for the labelling rules relating to packaged commodities.
(*iv*) AIDA Model is relevant to advertising as well as physical distribution.

Indicate the correct answer.
Codes:
A. All the above statements are false.
B. Only (*iii*) is true.
C. (*i*), (*iii*) and (*iv*) are true.
D. Only (*i*) is true.
E. Only (*ii*) is true.

16. Before performing the business analysis for developing a new product, a company should be engaged in:
A. Idea screening
B. Product development
C. Marketing strategy development
D. Product positioning
E. Marketing development

17. In the social-cultural arena, marketers may not understand:
A. People's views
B. Organisation's views
C. Society's views
D. Government's views
E. NGO's views

18. Which of the following is/are a type(s) of direct marketing?
A. Direct-Response Advertising
B. Personal Selling
C. Telemarketing
D. All of the above
E. None of these

19. Arrange the following stages involved in DBMS in proper sequence:
(*i*) Creating
(*ii*) Defining
(*iii*) Data structuring
(*iv*) Updating
(*v*) Interrogating

Codes:
A. (*i*), (*iii*), (*ii*), (*iv*) and (*v*)
B. (*ii*), (*i*), (*iii*), (*v*) and (*iv*)
C. (*iii*), (*ii*), (*v*), (*iv*) and (*i*)
D. (*ii*), (*iii*), (*i*), (*iv*) and (*v*)
E. None of these

20. The managerial process of developing and maintaining a viable fit between an organisation's objectives, skills, and resources, and its market opportunities is called:
A. Establishing strategic business units
B. Market-oriented strategic planning
C. Market research
D. Portfolio analysis
E. Marketing analysis

21. Low cost, product differentiation, and focused market are the examples of:
A. Corporate strategy
B. Business strategy
C. Functional strategy
D. Behavioural strategy
E. Marketing strategy

22. What kind of pricing strategy a firm should normally follow for marketing electronic goods?
A. Penetration pricing strategy
B. Skimming pricing strategy
C. Cost plus pricing strategy
D. All of the above
E. None of these

23. Which of the following function involved under marketing management's function?
1. Collection of market information
2. Marketing coordination
3. Marketing controlling
4. All the above

Codes:
A. 1 & 2 B. 2 & 3
C. 3 only D. 4 only
E. None of these

24. Match the following:

List-I	List-II
(*a*) Differentiation	1. How familiar and intimate consumers are with the brand.
(*b*) Esteem	2. The degree to which a brand is seen as different from others.
(*c*) Relevance	3. How well the brand is regarded and respected.
(*d*) Knowledge	4. The breadth of a brand's appeal.

Codes:

	(*a*)	(*b*)	(*c*)	(*d*)
A.	1	2	3	4
B.	2	3	4	1
C.	3	4	1	2
D.	4	3	2	1
E.	2	1	4	3

25. "Motivational research is a form of market research that attempts to discover the deeper reasons why people buy." Who said it?
A. Manson and Rath B. Stanton
C. Still and Scweff D. Philip Kotler
E. Ernest Dichter

26. In multi level channel arrangement Jobber stands in between ________.
A. manufacturer and wholesaler
B. wholesaler and retailer
C. retailer and consumer
D. none of these
E. manufacturing

27. A company following a strategy of advertising the product for a period followed by a period with no advertising is called:
A. Concentration B. Flighting
C. Pulsing D. Continuity
E. None of these

28. Franchise organization is an example of ______ vertical marketing system.
A. Corporate B. Administered
C. Contractual D. Co-operative
E. None of these

29. Match Item-I with Item-II:

Item-I (Type of Control)	Item-II (Prime Responsibility)
I. Annual Plan Control	1. Line and Staff Management or Marketing Controller

II. Profitability Control		2. Top/Middle Management
III. Efficiency Control		3. Marketing Controller
IV. Strategic Control		4. Top Management/ Marketing Auditor

Codes:

	(I)	(II)	(III)	(IV)
A.	2	3	1	4
B.	1	3	2	4
C.	2	1	4	3
D.	2	3	4	1
E.	1	2	3	4

30. Which of the following statement is true?
A. A brand name is a part of brand which can be vocalised.
B. A brand is usually composed of a name and mark of a product.
C. Brand means a name, term and symbol or a mix thereof used to identify the product of a firm and to distinguish.
D. All of the above
E. None of these

31. The term inventory includes:
A. the stock of raw materials only.
B. the stock of finished goods only.
C. the stock of raw materials and goods required for production in a factory or finished goods for sales.
D. none of the above
E. All of these

32. Brain storming is a group creativity exercise designed to come up with _______.
A. number of solutions to a single problem
B. two solutions to a single problem
C. three solutions to two problems
D. many solutions to many problems
E. three solutions to five solutions

33. The term Opportunity Cost refers to:
A. Variable Cost
B. Short-run cost
C. The cost forgone in favour of production of another product
D. Cost related to an optimum level of production
E. None of these

34. What is the characteristic of a purely competitive market?
A. Large number of buyers and sellers
B. A few sellers
C. A few buyers
D. Abnormal profit
E. Profit & Loss

35. Which of the following is not the stage of product life cycle?
A. Introduction
B. Growth
C. Market segmentation
D. Decline
E. Growth & Decline

36. For 'make or buy decision', which cost is to be considered?
A. Marginal cost
B. Total cost
C. Fixed cost
D. List of price
E. None of these

37. Who defines advertising as "any paid form of non-personal presentation and promotion of ideas, goods and services by an identified sponsor?
A. Philip Kotler
B. C.K. Prahlad
C. Chartered Institute of Marketing
D. American Marketing Association
E. H.L. Hansen

38. A market structure which consists of one buyer and one seller is referred as:
A. Monopsony
B. Bilateral monopoly
C. Monopoly
D. Duopoly
E. Personal selling

39. The four systems of Management in terms of Leadership styles are related to:
A. Blake and Mouton
B. Philip Kotler
C. Peter F. Drucker
D. Rensis Likert
E. Robert Lauterborn

40. Making profit by taking advantage of different prices prevailing in different markets is referred as:

A. Hedging B. Speculation
C. Arbitrage D. Gambling
E. None of these

41. The Branding strategy which uses a different brand name for each product is known as:
A. Overall Family Branding
B. Line Family Branding
C. Individual Branding
D. Brand Extension
E. None of these

42. Goods used by an organization in producing other goods is called:
A. Consumer called
B. Industrial goods
C. Speciality goods
D. Selling goods
E. None of these

43. Marketing information system gathers information from internal sources like marketing intelligence and marketing research to help the manager in:
A. Assessing the information needs
B. Developing the needed information
C. Distributing the information
D. All of the above
E. None of these

44. Giffen goods are those goods:
A. for which demand increases as price increases
B. which are in short supply
C. which have high elasticity of demand
D. which gives rise to a Cob-Web situation
E. None of these

45. Which of the following statement is true?
A. The essence of marketing is a transaction of an exchange.
B. Marketing–orientation is philosophy, which has to pervade the organisation structure.
C. Marketing is also a managerial function involving analysis, planning and control marketing activities in an organisation.
D. All of the above
E. None of these

46. Marketing research does not normally:
A. Gather environmental information
B. Provide a continuous source of information
C. Relate to all aspects of marketing operations
D. Describe the current situation
E. None of these

47. Globalization involves:
A. Free flow of technology from one country to another
B. Free flow of investment from one country to the other
C. Free flow of people from one country to the other
D. All of the above
E. None of these

48. Whistle-Blowers are:
A. to be removed from the jobs
B. to be promoted
C. to be rewarded for the organisational enrichment
D. to be protected since they intend to bring out truth
E. None of these

49. Selling the products only through a single wholesaler or retailer is called:
A. Extensive distribution strategy
B. Selective distribution strategy
C. Exclusive distribution strategy
D. Mass merchandise strategy
E. None of these

50. Marketing myopia concept was developed by:
A. Philip Kotler B. Peter Drucker
C. C.K. Prahlada D. Theodore Levitt
E. MC Carthy

51. Emerging market economies are:
A. A part of developed countries
B. Newly industrializing countries
C. A part of developing countries
D. A part of third world countries
E. All industrializing countries

52. Additional revenue generated by selling an additional unit is:
A. Incremental revenue
B. Marginal revenue

C. Total revenue
D. Average revenue
E. Total revenue and expenditure

53. The term "Grapevine Communication" is related to:
A. Formal Communication
B. Informal Communication
C. Written Communication
D. Vertical Communication
E. Formal & Informal communication

54. A company using high price and high promotion policy is adopting the following strategy:
A. Slow skimming B. Rapid Penetration
C. Slow Penetration D. Rapid Skimming
E. All of these

55. Which of the following is not a market oriented pricing technique?
A. Penetration pricing
B. Going rate pricing
C. Perceived value pricing
D. Early-cash recovery pricing
E. None of these

56. Which one of the following facilitates E-Commerce?
A. Public relations B. Direct marketing
C. Personal selling D. Product quality
E. Price Mix

57. Which of the variables is not used by marketers for demographic segmentation?
A. Age B. Income
C. Gender D. Poverty
E. None of these

58. Which pattern reflects a pure executive form of management?
A. Functional B. Line
C. Line and Staff D. Committee
E. All of these

59. The term financial engineering is related to:
A. Cost of production
B. Financial restructuring
C. Product planning
D. Capital issue
E. Product Pricing

60. "Make use of paper bags instead of plastic bags." It is related to:
A. Environmental Ethics
B. Green Marketing
C. Socially Responsible Marketing
D. Social Marketing
E. None of these

ANSWERS

1	**2**	**3**	**4**	**5**	**6**	**7**	**8**	**9**	**10**
B	D	C	A	D	A	D	C	C	A
11	**12**	**13**	**14**	**15**	**16**	**17**	**18**	**19**	**20**
A	B	C	D	B	C	D	D	C	B
21	**22**	**23**	**24**	**25**	**26**	**27**	**28**	**29**	**30**
B	*	D	B	A	B	B	C	A	D
31	**32**	**33**	**34**	**35**	**36**	**37**	**38**	**39**	**40**
C	A	C	A	C	A	D	B	D	C
41	**42**	**43**	**44**	**45**	**46**	**47**	**48**	**49**	**50**
C	B	D	*	D	B	D	D	C	D
51	**52**	**53**	**54**	**55**	**56**	**57**	**58**	**59**	**60**
C	B	B	D	D	B	D	A	B	A

Previous Paper (Solved)

Institute of Banking Personnel Selection [IBPS] Specialist (Marketing) Officer Scale-I Online Preliminary Exam, 2017*

REASONING

1. In the past, consumers would rarely walk into an ice cream store and order low-fat ice cream. But that isn't the case today. An increasing health conscious-ness combined with a much bigger selection of tasty low-fat foods in all categories has made low-fat ice cream a very profitable item for ice cream store owners.
Which of the following best support the statement?

A. low-fat ice cream produces more revenue than other low-fat foods.
B. ice cream store owners would be better off carrying only low-fat ice cream.
C. ice cream store owners no longer think that low-fat ice cream is an unpopular item.
D. low-fat ice cream is more popular than other kinds of ice cream.
E. consumers are fickle and it is impossible to please them.

2. Cause: All the major rivers in the state have been flowing way over the danger level for the past few weeks.
Which of the following is/are possible effect(s) of the above cause?

(*a*) Many villages situated near the river banks are submerged forcing residents to flee.
(*b*) Government has decided to provide alternate shelter to all the affected villagers residing near the river banks.
(*c*) The entire state has been put on high flood alert.

A. Only (*a*)
B. Only (*a*) and (*b*)
C. Only (*b*) and (*c*)
D. All (*a*), (*b*) and (*c*)
E. None of these

Directions (Qs. Nos. 3-6): *In these questions, relationship between different elements is shown in the statements. These statements are followed by two conclusions. Study the conclusions based on the given statement and select appropriate answer.*

Give answer—

A. If either conclusion I or II follows
B. If neither conclusion I nor II follows
C. If only conclusion II follows
D. If both conclusions I and II follow
E. If only conclusion I follows

3. Statements : $C \geq V \leq R = N \geq T > Q$; $Y \geq N < A$
Conclusions : I. $Q > V$ II. $Q < Y$

4. Statements : $C \geq V \leq R = N \geq T > Q$; $Y \geq N < A$
Conclusions : I. $Q \geq Y$ II. $A > Q$

5. Statements : $P \geq R < U \leq M < V$; $T \leq U$; $L < M$
Conclusions : I. $T < L$ II. $L > V$

6. Statements : $P \geq R < U \leq M < V$; $T \leq U$; $L < M$
Conclusions : I. $V > T$ II. $T \leq P$

* Based on Memory.

Direction (Qs. No. 7): *Study the given information carefully and answer the given question.*

Following are the observations of an experiment on 'sleep and memory' conducted on 18 healthy young adults (ages 18 to 25) and 18 healthy older adults (ages 61 to 81).

(*a*) The recall after 8 hours of sleep in younger adults was 65% more than that in the older adults.

(*b*) Night-sleep had higher negative impact on all of the participants as compared to that of day-sleep of equal duration.

(*c*) If a given set of words is memorised immediately before going to sleep, its recall after waking up was found to be better in younger adults than in the older adults.

7. Which of the following can be concluded from the given findings of the research?

I. As per the experiment, there is some correlation between sleep and memory.

II. The part of brain involved in memory is more active during the day as compared to that during the night.

III. A sleep of more than 8 hours can improve the memory in older adults.

IV. Memorising something immediately after waking up from an 8-hour long sleep will yield better results than memorising before sleep.

A. Only IV

B. All the given statements can be concluded from the given findings of the research.

C. Both I and III

D. Both II and IV

E. Only II

8. In this question, two statements I and II are given. These statements may be either independent causes or may be effects of independent causes or a common cause. One of those statements may be the effect of the other statement. Read both the statements and decide which of the given answer choice correctly depicts the relationship between these two statements.

Statements :

I. Company ABC, a leading automobile company in country G has decided to merge all its subsidiary companies into the parent company last week.

II. Company XYZ, a subsidiary of automobile company ABC, has opened five new branches in country F in the previous financial year.

A. Both the statements I and II are effects of some common cause.

B. Both the statements I and II are independent causes.

C. Statement II is the cause, and statement I is its effect.

D. Statement I is the cause and Statement II is its effect.

E. Both the statements I and II are effects of independent causes.

9. If all the letters in the word 'REGULATION' are arranged in English alphabetical order from left to right and then all the vowels are changed to the next alphabet in the English alphabetical series and all the consonants are changed to the previous alphabet in English alphabetical series, how will the word be written?

A. BFFJKOQQSV B. ZFFJKONSSV

C. ZDHHMONSUT D. BFHUKMPORV

E. BFFJKMPQSV

10. In Country A, it is mandatory for all government organizations to provide transportation facilities (home pick-up and drop) to employees if 75% or more number of total employees working in the organization reside more than 15 km away from office. The same, however, does not apply to XY enterprises as only 1500 of their employees travel more than 15 km to work.

Which of the following can be inferred from the given statement?

(*a*) The total number of employees in XY enterprises is definitely more than 2000.

(*b*) Only 25% employees of XY enterprises travel less than 15 km to office.

(*c*) If 25 new recruits who travel more than 15 km join XY enterprises, the XY enterprises will be definitely have to provide transportation facilities.

(*d*) XY enterprises is definitely not a government enterprise

A. Only (*a*) B. Only (*c*)
C. Both (*b*) and (*d*) D. Only (*d*)
E. (*a*), (*b*) and (*c*)

Directions (Qs. Nos. 11-15) : *Study the given information carefully to answer the given questions.*

Seven people — J, K, L, M, N, O and P have an interview on seven different days of the same week, starting from Monday and ending on Sunday, but not necessarily in the same order. Each one of them also likes different subjects namely — Statistics, Zoology, Sociology, English, Mathematics, Psychology and Economics, but not necessarily in the same order.

Only four people have their interview between N and the one who likes Zoology. Neither N nor the one who likes Zoology has an interview on Sunday. P has an interview immediately after the one who likes Zoology. Only two people have their interviews between P and J. The one who likes Psychology has an interview on one of the days before J but not on Wednesday. Neither N nor P likes Psychology. Only two people have their interviews between the one who likes Psychology and the one who likes Statistics. The one who likes Economics has an interview immediately before the one who likes Statistics. The number of people having interview between P and the one who likes Economics is same as that of the number of people between J and the one who likes English. N does not like English. Only one person has an interview between the one who likes English and K. The one who likes Sociology has an interview immediately after O. L has an interview on one of the days after M.

11. Four of the following five are alike in a certain way based on the given arrangement and hence form a group. Which of the following does not belong to the group?
A. K-English
B. Wednesday-K
C. Mathematics-Wednesday
D. Sociology-Statistics
E. Friday-L

12. How many people have their interviews between L and M?
A. Two B. Three
C. None D. One
E. More than three

13. Which of the following statements is TRUE as per the given arrangement?
A. None of the given statements is true
B. Only one person has an interview between K and J.
C. O likes Psychology.
D. M has an interview on Friday.
E. The one who likes Zoology has an interview on one of the day after M.

14. Who has an interview immediately after K?
A. M
B. The one who likes Zoology
C. The one who likes Statistics
D. J
E. P

15. How many people have their interview before the one who likes Mathematics?
A. One B. More than three
C. None D. Two
E. Three

Directions (Qs. Nos. 16-20) : *Study the following information and answer the given questions.*

Seven people namely, J, K, L, M, N, O and P like seven different movies namely, Twilight, Gladiator, Wanted, Dread, Hero, Jumanji and Signs but not necessarily in the same order. Each person also works in the same office but in a different department (on the basis of experience) namely Administration, Production, Marketing, HR, Finance, R & D and Client relations (CR), not necessarily in the same order.

(Please Note: Each person has been allocated to a department as per increasing order of experience with the one in Administration being the least experienced whilst the one in Client Relations (CR) being the most experienced).

Only two persons have less experience than K. P works in R & D. The one who likes Wanted has more experience than K but less than one who likes Jumanji. P neither likes Wanted nor Jumanji. The one who likes Wanted does not work in Finance.

J, who is more experienced than K, likes Twilight. The person who works in Production is less experienced than the person who likes Hero. K does not like Hero. The person who works in HR is more experienced than both L and N. N is not the least experienced person. The one who likes Signs has more experience than N. M is more experienced than J. L does not like Dread.

16. Four of the following five are alike in a certain way based on the given arrangement and so form a group. Which is the one that does not belong to that group?

A. MO B. NK
C. PK D. NJ
E. LO

17. Which combination represents the department in which O works and the movie he likes?

A. CR-Signs
B. CR-Gladiator
C. HR-Gladiator
D. Marketing-Wanted
E. HR-Wanted

18. Which of the following movies does M like?

A. Jumanji B. Hero
C. Gladiator D. Signs
E. Dread

19. As per the given arrangement, HR is related to Signs and CR is related to Hero in a certain way. To which of the following is Production related to in the same way?

A. Dread B. Jumanji
C. Wanted D. Gladiator
E. Twilight

20. Which of the following pairs represent the respective people who have more experience than J and less experience than K?

A. M, N B. P, O
C. O, J D. L, N
E. P, M

21. *Read the given information and answer the question.*

'Despite spending huge amount of money, we have not yet been able to find life on other planets. I am personally of the opinion that such research should stop with immediate effect as it is a waste of time and money as no good will ever come out of it. Instead it would be better to use this money to research other elements in space' Statement by a Scientist from Space Institute of Country X.

Which of the following does not weaken the statement of the scientist of space institute of country X?

A. Although life on other planets has not been discovered yet, such research has widened our knowledge and under-standing about other planets and has led to growth and development in science.
B. According to space scientists, if such efforts are continued, the probability of finding life in at least one other planet is much higher as compared to not finding life at all.
C. Various other research projects taken up by the said institute in the past have also failed despite spending huge amount of time as well as money on them.
D. With the amount of time and money that has already been invested in this research, shutting it now would lead to a greater loss than continuing the search.
E. None of the above

22. This question consists of information and two statements numbered I and II given below it. You have to decide which of the given statements weaken(s) or strengthen(s) the information and decide the appropriate answer.

In order to discourage crowd built-up at railway station X, the platform ticket (charged to all such priced at ₹ 10 should be increased to ₹ 20.

I. The price of ticket from X to nearest railway station is ₹ 12.
II. On an average, every railway station generates ₹ 24 lacs revenue by charging ₹ 10 for platform ticket while X generates ₹ 28 lacs.

A. Both statement I and statement II weaken the information.
B. Statement I weakens the information while Statement II is a neutral statement.
C. Statement I strengthens the information while statement II weakens the information.
D. Statement I weakens the information while Statement II strengthens the information.
E. Both statements I and II strengthen the information

23. Which of the following expressions will be definitely false if the given expression '$G > H = I \geq V \leq Y \leq Z \leq T$ is definitely true?

A. $I < G$ B. $T < V$
C. $Y \leq T$ D. $Z \geq V$
E. $V < G$

Directions (Qs. Nos. 24-28) : *A word and number arrangement machine when given an input line of words and numbers rearranges them following a particular rule in each step. The following is an illustration of input and rearrangement. (All the numbers are two-digit numbers.)*

Input: 42 prey burn 78 21 melt gulp 96 83 head
Step I : ban 23 42 prey 78 melt gulp 96 83 head
Step II : gap 44 ban 23 prey 78 melt 96 83 head
Step III : had 80 gap 44 ban 23 prey melt 96 83
Step IV : mat 85 had 80 gap 44 ban 23 prey 96
Step V : pay 98 mat 85 had 80 gap 44 ban 23

Step V is the last step of the above arrangement as the intended output of arrangement is obtained.

As per the rules followed in the given steps, find the appropriate steps for the given input.

Input: 61 rust 33 colt 86 four torn 28 49 leap

24. Which of the following is the fourth to the left of the eighth element from the left end of step II?

A. cat B. far
C. 35 D. rust
E. 30

25. Which of the following represents the element that is fifth to the right of 'cat' in step III?

A. torn B. 63
C. lap D. far
E. 86

26. In step III, how many elements are there between '86' and the third element from the left end?

A. More than three B. One
C. Three D. None
E. Two

27. What is the difference between the third element from the right end in step V and the fifth element from the left end in step II?

A. 31 B. 55
C. 26 D. 5
E. 16

28. 'torn' is related to 'rust' in step I in the same way as 'lap' is related to 'tan' in step V. Following the same pattern to which element is '86' related to in step IV?

A. cat B. 51
C. 35 D. far
E. 30

29. The question consists of a statement followed by two courses of action numbered I and II given below it. A course of action is an administrative decision to be taken for improvement, follow-up or further action in regard to the problem, policy etc. You have to assume everything in the statement to be true and then decide which of the suggested courses of action logically follow(s) from the given statement.

Statement: Most of the people looking for buying/renting properties these days complain of being taken to the same property by more than 6-7 brokers. So, even after contracting multiple agents, they end up having usually the same options.

Courses of action :

I. All the owners should strictly give the responsibility of their properties to only one.

II. The brokers should be instructed to mandatorily disclose the list of all the properties they will be showing the customers on a particular day before taking them to the actual site.
A. Both I and II follow
B. Only II follows
C. Only I follows
D. Neither I nor II follows
E. Either I or II follows

Directions (Qs. Nos. 30-34) : *Study the following information to answer the given questions.*

In a certain code language,

'economy and work related' is written as 'oj my bx st'

'work and employment today' is written as 'pk bx oj dy'

'employment for growth only' is written as 'el pk fd zn'

'growth is related today' is written as 'el dy gm my'

(All codes are two letter codes only)

30. If the code for 'related people only' is 'Id my xd' then what may be the code for 'people for decision' in the given code language?
A. to xd my B. zn xd fd
C. zn xd dy D. zn kz xd
E. kz fd xd

31. What does the code 'pk' stand for in the given code language?
A. growth B. employment
C. only D. economy
E. today

32. What may be the code for 'economy is boosting' in the given code language?
A. gm rc st B. zn gm st
C. ye st el D. cp st rc
E. st bx gm

33. Which of the following additional statements is required to definitely find the code of 'and' in the given code language?
A. 'work and prosper now' is written as 'bx yp jn oj'
B. 'work today also important' is written as 'iv en oj dy'
C. No additional statement is required to find the code
D. 'and more work today' is written as 'z1 oj dy bx'
E. 'related only for employment' is written as 'mv zn fd pk'

34. What is the code for 'growth today' in the given code language?
A. fd el B. dy fd
C. pk dy D. dy el
E. an fd

Directions (Qs. Nos. 35-39) : *Study the following information carefully to answer the given question:*

Ten persons from different companies viz Samsung, Bata, Microsoft, Google, Apple, HCL, ITC, Reliance, Airtel and Vodafone are sitting in two parallel rows containing five people each, in such a way that there is an equal distance between adjacent persons. In row 1-B, C, D, E and F are seated and all of them are facing south. In row-2 R, S, T, U and V are seated and all of them are facing north. Therefore, in the given seating arrangement, each member seated in a row faces another member of the other row. (All the information given above does not the order of seating as in give the final arrangement.)

- There people sit between R and the person from Apple. The person from Reliance is an immediate neighbour of the one who faces the person from Apple. V sits to the immediate left of the one who faces the person from Reliance.
- Only one person sits between V and T. The person from Bata sits second to the right of the one who faces T. F sits second to the left of the person from Google. The person from Google does not sit at an extreme end of the line.
- Only two people sit between F and D. The person from Samsung faces an immediate neighbour of D. U is an immediate neighbour of the person from Microsoft. V is not from Microsoft. B sits second to the left of C.

- The person from ITC is an immediate neighbour of the person from Vodafone. Neither V nor F is from ITC. The person from ITC faces the person from HCL.

35. F is related to ITC in the same way as T is related to HCL, based on the given arrangement. To who amongst the following is D related to following the same pattern?
A. Microsoft B. Samsung
C. Apple D. Bata
E. Reliance

36. Which of the following is true regarding E?
A. E is from ITC.
B. E is an immediate neighbour of the person from Samsung.
C. E sits at an extreme end of the line.
D. The person from Airtel faces E.
E. None of the given options is true.

37. Who amongst the following sit at extreme end of the rows?
A. The person from Apple and F.
B. V, E
C. The person from Samsung and C.
D. The person from HCL and Bata
E. R and the person from Reliance.

38. Four of the following five are alike in a certain way based on the given arrangement and so form a group. Which is the one that does not belong to that group.
A. R B. V
C. C D. F
E. B

39. Who amongst the following faces the person from Airtel?
A. The person from Google
B. B
C. The person from Reliance
D. E
E. The person from Bata

40. Which of the following symbols should replace the question mark (?) in the given expression in order to make the expressions '$H < R$' as well as '$D \geq M$' definitely true ?
$D \geq I \geq H = S \ ? \ M < P \leq R$
A. $\geq$ B. $\leq$
C. $<$ D. $>$
E. $=$

41. T is the father of M and P. P is the only daughter of V. M is married to N. A and B are children of M. How is V related to B?
A. Grandmother B. Uncle
C. Aunt D. Sister
E. Grandfather

42. A severe cyclonic storm hit the Eastern coastline last month resulting in huge loss of life and property on the entire east coast and the Government had to disburse a considerable amount for relief activities through the district administration machineries.

Which of the following may possibly be a follow up measure to be taken by the Government?
A. The Government may set up a task force to review the post relief scenario in all districts and also to confirm proper end user receipt of the relief supplies.
B. The Government may set up a committee for proper disbursement' of relief supplies in future.
C. The Government may empower the District magistrates to make all future disbursements of relief.
D. The Government may send relief supplies to the affected, people in future only after proper assessment of the damage caused by such calamities.
E. The government may need not to activate any follow up measure.

Directions (Qs. Nos. 43-47) : *These questions consist of a question and two statements numbered I and II given below it. You have to decide whether the data provided in the statements are sufficient to answer the question. Read both the statements and mark the appropriate answer.*

Give answer:
A. The data even in both statements I and II together are not sufficient to answer the question.

B. The data in statement I alone are sufficient to answer the question while the data in statement II alone are not sufficient to answer the question.
C. The data either in statement I alone or in statement II alone are sufficient to answer the question.
D. The data in both statements I and II together are necessary to answer the question.
E. The data in statement II alone are sufficient to answer the question while the data in statement I are not sufficient to answer the question.

43. In a building, the ground floor is numbered one, first floor is numbered two and so on till the topmost floor is numbered five. Amongst five people—M, N, O, P and Q, each living on a different floor, but not necessarily in the same order, on which floor does Q live?
I. O lives on an odd numbered floor. M lives immediately below O. Only two people live between M and P. N lives neither immediately below M nor immediately below P.
II. N lives on an even numbered floor. Only two people live between N and O. Only one person lives between O and Q.

44. Among people A, B, C, D, E and F, each having a different height, who is the second shortest?
I. Only two people are taller than A. E is taller than both B and C. F is shorter than E. F is taller than C.
II. Only two people are shorter than D. A is taller than D but shorter than E. F is neither the tallest nor the shortest. B is taller than C.

45. How many people are standing between A and D (Note: All are standing in a straight line facing north)?
I. K stands second from the left end of the line. Only four people stand between K and T. Y is an immediate neighbour of T. A stands second to the right of Y. As many people stand between K and D as between A and D.
II. A stands second from the right end of the line. Z stands third from the left end of the line. D stands exactly in the centre of the line. As many people stand between A and T as between D and Z.

46. How far and in which direction is Point M from Point S?
I. Point E is 2 m to the east of Point S. Point B is 4 m to the south of Point E. Point L is 10 m to the east of Point B. Point L forms a midpoint of the vertical straight line of 8 m formed by joining points Q and D. Point M is 5 m to the west of Point Q.
II. Point M is 8 m to the north of Point A. Point M forms the midpoint of the horizontal straight line formed by joining points O and F. Point F is 8 m to the west of Point O. Point S is 4 m to the west of Point F.

47. Amongst six people—P, Q R, S, T and U standing around a circle, some facing the centre while some facing outside (*i.e.,* opposite to the centre) but not necessarily in the same order, what is the position of T with respect to U ?
I. P stands second to the right of R. R faces the centre. Q stands second to the left of P. Q is an immediate neighbour of both U and T. U and P face opposite directions (*i.e.,* if U faces the centre then P faces outside and vice-versa.) Only two people stand between P and T.
II. Only two people stand between R and U. P stands to the immediate left of U. P faces outside. R is an immediate neighbour of T.

Directions (Qs. Nos. 48-50) : In these questions, two/three statements followed by two conclusions numbered I and II are given. You have to take the given statements to be true even if they seem to be at variance from commonly known facts and then decide which of the given conclusions logically follows from the given statements disregarding commonly known facts.

Give answer:
A. If either conclusion I or II follows
B. If neither conclusion I nor II follows
C. If only conclusion II follows

D. If both conclusions I and II follow
E. If only conclusion I follows

48. Statements : Some coffee is tea. All tea is water. All water is milk.
Conclusions :
I. All coffee being water is a possibility.
II. All milk is tea.

49. Statements : No sea is a sky. Some skies are kites. All kites are balloons.
Conclusions :
I. Some balloons are seas.
II. All balloons being skies is a possibility.

50. Statements : Some stars are planets. Some planets are galaxies. Some galaxies are suns.
Conclusions :
I. All suns being galaxies is a possibility.
II. Some galaxies are stars.

QUANTITATIVE APTITUDE

51. A can complete a project in 20 days and B can complete the same project in 30 days. If A and B start working on the project together and A quits 10 days before the project is completed, in how many days will the project be completed?
A. 18 days
B. 27 days
C. 26.67 days
D. 16 days
E. 12 days

52. A runs 25% faster than B and is able to allow B a lead of 7 metres to end a race in dead heat. What is the length of the race?
A. 10 metres
B. 25 metres
C. 45 metres
D. 15 metres
E. 35 metres

53. A train travelling at 100 kmph overtakes a motorbike travelling at 64 kmph in 40 seconds. What is the length of the train in metres?
A. 1777 metres
B. 1822 metres
C. 400 metres
D. 1111 metres
E. 520 metres

Directions (Qs. Nos. 54-58): *Study the following graph and table to answer the given questions.*

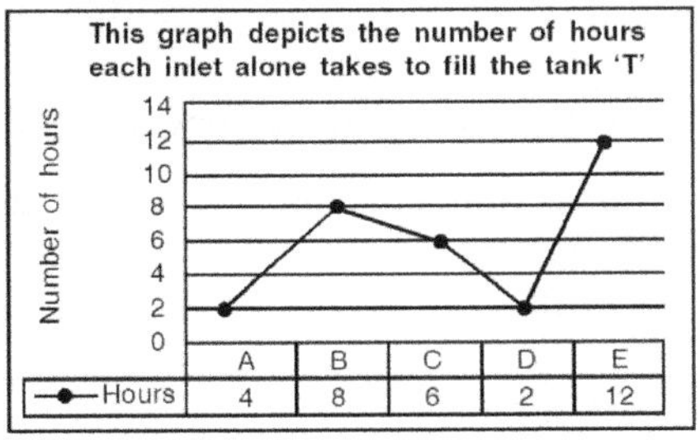

This table depicts the number of hours taken by each outlet alone to empty the full tank 'T'

Outlets	*Number of hours*
W	–
X	34
Y	–
Z	30

54. The time taken to fill the empty tank completely when inlet A and outlet X were opened together was 6 hours 40 minutes less than that taken by inlet B and outlet W together. How much time will outlet W alone take to completely empty the full tank? (in hours)
A. 26
B. 28
C. 20
D. 48
E. 24

55. When the tank was completely full, outlets X and Y were opened together for 8 hours 30 minutes. Both were then closed and inlet A was opened which filled the tank completely in 3 hours 30 minutes. In how much time (in hours) will outlet Y alone empty the full tank?
A. 15 hours
B. 13.6 hours
C. 13 hours
D. 14 hours
E. 15.5 hours

56. When the tank was completely full, outlets X and Z were opened together for 'H' hours. Had outlet Z been open alone, it would have taken 'H + 10' hours to empty the same quantity of water from the tank. What is the value of 'H'?

A. 10
B. 18
C. $11\frac{1}{3}$
D. $18\frac{1}{3}$
E. $10\frac{2}{3}$

57. Inlet E was open for 2 hours and then closed. If the remaining tank was filled by inlets B and C together, what was the total time (in hours) taken to fill the tank completely?

A. $5\frac{1}{7}$
B. $5\frac{4}{7}$
C. $4\frac{3}{7}$
D. $4\frac{6}{7}$
E. $5\frac{6}{7}$

58. When the tank was completely empty, inlets A, D and E were opened for one hour each and then closed. If after that outlet Z was opened, how much time (in hours) will it take to empty the tank completely?

A. $15\frac{2}{5}$
B. 18
C. 17
D. 20
E. 25

59. A boat running upstream takes 8 hours 48 minutes to cover a certain distance, while it takes 4 hours to cover the same distance running downstream. What is the ratio between the speed of the boat in still water and speed of the water current respectively?

A. 2 : 1
B. 3 : 2
C. 8 : 3
D. 3 : 5
E. 8 : 2

60. A, B and C jointly thought of engaging themselves in a business venture. It was agreed that A would invest ₹ 6,500 for 6 months, B, ₹ 8,400 for 5 months and C, ₹ 10,000 for 3 months. A wants to be the working member for which, he was to receive 5% of the profits. The profit earned was ₹ 7,400. What is the share of B in the profit?

A. ₹ 1,900
B. ₹ 2,660
C. ₹ 2,800
D. ₹ 2,840
E. ₹ 2,900

61. How much time will it take for an amount of ₹ 900 to yield ₹ 81 as interest at 4.5% per annum of simple interest?

A. 2 years
B. 3 years
C. 1 year
D. 4 years
E. 5 years

62. Mr. Thomas invested an amount of ₹ 13,900 divided in two different schemes A and B at the simple interest rate of 14% per annum and 11% per annum respectively. If the total amount of simple interest earned in 2 years be ₹ 3,508, what was the amount invested in scheme B?

A. ₹ 6,400
B. ₹ 7,200
C. ₹ 6,500
D. ₹ 7,500
E. ₹ 7,000

63. A bag contains 2 red, 3 green and 2 blue balls. Two balls are drawn at random. What is the probability that none of the balls drawn is blue?

A. $\frac{10}{21}$
B. $\frac{11}{21}$
C. $\frac{2}{7}$
D. $\frac{5}{7}$
E. $\frac{3}{7}$

64. A can contains a mixture of two liquids A and B in the ratio 7 : 5. When 9 litres of mixture is drawn off and the can is filled with B, the ratio of A and B becomes 7 : 9. How many litres of liquid A were contained by the can initially?

A. 10
B. 20
C. 21
D. 25
E. 29

65. A circular swimming pool is surrounded by a concrete wall 4 ft. wide. If the area of the concrete wall surrounding the pool is $\frac{11}{25}$ that of the pool, then the radius of the pool is:

A. 8 ft
B. 16 ft
C. 20 ft
D. 30 ft
E. None of these

Directions (Qs. Nos. 66-70): *In the given questions, two quantities are given, one as Quantity I and another as Quantity II. You have to determine relationship between two quantities and choose the appropriate option.*

A. If Quantity I ≥ Quantity II
B. If Quantity I > Quantity II
C. If Quantity I < Quantity II
D. If Quantity I = Quantity II or the relationship cannot be established from the information that is given.
E. If Quantity I ≤ Quantity II

66. The boat takes total time of 4 hours to travel 14 km upstream and 36 km downstream together. The boat takes total time of 5 hours to travel 20 km upstream and 24 km downstream together?

Quantity I : Speed of the boat in still water (in km/h).

Quantity II : 16 km/h.

67. M is an integer selected at random from the set.

(7, 14, 25, 27, 33, 29 and 30)

Quantity I : Probability that the average of 12, 9 and M is at least 17.

Quantity II : $\frac{1}{3}$.

68. $\left(\frac{x^2}{5}\right)+x+\left(\frac{4}{5}\right)=0$

$3y^2 + 4y + 1 = 0$

Quantity I : x

Quantity II : y

69. $mn \neq 0$

Quantity I : $m = n$

Quantity II : m/n.

70. A and B can together finish a piece of work in 20 days. If B starts working and after 15 days is replaced by A, A can finish the remaining work in 24 days.

Quantity I : Number of days taken by B alone to finish the same piece of work.

Quantity II : Number of days taken by A alone to finish the same piece of work.

Directions (Qs. Nos. 71-75): *Study the given information carefully and answer the given questions.*

The revenue of a given railway zone was collected from 4 primary sources—Offline Ticket Sales, Online Ticket Sales, Freight, Fines–during 3 Financial Years (FY 2013-14, FY 2014-15, FY 2015-16).

FY 2013-14 : Total revenue collected was ₹ 3,500 crore. Fines (₹ x crore) comprised $7\frac{6}{7}\%$ of the total revenue and revenue from online ticket sales was ₹ 'x + 300' crore. Revenue from freight was 12% more than that from offline ticket sales.

FY 2014-15 : Revenue from online ticket sales increased by ₹ 25 crore over FY 2013-14. Revenue from Offline ticket sales was 40% of the total revenue in FY 2014-15. Revenue from Freight and Fines was in the respective ratio of 5 : 1.

FY 2015-16 : Revenue from fines in FY 2013-14 was $\frac{11}{16}$th of that in FY 2015-16. Revenue from online ticket sales increased by 50% over that in FY 2014-15 and that from offline ticket sales was the average of that in FY 2013-14 and 2014-15. Revenue from freight has been and will continue to increase steadily by ₹ 250 crore every financial year.

71. Revenue from fines comprised two sources—vendors and passengers. Fines from passengers (₹ y crore) remained constant in FY 2013-14 and FY 2014-15. If the fine from vendors in FY 2013-14 was 55% of that in FY 2014-15, what was the value of y?

A. 180 B. 200
C. 218 D. 208
E. 220

72. If the railway profit in FY 2014-15 was 12.5% of the total expense, what was the total expense for FY 2014-15? (in ₹ crore)
A. 2900 B. 2400
C. 3200 D. 3000
E. 3822

73. In FY 2017-18, if the revenue from fines increases by 20% over FY 2015-16, what would be the ratio between the revenues from fines and freight in FY 2017-18?
A. 2 : 3 B. 1 : 5
C. 2 : 5 D. 3 : 4
E. 4 : 5

74. If the average revenue from online ticket sales in FY 2014-15, FY 2015-16 and FY 2016-17 was ₹ 1150 crore, by what per cent did the revenue from online ticket sales increase in FY 2016-17 as compared to that in 2014-15?
A. 250 B. 150
C. 300 D. 225
E. 230

75. If the average cost of a railway ticket was ₹ 300 in FY 2014-15, how many passengers (approx) travelled by railways in FY 2014-15? (in ₹ crore)
A. 4.8 B. 6.4
C. 6.2 D. 5.4
E. 7.73

Directions (Qs. Nos. 76-80): *Refer to the pie-charts to answer the given questions.*

Data regarding five villages—A, B, C, D and E—in a district in 2015.

Total village population = 18000

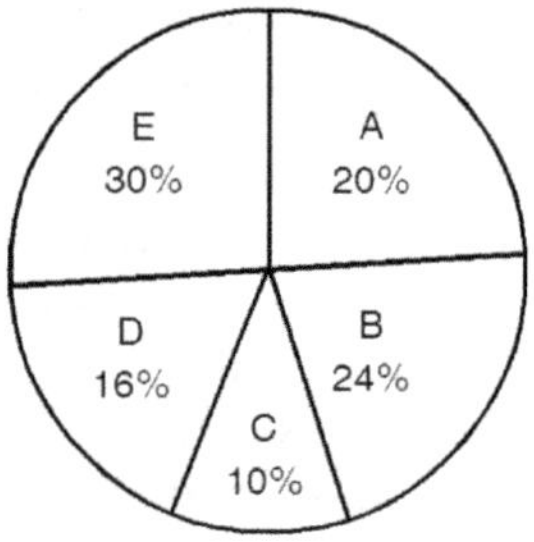

Total number of illiterates = 40% of Total village population

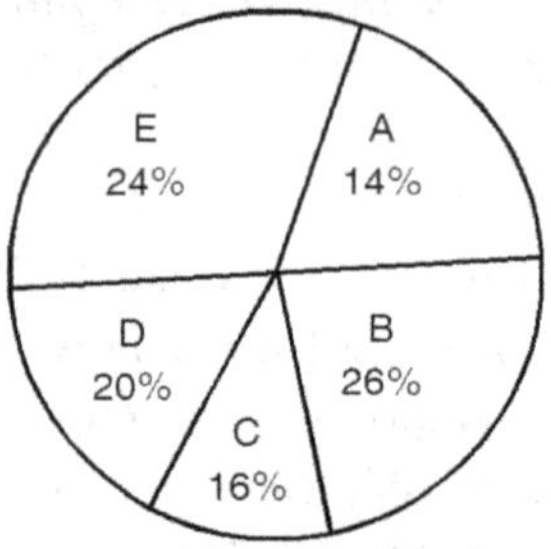

Total village population = Number of literates + Number of illiterates

76. In 2017, the population of village C remained the same as that in 2015, but the number of literates increased by 'x'. As a result, the total number of literates became 70% of that of illiterates. What is the approximate value of 'x'?
A. 620 B. 440
C. 680 D. 485
E. 430

77. The difference between the number of illiterates in villages D and E is approximately what per cent of that of literates in villages D and E?
A. 30% B. 20%
C. 35% D. 13%
E. 15%

78. In village D, the male to female ratio among the illiterates is 5 : 3 respectively. Out of the illiterates, if 'x' females and '$1.25x$' males work as farmers and the ratio between males and females who do not work as farmers is 5 : 2 respectively, what is the value of 'x'?
A. 240 B. 300
C. 360 D. 380
E. 280

79. The average number of illiterates in villages D, F and G is 1910. 40% and 30% of the population of villages F and G respectively are illiterates. If the ratio of the population of villages F and G is 4 : 5 respectively, what is the total population of villages F and G together?
A. 10000 B. 12000
C. 12456 D. 13000
E. 14000

80. In village A, if the respective ratio between number of males and females is 17 : 13 and there are 1000 male literates, what is the number of male illiterates in village A?
A. 480 B. 540
C. 940 D. 1040
E. 1140

Directions (Qs. Nos. 81-85) : *In this question, a number series is given. Only one number is wrong which doesn't fit in the series. Find out the wrong number?*

81. 6 4 5 8.5 18 48 139
A. 8.5 B. 4
C. 5 D. 18
E. 48

82. 10080 1440 240 48 12 3 2
A. 240 B. 3
C. 1440 D. 48
E. 12

83. 1 2 6 21 88 505 2676
A. 21 B. 6
C. 2 D. 505
E. 88

84. 18 21 25 35 52 78 115
A. 25 B. 21
C. 28 D. 35
E. 52

85. 120 137 178 222 290 375 477
A. 178 B. 137
C. 290 D. 375
E. 222

86. Area of a rectangle is 150 metre sq. When the breadth of the same rectangle is increased by 2 meter and the length decreased by 5 metre, the area of the rectangle decreases by 30 metre square. What is the perimeter of the square whose sides are equal to the length of the rectangle?
A. 76 m B. 72 m
C. 120 m D. 80 m
E. 60 m

87. A, B and C started a business with investments of ₹ 4200, ₹ 3600 and ₹ 2400 respectively. After 4 months from the start of the business, A invested ₹ 1000 more. After 6 months from the start of the business, B and C invested additional amounts in the respective ratio of 1 : 2. If at the end of 10 months they received a profit of ₹ 2820 and it's share in the profit was ₹ 1200, What was the additional amount that B invested?
A. ₹ 800 B. ₹ 200
C. ₹ 500 D. ₹ 600
E. ₹ 400

88. A vessel contains a mixture of milk and water in the respective ratio of 5 : 1. 24 litres of mixture was taken out and replaced with the same quantity of milk so that the resultant ratio between the quantities of milk and water in the mixture was 13 : 2 respectively. If 15 litres of the mixture is again taken out from the vessel, what is the resultant quantity of milk in the mixture? (in litres)
A. 97 B. 89
C. 91 D. 99
E. 84

Directions (Qs. Nos. 89-93) : *Refer to the table and answer the given question.* Data related to performance of 6 batsmen in a tournament:

Name of the batsman	Number of matches played in the tournament	Average runs scored in the tournament	Total balls faced in the tournament	Strike rate
A	8	-	-	129.6
B	20	81	-	-
C	-	38	400	114
D	-	-	-	72
E	28	55	1280	-
F	-	-	-	66

Note:

(*i*) Strike rate = (Total runs scored/Total balls faced) * 100

(*ii*) All the given batsmen could bat in all the given matches played by them.

(*iii*) Few values are missing in the table (indicated by –). A candidate is expected to calculate the missing value, if it is required to answer the given question, on the basis of the given data and information.

89. The respective ratio between total number of balls faced by D and that by F in the tournament is 3 : 4. Total number of runs scored by F in the tournament is what per cent more than the total runs scored by D in the tournament?

A. $22\frac{2}{9}$ B. $32\frac{4}{9}$

C. $18\frac{8}{9}$ D. $24\frac{4}{9}$

E. $28\frac{2}{9}$

90. If the runs scored by E in last 3 matches of the tournament are not considered, his average runs scored in the tournament will decrease by 9. If the runs scored by E in the 26th and 27th match are below 128 and no two scores among these 3 scores are equal, what are the minimum possible runs scored by E in the 28th match?

A. 137 B. 135

C. 141 D. 133

E. 139

91. In the tournament, the total number of balls faced by batsman A is 74 less than the total number of runs scored by him. What is the average run scored by batsman A in the tournament?

A. 42.5 B. 39.5

C. 38 D. 44

E. 40.5

92. Batsman B faced equal number of balls in first 10 matches he played in the tournament and last 10 matches he played in the tournament. If his strike rate in first 10 matches and last 10 matches of the tournament are 120 and 158 respectively, what is the total number of balls faced by him in the tournament?

A. 1150 B. 1400

C. 1200 D. 1000

E. 1500

93. What is the number of matches played by batsman C in the tournament?

A. 10 B. 16

C. 12 D. 18

E. 8

94. 10 men can complete a project in 12 days, 12 children can complete the same project in 16 days and 8 women can complete the same project in 20 days. 5 men and 12 children started working on the project. If after 4 days, 8 children were replaced by 4 women. In how many days the remaining project was completed?

A. $4\frac{2}{5}$ B. $5\frac{1}{2}$

C. $7\frac{1}{2}$ D. $3\frac{5}{9}$

E. $6\frac{2}{3}$

95. In a village, 60% registered voters cast their votes in the election. Only two candidates (A & B) were contesting the election. A won the election by 600 votes. Had B received 40% more votes, the result would have been a tie. How many registered voters are there in the village?

A. 4000 B. 3500

C. 3000 D. 3250

E. 3750

96. Eight years ago, Poorvi's age was equal to the sum of the present ages of her one son and one daughter. Five years hence, the respective ratio between the ages of her daughter and her son that time will be 7 : 6. If Poorvi's husband is 7 years elder to her and his present age is three times the present age of their son, what is the present age of the daughter? (in years)

A. 15 years
B. 23 years
C. 19 years
D. 27 years
E. 13 years

97. Boat A travels downstream from Point X to Point Y in 3 hours less than the time taken by Boat B to travel upstream from Point Y to Point Z. The distance between X and Y is 20 km, which is half of the distance between Y and Z. The speed of Boat B in still water is 10 km/h and the speed of Boat A in still water is equal to the speed of Boat B upstream. What is the speed of Boat A in still water? Consider the speed of the current to be the same?

A. 10 km/h
B. 16 km/h
C. 12 km/h
D. 8 km/h
E. 15 km/h

Directions (Qs. Nos. 98-100) : *Study the following information carefully and answer the given question.*

Data regarding number of applications received for various courses in University A and that in University B in the year 2001.

(Note : Universities A and B offer courses in six courses only, namely, Commerce, Science, Engineering, Arts, Management and Law.)

- In University A, applications received for Commerce, Science and Engineering together constituted 70% of the total number of applications received (for all the given courses together). Applications received for Arts, Management and Law were 800, 750 and 400 respectively. Applications received for management were 40% less than that for engineering. Applications received for Commerce were 20% more than that for Science.
- In University B, applications received for Science were 20% less than that for Science in University A.
- In University B, applications received for Arts were 780 and they constituted 15% of the total number of applications received (for all the given courses together). Also the applications received for arts were 40% less than that received for Commerce. Total number of applications received for engineering and management together, were double the total number of applications received for arts and law together. Applications received for engineering were equal to that for management.

98. What is the respective ratio between the total number of applications received for Engineering and Science together in University A and that for the same courses together in University B?

A. 50 : 47
B. 65 : 53
C. 52 : 37
D. 55 : 42
E. 43 : 36

99. Number of applications received for only Commerce in University B is what per cent less than that in University A?

A. 30
B. $27\frac{7}{9}$
C. 20
D. 15
E. $15\frac{5}{8}$

100. $\frac{5}{8}$th of the number of applications for Arts in University A were by female students. If the number of female applicants for the same course in University B is less than that in University A by 120, what is the number of male applications for Arts in University B?

A. 500
B. 420
C. 450
D. 360
E. 400

GENERAL ENGLISH

Directions (Qs. Nos. 101-110) : *Read the following passage carefully and answer the questions based on it. Some words have been printed in* ***bold*** *to help you locate them while answering some of the questions.*

Gross Domestic Savings (GDS) play a vital role in the economic growth of a country since it facilitates to provide requisite financial resources to undertake various developmental and welfare programs. A high level of savings helps the economy to progress on a continuous growth path as investment is mainly financed out of savings. GDS is one of the important economic indicators to measure financial regulation and soundness of the country. Absence of required savings rate may lead to external dependence, which may **jeopardize** the interests of the Nation.

Savings habit is an in-built culture of the Indian system and it has been growing consistently over the years. The GDS percentage to GDP has shown considerable improvement from 10% in 1950 to 33.70% in 2010, which is one of the highest globally. It is interesting to note that while the share of corporate sector increased from 10% to 24% during 1950 to 2010, the share of public sector has come down to 6% from 18% during the said period. The buoyancy of corporate sector in post reform era could be one of the reasons for increased share of corporates in GDS. While there is increasing trend in saving rate, marginal decline is observed under household sector *i.e.,* 72% to 70%.

Notwithstanding the fact that the share of household savings to GDS is showing decline, still this segment is the significant contributor to GDS with 70% share. Indian households are among the most frugal in the world. However, **commensurate** capital formation has not been taking place as a lion's share of household savings are being parked in physical assets compared to financial assets.

The pattern of disposition of saving is an important factor in determining how the saved amount is utilized for productive purposes. The proportion of household saving in financial assets determines the channelisation of saving for investment in other sectors of the economy. However, the volume of investment of saving in physical assets determines the productivity and generation of income in that sector itself.

Post independence era has witnessed a significant shift in deployment of household savings especially the share of financial assets increased from 26.39% in 1950 to 54.05% in 1990 may be on account of increased bank branch network across the country coupled with improved awareness of investors on various financial/banking products. However, contrast to common expectations, the share of financial assets in total household savings has come down from 54.05% to 50.21% especially in post-reform period *i.e.,* 1990 to 2010 despite providing easy access and availability of banking facilities compared to earlier years. The increased share of physical assets over financial assets (around 4%) during the last two decades is a cause of concern requires focused attention to arrest the trend.

Traditionally, the Indians are risk-averse and prefer to invest surplus funds in physical assets such as Gold, Silver and lands. Nevertheless, considerable share of savings also flowing to financial assets, which includes, Currency, Bank Deposits, Claims on Government, **Contractual** Savings, Equities.

The composition of household financial savings shows that the bank deposits (44%) continue to remain the major contributor along with the rise in the Contractual Savings, Claims on Government and Currency.

Though there was gradual decline in currency holdings by the households *i.e.,* 13.79% in 1970s to 9.30% in 2007, still the present currency holding level with households appears to be on high side compared to other countries. The primary reasons for higher currency holdings could be absence of banking facilities in majority villages (5.70 lakh villages) as well as hoarding of unaccounted money in the form of cash to circumvent tax laws. Though, cash is treated as financial asset, in reality, a major portion of currency is blocked and become unproductive.

Bank deposits seemed to be the preferred choice mainly on account of its inbuilt features such as Safety, Security and Liquidity. Traditionally, the Household sector has been playing a leading role in the landscape of bank deposits followed by the Government sector. However, the last two decades has witnessed significant shift in ownership of Bank deposits. While there was improvement in Corporate and Government sectors' share by 8.30% and 7.20% respectively during the period 1999 to 2009, household sector lost a share of 13.30% in the post reform period.

In the post-independence era, Indian financial system was characterized by poor infrastructure and low level of financial deepening. Savings in physical assets constituted the largest portion of the savings compared to the financial assets in the initial years of the planning periods. While rural households were keen on acquiring farm assets, the portfolio of urban households constituted consumer durables, gold, jewellry and house property.

Despite the fact that the household savings have been gradually moving from physical assets to financial assets over the years, still 49.79% of household savings are wrapped in unproductive physical assets, which is a cause of concern as the share of physical assets to total savings are very high in the recent years compared to emerging economies. This trend needs to be arrested as scarce funds are being diverted into unproductive segments.

Of course, investment in Real estate sector can be treated as productive provided construction activity is commenced within reasonable time, but it is regrettably note that many investors just buy and hold it for speculation leading to unproductive investments.

India has probably the largest fascination with gold than any other country in the world with a share of 9.50% of the world's total gold holdings. The World Gold Council believes that they are over 18000 tonnes of gold holding in the country. More impressive is the fact that current demand from India alone consumes 25% of the world's annual gold output. Large amount of capital is blocked in gold which resides in bank lockers and remain unproductive.

Indian economy would grow faster if the capital markets could attract more of the nation's savings and channel them into more productive areas, especially infrastructure. If the Indian market can develop and evolve into a more mature financial system, which persuades the middle class to put more of its money into equities, the potential is **mind-boggling.**

101. Which of the following statement (s) is/are correct tn the context of the given passage?

I. The GDS percentage GDP has shown considerable improvement from 10% in 1950 to 33.7% in 2010. which is one of the highest globally.

II. The saving rate however shows an increasing trend, marginal decline is observed under household sector.

III. The share of financial assets in total household savings have come down from 54.05% to 50.21% especially in post-reform era.

A. Only I
B. Only I and II
C. Only II and III
D. All I, II and III
E. None of these

102. Post-independence era has witnessed a significant shift in deployment of household savings especially the share of financial assets increased to 54.05% in 1990. Which of the following is/are supposed to be the prime cause of this shift?

A. It is due to bank branch network across the country
B. Government has made arrangements to aware the people
C. It is due to increase in bank branch network and awareness among investors on various banking products
D. Indian economy is growing at 8% and people are saving more than earlier
E. None of these

103. India has probably the largest fascination with gold than any other country in the world. Which of the following is incorrect in regard to this fascination as mentioned in the passage?
A. India shares 9.50% of the total gold holdings
B. According to the World Gold Council estimates, there are over 18000 tonnes of gold holding in India
C. The current demand from India alone consumes 25% of the world's annual gold output
D. A small amount of capital is blocked in gold in banks but is however productive
E. None of these

104. Which of the following are the primary reasons, cited in the passage, for higher currency holdings?
A. It is due to large banking network that stashes money.
B. It is due to absence of banking facilities in majority of villages and tendency to circumvent tax laws for unaccounted money.
C. People do not believe in banks and fear that government may take their money.
D. There is lack of awareness among people about savings in banks
E. None of these

105. Despite the fact that the household savings have been gradually moving from physical assets to financial assets over the years. What percentage of household savings is wrapped in unproductive physical assets?
A. 45% B. 46.79%
C. 58% D. 49.79%
E. None of these

106. Which of the following should be a suitable title of the passage?
A. Importance of Gross Domestic Savings
B. Growth of Indian economy
C. Fascination for Gold
D. Physical assets versus financial assets
E. None of these

Directions (Qs. Nos. 107 and 108) : *Choose the word/group of words which is* ***most nearly the same*** *in meaning to the word/group of words printed in bold.*

107. Contractual
A. promising B. agreeing
C. promissory D. agreeable
E. concord

108. Commensurate
A. matching B. commensal
C. commemorative D. unmatching
E. comfortable

Directions (Qs. Nos. 109 and 110) : *Choose the word(s) which is* ***most opposite*** *in meaning of the word printed in bold, as used in the passage.*

109. Jeopardize
A. severe B. endanger
C. saddle D. safeguard
E. saturate

110. Mind-bogging
A. conscious B. inclined
C. very difficult D. surprising
E. unsurprising

Directions (Qs. Nos. 111-115) : *In the following questions, a passage is given with a blank space in the beginning. Three statements are given following the passage. You are required to select which of the statement(s) may be the starter?*

111. .... It is so pleasant a profession that it is not surprising if a vast number of persons adopt it who have no qualifications for it. The writer is free to work in what he believes.
I. I am a writer.
II. I am a writer as I might have been a doctor or a lawyer.
III. I was a writer as I might have been a doctor.
A. Only I B. Only II
C. Only III D. Both I & II
E. Both II & III

112. .... It grew faster in year 2010. The conditions were favourable which helped in economic boom. The agriculture, tourism, export and mining helped in the growth of the economy.

I. Indian economy is not growing well.
II. The Indian economy grew fast as 10 per cent in 2008.
III. Due to economic reforms, economic growth of India was 8 per cent in 2009.

A. Only I B. Only II
C. Only III D. Both I & II
E. Both II & III

113. .... So, Anti Corruption campaign occupied centre stage during election season. Corruption prevailing in the high and mighty adversely impacts our nation and its global image.

I. Corruption is a big evil in India.
II. Corruption is not a big evil in India as propagated.
III. Anti corruption is a big challenge in India.

A. Only I B. Only II
C. Only III D. Both I & II
E. Both II & III

114. .... Roads are unsafe because of shortcomings in road and traffic engineer, old and non standard codes of traffic control devices, poor driver training and assessment, out dated legislations and a poor enforcement system.

I. Road safety is not a stand-along phenomenon.
II. Indian roads are unsafe not due to a single factor.
III. Road safety is a stand-along phenomenon.

A. Only I B. Only II
C. Only III D. Both I & II
E. Both II & III

115. .... Such an initiative was long overdue. India has been characterized as one of the most over regulated countries in the world. No central data base of all laws and regulations exists in the country.

I. The government was considering to prepare database.
II. The government is considering to prepare a database of all laws and regulations.
III. The government has considered to prepare a database.

A. Only I B. Only II
C. Only III D. Both I & II
E. Both II & III

Directions (Qs. Nos. 116-120) : *Rearrange the following six sentences (a), (b), (c), (d), (e) and (f) in the proper sequence to form a meaningful para-graph; then answer the questions given below them.*

(*a*) Arctic sea ice has been melting at break-neck speeds in the past few decades, driven by warming air temperature, warming air temperature, warming ocean water temperature, all of which are caused by or accelerated by man-made climate change.
(*b*) But there are other factors at play in the decline of ice in the Arctic Ocean.
(*c*) Sea ice is generally moderated by sunlight.
(*d*) Warm ocean currents travel north from the equator and usher in warmer and warmer water, making sea ice growth difficult.
(*e*) It grows in the winter and melts in the summer.
(*f*) Weather patterns over the high mid-latitudes and the Arctic can also affect sea ice growth.

116. Which of the following should be the **fourth** sentence after rearrangement?

A. (*e*) B. (*d*)
C. (*c*) D. (*b*)
E. (*a*)

117. Which of the following should be the **sixth** sentence after rearrangement?

A. (*a*) B. (*b*)
C. (*c*) D. (*d*)
E. (*e*)

118. Which of the following should be the **Second** sentence afer rearrangement?

A. (*e*) B. (*d*)
C. (*c*) D. (*b*)
E. (*a*)

119. Which of the following should be the **first** sentence afer rearrangement?

A. (*a*) B. (*b*)
C. (*c*) D. (*d*)
E. (*e*)

120. Which of the following should be the **third** sentence afer rearrangement?
A. (*a*) B. (*b*)
C. (*c*) D. (*d*)
E. (*f*)

Directions (Qs. Nos. 121-130) : *In the following passage there are blanks, each of which has been numbered. These numbers are printed below the passage and against each, five words are suggested, one of which fits the blank appropriately. Find out the appropriate word in each case.*

The rise of Asian manufacturers in the 1990s hit African firms hard; many were wiped out Northern Nigeria, which once had a **...(121)...** garments industry, was unable to **...(122)...** with low cost imports. South Africa has similar problems; its manufacturing failed to grow last year **...(123)...** the continental boom.

This is partly the **...(124)...** of governments. Buoyed by commodity income, they have neglected industry's needs, **...(125)...** for roads and electricity. But that, too, may at last be changing. Wolfgang Fengler, a World Bank economist says, "Africa is now in a good position to industrialise with the right mix of ingredients." This includes **...(126)...** demography, urbanisation, an emerging middle class and strong services. "For this to happen," he adds, "the continent will need to scale up its infrastructure **...(127)...** and improve the business climate and many [African] countries have started to **...(128)...** these challenges in recent years."

Kenya is not about to become **...(129)...** next South Korea. African countries are likely to follow a more diverse path, benefiting from the growth of countless small and medium-sized businesses, as well as some big ones. For the next decade or so, services will still generate more jobs and wealth in Africa than manufacturing, which is fine. India has **...(130)...** for more than two decades on the back of services, while steadily building a manufacturing sector from a very low base. Do not bet against Africa doing the same.

121. A. thriving B. flourish
C. detractive D. dooming
E. repulsive

122. A. competed B. compete
C. complete D. surrender
E. commensurate

123. A. inspite B. additional
C. in addition D. despite
E. despite of

124. A. fact B. quality
C. fault D. default
E. fiction

125. A. specific B. especially
C. particular D. partially
E. generally

126. A. favourable B. favourably
C. ferrocious D. special
E. contrast

127. A. expenditures B. disinvestment
C. investments D. development
E. developing

128. A. tackle B. tackling
C. decrease D. increase
E. improve

129. A. a B. an
C. the D. such
E. for

130. A. boomed B. booming
C. boom D. expand
E. plummeted

Directions (Qs. Nos. 131-135) : *In each of the question below, a sentence is broken into four parts. One of them may be grammatically or structurally wrong in the context of the sentence. The letter of that word is answer. If there is no wrong word or group of words, year answer will be "No error".*

131. Birthmarks on the back/could be signs of Tethered Spinal Cord Syndrome (TCS)/a neurological disorder/caused by tissue attachments.
A. Birthmarks on the back
B. could be signs of Tethered Spinal Cord Syndrome (TCS)

C. a neurological disorder
D. caused by tissue attachments
E. No error

132. As a part of the new survey,/if you says you are/unhappy, the city police may/call to ask you that reason.
A. As a part of the new survey,
B. if you says you are
C. unhappy, the city police may
D. call to ask you that reason.
E. No error

133. By keeping the brain/engaged, anyone can/become learn to/control immediate cravings.
A. By keeping the brain
B. engaged, anyone can
C. become learn to
D. control immediate cravings.
E. No error

134. Foodies have realised/that there is more to eating out/than switch restaurants that has/predictable menus and sterile decors.
A. Foodies have realised
B. that there is more to eating out
C. than switch restaurants that has
D. predictable menus and sterile decors.
E. No error

135. The doctors are been worried/that the ace cricketer will/suffer from a heart ailment/for the rest of his life.
A. The doctors are been worried
B. that the ace cricketer will
C. suffer from a heart ailment
D. for the rest of his life.
E. No error

Directions (Qs. Nos. 136-140) : *Rearrange the following seven sentences (a), (b), (c), (d), (e), (f) and (g) in the proper sequence to form a meaningful paragraph, then answer the given question.*

(*a*) These companies have long seen the US market as the scene of a battle for distribution, where they must secure placement for their products in the fastest growing retail channels just to maintain their share of a pie that's not getting bigger.
(*b*) Companies can thus generate above-average growth in the United States by not only taking market share from competitors, but also making targeted investments in these specific product categories.
(*c*) Somewhat surprisingly, a number of cities in developed markets, including the United States and Western Europe, are growing as rapidly as those in emerging markets.
(*d*) Our analysis forecasts that between 2014 and 2025, certain product categories will grow at almost twice the rate of overall US consumer spending.
(*e*) But this no-growth, or, at best, low-growth, picture isn't entirely accurate.
(*f*) Most CPG companies have had very low expectations for growth in the US market.
(*g*) Companies that ignore these cities could be missing out on opportunities, very close to home.

136. Which of the following should be the SECOND sentence after the rearrangement?
A. (*g*) B. (*a*)
C. (*e*) D. (*b*)
E. (*c*)

137. Which of the following should be the FIRST sentence after the rearrangement?
A. (*a*) B. (*b*)
C. (*f*) D. (*d*)
E. (*g*)

138. Which of the following should be the FOURTH sentence after the rearrangement?
A. (*g*) B. (*f*)
C. (*e*) D. (*d*)
E. (*c*)

139. Which of the following should be the THIRD sentence after the rearrangement?
A. (*a*) B. (*b*)
C. (*c*) D. (*d*)
E. (*e*)

140. Which of the following should be the LAST (SEVENTH) sentence after the rearrangement?
A. (*b*) B. (*g*)
C. (*d*) D. (*c*)
E. (*f*)

Directions (Qs. Nos. 141-150) : *In the following passage, there are blanks, each of which has been numbered. Against each, five words are suggested, one of which fits the blank appropriately. Find out the appropriate word in each case.*

Poverty is a perception–it is a status which is **...(141)...** on people who have relatively little-even in societies of plenty. That is why we **...(142)...** can never really ever "end" poverty. To see a world in which so many people have less than you and to want them to have more is, to many of us, human **...(143)....** It is why poverty in the UK matters as much as poverty elsewhere, despite the material differences. Relative poverty will always **...(144)...** and it should always be at the forefront of efforts to improve our world because it **...(145)...** more than the bare minimum solution. **...(146)...** this, the aid industry currently has quite a few eggs in the end poverty basket. We risk assuming that the public **...(147)...** between absolute and relative poverty. It probably doesn't especially not in austere times. Just look at the **...(148)...** political view on and to the middle income countries that contain hundreds of millions of desperately poor people. Too much negatively and we are **...(149)...** of not making any progress with aid money, too much task of progress and aid is no longer necessary. It shouldn't be a Catch 22 situation but in **...(150)...,** for some, it is.

141. A. subjected B. apprehended C. bestowed D. lifted E. labelled

142. A. spritely B. objectionably C. fatally D. continually E. probably

143. A. problem B. nature C. face D. being E. population

144. A. remainder B. leave C. allow D. exist E. touch

145. A. seek B. asks C. insists D. ensure E. demands

146. A. Along B. Added C. Despite D. Favouring E. Siding

147. A. understands B. distinguishes C. grasps D. separates E. draws

148. A. prevailing B. currently C. aimed D. lost E. multiple

149. A. accused B. alleged C. suspicion D. remarked E. stationed

150. A. actual B. now C. place D. reality E. form

ANSWERS

1	2	3	4	5	6	7	8	9	10
D	D	C	C	C	E	E	E	E	A
11	**12**	**13**	**14**	**15**	**16**	**17**	**18**	**19**	**20**
E	A	C	B	C	D	A	A	E	C
21	**22**	**23**	**24**	**25**	**26**	**27**	**28**	**29**	**30**
C	C	C	E	A	A	C	D	A	D
31	**32**	**33**	**34**	**35**	**36**	**37**	**38**	**39**	**40**
B	A	B	D	B	E	A	D	A	E
41	**42**	**43**	**44**	**45**	**46**	**47**	**48**	**49**	**50**
A	B	C	A	E	E	D	E	C	E

51	**52**	**53**	**54**	**55**	**56**	**57**	**58**	**59**	**60**
A	E	C	B	B	C	D	E	C	B
61	**62**	**63**	**64**	**65**	**66**	**67**	**68**	**69**	**70**
A	A	A	C	C	B	C	E	D	B
71	**72**	**73**	**74**	**75**	**76**	**77**	**78**	**79**	**80**
D	E	C	D	E	D	D	C	C	D
81	**82**	**83**	**84**	**85**	**86**	**87**	**88**	**89**	**90**
E	B	D	B	A	E	E	C	A	A
91	**92**	**93**	**94**	**95**	**96**	**97**	**98**	**99**	**100**
E	A	C	E	C	B	D	D	B	E
101	**102**	**103**	**104**	**105**	**106**	**107**	**108**	**109**	**110**
D	C	D	B	D	A	C	A	D	E
111	**112**	**113**	**114**	**115**	**116**	**117**	**118**	**119**	**120**
D	E	A	D	B	B	A	A	C	B
121	**122**	**123**	**124**	**125**	**126**	**127**	**128**	**129**	**130**
A	B	D	C	B	A	C	A	C	A
131	**132**	**133**	**134**	**135**	**136**	**137**	**138**	**139**	**140**
B	B	C	C	A	C	C	A	C	A
141	**142**	**143**	**144**	**145**	**146**	**147**	**148**	**149**	**150**
E	E	B	D	E	C	B	A	A	D

EXPLANATORY ANSWERS

51. Let the work be finished in x days

Then A's $(x - 10)$ day's work + B's x day's work = 1

$$\frac{x-10}{20}+\frac{x}{30} = 1$$

$$\Rightarrow \quad \frac{3(x-10)+2x}{60} = 1$$

$$\Rightarrow \quad 3x - 30 + 2x = 60$$

$$\Rightarrow \quad 5x = 90 \Rightarrow x = 18$$

Hence, the project will be completed in 18 days.

52. Let B runs 100 m then A runs 125 m

$$\text{Ratio of speed} = \frac{125}{100} = \frac{5}{4}$$

$$\text{Length of the race} = \frac{7\times 1}{\left(1-\frac{4}{5}\right)} = 7 \times 5 = 35 \text{ m}$$

53. Let length of the train = x m

Relative speed = (100 – 64) = 36 km/hr

$$= 36\times\frac{5}{18}\text{ m/s} = 10 \text{ m/s}$$

length of the train = speed × time

= 10 × 40 = 400 m.

54. $$\text{A's 1 hour work} = \frac{1}{4}$$

$$\text{X's 1 hour work} = \frac{1}{34}$$

(A + X)'s 1 hour work

$$= \frac{1}{4}-\frac{1}{34}=\frac{17-2}{68}=\frac{15}{68}$$

$\therefore$ Tank will fill in $\frac{68}{15}$ hours

Now, B's 1 hour work = $\frac{1}{8}$

W's 1 hour work = $\frac{1}{x}$

(B + W)'s 1 hour work = $\frac{1}{8}-\frac{1}{x}=\frac{x-8}{8x}$

$\therefore$ Tank will fill in $\frac{8x}{x-8}$ hours

But $\frac{8x}{x-8} = \frac{68}{15}+\frac{20}{3}$

$\Rightarrow \frac{8x}{x-8} = \frac{68+100}{15}=\frac{168}{15}=\frac{56}{5}$

$\Rightarrow 56x - 448 = 40x$

$\Rightarrow 56x - 40x = 448$

$\Rightarrow 16x = 448$

$\Rightarrow x = \frac{448}{16} = 28$

Hence, outlet W alone empty the full tank in 28 hours.

55. A's 1 hour work = $\frac{1}{4}$

A's $\frac{1}{2}$ hour work = $\frac{1}{4\times 2}=\frac{1}{8}$ part

$1-\frac{1}{8} = \frac{7}{8}$ part

$\because \frac{7}{8}$ part empty $(x + w)$ in $\frac{17}{2}$ hours

$\therefore$ 1 part can empty = $\frac{7}{8}\times\frac{2}{17}=\frac{7}{68}$ hours

$\therefore$ y can alone empty 1 part

$= \frac{7}{68}-\frac{1}{34}=\frac{7-2}{68}=\frac{5}{68}$

Hence, y can alone empty full tank in $\frac{68}{5}$ hours

$= 13\frac{3}{5}$ hours = 13.6 hours.

56. (X + Z)'s 1 hour work

$= \frac{1}{34}+\frac{1}{30}=\frac{15+17}{510}=\frac{32}{510}$

(X + Z)'s H hour work = $\frac{32\text{H}}{510}$

Z's 1 hour work = $\frac{1}{30}$

Z's (H + 10) hour work = $\frac{(\text{H}+10)}{30}$

$\frac{32\text{H}}{510} = \frac{\text{H}+10}{30}$

$32\text{H} = 17\text{H} + 170$

$15\text{H} = 170$

$\text{H} = \frac{170}{15}=\frac{34}{3}=11\frac{1}{3}$

Hence, value of H = $11\frac{1}{3}$ hours.

57. E's 1 hour work = $\frac{1}{12}$

E's 2 hours work = $\frac{1}{12}\times 2=\frac{1}{6}$

Remaining work = $1-\frac{1}{6}=\frac{5}{6}$

(B + C)'s 1 hour work

$= \frac{1}{8}+\frac{1}{6}=\frac{3+4}{24}=\frac{7}{24}$

$\because \frac{7}{24}$ part is filled in 1 hour

$\therefore \frac{5}{6}$ part is filled in $\frac{1}{\frac{7}{24}}\times\frac{5}{6}$ hours

$= \frac{24}{7}\times\frac{5}{6}=\frac{20}{7}$ hours

$\therefore$ Total time taken to fill the tank completely

$= 2+\frac{20}{7}=\frac{34}{7}=4\frac{6}{7}$ hours.

58. (A + D + E)'s 1 hour work

$$= \frac{1}{4}+\frac{1}{2}+\frac{1}{12} = \frac{3+6+1}{12} = \frac{10}{12} = \frac{5}{6}$$

Z's 1 hour work $= \frac{1}{30}$

$\because \frac{1}{30}$ part can empty in 1 hour

$\therefore$ 1 part can empty in $\frac{30}{1}$ hour

$\therefore \frac{5}{6}$ part can empty $= 30 \times \frac{5}{6}$ hours = 25 hr

Outlet Z can empty the tank completely in 25 hours.

59. Let the speed of the boat = x km/hr and speed of stream = y km/hr

Let distance = d km

$$\frac{d}{x+y} = 4$$

$$\Rightarrow \quad d = 4(x + y) \quad ...(i)$$

$$\frac{d}{x-y} = \frac{44}{5}$$

$$\Rightarrow \quad d = \frac{44(x-y)}{5} \quad ...(ii)$$

From (i) and (ii)

$$4(x + y) = \frac{44(x-y)}{5}$$

$$\Rightarrow \quad 20x + 20y = 44x - 44y$$

$$\Rightarrow \quad 24x = 64y$$

$$\Rightarrow \quad \frac{x}{y} = \frac{64}{24} = \frac{8}{3}$$

$$\therefore \frac{\text{Speed of boat}}{\text{Speed of stream}} = 8 : 3.$$

60. A : B : C = 6500 × 6 : 8400 × 5 : 10000 × 3

= 39000 : 42000 : 30000

= 39 : 42 : 30

= 13 : 14 : 10

$\because$ A is working member

$$\therefore \quad \frac{5}{100} \times 7400 = ₹\ 370$$

Profit = 7400 − 370

= ₹ 7030

Share of B in the profit

$$= \frac{14}{37} \times 7030$$

= ₹ 14 × 190

= ₹ 2660.

61. $\text{Time} = \frac{\text{S.I.} \times 100}{\text{P} \times r} = \frac{81 \times 100 \times 2}{900 \times 9} = 2 \text{ years.}$

62. Let Amount deposited in scheme A = ₹ x

$\therefore$ Amount deposited in scheme B

= ₹ 13900 − x

According to the question,

$$\frac{x \times 14 \times 2}{100} + \frac{(13900-x) \times 11 \times 2}{100} = 3508$$

$$\Rightarrow 28x + 13900 \times 22 - 22x = 3508 \times 100$$

$$\Rightarrow \quad 6x = 350800 - 305800$$

$$\Rightarrow \quad 6x = 45000$$

$$\Rightarrow \quad x = 7500$$

Hence, amount deposited in scheme B

= 13900 − 7500

= ₹ 6400.

63. Required probability $= \frac{10}{21}$.

64. Suppose the two liquids A and B are $7x$ litres and $5x$ litres respectively.

Now, when 9 litres of mixture are taken out,

$$\text{A remains} = 7x - 9\left(\frac{7}{7+5}\right)$$

$$= 7x - \frac{63}{12} = \left(7x - \frac{21}{4}\right) l$$

$$\text{and B remains} = 5x - 9\left(\frac{5}{7+5}\right)$$

$$= 5x - \frac{45}{12} = \left(5x - \frac{15}{4}\right) l$$

When 9 litres of liquid B are added

$$\left(7x - \frac{21}{4}\right) : \left(5x - \frac{15}{4} + 9\right) = 7 : 9$$

$$\Rightarrow \quad \frac{7x-\frac{21}{4}}{5x-\frac{15}{4}+9} = \frac{7}{9}$$

$$\Rightarrow \quad 63x-\frac{189}{4} = 35x-\frac{105}{4}+63$$

$$\Rightarrow \quad 28x = \frac{189}{4}-\frac{105}{4}+63$$

$$= 21 + 63 = 84$$

$$\Rightarrow \quad x = \frac{84}{28} = 3$$

$$\therefore \quad 7x = 7 \times 3$$

$$= 21 \text{ litres.}$$

65. $$\pi(r + 4)^2 - \pi r^2 = \frac{11}{25}\pi r^2$$

$$\Rightarrow \quad \pi(r^2 + 8r + 16 - r^2) = \frac{11}{25}\pi r^2$$

$$\Rightarrow \quad 8r + 16 = \frac{11}{25}r^2$$

$$\Rightarrow \quad 200r + 400 = 11r^2$$

$$\Rightarrow \quad 11r^2 - 200r - 400 = 0$$

$$\Rightarrow 11r^2 - 220r + 20r - 400 = 0$$

$$\Rightarrow 11r(r - 20) + 20(r - 20) = 0$$

$$(r - 20)(11r + 20) = 0$$

$$\Rightarrow \quad r = 20$$

or $$r = \frac{-20}{11}$$

Hence, radius of the swimming pool = 20 feet.

66. $$\frac{14}{x-y}+\frac{36}{x+y} = 4$$

$$\frac{20}{x-y}+\frac{24}{x+y} = 5$$

$$36a + 14b = 4 \quad] \times 2$$

$$24a + 20b = 5 \quad] \times 3$$

$$72a + 28b = 8$$

$$72a + 60b = 15$$

$$- \quad - \quad -$$

$$32b = 7 \Rightarrow b = \frac{7}{32}$$

$$24a+20 \times \frac{7}{32} = 5$$

$$\Rightarrow \quad 24a = 5-\frac{140}{32}$$

$$= \frac{160-140}{32} = \frac{20}{32}$$

$$\Rightarrow \quad a = \frac{20}{32 \times 24} = \frac{5}{192}$$

$$\frac{1}{x+y} = \frac{5}{192}$$

$$\Rightarrow \quad 5x + 5y = 192 \quad] \times 7$$

$$\frac{1}{x-y} = \frac{7}{32}$$

$$\Rightarrow \quad 7x - 7y = 32 \quad] \times 5$$

$$35x + 35y = 1344$$

$$35x - 35y = 160$$

$$70x = 1504$$

$$x = \frac{1504}{70} = 21 \text{ km/hr}$$

II speed of boat = 16 km/hr

$\therefore$ Quantity I > Quantity II

Hence, option (B) is correct.

68. $$\frac{x^2}{5}+x+\frac{4}{5} = 0$$

$$\Rightarrow \quad x^2 + 5x + 4 = 0$$

$$\Rightarrow \quad x^2 + 4x + x + 4 = 0$$

$$\Rightarrow \quad x(x + 4) + 1(x + 4) = 0$$

$$\Rightarrow \quad (x + 4)(x + 1) = 0$$

either $x = -4$ or $x = -1$

$$3y^2 + 4y + 1 = 0$$

$$\Rightarrow \quad 3y^2 + 3y + y + 1 = 0$$

$$\Rightarrow \quad 3y(y + 1) + 1(y + 1) = 0$$

$$\Rightarrow \quad (3y + 1)(y + 1) = 0$$

either $y = -1$ or $y = -\frac{1}{3}$

Quantity I ≤ Quantity II

Hence, option (E) is correct.

69. Quantity I ≥ Quantity II

Hence, option (D) is correct.

81. 6 → 4 → 5 → 8.5 → 18 → 48 [46] → 139

$\times\frac{1}{2}+1$, $\times 1+1$, $\times\frac{3}{2}+1$, $\times 2+1$, $\times\frac{5}{2}+1$, $\times 3+1$

Hence, wrong number is 48.

82. 10080 → 1440 → 240 → 48 → 12 → 3 [4] → 2

÷ 7, ÷ 6, ÷ 5, ÷ 4, ÷ 3, ÷ 2

Hence, wrong number is 3.

83. 1 → 2 → 6 → 21 → 88 → 505 [445] → 2676

× 1 + 1, × 2 + 2, × 3 + 3, × 4 + 4, × 5 + 5, × 6 + 6

Hence, wrong number is 505.

84. 18 → 21 [20] → 25 → 35 → 52 → 78 → 115

+ 2, + 5, + 10, + 17, + 26, + 37

+ 3, + 5, + 7, + 9, + 11

+ 2, + 2, + 2, + 2

Hence, wrong number is 21.

85. 120 → 137 → 178 [171] → 222 → 290 → 375 → 477

+ 17, + 34, + 51, + 68, + 85, + 102

↓ ↓ ↓ ↓ ↓ ↓

17 × 1, 17 × 2, 17 × 3, 17 × 4, 17 × 5, 17 × 6

Hence, wrong number is 178.

86. ∵ Area of rectangle = 150 m^2

$\Rightarrow \quad xy = 150$

$\Rightarrow \quad x = \frac{150}{y}$ ...(*i*)

Now, $(x - 5)(y + 2) = 120$

$\Rightarrow \quad xy + 2x - 5y - 10 = 120$

$\Rightarrow \quad 150 + 2x - 5y - 10 = 120$

$\Rightarrow \quad 2x - 5y = -20$

$\Rightarrow \quad 2\left(\frac{150}{y}\right) - 5y = -20$

$\Rightarrow \quad 300 - 5y^2 = -20y$

$\Rightarrow \quad 5y^2 - 20y - 300 = 0$

$\Rightarrow \quad y^2 - 4y - 60 = 0$

$\Rightarrow \quad (y - 10)(y + 6) = 0$

$\Rightarrow \quad y = 10$ or $y = -6$

which is not possible

∴ Breadth of rectangle = 10 m

Length of rectangle = 15 m

Side of square = 15 m

[∵ Length of rectangle = side of square given]

∴ Perimeter of square = 15 × 4 = 60 m.

87. Amount invested by A

$= 4200 \times 4 + 5200 \times 6 = 48000$

Amount invested by B

$= 3600 \times 6 + (3600 + x) \times 4$

$= 21600 + 14400 + 4x$

$= 4x + 36000$

Amount invested by C

$= 2400 \times 6 + (2400 + 2x)4$

$= 14400 + 9600 + 8x$

$= 24000 + 8x$

A : B : C = 48000 : 4x + 36000 : 8x + 24000

$$\text{A's share} = \left(\frac{48000}{48000 + 12x + 60000}\right) \times 2820$$

$$\Rightarrow \quad 1200 = \left(\frac{48000}{12x + 108000}\right) \times 2820$$

$\Rightarrow \quad 12x + 108000 = 282 \times 400 = 112800$

$\Rightarrow \quad 12x = 112800 - 10800 = 4800$

$$x = \frac{4800}{12} = 400$$

Hence, B invested additional amount = ₹ 400.

88.

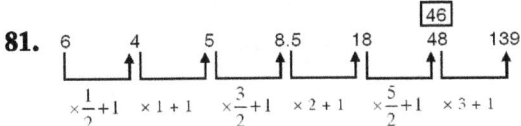

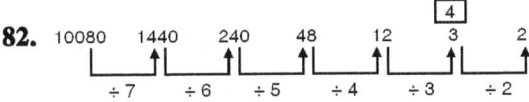

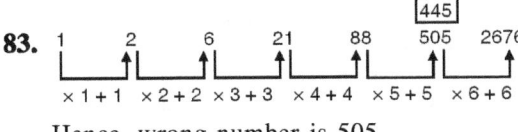

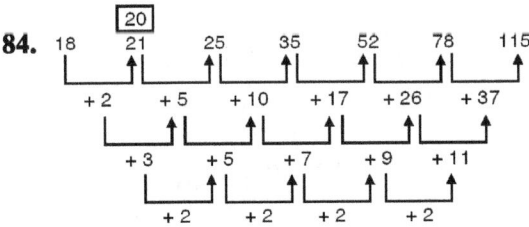

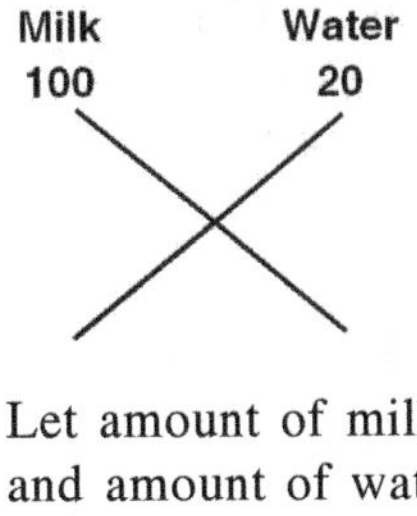

Let amount of milk = 100 *l*

and amount of water = 20 *l*

24 *l* mix taken out

Amount of milk in 24 *l* mix

$= \frac{5}{6} \times 24 = 20\,l$

Amount of water in 24 l mix

$$= \frac{1}{6} \times 24 = 4\,l$$

Now Amount of milk

$= 100\ l = 80\ l + 24\ l$ (added)

$= 104\ l$

Amount of water

$= 20 - 4 = 16\ l$

Again 15 l of mix taken out

Amount of milk in 15 l mix

$$= \frac{13}{15} \times 15 = 13\ l$$

Amount of water

$$= \frac{2}{15} \times 15 = 2\ l$$

Hence, the resultant quantity of milk in the mixture = 104 – 13 = 91 litres.

89. Let number of ball faced by D = 3x

then, number of ball faced by F = 4x

Total run scored by D = 72 × 3x

Total run scored by F = 66 × 4x

Per cent difference of run scored by F more than D

$$= \left(\frac{66 \times 4x - 72 \times 3x}{72 \times 3x}\right) \times 100$$

$$= \frac{4800}{216} = \frac{200}{9} = 22\frac{2}{9}\%.$$

90. Total run scored by E = 55 × 28 = 1540

Total run scored by E in first 25 matches

= 25 × (55 – 9) = 1150

Total run scored by E in last 3 matches

= 1540 – 1150 = 390

Minimum run scored by E in 28th match

$n \geq 390 - 127 - 126$

$n \geq 137$

$\therefore\ n = 137.$

91. Total run scored by A = $8x$

Total ball faced = $8x - 74$

$$\text{Strike rate of A} = \left(\frac{8x}{8x - 74}\right) \times 100$$

$$\Rightarrow \quad 129.6 = \frac{8x \times 100}{8x - 74}$$

$\Rightarrow 129.6 \times 8x - 8x \times 100 = 129.6 \times 74$

$\Rightarrow 8x(129.6 - 100) = 129.6 \times 74$

$$\Rightarrow \quad x = \frac{129.6 \times 74}{8 \times 29.6} = \frac{81}{2}$$

$$\Rightarrow \quad x = 40\frac{1}{2}$$

$\therefore$ Average runs scored by A = 40.5.

93. Let no. of matches played by C = x

Total runs scored = 38 x

$$\text{Strike rate} = \left(\frac{38x}{400}\right) \times 100$$

$$\Rightarrow \quad 114 = \frac{38x}{4}$$

$$\therefore \quad x = \frac{114 \times 4}{38} = 12$$

Hence, total number of matches played by batsman C = 12

94. $$1 \text{ man } 1 \text{ day work} = \frac{1}{10 \times 12} = \frac{1}{120}$$

$$1 \text{ child } 1 \text{ day work} = \frac{1}{12 \times 16} = \frac{1}{192}$$

$$1 \text{ women } 1 \text{ day work} = \frac{1}{8 \times 20} = \frac{1}{160}$$

(5 men + 12 children) 4 days work

$$= \left(\frac{5}{120} + \frac{12}{192}\right) \times 4$$

$$= \left(\frac{1}{24} + \frac{1}{16}\right) \times 4$$

$$= \left(\frac{2+3}{48}\right) \times 4 = \frac{5}{12}$$

$$\text{Remaining work} = 1 - \frac{5}{12} = \frac{7}{12}$$

(5 men + 4 women + 4 children) 1 day work

$$= \left(\frac{1}{24} + \frac{4}{160} + \frac{4}{192}\right) 1 \text{ day work}$$

$$= \left(\frac{1}{24}+\frac{1}{40}+\frac{1}{48}\right)$$

$$= \left(\frac{10+6+5}{240}\right)=\frac{21}{240} = \frac{7}{80}$$

$\because \frac{7}{80}$ part can do in 1 day

$\therefore \frac{7}{12}$ part can do in $\frac{80}{7}\times\frac{7}{12}=\frac{20}{3}=6\frac{2}{3}$ days.

95. 60% of x = 600

$$x = \frac{600\times100}{60} = 1000$$

$$(60 - 40)\% = 600$$

$$20\% \text{ of } x = 600$$

$$x = \frac{600\times100}{20} = 3000.$$

96. Let present ages of son and daughter are x and y years.

According to the question,

$$Z = x + y + 8$$

Where Z = Present age of mother

$$\frac{y+5}{x+5} = \frac{7}{6}$$

$\Rightarrow 7x + 35 = 6y + 30$

$\Rightarrow 7x - 6y = -5$

$\Rightarrow 7x + 5 = 6y$

$$y = \frac{7x+5}{6}$$

$$Z = x + y + 8 = x+\frac{7x+5}{6}+8$$

$$\Rightarrow \quad Z = \frac{6x+7x+5+48}{6} = \frac{13x+53}{6} \quad ...(i)$$

Now, Father's age is equal to three times son's ageZ + 7 = $3x$

$$\Rightarrow \quad Z = 3x - 7 \quad ...(ii)$$

From (i) and (ii)

$$\frac{13x+53}{6} = 3x - 7$$

$\Rightarrow \quad 13x + 53 = 18x - 42$

$\Rightarrow \quad 5x = 95$

$\Rightarrow \quad x = 19$

$$y = \frac{7\times19+5}{6} = \frac{138}{6} = 23$$

Hence, present age of the daughter = 23 years.

97. X —— Y —— Z (XY = 20 km, YZ = 40 km)

Let speed of the current = m km/hr

Speed of boat B in still water = 10 km/hr

Speed of B in upstream

= (10 – m) km/hr

Speed of boat A in still water

= (10 – m) km/hr

According to the question,

$$\frac{20}{10-m+m} = \frac{40}{10-m}-3$$

$$\Rightarrow \quad 2 = \frac{40}{10-m}-3$$

$$\Rightarrow \quad \frac{40}{10-m} = 5$$

$\Rightarrow \quad 10 - m = 8$

$m = 2$

$\therefore$ Speed of the current = 2 km/hr

Hence, the speed of boat A

= (10 – m) km/hr = (0-2) km/hr = 8 km/hr.

Previous Paper (Solved)

Institute of Banking Personnel Selection [IBPS]

Specialist (Marketing) Officer Scale-I

Online Main Exam 2017*

PROFESSIONAL KNOWLEDGE

1. Which of the following concepts holds that consumers prefer the products which are easily available and are inexpensive?
A. The product concept
B. The production concept
C. The selling concept
D. The marketing concept
E. None of these

2. .... is the added value endowed to a product or serice:
A. Brand equity
B. Brand image
C. Brand loyalty
D. Brand prefrence
E. None of these

3. The step after 'concept testing' in the new product development process is
A. Business analysis
B. Marketing strategy development
C. Product development
D. Test marketing
E. None of these

4. In India, Proctor & Gamble (P&G) (Home products division) is following the strategy of:
A. Cost leadership
B. Differentiation
C. Broad differentiation
D. Focussed differentiation
E. None of these

5. Producers of convenience goods typically prefer:
A. Exclusive distribution
B. Intensive distribution
C. Selective distribution
D. Intermittent distribution
E. None of these

6. A market penetration pricing strategy is suitable when:
A. lower price encourages actual competition.
B. the demand of the product is inelastic.
C. the production and distribution costs fall with increasing production.
D. a high price discourages competitors from entering the market.
E. None of these

7. Which one of the following is not included in the distribution logistics?
A. Order processing
B. Inventory
C. Warehousing
D. Wholesaler
E. None of these

8. 1. The last stage in the personal-selling process is 'closing the sale'.

* Based on Memory.

2. In India, companies spend much less on post-testing than on pre-testing of advertising.
3. Market targeting is currently the most popular marketing approves.
4. According to R.L. Stevenson, everybody lives by selling something.

The true statements are:
A. All of the above
B. None of the above
C. Only 2 and 3
D. Only 2, 3 and 4
E. Only 1

9. The attempt to build and/or maintain a good "corporate image" is referred to as:
A. Advertising
B. Public Relations
C. Personal selling
D. Sales promotion
E. None of these

10. The most significant advantage in the use of newspaper as an advertising medium is:
A. Audience selectivity
B. Flexibility
C. High attention
D. National market coverage
E. None of these

11. The promotional tool which is useful during the decline stage of product life cycle is:
A. Advertising
B. Personal selling
C. Public relation
D. Sales promotion
E. None of these

12. The most important factor in selecting advertising media is:
A. Media cost
B. Media preference of target audience
C. Nature of the product
D. Type of message
E. None of these

13. The most common form of organizing the marketing department is based on:
A. Customer
B. Functions
C. Geography
D. Product
E. None of these

14. In the model of consumer adoption of new products developed by Everitt M. Rogers, the first category of people to adopt a new product is called
A. Early adopters
B. Initial adopters
C. First users
D. Innovators
E. None of these

15. Pepsico used .... to enter the Indian market in the early 1980s.
A. Mega marketing
B. Meta marketing
C. Micro marketing
D. Multistage marketing
E. None of these

16. Pricing decisions are most complex at which stage of the product life cycle?
A. Decline stage
B. Growth
C. Introduction
D. Maturity
E. None of these

17. Branding seeks
A. to differentiate the product
B. to charge differential price
C. to sell the product in different countries
D. to give attractive name to a product
E. None of these

18. The components of E-business model are
(*i*) Web Server
(*ii*) Web Master
(*iii*) Internet
(*iv*) Web Administrator

Codes:

A. (*i*), (*ii*), (*iii*) and (*iv*)
B. (*i*), (*ii*) and (*iii*)
C. (*i*) and (*iii*) only
D. (*iii*) only
E. (*i*) and (*ii*) only

19. Personal influence is most important at the .... stage of the consumer adoption process.
A. Adoption B. Awareness
C. Evaluation D. Trial
E. None of these

20. The price setting method most closely corresponding of the concept of product positioning is
A. Cost-plus pricing
B. Psychological pricing
C. Going-rate pricing
D. Perceived-value pricing
E. None of these

21. Use of mail, telephone and other non-personal contact tools to communicate with, or solicit a response from, specific customers and prospects is called
A. Advertising B. Direct Marketing
C. Sales Promotion D. Public Relations
E. None of these

22. .... marketing describes the employees' skills in serving the clients.
A. External B. Interactive
C. Internal D. Relationship
E. None of these

23. Match the two sets of concepts:

List-I	***List-II***
(*i*) Evaluation of Alternatives	(*a*) Perception
(*ii*) Post-purchase behaviour	(*b*) Cognitive Dissonance
(*iii*) Selective distortion	(*c*) Life style
(*iv*) Psychographic segmentation	(*d*) Expectancy-value model

Codes:

	(*a*)	(*b*)	(*c*)	(*d*)
A.	(*i*)	(*ii*)	(*iii*)	(*iv*)
B.	(*ii*)	(*iii*)	(*iv*)	(*i*)
C.	(*iii*)	(*ii*)	(*iv*)	(*i*)
D.	(*iv*)	(*iii*)	(*ii*)	(*i*)
E.	(*i*)	(*iii*)	(*ii*)	(*iv*)

24. Which of the following is direct marketing?
A. Face-to-face marketing
B. Catalogue marketing
C. Direct mailing
D. Test marketing
E. None of these

25. In marketing research, primary data can be collected through
A. Observational Method
B. Survey Method
C. Experimental Method
D. All of the above
E. None of these

26. Holistic marketing does not include
A. Internal Marketing
B. Integrated Marketing
C. Performance Marketing
D. Financial Marketing
E. None of these

27. Which of the following is not a distinctive characteristics of services?
A. Transparency B. Intangibility
C. Inseparability D. Perishability
E. None of these

28. To remain dominant, a market leader looks for
A. ways to expand total market demand
B. attempting to protect its current share
C. increasing its market share
D. all of the above
E. None of these

29. Which method is least suited for forecasting the demand of a new product?
A. Survey of Buyers' Intentions

B. Composite Opinions of Sales Force
C. Test Marketing
D. Time-Series Analysis
E. None of these

30. TePP stands for
A. Technology for Promotion and Production
B. Trade for Profitability and Productivity
C. Technopreneur Promotion Programme
D. None of the above
E. All of the above

31. Consider the following statements:
(*i*) Brand equity is a function of brand awareness and brand preference.
(*ii*) Product lines tend to shorten over time.
(*iii*) The Standards of Weights and Measures (Packaged Commodities) Rules, 1977 provide for the labelling rules relating to packaged commodities.
(*iv*) AIDA Model is relevant to advertising as well as physical distribution.
Indicate the correct answer.
Codes :
A. All the above statements are false.
B. Only (*iii*) is true.
C. (*i*), (*iii*) and (*iv*) are true.
D. Only (*i*) is true.
E. None of these

32. A marketer developing a brand name that is easy to pronounce would conduct :
A. An association test
B. A memory test
C. A preference test
D. A recall test
E. None of these

33. Before performing the business analysis for developing a new product, a company should be engaged in
A. Idea screening
B. Product development
C. Marketing strategy development
D. Product positioning
E. None of these

34. Relationship marketing aims at building mutually satisfying long-term relations with
A. Customers
B. Employees
C. Marketing partners
D. All of the above
E. None of these

35. In the social-cultural arena, marketers may not understand
A. People's views
B. Organisation's views
C. Society's views
D. Government's views
E. None of these

36. A manufacturer of industrial goods would use ______ sales force structure.
A. Territorial
B. Matrix
C. Product
D. Market
E. None of these

37. Which of the following is/are a type(s) of direct marketing?
A. Direct-Response Advertising
B. Personal Selling
C. Telemarketing
D. All of the above
E. None of these

38. Arrange the following stages involved in DBMS in proper sequence :
(*i*) Creating
(*ii*) Defining
(*iii*) Data structuring
(*iv*) Updating
(*v*) Interrogating
Codes :
A. (*i*), (*iii*), (*ii*), (*iv*) and (*v*)
B. (*ii*), (*i*), (*iii*), (*v*) and (*iv*)
C. (*iii*), (*ii*), (*v*), (*iv*) and (*i*)

D. (*ii*), (*iii*), (*i*), (*iv*) and (*v*)
E. None of these

39. Which fact is true about on-line marketing ?
A. A website which is user-friendly.
B. A website which is user-friendly and regularly updated.
C. A website which is user-friendly, regularly updated and make product's graphical image available.
D. A website which is user-friendly, regularly updated, provides product's graphical image and product's price is competitive.
E. None of these

40. Which of the following function involved under marketing management's function?
1. Collection of market information
2. Marketing coordination
3. Marketing controlling
4. All the above

Codes :
A. 1 & 2
B. 2 & 3
C. 3 only
D. 4 only
E. None of these

41. Two statements are given below :
Statement–I : Product concept of marketing holds that consumers would favour those products that are available and highly affordable.
Statement–II : Production concept of marketing holds that consumers would not buy enough of the company's product unless the company undertakes a substantial promotional effort.

Choose the correct option from the four options given below :
A. Statement I is correct and II is wrong.
B. Statement II is correct and I is wrong.
C. Both statements are correct.
D. Both statements are wrong.
E. None of these

42. Match the following :

List-I	List-II
(*a*) Differentiation	1. How familiar and intimate consumers are with the brand.
(*b*) Esteem	2. The degree to which a brand is seen as different from others.
(*c*) Relevance	3. How well the brand is regarded and respected.
(*d*) Knowledge	4. The breadth of a brand's appeal.

Codes :

	(*a*)	(*b*)	(*c*)	(*d*)
A.	1	2	3	4
B.	2	3	4	1
C.	3	4	1	2
D.	4	3	2	1
E.	4	2	1	3

43. In multi level channel arrangement Jobber stands in between ________.
A. manufacturer and wholesaler
B. wholesaler and retailer
C. retailer and consumer
D. None of these
E. All of the above

44. A company following a strategy of advertising the product for a period followed by a period with no advertising is called
A. Concentration B. Flighting
C. Pulsing D. Continuity
E. None of these

45. Franchise organization is an example of ______ vertical marketing system.
A. Corporate
B. Administered
C. Contractual
D. Co-operative
E. None of these

46. Three statements are given below:

Statement–I: Introducing an existing product in the new market is called market development.

Statement–II: Introducing a new product in the existing market is called diversification.

Statement–III: Introducing an existing product in the existing market is called market penetration.

Choose the correct option about the statements from among the options given below:

A. Statements I & II are only correct.
B. Statements I & III are only correct.
C. Statements II & III are only correct.
D. Statements I, II & III are correct.

47. Making profit by taking advantage of different prices prevailing in different markets is referred as

A. Hedging
B. Speculation
C. Arbitrage
D. Gambling
E. None of these

48. A Marketing database is built as an aid to

A. Market research
B. Product-mix expansion
C. Reducing cost of production
D. Price hike
E. None of these

49. The Branding strategy which uses a different brand name for each product is known as

A. Overall Family Branding
B. Line Family Branding
C. Individual Branding
D. Brand Extension
E. None of these

50. Marketing information system gathers information from internal sources like marketing intelligence and marketing research to help the manager in

A. Assessing the information needs
B. Developing the needed information
C. Distributing the information
D. All of the above
E. None of these

51. One-level channel consists of

A. Producer-consumer
B. Producer-dealer-consumer
C. Producer-dealer-retailer-consumer
D. Producer-dealer-wholesaler-retailer-consumer
E. None of these

52. Which of the following statement is true?

A. The essence of marketing is a transaction of an exchange.
B. Marketing–orientation is philosophy, which has to pervade the organisation structure.
C. Marketing is also a managerial function involving analysis, planning and control marketing activities in an organisation.
D. All of the above
E. None of these

53. A marketing plan is composed of three basic components, namely

1. Objectives
2. Policies
3. Program
4. Procedure
5. Hints
6. Decision
7. Command
8. Periodic
9. Diversity

A. 1, 2 and 3 only
B. 6, 7 and 8 only
C. 5, 7 and 9 only
D. 2, 3 and 9 only
E. None of these

54. Which of the following is not the stage of new product development?

A. Idea Generation
B. Business Analysis
C. Test Marketing
D. Market Segmentation
E. None of these

55. Which of the following is not included in 7 P's of services marketing?
A. Physical evidence
B. People
C. Process
D. Marketing plan
E. None of these

56. Selling the products only through a single wholesaler or retailer is called
A. Extensive distribution strategy
B. Selective distribution strategy
C. Exclusive distribution strategy
D. Mass merchandise strategy
E. None of these

57. Marketing myopia concept was developed by
A. Philip Kotler B. Peter Drucker
C. C.K. Prahlada D. Theodore Levitt
E. None of these

58. Emerging market economies are
A. A part of developed countries
B. Newly industrializing countries
C. A part of developing countries
D. A part of third world countries
E. None of these

59. What describes the market, product and technological area of business?
A. Company's mission
B. Company's vision
C. Strategic plan
D. None of the above
E. None of these

60. Opportunity costs are also known as
A. Spill-over costs
B. Money costs
C. Alternative costs
D. Sunk costs
E. None of these

ANSWERS

1	**2**	**3**	**4**	**5**	**6**	**7**	**8**	**9**	**10**
B	A	B	C	B	C	D	D	B	B
11	**12**	**13**	**14**	**15**	**16**	**17**	**18**	**19**	**20**
D	B	B	D	A	D	A	C	C	D
21	**22**	**23**	**24**	**25**	**26**	**27**	**28**	**29**	**30**
B	B	C	A	D	D	A	D	D	C
31	**32**	**33**	**34**	**35**	**36**	**37**	**38**	**39**	**40**
B	D	C	D	D	D	D	C	D	D
41	**42**	**43**	**44**	**45**	**46**	**47**	**48**	**49**	**50**
D	B	B	B	C	B	C	A	C	D
51	**52**	**53**	**54**	**55**	**56**	**57**	**58**	**59**	**60**
B	D	A	D	D	C	D	C	A	C

Previous Year Paper (Solved)

IBPS–Specialist (Marketing) Officer Scale-I Online Examination 2016*

REASONING

Directions (Qs. Nos. 1 & 2) : *The questions consists of a question and two statements numbered I and II given below it. You have to decide whether the data given in the statements are sufficient to answer the questions. Read both the statements and choose the most appropriate option.*

A. If the data in statement I alone are sufficient to answer the question, while the data in statement II alone are not sufficient to answer the question.

B. If the data in statement II alone are sufficient to answer the question, while the data in statement I alone are not sufficient to answer the question.

C. If the data either in statement I alone or in statement II alone are sufficient to answer the question.

D. If the data given in both statements I and II together are not sufficient to answer the question and

E. If the data in both statements I and II together are necessary to answer the question.

1. How many people are standing in straight line (Note : All are facing North)?

I. Q stands third from the right end of the line. Only one person stands between Q and S. S stands at the extreme left end of the line.

II. Q stands exactly in the centre of the line. P and M are immediate neighbours of Q. Only one person stands to the left of P.

2. How far is point M from point Q?

I. Point S is 7 m to the south of point M. Point T is 4 m to the east of point S. Point P is 4 m to the north of Point T. Point Q is to the west of Point P. Point S is 4 m to the South of Point Q.

II. Point R is 4 m to the west of Point Q. Point R is 4 m to the north of Point Q. Point X is 4 m to the north of Point R. Point M is to the east of Point X.

Directions (Qs. Nos. 3-7) : *In each question below are three statements followed by two conclusions numbered I and II. You have to take the three given statements to be true even if they seem to be at variance from commonly known facts and then decide which of the given conclusions logically follows from the three statements disregarding commonly known facts.*

Give answer—

A. If only conclusion I follows.

B. If only conclusion II follows.

C. If either conclusion I or conclusion II follows.

D. If neither conclusion I nor conclusion II follows.

E. If both conclusion I and conclusion II follow.

3. Statements : All crafts are projects.
Some projects are missions.
No mission is a guide.

Conclusions : I. Some projects are guides.
II. No project is a guide.

* Online Exam held on 01-02-2016

4. Statements : Some outputs are results.
All outputs are products.
All products are yields.
Conclusions : **I.** No product is a result.
II. All yields are products.

5. Statements : Some outputs are results.
All outputs are products.
All products are yields.
Conclusions : **I.** All outputs are yields.
II. All results being yields is a possibility.

6. Statements : No price is a rate.
All rates are expenses.
Conclusions : **I.** No expense is a price.
II. All prices being expenses is a possibility.

7. Statements : All crafts are projects.
Some projects are missions.
No mission is a guide.
Conclusions : **I.** No guide is a craft.
II. At least some missions are crafts.

Directions (Qs. Nos. 8-12) : *Study the following information carefully and answer the question given.*

Eight friends P, Q, R, S, T, U, V and W are sitting around a square table in such a way that four of them sit at four corners while four sit in the middle of each of the four sides. The ones who sit at the four corners face the centre while those who sit in the middle of the sides face outside (*i.e.*, opposite to the centre).

- V sits second to the right of R. R sits in the middle of one of the sides of the table.
- Only two people sit between V and Q. S is one of the immediate neighbours of Q.
- T sits second to the left of S.
- P sits second to the left of U.
- V is not an immediate neighbour of U.

8. How many people sit between R and T when counted from the right of R?
A. None B. Four
C. One D. Three
E. Two

9. Which of the following is true regarding P?
A. Both T and R are immediate neighbours of P.
B. Only three people sit between P and S.
C. P sits at middle of one of the sides.
D. W sits second to the left of P.
E. None of the given options is true.

10. What is the position of V with respect to Q?
A. Second to the left
B. Third to the left
C. Third to the right
D. Fifth to the right
E. Fifth to the left

11. Four of the following five are alike in a certain way and so form a group. Which is the one that does not belong to that group?
A. Q B. T
C. S D. R
E. V

12. Who sits second to the left of W?
A. T B. U
C. V D. S
E. Q

Directions (Qs. Nos. 13-17) : *In these questions, relationship between different elements is shown in the statements. These statements are followed by two conclusions.*
Make answer if,
A. Only conclusion I follows.
B. Only conclusion II follows.
C. Either conclusion I or II follows.
D. Neither conclusion I nor II follows.
E. Both conclusions I and II follow.

13. Statements : $K \geq S = U \leq R; L < U \leq J$
Conclusions : **I.** $R > J$
II. $L = K$

14. Statements : $D > W \geq C \leq X; C \geq L; W < K$
Conclusions : **I.** $X > K$
II. $L \leq W$

15. Statements : $R \leq A < M \geq T \geq Y; M \leq S$
Conclusions : **I.** $S > R$
II. $Y \leq S$

16. Statements : $D > W \geq C \leq X; C \geq L; W < K$
Conclusions : **I.** $D > L$
II. $L > D$

17. Statements : $S > B = K \geq L; B = P \leq U$
Conclusions : **I.** $L < U$
II. $U = L$

Directions (Qs. No. 18) : *Study the following information and answer the question.*

In a recent performance approval done by Company X, more than 70% of the employees were found to be under-performing.

'I think that the restructuring done by the company in the previous year is responsible for the under-performance of the employees'–HR manager of company X.

18. Which of the following statements weakens the statement of HR Manager of Company X?
A. The incentives linked to performance were abolished upon restructuring creating dissatisfaction among employees.
B. After restructuring the decision making power was taken away from employees thus delaying the work by long hours.
C. The number of projects in Company X increased by 60% this year thereby increasing the burden on the existing employees this year.
D. After restructuring the employees were required to report to multiple bosses leading to ambiguity at the work place.
E. Adequate training was not provided to the employees transferred to different departments and locations after restructuring.

Directions (Qs. Nos. 19-24) : *Study the following information and answer the given question.*

Twelve people are sitting in two parallel rows containing six people each in such a way that there is an equal distance between adjacent persons. In row 1-J, K, L, M, N and O are seated (but not necessarily in the same order) and all of them are facing South. In row 2-U, V, W, X, Y and Z are seated (but not necessarily in the same order) and all of them are facing North. Therefore, in the given seating arrangement, each member seated in a row faces another member of the other row.

- M sits fourth to the left of J. The one facing J sits third to the left of Y.
- Only one person sits between Y and U. U does not sit at any of the extreme ends of the line.
- The one facing Z sits second to the right of K, Z does not sit at any of the extreme ends of the line.
- Only two people sit between K and O.
- The one facing K sits second to the left of X.
- V is not an immediate neighbour of Z. L is not immediate neighbour of M.

19. Which of the following groups of people represents the people sitting at extreme ends of both thc rows?
A. M, O, X, W
B. M, K, V, W
C. N, K, V, Y
D. J, N, U, V
E. J, O, Z, X

20. Who amongst the following faces V?
A. M
B. L
C. J
D. N
E. K

21. Which of the following is true with respect to the given information?
A. K faces one of the immediate neighbours of X
B. V sits exactly between W and U
C. None of the given options is true
D. J is an immediate neighbour of K
E. J faces Z

22. Which of the following is true regarding N?
A. K sits second to right of N.
B. V is an immediate neighbour of the person who faces N.
C. Both L and O are immediate neighbours of N.
D. Only one person sits between N and J.
E. None of the given option is true.

23. Who amongst the following sits second to the right of the person who faces L?

A. V B. Z
C. W D. U
E. Y

24. If '4' is subtracted from each digit at odd place and '1' is added to each digit at even place in the number 947658, which of the following numbers will appear twice in the new number thus formed?

A. Only 2 B. Both 1 and 7
C. Both 3 and 5 D. None
E. Only 5

Directions (Qs. No. 25) : *Read the given information and answer the question.*

The government of State D was recently criticised for accepting a proposal as per which schools in the State will not conduct exams up to standard nine. Rather, schools will promote all the students up to standard nine and from standard nine onwards the students would either be passed or failed depending upon their marks in the exams.

25. Which of the following may not be a reason for the criticism of the government of State D for accepting the proposal?

A. Several parents have raised concern that students would not be willing to pay attention in class and retain the information because they do not have to write exams.
B. Students learn to write exam papers in a stipulated period of time with practice of solving exam papers over the years and many students may not be able to grasp this directly in the standard nine.
C. Many teachers are of the opinion that students have become very competitive and are mainly focused on acquiring marks rather than gaining knowledge
D. Studies suggest that students become less prone to exam anxiety and exam fear when they get used to passing exams over the years as compared to when they do not appear for an exam at all.
E. Experts suggest that the special needs of children can be adequately assessed through education of their exam papers and early assessment helps initiate early intervention and major projects through exams.

Directions (Qs. Nos. 26-31) : *Study the following information and answer the question.*

Seven friends, namely P, Q, R, S, T, U and V visit seven different countries namely Japan, Germany, China, India, Nepal, Australia and Malaysia, not necessarily in the same order, starting from Monday to Sunday (of the same week).

R visits on Thursday. Only two people visit between R and the one who visits Germany. Only four people visit between the one who visits Germany and V. The one who visits Malaysia visits immediately before V. Only two people visit between the one who visits Malaysia and P. S visits on one of the days after the one who visits Malaysia. U visits immediately after the one who visits Japan. U does not visit Malaysia. Only three people visit between the one who visits Japan and the one who visits Nepal. The one who visits Australia visits immediately before the one who visits China. Q does not visit on Monday.

26. Which of the following countries does Q visit?

A. China B. Malaysia
C. Japan D. Nepal
E. Australia

27. On which of the following days does U visit a country?

A. Friday B. Saturday
C. Sunday D. Wednesday
E. Tuesday

28. Which of the following is true about T?

A. All the given options are true
B. T visits on Friday
C. T visits China
D. Only three people visit between T and R
E. T visits immediately before P

29. Who amongst the following visits India?

A. S B. T
C. P D. G
E. R

30. As per the given arrangement, P is related to the one who visits Japan in a certain way and V is related to the one who visits Nepal in the same way. To which of the following is R related to in the same way?
A. The one who visits Australia
B. The one who visits China
C. The one who visits India
D. The one who visits Malaysia
E. The one who visits Germany

31. Four of the following five are alike in a certain way and thus form a group as per the given arrangement. Which of the following does not belong to that group?
A. U-Friday
B. Q-Thursday
C. S-Saturday
D. V-Sunday
E. T-Tuesday

Directions (Qs. No. 32-35) : *Study the following information carefully and answer the given question.*

When a word and number arrangement machine is given an input line of words and numbers, it arranges them following a particular rule. The following is an illustration of input and rearrangement. (All the numbers are two digit numbers).

Input : 23 kinetic amount 64 nature 71 58 opium verdict 96 elderly 15

Step I : opium 23 kinetic amount 64 nature 71 verdict 96 elderly 15 58

Step II : elderly opium 23 kinetic amount nature 71 verdict 96 15 58 64

Step III : amount elderly opium 23 kinetic nature 71 verdict 15 58 84 96

Step IV : 15 amount elderly opium 23 kinetic nature 71 58 64 96 verdict

Step V : 23 15 amount elderly opium kinetic 71 58 64 96 verdict nature

Step VI : 71 23 15 amount elderly opium 58 84 96 verdict nature kinetic

Step VI is the last step of the above arrangement and as the intended arrangement is obtained.

As per the rules followed in the given steps, find out the appropriate steps for the given input.

Input : adverb 59 36 salient 81 idioms bakery 14 launch 47 umpire 62

32. Which elements come exactly between '59' and 'bakery' in Step II of the given input?
A. Only launch
B. Only 62
C. Only idioms
D. Both 81 and salient
E. Both adverb and 36

33. Which of the following combinations represents the first two and the last two element of the step VI of the given input?
A. 81, 59, launch, bakery
B. 81, 62, salient, launch
C. 50, 47, bakery, salient
D. 62, 14, idioms, umpire
E. 62, 81, umpire, launch

34. If in the step III, 'idioms' interchanges its position with '81' and 'salient' also interchanges its position with '14', then which element will be third to the left of '47'?
A. 14
B. salient
C. adverb
D. idioms
E. 81

35. Which step are the elements 'bakery launch 47 14' found in the same order?
A. Sixth
B. Third
C. Fourth
D. The given order of elements is not found in any step
E. Fifth

36. This consists of information and two statements numbered I and II given below it. You have to decide which of the given statements weakens or strengthens the information and decide the appropriate answer.

Information : Due to increased cases of kidnapping in its vicinity, school M has made it compulsory for parents or legal guardians of the students to give a duly signed authority letter to the person picking up the students from school.

I. Most working parents rely on their domestic help, for picking up their children from school, who can easily coerced into forging or misusing the authority letter for monetary plans.

II. There is no photograph on the authority letter making it difficult to identify the person who comes to pick up the child.

A. Both statement I and statement II strengthens the information.

B. Statement I strengthens the information while statement II weakens the information.

C. Both statement I and II weakens the information.

D. Both Statement I and II are neutral statements.

E. Statement I weakens the information while statement II strengthens the information.

37. How many such pairs of letters are there in the word 'PAINTED' each of which has as many letters between them in the word in both forward and backward directions, as there are between them in the English alphabetical series?

A. More than three B. Two
C. Three D. None
E. One

38. In a certain code language, FLUTE is coded as HJWRG and GIANT is coded as IGCLV. In the same code language, how will PLOTS be coded as?

A. RJMVU B. NUMRQ
C. QMPUT D. NNMVQ
E. RJQRU

Directions (Qs. Nos. 39-43) : *Study the given information carefully to answer the given question.*

In a certain code language,
'urban people prefer cars' is written as 've fm ab eg'
'profit for urban areas' is written as 'ab ep zi so'
'people demand for hike' is written as 'zi qr cd ve'
'hike in profit margin' is written as 'al jn ep cd'
(All codes are two letter codes only)

39. What will be the possible code for 'urban food demand' in the given code language?

A. qr ab nj B. qr cr ab
C. nj qr cd D. qr ab jn
E. zi ve nj

40. What is the code for areas in the given code language?

A. ab B. zi
C. ep D. qr
E. so

41. What does the code 'jn' stand for in the given code language?

A. either 'hike' or 'people'
B. either 'in' or 'margin'
C. profit
D. hike
E. demand

42. In the given code language, if 'small' is coded as 'wy', then how will 'prefer small cars' be coded as?

A. wy eg ab B. fm ve wy
C. eg wy fm D. ab eg fm
E. ab wy eg

43. What will be the code for 'hike' in the given code language?

A. xl
B. zi
C. other than those given as options
D. qr
E. jn

Directions (Qs. No. 44) : *Read the given information and answer the question.*

Long-term usage of antibiotics causes the disease. 'Cretosis' as it decreases the secretion of hormone X. While body can endure the level of hormone X dropping to half the required number of micrograms in levels dropping to 23-micrograms needs immediate medical attention.

44. Which of the following can be concluded from the given statement?

A. A patient can be said to have Cretosis

only if his/her hormone 'X' levels are 23 micrograms or low.

B. Usage of antibiotics on a short-term cannot cause 'Cretosis' ever to a minor extent.

C. All micrograms is exactly half of the amount of hormone X required daily by the body.

D. The normal numbers of micrograms of hormone X is more than all micrograms.

E. In a patient with hormone X level of 21 microgram, if administered another 23 micrograms would bring the level to absolute normal.

Directions (Qs. Nos. 45-49) : *Read the given information carefully to answer the given question.*

Eight people K, L, M, N, O, P, Q and R live on eight different floors of a building but not necessarily in the same order. The lowermost floor of the building is numbered one, the one above that is numbered two and so on till the topmost floor is numbered eight.

P lives on an even numbered floor but not on the topmost floor. Only three people live between L and P. L lives immediately below O. Only two people live between R and M. K lives immediately above Q. There are as many people between Q and R as are there between R and O.

45. If L and P interchanges their position and so do K and M, then who will live between M and L, as per the new arrangement?

A. Q　　B. O
C. N　　D. R
E. Other than those given as options.

46. Who amongst the following lives on the floor numbered six?

A. M　　B. P
C. Q　　D. R
E. L

47. On which of the following floor numbers does O live?

A. Eight　　B. Six
C. Three　　D. Seven
E. Two

48. As per the given arrangement, four of the following five are alike in a certain way and so form a group. Which one of the following does not belong to the group?

A. MR　　B. RP
C. QL　　D. LO
E. NK

49. Who amongst the following live exactly between K and N?

A. L, P
B. P, Q
C. Q, O
D. R, L
E. Q, R

Directions (Qs. No. 50) : *Study the given information carefully to answer the given question.*

The following are two findings of a one year long survey conducted on the employees of company K.

(*a*) Every time, an employee is rewarded for his/her work, he/she has performed better for at least next two years.

(*b*) The performance of none of the employees of company K has improved in the past ten months.

50. Which of the following can be inferred from the given information?
(NOTE : An inference is something by which you can logically deduce something to be true based on the known promises.)

A. More than 90% of company K's employees work to their highest potential only when they are rewarded.

B. All the employees of company K have been rewarded at least once in their work span.

C. The employees receive heavy incentives apart from being rewarded which drive them to perform better.

D. There are factors other than being rewarded which affect the performance of the employees.

E. No employee has been rewarded for his/her work in the last two quarters.

QUANTITATIVE APTITUDE

Directions (Qs. Nos. 51-60): *In each of the questions below consists of a question and two statements numbered I and II given below it. You have to decide whether the data provided in the statements are sufficient to answer the question. Read both the statements and give answer:*

A. If the data in statement I alone are sufficient to answer the question, while the data in statement II alone are not sufficient to answer the question.
B. If the data in statement II alone are sufficient to answer the question, while the data in statement I alone are not sufficient to answer the question.
C. If the data either in statement I alone or in statement II alone are sufficient to answer the question.
D. If the data given in both statements I and II together are not sufficient to answer the question and
E. If the data in both statements I and II together are necessary to answer the question.

51. What is the area of the circle?
I. Perimeter of the circle is 88 cms.
II. Diameter of the circle is 28 cms.

52. What is the rate of interest?
I. Simple interest accrued on an amount of ₹ 25,000 in two years is less than the compound interest for the same period by ₹ 250.
II. Simple interest accrued in 10 years is equal to the principal.

53. What is the number of trees planted in the field in rows and columns?
I. Number of columns is more than the number of rows by 4.
II. Number of columns in the field is 7.

54. What is the speed of the current?
I. A man can swim a distance of 9 kms in 1½ hrs downstream.
II. While coming back upstream it takes him 3 hours to cover the same distance.

55. What is the minimum passing percentage in a test?
I. Raman scored 25% marks in the test and Sunil scored 288 marks which is 128 more than Raman.
II. Raman scored 64 marks less than the minimum passing marks.

56. What is the value of $x^2 + y + z$?
I. $4x + 3y + 5z = 60$ and $2x = y$, $2y = z$
II. $3x + 3y + 2z = 34$ and $2x + 5y + 6z = 72$

57. Whose body weight is second highest among the five boys Arun, Vinay, Suraj, Raju and Pratap?
I. Average weight of Arun, Suraj and Vinay is 68 kg and average weight of Raju and Pratap is 72 kg. Also Suraj is 78 kg. Raju is 68 kg and Vinay is 46 kg.
II. Average weight of Arun, Suraj, Vinay and Raju is 68 kg and also Suraj is 78 kg. Raju is 68 kg and Vinay is 46 kg. All of them have different weight.

58. What is the marks obtained by Subodh in History?
I. The average marks of Subodh in History, Geography and Chemistry are 75.
II. His average marks in History, Geography and Physics are 78.

59. What is the population of the city A?
I. The ratio of the population of males and females in city A is 27 : 23 and the difference between their population is 100000.
II. The population of city A is 80% of that of city B. The difference of population of city A and city B is 312500.

60. How many students did participate in elocution?
I. The students who participate in dancing were 150% more than that who participated in elocution.
II. 150 students participated in dancing.

Directions (Qs. Nos. 61-65): *The following line graph gives the per cent profit earned by two Companies X and Y during the period 1996 - 2001.*

Percentage profit earned by Two Companies X and Y over the given Years

$$\% \text{ Profit} = \frac{\text{Income} - \text{Expenditure}}{\text{Expenditure}} \times 100$$

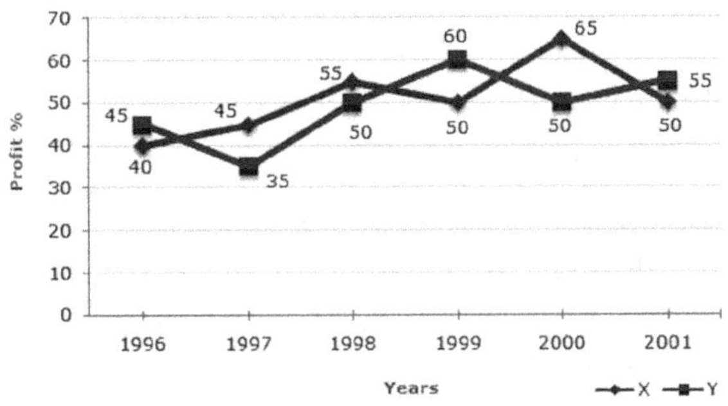

61. The incomes of two Companies X and Y in 2000 were in the ratio of 3:4 respectively. What was the respective ratio of their expenditures in 2000 ?

A. 7 : 22 B. 14 : 19
C. 15 : 22 D. 27 : 35
E. None of these

62. If the expenditure of Company Y in 1997 was ₹ 220 crores, what was its income in 1997?

A. ₹ 312 crores B. ₹ 297 crores
C. ₹ 283 crores D. ₹ 275 crores
E. None of these

63. If the expenditures of Company X and Y in 1996 were equal and the total income of the two Companies in 1996 was ₹ 342 crores, what was the total profit of the two Companies together in 1996? (Profit = Income – Expenditure)

A. ₹ 240 crores B. ₹ 171 crores
C. ₹ 120 crores D. ₹ 102 crores
E. None of these

64. The expenditure of Company X in the year 1998 was ₹ 200 crores and the income of Company X in 1998 was the same as its expenditure in 2001. The income of Company X in 2001 was.

A. ₹ 465 crores B. ₹ 385 crores
C. ₹ 335 crores D. ₹ 295 crores
E. None of these

65. If the income of two Comapanies were equal in 1999, then what was the ratio of expenditure of Company X to that of Company Y in 1999?

A. 6 : 5 B. 5 : 6
C. 11 : 6 D. 16 : 15
E. None of these

Directions (Qs. Nos. 66-70): *Study the following pie-graph carefully and answer the questions given below:*

A survey conducted on 5800 villagers staying in various villages and having various favourite fruits.

Favourite Fruits

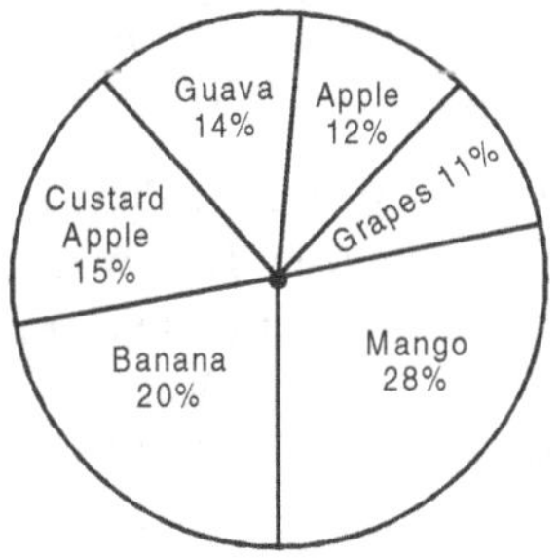

People Staying in Various Villages

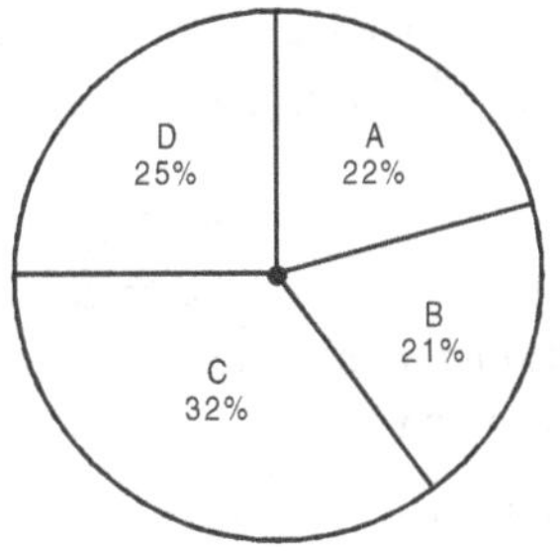

66. Mango is the favourite fruit of 50% of the people from village C. People having their favourite fruit as Mango from Village C form approximately what per cent of the people having their favourite fruit as Mango from all the villages together?

A. 48 B. 53
C. 57 D. 61
E. None of these

67. How many people in all have custard apple as their favourite fruit?
A. 812 B. 850
D. 864 D. 870
E. None of these

68. What is the total number of people having their favourite fruit as apples and grapes together?
A. 1286 B. 1300
C. 1334 D. 1420
E. None of these

69. 20% of the people from village D have banana as their favourite fruit and 12% of the people from the same village have guava as their favourite fruit. How many people from the village like other fruits?
A. 764 B. 896
C. 968 D. 986
E. None of these

70. 50% of the people from village B have banana as their favourite fruit. How many people from other villages have the same favourite fruit?
A. 551 B. 609
C. 1020 D. 1160
E. None of these

Directions (Qs. Nos. 71-80): *In each question, two equations numbered I and II are given. You have to solve both the equations and mark the appropriate answer.*
A. $x < y$ B. $x > y$
C. $x \geq y$ D. $x \leq y$
E. relationship between x and y cannot be established

71. I. $6x^2 + 5x + 1 = 0$
II. $15y^2 + 8y + 1 = 0$

72. I. $x^2 + 5x + 6 = 0$
II. $4y^2 + 24y + 35 = 0$

73. I. $2x^2 + 5x + 3 = 0$
II. $y^2 + 9y + 14 = 0$

74. I. $88x^2 - 19x + 1 = 0$
II. $132y^2 - 23y + 1 = 0$

75. I. $6x^2 - 7x + 2 = 0$
II. $20y^2 - 31y + 12 = 0$

76. I. $6x^2 + 23x + 20 = 0$
II. $6y^2 + 31y + 35 = 0$

77. I. $x^2 = 81$
II. $y^2 - 18y + 81 = 0$

78. I. $4x^2 + 20x + 21 = 0$
II. $2y^2 + 17y + 35 = 0$

79. I. $x^2 - 14x + 48 = 0$
II. $y^2 + 6 = 5y$

80. I. $38x^2 - 3x - 11 = 0$
II. $28y^2 + 32y + 9 = 0$

81. Two men P and Q start a journey from same place speed at a speed of 3 km/hr and 3½ km/hr respectively. If they move in the same direction then what is the distance between them after 4 hours?
A. 3 km B. 2½ km
C. 2 km D. 3½ km
E. None of these

Directions (Qs. Nos. 82-85): *What will come in place of question mark (?) in the given question?*

82. $14 * 627 \div \sqrt{(1089)} = (?)^3 + 141$
A. $5\sqrt{5}$ B. $(125)^3$
C. 25 D. 5
E. None of these

83. $2\frac{1.5}{5} + 2\frac{1}{6} - 1\frac{3.5}{15} = \left(\frac{(?)^{1/3}}{4}\right) + 1\frac{7}{30}$
A. 2 B. 8
C. 512 D. 324
E. None of these

84. $\left(\sqrt{(7)} + 11\right)^2 = (?)^{1/3} + 2\sqrt{(847)} + 122$
A. $36 + 44\sqrt{(7)}$ B. 6
C. 216 D. 36
E. None of these

85. $\left(\frac{18}{4}\right)^2 * \left(\frac{455}{19}\right) \div \left(\frac{61}{799}\right) = ?$

A. 6320 B. 6400
C. 6350 D. 6430
E. 6490

Directions (Qs. Nos. 86-90): *What will come in place of question mark (?) in the given number series?*

86. 28 39 63 102 158 ?
A. 232 B. 242
C. 233 D. 244
E. None of these

87. 7 16 141 190 919 ?
A. 1029 B. 1019
C. 1020 D. 1030
E. None of these

88. 12 17 32 57 92 ?
A. 198 B. 195
C. 137 D. 205
E. None of these

89. 19 25 45 87 159 ?
A. 254 B. 279
C. 284 D. 269
E. None of these

90. 83 124 206 370 698 ?
A. 1344 B. 1324
C. 1364 D. 1334
E. None of these

Directions (Qs. Nos. 91-95): *Study the table carefully and answer the given question.*

Publishing Houses	Number of books published	Ratio of Academic and Non-academic books	Percentage of books distributed	Number of distributors in publishing house
M	28200	7 : 3	81	17
N	32200	5 : 9	74	23
O	29700	6 : 5	92	18
P	31200	8 : 5	86	24
Q	33800	7 : 6	79	25
R	35700	11 : 6	82	21
S	37800	5 : 13	89	24

91. What is the difference between the number of academic books published by publishing house M and P?
A. 450 B. 640
C. 540 D. 504
E. None of these

92. How many books were given to each distributor by publisher Q if each publisher gets equal number of books?
A. 1806 B. 1068
C. 1608 D. 1308
E. None of these

93. What is the average number of non-academic books published by publishers R and S?
A. 18750 B. 18850
C. 19950 D. 18950
E. 19990

94. If the total number of books publishers P, Q and R is increased by 30% and the total number of books published by remaining publishers be decreased by 20%, what will be the new average of books published by all the publishers?
A. 33418 B. 33318
C. 32518 D. 33618
E. None of these

95. What is the total number of books distributed by publishers O and Q?
A. 26702 B. 27324
C. 55026 D. 54026
E. None of these

96. Meena Kumara goes to a shop and buys a saree, costing ₹ 5,225, including sales tax of 12%. The shopkeeper gives her a discount, so that the price is decreased by an amount equivalent to sales tax. The price is decreased by (nearest value).
A. ₹ 615 B. ₹ 650
C. ₹ 560 D. ₹ 580
E. ₹ 680

97. Mr. Phanse invests an amount of ₹ 24,200 at the rate of 4 p.c.p.a. for 6 years to obtain a simple interest, later he invests the principal amount as well as the amount obtained as simple interest for another 4 years at the same rate of interest. What amount of simple interest will be obtain at the end of the last 4 years?

A. ₹ 4,800
B. ₹ 4,850.32
C. ₹ 4,801.28
D. ₹ 4,700
E. ₹ 4,870.32

Directions (Qs. Nos. 98-100): *The questions are based on the following information:*

There are three different cable channels namely ahead, luck and bang. In a survey, it was found that 85% of viewers, respond to bang, 20% to luck and 30% of ahead, 20% of viewers respond to exactly two channels and 5% to none.

98. What percentage of the viewers responded to all three?

A. 10
B. 12
C. 14
D. 16
E. 11

99. Assuming 20% respond to ahead and bang, and 16% respond to bang and luck. What is the percentage of viewers. Who watch only luck?

A. 20
B. 10
C. 16
D. 18
E. 14

100. A milkman mixes 20 L of water with 80 L of milk. After selling one-fourth of this mixture, he adds water to replenish the quantity that he has sold. What is the current proportion of water to milk?

A. 2 : 3
B. 1 : 2
C. 1 : 3
D. 2 : 1
E. 3 : 4

ENGLISH LANGUAGE

Directions (Qs. Nos. 101-110): *Which of the phrases given against the sentence should replace the word/ phrase given in bold in the sentence to make it grammatically correct? If the sentence is correct as it is given and no correction is required. Mark* ***'No correction required'*** *as the answer.*

101. Ultimately, the only **way to sustained** a competitive advantage is to upgrade it.

A. ways to sustain
B. sustainable ways
C. way to sustainable
D. way to sustain
E. No correction required

102. What exactly have the managers **being doing wrong?**

A. doing wrong been
B. been doing wrong
C. been wrong doing
D. wrongly being doing
E. No correction required

103. Success in trade **is the result on** patent and meticulous preparations.

A. are result of
B. is resulting of
C. is the result of
D. results of the
E. No correction required

104. Competitors will eventually and inevitably overtake **any companies that** stops improving and innovating.

A. any company that
B. any companies who
C. any company
D. many company that
E. No correction required

105. The giant search engine has been flirting with virtual reality **but has never quite full** dived into it until now.

A. yet never fully quite
B. but has never quite fully
C. but ever fully
D. never has but full quietly
E. No correction required

106. Under the agreement, the government of Japan **committed to provide** a soft loan of 19,864 billion dollars to its neighbouring country.

A. committing to provide
B. provides to commit
C. provides committing
D. commitment to provide
E. No correction required

107. By its very nature, innovative design is initially destructive of capital-**either in the form for** labour skills or capital equipment.
A. either in the form and
B. in either forming of
C. neither form on
D. either in the form of
E. No correction required

108. A teenager **has work out** how germs travel on airplanes and what can be done to stop them.
A. has worked out
B. have worked on
C. worked in
D. has been worked out
E. No correction required

109. Ordinary salary is just one factor to consider **when it come to** choosing a university, exclaimed the Director of Civic University.
A. when it come to
B. when it comes to
C. when that comes to
D. when it coming to
E. No correction required

110. The research study is an eye-opener and **attempts to acquaint** us with the problems of the poor nations.
A. attempted to acquaint
B. attempts at acquainting
C. attempt to acquaint
D. attempting to acquaint
E. No correction required

Directions (Qs. Nos. 111-115): *Read the following passage carefully and answer the question. Certain words/phrases are given in bold to help you locate them while answering some of the questions.*

Today, the discipline of science that Sir Isaac Newton helped found in the second half of the 17th Century has **extended** humanity's horizons to a degree he could scarcely have envisaged. Even though Pluto was reclassified as a dwarf planet in 2006, with the discovery of other similarly sized bodies nearby, the latest mission of America's space agency NASA to Pluto is expected to produce plenty of data for planetary scientists to pore over. But then the stream of missions to the outer planets–namely Jupiter, Saturn, Uranus and Neptune—turns into a trickle. At the same time, Cassini was launched in 1997 to explore Saturn and its moons but by 2017 its propellant will be depleted and provided it survives a series of fly-bye through Saturn's rings–It will burn up as it plunges through the planet's thick atmosphere.

Sometimes, before 2025 even the stalwart voyage probes, both launched in 1977, will lack the power to continue sending back data. Voyage-1 now in intersteller areas is the most distant man-made object in the Universe, and Voyage-2 is not far behind. The upshot is that for a decade or so, discoveries will come mostly from objects closer to Earth, regular excursions to Mars are planned. There will also be plenty of instruments launched to look at Earth itself. The hiatus might not end until two proposed space missions are lunched in the early 2020s. It seems an abrupt slowdown after a golden age of missions by NASA and European Space Agency (ESA). But, building a space probe is both complicated and expensive, it takes years of planning and jostling for funds as well as hefty dose of lack to ensure that complex equipment works well. We are travelling today from some good science and good funding in the 1990s. And money has become much scarcer in recent years. In 1981, the recent high-water mark for NASA, the agency received $25 billion. Its budget fell to a low of $16.9 billion in 2013. Some of NASA's cash has been shifted to other projects. NASA's co-operation with ESA on future missions has also been scaled back as a result of budget cuts.

The Europeans, by contrast, have kept their funding fairly steady. But, ESA's budget is just £4.4 billion ($4.9 billion). Other countries are interested in space and have missions under way or in the making, including China, Japan and India. But so far they have no ambitions to venture beyond mars.

Does the coming gap in planetary exploration **matter**? Studying the geology, atmosphere and evolution of planets, and comets provides valuable science. Others have loftier ambitions. Keeping planetary science going is critical to the long-term survival of the species on this planet. Because space missions have such long lead times, the looming run of years will have deleterious effects even if budgets start to rise again. The concern is that when funding does get back, there will be a missing generation of valuable knowledge almost. It's really difficult to go through boom and bust cycles since you've got to keep the scientific community and the engineers ticking over to maintain the expertise they will have in outer solar-system exploration.

111. Which of the following is the central idea of the passage?
- A. Space travel is exclusive to developed countries and this is unlikely to change.
- B. We are too focused on studying the universe and proving the existence of extraterrestrial life.
- C. There has been a decline in the quality of scientific discovery in recent times.
- D. Despite huge leaps in planetary science in the past, exploration is unfortunately likely to dwindle now.
- E. Though we have physically explored various planets we are unable to make them habitable.

112. Which of the following can be said about the voyage probes?
- A. These have been obsolete for a long time and should be called as soon as possible.
- B. These probes have been damaged and are responsible for polluting the galaxy.
- C. These have travelled the furthest and provided invaluable insights in the field of planetary science.
- D. Scientists have lost contact with these and worryingly cannot prepare their exact location.
- E. Too many resources are diverted to maintaining these outdated probes.

113. Which of the following is/are (a) factor(s) which affect space missions today?
- (*a*) Funding from NASA and ESA to space programme in developing countries.
- (*b*) Scarcity of engineers in the field.
- (*c*) Budgets and advance planning of projects.

A. Only (*a*) B. Only (*c*)
C. All (*a*), (*b*) & (*c*) D. Only (*b*)
E. Only (*a*) & (*c*)

114. What does the phrase 'It's really difficult to go through boom-and-bust cycle' convey?
- A. Some economies are still trying to recover from exorbitant space funding in the year 1990s.
- B. Space exploration missions have had more failures than successes.
- C. Global economic mission since 2000 has resulted in lack of employment for engineers.
- D. Fluctuations in space exploration funding are not desirable.
- E. The durations for space missions should be more optimally planned to avoid wastage of resources.

115. Choose the word which is most nearly the same in meaning to the word MATTER given in bold as used in the passage.

A. substance B. theme
C. suitable D. count
E. question

116. What does the author suggest regarding countries such as China, Japan and India?
- (*a*) These countries should increase their budgets for space travel.
- (*b*) These should enter into agreements with developed countries for space exploration.
- (*c*) Their ideas of making Mars habitable are too lofty.

A. Only (*a*)
B. Only (*b*)
C. Only (*b*) & (*c*)
D. Only (*a*) & (*c*)
E. None of the given options (*a*), (*b*) & (*c*)

117. What is the author's view regarding reduction in funds for space exploration?

A. It is an appropriate step as the planet faces more pressing problems.
B. It will be detrimental as it will hamper scientific discovery and knowledge.
C. It is desirable as we have adequate evidence that sustaining life in some planets is too costly.
D. It is an unwelcome move as several space missions are scheduled this year.
E. Other than those given as options.

118. What do the statistics on space agency budgets cited in the passage indicate?

A. Space agency budgets vary across countries and within a country over time
B. Building spacecrafts is becoming more expensive over time.
C. Despite increasing space budgets, there is a lack of innovation in space exploration.
D. There have been many expensive failures in space incursions in recent times.
E. Asia's space budget is fast catching up to Europe's and America's till present.

119. Choose the word which is opposite in meaning to the word EXTENDED given in bold as used in the passage.

A. postponed
B. delayed
C. amplified
D. curtailed
E. relaxed

120. Which of the following is true in the context of the passage?

A. There is conflict among scientists about the classification of planetary bodies.
B. Collaborations among nations for space exploration has not really worked.
C. Studying outer space has implications for life on earth.
D. The number of space scientists has fallen since the 1990s.
E. None of the given options is true in the context of the passage.

Directions (Qs. Nos. 121-130): *Read each sentence to find out whether there is any error in it. The error, if any, will be in one part of the sentence. The number of that part is the answer. If there is no error, the answer is 'E'. (Ignore errors of punctuation, if any.)*

121. The next time you/are at the city airport,/apart of shopping for the usual,/you can also purchase a piece of art.

A. The next time you
B. art at the city airport,
C. apart of shopping for the usual,
D. you can also purchase a piece of art.
E. No error

122. Despite being laid low by illness/in the run-up to the event,/the sportsman intend to give his best/on the upcoming championship.

A. Despite being laid low by illness
B. in the run-up to the event,
C. the sportsman intend to give his best
D. on the upcoming championship.
E. No error

123. After staying together/for several years, the actress/finally separated from her huband/for good in 2004.

A. After staying together
B. for several years, the actress
C. finally separated from her husband
D. for good in 2004
E. No error

124. The city's young women/are going out and buying/diamonds themselves, as by gifted/diamonds by men is such passed.

A. The city's young women
B. are going out and buying
C. diamonds themselves, as by gifted
D. diamonds by men is such passed.
E. No error

125. After swung between playing/positive and negative characters,/the actor is set to attempt comedy/for the first time on small screen.

A. After swung between playing
B. positive and negative characters,
C. the actor is set to attempt comedy

D. for the first time on small screen.
E. No error

126. Research show that people/who are able to responding/more quickly to questions are/ perceived as more charismatic.
A. Research show that people
B. who are able to responding
C. more quickly to questions are
D. perceived as more charismatic.
E. No error

127. No sooner did/ the chairman begin speaking/ some participants started/ shouting slogans.
A. No sooner did
B. the chairman begin speaking
C. some participants started
D. shouting slogans.
E. No error

128. Staying healthy/and high spirited/is not/very difficult.
A. Staying healthy
B. and high spirited
C. is not
D. very difficult.
E. No error

129. Like against/a fixed interest rate loan,/a floating interest rate loan offers/flexibility to borrowers.
A. Like against
B. a fixed interest rate loan,
C. a floating interest rate loan offers
D. flexibility to borrowers.
E. No error

130. The director refused/to meet his critics/and did not respond to/any of their letters.
A. The director refused
B. to meet his critics
C. and did not respond to
D. any of their letters.
E. No error

Directions (Qs. Nos. 131-135): *In each of the following sentences, there are two blank spaces. Below each sentence there are five words/pairs of words denoted by number (A), (B), (C), (D) and (E). Find out which word/pair of words can be filled up in the blanks in the sentence in the same sequence to make the sentence meaningfully complete.*

131. Findings ______ that social intelligence is more than just ______ the right thing to do.
A. depict, making
B. state, letting
C. suggest, ascertaining
D. show, knowing
E. illustrate, allowing

132. Saunas are not only a good way to detox, but they also help you get _________ a cold quicker by opening up your sinus passage, and helping you ________ easily.
A. over, breathe
B. past, air
C. better, smell
D. leave, oxygenate
E. arrest, vacate

133. A fixed rate home loan is ________ for those who want to have a __________ monthly repayment schedule.
A. good, high
B. kept, limited
C. ideal, predictable
D. prime, logical
E. best, annual

134. Paintings are generally quite ________ , but by expanding art to forms and objects beyond paintings, we will make it ________ to the common man.
A. costly, limited
B. cheap, available
C. expensive, accessible
D. reasonable, pricey
E. steep, exorbitant

135. No ________ how big or small the piece of jewellery, it is the fact that you bought it with your own money that makes it _____ .
A. matter, special
B. doubt, unique
C. problem, stand
D. way, small
E. issue, dear

Directions (Qs. Nos. 136-140): *Rearrange the following six sentences (a), (b), (c), (d), (e) & (f) in a proper sequence to form a meaningful paragraph, then answer the given question.*

(*a*) At the same time, allowing restaurant drivers to take leftovers home in a 'doggy bag' is a common phenomenon in the US, but the practice is frowned upon in some EU countries.

(*b*) An approach to train waste-minimising habits is through cooking classes, for example, the local authority of Brussels trained 1900 people in 2009 on how to minimise waste.

(*c*) Caterers can minimise waste by anticipating demand, informed by reservations and customer feedback surveys.

(*d*) There are similar education opportunities in the hospitality industry as well.

(*e*) Societal efforts are needed to banish this embarrassment.

(*f*) The European Parliament has recommended that this practical training be incorporated in school curricula.

136. Which of the following should be the THIRD sentence after the rearrangement?

A. (*a*) B. (*b*)
C. (*f*) D. (*d*)
E. (*e*)

137. Which of the following should be the FOURTH sentence after the rearrangement?

A. (*a*) B. (*b*)
C. (*c*) D. (*e*)
E. (*d*)

138. Which of the following should be the LAST (SIXTH) sentence after the rearrangement?

A. (*a*) B. (*e*)
C. (*d*) D. (*c*)
E. (*b*)

139. Which of the following should be the FIRST sentence after the rearrangement?

A. (*a*) B. (*b*)
C. (*c*) D. (*d*)
E. (*e*)

140. Which of the following should be the FIFTH sentence after the rearrangement?

A. (*a*) B. (*b*)
C. (*c*) D. (*d*)
E. (*f*)

Directions (Qs. Nos. 141-150): *A passage is given below, there are a number of gaps each of which is numbered. The numbers given under each passage has five choices (A, B, C, D, E), for each number. You are to choose the best choice and write it in the box provided against each.*

Around the world, companies that have achieved international leadership employ strategies that **(141)** from each other in every respect. But, when every successful company will employ its own particular strategy, the **(142)** mode of operation–the character and trajectory of all successful companies is fundamentally the same.

Companies **(143)** competitive advantage through acts of innovation. They approach innovation in its broadest sense, including both new technologies and new ways of doing things. They perceive a new basis for competing or better means to competing in old ways. Innovation can be **(144)** in a new product design, a new production process, a new marketing approach or a new way of conducting training. Much innovation is mundane and incremental, depending more on accumulation of small insights and advances **(145)** on a single, major technological breakthrough. It often involves ideas that are not even 'new' ideas that have been **(146)**, but never vigorously pursued. It always involves investments in skill and knowledge, as well as in physical assets and brand reputations.

Some innovations create competitive advantage by perceiving an entirely new market opportunity or by serving a market segment that others have **(147)**. When competitors are slow to respond, such innovation **(148)** competitive advantage. For instance, in industries such as autos and home electronics, Japanese companies **(149)** this initial advantage by **(150)** on smaller more compact, lower capacity models that foreign competitors declared as less profitable, less important and less attractive.

141. A. offer B. deter
C. after D. contrast
E. vary

142. A. underlying B. basis
C. prima D. element
E. routed

143. A. compete B. work
C. follow D. achieve
E. dispatch

144. A. obviously B. seen
C. attached D. attested
E. noticeable

145. A. there B. the
C. that D. therefore
E. than

146. A. existed B. over
C. around D. all
E. universally

147. A. divergent B. noticed
C. ignored D. shut
E. detoured

148. A. profits B. yields
C. return D. felicitates
E. turns on

149. A. strengthens B. proceed
C. allowed D. gained
E. prove

150. A. heading B. indicating
C. touching D. focusing
E. hitting

PROFESSIONAL KNOWLEDGE (MARKETING)

151. A tangible product that the consumer feels comfortable purchasing without gathering additional information and then actually buys with minimum of effort is termed a(n)
A. Shopping good B. Convenience good
C. Business product D. Specially good
E. Unsought good

152. The process of dividing a market into distinct groups of buyers who have different needs, characteristics or behaviours and who might require separate products or marketing programs is called ______ .
A. Market segmentation
B. Market positioning
C. Market differentiation
D. Market targeting
E. Marketing mix

153. ______ is not a stage of product life cycle in marketing.
A. Introduction B. Maturity
C. Growth D. Decline
E. Planning

154. Which of the following is not a characteristic important in influencing an innovator's rate of adoption?
A. Organization type of the innovator
B. Compatibility
C. Divisibility
D. Communicability
E. Complexity

155. The Financial contracts whose values are obtained from the values of underlying assets are ______ .
A. Mortgage B. Commercial papers
C. Stocks D. Derivatives
E. Bonds

156. All of the following are considered to be broad market-follower strategies EXCEPT ______ .
A. innovator B. imitator
C. cloner D. counterteller
E. adapter

157. A company has four choices when it comes to developing brands. Which one of the following is not one among them?
A. New brands B. Multi brands
C. Brand extension D. Line extension
E. Brand sponsoring

158. ______ is a demand state where consumer may share a strong need that cannot be satisfied by an existing model?
A. Declining demand
B. Irregular demand
C. Negative demand
D. Non-existent demand
E. Latent demand

159. ________ is the development, design and implementation of marketing programme, processes and activities that recognises the breadth and interdependencies of today's marketing environment.
A. Niche marketing
B. Supply chain marketing
C. Holistic marketing
D. Relationship marketing
E. Demand-centred marketing

160. The _______ holds that marketing strategy should deliver value to customers in a way that maintain or improve both the consumer's and society's well-being.
A. societal marketing concept
B. society centered marketing
C. customer-centered marketing
D. focused business model
E. production centered business

161. Major oil producers carry an oil exploration, oil drilling, oil refining, chemical manufacture and service-station operation. When an organization does all of these separate tasks distribution channel they can be said to have achieved what is called ______ .
A. parallel marketing
B. horizontal integration
C. vertical integration
D. concentric integration
E. conglomerate marketing

162. Which of the following describes the tendency of people to interpret information in a way that will support what they already believe?
A. Selective creativity
B. Selective distortion
C. Selective matching
D. Selective attraction
E. Selective attribute

163. The _____ stage of a product is characterized as being one where there is period of rapid climb in sales and substantial profit improvement.
A. introduction
B. decline
C. maturity
D. saturation
E. growth

164. The discomfort caused by post purchase conflict is called ______ .
A. Dissatisfaction
B. Cognitive Dissonance
C. Post-purchase behaviour
D. Buyer's remorse
E. Comparative tension

165. _______ is the study of how individuals, groups and organizations select, buy, use and dispose of goods, services, ideas or experiences to satisfy their needs and wants.
A. Psychology
B. Product differentiation
C. Psychographic segmentation
D. Target marketing
E. Consumer behaviour

166. Mutual Funds are regulated in the country by______ .
A. IRDA
B. Association of Mutual Funds of India (AMFI)
C. NABARD
D. Securities and Exchange Board of India
E. Reserve Bank of India

167. Situation in which a firm introduces new products to stimulate sales but the profit comes at the expense of other products sold by that firm is called ______ .
A. Repositioning
B. Push marketing
C. Differentiated marketing
D. Cannibalization
E. Cartelization

168. Cultivating opinion leaders and getting them to spread information about a product or service to others in their communities is ______.
A. Buzz Marketing
B. Leader Marketing
C. Niche Marketing
D. Complex Marketing
E. Selective Marketing

169. Marketing management is defined as ______
A. monitoring the profitability of the company's products and services
B. the art and science of choosing target markets and building profitable relationships with them
C. managing the market process
D. developing marketing strategies to move the company forward
E. selecting target markets to deploy marketers.

170. The measures of the brand's ability to capture consumer performance and loyalty is termed ______ .
A. Brand superiority
B. Brand equity
C. Brand version
D. Brand loyalty
E. Brand preference

171. Mission statements are at their best when they reflect a ______ an almost impossible dream that provides direction for the next 10 to 30 years.
A. market
B. strength
C. competency
D. vision
E. value

172. A strategy in which the initial price of the product is set low in relation to the target market's range of expected prices is termed ______ .
A. Market skimming pricing
B. Old pricing
C. Discount market pricing
D. Market penetration pricing
E. Special market pricing

173. A group of tradition bound consumers who are the tool to adapt an innovation is called ______ .
A. Challengers
B. Leaders
C. Innovators
D. Laggards
E. Loyal agents

174. Low prices on products for which you have accurate price knowledge lets you know that the product has to be a bargain. This type of pricing is termed ______ .
A. Reference pricing
B. Psychological pricing
C. Volume pricing
D. Promotional pricing
E. Signpost pricing

175. The want satisfying power of a product is called its ______ .
A. Price B. Utility
C. Bond D. Purpose
E. Goal

176. Based on the rates firms play in the target market in a specific industry, they are classified as following except in a ______ .
A. Market challenger B. Market plotter
C. Market leader D. Market nicher
E. Market follower

177. TQM approach in which all the people of the company are involved in constantly improving the performance of products, services and business processes. TQM stands for ______ .
A. Total Quality Management
B. Total Quality Marketing
C. Total Quantity Management
D. Total Queries Management
E. Total Quality Manipulation

178. When backed by buying power, wants become ______ .
A. self-esteem needs
B. demands
C. exchanges
D. physical needs
E. social needs

179. The philosophy of product centered marketing concept is ______ .
A. Right products for the customers
B. Make and sell
C. Make what the market wants
D. Sense and respond
E. Selling on product benefits

180. The customer's evaluation of the difference between all the benefits and all the costs of a market offering relative to those of competing offers is called ______ .
A. Customer perceived value
B. Customer expectation
C. Customer satisfaction
D. Customer loyalty
E. Customer relationship

181. Button market is where ______ .
A. capital is disposed
B. gold is purchased and sold
C. shares are purchased
D. production of silver takes place
E. investment are made

182. Especially in large firms, a sales force frequently is specialized in some organizational fashion. Which of the following is not one of such specializations?
A. Customer specialization
B. Major accounts specialization
C. Product specialization
D. Geographic specialization
E. Economic order specialization

183. Greater consumer control means that, in building customer relationships, companies can no longer rely on marketing by intrusion. The most practice marketing is ______ .
A. Conversion B. Delivery
C. Retention D. Attraction
E. Attention

184. According to Maslow's Hierarchy of Needs, sense of belonging is grouped in ______ .
A. Esteem needs
B. Social needs
C. Safety needs
D. Physiological needs
E. Self-actualization needs

185. Michael Porter has identified five forces that determine the intrinsic long-run attractiveness of a market segment. Which of the following would not be among Porter's five forces?
A. Threat of buyers' growing bargaining power
B. Threat of substitute products
C. Threat of technological partners
D. Threat of intense segment rivalry
E. Threat of new entrants

186. The unplanned static or distortion during the communication process, which results in the receivers' getting a different message then the one that the sender sent is the ______ .
A. Response B. Feedback
C. Noise D. Decoding
E. Encoding

187. If a MNC like Nestle varied the elements of the marketing mix to suit the countries in which it sold its products, which type of strategy would it be following?
A. Differentiated
B. Undifferentiated
C. Standardized
D. Adapted
E. Concentrated

188. Under which of the following company orientations towards the market place would we expect to get 'better economical' talacy?
A. Marketing concept
B. Holistic marketing concept
C. Production concept
D. Selling concept
E. Product concept

189. If a company focuses on only one or a few market segments instead of small share of a large market, the same is ______ .
A. segment marketing
B. conceptual marketing
C. mass marketing
D. micro marketing
E. niche marketing

190. An estimate the total financial value of the brand is ______ .
A. Brand valuation
B. Brand tracking
C. Brand auditing
D. Brand partitioning
E. Brand equity

191. The total combined customer value of all the company's current and potential customers is called ______ .
A. Customer share
B. Customer delight
C. Customer loyalty
D. Customer orientation
E. Customer equity

192. We can say that a ___ has three characteristics.
1. It is a source of competitive advantage in that it makes a significant contribution to perceived customer benefits;
2. It has application in a wide variety of markets, and
3. It is difficult for competitors to imitate.

A. strategic business unit
B. core competency
C. business strategy
D. winning strategy
E. core technology

193. Which demographic segmentation divides buyers into different groups based on social class, lifestyle or personality characteristics?
A. Age and life cycle segmentation
B. Gender segmentation
C. Age segmentation
D. Psychographic segmentation
E. Income segmentation

194. The internet version of word of mouth marketing is termed ______ .
A. Viral marketing
B. Web marketing
C. Channel marketing
D. Network marketing
E. Virtual marketing

195. ______ is the development, interpretation and communication of decision oriented information to be used in all phases of marketing process.
A. Marketing forecast
B. Market intelligence
C. Market planning
D. Marketing research
E. Marketing Information system

196. GATT is more than 60 years old treaty designed to promote world trade by reducing tariff and other international trade barriers. GATT stands for ______ .
A. General Aspects on Tariff and Trade
B. General Agreement on Tariffs and Trade
C. Geneva Agreement on Trade and Tariff
D. General Allowance for Trade and Tariff
E. Geneva Agreement on Traffic or Trade

197. People differ greatly in their readiness to try new products. Which of the following do not belong to the adapter categorization on the basis of relation time of adopter of innovators?
A. Innovators
B. Laggards
C. Early majority
D. Late majority
E. Super majority

198. As per BCG Matrix of classification of SBUs of an organization, Cash cows are SBUs that typically generate ______ .
A. Large awareness levels but few sales
B. Problems for product managers often
C. High industry growth
D. More cash than that can be invested profitably in its own business
E. Paper losses in the long run

199. A strategy of ______ pricing involves using prick in a competitive weapon in order to push competitors out of market or eliminate competitors.
A. Bargain
B. Psychological
C. Premium
D. Advanced
E. Predatory

200. 'ECS' is a term associated with the ______.
A. Banking industry
B. Insurance industry
C. Mutual fund business
D. Capital market transactions
E. Microfinance activity

ANSWERS

1	**2**	**3**	**4**	**5**	**6**	**7**	**8**	**9**	**10**
C	A	C	D	E	B	D	D	D	C
11	**12**	**13**	**14**	**15**	**16**	**17**	**18**	**19**	**20**
A	E	D	B	E	A	C	C	A	E
21	**22**	**23**	**24**	**25**	**26**	**27**	**28**	**29**	**30**
E	B	E	E	D	B	D	E	A	B
31	**32**	**33**	**34**	**35**	**36**	**37**	**38**	**39**	**40**
A	D	A	D	B	A	C	E	A	E
41	**42**	**43**	**44**	**45**	**46**	**47**	**48**	**49**	**50**
B	C	C	A	A	E	D	D	B	E
51	**52**	**53**	**54**	**55**	**56**	**57**	**58**	**59**	**60**
C	C	E	E	E	A	A	D	C	E
61	**62**	**63**	**64**	**65**	**66**	**67**	**68**	**69**	**70**
C	B	D	A	D	C	D	C	D	A
71	**72**	**73**	**74**	**75**	**76**	**77**	**78**	**79**	**80**
D	E	B	C	A	E	D	C	B	C
81	**82**	**83**	**84**	**85**	**86**	**87**	**88**	**89**	**90**
C	D	C	C	C	C	E	C	D	E
91	**92**	**93**	**94**	**95**	**96**	**97**	**98**	**99**	**100**
C	E	C	B	D	C	C	A	C	A
101	**102**	**103**	**104**	**105**	**106**	**107**	**108**	**109**	**110**
D	B	C	A	B	E	D	A	B	B
111	**112**	**113**	**114**	**115**	**116**	**117**	**118**	**119**	**120**
D	C	B	D	D	E	B	A	D	B
121	**122**	**123**	**124**	**125**	**126**	**127**	**128**	**129**	**130**
C	D	A	C	A	C	C	D	A	C
131	**132**	**133**	**134**	**135**	**136**	**137**	**138**	**139**	**140**
D	A	C	C	A	A	D	C	B	E
141	**142**	**143**	**144**	**145**	**146**	**147**	**148**	**149**	**150**
E	A	D	A	E	C	C	B	D	D
151	**152**	**153**	**154**	**155**	**156**	**157**	**158**	**159**	**160**
B	A	E	A	D	A	E	E	C	A
161	**162**	**163**	**164**	**165**	**166**	**167**	**168**	**169**	**170**
C	B	E	B	E	D	D	E	C	D
171	**172**	**173**	**174**	**175**	**176**	**177**	**178**	**179**	**180**
D	D	C	A	B	B	A	B	E	A
181	**182**	**183**	**184**	**185**	**186**	**187**	**188**	**189**	**190**
E	D	D	B	C	C	D	C	E	A
191	**192**	**193**	**194**	**195**	**196**	**197**	**198**	**199**	**200**
E	B	D	D	A	B	B	C	E	A

EXPLANATORY ANSWERS

1. I.

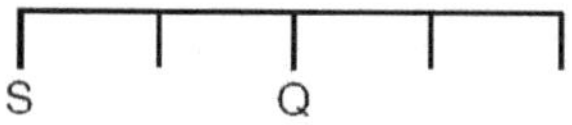

Number of Persons in the line = 5

II.

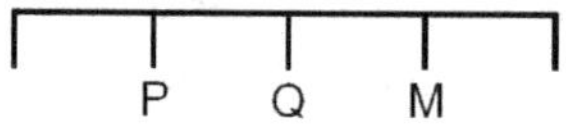

Number of Persons in the line = 5.

Hence, both I and II are sufficient to answer the question independently.

2. I.

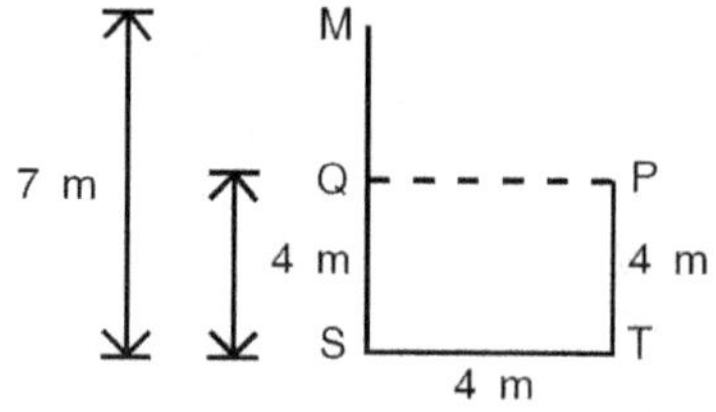

Hence, distance between points M and Q

$7 - 4 = 3$ m

Only statement I can answer the question.

3.

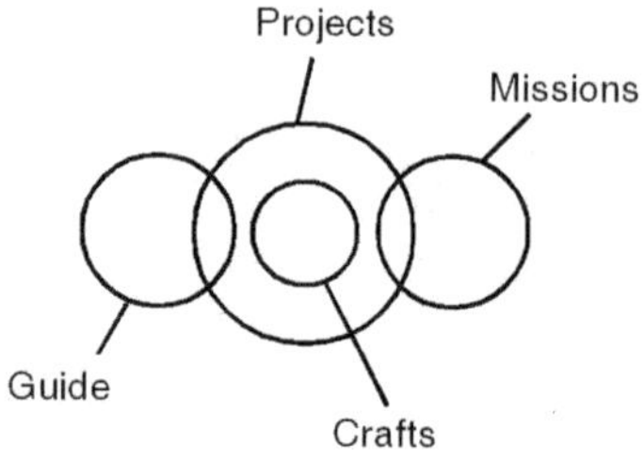

or

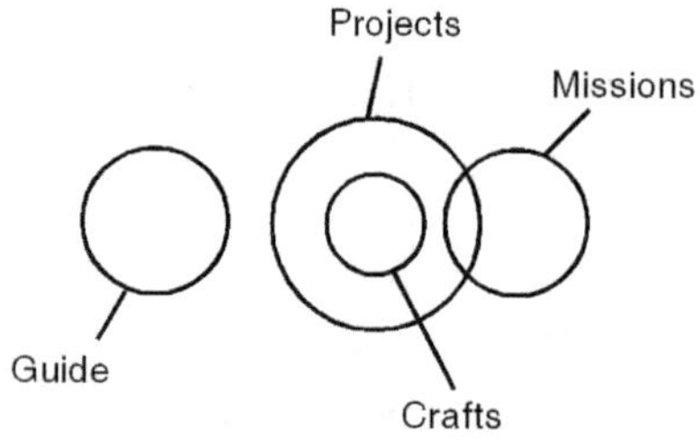

Hence, either conclusion I or II is true.

4.

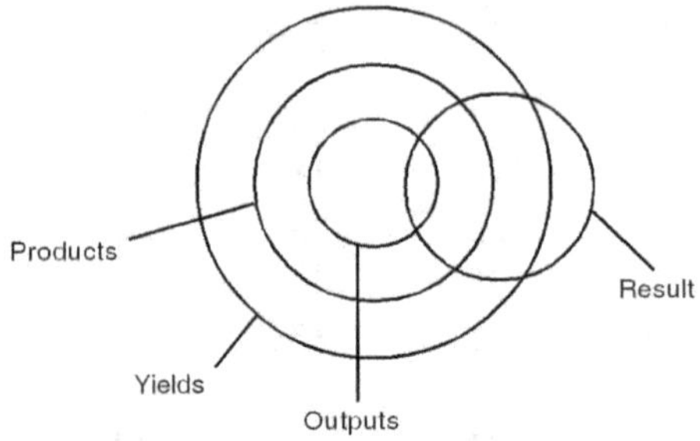

∴ Neither conclusions I nor II follow.

5.

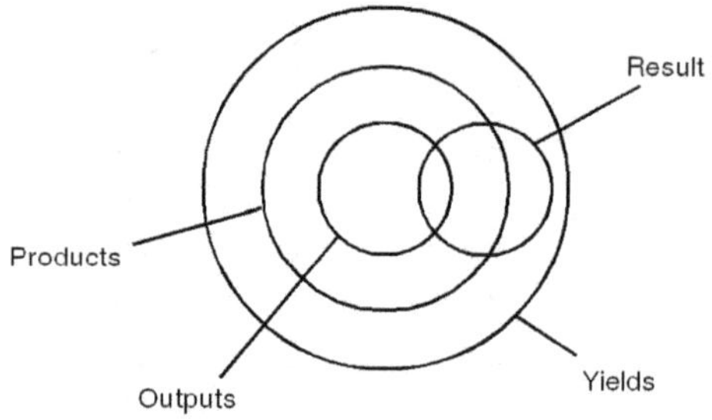

∴ Both conclusions I and II follow.

6.

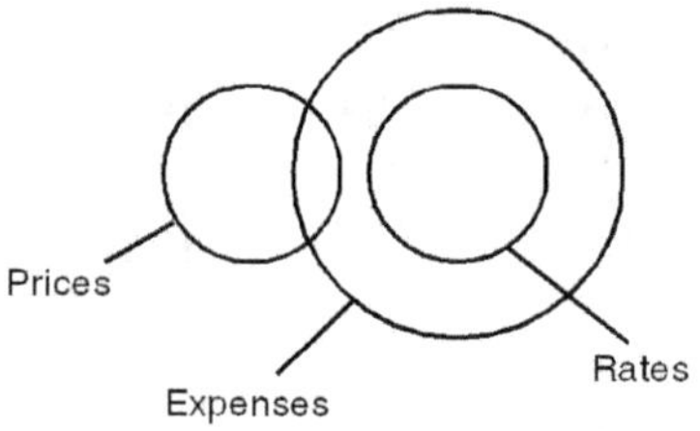

or

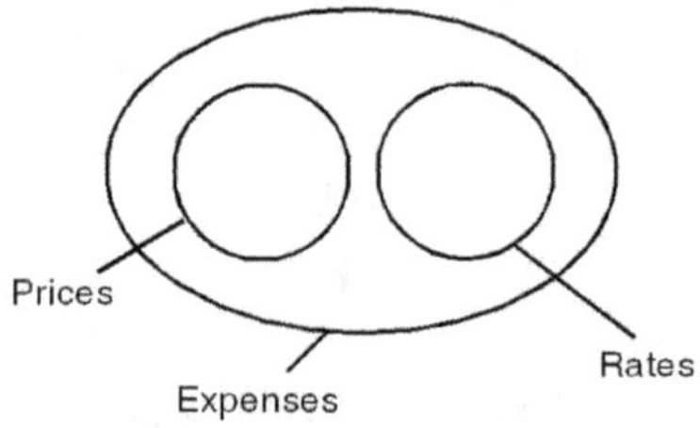

Hence, only conclusion II follows.

7.

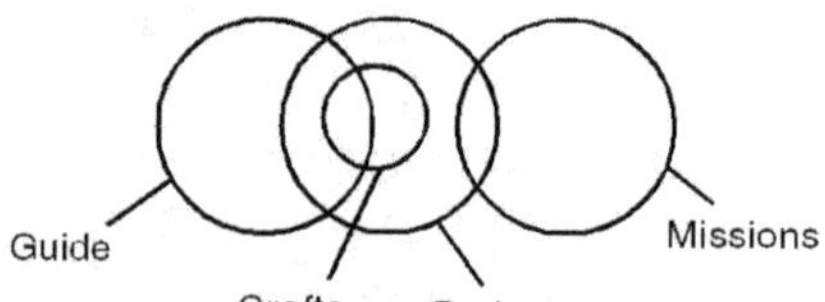

Hence, neither conclusion I nor II follows.

8-12. Sitting arrangement of 8 peoples around a square table:

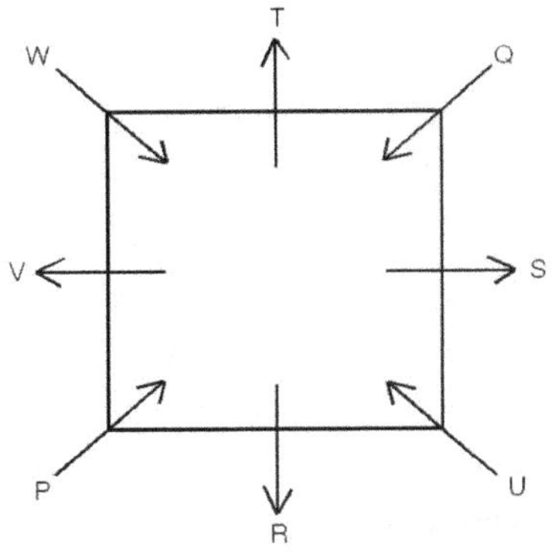

13. I. $R \geq U \leq J$

$\Rightarrow$ No relation between R & J

$\therefore$ $R > J$ {False}.

II. $K \geq S = U > L \Rightarrow K > L$

$\therefore$ $L = K$ {False}.

14. I. $X \geq C \leq W < K$

$\Rightarrow$ No relation between X and K

$\therefore$ $X > K$ {False}.

II. $W \geq C \geq L$

$\Rightarrow$ $W \geq L$ {True}.

15. I. $S \geq M > A \geq R$

$\Rightarrow S > R$ {True}.

II. $S \geq M \geq T \geq Y$

$\Rightarrow S \geq Y$ {True}.

16. I. $D > W \geq C \geq L$

$\Rightarrow D > L$ {True}.

II. $L > D$ {False}.

17. $U \geq P = B = K \geq L \Rightarrow U \geq L$

I. $U > L$ {True}

II. $U = L$ {True}

Hence, either I or II follows.

19-23. Row I :

Row II :

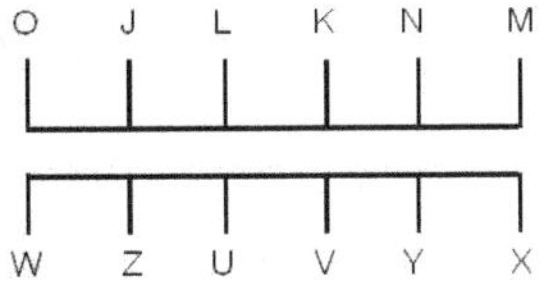

26-31.

Days	Persons	Countries
Monday	T	Germany
Tuesday	P	Japan
Wednesday	U	Australia
Thursday	R	China
Friday	Q	Malaysia
Saturday	V	Nepal
Sunday	S	India

32-35

Input : adverb 59 36 salient 81 idioms bakery 14 launch 47 umpire 62

Step-I : umpire adverb 59 36 salient 81 idioms bakery launch 47 62 14

Step-II : idioms umpire adverb 59 salient 81 bakery launch 47 62 14 36

Step-III : adverb idioms umpire 59 salient 81 bakery launch 47 14 36 62

Step-IV : 47 adverb idioms umpire 59 81 bakery launch 14 36 62 salient

Step-V : 59 47 adverb idioms umpire 81 bakery 14 36 62 salient launch

Step-VI : 81 59 47 adverb idioms umpire 14 36 62 salient launch bakery

37.

39-43.

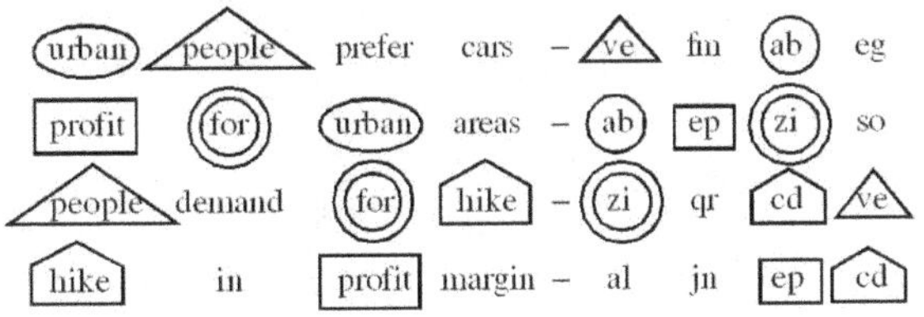

45-49. Floor No.

Floor No.	
8	M
7	O
6	L
5	R
4	K
3	Q
2	P
1	N

51. I. Area of circle = $\pi\ (r)^2$, where r = radius

$$\text{Perimeter} = 2\pi.r$$

$$\therefore \quad r = \frac{\text{Perimeter}}{2\pi}$$

$$= \frac{88}{2\times\frac{22}{7}}$$

$$= 14 \text{ cm}$$

$$\text{Area of circle} = \pi(r)^2$$

$$= \frac{22}{7}\times(14)^2$$

$$= 616 \text{ cm}^2$$

II. $$\text{Radius of circle} = \frac{\text{Diameter of circle}}{2}$$

$$= \frac{28}{2} = 14 \text{ cm}$$

$$\text{Area of circle} = \pi(14)^2 = 616 \text{ cm}^2$$

Statement I or II alone are sufficient to answer the question.

52. I. $$\text{C.I.} - \text{S.I.} = 250$$

$$25000\left[\left(1+\frac{r}{100}\right)^2 - 1\right] - \frac{25000\times r\times 2}{100} = 250$$

$$\left(1+\frac{r}{100}\right)^2 - 1 - \frac{2r}{100} = \frac{250}{25000}$$

$$\frac{r^2}{10000} = \frac{1}{100}$$

$$r = 10$$

Hence, rate of interest = 10%.

II. Simple Interest (in 10 years) = Principal

$$\text{P} = \frac{\text{P}\times r\times 10}{100}$$

$$\Rightarrow \quad r = 10$$

$\therefore$ rate of interest = 10%

Hence, either statement I or II alone are sufficient to answer.

54. From I & II, we have:

Let, swimming speed of man is u km/hr and speed of current is v km/hr

downstream speed = $(u + v)$ km/hr

upstream speed = $(u - v)$ km/hr

From question,

$$(u + v) = \frac{9}{\left(\frac{3}{2}\right)}$$

$$\Rightarrow \quad u + v = 6 \quad ...(i)$$

$$(u - v) = \frac{9}{3}$$

$$\Rightarrow \quad u - v = 3 \quad ...(ii)$$

From (*i*) and (*ii*), we have,

$$v = 1.5 \text{ km/hr}.$$

55. I. Let total marks = x.

Then, $$\text{Raman scores} = x\times\frac{25}{100}$$

$$= 0.25\,x$$

Again, $$\text{Sunil scores} = 288$$

From question, $288 - 128 = 0.25\,x$

$$0.25\,x = 160$$

$$x = \frac{160}{0.25} = 640$$

$\therefore$ Total marks = 640

Raman marks = 160

II. Minimum passing percentage

$$= \left(\frac{160+64}{640}\right)\times 100$$

$$= \frac{224}{640}\times 100 = 35\%.$$

56. I. $2x = y$, $2y = z \Rightarrow 4x = 2y = z$

$$\Rightarrow \quad x = \frac{z}{4}$$

$$y = \frac{z}{2}$$

Now, $4x + 3y + 5z = 60$ {given}

$$z + \frac{3}{2}z + 5z = 60$$

$$\frac{15z}{2} = 60$$

$$\Rightarrow \quad z = 8$$

$$y = \frac{z}{2} = \frac{8}{2} = 4$$

$$x = \frac{z}{4} = \frac{8}{2} = 2$$

$\therefore \quad x^2 + y + z = (2)^2 + 4 + 8 = 16.$

II. $3x + 3y + 2z = 34$

and $2x + 5y + 6z = 72$

There are three variables, so need three equation.

57. I. (Arun + Suraj + Vinay)'s weight

$= 68 \times 3$

$= 204$

(Raju + Pratap)'s weight = $72 \times 2 = 144$

From question,

Suraj's weight = 78 kg

Vinay's weight = 46 kg

$\therefore$ Arun's weight = 80 kg

Raju's weight = 68 kg

$\therefore$ Pratap's weight = 76 kg

So, second highest weight is Suraj.

59. I. From question,

$$27x - 23x = 100000$$
$$4x = 100000$$
$$x = 25000$$

Total population of the city A

$= 50x$

$= 50 \times 25000$

$= 1250000.$

II. Let population of city A = P_A

Population of city B = P_B

Then, $P_A = P_B \times \frac{80}{100}$

$\Rightarrow \quad P_A = 0.8\ P_B$

And $P_B - P_A = 312500$

$0.2\ P_B = 312500$

$P_B = 1562500$

$P_A = 1250000.$

60. From (I) and (II), we have

Let, Student participated in elocution = x

Then, $x\left(1+\frac{150}{100}\right) = 150$

$$x \times \frac{250}{100} = 150$$

$$x = \frac{150\times 100}{250} = 60$$

$\therefore$ Student participated in elocution = 60.

61. Let the incomes in 2000 of Companies X and Y be $3x$ and $4x$ respectively.

And let the expenditures in 2000 of Companies X and Y be E_1 and E_2 respectively.

Then, for Company X we have:

$$65 = \frac{3x - E_1}{E_1}\times 100$$

$$\Rightarrow \quad \frac{65}{100} = \frac{3x}{E_1} - 1$$

$$\Rightarrow \quad E_1 = 3x \times \left(\frac{100}{165}\right) \quad ...(i)$$

For Company Y we have:

$$50 = \frac{4x - E_2}{E_2} \times 100$$

$$\Rightarrow \quad \frac{50}{100} = \frac{4x}{E_2} - 1$$

$$\Rightarrow \quad E_2 = 4x \times \left(\frac{100}{150}\right) \quad ...(ii)$$

From (*i*) and (*ii*), we get:

$$\frac{E_1}{E_2} = \frac{3x \times \left(\frac{100}{165}\right)}{4x \times \left(\frac{100}{150}\right)}$$

$$= \frac{3 \times 150}{4 \times 165} = \frac{15}{22}$$

(Required ratio).

62. Profit percent of Company Y in 1997 = 35

Let the income of Company Y in 1997 be ₹ x crores.

Then, $$35 = \frac{x - 220}{220} \times 100$$

$$\Rightarrow \quad x = 297$$

∴ Income of Company Y in 1997

= ₹ 297 crores.

63. Let the expenditure of each companies X and Y in 1996 be ₹ x crores.

And left the income of Company X in 1996 be ₹ z crores

So that the income of Company Y in 1996 = ₹ (342 – z) crores

Then, for Company X we have:

$$40 = \frac{z - x}{x} \times 100$$

$$\Rightarrow \quad \frac{40}{100} = \frac{z}{x} - 1$$

$$\Rightarrow \quad x = \frac{100z}{140} \quad ...(i)$$

Also, for Company Y we have:

$$45 = \frac{(342 - z)}{x} \times 100$$

$$\Rightarrow \quad \frac{45}{100} = \frac{(342 - z)}{x} - 1$$

$$\Rightarrow \quad x = \frac{(342 - z) \times 100}{145} \quad ...(ii)$$

From (*i*) and (*ii*), we get:

$$\frac{100z}{140} = \frac{(342 - z) \times 100}{145}$$

$$\Rightarrow \quad z = 168$$

Substituting z = 168 in (*i*),

we get : x = 120

∴ Total expenditure of Companies X and Y in 1996 = $2x$ = ₹ 240 crores

Total income of Companies X and Y in 1996 = ₹ 342 crores

∴ Total profit = ₹ (342 – 240) crores

= ₹ 102 crores.

64. Let the income of Company X in 1998 be ₹ x crores.

Then, $$55 = \frac{x - 200}{200} \times 100$$

$$\Rightarrow \quad x = 310$$

∴ Expenditure of Company X in 2001 = Income of Company X in 1998

= ₹ 310 crores

Let the income of Company X in 2001 be ₹ z crores

Then, $$50 = \frac{z - 310}{310} \times 100$$

$\Rightarrow$ $z = 465$

$\therefore$ Income of Company X in 2001

= ₹ 465 crores.

65. Let the incomes of each of the two Companies X and Y in 1999 be ₹ x

And let the expenditure of Companies X and Y in 1999 be E_1 and E_2 respectively

Then, for Company X we have:

$$50 = \frac{x - E_1}{E_1} \times 100$$

$$\Rightarrow \quad \frac{50}{100} = \frac{x}{E_1} - 1$$

$$\Rightarrow \quad x = \frac{150}{100} E_1 \quad \text{...}(i)$$

Also, for Company Y we have:

$$60 = \frac{x - E_2}{E_2} \times 100$$

$$\Rightarrow \quad \frac{60}{100} = \frac{x}{E_2} - 1$$

$$\Rightarrow \quad x = \frac{160}{100} E_2 \quad \text{...}(ii)$$

From (*i*) and (*ii*), we get:

$$\frac{150}{100} E_1 = \frac{160}{100} E_2$$

$$\Rightarrow \quad \frac{E_1}{E_2} = \frac{160}{150}$$

$$= \frac{16}{15}$$

(Required ratio).

66. Percentage of people from village C, whose favourite fruit as Mango = 16%

Hence, required percentage

$$= \frac{16}{28} \times 100$$

$= 57.14 \approx 57\%$.

67. Number of people whose favourite fruit as custard apple

$$= \frac{15}{100} \times 5800$$

= 870.

68. Total number of people having their favourite fruit as apple and grapes together

$$= \frac{(12 + 11)}{100} \times 5800$$

$= 23 \times 58$

= 1334.

69. Percentage of people from village D having their favourite fruit as Banana and Guava together

= 20 + 12 = 32%

Since, percentage of people from village D having their other favourite fruit

= 100 – 32

= 68%

Hence, required number of people

$$= \frac{68}{100} \times \frac{25}{100} \times 5800$$

= 986.

70. Required number of people

$$= \frac{20}{100} \times 5800 - \frac{1}{2} \times \frac{21}{100} \times 5800$$

= 1160 – 609

= 551.

71. I. $6x^2 + 5x + 1 = 0$

$(2x + 1)(3x + 1) = 0$

$$x = -\frac{1}{2} \text{ or } -\frac{1}{3}$$

II. $15y^2 + 8y + 1 = 0$

$(5y + 1)(3y + 1) = 0$

$$y = -\frac{1}{3} \text{ or } -\frac{1}{5}$$

$\therefore$ $y \geq x$.

72. I. $x^2 + 5x + 6 = 0$

$(x + 3)(x + 2) = 0$

$x = -2$ or -3

II. $4y^2 + 24y + 35 = 0$

$4y^2 + 10y + 14y + 35 = 0$

$2y(2y + 5) + 7(2y + 5) = 0$

$(2y + 5)(2y + 7) = 0$

$\Rightarrow \quad y = -\frac{5}{2}$ or $-\frac{7}{2}$

No relation between x and y.

73. I. $2x^2 + 5x + 3 = 0$

$2x^2 + 2x + 3x + 3 = 0$

$(2x + 3)(x + 1) = 0$

$x = -1$ or $-\frac{3}{2}$.

II. $y^2 + 9y + 14 = 0$

$y^2 + 2y + 7y + 14 = 0$

$(y + 2)(y + 7) = 0$

$y = -2$ or -7

$\therefore \quad x > y$.

74. I. $88x^2 - 19x + 1 = 0$

$88x^2 - 8x - 11x + 1 = 0$

$(8x - 1)(11x - 1) = 0$

$x = \frac{1}{8}$ or $\frac{1}{11}$

II. $132y^2 - 23y + 1 = 0$

$132y^2 - 12y - 11y + 1 = 0$

$(12y - 1)(11y - 1) = 0$

$y = \frac{1}{11}$ or $\frac{1}{12}$

$\therefore \quad x \geq y$.

75. I. $6x^2 - 7x + 2 = 0$

$6x^2 - 3x - 4x + 2 = 0$

$(3x - 2)(2x - 1) = 0$

$x = \frac{2}{3}$ or $\frac{1}{2}$.

II. $20y^2 - 31y + 12 = 0$

$$y = \frac{31 \pm \sqrt{961 - 960}}{40}$$

$$y = \frac{31 \pm 1}{40}$$

$\Rightarrow \quad y = \frac{3}{4}$ or $\frac{4}{5}$

$\therefore \quad y > x$.

76. I. $6x^2 + 23x + 20 = 0$

$6x^2 + 8x + 15x + 20 = 0$

$(2x + 5)(3x + 4) = 0$

$x = -\frac{5}{2}$ or $-\frac{4}{3}$

II. $6y^2 + 31y + 35 = 0$

$6y^2 + 10y + 21y + 35 = 0$

$(3y + 5)(2y + 7) = 0$

$y = -\frac{5}{3}$ or $-\frac{7}{2}$

No relation between x and y.

77. I. $x^2 = 81$

$\Rightarrow \quad x = \pm 9$

II. $y^2 - 18y + 81 = 0$

$(y - 9)^2 = 0$

$\Rightarrow \quad y = 9$

$\therefore \quad y \geq x$.

78. I. $4x^2 + 20x + 21 = 0$

$(2x + 7)(2x + 3) = 0$

$x = -\frac{3}{2}$ or $-\frac{7}{2}$

II. $2y^2 + 174 + 35 = 0$

$2y^2 + 7y + 10y + 35 = 0$

$(2y + 7)(y + 5) = 0$

$y = -5$ or $-\frac{7}{2}$

$\therefore \quad x \geq y$.

79. I. $x^2 - 14x + 48 = 0$

$x^2 - 8x - 6x + 48 = 0$

$(x - 8)(x - 6) = 0$

$\Rightarrow \quad x = 6 \text{ or } 8$

II. $y^2 - 5y + 6 = 0$

$(y - 3)(y - 2) = 0$

$\Rightarrow \quad y = 2 \text{ or } 3$

$\therefore \quad x > y.$

80. I. $38x^2 - 3x - 11 = 0$

$$x = \frac{3 \pm \sqrt{9 + 4 \times 11 \times 38}}{2 \times 38}$$

$$= \frac{3 \pm 41}{76}$$

$$x = \frac{11}{19}$$

$$\text{or } -\frac{1}{2}$$

II. $28y^2 + 32y + 9 = 0$

$$y = \frac{-32 \pm \sqrt{(-32)^2 - 4.9.28}}{2 \times 28}$$

$$= \frac{-32 \pm 4}{56}$$

$$= -\frac{1}{2} \text{ or } -\frac{9}{14}$$

$\therefore \quad x \geq y.$

81. Distance between them is one hour

= 3.5 – 3

= 0.5 km

Distance betwen them in 4 hour

= 4 × 0.5

= 2 km.

86. 28 39 63 102 158 [233]

+11 +24 +39 +56 +75

+13 +15 +17 +19

87. 7 16 141 190 919 [1040]

$+(3)^2$ $+(5)^3$ $+(7)^2$ $+(9)^3$ $+(11)^2$

88. 12 17 32 57 92 [137]

+(5×1) +(5×3) +(5×5) +(5×7) +(5×9)

89. 19 25 45 87 159 [269]

+(2×3) +(4×5) +(6×7) +(8×9) +(10×11)

90. 83 124 206 370 698 [1354]

+(41) +(41×2) +(41×4) +(41×8) +(41×16)

91. Academic books published by M

$$= 28200 \times \frac{7}{(7+3)}$$

= 19740

Academic books published by P

$$= 31200 \times \frac{8}{(8+5)}$$

= 19200

Difference of books = 19740 – 19200

= 540.

92. Number of books given to each distributor by publisher Q

$$= \frac{33800}{25} = 1352.$$

93. Average of Non-academic books published by R and S

$$= \frac{35700 \times \frac{6}{17} + 37800 \times \frac{13}{18}}{2}$$

$$= \frac{12600 + 27300}{2}$$

= 19950.

94. Number of books by Publisher P, Q and R together when increases by 30%

$$= 100700 \times \frac{130}{100}$$

$$= 130910$$

Number of books by Remaining P, Q and R together when decreases by 20%

$$= 127900 \times \frac{80}{100}$$

$$= 102320$$

$$\text{New average} = \frac{130910 + 102320}{7}$$

$$= 33318.$$

95. Total number of books distributed by O and Q together

$$= 29700 \times \frac{92}{100} + 33800 \times \frac{79}{100}$$

$$= 27324 + 26702$$

$$= 54026.$$

96. Let cost price of the Saree is ₹ x from question,

$$x + x \times \frac{12}{100} = 5225$$

$$\frac{112x}{100} = 5225$$

$$x = 4665$$

Decrease in price = 5225 – 4665

= ₹ 560.

PROFESSIONAL KNOWLEDGE

MARKETING

☞ CHAPTER-1

INTRODUCTION TO MARKETING

MARKET

The term "market" originates from the Latin word "Marcatus" which means "a place where business is conducted". A layman regards market as a place where buyers and sellers personally interact and finalise deals.

According to Perreault and McCarthy, market is defined as a group of potential customers with similar needs or wants who are willing to exchange something of value with sellers offering various goods and/or services to satisfy those needs or wants. Of course, some negotiation will be needed. This can be done face-to-face at some physical location (for example, a farmer's market). Or it can be done indirectly through a complex network that links middlemen, buyers and sellers living far apart.

MARKETING

Numerous definitions were offered for marketing by different authors. Some of the definitions are as follows:

- Creation and delivery of a higher standard of living.
- Marketing is the process that seeks to influence voluntary exchange transactions between a customer and a marketer.
  —William G. Zikmund and Michael D'Amico
- Marketing is the process of discovering and translating consumer needs and wants into products and services, creating demand for these products and services and then in turn expanding this demand. *—H.L. Hansen*
- Marketing is the business process by which products are matched with markets and through which transfer of ownership are affected.
  —Edward W. Cundiff
- Marketing consists of the performance of business activities that direct the flow of goods and services from producers or suppliers to consumers or end-users.
  —American Marketing Association
- Marketing is a societal process by which individuals and groups obtain what they need and want through creating, offering and freely exchanging products and services of value with others. *—Philip Kotler*
- Marketing is the performance of activities that seek to accomplish an organization's objectives by anticipating customer or client needs and directing the flow of need satisfying goods and services from producer to customer or client.
  —William D. Perreault and E. Jerome McCarthy

Some other important definitions are:

- Marketing is a social and managerial process by which individuals and groups obtain what they need and want through creating, offering and exchanging products of value with others.
- Marketing is the process by which an organization relates creatively, productively and profitably to the market place.
- Marketing is the art of creating and satisfying customers at a profit.
- Marketing is getting the right goods and services to the right people at the right places at the right time at the right price with the right communication and promotion.

- Much of marketing is concerned with the problem of profitably disposing what is produced.
- Marketing is the phenomenon brought about by the pressures of mass production and increased spending power.
- Marketing is the performance of business activities that direct the flow of goods and services from the producer to the customer.
- Marketing is the economic process by which goods and services are exchanged between the maker and the user and their values determined in terms of money prices.
- Marketing is designed to bring about desired exchanges with target audiences for the purpose of mutual gain.
- Marketing activities are concerned with the demand stimulating and demand fulfilling efforts of the enterprise.
- Marketing is the function that adjusts an organization's offering to the changing needs of the market place.
- Marketing is a total system of interacting business activities designed to plan, promote, and distribute need satisfying products and services to existing and potential customers.
- Marketing origination with the recognition of a need on the part of a consumer and termination with the satisfaction of that need by the delivery of a usable product at the right time, at the right place, and at an acceptable price. The consumer is found both at the beginning and at the end of the marketing process.
- Marketing is a view point, which looks at the entire business process as a highly integrated effort to discovery, arouse and satisfy consumer needs.

It is obvious from the above definitions of marketing that marketing has been viewed from different perspective. Now it is imperative to discuss the important terms on which definition of marketing rests: needs, wants, and demands; products; value, cost, and satisfaction; exchange, transactions and relationships; markets; and marketers. These terms are also known as the core concepts in marketing.

Needs, Wants and Demands

Marketing starts with the human needs and wants. People need food, air, water, clothing and shelter to survive. They also have a strong desire for recreation, health, education, and other services. They have strong performances for particular versions and brands of basic goods and services. A human need is a state of felt deprivation of some basic satisfaction. People require food, clothing, shelter, safety, belonging, esteem and a few other things for survival. These needs are not created by their society or by marketers; they exist in the very texture of human biology and the human condition.

Wants are desires for specific satisfiers of these deeper needs. For example, one needs food and wants a pizza, needs clothing and wants a Raymond shirt. These needs are satisfied in different manners in different societies. While people's needs are few, their wants are unlimited. Human wants are continually shaped and reshaped by social forces and institutions.

Demands are wants for specific products that are backed up by an ability and willingness to buy them. For example, many people want to buy a luxury car but they lack in purchasing power. Companies must therefore measure not only how many people want their products, but, how many would actually be willing to buy and finally able to buy it.

Marketers do not create need, they simply influence wants. They suggest to consumers that a particular product or brand would satisfy a person's need for social status. They do not create the need for social status but try to point out that a particular product would satisfy that need. They try to influence demand by making the product attractive, affordable, and easily available.

Products

People satisfy their needs and wants with products. Product can be defined as anything that can be offered to someone to satisfy a need or want. The word product brings to mind a physical object, such as T.V., Car, and Camera etc. The expression products and services are used distinguish between physical objects and intangible ones. The importance of physical products does not lie in owning them rather using them to satisfy our wants. People do not buy beautiful cars to look at, but because it provides transportation service. Thus, physical products are really vehicles that deliver services to people. Services are also supplied by other vehicles such as persons, places, activities, organizations and ideas. If people are bored, they can go to a musical concert (persons) for entertainment, travel to beautiful destination like Shimla (place), engage in physical exercise (activity) in health clubs, join a laughing club (organization) or adopt a different philosophy about life (idea). Services can be delivered through physical objects and other vehicles. The term product covers physical products, service products, and other vehicles that are capable of delivering satisfaction of a need or want. The other terms also used for products are offers, satisfiers, or resources.

Manufacturers pay more attention to their physical products than to the services produced by these products. They love their products but forget that customers buy them to satisfy their need. People do not buy physical object for their own sake. A tube of lipstick is bought to supply a service: helping the person to look better. A drill is bought to supply a service: producing holes. The marketers job is to sell the benefits or services built into physical products rather than just describe their physical features.

Value, Cost, and Satisfaction

How do consumers choose among the various products that may satisfy a given need is very interesting phenomenon. If a student needs to travel five kilometers to his college every day, he may choose a number of products that will satisfy this need: a bicycle, a motorcycle, automobile and a bus. These alternatives constitute product choice set. Assume that the student wants to satisfy different needs in traveling to his college, namely speed, safety, ease and economy. These are called the need set. Each product has a different capacity to satisfy different needs. For example, bicycle will be slower, less safe and more effortful than an automobile, but it would be more economical. Now, the student has to decide on which product delivers the most satisfaction.

Here comes the concept of value. The student will form an estimate of the value of each product in satisfying his needs. He might rank the products from the most need satisfying to the least need satisfying. Value is the consumer's estimate of the product's overall capacity to satisfy his or her needs. The student can imagine the characteristics of an ideal product that would take him to his college in a split second with absolute safety, no effort and zero cost. The value of each actual product would depend on how close it came to this ideal product.

Assume the student is primarily interested in the speed and case of getting to college. If the student was offered any of the above mentioned products at no cost, one can predict that he would choose an automobile. Here comes the concept of cost. Since each product involves a cost, the student will not necessarily buy automobile. The automobile costs substantially more than bicycle or motorcycle. Therefore, he will consider the product's value and price before making a choice. He will choose the product that will produce the most value per rupee.

Today's consumer behaviour theorists have gone beyond narrow economic assumptions of how consumers form value in this mind and make product choices. These modern theories on consumer behaviour are important to marketers because the whole marketing plan rests on assumptions about how customers make choices. Therefore the concept of value, cost and satisfaction are crucial to the discipline of marketing.

Exchange, Transactions and Relationships

The fact that people have needs and wants and can place value on products does not fully explain the concept of marketing. Marketing emerges when people decide to satisfy needs and wants through exchange. Exchange is one of the four ways people can obtain products they want. The first way is self production. People can relieve hunger through hunting, fishing, or fruit gathering. In this case there is no market or marketing. The second way is coercion. Hungry people can steal food from others. The third way is begging. Hungry people can approach others and beg for food. They have nothing tangible to offer except gratitude. The fourth way is exchange. Hungry people can approach others and offer some resource in exchange, such as money, another food, or service.

Marketing arises from this last approach to acquire products. Exchange is the act of obtaining a desired product from someone by offering something in return. For exchange to take place, five conditions must be satisfied:

- There are at least two parties.
- Each party has something that might be of value to the other party.
- Each party is capable of communication and delivery.
- Each party is free to accept or reject the offer.
- Each party believes it is appropriate or desirable to deal with the other party.

If the above conditions exist, there is a potential for exchange. Exchange is described as a value creating process and normally leaves both the parties better off than before the exchange. Two parties are said to be engaged in exchange if they are negotiating and moving towards an agreement. The process of trying to arrive at naturally agreeable terms is called negotiation. If an agreement is reached, we say that a transaction takes place. Transactions are the basic unit of exchange. A transaction consists of a trade of values between two parties. A transaction involves several dimensions; at least two things of value, agreed upon conditions, a time of agreement, and a place of agreement. Usually a legal system arises to support and enforce compliance on the part of the transaction. A transaction differs from a transfer. In a transfer A gives X to B but does not receive anything tangible in return. When A gives B a gift, a subsidy, or a charitable contribution, we call this a transfer.

Transaction marketing is a part of longer idea, that of relationship marketing. Smart marketers try to build up long-term, trusting, 'win-win' relationships with customers, distributors, dealers and suppliers. This is accomplished by promising and delivering high quality, good service and fair prices to the other party over time. It is accomplished by strengthening the economic, technical, and social ties between members of the two organizations. The two parties grow more trusting, more knowledgeable, and more interested in helping each other. Relationship marketing cuts down on transaction costs and time. The ultimate outcome of relationship marketing is the building of a unique company asset called a marketing network. A marketing network consists of the company and the firms with which it has built solid, dependable business relationships.

MARKETS

The concept of exchange leads to the concept of market. A market consists of all the potential customers sharing a particular need or want who might be willing and able to engage in exchange to satisfy that need or want. The size of market depends upon the number of persons who exhibit the need, have resources that interest others, and are willing to offer these resources in exchange for what they want.

Originally the term market stood for the place where buyers and sellers gathered to exchange their goods, such as a village square. Economists use the term, 'market' to refer to a collection of buyers and sellers who transact over a particular product or product class; i.e. the housing market, the grain market, and so on. Marketers, however, see the sellers as constituting the industry and the buyers as constituting the market. Business people use the term, 'markets' colloquially to cover various groupings of customers. They talk about need markets (such as diet-seeking market); product markets (such as the shoe market); demographic markets (such as the youth market); and geographic markets (such as the Indian market). The concept is extended to cover non-customer groupings as well, such as voter markets, labour markets, and donor markets.

Marketing, Marketers, and Marketing Management

The concept of markets bring the full circle to the concept of marketing. Marketing means human activities taking place in relation to markets. Marketing means working with markets to actualize potential exchanges for the purpose of satisfying human needs and wants. If one party is more actively seeking an exchange than the other party, we call the first party a marketer and the second party a prospect. A marketer is someone seeking a resource from someone else and willing to offer something of value in exchange. The marketer is seeking a response from the other party, either to sell something or to buy something. Marketer can be a seller or a buyer. Suppose several persons want to buy an attractive house that has just become available. Each buyer will try to market himself or herself to be the one the seller selects. These buyers are doing the marketing. In the event that both parties actively seek an exchange, we say that both of them are marketers and call the situation one of reciprocal marketing.

In the normal situation, the marketer is a company serving a market of end users in the face of competitors. The company and the competitors send their respective products and messages directly and/or through marketing intermediaries i.e. middlemen and facilitators to the end users.

Marketing management takes place when at least one party to a potential exchange gives thought to objectives and means of achieving desired responses from other parties. According to American Marketing Association, 'Marketing Management is the process of planning and executing the conception, pricing, promotion, and distribution of ideas, goods, and services to create exchanges that satisfy individual and organizational objectives'. This definition recognizes that marketing management is a process involving analysis, planning, implementation, and control; that it covers ideas, goods and services; that it rests on the notion of exchange; and that the goal is to produce satisfaction for the parties involved.

NATURE OF MARKETING

- Marketing is both consumer-oriented and competitor-oriented. The consumer and competitor orientations can be easily understood by the following diagram.

		Competitor emphasis ← Minor	Major →
Customer Emphasis ↕	Minor	Self-centred	Competitor Oriented
	Major	Customer Oriented	Market driven

(*a*) Self-centred companies do not give any concern to the consumers and competitors. This type of companies can exist in the situation of monopoly. In the competitive economy, these companies cannot remain in thc business for long.

(*b*) Competitor-oriented companies mainly focus on competitor's activities, what the competitors are doing and what they are likely to do in the near future are the major areas of concern. The companies can be either reactive or proactive. The reactive companies will follow the moves of competitors. For example, if the competitors reduce price of its product or service then the reactive competitor-oriented companies will also reduce its prices. Whereas the proactive competitor oriented companies will try to identify what its major competitor is going to do.

(*c*) Customer-oriented companies believe in satisfying the customers at any cost. These companies obtain inputs from the customers and then develop their product or service as per customers' requirements and then earn profit through-customer satisfaction. The biggest problem is that they don't consider what their competitors are doing and in the long run it might prove counter-productive.

(*d*) Market driven companies are concerned about customers as well as competitors.

These companies regularly interact with the customers to know about their satisfaction levels and their future requirements and then try to develop the product or service which is better than their competitors. In the era of cut throat competition, these companies one more likely to be successful than the other companies.

- Marketing is a dynamic activity because a number of variables keep changing. For example marketing environment, customer's requirements, competitor's actions etc. keep changing thereby necessitating the changes in the company's offer. The companies may have to modify product, price, place or promotion due to changes in any of the numerous variables. For example, Indian manufacturer's either have to improve the quality or reduce the cost to meet the competition from foreign companies.
- Long-term objective of marketing is profit maximization through customer satisfaction. This is so because a satisfied customer will come back again for the same or different needs to the company. Apart from this, the satisfied customer is the company's best advertisement because word of mouth communication by the customer has more credibility than any other form of marketing communication and he'll recommend the company's products/services to his friends and relatives.
- Marketing is an integrated function and all the marketing decisions are linked with each other. One decision will automatically lead to another decision. For example if a company has decided to launch a product for limited number of customers then its price will be high and that product will be available through exclusive distribution system and the promotion strategy will depend on the media preferred by the target market. So, if a company decides the first step then decisions regarding the remaining steps will follow automatically.
- Marketing is the core functional area of modern day organisations and is the driving force behind every organisation. Marketing provides the vital input for corporate planning which in turn dictates the plans for other functional areas.
- Marketing is interlinked with other functional areas of the organisation. Marketing people collects the information regarding (customer's requirements and pass it to) the research and development and engineering people who'll turn the customer requirements into the product or service features. The finance and accounts people help in obtaining the money for the development of new product and also help in arriving at the final price decision. The human resource department provides the necessary manpower for carrying out various activities not only in the marketing area but also in the other functional areas.

IMPORTANCE OF MARKETING

Marketing is an important component of business. It satisfies human wants and also serves as an instrument for economic growth and social welfare. Even large-scale production is possible because of the support of marketing system. As marketing is growing all over the world, all countries are participating in global marketing and sharing benefits of such participation. In short, we can say now-a-days marketing has become important in every stage of business and in every walk of the common people's life. Some of the points which can explain its importance are as under:

- **Satisfies human wants:** The essence of marketing is to understand the needs and wants of consumers. It identifies unfulfilled human needs, convert them into business opportunities and as it involves in production and distribution process, through the exchange process satisfies the customers.
- **Generates Employment:** Marketing generates job opportunities directly or indirectly. Marketing involves in various functions like production, distribution, promotion etc. Thousands of people are employed in these sectors. Thus, people gets work for their hands.

- **Improves standard of living:** Marketing facilitates introduction of new and better products and also as per needs of consumers. It also intensifies competition forcing the marketers to improve the quality of their products and offers those at reasonable price. This raises the standard of living of the people. Consumers may start consuming good quality products as marketing has converted "yesterday's" luxuries into today's necessities. This leads towards standard of living.
- **Creates utility:** Marketing is important as it creates form, time, place and possession utilities. Such utility creation gives satisfaction and pleasure to consumers.
- **Introduction of new products:** In order to stay ahead in competition, it is necessary for an organisation to develop new products frequently. Marketing functions like research, product development etc. facilitate introduction of new products. As marketing starts with customer and ends with it also indentifies exact need of the people and accordingly introduces the product.
- **Achieves objectives:** With the help of the marketing activities, business firms can earn good amount of profit. This helps them achieve business objectives like increase in market share, creating goodwill, expanding business and so on.
- **Widens Markets:** Marketing widens market through large-scale movement of goods throughout the country. Marketing includes various promotional tools like advertising personal selling, sales promotion, direct marketing etc. These promotional tools help a firm expand its market from local to regional to national and at international level.
- **Facilitates specialisation and division of labour:** Marketing functions, if performed successfully, lead to specialisation, division of a labour and efficient performance of production of functions. Marketing gives basic ideas about customer's needs and requirements, business can arrange and allocate resources accordingly which leads to division of labour.
- **Economic growth:** Marketing brings industrial and economic growth as it creates new demands for goods and thereby encourages production activities. This leads to the creation of massive employment opportunities. Thus, marketing is the kingpin that sets revolving of the whole economy.

MARKETING CONCEPTS

Firms vary in their perceptions about business, and their orientations to the market place. This has led to the emergence of many different concepts of marketing. Marketing activities should be carried out under some well-thought out philosophy of efficient, effective, and responsible marketing. There are six competing concepts under which organisations conduct their marketing activity.

Exchange Concept

The exchange concept of marketing, as the very name indicates, holds that the exchange of a product between the seller and the buyer is the central idea of marketing. While exchange does form a significant part of marketing, to view marketing as more exchange will result in missing out the essence of marketing. Marketing is much broader than exchange. Exchange, at best, covers the distribution aspect and the price mechanism. The other important aspects of marketing, such as, concern for the customer, generation of value satisfactions, creative selling and integrated action for serving customer, are completely overshadowed in exchange concept.

Production Concept

It is one of the oldest concepts guiding sellers. The production concept holds that customers will favour those products that are widely available and low in cost. Managers of production-oriented organisations concentrate on achieving high production efficiency and wide distribution coverage.

The assumption that consumers are primarily interested in product availability and low price holds in at least two types of situations. The first is where the demand for a product exceeds supply. Here consumers are more interested in obtaining the product than in its fine points. The suppliers will concentrate on finding ways to increase production. The second situation is where the product's cost is high and has to be brought down through increased productivity to expand the market.

The Product Concept

The product concept holds that consumers will favour those products that offer quality or performance. Managers in these product-oriented organisations focus their energy on making good products and improving them over time.

These managers assume that buyers admire well-made product and can appraise product quality and performance. These managers are caught up in a love affair with their product and fail to appreciate that the market may be less "turned on" and may even be moving in different direction.

The product concept leads to "marketing myopia", an undue concentration on the product rather than the need. Railroad management thought that users wanted trains rather than transportation and overlooked the growing challenge of the airlines, buses, trucks, and automobiles. Slide-rule manufacturers thought that engineers wanted slide rules rather than the calculating capacity and overlooked the challenge of pocket calculators.

The Selling Concept

The selling concept holds that consumers, if left alone, will ordinarily not buy enough of the organization's products. The organization must therefore put an aggressive selling and promotion effort.

The concept assumes that consumers typically show buying inertia or resistance and have to be coaxed into buying more, and that the company has available a whole battery of effective selling and promotion tools to stimulate more buying.

The selling concept is practiced most aggressively with "sought goods", those goods that buyers normally do not think of buying, such as insurance, encyclopedias, and funeral plots. These industries have perfected various sales techniques to locate prospects and hard-sell them on the benefits of their product. Hard selling also occurs with sought goods, such as automobiles. Most firms practice the selling concept when they have overcapacity. Their aim is to sell what they make rather than make what they can sell.

Thus selling, to be effective, must be preceded by several marketing activities such as needs assessment, marketing research, product development, pricing, and distribution. If the marketer does a good job of identifying consumer needs, developing appropriate products, and pricing, distributing, and promoting them effectively, these products will be sold very easily. When Atari designed its first video game, and when Mazda introduced its RX-7 sports car, these manufacturers were swamped with orders because they had designed the "right" product based on careful marketing homework.

Indeed, marketing based on hard selling carries high risks. It assumes that customers who are coaxed into buying the product will like it; and if they don't, they won't bad-mouth it to friends or complain to consumer organizations. And they will possibly forget their disappointment and buy it again. These are indefensible assumptions to make about buyers. One study showed that disappointed customers bad-mouth the product to eleven acquaintances, while satisfied customers may good-mouth the product to only three.

The Marketing Concept

The marketing concept holds that the key to achieving organizational goals consists in determining the needs and wants of target markets and delivering the desired satisfactions more effectively and efficiently than competitors.

Theodore Levitt drew a perceptive contrast between the selling and marketing concepts. Selling focuses on the needs of the seller; marketing on the needs of the buyer. Selling is preoccupied with the seller's need to convert his product into cash; marketing with the idea of satisfying the needs of the customer by means of the product and the whole cluster of things associated with creating, delivering and finally consuming it.

Market focus: No company can operate in every market and satisfy every need. Nor can it even do a good job within one broad market: Even the mighty IBM cannot offer the best customer solution for every computer need. Companies do best when they define their target markets carefully. They do best when they prepare a tailored marketing program for each target market.

Customer orientation: A company can define its market carefully and still fail at customer-oriented thinking. Customer-oriented thinking requires the company to define customer needs from the customer point of view, not from its own point of view. Every product involves tradeoffs, and management cannot know what these are without talking to and researching customers. Thus, a car buyer would like a high-performance car that never breaks down, that is safe, attractively styled, and cheap. Since all of these virtues cannot be combined in one car, the car designers must make hard choices not on what pleases them but rather on what customers prefer or expect. The aim, after all, is to make a sale through meeting the customer's needs.

Why is it supremely important to satisfy the customer? Basically because a company's sales in each period come from two groups: customers and repeat customers. It always costs more to attract new customers than to retain current customers. Therefore, customer retention is more critical than customer attraction.

Coordinated marketing: Unfortunately, not all the employees in a company are trained or motivated to pull together for the customer. Coordinated marketing means two things. First, the various marketing functions-sales-force, advertising, product management, marketing research, and so on- must be coordinated among themselves. Too often the sales-force is made at the product managers for setting "too high a price" or "too high a volume target", or the advertising director and a brand manager cannot agree on the best advertising campaign for the brand. These marketing functions must be coordinated from the customer point of view. Second, marketing must be well coordinated with other departments. Marketing does not work when it is merely a department; it only works when all employees appreciate the effect they have on customer satisfaction.

Profitability: The purpose of the marketing concept is to help organizations achieve their goals. In the case of private firms, the major goal is profit; in the case of non-profit and public organizations, it is surviving and attracting enough funds to perform their work. Now the key is not to aim for profits as such but to achieve them as a byproduct of doing the job well.

This is not to say that marketers are unconcerned with profits. Quite the contrary, they are highly involved in analyzing the profit potential of different marketing opportunities. Whereas salespeople focus on achieving sales-volume goals, marketing people focus on identifying profit-making opportunities.

The Societal Marketing Concept

In recent years, some people have questioned whether the marketing concept is appropriate organizational philosophy in an age of environmental deterioration, resource shortages, explosive population growth, world hunger and poverty, and neglected social services. The question is whether companies that do an excellent job of sensing, serving, and satisfying individual consumer wants are necessarily acting in then best long-run interests of consumers and society.

The societal marketing concept holds that the organization's task is to determine the needs, wants, and interests of target markets and to deliver the desired satisfactions more effectively and efficiently than competitors in a way that preserves or enhances the consumer's and the society's well-being.

The societal marketing concept calls upon marketers to balance three considerations in setting their marketing policies, namely, company profits, consumer wants satisfaction, and public interest. Originally, companies based their marketing decisions largely on immediate company profit calculations. Then they began to recognize the long-run importance of satisfying consumer wants, and this introduced the marketing concept. Now they are beginning to factor in society's interests in their decision-making. The societal marketing concept calls for balancing all three considerations. A number of companies have achieved notable sales and profit gains through adopting and practicing the societal marketing concept.

The Difference Between Selling and Marketing

Marketing is much wider than selling, and much more dynamic. In fact, there is a fundamental difference between the two. Selling revolves around the needs and interests of the seller; marketing revolves around the needs and interests of the buyer. Selling starts with the existing products of the corporation and views business as a task of somehow promoting these products. Marketing, on the contrary starts with the customers-present and potential-and views business as a task of meeting the needs of the customers by producing and supplying those products and services that would meet such needs. Selling seeks profits by 'pushing' the products on the buyers. Marketing too, seeks profits, but not through aggressive pushing of products, but by meeting the needs of customers and by creating value satisfactions for them. In other words, marketing calls upon the corporation to choose products, prices and methods of distribution and promotion, which will meet the needs of the customers. It does not unwisely limit its role to persuading the customers to accept what the corporation already has or what it can offer readily.

To quote Theodore Levitt, "The difference between selling and marketing is more than semantic. A truly marketing-minded firm tries to create value-satisfying goods and services which the consumers will want to buy. What it offers for sale is determined not by the seller but by the buyer. The seller takes his cues from the buyer and the product becomes the consequence of the marketing effort, not vice-versa. Selling merely concerns itself with the tricks and techniques of getting the customers to exchange their cash for the company's products; it does not bother about the value satisfactions that the exchange is all about. On the contrary, marketing views the entire business as consisting of a tightly integrated effort to discover, create, arouse and satisfy customer needs."

The Difference Between Selling and Marketing

Selling	Marketing
Selling starts with the seller, and is preoccupied all the time with the needs of the seller.	Marketing starts with the buyer and focuses constantly on the needs of the buyer.
Seller is the centre of the business universe; activities start with the sellers.existing products.	Buyer is the centre of the business universe; activities follow the buyer and his needs.
Emphasises on saleable surplus available within the corporation.	Emphasises on identification of a market opportunity.
Seeks to quickly convert 'products' into 'cash'.	Seeks to convert customer 'needs' into 'products'.
Concerns itself with the tricks and techniques of getting the customers to part with their cash for the products available with the salesman.	Emphasises on fulfilling the needs of the customers.
Views business as a 'goods producing process'.	Views business as a 'customer satisfying process'.
Overemphasises the 'exchange' aspect, without caring for the 'value satisfactions' inherent in the exchange.	Concerns itself primarily and truly with the 'value satisfactions' that should flow to the customer from the exchange.
Sellers' preference dominates the formulation of the 'marketing mix'.	Buyer determines the shape the 'marketing mix' should take.
The firm makes the product first and then figures out how to sell it and make profit.	What is to be offered as a product is determined by the customer.

Selling	Marketing
Emphasises on staying with the existing technology and reducing costs.	The firm makes a 'total product offering' that will match and satisfy the identified needs of the customer.
Sellers' motives dominate marketing communications.	The 'product' is the consequence of the marketing effort; the marketing effort leads to products that the customers actually want to buy in their own interest.
Cost determines the price.	Emphasises on innovation in every sphere; on providing better value to the customer by adopting better technology.
Transportation, storage and other distribution functions are perceived as mere extensions of the production function.	Marketing communications is looked upon as the tool for communicating the benefits/satisfactions provided by the product.
Emphasis is laid on 'somehow selling' : there is no coordination among the different functions of the total marketing task.	Consumer determines price; price determines costs.
Different departments of the business operate as separate watertight compartments.	They are seen as vital services to be provided to the customer, keeping customer's convenience in focus.
In firms practising 'selling', production is the central function of the business.	Emphasis is laid on integrated marketing; an integrated strategy covering product, promotion, pricing and distribution.
'Selling' views the customer as the last link in the business.	All departments of the business operate in a highly integrated manner, the sole purpose being generation of consumer satisfaction. In firms practising 'marketing', marketing is the central function of the business; the entire company or business is organised around the marketing function. 'Marketing' views the customer as the very purpose of the business; sees the business from the point of view of the customer; customer consciousness permeates the entire organisation-all departments and all people in the organisation-all the time.

ROLE OF MARKETING MANAGERS IN CHANGING MARKETING ENVIRONMENT

Marketing activity of a business is the base of its success. So marketing manager must be very much cautions about each and every aspect of marketing and accordingly need to modify, change and adopt marketing activity, so that he can do well in existing condition. In facts marketing manager is basically responsible to earn more revenue through successful accomplishment of marketing objectives. Therefore, he must have doctrine over marketing environment, with which he can meet (solve) internal challenges and at the same time avoid socially undesirable external consequences. The marketing manager must be aware of the inter-relationship of the firm and the system and an appreciation of forces operating in both directions. The marketing environment may create new opportunities along with new threats. So the marketing managers' challenges are to study and understand the complex human behaviour and adjust his marketing activities accordingly. Following are some of the challenges faced by marketing managers, which have arisen in changing marketing environment. These include:

- **Product planning and development:** The marketing manager is very much associated with product planning and development.

  Product planning means devising products for the markets. It must satisfy the needs and expectations of consumers.

  Product development means introducing modifications to the existing product and bringing it into new form in the market.

  Nowadays, in a tough competition, the products have very small life, products need to have changes periodically. So marketing manager's responsibility to keep this in mind and accordingly he has to act, then only he can survive well in the market.

- **Processing knowledge of marketing environment:** Marketing environment is dynamic in nature. It plays a crucial role in securing balance between consumers and the firm using marketing techniques. Here marketing manager should see or visualize that where the environment is heading, what new trends are coming up and in what way it should be responded. This can be done by only knowledgeable marketing manager and justifying the situation.
- **Development marketing policy:** Marketing manager needs to develop his marketing policies. While developing, he should see the framework of organisational philosophy. Here based on his rich experiences, he can contribute in formulating a progressive, forward-looking, and result-oriented marketing policy in the light of changing marketing environment.
- **Optimum utilization of resources:** To attain the organisational objectives a marketing manager needs to handle and mobilize all types of resources in tune of organisational requirements. Then the resources may be manpower (personnel) time, finance, machinery or other physical assets. If he is able to find out the exact use of each of resources and without any surpluses or shortages of resources he deploy it and utilise upto maximum limit of it, is called proper utilization of resources.
- **To follow government legislations:** The marketing manager must be competent to operate the business within the limits prescribed by various laws. This will help the business earn goodwill respect and will avoid, undesirable circumstances, controversy and penalty. The ethical business activities will be carried out by the business. For this manager's needs to be well conversant with existing rules, laws etc.
- **Diversified rules:** Marketing manager's role is not restricted to selling and marketing area of the business. He has to deal and maintain vital link between different parties like customers, distributors, retailers, other firm and at society. Here he has to play different roles in different capacities so that he can enhance business activity well and maintain relation with each of them very co-cordially.
- **To adopt improved technology:** Technology is not a static element of business, Often one or the other way there is change in technological environment. This is sometimes directly or indirectly affecting to the business. Here marketing manager's responsibility is to see such type of changes are taking place and accordingly on the basis of business requirements need to adopt, If he is able to do so, then only he can stand as a successful manager.
- **Recognising changes in environment:** Business can't survive in its isolation. It needs support from all aspects of its surroundings. It includes natural, political, social, economical, cultural and demographical environment. At the time of managing organisation effectively, marketing manager should take note of the changes taking place and accordingly re-conceal or re-adjust resources, so that he can do well. Doing such type of changes is a very crucial job.

MULTIPLE CHOICE QUESTIONS

1. Good marketing is no accident, but a result of careful planning and ....

(*a*) Execution (*b*) Selling
(*c*) Research (*d*) Strategies
(*e*) None of these

2. Marketing is both an "art" and a "science" there is constant tension between the formulated side of marketing and the .... side.

(*a*) Creative (*b*) Management
(*c*) Selling (*d*) Behavior
(*e*) None of these

3. The most formal definition of marketing is ....
(*a*) Meeting needs profitability
(*b*) Improving the quality of life for consumers
(*c*) The 4Ps
(*d*) An organizational function and a set of process for creating, communicating and delivering, value to customers and that benefit the organization
(*e*) None of these

4. Marketing is a process which aims at ....
(*a*) Satisfaction of customer needs
(*b*) Selling products
(*c*) Production
(*d*) Profit making
(*e*) None of these

5. Marketing is a .... function of transferring goods from producers to consumers.
(*a*) Systematic (*b*) Economic
(*c*) Management (*d*) Commercial
(*e*) None of these

6. Marketing helps firms to increase their profits by ....
(*a*) Increase in sales
(*b*) Increase in production
(*c*) Increase in price
(*d*) Increase in customer
(*e*) None of these

7. The .... function of marketing makes the products available in different geographic regions.
(*a*) Production (*b*) Selling
(*c*) Distribution (*d*) Promotion
(*e*) All of these

8. Ensuring the availability of the products and services as and when required by the customers is .... utility.
(*a*) Time (*b*) Place
(*c*) Form (*d*) Possession
(*e*) None of these

9. Transportation belongs to .... function of marketing.
(*a*) Research (*b*) Exchange
(*c*) Physical supply (*d*) Facilitating
(*e*) None of these

10. The traditional view of marketing is that the firm makes something and then .... it.
(*a*) Markets (*b*) Sells
(*c*) Prices (*d*) Services
(*e*) None of these

11. Logistics means ....
(*a*) Production (*b*) Flow of goods
(*c*) Consumption (*d*) Marketing channel
(*e*) None of these

12. Marketing buzz means ....
(*a*) Viral marketing (*b*) Virtual marketing
(*c*) De-marketing (*d*) Social marketing
(*e*) None of these

13. .... is an attempt to reduce the demand for consumption of a specific product or service on permanent or temporary basis.
(*a*) De-Marketing
(*b*) Re-Marketing
(*c*) Ostensible Marketing
(*d*) Synchronic Marketing
(*e*) None of these

14. The customer focused philosophy is known as the .... concept.
(*a*) Production (*b*) Product
(*c*) Selling (*d*) Marketing
(*e*) Services

15. Which of the following is central to any definition of marketing?
(*a*) Marketing a profit
(*b*) Marketing a sale
(*c*) customer relationship
(*d*) Transaction
(*e*) None of these

16. When backed by buying power, wants become ....
(*a*) Social needs (*b*) Exchanges
(*c*) Demands (*d*) Physical needs
(*e*) None of these

17. Modern marketing begins and ends with the ....
(*a*) Sales (*b*) Products
(*c*) Customers (*d*) Price
(*e*) All of these

18. In selling concept, maximization of profit of the firm is done through ....
(*a*) Sales volume
(*b*) Increasing production
(*c*) quality
(*d*) Services
(*e*) None of these

19. Marketing is a .... function of transferring goods from producers to consumers.
(*a*) Systematic (*b*) Commercial
(*c*) Management (*d*) Economic
(*e*) None of these

20. Marketing evaluation and .... process are necessary to understand the efficiency and effectiveness of marketing activities and how both could be improve.
(*a*) Control
(*b*) Feedback
(*c*) Consumer behavior
(*d*) Measurement
(*e*) None of these

21. Marketing is a process of convincing one potential customer into .... customers.
(*a*) Rare (*b*) Actual
(*c*) Future (*d*) New
(*e*) None of these

22. Modern marketing begins and ends with ....
(*a*) Business (*b*) Consumers
(*c*) Economic (*d*) Company
(*e*) None of these

23. Marketing is a .... process.
(*a*) Goal oriented (*b*) Social
(*c*) Exchange (*d*) All of these
(*e*) None of these

24. The term Meta marketing was first used by ....
(*a*) Eugene J. Kelly (*b*) N. H. Borden
(*c*) Wendell (*d*) Philip Kotler
(*e*) Edward W. Cundiff

25. Marketing management covers not only the market of goods but also the marketing of ....
(*a*) Products (*b*) Services
(*c*) Quality (*d*) Sales volume
(*e*) None of these

26. Marketing utility consists of ....
(*a*) Price
(*b*) Place, price
(*c*) Product, place, price and profit
(*d*) Price, place, promotion and product
(*e*) Marketing management

27. A place for buying and selling activities is called ....
(*a*) Market (*b*) Marketing
(*c*) Market research (*d*) Market information
(*e*) None of these

28. The exchange value of a good service in terms of money is ....
(*a*) Price (*b*) Product
(*c*) Buying (*d*) Selling
(*e*) None of these

29. Selling the same product at different prices is known as ....
(*a*) Price lining
(*b*) Dual pricing
(*c*) Geographical pricing
(*d*) Monopoly pricing
(*e*) None of these

30. The social aspect of marketing is to ensure ....
(*a*) Price
(*b*) Demand
(*c*) Low price with high quality
(*d*) Service goods
(*e*) None of these

31. Marketing creates profit by creating .... to the buyer.
(*a*) Value (*b*) Money
(*c*) Product (*d*) Price
(*e*) None of these

32. .... includes the configuration of benefits, value, cost and satisfaction:
(*a*) Demand (*b*) Innovation
(*c*) Creativity (*d*) Invention
(*e*) None of these

33. Which of the following best identifies how marketing must be understood today?
(*a*) Satisfy customer needs
(*b*) Marketing
(*c*) Selling
(*d*) Behaviour
(*e*) None of these

34. .... consists of a group of customers who share a similar set of wants:
(*a*) Micro Marketing
(*b*) Mass Marketing
(*c*) Market Segment
(*d*) Market targeting
(*e*) None of these

35. A marketer is someone seeking a response from another party called ....
(*a*) Marketer (*b*) Prospect
(*c*) Supplier (*d*) Distributor
(*e*) All of these

36. .... are wants for specific products that are backed up an ability and willingness to buy them.
(*a*) Demand (*b*) Wants
(*c*) Needs (*d*) Desire
(*e*) None of these

37. A .... is someone seeking a response (attention, a purchase, a vote, a donation) from another party, called the ....
(*a*) salesperson, customer
(*b*) fund raiser, contributor
(*c*) politician, voter
(*d*) marketer, prospect
(*e*) celebrity, audience

38. The .... is practiced most aggressively with unsought goods, goods that buyers normally do not think of buying, such as insurance, encyclopedias, and funeral plots.
(*a*) marketing concept
(*b*) selling concept
(*c*) production concept
(*d*) product concept
(*e*) holistic marketing concept

39. The .... concept holds that consumers and businesses, if left alone, will ordinarily not buy enough of the organization's products.
(*a*) production (*b*) selling
(*c*) marketing (*d*) product
(*e*) holistic marketing

40. According to Theodore Levitt, who drew a perceptive contrast between the selling and marketing concepts, ... is preoccupied with the need to convert products into cash.
(*a*) marketing (*b*) selling
(*c*) direct marketing (*d*) holistic marketing
(*e*) service marketing

41. Marketing Concept is based on:
(*a*) Profit
(*b*) Loss
(*c*) Customer-Oriented
(*d*) Product-Oriented and Centred
(*e*) None of these

42. Which is centre point of marketing concept?
(*a*) Large scale organisation
(*b*) Production on large scale
(*c*) Profit
(*d*) Customer
(*e*) None of these

43. Which is centred point of Bank?
(*a*) Staff
(*b*) Profit
(*c*) Loan
(*d*) Present and potential customer of Bank
(*e*) None of these

44. .... is an integration of marketing activities directed towards customer satisfaction.
(*a*) Service
(*b*) Product
(*c*) Marketing Concept
(*d*) Marketing Planning and Controlling
(*e*) None of these

45. The marketing concept is based on .... period.
(*a*) Short run success
(*b*) Output
(*c*) Long run success
(*d*) Short & Long run success
(*e*) None of these

46. Which is the element of Marketing Concept?
(*a*) Goal of the organisation
(*b*) Marketing of product with coordinated efforts
(*c*) Consumer satisfaction
(*d*) All of these
(*e*) None of these

47. Who is the king of a bank?
(*a*) Bank's chartered accountant
(*b*) Bank's employee
(*c*) Bank's customers
(*d*) All of these
(*e*) None of these

48. Marketing Concept includes—
(*a*) Product planning and development
(*b*) A comprehensive philosophy
(*c*) Long run success
(*d*) All of these
(*e*) None of these

49. Bank marketing concept is a—
(*a*) Advances
(*b*) Loan
(*c*) Customer-oriented philosophy
(*d*) Product planning
(*e*) None of these

50. ''Marketing Concept is a Company wide consumer-orientation with the objective of achieving long run success.'' Who said?
(*a*) Lawrence A. Klatt
(*b*) Stanton, Etzel and Walker
(*c*) Robert
(*d*) Hills
(*e*) None of these

51. Match the following—

List-I

1. Production Concept
2. Product Concept
3. Selling Concept
4. Marketing Concept

List-II

A. Production-oriented
B. Product-oriented
C. Sales-oriented
D. Customer-oriented
E. Plant-oriented

Codes :

	1	2	3	4
(*a*)	A	D	C	E
(*b*)	A	B	C	D
(*c*)	E	A	B	D
(*d*)	B	D	E	A
(*e*)	B	E	A	D

52. The Selling Concept applies on:
(*a*) Insurance
(*b*) Water Supply
(*c*) Bank and other Financial Institution
(*d*) All of these
(*e*) None of these

53. Which is the part of Selling Concept?
(*a*) Profit by Sales
(*b*) Sales/Promotional Efforts
(*c*) Production of Present Product
(*d*) All of these
(*e*) None of these

54. Which concept of market is based on customer welfare and satisfaction?
(*a*) Marketing Concept
(*b*) Social Marketing Concept
(*c*) Production Concept
(*d*) Product Concept
(*e*) None of these

55. Societal Marketing Concept involves:
(*a*) Long run satisfaction of customers
(*b*) Long run welfare of society
(*c*) Research and Development
(*d*) All of these
(*e*) None of these

56. Which is customer and Society-Oriented Concept of Marketing?
(*a*) Selling Concept
(*b*) Marketing Concept
(*c*) Production Concept of Marketing
(*d*) Societal Marketing Concept
(*e*) All of these

57. Which is the pillar of marketing concept?
(*a*) Sales
(*b*) Plant
(*c*) Customer-orientation

(*d*) Fixed cost
(*e*) None of these

58. Which is/are marketing activities?
(*a*) Pricing
(*b*) Transportation
(*c*) Product Planning and Pricing
(*d*) All of these
(*e*) None of these

59. Customerisation means:
(*a*) Goods offer on various conditions
(*b*) Sales
(*c*) Promotion
(*d*) Customer Information
(*e*) None of these

60. Individualisation is the process of:
(*a*) Customerisation
(*b*) Storage
(*c*) Transport
(*d*) Customer Information
(*e*) None of these

61. .... consists of those efforts which effect transfers in the ownership of goods and services which provide for physical distribution.
(*a*) Marketing (*b*) Financing
(*c*) Accounting (*d*) Size
(*e*) None of these

62. CRM is helpful in:
(*a*) Risk creation
(*b*) System
(*c*) New product development and planning
(*d*) Production
(*e*) None of these

63. Sales promotion is a tool of:
(*a*) Accounting
(*b*) Cost
(*c*) Budget
(*d*) New, concept of marketing
(*e*) None of these

64. Profit by customer satisfaction is a tool of:
(*a*) Old concept of marketing
(*b*) New concept of marketing
(*c*) Production
(*d*) Price
(*e*) Marketing

65. Social marketing:
(*a*) is tool of social transaction
(*b*) is a social product
(*c*) is marketing of social assets
(*d*) is the design, implementation and control of programme seeking increase the acceptability of a social idea or practice in a target
(*e*) None of these

66. Which factor is responsible for development of marketing?
(*a*) Barter system
(*b*) Marketing-orientation
(*c*) Sales-orientation
(*d*) All of these
(*e*) None of these

67. Which is the mode of payment in the contract of sale?
(*a*) Product (*b*) Service
(*c*) Money (*d*) Sales
(*e*) All of these

68. Which is the decision of marketing?
(*a*) Marketing
(*b*) Information
(*c*) Promotion decision
(*d*) Nature and scope of marketing
(*e*) None of these

69. Which is the function of marketing?
(*a*) Pricing
(*b*) Product Designing
(*c*) Labelling
(*d*) All of these
(*e*) None of these

70. The nature of marketing involves:
(*a*) Promotion decision
(*b*) Determination of distribution channel
(*c*) After sale service
(*d*) All of these
(*e*) None of these

71. Which is the P of marketing?
(*a*) Premium (*b*) Programme
(*c*) Place (*d*) Price
(*e*) Product

72. Which is the benefit of marketing?
(*a*) Reduction in per unit cost
(*b*) Maximum profit
(*c*) Maximum production and sales
(*d*) All of these
(*e*) None of these

73. Marketing includes:
(*a*) Branding (*b*) Pricing
(*c*) Packaging (*d*) All of these
(*e*) None of these

74. Marketing comprises:
(*a*) Harvesting
(*b*) Production
(*c*) Buying and Selling activities
(*d*) Pricing
(*e*) None of these

75. Marketing Planning includes:
(*a*) Price Policy
(*b*) Productional Policy
(*c*) Product Policy
(*d*) All of these
(*e*) None of these

76. Long range planning is concerned with:
(*a*) Market expension
(*b*) Planning for product expension
(*c*) Plant extension
(*d*) All of these
(*e*) None of these

77. Short range planning is suitable for:
(*a*) Adjustment in prices
(*b*) Seasonal purchasing
(*c*) Regular advertisement
(*d*) All of these
(*e*) None of these

78. Which factor affecting marketing planning?
(*a*) Price Trend
(*b*) Monetary Policy
(*c*) National Production and National Income
(*d*) All of these
(*e*) None of these

79. Which is the stage of Marketing Planning?
(*a*) Setting the goal or objectives
(*b*) Analysis of Problem
(*c*) Programme Preparation
(*d*) All of these
(*e*) None of these

80. Marketing Planning in the product oriented organisation includes:
(*a*) Advertisement
(*b*) Sales Promotion
(*c*) Product development and Marketing Research
(*d*) All of these
(*e*) None of these

81. Marketing Planning in function oriented organisation includes:
(*a*) Physical distribution
(*b*) Marketing Research
(*c*) Sales Promotion
(*d*) All of these
(*e*) None of these

82. Which is Internal variable of marketing programme?
(*a*) Packaging (*b*) Price
(*c*) Design (*d*) All of these
(*e*) None of these

83. Which point should be considered at the time of Sales Planning?
(*a*) Good Packing
(*b*) Good Product Shape and Style
(*c*) Trademark must be attractive
(*d*) All of these
(*e*) None of these

84. EOQ stands for:
(*a*) Evaluation-on-Quantity
(*b*) Even-on-Quality
(*c*) Economic Order Quantity
(*d*) Economic on Quality
(*e*) None of these

85. Bank's Sales Planning includes:
(*a*) Sales Promotion
(*b*) ATM Sales decision
(*c*) Distribution Channel of ATM Card
(*d*) All of these
(*e*) None of these

86. Which is the part of process of marketing control?
(*a*) Marketing Cost Analysis
(*b*) Marketing Budget
(*c*) Bazar forecasting
(*d*) All of these
(*e*) None of these

87. Which is the technique of marketing control?
(*a*) Attitude Study
(*b*) Sales Analysis
(*c*) Market Share Analysis
(*d*) All of these
(*e*) None of these

88. Which System may be involved in bank?
(*a*) Internal Audit System
(*b*) Internal Check System
(*c*) Internal Control System
(*d*) All of these
(*e*) None of these

89. Price policy is related with:
(*a*) Purchasing
(*b*) Investing
(*c*) Pricing of Product and Services
(*d*) All of these
(*e*) None of these

90. Which is the element of marketing plan?
(*a*) Marketing Programme
(*b*) Completion Schedule
(*c*) Statement of Goals
(*d*) All of these
(*e*) None of these

ANSWERS

1	**2**	**3**	**4**	**5**	**6**	**7**	**8**	**9**	**10**
(*a*)	(*a*)	(*d*)	(*a*)	(*d*)	(*d*)	(*c*)	(*a*)	(*c*)	(*b*)
11	**12**	**13**	**14**	**15**	**16**	**17**	**18**	**19**	**20**
(*b*)	(*a*)	(*a*)	(*d*)	(*c*)	(*c*)	(*c*)	(*a*)	(*b*)	(*a*)
21	**22**	**23**	**24**	**25**	**26**	**27**	**28**	**29**	**30**
(*b*)	(*b*)	(*d*)	(*a*)	(*b*)	(*d*)	(*a*)	(*a*)	(*b*)	(*c*)
31	**32**	**33**	**34**	**35**	**36**	**37**	**38**	**39**	**40**
(*a*)	(*d*)	(*a*)	(*a*)	(*b*)	(*a*)	(*d*)	(*b*)	(*b*)	(*b*)
41	**42**	**43**	**44**	**45**	**46**	**47**	**48**	**49**	**50**
(*c*)	(*d*)	(*d*)	(*c*)	(*c*)	(*d*)	(*c*)	(*d*)	(*c*)	(*b*)
51	**52**	**53**	**54**	**55**	**56**	**57**	**58**	**59**	**60**
(*b*)	(*d*)	(*d*)	(*b*)	(*d*)	(*d*)	(*c*)	(*d*)	(*a*)	(*a*)
61	**62**	**63**	**64**	**65**	**66**	**67**	**68**	**69**	**70**
(*a*)	(*c*)	(*d*)	(*b*)	(*d*)	(*d*)	(*c*)	(*c*)	(*d*)	(*d*)
71	**72**	**73**	**74**	**75**	**76**	**77**	**78**	**79**	**80**
(*c*)	(*d*)	(*d*)	(*c*)	(*d*)	(*d*)	(*d*)	(*d*)	(*d*)	(*d*)
81	**82**	**83**	**84**	**85**	**86**	**87**	**88**	**89**	**90**
(*d*)	(*d*)	(*d*)	(*c*)	(*d*)	(*d*)	(*d*)	(*d*)	(*c*)	(*d*)

☞ CHAPTER-2

MARKETING ENVIRONMENT

WHY ANALYSE THE MARKETING ENVIRONMENT?

Knowledge of Marketing Environment is Central to Marketing Management

Marketing management rests squarely on the knowledge of the marketing environment. Environment plays a crucial role in marketing and that securing the right fit between the environment and the firm, using the marketing mix as the tool, is the crux of marketing. The firm has to know where the environment is heading, what trends are emerging therein and what should be its response to the environmental changes. Only by analysing the environment, can the firm grapple with these issues.

Strategic Response to Environment is Possible only with Proper Environment Analysis

Facilitating the corporation's strategic response to the changes taking place in environmental factors is the ultimate purpose of environment analysis. The firm has to come up with alternative programmes and strategies in line with environmental realities. This is possible only with proper environment analysis. It helps strategic response by highlighting opportunities, the pursuit of which will help the firm attain its objectives. It helps assess the attractiveness and profitability position of these opportunities, and helps prepare a shortlist of those which are relevant to the firm and which can be pursued by it.

The marketing environment can be divided into two parts:

- The Micro-environment
- The Macro-environment

The Micro Environment

The micro environment consists of the actors in the company's immediate environment that affects the ability of the marketers to serve their customers. These include the suppliers, marketing intermediaries, competitors, customers and publics.

- **Suppliers:** Suppliers are those who supply the inputs like raw materials and components etc. to the company. Uncertainty regarding the supply or other supply constraints often compels companies to maintain high inventories causing cost increases. It has been pointed out that factories in India maintain indigenous stocks of 3-4 months and imported stocks of 9 months as against on average of a few hours to two weeks in Japan.

  It is very risky to depend on a single supplier because a strike, lockout or any other production problem with that supplier may seriously affect the company. Hence, multiple sources of supply often help reduce such risks.

- **Customers:** The major task of a business is to create and sustain customers. A business exists only because of its customers and hence monitoring the customer sensitivity is a prerequisite for the business to succeed.

  A company may have different categories of consumers like individuals, households, industries, commercial establishments, governmental and other institutions etc. Depending on a single customer is often too risky because it may place the company in a poor bargaining position. Thus, the choice of the customer segments should be made by considering a number of factors like relative profitability, dependability, growth prospects, demand stability, degree of competition etc.

- **Competitors:** A firm's competitors include not only the other firms which market the same or similar products but also all those who compete for the discretionary income of the consumers. For example, the competition for a company making televisions may come not only from other TV manufacturers but also from refrigerators, stereo sets, two-wheelers, etc. This competition among these products may be described as desire competition as the primary task here is to influence the basic desire of the consumer.

  If the consumer decides to spend his disposable income on recreation, he will still be confronted with a number of alternatives to choose from like T.V., stereo, radio, C.D. player etc. the competition among such alternatives which satisfy a particular category of desire is called generic competition.

  If the consumer decides to go in for a T.V., the next question is which form of T.V. - black and white, color, with remote or without etc. this is called 'product form competition'. Finally, the consumer encounters brand competition, i.e. competition between different brands like Philips, B.P.L., Onida, Videocon, Coldstar etc.

  An implication of these different brands is that a marketer should strive to create primary and selective demand for his products.

- **Marketing intermediaries:** The immediate environment of a company may consist of a number of marketing intermediaries which are "firms that aid the company in promoting, selling and distributing its goods to final buyers.

  The marketing intermediaries include middlemen such as agents and merchants, who help the company find customers or close sales with them; physical distribution firms which assist the company in stocking and moving goods from their origin to their destination such as warehouses and transportation firms; marketing service agencies which assist the company in targeting and promoting its products to the right markets such as advertising agencies; consulting firms, and finally financial intermediaries which finance marketing activities and insure business risks.

  Marketing intermediaries are vital link between the company and final consumers. A dislocation or disturbance of this link, or a wrong choice of the link, may cost the company very heavily.

- **Public:** A company may encounter certain publics in its environment. "A public is any group that has actual or potential interest in or impact on an organisation's ability to achieve its interests". Media, citizens, action publics and local publics are some examples.

  Some companies are seriously affected by such publics, e.g. one of the leading daily that was allegedly bent on bringing down the share price of the company by tarnishing its image. Many companies are also affected by local publics. Environmental pollution is an issue often taken up by a number of local publics. Action by local publics on this issue has caused some companies to suspend operations and/or take pollution control measures.

  However, it is wrong to think that all publics are threats to business. Some publics are opportunity for business. Some businessmen e.g. regard consumerism as an opportunity for their business. The media public may be used to disseminate useful information. Similarly, fruitful symbiotic cooperation between a company and the local publics may be established for the benefit of the company and the local community.

Macro environment

The macro forces are, generally, more uncontrollable than the micro forces. The macro environmental forces are given below:

- **Economic environment:** Economic conditions, economic policies and the economic system are the important external factors that constitute the economic environment of a business.

The economic conditions of a country e.g., the nature of the economy, the stage of development of the economy, economic resources, the level of income, the distribution of income and assets etc. are among the very important determinants of business strategies.

In a developing economy, the low income may be the reason for the very low demand for a product. In countries where investment and income are steadily and rapidly rising, business prospects are generally bright, and further investments are encouraged.

The economic policy of the government, needless to say, has a very strong impact on business. Some types of businesses are favorably affected by government policy, some adversely affected, while it is neutral in respect of others, e.g. in case of India, the priority sector and the small-scale sector get a number of incentives and positive support from the government, whereas those industries which are regarded as inessential may find the odds against them.

The monetary and fiscal policies by way of incentives and disincentives they offer and by their neutrality, also affect the business in different ways. The scope of private business depends, to a large extent, on the economic system. At one end, there are the free market economies, or capitalist economies, and at the other, are the centrally planned economies or communist economies. In between, these two extremes are the mixed economies.

A completely free economy is an abstract rather than a real system because some amount of government regulations always exist. Countries like the United States, Japan, Canada, Australia etc. are regarded as free market economies.

The communist countries have, by and large, a centrally planned economic system. The State, under this system, owns all the means of production, determines the goals of production and controls the economy. China, Hungary, Poland etc. had centrally planned economies. However, recently, several of these countries have discarded communist system and have moved towards the market economy.

In a mixed economy, both public and private sectors co-exist, as in India. The extent of state participation varies widely across different mixed economies. However, in many mixed economies, the strategic and other nationally very important industries are fully owned or dominated by the state.

The economic system, thus, is a very important determinant of the scope of business.

- **Political and Government environment:** Political and government environment has a close relationship with the economic system and economic policy. In most countries, there are a number of laws that regulate the conduct of the business. These laws cover such matters as standards of product, packaging, promotion etc. In many countries, with a view to protecting consumer interests, regulations have become stronger. Regulations to protect the purity of the environment and preserve the ecological balance have assumed great importance in many countries.

  In most nations, promotional activities are subject to various types of controls. Media advertising is not permitted in Libya. In India too, till recently advertisements of liquor, cigarettes, gold, silver etc. were prohibited. There is a host of statutory control on business in India. MRTP commission, industrial licensing, FEMA regulations etc. kept a strict check on the expansion of private enterprises till recently. Recent changes in the statutes and policies have had a profound and positive impact on business.

  Thus, marketing policies are definitely influenced by government policies and controls throughout the world.

- **Socio-cultural environment:** The socio-cultural environment includes the customs, traditions, taboos, tastes, preferences etc. of the members of the society, which cannot be ignored at any cost by any business unit. For a business to be successful, its strategy should be the one that is appropriate in the socio-cultural environment. The marketing-mix will have to be so designed as to suit the environmental characteristics of the market. Nestle, a Swiss multinational company, today brews more than forty varieties of instant coffee to satisfy different national tastes.

Even when people of different cultures use the same basic product, the mode of consumption, conditions of use, purpose of use or the perceptions of the product attributes may vary so much so that the product attributes, method of presentation, or promotion etc. may have to be varied to suit the characteristics of different markets.

The differences in language sometimes pose a serious challenge and even necessitate a change in the brand name. The values and beliefs associated with color vary significantly across different cultures e.g. white is a color which indicates death and mourning in countries like China, Korea and India but in many countries it is a color expressing happiness and often used as a wedding dress color.

While dealing with the social environment, it is important to remember that the social environment of business also encompasses its social responsibility, alertness or vigilance of the consumers and the society's interests and well-being at large.

- **Demographic environment:** Demographic factors like the size, growth rate, age composition, sex composition, family size, economic stratification of the population, educational levels, language, caste, religion etc. are all factors relevant to business. All these demographic variables affect the demand for goods and services. Markets with growing population and income are growth markets. But the decline in birth rates in countries like United States, etc. has affected the demand for baby products. Johnson & Johnson had to overcome this problem by repositioning their products like baby shampoo and baby soaps, and promoting them to the adult segment particularly females.

  A rapidly increasing population indicates a growing demand for many products. High population growth rates also indicate an enormous increase in labor supply. Cheap labor and a growing market have encouraged many multinational corporations to invest in developing countries like India.

- **Natural environment:** Geographical and ecological factors such as natural resources endowments, weather and climate conditions, topographical factors, location aspects in the global context, port facilities etc. are all relevant to business. Geographical and ecological factors also influence the location of certain industries, e.g. industries with high material index tend to be located near the raw material sources. Climate and weather conditions affect the location of certain industries like the cotton textile industry. Topographical factors may affect the demand pattern, e.g. in hilly areas with a difficult terrain, jeeps may be in greater demand than cars.

  Ecological factors have recently assumed greater importance. The depletion of natural resources, environmental pollution and the disturbance of the ecological balance has caused great concern. Government policies aimed at the preservation of environmental purity and ecological balance, conservation of non-replenishable resources etc. have resulted in additional responsibilities and problems for business, and some of these have the effect of increasing the cost of production and marketing.

- **Physical facilities and technological environment:** Business prospects depend on the availability of certain physical facilities. The sale of television sets e.g. is limited by the extent of coverage of telecasting. Similarly, the demand for refrigerators and other electrical appliances is affected by the extent of electrification and the reliability of power supply.

  Technological factors sometimes pose problems. A firm which is unable to cope with the technological changes may not survive. Further, the different technological environment of different markets or countries may call for product modifications, e.g. many appliances and instruments in the U.S.A. are designed for 110 volts but this needs to be converted into 240 volts in countries which have that power system.

- **International environment:** The international environment is very important from the point of view of certain categories of business. It is particularly important for industries directly depending on exports or imports. E.g. a recession in foreign markets or the adoption of protectionist policies may help the export-oriented industries. Similarly, liberalization of imports may help some industries which use imported items, but may adversely affect import-competing industries.

  Similarly, international bodies like WTO, IMF, WHO, ILO etc. have had a major impact on influencing the policies and trade of many countries, especially India.

SWOT ANALYSIS

SWOT analysis is a tool for auditing an organization and its environment. SWOT stands for strengths, weaknesses, opportunities, and threats. Strengths and weaknesses are internal factors. Opportunities and threats are external factors.

In SWOT, strengths and weaknesses are internal factors.

For example:

A strength could be:

- Specialist marketing expertise.
- A new, innovative product or service.
- Location of your business.
- Quality processes and procedures.
- Any other aspect of business that adds value to your product or service.

A weakness could be:

- Lack of marketing expertise.
- Undifferentiated products or services (i.e. in relation to your competitors).
- Location of your business.
- Poor quality goods or services.
- Damaged reputation.

In SWOT, opportunities and threats are external factors:

For example:

An opportunity could be:

- A developing market such as the Internet.
- Mergers, joint ventures or strategic alliances.
- Moving into new market segments that offer improved profits.
- A new international market.
- A market vacated by an ineffective competitor.

A threat could be:

- A new competitor in your home market.
- Price wars with competitors.
- A competitor has a new, innovative product or service.
- Competitors have superior access to channels of distribution.
- Taxation is introduced on your product or service.

PEST Analysis

It is very important that an organization considers its environment before beginning the marketing process. In fact, environmental analysis should be continuous and feed all aspects of planning.

The organization's marketing environment is made up of:

1. The internal environment example staff (or internal customers), office technology, wages and finance, etc.
2. The micro-environment example our external customers, agents and distributors, suppliers, our competitors, etc.
3. The macro-environment example Political (and legal) forces, Economic forces, Sociocultural forces, and Technological forces. These are known as PEST factors.

Political Factors:

The political arena has a huge influence upon the regulation of businesses, and the spending power of consumers and other businesses. You must consider issues such as:

1. How stable is the political environment?
2. Will government policy influence laws that regulate or tax your business?
3. What is the government's position on marketing ethics?
4. What is the government's policy on the economy?
5. Does the government have a view on culture and religion?
6. Is the government involved in trading agreements such as EU, NAFTA, ASEAN, or others?

Economic Factors:

Marketers need to consider the state of a trading economy in the short and long-terms. This is especially true when planning for international marketing. You need to look at:

1. Interest rates.
2. The level of inflation Employment level per capita.
3. Long-term prospects for the economy Gross Domestic Product (GDP) per capita, and so on.

Sociocultural Factors:

The social and cultural influences on business vary from country to country. It is very important that such factors are considered. Factors include:

1. What is the dominant religion?
2. What are attitudes to foreign products and services?
3. Does language impact upon the diffusion of products onto markets?
4. How much time do consumers have for leisure?
5. What are the roles of men and women within society?
6. How long are the population living? Are the older generations wealthy?
7. Do the population have a strong/weak opinion on green issues?

Technological Factors:

Technology is vital for competitive advantage, and is a major driver of globalization. Consider the following points:

1. Does technology allow for products and services to be made more cheaply and to a better standard of quality?
2. Do the technologies offer consumers and businesses more innovative products and services such as Internet banking, new generation mobile telephones, etc?
3. How is distribution changed by new technologies e.g. books via the Internet, flight tickets, auctions, etc?
4. Does technology offer companies a new way of communicating with consumers e.g. banners, Customer Relationship Management (CRM), etc?

Five Forces Analysis

Five Forces Analysis helps the marketer to contrast a competitive environment. It has similarities with other tools for environmental audit, such as PEST analysis, but tends to focus on the single, stand alone, business or SBU (Strategic Business Unit) rather than a single product or range of products. For example, Dell would analyse the market for Business Computers i.e. one of its SBUs Five forces analsysis looks at five key areas namely the threat of entry, the power of buyers, the power of suppliers, the threat of substitutes, and competitive rivalry.

The threat of entry:

- Economies of scale e.g. the benefits associated with bulk purchasing.
- The high or low cost of entry example how much will it cost for the latest technology?
- Ease of access to distribution channels example Do our competitors have the distribution channels sewn up?
- Cost advantages not related to the size of the company example personal contacts or

knowledge that larger companies do not own or learning curve effects.

- Will competitors retaliate?
- Government action e.g. will new laws be introduced that will weaken our competitive position?
- How important is differentiation? example the Champagne brand cannot be copied. This desensitises the influence of the environment.

The power of buyers:

- This is high where there a few, large players in a market example the large grocery chains.
- If there are a large number of undifferentiated, small suppliers example small farming businesses supplying the large grocery chains.
- The cost of switching between suppliers is low example from one fleet supplier of trucks to another.

The power of suppliers:

The power of suppliers tends to be a reversal of the power of buyers.

- Where the switching costs are high example Switching from one software supplier to another.
- Power is high where the brand is powerful example Cadillac, Pizza Hut, Microsoft.
- There is a possibility of the supplier integrating forward example Brewers buying bars.
- Customers are fragmented (not in clusters) so that they have little bargaining power example Gas/Petrol stations in remote places.

The threat of substitutes:

- Where there is product-for-product substitution example email for fax. Where there is substitution of need e.g. better toothpaste reduces the need for dentists.
- Where there is generic substitution (competing for the currency in your pocket) example Video suppliers compete with travel companies.
- We could always do without example cigarettes.

Competitive Rivalry:

- This is most likely to be high where entry is likely; there is the threat of substitute products, and suppliers and buyers in the market attempt to control. This is why it is always seen in the center of the diagram.

Importance of Environmental Analysis

The marketing manager needs to be dynamic to effectively deal with the challenges of environment. The environment of business is not static. It is changing with fast speed. The following benefits of environment scanning can be discussed:

1. It guides with greater effectiveness in matters relating to government.
2. It helps in marketing analysis.
3. It creates an increased general awareness of environmental changes on the part of management.
4. It suggests improvement in diversification and resource allocations
5. It provides a base of objective qualitative information about the business that can subsequently be of value in designing the strategies.
6. It helps firms to identify and capitalize upon opportunities rather than losing out to competitors.
7. It provides a continuing broad-based education for executives in general and the strategies in particular.

The environmental conditions faced by an organization are capable of varying greatly in their complexity and need to be reflected both in the warp in which environment analysis is conducted and in the ways in which strategy is subsequently developed. It is widely recognized that the pace of environmental changes in increasing and this requires the organization to develop a structured approach to environmental analysis with the results than being fed into the marketing planning process in a greater degree than ever before.

MULTIPLE CHOICE QUESTIONS

1. Political Environment of marketing includes:
(*a*) Foreign Policy
(*b*) Public Welfare and Social Justice
(*c*) Democracy
(*d*) All of these
(*e*) None of these

2. Meaning of R and D is:
(*a*) Rate and Division
(*b*) Research and Development
(*c*) Research and Department
(*d*) Rate and Department
(*e*) None of these

3. Industrial Law includes:
(*a*) Income Tax Act (*b*) Factory Act
(*c*) Companies Act (*d*) Both (*b*) and (*c*)
(*e*) None of these

4. Matching the following:

List-I	List-II
1. Indian Contract Act	A. 1872
2. Companies Act	B. 1956
3. Banking Regulation Act	C. 1949
4. Indian Partnership Act	D. 1932
	E. 1930

Codes :

	1	2	3	4
(*a*)	E	D	A	C
(*b*)	A	C	B	D
(*c*)	C	A	B	D
(*d*)	A	D	E	B
(*e*)	D	A	B	E

5. Nature of marketing environment includes:
(*a*) Communication
(*b*) Challenges
(*c*) Changes as per environment
(*d*) Above all
(*e*) None of these

6. In India, bank is regulated by:
(*a*) Indian Contract Act, 1872
(*b*) Banking Regulation Act, 1949
(*c*) Indian Companies Act, 1956
(*d*) Indian Partnership Act, 1956
(*e*) None of these

7. Result of marketing environment is:
(*a*) Knowledge of Challenge
(*b*) Innovation
(*c*) Development of competitive ability
(*d*) Above all
(*e*) None of these

8. Source of short-term credits in Banking is:
(*a*) Short Term Loan
(*b*) Bank Credit
(*c*) Only (*a*)
(*d*) Both (*a*) and (*b*)
(*e*) None of these

9. Internal factors of marketing includes:
(*a*) Target of organisation
(*b*) Production method
(*c*) Resource of organisation
(*d*) Above all
(*e*) None of these

10. In Banking, factor at external marketing is:
(*a*) Assets (*b*) Consumers
(*c*) Loans (*d*) All of these
(*e*) None of these

11. Controllable factors of marketing environment includes:
(*a*) Organisational Structure
(*b*) Marketing Policy
(*c*) Methods of production
(*d*) All of these
(*e*) None of these

12. Match the following:

List I (Type of Customers)	List II (Example)
1. Consumer	A. Educational Loan
2. Industrial Customer	B. Loan for production works
3. Reseller	C. Fund from the bank for re-financing
4. International consumer	D. Purchasing of bank's product by a foreigner
	E. Production price

Codes :

	1	2	3	4
(*a*)	B	D	C	E
(*b*)	A	B	C	D
(*c*)	E	A	B	D
(*d*)	A	C	E	D
(*e*)	B	D	E	A

13. Organisation's Policy includes:
(*a*) Accounting Policy
(*b*) Production and Purchasing Policy
(*c*) R and D
(*d*) Above all
(*e*) None of these

14. Market demand is affected by:
(*a*) Change in population
(*b*) Change in taste
(*c*) Change in income
(*d*) Above all
(*e*) None of these

15. Macro environment includes:
(*a*) Demography (*b*) Economy
(*c*) Technology (*d*) Above all
(*e*) None of these

16. Micro environment includes:
(*a*) Market demand (*b*) Consumer
(*c*) Competition (*d*) Above all
(*e*) None of these

17. In PEST analysis, 'P' represents:
(*a*) Political (*b*) Place
(*c*) Promotion (*d*) Price
(*e*) None of these

18. In SWOT analysis, 'S' stands for:
(*a*) Strengths (*b*) Strategies
(*c*) Smart card (*d*) Sales
(*e*) None of these

19. 'PEST Analysis' related with:
(*a*) Micro Environment
(*b*) Macro Environment
(*c*) Economic Environment
(*d*) Legal Environment
(*e*) Natural Environment

20. Which of the following is Marketing Intermediaries?
(*a*) Wholesaler (*b*) Advertisement
(*c*) Government (*d*) Reseller
(*e*) None of these

21. Social environment of a Bank includes:
(*a*) Quality of life (*b*) Life style
(*c*) Tradition (*d*) All of these
(*e*) None of these

22. Cultural Environment includes:
(*a*) Perception
(*b*) Respect of old citizens
(*c*) Cultural values
(*d*) Above all
(*e*) None of these

23. Natural environment of marketing includes:
(*a*) Climate
(*b*) Ecology
(*c*) Natural Resources
(*d*) Above all
(*e*) None of these

24. Technology environment includes:
(*a*) Cost of technology
(*b*) Status of technology
(*c*) Improvement of technology
(*d*) Above all
(*e*) None of these

25. 'Pricing' is a factor of:
(*a*) Demographic Environment
(*b*) Economic Environment
(*c*) Natural Environment
(*d*) Technology Environment
(*e*) None of these

26. 'Location' is a component of:
(*a*) Demographic Environment
(*b*) Economic Environment
(*c*) Political Environment
(*d*) Natural Environment
(*e*) Technology Environment

27. 'Law of Taxation' is a component of:
(*a*) Legal Environment
(*b*) Natural Environment
(*c*) Economic Environment

(*d*) Political Environment
(*e*) None of these

28. 'Competition' is a component of:
(*a*) Macro Environment
(*b*) Micro Environment
(*c*) Both (*a*) and (*b*)
(*d*) Legal Environment
(*e*) None of these

29. In PEST analysis, 'T' stands for:
(*a*) Target Customer
(*b*) Technological Environment
(*c*) Terms and Conditions
(*d*) All of these
(*e*) None of these

30. The .... is defined as the external forces that directly or indirectly influence an organisation's capability to under take its business.
(*a*) Marketing Strategy
(*b*) Marketing Environment
(*c*) Sales Forecasting
(*d*) Production strategy
(*e*) None of these

31. Resoure should be obtained at:
(*a*) Minimum cost
(*b*) Maximum cost
(*c*) No cost no profit
(*d*) All of these
(*e*) None of these

32. Put option is available for:
(*a*) Buyer
(*b*) Seller
(*c*) Buyer or Seller
(*d*) All of these
(*e*) None of these

33. The dynamic factors are:
(*a*) Social and Political factors
(*b*) Cultural factor
(*c*) Economic factor
(*d*) All of these
(*e*) None of these

34. Tax structures includes:
(*a*) Tradition (*b*) Custom Tax
(*c*) Brand (*d*) Price
(*e*) None of these

ANSWERS

1	**2**	**3**	**4**	**5**	**6**	**7**	**8**	**9**	**10**
(*d*)	(*b*)	(*d*)	(*b*)	(*d*)	(*b*)	(*d*)	(*d*)	(*d*)	(*b*)
11	**12**	**13**	**14**	**15**	**16**	**17**	**18**	**19**	**20**
(*d*)	(*b*)	(*d*)	(*d*)	(*d*)	(*d*)	(*a*)	(*a*)	(*b*)	(*a*)
21	**22**	**23**	**24**	**25**	**26**	**27**	**28**	**29**	**30**
(*d*)	(*d*)	(*d*)	(*d*)	(*b*)	(*a*)	(*a*)	(*b*)	(*b*)	(*b*)
31	**32**	**33**	**34**						
(*a*)	(*a*)	(*d*)	(*b*)						

☞ CHAPTER-3

MARKETING MIX

INTRODUCTION

The marketer delivers value to the customer basically through his market offer. He takes care to see that the offer fulfils the needs of the customer. He also ensures that the customer perceives the terms and conditions of the offer as more attractive vis-à-vis other competing offers. Marketing Mix is the set of marketing tools that the firm uses to pursue its marketing objectives in the target market. It is the sole vehicle for creating and delivering customer value.

It was James Culliton, a noted marketing expert, who coined the expression marketing mix and described the marketing manager as a mixer of ingredients. To quote him, "The marketing man is a decider and an artist – a mixer of ingredients, who sometimes follow a recipe developed by others and sometimes prepares his own recipe. And, sometimes he adapts his recipe to the ingredients that are readily available and sometimes invents some new ingredients, or, experiments with ingredients as no one else has tried before'. The dynamics of the marketing process and the versatility of the marketing process and the versatility of the marketing mix tool cannot be described any better. Subsequently Niel H. Borden, another noted marketing expert, popularized the concept of marketing mix. It was Jerome McCarthy, the well known American Professor of marketing, who first described the marketing mix in terms of the four Ps. The classified the marketing mix variables under four heads, each beginning with the alphabet 'p'.

- Product
- Price
- Place (referring to distribution)
- Promotion

McCarthy has provided an easy to remember description of the marketing mix variables. Over the years, the terms-Marketing mix and four Ps of marketing-have come to be used synonymously.

- **Product:** The most basic marketing mix tool is product, which stands for the firm's tangible offer to the market including the product quality, design, variety features, branding, packaging, services, warranties etc.
- **Price:** A critical marketing mix tool is price, namely, the amount of money that customers have to pay for the product. It includes deciding on wholesale and retail prices, discounts, allowances, and credit terms. Price should be commensurate with the perceived value of the offer, or else buyer will turn to competitors in choosing their products.
- **Place:** This marketing mix tool refers to distribution. It stands for various activities the company undertakes to make the product easily available and accessible to target customers. It includes deciding on identify, recruit, and link various middlemen and marketing facilitators so that products are efficiently supplied to the target market.
- **Promotion:** The fourth marketing mix tool, stands for the various activities the company undertakes to communicate its products' merits and to persuade target customers to buy them. It includes deciding on hire, train, and motivate salespeople to promote its products to middlemen and other buyers. It also includes setting up communication and promotion programs consisting of advertising, personal selling, sales promotion, and public relations.

Marketing mix or 4 Ps of marketing is the combination of a product, its price, distribution and promotion. It must be designed by marketers in such a manner that these four elements together must satisfy the needs of the organisation's target market, and at the same time, achieve its marketing objectives.

Note that the four Ps represent the sellers' view of the marketing tools available for influencing buyers. From a buyer's point of view, each marketing tool is designed to deliver a customer benefit. Robert Lauterborn suggested that the sellers' four Ps correspond to the customers' four Cs.

Four Ps	Four Cs
Product	Customer solution
Price	Customer cost
Place	Convenience
Promotion	Communication

NATURE OF MARKETING MIX

Following are the points with which we can understand the nature/features of marketing mix.

1. **It is a combination of 4 marketing variables:** Marketing mix involves a fine combination of its four variables i.e. product, price, place and promotion. It is a creative work and should be combining in such a way it should stand as winning marketing strategy. It should be in accordance with demand situation.
2. **Target-oriented concept:** Marketing mix aims at achieving marketing target in terms of sales, profit and consumer satisfaction. Marketing mix is the marketing manager's instrument for achieving marketing target.
3. **Dynamic concept:** Marketing mix concept is dynamic in nature. It has constant changes in its components. The components cannot fix at one standard or by any one parameter. It becomes necessary in order to adjust and respond to the changes in the environmental factors like political, social, technological etc. For example in a recessionary period marketer must have to reduce the price of the product or spent more on promotion so that the business can survive.
4. **Customer is the focus points:** The main focus of marketing mix is the customer. The marketing mixer is to be made as per customers' satisfaction and support. If the marketing manager is able to do so then he will be the successful marketing manager because customers' satisfaction is the core of modern marketing concept.
5. **Marketing mix variables are inter-related and interdependent:** Marketing mix variables are interlinked to one another. A change in one variable, invariably leads to a change in the other variables; for example when a new product introduced in the market, the firm has to spend more on promotion of that product or qualitative product always leads to good prices etc.
6. **Wide applicability:** The concept of marketing mix has wide applicability. In other words, it is applicable to business as well as non-business organizations such as clubs and associations, hospitals and educational institutions etc.

IMPORTANCE OF MARKETING MIX

Marketing mix plays very important role in marketing to study the nature or various elements of market. It promotes better utilization of limited resources by focusing attention on the need for proper blend of policies, with Limited Components at its disposal. It attempts to gain best possible results. Marketing mix is an effective tool for problem solving. It reminds marketer that on one side he should be careful to consider the market forces and on the other side he should think of a total marketing programms instead of relying heavenly on one particular aspects of market.

1. **Increases Profit:** Marketing mix helps the organization to increase the profit by avoiding inappropriate mixes, which are adversely affecting the profit of the organization.

2. **Ensures Survival:** Every organization's ultimate aim is to survive successfully in the market. For this organisation has to give a Right Product at the Right Price and Place through right medium of promotion. It is possible only with the help of appropriate marketing mix.
3. **Optimum Utilization of Resources:** Optimum Utilization of resources means using resources at the most of its capacity or taking maximum output from the resources. For this purpose the appropriate marketing mix will guide the business to produce the product which are profitable and suitable from the view point of customers as well as organizations. This may leads to the effectives utilizations of existing resources.
4. **Corporate Image:** Every organization tries to build a good image. This depends on the polices and practices followed by the organization. Charging fair prices to the products and services and selling quality goods, making goods available regularly and providing proper after sale services etc. are some of the elements which are the parts of appropriate marketing mix. This form of services leads to create good image among the people towards that organization for e.g. Tata fulfills social obligation. A business organization has to fulfill social obligation like giving donation to the charitable institutions, sponsoring cultural events etc. This is possible only when if the company earns good profit consistently. It is possible only by having an appropriate marketing mix.
5. **Customer Satisfaction:** An appropriate marketing mix involves offering the product according to consumer requirements, which would inevitably lead to consumer satisfaction. A satisfied consumer is the best brand ambassador of the organization.

MULTIPLE CHOICE QUESTIONS

1. What is the First 'P' of the 4 P's of marketing?
   (*a*) Product (*b*) Price
   (*c*) Promotion (*d*) Place
   (*e*) None of these
2. Product line means:
   (*a*) Expansion of product mix
   (*b*) Production technology
   (*c*) Pricing
   (*d*) Packaging
   (*e*) None of these
3. Who propounded the theory of 4 P's of marketing?
   (*a*) Stanton (*b*) Philip Kotler
   (*c*) Mc Carthy (*d*) Edward W. Cundiff
   (*e*) H.L. Hansen
4. Which is correct about the Marketing Mix?
   (*a*) Regular process
   (*b*) Mix of organisational policies
   (*c*) It is a function of Marketing Manager
   (*d*) Above all
   (*e*) None of these
5. Product mix includes:
   (*a*) Style (*b*) Brand name
   (*c*) Packaging (*d*) Above all
   (*e*) None of these
6. Distribution is also known as:
   (*a*) Product (*b*) Place
   (*c*) Promotion (*d*) Packaging
   (*e*) None of these
7. Distribution of marketing mix involves:
   (*a*) Retailer (*b*) Wholesaler
   (*c*) Agent (*d*) Above all
   (*e*) None of these
8. DSA of a Bank is a sub-element of:
   (*a*) Price mix
   (*b*) Distribution mix
   (*c*) Promotion mix
   (*d*) Expansion of product mix
   (*e*) None of these

9. Retailer is a sub-element of:
(*a*) Place mix (*b*) Product mix
(*c*) Price mix (*d*) All of these
(*e*) None of these

10. Promotion tools are:
(*a*) Advertising (*b*) Public relations
(*c*) Personal selling (*d*) Above all
(*e*) None of these

11. 4 C's of marketing includes:
(*a*) Customer solution
(*b*) Customer cost
(*c*) Convenience
(*d*) Above all
(*e*) None of these

12. Four C's of marketing theory was propounded by:
(*a*) Robert Lauterborn
(*b*) Philip Kotler
(*c*) Clark
(*d*) H.L. Hansen
(*e*) None of these

13. Which is the example of product of Bank?
(*a*) Bank's Building
(*b*) Fixed Term Deposits
(*c*) Bank's Staff
(*d*) All of these
(*e*) None of these

14. Match the following:
List-I: (Marketing Mix's Elements)
1. Product 2. Price
3. Place 4. Promotion
List-II: (Sub-Elements)
A. Style
B. List of Price
C. Inventory Level
D. Personal Selling
E. Personal Loan

Codes :

	1	2	3	4
(*a*)	A	B	C	D
(*b*)	E	D	B	C
(*c*)	B	D	A	E
(*d*)	C	E	B	D
(*e*)	D	B	E	A

15. Physical distribution of a product involves:
(*a*) Packaging (*b*) Transportation
(*c*) Storage (*d*) Above all
(*e*) None of these

16. First element of the marketing mix is:
(*a*) Product (*b*) Price
(*c*) Place (*d*) Promotion
(*e*) None of these

17. Example of tangible product is:
(*a*) Car
(*b*) Computer Repair
(*c*) Income Tax Preparation
(*d*) Customer Solution
(*e*) None of these

18. Example of intangible product is:
(*a*) Computer Repair (*b*) Bicycle
(*c*) T.V. (*d*) None of these
(*e*) All of these

19. Warranty is a sub-element of:
(*a*) Place (*b*) Product
(*c*) Price (*d*) Promotion
(*e*) None of these

20. Discounts and rebates is a sub-element of:
(*a*) Product (*b*) Price
(*c*) Promotion (*d*) Place
(*e*) None of these

21. Personal selling is a part of:
(*a*) Promotion (*b*) Place
(*c*) Price (*d*) Product
(*e*) All of these

22. Public relations is a part of:
(*a*) Promotion (*b*) Place
(*c*) Price (*d*) Product
(*e*) None of these

23. Channels of distribution is a part of:
(*a*) Place (*b*) Price
(*c*) Promotion (*d*) Product
(*e*) None of these

24. Warehousing is a component of:
(*a*) Physical distribution
(*b*) Price
(*c*) Promotion

(*d*) All of these
(*e*) None of these

25. Price element of marketing mix includes:
(*a*) Pricing Policies (*b*) Terms of Delivery
(*c*) Payment terms (*d*) Above all
(*e*) None of these

26. Physical features of product is:
(*a*) Size of product
(*b*) Colour of product
(*c*) Packaging of product
(*d*) Above all
(*e*) None of these

27. Intangible features of a product is:
(*a*) After sale services
(*b*) Performance of product
(*c*) Goodwill of product
(*d*) Above all
(*e*) None of these

ANSWERS

1	**2**	**3**	**4**	**5**	**6**	**7**	**8**	**9**	**10**
(*a*)	(*a*)	(*c*)	(*d*)	(*d*)	(*b*)	(*d*)	(*b*)	(*a*)	(*d*)
11	**12**	**13**	**14**	**15**	**16**	**17**	**18**	**19**	**20**
(*d*)	(*a*)	(*b*)	(*a*)	(*d*)	(*a*)	(*a*)	(*d*)	(*b*)	(*b*)
21	**22**	**23**	**24**	**25**	**26**	**27**			
(*a*)	(*a*)	(*a*)	(*a*)	(*d*)	(*d*)	(*d*)			

CHAPTER-4

MARKETING SEGMENTATION, TARGETING AND POSITIONING

SEGMENTATION

Market segmentation is defined as "the process of taking the total, heterogeneous market for a product and dividing it into several submarkets or segments, each of which tends to be homogeneous in all significance". The markets could be segmented in different ways. For instance, instead of mentioning a single market for 'shoes', it may be segmented into several sub-markets, e.g., shoes for executives, doctors college students etc. Geographical segmentation on the very similar lines is also possible for certain products.

Requirements for Markets Segmentation

For market segmentation to become effective and result-oriented, the following principles are to be observed: (1) Measurability of segments, (2) Accessibility of the segments, and (3) Represent ability of the segments.

The main purpose of market segmentation is to measure the changing behaviour patterns of consumers. It should also be remembered that variation in consumer behavior are both numerous and complex.

Therefore, the segments should be capable of giving accurate measurements. But this is often a difficult task and the segments are to be under constant review.

The second condition, accessibility, is comparatively easier because of distribution, advertising media, salesmen, etc. Newspaper and magazines also offer some help in this direction. For examples, there are magazines meant exclusively for the youth, for the professional people, etc.

The third condition in the represent ability of each segment. The segments should be large and profitable enough to be considered as separate markets. Such segments must have individuality of their own. The segment is usually small in case of industrial markets and comparatively larger in respect of consumer products.

Benefits of Segmentation

1. The manufacturer is in a better position to find out and compare the marketing potentialities of his products. He is able to judge product acceptance or to assess the resistance to his product.
2. The result obtained from market segmentation is an indicator to adjust the production, using man, materials and other resources in the most profitable manner. In other words, the organization can allocate and appropriate its efforts in a most useful manner.
3. Change required may be studied and implemented without losing markets. As such, as product line could be diversified or even discontinued.
4. It helps in determining the kinds of promotional devices that are more effective and also their results.
5. Appropriate timing for the introduction of new products, advertising etc., could be easily determined.

Aggregation and Segmentation

Market aggregation is just the opposite of segmentation. Aggregation implies the policy of lumping together into one mass all the markets for the products. Production-oriented firms usually adopt the method of aggregation instead of segmentation. Under this concept, management having only one product, considers the entire buyers as one group. Market aggregation enables an organization to maximize its economies of scale of production, pricing, physical distribution and promotion. However, the applicability of this concept in consumer-oriented market is doubtful. The 'total market' concept as envisaged by market aggregation may not be realistic in the present-day marketing when consumers fall under heterogeneous groups.

Basis of Market Segmentation

There is no single way to segment a market. A marketer has to try different segmentation variables, alone and in combination, to find the best way to view the market structure. There are major variables that might be used in segmenting consumers markets. Like geographic demographic, psychographic and behavioural variables.

Bases of Market Segmentation

Geographical	Demographic	Socio-Economic	Psychographic	Behavioral
- Local - Regional - National etc.	- Age - Sex - Income - Education - Language - Occupation - Religion etc.	- Socio class - Cultural background - Upper class - Middle class - Lower class etc.	- lifestyle - Personality Traits - Social Status etc.	Occasion - Benefit - User status - User rare etc.

Geographic Market Segmentation

Geographic market segmentation is related to the geographical area of the market. It divides the market into different geographical units such as nations, states, regions, cities etc. A company may decide to operate in one or few geographical areas or to operate in all areas but could not pay attention to all geographical differences and needs and wants. The assumption for doing this type of segmentation is that consumer needs and responses vary geographically. Here, regional difference in term of topography, climate, population and its density are used as base for market segmentation. This type of segmentation is commonly used for preparation of marketing plans and for the allocation of territories of salesmen or distribution. For example people in South India prefer coffee while those in North India prefer tea. Hence, companies prepare separate marketing mix for different region. People staying within the same region tend to share same values, attitudes, beliefs, and preferences. Again, there may be difference between urban people and rural people. For example, people residing in urban areas are more conscious, exposed to different media and having greater awareness of the products so better quality and novel expensive product can be sold here easily, whereas in rural area, people's income being limited, they are price-conscious; gifts, discounts, and other promotional tools can be very effective.

Demographic Segmentation

Demographic segmentation is related to people or people's characteristics such as age composition, gender, education, income, language, family size etc. It is the most popular form of market segmentation. Adequate information regarding the people can be easily made available, by going through consumer reports or other publications. Therefore, most of the companies adopt this type of segmentation for example HMT have segmented its market on the basis of sex and manufactured separate watches for male and female. In the same way, bicycle manufactures use this base. Again, marketer can segment market on the basis of age considering people belonging to 15 years and below or young adults between 18-25 years etc. Family life cycle can be a base as bachelors, newly married, married with children etc. for different purposes (Motor bike or LIC Policy) etc. Education can be a base for some products like newspaper, magazines, computers etc.

Race and religion is also one more important base for segmenting market like Hindus, Muslim, Parsi, etc. Products like garments, meat, alcohol, etc are sold on this basis.

Socio-Economic Segmentation

Under this type of segmentation, differences amongst population in terms of income consumption level, castes, communities and other cultural aspects are taken as variable for dividing the consumers in different groups. In India it is necessary as the society is divided into different groups on this factor. Lower class, middle class, working class is one example of economic classification.

Psychographic Segmentation

Psychographic segmentation divides buyers into different groups based on social class, lifestyle, or personality characteristics. People in the same demographic group can have very different psychographic make ups.

In the case of psychographic variables, relevant information for segmentation is not readily available and has to be collected through behavioural research. It is complicated as it is always difficult to expose individuals to a battery of psychographic test and to find out their specific personality traits.

Generally, manufacturers of cars, textiles and home furnishings divide their customers on the basis of lifestyle. Here marketing efforts are adjusted according to variables (reading habit of leisure activity, lifestyle).

So far as the personality traits are considered, like leadership, self-confidence ambitious, aggressive etc. Marketers positions their products in such way that consumers are tempted to use them in order to enhance their personality.

Behavioural Segmentation

Behavioural segmentation divides buyers into groups based on their knowledge, attitude, use or responses to a product. Many marketers believe that behaviour variables are the best starting point for building market segment. Dividing the market into groups according to occasion when buyers get the idea to buy and it is the actual time when they make purchase or use the purchased item. Here while segmenting market, consumers will be grouped on user's status like, user, non-user, ex-user, potential users, first time user, regular user etc. and accordingly segment the market. Then it will be segmented on the basis of benefit sought by the consumer on the part of product. E.g. soap may be purchased by some for economy, some for fragrance, some for medicinal value, fairness or health purpose. The behaviour can be of readiness stage of product. Like, purchasing products on the basis of unawareness of the products some are aware, some are informed about the product, or some may be interested in buying the product. Any one of readiness stage compel to them to purchase the product and finally the behavioural segmentation will be made on buying motives basis as motives may be convenience, comfort, economy, love and affection and prestige. Here marketer as per the above variables, uses to design marketing mix.

Markets on the Basis of Segmentation

It is now certain that any market could be segmented to a considerable extent because buyers' characteristics are never similar. This, however, does not mean that manufacturers may always try to segment their market. On the basis of the intensity of segmentation, marketing strategies to be adopted may be classified into:

1. Undifferentiated marketing: When the economies of organization do not permit the division of market into segments, they conceive of the total market concept. In the

case of fully standardized products and where substitutes are not available, differentiation need not be undertaken. Under such circumstances, firms may adopt mass advertising and other mass methods in marketing, e.g., Coca Cola.

2. Differentiated marketing: A firm may decide to operate in several or all segments of the market and devise separate product-marketing programmes. This also helps in developing intimacy between the producer and the consumer. In recent years most firms have preferred a strategy of differentiated marketing, mainly because consumer demand is quite diversified. For example, cigarettes are now manufactured in a variety of lengths and filter types. This provides the customer an opportunity to select his or her choice from filtered, unfiltered, long or short cigarettes. Each kind offers a basis for segmentation also. Though the differentiated marketing is sales-oriented, it should also be borne in mind that it is a costly affair for the organization.
3. Concentrated marketing: Both the concepts explained above imply the approach of total market either with segmentation or without it. Yet another option is to have concentrated efforts in a few markets capable of affording opportunities. Put in another way, instead of spreading itself in many parts of the market, it concentrates its forces to gain a good market position in a few areas. Then new products are introduced and test marketing is conducted, and this method is adopted. For a consumer product 'Boost' produced by the manufacturers of Horlicks, this method was adopted. The principle involved here is 'specialization' in markets which have real potential. Another notable feature of this method is the advantage of one segment is never offset by the other. But in the case of the first two types, good and poor segments are averaged.

TARGETING

Target marketing is the process of assessing the relative worth of different market segments and selecting one or more segments in which to compete. These become the target segments. Titan is using the target marketing strategy very effectively. German car manufacturer Mercedes targets high status consumers with experience and prestigious motor cars.

According to David Cravens and others, "Target market is a group of existing or potential customers within a particular product market towards which an organisation directs its marketing efforts".

Target Marketing Strategies

- **Total market approach:** A company develops a single marketing mix and directs it at the entire market for a particular product. This approach is used when an organisation defines the total market for a particular product as its target market.
- **Concentration approach:** An organisation directs its marketing efforts toward a single market segment through a single marketing mix. The total market may consist of several segments, but the organisation selects only one of the segments as its target market.
- **Multi-segment approach:** An organisation directs its marketing efforts at two or more segments by developing a marketing mix for each segment.

Steps in Target Marketing

It involves the following four major steps:

1. Market segmentation: Markets are segmented on the basis of certain characteristic such as sex, education, income, age etc.
2. Market targeting: It refers to evaluating each market segment's attractiveness and selecting one or more of the segments to enter. Thus, target marketing and market targeting are not one and the same. Market targeting is only a step in target marketing.

3. Designing the marketing mix: After selecting the segment, the next step is to design a suitable product and other marketing mix elements for each segment selected.
4. Product Positioning: Market segmentation strategy and market positioning strategy are like two sides of a coin. Target marketing begins with segmentation and ends with positioning.

Evaluating the market segments

In evaluation of different market segments, the firm must look at three factors, namely segment size and growth, segment structural attractiveness and company objectives and resources.

(a) Segment Size and Growth: The first question that a company should ask is whether a potential segment has the right size and growth characteristics. Large companies prefer segments with large sales volumes and overlook small segments. Small companies in turn avoid large segments because they would require too many resources. Segment growth is a desirable characteristic since companies generally want growing sales and profits.

(b) Segment Structural Attractiveness: A segment might have desirable size and growth and still not be attractive from a profitability point of view. The five threats that a company might face are:

(i) *Threat from industry competitors:* A segment is unattractive if it already contains numerous and aggressive competitors. This condition may lead to frequent price wars.

(ii) *Threats from potential entrants:* i.e. from new competitors who, if enter the segment at a later stage, bring in new capacity, substantial resources and would soon steal a part of the market share.

(iii) *Threat of substitute products:* A segment is unattractive if there exists too many substitutive products because it would result in brand switching, price wars, low profits etc.

(iv) *Threat of growing bargaining power of buyers:* A segment is unattractive if the buyers possess strong bargaining power. Buyers will try to force price down, demand more quality or services, all at the expense of the seller's profitability.

(v) *Threat of growing bargaining power of suppliers:* A segment is unattractive if the company's suppliers of raw materials, equipment, finance etc., are able to raise prices or reduce the quality or quantity of ordered goods.

(c) Company objectives and resources: Even if a segment has positive size and growth and is structurally attractive, the company needs to consider its own objectives and resources in relation to that segment. Some attractive segments could be dismissed because they do not match with the company's long-run objectives. Even if the segment fits the company's objectives, the company has to consider whether it possesses the requisite skills and resources to succeed in that segment. The segment should be dismissed if the company lacks one or more necessary competences needed to develop superior competitive advantages.

Selecting the Market Segments

As a result of evaluating different segments, the company hopes to find one or more market segments worth entering. The company must decide which and how many segments to serve. This is the problem of target market selection. A target market consists of a set of buyers sharing common needs or characteristics that the company decides to serve. The company can consider five patterns of target market selection.

1. **Single segment concentration:** In the simplest case, the company selects a single segment. This company may have limited funds and may want to operate only in one segment, it might be a segment with no competitor, and it might be a segment that

is a logical launching pad for further segment expansion.

2. **Selective specialization:** Here a firm selects a number of segments, each of which is attractive and matches the firm's objectives and resources. This strategy of 'multi-segment coverage' has the advantage over 'single-segment coverage' in terms of diversifying the firm's risk i.e. even if one segment becomes unattractive, the firm can continue to earn money in other segments.
3. **Product specialization:** Here the firm concentrates on marketing a certain product that it sells to several segments. Through this strategy, the firm builds a strong reputation in the specific product area.
4. **Market specialization:** Here the firm concentrates on serving many needs of a particular customer group. The firm gains a strong reputation for specializing in serving this customer group and becomes a channel agent for all new products that this customer group could feasibly use.
5. **Full market coverage:** Here the firm attempts to serve all customer groups with all the products that they might need. Only large firms can undertake a full market coverage strategy. e.g. Philips (Electronics), HLL (Consumer non-durables). Large firms going in for whole market can do so in two broad ways— through undifferentiated marketing or differentiated marketing.

PRODUCT POSITIONING

The act of creating an image about a product or brand in the consumers' mind is known as positioning.

In the words of Kotler, "Positioning is the act of designing the company's offer and image so that it occupies a distinct and valued place in the target consumers' minds." In short, the process of creating an image for a product in the minds of targeted customers is known as product positioning. Close-up toothpaste is looked upon by the consumers more as a mouthwash than a teeth cleaner, while 'Pepsodent' has created an impression of germ killer in the consumers' minds.

Steps in Product Positioning

1. **Identifying potential competitive advantages:** Consumers generally choose products and services which give them greatest value. The key to winning and keeping customers is to understand their needs and buying processes far better than the competitors do and deliver more values.
2. **Identifying the competitors position:** When the firm understands how its customers view its brand relative to competitors, it must study how those same competitors position themselves.
3. **Choosing the right competitive advantages:** It refers to an advantage over competitors gained by offering consumers greater value either through lower price or by providing more benefits.
4. **Communicating the competitive advantage:** The company should take specific steps to advertise the competitive advantage it has chosen so that it can impress upon the minds of consumers about the superiority claimed in respect of the product over its competing brands.
5. **Monitoring the positioning strategy:** Markets are not stagnant. They keep on changing. Consumer tastes shift and competitors react to those shifts. After a desired position is developed, the marketer should continue to monitor its position through brand tracking and monitoring.

Elements of Positioning

It is concerned with the following four elements.

1. **The Product:** Design, special feature, attributes, quality, package etc. of product create its own image in the minds of the consumers. Material ingredient of a product is also important in the process of product positioning.

2. **The Company:** The goodwill of a company lends an aura to its brand. For example, Tata, Godrej, Bajaj etc have very good reputation in the market
3. **The Competitors:** Product image is built in consumers mind in relation to the competing product. Thus, a careful study of competition is required.
4. **The Consumer:** Ultimate aim of positioning policy is to create a place for the product in consumers' minds. Therefore, it becomes necessary to study the consumer behaviour towards the product.

Techniques of Product Positioning

Following techniques are used in positioning a product in the market:

- **Positioning by Corporate Identity:** The companies that have become a tried and trusted household name. For example, Tata, Sony etc.
- **Positioning by Brand Endorsement:** Marketers use the names of company's powerful brands for line extentions or while entering another product category. Lux, Surf, Dettol etc.
- **Positioning by Product Attributes and Benefits:** It emphasizes the special attributes and benefits of the product. Close-up is positioned on fresh breath and cosmetics benefits.
- **Positioning by use, Occasion and Time:** It is to find an occasion or time of use and sit on it. For example, Vicks vaporub is to be used for child's cold at night.
- **Positioning by Price and Quality:** Company position its brand by emphasizing its price and quality. E.g. Nirma detergent powder.
- **Positioning by Product Category:** Brand is perceived to be another product category. E.g. Maruti positioned its van as *Omni*, family car.
- **Positioning by Product User:** Positioning the product as an exclusive product for a particular class of customers. E.g. Scooty as a two wheeler for teenagers.
- **Positioning by Competitor:** An offensive positioning strategy and is often seen in cases of comparative advertising. E.g. Tide and Rin.
- **Positioning by Symbols:** Some companies use some symbols for positioning their products. E.g. Vodafone symbol.

MULTIPLE CHOICE QUESTIONS

1. Objective of Market Segmentation is:
(*a*) To select the best market
(*b*) To make subset of market
(*c*) To set the correct form of market
(*d*) All of these
(*e*) None of these

2. The benefits of market segmentation includes:
(*a*) To determine the product mix
(*b*) To select the targeted market
(*c*) To search attractive marketing options
(*d*) Above all
(*e*) None of these

3. Heterogeneous customer is related with:
(*a*) Market Segmentation
(*b*) Pricing
(*c*) Product Mix
(*d*) Custom
(*e*) None of these

4. According to Philip Kotler, the basis of Market Segmentation is:
(*a*) Demographic Basis
(*b*) Geographical Basis
(*c*) Psychographic Basis
(*d*) Above all
(*e*) None of these

5. Brand loyalty means:
(*a*) Product without name
(*b*) Loyalty is product quality
(*c*) Attitude
(*d*) Social responsibility
(*e*) None of these

6. Behavioural basis of Market Segmentation includes:
(*a*) Loyalty (*b*) Buying Occasions
(*c*) Attitude (*d*) Above all
(*e*) None of these

7. Essential of effective segmentation is:
(*a*) Pricing
(*b*) Measurable
(*c*) Identifiable and distinguishable
(*d*) Both (*b*) and (*c*)
(*e*) None of these

8. Factors of target market involves:
(*a*) Competitors strategies
(*b*) Market variability
(*c*) Social responsibility
(*d*) Above all
(*e*) None of these

9. Social responsibility of a bank includes:
(*a*) Water facility
(*b*) Training to the bank employees
(*c*) Deposits
(*d*) Both (*a*) and (*b*)
(*e*) None of these

10. Requirement of effective Segmentation is:
(*a*) Measurable (*b*) Easy accessibility
(*c*) Substantiality (*d*) Above all
(*e*) None of these

11. Important method of Market Segmentation is:
(*a*) Cost method
(*b*) Discount
(*c*) Each buyer a separate market
(*d*) Pricing
(*e*) None of these

12. Sub market is also known as:
(*a*) Origin of market
(*b*) Merging of market
(*c*) Market segment
(*d*) All of these
(*e*) None of these

13. Grouping of buyers is described as:
(*a*) Market Segmentation
(*b*) Product Planning
(*c*) Customer Planning
(*d*) Market planning
(*e*) None of these

14. .... is the process of dividing the market according to similarities that exist among the various sub groups within the market.
(*a*) Marketing Mix
(*b*) Product Mix
(*c*) Market Segmentation
(*d*) Customer Planning
(*e*) None of these

15. Identifiable, accessible, substantial, unique needs and durable are requirements of ....
(*a*) Product Mix
(*b*) Marketing Mix
(*c*) Market Segments
(*d*) Competitors Strategies
(*e*) None of these

16. Segmentation of consumers based on climatic zone is known as:
(*a*) Geographic Segmentation
(*b*) Demographic Segmentation
(*c*) Psychographic Segmentation
(*d*) Market Segmentation
(*e*) None of these

17. .... Segmentation is based on traits, attitudes, interests and lifestyles of potential customer groups.
(*a*) Psychographic (*b*) Demographic
(*c*) Behaviouralistic (*d*) Geographic
(*e*) None of these

18. Marketing Gridding is based on:
(*a*) Product (*b*) Customer
(*c*) Age (*d*) Cost method
(*e*) None of these

19. Segmentation of consumers on brand loyalty is known as:
(*a*) Demographic Segmentation
(*b*) Psychographic Segmentation

(*c*) Geographic Segmentation
(*d*) Behaviouralistic Segmentation
(*e*) None of these

20. Match the following:

List-I (Bases of Segmentation)	**List-II (Examples)**
A. Geographic Segmentation	1. Region
B. Demographic Segmentation	2. Occupation
C. Psychographic Segmentation	3. Traits
D. Behaviouralistic Segmentation	4. User Status
	5. Place

Codes :

	A	B	C	D
(*a*)	1	2	3	4
(*b*)	2	3	5	4
(*c*)	5	3	2	4
(*d*)	2	1	4	5
(*e*)	2	5	3	1

ANSWERS

1	2	3	4	5	6	7	8	9	10
(*d*)	(*d*)	(*a*)	(*d*)	(*b*)	(*d*)	(*d*)	(*d*)	(*d*)	(*d*)
11	**12**	**13**	**14**	**15**	**16**	**17**	**18**	**19**	**20**
(*c*)	(*c*)	(*a*)	(*c*)	(*c*)	(*a*)	(*e*)	(*a*)	(*d*)	(*a*)

CHAPTER-5

PRODUCT, PRODUCT MIX AND NEW PRODUCT DEVELOPMENT

INTRODUCTION

The marketing mix, which is the means by which an organisation reaches its target market, is made up of product, pricing, distribution, promotion and people decisions. These are usually shortened to the acronym "5P's". Product decisions revolve around decisions regarding the physical product (size, style, specification, etc.) and product line management.

Difinition

A product can be defined as a collection of physical, service and symbolic attributes which yield satisfaction or benefits to a user or buyer. A product is a combination of physical attributes say, size and shape; and subjective attributes say image or "quality". A customer purchases on both dimensions

According to Jobber(2004), "A product is anything that has the ability to satisfy a consumer need." In the words of Dibb et al, "A product is anything, favourable and unfavourable that is received in exchange."

Classification of Products

A product's physical properties are characterized the same the world over. They can be convenience or shopping goods or durables and nondurables; however, one can also classify products according to their degree of potential for global marketing:

(*i*) **Local Products:** seen as only suitable in one single market.

(*ii*) **International Products:** seen as having extension potential into other markets.

(*iii*) **Multinational Products:** products adapted to the perceived unique characteristics of national markets.

(*iv*) **Global Products:** products designed to meet global segments.

Products and services fall into two broad classes based on the types of consumers that use them

1. Consumer Product
2. Industrial Product

1. Consumer Product: "Product bought by final consumer for personal consumption". Consumer products divided into four classes.

- Convenience Product
- Shopping Product
- Specially Products
- Unsought Product

(*i*) **Convenience Product:** Consumer product that the customer usually buys frequently, immediately, and with a minimum of comparison and buying effort consumer products can be divided further into staples, impulse products, and emergency products.

Staples Products are those product that consumers buy on a regular basis, such as ketchup, toothpaste etc. *Impulse* products are those product that purchased with little planning or search effort, such as Candy bar, and magazine, *Emergency* product is those when consumers' need is urgent, e.g. umbrellas during a rainstorm etc.

(ii) **Shopping Product:** Consumer good that the consumer, in the process of selection and purchase, characteristically compares on such bases as suitability, quality, price, and style. Example: Furniture, clothing, used cars, major appliances and hotel and motel services.

(iii) **Specialty Products:** Consumer product with unique characteristics or brand identification for which a significant group of buyers is willing to make a special purchase effort. E.g. Specific brands and types of cars, high-priced photographic equipment, designer clothes etc.

(iv) **Unsought Products:** Unsought products are consumer products that the consumer either does not know about or knows about but does not normally think of buying. Most major new inventions are unsought until the consumers become aware of them through advertising. E.g. Life Insurance and blood donations to the Red Cross.

2. Industrial Goods: It is meant for use in the production of other goods or for some business or institutional purposes. Industrial goods are classified into four- production facilities and equipment, production materials, production supplies and management materials.

Product Line

Product lining is the marketing strategy of offering for sale several related products. Unlike product bundling, where several products are combined into one, lining involves offering several related products individually. A line can comprise related products of various sizes, types, colors, qualities, or prices. Line depth refers to the number of product variants in a line. Line consistency refers to how closely related the products that make up the line are. Line vulnerability refers to the percentage of sales or profits that are derived from only a few products in the line. If a line of products is sold with the same brand name, this is referred to as family branding.

Product Line Modification

When you add a new product to a line, it is referred to as a line extension. When you add a line extension that is of better quality than the other products in the line, this is referred to as trading up or brand leveraging. When you add a line extension that is of lower quality than the other products of the line, this is referred to as trading down. When you trade down, you will likely reduce your brand equity. You are gaining short-term sales at the expense of long-term sales.

- Product Line Contraction
- Product Line Expansion
- Changing Models or Styles of the Existing Products

Product Simplifcation

Product Simplification means limiting the number of products a dealer deals. Sometimes it becomes necessary for a company to stop the production of unprofitable products.

Product Diversification

Product diversification means adding a new product or products to the existing product. It is a strategy for growth and survival in the highly complex marketing environment.

Product Differentiation

Product differentiation involves developing and promoting an awareness in the minds of customers that the company's products differ from the products of competitors. This is made by using trade mark, brand name, packaging, labeling etc.

Product Levels

In planning its market offering, the marketer needs to think through five levels of the product (Fig 1). Each level adds more customer value, and the five constitute a customer value hierarchy. The most fundamental level is the core benefit : the fundamental service or benefit that the customer is really buying. A hotel guest is buying "rest and sleep". The purchaser of a drill is buying "holes". Marketers must see themselves as benefit providers.

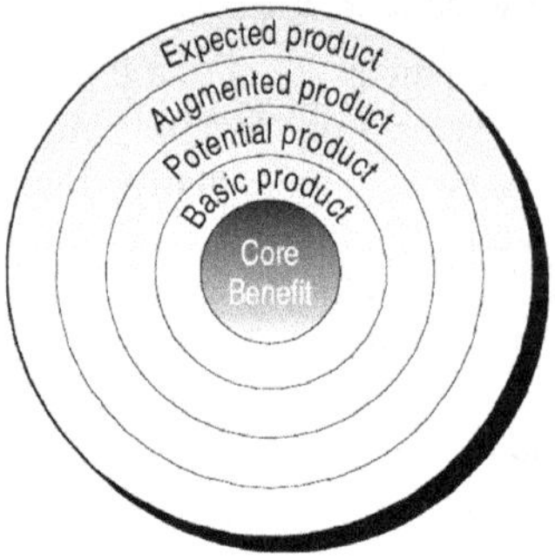

Fig. 1: *Five Product Levels*

At the second level, the marketer has to turn the core benefit into a basic product. Thus, a hotel room includes a bed, bathroom, towels, desk, dresser, and closet.

At the third level, the marketer prepares an expected product, a set of attributes and conditions buyers normally expect when they purchase this product. Hotel guests expect a clean bed, fresh towels, working lamps, and a relative degree of quiet. Because most hotels can meet this minimum expectation, the traveler normally will settle for whichever hotel is most convenient or least expensive.

At the fourth level, the marketer prepares an augmented product that exceeds customer's expectations. A hotel can include a remote-control television set, fresh flowers, rapid check-in, express checkout and fine dining and room service. Elmer Wheeler once observed, "Don't sell the steak—sell the sizzle."

Today's competition essentially takes place at the product-augmentation level. (In less developed countries, competition takes place mostly at the expected product level.) Product augmentation leads the marketer to look at the user's total consumption system: the way the user performs the tasks of getting, using, fixing and disposing of the product. According to Levitt:

The new competition is not between what companies produce in their factories, but between what they add to their factory output in the form of packaging, services, advertising, customer advice, financing, delivery arrangements, warehousing and other things that people value.

Some things should be noted about product-augmentation strategy. First, each augmentation adds cost. The marketer has to ask whether customers will pay enough to cover the extra cost. Second, augmented benefits soon become expected benefits. Today's hotel guests expect a remote-control television set and other amenities. This means that competitors will have to search for still other features and benefits. Third, as companies raise the price of their augmented product, some competitors can offer a "stripped-down" version at a much lower price. Thus, alongside the growth of fine hotels like Four Seasons and Ritz Carlton, we see the emergence of lower-cost hotels and motels (Motel Six, Comfort Inn) catering to clients who simply want the basic product.

At the fifth level stands the potential product, which encompasses all the possible agmentations and transformations the product might undergo in the future. Here is where companies search for new ways to satisfy customers and distinguish their offer. All-suite hotels where the guest occupies a set of rooms represent an innovative transformation of the traditional hotel product.

Successful companies add benefits to their offering that not only satisfy customers but also surprise and delight them. Delighting is a matter of exceeding expectations. Thus, the hotel guest finds candy on the pillow or a bowl of fruit or a video recorder with optional videotapes. Ritz-Carlton hotels, for example, remember individual guests. preferences and prepare rooms with these preferences in mind.

Product Offer Can Range from the Generic to the Potential

At the beginning of this chapter, we made a simple definition of product as a "need satisfying entity". Now, after analysing the various components that actually build up the product, we have a better idea of what a product means. A product has a personality consisting of several components–the basic material, its associated features, the brand name, the package and the labelling, the price range, the positioning, speciality of the sale outlets, the quality of promotion and the corporate image and prestige. A product that is finally offered in the market is a combination of all these elements.

In fact, the crucial task in product management lies in working out the best possible alignment among the myriad factors mentioned above. The marketing man is constantly at it, always engaged in enriching his product offer. In his attempt to satisfy the customer and score over competition, he brings out refinement upon refinement on his basic product offer, and takes the product to higher levels of evolution. Theodore Levitt explains this idea beautifully in his HBR article: "Marketing Success Through Differentiation of Anything". According to Levitt, a product offer can be conceived at four levels: the generic product, the expected product, the augmented product and the potential product. To make this evolution easier to understand, we go by a six-level approach, as shown:

Product Offer can Range from the Generic to the Potential

- The generic product
- The branded product
- The differentiated product
- The customised product
- The augmented product
- The potential product

The Generic Product: The generic product is the unbranded and undifferentiated commodity like rice, bread, flour, or cloth. Here, the product does not have an identity through a name and is not linked to any one maker or owner.

The Branded Product: The branded product gets an identity through a 'name', Lalkila basmati rice, Modern bread, and Annapurna atta are branded products.

The Differentiated Product: The differentiated product enjoys further distinction from other similar products/brands in the market. The marketer endows his brand with some special attributes/qualities and claims uniqueness for his offer. The differentiation claimed may be 'tangible', with a distinction on ingredient, quality, utility or service. It may also be intangible or 'psychological', highlighted by subtle sales appeals.

Maggi noodles, and Dettol soap are examples of differentiated products with tangible differentiation. Maggi claims a tangible distinction over other brands of noodles. It is ready in two minutes and involves very little cooking. It is available with different 'taste makers' for the vegetarian and the non-vegetarian users. The differentiation is tangible and rests on the planks of convenience and variety. Among bath soaps, Dettol is differentiated on the basis of its ability to provide total protection from germs.

The scope for differentiation is immense; and to win over cutomers, firms seek higher levels of differentiation through customising and augmenting of the product.

The Customised Product: A product that is adapted to the requirements of the individual customer is a customised product. Today, many products coming from the IT and telecom industries have large degree of customisation built into them. For example, the telephone 'knows' which language a given user would like to use while calling a long-distance operator. It will also allow him to create a distinctive ring so that his best friend knows that he is calling. And, it can also recognise his most frequently called numbers, not just by number, but by name as well.

The Augmented Product: The augmented product is the result of voluntary improvements brought about by the manufacturer in order to enhance the value of the product. The firm goes beyond all expectations of the consumers. It finds out through market research how the value of its product can be enhanced. Using the insights so gathered, the firm augments the product by adding extra features and functions to it.

Examples of augmented products: Titan, added protective packing to its alarm clocks and claimed, 'Here is a travel clock with a protective shutter. Available in 3 dial options and 4 elegant colours'. Aristocrat introduced suitcases with wheels. The wheel was an extra facility, an augmentation to the luggage. Instead of lifting and carrying the suitcase, the users could now pull it on its wheels. Hindustan Motors augmented its Ambassador car and offered the Ambassador 1800 ISZ, incorporating into the car, the 1817 cc, 74 HP, Isuzu engine, 5 synchromeshed gears with an overdrive, power-assisted brakes, progressive suspension, diaphragm clutch, a new dashboard and bucket seats. The augmentations translated into faster pick-up, greater speed, sure stopping and greater comfort.

Companies resorting to the product development route in their marketing strategy are basically in the game of continuous augmentation of products.

The Potential Product: The potential product is "tomorrow's product", carrying all the improvement and finesse that is possible under the given technological, economic and competitive conditions. For example, today, a robot available for domestic help can be considered a potential product. In actual practice, development of potential products is the forte of big companies, since heavy resources are required for this task.

Product Mix

The number of different product lines sold by a company is referred to as width of product mix. The total number of products sold in all lines is referred to as length of product mix.

Factors Influencing Product Mix

- Change in demand.
- Marketing influences.
- Production efficiencies.
- Financial influence.
- Use of waste.
- Competitor's strategy.
- Profitability.

A Company's Product Mix Includes:

I. Product Width: Means the number of different products the organization offers (E.g. Hindustan Lever Ltd. has soaps, cosmetics, ice-cream, Atta, etc).

II. Product Length: It means the total number of items in each product category. For example HLL's product length is: brands like Lux, Liril, Lifebuoy and so on.

III. Product Depth: It means the number of variants of each product in the line, e.g. Colgate has Colgate Total and Colgate Gel and these are available with three sizes, it means it has depth of six.

IV. Consistency (product consistency): It refers to how closely related the various product lines are in end use, production requirements, distribution channels or in some other way.

Product mix dimensions, as explained above, help to define the company's product strategy. A company can add new product line there by widening its product mix. This decision will add to the company's reputation on the existing product lines. A company can also lengthen its existing product lines to become a full line company serving diversified needs of consumers. Product mix decision indicates whether a company wants to have a strong reputation in single field or in several fields.

Components of Product Mix

The product mix has various sub mixes with which the product mix can be made more effective, and impressive and more saleable one. Such subvariables are as under:

(i) **Brand:** It is a name and/or mark intended to identify the product of one seller and differentiate the product from competing products. So it should be designed with thorough consideration

(ii) **Labeling:** It is the part of a product that carries information about the product and the seller. As it provides all information of the product, it helps the buyer to take decision. It is always attached with packaging.

(iii) **Packaging:** It is actual container, covering or wrapper to protect the product. Its intension is to protect product, from external effects on product.

(*iv*) **Product design:** Design refers to the arrangement of element that collectively form a product. It includes usability, aesthetics, reliability, functionality, and appropriateness. So the design should be in such a way that it can easily be used by the consumers.

(*v*) **Product quality:** Product quality means the set of characteristics of a product or service that determines its ability to satisfy needs.

(*vi*) **Products colour:** It is also important in selection or rejection of product.

(*vii*) **Warranties:** It is an assurance given by a manufacturer to the buyers that they would be compensated in case the product does not perform up to reasonable expectations.

(*viii*) **After sale service:** Some product require after sale services means regular checking is required whether the product is not working properly or servicing of the product or maintenance etc.

New Product Development

Once a company has carefully segmented the market, chosen its target customers, identified their needs, and determined its market positioning, it is better able to develop new products. Marketers play a key role in the new-product process, by identifying and evaluating new-product and working with R & D and others in every stage of development.

Every company must develop new products. New-product development shapes the company's future. Replacement products must be created to maintain or build sales. Customers want new products, and competitors will do their best to supply them. Each year over 16,000 new products (including line extensions and new brands) are introduced into groceries and drugstores.

A company can add new products through acquisition or development. The acquisition route can take three forms. The company can buy other companies, it can acquire patents from other companies, or it can but a licence or franchise from another company. The development route can take two forms. The company can develop new products in its own laboratories. Or it can contract with independent researchers or new-product development firms to develop specific new products.

Booz, Allen and Hamilton had identified six categories of new products:

1. **New-to-the-world products:** New products that create an entirely new market.
2. **New product lines:** New products that allow a company to enter an established market for the first time.
3. **Additions to existing product lines:** New products that supplement a company's established product lines (package sizes, flavours, and so on).
4. **Improvements and revisions of existing products:** New products that provide improved performance or greater perceived value and replace existing products.
5. **Repositionings:** Existing products that are targeted to new markets or market segments.
6. **Cost reductions:** New products that provide similar performance at lower cost.

Management's Perspective on New Products

Managers may consider a product new if it is new to the market or simply new to the company. Products can be either new-to-the-world products, product category extensions, product line extensions, or product modifications. Companies have considerable experience marketing product modifications but far less experience with products in the first three categories.

- New-to-the-world products are inventions that create an entirely new market. These are the highest-risk products, because they are new to both, the company and the market. The technology for producing these innovative products, which is itself new to the company, is often the result of a large investment in research and development.

- Product category extensions are new products that, for the first time, allow a company to diversify and enter an established market for an existing product category. These products are not entirely new to the market, but the company has had no previous technological or marketing experience with them. If these products imitate competitive products with identical features, they can be described as "me, too" products.
- Product line extensions are additions to an existing product line that supplement the basic items in the established line. Line extensions include enhanced models, low-price economy models, and variations in colour, flavour, design, and so on. These new products may be family branded or marketed under a new brand name, perhaps a private label that appeals to a different market segment.
- Product modifications include product improvements, cost reductions, and repositionings. New and improved versions replace existing products and are intended to provide improved performance, enhanced features, or greater perceived value. Cost reductions replace existing products by providing similar performance at a lower cost. Repositionings may modify existing products by targeting new market segments, offering a new benefit, or assuming a different competitive position. The marketing task for these products often is to communicate the benefits of product modifications to consumers who do not see the product as unique or strikingly different from past offerings.

The Consumer's Perspective on Newness

From a consumer's perspective, new products vary in degree of newness. There are three types of innovations: discontinuous, dynamically continuous, and continuous, as shown in Fig. 2.

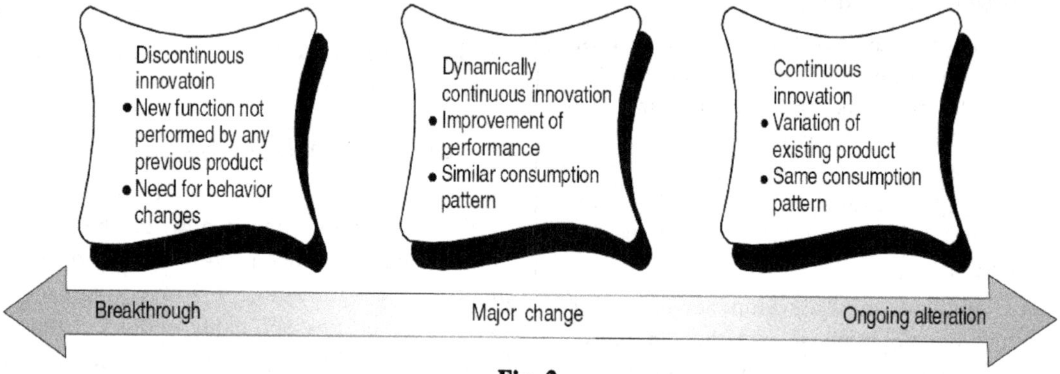

Fig. 2

Discontinuous Innovation

Discontinuous innovation: *A product so new that no previous product performed an equivalent function. Such a product requires the development of new consumption or usage patterns.*

Discontinuous innovations are pioneering products so new that no previous product performed an equivalent function. As a result of this near-complete newness, new consumption or usage patterns are required. The lithium battery pacemaker implanted in heart patients was a discontinuous innovation. The fax machine was another. These products, once new to the world, did things no products before them had done, and to use them properly, people had to make extensive behaviour changes. Artificial hearts and a drug to cure AIDS are still in their developmental stages, but once perfected and made available, they, too, will be discontinuous innovations.

Dynamically Continuous Innovation

Dynamically continuous innovation: *A product that is different from previously available products but that does not strikingly change buying or usage patterns.*

In the newness continuum, somewhere between the breakthrough achieved with the perfected artificial heart and the commonplace newness of the new and improved consumer product, is the dynamically continuous innovation. New products in this middle range represent changes and improvements that do not strikingly change buying and usage patterns.

The hybrid gasoline engine/electric motor car is an example of a dynamically continuous innovation. The buying habits of those purchasing cars and fuel may be altered by successful and appealing hybrid gas/electric automobiles, but virtually all driving behaviour will remain as it is. Compare this situation with the way the Model T Ford affected society. Similarly, although TiVo's personal video recorder system, is genuinely new, its effect on buyers and users is nothing like the effect of the first video-tape recorder.

Continuous Innovation

Continuous innovation: *A new product that is characterized by minor alterations or improvements to existing products and that produces little change in consumption patterns.*

A continuous innovation is a commonplace change that is part of an ongoing product modification effort, such as a minor alteration of a product or the introduction of an imitative product. The flat-panel computer monitor is an example of a continuous innovation. This new product is an improvement over existing monitors because it takes up less space. Although the product has a new form, it is used in the traditional manner, so consumers do not have to change their consumption behaviour. This is a key characteristic of a continuous innovation. Marketers constantly strive to improve products, because even minor improvements, such as reducing calories or salt, can provide a competitive advantage. Although this approach may be viewed as finetuning the product, the new product is an innovation of a sort.

The Characteristics of Success

Five characteristics influence a new product's chances for success in the market place: relative advantage, compatibility with existing consumption patterns, trialability, observability, and simplicity of usage. When a product lacks one or more of these characteristics, the others may be used effectively to make up for the deficiency. Non-product elements of the marketing mix-price, promotion, and distribution-must be developed and adjusted with these same characteristics in mind.

Stages of New Product Development

New product development tends to happen in stages. Although firms often go back and forth between these idealized stages, the following sequence is illustrative of the development of a new product:

- **New Product Strategy Development:** Different firms will have different strategies on how to approach new products. Some firms have stockholders who want to minimize risk and avoid investing in too many new innovations. Some firms can only survive if they innovate frequently and have stockholders who are willing to take this risk. For example, Hewlett-Packard has to constantly invent new products since competitors learn to work around its patents and will be able to manufacture the products at a lower cost.
- **Idea Generation:** Firms solicit ideas as to new products it can make. Ideas might come from customers, employees, consultants, or engineers. Many firms receive a large number of ideas each year and can only invest in some of them.

- **Screening and Evaluation:** Some products that after some analysis are clearly not feasible or are not consistent with the core competencies of the firm are eliminated.
- **Business Analysis:** Ideas are now exposed to more rigorous analysis. Profit projections, risks, market size, and competitive response are considered. If promising, market research may be done.
- **Development:** The product is designed and manufacturing facilities are planned.
- **Market Testing:** Frequently, firms will try to "test" a product in one region to see if it will sell in reality before it is released nationally and internationally. There is a lesser risk if the firm only commits money to advertising and other marketing efforts in one region. Retailers will also be more receptive in other parts of the country and world if it has been demonstrated that the product sold well in one region. The firm may also experiment with different prices for the product.
- **Commercialization:** Facilities to manufacture the product on a larger scale are now put into operation and the firm starts a national marketing campaign and distribution effort.

New Product Development Process

1. Its the idea generation the idea worth considering?

↓

2. Is idea screening the product idea compatible with company objectives, strategies, and resources?

↓

3. Can we find concept development and testing a good concept for the product that consumers say they would try?

↓

4. Can we find Marketing strategy development a cost-effective, of fordable marketing strategy?

↓

5. Business analysis: Will the product meet our profit god?

↓

6. Product development: Have we developed a technically and commercially sound product?

↓

7. Market testing: Have product sales met expectations?

↓

8. Commercialization: Are prodcut sales meeting expectations?

MULTIPLE CHOICE QUESTIONS

1. Which of the following is the stage of product development?
(*a*) New Ideas (*b*) Business Analysis
(*c*) Test marketing (*d*) Above all
(*e*) None of these

2. In product development, we include:
(*a*) Guarantee and condition on the product
(*b*) Brand
(*c*) Label
(*d*) Above all
(*e*) None of these

3. Which of the following is the principle of product development?
(*a*) Principle of Simplification
(*b*) Principle of Standardisation
(*c*) Principle of Specialisation
(*d*) Above all
(*e*) None of these

4. The scope of product planning and development includes:
(*a*) Product decision
(*b*) Design and size of the product
(*c*) Colour of the product
(*d*) Above all
(*e*) None of these

5. Product development's activities are:
(*a*) Engineering activity
(*b*) Functional activity
(*c*) Attributes determination
(*d*) Above all
(*e*) None of these

6. Business analysis includes:
(*a*) Demand analysis
(*b*) Cost analysis
(*c*) Profitability analysis
(*d*) Above all
(*e*) None of these

7. Which of the following is the sources of generation of ideas?
(*a*) Investors (*b*) Competitor
(*c*) Employees (*d*) Above all
(*e*) None of these

8. Which is the stage of product development process?
(*a*) Generation of ideas
(*b*) Screening of the ideas
(*c*) Business analysis
(*d*) Above all
(*e*) None of these

9. .... is a product growth strategy in which a company develops new product to sell to its existing markets.
(*a*) Product Simplification
(*b*) Product Development
(*c*) Market Segmentation
(*d*) Personal Selling
(*e*) None of these

10. Product innovation includes:
(*a*) Development of shape of product and services
(*b*) Development of new product or new services
(*c*) Improvement in existing production process
(*d*) Above all
(*e*) None of these

11. Legal protection includes:
(*a*) Patent of product
(*b*) Planning and product style
(*c*) Wage
(*d*)
(*e*) None of these

12. Which of the following is the type of goods?
(*a*) Contingent goods (*b*) Specific goods
(*c*) Existing goods (*d*) Above all
(*e*) None of these

13. .... is basically a method of communication.
(*a*) Product Development
(*b*) Product Planning
(*c*) Personal Selling
(*d*) Above all
(*e*) None of these

14. Job description involves:
(*a*) Training (*b*) Working conditions
(*c*) Job-Summary (*d*) Above all
(*e*) None of these

15. Product planning and development function includes:
(*a*) Branding (*b*) Financial transaction
(*c*) Audit (*d*) Resources
(*e*) None of these

16. Creation of demand is important function of:
(*a*) Marketing organization
(*b*) Selling
(*c*) EOQ
(*d*) Demand of product
(*e*) None of these

17. Economic activity involves:
(*a*) Demand of product
(*b*) Investment
(*c*) Employment
(*d*) Above all
(*e*) None of these

18. Sales territories increases:
(*a*) Profit of the organisation
(*b*) Individual satisfaction
(*c*) Efficient services
(*d*) Above all
(*e*) None of these

19. Consumer co-operative stores is based on:
(*a*) Democracy system (*b*) Partnership system
(*c*) Companies system (*d*) Marketing system
(*e*) None of these

20. Corporate culture is a result of:
(*a*) Old concept of marketing
(*b*) Profit based marketing
(*c*) Ethical aspect of marketing
(*d*) Profit and Loss based marketing
(*e*) None of these

21. The planning, direction and control of all stages in the life of a product from the time of its creation to the time of its removal from the company's line of product is known as:
(*a*) Product Pricing (*b*) Product Planning
(*c*) Wage (*d*) Product Costing
(*e*) None of these

22. Elements of product planning is:
(*a*) Proper utilisation of resources
(*b*) Increasing in sales and profits
(*c*) Cost reduction
(*d*) Above all
(*e*) None of these

23. Match the following:

List-I
1. Product dropping
2. Product modification
3. Product simplification
4. Product diversification

List-II
A. Marginal Product
B. Change in the shape of product
C. Single product
D. Different product
E. Same product

Codes :

	1	2	3	4
(*a*)	A	C	B	E
(*b*)	E	D	C	B
(*c*)	A	B	C	D
(*d*)	C	D	E	A
(*e*)	E	B	C	A

24. Product planning is essential for:
(*a*) Minimisation of risk
(*b*) Basis of marketing programme
(*c*) Instrumental in growth
(*d*) Above all
(*e*) None of these

25. Which of the following is compulsory for product planning and development?
(*a*) Innovation (*b*) Company Manager
(*c*) Cost (*d*) Product Planning
(*e*) None of these

26. In nature of product planning, we include:
(*a*) Planning of product
(*b*) RD
(*c*) Primary work of marketing
(*d*) Above all
(*e*) None of these

27. ... is the starting point for the entire marketing programme in a firm.
(*a*) Product Planning (*b*) Marketing
(*c*) Pricing (*d*) Financing
(*e*) None of these

28. Main target of product planning is:
(*a*) Profit Maximisation
(*b*) Customer Satisfaction and Welfare
(*c*) Cost Minimisation
(*d*) Loss Minimisation
(*e*) None of these

29. Product planning includes:
(*a*) Test Marketing
(*b*) Product Control
(*c*) Research and development of production
(*d*) Above all
(*e*) None of these

30. Which of the following is product attributes?
(*a*) Product design (*b*) Product size
(*c*) Product trade mark (*d*) Above all
(*e*) None of these

31. Product attributes include:
(*a*) Production
(*b*) Sales
(*c*) Guarantees and warranties
(*d*) Above all
(*e*) None of these

32. Test marketing means:
(*a*) Test the product before the commercialisation
(*b*) Valuation
(*c*) Vouching
(*d*) Product control
(*e*) None of these

33. Commercialisation of product is based on:
(*a*) Production (*b*) Test Marketing
(*c*) Pricing (*d*) Wages
(*e*) None of these

34. Product diversification can be defined as:
(*a*) A sales promotion technique
(*b*) A brand of product
(*c*) The introduction of products that are a different type from those previously produced by the company
(*d*) All of these
(*e*) None of these

35. Bye-product is a result of:
(*a*) Product diversification
(*b*) Product simplification
(*c*) Product identification
(*d*) Product attributes
(*e*) None of these

36. Which of the following is the example of product diversification of Bank?
(*a*) Credit Card
(*b*) International Credit Card
(*c*) Debit Card
(*d*) Above all
(*e*) None of these

37. Product Innovation is a part of:
(*a*) Product Pricing
(*b*) Product Modification
(*c*) Cost
(*d*) Product simplification
(*e*) None of these

38. Product Modification Strategies includes:
(*a*) Style Improvement Strategy
(*b*) Quality Improvement Strategy
(*c*) Functional Features Improvement Strategy
(*d*) Above all
(*e*) None of these

39. Main reason of product innovation is:
(*a*) Market Strategy (*b*) Risk
(*c*) Competition (*d*) Above all
(*e*) None of these

40. VAT stands for:
(*a*) Value Added Tax (*b*) Value After Tax
(*c*) Volume And Tax (*d*) All of these
(*e*) None of these

41. Products that are marketed include:
(*a*) Physical goods and services
(*b*) Persons
(*c*) Places
(*d*) All of these
(*e*) None of these

42. Market Plan is a:
(*a*) Selling process
(*b*) Year-end-budget
(*c*) Business document for marketing strategies
(*d*) All of these
(*e*) None of these

ANSWERS

1	2	3	4	5	6	7	8	9	10
(*d*)	(*d*)	(*d*)	(*d*)	(*d*)	(*d*)	(*d*)	(*d*)	(*b*)	(*b*)
11	**12**	**13**	**14**	**15**	**16**	**17**	**18**	**19**	**20**
(*a*)	(*d*)	(*c*)	(*d*)	(*a*)	(*b*)	(*d*)	(*d*)	(*a*)	(*c*)
21	**22**	**23**	**24**	**25**	**26**	**27**	**28**	**29**	**30**
(*b*)	(*d*)	(*c*)	(*d*)	(*a*)	(*d*)	(*a*)	(*b*)	(*d*)	(*d*)
31	**32**	**33**	**34**	**35**	**36**	**37**	**38**	**39**	**40**
(*d*)	(*a*)	(*b*)	(*c*)	(*a*)	(*d*)	(*b*)	(*d*)	(*d*)	(*a*)
41	**42**								
(*d*)	(*a*)								

☞ CHAPTER-6

PRODUCT LIFE CYCLE

INTRODUCTION

All products withness a Life Cycle. A product life cycle, abbreviated as PLC, consists of a series of stages, beginning with its introduction into the market and ending with its decline. As a product passess through its life cycle, its sales and profitability change as it faces changing environment pressures. Understanding the Product Life Cycle (PLC) is of critical importance to a firm launching a new product. It helps a firm to manage the risk of launching a new product more effectively, whilst simultaneously maximizing the sales and profits that could be achieved throughout the product's life cycle.

We can define Product Life Cycle as. "It is a series of successive stages a product class or product goes through from the time it is put in the market till it is withdrawn from the market. Thus, the PLC indicates that products have four things in common. Following are the characteristics of PLC....

1. They have a limited lifespan;
2. Their sales pass through a number of distinct stages, each of which has different characteristics, challenges, and opportunities;
3. Their profits are not static but increase decrease through these stages; and
4. It needs di-financial, human resource, manufacturing, marketing and purchasing strategies.

At diffrent stages in the life cycle. Whilst there is a common pattern to a product's life cycle, which is bell-shaped in nature, this pattern does vary depending on the specific characteristics of a given product. These life cycle patterns are illustrated and discussed in the subsequent section.

Stages of the Product Life Cycle

The PLC concept shows the sales history of a typical product as following a bell –shaped curve, depicting the five different stages.

1. Product Development,
2. Introduction,
3. Growth,
4. Maturity; and
5. Decline.

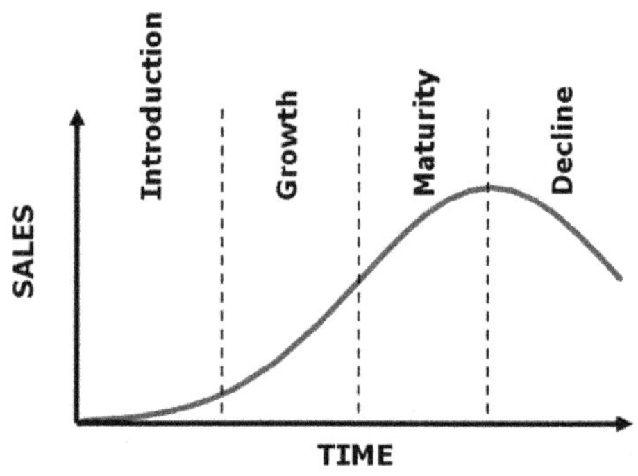

Fig. 1: *Product Life Cycle Curve*

1. Product Development: The PLC begins with product development, during which time the firm devises and creates a new product. Whilst the end aim of this development process is to have a profitable, well-performing product on the market, this initial stage is characterized by zero sales, the firm bearing the costs of such development, typically resulting in negative profitability (Kotler and Armstrong, 2004). However, despite the importance of the product development process, the PLC literature tends to focus on the subsequent four stages, which are discussed in more detail below.

2. Introduction Stage: The introduction of a new product onto the market is typically characterized by very slow sales, which may grow only very slightly over a long period of time. Whilst profits will gradually improve during this stage, it may take until near the completion of the introductory stage in the PLC before the company witnesses positive profitability.

The reason for such low profitability during this stage is not so much the limited success of the product – measured in terms of low, albeit growing, sales – but the high costs of production and promotion that are required to try to develop customer awareness. Depending on the nature of the product, the firm may need to invest in building inventories or acquiring fixed assets such as plant and machinery. Whilst this stage in the process can take a long time and consume considerable resources, firms must not be tempted to try to obtain early profitability at the expense of long-term product viability. For example, introducing a new product at a low price may encourage a lot of consumers to make an immediate purchase, but the firm not only sacrifices long-term sales because too many people have bought the product early on but also may considerably reduce its margins, making it more difficult and time consuming before the product first becomes profitable and hits its break-even level. As such, firms must make careful choices over their marketing strategies; in particular, their pricing, promotional and placement decisions.

During the introduction stage, the primary goal is to establish a market and build primary demand for the product class. The following are some of the marketing mix implications of the introduction stage:

- **Product:** one or few products, relatively undifferentiated.
- **Price:** Generally high, assuming a skim pricing strategy for a high profit margin as the early adopters buy the product and the firm seeks to recoup development costs quickly. In some cases a penetration pricing strategy is used and introductory prices are set low to gain market share rapidly.
- **Place :** Place (Distribution) is selective and scattered as the firm commences implementation of the distribution plan.
- **Promotion :** Promotion is aimed at building brand awareness. Samples or trial incentives may be directed toward early adopters. The introductory promotion also is intended to convince potential resellers to carry the product.

Marketing Strategies during Introduction Stage:

While launching a new product, marketing can set a high or a low level for each marketing variable, such as price, promotion, distribution and product quality. Considering only price and promotion, marketing management can pursue one of the four strategies as below:

- **Rapid skimming strategy:** This consists of launching the new product at a high price and high promotion level to skim the market.
- **Slow skimming strategy:** This consists of launching the new product at a high price and low promotion.
- **Rapid penetration strategy:** This consists of launching the new product at a lower price and high promotion level to skim the market.
- **Slow penetration strategy:** This consists of launching the new product at a lower price and lower promotion level to skim the market.

During introduction, particularly for mass market, small value products, promotion for advertising, sales promotion and sales force are high in terms of percentage of total sales. The foremost communication task at this stage is to build awareness about the unique features and benefits and ensure product availability.

3. Growth Stage: The growth stage in the PLC typically involves a rapid growth in sales as early adopters replace pioneers as the main consumer group. Whilst pioneers are characterized as those consumers who purchase products almost immediately when new products are launched, early adopters wait until the price starts to fall and some of the product's potential weaknesses are ironed out. Nonetheless, over time the risk of purchasing a new product – one that is not as well tested and supported – decreases and increasing numbers of people become interested in, and purchase, the product. Towards the second half of the growth stage, later buyers will start to adopt the product as they receive positive word-of-mouth recommendations from people they trust. Whilst profits start to increase during this period, they do not match the growth in sales. This is because the awareness of the new product and growth in product sales make the market for the product more attractive to potential new entrants and competitors.

During this period of high sales growth, many competitors may choose to enter the market, reducing the company's relative market share and, in the process, its profitability. As the sales volume increases, the manufacturing and promotional spend per unit decreases, which also helps to increase profitability. Nonetheless, if the firm wants this growth phase to continue rapidly without petering out, it must invest in adding new product features or improving the quality of the product. This may not only attract existing customers to upgrade their current product purchase but it may also attract different customer demographics that would ordinarily not have been drawn to the product's features and functionality. Alternatively, improvements in customer support or the creation of easy-to-use functionality can help the firm acquire more risk-averse consumers who require greater product support. Over time, the company may choose to reduce prices considerably in an attempt to attract more customers, or bundle the product with other offerings that may be approaching the end of their growth stage.

During the growth stage, the goal is to gain consumer preference and increase sales. The marketing mix may be modified as follows:

- **Product:** New product features and packaging options; improvement of product quality.
- **Price:** Maintained at a high level if demand is high, or reduced to capture additional customers.
- **Place:** Place (Distribution) becomes more intensive. Trade discounts are minimal if resellers show a strong interest in the product.
- **Promotion:** Increased advertising to build brand preference.

Marketing Strategy during Growth stage: At the product level, the line expands by making available products with differing features, and at different prices. The main focus now is on creating meaningful and persuasive differentiation relative to other competing brands in the category. The prices tend to decline, more so during competitive turbulence period because of price competition. Generally price differences among different brands narrow down. Promotion expenditure cover advertising, sales promotion, personal selling etc. apart from this companies try to develop their distribution channel also.

4. Maturity Stage: The maturity stage in the PLC is a key point for a firm because it marks the turning point in the product's success. Typically, the growth in sales decreases quite significantly and manufacturer's over-capacity (that is, larger than required inventories) results in a reaction by the firm and its competitors to slash prices. Whilst this prolongs the maturity stage and the total number of sales for some time, the drop in prices has an adverse effect on the product's profitability, and profit level, whilst still positive, starts a downward slide. Many firms, especially single-product firms, will look to every possible marketing management technique known to revitalize product sales, whether this involves starting new users or market segments, or making significant modifications to the product, perhaps improving its quality, reliability or some aesthetic feature.

Ultimately, the maturity stage becomes the key turning point for companies because at some point during this period, sales will start to decrease and potentially never experience positive growth again. In most cases this eventually leads to the decline stage during which time the product's sales drop significantly and in some cases, rapidly, with profits continuing to fall until profitability becomes so low that the product is discontinued or company leaves sales to continue but accepts that the product has passed its core selling years. During this stage, a few laggards adopt the product but these are rarely a profitable customer group. Such a decline may be the result of technological developments, changes in consumer purchasing behaviour or significant increases in competition. In the case of the latter, international products may suffer from the loss of a patent license or import protections that have otherwise kept a product's sales high long after its offering became relatively uncompetitive.

As such, barriers to entry decrease; products may be substituted by cheap imports that benefit from lower costs of production and an established distribution network. During this period, firms in more advanced nations tend to refocus their efforts on creating new, high-value, technology-backed products that can again achieve a high price and start another PLC for the company.

During the maturity stage, the primary goal is to maintain market share and extend the product life cycle. Marketing mix decisions may include:

- **Product:** Modifications are made and features are added in order to differentiate the product from competing products that may have been introduced.
- **Price:** Possible price reductions in response to competition while avoiding a price war.
- **Place:** New distribution channels and incentives to resellers in order to avoid losing shelf space.
- **Promotion:** Emphasis on differentiation and building of brand loyalty. Incentives to get competitors' customers to switch.

Marketing strategy during Maturity Stage:

In this stage if the decline is slow and exist barriers are low, prices tend to remain stable because there are still some enduring profitable segments, customers are fragmented and weak in bargaining power, and there are only few single product competitors. In case the exist barriers are high and decline is fast and erratic, price-cuts are stiff.

The marketing mix may be modified as follows:

- **Product:** The number of products in the product line may be reduced. Rejuvenate surviving products to make them look new again.
- **Price:** Prices may be lowered to liquidate inventory of discontinued products. Prices may be maintained for continued products serving a niche market.
- **Place:** Distribution becomes more selective. Channels that no longer are profitable are phased out.
- **Promotion:** Expenditures are lower and aimed at reinforcing the brand image for continued products.

5. Decline Stage: At this point there is a downturn in the market. For example more innovative products are introduced or consumer tastes have changed. There is intense price-cutting and many more products are withdrawn from the market. Profits can be improved by reducing marketing spend and cost cutting

Marketing Strategies during decline stage:

During the decline phase, the firm generally has three options:

- Maintain the product in hopes that competitors will exit. Reduce costs and find new uses for the product.
- Harvest it, reducing marketing support and coasting along until no more profit can be made.
- Discontinue the product when no more profit can be made or there is a successor product.

Product Life Cycle Analysis

The term "life cycle" implies a well-defined life cycle as observed in living organisms, but products do not have such a predictable life and the specific life cycle curves followed by different products vary substantially. Consequently, the life cycle concept is not well-suited for the forecasting of product sales. Furthermore, critics have argued that the product life cycle may become self-fulfilling. For example, if sales peak and then decline, managers may conclude that the product is in the decline phase and therefore cut the advertising budget, thus precipitating a further decline.

"Not all products follow the classic introduction, growth, maturity and decline cycles. Some products are able to find ways to re-invest themselves at the end of their growth stage or before they witness the negative side of the maturity stage. In doing so, they achieve what Kotler and Keller (2006) call a scalloped pattern. As a classic example, they point to nylon sales which have found numerous need users, such as car tyre is, carpeting, hosiery, parachutes and shirts, amongst others. For example, companies such as Levi's have managed to re-invent their jeans brand through the use of different fabrics and cuts that have given their product a new, youthful look. In addition to those variations to the common PLC, the concept can also be used to describe (1) fads, (2) fashion, and (3) style.

Fads are fashions that are introduced and adopted very quickly, but just as quickly they fall. They typically have a limited following, but are nonetheless adopted with real zeal, such as the hula-hoop. Fashions grow more slowly but still quite quickly before eventually witnessing a decline. However, in some cases these become a style; that is, they come back into fashion. For example, Beanies and Yo-Yos were in fashion during the 1950s and 1960s respectively before largely dropping off the radar until the 1990s when both products witnessed a revival.

PLC analysis can be used both proactively and retrospectively. Proactively, companies need to assess how they think that their product will perform through its PLC and the marketing strategies and marketing mix that should accompany each stage. After all, a company should aim to prolong the growth stage of its product and look at ways of revitalizing the product during its maturity stage. However, firms should assess how they are going to do this well before they reach each stage. The proactive approach is particularly useful for market pioneers, such as Amazon.com, Coca-Cola and Hallmark because they are often not only introducing a new product, but also creating a whole new market. Alternatively, the PLC can be used as a retrospective tool to assess when a firm should enter an existing market with a new product. This is important because firms need to examine what marketing strategies and marketing mix will enable them to differentiate their product offering from those of existing firms. If implemented effectively, imitators and later entrants can make significant inroads into a market and, in some cases, overtake incumbents. Classic examples include Compaq, Dell and Gateway.

Implications of Product Life Cycle

Product life cycle concept shows a framework to spot the occurrence of opportunities and threats in a product market and the industry. This concept can help firms to reassess their objectives, strategies and different elements of marketing programme.

When a firm is launching a new product it requires investment of considerable resources, and most companies have no contend with substantial short-term losses. During the growth stage, sales rise rapidly and competition increases and large investment are required. The company that captures largest share of the market should have lowest per unit cost because of economies of scale and experience. If the market leader reduces the price, it discourages aspiring new entrants and low share firms. Thus, a PLC can be very helpful for a firm while launching or rather taking any decision in any phase of the product life cycle.

On the other hand, the major weakness of product life cycle concept is that it is prescriptive in nature and focuses on strategies based on assumption about different life cycle stages. Apart form this, it is difficult to tell what stage the product is in. A product may seem to have reached the maturity stage but it might be a temporary phase before it takes another upsurge.

MULTIPLE CHOICE QUESTIONS

1. Bata Shoe is an example of:
(*a*) Product Mix
(*b*) Product Line
(*c*) Product Planning
(*d*) Product Development
(*e*) None of these

2. Which is not the Product Line Policy?
(*a*) Contraction of Product Mix
(*b*) Alteration of Existing Products
(*c*) Development of New Uses for Existing Products
(*d*) Costing
(*e*) None of these

3. Match the following:

List-I (Product Line Policies)	**List-II (Example)**
1. Expansion of Product Mix	A. Making a New Product
2. Contraction of Product Mix	B. Closed the Product
3. Alteration of Existing Product	C. Changing in Packing of the Product
4. Development of New Uses for Existing Products	D. Changes in the Utility of Product
	E. Product Advertising

Codes :

	1	2	3	4
(*a*)	A	C	B	E
(*b*)	B	E	A	C
(*c*)	A	B	C	D
(*d*)	A	D	E	C
(*e*)	E	B	C	D

4. Product mix is/are:
(*a*) Style (*b*) Packaging
(*c*) Brand name (*d*) Above all
(*e*) None of these

5. Which is product line of a bank?
(*a*) Credit Card
(*b*) Debit Card
(*c*) International Debit Card
(*d*) Above all
(*e*) None of these

6. Which of the following is the product of bank?
(*a*) Fixed Term Deposits
(*b*) Bank's Building
(*c*) Bank Staff
(*d*) Cash
(*e*) None of these

7. Example of convenience product is:
(*a*) Truck
(*b*) Bank's Furniture
(*c*) Magazine and Newspaper
(*d*) Television
(*e*) None of these

8. Which of the following is the example of staple product?
(*a*) Fruits (*b*) Television
(*c*) Computer (*d*) Truck
(*e*) None of these

9. Example of durable product is:
(*a*) Milk (*b*) Car
(*c*) Butter (*d*) Fruits
(*e*) None of these

10. Which of the following is the example of intangible services?
(*a*) Hospital (*b*) Entertainment
(*c*) Insurance (*d*) Above all
(*e*) None of these

11. Example of non-durable product is:
(*a*) Salt (*b*) Mobile
(*c*) Computer (*d*) Sugar
(*e*) None of these

12. Examples of the industrial product is:
(*a*) Raw Material
(*b*) Component Parts
(*c*) Process Materials
(*d*) Above all
(*e*) None of these

13. Which of the following is the durable product?
(*a*) Car (*b*) Washing Machine
(*c*) Furniture (*d*) Above all
(*e*) None of these

14. 'MRO' means:
(*a*) Money Rate Over
(*b*) Maintenance Repair and Operating
(*c*) More Rate Over
(*d*) All of these
(*e*) None of these

15. Full form of FDR is:
(*a*) Fixed Deposits Receipts
(*b*) Full Division Rate
(*c*) Full Document Roll
(*d*) All of these
(*e*) None of these

16. Example of Capital Product is:
(*a*) Machine (*b*) Home
(*c*) Car (*d*) Above all
(*e*) None of these

17. 'PLC' represents:
(*a*) Product Life Cycle
(*b*) Product Life Cost
(*c*) Product Long Cost
(*d*) Product Loss Cost
(*e*) None of these

18. .... is the course of a product's sales and profits over its life time.
(*a*) Product Life Cycle
(*b*) R and D
(*c*) Brand Planning
(*d*) Product Life Cost
(*e*) None of these

19. Characteristics of introduction stage of PLC is:
(*a*) Lower demand
(*b*) Low growth rate in demand
(*c*) Limited customer
(*d*) Above all
(*e*) None of these

20. Products that are marketed include:
(*a*) Physical goods and services
(*b*) Experiences and events
(*c*) Persons
(*d*) Above all
(*e*) None of these

21. Example of tangible product is:
(*a*) House (*b*) T.V.
(*c*) Car (*d*) Above all
(*e*) None of these

22. A product represents a marketer's offering as it is perceived by:
(*a*) Present customers
(*b*) Potential customers
(*c*) Company
(*d*) Above all
(*e*) None of these

23. Physical features aspect of product is:
(*a*) Brand
(*b*) Colour and size of product
(*c*) Packaging
(*d*) Above all
(*e*) None of these

24. Influencial factors of product life cycle is/are:
(*a*) Speed of technological change and development
(*b*) Competition
(*c*) Goodwill
(*d*) Above all
(*e*) None of these

25. Product control involves:
(*a*) Quality control of the product
(*b*) Price control
(*c*) Supply control
(*d*) Above all
(*e*) None of these

26. The importance of product life cycle includes:
(*a*) Help in promotional decision
(*b*) Help in product control
(*c*) Facilitates sales forecasting
(*d*) Above all
(*e*) None of these

27. Promotional decision involves:
(*a*) Publicity
(*b*) Public relations

(*c*) Advertisement and Sales promotion
(*d*) Above all
(*e*) None of these

28. In introduction stage of PLC:
(*a*) Advertisement is required
(*b*) Sales promotion is required
(*c*) R and D is required
(*d*) Both (*a*) and (*b*)
(*e*) None of these

29. Micro finance of banking services falls in:
(*a*) Introduction Stage of PLC
(*b*) Growth Stage of PLC
(*c*) Maturity Stage of PLC
(*d*) All of these
(*e*) None of these

30. Example of the product line of a Bank is:
(*a*) Car loan (*b*) Personal loan
(*c*) Home loan (*d*) Above all
(*e*) None of these

31. .... is the unbranded and undifferentiated product.
(*a*) Generic Product
(*b*) Branded Product
(*c*) Customised Product
(*d*) All of these
(*e*) None of these

ANSWERS

1	2	3	4	5	6	7	8	9	10
(*a*)	(*d*)	(*c*)	(*d*)	(*d*)	(*a*)	(*c*)	(*a*)	(*b*)	(*d*)
11	**12**	**13**	**14**	**15**	**16**	**17**	**18**	**19**	**20**
(*a*)	(*d*)	(*d*)	(*b*)	(*a*)	(*d*)	(*a*)	(*a*)	(*d*)	(*d*)
21	**22**	**23**	**24**	**25**	**26**	**27**	**28**	**29**	**30**
(*d*)	(*b*)	(*d*)	(*d*)	(*d*)	(*d*)	(*d*)	(*d*)	(*a*)	(*d*)
31									
(*a*)									

CHAPTER-7

PRICING DECISIONS

INTRODUCTION

Price is one of the four elements of marketing mix. Price is the only element in the marketing mix that produces revenue whereas the other elements spend money. Price directly affects the income and profit of the organization. If a company charges low for its products than it may, it will not earn adequate profits as contribution per product will be low. And if a company charges high for its products than it may, it will not achieve sufficient sales because overall unit sales may be low. Further, with some product categories, price works as the major determinant of buyer choice. Although, today non-price factors have become more important in buyer behavior, price still remains one of the important elements determining company market share and profitability. However, at the same time, pricing and price competition is the number-one problem facing many marketing executives.

Companies handle pricing in a variety of ways. In small companies, prices are often set by top management rather than by marketing or salespeople. In large companies, top management sets the pricing guidelines and the middle level managers set the prices. In the industries, where pricing is a key factor for success, companies establish a pricing department to set prices or assist others in determining appropriate prices.

MEANING OF PRICE

Price is the amount of money and/or other items a buyer pays to acquire products from a seller. In another words, when an exchange or transaction takes place between two parties, price refers to what must be given by one party (buyer) in order to obtain something offered by another party (seller). Different parties involved in exchange have different meanings of price:

- For final customers, price refers to what must be given to obtain benefits. In most cases, money is given in exchange for acquiring access to a good or service. But sometimes, in a barter situation, a buyer may acquire a product by exchanging their own product.
- For sellers, price reflects the revenue generated for each product sold. For companies, price also serves as a marketing tool and is a key element in marketing promotions. For example, many companies highlight their product prices in the advertising campaigns.

Price has various forms and is known by many names. Table shows the different names of price associated with different products.

Price Versus Value

Value can be defined as bundle of benefits a customer expects from a given product. It can be seen as a combination of three things; product quality, services associated with product and price. The value increases with quality and service and decreases with price. Therefore, for many customers price itself is not the key factor while making purchase decision. This is because they compare the entire marketing offering and price is one of several variables customers evaluate when they mentally assess a product's overall value.

Perceived value of a product is affected by a marketer's pricing decision. The relationship among value, price and benefits of a product can be represented as:

$$\text{Value} = \frac{\text{Perceived Benefits Received}}{\text{Perceived Price Paid}}$$

For the buyer, value of a product will change as perceived price paid and (or) perceived benefits received change.

Importance of Price

Pricing decisions have important consequences for the marketing organization and it is as important as the other marketing mix variables. They are as follows:

1. A product's price is a major determinant of the demand for it. To earn a profit, managers must choose a price that is not too high or too low. The price of a product should be equal to perceived value of product by target consumers.
2. Price is one of the most flexible elements of the marketing mix. The other elements of marketing mix; product, or distribution channel, can take months or years to change, or some forms of promotion can be time consuming to alter (e.g., television advertisement), but price can be changed very rapidly. For instance, company can agree to a field salesperson's request to lower the price of a product for a big customer during a phone conversation.
3. Pricing decisions made in a hurry without sufficient research, analysis, and strategic evaluation can lead to revenue loss. Prices set too low may mean the company is missing out on additional profits that could be earned if the target market is willing to spend more to acquire the product. Prices set too high can also impact revenue as it prevents interested customers from purchasing the product.
4. Price helps in creating image of the product. Customers' perception of a product is also influenced by price of product, such as high price downfall high quality of product.
5. Price affects the purchase decision of customers. It is important for marketers to know if customers are more likely to purchase or dismiss a product after learning about the price of a product. In such cases, pricing may become the most important of all marketing decisions.
6. Price also plays an important role in the sales promotion plan of a company. Many times price adjustments are part of sales promotions that lower price for a short term to stimulate interest in the product, e.g. cash discounts.

FACTORS AFFECTING PRICING DECISIONS

The final price for a product is influenced by many factors. They are:

(i) Business and Marketing Objectives: Marketing decisions are guided by the overall objectives of the company. Pricing decisions are influenced by many types of objectives set up for the marketing functional area. Mainly they include; profit maximization, sales maximization, increase in market share, targeted return on investment (ROI) of marketing expenditure, etc. These marketing objectives are discussed later in detail.

(ii) Marketing Strategy of Company: In an effective marketing strategy, all marketing mix variables must work together and properly integrate. Hence Price, as one element of the marketing mix, is impacted by other ingredients of marketing mix. For instance, a company producing high quality product would be expected to keep price high so that it also communicate the high quality of the product. Also, marketing strategy concerns with that how the company is going to compete in the marketplace. If the basis of the competition is price, and competitors are using it as a key weapon, it affects the firm's pricing decision also.

(iii) Demand: Demand is the quantity of product that will be sold in the market at various price levels for a specified period. Demand of a product greatly affects the pricing decision of a company. A typical demand schedule shows an inverse relationship between quantity demanded and price. The companies need to understand the 'elasticity of demand' which can be defined as effect of price changes on the demand and relates to how purchase quantity changes as prices change.

Elasticity deals with three types of demand scenarios:

- **Elastic Demand:** Demand is elastic when a certain percentage change in price results in a larger and opposite percentage change in demand.
- **Inelastic Demand:** Demand is inelastic when a certain percentage change in price results in a smaller and opposite percentage change in demand.
- **Unitary Demand:** This demand occurs when a percentage change in price results in an equal and opposite percentage change in demand.

  For marketers the important issue with elasticity of demand is to understand how it impacts company revenue. In general, the following scenarios apply to making price changes for a given type of market demand:

- **For elastic markets:** Increasing price lowers total revenue while decreasing price increases total revenue.
- **For inelastic markets:** increasing price raises total revenue while decreasing price lowers total revenue.
- **For unitary markets:** there is no change in revenue when price is changed.

(iv) Costs: Another major factor that affects pricing decisions is cost. To earn profit or for sustainable business, the price paid by customers must exceed the cost of producing a good or delivering a service. Costs can be broadly divided into following categories:

- **Fixed Costs:** Fixed costs, also known as overhead costs, are not affected by level of production or sales. For example, a manufacturer of pens, whether produces one pen or one lac pen, will be required to pay the full monthly rent for the building.
- **Variable Costs:** These costs are directly associated with the production levels of products. They are called variable because their total varies with the number of units produced. Typically variable costs are evaluated on a per-unit basis. For example, cost of raw material, parts, direct labor etc.
- **Total Cost:** Total cost in the sum of total fixed cost and total variable cost for a specific quantity of products produced.
- **Average Costs:** Average cost is the cost per unit at a particular level of production. It is equal to total costs divided by production (number of units produced).

(v) Competitive Environment: Intensity of competition, offerings of competitors, their price structure, competitors' reaction, as pay etc. affect the price of a company's product. Marketers must research competitive prices as well as pay close attention to how these companies will respond to the marketer's pricing decisions. For instance, products that dominate markets and are viewed as market leaders may not be heavily influenced by competitor pricing since they are in a commanding position to set prices as they see fit. On the other hand, in markets where a clear leader does not exist, the pricing of competitive products will be carefully considered.

(vi) Government Regulation: Marketers must be aware of regulations that impact how price is set in the markets in which their products are sold. These regulations are primarily government enacted and there may be legal ramifications if the rules are not followed. For instance, in some industries, government regulation may set price ceilings (highest price) while in other industries there may be price floors (lowest price).

(vii) Other Factors: Customer expectations is one very obvious factor that influences price setting. As it has been discussed earlier that, while making a purchase decision, customers assess the overall "value" of a product much more than they assess the price. Therefore, marketers need to conduct customer research to determine what "price points" are acceptable to customers.

Product life-cycle also affects the pricing decisions. Price of a product normally changes as product moves through different stages of life-cycle. Companies often sets a higher price during introductory stage, which gradually come down when competitors enter into the market.

SETTING THE PRICE

A firm must set a price for the first time when the firm develops or acquires a new product, when it introduces its regular product into a new distribution channel or geographical area, and when it enters bids on new contract work. The firm has to consider many factors in setting its pricing policy, which are already discussed earlier. In the current section, six-step procedure for pricing setting is discussed:

Step 1: Selecting the Pricing Objective

First, the company has to decide what it wants to accomplish with its particular product offer. If the company has selected its target market and market positioning carefully, then its marketing-mix strategy-including price will be fairly straightforward. The clearer a firm's objectives, the easier it is to set the price. A company can pursue any of the below mentioned major objectives through its pricing, which are: survival, maximum current profit, maximum current revenue, maximum sales growth, maximum market skimming, or product-quality leadership.

(i) Survival: Companies pursue survival as their major objective if they have overcapacity, face intense competition, or change in consumer wants. In such situations, survival of organization becomes more important as compared to earn profits. To keep the plant operating, companies will cut prices. As long as prices cover variable costs and some fixed costs, the companies stay in business. However, survival is only a short-run objective. No company can exist in the market in the long run by setting prices merely for survival. It has to focus on attaining profits by improving its performance and capabilities.

(ii) Maximum Profit: Many companies try to set the price that will maximize current profit. Price being a controllable factor in the profit equation, can be adjusted such that it maximises the current profit of organisation. Companies estimate the demand and costs associated with alternative prices and choose the price that produces maximum current profit. This strategy assumes that the firm has knowledge of its demand and cost functions; whereas in reality, these are difficult to estimate.

(iii) Return on Investment (ROI): The objective of pricing in an organisation can be to attain a specified return on their investments (ROI). Company should like to have certain level of ROI on marketing investments, new product development cost, or overall investment in business. Usually, data used to calculate ROI are not available at the time when prices are set. Therefore, organisations adopt a trial and error method to arrive at the best price alternatives to leverage maximum ROI.

(iv) Maximum Current Revenue: Some companies set a price that maximizes sales revenue. Revenue is the multiplication of price charged and the number of units sold (i.e. Revenue = Price × Sales Units). Revenue maximization requires estimating only the demand function. Many managers believe that revenue maximization will lead to long-run profit maximization and growth in market share.

(v) Maximum Sales Growth: Some companies want to maximize unit sales. They believe that a higher sales volume will lead to lower unit costs because of economies of scale and then company will earn high profit in the long-run. They set the lowest price, assuming the market is price sensitive. This practice is called **market-penetration pricing**. The following conditions favour setting a low price

(a) The market is highly price sensitive, and a low price stimulates market growth;

(b) Production and distribution costs fall with accumulated production experience; and

(c) A low price discourages actual and potential competition.

(vi) Maximum Market Skimming: Setting the price of a new product at the highest possible level is referred as market-skimming pricing. Ordinarily, the price is high in relation to the target market's range of expected prices. The main purpose of this strategy is to recover research and development costs as quickly as possible. Market skimming makes sense under the following conditions:

(a) A sufficient number of buyers have a high current demand,

(b) The unit costs of producing a small volume are not so high that they cancel the advantage of charging what the consumers will bear,

(c) The high initial price does not attract more competitors to the market,

(d) The high price communicates the image of a superior product.

(vii) Product Quality: A company may set prices in relation to its product quality. There are possible nine price-quality strategies a company can pursue. They are shown below:

Product Quality \ Price	High	Medium	Low
High	1. Premium Strategy	2. High Value Strategy	3. Super Value Strategy
Med.	4. Over charging Strategy	5. Medium Water Strategy	6. Good Value Strategy
Low	7. Rip-off Strategy	8. False Economy Strategy	9. Economy Strategy

The diagonal strategies 1, 5 and 9 can all coexist in the same market; that is one firm offers a high quality product at a high price, another firm offers an average quality product at an average price, and still another firm offers a low quality product at a low price. All the three competitors can coexist as long as the market consists of three groups of buyers: those who insist on quality, those who insist on price, and those who balance the two considerations. Positioning strategies 2, 3 and 6 represent the ways to attack the diagonal position. Positioning strategies 4, 7 and 8 lead to overpricing the product in relation to its quality.

(viii) Other Pricing Objectives: Companies can follow other price related objectives also. For example, nonprofit and public organisations may aim for partial cost recovery and rely on public grants and donations to cover the remaining costs. Some non-profit organisations may aim for full cost recovery in its pricing.

Step 2 : Demand Measurement

Next step in setting the price for its product is assessment of the demand for company's product. They can determine the demand through market research and using sales forecasting techniques. Companies should also understand the relationship between alternative prices that might be charged in the current time period and the resulting current demand, which can be shown through demand curves. In the normal case, demand and price are inversely related. i.e., the higher the price, the lower the demand, and vice-versa.

The first step in estimating demand is understanding the factors that affect buyers' price sensitivity as under:

(i) Price Sensitivity: Price sensitivity can be defined as impact of price changes on demand. If small change in price greatly affect the demand then the market (customer) would be considered as price sensitive. There are nine factors that affect price sensitivity:

(a) *Unique-value effect:* Buyers are less price sensitive when the product is more distinctive.

(b) *Substitute-awareness effect:* Buyers are less price sensitive when they are not aware of substitutes.

(c) *Difficult-comparison effect:* Buyers are less price sensitive when they cannot easily compare the quality of substitutes.

(d) *Total-expenditure effect:* Buyers are less price sensitive when expenditure on product is lower as compared to their total income.

(e) *End-benefit effect:* Buyers are less price sensitive when the smaller the expenditure is to the total cost of the end product.

(f) *Shared-cost effect:* Buyers are less price sensitive when part of the cost is borne by another party.

(g) *Sunk-investment effect:* Buyers are less price sensitive when the products are purchased as an extension of products that were purchased in the past.

(h) *Price-quality effect:* Buyers are less price sensitive when the product is assumed to have more quality, prestige, or exclusiveness.

(i) *Inventory effect:* Buyers are less price sensitive when they cannot store the product.

(ii) Estimating Demand Curves: The demand curve shows the market's purchase quantity at alternative prices. It sums the reactions of many individuals who have different price sensitivities. There are various methods to estimate the demand curve of a product. The first involves statistically analyzing existing data on past prices, quantities sold, and other factors to estimate their relationships. Building the appropriate model and fitting the data with the proper statistical techniques will produce the demand curves. The second approach is to conduct price experiments, i.e. charge different prices in similar territories to see how sales are affected. The third approach is to ask buyers to state how many units they would buy at different proposed prices.

In measuring the price/demand relationship, the market researcher must control for various factors such as competitors response and external environmental factors.

Step 3: Estimating Costs

For many companies, the starting point for setting a product's price is to first determine how much it will cost to get the product to their customers. Demand of a product sets a ceiling (maximum price) on the price that the company can charge and company costs set the floor (minimum price). The company wants to charge a price that covers its cost of producing, distributing, and selling the product, including a fair return for its effort and risk. Companies need to estimate fixed costs, variable cost, total cost and average cost for its products before setting up the price. We have already discussed the meaning of these types of costs in earlier section. Calculation of these costs and total cost of a product is must because it will clear the picture that what should be the minimum price that will at least cover the total production costs at a given level of production.

Step 4 : Analysing Competitors' Costs, Prices and Offers

After identifying the range of possible prices determined by market demand and costs; company should identify and analyse the competitors' costs, prices and their possible price reactions. The company needs to benchmark its costs against its competitors costs to learn whether it is operating at a cost advantage or disadvantage. The company also needs to learn the price and quality of competitors' offers. The firm can send out comparison shoppers to assess competitors offers, acquire competitors' price lists, buy competitors' equipment and take it apart, and ask buyers how they perceive the price and quality of each competitors' offer.

Once the company is aware of competitors' prices and offers, it can use them as an orienting point for its own pricing. If the firm's offer is similar to a major competitors' offer, then the firm will have to price close to the competitor otherwise it may lose sales. If the firm's offer is inferior, the firm will not be able to charge more than the competitor. If the firm's offer is superior, the firm can charge more than the competitor. The firm must be aware, however, that the competitors might change their prices in response to the firm's price.

Apart from these issues, the pricing policies of a company might attract a new competitior into the market or may force the existing competitors to leave the industry. Therefore, marketers should be careful about potential and future competition. Further, company's pricing policies also influence the competitors pricing policy. Competitors may react to firm's prices in various ways which we have discussed in another section.

Step 5 : Selecting a Pricing Method

When the company has idea for demand of its product, the cost function of its product and competitors price; it is now ready to select a price. There are various methods exist for selecting and finalizing the price of company's product, they are: markup pricing, target pricing, perceived-value pricing, value pricing, going-rate pricing, sealed-bid pricing and add pricing.

(i) **Markup Pricing:** This is the most elementary pricing method used by companies. In this type of pricing, a marketer adds a mark-up on its cost of the product, sometimes also referred as mark-on. Markups are expressed as a percentage of either the cost or selling price. This type of pricing method is usually used by retailers and wholesalers, who add markup percentages to the cost of acquiring product. Lets say we want to determine the selling price of a calculators, following example will clarify the markup method:

Variable cost per calculator	₹ 100
Fixed cost	₹ 30,00,000
Expected unit sales	₹ 50,000

The unit cost of calculator for manufactures can be calculated by

$$\text{Unit cost} = \text{Variable cost} + \frac{\text{Fixed cost}}{\text{Unit sales}}$$

$$= 100 + \frac{30,00,000}{50,000} = ₹\ 160$$

Now assume the manufacturer wants to earn a 20% markup on sales. The manufacturer's markup price is given by

$$\text{Markup price} = \frac{\text{Unit cost}}{\text{(1-markup percentage)}}$$

$$= \frac{160}{1-0.2} = ₹\ 200$$

Hence, the cost of a calculator is ₹ 160/unit to manufacturer and it will be priced at ₹ 200/Unit to earn 20% markup on cost. Here the manufacturer would make a profit of ₹ 40 per unit.

Markups vary considerably across different goods. Markups are generally higher on seasonal items (to cover the risk of not selling), speciality items, slower moving items, items with high storage and handling costs, and demand-inelastic items. In addition, companies sometimes use higher markup when hidden or highly variable costs are involved.

(ii) Target Return Pricing: Another cost based pricing approach is target-return pricing. Here, firm wants to have certain level of return on its total investment in business, known on return as investment (ROI). The firm determines the price that would yield its target rate of return. The target-return price is given by the following formula:

$$\text{Target return price} = \text{Unit cost} + \frac{\text{desired return} \times \text{invested capital}}{\text{Unit sales}}$$

For our earlier example of calculator, if manufacturer has invested ₹ 2 crore in plants and machinery and wants to earn 20% ROI on invested capital than

$$\text{Price} = 160 + \frac{0.20 \times 200,00,000}{50,000}$$

$$= 160 + 80 = ₹\ 240$$

Therefore, manufacturer should charge ₹ 240 per unit of calculator to earn 20% return on invested capital of ₹ 2 crore. This return will be realised under the condition that costs and estimated sales turn out to be accurate.

(iii) Perceived Value Pricing: In this method, prices are decided on the basis of customer's perceived value of the product. Companies see the buyers' perceptions of value, not the seller's cost, as the key to pricing and use the non-price variable such as, advertising in the marketing mix to build up perceived value in the buyers' minds.

Perceived-value pricing fits well with product-positioning philosophy. A company develops a product concept for a particular target market with a planned quality and price. Then management estimates the volume it hopes to sell at this price. The estimate indicates the needed plant capacity, investments and unit costs. Management then works out whether product will reach a satisfactory profit at the planned price and cost. If the answer is yes, the company goes ahead with product development. Otherwise, the company drops the idea.

The key to perceived-value pricing is to accurately determine the market's perception of the product's value. Sellers with an inflated view of their product's value will overprice their product. Sellers with an underestimated view will charge less than they could. Companies should use market research to establish the market's perception of value as a guide to effective pricing.

(iv) Value Pricing: In value pricing, companies charge a fairly low price for a high-quality offering. Value pricing says that the price should represent a high-value offer to consumers. Value pricing involves re-engineering the company's operations to truly become the low-cost producer without sacrificing quality, and consequently lowering the prices significantly to attract a large number of value conscious customers.

An important type of value pricing is everyday low pricing (EDLP), which is used by large retail stores. A retailer who holds to an EDLP policy charges a constant, everyday low price with no temporary price discounts. Retailers adopt EDLP for a number of reasons, the most important of which is that constant sales and promotions are costly. Also, consumers have low confidence in the credibility of sales promotional schemes. Consumers also have less time and patience for waiting the supermarket special deals and discounts.

(v) Going Rate Pricing: In going rate pricing, the firm pays less attention to its own costs or demand and bases its price largely on competitors price. The firm might charge the same, more, or less than its major competitor(s). In industries that sell a commodity such as steel, paper, or fertilizer, firms normally charge the same price. The smaller firms also follow the leader and change their prices when the market leader's prices change. Going rate pricing is quite popular. Where costs are difficult to measure or competitive response is uncertain, firms feel that the going price represents a good solution.

(vi) Sealed Bid Pricing: In some markets, especially industrial markets and government purchases business is carried out on the basis of sealed bids rather than on the basis of openly setting prices for products. This type of pricing is more suitable for industrial products. Many companies complete in this process, where the price of the product of service is usually quoted in a sealed cover. In this method, the firms submit bids in sealed covers for the price of the job or the service. This is based on firm's expectation about the level at which the competitor is likely to set up prices rather than on the cost structure of the firm. The firm wants to win the contract, and winning normally requires submitting a lower price than competitors. The sealed bid method is usually followed in government organizations. Whenever a government organisation needs to purchase a product or service, it is required to call for bids and several companies are invited to quote their prices in a sealed form. After receiving the sealed bids, the organisation will normally purchase the product or service from the company, which has bid the least price.

Step 6 : Selecting the Final Price

After deciding the method of pricing, company must select its final price. In selecting the final price, the company must consider additional factors, including psychological pricing, the influence of other marketingmix elements on price, company pricing policies and the impact of price on other parties.

(i) Psychological Pricing: Sellers should consider the psychology of prices in addition to their economics. Many consumers use price as an indicator of quality. When alternative information about true quality is available, price becomes a less significant indicator of quality. When this information is not available, price acts as a quality signal. For example, in a study of the relationship between price and quality perceptions of cars, it has been found that higher-priced cars were perceived as high quality cars. Also, higher quality cars were perceived to be higher priced. Another issue under psychological pricing is that when looking at a particular product, buyers carry in their minds a reference price that might have been formed by noticing current prices, past prices, or the buying context. Sellers should consider these reference prices in pricing their product.

(ii) The Influence of other Marketing: Mix Elements : The relationship between price and other marketing mix variables has been discussed earlier. The final price must take into account the rest of marketing mix variables such as; advertising, sales promotion, product quality, distribution strategy etc.

(iii) Company Pricing Policies: The final price must be consistent with company pricing policies. Many companies set up a pricing department to develop pricing policies and establish or approve pricing decisions. Their aim is to ensure that the salespeople quote prices that are reasonable to customers and profitable to the company.

(iv) Impact of Price on Other Parties: Companies must also consider the reactions of other parties to the intended price. For example, management should try to seek answers of following questions, while selecting final price : How will the distributors and dealers feel about it? Will the company sales force be willing to sell at that price or complain that the price is too high? How will competitors react to this price? Will the government intervene and prevent this price from being charged?

PRICING STRATEGIES

In price related decisions of a company's marketing mix, after deciding the pricing objectives and identifying the base price for its product; the next major task is to design pricing strategies that are compatible with the rest of the marketing mix. Companies face many strategic issues related to price, such as:

1. Is company going to compete primarily on the basis of price? (Price versus non-price competition).
2. How to price company's product according to different customers in different geographic locations/countries? (Geographical Pricing Strategies)
3. What kind of discount schedule should be adopted? (Price discounts and allowances).
4. What adjustments need to be made in final price of a product because of sales promotion? (Promotional pricing).
5. What should be pricing policy for product lines and product mix? (Product mix strategies).

These issues are discussed below:

(i) Price versus Non-price Competition: In developing a marketing program, companies need to decide whether to compete primarily on the basis of price or the non-price elements of marketing mix. A company will engage in price competition when it markets its product on lowest possible prices. In this strategy, product accompanied few services or no services. With price competition, there is little customers loyalty and consumers buy a brand which has lowest price.

In non-price competition, companies maintain stable prices and emphasize more on other aspects of marketing program. Although while deciding price of the product, competitors prices are taken into consideration. In this strategy, companies attempt to compete by the means of product differentiation, promotional activities, product quality, variety, more features or on some other element of marketing mix.

(ii) Geographical Pricing Strategies: Under geographical pricing, managers need to make decision about price of its products according to different customers in different locations and countries. The main issue is whether the company should charge higher prices to distant customers to cover the higher shipping costs or should it charge a similar prices to all geographic locations.

Companies can establish different pricing policies whereby buyer pays the entire freight expense, the seller bears the whole burden, or the seller and buyer share this expense. The chosen strategy can influence the geographic limits of a firm's market, location of its production facilities, sources of its raw material, and its competitive strength in various geographic markets. Following are different pricing mechanism a company can follow under geographical pricing strategy:

- **Point of production pricing:** In this strategy, company quotes the selling price at the factory gate (point of production) and the buyer selects the mode of transportation and pays all freight costs.
- **Uniform delivered pricing:** Under this, the same price is quoted to all buyers regardless of their geographical location.
- **Zone-delivered pricing:** Here, company divides a market into a limited number of broad geographical zones and then sets a uniform delivery price for each zone.
- **Freight-Absorption pricing:** Company quotes a price equal to its factory price plus the shipping costs that would be charged by a competitive seller located near the customers.

(iii) Price Discounts and Allowance: Companies provide discounts and allowances on their basic price to reward customers for such acts as early payment, volume purchases, and off-season buying. The discounts and allowances may be in the various forms, which are:

- **Cash Discount:** A cash discount is a price reduction to buyers who pay their bills within a specified time. The cash discount is computed on the net amount due. Every cash discount includes three elements which are:

  (a) The percentage (%) discount;

  (b) The period during which discount is applicable; and

(c) The time when the bill becomes overdue.

- **Quantity Discount:** A quantity discount is a price reduction to buyers who buy in large volumes. Quantity discounts can be offered on a noncumulative basis (on each order placed) or on a cumulative basis (on the number of units ordered over a given period). The objective of quantity discount is to encourage customers to buy in larger amounts or provide an incentive to the customers to purchase from one seller rather than buy from multiple sellers.
- **Functional Discounts:** Functional discounts (also called trade discounts) are offered by the manufacturer to trade-channel members (wholeseller, retailer etc.) if they perform certain functions, such as; selling, storing and record-keeping. Manufacturers may offer different functional discounts to different trade channels because of their varying functions.
- **Seasonal Discounts:** A seasonal discount is a price reduction to buyers who buy products during off season. Seasonal discounts allow the seller to maintain uniform production during the year. For example, hotels, motels and airlines offer seasonal discounts in their slow moving season or off season.
- **Allowances:** Allowances are other types of reduction from the list price of a product. Trade-in allowances are price reduction granted for exchanging an old item when buying a new one. For instance, Maruti Automobiles offers exchange bonus to its customers for exchanging old Maruti cars with newer one. Promotional allowances are payments or price reductions to reward dealers for performing promotional services, such as advertising and sales support programs.

Besides this, companies can adjust pricing by offering low-interest finance, longer payment terms and additional warranties and service contracts.

(iv) Promotional Pricing Strategies: The main objective of promotional pricing is to stimulate product demand. The options for promotional pricing include: Markdowns, Loss Leaders, and Sales Promotions.

- **Markdowns:** The most common method for stimulating customer interest using price is the promotional markdown method, which offers the product at a price that is lower than the product's normal selling price.
- **Loss Leader:** This kind of pricing strategy is adopted by large retailers. Here supermarkets and department stores sell the well-known brands at equal or below the cost of acquisition. The idea is that offering such a low price will entice a high level of customer traffic to visit a retailer's store.
- **Sales Promotion:** Under this, marketers may offer several types of pricing promotions to simulate demand. These include rebates, coupons, trade-in, and loyalty programs, etc.

(v) Discriminatory Pricing: Discriminatory pricing (also called price discrimination) occurs when a company sells a product or service at two or more prices that do not reflect a proportional difference in costs. Discriminatory pricing takes several forms:

- **Customer-segment pricing:** Different customer groups are charged different prices for the same product or service.
- **Product-form pricing:** Different versions of the product are priced differently but not proportionately to their respective costs.
- **Image Pricing:** Some companies price the same product at two different levels based on image differences.
- **Location pricing:** The same product is priced differently at different locations

even though the cost of offering at each location is the same.

- **Time Pricing:** Prices are varied by season, day, or hour. For example, cinema halls vary their ticket rates to by time of day and weekend versus weekday.

(vi) Product Mix Pricing: In this case, the firm searches for a set of prices that maximizes the profits on the total product mix. Pricing is difficult because the various products have demand and cost interrelationship and are subject to different degrees of competition. There are six situations involving product-mix pricing : product-line pricing, optional-feature pricing, capture-product pricing, two-part pricing, by product pricing, and product-bundling pricing.

- **Product line pricing:** When marketers offer more than one product item in a product line, they usually set prices for product lines instead of individual products. In such a pricing, the sales of one product in the product line may affect others. Marketers usually try to offer products that will increase the sales of other products as well. But, in an efforts to provide variety to the customers, they offer directly competitive products. Marketers can adopt different price points within a product line so that customers perceive the quality of these products on the basis of these price points.
- **Optional feature pricing:** Many companies offer optional products or features along with their main products. For example, during the purchase of a car, accessories such as seat covers, floor mats, metal guards, air-conditioner, music system, etc., do not form a part of standard features and are priced separately. Pricing these options is a sticky problems, because automobile companies must decide which items to include in the sticker price and which to offer as options.
- **Captive-Product Pricing:** Some products require the use of ancillary or captive products. Examples of captive products are razor blades (razors are useless with them) and camera film (cameras are useless without film). When manufacturers price the ancillary products or spare parts relatively higher than the basic product to overcome the low profits earned on the basic product, it is termed as captive product pricing. For example, Gillette follows this strategy for its Mach III blades. The original razor comes at an attractive price, but the blades that have to be used along with the razor are priced higher.
- **Two-part pricing:** Service firms often engage in two-part pricing. That is they charge a fixed fee plus a variable usage fee. Thus, telephone users pay a minimum monthly fee plus charges for calls beyond a certain limit. The services firm faces a problem similar to captive-product pricing- namely, how much to charge for the basic service and how much for the variable usage. The fixed fee should be low enough to induce purchase of the service; the profit can then be made on the usage fees.
- **By Product Pricing:** The production of certain goods often results in by products. For example, refining of crude petroleum oil produces petrol as well by products also, such as; diesel, kerosene, wax etc. If the by products have value to a customer group, then they should be priced on their value. Income earned on the by-products make it easier for the company to charge a lower price on its main product.
- **Product-bundling pricing:** Product bundling pricing is a procedure where the manufacturer provides a set of related products at a price. In this pricing strategy, marketers anticipate customer needs and accordingly bundle either accessories or other related products with the main product. For example, most PC manufacturers bundle free software (antivirus, office suites, etc.) with PCs.

PRICE CHANGES AND ADJUSTMENTS

Pricing is not a one-time decision, rather it is a continuous one. A company faces many situations under which it is required to change and adjust the price of its product. In some situations, companies initiate price cuts or price increase and in another situation they need to react towards price changes by competitors. While initating or reacting towards price changes, companies should also gauge the competitotrs' and customers' responses to price change.

Company's Initiation to Price Changes

Company may initate to reduce the price of its products as raise the price under several circumstances. They are discussed below:

(i) Price Cuts: Companies may initiate price cuts under following situations:

- Company has excess plant capacity and want to generate additional business through price cuts.
- When company's market share is declining and decide to protect its market by cutting the prices.
- When company want to dominant in market through increasing its market share, than it initiates price cuts in the hope of gaining market share, which would lead to falling costs through larger volume and more experience.
- Companies also cut their prices in a period of economic recession.

(ii) Price Increases: While increasing the price of a product, a company need to decide whether to raise the price sharply on a one-time basis or to raise it by small amounts several times. Generally, consumers prefer small price increases on a regular basis to sharp price increases. Companies may initiate price increase under following conditions:

- A successful price increase can increase profits considerably. For example, if the company's profit margin is 3% of sales, a 1% price increase will increase profits by 33% if sales volume remains the same.
- Another major circumstance provoking price increases is rising costs of raw material, parts or other resources used for production.
- Another factor leading to price increase is over demand. When a company cannot supply all of its customers, it can raise its prices, ration the supplies to customers or can do both the things.

Responding to Competitors Price Change

Many times competitors may initiate price changes and then company is required to respond to this price change. The company's response is affected by many factors, such as; market characteristics, product characteristics, etc. For example, in the markets characterized by high product homogeneity, the firm has little choice but to meet a competitor's price cut. In non-homogeneous-product markets, a firm has more choice in reacting to a competitors price change when buyers choose the product on other considerations; such as; service, quality, reliability etc. then these factors desensitize buyers to minor price difference. Another factor which affects the company's response is its leading position in the market. Market leaders frequently face aggressive price cutting by smaller firms trying to build market share. When the attacking firm's product is comparable to the leaders, its lower price will cut into the leader's share. The leader at this point has several options and the best response varies with situation. The company under attack has to consider the product's stage in the life cycle, its importance in the company's product portfolio, the competiters intentions and resources, the market's price and quality sensitivity, the behaviour of costs with volume, and the company's alternative opportunities following are possible responses:

(i) Maintain price: The leader might maintain its price and profit margin, believing that

- it would lose too much profit if it reduced its price
- it would not lose much market share, and

- it could regain market share when necessary. The leader believes that it could hold on to good customers, giving up the poorer ones to the competitor.

(ii) Raise perceived quality: The leader could maintain price but strengthen the value of its offer. It could improve its product, service and communications. It could stress the relative quality of its product over that of the low-price competitor.

(iii) Reduce price: The leader might drop its price to the competitor's price. It might do so because

(a) its costs fall with volume.

(b) it would lose market share because the market is price sensitive, and

(c) it would be hard to rebuild market share once it is lost.

(iv) Increase price and improve quality: The leader might raise its price and introduce new brands to counter the attacking brand.

(v) Launch low-price fighter line: One of the best responses is to add lower-price items to the product line or to create a separate lower-price brand. This is necessary if the particular market segment is price sensitive and do not respond to arguments of higher quality. This is what some major brands are doing to fight back against lower price store brands.

Reactions to Price Changes

Any price change affects customers, competitors, distributors, and suppliers and may provoke government reaction as well.

(i) Customers' Reactions: When companies change price of their products, customers would like to know the motivation behind price changes. Companies should understand that customers are very price sensitive to products that cost a lot and/or are bought frequently. Whereas they hardly notice higher prices on low-cost items that they buy infrequently. Whatever may be the reasons, for price changes marketers need to make sure that they convince the customers about the necessity of making price changes in the products and services they offer, otherwise they will face losing customer loyalty forever.

(ii) Competitors' Reactions: Companies should assess the competitors' reactions before going for any price change. Competitors are most likely to react when the number of firms in the industry is small, the product is homogeneous, and the buyers are highly informed. The firm can estimate its competitor's reaction from two points. One is to assume that the competitor reacts in a set way to price changes. The other is to assume that the competitor treats each price change as a fresh challenge and reacts according to self-interest at the time. In this case, the company will have to figure out what lies in the competitors self-interest.

When there are several competitors, the company must estimate each close competitor's likely reaction. If all competitors behave alike, that analysis of a typical competitors would be sufficient enough. It the competitors do not react uniformly because of differences in size, market shares, or policies, then separate analyses are necessary.

MULTIPLE CHOICE QUESTIONS

1. Which of the following is the internal factors of pricing?

(*a*) Elasticity of demand
(*b*) Use pattern
(*c*) Characteristics of the product
(*d*) Above all
(*e*) None of these

2. Which of the following is the external factor of pricing?

(*a*) Condition of economy
(*b*) Nature of competitions
(*c*) Purchasing power of the consumers
(*d*) Government policy
(*e*) Above all

3. Which of the following is the cost-based pricing method?
(*a*) Mark up pricing
(*b*) Cost plus pricing
(*c*) Target rate of return pricing
(*d*) Marginal cost pricing
(*e*) Above all

4. Which of the following is the Demand-based pricing method?
(*a*) Skimming pricing
(*b*) Penetration pricing
(*c*) Value pricing
(*d*) Both (*a*) and (*b*)
(*e*) None of these

5. Which of the following is the competition-oriented pricing method?
(*a*) Premium pricing
(*b*) Discount pricing
(*c*) Parity pricing
(*d*) Above all
(*e*) None of these

6. Which of the following is the sales oriented objectives of pricing?
(*a*) Maximising market share
(*b*) Maximising number of customers
(*c*) Maximising sales volume
(*d*) Above all
(*e*) None of these

7. Which of the following is the example of Variable Cost (VC) of the product?
(*a*) Rent
(*b*) Insurance Premium
(*c*) Interest
(*d*) Loan
(*e*) None of these

8. Cost of raw materials is the example of:
(*a*) Fixed cost (*b*) Variable cost
(*c*) Marginal cost (*d*) None of these
(*e*) None of these

9. Which of the following is the influencing factor of price determination?
(*a*) Marketing mix
(*b*) Cost of the product
(*c*) Organisational factors
(*d*) Above all
(*e*) None of these

10. Skimming is the:
(*a*) Pricing method
(*b*) Sales promotion method
(*c*) Wage method
(*d*) Cost method
(*e*) None of these

11. .... means high price in the early stage of marketing the product.
(*a*) Penetration pricing
(*b*) Skimming pricing
(*c*) Psychological pricing
(*d*) Discount pricing
(*e*) None of these

12. .... seeks to achieve greater market penetration through relatively too prices.
(*a*) Skimming pricing
(*b*) Psychological pricing
(*c*) Penetration pricing
(*d*) Above all
(*e*) None of these

13. Objective of pricing includes—
(*a*) Profit oriented objective
(*b*) Sales oriented objective
(*c*) Customer oriented objective
(*d*) Both (*a*) and (*b*)
(*e*) None of these

14. Which of the following is the variable cost?
(*a*) Cost of raw material
(*b*) Cost of labour charge
(*c*) Cost of energy
(*d*) Above all
(*e*) None of these

15. Which of the following is the type of price policy?
(*a*) Single price policy
(*b*) One price policy
(*c*) Price lining policy
(*d*) Above all
(*e*) None of these

16. Policy of leader pricing policy is adopted by:
(*a*) Retailer (*b*) Wholesaler
(*c*) Producer (*d*) All of these
(*e*) None of these

17. Which of the following is the psychological pricing policy?
(*a*) Reference pricing policy
(*b*) Higher prices with better policy
(*c*) Odd price policy
(*d*) Above all
(*e*) None of these

18. Which of the following is the determinant of Pricing Decision?
(*a*) Demand of the product
(*b*) Government control
(*c*) Customer's behaviour
(*d*) Above all
(*e*) None of these

19. At Break-Even-Point:
(*a*) No profit no loss
(*b*) Maximisation profit
(*c*) Maximum sales
(*d*) Minimum loss
(*e*) None of these

20. MOS means:
(*a*) Marginal Operation System
(*b*) Margin of Safety
(*c*) Margin on sale
(*d*) All of these
(*e*) None of these

21. The act of selling the same article product under a single control, at different prices to different buyers is known as:
(*a*) Wage discrimination
(*b*) Price discrimination
(*c*) Product simplification
(*d*) All of these
(*e*) None of these

22. What is the Price?
(*a*) It is monetary value
(*b*) It is a product
(*c*) It is a loss
(*d*) All of these
(*e*) None of these

23. Ethical values includes:
(*a*) Pollution
(*b*) Block money
(*c*) Be honest and be social
(*d*) Black money
(*e*) None of these

ANSWERS

1	2	3	4	5	6	7	8	9	10
(*d*)	(*e*)	(*e*)	(*d*)	(*d*)	(*d*)	(*d*)	(*b*)	(*d*)	(*a*)
11	**12**	**13**	**14**	**15**	**16**	**17**	**18**	**19**	**20**
(*b*)	(*c*)	(*d*)	(*d*)	(*d*)	(*a*)	(*d*)	(*d*)	(*a*)	(*b*)
21	**22**	**23**							
(*b*)	(*a*)	(*c*)							

CHAPTER-8

MARKETING COMMUNICATION

INTRODUCTION

In the past, a number of terms have been used in the field of marketing communications the most common of which appear to be 'advertising' and 'promotion'. The origin of these two words help us to define what marketing communications entails, namely the pushing forward of products or services and the turning of the consumer towards the product or service. Once these two elements are met, there is a chance of a sale. Marketing communications includes a number of elements that make up the marketing communication mix: advertising, personal selling, sales promotion, publicity, direct marketing and cyber marketing.

Marketing communication is an integral part of a marketing strategy and often forms a very significant linkage between the firm and the market. Thus, it is a continuing dialogue between buyers and sellers in a market place. Marketing communication can be defined as:

"Marketing communication is the process of presenting an integrated set of stimuli to a target with the intent of evoking a desired set of responses within the target market and setting a channel to receive, interpret and act upon messages and identifying new communication opportunities." Thus, we can say that marketing communication is focused on the creation and execution of message and other related media used to communicate with a market.

The basic objective of marketing communication is to generate demand in the market, product positioning by the optimal combination of communication elements in order to minimize effect in the target market.

Marketing communications are the messages and related media used to communicate with a market. Those who practise advertising, branding, direct marketing, graphic design, marketing, packaging, promotion, publicity, sponsorship, public relations, sales, sales promotion and online marketing are termed marketing communicators, marketing communication managers.

Marketing communications is focused on product/produce/service as opposed to corporate communications where the focus of communications work is the company/enterprise itself. Marketing communication is primarily concerned with demand generation, product/produce/service positioning while corporate communications deal with issue management, mergers and acquisitions, litigation etc.

Marketing Communications is a term used to describe a holistic approach to communication. It aims to ensure consistency of message and the complementary use of media. The concept includes online and offline marketing channels. Online marketing channels include any e-marketing campaigns or programs, from search engine optimization (SEO), pay-per-click, affiliate, email, banner to latest web related channels for webinar, blog, micro-blogging, RSS, podcast, internet radio and internet television. Offline marketing channels are traditional print (newspaper, magazine), mail order, public relations, industry relations, billboard, radio, and television. A company develops its integrated marketing communication programme

1795 (Mkt.)–11-II

using all the elements of the marketing mix (product, price, place, and promotion).

Thus, we can say that the marketing communication is integration of all marketing tools, approaches, and resources within a company which maximizes impact on consumer mind and which results into maximum profit at minimum cost.

MEANING AND DEFINITION OF COMMUNICATION

Communication is something so simple and difficult that we can never put it in simple words, says T. S. Matthews. Peter Little defines communication as follows:

Communication is the process by which information is transmitted between individuals and/or organisations so that an understanding response results. Another very simple definition of 'communication' has been provided by W. H. Newman and C. F. Summer Jr.: "Communication is an exchange of facts, ideas, opinions, or emotions by two or more persons". William Scott defined communication in his Organisation Theory: "Administrative communication is a process which involves the transmission and accurate replication of insured by feedback for the purpose of eliciting actions which will accomplish organizational goals".

These definitions emphasize four important points:

1. The process of communication involves the communication of ideas.
2. The ideas should be accurately replicated (reproduced) in the receiver's mind, i.e., the receiver should get exactly the same ideas as were transmitted. If the process of communication is perfect, there will be no dilution, exaggeration or distortion of the ideas.
3. The transmitter is assured of the accurate replication of the ideas by feedback, i.e., by the receiver's response which is communicated back to the transmitter. Here it is suggested that communication is a two way process including transmission of feedback.
4. The purpose of all communication is to elicit action.

OBJECTIVES OF MARKETING COMMUNICATION

As we have discussed that marketing communication is an integral part of marketing strategy and plays a vital role for bringing the marketer and the consumer closer to each other to achieve their respective objective.

These objectives are derived from the marketing objectives and there is a clear distinction between them. Marketing communication objectives can be formulated from the answers to four basic questions and there are a number of guidelines that will help this formulation.

- To communicate features of goods and services
- To introduce the new product
- To induce present customer to buy more
- To attract new customers
- To confront competition
- To maintain sales in off-seasons
- To explain where goods and services can be purchased
- To generate enthusiasm in channel members
- To increase retail inventories so more goods could be sold
- To establish close rapport with the customers

Marketing versus Communications Objectives: It is very important to emphasize the differences between marketing versus communications objectives. Marketing objectives are generally stated in the firms marketing plan and are statements of what is to be accomplished by the overall marketing program within a given time period. Marketing objectives are usually defined in terms of specific, measurable outcomes such as sales volume, market share, profits, or return on investment. The achievement of marketing objectives will depend upon the proper coordination and execution of all the marketing mix elements, not just promotion.

Your marketing communication objective should describe what you want your target audience to think, feel, and do after they are exposed to your marketing message. It should answer the fundamental question, "What's in it for me?". To often, marketing messages fail to deliver the benefits the target audience will get if the target uses the companies product or service. People make purchases based on what they will receive out of the purchase or service. This is why it's important to include the benefit the target will receive, in your marketing message.

We can say that broadly, marketing communication objectives include:

1. Create a brand awareness for your company
2. Defining a need the product or service can fulfill
3. Encouraging action from the target

Defining your objectives may be a challenge at first, however, once you have a clear objective, then you will be able to move forward with your marketing communication strategy.

MEDIA OF COMMUNICATION

These days communication is possible through a vast variety of media. The Managing Director desirous of communicating with the sales manager can summon him to his room, talk to him over the telephone, or send him a memo. If he wants to consult all the departmental heads, he would most probably convene a meeting. If information is to be transmitted to all the employees, a notice may be put on the notice board or a peon may circulate it among them, a senior officer may announce it over the public address system, or it may be printed in the office bulletin. Posters may be used to issue warnings. Communication with Government departments and other agencies is mostly conducted through written letters. General public can be reached through advertisements on the radio, the television, the cinema screen, or in the newspapers and popular journals. For communication to be effective, the communicator has to be very careful and judicious in the choice of media, which will depend on various factors like the urgency of the message, the time available, the expenditure involved and the intellectual and emotional level of the receivers. All the media available can be broadly classified into five groups:

(i) *Written communication:* It includes letters, circulars, memos, telegrams, reports, minutes, forms and questionnaires, manuals, etc. Everything that has to be written and transmitted in the written form falls in the area of written communication.

(ii) *Oral communication:* It includes face-to-face conversation, conversation over the telephone, radio broadcasts, interviews, group discussions, meetings, conferences and seminars, announcements over the public address system, speeches, etc.

(iii) *Visual communication:* It encompasses gestures and facial expressions, tables and charts, graphs, diagrams, posters, slides, film strips, etc.

(iv) Audio-visual communication encompasses television and cinema films that combine the visual impact with narration.

(v) Computer-based communication includes E-mail, voice mail, cellular phones, fax, etc.

Most often more than one medium may have to be simultaneously employed to make the communication effective. Face-to-face communication combines the oral form with the visual. Graphs and posters often combine the visual with the written form. A manager giving written instructions may also take pains to explain them to a subordinate: he is simultaneously using the oral and the written form of communication. And a great deal can be communicated by the absence of communication, that is, by maintaining total silence.

BARRIERS TO COMMUNICATION

In the earlier paragraph, we have discussed the various media of communication available to us - oral, written visual, audio-visual, computer-based, etc. While a properly chosen medium can add to the effectiveness of communication, an unsuitable medium may act as a barrier to it. Each communication must be transmitted through an appropriate medium. An unsuitable medium is one of the biggest barriers to communication. In addition, some of the barriers of communications are as follows:

Physical Barriers

Noise: Noise is quite often a barrier to communication. In factories, oral communication is rendered difficult by the loud noise of machines. Electronic noise like blaring often interferes in communication by telephone or loudspeaker system. The word noise is also use to refer to all kids of physical interference like illegible handwriting, smudged typescript, poor telephone connections, etc.

Time and Distance: Time and distance also act as barriers to the smooth flow of communication. The use of telephone along with computer technology has made communication very fast and has; to a large extent overcome the space barrier. However, sometimes mechanical breakdowns render these facilities ineffective. In such cases, the distance between the transmitter and the receiver becomes a mighty barrier. Some factories run in shifts. There is a kind of communication gap between persons working in different shifts. Faulty seating arrangement in the room can also become a barrier to effective communication, for whichever seats the employees may be occupying; they definitely want an eye contact with one another.

Semantic Barriers

Interpretation of words: Most of the communications is carried on through words, whether spoken or written. But words are capable of communicating a variety of meanings. It is quite possible that the receiver of a message does not assign the same meaning to a word as the transmitter had intended. This may lead to miscommunication.

Bypassed instruction: Bypassing is said to have occurred if the sender and the receiver of the message attribute different meanings to the same word or use different words for the same meaning. Murphy and Pack have given a classic example of how bypassed instructions can play havoc with the communication process: An office manager handed to a new assistant one letter with the instruction. "Take it to our stockroom and burn it". In the office manager's mind (and in the firm's jargon) the word "burn'' meant to make a copy on a company machine which operated by a heat process. As the letter was extremely important, she wanted an extra copy. However, the puzzled new employee, afraid to ask questions, burned the letter with a lighted match and thus destroyed the only existing copy.

Socio-psychological Barriers

Attitudes and opinions: Personal attitudes and opinions often act as barriers to effective communication. If information agrees with our opinions and attitudes, we tend to receive it favourably. It fits comfortably in the filter of our mind. But if information disagrees with-our views or tends to run contrary to our accepted beliefs, we do not react favourably. If a change in the policy of an organisation proves advantageous to an employee, he welcomes it as good; if it affects him adversely, he rejects it as the whim of the Director.

Emotions: Emotional state of mind plays an important role in the act of communication. If the sender is perplexed, worried, excited, afraid, nervous, his thinking will be blurred and he will not be able to organise his message properly. The state of his mind is sure to be reflected in his message. It is a matter of common observation that people caught in a moment of fury succeed only in violent gesticulation. If they try to speak, they falter and keep on repeating the same words. In the same way, the emotions of the receiver also affect the communication process. If he is angry, he will not take the message in proper light. It is extremely important that emotions are not allowed to impede the smooth flow of communication. The communicator should not try to communicate while in a state of emotional excitement. He should first cool down. In the same way, the receiver should not react to the message if his mind is perturbed.

Closed mind: A person with a closed mind is very difficult to communicate with. He is a man with deeply ingrained prejudices. And he is not prepared' to reconsider his opinions. If closed-minded people can be encouraged to state their reasons for rejecting a message or a proposal, they may reveal deep-rooted, prejudices, opinions and emotions. Perhaps, one can make an attempt to counteract those prejudices, opinions, etc. But if they react only with anger and give a sharp rebuff to anyone who tries to argue with them, they preclude all possibility of communication.

Status-consciousness: Status consciousness exists in every organisation and is one of the major barriers to effective communication. Subordinates are afraid of communicating upward any unpleasant information. They are either too conscious of their inferior status or too afraid of being snubbed. Status-conscious superiors think that consulting their juniors would be compromising their dignity. Status consciousness proves to be a very serious barrier to face-to-face communication. The subordinate feels jittery and nervous, fidgets about where he is standing, falters in his speech and fails in communicating what exactly he wanted to say. The officer, on the other hand, reveals impatience and starts giving comments or advice before he fully hears his subordinate. Consequently, there is a total failure of communication; the subordinate returns to his seat dissatisfied and simmering inside, while the officer resumes his work with the feeling that his employees have no consideration for the value of his time and keep on pestering him for nothing.

Such communication failures can be averted if the managers and other persons in authority rise above the consciousness of their status and encourage their employees to talk freely.

The source of communication: If the receiver has a suspicion about or prejudice against the source of communication, there is likely to be a barrier of communication. People often tend to react more according to their attitude to the source of facts than to the facts themselves. Think of an executive in the habit of finding fault with his employees. If once in a while he begins with a compliment, the employees immediately become suspicious and start attributing motives to the compliment. If a statement emanates from the grapevine, the manager will not give credence to it, but the same state coming from a trusted supervisor will immediately be believed.

Inattentiveness: People often become inattentive while receiving a message, in particular, if the message contains a new idea. The adult human mind usually resists change, for change makes things uncertain. It also threatens security and stability. So the moment a new idea is presented to them, they unconsciously become inattentive. Sometimes a person becomes inattentive because of some distraction. It is possible that an employee does not listen to the supervisor's instructions attentively because he is being distracted by the lady typist who has chosen exactly this moment to repair her make-up, or because he is feeling amused at the supervisor's artificial accent and finds it difficult to concentrate on his words. Sometimes when the listener has received a part of the message, his mind gets busy in framing a reply to it, or in guessing the next part of the message. It is quite likely that in thinking of what has been said or that might be said later, the listener misses a part of what is actually being said at the present moment.

Faulty transmission: A message is never communicated from one person to another in its entirety. This is true in particular of oral messages. If a decision has been taken by the Board of Directors, it must be in the form of a lengthy resolution. This resolution cannot be passed on to the factory workers in the same form. It has to be translated in simple language so that they may easily understand it. But translation can never be perfect. In the process of interpretation, simplification and translation, a part of the message gets lost or distorted. A scientific study of the communication process has revealed that successive transmissions of the same message are decreasingly accurate. In oral communications, something in the order of 30 per cent of the information is lost in each transmission.

Poor retention: Poor retention of communication also acts as a barrier. Studies show that employees retain only about 50 per cent of the information communicated to them. The rest is lost. Thus if information is communicated through three or four stages, very little reaches the destination, and of that very little also only a fraction is likely to be retained poor retention may lead to imperfect responses, which may further hamper the communication process.

Unsolicited communication: Unsolicited communication has to face stronger barriers than solicited communication. If I seek advice, it should be presumed that I will listen to it. But if a sales letter comes to me unsolicited, it is not very sure that I will pay much attention to it.

MARKETING COMMUNICATION PROCESS

Communication has been variously defined as the passing of information, the exchange of ideas, or the process of establishing a communication or oneness of thought between the sender and a receiver. Thus, marketing communication is the link between the sender and receiver.

The marketing communication process can be very complex but it is based on the universal model used in all forms of communication which includes a sender, the message, receivers, a medium and, in the case of two-way communication, feedback. However, this universal model needs to be presented in the context of marketing communications in order that its relevance to marketing is understood. The purpose of a marketing communication campaign can best be described by reference to the hierarchy of communication effects represented by a four-phase model.

Marketing Communication Process: Marketing communication is the message that deals with the buyer-seller relationship. True communication takes place only when the proper message reaches from the sender to the receiver. Such an exchange could be oral or written, personal or public, using words, figures, symbols or combination thereof. Therefore, it is essential for the marketer to communicate his prospective buyer and provide them relevant information in a pursuasive language. The whole communication process contains various elements as shown in the given figure.

Communication can be defined as the sharing of a common meaning, i.e., sharing of an orientation toward a set of informational signs. All communications are action-oriented. For the

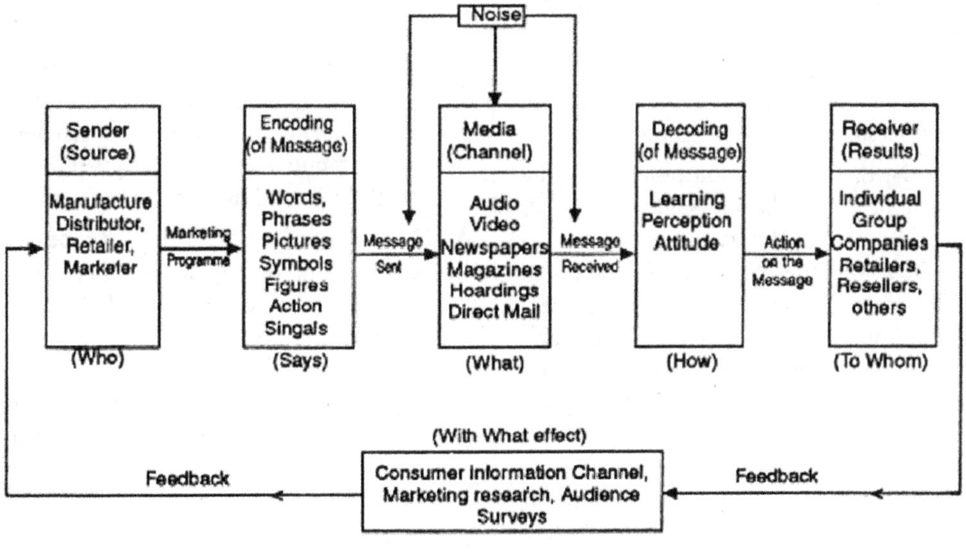

Fig.: *Marketing Communication System*

communication to be effective, there should be a common understanding between the sender and the receiver. Both have to be actively involved-the sender in sending the messages and receiver in receiving them and giving feedback to the sender. Communication is a social process which varies as societal factor varies. The process, the message, the objectives, etc. change as the social values change. Culture, tradition, social institutions etc. have a wide impact on the communication process.

Components of Communication Process: The main components of communication-mix are communicator who is the first component and communicate or sends the message. Sender must have clear objectives as to what he seeks to communicate. It is difficult to find the right mix of communicators. There may be copywriters, artists, merchandising specialists and other specialists who have helped the communicator to perform his job satisfactorily. This is two-way communication whereby the sender and the receiver talk face-to-face. Each evaluates the other's attitude and desire. At the time of sending the message, the communicator must see, whether the receiver is capable at understanding and decoding the message as well as his willingness to listen. The communicator or salesman has more knowledge of the area, people, stratum, culture and other factors affecting the needs of the people. The role of the sale communicator is like that of marketing researcher who can arouse awareness, interest and encourage for adopting the new product.

Message is the second component in the communication process. The message may either visual or verbal. The effectiveness of any ad depends on how the messages are created and arranged. The message may be commercial idea, sales story and cow theme. The word, the picture, the symbol and other communicative elements are the bases of the message. The media of communication or ads are newspapers, magazines, television, radio etc. which create the interrelationship between receiver and sender. If there is a choice of channel the most effective message channel must be selected.

In the marketing communication process, a sender sends the encoded through a medium for a receiver to receive and decode. Normally, the marketing communication process has some dorm of feedback. As diagram shows Marketing communication process has five major components as described below:

1. Source
2. Encoding
3. The Medium
4. Decoding
5. Feed back

1. **Source:** Communication process starts when an individual, group of individual or an organization wants to communicate some message to the target audience. Therefore, the sender of the message is the source of communication destination through a medium. The communication destination in the process is called the receiver. This communication can take place in many ways ranging from face-to-face communication to communication through electronic media such as television, the internet, radio or the print media. Thus, it is essential for the sender to communicate in such a way as to ensure the message is perceived by the receiver in the way it was intended to be.

2. **Receiver:** The receiver ,the destination of the communicated message, receives the message transmitted by the sender. The manner in which the communication is received is dependent on the perception of the receiver.

3. **Encoding:** The encoding process involves selection of the right amount of information, the type of information and the organization of information that has to be sent to the receiver. The sender has to ensure that the right amount of information is communicated to the receiver. Too much information may confuse the receiver and vice-versa is also possible.

4. **The Medium:** The medium of transmission is the interface between the sender and the

receiver. It acts as a carrier for information from the source to the final destination i.e. receiver. Thus, the organization should choose the right medium on the basis of the type of the information that has to be communicated, the location of the receiver, frequency of the information etc.

5. **Decoding:** Decoding is the process in which the receiver analyses or interprets the information that has been sent by a sender. The decoding process is successful only when the receiver interprets the message as it was intended to be interpreted by the sender.

6. **Feedback:** This is a very important step in the communication process, as it helps in the continuation of the communication process. The feedback given by the receiver forms the basis for further communication. The feedback also helps in analysing the way in which the receiver interprets the information and thus help the sender take corrective action, if desired.

ELEMENTS OF MARKETING COMMUNICATION

Marketing communication is an element of the marketing mix and as such is probably the most visible. Being part of the marketing mix means that as a variable it should never by managed in isolation from the other elements. This means that in terms of planning the marketing communication, plan should be aligned with and supportive of both the short-term and long-term objectives of the wider marketing plan. The marketing communication plan will contain a number of steps. Marketing Communication comprises the following elements.

1. Personal selling
2. Advertising
3. Sales Promotion
4. Public Relations
5. Publicity

MARKETING COMMUNICATION AND THE TARGET AUDIENCE

The marketing communication process really begins with identifying the audience that will be the focus of the firm's advertising and promotional efforts. The target audience may consist of individuals, groups, niche markets, market segments, or a general public or mass audience. Marketers approach each of these audiences differently. The target market may consist of individuals who have specific needs and for whom the communication must be specifically tailored. This often requires person-to-person communication and is generally accomplished through personal selling. Other forms of communication, such as advertising, may be used to attract the audience's attention to the firm, but the detailed message is carried by a salesperson that can respond to the specific needs of the individual customer. Life insurance, financial services, and real estate are examples of products and services promoted this way.

The group represents a second level of audience aggregation. Marketers often must communicate with a group of people who make or influence the purchase decision. For example, organizational purchasing often involves buying centers or committees that vary in size and composition. Companies marketing their products and services to other businesses or organizations must understand who are on the purchase committee, what aspect of the decision each individual influence, and the criteria each member uses to evaluate a product. Advertising may be directed at each member of the buying center, and multilevel personal selling may be necessary to reach those individuals who influence or actually make decisions.

Marketers look for customers who have similar needs and wants and thus represent some type of market segment that can be reached with the same basic communication strategy. Very small, well-defined groups of customers are often referred to as market niches. They can usually be reached through personal selling efforts or highly targeted media such as direct mail. The next level of audience aggregation is market segments, broader classes of buyers who have similar needs and can be reached with similar messages. There are various ways of segmenting markets and reaching the customers in these segments. As market segments get larger, marketers usually turn to broader-based media such as newspapers, magazines, and TV to reach them. Marketers of most consumer products attempt to attract the attention of large numbers of present or potential customers (mass markets) through mass communication, such as advertising or publicity. Mass communication is a one-way flow of information from the marketer to the consumer. Feedback on the audience's reactions to the message is generally indirect and difficult to measure.

THE RESPONSE PROCESS IN MARKETING COMMUNICATION

Perhaps the most important aspect of developing effective communication programs involves understand the response process the receiver may go through in moving toward a specific behavior (like purchasing a product) and how the promotional efforts of the marketer influence consumer responses. In many instances, the marketer's only objective may be to create awareness of the company or brand name, which may trigger interest in the product. In other situations, the marketer may want to convey detailed information to change consumers' knowledge of and attitudes toward the brand and ultimately change their behavior.

The function of all elements of the promotional mix is to communicate; so promotional planners must understand the communication process. This process can be very complex; successful marketing communications depend on a number of factors, including the nature of the message, the audience's interpretation of it, and the environment in which it is received. For effective communication to occur, the sender must encode a message in such a way that the receiver will decode it in the intended manner. Feedback from the receiver helps the sender determine whether proper decoding has occurred or whether noise has interfered with the communication process. Promotional planning begins with the receiver or target audience, as marketers must understand how the audience is likely to respond to various sources of communication or types of messages. For promotional planning, the receiver can be analysed with respect to both its composition (i.e., individual, group, or mass audiences) and the response process it goes through. Different orderings of the traditional response hierarchy include the standard learning, dissonance/attribution, and low-involvement models. The information response model integrates concepts from both the high- and low-involvement response hierarchy perspectives and recognises the effects of direct experience with a product.

MULTIPLE CHOICE QUESTIONS

1. Which of the following terms best fits the activity of marketing communications?
   (*a*) Making product available
   (*b*) Convenience of location
   (*c*) High level of regulation
   (*d*) Communication between stakeholders
   (*e*) None of these

2. The marketing communications strategy of the marketing mix deals exclusively with:
   (*a*) personal selling and advertising
   (*b*) advertising and public relations
   (*c*) advertising, publicity and pricing
   (*d*) personal selling, advertising, sales promotion, and public relations
   (*e*) None of these

3. This model is similar to the two-step model, but in this interpretation the parties are seen to interact among themselves. Communication

flows among all the members in what is regarded as a communication network. This is known as:
(*a*) the Interaction Model of Communication
(*b*) the Two-Step Model of Communication
(*c*) the Linear Model of Communication
(*d*) the HoE model
(*e*) None of these

4. This is a hierarchy of effects or sequential model used to explain how advertising works:
(*a*) ADD (*b*) AIDA
(*c*) PESTLE (*d*) SWOT
(*e*) None of these

5. AIDA stands for awareness, ..., desire and ....
(*a*) interest; action
(*b*) intensity; appeal
(*c*) involvement; action
(*d*) Involvement; appeal
(*e*) None of these

6. Marketing communications is used to achieve one of two principal goals. The first concerns the development of brand values. What is the other goal?
(*a*) Increasing sales
(*b*) Informing about products
(*c*) Changing the behaviour of target audiences
(*d*) Channelling communication tools
(*e*) None of these

7. This is the sharing of meaning created through the transmission of information:
(*a*) Communication (*b*) Noise
(*c*) Transfer (*d*) Understanding
(*e*) None of these

8. This is a series of economic transactions between parties, who have a long-term orientation towards, and are primarily motivated by, concern for each other:
(*a*) Partner exchanges
(*b*) Collaborative exchanges
(*c*) Co-operative transfer
(*d*) Partner exchange
(*e*) None of these

9. The role of marketing communications is to engage audiences and there are four main tasks that it can be used to complete. Which of the following is not part of the four main tasks?
(*a*) Differentiate (*b*) Participate
(*c*) Reinforce (*d*) Inform
(*e*) None of these

10. .... is an important element in the communication process. It recognizes that successful communications are more likely to be achieved if the source and the receiver understand each other.
(*a*) The realm of understanding
(*b*) Personal selling
(*c*) Noise
(*d*) Feedback
(*e*) None of these

11. This is part of the communication process where receivers unpack the various components of the message, and begin to make sense and give the message meaning:
(*a*) Encoding (*b*) Decoding
(*c*) Transfer (*d*) Noise
(*e*) None of these

12. This is a part of the communication process where the sender selects a combination of appropriate words, pictures, symbols and music to represent a message to be transmitted:
(*a*) Encoding (*b*) Decoding
(*c*) Transfer (*d*) Feedback
(*e*) None of these

13. This is part of the communication process and refers to the responses offered by receivers:
(*a*) Encoding (*b*) Decoding
(*c*) Transfer (*d*) Feedback
(*e*) None of these

14. .... is concerned with the development of knowledge that is specific to the parties involved and is referred to as 'learning together'.
(*a*) Dialogue
(*b*) Personal influencer
(*c*) Feedback
(*d*) Message
(*e*) None of these

15. This approach has been used to convey particular information and help educate large target audiences through television and radio programmes. This approach is referred to as:
(*a*) Opinion followers
(*b*) Opinion formers
(*c*) Public relations
(*d*) Opinion leaders
(*e*) None of these

16. They are not part of the same peer group as the people they influence. Their defining characteristic is that they exert personal influence because of their profession, authority, education, or status associated with the object of the communication process. This is referred to as:
(*a*) Opinion aggregators
(*b*) Opinion followers
(*c*) Opinion formers
(*d*) Opinion gatherers
(*e*) None of these

17. The success of marketing communication depends upon the extent to which messages engage their audiences. These audiences can be seen to fall into three main groups:
(*a*) Customers, general public, and sales personnel
(*b*) Customers, channel members, and general stakeholders
(*c*) Customers, general stakeholders, and club members
(*d*) General public, club members, and general stakeholders
(*e*) None of these

18. Each organization is part of a network of other organizations such as suppliers, retailers, wholesalers, value added resellers, distributors, and other retailers, who join together, often freely, to make the product or service available to end users. This is referred to as:
(*a*) Channel members
(*b*) Customers
(*c*) Stakeholders
(*d*) Community
(*e*) None of these

19. Which of the following is the communication model that depicts information flowing via various media channels, to particular types of people to whom other members of the audience refer for information and guidance?
(*a*) Two-step (*b*) Three-step
(*c*) Multi-step (*d*) One-step
(*e*) None of these

20. Which of the following is the interpersonal communication about products or services where a receiver regards the communicator as impartial and is not attempting to sell products or services?
(*a*) Word of Mouth (WOM)
(*b*) Personal Selling (PS)
(*c*) Direct Marketing (DM)
(*d*) Customer Service (CS)
(*e*) None of these

21. This is a form of non-personal communication, by an identified sponsor, that is transmitted through the use of paid-for media:
(*a*) Advertising (*b*) Personal selling
(*c*) Public relations (*d*) Publicity
(*e*) None of these

22. .... is very effective at delivering messages to target audiences as it allows for explanation in a way that most other media cannot.
(*a*) Digital (*b*) Print
(*c*) Broadcast (*d*) Outdoor
(*e*) None of these

23. .... is content that is created by general users, not producers, although this begs the question about who is the producer.
(*a*) PR-generated content
(*b*) Organisation-generated content
(*c*) User-generated content
(*d*) Customer-generated content
(*e*) None of these

24. Rather than trawl all relevant web pages to find new content and updates, ... allows for specific content to be brought together and made available to an individual without themalways having to return to numerous sites.
(*a*) Social networks (*b*) Podcasting

(*c*) Blogs (*d*) RSS
(*e*) None of these

25. Users are able to create content and become more involved with a brand through:
(*a*) Door to door (*b*) Online communities
(*c*) Direct mail (*d*) Telemarketing
(*e*) None of these

26. A commercial activity, whereby one party permits another an opportunity to exploit an association with a target audience in return for funds, services, or resources is referred to as:
(*a*) Advertising (*b*) Exchange
(*c*) Sponsorship (*d*) Public relations
(*e*) None of these

27. This is a marketing communication tool that uses non-personal media to create and sustain a personal and intermediary free communication with customers, potential customers and other significant stakeholders:
(*a*) Direct marketing (*b*) Advertising
(*c*) Public relations (*d*) Sales promotion
(*e*) None of these

28. This includes advertisements that contain 'call-to-response' mechanisms such as telephone numbers, website addresses, email and postal addresses:
(*a*) Direct response advertising
(*b*) Sales promotions
(*c*) Mass media advertising
(*d*) Public relations
(*e*) None of these

29. These are events when groups of sellers meet collectively with the key purpose of attracting buyers:
(*a*) Exhibitions
(*b*) Sales promotions
(*c*) Mass media advertising
(*d*) Press conference
(*e*) None of these

30. This is a marketing communications activity concerned with providing support for the sales force and merchandising personnel:
(*a*) Store marketing (*b*) Field marketing
(*c*) Sales promotions (*d*) Personal selling
(*e*) None of these

31. This is a systematic process involving a series of procedures and activities that lead to the setting of marketing communication objectives and the formulation of plans for achieving them:
(*a*) Key account communication
(*b*) Corporate communication management
(*c*) Marketing communication planning
(*d*) Customer account management
(*e*) None of these

32. Which of the following is not an element of the Marketing Communication Planning Framework (MCPF)?
(*a*) Mission (*b*) Context analysis
(*c*) Resources (*d*) Feedback
(*e*) None of these

33. This term encompasses the five key communication tools used by organizations to reach consumers and other organizations with product and organization-based messages. The tools covered are advertising, sales promotions, public relations, direct marketing and personal selling:
(*a*) Marketing communications mix
(*b*) Marketing mix
(*c*) Pricing mix
(*d*) Media mix
(*e*) None of these

34. This marketing and communication tool offers a direct inducement or an incentive to encourage customers to buy a product/service:
(*a*) Advertising (*b*) Public relations
(*c*) Sales promotion (*d*) Direct marketing
(*e*) None of these

35. This is the use of inter-personal communications with the aim of developing positive feelings and stimulating behaviour.
(*a*) Direct marketing (*b*) Personal selling
(*c*) Sale promotions (*d*) Advertising
(*e*) None of these

36. .... is used to influence the way an organization is perceived by various groups of stakeholders.
(*a*) Direct marketing (*b*) Public relations
(*c*) Sale promotion (*d*) Advertising
(*e*) None of these

37. This is the unpaid peer-to-peer communication of often provocative content originating from an identified sponsor using the Internet to persuade or influence an audience to pass along the content to others:
(*a*) Viral marketing
(*b*) Word-of-mouth marketing
(*c*) Direct-response advertising
(*d*) Peer-to-peer marketing
(*e*) None of these

38. A means of orchestrating the tools of the marketing communications mix, so that audiences perceive a single, consistent, unified message whenever they have contact with a brand, is referred to as:
(*a*) Integrated Marketing Communications (IMC)
(*b*) Personal Selling (PS)
(*c*) Direct Marketing (DM)
(*d*) Customer Service (CS)
(*e*) None of these

39. What type of media helps advertisers demonstrate the benefits of using a particular product and can bring life and energy to an advertiser's message?
(*a*) Broadcast media (*b*) Interactive media
(*c*) Print media (*d*) Support media
(*e*) None of these

40. What type of media has the primary objective to get the attention of shoppers and to stimulate them to make a purchase? (Examples include point-of-purchase displays and packaging.)
(*a*) Broadcast media
(*b*) Interactive media
(*c*) In-store media
(*d*) Support media
(*e*) None of these

ANSWERS

1	**2**	**3**	**4**	**5**	**6**	**7**	**8**	**9**	**10**
(*d*)	(*d*)	(*a*)	(*b*)	(*a*)	(*c*)	(*a*)	(*b*)	(*b*)	(*a*)
11	**12**	**13**	**14**	**15**	**16**	**17**	**18**	**19**	**20**
(*b*)	(*a*)	(*d*)	(*a*)	(*d*)	(*c*)	(*b*)	(*a*)	(*a*)	(*a*)
21	**22**	**23**	**24**	**25**	**26**	**27**	**28**	**29**	**30**
(*a*)	(*b*)	(*c*)	(*d*)	(*b*)	(*c*)	(*a*)	(*a*)	(*a*)	(*b*)
31	**32**	**33**	**34**	**35**	**36**	**37**	**38**	**39**	**40**
(*c*)	(*a*)	(*a*)	(*c*)	(*b*)	(*b*)	(*a*)	(*a*)	(*a*)	(*c*)

CHAPTER-9

PROMOTION MIX: DIRECT SELLING, ADVERTISING, SALES PROMOTION AND PUBLIC RELATIONS

INTRODUCTION

Broadly speaking, promotion means to push forward or to advance an idea to gain its acceptance and approval. Promotion is any communicative activity whose main object is to move forward a product, service or idea in a chain of distribution. It is an effort by a marketer to inform and persuade buyers to accept, use, recommend, and repurchase the idea, good or service which is being promoted. Thus, promotion is a form of communication with an additional element of persuasion. The promotional activities always attempt to affect knowledge, attitudes, preferences, and behavior of recipients i.e. buyers.

In any exchange activity, communication is absolutely necessary. The company may have the best product, package etc. but still people may not buy the product if they haven't heard of it. The marketer must communicate to his prospective buyers and provide them with adequate information in a persuasive language. People must know that the right product is available at the right place and at the right price. This is the job of promotion in marketing.

Thus, promotion is the process of marketing communication involving information, persuasion and influence. Promotion has three specific purposes.

1. It communicates marketing information to consumers, users, and prospects.
2. Besides just communication, promotion also persuades and convinces the buyers.
3. Promotional efforts act as powerful tools of communication. Providing the cutting edge to its entire marketing programmed. Thus, promotion is a form of non-price competition.

Promotion is thus responsible for awakening and stimulating demand, capturing demand from rivals and maintaining demand for products even against keen competition.

Every company can choose from the following tools of promotion, popularly known as the promotion-mix variables:

1. Advertising,
2. Sales Promotion,
3. Personal Selling,
4. Public Relations.

Advertising

The word 'advertising' is derived from a Latin word "advertere" which means to turn attention towards a specific thing. The dictionary meaning of the word 'advertising' is to announce publicly or to give public notice. In other words, it may be interpreted as to turn the attention of the people concerned to a specific thing which has been announced by the advertiser publicly in order to inform and to influence them with the ideas which the advertisement carries. In this way, advertising is turning the attention of the people towards products, services, ideas by an identified sponsor. It is intended to influence the prospective customers in the market and increase sales. Advertising is thus the method or mode of carrying a message to the prospective customer to buy a particular product.

Although advertising has been variously defined by different authors, the basic theme has more or less remained the same. Some of the widely accepted definitions of advertising are as follows:

1. According to Definitions Committee of the American Marketing Association, "Advertising is any paid form of non-personal presentation and promotion of ideas, goods and services by an Identified sponsor."
2. According to William J. Stanton, "Advertising consists of all the activities involved in presenting to a group a non-personal, oral or visual, openly sponsored message regarding a product, service or idea."
3. According to Philip Kotler, "Advertising is non-personal form of communication conducted through paid media under clear sponsorship."
4. According to Wheeler, "Advertising is any form of paid non-personal presentation of ideas, goods or services for the purpose of inducing people to buy."

From the above definitions we conclude that "advertising is personal presentation of ideas, goods or services by an identified sponsor for the purpose of inducing the prospects to buy them."

Characteristics: The main characteristics or elements of advertising are as follows:

1. It is non-personal communication to specific audience or consumers.
2. It is a paid form of communication by an identified sponsor.
3. It may be visual, spoken or written.
4. It disseminates information or products or services to the consumer.
5. It presents the message about product availability in the market.
6. It persuades people to buy a product by creating interest of the prospective buyers in the product.
7. It is the promotion of ideas, goods and services.
8. It supplements the voice and personality of individual salesman. It is a salesmanship in print.
9. It is a general term used for any and all types of publicity.
10. It is an essential form of communication through different media to inform the customer about the product and its features.
11. It stimulates sales or patronage for the product.
12. It helps in positioning the product in the market.
13. It carries the message of the manufacturer or the seller to the target audience for which it is intended.

Development of Advertising

The potentialities of advertising multiplied when the handpress was invented at the end of the 15th century. By Shakespeare's time, posters had made their appearance and there is evidence to prove that advertising had assumed the function of fostering demand for existing products. Another important development at this time was emergence of the pamphlet as an advertising medium. The early examples of example of these pamphlets disclose their sponsorship by companies intent on generating goodwill for their activities.

It was in the later half of the 19th century that with the advert of mass advertising, as we know it today, came into being. Mass production became a reality and channels of distribution had to be developed to cope with the physical movements of goods, creating a need for mass communication to inform the consumers of the choices available to them. In short, the speedy development of advertising was accelerated on account of the following factors:

1. The industrial production led to mass production on account of use of machines and necessitated the need of advertising for selling the same.
2. With the development of improved means of transport and communication the world was getting closer day-by-day leading to widening of the market from local to regional and national levels etc. Advertising gave the needed communication vehicle for contacting the consumers.

3. Increasing literacy was also responsible for the development of advertising media.
4. With the increase in literacy rate, the number of newspapers and magazines increased. They carried the message about new products to consumers.
5. The advent and development of advertising agencies in the beginning of the 20th century gave inpetus to the rapid development of advertising.
6. Finally, the advent of radio, television, telephone etc. added impetus to the development of advertising. And now one step more, the colour transmission has made advertising more attractive. This medium is second only to newspapers.

So far as India is concerned, advertising as a potent and recognised means of sales promotion was accepted only two decades ago. The delay is obviously attributable to late industrialisation in our country. But today India has emerged as an industrial nation which is quite evident from the nature of the advertisements that appear regularly in local, national as well as international newspapers and magazines.

Objectives of Advertising : The following are the main objectives of advertising

1. **Preparation of ground for sale of the new Product:** When a new product is to be introduced in the market, advertising is necessary. The potential consumers can be informed only by means of advertising. In this way, advertising may be used for preparing a ground for the sale of a new product. The mass media like radio, television and cinema-halls are used for this purpose.
2. **Creation of demand:** Another main objective of advertising is to create demand for a product or service. Advertising creates a favourable atmosphere for maintaining or improving sales. Customers are regularly reminded about the product, brand etc. The prospective customers may be induced to buy a product by informing them about the comparative quality, price and other attributes of that product. The object is to change the habit of the consumer, to shift from a rival product.
3. **Educate the consumers and the users:** Another objective of the advertising is to educate the consumers and the users about the uses and utility of the product. Unless information reaches the consumers and the users, they cannot decide and make good choice.
4. **Building up brand image and brand loyalty:** Another objective is to build up brand image. This objective can be achieved through constant and repeated advertisements about the brand. For instance, today everybody knows about Bata's Shoes, Philips Radios etc.
5. **Facing the competition:** Another objective of the advertising is to face the existing competition The producer informs the consumers about the price, quality and availability of the product in relation to the competitiors.
6. **Informing about the changes to the Consumers and the Users:** Another objective of advertisement is to inform the consumers and users about the changes in quality, packing, design, size, brand, price, weight packing etc.
7. **Forcing middlemen to deal in the product:** The objective of advertising is also to force the middlemen to deal in a particular product or products only. It is possible when the consumers and the users approach the middlemen for purchasing a product through the influence of advertisements of that product.
8. **Neutralising competitor's advertising:** Another objective of advertising is to neutralise competitors' advertising. It is essential to follow similar practices to neutralise their effects.
9. **Enhancing goodwill of the firm:** The objective of advertising is also to enhance goodwill and reputation of the firm in the minds of middlemen, consumers and the users. In this context, constant and repeated advertisements are of great importance.

10. **Performing selling job:** The object of advertising is also to perform selling function, e.g., in mail order business the selling function is performed by advertisement.
11. **Acquaint buyers with new uses:** The objective of advertising is also to acquaint buyers and users with the new uses of a product.
12. **Assisting salesman's efforts:** The objective of advertising is also to assist the salesman's efforts in increasing the sales of a product or products. Since the advertising educates the customers about the product, the function of the salesman remains simply to sell the product.
13. **Reduction in production and distribution Costs:** The objective of advertising is also to assist a producer in reducing production and distribution costs. Advertisement helps in increasing sales and also in informing prospective customers about the product. This causes large-scale production resulting in overall reduction in cost of production and distribution.
14. **Maintenance of demand:** The objective of advertising is not only to increase the demand but also to maintain the demand of existing product or products.
15. **Rationalizations for buying:** The objective of advertising is also to provide rationalization for buying to the buyers so as to make right selection of the product needed by them.

According to Mathews, Buzzell and Frank, objectives of advertising are:

(i) To make an immediate sale,
(ii) To build primary market,
(iii) To introduce a price deal,
(iv) To inform about a product availability,
(v) To build brand recognition or brand-insistance,
(vi) To help salesman by building an awareness of a product among retailers,
(vii) To create a reputation for service, reliability or research strength,
(viii) To increase market share,
(ix) To modify existing product appeals and buying motives,
(x) To inform about the availability of new products or features or price,
(xi) To increase the frequency of use of a product,
(xii) To increase the number or quality of retail outlets,
(xiii) To build overall company image,
(xiv) To effect immediate buying action,
(xv) To reach new areas or new segments of population within existing areas, and
(xvi) To develop overseas markets.

Sales Promotion

Sales promotion is another way of promoting of increasing sales. It includes all those activities which are used for increasing sales. It is a special type of promotional activity carried on in such a way as to attract consumers for buying. Sales promotion activities consist of displays, shows, expositions, demonstrations and other special efforts such as bonus, off-season discount, contests, coupons etc. that are intended to attract consumers and create more sales. Some important definitions of sales promotion are as follows:

1. According to H. R. Delens, "Sales promotion means any steps that are taken for the purpose of obtaining or increasing sales. Often this term refers specially to selling efforts that are designed to supplement personal selling and advertising and by coordination help them to become more effective."
2. According to the American Marketing Association, "Sales promotion refers to those marketing activities connected with the promotion of sales other than personal selling, advertising and publicity, that stimulate consumer purchasing and dealer effectiveness such as displays, shows and expositions, demonstrations and various non-recurrent selling efforts not in the ordinary routine."

3. According to L. K. Johnson, "Sales promotion consists of all those activities whose purpose is to supplement, to coordinate and to make more effective the efforts of the sales force, of the advertising department, and of the distributors and dealers to increase sales and otherwise stimulate consumers to take greater initiative in buying."

From the above study, we may conclude that sales promotion includes all those activities other than advertising and personal selling which are designed to increase sales.

Objectives of Sales Promotion

Sales promotion activities are mainly intended to supplement personal selling, advertising and to increase the sale of the product. Sales promotion activities help the trader and the sales force to represent the product to the consumers effectively and induce them to buy. The main objectives of sales promotion are as follows:

1. To attract customers.
2. To stimulate the demand by popularising the products.
3. To face competition effectively.
4. To keep the memory of the product in the minds of the consumers.
5. To supplement personal selling and advertising.
6. To establish and maintain communication with large market segments.
7. To induce middlemen-wholesalers and retailers to purchase goods in large quantity by offering more facilities such as credit facilities, higher trade and cash discounts, free gifts, bonus etc.
8. To arrest seasonal demand in sale
9. To assist salesmen in increasing sales, achieving, sales targets and salesmen's activities to promote sales.
10. To help in introducing new products in the market.
11. To introduce such sales promotion methods as to adopt aggressive selling and thereby increase sales.
12. To stimulate market research.

Methods of Sales Promotion

Various methods of sales promotion arc being adopted by modern entrepreneurs nowadays. They may be grouped or classified under the following heads:

(i) Consumer Sales Promotion Methods.

(ii) Trade Sales Promotion Methods.

(iii) Sales Force Promotion Methods.

(i) Consumer Sales Promotion Methods: These methods are directed at consumers to induce or persuade them to buy the company's product. Under this method consumers are given incentives directly by the company to buy a product.

Methods: Prominent consumer sales promotion methods or devices are as follows:

1. **Coupon:** Coupon is a chit of a given value and mostly kept inside the package. Coupons are given directly to the consumer at the time of purchasing the product. It entitles the bearer (purchaser) to purchase a product at the reduced price. The buyer is required to surrender the coupon and get reduction of the slated value in the coupon. Thus, the consumer gets the benefit of reduced price to the extent of the value of that coupon. Coupons attract the consumers to buy a product. Coupons also encourage retailers to stock the product. Coupons provide short-term stimulus to the sales of the product. Coupon offers are less expensive as compared with other consumer sales promotion methods.
2. **Samples:** Samples are given free of cost to the potential customers at the time of introducing a new product in the market. Samples are given or distributed with a view to allowing the customer to test the quality of the product before purchasing the same. The samples may be distributed door to door, offered in a retail store, given to professionals (e.g. doctor) for

recommendation or may be sent by post. Samples are also given to prospective buyers when sales contracts are entered into with them. The seller guarantees that the goods will be delivered as per the sample given or shown to the prospective buyers.

3. **Premium:** According to Gross and Houghton, "A premium is defined as an article of merchandise or other thing of value which is offered as an inducement to purchase a product or service." Premium is an item of merchandise that is offered at cost or relatively at low cost as bonus to purchase a particular product.

   Premium is of four types:

   - **Factory in-pack premium:** This is a gift of low value article packed by the company in the box or package itself. It is very popular in case of baby food and tin food items. Spoons, cups etc. are generally packed with the product inside the package.
   - **Reusable container:** It is a container that has value to the consumer after the product is consumed, such as, a glass jar or a plastic container.
   - **Free-in-the-mail premium:** It is a gift which will be sent free of cost by the manufacturer to the buyer by mail after the purchaser sends the proof of purchase, such as a box-top or/and labels etc.
   - **Self-liquidating premium:** A self-liquidating premium is a method of sending an item by mail to the customers at a considerably low price. It is offered only to those customers who purchase goods from the company. This becomes possible because the company purchases these items in bulk at a low price. It is called self-liquidating premium because the company usually recovers the cost of the item from the buyer.

4. **Price-off:** It is an offer to the consumer of a certain amount of money off the regular price of a product. In this case, the consumer is offered a price reduction over the printed or list price on purchases made during a fixed period. This is done to attract consumers of other brands to this brand or when a new product or brand enters the market.

5. **Money refund offer:** This is an offer to the consumer that if he is not satisfied with the quality of the product, the manufacturer will return the purchase price within a stated period. This offer is generally stated on the package itself in the media advertising.

6. **Competitions-contest calls:** Competitions-contest calls are arranged with a view to attracting the customers, preferably new customers, to participate in the contest and win cash prizes trips or tours or goods. Generally, the consumers may be asked to send along with entries for contest box-tops or certain flaps or even packages. The entry forms are available with the retailers free of cost. Contest calls are also made without any restrictions or enclosures to entries. The Contestants are asked to answer the puzzles or write a slogan on the product. It is an indirect method of introducing a new product in the market or stimulating the sales of an existing product. This method is quite popular these days.

7. **Trading or bonus stamps:** A premium in the form of stamps is given by the seller along with purchases to the consumers. The number and value of stamps received by the consumer depends upon the, value of purchases made by the consumer. The consumer goes on collecting stamps unless he has sufficient quantity so as to obtain a desired merchandise in exchange for the stamps from the stamp redemption centres.

8. **Demonstration:** This consumer sales promotion method is used for promoting the sales of a new brand or new product in the market. The product is demonstrated in manufacturer's or seller's premises at fairs and exhibitions, religious festivals or even on door-to-door basis depending upon the size and value of the product. This method is popular mostly for the

sales of household appliances such as detergent powders, small machines etc.

9. **Reduction sale:** Under this method, products are sold at reduced prices by the company. It is also called 'Clearance Sale' or 'Washing Sale'. This method is particularly employed when a large stock of products accumulates with the seller and then the offer is made to the consumers to purchase the same at concessional rates. For instance, this method is employed by Bata Shoe Company or Delhi Cloth Mills to clear up the old stocks at their stores (shops) on particular occasions such as Diwali, Holi etc. In this case, new as well as old customers are attracted to purchase the products at reduced prices.

(ii) Trade Sales Promotion Methods: Trade sales promotion is an incentive given to middlemen (wholesalers, retailers, stockiest etc) to buy goods in large quantity from the producer/manufacturer. The methods adopted for making bulk sales are called trade sales promotion methods. This incentive is to encourage or motivate the middlemen to store the company's product in large quantity.

Methods of Trade Sales Promotion: The main trade sales promotion methods or techniques are as follows:

1. **Buying allowance or discount:** In this case, the buying allowance or discount on purchases is offered to the dealers to induce them to purchase company's product during a stated period of time. This is to encourage buying in large quantities. It increases the sales of the manufacturer and profits of the dealer.

2 **Display and advertising allowance:** In this method, dealers display company's product at their premises and for this they are given display and advertising allowance by the company. The display and advertising allowance is paid on the basis of the space provided to display the company's product at their premises.

3. **Buy-back allowance:** In this method, the dealer is offered by the company an allowance of certain amount of money at the time of each purchase on the basis of purchase made on earlier trade deals. This extends the life of a trade deal and prevents a decline in post deal.

4. **Merchandise allowance:** In this method, an agreement is entered between the dealer and the company to compensate the dealer for featuring the company's product in newspaper (preferably local newspaper), handbills, wall-writing etc.

5. **Store demonstration:** In this method, demonstrations are arranged in the premises of dealers (both wholesalers and retailers) by the company's sales force. This method is used particularly in case of a new product. This demonstration is done to attract new customers in particular, to explain to them the peculiarities of the product and also to sense the doubts of the prospects on the spot. The dealers are paid by the company for store demonstration.

6. **Free advertising material:** In this method, dealers are-provided free advertising material by the company, such as signboards, store signs, bill books etc. with the dealer's name. Other free goods include fountain-pens, pencils, diaries, calendars and their publicity materials with the dealer's name etc.

7. **Free goods:** In this method, the company offers a certain quantity of the product free of cost to the dealers depending on their purchases of the same or some other product.

8. **Special sales contest:** In this method, special sales contests are conducted by the sales force of the company at different places. This is to stimulate and motivate the 'dealers to increase sales'. The dealers participate in the same. Such sales contests may take the funs of window display, internal store display etc. Cash prices are offered to those who win the contest or make the highest sales during a stated period.

9. **Count and re-count allowance:** In this method, an offer is made by the company to the wholesaler of a certain amount of money for the goods that move out of the wholesaler's godown during a stated period of time. The object of this incentive is to clear the old stock and achieve quick turnover.

10. **Free tours:** In this method, dealers who achieve more than target sales during a given period or for a certain continuous period are offered free tours to hill stations or big cities. It includes railway/bus fare, hotel charges (boarding and lodging both) and other miscellaneous expenses incurred during a given period. Some companies also provide free foreign tours.

11. **Dealers conference:** In this method, dealers' conferences are arranged by the company preferably at hill-stations or sight-seeing places. Only leading dealers are invited to attend these conferences. All the expenses of the dealers are paid by the company. Such conferences provide a platform to the company to educate the dealers about the nature of the product, policy of the company, mutual exchange of ideas and opinions and providing necessary information about their future incentive plans.

(iii) Sales force promotion methods: Sales force promotion methods are those methods which are intended to motivate the sales force to increase sales. The sales force promotion methods support a salesman to perform his job more effectively and sincerely.

Methods : The main techniques or methods of sales force promotion are as follows:

1. **Sales force contests:** In this method, special incentives in the form of prize or awards are offered over and above those provided under the regular compensation plans to sales force. The main object of organising sales force contests is to spur the sales force to increase sales and bring more profits to the company. According to Herzberg, 'Sales force contests aim at fulfilling the needs of individuals for achievement and recognition." The sales force contests are planned, organised and arranged by the company from time to time so as to motivate the sales force to increase sales.

2. **Bonus to sales force:** In this method, a sales quota is fixed to each salesman to be achieved during a fixed stated period. In case the sales during a given period exceeds the quota, the salesman is allowed a bonus on the excessive sales only. This method also induces the salesman to increase sales to the maximum. This method is employed by leading companies such as Asian Paints.

3. **Sales meetings conventions, and conferences:** In this method, sales meetings, conventions and conferences are organised by the company from time to time for the purpose of educating, inspiring and rewarding the salesmen. The new techniques of increasing sales are also discussed in such meetings and conferences.

Personal Selling

Selling may be personal or impersonal. Personal selling is a highly distinctive word and the only form of direct sales promotion involving face-to-face relationship between seller and potential customers. Personal selling is flexible and extremely effective but costly form of sales promotion. Personal selling is a two-way communication or mutual communication.

According to American Marketing Association, 'Personal selling is an oral presentation in a conversation with one or more prospective purchasers for the purpose of making sales.' According to Richard Bwhirk, 'Personal selling consists of contacting prospective buyers personally.' Personal selling is a direct, face to face, seller to buyer conversation which can communicate relevant facts about the product and the firm to the prospect so that he or she may take buying decision. Personal selling can use the psychology of persuasion most effectively so as to encourage a buying decision.

Difference Between Personal Selling and Salesmanship

Most of us think that these two terms, i.e. personal selling and salesmanship are synonymous to each other and are used without any distinction. There is a vital difference between these two terms. Personal selling is a broader concept and involves oral presentation in conversation with one or more prospective buyers for making sales. The main purpose of personal selling is to bring the product and the company to the knowledge of the prospective buyers and to convince them about the quality of the product and make certain that ownership transfer will take place. It is an effective form of sales promotion. On the contrary, salesmanship is an art of selling goods or services to the prospective buyer or buyers. It is an attempt to induce the prospective buyer to buy goods. Personal skill of the salesman is used in salesmanship. Salesmanship may be employed both in personal selling and impersonal selling (such as advertising).

Importance of Personal Selling

Personal selling is the most important ingredient in the promotion-mix. It renders valuable services to consumers, producers and the society. It is an effective form of sales promotion. Unlike advertising, personal selling is present in all the three phases of buying, namely, pre-transactional, transactional, and post-transactional. It cultivates the market, negotiates the transaction and reduces post-purchase dissonance. Personal selling in an effective medium of selling. It is the largest single cost accounting, say for 20% of net sales in several business enterprises. Besides this, there are other advantages of personal selling also. The main advantages are as follows:

1. Personal selling is more flexible and adaptable to the varying purchasing situations. Under personal selling, it is possible for the salesman to adopt himself to the needs, motives, impulses and other behavioural traits of the prospective buyers so as to communicate the message and clinch the deal.
2. In personal selling, there is minimum waste of effort and expenditure because the whole effort is focused on a qualified target, consumer/consumers. Also, there is minimum possibility of message distortion.
3. Personal selling is two-way communication between the company and its customers. Top sales management can be fully informed about many vital matters, such as, customer's reaction, market trend, competition, dealer's demand etc.
4. In personal selling, it is possible for the salesman to carry the qualified target consumer through a logical and persuasive reasoning process so as to consummate sale.
5. In personal selling, it is possible for the salesman to detect loss of consumer's attention and interest and regenerate them by frequent repetitions and reinforcements.
6. In personal selling, it is possible to develop durable relationship between salesman and the consumer which makes future sale exploration much more effective.
7. Personal selling is a powerful means of convincing the prospective buyer by presenting actual demonstration of the product or its use. Salesman is in a position to remove every possible doubt of the prospective buyers and convince them about the quality of goods and transfer of title.
8. Personal selling helps in increasing the volume of sales. It results in large-scale production and thereby reduction in cost and prices. In this way, the society may get better quality goods at a comparatively cheaper rate. Thus, "personal selling is as basic to our society as metabolism is to life."

The main objectives of personal selling

Personal selling objectives may be of short-term and long-term duration. Short-term personal selling objectives are more specific and of short-term duration. These objectives change very frequently as soon as there is change in promotion-mix. Further, they are usually quantitative objectives. On the contrary, long-term personal selling objectives are broad and general. There is very little scope of change in long-term objectives. They are usually qualitative objectives.

According to Cundiff, Still and Govani, the personal selling objectives are as follows:

1. To undertake selling job.

2. To make search for new customers.
3. To maintain regular communication with present customers.
4. To assist the customers in selling the product line.
5. To keep the customers informed about the changes in the product line and other aspects of marketing strategy.
6. To maintain and secure effective cooperation with the customers in stocking and promoting the product line.
7. To assist or handle the training of middlemen's sales - personnel.
8. To obtain the desired market information.
9. To provide necessary assistance to middlemen on various management problems.
10. To provide technical assistance to customers where the products are complicated.

    Besides the above, there are certain other personal selling objectives which may be summarised as under:

11. To increase the overall volume of sales.
12. To convince the customers about the quality of the product or products and creditability of the company.
13. To remove the doubts from the mind of the customer.
14. To keep the personal selling expenses within controllable limits.
15. To secure and retain a certain share of the market.

Public Relations

We have seen that both salesmanship and advertising help in creating in the prospect's mind a favourable image of the company and its products. This image building has become particularly important in recent years. This movement of image building activities, whether done through salesmanship, advertising or otherwise, are termed as Public Relations activities. Public relations is a new term which got momentum in 1940 and ever since it is gaining popularity in the field of commerce and industry.

According to Mr. Edward Bareney, "Public relation is the attempt by information persuasion and adjustment to engineer public support for an activity, cause, movement or institution" Thus in short, public relation is a technique of getting public support for activity, cause or movement. The most widely accepted and popular definition of public relation has been given by the Institute of Public Relations in the following words:

"Public relations practice is the deliberate, planned and sustained effort to establish and maintain mutual understanding between the organisation and the general public." Thus in short, public relations is a duly planned effort to develop the mutual understanding between the organisation (business house) and the general public. General public is a wide term and thus includes customers, dealers, shareholders, suppliers, employees, government and the community at large. Experts have identified five significant targets for public relations efforts:

(i) Consumers,

(ii) Dealers,

(iii) Employees,

(iv) Share-holders, and

(v) Community.

Besides these, there may be other target groups with which the company (business house) might wish to communicate. The main object of public relations is to secure the goodwill of the public by behaving in a manner as to please those with whom the company (business house), through its representatives, comes in contact. It is an image building activity of the company in the mind of the general public. It is, therefore, increasingly recognised that not only a business house requires good products and efficient employees, but it also needs good public relations.

The Communication Functions of Public Relations

The primary function of the public relations is to create a favourable image of the company and its products in the mind of the public by communicating the policies, practices, performances and achievements to the public. Public is a very wide term which includes consumers, dealers, employees, share-holders, government and the community at large. Now we shall discuss how the public relations communicates with the various sections of the public.

1. **Communicating with Consumers:** The goodwill and image of the company and its products in the mind of the consumers is a dominant factor for the success of the business enterprise. A favourable image must be created both about the product of the company as well as the company itself in the mind of the consumers. Consumer relations activities include providing proper information regarding company's history, background, policies, objectives and nature as well as quality of products. The knowledge of consumer's mind about the company and its products can be studied through surveys, research and project etc. The consumers should be kept well informed from time to time about the availability and the quality of the products. Attempts should also be made to adjust the company's products, policies and practices to meet the consumer's preference. Every possible effort should be made to find out the consumer's need and then indicate how a suitable product will meet that need and provide satisfaction to the consumers. It should also be noted that the total personality or image of a company as well as its products not only lies in product's advertising, packaging and the appearance of the products but also in institutional advertising and public relation activities.

2. **Communicating with Dealers:** Since it is neither possible nor practicable for any company to contact each and every consumer directly for the sale of its products, the communication with dealers by the company is called for. It is true, particularly in case of large manufacturers, who totally depend on dealers to sell their products. The dealers represent the manufacturers to the public and to the community at large of which he is a part. Therefore, good dealer relationship becomes most important for them. Thus dealer's relations are a key note in any company's public relations programme mainly in India.

3. **Communicating with Employees:** Strikes, lockouts, gheraos are a clear-cut indication of poor employer-employee relations. It affects the production and the progress adversely. It is mainly due to communication gap between the employer and the employees. No doubt, this is the area of personnel department, but the public relation can also play an important role in this connection. A good company always tries to build up loyalty amongst its employees and motivates them to higher productivity or better performance. The public relations department can assist the personnel department in its efforts to bring about improved working conditions, grievance procedures, promotional policies, employee's - training, career-planning, education, health and other welfare activities.

4. **Communicating with Share-holders:** A share-holder is a person who has invested money in the company. He, therefore, naturally expects a reasonable return on his investment, keeping in view the risk he is taking by investing his money in the company. Thus, good company-shareholders relationship cannot be built up if the company is not fair to them in the declaration of proper dividends every year besides holding regular meetings etc. Besides the declaration and payment of dividends regularly, good companies also try in different ways to build up better company-shareholders relations. For instance, the attractive annual report, which is an important means of communication, creates good image of the company in the mind of the share-holders. Some companies (such as Reliance Industries) even send coupons to their share-holders which entitle them to purchase the company's products at a special discount.

5. Communicating with the Community: Communication with the community is most essential for developing goodwill and favourable image of the company in the minds of the general public. It is, therefore, necessary for every company to realise its social responsibility towards the community at large. After all, the share-holders, consumers, dealers, employees or even the company itself is an integral part of the community. Effective communication with the community can be established through:

(i) Providing donations to charitable institutions

(ii) Providing educational facilities by establishing schools and colleges and also providing scholarships to poor and brilliant students

(iii) Encouraging family planning programmes

(iv) Adoption of a code of fair trade practices

(v) Assisting in the removal poverty, backwardness and ignorance etc.

Publicity

Publicity is a part of marketing and customer relations. Publicity is also non-personal communication about an organization or its products that is transmitted through a mass medium in the form of news but is not paid for by the organization. Publicity comes from news reporters, columnists and journalists. Publicity is a part of a larger set of communication activities called public relation, which is designed to create and maintain a favourable image of an organization and may be paid or non-paid. Public relation and publicity taken together are one of the four major ingredients of promotion-mix.

Difference between Advertising and Publicity

1. Advertising is informative as well as persuasive.	1. Publicity is informative but not persuasive.
2. Advertising is a paid form of communication.	2. Publicity is a non-paid mention of an organisation.
3. Advertisement is issued by an identified sponsor.	3. Publicity does not need an identified sponsor.
4. Control over the type, size, duration and frequency of the message lies with advertiser.	4. Control lies with the publicity media.
5. Advertisements are generally repeated.	5. Publicity messages are generally not repeated.

Every firm tries to create a good public relation so as to get good publicity through press and electronic media. Publicity is mainly due to good response of customers, or due to quality or can be even due to some controversies.

Forms of Publicity

The various forms of publicity used by an organization are new release which is a form of publicity that is usually a single page of typewritten copy about a news worthy event and is sent to news editors for possible publication. Feature article is a form of publicity that is upto three thousand words in length and is usually prepared for a specific publication. Captioned photograph is a photograph with a brief description explaining the people or event pictured. News conference is a meeting with media representatives to give major news events. Editorial film or tape is a tape or film distributed to broadcast station or newspapers in the hope that its contents will be used in news stories.

DIRECT MARKETING

Direct marketing is a form of advertising that reaches its audience without using traditional formal channels of advertising such as TV, newspapers or radio. Businesses communicate straight to the consumer with advertising techniques such as fliers, catalogue distribution, promotional letters, and street advertising.

Direct Advertising is a sub-discipline and type of marketing. There are two main definitional characteristics which distinguish it from other types of marketing. The first is that it sends its message directly to consumers, without the use of intervening commercial communication media. The second characteristic is the core principle of successful advertising driving a specific "call to action." This aspect of direct marketing involves an emphasis on trackable, measurable, positive responses from consumers (known simply as "response" in the industry) regardless of medium.

If the advertisement asks the prospect to take a specific action, for instance call a free phone number or visit a website, then the effort is considered to be direct response advertising. Direct marketing is predominantly used by small to medium-size enterprises with limited advertising budgets that do not have a well-recognized brand message. A well-executed direct advertising campaign can offer a positive return on investment as the message is not hidden with overcomplicated branding. Instead, direct advertising is straight to the point offers a product, service, or event; and explains how to get the offered product, service, or event.

Advantages and disadvantages

Direct marketing is attractive to many marketers, because in many cases its positive effect (but not negative results) can be measured directly. For example, if a marketer sends out 1,000 solicitations by mail, and 100 respond to the promotion, the marketer can say with confidence that campaign led directly to 10% direct responses. The number of recipients who are offended by junk mail/spam, however, is not easily measured. By contrast, measurement of other media must often be indirect, since there is no direct response from a consumer.

The Internet has made it easier for marketing managers to measure the results of a campaign. This is often achieved by using a specific website landing page directly relating to the promotional material, a call to action will ask the consumer to visit the landing page, and the effectiveness of the campaign can be measured by taking the number of promotional messages distributed (e.g., 1,000) and dividing it by the number of responses (people visiting the unique web site page). Another way to measure the results is to compare the projected sales for a given term with the actual sales after a direct advertising campaign.

While many marketers recognise the financial benefits of increasing targeted awareness, some direct marketing efforts using particular media have been criticised for generating unwanted solicitations, not due to the method of communication but because of poorly compiled demographic databases, advertisers do not wish to waste money on communicating with consumers not interested in their products. For example, direct mail that is irrelevant to the recipient is considered "junk mail," and unwanted e-mail messages are considered "spam." Some consumers are demanding an end to direct marketing for privacy and environmental reasons, which direct marketers are able to do to some extent by using "opt-out" lists, variable printing, and more-targeted mailing lists. In response to consumer demand and increasing business pressure to increase the effectiveness of reaching the right consumer with direct marketing, companies such as Ireland Advertising specialises in targeted direct advertising to great effect, reducing advertising budget waste and increasing the effectiveness of delivering a marketing message with better geodemography information, delivering the advertising message to only the consumers interested in the product, service, or event on offer.

Tools of Direct Marketing

- Direct Mail
- Telemarketing
- Email Marketing
- Door-to-Door Leaflet Marketing
- Broadcast faxing
- Voicemail Marketing
- Couponing
- Direct-response television marketing
- Direct selling

MULTIPLE CHOICE QUESTIONS

1. .... includes those sales activities that supplement both personal selling and advertising and coordinate them and make them effective such as displays, shows, demonstrations and other non-recurrent selling efforts not in the ordinary routine.
(*a*) Advertising (*b*) Sales promotion
(*c*) Product mix (*d*) All of these
(*e*) None of these

2. Selling is:
(*a*) Impersonal Activity
(*b*) Personal Activity
(*c*) Both (*a*) and (*b*)
(*d*) Public Activity
(*e*) None of these

3. Which of the following is the function of selling?
(*a*) Customer Services
(*b*) Sale Contract
(*c*) Contractual Function
(*d*) Above all
(*e*) None of these

4. Which of the following is true about selling?
(*a*) It is a product
(*a*) It is a productive activity
(*c*) It is a technique of production
(*d*) All of these
(*e*) None of these

5. Match the following:

List-I	**List-II**
1. Advertising	A. TV
2. Packaging	B. Colour
3. Sales promotion	C. Coupon
4. Public Relation	D. Physical Control
	E. Economic Control

Codes:

	1	2	3	4
(*a*)	A	B	C	D
(*b*)	B	A	C	E
(*c*)	A	E	D	C
(*d*)	E	C	A	B
(*e*)	A	E	D	C

6. Selling includes:
(*a*) Advertising (*b*) Sales promotion
(*c*) Publicity (*d*) Above all
(*e*) None of these

7. ... Selling is informing and persuading a market about a:
(*a*) Product (*b*) Cost
(*c*) Price (*d*) Sale
(*e*) None of these

8. Sales promotion is essential due to:
(*a)* Maximisation of sales
(*b)* Employment
(*c*) Production
(*d)* All of these
(*e*) None of these

9. Tools of sales promotion include:
(*a*) Packaging
(*b*) Advertising
(*c*) Personal Selling
(*d*) Above all
(*e*) None of these

10. Determinant of sales promotion is:
(*a*) Nature of Market
(*b*) Product Life Cycle
(*c*) Nature of Product
(*d*) Above all
(*e*) None of these

11. Which of the following is the objective of sales promotion?
(*a*) To attract new customer
(*b*) To introduce new products
(*c*) Expansion of sales
(*d*) Above all
(*e*) None of these

12. Which of the following is the tool of sales promotion in marketing?
(*a*) Premium (*b*) Coupons
(*c*) Free Samples (*d*) Above all
(*e*) None of these

13. Example of middlemen is:
(*a*) Wholesaler (*b*) Customer
(*c*) Producer (*d*) All of these
(*e*) None of these

14. Which of the following is the advantage of sales promotion?
(*a*) Low price product
(*b*) Thrill in the life due to contests
(*c*) Skill development of the users
(*d*) Above all
(*e*) None of these

15. Example of defective product is:
(*a*) Better quality product
(*b*) Eco-friendly product
(*c*) Power wastages machine
(*d*) Low price product
(*e*) None of these

16. Performance of salesmen can be evaluated by:
(*a*) Report on lost of business
(*b*) Report on future activities
(*c*) Report on expenses
(*d*) Above all
(*e*) None of these

17. The right of patent's use is known as:
(*a*) Assets (*b*) Royalty
(*c*) Commission (*d*) Producer
(*e*) None of these

18. Who is Prospect Customers?
(*a*) Potential Customer
(*b*) Present Customer
(*c*) Staff
(*d*) Past & Present Customer
(*e*) None of these

19. Selling cost is:
(*a*) Selling Expenses
(*b*) Incremental Cost
(*c*) Salary of Salesman
(*d*) Above all
(*e*) None of these

20. Consumer loan taken by a customer on any consumer item, it is a contract of:
(*a*) Hire Purchase Agreement
(*b*) Contract of Sale
(*c*) Capital
(*d*) Control of Price
(*e*) None of these

21. Which of the following is the promotional media?
(*a*) Publication
(*b*) Printing
(*c*) Internet marketing
(*d*) Above all
(*e*) None of these

22. E-CRM stands for:
(*a*) E-Cost Rate Mail
(*b*) E-Cost Roll Mail
(*c*) Electronic Customer Relationship Management
(*d*) All of these
(*e*) None of these

23. 'AIDA' is related to:
(*a*) Advertising (*b*) Branding
(*c*) Packaging (*d*) Selling
(*e*) None of these

24. Which of the following is the source of outdoor advertising?
(*a*) Hoarding (*b*) Posters
(*c*) Neon Signs (*d*) Above all
(*e*) None of these

25. Which of the following is the source of print media?
(*a*) News papers (*b*) Magazines
(*c*) Trade Journals (*d*) Above all
(*e*) None of these

26. Which of the following is the source of electronic media?
(*a*) Radio (*b*) Television
(*c*) Internet (*d*) Above all
(*e*) None of these

27. Publicity is a:
(*a*) Promotional mix
(*b*) Advertising devices
(*c*) Production and development tool
(*d*) All of these
(*e*) None of these

28. Which of the following is the consumer promotion device?
(*a*) Exchange of Coupons
(*b*) Consumer Contests
(*c*) Premium
(*d*) Above all
(*e*) None of these

29. Match the following:

List-I (Factors of Selling)	**List-II (Nature)**
1. Advertising	A. Radio
2. Publicity	B. No Paid Mode
3. Sales Promotion	C. Coupon
4. Public Relations	D. Physical Contract
	E. Car

Codes :

	1	2	3	4
(*a*)	A	B	C	D
(*b*)	E	D	C	A
(*c*)	C	A	E	D
(*d*)	C	E	B	A
(*e*)	A	B	E	C

30. .... has been defined as any paid form of non-personal presentation and promotion of ideas, goods or services by an identified sponsor.
(*a*) Advertising (*b*) Packaging
(*c*) Branding (*d*) Selling
(*e*) None of these

31. Which of the following is the objective of Advertising?
(*a*) To introduce new product
(*b*) To remind the customers
(*c*) To build brand preference
(*d*) Above all
(*e*) None of these

32. Which of the following is the component of advertising planning?
(*a*) Research
(*b*) Cost
(*c*) Selection of media
(*d*) Above all
(*e*) None of these

33. Which of the following is the source of Bank advertising?
(*a*) Television (*b*) Posters
(*c*) Magazine (*d*) Above all
(*e*) None of these

34. Requirements of a good advertising policy is:
(*a*) Understandable (*b*) Believable
(*c*) Arousing Interest (*d*) Above all
(*e*) None of these

35. In advertising selection of media depends on:
(*a*) Cost of media (*b*) Nature of market
(*c*) Nature of product (*d*) Above all
(*e*) None of these

36. Which of the following is the demerits of advertising?
(*a*) Wastage of money
(*b*) Reduction of ethics
(*c*) False information
(*d*) Above all
(*e*) None of these

37. Budget of advertising depends on:
(*a*) Types of media
(*b*) Period of advertising
(*c*) Area of advertising
(*d*) Above all
(*e*) None of these

38. Match the following:

List-I	**List-II**
1. Purchase Point Advertising	A. Window display
2. Mail advertising	B. Sales letter
3. Outdoor advertising	C. Mural or wall writing
4. Press advertising	D. Magazine
	E. Advertising

Codes :

	1	2	3	4
(*a*)	A	B	C	D
(*b*)	B	A	D	E
(*c*)	E	B	D	C
(*d*)	B	A	E	D
(*e*)	C	A	D	E

39. Which of the following is the principle of effective advertising?
(*a*) Attractive headline
(*b*) Using of pictures
(*c*) Simple language
(*d*) Above all
(*e*) None of these

40. Selection of media of advertising is based on:
(*a*) Nature of product
(*b*) Nature of market
(*c*) Nature of demand
(*d*) Above all
(*e*) None of these

41. Media of advertising is affected by:
(*a*) Quality of product
(*b*) Cost of media
(*c*) Nature of market
(*d*) Above all
(*e*) None of these

42. Advertising derived from:
(*a*) Credere (*b*) Advertere
(*c*) Adre (*d*) Net
(*e*) None of these

43. Advertising may be:
(*a*) Non-personal presentation
(*b*) Personal presentation
(*c*) Negative
(*d*) Positive
(*e*) None of these

ANSWERS

1	**2**	**3**	**4**	**5**	**6**	**7**	**8**	**9**	**10**
(*b*)	(*c*)	(*d*)	(*b*)	(*a*)	(*d*)	(*a*)	(*a*)	(*d*)	(*d*)
11	**12**	**13**	**14**	**15**	**16**	**17**	**18**	**19**	**20**
(*d*)	(*d*)	(*a*)	(*d*)	(*c*)	(*d*)	(*b*)	(*a*)	(*d*)	(*a*)
21	**22**	**23**	**24**	**25**	**26**	**27**	**28**	**29**	**30**
(*d*)	(*c*)	(*a*)	(*d*)	(*d*)	(*d*)	(*a*)	(*d*)	(*a*)	(*a*)
31	**32**	**33**	**34**	**35**	**36**	**37**	**38**	**39**	**40**
(*d*)	(*d*)	(*d*)	(*d*)	(*d*)	(*d*)	(*d*)	(*a*)	(*d*)	(*d*)
41	**42**	**43**							
(*d*)	(*b*)	(*a*)							

☞ CHAPTER-10

BRANDING

INTRODUCTION

Products are what companies make, but customers buy the brands and therefore, marketers resort to branding in order to distinguish their offering from similar products and services provided by their competitors. Additionally, it carries an inherent assurance to the customers that the quality of a purchase will be similar to earlier purchases of the same brand.

The branding of a product is like a new born child at it basically serves to identify the new kid. Since the early times, producers of goods have used their brands or marks to distinguish their products. Pride in their products has no doubt played a part in this. More particularly, by identifying their products they have provided purchasers with a means of recognising and specifying them, should they wish to repurchases or recommend the products to others,

Branding has been around for centuries as a means of distinguishing the goods of one producer from those of another. In fact, the word brand is derived from the old Norse word "brandr" which means to burn. As brands were and still are the means by which owners of livestock mark their animals to identify them.

The use of brands has developed considerably, especially in the last century. Indeed, the words 'brand' and branding are now such common currency that their original meaning is in danger of being wreaked. However, the function of a brand as distinguishing the goods of one produce from those of another and of thus allowing consumer freedom of choice has remained unaltered.

The word **"Branding"** immediately reminds us of Sony, Samsung, Whirlpool, LG., Reliance, Tata, The Times of India, Raymond's, Coca-Cola and many others. It is commonly felt that the brand is related with the big corporates only, but the fact is something else. Even the street tailor or the namkeen wala needs Branding. Because it is the only way through which these people can survive in present highly competitive market.

Buying decisions of the consumers up to a great extent are based on brand perception. Branding has a unique and vital role in the effective marketing of products. A brand is associated with a familiar logo. Whenever we come across this logo, we think of the brand and the whole value package it represents and the promise it carries. This is the way it is supposed to work. A brand starts as a product and a name. But much can be built on that name.

Definitions

A brand by definition, is a short hand description of a package of value, on which consumers can rely to be consistently the same or better over a period of time. A brand distinguishing a product or services from competitive offering

Branding is the process by which a marketer tries to build a long-term relationship with the customers by learning their needs and wants so that the offering (Brand) could satisfy their mutual aspirations. Branding can be viewed as a tool to position a product or a services, with a consistent image of quality and value for money, to ensure the development of a recurring preferences by the consumer.

According to American Marketing Association (AMA), a brand is a name, term, sign, symbol or design or a combination of them ,intended to identify the goods and services of one seller or group of seller and to differentiate them form those of competition.

David Ogilvy defines brand as "the consumer idea of a product". A brand distinguishes a product or services from similar offering on the basis of unique features perceived by the consumers. The best examples of brand names are Lux, Liril, Rexona, Evita, Hamam in case of toilet soap, Surf and Nirma in case of detergent and Nivea, Charmis and Fair Lovely in case of vanishing cream. Other examples of successful brand are; Sunsilk, Surf, Wheel, Brooke Bond, Pond's etc.

According to Al Ries and Laura Ries (1998), "a brand is a singular idea or concept that you own inside the mind of the prospect." A commonly accepted definition by David Aaker is " A brand is distinguishing name and /or symbol such as a logo, trademark or package design intended to indentify goods or services of either one seller or group of seller and to differentiate those from competitor. Technically, whenever a marketer creates a new logo or symbol for a new product, he or she has created brand. A brand is therefore a product but one that adds other dimensions that differentiate it in some way from other products designed to satisfy the same need. Ultimately a brand is something that resides in the minds of consumer.

From the analysis of above definitions the following characteristics may be identified with regard to brand:

- It is the name of the product.
- It includes any symbol, term, design or a combination of them.
- It is used for the purpose of identification of marketer's products or services.
- It is used to differentiate the products or services from those of competitors.
- Brand name is vocalised part of brand and has its own personality.
- When name is registered, it becomes trade mark.

EVOLUTION OF BRANDS

Branding is the technique of marketing process to a specific product, product line, or brand. It seeks to increase the product's perceived value to the customer and thereby increase brand franchise and brand equity. Marketers see a brand as an implied promise that the level of quality people have come to expect from a brand will continue with future purchases of the same product. This may increase sales by making a comparison with competing products more favourable. It may also enable the manufacturer to charge more for the product. Thus, the value of the brand is determined by the amount of profit it generates for the manufacturer. This can result from a combination of increased sales and increased price, and/or reduced COGS (cost of goods sold), and/or reduced or more efficient marketing investment. All of these enhancements may improve the profitability of a brand, and thus, "Brand Managers" often carry line management accountability for a brand's P&L (Profit and Loss) profitability, in contrast to marketing staff manager roles, which are allocated budgets from above, to manage and execute. In this regard, Brand Management is often viewed in organisations as a broader and more strategic role than Marketing alone.

Although connected with the history of trademarks and including earlier examples which could be deemed "protobrands" (such as the marketing puns of the "Vesuvinum" wine jars found at Pompeii), brands in the field of mass-marketing originated in the 19th century with the advent of packaged goods. Industrialisation moved the production of many household items, such as soap, from local communities to centralised factories. When shipping their items, the factories would literally brand their logo or insignia on the barrels used, extending the meaning of "brand" to that of trademark. Bass & Company, the British brewery, claims their red triangle brand was the world's first trademark. Lyle's Golden Syrup makes a similar claim, having been named as Britain's oldest brand, with its green and gold packaging having remained almost unchanged since 1885. Cattle were branded long before this; the term "maverick", originally meaning an unbranded calf, comes from Texas rancher Samuel Augustus Maverick who, following the American Civil War, decided that since all other cattle were branded, his would be identified by having no markings at all. Even the signatures on paintings of famous artists like Leonardo Da Vinci can be viewed as an early branding tool.

Factories established during the Industrial Revolution introduced mass-produced goods and needed to sell their products to a wider market, to customers previously familiar only with locally-produced goods. It quickly became apparent that a generic package of soap had difficulty competing with familiar, local products. The packaged goods manufacturers needed to convince the market that the public could place just as much trust in the non-local product. Campbell soup, Coca-Cola, Juicy Fruit gum, Aunt Jemima, and Quaker Oats were among the first products to be 'branded', in an effort to increase the consumer's familiarity with their products. Many brands of that era, such as Uncle Ben's rice and Kellogg's breakfast cereal furnish illustrations of the problem.

Around 1900, James Walter Thompson published a house ad explaining trademark advertising. This was an early commercial explanation of what we now know as branding. Companies soon adopted slogans, mascots, and jingles that began to appear on radio and early television. By the 1940s, manufacturers began to recognise the way in which consumers were developing relationships with their brands in a social/psychological/anthropological sense.

From there, manufacturers quickly learnt to build their brand's identity and personality such as youthfulness, fun or luxury. This began the practice we now know as "branding" today, where the consumers buy "the brand" instead of the product. This trend continued to the 1980s, and is now quantified in concepts such as **brand value** and **brand equity**. Naomi Klein has described this development as "brand equity mania". In 1988, for example, Philip Morris purchased Kraft for six times what the company was worth on paper; it was felt that what they really purchased was its **brand name**.

Marlboro Friday: April 2, 1993 - marked by some as the death of the brand - the day Philip Morris declared that they were to cut the price of Marlboro cigarettes by 20%, in order to compete with bargain cigarettes. Marlboro cigarettes were notorious at the time for their heavy advertising campaigns, and well-nuanced brand image. In response to the announcement Wall Street stocks nose-dived for a large number of 'branded' companies: Heinz, Coca Cola, Quaker Oats, PepsiCo. Many thought the event signalled the beginning of a trend towards "brand blindness" (Klein 13), questioning the power of "brand value".

Thus, branding involves decisions that establish an identity for a product with the goal of distinguishing it from competitors' offerings. In markets where competition is fierce and where customers may select from among many competitive products, creating an identity through branding is essential. It is particularly important in helping position the product (see discussion of product position) in the minds of the product's target market.

While consumer products companies have long recognised the value of branding, it has only been within the last 10-15 years that organisations selling component products in the business-to-business market have begun to focus on brand building strategies. The most well-known company to brand components is Intel with its now famous "Intel Inside" slogan. Intel's success has led many other b-to-b companies and even non-profits to incorporate branding within their overall marketing strategy.

LEVELS OF BRAND

As we have discussed that a brand is a "name, term, sign, symbol or design or a combination of them, intended to identify the goods and services of one seller or group of sellers and to differentiate them from those of competition. In other sense, a brand is the proprietary, visual, emotional, rational and cultural image that one associates with a company or a product. It is always clubbed with a communication message, which it wants to be communicated to the consumers.

Levels of Brand

As Brand can also be considered in terms of four levels:

(i) Generic: It is the commodity level which satisfies the basic needs such as transportations. It is so easy to imitate a generic product. A brand continues to add values so as to reach the expected level

(ii) Expected: generic is modified to satisfy some minimum buying conditions such as functional performance, pricing, availability etc.

(iii) Augmented: Brand is refined further by adding non functional values along with the functional ones. We may direct advertising to the social prestige, the possessor of the brand is likely to enjoy.

(iv) Potential: As brand evolves, we become more critical. Creativity plays an important role to grow up the brand to its full potential. If no creative effort is taken, there is danger of the brand relapsing to its augmented or expected level.

Consumers are rarely prepared to pay a premium for products or services that simply deliver core benefits – they are the expected elements of that justify a core price. Successful brands are those that deliver added value in addition to the core benefits. These added values enable the brand to differentiate itself from the competition. When done well, the customer recognises the added value in an augmented product and chooses that brand in preference. For example, a consumer may be looking for reassurance or a guarantee of quality in a situation where he or she is unsure about what to buy. A brand like Mercedes, Sony or Microsoft can offer this reassurance or guarantee.

Alternatively, the consumer may be looking for the brand to add meaning to his or her life in terms of lifestyle or personal image. Brands such as Nike, Porsche or Timberland do this. A brand can usefully be represented in the classic "fried-egg" format shown below, where the brand is shown to have core features that are surrounded (or "augmented") by less tangible features.

SIGNIFICANCE OF BRANDING

Branding generally communicates following aspects to enhance the brand image, personality and loyalty.

Thus, a brand communicates:

- Attributes
- Benefits
- Values
- Culture
- Personality
- Target User
- **Attributes:** Brands highlight the product attributes to inform existing customers and to attract potential customers. For example Style, Fashion, and high quality premium clothing are the attributes of the Raymond's.
- **Benefits:** As we know that customers buys the benefits rather than attributes thus the attributes eventually transform into emotional and functional benefits, for the brand to be successful. with the same example of Raymond's if we consider the above attributes, style fashion and modernity will transform into emotional benefits, while high quality will transform into functional benefits like the consumers not having to spend frequently on clothes.
- **Values:** Most brands associate some value with themselves. for instances, the baseline of Raymond's The Complete Man,' communicates a value preposition that their clothing makes a man complete and perfect.
- **Culture:** Brands also represents a certain culture, again Raymond's projects a culture of family bonding (Father, son, husband and wife) and no above all Indian-ness in its advertisement.
- **Personality:** Further brand communicates a type of personality. Raymond's suggest that it is a brand for a man, who cares for his family, society, and himself.
- **Target user:** Brands clearly states their user segments. Raymond's a target the upper middle and upper class customers.

FEATURES OF A BRANDING

Selection of brand name is crucial for the success for a brand. There were several factors that have to be considered before the brand is selected. Thus, it is necessary to ensure that the brand name should be acceptable, pronounceable, memorisable and recognisable in the language of the target audience. A good brand name should possess as many of the following characteristics as possible.

- **It should be distinctive:** The market is filled with over-worked names and over-used symbols. A unique and distinctive symbol is not only easy to remember but also is a distinguishing features. Adidas shoes and Kodak films are distinctive names.
- **It should be simple:** It is desirable to have short names which are easy to read, speak and understand. It should be easy to pronounce and spell. Tide and Surf are examples of such names. With limited capacity to process names, consumers find it easy to encode short words in in their memory. Consumers even tend to shorten long names, e.g. Coca-Cola becomes Coke and Pepsi Cola, Pepsi. Even when consumers become emotionally involved with the brand, they shorten its name, e.g. Merc for Mercedes.
- **It should be meaningful:** brand name should be suggestive of quality, superiority or personality or such attributes. They should communicate consumer benefits. Creativity should be encouraged. Promise is suggestive of an assurance of toothpaste. VIP classic for travel wares of a superior quality for distinctiveness class of people.
- **It should be flexible:** In a hanging market, a brand name should be flexible and should adopt to the new situation of changing market needs. Thus, Caterpillar tractor dropped tractor from the brand names to diversify into earth moving equipment. Videocon is not a nickname for washing machines and air-conditioners. Hotline is good for gas burners, but not for TV.
- **It should be registrable:** Brand name must be prosecutable under the Indian laws of Trademark and copyright. There should be a search to confirm whether the chosen name is available.
- **It should be universally valid:** While naming a brand, its geographically market must be considered. When limited to a nation with a homogeneous culture, it is easier to understand its cultural association. But when it goes to across the cultures, it is necessary to understand the culture diversity. Big Macs form Mc Donald's is Canadian slang for big breast.

Thus, brand name should be shortlisted. It is necessary to do some consumer research. There is debate and discussion. Then finally name is chosen. There should be regular audit of the name chosen. It may be necessary to change the name considering the changing environment. Further, a brand name can be descriptive such as Close-up, Frooti, Fair and Lovely or suggestive such as Pampers, surf or free-standing such as Xerox Kodak.

ADVANTAGES AND DISADVANTAGES OF BRANDING

There are many advantages to a company that build the successful brands. Traditionally, a brand provides the following advantages to the company:

- Higher prices
- Higher profit margins
- Better distribution
- Customer loyalty

But apart from these, a strong brand also offers many advantages and disadvantages to marketers and customers both; these includes:

Advantages to Marketers

(i) **Customer recognition:** Brands provide multiple sensory stimuli to enhance customer recognition. For example, a brand can be visually recognisable from its packaging, logo, shape, etc. It can also be recognisable via sound, such as hearing the name on a radio advertisement or talking with someone who mentions the product.

(ii) Brand Loyalty: Customers who are frequent and enthusiastic purchasers of a particular brand are likely to become brand loyal. Cultivating brand loyalty among customers is the ultimate reward for successful marketers since these customers are far less likely to be enticed to switch to other brands compared to non-loyal customers.

(iii) Effective positioning: Well-developed and promoted brands make product positioning efforts more effective. The result is that upon exposure to a brand (e.g., hearing it, seeing it) customers conjure up mental images or feelings of the benefits they receive from using that brand. When customers associate benefits with a particular brand, the brand may have attained a significant competitive advantage. In these situations the customer who recognises the needs of a solution to problem (e.g., needs to bleach clothes) may automatically think of one brand that offers the solution to the problem (e.g., Clorox). This "benefit = brand" association provides a significant advantage for the brand that the customer associates with the benefit sought.

(iv) Extension of brand image: Firms that establish a successful brand can extend the brand by adding new products under the same "family" brand. Such branding may allow companies to introduce new products more easily since the brand is already recognised within the market.

(v) Financial advantage: Strong brands can lead to financial advantages through the concept of Brand Equity in which the brand itself becomes valuable. Such gains can be realised through the out-right sale of a brand or through licensing arrangements.

Advantages and Disadvantage to buyers

Advantages to buyers

(i) A brand name denotes uniform quality. With it the consumers have the assurance of quality when they buy the products having a particular name.

(ii) Brand names make shopping easier. The customer has to spend less time and energy in buying as brand names make product identification easier. Moreover, the customer has to go to the market and buy the products for the brands he prefers without wasting time.

(iii) Purchasing a socially visible brand gives immense psychological satisfaction to the buyer.

(iv) Competition among brands can and does, in due course of time, lead to quality improvement.

Disadvantages to buyers:

(i) The product price tends to go up.

(ii) Manufactures, taking advantages of the popularity of their brand names, may reduce the quality gradually.

(iii) Branding creates confusion. Consumers are not able to decide which brand is the best in quality, because all the brands claim to be best ever in quality.

BRANDING POLICY

Major branding policies may be discussed under the following heads:

(i) Non Branding Policy: As the name suggests, under this policy the marketing company opts not to use a brand name for its products. Marketing company use this policy when conducive conditions for branding is not prevailing. In this situation, the marketing company sells its products without using brand name.

(ii) Individual Branding Policy: This is also known as multi-branding. In this policy, the marketing company adopts distinctive brand name for each of its products. For example **HLL and Nestle,** which are the mega multi-national companies, generally use individual branding for their products. Individual branding has certain advantages and disadvantages also:

Advantages of Individual Branding:

1. The personality of each brand can be generated through superior promotional campaign for distinctive characteristics of each product.
2. Failure of any brand does not make any effect on other brands.
3. Company can acquire large sales with so many individual brands.
4. Individual branding provides enormous help in maintaining overall profitability; because decline in sales of one brand can be offset by growth of sales of another brand.

Disadvantages of Individual Branding:

1. The use of individual branding requires huge funds to promote each brand separately in the target market.
2. Not only to promote, but funds are continuously required for maintenance and growth of all brands.
3. It is uneconomical for small marketing companies.
4. It is also difficult to find suitable brand names, where the product-mix of the firm is very large.

(iii) Family Branding Policy: This is also known as umbrella branding. In this family branding policy, the marketing company generally use single brand for its entire product-mix. The firm may adopt different branding approaches for its different product lines. For example Tata, Godrej, Bata,Videocon, BPL etc.

Advantages of Family Branding:

1. The market acceptance of a new product becomes easier due to already earned image and reputation of the marketing company.
2. Family branding increase the speed of product adoption, because customers do not hesitate in buying the new product of their trusted company.
3. Promotional cost are very low as number of products may be advertised simultaneously.
4. This branding policy provides co-operation to form the members of channels of distribution. Retailers find it easier to push new products having a popular brand name.

Disadvantages of Family Branding:

1. Under this policy it becomes difficult to develop an individual personality for the each brand.
2. Products offered under the family brand name have to maintain equal quality standards, which is not an easy task.
3. Negative brand image of one product can make adverse impact on the other products of the company.

(iv) Combination Branding Policy: This is also known as mixed branding. In this policy, company markets some products by its own brands and hands over the remaining part to middlemen for branding. A combination brand name brings together a family brand name and an individual brand name. The idea here is to provide some association for the product with a strong family brand name but maintaining some distinctiveness so that customers know what they are getting. Examples of combination brand names include Microsoft XP and Microsoft Office in personal computing software and Heinz Tomato Ketchup and Heinz Pet Foods.

BRANDING DECISIONS

Branding strategy starts from the decision whether to put the brand name on a product or not. It is usually believed that for homogeneous and non differentiated products. Branding does not make sense. Salt was previously considered a generic product till Tata started branding it as Tata salt. Now the market is flooded with branded salt. Similarly, sugar, a non differentiated product may well become a branded product soon. Previously, we also knew Bharat Sanchar Nigam Limited (BSNL) as only telecom services provider, now the market is replete with telecom service providers such as Idea Reliance, Vodafone, Airtel and Tata Telecom. Even branding is slowly catching up in the staple food markets, too, where rice, vegetable, bread are branded into packaged of local/global chain retailers like Walmart and Food World.

Branding poses several challenges to the marketer. The first is whether or not to brand, the second is how to handle brand sponsorship, the third is choosing a brand name, the fourth is deciding on brand strategy, and the fifth is whether to reposition a brand later on.

To Brand or Not to Brand?

The first decision is whether the company should develop a brand name for its product. Branding is such a strong force today that hardly anything goes unbranded, including salt, oranges, nuts and bolts, and a growing number of fresh food products such as chicken and turkey. In some cases, there has been a return to **"no branding"** of certain staple consumer goods and pharmaceuticals. *Generics* are unbranded, plainly packaged, less expensive versions of common products such as spaghetti or paper towels. They offer standard or lower quality at a price that may be as much as 20 percent to 40 percent lower than nationally advertised brands and 10 percent to 20 percent lower than retailer private-label brands. The lower price is made possible by lower-quality ingredients, lower-cost labeling and packaging, and minimal advertising.

Sellers brand their products, despite the costs, because they gain a number of advantages: The brand makes it easier for the seller to process orders; the seller's brand name and trademark legally protect unique product features; branding allows sellers to attract loyal, profitable customers and offers some protection from competition; branding helps the seller segment markets by offering different brands with different features for different benefit-seeking segments; and strong brands help build the corporate image, easing the way for new brands and wider acceptance by distributors and customers.

Distributors and retailers want brands because they make the product easier to handle, indicate certain quality standards, strengthen buyer preferences, and make it easier to identify suppliers. For their part, customers find that brand names help them distinguish quality differences and shop more efficiently.

Brand-Sponsor Decision

A manufacturer has several options with respect to brand sponsorship. The product may be launched as a manufacturer brand (sometimes called a national brand), a distributor brand (also called reseller, store, house, or private brand), or a licensed brand name. Another alternative is for the manufacturer to produce some output under its own name and some under reseller labels. Kellogg, John Deere, and IBM sell virtually all of their output under their own brand names, whereas Whirlpool produces both under its own name and under distributors' names (Sears Kenmore appliances).

Although manufacturers' brands dominate, large retailers and wholesalers have been developing their own brands by contracting production from willing manufacturers. Sears has created several names—Diehard batteries, Craftsman tools, Kenmore appliances—that command brand preference and even brand loyalty. Retailers such as The Body Shop and Gap sell mostly own-brand merchandise. Sainsbury, Britain's largest food chain, sells 50 percent store-label goods, and its operating margins are six times those of U.S. retailers (U.S. supermarkets average 19.7 percent private-brand sales).

Why do middlemen sponsor their own brands? First, these brands are more profitable, since they are produced at a low cost by manufacturers with excess capacity. Other costs, such as research and development, advertising, sales promotion, and physical distribution, are also much lower. This means that the private brander can charge a lower price and yet make a higher profit margin. Second, retailers develop exclusive store brands to differentiate themselves from competitors. In years past, consumers viewed the brands in a category arranged in a brand ladder, with their favourite brand at the top and remaining brands in descending order of preference. There are now signs that this ladder is being replaced with a consumer perception of brand parity—that many brands are equivalent. Instead of a strongly preferred brand, consumers buy from a set of acceptable brands, choosing whichever is on sale that day.

Today's consumers are also more price sensitive, because a steady barrage of coupons and price specials has trained them to buy on price. In fact, over time, companies have reduced advertising to 30 per cent of their total promotion budget, weakening brand equity. Moreover, the endless stream of brand extensions and line extensions has blurred brand identity and led to a confusing amount of product proliferation. Further, consumers see little difference in quality among brands now that competing manufacturers and retailers are copying and duplicating the qualities of the best brands.

Of course, one of the factors that is changing the entire branding landscape is the Internet. While some "born digital" companies like America Online (AOL) and Amazon.com have used the Internet to gain brand recognition seemingly overnight, other companies have poured millions of dollars into on-line advertising with little effect on brand awareness or preference. For some low-price, low-involvement products, such as soap, the Internet offers little potential as a commerce vehicle. Still, the packaged-goods powerhouses are trying different approaches to Web marketing.

Procter & Gamble, for example, has put much of its online marketing budget behind brands like Always Panty Liners, Tampax tampons, and Pampers diapers, which have narrow target audiences with more personal subject matter. With this strategy, the company has turned Pampers.com into Pampers Parenting Institute, reaching out to customers by addressing various issues of concern to new or expectant parents.

All companies that have powerful brand awareness on the Web have sites that help customers do something—whether it's configuring a computer system online at Dell.com or offering customisation options for services at Yahoo.com. Yet some of the biggest superstars of e-commerce conduct most of their branding efforts off-line: Cisco advertises in business publications, while Dell advertises in tech trade magazines and on television.

AOL, like many high-tech companies, has been adept at achieving solid brand recognition through less conventional marketing approaches. Today, over half of all U.S. households are familiar with AOL brand. That's because AOL has blanketed the country for years with free software and free trial offers. The company has also cut deals to put its product in some unlikely places: inside Rice Chex cereal boxes, United Airlines in-flight meals, and Omaha Steaks packages, to name a few. AOL's marketers believe that novices need to try the service to appreciate its benefits. Then, once consumers start using AOL, the company reasons that the user-friendly program will lure them to subscribe. Also, on AOL's side is sheer inertia, which prevents many people from switching to another Internet service provider.

Brand-Name Decision

Manufacturers and service companies who brand their products must choose which brand names to use. Once a company decides on its brand-name strategy, it must choose a specific brand name. The company could choose the name of a person (Honda, Estée Lauder), location (American Airlines, Kentucky Fried Chicken), quality (Safeway, Duracell), lifestyle (Weight Watchers, Healthy Choice), or an artificial name (Exxon, eBay). Among the desirable qualities for a brand name are the following:

- It should suggest something about the product's benefits. Examples: Beauty-rest, Priceline.com
- It should suggest product qualities. Examples: Spic and Span, Jiffy Lube
- It should be easy to pronounce, recognise, and remember. Examples: Tide, Amazon.com

- It should be distinctive. Examples: Kodak, Yahoo!
- It should not carry poor meanings in other countries and languages. Example: Nova is a poor name for a car to be sold in Spanish-speaking countries because it means "doesn't go."

Many firms strive to build a unique brand name that eventually will become intimately identified with the product category. Examples are Frigidaire, Kleenex, Kitty Litter, Levis, Jell-O, Popsicle, Scotch Tape, Xerox, and Fiberglas. In 1994, Federal Express officially shortened its marketing identity to FedEx, a term that has become a synonym for "to ship overnight." Yet identifying a brand name with a product category may threaten the company's exclusive rights to that name. For example, cellophane

Individual names General Mills (Bisquick, The firm does not tie its Gold Medal, Betty Crocker) reputation to the product's; if the product fails or seems low quality, the company's name or image is not hurt.

Blanket family names Campbell's, Heinz, General The firm spends less on Electric development because there is no need for "name" research or heavy ad spending to create brand-name recognition; also, product sales are likely to be strong if the manufacturer's name is good. Separate family names Sears (Kenmore for appliances, where a firm offers quite for all products Craftsman for tools); Bank different products, separate One (Bank One for the family names are more physical branches, appropriate than one blanket WingspanBank.com for the family name. Internet-based bank) Company trade name Kellogg (Kellogg's Rice Krispies, The company name legitimises with individual product Kellogg's Raisin Bran) while the individual name names individualises each product.

Given the rapid growth of the global marketplace, successful companies and e-businesses are careful to choose brand names that are meaningful worldwide and pronounceable in other languages. One thing Compaq liked about the name Presario for its line of home computers is that it conjures up similar meanings in various Latin influenced languages. In French, Spanish, Latin, or Portuguese, Presario has the same, or similar, association that it does in English: It suggests an "Impresario," the magical master of the whirl and fantasy of a stage production.

Brand Strategy Decisions

A company has five choices when it comes to brand strategy. The company can introduce:

- **Line Extensions:** Line extensions introduce additional items in the same product category under the same brand name, such as new flavors, forms, colors, added ingredients, and package sizes. Dannon introduced several Dannon yogurt line extensions, including fat-free "light" yogurt and dessert flavors such as "mint chocolate cream pie." The vast majority of new products are actually line extensions.

  Line extension involves risks and has provoked heated debate among marketing professionals. On the downside, extensions may lead to the brand name losing its specific meaning; Ries and Trout call this the "line-extension trap." A consumer asking for a Coke in the past would receive a 6.5-ounce bottle. Today the seller will have to ask: New, Classic, or Cherry Coke? Regular or Diet? With or without caffeine? Bottle or can? Sometimes the original brand identity is so strong that its line extensions serve only to confuse and do not sell enough to cover development and promotion costs.

  A line extension works best when it takes sales away from rivals, not when it deflates or cannibalises the company's other items. On the upside, line extensions have a much higher chance of survival than do brand-new products. In fact, some marketing executives defend line extensions as the best way to build a business. Kimberly-Clark's Kleenex unit has had great success with line extensions. "We try to get facial tissue in every room of the home," says one Kimberly-Clark executive. "If it is there, it will get used." This philosophy led to 20 varieties of Kleenex facial tissues, including a line packaged for children.

- **Brand Extensions:** A company may use its existing brand name to launch new products in other categories. Autobytel.com, a pioneer of Internet-based car sales, used brand extensions to introduce automotive financing, insurance, and car repairs on its Website. A recent trend in corporate brandbuilding is corporations licensing their names to manufacturers of a wide range of products—from bedding to shoes. Harley- Davidson, for example, uses licensing to reach audiences that are not part of its core market, with branded armchairs for women and branded a Barbie doll for the future generation of Harley purchasers.

  Brand-extension strategy offers many of the same advantages as line extensions— but it also involves greater risks. One risk is that the new product might disappoint buyers and damage their respect for the company's other products. Another is that the brand name may be inappropriate to the new product—consider Bic perfume, a classic failure because buyers did not associate the Bic brand with fragrance products. A third risk is brand dilution, which occurs when consumers no longer associate a brand with a specific product or highly similar products.

- **Multibrands:** A company will often introduce additional brands in the same product category. Sometimes the firm is trying to establish different features or appeal to different buying motives. Multibranding also enables the company to lock up more distributor shelf space and to protect its major brand by setting up flanker brands. For example, Seiko uses one brand for higher-priced watches (Seiko Lasalle) and another for lower-priced watches (Pulsar) to protect its flanks. Ideally, a company's brands within a category should cannibalise the competitors' brands and not each other. At the very least, net profits from multibrands should be larger despite some cannibalism.

- **New Brands:** When a company launches products in a new category, it may find that none of its current brand names are appropriate. If Timex decides to make toothbrushes, it is not likely to call them Timex toothbrushes. Yet establishing a new brand name in the U.S. marketplace for a massconsumer- packaged good can cost anywhere from \$50 million to \$100 million, making this an extremely critical decision.

- **Co-brands:** A rising phenomenon is the emergence of co-branding (also called dual branding), in which two or more well-known brands are combined in an offer. Each brand sponsor expects that the other brand name will strengthen preference or purchase intention. In the case of co-packaged products, each brand hopes it might be reaching a new audience by associating with the other brand. Co-branding takes a variety of forms. One is ingredient co-branding, as when Volvo advertises that it uses Michelin tires or Betty Crocker's brownie mix includes Hershey's chocolate syrup. Another form is same-company co-branding, as when General Mills advertises Trix and Yoplait yogurt. Still another form is joint venture co-branding, as in the case of General Electric and Hitachi lightbulbs in Japan and the MSNBC Website from Microsoft and NBC. Finally, there is *multiple*—sponsor co-branding, as in the case of Taligent, a technological alliance of Apple, IBM, and Motorola. Many manufacturers make components—motors, computer chips, carpet fibres—that enter into final branded products, and whose individual identity normally gets lost. These manufacturers hope their brand will be featured as part of the final product. Intel's consumer-directed brand campaign convinced many people to buy only PCs with "Intel Inside." As a result, many PC manufacturers buy chips from Intel at a premium price rather than buying equivalent chips from other suppliers.

Brand Repositioning

However well a brand is currently positioned, the company may have to reposition it later when facing new competitors or changing customer preferences. Consider 7-Up, which was one of several soft drinks bought primarily by older people who wanted a bland, lemon-flavored drink. Research indicated that although a majority of soft-drink consumers preferred a cola, they did not prefer it all of the time, and many other consumers were non-cola drinkers. 7-Up sought leadership in the non-cola market by call Packaging and Labelling itself the Uncola and positioning itself as a youthful and refreshing drink, the one to reach for instead of a cola. Thus, 7-Up successfully established itself as the alternative to colas, not just another soft drink.

BRAND EQUITY

A brand is an intangible asset for organisation. The concept of brand equity originated in order to measure the financial worth of this significant, yet intangible entity. Brand equity is one of the popular and potentially important concepts in making the emerged in the 1980s. It has raised the importance of the brand in marketing strategy.

Brand equity is defined as the main concern in brand management and IMC campaign. Every marketer should pursue the long-term equity and pay attention to every strategy in detail. Because a small message dissonance would cause great failure of brand extension. On the other hand, consumer has his psychology process in mind. The moderating variable is a useful indication to evaluate consumer evaluation of brand extension.

Throughout the categorisation theory and associative network theory, consumer does have the ability to process information into useful knowledge for them. They would measure and compare the difference between core brand and extension product through quality of core brand, fit in category, former experience and knowledge, and difficulty of making. Some points about consumer evaluation of brand extension are as follows:

1. Quality of core brand creates a strong position for brand and low the impact of fit in consumer evaluation.
2. Similarity between core brand and extension is the main concern of consumer perception of fit. The higher the similarity, the higher perception of fit.
3. Consumer's knowledge and experience affect the evaluation before extension product trails.
4. The more innovation of extension product, the greater positive fit can perceive. A successful brand message strategy relies on a congruent communication and a clear brand image. The negative impact of brand extension would cause a great damage to parent brand and brand family. From a manager and marketer's perspective, an operation of branding should maintain brand messages and associations within a consistency and continuum in the long way. Because the effects of negative impact from brand extension are tremendous and permanently. Every messages or brand extension can dilute the brand in nature.

David A. Aaker defines brand equity in the following words:

"Brands have equity because they have high awareness many loyal consumers, a high reputation for perceived quality, proprietary assets such as access to distribution channels or to agents, or the kind of brand association (such as personality association)"

In other words, we can say that set of assets and liabilities of a organisation is known as brand equity. Brand equity comprises the following elements:

1. **Brand awareness:** Awareness of the brand name among target customer is the first step in the equity building process. Awareness essentially means that customers know about the existence of the brand, and also recall what categories the brand is in.
2. **Brand association:** Anything that connects to the customer's memory about the brand is an association. Customers form association on the basis of quality perception, their interactions with employees and the organisation, advertisements of the brand, price points at which

the brand is sold, product categories that the brand is in, product displays in retail stores, publicity in various media, offering of competitors, celebrity association and from what others tell them about the brand.

3. **Perceived quality:** Perceived quality is also a brand association, though because of its significance, it is accorded a distinct status while studying brand equity. Perceived quality is the perception of the customers about the over all quality of a brand.

4. **Brand loyalty:** Brand loyalty is a consumer's preference to buy a particular brand in a product category. It occurs because consumers perceive that the brand offers the right product features, images, or level of quality at the right price. This perception becomes the foundation for a new buying habit. Basically, consumers initially will make a trial purchase of the brand and, after satisfaction, tend to form habits and continue purchasing the same brand because the product is safe and familiar.

5. **Other proprietary brand assets:** Proprietary assets include patents, trademarks and channel relationship. These assets are valuable as they prevent competitors from attacking the company, and prevent erosion of competitive advantages and loyal customer base.

MULTIPLE CHOICE QUESTIONS

1. Brand loyalty means:
(*a*) No storage cost
(*b*) Loyalty in product quality
(*c*) No profit no loss
(*d*) All of these
(*e*) None of these

2. Brand loyalty may be used for:
(*a*) Customer of a bank
(*b*) Product planning and controlling
(*c*) Place mix
(*d*) Advertisement
(*e*) None of these

3. Maruti-Alto is a:
(*a*) Brand name
(*b*) Company
(*c*) RD stage of product
(*d*) Symbol
(*e*) None of these

4. Micro Finance is related to:
(*a*) Poor class (*b*) Rich class
(*c*) Industry (*d*) Farmer's
(*e*) None of these

5. Which of the following is the example of the brand of SBI?
(*a*) SBI Mutual Fund
(*b*) Saving and Current Deposits
(*c*) Car Loan
(*d*) Home Loan
(*e*) None of these

6. A.......is a brand that has been given legal protection, these ensuring its use exclusively by one seller.
(*a*) Trademark (*b*) Advertisement
(*c*) Product (*d*) Company
(*e*) None of these

7. A logo is a:
(*a*) Symbol or a word (*b*) Service
(*c*) Cost (*d*) Production
(*e*) None of these

8. Which of the following is the example of brand?
(*a*) Nokia (*b*) Samsung
(*c*) LG (*d*) Above all
(*e*) None of these

9. Which of the following is the example of brand of bank?
(*a*) HDFC Standard Life Insurance
(*b*) SBI Mutual Fund
(*c*) PAN Card
(*d*) Above all
(*e*) None of these

10. Match the following:

List-I	**List-II**
1. Combination Brand	A. Maruti Alto
2. Family Brand	B. Himani Products
3. National Brand	C. Parle
4. Individual Brand	D. VIM
	E. E. Maruti Suzuki

Codes :

	1	2	3	4
(*a*)	A	C	B	E
(*b*)	E	D	B	A
(*c*)	A	D	C	B
(*d*)	A	B	C	D
(*e*)	A	C	E	B

11. Which of the following is Brand Testing Mode?
(*a*) Learning Test (*b*) Association Test
(*c*) Preference Test (*d*) Above all
(*e*) None of these

12. Branding is essential because:
(*a*) Demand stimulation
(*b*) Difficulty in Differentiation
(*c*) Customer's Dissatisfaction
(*d*) Above all
(*e*) None of these

13. .... is the value or the worth of the brand.
(*a*) Logo (*b*) Brand Equity
(*c*) Trademark (*d*) All of these
(*e*) None of these

14. DSA stands for:
(*a*) Division Sales Act
(*b*) Direct Selling Agent
(*c*) Direct Sales Association
(*d*) Direct Sales Division
(*e*) None of these

15. The product of HDFC Bank includes:
(*a*) Credit Card (*b*) Personal Loan
(*c*) Life Insurance (*d*) Above all
(*e*) None of these

16. Match the following:

List-I	**List-II**
1. Tangible Product	A. Debit Card
2. Special Quality	B. Zero rate of interest
3. Generic name of product	C. FDR
4. Brand Name	D. SBI Mutual Fund
	E. HDR

Codes :

	1	2	3	4
(*a*)	A	C	B	E
(*b*)	A	B	C	D
(*c*)	E	C	D	B
(*d*)	B	A	E	D
(*e*)	C	D	A	E

17. Which of the following is the internal factor of organisation?
(*a*) Fund Available
(b) Status of Raw Material
(*c*) Production Knowledge and Skill
(*d*) Above all
(*e*) None of these

18. Which of the following is the variable of marketing programme?
(*a*) Demand variable
(*b*) Distribution system and its role
(*c*) Price
(*d*) Above all
(*e*) None of these

19. Sales Performance of Bank includes:
(*a*) To introduce ATM card
(*b*) To sanctioning the bank loan
(*c*) To open new ATM centre
(*d*) To sanctioning the home loan
(*e*) None of these

20. SEM stands for:
(*a*) Search-Engine-Marketing
(*b*) Sales-Even-Method
(*c*) Sales-Even-Organisation
(*d*) All of these
(*e*) None of these

ANSWERS

1	2	3	4	5	6	7	8	9	10
(*b*)	(*a*)	(*a*)	(*a*)	(*a*)	(*a*)	(*a*)	(*d*)	(*d*)	(*d*)
11	**12**	**13**	**14**	**15**	**16**	**17**	**18**	**19**	**20**
(*d*)	(*d*)	(*b*)	(*b*)	(*d*)	(*b*)	(*d*)	(*d*)	(*b*)	(*a*)

☞ CHAPTER-11

PACKAGING AND LABELLING

INTRODUCTION

In modern times, packaging has become so important that it is called fifty. With increasing competition, marketers are turning to innovative packaging to gain a distinctive edge to their overall product offers. This is especially true in the marketing of consumer products like processed foods, soft drinks, toiletries, cosmetics and other personal care products. In such product categories, packaging has become a powerful marketing tool. Marketers are providing value-addition to the products and greater benefits to the consumers through the packaging route.

All consumer products we find in the market are sold either in a container or wrapper and the idea behind the use of container or wrapper is to store the product in the packed condition, protect the product from the environment and keep its vital attributes and features safe and also to protect the product from handling during its transportation. Another important aspect of using an attractive pack is to enhance its marketing appeal. Products like shampoo, soap, toothpaste, detergent, wrist watches, shoes, garments, food products are well packed in glossy printed containers or wrappers that the product appeals to the consumers and helps in making a favourable decision for the product or the brand. Thus, a package is a container or wrapper in which a product is enclosed, encased or sealed.

Packaging can be defined as an act of a designing and producing a suitable and attractive package for the product, to protect and safe delivery of the product to be sold in the market. However, there are many definitions of packaging, the two widely quoted are:

1. Packaging is the art, science and technology of preparing goods for transport and sales.
2. It may be defined as the means of ensuring the safe delivery of products to the ultimate consumer in sound conditions, at the minimum overall cost.

There is another definition which sets out to explain what packing is by saying what is does- "Packing must protect what it sells and sell what is protects". This adds to the first two definitions and is the important subject of sales appeal.

FUNCTIONS OF PACKAGING

Packaging, apart from adding marketing appeal has some very important primary functions to perform and failure of these functions may lead to either loss of product or damage to product and financial loss to the company. Packaging also plays an important role in product display and the shape of the packaging design is very crucial. It performs the following important functions:

Utilitarian Functions

Package performs a utilitarian function by retaining and enhancing the product value to consumers in the following ways:

1. **Protection of Product:** Package protects a product from deterioration due to moisture and sunlight, for instance tea, hygroscopic material like salt, chemicals, pharmaceutical products, food products, spilling oil or chemical in drums, liquid products in bottles leading to spoilage. Some time the product is to be protected from evaporation during transportation.

2. **Convenience in Product Usage:** It enhances convenience of product use by keeping it clean and undisturbed.
3. **Product or Brand Identification:** It helps in easy brand identification. Brands like Coca Cola, Pepsi soft drink bottles, Dettol or Savlon bottle, Horlicks bottle, Fair & Lovely Skin Care, Colgate toothpaste, Nirma detergent and Lifebuoy soap - can be easily identified by consumers and the retail people.
4. **Easy and Safe to Handle:** It makes product handling easier and safe on the retail store shelves. Hair oil, shampoo, medicines, and cornflakes can be safely and quickly handled in a well-packed container.

Communication Function

Packing performs the function of communication by becoming an important adjunct to the components of communication mix, namely through advertising and sales promotion such as:

1. It makes product's identification and differentiation both easy and effective. In a competitive market when differences in tangible products attributes are not conspicuous, it is the package's unique presentation that makes a product look different from competing brands. Different brands of hair oil, shampoo, detergent, soap, liquor have different design and colour of glass or plastic or paper containers resulting in easy identification and the package becomes an integral part of the total product. The consumers visualise the product along with the package and these days they prefer a good, appealing and attractive packaging.
2. Package features communicate product message and motivate consumers to buy i.e., Liril soap and Kelloggs breakfast cereals, Keo Karpin hair oil and Dettol etc. This is particularly true for food and pharmaceutical products as the information and instructions on the label of the package focuses on important attributes or contents of the product and product application.
3. A change in product package design and message considerably facilitates implementation of product/brand repositioning strategy of a company. This is particularly relevant for regular consumer products like baby powder, toothpaste, soaps, detergent, shampoo.
4. Package repeats the selling message printed on it before a consumer when it is repeatedly handled during a series of uses. This encourages repeat and replacement purchases. This is also true for househlod products and fast moving consumer products like Maggi Noodles, Lifebuoy liquid soap and Mobil car lubricants.
5. The product display at the dealer's shop becomes more relevant and useful and consumers are drawn towards products or brands occupying prominent shelf space like Lux, Liril, Lifebuoy soaps, Kelloggs.
6. It promotes products at the point of purchase and usually helps in the purchase decision process. New brands or products are easily identified by consumers leading to communication with the dealer and may result in ultimate purchase. New products like Philips electric shaver, 7'o' clock twin blades, Maggi tomato ketchup are some examples which are easy to see or locate at the point of purchase.

Purchase and Marketing Functions

Two of the major functions of packaging activity are purchasing and marketing. The purchasing function is responsible for all packaging purchases and because of this, it needs to be familiar with all work on development projects. Liaison with outside suppliers is also the main responsibility of the purchasing function. When personnel are involved in packaging work directly with external suppliers, they need to keep their company buyers fully informed.

During the initial stages of new product development, the marketing and consumer research functions together with external designers, work with the packaging team to develop and assess package shape and surface design. Legal experts are called in to advise on the validity of pack copy and on matters affecting trademarks. On the technical side, development of the product, packaging and filling equipment involve liaison with the research and development and engineering functions. It will be seen, therefore, that to operate efficiently, the packaging man needs knowledge of the disciplines and techniques used in the departments with which he is in regular contact. Equally important, he needs to be able to communicate clearly, both verbally and in writing. Effectively designed packages sustain the cost of handling and transportation and protect product from transit damages or the damages during handling and storage. Extra care has to be taken if the condition of roads and age of transport vehicle is old as they contribute to excessive transit damages.

Profit Functions

Package also performs a profit functions in two ways:

1. Consumers assigning relatively higher value to a package are usually prepared to pay higher price for the product's attribute. As a result, higher contribution to profit flows from package. Food products, cosmetics and other consumer products have cheap quality, medium quality, super quality or premium quality products and these products are packed in different type of packages, depending upon the price of the product and segment of the market to which it caters.
2. Effective package cuts cost of handling and transportation and protects product from damage, thereby saving a company from cuts in profits. Products are packed in cartons and are transported safely to their destined markets.

The consumer products are distributed to different territories and hence go through loading, unloading, transportation and stocking in godowns and all this handing gives a probability of loss of material or breakage of product and therefore, effective package reduces considerably the incidence of breakage during handling and transportation. The higher loss of material or breakage during handling, transportation and storage result in dealer and consumer dissatisfaction also, which may affect sale of company's product. Therefore, effective and good package avoids dilution of profit and customer satisfaction. This is relevant for table salt, tea or coffee, fertilisers and cement.

Marketing Mix Function

Package is an integral part of the product but good and effective packaging could give an added product or brand value and thereby improving the probability of the brand's sale. The effective package can tie the brand to the rest of the marketing strategy. Expensive perfume or a cosmetic product may be packed in crystal or classic designed glass bottle improving its storage appeal. Sometimes a good package gives firm more promotional effect than it could do with advertising. The package is seen in stores or retail outlets when customers are actually doing the buying activity. This is very relevant at the point of purchase sale. Therefore, some marketing experts feel packaging should be treated as the fifth 'P' of marketing mix and the package can bring in the much desired product differentiation. Therefore, it can act as an important input into the marketing effort and should be an equally significant element of marketing mix. A well-designed attractive packaging improves not only marketing appeals but also gives positive evaluation of the behaviour of the consumers. This is likely to improve sales turnover and give additional profit margin and may also result in higher market share.

PACKAGING CRITERIA

The final form of any package is influenced by many factors but logical packaging development can be achieved by considering various packaging criteria. There are basically seven important criteria:

1. Appearance
2. Protection
3. Functions
4. Cost
5. Disposability

6. Ecofriendly or biodegradable features
7. Marketing appeal

These are the main considerations when developing a pack. The relative emphasis placed on them depends on the product and on its marketing requirements. Some examples are listed below:

1. A cosmetic product; the most important criterion likely to be is appearance. For example, shampoo, perfume or hair oil.
2. Aerosol hair spray; the most important criterion is usage function.
3. Ethical pharmacy; the most important criterion is protection.
4. For buying one bottle of milk or soft drink, the most important criteria are cost and disposability.

This is not to say that the other criteria are ignored. For example, the most exotic cosmetic product must have some cost limitations attached to its packaging requirements and the most humble household product like edible oil or table salt will need to have some attention paid to its appearance. One thing is sure and that is disposability among consumers is growing in importance.

1. *Appearance*

This criterion is growing in importance with the growth of supermarkets and cash and carry system. The appearance of a package is important for a number of reasons:

- It has to help in identifying the product throughout the distribution chain.
- It may have to carry instructions for use like liquid hair dye or an eye ointment.
- It may have to carry information about the contents in order to satisfy legal requirements (as with poisons, or with most foodstuffs or pharma products)
- It will usually carry the brand name and the name of the manufacturer or both.
- It can act as an important sales aid particularly for personal products.

The appearance of package is dependent on two main elements: shape and surface appearance. There are often conflicting requirements for package shape. On the one hand, the market requirements may be for a complex shape to fit the product image, whereas the retailer's requirements are for stability on stocking and efficient use of shelf space. One example of a special limitation is to provide positive identification in the dark.

Surface appearance may be achieved either by labelling or by direct printing on the package. An important aspect of appearance is that it must be durable. In the case of retail foods, this means that the appearance must still be attractive enough to sell goods as well as to identify them. In the case of industrial foods, the identification factor is often more important than sales appeal, but even here, any deterioration in appearance should be then avoided. The function of identification achieves paramount importance when the subject of packaging for the defence or telecom series is considered. If military equipment (ammunition, etc.) is wanted in a hurry, the packages must be capable of giving instant and positive identification. The other factor is that of time, packaging for the services is designed for long life (of the order of five years or more) and the identification must be equally long.

2. *Protection*

Although protection may not always be the most important criterion for every packaging situation, it is requirement that is rarely completely absent. The protection required by the product will vary enormously with the nature of the product itself, the final destination, the distribution system and the total time that protection is required. Protection is normally required against two main hazards - chemical and physical.

Product Packaging and Material Compatibility: Chemical interaction between the product, and its container is undesirable. Not only it may lead to undesirable changes in the product, but it may cause a weakening of the container with consequent failure in service.

One of the most common examples of product package incompatibility is packaging of acidic or alkaline products in tin plate containers. Both types of interaction can be found in this situation. For example, certain detergents corrode tin plate and eventually cause leakage of the product. The answer is to prevent contact of the product and the tin plate by lacquering of the surface. This solution is more likely to be successful in the case of preventing deterioration of the product since even if pin holes or other imperfections occur in the lacquer, the area of contact will be very small, in relation to the volume of the product.

Some effects of product package incompatibility are more subtle than the ones just considered. It has been known for glass, which is normally considered to be extremely inert, to affect certain products. Aqueous liquids acquire an alkaline reaction very slowly when stored in glass and this can adversely affect certain alkali-sensitive drugged or transfusion liquids. Specially treated glass (sulphated glass) is available for the packaging of such liquids.

Ingress of Liquids and Vapours: The packaging material is used to act as a barrier against any form of entry into the package. One of the commonest causes of product deterioration is water, either in the form of moisture or vapour. Many granular or powdered chemicals, for instance, cake badly under humid conditions, while others become extremely corrosive when damp. Paper is normally not a barrier to moisture or vapour but glass, tin plate and aluminium are. It should be remembered, incidentally, that even the best container is only as good as its closure or seal. The hazard of liquid ingressing may arise when a product is shipped through deck cargo or climatic to provide an outer, water-proof package using a plastics film or a varnished fibre-board case.

Many products require protection against the ingress of gases, particularly of oxygen. Fatty foods, for instance, get affected when the fat is oxidised. Also, many medicines are adversely affected by reaction with oxygen. Once again, the best barriers are glass and metals (subject to the provision of efficient closures). Some plastics have quite low permeabilities of oxygen while others have high ones. The success of materials with an appreciable permeability will depend on external conditions, such as temperature and humidity and on the shelf life required.

Finally, many foodstuffs can be adversely affected by pick-up of external odours or flavours during transit and storage. The package, therefore, act as a barrier in such cases. Metal and glass are complete barriers but paper, board and plastics are not. Plastics vary a great deal in their permeability to odours and flavours but one of the highest permeabilities to essential oils (which constitute a high proportion of odours or flavours) is possessed by low-density polythylene. This material should not, therefore, be used alone where it is thought to be a real danger of odour or flavour pick-up, particularly if the product itself has only a slight odour or flavour of its own. Plastic coated paper material is widely used for such needs.

Loss of liquid or vapour can also lead to adverse changes in the product. Examples include the drying out of tobacco or cigarettes, loss of solvents from shoe polish (leading to hardening of the product), loss of flavour from foodstuffs and the loss of perfume from cosmetics. The problems are much the same as those discussed above and the types of barrier materials are the same. The provision of an efficient closure is equally important. The importance of leak proof mouth or pilfer proof guala cap is being seen these days.

Micro-organisms: Where the product is food or pharmaceutical which has to be sterilised (usually by heat) either prior to packaging or in package, then the function of the package is to prevent the ingress of fresh micro-organisms. Suitable packaging materials are tin plate, aluminum, glass and some plastics or plastic-coated paper or aluminum foil.

For dry foods which have not been sterilised the package has to prevent the increase of moisture which would subsequently promote microbial growth of organisms already present. The importance of efficient packaging in such instances cannot be overlooked. Apart from spoilage of the contents, some bacteria produce toxins which can be deadly. It is not only edible products which have to be protected from attack by micro-organisms. Glass is attacked by the enzymes produced by certain moths so that the glass jar and the glass covers for instrument dials are both susceptible to damage. Similarly, aluminum is attacked by an acid produced by moth growth. In addition, outer cases of wood or fibre board may have to be treated with a fungicide for export to tropical regions because of possible attack by fungi and bacteria.

Physical hazards in distribution may be static or dynamic and may be summarised under the following headings:

Impression: This arises from stocking in transit or in storage. If the primary pack is sufficiently stout (for example, a cylindrical tin plate container with flat ends), the outer pack needs no more than the primary packs which can take the stocking load themselves. For weaker primary packs such as corrugated carton or flexible plastic packs, the outer container must be constructed to take a large promotion of the maximum stocking load likely to be encountered. It must be emphasised that damage to the bottom containers in the stack is not the only danger. More serious is the risk of stack instability, with possible damage to many more containers as well as risk to life or limb.

Impact: Damage due to impact can arise through dropping of the package or shunting of rail cars, or bad roads in certain parts of India etc. In addition to breakage of containers, leading to leakage there is also the risk of damage to equipment by distortion.

Puncturing: Puncturing can occur through similar hazards to those outlined above for impact, The main risk is leakage of liquid or powdered contents but punctures may also provide inlets for moisture vapour, with consequent corrosion of metallic products.

Vibration: Vibration can cause a multitude of problems from abrasion and scratching of the outside of the containers (perhaps with loss of identification) to breakage of the contents. The package has a vital role to play a cushion when transporting fragile goods like glass tumblers, medicine (liquid preparation), sheet glass and horticulture products.

Effect of Temperature: The effects of high temperature on a product are usually more serious than those of low temperature. Corrosion effects, for example, are accelerated by high temperature as are other chemical changes and biological spoilage. It is also necessary to consider the effect of changes in temperature even when the extremes likely to be encountered are not thought to be harmful. Thus, cooling of a warm, moist atmosphere will lead to deposition of some moisture and condensation and this liquid water can then cause corrosion of metal parts or deterioration of water-sensitive chemicals, foodstuffs, etc. Examples of products likely to be adversely affected by an increase in temperature include chocolate, (which softens and melts at elevated temperatures and become unsaleable): fish, (which rapidly develops a strong off-odour and start decomposing and then becomes inedible), frozen foods start to deteriorate biologically; and many pharmaceutical products which lose their therapeutic activity (or many even become biologically inimical) if stored at high temperatures.

Fall in temperatures is not normally so important and will, in fact, often increase the shelflife. One important exception is emulsion paints which consist of a dispersion of pigments and synthetic resins in water. Too low a temperature will freeze the water component and thus break the emulsion, making it unsaleable. Tins of emulsion paint exported to low temperature countries should therefore, be placed in another packing giving adequate heat insulation. Similar remarks apply to many adhesives as these tend to undergo physical changes at low temperatures; such changes are difficult to reverse by the consumer.

It should be noted that very low temperatures are not only encountered by products exported to cold countries but also by products taken by aircraft. These days refrigerated vans and containers are used for transportation of temperature-sensitive products.

Effect of light: Light may adversely affect many light-sensitive product like films. The effect varies from changes to colour, embrittlement of some plastic and catalysis of chemical reactions (such as "oxidation of fats, giving rancidity). Many pharmaceutical products are affected by visible or ultraviolet light and must, therefore, be packed in opaque containers or coloured glass bottles to prevent ultra violet (UV) ray penetration.

Pilferage: Although no package is a complete defence against pilferage, some can often make the job of the thief much more difficult. One way of reducing pilferage is by containerisation, whereby a large number of normal shipping containers are put into a large van type container. These large containers are solidly built and can be padlocked. The shrink wrapping of whole pallet loads can also be of help in this area. The shrink wrapping of glass containers and carton trays and boxes are used. The oil-proof caps are also used in pharmaceutical and liquor products.

3. *Functions*

The functions which a container may be called upon to perform can be divided into two main classes:

1. Those concerned with its end use, and
2. Those concerned with its behaviour on the packaging or on filling line.

End-use performance: This is obviously important since faulty performance will lead to dissatisfaction with the product itself despite good attributes and, hence, to a reduction in sales. End-use package functions include:

Display: The package may be used for displaying on item in its own right by means of an attractive surface decoration or it may act as a display item for the product. The former has already been dealt with under the heading "Appearance". The second factor i.e., product visibility is not always desirable; of course, especially where the product is sensitive to light or ultraviolet rays. When visibility is required, it is usually an aid to identification or to add sales appeal to the finished pack. The latter is an increasing trend in large chain stores. This is true for jams, pickles, squashes, edible oils, transfusion solutions and cold drinks.

In the case of flexible packaging, there are many plastic films together with regenerated cellulose films, which can be obtained in a fully transparent form. For rigid packs the choice lies between glass or certain plastic packs such as PVC bottles. One other possibility exists where the product does not have to be protected from the environment and that is the use of a cut-away or some other form of open container. One example is the use of cotton or plastic nets for the packaging of eggs where a cut-away mould pulp container can be used which will give sufficient visibility while still maintaining mechanical protection. Until the advent of translucent polystyrene egg packs, this was the only way of obtaining product visibility plus mechanical protection.

Easy in Opening: This is a very difficult function to satisfy since it is generally combined with the necessity for the pack to maintain its seal or closure integrity until the customer wants to open it. E.g. Tear tapes in the case of film overwraps while there are now a number of easy opening devices for metal cans, such as or coke cans. The most difficult field is probably that of plastic pouches, especially those containing liquid products. Tearing plastic films is not easy, even with solid products inside but to tear open a plastic pouch of liquid without spilling the contents is extremely difficult and generally they are cut to opened.

Convenience: The need for convenience in packaging has led to the growth of packs where the package and the product are completely integrated and where it is difficult to separate product and package performance.

An excellent example of this type of product and package integration is the aerosol or pressurized pack. The product as used by the consumer (for example, an insecticidal mist or a shaving foam) is not actually contained by the package but is produced at the moment it is required. The production of the mist, foam, etc is function of the complete pack. With the shaving foam, the container has to be strong enough to withstand the high internal pressures generated by the mixture of soap solution and liquefied gas propellant while the value, part of which is an actuating button, also provides an expansion chamber in which the foam is formed as the pressure is released on the mixture of the soap solution and propellant.

A number of examples from western countries can be quoted from the food industry including boil-in-the bag pack (the pouch and its contents), are placed into boiling water or put in a micro-wave oven for a few minutes, the package is removed and the cooked food is dispensed ready for eating by cutting open the pouch. This type of pack has to be able to contain the food during transit and storage, resist the temperature of boiling water and be readily opened when required. The main convenience factors are, absence of cooking smell, absence of the need to clean saucepans after cooking and ease of preparation of a complete meal.

Dispensing: This is allied in some ways to ease of opening and convenience. A great number of advances made in dispensing devices, such as pourers, spouts and taps have been made with the aid of plastics because of the flexibility of design offered by these materials. Dispensing aids range from a plastic cap which is easily punctured to give a hole through which a liquid can be shaken, to complicated retractable taps for drums which can then be rolled along the ground without breaking off the tap. Liquid soap solution, vinegar, pest control liquids and skin treatment medicines, perfumes, and lotions etc. Use such dispensing systems. Recently HLL has added this dispensing device in its packing for its brand surf at higher price.

Performance of Packaging on filling line: This can be important aspect of container design. Examples of container designs which can affect speed or types of filling equipment are neck diameter, stability (relationship between base diameter and diameter at top of container), rigidity of container wall (a certain amount of rigidity is necessary for vacuum filling) and variations in container weight (which affects reproduction of weight filling).

A change from one type of container to another may necessitate change in filling equipment ranging from a simple modification to a complete new filling line. Thus, a lube oil line designed to run full aperture metal cans with double seamed lids, would need major alterations to run on light weight plastic bottles with narrow necks and screw-on caps. Plastic containers can be used, however, in the form of full aperture plastic bodies with metal lids fixed to the plastic bodies with slightly modified equipment but the filling could then be carried on as before (at high speeds) because the aperture of the containers was unchanged.

It is difficult to delink the package from the machinery which is needed to fill it and handle it on production line. Package design and machinery design are often inter-dependent and thus the packaging and machinery design and selection must be taken into consideration from the initial stages.

In particular, new packaging materials usually pose problems in use on high speed equipment developed primarily for more established materials. The case of low-density polyethylene film was an excellent example in this connection. Wrapping equipment had previously been designed to deal with paper or with regenerated cellulose film, both of which are stiff, even in these gauges. Polyethylene film on the other hand through the wrapping machine usually worked on the principle of mechanical fingers, pushing the material along and new equipment had to be developed before the polyethylene film could capture an appreciable share of the wrapping market. The packaging and machinery interface is sometimes difficult to distinguish. Many modem packaging machines produce filled packages from film or sheet without any intermediate package being formed.

These form, if and seal (FFS) machines bring package making into the product manufacturer's plant and have been used in intravenous transfusion (IV) filling. Different types of expertise also have to be employed and it may create difficulties for industries such as dairies which are confronted with the problems of plastic technology in the form of bottle blowing. This would be so in the case of the form, fill and seal technique where bottles are blown from plastic granules, filled and head sealed, all on one machine.

4. *Cost*

Cost of packaging is an important criterion for selection of packaging material and its design. The selection of material for packaging will depend upon function of packaging. Expensive well designed packaging is used for premium or luxury products like expensive perfumes, cigarettes, beverages, personal products and electronic household gadgets. The desire to reduce prices to be competitive in the market leads to explore cheap packaging for non-premium products. However, well-designed packaging gives rise to better marketing appeal and higher cost of packaging can be feasible for premium and luxury products meant for upmarket consumer segment. The expensive products also yield higher profit margins.

The cost of packaging is decided by the weight of packaging material and the design and moulding or fabrication charges. The packaging development is done keeping the environmental laws in mind and it is desirable to use ecofriendly materials.

5. *Disposability*

In most of the cases, packaging material is disposed once the product is exhausted or consumed. Therefore, factor of disposability is an essential criterion in the selection of packaging material. The disposal plastic materials is difficult in view of its non biodegradable nature. The glass should be disposed off properly otherwise broken glass may be unsafe for general consumers. The disposal of one time throw away bottles for beverage caused serious concern for disposal of bottles.

6. *Ecofriendly or biodegradable Features*

The packaging material and its disposability is becoming extremely significant in view of environmental problems. Products like metal and plastic are non-biodegradable and therefore becoming serious concern for environmentalists. The emphasis is on using bio-degradable or ecofriendly material like paper cuttings or shavings, wooden material, glass or any other packaging material. The companies are therefore shifting their stand on non-biodegradable and moving towards using material which are ecofriendly. The Green Dot Scheme in Germany, does not allow companies to import materials into Germany which are packed with such non-biodegradable material.

7. *Marketing Appeal*

The consumer attitude towards packaging is changing and manufacturing firms are giving special importance to designs of the pack. The consumer products in well-designed and well-shaped containers give better appeal to consumers when products are displayed. The impulsive buyers may go for well-designed attractive packed products like cosmetics, skin treatment and hair treatment products, beverages, alcohols and cigarettes etc. Packaging is a great asset for some expensive consumer goods and has tremendous marketing appeal. It leads to positive evaluation and ultimately purchase decision. There are consumers who even retain empty packaging material or containers as souvenir as they like the design and shape of the container.

PACKAGING DECISIONS

Decisions on packaging have to cover areas like package design, packaging materials, packaging processes, testing and evaluation, marketing economics, and environmental issues.

We shall take up the following areas for discussion:

Package Materials

Changing trends - from wood to paper: Over the years, a great deal of changes have taken place in the materials used for packaging. In the earlier days, wood was the main material used. It has slowly given place to paper and paperboard, especially on account of the shortage in wood supplies. Paperboard cartons, paper bags and corrugated boards have become popular forms of packaging for a variety of products, from groceries to garments.

Metal containers are also popular: Metal containers are an excellent packaging medium for processed foods, fruit, vegetables, meat products, oil, paint, etc. However, the acute shortage of tin in India makes metal packaging radier costly. In recent years, aluminium-based packaging has become popular. It is used in the form of foil, foil-based laminates, cans, pilfer-proof caps, etc. Products like tea, coffee, and spices have adopted aluminium foil packaging.

Plastics: The synthetic packaging material, 'plastics', has several merits such as:

(i) Water/moisture proof property,

(ii) Capacity to provide barrier to vapour,

(iii) Greater resistance to sun exposure,

(iv) Thermal stability,

(v) Light weight,

(vi) Alkali and acid proof property, and

(vii) Attractiveness and transparency.

They also allow attractive printing/labelling on them. Plastics, as a group, are now dominating the packaging field in India and are used in a variety of packaging applications - from simple grocery bags to sophisticated stretch blown bottles. Well-known brands like Tata Tea, Nescafe", Amul milk chocolates, and even agricultural inputs like chemical feertilisers, have all gone in for plastic packaging materials. However, in recent years, a resistance to plastic packages has been building up due to the problems it creates to environmental cleanliness.

Tetra packs: Tetra packs or aseptic packaging is one such innovation. It has revolutionised food packaging. Here, the packages as well as the contents are sterilised and human handling dispensed with. The package consists of several thin layers of polyethylene foil and paper. Several manufacturers of fruit juices and fruit drinks are now using tetra packs. Tetra packs have an edge over cans since their contents have a shelf life of three months without the addition of preservatives.

Innovations in packaging: The continuous search for improved types of packing has led to a stream of innovations. Reducing the cost of packaging, enhancing the shelf life of the product, increasing the handling convenience and enhancing the overall product appeal, were central concerns behind these innovations.

Package Aesthetics: For enhancing the sales appeal of the product, more and more attention is now being given to package aesthetics. Packaging material, package designs, package size and shape, are all elements that decide the charm of the package and consequently the sales appeal of the product. Marketers of products rely heavily on package aesthetics as a tool for sales appeal, brand identification and product differentiation.

Innovative packaging can greatly help in generating trials. It facilitates merchandising. The role of package aesthetics in rendering the package a silent salesman, projecting a right image about the product is discussed in the chapter on Marketing Communications. Here it is sufficient to say that the size and shape of the package, the material used, the finish, the colour, the labelling, etc., are all influential components of the total sales appeal of the product.

Handling Convenience: Handling convenience is an important feature of the package. It contributes greatly to the success of the product. In fact, in many cases, it functions as a useful differentiator. The various attributes of the package-material, design, shape, size, etc., together should make the handling and use of the product convenient for the customer.

Pond's cold cream and Brylcreem in tubes. Earlier Pond's cold cream was coming in a bottle container and it was intended and used as a dressing table item. Subsequently, Pond's introduced the cream in a handy plastic tube. The new package changed the very perception of the product. From a dressing table item it also became a carry-along product. This change in package increased the sales of Pond's cold cream. The same was the case with Brylcreem. Earlier, this hair-cream used to come only in bottle containers. Later, Brylcreem appeared in a convenient tube. Brylcreem in the new package became a convenient, carry-along, dressing item.

Application convenience of Harpic liquid toilet cleaner is another product that has successfully exploited the concept of customer convenience in packaging. With Harpic, it is a case of application convenience. The container fitted with a nozzle for cleaning the toilet gives Harpic an advantage as it solves the application problem for the consumers.

The soft drink, beer can serves as one of the best examples of packaging convenience. The design of the can makes opening the can so simple an action, requiring no instructions whatsoever. The design is based on an understanding of people's basic pattern of expectations. Confronted with the ring around the neck of the can, what would you do but pull it and open it!

Package Size: Package size is another critical feature influencing consumers' purchase decision. Marketers have all along been using it as a convenient pricing and marketing tool. That is how Jumbo packs, family packs, economy packs, refill packs, etc., came into play. And the marketers' aim here has been to hook the customer to as large a pack as possible by offering a concessional price for the larger pack.

Economy pack: The economy or family pack makes the product available in larger size. Households with several members can buy economy packs and avoid the inconvenience of repeat purchases making a saving in the bargain.

Refill packs: Refill packaging is also related to customer convenience and economy. Several product categories like health drinks, coffee, tea and cooking oils are now coming in refill packs. Brands like Nescafe, Bru, Bournvita, Maltova, Saffola, Sundrop, Dhara, etc., are examples. The refill packs are sold at a slightly lesser price than the regular package and that itself serves as a sales promotion support.

Reusable containers: Providing reusable containers is another way by which marketers try to enhance the appeal of product. Nescafel at a point of time came in a glass jar, which could be later used as a glass. And the Nescafel campaigns persuaded the customers to collect a set of such glasses. Plastic containers lend themselves for reuse in the kitchen store. Bournvita in the 200 gm handle-jar was much sought after by the housewife. Bournvita was also sold in packs constituting drinking mugs and pet jars. Cadbury's cocoa powder was introduced in a special 'measuring glass cup'.

The Sachet sweep: In more recent times, instead of larger packs, a reverse revolution is taking place in packaging. The sachet is dominating the packaging scene. Every marketer is becoming part of this new packaging-cum-marketing initiative. It started with pan masalas and shampoos; it is now spreading to all kinds of products ranging from hair oil, tea and coffee to soups, candy, toothpaste and even cough syrup. Fair & Lovely has affaired phenomenal results through soft packs.

Using Package for Product Renovation: Marketers also use packaging as a device for renovating the product. When a declining trend in the sale of the product is noticed, marketers often use the packing to arrest the decline. They change the package and give a new look to the product without bringing about any substantive change in the product. The product is then advertised as new on the strength of the newness of the packing. In some other cases, the package is changed even when the sales go up. The intention is to retain the interest of the existing customers and to attract new customers.

After packaging is designed, it must be tested. Engineering tests are conducted to ensure that the package stands up under normal conditions; visual tests, to ensure that the script is legible and the colours harmonious; dealer tests, to ensure that dealers find the packages attractive and easy to handle; and consumer tests, to ensure favourable consumer response.

PACKAGING AS A MARKETING TOOL

Marketing can be defined as the overall strategy or complex which moves goods from the source of production into the hands of the consumer. Within this definition several functions can be identified; these are exchange (buying and selling), supply (transport and storage), standardisation and grading, financing, risk-taking, and the provision of market information. Packaging is deeply involved in many of the above functions and should be taken into account at an early stage in any marketing plan.

The importance of the pack in relation to the product is generally accepted insofar as luxury or semi-luxury items are concerned. In the cosmetics industry, for example, the pack plays a vital role in promoting sales and a great deal of time and money is spent on pack design. A similar situation exists in the expensive end of the chocolate trade, especially for gift packs designed for seasonal promotions at Christmas, Diwali or New Year time.

The pack should be recognised as an important marketing tool in many other fields, especially in the light of the increasing emphasis being placed on self-service, selling, advertising and sales however, promotional schemes.

The importance of packaging as a marketing tool will be seen more clearly if its various interactions with other marketing functions are analysed.

Retail Marketing Trends

The growth of packaging has had a tremendous impact on retailing methods. Packaging in its turn has itself been affected by changes in retail marketing. The first major change was, of course, from a state of minimum packaging to one where a majority of items were packed and of these, most were packed by the manufacturer. There was a gradual transition during post World War II period - from packaging which was meant only as a container, to packaging with a definite emphasis on sales appeal as an important aid to sales.

Packaging had two main effects on retail marketing during this period. It enabled manufacturers to sell more and more goods under brand names and it changed the character of the retail shops. The interiors of shops became less cluttered, while allowing the display of a greater number of products and window display was revolutionised from chemist's shop to readymade garments and from white goods to electronic entertainment products.

Radical changes were brought about using old and established packaging materials such as glass, tin plate and paper or board but there was a new material which contributed a great deal to sales appeal and that was cellulose film. There is little doubt that its combination, clarity, colour and protection against moisture, vapour did a great deal to speed up the packaging revolution.

Self-service and Supermarkets

Since the end of World War II, the biggest change in retail marketing has been the growth of self-service. Self-service on any large scale is completely dependent on packaging, although it is also true to say that the growth of self-service in departmental stores and supermarkets has had a corresponding great impact on packaging developments. Having once established the concept of supermarkets, it was natural to bring under their wing the marketing of products not normally packaged. One large area affected was that of fruits, vegetables, gift items and books.

The desire to round out the product range with fresh products led not only to developments in the packaging of such commodities but also led to changes in distribution. Certain chain stores and supermarkets have their own central pre-packaging facilities and so buy in bulk either from local farmers or from the usual fruits and vegetable market. Other supermarkets and self-service stores buy from packing stations who are themselves supplied with produce from a number of farmers in their locality.

Supermarkets also had a direct effect on the packaging of confectionery. At one time, most confectioneries were sold unpackaged but the practice of placing confectionery near check-out points of supermarkets for impulse sales soon led to the packaging of chocolates, toffees, boiled sweets, cakes and pastries, other items in cartons or film sachets, in order to obtain the benefit of increased sales.

One important influence of supermarket selling on packaging is geographies of the package. In the self-service environment, the package acts as the product's only salesman and quite small differences in shape or surface may mean the difference between 'sale and no sale'. The question is not just the simple one of designing a package which will attract the maximum amount of attention and one which will project the correct image. The use of a completely different shape may be a solution but this may bring problems in stocking on the supermarket shelves. Selling space is extremely limited and valuable in a self-service store and the store owner is not anxious to stock products which make inefficient use of his valuable space.

Supermarket selling has another influence on package appearance. Because of the emphasis it places on the package acting as a silent salesman, it is essential that brand recognition be made possible from as many different viewpoints as possible.

LABELLING

Sellers must label products. The label may be a simple tag attached to the product or an elaborately designed graphic that is part of the package. The label might carry only the brand name or a great deal of information. Even if the seller prefers a simple label, the law may require additional information.

Labels perform several functions. First, the label *identifies* the product or brand—for instance, the name Sunkist stamped on oranges. The label might also *grade* the product; canned peaches are grade labelled A, B and C. The label might *describe* the product: who made it, where it was made, when it was made, what it contains, how it is to be used, and how to use it safely. Finally, the label *promotes* the product through its attractive graphics.

Labels eventually become outmoded and need freshening up. The label on Ivory soap has been redone 18 times since the 1890s, with gradual changes in the size and design of the letters. The label on Orange Crush soft drink was substantially changed when competitors' labels began to picture fresh fruits, thereby pulling in more sales. In response, Orange Crush developed a label with new symbols to suggest freshness and with much stronger and deeper colours.

There is a long history of legal concerns surrounding labels, as well as packaging. In 1914, the Federal Trade Commission Act held that false, misleading, or deceptive labels or packages constitute unfair competition. The Fair Packaging and Labelling Act, passed by Congress in 1967, set mandatory labelling requirements, encouraged voluntary industry packaging standards, and allowed federal agencies to set packaging regulations in specific industries. The Food and Drug Adminstration (FDA) has required processed-food producers to include nutritional labelling that clearly states the amounts of protein, fat, carbohydrates, and calories contained in products, as well as their vitamin and mineral content as a percentage of the recommended daily allowance. The FDA recently launched a drive to control health claims in food labelling by taking action against the potentially misleading use of such descriptions as "light", "high fibre" and "low fat". Consumerists have lobbied for additional labelling laws to require *open dating* (to describe product freshness), *unit pricing* (to state the product cost in standard measurement units), *grade labelling* (to rate the quality level), and *percentage labelling* (to show the percentage of each important ingredient).

Labelling—Telling About the Product

The paper or plastic sticker attached to a can of peas or a mustard jar is technically called a **label**. But as packaging technology improves and cans and bottles become less prominent, labels become incorporated into the protective aspects of the package. In the case of a box of frozen broccoli, for example, a good portion of the vegetable's protection comes from the label, which is more properly called, in this case, the *wrapper*.

Whether the label is a separate entity affixed to a package or is, in effect, the package itself, it must perform certain tasks. It carries the brand name and information concerning the contents of the package, such as cooking instructions and information relating to safe and proper use of the product. A label may also carry instructions for the proper disposal of the product and its package, or at least a plea to consumers to avoid littering.

The label must contain any specific nutritional information, warnings, or legal restrictions required by law. Some labels, such as those of Procter & Gamble, also give an 800 telephone number that customers with ideas or complaints can use. Consumers, calls are a major source of Procter & Gamble's product improvement ideas.

Universal Product Code (UPC): The array of black bars, readable by optical scanners, found on many products. The UPC permits computerisation of tasks such as checkout and compilation of sales volume information.

Most consumer packaged goods are labelled with an appropriate **Universal Product Code (UPC),** and array of black bars readable by optical scanners. The advantages of the UPC—which allow computerised checkout and compiling of computer-generated sales volume information—have become clear to distributors, retailers and consumers in recent years.

MULTIPLE CHOICE QUESTIONS

1. A.........provides written information about the product.
(*a*) Label (*b*) Packaging
(*c*) Branding (*d*) Pricing
(*e*) None of these

2. Main decision areas in packaging is:
(*a*) Package Materials
(*b*) Package Aesthetics
(*c*) Package size and convenience
(*d*) Above all
(*e*) None of these

3. In........, all activities of designing and producing the container for a product are included.
(*a*) Packaging (*b*) Costing
(*c*) Pricing (*d*) Lebelling
(*e*) None of these

4. The main objective of packaging is:
(*a*) Identification of Product
(*b*) Protection of Product
(*c*) Maintaining the Quality of Product
(*d*) Above all
(*e*) None of these

5. Characteristics of good packaging is:
(*a*) Convenient
(*b*) Interesting
(*c*) Attractive and Protective
(*d*) Above all
(*e*) None of these

6. Match the following:

List-I (Characteristics of Good Packaging)	List-II (Example)
1. Attractive	A. Colour and design
2. Interesting	B. For Purchase
3. Reusable	C. Packet
4. Pollution free and durable	D. Disposal
	E. Design & Price

Codes :

	1	2	3	4
(*a*)	A	B	C	D
(*b*)	B	C	D	E
(*c*)	E	A	B	D
(*d*)	A	D	C	B
(*e*)	A	C	E	D

7. Product Identification involves:
(*a*) Branding (*b*) Packaging
(*c*) Labelling (*d*) Above all
(*e*) None of these

8. The........is an informative tag, wrapper or seal attached to a product or product's package.

(*a*) Label (*b*) Brand
(*c*) Trade mark (*d*) Quality
(*e*) None of these

9. Grade labels identify by:
(*a*) Letter (*b*) Number
(*c*) Quality (*d*) Above all
(*e*) None of these

10. The......is the part of a product which carries verbal information about the product.
(*a*) Packaging (*b*) Branding
(*c*) Label (*d*) Advertising
(*e*) None of these

11. Trickle Down Theory is associated with:
(*a*) Brand (*b*) Fashion
(*c*) Patent (*d*) Quality
(*e*) None of these

12. A.........is any style which is popularly accepted and purchased by several successive groups of people over reasonably period of time.
(*a*) Fashion
(*b*) Product Planning
(*c*) Product Identification
(*d*) Product Advertising
(*e*) None of these

13. BPO stands for:
(*a*) Budget Product Online
(*b*) Balance of Payment
(*c*) Business Process Outsourcing
(*d*) All of these
(*e*) None of these

14. Redical marketing is related with:
(*a*) Individualisation
(*b*) Product Planning
(*c*) Cost Management
(*d*) Market Management
(*e*) None of these

15. Which is the area of ethical aspect of marketing?
(*a*) True Information
(*b*) Fair Pricing
(*c*) False and Misleading Advertising
(*d*) True Advertising
(*e*) None of these

16. Marketing is successful when:
(*a*) Demand exceeds supply
(*b*) Supply exceeds demand
(*c*) Salesmen are effectively trained
(*d*) All of these
(*e*) None of these

17. In marketing, Market Penetration means:
(*a*) Entry likely purchasers houses
(*b*) Entering stores and shops
(*c*) Covering a wide area of the market
(*d*) Above all
(*e*) None of these

18. Diversification means:
(*a*) Marketing in diverse countries
(*b*) Marketing in diverse companies
(*c*) Marketing of new diverse products
(*d*) None of these

19. Personal Banking includes:
(*a*) Deposits (*b*) Insurance
(*c*) Investment (*d*) Above all
(*e*) None of these

20. Global marketing is a result of:
(*a*) Domestic changes
(*b*) Globalisation
(*c*) Privatisation
(*d*) All of these
(*e*) None of these

ANSWERS

1	2	3	4	5	6	7	8	9	10
(*a*)	(*d*)	(*a*)	(*d*)	(*d*)	(*a*)	(*d*)	(*a*)	(*d*)	(*c*)
11	**12**	**13**	**14**	**15**	**16**	**17**	**18**	**19**	**20**
(*b*)	(*a*)	(*c*)	(*a*)	(*c*)	(*c*)	(*d*)	(*c*)	(*d*)	(*b*)

☞ CHAPTER-12

DISTRIBUTION CHANNEL

INTRODUCTION

Progress and prosperity of a manufacturing concern depend on efficient performance of production and distribution functions. For the manufacturers, production has always remained an area of attention whereas distribution has assumed greater importance because of mass production. In this competitive business world, the production function is commenced with the complete plan of distribution of products.

Distribution is an integrat part of marketing. It includes formulating distribution policies and strategies, selection of distribution channels, motivation of middlemen, managing channel conflicts, etc. Various activities involved in distribution function can be divided into two parts:

(i) Organisational Activities: These activities are concerned with the following issues:

- Will the direct selling to the consumers be advantageous?
- Through what channels the products are to be distributed?
- How the channels are to be selected?
- Should a particular middleman be used or not?
- Should selling agents be employed?

(ii) Operational Activities: These activities refer to physical distribution of products and include all physical operations involved in moving products from one place to another. Transportation, warehousing, storage etc. are also included in these activities.

DISTRIBUTION CHANNEL

For understanding channels of distribution a clear understanding of 'Distribution' and 'Channel' is necessary.

- **Distribution:** The word distribution refers to an activity or series of activities which physically bring the products of a particular manufacturer in the hands of final consumers or industrial users.
- **Channel:** The term 'channel' refers to canal or path through which the products flow from producers to consumers or industrial users. In other words, the channel is a link between producers and consumers or industrial users.
- **Channel of Distribution:** A channel of distribution consists of a producer, consumer and various middlemen. For example, Producers—Wholesalers—Retailers— Consumer is one channel of distribution.

The success of a markets depends on the soundness of decisions pertaining to channels of distribution which are carefully taken by the management before starting the production on commercial scale. These decisions include analysing customer needs, establishing distribution channel objectives, identifying major channel alternatives, deciding the number of intermediaries to be used at each channel level, determination of terms and responsibilities of channel members, evaluation of channel alternatives for making channel-choice, and management of the selected channels, and management of channel conflict. These are the most critical decisions to be taken by the managers these days.

ANALYSING CUSTOMERS' NEEDS

For making distribution channel decision, it is necessary for a marketer to understand the customers' needs and expectations. Generally speaking, the customers need greater service outputs at lower price. It is a fact that providing greater service outputs requires high channel costs resulting into higher prices for customers. It is also true that service needs of various customers differ. All customers cannot or do not pay high prices. Many customers accept smaller service outputs if they get the product at lower price. Various service outputs provided by channels and customers' needs are as under:

- **Number of Units:** The number of units also called lot size, allowed to be purchased by a channel at one time influence customers' buying decisions. Some customers want a channel that allows buying a small lot size whereas others, particularly institutional buyers, prefer a channel from which large lot size can be bought.
- **Time taken for delivery:** It refers to the average time the customers of a particular channel are required to wait for receiving goods. Nowadays no one likes to wait. Every customer prefers faster delivery channels reducing customers' waiting time.
- **Convenience in purchasing:** It is the degree to which a distribution channel makes the purchase of products easier. The customers prefer to avoid difficulties in purchasing products.
- **Product variety:** Technically known as assortment breadth, it refers to the group or set of products provided by the distribution channel. The customers need greater assortment to be able to find what they like from large variety of products.
- **Services provided:** Various services such as credit facility, repair, installation help etc., provided by a distribution channel influence customers' purchase decision. In other words, greater the service backup, more the customers' preference for the channel.

In a nutshell, clear understanding of customers' needs enables a manufacturer to make right distribution channel decision. Moreover, in the light of customers' needs, manufacturers have to plan service output levels.

ESTABLISHING DISTRIBUTION CHANNEL OBJECTIVES

Manufacturers have to state channel objectives in terms of targeted service output levels. On the basis of product characteristics, the channel objectives also vary. More direct distribution is required in case of perishable products. Bulky products require channels that minimise the amount of handling. Products requiring technical services such as installation and maintenance are required to be sold by the franchised dealers or by manufacturers directly. The broad objectives of distribution channels may be:

- To ensure trade product availability in the market place.
- To create uninterrupted relationships with the middlemen.
- To minimise channel costs and still provide desired levels of services output.

In a nutshell, the channel objectives vary with product characteristics, competitive conditions, economic conditions, legal regulations and restrictions, etc.

LEVELS OF CHANNEL

This indicates the number of intermediaries between the manufactures and consumers. Mainly there are four channel levels. They are:

1. **Zero level channel:** Here the goods move directly from producer to consumer. That is, no intermediary is involved. This channel is preferred by manufactures of industrial and consumer durable goods.
2. **One level channel:** In this case there will be one sales intermediary i.e., retailer. This is the most common channel in case of consumer durable such as textiles, shoes, ready garments etc.

3. **Two level channel:** This channel option has two intermediaries, namely wholesaler and retailer. The companies producing consumer non-durable items use this level.

4. **Three level channel:** This contains three intermediaries. Here goods moves from manufacture to agent to wholesalers to retailers to consumers. It is the longest indirect channel option that a company has.

MAJOR CHANNEL ALTERNATIVES

Manufacturers can reach the customers through a wide variety of channels from sales force to agents, distributors, dealers, direct mail, telemarketing, and the internet. Each channel has its pros and cons. Some channels are expensive but very suitable whereas other channels may be less expensive but having some limitations. For example, internet is less expensive but it cannot handle complex products.

Therefore, manufacturers have to identify existing channels and also search for innovative channels of distribution. A channel of distribution consists of a producer, consumer and various intermediaries. The intermediaries transfer title or possession of the products from producers to customers. There are direct, indirect and mixed channels of distribution. Manufacturer's own system of delivery of products to the consumers/users is called direct channel. Indirect channel refers to the distribution of products through intermediaries. Mixed channel is a combination of direct and indirect channels.

In a competitive market, the success of a manufacturer depends upon the selection of most appropriate and economical channels of distribution. A marketer should therefore have clear understanding of various channels of distribution described below:

- **Direct channel:** It is known as Manufacturer-Consumer channel. Under this channel the producer makes direct contact with the consumer/users. In case of industrial goods, this channel is very common.

Heavy machinery, industrial chemical etc. are all marketed through direct channel. In a direct way the manufacturer reaches the customers in any of the following ways:

(a) Mail order selling

(b) Door-to-door selling through sales force.

(c) Multiple-shop selling i.e. by opening retail shops.

(d) Vending machines

(e) Computer-interactive retailing

Advantages: This is the shortest channel of distribution beneficial for both manufacturers and consumer/users in the following ways:

(i) Original and unadulterated products reach the customers at comparatively low rates, and

(ii) Manufacturers can directly get the desired information about the customers. Moreover, they can exercise price control and face competition in an effective way.

Limitation: The limitations of direct channels are:

(i) The customers have no opportunity of comparative choice and bargaining.

(ii) Distribution becomes burdensome for the marketer.

(iii) Fixed cost of distribution cannot be reduced in case there is sales reduction.

Indirect Channels: The manufacturers can also reach the customers through intermediaries i.e. through indirect channels which are described as follows:

Distribution Channels for Consumer Goods

(i) Producer-Retailer-Ultimate Consumer Channel: In this channel, the wholesales are avoided totally as the manufacturer assumes the functions of wholesalers as well. This channel is very suitable in case the buyers are big retailers like departmental stores. If the product needs speedy distribution due to its perishable nature, this channel is again very suitable.

(ii) Producer-Wholesaler-Retailer-Consumer Channel: It is a traditional channel. The wholesalers, in this channel, buy in large quantities and sell in small quantities to large number of retailers. The wholesalers sell at a price higher than the purchase price to make profit. The channel is very good for medicines, groceries and many other consumer goods. This distribution channel is suitable for the manufacturers whose products are durables and not subject to physical deterioration. But this channel is not free from limitations. Manufacturers lose contact with dealers due to over dependence on wholesalers. Moreover, the wholesalers sometimes cannot increase sales as they have different products of different producers to sell.

(iii) Producer-Agent-Wholesaler-Retailer-Consumer Channel: In this channel, the services of an agent middleman are used who sells to the wholesalers or large retailers. Manufacturer uses this channel when – (a) there are limited resources to employ sales force, or (b) the management has decided to get rid of marketing tasks.

(iv) Producer-Wholesaler-Consumer Channel: No retailers are used in this channel. The manufacturer sells to wholesalers who sell to the consumers directly without involving retailers. This channel is used only if large buyers are there such as industrial houses, institutions, government, etc.

Distribution Channels for Industrial Goods

The distribution of industrial goods takes place through the channels which are shorter as compared to those used for consumer goods. A brief description follows:

1. **Producer-Industrial User:** The manufacturer of large installations such as generators, locomotives, etc. sell to the users directly.
2. **Producer-Distributors-Industrial User:** To reach the industrial users this channel is used by the manufacturers of operating supplies and small accessory equipment.
3. **Producer-Agent-Industrial User:** This channel is useful for the manufacturers not having their own marketing department. Some manufacturers may use agents rather than their sales force to introduce a new product in the market.
4. **Producer-Agent-Distributor-Industrial User:** In case it is not possible to reach the users directly through the agents, the services of industrial distributors are also utilised.

CLASSIFICATION OF INTERMEDIARIES

Manufacturers have to make a strategic decision regarding the number of intermediaries to be used at each channel level. Three alternative strategies are available:

1. **Exclusive Distribution:** It involves the use of limited number of intermediaries for maintaining control over the service output levels. It is a sort of exclusive selling agreement with the distributor selected for one particular area called 'territory'. The distributor is given the exclusive right to sell in that particular territory. There is an agreement of the manufacturer with the distributor not to sell the goods to any one else in that territory. The distributor also agrees not to sell any competing. Exclusive distribution is ideal for products which are frequently purchased, consumed over a long time and require service/information for use. Scooters, motor cycles, motor cars etc. are the examples of products marketed through exclusive distribution strategy.
2. **Selective Distribution:** It involves the use of that number of intermediaries which is more than a few but less than all of those who are ready to sell the particular product. The manufacturers using selective distribution need not to worry about so many outlets for controlling them. Moreover, market can be sufficiently covered at the cost comparatively less than intensive distribution. However, there is a limitation that a large city market cannot be entirely covered through selective distribution.

The suitability of this strategy is for the products which are not purchased frequently like convenience goods and also which are of higher unit price.

3. **Intensive Distribution:** It involves the use of maximum number of intermediaries to place the products in maximum possible outlets. The idea is to make the product readily available to the prospective buyers as they frequently purchase these convenience goods. The intermediaries therefore, maintain high stock of these products. Intensive distribution is suitable for tobacco products, newspapers, soft drinks, bread, shaving blades, soap, etc.

All these distribution strategies have their own strengths and weaknesses. However, the manufactures are attracted by intensive distribution to increase sales and market coverage. For marketers it is a field of strategic decision-making.

It will not be out of place to know about various intermediaries in channels of distribution. There are two categories of intermediaries on the basis of the fact "Whether the title to the goods is taken by them or not." They are described as under:

(A) Merchant Middlemen: These are those middlemen who take title to the goods and later sell them. Wholesalers and retailers are the best examples of merchant middlemen.

(B) Agent Middlemen: These middlemen do not take title to the goods. They simply get orders from the buyers and pass them on to the sellers. They function on behalf of their principals to help in negotiating sales or purchases or both in return of commission. Some agent middlemen are:

1. **Commission Agents:** Commission agents on being appointed on the principals buy and sell goods at the best possible terms and conditions without taking title to the goods. They take possession of the goods and enjoy broad powers as to prices, terms of sale etc, no doubt the instructions of the principals are obeyed by them.
2. **Brokers:** The agents who negotiate the sale or make contracts for the sale and purchase of goods without having physical control of goods are known as brokers. Obviously they act on behalf of their principals and get commission for rendering the services. The commission of a broker is called brokerage.
3. **Selling Agents:** A selling agent is a middleman who takes over all the selling activities of the goods produced by his principal and enjoys authority and control over prices and other terms and conditions of sale. He negotiates sales of the goods produced by his principal. He sometimes advertises the products he sells and organises his own sales department. He may also advise his principal on what kind of products should be produced.
4. **Manufacture's Agent:** He is an agent appointed by the manufacturer to sell his products in new territories or in an area where his sales are limited. The manufacturer appoints such an agent to create demand for his product in that particular area as the agent can popularise his product being already active in selling other products there. The electric goods, furniture, domestic equipment, etc. are sold through such agents.
5. **Auctioneer:** There is an auction method of sale under which the auctioneers take possession of the goods, display them and sell to the highest bidder thereby transferring ownership to the buyers. As such, the auctioneers sell to the highest bidder, subject to any minimum price fixed by the seller. The agricultural producers employ the auctioneers who provide many services such as providing location for bidding, provide temporary storage, making advertisements, etc. The auctioneers take commission on the sale proceeds of goods.
6. **Export and Import Agent:** These agents are experts in Foreign trade operating in port cities. They provide number of services in connection with export/import trade. These agents act as selling agents, commission agents, brokers etc.

DETERMINATION OF TERMS AND RESPONSIBILITIES

Determination of rights and responsibilities of various channels members is also an important task before the marketers. Respectful and profitable participation of channel members is to be ensured for the success of the channel. Sound decisions are, therefore to be made on the following elements of trade-relations mix:

1. **Price policy:** Manufacturers need to prepare price list. Sufficient discount offers are also to be communicated to the intermediaries.
2. **Conditions of sale:** Terms related to cash discounts to ensure early payments are to be made clear. Gurantee against defective products or price declines is also necessary to be provided.
3. **Territorial rights of intermediaries:** It refers to clarifying distributor's territories and the terms of credit etc.
4. **Mutual services and responsibilities:** The services and responsibilities of manufacturers and interdediaries must be carefully decided particularly in franchised and exclusive agency channels.

EVALUATION OF CHANNEL ALTERNATIVES

As a large number of channels of distribution are available to the manufacturer for bringing products to ultimate consumers, a most suitable channel has to be selected having evaluated all channel alternatives. There are number of factors which influence the choice of channels. Therefore, different channel alternatives have to be evaluated against the following factors:

Economic factors: Cost of distribution reflects in price of the product. Therefore, the cost involvement and the level of possible sales through each channel are two important economic criteria against which channel alternatives are to be evaluated. A comparison of probable sales levels and estimated costs of various channels is to be made to decide about the suitability or otherwise of different channels.

Control consideration: Direct channels of distribution are good from control point of view but using a sales agency poses a control problem. Middlemen have their own object of maximising profits which may result into their behaviour undesirable from manufacturer's point of view.

Adaptiveness: Everything is changing in this world and product markets are no exceptions. Therefore, the channels and the distribution policies must have high degree of adaptability so that a manufacturer is able to respond to the changing markets.

The Nature of the product: The nature of the product refers to physical characteristice of the product. The choice of the distribution channels is greatly influenced by the nature of the product and other product considerations which are explained below:

(a) **Product perishability:** It refers to physical or fashion perishability. Perishable products require speedy distribution through short channels as delays result into persihability/ obsolesence of products fetching little or no returns.

(b) **Product standardisation:** Standardised products need direct contact between producers and users so they require short channels.

(c) **Highly technical nature of product:** Highly technical industrial products need to be distributed directly to the industrial users because pre-sale and post-sale services are to be provided to the users which is normally not possible for the middlemen. However in case of consumer products, no doubt some middlemen are involved yet services are provided by the producers.

(d) **Heavy weight and bulky products:** In case of such products, direct distribution through trucks/wagons is preferred to minimise distribution cost by minimising physical handling.

(e) **Unit value of product:** The product with low unit value reach the consumers/users through longer channels of distribution. High unit value products can be directly sold as we see in case of high unit value industrial products.

The Nature of the market: It is very important factor influencing the choice of channels of distribution as the number and type of customers really influence the channel decision. Various market factors are as under:

(a) Consumer/Industrial market: If the products are intended for industrial market, the retailers will not be included in the distribution channel. If the product is meant for consumer market, the services of the retailers will have to be utilised. More than one channel will have to be utilised if the product is intended for both consumer and industrial markets.

(b) Size of the market: In case of large number of potential customers, more middlemen are required. If there is small size of the market, it is possible for the company to sell directly.

(c) Geographic nature of market: Concentration of buyers in few areas encourages direct sales. On the other hand, widely scattered buyers can be reached through a large number of middlemen.

(d) Size and frequency of orders: Channel choice is also influenced by the size and frequency of the customers' orders. Direct selling is more economical if the size of the order is bigger i.e. if the volume of sales is large. Small qunatity order can be conveniently executed through the services of retailers and other middlemen.

(e) Consumer factors: The consumers' ability to pay, willingness to pay, buying motives and habits, desire for credit, age, sex, religion, living style, etc., all have the bearing on the channel policies.

Factors pertaining to intermediaries: The selection of suitable distribution channel is also affected by the factors pertaining to the middlemen. These factors are as under:

(a) Marketing services provided by middlemen: Sometimes the middlemen can provide the special marketing services which are urgently needed by the producers. For example, for a new product an agent can provide comparatively better aggressive promotion services. A wholesaler can comparatively provide better storage facilities. Therefore, the choice of middlemen will definitely depend on the consderation of various marketing services provided by middlemen.

(b) Availability of appropriate middlemen: Sometimes suitable middlemen are not available or they may be dealing in competitive products not willing to add another line of product. In such cases, obviously the direct selling is the only choice.

Company Consideration: The channel choice/ decision is also influenced by the size of the company. Generally a large company is more likely to select shorter channels. Various company/ enterprise factors are:

(a) Experience of management: A new company heavily relies on middlemen because of little or no marketing experience of the management.

(b) Financial resources: An enterprise with sound financial position can afford to reduce the levels of distribution. Such a business enterprise can grant credit, employ its own sales force, establish its own branches, warehouse its own products, etc. But the business house with inadequate financial resources will have to rely on various middlemen for their services.

(c) Reputation: For well-reputed companies, there is always scope for availability of channels and middlemen of their choice. For the companies with little/no reputation, it is a difficult task to acquire a channel of their choice.

(d) Marketing Services provided by the company: The channel decision is also influenced by the quantity and quality of marketing services which can be provided by the company itself. Frequently the middlemen demand for heavy advertising, in-store display, missionery salesmen, etc.

Environmental Factors: The decision of selection of the suitable distribution channel is also influenced by the overall marketing environment. In recessionery phase, shorter and economical channels are selected. Prosperity encourages for relatively costlier longer channels.

Legal/regulatory Factors: The distribution channel decisions are also influenced by governmental regulations in case of some products. The regulations pertaining to special taxes, inspection requirements, restrictions on markets where the products can be sold etc. need consideration before selection of the channel. Drugs, alcoholic beverages etc. are examples of the products under regulatory influence.

Competition: The nature and extent of competition in the industry needs careful analysis while making the channel decision. When products with minor differences are offered to the same markets, the same type of channels are used by the competitors. It is so because the channels are already familiar to the buyers. Moreover, the selection of totally different channel may decrease the sales and /or increase the cost of distribution. However, if the producer is convinced that a particular new channel could be more efficient and effective, there is no harm in optional for that particular channel.

In a nutshell, a producer has to carefully consider a number of factors to select a right channel of distribution. It is an age of global competition and the law of 'the survival of the fittest' applies. The products must reach the consumer/users in an economical, efficient and effective way. There is need to make wise blend of pro-producer factors and pro-consumer/user factors. The world is fastly changing. The internal and external business environment analysis can guide in the field of making distribution channel decsions and reviewing them constantly.

CHANNEL MANAGEMENT DECISIONS

When a particular channel alternative is selected by the manufacturer, the need arises for channel management which involves the following decisions:

1. **Selecting Channel Members:** After selecting a channel alternative, companies are required to select individual intermediaries carefully. An intermediary being index of company for the customers, the company requires a lot of information about the channel members for making right selection. The intermediary's number of years in business, growth and profit record, other lines carried, reputation, cooperativeness, financial soundness etc., are to be evaluated for the purpose of channel member selection. If the intermediaries are departmental stores, the information regarding their locations, type of customers served etc. influence the channel member selection decision.
2. **Training Channel Members:** The companies are required to formulate training programmes for the intermediaries to make them aware of company plans and policies, knowledge of the product, technical details of the product, laws pertaining the products, etc., to ensure success of the channel members.
3. **Motivating Channel Members:** No channel of distribution can be successful unless all the channel members function efficientlty and effectively with enthusiasm. The companies, therefore, need to motivate the channel members by giving them various incentives having understood their needs and wants. Negative and positive motivators can work in this direction:
   - Negative motivators include threat to withdraw a facility, terminate a relationship, reduce margins, slow down delivery etc. These motivators are no doubt effective but they result into presenting and conflicting behaviour of channel members.
   - Positive Motivators include giving higher trade margins and allowances, training in accounting, providing display stands etc. A number of positive incentives can emerge from creative thinking of the management. Motivating channel members require manufacturers to develop channel power which refer to the ability to alter channel member's behaviour from undesirable to desirable actions.

4. **Evalutaion of channel members:** The channel members being outside the organisation need to be closely watched and their performance must be periodically evaluated against the expectations and already laid down standards such as attainment of sales quota, maintenance of inventory levels, cooperation in promotional and training programs etc. Underperformers need to be motivated, trained, counselled, or terminated.
5. **Modifying channel Arrangements:** The business world is fastly changing. The consumer buying behaviour changes, new rivals enter the market, new channels of distribution emerge, new discoveries and inventions take place etc. With such changes the existing channels sometimes fail to keep pace with time, and their performance remains below the planned level. The manufacturer must, therefore, periodically review and modify its existing channel arrangements. In other words, the manufacturers have to add or drop individual channel members, add or drop particular channel of distribution, or make totally new channel arrangement.

   In a nutshell, the success of channel members depends upon the proper selection, training, motivation, evaluation and modification to keep pace with new expectations of the markets.

MANAGEMENT OF CHANNEL CONFLICT

Channel Conflict: Conflict is part and parcel of human life. There is presence of conflict in some form or degree in all organisations. A situation in which two or more parties feel themselves in opposition is known as conflict. When a person perceives that another person has negatively affected the interest of the first person, conflict is said to be there.

The marketers, select and manage channels of distribution with lot of care, but they cannot make channels free of conflict. It is so because the interests of various business houses in the channels of distribution are different and the behaviour of one may go against the interests of other/s. When actions of one channel member do not allow a channel to achieve its goals, channel conflict is said to have started.

Types of channel Conflict: The channel conflict may be

Vertical conflict: When within the same channel, there is conflict between different levels, a vertical channel conflict is there. The examples are the conflict between wholesalers and retailers or conflict between producers and wholesalers. Lack of clarity of terms and responsibilities of various channel members sometimes results into the actions of the members going against the interests of each other.

Horizontal channel conflict: It refers to conflict between channel members functioning at the same level within the channel. For example, the conflict between various wholesalers or retailers.

Multichannel conflict: As it is clear from the heading, when two or more channels are selected to sell to the same market, there exists multichannel conflict. Sometimes members of one channel are treated better as compared to the members of another channel because of more quantity of purchases made by them. This gives rise to conflict between different channels.

Causes of Channel Conflict: The members must have deep understanding of various causes of channel confict to equip themselves fully to manage distribution channel conflict. Their causes are:

- **Role ambiguity:** Role ambiguity is one of the reasons for channel conflict. When roles and rights of various channel members are not clearly defined, conflict is bound to occur. The marketer himself is responsible for such conflicts.
- **Goal incompatibility:** The goal of various channel members have a powerful impact on their relationships. Inter member conflict in a channel arises because of goal incompatibility i.e., goal attainment by one member may prevent or reduce the level of goal attainment by one or more other channel members. For example, the manufacturer may decide low-price policy and dealers may prefer high margins to earn high profits in the short-run.

- **Difference in perception:** The perception varies from man to man. The manufacturers may perceive favourable economic environment in the long-run whereas the dealers may have pessimistic outlook resulting into different behaviour giving rise to disputes.
- **Attitude of Channel Members:** The attitudes that channel members hold towards each other can be cause of the nature of their relationship. If the channel members' relations begin with the attitude of distrust, secrecy, closed communications, etc., the result will, obviously, be channel conflict.

Effective Conflict Management

Generally, conflict is perceived to have negative connotations. But nowadays, there is belief that conflict is necessary positive force for channel success. Conflict is bad when it becomes dysfunctional. It is a fact that despite all efforts channel conflict cannot be eliminated. It is, therefore, necessary to manage the conflict effectively.

There may be two approaches for managing channel conflict. Preventive measures and curative measures. In the preventive measures, the marketers try to create an environment where dysfunctional conflicts do not take place. The curative measures include the resolution of conflicts when they take place and become dysfunctional. Such preventive and curative mechanisms for effective conflict management are as under:

1. **Establishing Common Goals:** Most of the conflicts are the results of incompatible goals of channel members. The setting of common goals can reduce the occurrence of dysfunctional conflicts. The channel members, when the channel faces an outside threat, set the common goals in the form of survival, market share, customer satisfaction etc., and jointly seek the goals leaving no room for conflict.
2. **Exchanging persons between two or more channel levels:** When the persons are exchanged between two or more channel levels, the cooperation and coordination take place. The misunderstanding, if any, between the channel member is gone and better and healthy relations develop.
3. **Co-optation:** Sometimes, one organisation includes the leaders of another organisation in advisory boards, boards of directors, etc., to win their support. This is done to reduce conflicts by gaining their support.
4. **Encouraging joint membership in trade associations:** Conflicts can also be minimised by encouraging joint membership in and between trade associations.
5. **Diplomacy, Mediation and Arbitration:** These are applicable when conflict is chronic or more intense. In case of diplomacy, the conflicting parties send their representatives to meet and resolve the conflict. Mediation is resorting to a neutral third party who works for the acceptable solution of the problem for both the parties. In case of arbitration the disputing parties agree to present their arguments to one or more arbitrators. The parties then accept the decision of arbitrator/s.
6. **Filing Suit in the Court:** When all the above mentioned conflict management mechanisms fail, a lawsuit can be filed which is the last resort. The disputing channel parties can fight legal battle to seek justice and safeguard their interests.

In a nutshell, it is a big challenge for the managers to ensure effective conflict management before it becomes dysfunctional. It is possible if channel members are brought together to ensure achievement of channel goals. If channel cooperation and coordination is there, no channel conflict can exist in the organisation.

MULTIPLE CHOICE QUESTIONS

1. A .... is defined as the path or route along which goods move from producers or manufacturers to ultimate consumers or industrial users.
(*a*) Product Planning
(*b*) Channel of Distribution
(*c*) Marketing Mix
(*d*) All of these
(*e*) None of these

2. .... is the process of delivering the product to the marketing channels and consumers.
(*a*) Physical Distribution
(*b*) Advertising
(*c*) Branding
(*d*) Producer
(*e*) None of these

3. Which of the following is the component of physical distribution?
(*a*) Transportation
(*b*) Warehousing
(*c*) Inventory Management
(*d*) Above all
(*e*) None of these

4. A .... is a commercial building for storage of goods. These are used by manufacturers, importers, exporters, wholesalers and customs.
(*a*) Godowns (*b*) Warehouse
(*c*) Store house (*d*) Retailer
(*e*) None of these

5. Which of the following is the example of market intermediaries?
(*a*) Wholesaler (*b*) CFAs
(*c*) Retailer (*d*) Above all
(*e*) None of these

6. .... is a business model in which an individual purchase a license of a specific business.
(*a*) Franchising (*b*) Wholesaler
(*c*) Retailer (*d*) All of these
(*e*) None of these

7. Which of the following is the function of Retail Marketing?
(*a*) Estimating demand
(*b*) Selling of products to consumer
(*c*) Credit selling
(*d*) Above all
(*e*) None of these

8. Super market is the example of:
(*a*) Wholesaler (*b*) Retailer
(*c*) Producer (*d*) Distribution
(*e*) None of these

9. Departmental store is an example of:
(*a*) Large Retailer (*b*) Small Retailer
(*c*) Wholesaler (*d*) All to these
(*e*) None of these

10. Retailing by manufacturers includes:
(*a*) House-to-House selling
(*b*) Own Retail Stores
(*c*) Mail order Retailing
(*d*) Above all
(*e*) None of these

11. 'Big Bazar' is an example of:
(*a*) Producer (*b*) Retailer
(*c*) Agent (*d*) Wholesaler
(*e*) None of these

12. Malls is an example of:
(*a*) Wholesaler (*b*) Retailer
(*c*) Producer (*d*) Agent
(*e*) None of these

13. Inventory decision is based on:
(*a*) Economic order quantity
(*b*) Order lead time
(*c*) Usage rate
(*d*) Above all
(*e*) None of these

14. Which of the following is the function of marketing channel?
(*a*) Distributional activities
(*b*) Promotional activities
(*c*) Managing finances

(*d*) Above all
(*e*) None of these

15. Which of the following is the part of direct distribution?
(*a*) Own salesmen
(*b*) Own sales showroom
(*c*) Mail order
(*d*) Above all
(*e*) None of these

16. Which of the following is the sequence of direct distribution channel?
(*a*) Producer → Wholesaler → Agent → Consumer
(*b*) Producer → Consumer
(*c*) Producer → Wholesaler-Retailer → Consumer
(*d*) Producer → Retailer → Consumer
(*e*) None of these

17. Which of the following is the affecting factor of distribution channel?
(*a*) Product weight
(*b*) Perishability
(*c*) Number of customer
(*d*) Above all
(*e*) None of these

18. Wholesaler sales his product to:
(*a*) Retailers
(*b*) Institutional users
(*c*) Industrial users
(*d*) Above all
(*e*) None of these

19. .... is selling of final consumer products to households.
(*a*) Retail business
(*b*) Wholesaler
(*c*) Manufacturer
(*d*) Storing
(*e*) None of these

20. Assembling of goods means:
(*a*) Storing
(*b*) Grading
(*c*) Collecting the goods from various producer
(*d*) Manufacture
(*e*) None of these

21. Grading is related to:
(*a*) Pricing
(*b*) Marketing mix
(*c*) Different product
(*d*) Selling
(*e*) None of these

22. Which of the following is the function of distribution channel?
(*a*) Transfer of title
(*b*) Creation of utility
(*c*) Demand forecasting
(*d*) Above all
(*e*) None of these

23. DSA is an example of:
(*a*) Distribution Channel in Bank
(*b*) Product Planning
(*c*) Marketing Planning
(*d*) All of these
(*e*) None of these

24. Which of the following is the example of middlemen?
(*a*) Warehousing agent
(*b*) Clearing agent
(*c*) Forwarding agent
(*d*) Above all
(*e*) None of these

25. Wholesaling agency is:
(*a*) Distributors (*b*) Stockist
(*c*) Both (*a*) and (*b*) (*d*) Storing
(*e*) None of these

26. Relationship marketing is related with:
(*a*) Brand Management
(*b*) Customer Relationship Management
(*c*) Brand Marketing
(*d*) Market Management
(*e*) None of these

27. Marketing channels mean:
(*a*) Delivery Period
(*b*) Delivery Time
(*c*) Delivery Outlets
(*d*) All of these
(*e*) None of these

28. Which is the element of marketing plan?
(*a*) Marketing Programme
(*b*) Completion Schedule
(*c*) Statement of Goals
(*d*) Above all
(*e*) None of these

29. A marketing programme is:
(*a*) a set of policy decisions on the level, allocation and mix of marketing efforts
(*b*) a structure of production
(*c*) a plan of purchasing
(*d*) a plan of selling
(*e*) None of these

30. Which of the following is the part of distribution of sales territory?
(*a*) Sales persons (*b*) Sales department
(*c*) Dealers (*d*) Above all
(*e*) None of these

ANSWERS

1	**2**	**3**	**4**	**5**	**6**	**7**	**8**	**9**	**10**
(*b*)	(*a*)	(*d*)	(*b*)	(*d*)	(*a*)	(*b*)	(*b*)	(*a*)	(*d*)
11	**12**	**13**	**14**	**15**	**16**	**17**	**18**	**19**	**20**
(*b*)	(*a*)	(*d*)	(*a*)	(*d*)	(*b*)	(*d*)	(*d*)	(*a*)	(*c*)
21	**22**	**23**	**24**	**25**	**26**	**27**	**28**	**29**	**30**
(*c*)	(*d*)	(*a*)	(*d*)	(*c*)	(*b*)	(*d*)	(*d*)	(*a*)	(*d*)

CHAPTER-13

CONSUMER BEHAVIOUR

INTRODUCTION

Consumers have so many choices to make, compared to ten or even twenty years ago. Today as always, business growth depends heavily on loyal customers who return because they are satisfied with the product and/or service they have received. The study of consumers helps firms improve their marketing strategies by understanding how consumers think, feel, reason, and select between different alternatives such as brands, products, and services that are used or bought for use primarily for personal, family, or household purposes. Consumer behaviour is the study of individuals, groups, or organisations and the processes they use to select, secure, use, and dispose of products, services, experiences, or ideas to satisfy needs and the impacts that these processes have on the consumer and society. Behaviour occurs either for the individual, or in the context of a group. For example, friends influence us in deciding what kinds of clothes she wears or one finds individuals on the job make decisions as to which products the company should use. It involves services and ideas as well as tangible products. The impact of consumer behaviour on society is also of relevance. For example, aggressive marketing of high fat foods, or aggressive marketing of easy credit, may have serious repercussions for the national health and economy. The reason for a business firm to come into being is the existence of a consumer who has unfulfilled needs and wants. To fulfill these consumer needs an organisation is set up. An in-depth knowledge of consumers and an understanding of their behaviour are highly essential for survival and growth of the business.

MEANING, DEFINITION AND NATURE

Consumer behaviour has been defined as the decision process and physical activity engaged in when evaluating, acquiring, using or disposing of goods and services. This definition raises a few queries in our minds-what or who are consumers? What is the decision process that they engage in? Answers to these questions help define the broad nature of consumer behaviour. According to Ostrow and Smith's Dictionary of marketing, the term 'consumer behaviour' consists of the actions of consumers in the market place and the underlying motives for those actions. Marketers expect that by understanding what causes consumer to buy particular goods and services the marketrs will be able to determine which products are needed in the market place, which are obsolete, and how best to present the goods to the consumers. According to Loudon and Della Bitta, it is the decision process and physical activity individuals engage in while evaluating, acquiring, using, or disposing of goods and services. As per the opinion of Schiffman and Kanuk, consumer behaviour refers to how consumer behaves in searching for, purchasing, using, evaluating and disposing of products and services that they expect will satisfy their needs. It is the study of how individuals make decisions to spend their available resources-like time, effort, money- on the consumption related items. According to James F. Engel, Roger D Blackwell& Paul Miniard, consumer behaviour refers to the actions and decision process of people, who purchase goods and services for personal consumption. According to Bearden and others, Marketing Principles and perspectives, consumer behaviour is the mental and emotional processes and the physical activities of people who purchase and use goods and services to satisfy particular needs and wants. Satish K Batra &, S H Kazami have defined consumer behaviour as the mental and emotional processes and the observable behaviour of consumers during searching purchasing and post-consumption of products and services.

PARTICIPANTS IN THE BUYING PROCESS

It mainly consists of following:

Initiator: The initiator is a person who first suggests or thinks of the idea of buying a particular product. She is the person who determines that some need or want is not being met

Influencer: The influencer is a person who explicitly or implicitly has some influence on the final buying decision of other. She intentionally or unintentionally influences the decision to buy the actual purchase and/or use of product or service.

Decider: The decider is a person who ultimately decides any part or whole of the buying decision, that is whether to buy, what to buy, how to buy, when to buy or where to buy.

Buyer: The buyer is a person who actually makes the purchase.

User: The person who actually uses or consumes the product or service.

SCOPE OF CONSUMER BEHAVIOUR

The scope of consumer behaviour includes not only the actual buyer and his act of buying but also the various roles played by different individuals and the influence they exert on the final purchase decision.

The following figure subdivided into three parts of the decision process provides a brief sketch of the scope of consumer behaviour.

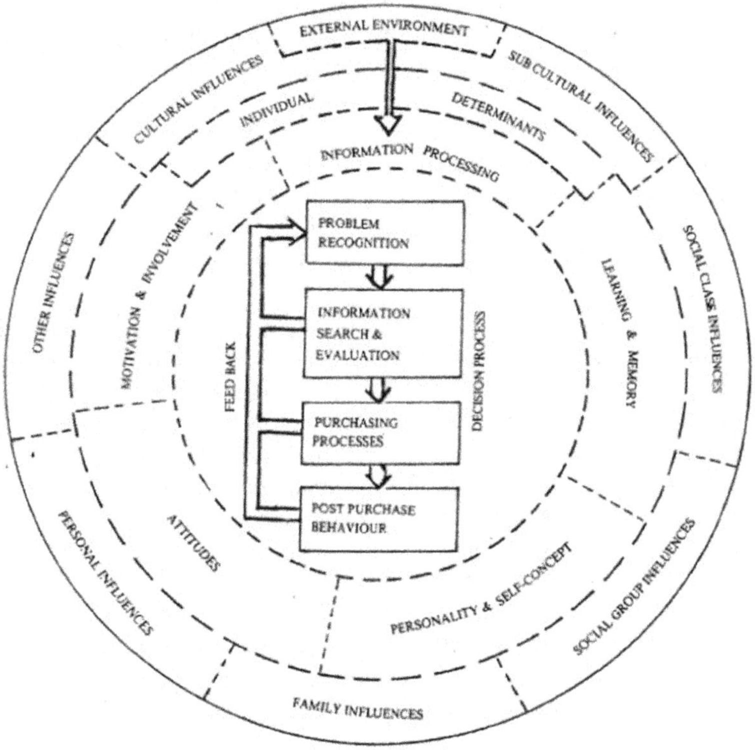

Fig.: *A Simplified Framework for Studying Consumer Behaviour*

Consumer behaviour is the decision process and physical activity engaged in by individuals. The physical activity focuses upon actual visible purchase which is complex one because of interplay of multiple influences on individuals. The final purchase is an end activity of the whole of the buying decision process. Depending on the nature of product or service in question, the mental decision process accompanying the physical act of purchase may vary from very simple to extremely complex, and from being instantaneous in nature to time consuming and elaborate. But they all constitute consumer behaviour. Thus, not only the overt, observable physical behaviour exhibited in the art of making a purchase, but all the accompanying, preceding and following mental processes and activities also are an integral part of consumer behaviour. The decision process comprises a number of steps.

The first step is when the consumer becomes aware of the fact that s/he has a problem such as that she has run out of shampoo or that she needs new set of furniture for the drawing room or that she needs to engage the services of a computer expert to help him or her in purchase of a Personal Computer System. Problem recognition thus occurs when the consumer recognises that she has an unfulfilled need. The desire to fulfill this need triggers off the other steps of information; search and evaluation and finally results in the purchase process. A consumer may recognise the need for a Mobile Phone for communication activities. But, if she lacks the means to buy a mobile phone despite of its recognition might be because of the constraints of lack of availability and ability to buy. Only after due care of all probable constraints taken by customers, s/he will look for information search which may take the form of a deliberate, prolonged search. Having gathered the relevant information, the consumer needs to evaluate it to arrive at the decision regarding which toothpaste best fulfils his need. Having arrived at the decision, she shall be ready to make the purchase.

At this point, she has to make a choice regarding which outlet to buy from. After the purchase when she uses the product she either feels satisfied with-it and shall conclude that she has made the right decision or the feels dissatisfied and decides that his or her decision was not correct. This dissatisfaction-set in motion a search for alternative choices and fresh evaluation. It is thus a continuing cycle of decision process.

TYPES OF CONSUMER BEHAVIOUR

There are four types of consumer behaviour. They are:

Complex Buying Behaviour: Consumers go through complex buying behaviour when they are highly involved in a purchase and aware of significant differences among brands. Consumers are highly involved when the product is expensive, bought infrequently, risky and self-expensive. Here consumers go through a rational/logical thinking process to collect as much information as possible about the available brands. Behaviour exhibited while purchasing a car is an example of complex buying behaviour.

Dissonance Reduction Buying Behaviour: Sometimes consumers are highly involved in purchases but see little difference in the brands. After the purchase they feel that the product does not perform to their expectations. They may think about alternative brand which has forgone in the brand selection process. As a result, they feel some discomfort. This mental condition is known as *Cognitive Dissonance.*

Variety Seeking Buying Behaviour: Here consumers have a lot more brand options to choose. At the same time there are significant brand differences. Unit price of product is low. Consumer involvement is also low. But consumer show brand switching behaviour. They go on changing from one brand to another. They like experiments for the sake of variety satisfaction. They exhibit variety seeking behaviour in case of products like soap, detergents, toothpaste etc.

Habitual Buying Behaviour: In this situation consumers buy their products on regular basis. Brand switching behaviour is quite common here. Variations among brands are significant. Products are usually low priced. Gathering product knowledge is not so important. Consumers show habitual buying behaviour in case of products like salt, matches etc.

WHY UNDERSTANDING CONSUMER BEHAVIOUR

This part of unit explains why the study of Consumer Behaviour is important for marketers? An understanding of consumer behaviour is important to: (1) Satisfy the Customers (2) Adoption of the Marketing Concept, and to (3) Gain legitimacy in Society explained in brief as follows:

1. **Satisfy the Customers:** According to Peter F. Drucker, the purpose of business is to create and then retain a satisfied customer because companies make a profit, which is a necessity, not a purpose. In order to satisfy customers, companies should adopt a Customer Culture which is a culture that incorporates customer satisfaction as an integral part of the corporate mission and utilises an understanding of consumer behaviour as an input to all its marketing plans and decision. If marketer does not keep the customer for several years, they don't make money. Nowadays, customers have become more demanding, time-driven, more information-intensive, and highly individualistic, and therefore, satisfying customer becomes very important and it is only possible by understanding their behaviour.
2. **Adoption of the Marketing Concept:** According to Philip Kotler Marketing is the improvement over the Selling Concept. In selling concept, the company's principal focus is on finding a buyer for the product it makes and somehow selling that customer in to parting with his/her cash in exchange for the product the firm has to offer. Whereas, in marketing concept the firm's obsession is to make what the customer needs or wants. It is presumed that under the Marketing Concept, it plays a consultative role, helping customers identify products and services that would best meet their needs.
3. **Gaining Legitimacy in Societies:** A society supports business because it serves its members by catering to their needs and wants.

Focusing on the customer leads to better serving the society's needs. Paying attention to consumer behavior and fashioning a business to respond to customer needs, desires and preferences amounts to business' democracy for a nation's citizens and serves both public and private interest.

In summary, consumers do not always act or react as the theory would suggest. Consumers preferences are changing and becoming highly diversified. Consumers' research has vividly pointed out that customers dislike using identical products and prefer differentiated products. Meeting of special needs of customers requires market segmentation which needs to study consumer behaviour. Rapid introduction of new products with technological advancements has made the job of studying consumer behaviour more imperative.

APPLICATIONS OF CONSUMER BEHAVIOUR

The marketing activities begin with identifying unsatisfied human needs in order to understand the kind of activities in which people engage to fulfill their needs. Thus, Marketing is defined by Philip Kotler as human activity directed at satisfying needs and wants of people through exchange processes. This definition clearly states the importance and application of understanding consumer behaviour.

The major applications of the Consumer Behaviour are summarised as follows:

(a) **Identification & Analysis of Market Opportunities:** Unfulfilled needs and wants of consumers can be identified easily with the help of understanding of consumer behaviour which can be done by examining trends in income, consumers' lifestyles and emerging influences. For example, the change in behaviour of consumer is reflected in terms of increasing number of working wives, and more focus on convenience which gives rise to needs of washing machine, vacuum cleaner, mixer grinder etc.

(b) **Selection of the Target Market:** The understanding of the needs of consumers would help in identifying different groups of consumers with very distinct needs and wants; how they decide to buy product or services; how they behave, who are involved in buying decision. This enables the marketer to market products/services especially suited to needs of different groups of customers. For example, a study conducted by marketer of soaps and shampoo found that there was a class of consumers who would like to use shampoo only on special occasions and who otherwise use soap to wash their hair. So the marketer has launched their shampoos in small sachets containing enough quantity for one wash and priced just at two or three rupees to meet the need of this target market.

(c) **Determination of the Marketing Mix:** Once the marketer has identified the unfulfilled needs of group of customers and having modified the product to suit differing consumer tastes, the marketer now has to determine the right mix of marketing mix elements i.e. product, price, place, promotion and advertising.

- **Product:** The marketer should offer the product that will not only satisfy unfulfilled consumer need, but the marketer must decide the size, shape, packaging, guarantee, after sale service, attributes of the product. And whether it is better to have one single product or a number of products. For example, the study of consumer needs revealed the need for a water storage facility in the kitchen and bathroom but which didn't occupy floor space. In response to this need, Sintex added the overhead indoor loft tank to their existing range of outdoor rooftop water storage tanks.
- **Price:** What price should be charged is very important decision the marketer needs to take. Should the charged price be the same high or low as that of the competeting product? Should the price be marked on the product or left to the discretion of the retailer to charge from customer? Should any price discounts be offered? What is the customer perception of a lower or higher price? These are the kinds of questions facing a marketer when taking a decision regarding pricing. The marketer has to determine the price level which makes the image of the product and which also maximises the sales revenue.
- **Place:** After determining product and its attributes and fixing the price, the marketer needs to decide regarding the distribution channel; the type of retail outlets should sell the products; the territorial right of retail; decision regarding convenient location of retail outlets; decision regarding selective, exclusive, or intensive distribution of product etc. The answers to all these questions can only be found when the marketer has a good understanding of the consumers' needs which are being fulfilled by his product and the manner in which consumers arrive at the decision to buy.
- **Promotion:** The basic concern of marketer now is to find out the most effective methods of promotion which will make the product stand out amongst the clutter of so many other brands: and products, which will help increase the sales objective and yet be within the budget. This is possible only when the marketer knows who his target consumers are, where are they located, what media do they have access to, what is their preferred media and what role does advertising play in influencing the purchase decision? Today, TV is the most powerful advertising medium in the country. And many brands spend the greater part of their promotion and advertising budget on TV. In so many cases of industrial product, media advertising is very negligible, instead, brochures or leaflets containing detailed product specification and information are directly mailed to the actual consumer, and sometimes followed up by a salesman making a call to clinch the deal.

(d) **Applications of Consumer Behaviour in Not-for-Profit Organisations:** The knowledge of consumer behaviour is also useful in the marketing of non-profit or social or governmental services of institution such as hospitals, voluntary agencies, law enforcement and tax collection agencies.

INFLUENCES ON CONSUMER BUYING BEHAVIOUR

Consumer buying behaviour is influenced by various factors which can be grouped as Cultural, Social, Personal, and Psychological factors.

(a) Cultural Factors: The marketer needs to understand the role played by the consumer's culture, sub-culture and social class.

- **Culture:** Culture is the set of basic values, perceptions, wants and behaviours learned by a member of society from family and other important institutions. Culture is defined as the complex, sum total of knowledge, belief, traditions, customs, art, morals, law and any other habits acquired by people as members of a society. Culture is the most basic cause of a person's wants and behaviour. Culture of one society differs from that of another. Many of our actions and behaviour as consumers stem from our cultural background. Cultural factors exert the broadest and deepest influence on consumer behaviour. The marketer needs to understand the role played by the buyer's culture, subculture and social class.
- **Sub-Cultural Influences:** Within a given culture, there are many groups or segments of people with distinct customs, tradition and behaviour, which set them apart from other people. Each of these people, within one cultural mainstream, has uniquely distinct sub-cultures. They have their style of dress, food habits, religious traditions and rites all of which have implication for the marketer. Each culture contains smaller subcultures or groups of people with shared value systems based on common life experiences and situations. Subcultures include nationalities, religions, racial groups and geographic regions. Many subcultures make up important market segments and marketers often design products and marketing programmes tailored to their needs.
- **Social Class Influences:** Social classes are relatively permanent and ordered divisions in a society whose members share similar values, interests and behaviours. Social class is not determined by a single factor, such as income, but is measured as a combination of occupation, income, education, wealth and other variables. Not only do class systems differ in various parts of the world: the relative sizes of the classes vary with the relative prosperity of countries. Social class is a group consisting of a number of people who share more or less equal position in a society. Within a social class people tend to share same values, beliefs, and exhibit similar patterns of behaviour and consumption. Some social classes are ranked as higher and lower. Social classes differ from one society to another, and their standing in society may also change over time.

(b) Social Factors: A consumer's behaviour is also influenced by social factors, such as the consumer's reference groups, family, and social roles and status. Because these social factors can strongly affect consumer responses, companies must take into account when designing their marketing strategies.

- **Reference Groups:** A social reference group is a collection of individuals who share some common attitudes and a sense of relationship as a result of interaction with each other. Social groups may be primary where face-to-face interaction takes place frequently, such as families, friends, neighbours, work groups and study groups. Secondary groups are those where the relationship is a more formalised and less personal in nature. These include organisations like religious groups, professional associations and trade unions. The behaviour of individuals as consumer is greatly influenced by other members of the group. If executives of an office normally wear a safari suit to work, it is most likely that a newcomer to the office would tend to conform to this pattern even though he may have been dressing very differently in his earlier work situation.

Marketers try to identify the reference groups of their target markets. At least there are three ways in which reference groups influence persons' behaviour. They expose the person to new behaviours and lifestyles. They influence the person's attitudes and self-concept because he or she wants to 'fit in'. They also create pressures to conform that may affect the person's product and brand choices. The importance of group influence varies across products and brands.

- **Family:** Family is a social group which can be defined as a primary group. The first and strongest influence on a child is that of his family. Family members strongly influence buyer behaviour. Parents provide a person with an orientation towards religion, politics and economies, and a sense of personal ambition, self-worth and love. In countries, where parents continue to live with their children, their influence can be crucial. The buyer's spouse and children have a more direct influence on everyday buying behaviour. In the case of expensive products and services, husbands and wives more often make joint decisions. Marketers are interested in the roles and relative influence of the husband, wife and children on the purchase of a large variety of products and services.
- **Role & Status:** A person belongs to many groups such as family, clubs, and organisations. The person's position in each group can be defined in terms of both role and status. A role consists of the activities that people are expected to perform according to the persons around them. Each role carries a status reflecting the general esteem given to it by society. People often choose the products that show their status in society. For example, the role of executive has more status in our society than the role of worker in an organisation and accordingly, they choose the products.

(c) Personal Factors: Even if two individuals brought up in one family environment with exactly the same educational background living in one house and yet exhibiting very different tastes and purchase decisions. What is it that accounts for the vast differences of consumer behaviour? It is because of personal motivation and involvement, attitudes, self-concept and personality, learning, memory and information processing is different from one individual to another individual. A buyer's decisions are also influenced by personal characteristics such as the buyer's age and life-cycle stage, occupation, economic situation, lifestyle, and personality and self-concept.

- **Age and Life-Cycle Stage:** People change the goods and services they buy over their lifetimes. Tastes in food, clothes, furniture and recreation are often age related. Buying is also shaped by the family life cycle, i.e. unmarried, married, married with children, old aged etc., stages through which families might pass as they mature over time. Marketers often define their target markets in terms of life-cycle stage and develop appropriate products and marketing plans for each stage.
- **Occupation:** A person's occupation affects the goods and services bought. Blue-collar workers tend to buy more work clothes, whereas white-collar workers buy more suits and ties. Marketers try to identify the occupational groups that have an above-average interest in their products and services.
- **Economic Circumstances:** A person's economic situation will affect product choice. Consumer can consider buying expensive products if he/she has enough disposable income, savings or borrowing

power. Marketers of income sensitive goods closely watch trends in personal income, savings and interest rates.

- **Lifestyle:** A person's pattern of living an expressed in his or her activities, interests and opinions. People coming from the same subculture, social class and occupation may have quite different lifestyles. Lifestyle captures something more than the person's social class or personality. It refers to a distinctive or characteristic mode of living, in its aggregate and broadest sense, of a whole society or segment thereof. The aggregate of consumer purchases, and the manner in which they are consumed, reflect a society's or consumer's lifestyle. It can be defined as unified patterns of behaviour that both determine and are determined by consumption. The term unified patterns of behaviour thus refers to behaviour in its broadest sense. Attitude formation and other types of subjective activity are not readily observable, but are behaviours' nonetheless.
- **Personality and Self-Concept:** Personality is the sum total of the unique individual characteristics that make each one of us what we are. It provides a framework within which a consistent behaviour can be developed. Each person's distinct personality influences his or her buying behaviour. Personality is usually described in terms of traits such as self-confidence, dominance, sociability, autonomy, defensiveness, adaptability and aggressiveness. Personality can be useful in analysing consumer behaviour for certain product or brand choices. Self-concept or self-image is the way we perceive ourselves in a social framework. We always tend to buy only those products and services which we think fit or match with our personality. Marketers also try to give a distinct image or personality to their products which is as close as possible to that of the target consumers.

(d) Psychological Factors: The important psychological factors such as motivation, perception, learning, and beliefs and attitudes affect consumer's buying choices.

- **Motivation:** Motivation is that internal force which arouses or activates some need and provides direction of behaviour towards fulfillment of the need. A motivation may be physiological or most of these needs will not be strong enough to motivate the person to act at a given point in time. A need becomes a motive when it is aroused to a sufficient level of intensity. A motive (or drive) is a need that is sufficiently pressing to direct the person to seek satisfaction. Everyone has both physiological and psychological motivations, but we each fulfill them in different ways. One consumer satisfies his thirst by drinking water, the second quenches it by having a soft drink, the third drinks Bisleri Mineral Water bottle a fourth prefers soda. For one consumer, buying a luxary car is a way of seeking status, another satisfies his want for status by becoming a member of the best club in town. The reason why marketer adopts different methods of satisfaction of our motivations is because of the differing level of personal involvement in various activities. Involvement refers to the personal relevance or importance of a product or service that a consumer perceives in a given situation.
- **Perception:** A motivated person is ready to act. How the person acts is influenced by his or her perception of the situation. Two people with the same motivation and in the same situation may act quite differently because they perceive the situation differently. Thus, perception is the process by which people select, organise and interpret information to form a meaningful picture of the world. People perceive the same situation differently because all consumers learn by the flow of information through our five senses: sight, hearing, smell, touch and taste. However, each one of us receives, organises and interprets this sensory information in an individual way.

- **Learning:** Learning is changes in an individual's behaviour arising from experience. If the experience of consumer is rewarding, he/she will probably use that product more and more. His/her response to product will be reinforced. In case of dissatisfaction from product consumption, consumer will speak and spread negative aspects of product. The practical significance of learning theory for marketers is that they can build up demand for a product by associating it with strong drives, using motivating cues and providing positive reinforcement.
- **Beliefs and Attitudes:** Through doing and learning, people acquire their beliefs and attitudes. These, in turn, influence their buying behaviour. A belief is a descriptive thought that a person holds about something. These beliefs may be based on real knowledge, opinion or faith, and may or may not carry an emotional charge. Marketers are interested in the beliefs that people formulate about specific products and services, because these beliefs make up product and brand images that affect buying behaviour. Attitudes are our learned predispositions towards objects, people and events.

  Attitudes guide consumer's orientation towards products and services. Attitude can be defined as a person's consistently favourable or unfavourable evaluations, feelings and tendencies towards an object or idea. People have attitudes regarding religion, politics, clothes, music, food and almost everything else. Attitudes put people into a frame of mind of liking or disliking things, of moving towards or away from them. Attitudes are difficult to change. A person's attitudes fit into a pattern and to change one attitude may require difficult adjustments in many others. Thus, a company should usually try to fit its products into existing attitudes rather than try to change attitudes.

CONSUMER BUYING DECISION PROCESS

In order to understand how consumers buy, an attempt should be made to know the actual stages they pass through to reach their buying decisions. A model buying process through which a consumer passes has five stages which are as follows:

Table: "Consumer Buying Decision Process"

1. PROBLEM RECOGNITION OR NEED AROUSAL
   (a) Internal stimulus
   (b) External stimulus

↓

2. INFORMATION SEARCH
   (a) Heightened attention
   (b) Active Information Search: through (i) personal sources (ii) commercial sources (iii) public sources (iv) Experiential sources

↓

3. EVALUATION OF ALTERNATIVES
   (a) Product Attributes
   (b) Rating information (For developing brand mage on the basis of brand beliefs
   (c) Assign weights
   (d) Utility of Products
   (e) Making judgement or forming Attitude

↓

4. PURCHASE DECISION
   (a) Attitude of Others
   (b) Anticipated Situational Factor
   (c) Unanticipated Situational Factor

↓

5. POST PURCHASE BEHAVIOURS
   (a) Post Purchase Satisfaction
   (b) Post Purchase Action
   (c) Post Purchase Use or Disposal

This buying process suggests that buying process starts long before actual purchase and has consequences long after the purchase. It suggest that consumer pass through all five stages, but it is not always true. Consumer buying process varies in buying special or expensive items than routine or inexpensive items.

1. **Problem Recognition or Need Arousal:** Consumer buying process starts with need arousal. Need gets aroused when consumers feel that there is a difference between his actual and desired state. A need can be activated through internal or external stimuli.
   - **Internal Stimuli:** Due to his biogenic conditions when person feels hungry, thirsty, desire for sex, the need gets aroused which creates tension to person and it becomes a drive, the person know how to cope with such drive from his previous experience and is motivated to buy a product which satisfy his desire.
   - **External Stimuli:** Person's need gets aroused by external stimulus, for example a woman has seen the advertisement of ornaments, or person passing near restaurants may have look at fresh foods which increase his appetite (hunger) and he decides to buy a food.
2. **Information Search:** If an aroused need is intense and product is affordable and easily available consumer buys it and satisfies his need, for example hungry person sees a food, buys it and consumes it immediately. In more cases need is not intense or product is not easily available, it enters consumer's memory and will be satisfied in future. Depending upon the intensity of need, the need produces two types of behaviour (a) Heightened Attention (b) Active Information Search.

   (a) Heightened Attention: Here, consumer, in his normal routine life, becomes alert to any information which can help him in satisfying his need. Consumer pays his attention to advertisement, views of his friends etc.

   (b) Active Information Search: Here, consumer need is intense and he actively starts collecting information for satisfying his or her need from following sources:
   - Personal Sources, such as family, neighbours, friends, colleagues etc.
   - Public Sources, such as mass media (TV, Newspaper) etc.
   - Experiential Sources, such as using the product, examining the product, testing the product, product trial etc.
   - Commercial Source, such as advertisements, information from dealers, packing of the product, display etc.

   The relative influence and importance of these information sources depends on type of product and characteristics of buyer. Generally, consumer receives information from commercial sources.
3. **Evaluation of Alternatives:** Information collected for different products helps consumers evaluate the alternatives. There is not a simple and single evaluation process used by all consumers or even by one consumer in all buying situations. Normally, consumer takes judgement about product on conscious and rational basis. Certain basic concepts help in understanding consumer evaluation process are given below:

   (a) Product Attributes: Consumer perceived product in terms of its attributes relevant to that product class or category. The attributes of normal interest in some familiar products are: (i) Hotel: Housekeeping, Location, Atmosphere, Cost etc. (ii) TV : Screen Size, Sound Quality, Picture Clarity, Price, colour etc.

   (b) Rating Information: Consumer gives ratings to information collected.

   (c) Assign Weightage: Consumer assigns different weight to different attributes of products.

   (d) Utility Function: Consumers also consider the quality of different products with each of its attributes.

   (e) Judgement Preference: The product that carries maximum attributes.

4. **Purchase Decision:** Once evaluation of alternative is done, consumer forms ranked preference among alternative brands. The consumer's evaluation will lead to an intention to purchase one of the products. Before actual purchase decision, additional three factors influence the buying decision.

   (a) **Attitude of Others:** Attitude of family members, wife, children, friends etc. affect the buying decision. Suppose a person has decided to buy Maruti 800, whereas his wife attitude towards Maruti 800 is negative, and if he gives importance to his wife's preference, his decision to buy Maruti 800 will be changed.

   (b) **Anticipated Situational Factors:** Consumer's purchase intention is also influenced by anticipated circumstances. Consumer forms a purchase intention on the basis of expected family income, expected total cost of product, expected benefits of products etc. any change in this factors will affect their purchase intention.

   (c) **Unanticipated Situational Factors:** The unanticipated factors prevent the consumer to fulfill his purchase intension. For example, buyer may not be able to negotiate desirable terms, he may not like behaviour of sales person, language of shopkeeper etc. so buyer changes his decision to buy preferred product.

5. **Post-purchase Behaviour:** After buying and trying the product, consumer will feel either satisfied or dissatisfied. Consumer satisfaction therefore depends upon consumers' expectations and products' perceived performance.

   (a) **Post-Purchase Satisfaction:** If, consumer feels satisfied, i.e. if product matches Consumers' expectations, consumer shall be satisfied. If product's performance exceeds consumers' expectations, consumer shall be highly satisfied. When product's performance is less than expectations then consumer shall be dissatisfied.

   (b) **Post-Purchase Action:** If consumer is satisfied with product's performance, he shall continue to buy the same product and might also influence others' decision of buying that particular product. If consumer is dissatisfied, he will not make repeat purchase and even does not communicate with others in regard of buying that particular product.

   (c) **Post-Purchase Use and Disposal:** Some consumers also find new uses of product so the preserve it. Some other buyers, on the other hand throw out the product after its use, and some consumers retain the packaging of the product or its containers for some other use.

MODELS OF CONSUMER BEHVIOUR

The traditional way to understand the consumers by the marketers is tracing daily experience of selling to consumers. But, with the development and growth in the size of markets/business, many marketers found it difficult to have direct contact with their customers and therefore, marketing decisions of marketer now turn to consumer research. Marketers spend huge than ever before to study consumers in order to learn more about behaviour of consumers which help in getting answers for certain important questions encountered by marketers. Such questions include: Who buys? How do they buy? When do they buy? Where do they buy? Why do they buy? The most important question for marketers is related with consumer response to marketers' efforts, i.e. how do consumers respond to various marketing stimuli that the company might use? Only those companies have a great advantage over its competitors that really understands how consumers will respond to different product features, prices and advertising appeals. Attempts to understand why a consumer behaves the way he does, have always been a continuous activity. Three major models are discussed below in brief:

Nicosia Model

Nicosia model explains the consumer behaviour on the basis of four fields in which the output of field one becomes the input to next field.

Field One: In order to explain consumer behaviour, this model starts with field one which is concerned with attributes of firm and attributes of consumer and exposure with message. So mainly it includes two subfields (a) Firms Attributes (b) Consumer attributes.

(a) Firms Attributes: It includes the characteristics of firm and its products. Generally, the firm name, firm characteristics, its products etc. will be considered by consumers for making a purchase decision. Consumers confront various stimulus i.e., products, packages, brand names, advertisements and commercials etc. Such exposure to messages of companies will have effect on consumer attributes and their choice.

(b) Consumer Attributes: It includes the consumer predisposition and his own characteristics and attributes. Predisposition means person is preoccupied with own thinking before he perceived something and it is based on his background, value orientation, prejudices, belief, attitudes, personality etc. This consumer predisposition and attributes are affected by his exposure to messages of various firms and this in turn is responsible for building of attitude of the consumer.

Field Two: It is a pre-action field, i.e. consumer takes action before purchasing. In this, consumer do the research i.e. collect further information from various sources and evaluate it through various means and various criteria which help him in relating the alternative with his requirement.

Field Three: Field three is an act of purchase or the decision-making to buy the product. The consumer buys the product and uses it.

Field Four: Field four is concerned with post purchase behaviour i.e. how the product is used (purpose) by consumer, the storage and preservation of product, the consumption behaviour of consumer for product i.e. whether after consumption whether consumer gets satisfaction or dissatisfaction. All such information about consumer use, storage, preservation and consumption behaviour will be collected by a firm as such feedback is used to make changes in the firms' product attributes. At the same time this feedback in the form of product use experience will be responsible for changing the predisposition of the consumer and it will also determine later attitude of consumer towards product.

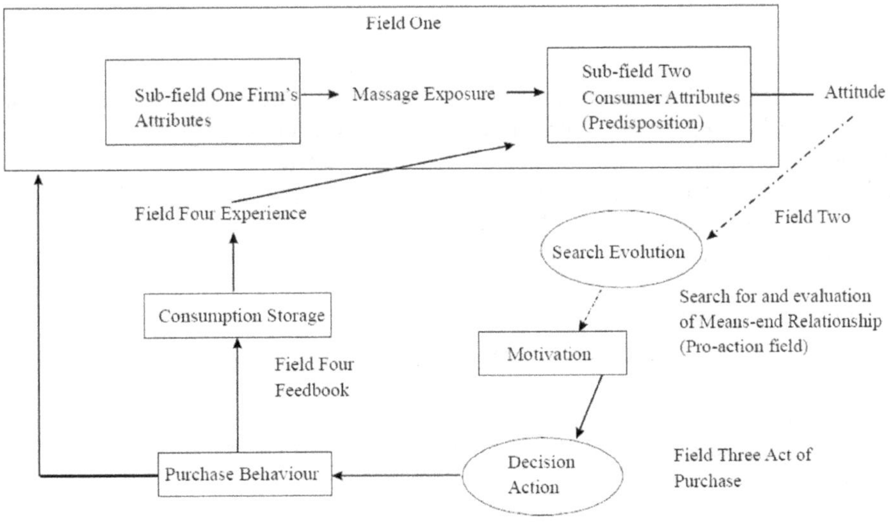

Fig.: *"Nicosia Model"*

Howard-sheth Model

In the literature of consumer behaviour, one of the major contributions was the theory of buyer behaviour by "John A. Howard" and "Jagdish N. Sheth" in 1969. They take some years and model of consumer behaviour was appeared in 1974. "John Howard" has revised the "Howard-Sheth" model further in their volume published in 1977, entitled "consumer behaviour: Application of Theory".

Simplified version of the Howad-Sheth Model of Buyer behaviour

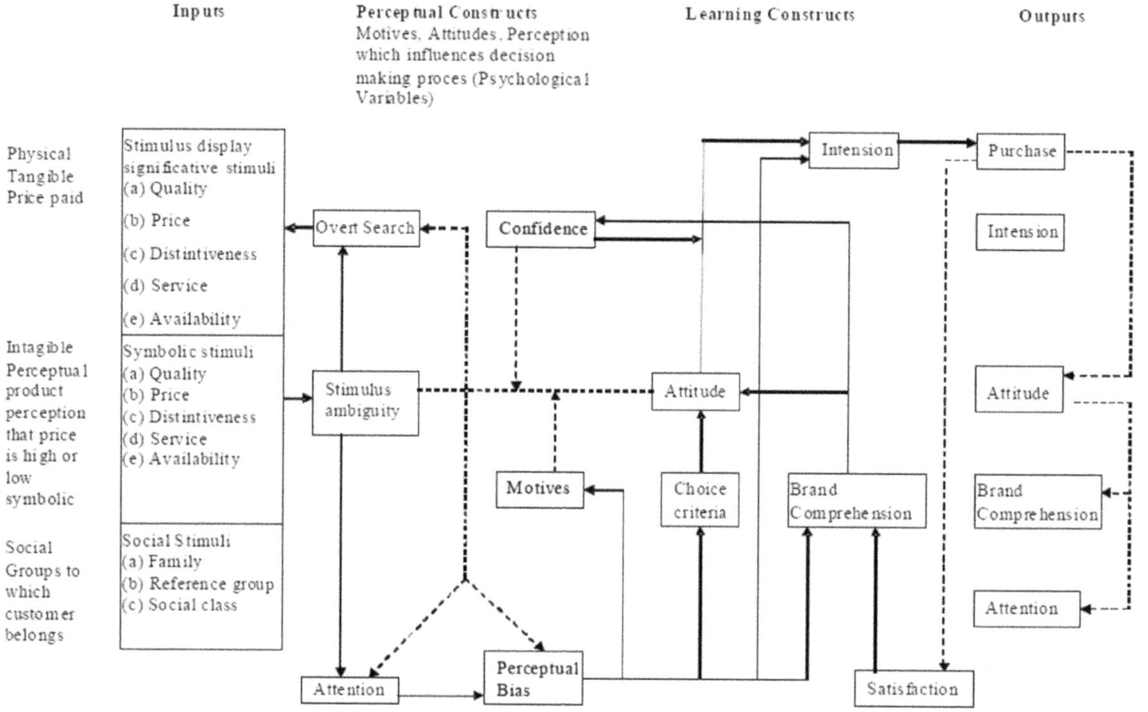

Fig.: *"Howard-Sheth Model"*

In a model, the dotted lines designated as feedback or indirect influence, whereas solid line shows direct influence or flow of information. This model is slightly complicated and shows that consumer behaviour is a complex process. Model has incorporated that the learning, perception and attitudes influence the consumer behaviour. In this model, four sets of variables are shown (i) Input (ii) Perceptual & Learning constructs (iii) Outputs (iv) Exogenous or External variables.

(i) Input: This model starts with inputs i.e. information consumer has acquired for making decisions. This model is totally information-based and it focuses more information which consumer uses to make a purchase decision. These inputs are provided by three types of stimuli (1) Significative stimuli (2) Symbolic stimuli (3) Social stimuli.

- **Significative Stimuli:** It is concerned with information about physical tangible characteristics of product i.e. Price, Quality, Distinctiveness of product, Services rendered and availability of product. Such information is essential for making decision. Here the consumer considers only what the physical characteristics in the product are.
- **Symbolic Stimuli:** These stimuli are same as significative characteristics, but this includes the perception of intangible characteristics of product by the individual

consumer, i.e. how the consumer perceive price? Whether price is high or low? Consumer will consider whether the quality is up to the mark or below average? How the product is different from other products? What services the product render? What is the position of after sales service? How quickly and easily product is available & from where the product is available.

- **Social Stimuli:** Social stimuli includes the stimuli provided by family, reference groups (primary groups, secondary groups, aspirational groups, dissociative groups), and social class (Upper class, Middle class, Lower class). So these informational cues may come from the buyer's social environment, comprising his family, reference groups, social class, culture etc. This source is not only non-commercial and non-controllable by the firm, but it is also a personal source of information input.

(ii) Perceptual and learning constructs: These constructs have been classified as the perceptual constructs and the learning constructs. These constructs are psychological variables, e.g. motives, attitudes, perception and its influence on buyer behaviour. The Perceptual constructs deal with the way the individual perceives and responds to the information from the input variables. All the information that is received may not attract the attention as it is subject to perceived uncertainty and lack of meaningfulness of information received. In this two type of search, consumer makes i.e. Overt and Latent. Overt search which is reflected in the direct behaviour of consumer, such behaviour openly manifests itself that what actually consumer is searching. Latent search which is hidden research and it does not reflect itself. Hidden research for searching the root cause of information searching behaviour of consumer. Through search behaviour, consumer receives the stimuli and try to interpret it. Two factors that influence this understanding of stimuli are (a) Stimulus ambiguity (b) Perceptual bias.

(a) Stimulus Ambiguity: It occurs when the person cannot interpret or fully understand the stimuli, or as a result of this he does not know how to respond it.

(b) Perceptual Bias: It occurs when an individual distorts the information according to his needs and experiences. Individual always would like to perceive the things in which he is interested and has three types of behaviour (i) Selective attention (ii) Selective distortion (iii) Selective retention. Clear perception of stimuli by individual is affected by perceptual bias.

The learning constructs deal with the stages from the buyer moves to his satisfaction in a buying situation. The purchase intention is an outcome of the interplay of buyer motives, choice criteria, brand comprehension, resultant brand attitude and the confidence associated with the purchase decision. The motives are representative of the goals that the buyer seeks to achieve in the buying exercise; these may originate from the basis of learned needs. These stimuli ambiguity and perceptual bias affect the individual in comprehending and ratings the brands. If brand is rated at higher level by consumer, he develops confidence in brand (confidence means ability to judge the product). Person's perceptual bias affects the brand comprehension, choice, criteria and his attitude. With the positive attitude and confidence in judging product the individual will form the intention i.e. firmness of an individual to purchase a particular product.

(iii) Output: Output means the purchase decision-person intention will make him to purchase the brand. After purchase an individual may have satisfaction or dissatisfaction, where satisfaction leads to positive attitude and person brand comprehension increases. With dissatisfaction person will have a negative attitude about product.

(iv) Exogenous or External Variables: The model also includes some exogenous variables which are not defined but are taken as constant. The external factors which are not shown in model but they indirectly influence the buyer's choice. These external variables vary from individual to individual. Such factors are (a) personality traits (b) Social class (c) Importance of purchase (d) Financial status (e) personality traits etc. All factors are interdependent and have influence on the decision-making process of individual. The model though complicated, deals with the purchase behaviour in an exhaustive manner.

The amount of attention that stimulus invokes depends upon the stimulus ambiguity and perceptual bias which motivates a search for further information. These informational inputs may alter the existing configuration of motives and choice criteria and thereby modify or disturb the brand attitude, brand comprehension, purchase intention and/or action.

The major advantage and strength of the theory lies in the precision with which a large number of variables have been linked in the working relationships to cover most aspects of the purchase decision and the effective utilisation of contribution from the behavioural sciences. The weakness stems from the fact that, there being substantial measurement error, the theory cannot be realistically tested. The distinction between the exogenous and endogenous variables is not clear cut. Inspite of all these limitations, the model because of its comprehensive coverage of almost all aspects of the purchase decision and operational explanation of the underlying stimuli and responses have given a useful frame of reference for the study of the buying decision over time.

EKB Model

The authors first began to work in 1965 at the Ohio State University in the field of Consumer Behaviour. The 1968 version of their books was the first text on Consumer Behaviour. Later on,

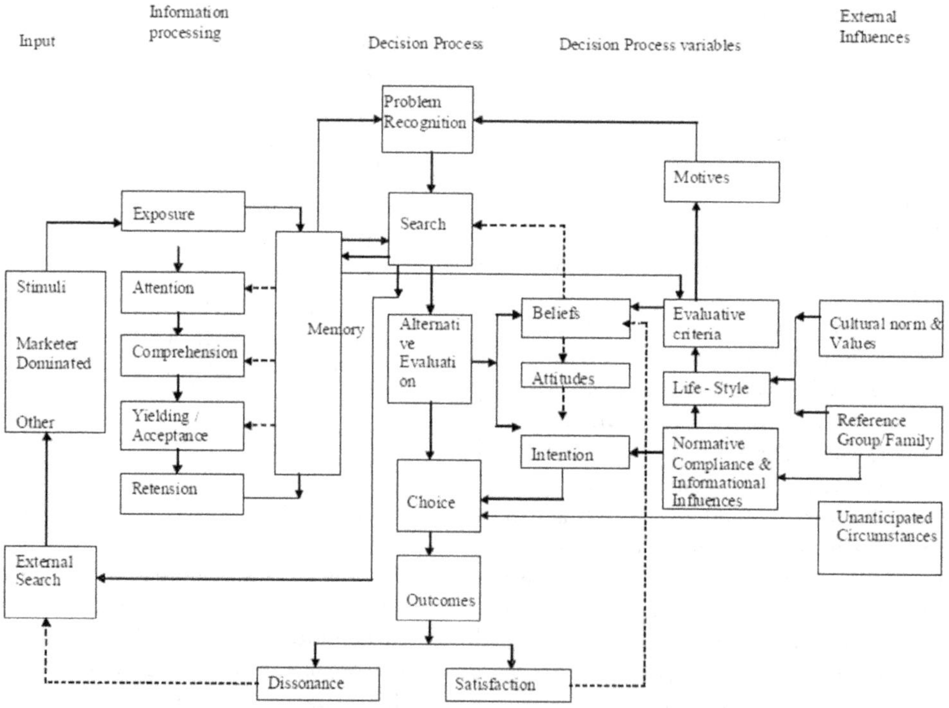

Fig.: *"EKB Model"*

when the book was revised for the first time, the authors had the benefit of the Nicosia model, the Howard-Sheth model and benefits from a growing body of published research in this field. The EKB Model had several distinct purposes: (a) To highlight more clearly the interrelationships between different stages in the decision process and the various endogenous and exogenous variables. (b) To clarify the relationships between attitude and behaviour, beliefs and intentions were introduced as decision variables for the first time (c) To define the variables and their relationships with greater precision, the consumer decision process can be divided into five steps. (1) Problem Recognition (2) Search stage (3) Alternative evaluation (4) Choice, and (5) Outcomes.

(I) Problem Recognition

The first step in the consumer behaviour decision process is problem recognition. This occurs when an individual perceives a difference between an ideal and actual state of affairs at the given point of time. It can be activated by motive activation; references' influence; the influence of other decisions, and marketing efforts. For a marketer, it is common to view the role of advertisements only as a trigger to immediate buyers' action. Advertisements have a major effect in stimulating initial awareness which will result in purchase at a later time. Advertisers that do not generate this outcome will be considered as failures.

Stimuli: A stimuli is any unit of input to any of the senses (such as products, purchases, brand names, advertisements and commercials) or stimuli may be marketer dominated (advertisements or display) or other sources, which are beyond the concern of business (i.e., comment from recent purchasers). But how the individual recognises, selects, organises and interprets these stimuli depends upon each person's needs and expectations and his sensations.

Sensation: Sensation is the immediate and direct response of the sensory organs (sensory receptors) to simple stimuli (advertisement, package, brand name, etc.). Sensory receptors (organs) are the human organs that receive sensory inputs i.e., eyes, ears, nose, mouth and skin. Human sensitivity refers to the experience of sensation, and sensitivity to stimuli varies with the quality of an individual's sensory receptors; with the amount or intensity of the stimuli to which he/she is exposed. It also varies with the energy change, e.g., differentiation of input {a perfectly bland (mild, gentle, polite) or unchanging environment, regardless of the strength of the sensory input, provides little or no sensation at all. e.g., a person standing on a very busy traffic street will probably receive little or no sensation from the inputs of noisy stimuli}. Situations in which there is a great deal of sensory input, the senses do not detect small changes or differences in input. As sensory input decreases, our ability to detect changes in input or intensity of input increases, e.g., "it was so quiet; I could hear a pin drop." So the human organism is able to adjust itself as external conditions vary, i.e., it provides more sensitivity when it is needed but also protects from damages when input is high.

Absolute Threshold: The lowest level (minimum level) at which an individual can perceive a specific stimulus or can experience a sensation is called the absolute threshold. E.g., the distance at which a driver can note a specific billboard on the highway is that individual's absolute threshold. Under the conditions of constant stimulation such as driving through a corridor of billboards, after an hour of driving through billboards, it is doubtful if any one billboard will make an impression. This happens due to the adaptation or getting used to certain sensations or stimulus. So "sensory adaptation" is a problem for many advertisers. The advertisers try to change their advertising campaigns regularly to provide sufficient sensory inputs. In an effort to ensure that consumers note their ads: Some marketers try to increase sensory input; some marketers use unusual media to advertise their product to gain attention; some marketers advertise their products in buses, parking places, TV programmes and movies.

Differential Threshold: "The minimal difference that can be detected between two similar stimuli is called the differential threshold or J.N.D. (just noticeable difference). In the 19th century, a German scientist named Ernst Weber developed "Weber's Law". Weber discovered that the J.N.D. between two stimuli was not an absolute amount, but an amount relative to the intensity of the first stimuli. Weber's law states that the stronger the initial stimulus, the greater the additional intensity needed for the second stimuli to be perceived as different. According to Weber's law, an additional level of stimulus equivalent to the J.N.D. must be added for the majority of people to perceive a difference between the resulting stimulus and the initial stimulus.

Weber's law holds true for all the senses. Weber's law has important applications in marketing. Marketers often want to update their existing package designs without losing the ready recognition of consumers who have been exposed to years of cumulative advertising impact. Marketers usually make a number of small changes, each carefully designed to fall below the J.N.D. so that consumers will perceive minimal difference.

A. **Exposure:** When the person confronts with the stimuli, the message must be gotten to the consumer, message is noticed by is brain, this is known as exposure, the first step in information processing of the consumer.

B. **Attention:** The exposure to message activates on or more senses and preliminary information processing takes place. It may or may not attract attention. If exposure is voluntary, it is much more likely that attention will be attracted.

C. **Comprehension:** Once the person's attention is attracted, the message is further processed in short-term memory in order to clarify the meaning of the message.

D. **Yielding Acceptance:** If the message is understood by the person, it may yield acceptance of the same. Acceptance is concerned with the extent to which a person is persuaded by the information; such persuasion is reflected by either the creation of new beliefs and attitudes or modification of existing beliefs and attitudes. Message comprehension is not equivalent to message acceptance. A person may understand all that is communicated but he/she may not agree with the message.

E. **Retention:** Retention is concerned with storing the information in the memory. Memory consists of three different storage systems. (1) Sensory memory (2) Short-term memory (3) Long-term memory.

1. Sensory memory where incoming information receives an initial analysis for meaning, based on physical properties such as loudness, colour, pitch. No meaning is attributed at this stage.
2. In Short-term memory, once the stimulus passes through sensory processing, it enters short-term memory, where it is held briefly and analysed for meaning. In effect, short-term memory combines sensory input with the contents of long-term memory, in that the new input is categorised and interpreter. Short-term memory is limited in its capacity to process information at any given point of time.
3. In Long-term memory, information is rehearsed and transferred to long-term memory where it is stored permanently and may be retrieved later if certain conditions are made. Long-term memory is viewed as an unlimited permanent store house containing all of our knowledge. Own information, experience, knowledge of how to use own information and experience in situation, visual images etc.

(II) Search

Once a problem is recognised, the consumer searches for information. The initial step is an internal search within the memory to determine whether or not enough information is known about the alternatives to make a choice. Often one brand will be strongly preferred over others based on a past experience, and a decision will be made on the spot. This is an example of routinised consumer behaviour. But this is not the case with all product decisions. For expensive and high involvement products, it is necessary to make external search and use of variety of information sources. There always will be individual differences in the propensity to engage in search, because perceived risk of making the wrong choice is high, further information as additional justification is necessary for expensive items. Some consumers are more willing to act on hunch and intuition. The extent of the search is governed by the balance between expected gains and the cost of time, energy and finance. etc. In case of automobile buying, dealer visits and test drives are a part of the search process. So many factors like quality of workmanship, reputation of the manufacturer, the previous positive experience with its product etc. are considered by the buyer in the search stage.

(III) Alternative Evaluation

Once search has been completed, the buyer must evaluate competing alternatives to arrive at a purchase intention. This involves the interactions of several types of variables.

Evaluative Criteria: Alternative evaluations begin with evaluative criteria. These evaluative criteria are specifications and standards used by consumers to evaluate the products and brands. Criteria are desires and outcomes from choice and preferred product benefits; the general evaluative criteria are price, quality, manufacturer's reputation etc.

Beliefs: Consumer compares the information gained through search process against these evaluative criteria and outcomes, is the formation of belief, Belief is a "strong attitude" or "belief is a descriptive thought which people carry in their mind about a particular product". Belief means whatever the individual believes to be true about various alternatives.

Attitude: Attitudes are emotionally loaded belief. Once beliefs have been formed or changed, attitudes towards the act of purchasing a given alternative will also change (all things being equal). An attitude is a positive or negative evaluation of the consequences of buying and using a particular produce or brand. An attitude is an enduring (stable), favourable or unfavourable, emotional feeling, or action towards particular object or events.

Intention: If attitude is favourable i.e. then followed by formation of a purchase intention. Purchase intention is the subjective probability that a given product or brand will be purchased. It is necessary to assume that "all things being equal" because intensions as well as attitudes can be affected by outside social, and environmental influences.

Cultural Norms and Values: Culture is a complete set of values, beliefs, attitudes which people share commonly in a particular group or culture.

Reference Groups: Reference groups have direct or indirect influence on behaviour of people such as primary groups, secondary groups, aspirational groups, dissociative groups, opinion leaders.

Normative Compliance: Normative Compliance or normative social influences can be defined as confirming with the expectations of others in order to avoid particular outcomes that are under the control of others. Example, an employee may comply with the demands of his or her employer because of the desire to attain positive (e.g. a pay rise) and/or avoid negative (e.g. being fired) outcomes that the boss controls. Marketers also use normative social influence to their advantage by focusing on the unfavourable social consequences that can occur if the consumer does not use the product example ads shows that others reacting in a less than desirable manner to non-user with dandruff.

Informational Social Influence: It refers to information accepted from others as evidence about reality. The others do not control valued outcomes, but people conform to others because others are perceived as possessing superior knowledge or information, e.g. we follow the pharmacist's or doctor's advice as of which medicine to buy, simply because we believe he or she knows more than us. Consumers repeatedly rely on others' opinions and experiences as valuable inputs for forming their product beliefs and attitudes.

(IV) Choice and Outcomes

A choice is the outcome of two determinants (i) intentions (ii) unanticipated circumstances. The intentions are the subjective probability that given brand will be purchased. It is the firmness of buyer. Unanticipated circumstances could be endless. Even if lack of funds at the moment of purchase, display or exposure to other substitute may lead to brand substitution. This new formation, causes the consumers re-evaluate the established beliefs and attitudes, with the result that intention to act changes.

The outcome of choice is dissonance satisfaction and dissatisfaction. Dissonance is doubt that a correct decision was made person is not comfortable with product for any reason. Satisfaction is defined as an evaluation that the chosen alternative is consistent with prior beliefs with respect to that alternative. Dissatisfaction is outcome when chosen alternative is not consistent with prior beliefs. Favourable experience of course, reinforces future intentions and dissatisfaction will have the adverse effect.

MULTIPLE CHOICE QUESTIONS

1. Psychology of consumer includes:
(*a*) Intentions
(*b*) Desires
(*c*) Consumer attitudes
(*d*) All of these
(*e*) None of these

2. Today, marketing is:
(*a*) Consumer Oriented
(*b*) Profit Oriented
(*c*) Cost Oriented
(*d*) Product Oriented
(*e*) Loss and Profit Oriented

3. A ...... is the inner state that energizes activates, or moves and that directs or channels behaviour toward goals.
(*a*) Research and Development
(*b*) Market Research
(*c*) Motive
(*d*) Plan
(*e*) None of these

4. Which is Psychological Buying Motives?
(*a*) Thirst (*b*) Sleeping
(*c*) Hungry (*d*) All of these
(*e*) None of these

5. Emotional Buying motive includes:
(*a*) Fashion (*b*) Operating efficiency
(*c*) Law (*d*) Affection
(*e*) None of these

6. An Acquired buying motive is:
(*a*) Profit and cleanliness
(*b*) Fashion
(*c*) Economy
(*d*) All of these
(*e*) None of these

7. The stepes of decision making process in buying includes:
(*a*) Identification of options
(*b*) Evaluation of options
(*c*) Purchase decision
(*d*) All of these
(*e*) None of these

8. Which is the impact of buying motives?
(*a*) Promotional Policies
(*b*) Price Policies
(*c*) Product Planning
(*d*) All of these
(*e*) None of these

9. Which are motivation models?
(*a*) Learning Model
(*b*) Economic Model
(*c*) Socio-Psychological Model
(*d*) All of these
(*e*) None of these

10. The type of consumer is:
(*a*) Emotional Reactors Groups
(*b*) Cognitive group
(*c*) Habit determined
(*d*) All of these
(*e*) None of these

11. Match the following:

List-I : (Type Term Depositor)

1. Fixed Term depositor
2. Saving depositor
3. Emotional Research Group
4. Impulsive Group

List-II : (Nature)

A. Habit Determined Group
B. Congnitive Group
C. Credit Card holder
D. Loan
E. Tax

Codes:

	1	2	3	4
(*a*)	E	A	B	D
(*b*)	C	A	B	D
(*c*)	A	B	C	D
(*d*)	B	E	C	A
(*e*)	A	D	C	B

12. Which is the Psychological Product?
(*a*) Maturity Products
(*b*) Functional Products
(*c*) Prestige Products
(*d*) All of these
(*e*) None of these

13. Which is Prestige product of a bank?
(*a*) International Debit and Credit Card
(*b*) Credit Card
(*c*) ATM Card
(*d*) All of these
(*e*) None of these

14. Which is the Psychological factors?
(*a*) Physiological needs
(*b*) Need for self actualization
(*c*) Basic needs
(*d*) All of these
(*e*) None of these

15. Which are the features of buying behaviour of Indian Consumers?
(*a*) Charging consumption pattern
(*b*) Bargaining
(*c*) Trademark consciousness
(*d*) All of these
(*e*) None of these

16. Purchase made without very much advance planning are:
(*a*) Cash Purchasing
(*b*) Desire for Convenience
(*c*) Impulse buying
(*d*) Marketing
(*e*) None of these

17. In India, who plays a vital role in buying decision?
(*a*) Staff
(*b*) Man with their friends
(*c*) Woman
(*d*) Men with their boss
(*e*) None of these

18. ..... is the process whereby individuals decide whether, what, when, where, how and from whom to purchase goods and services.
(*a*) Budget
(*b*) Trademark
(*c*) Consumer behaviour
(*d*) Brand
(*e*) None of these

19. Buyer behaviour is:
(*a*) A tool of advertising
(*b*) All Psychological, Social and Physical behaviour of potential customers as they become aware of evaluate purchase consumer and tell other people about products and services
(*c*) A technique of purchase
(*d*) All of these
(*e*) None of these

20. Which is the environment of Buying Stimuli?
(*a*) Economic Factors
(*b*) Political Factors
(*c*) Social and Cultural Factors
(*d*) All of these
(*e*) None of these

21. Which is not the step of consumer decision process?
(*a*) Re-purchase decision
(*b*) Production style
(*c*) Brand selection
(*d*) Selection of distribution channel
(*e*) None of these

22. Who may be Product Influencer?
(*a*) Buyer of product (*b*) User
(*c*) Decider (*d*) All of these
(*e*) None of these

23. What is advantage of studying consumer behaviour?
(*a*) Help in marketing forecasting
(*b*) Help in Marketing planning
(*c*) Product development and planning
(*d*) All of these
(*e*) None of these

24. Liquid assets includes:
(*a*) Bills payable (*b*) Cash in hand
(*c*) Cash at Bank (*d*) All of these
(*e*) None of these

25. Attitude of the Customer is:
(*a*) Social factors
(*b*) Personal factors
(*c*) Psychological factors
(*d*) Cultural factors
(*e*) None of these

26. Need hierarchy of motivation is developed by:
(*a*) Clark (*b*) Rath
(*c*) Abraham Maslow (*d*) Stanton
(*e*) Herzberg

ANSWERS

1	**2**	**3**	**4**	**5**	**6**	**7**	**8**	**9**	**10**
(*d*)	(*a*)	(*c*)	(*d*)	(*b*)	(*d*)	(*d*)	(*d*)	(*d*)	(*d*)
11	**12**	**13**	**14**	**15**	**16**	**17**	**18**	**19**	**20**
(*c*)	(*d*)	(*d*)	(*d*)	(*d*)	(*c*)	(*c*)	(*c*)	(*b*)	(*d*)
21	**22**	**23**	**24**	**25**	**26**				
(*b*)	(*d*)	(*d*)	(*d*)	(*c*)	(*c*)				

CHAPTER-14

MARKETING INFORMATION SYSTEM (MIS) AND MARKETING RESEARCH

CONCEPT AND DEFINITION

Marketing information system is system of collecting and analysing information related to marketing of goods and services. It consists of people, equipment, and procedures to gather, sort, analyse, evaluate, and distribute pertinent, timely and accurate information for use by marketing decision-makers. A marketing information system collects the information on various related aspects of marketing environment such as marketing channels, competitors, prices, arrivals, grades, standards etc. For international marketing, it collects information on prices, quality, standard, grades and legal aspects for products sale in importing countries. It combines this external information with its own business information including its capacity and capability (internal) to take the right decision on what, where, when and how to sell (from farmer's point of view or any other seller's/manufacturer's point of view).

Market information may be defined as a information on all marketing aspects important from selling or buying point of view. It includes all facts, estimates, opinions and other information which affect the marketing of goods and services. Authentic market information is the life blood for profitable marketing/sales. Market information agencies judge the pulse of market (whether price is high and sale is active or sluggish?), measure the temperature of markets (prices whether rising or fallings?), and monitor the market's pressure (whether supplies are adequate, short or in glut?). The market's history is recorded in statistical data series, and agencies offer a prognosis or estimate of the markets' future health.

Market information is a facilitating marketing function, and market intelligence is essential to a smooth and efficiently operating marketing system. Accurate and timely market information facilitates market decision, regulates the competitive market process and lubricates the marketing machinery. All those who produce, buy and sell agricultural products are continuously amassing, revising and using market information on prices, supplies, demand, and other market conditions. According to Kotler, "A marketing information system (MIS) consists of people, equipment, and procedures to gather, sort, analyse, evaluate, and distribute needed, timely, and accurate information to marketing decision-makers."

Importance and Need of Marketing Information System

During the past century three developments have taken place that necessitated need for more and better marketing information system.

(a) **Markets expanded from local to national and international marketing:** The fast infrastructure development has remarkably expanded the market. The producers can take the advantage of this expanded market. When the commercial farmers expand their business or area of operation to meet demand, they need more formal system for collecting market information and analysing it. The WTO has opened a new chapter for developing countries for export of agricultural products in global market provided developed countries do follow the code of conduct and help in establishing fair trading system.

(b) Change from buyers needs to buyer wants: As the income of the buyers increases, they become more choosy and need variety of goods. In fact, today, consumers need more diversified food basket. The increase in number of buyer also result in large opportunities. However, seller find it harder to predict buyers, response to different features. Obviously, more detailed information on consumers' wants can help the business enterprises.

(c) Change from price to non-price competition: As sellers increase the use of branding, products differentiation, advertising and sales promotion, they require more information on effectiveness of these marketing tools.

Marketing information need can be assessed through the following questions:

- What type of decision are you normally required to take?
- What type of information do you need to take these decisions?
- What type of information do you regularly get?
- What additional type of information do you need?
- What information do you want daily, weekly, monthly and annually?
- What five most important improvements can be made in the present marketing information system?
- What information do you need for export of specific product?

Both government and non-government organisations are engaged in collecting and disseminating the information worldwide. Better endowed farmers/traders/ firms collect the market information through their own resources. Recent advances in information technology will help small farmers, large farmers or traders with the marketing information they need to make right decision. However, farmers may not benefit from sophisticated facilities, if the system is poorly managed or not designed for their needs in terms of infrastructure. It is not enough for marketing information to be collected: it must also be disseminated in a form accessible to clients and adapted in their decisions. In many marketing information systems, regional data is transmitted to a central national facility where it is processed and amalgamated with similar data from all over the country. The result is useful to those working for central government agencies, who need to know what is happening over the whole country. It is of less value to the farmers or consumers in the rural areas. Farmers are interested mainly in prices in local markets where they sell their goods. Big traders, associations/ houses take advantage of such national and international marketing information.

Making decisions is not a single event but a series of activities taking place over time. For example, the Operations Manager for the National Milling Corporation is faced with a decision as to whether to establish buying points in rural locations for the grain crop. It soon becomes apparent that the decisions are likely to be made over a period of time, have several influences, use many sources of information and have to go through several stages. It is worth considering the question of how, if at all, information systems could assist in making such a decision. To arrive at some answer, it is helpful to break down decision-making into its component parts.

The literature has described four stages in decision-making: intelligence, design, choice and implementation. That is, problems have to be perceived and understood; once perceived solutions must be designed; once solutions are designed, choices have to be made about a particular solution; finally, the solution has to be implemented. Intelligence involves identifying the problems in the organisation: why and where they occur with what effects. This broad set of information gathering activities is required to inform the managers how well the organisation is performing and where the problems exist. Management information systems that deliver a wide variety of detailed information can be useful, especially if they are designed to report exceptions. For instance, consider a commercial organisation marketing a large number of different products and product variations. Management will want to know, at frequent intervals, whether sales targets are being achieved. Ideally, the information system will report only those products/product variations which are performing substantially above or below target.

Designing many possible solutions to the problems is the second phase of decision-making. This phase may require more intelligence to decide if a particular solution is appropriate. Here, more carefully specified and directed information activities and capabilities focused on specific designs are required. Choosing among alternative solutions is the third step in the decision-making process. Here a manager needs an information system which can estimate the costs, opportunities and consequences of each alternative problem solution. The information system required at this stage is likely to be fairly complex, possibly also fairly large, because of the detailed analytic models required to calculate the outcomes of the various alternatives. Of course, human beings are used to making such calculations for themselves, but without the aid of a formal information system, we rely upon generalisation and/or intuition.

Implementing is the final stage in the decision-making process. Here, managers can install a reporting system that delivers routine reports on the progress of a specific solution, some of the difficulties that arise, resource constraints, and possible remedial actions.

COMPONENTS OF A MARKETING INFORMATION SYSTEM

A Marketing Information System (MIS) is intended to bring together disparate items of data into a coherent body of information. An MIS is more than raw data or information suitable for the purposes of decision-making. An MIS also provides methods for interpreting the information the MIS provides. Moreover, as Kotler's definition says, an MIS is more than a system of data collection or a set of information technologies: "A marketing information system is a continuing and interacting structure of people, equipment and procedures to gather, sort, analyse, evaluate, and distribute pertinent, timely and accurate information for use by marketing decision-makers to improve their marketing planning, implementation, and control".

Instead of a plethora of unrelated data on market information, one needs pinpointed information which farmers/traders/firms combine various inputs

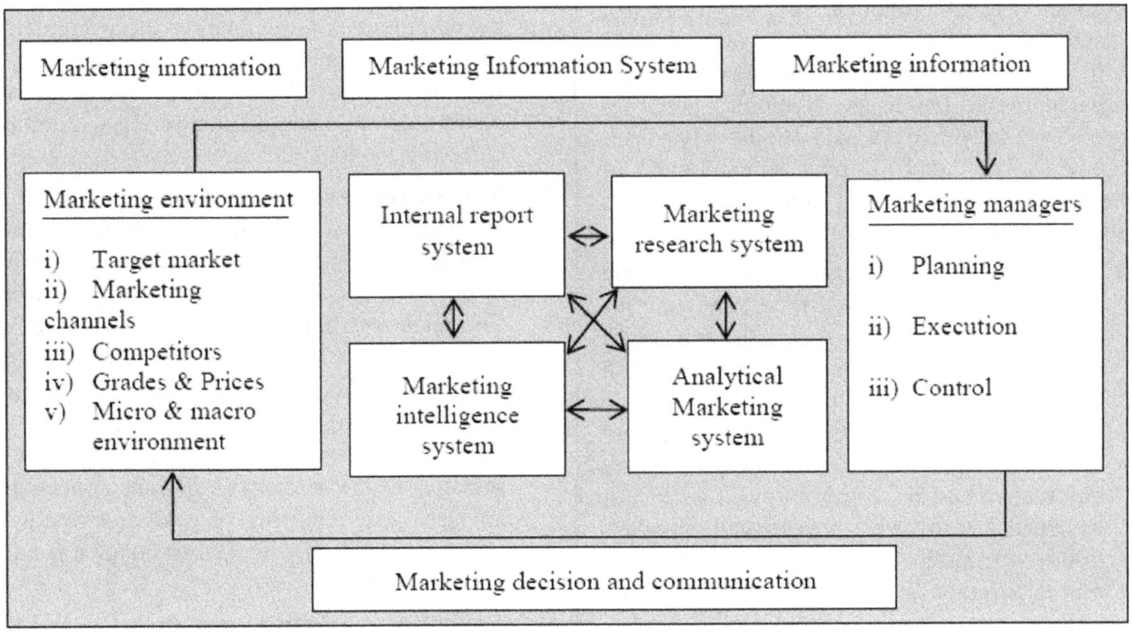

Fig.: *The marketing information systems and its subsystems*

with internal information and presents integrated report for him. Thus, every farmer or trader must organise a rich flow of information or they must search for relevant information. Conceptually in a competitive world they must study the information need and design marketing information system to meet its demand. The various components of marketing environment are:

- Target market
- Marketing channels
- Competitors
- Publics
- Micro-environment forces and
- Macro-environment forces.

They must collect and monitor marketing environment and market trend information and analyse through four subsystems making up the Marketing Information System. These subsystems are presented in the diagram given previous page.

The explanation of this model of an MIS begins with a description of each of its four main constituent parts: the internal reporting systems, marketing research system, marketing intelligence system and marketing models. It is suggested that whilst the MIS varies in its degree of sophistication - with many in the industrialised countries being computerised and few in the developing countries being so - a fully fledged MIS should have these components, the methods (and technologies) of collection, storing, retrieving and processing data notwithstanding.

(i) Internal report system: Every farm/firm manager produces internal report showing his current production, sales, cost, inventory, profit and capabilities. He plans the information need and designs to collect it. Internal company records are used to know about the market. Internal reports are made which includes reports on orders, sales, price, costs, inventory levels, payments etc. to keep tab and handle the day-to-day operations of the company. Internal report formats and designs are driven by business processes followed by various departments. For example finance department will have its own set of reports while sales department will have its own different set to meet its requirements. Marketing managers require the latest and updated information about the market. Using this information, they can analyse data about the prospects/customers and immediately send feedback/sales reports to the sales staff at the front end for taking necessary action to either increase sales or stop fall in sales.

(ii) Market Intelligence System: This system provides the firm with happenings data in the commercial environment. The farm managers get the information through reading newspaper, reports, internet, telephone/mobiles, telegraph, suppliers, distributors, specialist, panel of experts, even purchase the intelligent from outside, or keep their own staff to get information. Farmers normally need the information of standard/grades, prices, transport, channels, strategies, legal system, institutions and competitiveness. According to Kotler, "A marketing intelligence system is a set of procedures and sources used by managers to obtain everyday information about developments in the market environment." Information is gained through various sources like reading articles, talking to customers, distributors, and suppliers, meeting with other company persons etc.

(iii) Marketing research system: It is the systematic design, collection, analysis and reporting of data and finding relevant information specific to situation facing the firm. The managers either get the data analysed or study the specific situation himself. They measure market potential based on various marketing components and analyse it to take decision. According to Kotler, "Marketing research is the systematic design, collection, analysis, and reporting of data and findings relevant to a specific marketing situation facing the company".

(iv) Analytical marketing system: It consists of advanced techniques for analysing marketing data and problems. The data is available in the farm records/firms data bank. Farm/firm managers try to find out major variables (and their significance) which affect the sales potential. They thus find the potential markets and the segment of the markets through analytical system. Then they plan for marketing of produce. They choose the mode of transport, distributor and channels. Marketing decision support system is a collection of data, tools, techniques that helps the marketing managers to take important decisions. These are customised internal as well as external reports that help a manager get a bird's eye view of the business. Marketing decision support system will be discussed later in the same chapter.

DESIGNING MIS

The process consists of:

- Identifying the broad information requirement of the organisation.
- Classifying the information requirement and identifying whether it is for planning purposes or control purpose.
- Evaluating the cost of collecting and processing the information.
- Comparing the cost verses benefits.
- Decoding the frequency and timing of collection of information.
- Identifying the sources of information.
- Designing the mechanism/procedure for gathering, processing, storing and retrieval of information.
- Analysing and interpreting the information and disseminating it to the right persons at the right time and in the right manner.
- Monitoring, maintaining, reviewing and improving the system

Marketing Information Benefits

Various benefits that flow from marketing information are listed below:

- It helps marketing planning by making available reliable information on the external environment and the internal realities of the company.
- It helps effective tapping of marketing opportunities and provides effective defence against emerging marketing threats.
- It helps early spotting of changing trends; it provides market intelligence to the firm.
- It facilitates the development of action programmes for achieving goals.
- It helps the farmers/traders adjust their products and services to the needs and tastes of customers.
- It helps the farmers/traders control their marketing activities.

The quality of marketing decisions are decided to a great extent by the quality of marketing information available to the decision-maker.

Criteria for Evaluating Market Information

For maximum benefits, the market information must meet a number of criteria. Some of those are described below:

1. **Comprehensive information:** The information must cover all agricultural commodities and markets, including international markets. A reasonable and comprehensive information includes prices, price trends, production, supply movements, stocks, and demand conditions at each level of the market for a product. Providing such a mass of information, especially under the constantly changing conditions is a formidable and expensive task.
2. **Accuracy and trustworthiness:** Information must be accurate and trustworthy. However by nature, market information can never be 100 per cent accurate, but it must be an honest market appraisal in order to earn the trust of information users. Constant efforts are made to improve the accuracy of market information and news services.
3. **Usability:** Information also must be relevant and in usable form. It is not enough to simply collect a number of reports. Information must

be collected, packaged, and disseminated with the user's interests in mind. Much market information goes unused because it is not in usable form. In such case the efforts made in collecting the information go waste.

4. **Confidentiality:** The information should be confidential to whom it is collected. The information revealed under this situation of confidentiality will be more correct and may assist in drawing policy implications. The names of firms, to whom the market information is collected, should not be leaked out.
5. **Timeliness:** Market information must be timely, in the sense of being relevant to current decisions, and must be speedily transmitted to users. Much market information is unusable. Futures market traders require minute-to-minute market information.
6. **Accessibility:** Each interested party like farmers, consumers, government officials and marketing agencies should have equal access to all the information relevant to the bargaining and marketing processes.
7. **Relevance and clarity:** Market information must be relevant and clear.
8. **Objectivity:** It should convey objective message.
9. **Strategic value:** It should be conceived and used as a marketing decision support system.
10. **Economic:** It must be economical. In other words, it should be cost-effective.

MARKETING RESEARCH

A marketing research starts with an information need. It ends with an actionable report or presentation or both. In between, there are various steps to ensure that the marketing research report achieves what we set out to do. The marketing research process includes the systematic identification, collection, analysis and distribution of information for the purpose of knowledge devlopement and decision-making. The reasons and times at which any company or organisation might consider performing marketing research varies, but the general purpose of gaining intelligence for decision-making remains constant throughout. As a company or organisation, the overwhelming majority of researches is currently considering what likely revolves around the coustomer.

Marketing research process varies with the nature of problem, the accuracy of the results and the sum of money spent. Marketing research process consists of the interwoven and frequently overlapping seven steps in proper sequence.

1. *Defining Problem*

The first step in marketing research is identifying and understanding the marketing problem. What is the problem? What type of information is required to solve it? What segments of the related information are already available? Marketing research also makes use of the available literature for an in-depth background study of the problem and a marketing researcher must define the research objectives clearly. The marketing research problem undertaken for study must be carefully selected. The task is a difficult one, although it may not appear to be so. Sometimes further definition of the issue or problem is needed, and for that there are several tools you can use. The most common tools are internal and external secondary research. Secondary research intelligence consists of information that was collected for another purpose, but can be useful for other purposes. Examples of internal secondary research are sales revenues, sales forecasts, customer demographics, purchase patterns, and other information that have been collected about the customer. Often referred to as data mining, this information can be critical in diagnosing the problem for further exploration and should be leveraged when available and appropriate. The amount of internal secondary information that can be applied is typically limited.

External secondary research is typically far more available, especially so since the internet age. Most external secondary information are produced via research conducted for other purposes, financial performance data, expert opinions and analysis, corporate executive interviews, legal proceedings, competitive intelligence firms etc.

Leading sources for external secondary research resources include:

- Newspapers/Magazine Articles (business and vertical trades)
- Television
- Newsletters
- Competitive Intelligence firms
- Industry Reports
- Trade Associations
- Business Directories
- Government publications & Websites
- Search Engines
- Competitive Websites
- Friends & Colleagues

Nevertheless, every researcher must find out his own salvation for research, as problems cannot be borrowed. How to define a marketing research problem? How to define marketing research problem is undoubtedly a Herculean task. However, it is a task that must be tackled intelligently to avoid the perplexity encountered in a research operation. The usual approach is that the researchers should themselves pose a question and set up techniques and procedures for throwing light on the question concerned. Formulating or defining the research problem properly and clearly is a crucial part of a research study and must in no case be accomplished hurriedly. Poorly defined problems cause confusion and do not allowed the researcher to develop a good research design.

To find out the problem, three categories of symptomatic situations, namely over difficulties, latent difficulties and unnoticed opportunities should be studied. Over difficulties are those which are quite apparent and which manifest themselves example, if a firm has been witnessing a decline in its sales for sometime, this will be called over difficulties. Latent difficulties on the other hand, are those which are not so apparent and which if not checked, would soon become evident. For example, declining sale may, in due course, demoralise the sales staff. Unnoticed opportunities indicate the potential for growth in a certain area of marketing. Such opportunities are not clearly seen and some effort is required to explore them. After a problem has been chosen, the next task is to formulate it precisely. Formulation implies a clear statement or definition of the problem. A complete problem definition must specify each of the following:

- **Unit of Analysis:** The individual or objects whose characteristics are to be measured are called the units of analysis. The units always identify the object to be studied. It is necessary that the universe is well-defined. For example, "Women's dress buyers in Delhi stores on May 31st, 2004''. This specifies a particular universe, provided that clear definitions are given for 'Women dress buyers', and 'Delhi stores.'
- **Times and Space Boundaries:** We find that two universe are again different. In the first instance, a precise date, viz. 31st May, 2004 is given while in the second instance the entire month of May is given. Similarly, the two universe are different in terms of space-the 'buyers universe specifies stores located in Delhi while the 'shoppers' universe specifies the Delhi Metropolitan area which should be a larger territory than the former.
- **Characteristics of Interest:** Characteristics of interest can be style and colour preference, buying behaviour, personality traits, etc. It is necessary that the problem definition specifies one or more characteristics to be measured and the fact that the nature of relationships amongst them is to be determined.
- **Environmental Conditions:** It indicates the uniqueness or generality of the problem. The problem definition must specify the environment for which the company wants research results. It may also spell out the possibilities of changes as well as the direction of change in the environment so that the results of the research study do not become irrelevant. For example, if the management is interested in knowing how the units respond to price changes, then the problem definition should specify the prices to be researched.

- **Hypothesis Development:** A hypothesis is a proposition which the researcher wants to verfiy. Often there may be several competing hypotheses, either specified or implied. One objective of research is to select to among the possible hypothesis and to test them empirically with the help of statistical tools in order to ascertain whether they are true or false.

2. *Developing Marketing Research Plan*

Once the marketing problem is clearly defined, researcher can move on to developing his approach, which will generally be around a defined set of objectives. Clear objectives developed in step 1 will help better approach development. Developing marketing research plan should consist of honestly assessing and market research skills, establishing of a budget, understanding environment and its influencing factors, developing an analysis model, and formulating hypothesis. While developing the research plan, he should also familiarise himself with the existing research findings. He can also take the help of library sources as well as experienced consultants, persons with practical knowledge, etc.

Project Analysis:

- How difficult is the project to execute?
- Is it a large sample (500+) or small sample (<200)?
- Will the project need advanced analysis?
- What are the likely methodological approaches?
- Is in-depth and detailed reporting or executive summary reporting needed?

Skills Analysis:

- Is there in-house market research available to meet project needs?
- Is the in-house market research expertise available during the given time frame?
- What parts of the market research process can be handled internally?

Budget Analysis

- Is this a strategic problem/issue or a tactical one?
- Is it a $20,000 project or $200,000 project- what is the information worth?
- Where will the budget come from, and can it be shared between departments?
- Who are those most likely to benefit from the research, and likely those most willing to fund the project?
- In what time frame will budget be available?

Environment

- What is the overall economic environment?
- What is the economic environment relative to your products/services?
- What is the government environment (regulatory, etc.)?

Overall Theory

- What is your overall theory and hypothesis?
- What do you intend to prove or disprove?
- What actions is your company willing to take based upon survey results?
- What are the internal/external roadblocks that will need to be overcome to drive results?

3. *Designing Marketing Research Strategy*

Based upon a well-defined approach from step 2, a framework for the designing your marketing research programme should be apparent. This step is the most encompassing of all steps in the research process, requiring the greatest amount of thought, time and expertise, is the point at which those less experienced in market research will obtain assistance from an internal market research expert or perhaps partner with an external marketing research provider. Since the intelligence eventually gained from the research is so closely related to the selected research design, this is the single most important step in the research process and the step most vulnerable to the typical research errors. Research design includes secondary, question measurement & scale selection, questionnaire design, sample design & size and determining data analysis to be used. Elements of Research Design include:

The Questionnaire Design Process: Every company or organisation that considers performing market research will have different issues, that is why it is so difficult to find a single questionnaire design sample. It is highly recommended that team go through the entire questionnaire design process to make sure that any survery instrument created will be an effective tool for gatherinig the information you need. The Questionnaire Design Process consists of:

- Determine the information needed.
- Determine which survey methodology is most appropriate for your needs.
- Specify individual questions to be asked.
- Decide what question structure, scale, and wording is appropriate.
- Properly order the questions within the questionnaire.
- Proof and pretest survey with small sample to check performance.
- Make changes based on pretest and execute survey.

Measuring and Scaling: Creating a survey questionnaire that is capable of effectively collecting accurate data is a difficult process with many opportunities for making some of the more common market research errors. Many less experienced market researchers may believe that creating a questionnaire is simply the act of coming up with questions and putting a pen to paper, but that is a dangerous assumption.

Creating a questionnaire requires as much science as art, and incorporating those two elements into a high quality survey that will draw good response rates while effectively collecting accurate data often takes time and experience.

What creating a survey questionnaire, there are basic types of scale questions to have in your tool box. They are:

- **Nominal:** When numbers are used to identify objects, such as social security number, license numbers or daily customers. In this case, the number acts mostly as a data tag, typically for identification.
- **Ordinal:** When numbers are used to indicate the relative position, but not indicate the magnitude of the difference between those positions. An example of this would be rankings in which items are listed by priority, say first through fifth, or competitive events where the quantifiable difference in perception between #1 And #2 is Unknown.
- **Interval:** When a rating scale is used and the zero point is arbitrary. An example of this is satisfactional scores (satisfaction of 3 on a scale of 1 to 5) as well as most other attitude and opinion questions, regarddless of the scale used (3, 5 or 10 point). Unlike ordinal, the difference between each data point is fixed.
- **Ratio:** The most useful of all of the scales, ratio scales allow the researcher to incorporate each of the above listed scales into one (nominal, ordinal and interval). The key difference with ratio is that unlike the interval scale, it is anchored with an absolute zero point. Examples of ratio questions are market share, income group, age gourp, etc.

4. *Collection of Data*

To collect the data there must be some communication between the research and the respondent, or alternatively, the researcher observes the respondent and records (mechanically manual, or electronically) the observations. A marketing researcher has to make a plan for collecting secondary data, primary data or both, as the case may be. Primary data gives the original information for specific purposes whereas secondary data consists of information that already exists.

The marketing researcher would either select one of the above-mentioned methods or both. His decision depends upon on the nature of the study, financial resource available, availability of time and the desired dgree of accuracy. Primary data can be collected through experiment or through survey. If the researcher conducts an experiment, he requires some quantititative measurements, or the data, with the help of which he examines the truth contained in marketing researcher hypothesis. But in the case of a survey, data can be colleted by any one or more following ways:

- Questionnaire method
- Telephonic interview method
- Personal interview method
- Observation method

5. *Data Processing*

Data collection is incomplete unless that collection process incorporates the procedure to code the data for computer analysis. The data is coded with numbers and edited wherever the respondent has not provided consistent information. And then the data, once coded into numbers, goes into the computer for entry into relevant files. Once the field survey is over and questionnaires have been received, the next task is to aggregate the data in a meaningful manner. A number of tables are prepared to bring out the main characteristics of the data. The researcher should have a well thought out framework for processing and analysing data, and this should be done prior to the collection. It is advisable to prepare dummy tables, as such an exercise would indicate the nature and prepare dummy tables, as such an exercise would indicate the nature and extent of tabulation as also the comparisons of data that can be undertaken.

In order to derive meaningful results from the statistical table, the researcher may use one or more of the following four steps:

The first step is to calculate relevant majors of central tendency as also of dispersionn, highlighting the major aspects of the data. The second is to cross tabulate the data to ascertain some useful ralationships. The third is to calculate the correlation coefficient and undertake a regression analysis betwen variables. The fourth is to undertake a multivariate analysis. Such an analysis uses a veriety of techniques to determine important relationships amongst several variables.

While data analysis, a researcher should give adequate thought to the use of particular analytical techniques. In the recent year, many such analytical techniques have prolifearted due to the emergence of the computer. The researcher now has access to an increasing assortment of techniques and it is desirable to know well in advance as to what analytical techniques are going to be used, so that the data can be collected accordingly. It is necessary that the researcher gives as much importance to the analysis and interpretation of the data as he has given to their collection in the absence of proper analysis, data may be rendered useless resulting in waste of time and money.

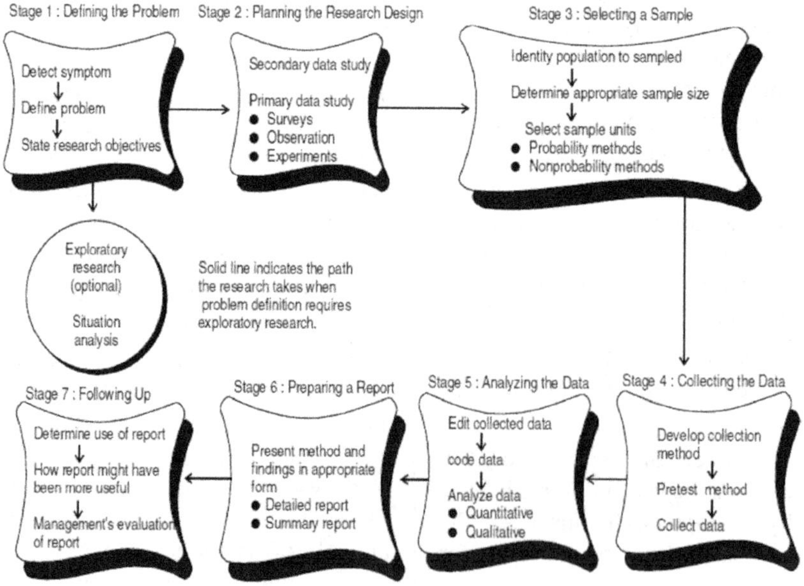

Fig.: *The Marketing Research Process*

Preparing the Research Report

Once the data have been tabulated, interpreted and analysed, the marketing researcher is required to prepare his report embodying the findings of the research study and recommendations. As a poor report on an otherwise good research will considerably undermine its utility, it is necessary that the researcher gives sufficient thought and care to its perparation.

Although report writing needs some skill, which can be developed with practice, the researcher should follow the main principles of writing a report. Some of these principles are objectively, coherence, clarity in the presentations of ideas and use of charts and diagrams. The essence of a good research report is that it effectively communicates its reasearch findings. As management is generally not interested in details of the research design and statistical findings, the research report should not be loaded with such details, otherwise there is a strong likelihood of its remaining unattended on the manager's desk. In view of this, the researcher has to exercise extra care to make the report a useful and a worthwhile document for the management. Sometimes, a detailed marketing research study throws up one or more areas where further investigation is needed. Since research on those areas or aspects could have been fitted into the original project, a sperate follow-up study has to be attempted.

The marketing research process, as described above, involves various steps, though strict adherence to each of these steps may not be necessary. A researcher may deviate from the above sequence and steps depending on his specific needs. It should be remembered that as research proceeds from the selection on the theme through the collection and analysis of data to the preparation of a report, the focus of attention will move from one activity to the other. This implies that the researcher does not always concentrate exclusively on one particular phase of research untill its completion.

Further, while it is beneficial to draw a detailed plan and sequence of various activities in marketing research, it is hardly so if it requires such kind of financial backing which the firm cannot afford. There is no point in attempting something which cannot be completed on account of financial constraints or limitations of time. Another point worth emphasising is that howsoever elaborate a research design may be, its management in fact, research management, whether in marketing or in any other field, is of great importance.

IMPORTANCE OF MARKETING RESEARCH

- It facilitates planned production by forecasting probable sales.
- It helps in identifying the reasons for consumer resistance to existing or new products.
- It reveals the nature of demand for the product i.e. whether the product is in demand throughout the year or has a seasonal demand.
- It indicates the product utility as well as the effectiveness of existing channels of distribution.
- It may reveal certain new uses for the existing products.
- It provides information about potential or future markets.
- It helps in the discovery of new lines of production.

MULTIPLE CHOICE QUESTIONS

1. R & D means:
(*a*) Rate and Division
(*b*) Research and Development
(*c*) Research and Department
(*d*) Rate and Department
(*e*) None of these

2. Research involves:
(*a*) Consumer Research
(*b*) Product Research
(*c*) Consumer Motivation Research
(*d*) Above all
(*e*) None of these

3. Innovation means:
(*a*) New idea (*b*) New raw material
(*c*) New Product (*d*) Above all
(*e*) None of these

4. Product Innovation is a part of:
(*a*) Product pricing
(*b*) Product modification
(*c*) Cost
(*d*) Production
(*e*) None of these

5. Business Analysis includes:
(*a*) Estimating Future Profits
(*b*) Estimating Future Costs
(*c*) Estimating Future Sales
(*d*) Above all
(*e*) None of these

6. Market Research includes:
(*a*) Product Survey
(*b*) Market Survey
(*c*) Survey of Customers
(*d*) Above all
(*e*) None of these

7. Match the following:

List-I (Marketing Research)	**List-II (Example)**
1. Customers Survey	A. Income of the Customer
2. Product Survey	B. Quality of the Producer
3. Market Survey	C. Potential Customer
4. Price Survey	D. Discount
	E. Quality of the product

Codes:

	1	2	3	4
(*a*)	A	D	B	C
(*b*)	A	B	C	D
(*c*)	E	D	A	C
(*d*)	C	A	B	D
(*e*)	D	E	B	C

8. Which of the following is MR Agencies in India?
(*a*) AC Nielsen (*b*) ORG-MARG
(*c*) IMRB (*d*) Above all
(*e*) None of these

9. .... is a method of collecting marketing information required for a given marketing research assignment.
(*a*) Marketing Survey
(*b*) Marketing Planning
(*c*) Marketing Mix
(*d*) Marketing value
(*e*) None of these

10. .... is systematic problem analysis, model building and fact finding for the purposes of decision-making control in the marketing of goods and services.
(*a*) Marketing Survey
(*b*) Marketing Research
(*c*) Marketing Planning
(*d*) Above all
(*e*) None of these

11. A marketing information system (MIS) caters to the needs of ....
(*a*) Marketing decision
(*b*) Databases
(*c*) Safeguard
(*d*) Customized
(*e*) None of these

12. .... is the oral presentation in a conversation with one or more prospective buyers for the purpose of making sales.
(*a*) Samples (*b*) Rebates
(*c*) Coupons (*d*) Money refund offer
(*e*) None of these

13. Marketing research data is gathered by ....
(*a*) Observation
(*b*) In depth interviews
(*c*) Controlled experiment
(*d*) All the above
(*e*) None of these

14. MIS stands for ....
(*a*) Marketing Information System.
(*b*) Management information System.

(*c*) Management interface system.
(*d*) Market Interface system.
(*e*) None of these

15. Customers are showing greater price sensitivity in their search for ....
(*a*) the right product
(*b*) the right service
(*c*) the right store
(*d*) value
(*e*) None of these

16. Companies who form a .... collect information on each customer's past transactions, demographics, psychographics, and media and distribution preferences.
(*a*) sales network
(*b*) holistic union
(*c*) marketing network
(*d*) supply-chain network
(*e*) None of these

17. Companies see .... as an opportunity to enhance their corporate reputation, raise brand awareness, increase customer loyalty, build sales, and increase press coverage.
(*a*) cause-related marketing
(*b*) brand marketing
(*c*) equity marketing
(*d*) direct marketing
(*e*) None of these

18. For each target market, the firm develops a .... The offering is positioned in the minds of the target buyers as delivering some central benefit(s).
(*a*) value offering (*b*) niche offering
(*c*) market offering (*d*) segment offering
(*e*) None of these

19. .... includes all the actual and potential rival offerings and substitutes that a buyer might consider.
(*a*) Competition
(*b*) The product offering
(*c*) A value proposition
(*d*) The supply chain
(*e*) None of these

ANSWERS

1	2	3	4	5	6	7	8	9	10
(*c*)	(*d*)	(*d*)	(*b*)	(*d*)	(*d*)	(*b*)	(*d*)	(*a*)	(*b*)
11	**12**	**13**	**14**	**15**	**16**	**17**	**18**	**19**	
(*a*)	(*c*)	(*d*)	(*b*)	(*d*)	(*c*)	(*a*)	(*c*)	(*a*)	

CHAPTER-15

MARKETING STRATEGIES

INTRODUCTION

How are the marketing objectives going to be achieved? This is the burden of marketing strategy. In fact, marketing strategy formulation is the core of marketing planning. After all, it is the strategy that brings home the income and profits expected of the business. And it is strategy that renders one firm distinct from another and makes its offerings unique, compared to those of its competitors. The unit that follows explains elaborately the scope and significance of marketing strategy and the process of formulating it. When the business unit is through with the strategy formulation, it is ready with the game plan on what to do with each product/ brand in its fold and how to go about it.

Marketing Strategy and plan can be prepared in a few weeks or a couple of months, but its implementation takes place over years. Moreover, Strategy execution involves more people at various levels, across the organisation. To facilitate execution, strategic plans must be translated into detailed functional plans and short-term operating plans whose fulfillment must be tracked using suitable metrics. In other words, it is the quality of the functional plans and the efficiency in monitoring its implementation, that finally decide the success of marketing plan/strategy.

THE SIGNIFICANCE OF MARKETING STRATEGY

- **Instrument for Value Delivery:** Marketing strategy represents the plan by which the firm delivers its value to the customers. It also specifies how the firm would be enabled/ empowered to deliver that value. It is marketing strategy that specifies how the firm would go about its value selection, value creation, and value communication. In the sections that follows we are going to see that the firm's marketing mix is the carrier of value and it is the marketing strategy that assembles this mix. Marketing strategy thus works as the key in value delivery. It clarifies what benefit/value the consumer seeks, how much he can afford to pay for it, and how much of the value the firm could provide to him **(the value to him - cost to us** analysis). It also serves as the guide for the firm in creating, delivering, and communicating that value.
- **Helps Realising Marketing Objectives:** Marketing strategy enables the business units attain there marketing objectives. The objectives indicate what the firm wants to achieve; the strategy provides the design for achieving them. Put differently, the objectives tell where the firm wants to go and the strategy shows how it will reach there.
- **Helps in Realising the Targeted Income and Profit:** In particular, marketing strategy enables the unit realise its targeted sales income and profits pertaining to a brand/product. For example, if the marketing objective of the unit is to achieve a sales of ₹ 1,000 crore and a net profit of 12 per cent on that sale, the marketing strategy would indicate how and wherefrom this sale and profit will come, which brand will accomplish what portion of this objective and how. Let us understand this dimension in detail through the example of Lifebuoy.

Suppose, in accordance with the corporate growth objective (fixed by HUL in FY 06), all the businesses of HUL together have to achieve in FY 2007 a sales income of ₹ 12,700 crore (a 5 per cent increase over previous year) and a profit of ₹ 1,270 crore (10 percent of the projected sale). The three SBUs of HUL - soaps & detergents, foods & beverages and personal care products - have to collectively deliver this income and profit to the company. According to the ongoing pattern, soaps and detergents account for 45 per cent of the corporate income and the balance is met by the other SBUs. HUL may opt to continue the same pattern and allot 45 per cent of the corporate turnover target to the soaps and detergents business. That means, the business has to achieve a sales income of ₹ 5,715 crore for the year. The soaps and detergents SBU has three product lines: Bathing soaps, Washing soaps, Detergents (powder and cake). The SBU has to decide: How much contribution can be expected of each product line- from bathing soaps, washing soaps and detergents? The SBU has to extend the question to the brand level in each line and fix how much income has to come from a particular brand.

- **Specifies the Position:** A company needs to clarify the position it seeks in the industry. Does it want to be the market leader in the long term? Or, is it satisfied with a less aggressive profile? Strategy provides this clarification. The marketing programme to be developed will based on this posture. For example, when GE Capital entered the Indian consumer finance market in the early 1990s, its strategic intent was to become the leader in the consumer finance business. It proclaimed that the position it was seeking was that of No. 1. All its activities were woven around this intent. To secure a fast spread throughout the national market, GE Capital straightaway set up three consumer-finance JVs in collaboration with Godrej, HDFC and Maruti Udyog. The takeover of SRF Finance, which had 10 branch offices, a 136,000 strong depositor-base and a distinctive strength in the businesses proposed by GE Caps was another major move to ensure wide reach and deep penetration of the market. In short, GE Caps was putting in place a ready marketing organisation to secure its objective of becoming the leader in the Indian consumer finance market.

  Obviously, all firms in an industry cannot and do not seek the No. 1 position. Many are content with a follower's position while a few prefer to be niche players. Whatever be the case, marketing strategy will clearly specify the position that a unit seeks in the industry.

- **Specifies the Products to Offer:** The strategy also clarifies what market segments the business unit will serve and what product offers it will make to the selected segments. In other words, it has to state its product-market scope. For example, when ICICI Bank commenced its activities, it decided to exclusively serve urban India. It sets up offices only in the major cities. Its target market consisted of corporates and high net worth individuals in cities. It also decided to offer several new banking products for the chosen clientele. It chose not to target the rural markets. When Motorola entered the emerging mobile phone market of India, its choice was to serve the upper-end consumer with high priced, feature packed models. Nokia on the other hand decided to serve varied segments ranging from entry-level users to middle, upper and lifestyle segments.

- **Specifies Firm's Competitors:** The firm has to reckon who the major players in the industry are and against whom it will have to compete. It also has to decide which players it would choose to avoid competing with. Strategy specifies whom to confront and whom to exclude. For example, when the US car major, Ford, entered the Indian car market, Maruti was the dominant player here, with its Maruti 800 model holding a 70 per cent plus share. Ford decided to cultivate the higher B+ and C segment, with models like Ford Ikon. Ford was thus opting to compete with players like GM, who were competing in this segment with models like Opel Astra and Corsa. Ford chose not to compete with Maruti in the small/

compact car segment. So, whom to compete with and whom to avoid is a vital issue in marketing strategy.

- **Specifies the Growth Path:** The strategy also specifies the unit's path for achieving the growth envisaged: **market penetration, market development, or product development?** For example, when Maruti Udyog commenced its activities in the Indian passenger car market, in the initial stages it resorted to market penetration and in the later stages, it employed a combination of market penetration and product development strategies. The global IT software firm, Microsoft, always chooses the product development route as its growth path. It consistently brings out new software programs, each a significant improvement over the previous one and competes in the market.
- **Specifies the Differentiation of Strengths:** The next issue is: On what distinctive capability/ differentiation strength, will the business unit compete in its industry? On what unique strengths will it launch its products/brands and wage the marketplace battles? Kellogg, for example, entered the Indian breakfast cereal market heavily banking on the company's brand clout. Apple's iPhone relied on product (technology) superiority. Nirma acquired its place in the detergent market on the strength of an attractive price. Kingfisher Airlines based its fight on high-class service.
- **Specifies the Competitive Advantages:** Marketing strategy specifies on what competitive advantage it will base its fight and how it will build that advantage. What competencies and facilities should it develop? For marketing its TVs, Videocon, a major player in the Indian TV market, relies heavily on its integrated manufacturing facilities. Videocon makes all components of its TV in-house, and uses this facility to offer a quality product at competitive prices. It has control over both cost and process quality. In other words, Videocon plays the marketing game with the competitive advantages arising out of integration.
- **Specifies the Resources:** The business unit has to assess the resources available to it for putting the strategy into action and for developing the intended competencies. Resources available to the unit - money, people and facilities delimit the scope of the strategy that can be employed. Formulation of competitive/marketing strategy for a product/brand involves sorting out all such issues. In fact, the answers to them would constitute the strategy.

FORMULATING MARKETING STRATEGY

Formulating STP Strategy

The marketing strategy for a given product/brand takes shape when these two steps are completed. As segmentation, targeting, and positioning form one homogeneous group of tasks in this process, they are grouped as one step and referred to by the acronym STP. Assembling the marketing mix/4Ps is the other step. STP and marketing mix together constitute the marketing strategy of the given product. Segmentation serves as the prelude to target market selection. It brings to the fore the various possibilities lying within a heterogeneous market. The target market that is arrived at through segmentation shows *to whom,* the unit intends to sell the product. Positioning and marketing mix together show *how* - using what uniqueness or distinction - the unit intends to sell it.

(a) Segmentation of the market

Segmentation of the market is the starting point of the whole exercise. The market for any product is a heterogeneous entity. In fact, it is stratified-based on several characteristics. Segmentation is a process by which you try to understand the heterogeneous market by viewing it from different angles and grasping the commonalities as well as differences contained therein, and then divide the whole market into segments, each homogeneous within itself, sharing certain common characteristics.

(b) Targeting (picking the appropriate segments)

From segmentation, we proceed to target market selection. The latter essentially means picking up of the appropriate market segments. The process of segmentation throws up not one but several market segments, with varying potential, profitability and risks. The firm may not be interested in all the segments. There may be segments that are sizeable and the ones that are not so sizeable. There may be segments assuring immediate profits and the ones that call for heavy investment in market development. There may also be segments that show great potential, but display tough barriers to entry. As such, the question - which segment/ segments the firm should select as its target market - assumes crucial importance.

To say that target market selection is a part of marketing strategy formulation is just stating the obvious. One has to appreciate the total linkage between the two. With the selection of the target market, a major part of the marketing strategy of the product is determined, defined and expressed.

How Reliance Textiles chose its target market: To cite an example, when Reliance Textiles, subsequently a part of the Reliance Industries, entered the Indian textile market in 1967, it found that this market consisted of many distinct segments. And it was spread over entire rural and urban India. It was a ₹ 5,000 crore market, with cotton textiles taking more than 70 per cent share and the rest taken up by silks and synthetics. Reliance was coming out with premium products - high quality synthetic fabrics - sarees, suitings, shirtings and dress materials. Reliance had to select its target market for this product. It spotted the well-to-do and fashion loving upper middle class of urban India as its target market. The decision came through a combined process of analytical exercise and executive judgement. Of the many distinct segments, the company deliberately chose the one that was most profitable and was also most suited to its offer.

What part of the market do we serve? What part we choose not to serve: In effect, target market selection boils down to deciding - what parts of the market are we going to serve? What parts of the market we choose not to serve? And, what is the logic of selecting a particular segment? In other words, it is basically a question of balancing the attractiveness of the various segments with the objectives and resources of the firm. Target market selection is, therefore, the first burden of marketing strategy formulation.

When the target market for the product is selected the right way, ('rightness' obviously gets proved only subsequently) half the job of marketing strategy formulation is over. The firm decides: This is the arena we will play in. So, target market selection becomes fundamental to marketing strategy formulation; in fact, it becomes fundamental to the marketing game as a whole. Target market determines the broad contours of the marketing strategy. After all, the whole purpose of marketing strategy is only to serve the target market effectively and successfully. In fact, it is incorrect to treat target market selection and marketing strategy as two different entities. They are parts of a unified process.

(c) Positioning the offer

The next major dimension of marketing strategy relates to the positioning of the offer. The firm has already selected the target market and decided its basic offer. For example, it has selected the well-to-do fashion loving upper-middle class of urban India as its target market, and high-quality synthetic fabrics as its product offering. Now, what is the conjunction between these two entities? How do they get connected? What is the interface? In other words:

- What is the locus the firm seeks in the minds of the chosen customers/target market with its offering?
- How would the firm want the consumer to view and receive the offer? For example, does the firm want to lodge the intended product as the most distinctive offer in the market?
- Does it want to lodge it as the latest, with certain unique functional benefits?

- Is the firm seeking the leader position with its product offer? Or, is it occupying the challenger's role, with the promise that the customer can expect a performance that is one better than that of the present leader?

The point is that the firm has to clarify what it proposes to do with its offering, how it wants the offer to be perceived by the customer, what position it seeks in the minds of the customers and what image it proposes to build for its offer.

Assembling the Marketing Mix

Once STP is decided on, assembling the marketing mix becomes the main task in marketing strategy formulation. In the execution of the strategy too, the marketing mix plays the lead role. It is by operating the marketing mix that a marketing man executes his marketing strategy. Assembling the marketing mix means making the best combination of the 4Ps. Best combination implies one that delivers the best possible value to the target market and in turn brings the best possible value back into the firm's kitty. Involved in this process is the choice of appropriate marketing activities and allocation of the appropriate portion of the marketing effort/resources to each of them. The marketing man basically tries to know how he can generate the targeted sales and profit. He considers different marketing mixes with varying levels of expenditure assigned to each marketing activity and tries to figure out the effectiveness of the different combinations in terms of the possible sales and profits. He then chooses the combination/mix that is best according to his judgement.

Assembling the marketing mix involves decisions relating to each of the marketing mix elements, product, price, channel and promotion and the linkages among them. For example, one has to decide:

- Which product should be offered to an identified target market?
- What should be the price structure?
- Which channel has to be used?
- What is the right promotion strategy?
- How should the marketing effort/resources of the firm be apportioned among the 4 Ps?
- What is the best combination in the given situation?
- How to balance the impact of an increase or decrease in the allocation to a particular element on the other elements?

It is obvious that theoretically the marketing mix elements can be combined in an infinite number of ways. In practice too, marketing managers usually consider many different combinations and select the best. The marketing mix elements are substitutable by one another to some extent. Marketing managers can achieve superior result with a carefully selected mix. And, they can also achieve the same objective, using different marketing mix. They can take away some resources from one element and assign them to another and achieve superior result.

The name of the game is to select a combination, which will have the desired impact on the target market and will also be cost-effective. The marketing objective and context decide the weightage to be assigned to each element and sub-element. For example, within promotion, advertising may get a higher weightage if the objective is brand building, and sales promotion may get a higher weightage if the objective is quicker sales in the immediate run. The marketing manager works out different combinations of sales levels and marketing mix spending and chooses the optimum one.

The effectiveness of any marketing programme depends directly on the extent to which the marketing mix is able to harmonise and synthesise the different elements into a unified entity.

(a) Deciding the weightage for each P: Earlier we saw that deciding the weightage to be assigned to each of the 4Ps is the crux of marketing mix formulation. There is no standard formula in this respect. One firm may assign maximum weightage to the product, and build up its technological superiority and functional benefits. It may opt for a better design or an improved formula and bring out a product with a significant specialty. It may provide only an average weightage to distribution and promotion. In other words, the firm puts in extra effort and investment on product and product superiority forms the mainstay of its marketing mix. Another firm in the same industry may assign a greater weightage to distribution, and yet another firm, to promotion.

- **Godrej Storwel gives higher weightage to product :** In formulating the marketing mix for its steel cupboard, Storwel, Godrej gave maximum weightage to product. Using quality steel, more steel per sq inch, and a design that gave convenient inside-space, Godrej offered a superior product. Safe locking certainly was a product-strength, as Godrej had great expertise in locking systems. In distribution and promotion, it was almost on par with the other players in the industry. And, commensurate with the superiority of the product, Godrej also fixed a higher price for it. Godrej explained the proposition to the consumer like this:
  - You are paying just a little extra for
  - all these extras ...
  - extra strength
  - extra security
  - extra options
  - extra life...
- **Asian Paints places higher emphasis on distribution :** Asian Paints, in formulating the marketing mix for its paints, placed high emphasis on distribution. While other players in the industry were relying on the wholesale trade, Asian Paints bypassed the wholesale trade and went retail. Again, while the other players were concentrating on the urban markets, Asian Paints went national, serving the semi-urban and rural markets through its nationwide retail marketing set-up consisting of 14,000 retailers.

(b) The mix has to take its cue from the customers: The marketing mix of a firm corresponds to its total product offering. And, this total product offering is supposed to provide the best value to the customer. So, it follows that marketing mix formulation has to take its cue totally from the customer. One has to carry out an in-depth customer analysis and give appropriate weightage to different elements based on what the customer considers as important.

(c) Marketing mix cannot be a static thing; it has to be juggled as required : It is not as though a firm can rest once it has assembled and put through a marketing mix for a product. Assembling the marketing mix is not a one-shot assignment. No marketing manager can assume that his job is over once a marketing mix is put in place. The marketing mix is a dynamic entity. It is to be monitored closely and modified and manipulated, depending on requirements. Since the task of marketing is to meet the changes taking place in the market, marketing mix has got to be a flexible and dynamic entity. The marketing manager monitors the conditions in the market and keeps juggling the mix. There is no such thing as a for-ever-valid marketing mix. The optimum combination is no permanent thing. Whereas decisions relating to STP are more durable and are not tinkered with every now and then, mix decisions are modified as warranted by the environment. Within a certain framework, the elements are ingeniously juggled to accommodate the changes taking place in the relevant external environment and within the firm.

(d) Change in environmental variables warrants the mix to be juggled: Constant flux in environmental variables is the main reason why the mix needs constant juggling. The marketing man has to respond properly to the changes. Competitors will naturally be making their tactical manoeuvres in the market all the time. They will introduce a new product, or initiate an aggressive promotion campaign, or announce a price reduction. The competing marketing manager has to meet all these manoeuvres and take care of the competitive position of his firm/brand in the market. The only way he can achieve this is by juggling his own marketing mix. Similar is the case with other major environmental variables like economic conditions and government policies. All of them keep changing and the marketing man has to keep adjusting the marketing mix accordingly.

(e) **In particular, change in customer preference warrants the juggling:** In many businesses, customer is the most fluctuating environmental variable. Customer tastes and preferences change very fast. Brand loyalty shifts equally fast; customers' purchasing power too changes over time. The marketing manager is vitally concerned with these changes. He has to gather timely insights about these changes and respond to them through appropriate modification of his marketing mix.

(f) **Change in PLC stage too demands change in the mix:** The growth of a product/ brand over different stages of its growth cycle (Product Life Cycle) is another criterion influencing change in its marketing mix. As a product evolves from its launch period towards different stages of growth, maturity and decline, it will demand different treatments from the point of view of pricing, distribution, promotion and even product attributes. In fact, not only the 4P-combination but, even the target market and positioning - i.e. the entire marketing strategy - will change through this life cycle.

(g) **Changes within the firm too necessitate modifications in the mix:** Changes taking place within the firm too, necessitate modifications in the marketing mix. Changes in the corporate/ competitive strategy of the firm, changes in its product lines, organisation structure, resource level, will all necessitate changes in the marketing mix for a given product/brand.

(h) **Freezing the marketing mix would mean marketing inertia:** The very fact that the elements of marketing mix (4P) are a set of adjustable values between the firm and the consumer makes it clear that the marketing mix cannot be a static thing and that it has to be juggled as required. A set of adjustable values cannot obviously be frozen. It has to be left flexible. It is marketing inertia on the part of the marketing man that freezes those values in positions found appropriate in the past. And that, is a sure recipe for disaster. In today's conditions in particular, flexibility with the elements of the marketing mix is inescapable. In fact, today, the marketing men are required to make pre-emptive and not just reactive changes in their marketing mix.

(i) **The marketing mix has to be separately worked out for each brand:** A multi-product firm has to develop a marketing mix for each of its products. In fact, the mix has to be worked out for every brand because the market fight is finally at the brand level. And it is the marketing mix that decides how much leeway and resources the brand has at its disposal in this fight. For example, Lifebuoy and Lux, two brands of HUL in bath soaps, operate with vastly differing marketing mix. This is natural because they are addressed to two vastly differing target markets. Lifebuoy is the anti-germ, health-highlighting popular soap, mainly targeted at the rural buyer, whereas Lux is the beauty soap targeted at the complexion conscious city woman. Lifebuoy is low priced, (₹ 10 per 100 gm pack), having just protective packing, and no frills, and promoted through outdoor, vernacular print and regional TV. Lux is high priced (₹ 15 per 75 gm), product with fine finish, silky, creamy lather, fine fragrance, double protection packing and promoted through urban-oriented magazines and TV channels.

(j) **Marketing mix is the visible part of marketing strategy:** An interesting fact about the marketing mix is that it is the visible part of the marketing strategy of a firm. After all, no firm notifies its marketing strategy in black and white, to the outside world. But the outside world does have the means of deciphering the marketing strategy of a firm. The strategy manifests through marketing mix of the firm, i.e. through what the firm does with its product, promotion, price and channel. The outside world, whether it is the customer, or the competition, or the trade, acquires an idea of the marketing strategy of a firm, once the latter finalises its marketing mix and puts it in the market in the form of a marketing programme. In other words, the marketing mix of a firm is actually the marketplace manifestation of its marketing strategy. The understanding that the marketing mix is the visible representation of the marketing strategy of a firm will come handy in formulating one's own competitive/ marketing strategy. Because, the strategies of the competitors can be discerned through their marketing mix, and then, one's own strategy can be appropriately formulated.

(k) **Both quantitative analysis and judgement have a role in finalising marketing mix:** Assembling the marketing mix requires knowledge of the effect of each mix element on sales, and the interrelationship of the various elements. There is a need to predict the final outcome of the different options. In this exercise, marketing managers employ quantitative techniques/field experiments as well as their judgement. Both have their due roles in deciding an optimal mix.

(l) **The interaction between marketing mix variables and environment variables:** They include consumer, competition, trade and the mega environment. At this juncture, it would be appropriate to highlight that the two sets of variables together complete the marketing process. The marketing man encounters the environmental variables with his marketing mix variables.

(m) **The controllable and the non-controllable variables of marketing:** While a marketing man can choose, alter and control the marketing mix variables, he cannot choose or alter or dictate to the environmental variables.

The marketing man intelligently selects and adjusts the marketing mix variables, and brings them in alignment with the environmental variables. In fact, the crux of marketing lies in choosing and configuring the marketing mix variables in alignment with the environmental variables. And by using the marketing mix variables the marketing man harnesses the opportunities in the environment. So, marketing can be viewed as the interaction between marketing mix variables and environmental variables. The two sets of variables are the two parts of the marketing process.

(n) **Linkage between marketing mix, marketing effort and marketing budget:** Marketing mix, in effect, signifies the manner in which the marketing effort or marketing budget of the firm is distributed over the different components of the marketing job. The marketing effort required for achieving the targeted sales, translates itself into the marketing expense budget; and the distribution of this budget over the four Ps, indicates the marketing mix position. When the marketing manager has completed assembling the marketing mix, it means that he has, on his hands the marketing budget. He has decided the marketing effort/ marketing expenditure; he has also decided how it should be allocated over four Ps. When he expresses the marketing mix in rupee terms, it becomes the marketing budget.

(o) **Assembling and managing the marketing mix is the main task in marketing:** Assembling and executing the marketing mix accounts for the bulk of the marketing task. It is by assembling and operating its marketing mix that a firm executes its marketing strategy. And all the decisions on marketing mix form an integral part of the marketing strategy. The marketing mix is both a creation of the marketing strategy, and the instrument with which the marketing strategy is executed. Effectiveness of a marketing programme depends on the extent to which the marketing mix elements are harmonised and synthesised into a unified entity. It is to be particularly noted that the 4Ps are no independent silos but constitute one unified, logically related, value-creation set.

(p) 'STP plus marketing-mix' sums up marketing strategy: 'STP plus marketing-mix', or 'STP plus 4Ps' constitutes an easy-to-grasp description of marketing strategy. No other clue than these two steps is required to understand it. STP is the preparatory part of strategy formulation and the strategy takes shape when the marketing mix/4P is constructed upon the STP. In fact, the entire marketing can be explained in terms of STP and marketing mix. If you decide the STP and the mix and implement the mix - you have completed marketing. It then follows that it should be possible to state, in precise terms, the marketing strategy of any firm in terms of STP and marketing mix. Exhibit 14.3 gives an illustrative marketing statement based on the target market, positioning and marketing Mix.

(q) Firms do change their marketing strategy when required: Marketing strategy for a product/brand is not a permanent fixture. It has to undergo appropriate changes to meet the shifts in consumer behaviour, competition and market evolution. The competitive posture a company takes in the first instance and the extent of realisation/non-realisation of that objective too is a factor in deciding whether a change has to be made or not.

Another factor influencing change in strategy for a product/brand is the change in its life cycle stage. As the market for a given product evolves, grows, and declines, the strategies have to necessarily change. Product life cycle and market evolution are concurrent phenomena demanding monitoring by the marketer.

The strategies aimed at a novice buyer in a newly unfolding market, and the strategies needed when he becomes an experienced user of the product in an arrived market, fully backed by his **learning curve** have to be different.

MARKETING STRATEGIES VARIED APPROACHES

Porter's threefold categorisation

Michael Porter speaks of three broad generic strategies in relation to competitive strategy - **cost leadership, differentiation,** and **focus.** We take the view that ultimately there are just two categories of strategies **-cost leadership,** and **differentiation** - because the third one propounded by Porter viz., **focus** does not represent a distinct category, but just a variant of either cost or differentiation. Even Porter appreciates and grants this fact. According to him, the focus strategy has two variants - **cost focus** and **differentiation focus. In cost focus,** a firm seeks a cost advantage in its target segment, while in **differentiation focus** a firm seeks differentiation in its target segment. Focus rests on the scope of a narrow competitive choice within an industry. The focuser selects a segment in the industry and tailors his strategy to serve it to the exclusion of the others. It is therefore appropriate to vote for a two-fold categorisation.

A. Price-oriented marketing strategy

Firms taking to the price route in marketing strategy compete on the strength of competitive/lower pricing. They use price as their competitive lever. They juggle the price of their product to suit the prevailing competitive reality. They can afford to offer lower prices and still make the targeted profits, in view of their cost advantage. They elbow out competition with the cushion they enjoy in the matter of pricing.

A firm opting for the price route will have to have a substantial cost advantage in their operations, vis-à-vis the competition. It should be enjoying an overall cost leadership in the given industry and its lower cost should enable it to secure above average returns in spite of the compulsion to lower prices to meet the competition. In the absence of such cost advantage, it cannot offer a lower price compared to competition over the long term. The cost advantage can emanate from different factors like, scale economies, early entry, a large market share built over a period of time, locational advantage, or synergy among the different businesses. The firm's whole strategy, in fact, will revolve around building such cost advantage; it will always be looking for opportunities for cost reduction. For example, it may drop unprofitable customers/ segments, it may minimise its expenditure on R&D, it may practice just-in-time inventory. And, with the cumulative support of such strategies, it will fight on the cost/ price front. In short, developing such a cost leadership is the main task of firms that vote for a price-led strategy.

In cost leadership, a firm sets out to become the low-cost producer in its industry. The sources of cost advantage include the pursuit of economies of scale, proprietary technology, preferential access to raw materials, and other factors. A cost leader must achieve parity or proximity in the bases of differentiation relative to its competitors to be an above-average performer, even though it relies on cost leadership for its competitive advantage. Parity in the bases of differentiation allows a cost leader to translate its cost advantage directly into higher profits than competitors. Proximity in differentiation means that the price discount necessary to achieve an acceptable market share does not offset a cost leader's cost advantage and hence the cost leader earns above-average returns. The strategic logic of cost leadership usually requires that a firm be the cost leader, not one of several firms vying for this position.

To successfully practise such a price-led strategy, a firm should have consciously taken to the idea sufficiently early in its evolutionary process and prepared itself for adopting such a strategy. The firm cannot opt for the strategy midway, after getting stuck in the face of competition. Right from the beginning, it must have voted for cost-effective technologies/processes, scale economies, cost reduction programmes, a steady pursuit of automation, a constant vigil to exploit learning curve effects, best inventory practices, and a company-wide commitment to cost reduction. Without obtaining a cost leadership in the industry through resorting to such steps early on, it is difficult for a firm to compete on the basis of price.

Nirma: Case study of Nirma Chemicals provides a fine example for a price-led marketing strategy. Nirma entered the detergent market of India at a time when HUL, with its Surf, had established a near monopoly in the business. And, Nirma succeeded through its price-led strategy. HUL marketed Surf, taking to the differentiation route; the differentiation theme was 'Surf washes whitest.' Nirma had built cost leadership right from the beginning. And, it was this cost leadership built early on that enabled Nirma to follow the price-based marketing strategy. Taking advantage of the concessions as an SSI unit and choosing the price conscious segment as its market, Nirma Chemicals offered a low price brand and promoted it aggressively. While Surf was sold at a price of over ₹ 32 per kg. Nirma priced its detergent at ₹ 10.50 per kg. It relied on low cost technology, process and raw materials. In just about 10 years, Nirma became a ₹ 1,000 crore business.

Nirma's strategy led to a churning process in the detergent industry. Market shares changed drastically. Nirma kept growing both in volume and marketshare. HUL defended Surf. It stepped up promotion and boosted its differentiation theme further. But, all this did not arrest the growth of Nirma. Finally, HUL was forced to adopt the strategy. 'If you can't beat them, join them'. It started playing in the segment, which Nirma had chosen, with Nirma-like strategy. It introduced Wheel, a low priced brand and positioned it directly against Nirma in the same segment. Wheel was priced at Rs 11 per kg. The point is that Nirma's price-led strategy was so successful that even the market leader, who was all along following the differentiation- led route, was forced to review its strategy.

Case Study of Maruti 800: Maruti's strategy for its 800 car is another example of a successful price-led marketing strategy. Here, for about a decade, the price-led strategy was actually used more as an entry barrier to other aspiring players than as a competitive strategy for competing with existing players. Subsequently, it was used as an entry barrier as well as a competitive strategy for competing with existing players. At a time when passenger car was a luxury item in India, Maruti Suzuki entered with its small car and made it affordable for the fast growing middle class of the country. On the strength of an affordable price, easy availability, and high fuel efficiency, Maruti soon cornered more than 70 per cent share of the expanded passenger car market of the country. And simultaneously, it became a household name in the country.

Like Nirma, Maruti too, enjoyed substantial cost advantage to wage and win such a price-based strategy. First of all, Maruti had considerable **size advantage.** Its large production capacity - 2,25,000 to start with - gave it a relatively low unit cost and conferred on it an enviable pricing cushion. Maruti also had cost advantage independent of size. Low initial investment was one source of such cost advantage. Investment costs steeply went up in subsequent years. Unique concessions from the government were another source of cost advantage. As the early bird, and as a public sector firm, Maruti received several concessions from the government, which were not available to later day players. Moreover, Maruti's first set of plants was fully depreciated by 1998. Maruti also indigenised its manufacturing rapidly and achieved cost competitiveness. Consistent capacity expansions completed on schedule, further supported the pricing freedom.

New players have found it difficult to compete against Maruti (in the entry level segment), with its large production capacity, depreciated low cost plant and highly indigenized sourcing of components.

B. Differentiation-Oriented Marketing Strategy

The differentiation strategy revolves around aspects other than price. It works on the principle that a firm can make its offer distinctive from all competing offers and win through the distinctiveness. And, a firm adopting such route can price its product on the perceived value of the attributes of the offer and not necessarily on competition-parity basis.

The interesting point is that an offer can be differentiated on any of the multitude of attributes that form part of the offer. Any of the ever so many activities performed by the firm, tangible and intangible can also constitute the source of differentiation. The product with its innumerable features, the service and the other functions performed by the firm are all possible sources of differentiation.

The potential of the differentiation-led strategy is vividly explained by Theodore Levitt in his article in Harvard Business Review 'Marketing Success, Through Differentiation of Anything'. In this article, Levitt elaborates that there is practically no such thing as a commodity. All goods and services are differentiable. In the marketplace, differentiation is everywhere. Everybody - the producer, fabricator, seller, broker, the agent and the merchant - tries constantly to distinguish his offer from that of his competitors. This is true even of those who produce and deal in primary metals, grains, chemicals, plastics and money. Through an array of examples, Levitt explains how, from the simplest of commodities to the most complicated of products, differentiation can be put to use.

In the marketplace today, companies do try to 'achieve marketing success through differentiation of anything'. They not only differentiate on the unique features of their product, but even on plain facts like the collaboration with a valuable partner, or the location of the plant, as differentiation themes. They use any fact/theme that gives them a relative advantage.

Examples of differentiation route

IBM uses its service strength and technology strength as its differentiation themes.

Garden Silks uses its strength in design as the differentiation plank.

Eureka Forbes has successfully used home selling as its distinctiveness.

Citibank differentiates on its personalised service. It claims that it employs only professionally qualified people and the person who answers a customer's phone call will be competent to solve all the problems raised by the customer.

Caterpillar Tractor uses its service strength/ global dealer network as the differentiation plank.

Rolls Royce highlights its engineering quality as its major strength.

The differentiation route is a more dynamic and powerful route to competitive strategy. Most business battles are fought on the strength of differentiation rather than that of price. The major attraction of the differentiation-based strategy is that it allows a firm to move away from the disadvantage of a wholly price-based fight and allows it the flexibility of fighting on the non-price front, on the strength of the uniqueness and specialty of its offer. The differentiation route is thus a crucial option for a firm in its search for a rewarding competitive strategy.

In a differentiation-oriented strategy, a firm seeks to be unique along some dimensions that are valued by the buyers. It selects one or more attributes that buyers perceive as important, and positions itself uniquely to meet those attributes. It gets the due reward for its uniqueness through an appropriate, premium price. By and large, a firm following a differentiation strategy will be an above average performer in its industry. One basic requirement is that it should keep the cost of the differentiation below the premium price it can command from the differentiation. The differentiation-oriented strategy requires the firm to choose the attributes of differentiation very carefully. A firm must be truly unique at something or be perceived so, if it is to expect a premium price. It also has to see that the price premium is justified by the value generated by its differentiation. In contrast to price-oriented strategy where everything works around the price, in the case of differentiation-oriented one, there will be many different possibilities.

Differentiation does not imply that any cost level is okay. A differentiator cannot ignore his cost position. No firm can afford to have an unjustified cost position and jack up its price to cover that. A differentiator thus aims at cost parity or proximity relative to its competitors, by reducing cost in all areas that do not affect the differentiation.

Different possibilities within Differentiation-oriented strategy: Since differentiation can be shaped around a large variety of factors, there can be many different types of differentiation-oriented strategies. They can be grouped under three broad categories, as shown below:

It can be seen that the three categories relate to the three Ps of the 4P framework of the marketing mix, the fourth, Price, servicing as a separate route for strategy. It is by drawing from all the 4P's that any marketing strategy is shaped. Depending on the context in which they are placed, firms rely relatively more on one particular element. So, when we talk of strategies with emphasis on, say, **Product,** it does not imply that only the Product matters in this strategy. It cannot be so. All the four Ps are judiciously utilised in forging the strategy. But the product is more heavily leaned on by the firm. In other words here, the **Product** is the centerpiece of the strategy, the other 3Ps playing their assigned supportive roles. Same is the case with **Place, Promotion** and **Price.** One element may get prominence over the other in the marketing strategy; but no element gets ignored.

(i) Differentiation with emphasis on product: **Product** covers attributes such as its functionality, packing convenience etc. It also covers service and experience delivered by the offer.

- **Differentiating with emphasis on experience:** Since value is the crux in marketing, anything that is of value to the customer can be used as a base for differentiating an offer. So, where experience forms a significant part of offer, firms do try to differentiate their offer by differentiating the experience.
- **Experience brands:** In fact, where experience forms a significant part of the offer and the firms differentiate it on the experience, the brands concerned become experiential brands. To quote Alice M. Tybout and Gregory S. Carpenter, 'Experiential brands focus on how consumers feel when interacting with the brand. Products, environments and services are combined to create multisensory

encounters with the brand. These encounters may be recurring or may involve extended contact with the customer. Consequently, the "place" and "people" components of service delivery are particularly important in creating strong experiential brands. One hallmark of any great experience brand really, is consistency. Delivering a consistently good experience is a challenge.''

- **The new generation coffee cafes:** The new generation coffee cafes in our cities is a good example of 'differentiating on experience'. These cafes are essentially experiential brands. They rely on creating a unique, engaging experience - a memorable experience - that extends well beyond the actual sipping of the coffee at the cafe. They differentiate themselves as a class, from the general category hotels/coffee shops/ restaurants. They also differentiate among themselves. In both cases, they differentiate on 'experience'.

(ii) Differentiation-oriented strategies with emphasis on distribution: Reaching India's village markets has always remained a problem for business firms. The best they could do was to set up a three-tier distribution system and reach some village shops for storing and selling their products. Most of the companies stop with the towns. One of the maximum penetrating retail network in rural India belongs to HUL. But even this is found inadequate to reach the interior markets. It is in this context, we have to see the e-Choupal, the new retail channel being built by ITC. ITC markets a number of products like *agarbattis,* salt, matchbox, seeds, *atta,* notebooks, cigarettes etc in remote villages. But ITC found the existing channel penetration grossly insufficient to unblock the demands lying in rural India.

(iii) Differentiation-oriented strategy with emphasis on promotion: There are many companies/brands who wage their differentiation-oriented strategy relying largely on the power of **Promotion.** It is not that they are devoid of product strength, distribution reach, and pricing options. They resort more to promotion and rely more on appeals with psychological/emotional/prestige/status orientation than the rational, tangible, and benefit oriented ones.

- **Selling more of image/status than a product:** These companies/brands build around their offerings a halo/image, and sell them through persuasive marketing communications, especially advertising. Quite often, they sell the offer and build the brand by using celebrities in the respective fields and portraying an intimate bond between them and the product. They deliver the theme through message/media appealing to the target, and repeating the campaigns for the best reach and impact.

  Many of the global brands we see today, especially those in categories like personal care, cosmetics, food and drinks and personal wear have been built through sustained, high power, promotional effort over years. Brands like Dove, Lux, Eau de Cologne, Nike, Coca-Cola, Pepsi and De Beers are some examples. They have not been built through the product-functionality appeal but on the *image* appeal. The customer is invited to become part of this image.

- **Showcasing the user:** The equation between the brand and the endorser or the unique setting with which the brand is associated, is the selling point here. The consumer enjoys being a part of this setting. Through the brand, he is also projecting a new image of himself; the brand becomes a style statement for him.

- **Suits image brands more:** As a general rule, differentiation strategy with emphasis on promotion, works well with image brands. To quote Tybout and Carpenter, 'Image brands create value, principally by projecting an image. The value of these brands stem, in large measure, from a shared interpretation of what using the brand represents rather than the product features'. Since image is the basis for differentiation here, and social and esteem needs are addressed more, promotion/communication works out as an apt route.

- **Promotion contributes to brand equity over time:** Well-conceived promotion strategies, executed appropriately and in a sustained manner go a long way in adding to a brand's equity. Here, it suffices to emphasise that promotion has an important role in investing brands with great value. Exhibit 15.4 presents a few examples of companies/ brands using promotion as the main of their differentiation-oriented strategy.

Example:

Reid & Taylor: In the same product category of suitings, Reid & Taylor uses the same approach for differentiation, with even more telling effect. Here 'James Bond' is the prestigious endorser. The ad message links the prestige of Bond and the brand: Reid & Taylor... the legend of a cloth ... James Bond ... the legend of a man Luxury Suitings .. . Bond with the best. The suiting is a *legend* like the endorser, not a piece of cloth!

Ray-Ban: Ray-Ban sunglasses does not build a differentiation on the functional characteristics/ special properties of the glass it uses. Instead, it projects aesthetics, and claims, 'Ray-Ban ... for exhilaration!' It is the lifestyle that is played up. Ray-Ban is promoted through high outlay ad campaigns.

Nike: In the case of Nike, the marketing is built almost wholly around the brand name and promotion. By consistently using sport stars from the initial years till date - from Michael Jordan and John McEnroe in the 1970's and Roger Federrer today - Nike has been projecting the image of a winner and high performer. Nike and success go together; that is the equation between the brand and whoever uses it. You are made to feel that by wearing Nike, you are in the league of those very special sports personalities whom you admire. In addition to its regular high budget ad campaigns, Nike puts its logo, the swoosh, on every possible medium/vehicle - MP3 players, watches, walkie-talkies, and even portable heart monitors.

(iv) Price-oriented strategy: A firm opting for the price route should be enjoying an overall cost leadership in the given industry. Its lower cost vis-à-vis the competition should enable it to secure above average returns, even when it lowers its prices as required to meet the competition. It is obvious that in the absence of such cost advantage, it cannot keep offering a lower price over the long term.

Maruti's strategy for its 800 car is an apt example of a successful price-led marketing strategy. Its cost leadership in the industry and in the given segment in particular, was its anchor in playing such a strategy. Even in industries that are not so capital intensive, cost advantage is a basic requirement for firms playing such a strategy. More importantly, for these firms it is essential to get the customer value equation right. It is by picking the right target market and the optimum price point, that these firms win. Recent experiences from Indian markets show that if firms want large volume, they have to offer affordably priced, adequately performing products. Whenever such offerings happen - televisions, and cell phones are apt examples - the market has always embraced them in a big way. The smart marketers who had got their customer value equation right, and had the competence for cost-cum-quality management, had been the winners. It enabled them to make a handsome profit despite their extending affordable prices to the consumers.

Example of Maruti-Suzuki:

Relying on the price route, Maruti achieved a phenomenal success in the small car segment of the passenger car industry of India. Of course, there were other elements besides competitive price, playing their parts in the strategy. But the trump was the difficult-to-match price.

Maruti created all the necessary settings for successfully playing a price-oriented strategy. Its early entry, large production capacity, relatively low initial investment, depreciated low cost plants by the time the others entered, and high level of indigenisation in sourcing of components, all supported such a strategy. In the chosen segment, Maruti did face all the challenges a leader usually faces in retaining his leadership. There were the aggressive No. 2s trying to take over the No. 1 slot. But Maruti, with its cost leadership, held on and did not have to yield the No. 1 slot to anyone else. It is relatively easy for a firm to achieve the No. 1 spot, but not that easy to stay there.

CONDITIONS FOR SUCCESS OF MARKETING STRATEGY

- **Correct Sizing up of the Competitive Forces:** Sizing up competition/the forces that shape competition in the industry, is a component task of marketing strategy formulation. Sizing up the competitive forces in the industry is fundamental to strategy formulation. Because, in competitive strategy, the basic requirement for a firm is to find a position in the industry wherefrom it can defend itself against competitive forces, and, wherever possible, influence these forces in its favour.
- **Strategy and forces of competition impact mutually; strategy reflects as well as shapes forces of competition:** Strategy is a response to and a reflector of the forces of competition in the industry. Interestingly, strategy also shapes the competitive forces in an industry. The main aim of strategy is actually to cope with the forces of competition.
- **Possession of Relevant Competitive Advantages:** For marketing strategy to work - whatever might be the strategy - the firm must posses relevant competitive advantages and it must weave the strategy around them. Any strategy becomes worthwhile only when it is executed and yields the intended results. And, to execute strategies, the firm should have the relevant capabilities/expertise. Since, marketing strategies have to operate in the competitive context, the capabilities/expertise have to be superior compared to the competition. In the absence of the relevant competitive advantages, all strategies will fail.
- **While price route requires cost advantage, differentiation requires relevant competitive advantages:** In the previous section, we saw that the price route to strategy requires cost leadership. It means the firm should have the competitive advantage in terms of cost for playing this strategy. The differentiation route too requires competitive advantage. In fact, this route often needs multiple competitive advantages. Brand image, channel clout, strong collaborations, unique process, integrated production facilities, flexible production facilities, and advanced R&D facilities, are some of them.
- **Cost advantage desirable whether the strategy is price-oriented or differentiation oriented:** It is not as if it is only the price route that requires cost advantage. Cost advantage is quite a desirable strength in respect of differentiation-oriented strategies too.
- **Price and Differentiation routes cannot remain mutually exclusive:** Though the two strategy routes are distinct from one another, it does not mean that the two routes are mutually exclusive. In a highly competitive and complex market, firms are often compelled to embrace both the routes. They cannot totally ignore the price aspect and wage their marketing warfare on differentiation alone. Nor can they afford to totally ignore distinctiveness and go solely by the advantage of a low price. In their effort at staying ahead of competition, they use both the cards.
- **Neither Price Competitiveness, nor Differentiation is sufficient; the firm has to be Value Competitive:** Especially in the present times of global, no-holds-barred competition, business firms are compelled to extract the benefits of both the routes in their marketing

strategies and offer the customer maximum benefits at the most attractive price, so that the offer is irresistible to the customers. Jack Welch, the former CEO of GE, aptly captures this idea when he says that in a highly competitive market, a firm has to offer the best product, coming out of the best technology, at the lowest price. So, the winner in the marketplace is the one whose offer is distinct and also price competitive. The name of the game, in marketing strategy, is to make the offer distinct, (superior) and price competitive.

MULTIPLE CHOICE QUESTIONS

1. The .... process commences at corporate level. Here the organisation sets out its overall mission, purpose, and values.
(*a*) researching (*b*) strategic planning
(*c*) controlling (*d*) managing
(*e*) None of these

2. A statement about what an organisation wants to become, which sets out an organisation's future, is referred to as:
(*a*) mission
(*b*) values
(*c*) organisational goals
(*d*) vision
(*e*) None of these

3. A statement that sets out what the organisation wishes to achieve in the long term is referred to as:
(*a*) mission (*b*) vision
(*c*) values (*d*) strategic context
(*e*) None of these

4. Organisational values are important because they:
(*a*) help shape mission statements
(*b*) help increase sales
(*c*) help guide behaviour and the recruitment and selection decisions
(*d*) help define market research
(*e*) None of these

5. Large organisations create ...., which assume the role of a separate company and create their own strategies and plans in order to achieve their corporate goals and contribution to the overall organization.
(*a*) marketing objectives
(*b*) strategic business units
(*c*) marketing activities
(*d*) business development units
(*e*) None of these

6. The Strategic Marketing Planning process consists of a series of logical steps and these steps can be aggregated into four phases. Which of the following is not included in the phases of the strategic marketing planning?
(*a*) Defining marketing strategy
(*b*) Setting the right mission and corporate goals
(*c*) Reviewing the current situation
(*d*) Formulating strategy
(*e*) None of these

7. Which of the following firms has often followed a market challenger (second-mover) strategy?
(*a*) Apple Computer (*b*) eBay
(*c*) Sainsbury's (*d*) Amazon.com
(*e*) None of these

8. SWOT is an acronym for:
(*a*) strategy, working, opinion, tactical
(*b*) strengths, weaknesses, opportunities, threats
(*c*) strategy, work, openness, toughness
(*d*) strategy, weakness, opinions, tactics
(*e*) None of these

9. In SWOT analysis, situations where organisations are able to convert weaknesses into strengths and threats into opportunities, are called:
(*a*) strategic windows
(*b*) strategic leverage
(*c*) conversion strategies
(*d*) Vulnerability
(*e*) None of these

10. This is something that at some time in the future may destabilise and/or reduce the potential performance of the organisation.
(*a*) Threat (*b*) Strength
(*c*) Weakness (*d*) Opportunities
(*e*) None of these

11. .... is the process that helps managers understand the nature of the industry, the way firms behave competitively within the industry, and how competition is generally undertaken.
(*a*) Market needs analysis
(*b*) Portfolio analysis
(*c*) Strategic market analysis
(*d*) Organisational analysis
(*e*) None of these

12. These objectives are often employed in mature markets as firms/products enter a decline phase. The goal is to maximise short-term profits and stimulate a positive cash flow.
(*a*) Harvest objectives (*b*) Divest objectives
(*c*) Hold objectives (*d*) Growth objectives
(*e*) None of these

13. Which of the following is not the condition necessary for the achievement of sustainable competitive advantage (SCA)?
(*a*) The perceived difference results from cheaper price
(*b*) The customer consistently perceives a positive difference between the products and services offered by a company and its competitors
(*c*) The perceived difference results from the company's relatively greater capability
(*d*) The perceived difference persists for a reasonable period of time
(*e*) None of these

14. These objectives are often the most suitable when firms operate in a market dominated by a major competitor and where their financial resources are limited.
(*a*) Niche objectives (*b*) Hold objectives
(*c*) Harvest objectives (*d*) Divest objectives
(*e*) None of these

15. This type of growth refers to concentrating activities on markets and/or products that are familiar.
(*a*) Diversification (*b*) Condensive
(*c*) Integrative (*d*) Intensive
(*e*) None of these

16. An organisation can offer standard products at acceptable levels of quality, yet still generate above-average profit margin by adopting ....
(*a*) differentiation
(*b*) focus strategy
(*c*) cost leadership
(*d*) market follower strategy
(*e*) None of these

17. .... are about organisations seeking gaps in broad market segments or finding gaps in competitors' product ranges.
(*a*) Market niche strategies
(*b*) Differentiation
(*c*) Cost leadership
(*d*) Focus strategies
(*e*) None of these

18. These products and brands can shape the nature of competition in the market, set out standards relating to price, quality, speed of innovation, communications, as well as influencing the key distribution channels. This market positioning is called:
(*a*) market challenger (*b*) market leader
(*c*) market follower (*d*) market nicher
(*e*) None of these

19. Diversification is best described as which of the following?
(*a*) Existing products in new markets
(*b*) Existing products in existing markets
(*c*) New products for new markets
(*d*) New products for existing markets
(*e*) None of these

20. Key performance indicators, which companies set and measure their progress towards in order to determine whether or not they have improved or maintained their performance over a given period of time, are referred to as:
(*a*) marketing implementation
(*b*) marketing programmes
(*c*) budgetting
(*d*) marketing metrics
(*e*) None of these

ANSWERS

1	**2**	**3**	**4**	**5**	**6**	**7**	**8**	**9**	**10**
(*b*)	(*d*)	(*a*)	(*c*)	(*b*)	(*a*)	(*c*)	(*b*)	(*c*)	(*a*)
11	**12**	**13**	**14**	**15**	**16**	**17**	**18**	**19**	**20**
(*c*)	(*a*)	(*a*)	(*a*)	(*d*)	(*c*)	(*d*)	(*b*)	(*c*)	(*d*)

CHAPTER-16

MARKETING CONTROL

Following Table lists four types of marketing control needed by companies : annual-plan control, profitability control, efficiency control, and strategic control.

Types of Marketing Control

Type of Control	Prime Responsibility	Purpose of Control	Approaches
I. Annual-plan control	Top management Middle management	To examine whether the planned results are being achieved.	• Sales analysis • Market-share analysis • Marketing expense-to-sales analysis • Financial analysis • Market-based scorecard analysis
II. Profitability control	Marketing controller	To examine where the company is making or losing money	Profitability by : • product • territory • customer • segment • trade channel • order size
III. Efficiency control	Line and staff management Marketing controller	To evaluate and improve the spending efficiency and impact of marketing expenditures	Efficiency of : • sales force • advertising • sales promotion • distribution
IV. Strategic control	Top management Marketing auditor	To examine whether the company is pursuing its best opportunities in markets, products, and channels review	• Marketing-effectiveness review • Marketing audit • Marketing excellence review • Company ethical and social responsibility

ANNUAL-PLAN CONTROL

The purpose of annual-plan control is to ensure that the company achieves the sales profits, and other goals established in its annual plan. The heart of annual-plan control is *management by objectives.* Four steps are involved (given Figure). First management sets monthly or quarterly goals. Second, management monitors its performance in the marketplace. Third, management determines the cause of serious performance deviations. Fourth, management takes corrective action to close the gaps between goals and performance.

This control model applies to all levels of the organisation. Top management sets sales and profit goals for the year that are elaborated into specific goals for each lower level of management. Each product manager is committed to attaining specified levels of sales and costs; each regional and district sales manager and each sales representative is also committed to specific goals. Each period, top management reviews and interprets the results.

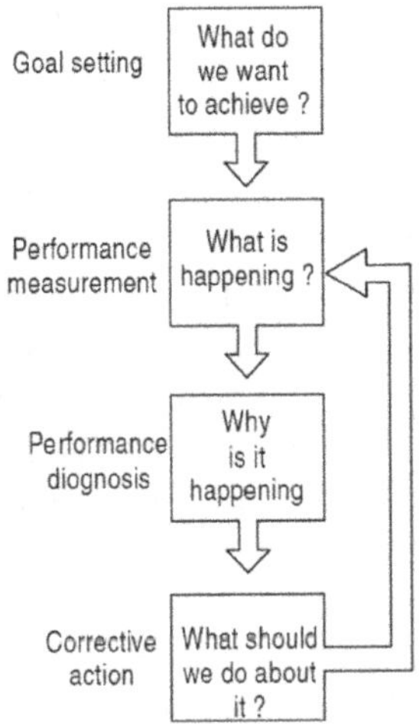

Fig. *The Control Process*

Managers use five tools to check on planned performance: Sales analysis, market share analysis, marketing expense-to-sales analysis, financial analysis, and market-based scorecard analysis.

Sales Analysis

Sales analysis consists of measuring and evaluating actual sales in relation to sales goals. Two specific tools are used in sales analysis.

Sales-variance analysis measures the relative contribution of different factors to a gap in sales performance. Suppose the annual plan called for selling 6,000 units in the first quarter at ₹ 15/- per unit, for total revenue of ₹ 90,000/-. At quarter's end, only 5,000 units were sold at ₹ 13/- per unit, for total revenue of ₹ 65,000/-. The sales performance variance is ₹ 25,000, or 27.8% of expected sales. How much of this underperformance is due to the price decline and how much to the volume decline?

The following calculation answers these questions:

Variance due to price decline

= (₹ 15 – ₹ 13) (5,000)

= ₹ 10,000 40%

Variance due to volume decline

= (₹ 15) (6,000 – 5,000)

= ₹ 15,000 60%

₹ 25,000 100.0%

Almost three-fifth of the variance is due to failure to achieve the volume target. The company should look closely at why it failed to achieve expected sales volume.

Microsales analysis looks at specific products, territories, and so forth that failed to produce expected sales. Suppose the company sells in three territories and expected sales were 1,500 units, 500 units, and 2,000 units respectively. The actual sales volume was 1,400 units, 525 units, and 1,075 units, respectively. Thus, territory 1 showed a 7 per cent shortfall in terms of expected sales; territory 2, a 5 per cent improvement over expectations; and territory 3, a 46 per cent shortfall! Territory 3 is causing most of the trouble. The sales vice president can check into territory 3 to see what explains the poor performance. Territory 3's sales representative is loafing or has a personal problem; a major competitor has entered this territory; or business is a recession in this territory or customer's tastes and preferences have changed in this territory.

Market-Share Analysis

Company sales do not reveal how well the company is performing relative to competitors. For this purpose, management needs to track its market share. Market share can be measured in three ways: Overall market share is the company's sales expressed as a percentage of total market sales. Served market share is its sales expressed as a percentage of the total sales to its served market. Its *served market* is all the buyers who are able and willing to buy its product. Served market share is always larger than overall market share. A company could capture 100 per cent of its served market and yet have a relatively small share of the total market. Relative market share can be expressed as market share in relation to its largest competitor. A relative market share over 100 per cent indicates a market leader. A relative market share of exactly 100 per cent means that the company is tied for the lead. A rise in relative market share means a company is gaining on its leading competitor.

Conclusions from market-share analysis, however, are subject to certain qualifications:

- *The assumption that outside forces affect all companies in the same way is often not true:* The U.S. Surgeon General's Report on the harmful consequences of cigarette smoking caused total cigarette sales to falter, but not equally for all companies.
- *The assumption that a company's performance should be judged against the average performance of all companies is not always valid :* A company's performance should be judged against the performance of its closests competitors or the best in the industry, if it wants to survive and grow.
- *If a new firm enters the industry, then every existing firm's market share might fall:* A decline in market share might not mean that the company is performing any worse than other companies. Share loss depends on the degree to which the new firm hits the company's specific markets. If the new firm's offer is superior than the rest of the companies, then the assumption will be true.
- *Sometimes a market-share decline is deliberately engineered to improve profits:* For example, management might drop unprofitable customers or products to improve its profits. Although total sales and market share will decline but the gross profits and net profits will improve.
- *Market share can fluctuate for many minor reasons*: For example, market share can be affected by whether a large sale occurs on the last day of the month or at the beginning of the next month. Not all shifts in market share have marketing significance.

Managers must carefully interpret market-share movements by product line, customer type, region, and other breakdowns.

Marketing Expense-to-Sales Analysis

Annual-plan control requires making sure that the company is not overspending to achieve sales goals. The key ratio to watch is *marketing expense-to-sales.* In one company, this ratio was 30 percent and consisted of five component expense-to-sales ratios : sales force-to-sales (15 per cent); advertising-to-sales (5 per cent); sales promotion-to-sales (6 per cent); marketing research-to-sales (1 per cent); and sales administration-to-sales (3 per cent).

Management needs to monitor these ratios, which will normally exhibit small fluctuations that can be ignored. Fluctuations outside the normal range are a cause for concern. The period-to-period fluctuations in each ratio can be tracked on a *control chart* (given Figure). This chart shows that the advertising expense-to-sales ration normally fluctuates between 8 per cent and 12 per cent, say 99 out of 100 times. In the fifteenth period, however, the ratio exceeded the upper control limit. One of two hypotheses can explain this occurrence: (1) The company still has good expense control, and this situation represents rare chance event. (2) The company has lost control over this expense and should find the cause. If no investigation is made to determine whether the environment has changed, the risk is that some real change might have occurred, and the company will fall behind. If the environment is investigated, the risk is that the investigation will uncover nothing and be a waste of time and effort.

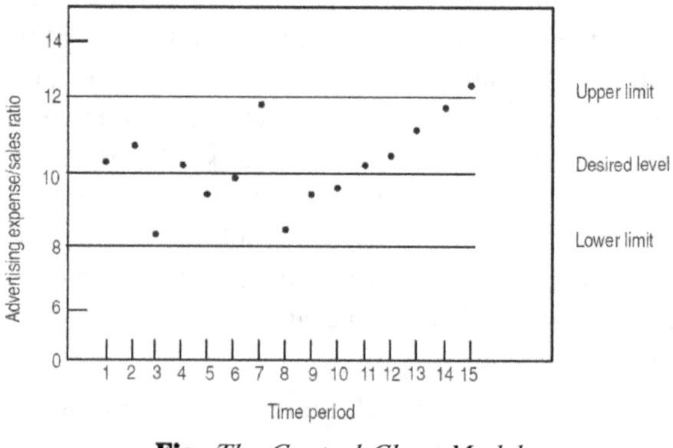

Fig. *The Control-Chart Model*

The behaviour of successive observations even within the upper and lower control limits should be watched. Note in Figure given above that the level of the expense-to-sales ratio rose steadily from the ninth period onward. The probability of encountering six successive increases in what should be independent events is only 1 in 64. This unusual pattern should have led to an investigation sometime before the fifteenth observation.

Financial Analysis

The expense-to-sales ratios should be analysed in an overall financial framework to determine how and where the company is making its money. Marketers are increasingly using financial analysis to find profitable strategies beyond sales building. Management uses financial analysis to identify the factors that affect the company's *rate of return on net worth.* The main factors are shown in Figure, along with illustrative numbers for a large chain-store retailer. The retailer is earning a 12.5 per cent return on net worth. The return on net worth is the product of two ratios, the company's *return on assets* and its *financial leverage.* To improve its return on net worth, the company must increase the ratio of its net profits to its assets or increase the ratio of its assets to its net worth. The company should analyse the composition of its assets (*i.e.,* cash, accounts receivable, inventory, and plant and equipment) and see if it can improve its asset management.

The return on assets is the product of two ratios, the *profit margin* and the *asset turnover.* The profit margin in following figure, seems low, whereas the asset turnover is more normal for retailing. The marketing executive can seek to improve performance in two ways: (1) Increase the profit margin by increasing sales or cutting costs; and (2) increase the asset turnover by increasing sales or reducing the assets (*e.g.,* inventory, receivables) that are held against a given level of sales.

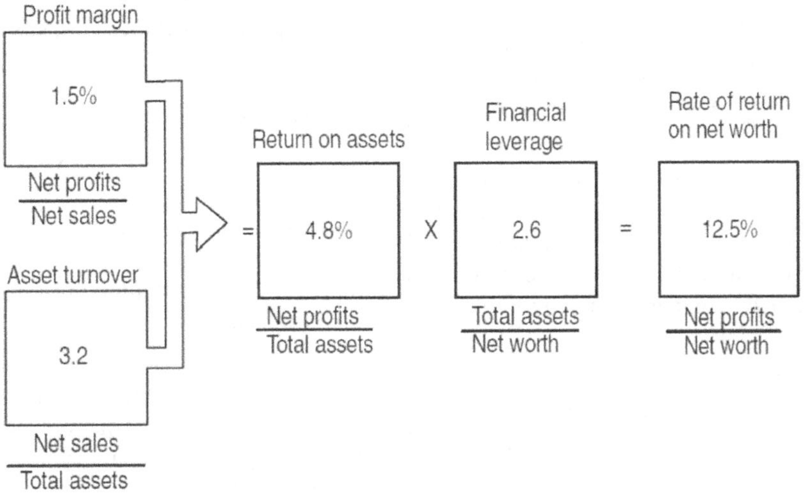

Fig. *Financial Model of Return or Net Worth.*

Market-Based Scorecard Analysis

Most company measurement systems amount to preparing a financial-performance scorecard at the expense of more qualitative measures. Companies would do well to prepare two market-based scorecards that reflect performance and provide possible early warning signals.

A *customer-performance* score-card records how well the company is doing year after year on such customer-based measures as:

- New customers
- Target market preference

- Dissatisfied customers
- Relative product quality
- Lost customers
- Relative service quality
- Target market awareness

Norms should be set for each measures and management should take action when results get out of bounds.

The second measure is called a *stakeholder-performance scorecard.* Companies need to track the satisfaction of various constituencies who have a critical interest in and impact on the company's performance: employees, suppliers, banks, distributors, retailers, stockholders. Again, norms should be set for each group and management should take action when one or more groups register increased levels of dissatisfaction.

PROFITABILITY CONTROL

Here are some disconcerting findings from a bank profitability study :

We have found that anywhere from 20 to 40 per cent of an individual institution's products are unprofitable, and up to 60 per cent of their accounts generate losses.

Our research has shown that, in most firms, more than half of all customer relationships are not profitable, and 30 to 40 per cent are only marginally so. It is frequently a mere 10 to 15 per cent of a firm's relationships that generate the bulk of its profits.

Out profitability research into the branch system of a regional bank produced some surprising results .... 30 per cent of the bank's branches were unprofitable.

Clearly, companies need to measure the profitability of their products, territories, customer groups, segments, trade channels, and order sizes. This information will help management determine whether any products or marketing activities should be expanded, reduced, or eliminated.

In general, marketing-profitability analysis indicates the relative profitability of different channels, products, territories, or other marketing entities. It does not prove that the best course of action is to drop the unprofitable marketing entities, nor does it capture the likely profit improvement if these marginal marketing entities are dropped. Companies are showing a growing interest in using marketing-profitability analysis or its broader version, *activity-based cost accounting* (ABC), to quantify the true profitability of different activities. According to Cooper and Kaplan, ABC "can give managers a clear picture of how products, brands, customers, facilities, regions, or distribution channels both generate revenues and consume resources". To improve profitability, managers can then examine ways to reduce the resources required to perform various activities, or make the resources more productive or acquire them at a lower cost. Alternatively, management may raise prices on products that consume heavy amounts of support resources. The contribution of ABC is to refocus management's attention away from using only labour or material standard costs to allocate full cost, and toward capturing the actual cost of supporting individual products, customers, and other entities.

EFFICIENCY CONTROL

Suppose a profitability analysis reveals that the company is earning poor profits in certain products, territories, or markets. Are there more efficient ways to manage the sales force, advertising, sales promotion, and distribution in connection with these marketing entities?

Some companies have established a *marketing controller* position to improve marketing efficiency. Marketing controllers work out of the controller's office but specialise in the marketing side of the business. At the leading companies they perform a sophisticated financial analysis of marketing expenditures and results. They examine adherence to profit plans, help prepare brand managers budgets, measure the efficiency of promotions, analyse media production costs, evaluate customer and geographic profitability and educate marketing personnel on the financial implications of marketing decisions.

Sales Force Efficiency

Sales managers need to monitor the following key indicators of efficiency in their territory:

- Average number of calls per salesperson per day
- Percentage of orders per 100 sales calls
- Average sales call time per contact
- Number of new customers per period
- Average revenue per sales call
- Number of lost customers per period
- Average cost per sales call
- Sales force cost as a percentage of total sales
- Entertainment cost per sales call

When a company starts investigating sales force efficiency, it often finds areas for improvement. General Electrical reduced the size of one of its divisional sales force after discovering that its salespeople were calling on customers too often. When a large airline found that its salespeople were both selling and servicing, they transferred the servicing function to lower-paid clerks. Another company conducted time-and duty studies and found ways to reduce the ratio of idle-to-productive time.

Advertising Efficiency

Many managers believe it is almost impossible to measure what they are getting for their advertising expenditure. But they should try to keep track of at least the following statistics:

- Advertising cost per thousand target buyers reached by media vehicle
- Percentage of audience who noted, saw or associated, and read most of each print ad
- Consumer opinions on the ad's content and effectiveness
- Before and after measures of attitude toward the product
- Number of inquiries stimulated by the ad
- Cost per inquiry

Management can take a number of steps to improve advertising efficiency, including doing a better job of positioning the product, defining objectives, pretesting messages, using computer technology to guide the selection of media, looking for better media buys, and doing posttesting.

Sales-Promotion Efficiency

Sales promotion includes dozens of devices for stimulating buyer interest and product trial. To improve sales promotion efficiency, management should record the costs and sales impact of each promotion. Management should watch the following statistics:

- Percentage of sales sold on deal
- Display costs per sales dollar
- Percentage of total amount of coupons redeemed to the total sales involving coupons.
- Number of inquiries resulting from a demonstration.

A sales-promotion manager can analyse the results of different sales promotions and advise product managers on the most cost-effective promotions to use.

Distribution Efficiency

Management needs to search for distribution economies in inventory control, warehouse locations, and transportation modes. One problem is that distribution efficiency declines when the company experiences strong sales increases. Peter Senge describes a situation in which a strong sales surge causes the company to fall behind in meeting delivery dates (given Figure). This leads-customers to bad-mouth the company and eventually sales fall. Management responds by increasing sales force incentives to secure more orders. The sales force succeeds but once again the company slips in meeting delivery dates. Management needs to identify the real bottleneck and invest in more production and distribution capacity.

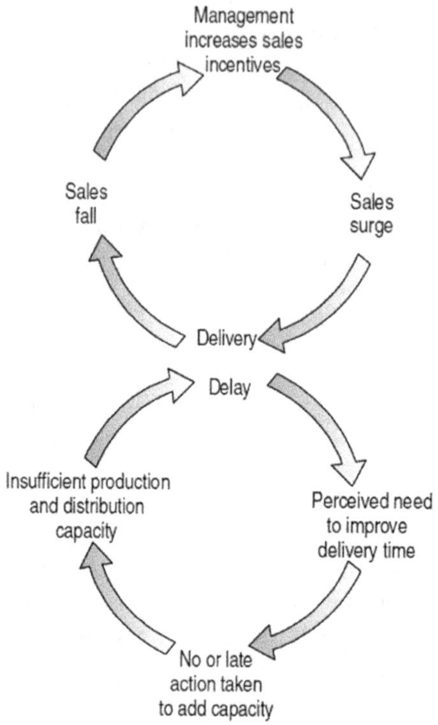

Fig. *Dynamic Interactions Between Sales Orders and Distribution Efficiency*

STRATEGIC CONTROL

From time to time, companies need to undertake a critical review of overall marketing goals and effectiveness. Each company should periodically reassess its strategic approach to the marketplace with marketing-effectiveness reviews and marketing audits. Companies can also perform marketing excellence reviews and ethical-social responsibility reviews.

MULTIPLE CHOICE QUESTIONS

1. The EPRG framework of management orientations in global marketing refers to:
(*a*) ethnocentrism, Polycentrism, Regionalism and Geocentrism
(*b*) ethnocentrism, Polycentrism, Regiocentrism and Geocentrism
(*c*) environmental, Political, Regional and Geographical
(*d*) environmental, Political, Regiocentric and Geological
(*e*) None of these

2. The .... management style sees each host country as unique and sees real differences in these countries to the domestic one.
(*a*) ethnocentric (*b*) regiocentric
(*c*) polycentric (*d*) geocentric
(*e*) None of these

3. Which of the following factors affect the development of a marketing control system?
(*i*) Domestic practices and values
(*ii*) Communication systems
(*iii*) Distance

(*iv*) The product
(*v*) Environmental differences

Code:

(*a*) (*i*), (*ii*) and (*iii*)
(*b*) (*ii*), (*iii*) and (*iv*)
(*c*) (*iii*), (*iv*) and (*v*)
(*d*) All of the above
(*e*) None of these

4. An international marketing control system has four elements, which are:
(*a*) performance standards, performance measurement, analysis of deviations and corrective actions.
(*b*) performance standards, performance measurement, analysis of data and corrective actions.
(*c*) quantitative data, qualitative data, analysis of data and efficiency measures.
(*d*) quality standards, corrective measurement, analysis of defects and effectiveness control.
(*e*) None of these

5. A global marketing audit is:
(*a*) a crucial mechanism for the evaluation of customer response.
(*b*) a technique aimed at evaluating and improving an organisation's global marketing operations.
(*c*) a set of organisational procedures for controlling the effectiveness of productivity.
(*d*) an important process to collect information on the key target markets.
(*e*) None of these

6. Which are the following are examples of traditional marketing control methods?
(*i*) Strategic control
(*ii*) Efficiency control
(*iii*) Financial control
(*iv*) Communication control

Code:

(*a*) (*i*), (*ii*) and (*iii*)
(*b*) (*ii*), (*iii*) and (*iv*)
(*c*) (*i*), (*iii*) and (*iv*)
(*d*) (*ii*) and (*iv*)
(*e*) (*i*), (*ii*), (*iii*) and (*iv*)

7. Which are the following are examples of non-traditional marketing control methods?
(*i*) Financial ratio
(*ii*) Benchmarking and best practice
(*iii*) Self-assessment
(*iv*) Double loop learning

Code:

(*a*) (*i*), (*ii*) and (*iii*)
(*b*) (*ii*), (*iii*) and (*iv*)
(*c*) (*i*), (*iii*) and (*iv*)
(*d*) (*ii*) and (*iv*)
(*e*) (*i*), (*ii*), (*iii*) and (*iv*)

8. Manufacturers today face the dual challenge of trying to fight off the competitive challenge as well as satisfy ever demanding customers. What has been their main strategic response?
(*a*) Development of new strategies to capture knowledge and organisational learning.
(*b*) Increase investment in research for the development of genuine innovations.
(*c*) Development of strategies to improve employees' effectiveness in managing customer relationships
(*d*) The rationalisation of global manufacturing for greater internal operating efficiencies
(*e*) None of these

9. A virtual organisational structure can be defined as:
(*a*) a virtual structure of company functions which come together to serve a specific purpose and then disappear.
(*b*) a temporary network of company functions which come together to serve a specific purpose and then disappear.
(*c*) a non-permanent form of organisation encourages the growth of regional groupings, thus allowing a degree of autonomy.
(*d*) an organisational form based on a functional corporate structure with a mainly 'domestic' focus and have a small international division.
(*e*) None of these

10. When screening a strategy for potential implementation problems, which of the following step is NOT included?
(*a*) Identification of strategy and objectives
(*b*) Identify and evaluate all key players
(*c*) Internal marketing
(*d*) External marketing
(*e*) None of these

ANSWERS

1	2	3	4	5	6	7	8	9	10
(*b*)	(*c*)	(*d*)	(*a*)	(*b*)	(*a*)	(*b*)	(*d*)	(*b*)	(*d*)

EMERGING TRENDS IN MARKETING

INTRODUCTION

Marketing is the process by which companies create customer interest in goods or services. It generates the strategy that underlies sales techniques, business communication, and business developments. It is an integrated process through which companies build strong customer relationships and creates value for their customers and for themselves.

It is a fundamental idea of marketing that organisations survive and prosper through meeting the needs and wants of customers. This important perspective is commonly known as the marketing concept. The marketing concept is about matching a company's capabilities with customer wants. This matching process takes place in what is called the marketing environment.

SERVICE MARKETING

Services are activities and benefits provided by an organisation that satisfy the buyer's needs while providing little or no new ownership of physical or tangible goods. Physical items may or may not be involved in the production of the service; the primary customer benefit is from the usefulness or enjoyment derived from the service. It is possible for customers to purchase services that they will never be able to touch or even define clearly, as in the case of life insurance or inoculation against disease.

The process of marketing services and marketing tangible goods is fundamentally the same the process of planning, implementing and controlling the marketing mix are carried out in. Because of their intangibility, services present special problems and challenges to marketer. In marketing the service of an airline company for example, it may be as important to stress the politeness, friendliness and neatness of the employees as it to emphasise their competence. The environment in which a service is sold and the image consumers have of service providers can be as important as the service itself in obtaining the acceptance of buyers.

CHARACTERISTICS OF SERVICES AND THEIR MARKETING IMPLICATIONS

Services have four major characteristics that greatly affect the design of marketing programs: intangibility, inseparability, variability, and perishability.

Intangibility

Services are intangible. Unlike physical products, they cannot be seen, tasted, felt, heard, or smelled before they are bought. The person getting a face lift cannot see the exact results before the purchase, and the patient in the psychiatrist's office cannot know the exact outcome.

To reduce uncertainty, buyers will look for signs or evidence of the service quality. They will draw inferences about quality from the place, people, equipment, communication material, symbols, and price that they see. Therefore, the service provider's task is to "manage the evidence," to "tangibilise the intangible". Whereas product marketers are challenged to add abstract ideas, service marketers are challenged to add physical evidence and imagery to abstract offer.

Suppose a bank wants to position itself as the "fast" bank. It could tangibilise this positioning strategy through a number of marketing tools:

1. *Place:* The physical setting must connote quick service. The exterior and interior should have clean lines. The layout of the desks and the traffic flow should be planned carefully. Waiting lines should not get overly long.
2. *People:* Personnel should be busy. There should be a sufficient number of employees to manage the workload.
3. *Equipment:* Equipment—computers, copying machines, desks—should be and look "state of the art".
4. *Communication material:* Communication materials—text and photos—should suggest efficiency and speed.
5. *Symbols:* The name and symbol should suggest fast service.
6. *Price:* The bank could advertise that it will deposit ₹ 50/- in the account of any customer who waits in line for more than five minutes.

Service marketers must be able to transform intangible services into concrete benefits.

Inseparability

Services are typically produced and consumed simultaneously. This is not true of physical goods, which are manufactured, put into inventory, distributed through multiple resellers, and consumed later. If a person renders the service, then the provider is part of the service. Because the client is also present as the service is produced, provider-client interactions is a special feature of services marketing. Both provider and client affect the outcome.

In the case of entertainment and professional services, buyers are very interested in the specific provider. It is not the same concert if Ghulam Ali is indisposed and replaced by Kumar Sanu, or if a legal defense will be supplied by John Nobody because Ram Jethmalani is unavailable. When clients have strong provider preferences, Price is raised to ration the preferred provider's limited time.

Several strategies exist for getting around this limitation. The service provider can learn to work with larger groups. Psychotherapists and Yoga Instructors have moved from one-on-one therapy to small-group therapy to groups of over 300 people in a large hotel conference room. The service provider can learn to work faster—the psychotherapist can spend 30 minutes with each patient instead of 50 minutes and can see more patients. The service organisation can train more service providers and build up client confidence.

Variability

Because they depend on who provides them and when and where they are provided, services are highly variable. Some doctors have excellent bedside manner; others are less patient with their patients. Some surgeons are very successful in performing a certain operation; others are less successful. Service buyers are aware of this variability and often talk to others before selecting a service provider.

Service firms can take three steps toward quality control. The first is investing in good hiring and training procedures. Recruiting the right service employees and providing them with excellent training is crucial regardless of whether employees are highly skilled professionals or low-skilled workers.

The second step is standardising the service-performance process throughout the organisation. This is helped by preparing a service blueprint that depicts events and processes in a flowchart, with the objective of recognising potential fail points. Figure shows a service blueprint for a nationwide floral-delivery organisation. The customer's experience is limited to dialing the phone, making choices and placing an order. Behind the scenes, the floral organisation gathers the flowers, places them in a vase, deliver them, and collects payment. Any one of these activities can be done well or poorly.

The third step is monitoring customer satisfaction through suggestion and complaint systems, customer surveys, and comparison shopping.

Perishability

Services cannot be stored. Some doctors charge patients for missed appointments because the service value existed only at that point. The perishability of services is not a problem when demand is steady. When demand fluctuates, service firms have problems. For example, public-transportation companies have to own much more equipment because of morning and evening rush-hour demand than if demand were even throughout the day.

Sasser has described several strategies for producing a better match between demand and supply in a service business.

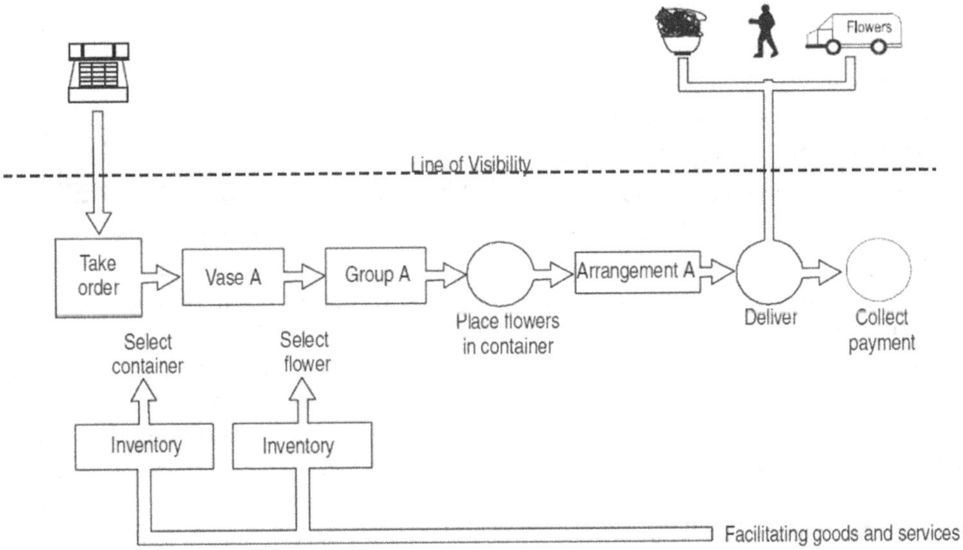

Fig. *A Service-Performance-Process Map: Nationwide Floral Delivery*

On the demand side :

- *Differential Pricing* will shift some demand from peak to off-peak periods. Examples include low night telephone tariffs and weekend discount prices for car rentals.
- *Nonpeak demand* can be cultivated. McDonald's opened a breakfast service, and hotels reduces their tariffs during off-season.
- *Complementary services* can be developed during peak time to provide alternatives to waiting customers, such as cocktail lounges in restaurants and automatic teller machines in banks.
- *Reservation systems* are a way to manage the demand level. Airlines, railways, hotels, and physicians employ them extensively.

On the supply side :

- *Part-time employees* can be hired to serve peak demand. Colleges add part-time teachers when enrollment goes up, and restaurants call in part-time servers when needed.
- *Peak-time efficiency routines* can be introduced. Employees perform only essential tasks during peak periods. Paramedics assist physicians during busy periods.
- *Increased consumer participation* can be encouraged. Consumers fill out their own medical records or bag their own groceries.
- *Shared services* can be developed. Several hospitals can share medical-equipment purchases.

- *Facilities for future expansion* can be developed. An amusement park buys surrounding land for later development.

Five R's of Customer Service

Customer service gets a lot of lip service these days. For giving really a good customer service, service-oriented sales people always follow the five R's, i.e.,

1. *Reachable:* We should be reachable when the customer needs our help.
2. *Responsive:* We should always handle a customer's problem or request promptly.
3. *Readable:* Communicating clearly and concisely, whether in person, by phone or by mail.
4. *Reliable:* Reliability means customers known they can count on us to do what we promise.
5. *Reasonable:* We should always open to customer's question and concerns. We should always be first to admit a mistake.

SOCIAL MARKETING

MEANING

The concept of social marketing was introduced by Philip Kotlar in the year 1971. It combines traditional approaches to social change with commercial marketing & advertising techniques. Marketing principles can be used for propagating social causes like family planning, child care, abolition of dowry, AIDS awareness, and so on. They can be used as tools for correcting attitudes of the people, such type of marketing is understood by government, social organisation, religious institutions and NGO's.

In a country like India, where people are still ignorant and illiterate, marketers should support the government to market social causes. In short, social marketing aims to influence people, idea and behaviour. To make it more clear, we will consider same examples and social marketing undertaken by a some businesses.

1. Britannia Industries have undertaken the social cause of 'Save Tiger' supported by its tiger brands of biscuits.
2. Marico has taken up the social cause of preventing heart care through the promotion and its brand Saffola etc.

Definition

"Social marketing is the design, implementation and control of programmes seeking to increase the acceptability of a social ideas, cause or practice in a target group" **—Philip Kotlar**

FEATURES OF SOCIAL MARKETING

(i) Initiated by any group: Any group or organisation devoted to a cause can adopt social marketing. The idea is to do good to the people. The intension of this is to make aware of its merits and demerits, so that customer will take care and protect that aspect. For example, Close-up product. Manufacturer organises teeth care week for school going children's and tells them about do's and don'ts to preserve teeth.

(ii) Comprehensive presentation: social marketing does not cover only one aspect of a problem. it is also comprehensive in presentation and includes all sides of an issue. So it can be used by both the parties arguing in favour and against. For example family planning. People who take excuse of religion and are against. Family planners are told to plan their life and that of their children. By quoting To lead quality life, one needs to have small family.

(iii) Different from social advertising: social advertising leads with the communication and public interest causes. Whereas social marketing covers issues of public good which are mostly not attended like issues of public good which are mostly not attended. Like danger of overheating, resources conservation, women's right etc.

Social marketing has been defined as "the application of commercial marketing technologies to the analysis, planning, execution, and evaluation of programmes designed to influence the voluntary behaviour of target audiences in order to improve their personal welfare and that of their society" (Andreasen, 1995). This definition encompasses several key aspects of the social marketing approach;

GREEN MARKETING

MEANING OF GREEN MARKETING

In late (eighties) 1980s, a document prepared by the World Commission on Environment and Development, defined sustainable development as meeting the needs of the present without compromising the ability of future generation to meet their own need. This makes essential to have environment-friendly products.

Green marketing means promotion of products with environmental characteristics e.g. recyclable, refillable, ozone-friendly, phosphate-free and environment-friendly. But it is not limited to it. It is much wider concept and applicable to consumer goods, industrial goods, and even services some like hotels and resorts. In short, green marketing includes a broad range of activities like, product modification, changes in the production process, changes in packaging and truthful advertising.

As we know, pollution is the price we pay for our industrial progress, and everyone is affected by it. Industrilisation is mainly responsible for the problem of environmental pollution. It disturbed the ecological balance and gives very visible adverse effects. Here every businessman's efforts are to be directed and diverted to maintain clean and healthy environment to fulfill their social responsibilities.

Definition: "Green marketing is the marketing of products that are presumed to be environmentally safe". **—American Marketing Association**

IMPORTANCE OF GREEN MARKETING

1. **Sustainable Development:** The benefit of green marketing is sustainable development. Nature's resources should be used for development and improving the quality of life of not only present generation, but also to ensure that the environment is not degraded so that the future generation does not suffer.
2. **Less Pollution:** Green marketing helps in reducing pollution. The technologies that are used under green technology keep pollution to the minimum and make the life comfortable and suitable to live.
3. **Less Government Control:** There are certain regulations made by government to protect the consumer in a different ways. There are some regulations relating to environmental marketing like, Reduction of harmful goods, Modifying consumer & industries consumption of harmful goods & ensure that consumers have the ability to evaluate the environmental consumption of goods. The organisation which produces goods are in the interest of the society then there are less control of government as organisation hare taken care of societies expectation.

Capital Influence

A company adopting green technology is likely to receive more capital influence not only from people within the country but also from outside. With such a good inflows of capital, organisation can further or for better technology which is environmental friendly

EVENT MARKETING

Event marketing refers to building a product marketing programme around sponsored event. It includes designing or developing live themed activity, occasions, displays or exhibit such as sporting event, music festival, fair or concert to promote a product. It is recently pioneered in India but has taken off very well with the Indian consumers.

The above noted event are golden opportunities to the marketers to build brand associations and to improve perceived value of brand in consumers' mind. The basic idea of this is to make the brand much visible as possible. Generally, company decides on event marketing through the sponsorship in its effort to support causes that are close to people.

Event management companies organisations services of variety of causes including corporate events. Like product launches, press conferences, corporate meetings and conferences, marketing programmes like road shows, grand opening events, and special corporate hospitality events like concerts, award ceremonies, film premises, Launch/ Release parties, fashion shows, commercial events, private events such as weddings etc.

While doing event marketing there is need to follow some guidelines to ensure that the event gains the maximum response and the event is to manage at minimum cost. The guidelines are:

1. **Attendance of potential customer:** If event is meant to market a product then it has to ensure that the purchase decision maker attended the events. For this purpose it is important to keep the message across the target audience and the adequate research is to be carried out from the viewpoint of attenuation profiles.
2. **Ensure value addition:** Value addition means the benefit which is gained on the part of venue or trade show organiser.
3. **Undertake cost benefit analysis:** Before the event is undertaken, the cost-effectiveness of promoting product should be questioned and it is essential to analyst. Cost-benefit of the entire event.

Recent Trends in event marketing

In India, day-by-day event marketing is becoming more popular. The sponsorers are ready to spend lacks of rupees, for the purpose of circulating, the name within the country and abroad within no time. E.g. filmfare night event. This event marketing is not only important or restricted to profit-oriented companies but also made open to non-profit making organisation. E.g. Health for all can be achieved when people understand the health's priority. Therefore, hospitals are beginning to treat such type of marketing as serious issues. The objectives of hospital are intangible like patients' satisfaction is our satisfaction. Event like free health check-up for senior citizens are sponsored by WOCKHARDT.

TELEMARKETING

Meaning of Telemarketing

Telemarketing is a form of direct marketing. It is one of marketing strategies. It is very well to use the phone to sell products and services. It is also known as phone sales or cold calls. Cold calls means the recipient of the call has not requested that the telemarketer should contract them.

Telemarketing comprises the integrated and systematic application of tele-communications. It retains personalised customer relations. Though it is non-face-to-face customer contract, but it is economical and time-saving and quick problem solving marketing activity. Generally, manufacturers use to establish this type to marketing for the purpose of answering dealers' questions, about inventory management, service and replacement of parts. Under this type of marketing, customers have given toll-free number to dial & deal. In short, user can say telemarketing is nothing but marketing conducted over the telephone.

Advantages of Telemarketing

Telemarketing has the following advantages

I. **Building customer relationship:** Telephone marketing helps to build customer relationship. The marketer can have a dialogue with the customers and learn about their specific needs. Such interaction helps the marketer to offer individualised offer of product and incentives.

II. **Reduced cost:** Here marketer is getting all information at one dial or click, which reduces sales cost greatly. Here marketer need not send his staff on visit or maintain a store and bear the cost on rent, insurance and facilities. They can also produce digital catalogue for less cost.

TECHNOLOGY MARKETING

Success with high tech products requires a confluence of technical understanding and marketing skills with conventional products, the general need or desire is well known while with the new technological possibilities, the need or desire is not always known. Therefore, the technological marketer must take one step backward to identify the fundamental role that his product can fulfill in the marketplace. The fundamental approach for new technology marketing can be modelled as the P's and Q's of marketing. The P's are people, product, place, price, packaging and promotion, and the Q's are quantity, quality and quickness.

Technological marketing focuses on inducing substitution or reducing the buyer to purchase the new product or service instead of something else. Unplanned babies come out of using technology to modernise something that has a well-established place in everyday life. One common example is the use of automatic teller machines (ATMs). The original idea was that machines could carry out the old cash dispensing function more efficiently –i.e., Phase-I-deciding to use new technology for an old function.

But a new way of doing things is always subtly different from what has been done before. There is always at least an aspect that has changed. In the case of dispensing ATM's changed two things where the cash was available and when. And there two aspects caused a fundamental change in the utility of the service received by customers. For the first time, they could get cash out of bank working hours and away from bank premises, which was indeed a new bank service. The customers were delighted with it and demanded more. This led to Phase-II- i.e., where in new technology used for an old purpose give rise to a new market situation.

The Phase-III is that the marketer stands back from such a situation and reappraises it objectively as it gives him the opportunity to gain a much deeper understanding of the needs and desires of potential customers that have arisen out of the reappraisal.

In the case of ATMs, the numbers of banks around the world have entered this phase by introducing new type of customers that are accessed entirely by ATM cards. Microprocessor technology is another example of unexpected multidimensional changes leading to a large range of new products embodying multifarious market desires.

In essence, it can be said that technology marketing comprises analysing existing market demands through technology, reappraising and redefining market needs and desires in the light of the response to the new technology and, accordingly fine-tuning products for the developing marketplace.

POLITICAL MARKETING

In a Democracy like India, the public has to go through the elections for electing office bearers in every few years. These are for national, state or local offices. In India, there are the Parliament, Assembly, the local Zila Parishad, Municipal bodies and Panchayats. Political parties' candidates and independent candidates contest the elections. Each one wants to win the election and for this one has to pull voters. For this purpose, candidates are involved in the process of political marketing.

Political marketing has become a major industry and area of specialisation. In India in 1989 parliamentary elections, roughly ₹ 1000 crore were spent on media advertising, outdoor advertising, video and audio cassettes, posters, stickers and other ways. The major marketing input in case of political marketing includes:

1. Marketing research through opinion pools.
2. Employing professional advertising for campaign development.

E-COMMERCE

In the series of latest developments that marked the progress of technology are the internet and the

World Wide Web (WWW). At par with the earlier discoveries such as fire, steam engine and the proliferation of telephone lines, the world wide web ushers revolutionary changes relating to how the human beings communicate, educate, entertain and the way how they carry on business. Companies all over the world are finding e-commerce as the new platform for the business in the years to come. The revolution in information technology has brought many changes in the business practices and its performance. E-commerce is the latest concept which helps to develop their competitive edge.

Commercial transactions over an electronic medium are known as e-commerce. E' stands for Electronic and Commerce' stands for trade and practices. Though there is no official definition of e-commerce, different experts have defined it differently and as under:

The sharing of business information, maintaining business relationships and conducting business transactions by means of telecommunication networks.

E-commerce is more than simply buying and selling goods electronically. It involves using network communication technology to engage range of activities up and down the value added chain, both within and outside the Objectives of e-commerce.

The system of e-commerce is designed to fulfill the following objectives:

1. To bring paradigm in shift in business performance and to develop their competitive edge.
2. To develop business relationship on strong footing.
3. To find out and analyse market potential.
4. To provide better service and delight to customers.

Models of E-commerce

There are several ways in which E-commerce products and services can be sold. But all these kinds of selling is a part of five levels of E-commerce

1. Business to Business (B 2 B)
2. Business to Consumer (B 2 C)
3. Consumer to Consumer (C 2 C)
4. Consumer to Business (C 2 B)
5. Government to Consumers (G 2 C)

RELATIONSHIP MARKETING

Today the process of globalisation, privatisation and liberalisation coupled with faster urbanisation has created the marketing environment highly competitive and sensitive. Gone are the days when the companies were supplying their products to the customers and the customers were willing or unwillingly forced to accept the product at services, reason being that the customers were having option. Today a lot of water has flown through river. A new age marketing aims at winning customers forever, where, companies greet the customers, create products to suit their needs, work hard to develop lifetime customers through the principle of customer delight, customer approval, customer enthusiasm etc.

Modern marketing calls for building trust, a binding force and a value added relationship with the customer to win their hearts. Marketers care, acknowledge, appreciate and empower the customer in a number of ways like sending thank you cards, special occasion cards, frequency rewards. Hence, relationship marketing is aimed to create strong, long-lasting, fruitful relationship by developing long-term bonds through its various instruments of personal connections, as a result, customers start identifying associating themselves with the product, prefer and accept company's product and service over competitors' offerings, and buy again and again, recommend others to buy. Thus, they become loyal to the product and feel a kind of kinship with it.

Benefits and Importance

1. Relationship marketing builds goodwill in the market which in turn generates additional traffic to the outlet.
2. Relationship marketing is a highly effective technique to keep track of buying habits,

intensions, self images & spending patterns.

3. Relationship marketing leads to the development of loyalty and satisfaction which in turn increases transactions with the same customers, again and again.
4. Relationship marketing can stop-customers switching to another brand.
5. Relationship marketing results in positive image projection and enhanced brand equity on account of high degree of customer relation and loyalty.
6. Relationship marketing calls for listening and caring for the customers which in turn develop a sense of belongingness and a soft corner for the company itself in the mind of customers.
7. Relationship marketing leads to develop a positive relation with the customers and in this way it becomes an effective tool to keep the competitors away from our customers' sight.

Principles of Relationship Marketing:

Following guidelines help in developing a positive and long-term relationship with the customers:

1. Marketing system should be an integrative marketing system with the open system approach which takes into consideration the environmental forces.
2. Companies should continuously search for value building approaches through a system of quality management review process because only by exceeding customers' expectations, marketers can build a value laden relationship with customers.
3. Marketing organisation should establish a separate relationship cell to prepare, implement and monitor their relationship marketing programme.
4. A provision of additional compensation and incentive system should be made for the sales people working with important charts.
5. Developing the relationship is a specialised job and the companies should not totally rely on technical people. Instead, relationship managers should be employed who are specialised in marketing, communication and interpersonal skills.

Information Technology and Customer relationship Management

Information technology holds the key of future of customer relationship management. Now, marketers with technical capabilities are keeping track of individualised behaviour and purchases, directly interacting with the customers through electronic links and developing data bases to recognise unexpected patterns for marketing adaptation and using software to manipulate and update data quickly for best marketing results.

Information technology is playing a highly significant role in building on the established customer base on the battleground of 21st century marketplace. Marketers are using information technology in the following different ways to recognise, respect, reward and retain their key customers.

1. **Capturing customer perception in real time:** This is the most effective way of being truly responsive to customers and allows organisations to take quick actions. Encouraging customers to comment and complain on the spot and then empowering the markets to respond in the desired fashion. Companies are using variety of devices for this purpose like video cameras, tape recorders etc. To collect first hand information any time about customer perception, a portable computer system called 'Q' is being developed. It is freestanding mobile computer that can read and analyse customer feedbacks.
2. **Data base Marketing:** Companies are using state of the art database marketing techniques, which allow marketers to analyse customers past buying patterns and compare them with demographic and psychographic

data to determine future purchase behaviour. Marketers are shifting their focus from product and brand management to customer/ account management.

3. **Creating virtual dialogue:** Marketers are developing databases to keep a record of their spending patterns and other behavioural aspects of customers. By monitoring the behaviour over a period of time the marketer may interact in the most effective way to inform the customers about the new product or service offerings best suited to their personality type, lifestyle and other behavioural characteristics.
4. **Electronic and infra red surveillance equipment:** These equipment provide retailers with improved data about customer's traffic patterns and buying habits while they shop in stores.
5. **Z-axis:** Using PCs and a customerised software program called 'Z-axis'; sales people can design and generate proposals in no time.
6. **Electronic relationship marketing program:** Marketers are developing and implementing electronic relationship marketing program involving frequently shopper cards, customer profile and intention forms.
7. **Use of software, enhancing marketing effectiveness:** Marketers are using a number of softwares like BMW's Retail 2000 relationship marketing uses sales person empowerment and desktop technology to bland sales and service into a seamless process. It enhances customer satisfaction and help dealers to retain customers and employees. Ford Motors uses focal point technology to guide employees through sales and service transactions.
8. **Software installation:** Marketers are locking customers into the services of product offerings by installing softwares for the customer's. Thus, they are not only providing them an ease or convenience in communicating with the marketers but also restricting in their switching over the competitors by developing a kind of kinship with them.
9. **Infrared sensors:** Retailers are using infra red sensors in the store ceilings to track shopping carts and to get an insight into customer's purchase patterns.
10. **Networking of devices:** The networking of devices has enabled organisations to collect information in detail about spending patterns, spending preferences, cross sales etc. from the point where the transaction occurs. Electronic data devices are used to collect information, which are then transmitted back to a central computer so that customer's actions can be monitored. The most commonly systems in use are:
    (a) **Market Basket Analysis:** This technique is used to build profiles of the individuals shopping in the store. The collected information can be used to target with marketing materials and specifically aimed at encouraging them to spend more.
    (b) **Electronic Point of Sale System (EPOS):** Through a regular interaction with the customers' marketers are collecting information on the customer's preferences for particular product or service and then trying to match them with the total population of customers. By identifying the suggestions to the potential and existing customers about the purchase patterns and satisfaction levels of the customers who have already purchased or consumed the given offerings. Thus, marketers are trying to add new opportunity to the existing shopping experience, enabling customers to access the views of people with similar tastes and interests and automating the word of mouth experience.

11. **Automating the word of mouth experience:** Through a regular interaction with the customers, marketers are collecting information on the customer's preferences for particular product or service and then trying to match them with the total population of customers. By identifying the customers on their database who have the most similar preferences and tastes, marketers are offering suggestions to the potential and existing customers about the purchase patterns and satisfaction levels of the customers who have already purchased or consumed the given offerings. Thus, marketers are trying to add new opportunity to the existing shopping experience, enabling customers to access the views of people with similar tastes and interests and automating the word of mouth experience.
12. **Online analytical processing (OLAP):** The process of quarrying and analysing with multiple dimensions is the core principle of these tools. OLAP tools are used for finding out the relationship with customer related variables. The drills down facilities are there in the tools to concentrate on much deeper trend analysis.
13. **Data warehousing:** Marketers are employing data warehousing techniques to develop customer profile and check the patterns of retention and loyalty.
14. **Automated telephone service:** Customers are being provided by the marketers with the facility of automated telephone services to empower the customers by having an instant access to information about the availability of product.
15. **CRM:** It is asset of discrete software and technologies which focuses on automating and improving the business processes associated with managing customer relationships in the area of sales, marketing, customer service and support. CRM applications coordinate multiple channels of communication with the customers such as face-to-face, the web, and the telephony.
16. **Internet:** These contain sales and marketing information such as catalogues, price lists, customer information and order status to let sales representative quickly answer the customer's questions and take orders without call backs.
17. **Customer information system:** Marketers are developing a separate customer information system to gather, process and analyse all sorts of information about individual customers and thus enable the organisation to customise to the individual level, remain up to data with the satisfaction, loyalty, retention level and other relevant information needed for strategic purposes.
18. **Point of sale system:** Companies have developed point of sale systems—a software integration to capture the information in real time and building a data warehouse.
19. **Information technology enabling all time all days working:** Use of Information technology (telephone, interactive T.V., and other sophisticated technology) in marketing and purchase related activities not only means that geographical presence is unimportant but also offers a way of enhancing the value attached with the product and service offerings.
20. **Internet:** In the modern marketing environment, customer can interact in any business at any state in a number of ways like product designing, tracking information search etc. through internet-a most important tool forcing both the marketers customers to understand and value each other activities.
21. **Internet based knowledge management systems:** These incorporate subject matter expertise on various customer care issues and make all that knowledge available to customer care representatives as they work to solve the problems.
22. **Computer networking:** Devices like E-mail, videoconferencing, groupware etc. facilitate horizontal communication. When a customer

reports a problem, the call automatically goes to the person specialising in the field. Operator gets a description of the problem and its urgency, type the information into the database and zap the file to the place where the related person is located.

23. **Mass customisation of Product/Services:** Marketers are making strategic use of sophisticated customer information gathered from key customers and complied in the form of database. The database is then used to determine an individualised communication strategy and customised product or service for high potential relationship customers. Through I.T., marketers are differentiating and improving offerings also for their key customers.

24. **Mass customised advertising:** Marketers are now making use of mass customised advertising-advertisements specially designed for individual prospects to catch their attention.

25. **Electronic communication systems:** Prompt response requires electronic communication program like interactive voice response program to touch and feel, fax on demand to answer the raised queries, restricted access internet site to make information available under all heads and live customer service representative answering the raised questions.

26. **Business intelligence solutions:** A few marketers are hiring consultants, installing softwares and developing software technology labs, providing analytical tools aimed at addressing business efforts. Business intelligence solutions are becoming mission critical systems for managing customer relationship.

27. **Collaborative filtering:** It compares individual purchase behaviour with every other individual purchase behaviours.

28. **Internet based knowledge management systems:** Companies are developing internet based knowledge management systems that incorporate subject matter expertise on various customer care issues and make all that knowledge available to customer care representatives as they work to solve the problems within no time.

29. **Customer smart card:** Marketers are providing key customers a card called as smart card which carries all relevant information, details or previous and repeat purchases etc. to make it convenient for the customers to recall and for the marketers to keep a track of the behavioural and purchase trends.

30. **Virtual reality:** It encompasses a wide variety of computer technology application and conveys multiple sensory informational and thus allows the customers to interact with the offerings. It offers potential for effective design and marketing of service scopes.

31. **Data mining:** Data mining tools extracts the hidden, unexpected trends from large databases to predict future trends and behaviour, allowing business to make proactive knowledge-driven decisions in the areas like market segmentation, targeting and positioning, development of customer-oriented marketing strategies etc.

32. **Toll free numbers:** Marketers are making use of toll free numbers to solicit buyers' feedback about the offerings.

33. **Extranet:** Development of extranet enables sharing selected information directly with the customers by linking themselves the customers. Marketers are installing software so that customers can examine about the availability of the product and also order at the same time.

34. **In-touch programs:** The in-touch programs like fax on demand keeps the relationship on the providing timely support material, quotes, delivery dates and so on.

35. **Call centers and answer centers:** These are being designed to answer the specific queries

before and after the purchase made by the buyer.

36. **Firefly:** A software designed to track consumer preferences and make suggestion to customers based on their previous and those of people with similar preferences.

37. **Infomediaries/information based brands:** The amount of information marketers have on a customer's previous purchases based on which they recommended recipes on individual preferences.

38. **Imaging systems:** They allow organising all incoming mails and automatic filing into the appropriate customer file.

39. **Online Information Tracking Programs:** Programs like Cosmos IIB track and process online data to provide real time information on net to customers.

Relationship Marketing and Indian Environment

Indian marketers are striving hard to create strong lasting relationship with the customers through various instruments of personal connections. Indian marketers seem to be in the responsive marketing stages in case of product and in the stage of accountable marketing in case of services.

1. **Special Facilities:** Opel Astra card to car owners to provide special facilities like 24 hours service breakdown service etc.
2. **Customer Training:** Hawkins with a dealer network of more than 500 dealers provides training to customers as how to cook effectively and variedly in Hawkins pressure cooker.
3. **Mystery shopping program:** Bank of America is using mystery shopping to identify, appraise and reward on interpersonal skills and relationship-building abilities of marketing personnel.
4. **Frequent marketing programs:** Free flights to frequent fliers by British Airways.
5. **Club information:** Magic Club, Barbie Club, Saffola Healthy Heart Club etc.
6. **Relationship cells:** Apollo Tyres have developed a separate relationship marketing cell specially functioning to develop and maintain relationship with the customers.
7. **Awards:** Welcome group gives away awards to the most loyal customers.

Environmental Marketing

Environment is a dynamic word. It stands differently for various people. A marketing man defines it as a marketing environment, financial man has his introspective definition, yet a business environment has different meaning. Here environment refers to natural environment which is defined as surroundings around of us, where we brought up, survive and end our breath.

Environment is a core requirement for survival and growth of any living or non-living thing. In the absence of environment, it is unthinkable about survival of any creature, subsequently question does not arising in conceiving a business corporation and marketing its products.

These days there is an increasing focus on ecological trade-off and environmental protection. There is great alertness in the mind of not only environmentalists but also every citizen of the planet. All of us are fully aware and concern about environmental problems whenever they make any purchase right from cosmetic to automobile, pay meticulous heed at environment.

Morph Marketing

In today's time of competition, the products' attributes are not much important for differentiation but the service features especially for the marketing of consumer semi-durables and durables. Today product and services are exchanging features more closely than ever before. A new powerful tool of selling-Morph Marketing is shaping this transformation. The important is not what marketer is selling but how he develops the long-term relationships with customer and up to what level he is able to reduce customer's dissonance.

Benefits of Morph Marketing

1. Bundling services with the product help to rewrite customer expectations. Customer will use the services as a measuring stick with which they judge the value of the product.
2. Product-service envelop will embellish branded value, keeping it contemporary.
3. Differentiating through service will deliver unexpected value to customer and boost sales.
4. Spear heading the marketing through a service will make mass customisation possible as in case of Videocon the company maintains a direct relationship between brand and consumer by dispatching a company engineer to the customer's home.
5. Enriching the product with the service envelop enables quick responses to changing customer needs. As by Philip 24 hours complaint registration facility and giving information facility.
6. A service product combination allows overcoming the non-involvement barrier. Low excitement product can seldom generate sufficient enthusiasm after purchase to induce the customer to choose the one brand over another. To overcome this situation, CEAT renamed its showrooms Ceat Shoppe and provided the services like inspection, wheel-alignment, pick up and delivery and general auto maintenance advise free of cost.

MULTIPLE CHOICE QUESTIONS

1. A market where goods are sold in bulk quantities to the customers is known as ....
(*a*) Retail market (*b*) Wholesale market
(*c*) Product market (*d*) Service market
(*e*) None of these

2. The process of supplying products to all retail outlets is known as ....
(*a*) Selective distribution
(*b*) Exclusive distribution
(*c*) Channel configuration
(*d*) Intensive distribution
(*e*) None of these

3. Inside sales is known as ....
(*a*) Direct marketing (*b*) Tele-marketing
(*c*) Social marketing (*d*) Viral marketing
(*e*) None of these

4. Which is the feature of direct marketing ....
(*a*) Open dialogue
(*b*) One-to-one communication
(*c*) Personal relationship
(*d*) All of the above
(*e*) None of these

5. Direct marketing refers to a communication between the .... and .... directly.
(*a*) Seller, buyer
(*b*) Firm, suppliers
(*c*) Society, target market
(*d*) Price, services
(*e*) None of these

6. Super market is also known as ....
(*a*) Self service store
(*b*) Hyper market
(*c*) Co-operative societies
(*d*) All of these
(*e*) None of these

7. Direct marketing is sometimes called ....
(*a*) Self service
(*b*) Retail stores
(*c*) Armchair shopping
(*d*) Social marketing
(*e*) None of these

8. Which of the following is the largest retail enterprise in the world?
(*a*) K mart (*b*) Wall mart
(*c*) Shoppers stops (*d*) Alibaba
(*e*) None of these

9. Which of the following is not a non-store retailing?
(*a*) Tele-marketing (*b*) Direct marketing
(*c*) Kiosk marketing (*d*) Retail chains
(*e*) None of these

10. Direct marketing is found more suitable to which of the following products?
(*a*) Agricultural products
(*b*) TV
(*c*) Shoes
(*d*) Vacuum cleaner
(*e*) None of these

11. Which company is the pioneer in direct marketing?
(*a*) Johnson & Johnson (*b*) Eureka forbs
(*c*) Avon cosmetics (*d*) Cypla
(*e*) None of these

12. The best channel of distribution for vacuum cleaner is ....
(*a*) Direct marketing (*b*) Tele-marketing
(*c*) Retail marketing (*d*) Kiosk marketing
(*e*) None of these

13. A .... operates multiple retail outlets under common ownership in different cities and town
(*a*) Retail chains (*b*) Destination store
(*c*) Shopping malls (*d*) Retail chain
(*e*) None of these

14. The process of direct communication between the sales person and a prospect is called
(*a*) Direct marketing (*b*) Personal selling
(*c*) Advertising (*d*) Retail marketing
(*e*) None of these

15. Department stores generally serves .... class.
(*a*) Poor (*b*) Middle
(*c*) Rich (*d*) All of the above
(*e*) None of these

16. Tenant farmers are ....
(*a*) Zamindars
(*b*) Small peasants
(*c*) Marginal farmers
(*d*) Farmers who operate on rented lands
(*e*) None of these

17. Rural rich consumers are sub-divided into .... and ....
(*a*) Consumers around rural and urban area
(*b*) Consumers above poverty and below poverty line
(*c*) Concentrate Rich consumers and Scattered rich consumers
(*d*) Aspirants and climbers
(*e*) None of these

18. In a village haat CoCo Cola competes with ....
(*a*) Pepsi (*b*) Nimboo Panni
(*c*) Jalzeera (*d*) All of the above
(*e*) None of these

19. The urban buyer's behavior is individual or at the most family –driven, whereas in rural areas the decision making is a ....
(*a*) Collective Process
(*b*) Long Process
(*c*) Experience Process
(*d*) Conformance Process
(*e*) None of these

20. Rural markets remain untapped because of three Ds, they are ....
(*a*) Distribution, distance and delivery
(*b*) Distance, diversity and dispersion
(*c*) Difference, distance and delivery
(*d*) Diversity, Difference and distribution
(*e*) None of these

21. The rural consumers recognize the brands using ....
(*a*) Words
(*b*) Company name
(*c*) Logos and symbols
(*d*) Brand ambassadors
(*e*) None of these

22. The highest incidence of fake products in rural markets is at ....
(*a*) village retailer (*b*) haats
(*c*) village wholesaler (*d*) village distributor
(*e*) None of these

23. Project Jagruti is the marketing effort of ....

(*a*) HLL (*b*) ITC
(*c*) Escorts (*d*) Colgate
(*e*) None of these

24. The rural consumers in the south are ....
(*a*) More brand conscious.
(*b*) Less brand conscious.
(*c*) More willing to accept high-tech products.
(*d*) Both (*a*) & (*c*)
(*e*) None of these

25. .... is the hall mark of the rural market.
(*a*) Homogenity (*b*) Heterogenity
(*c*) Diversity (*d*) Difference
(*e*) None of these

26. "The future lies with companies who see poor as their customers" The above quote was said by the management guru ....
(*a*) Peter F. Drucker (*b*) Michel Porter
(*c*) C.K. Prahalad (*d*) Garry Hamel
(*e*) None of these

27. The concept of using video vans as an effective means of reaching out to rural markets was pioneered by ....
(*a*) HLL (*b*) Philips
(*c*) Political parties (*d*) Marico
(*e*) None of these

28. Cash –rich farmers can be directly contacted by setting up brand stalls in ....
(*a*) Melas (*b*) Haats
(*c*) Mandis (*d*) Village fairs
(*e*) None of these

29. Many companies congregate at the Ganges river for the .... festival, where about 3 crore people, mostly from rural areas are expected to come over a span of one month.
(*a*) Sonepur mela (*b*) Kumbh mela
(*c*) Pushkar mela (*d*)
(*e*) None of these

30. .... has 250 most popular festivals in the year, which include sports festival, agricultural as well as cultural festivals.
(*a*) Hariyana (*b*) Bihar
(*c*) Punjab (*d*) Rajasthan
(*e*) Jharkhand

31. Swasthya Chetna is a campaign to promote the habits of washing hands by ....
(*a*) P&G (*b*) CavinKare
(*c*) HLL (*d*) Nirma
(*e*) Colgate

32. Shakthi Ammas are the personal selling agents of ....
(*a*) Marico (*b*) ACC
(*c*) HUL (*d*) P&G
(*e*) None of these

33. Main cropping season in India are ....
(*a*) Kharif (October-November)
(*b*) Rabi (June–July)
(*c*) Garma (May-June)
(*d*) All of these
(*e*) None of these

34. Corporate farm service centers named as "Kisan Sansars" is the project of ....
(*a*) EID-Parry (*b*) Rallis
(*c*) ITC (*d*) TATA
(*e*) None of these

35. .... provides the largest compilation of rural demographic data.
(*a*) NCAER (*b*) Census of India
(*c*) ICDS (*d*) Panchayat Office
(*e*) None of these

36. DRDA refers to ....
(*a*) Development and Rural Distribution Authority
(*b*) Distribution and Rural Development Authority
(*c*) Distribution and Rural Authority
(*d*) District Rural Development Authority
(*e*) None of these

37. Rural people are very .... in their living style and communication.
(*a*) Suspicious (*b*) Simple
(*c*) Harsh (*d*) Skeptical
(*e*) None of these

38. The rural researcher is advised to ....
(*a*) Carry writing material
(*b*) Carry recorders

(*c*) Memorize all relevant information
(*d*) Carry pen recorders
(*e*) None of these

39. Rural consumers buy clothes and cheap jewellery from ....
(*a*) village shop (*b*) shanty
(*c*) nearest town (*d*) mela and jatra
(*e*) None of these

40. Which private Insurance company tied up with NGOs and offered reasonably priced policies in the nature of group insurance covers in rural areas?
(*a*) Birla Sunlife
(*b*) HDFC Standard Life
(*c*) SBI Life
(*d*) Bajaj-Allianz
(*e*) None of these

41. Farmers preferred .... torches such as 'Jeevan Saathi' from Eveready.
(*a*) plastic (*b*) dry cell
(*c*) heavy brass (*d*) chargeable
(*e*) None of these

42. Which is the company based at Chennai who is a major player in the FMCG category in rural markets?
(*a*) HUL (*b*) Dabur
(*c*) Marico (*d*) Cavinkare
(*e*) None of these

43. .... is the detergent powder which is a generic brand in rural India.
(*a*) Wheel (*b*) Nirma
(*c*) Surf (*d*) Rin
(*e*) None of these

44. .... is the name of the tractor which is associated with the head of the village.
(*a*) Sonalika
(*b*) Escorts
(*c*) Bhumiputra
(*d*) Mahindra & Mahindra - Sarpanch
(*e*) None of these

45. Which is the fake brand for Tiger Biscuits in rural markets?
(*a*) Leopard (*b*) Fighter
(*c*) Lion (*d*) Cheetah
(*e*) None of these

46. 'LUP' refers to ....
(*a*) Low Unit Packs
(*b*) Light Utility Packs
(*c*) Low Utility Packs
(*d*)
(*e*) None of these

47. .... is the name of the economy brand of tea launched by Tata Tea in rural areas to compete with loose tea powder.
(*a*) Tajmahal (*b*) A 1
(*c*) Agni (*d*) Kannan Devan
(*e*) None of these

48. There are .... layers of distribution channels for the movements of products from the company depot to the interior village markets.
(*a*) 4 (*b*) 5
(*c*) 3 (*d*) 6
(*e*) None of these

49. .... are the last–mile distribution in rural markets.
(*a*) Haats (*b*) Melas
(*c*) Distribution Vans (*d*) Mobile traders
(*e*) None of these

50. PDS is a system of distribution for essential commodities to a large number of people through a network of ....
(*a*) Margin Free Markets
(*b*) Fair Price Shops
(*c*) Ration Shops
(*d*) Both (*b*) & (*c*)
(*e*) None of these

51. .... function like mini super markets for rural consumers.
(*a*) Haats
(*b*) Melas
(*c*) Farmers' Services Cooperative Societies
(*d*) Ration shops
(*e*) None of these

52. Kisan Credit Card scheme was introduced by ....

(*a*) KVIC
(*b*) State Bank of India
(*c*) Indian Government
(*d*) Canara Bank
(*e*) None of these

53. KAP in rural marketing refers to ....
(*a*) Knowledge, Awareness and Personality
(*b*) Knowledge, Attitude and Personality
(*c*) Knowledge, Attitude and Practices
(*d*) None of the above
(*e*) None of these

54. Data Collection in rural area is ....
(*a*) easy (*b*) difficult
(*c*) scattered (*d*) remote
(*e*) None of these

55. Challenges to reach the small & scattered rural market places need to be addressed by marketers by adopting ....
(*a*) out-of-box thinking
(*b*) discovering innovative solutions
(*c*) understanding the challenges to rural distribution
(*d*) all the above
(*e*) None of these

56. In villages, small shops alone are the backbone of the ....
(*a*) local retail network
(*b*) regional retail network
(*c*) national retail network
(*d*) neighbourhood retail stores
(*e*) None of these

57. More than 70% of the rural market is still beyond the reach of ....
(*a*) promotional activities
(*b*) stocking pattern
(*c*) price discipline
(*d*) direct distribution
(*e*) None of these

58. Galla Kirana merchant in India often acts as a ....
(*a*) speculator (*b*) distributor
(*c*) trader (*d*) marketer
(*e*) None of these

59. Rural shops in India have the .... per capita in the world.
(*a*) lowest retail space
(*b*) medium retail space
(*c*) highest retail space
(*d*) none of the above
(*e*) None of these

60. Rural retailers stock a particular item usually because of ....
(*a*) consumers demand
(*b*) wholesaler's push
(*c*) competitor stocks the same item
(*d*) all the above
(*e*) None of these

61. .... have an important place in the distribution and promotion of products in villages.
(*a*) Mobile vans (*b*) Retailers
(*c*) Festival melas (*d*) Haats
(*e*) None of these

62. Initiative to reach rural consumers through e-choupal model for backward & forward linkages for agri-related business was taken by ....
(*a*) HLL (*b*) P&G
(*c*) ITC (*d*) LG
(*e*) None of these

63. .... is the spinal cord of a company.
(*a*) Distribution (*b*) Innovation
(*c*) Marketing (*d*) Market share
(*e*) None of these

64. .... is otherwise called as the hub-and-spoke system.
(*a*) Syndicate distribution
(*b*) Satellite distribution
(*c*) Corporate-SHG linkage
(*d*) Distribution model of durable goods companies
(*e*) None of these

65. Expand FSCS ....
(*a*) Fertilizer's Services Coordinating Societies
(*b*) Farmer's Services Coordinating Societies

(*c*) Fertilizer's Services Cooperating Societies
(*d*) Farmer's Services Cooperating Societies
(*e*) None of these

66. Rural communication is not a ....
(*a*) peripheral activity
(*b*) comprehensive activity
(*c*) normal activity
(*d*) easy task
(*e*) None of these

67. Rural India has traditionally been a society based on ....
(*a*) written communication
(*b*) oral communication
(*c*) interpersonal communication
(*d*) grapevine communication
(*e*) None of these

68. 'Knowing your customer' is one of the cardinal principle of ...., be it rural or urban India.
(*a*) advertising (*b*) promotion
(*c*) marketing (*d*) all the above
(*e*) None of these

69. Expand AICDA ....
(*a*) Awareness, Intention, Conviction, Desire, Action
(*b*) Awareness, Intention, Catch, Determination, Action
(*c*) Awareness, Interest, Conviction, Desire, Action
(*d*) Attention, Intention, Conviction, Desire, Action
(*e*) None of these

70. In rural context, ... is the first channel to which potential consumers automatically turn, before they solicit views and opinions from the outside world.
(*a*) the social channel
(*b*) the advocate channel
(*c*) the expert channel
(*d*) the personal channel
(*e*) None of these

71. Which one among the following medium is largely used by most of the fertilizer, tractor and FMCG companies for advertising?
(*a*) Personal selling (*b*) Radio
(*c*) Television (*d*) Cinema
(*e*) None of these

72. .... is the fastest growing, most powerful and most popular medium both in rural and urban media.
(*a*) radio (*b*) television
(*c*) cinema (*d*) all the above
(*e*) None of these

73. In rural areas the .... medium faces problems of both reach and access coupled with low literacy levels.
(*a*) radio (*b*) television
(*c*) cinema (*d*) print
(*e*) None of these

74. The haat, better known as the .... of rural India, is the oldest marketing channel in the country.
(*a*) cooperative stores
(*b*) mobile supermarket
(*c*) barefoot agents
(*d*) online supermarket
(*e*) None of these

75. "The rural market is not for all ,but for those with the guts, the skin of an elephant and the mind of an evangelist."
(*a*) Mr.Karthik Raina (*b*) Kotler
(*c*) C.K.Prahalad (*d*) Adi Godrej
(*e*) None of these

76. "A dissatisfied customer tells to 11 persons, a satisfied customer tells to 3 persons" The above quote was said by ....
(*a*) Peter F.Drucker
(*b*) Kotler
(*c*) C.K.Prahalad
(*d*) None of the above
(*e*) None of these

77. MPV refers to ....
(*a*) Maximum personal value
(*b*) Market potential value
(*c*) Market premium value
(*d*) None of the above
(*e*) None of these

78. Tele-marketing is a part of ....
(*a*) Direct marketing
(*b*) Social marketing
(*c*) Viral marketing
(*d*) Relationship marketing
(*e*) None of these

79. Television is a type of .... media.
(*a*) Broadcast (*b*) Print
(*c*) Outdoor (*d*) Online
(*e*) None of these

80. Organisations which sell their produces on the internet directly to consumers are called.
(*a*) B2B
(*b*) B2C
(*c*) Re-marketing
(*d*) Service marketing
(*e*) None of these

81. Which of the following is for an e-marketing tool?
(*a*) I-radio (*b*) Mobile phone
(*c*) I-kiosks (*d*) Cinema
(*e*) None of these

82. A financial instrument which can be used more than once to borrow money or buy goods and services on credit is :
(*a*) Debit card (*b*) Credit card
(*c*) Smart card (*d*)
(*e*) None of these

83. Which of the following is not a risk in internet based transaction.
(*a*) Ears-dropping (*b*) Spoofing
(*c*) Encryption (*d*) Unauthorized action
(*e*) None of these

84. A security tool to verify the authenticity of the message and claimed identify of the sender and to verify the message integrity is
(*a*) Encryption (*b*) Firewalls
(*c*) Digital certificate (*d*) Digital signature
(*e*) None of these

85. E-marketing is a part of ....
(*a*) E-commerce (*b*) E-cash
(*c*) E-payment (*d*) E-mail
(*e*) None of these

86. .... refers to word of mouth through electronic channels.
(*a*) E-advertising (*b*) E-Commerce
(*c*) E-cash (*d*) Viral marketing
(*e*) None of these

87. Internet advertising includes web advertising, ... etc.
(*a*) Transaction (*b*) Encryption
(*c*) E-mail (*d*)
(*e*) None of these

88. .... advertisement is a small, graph links placed on a web page.
(*a*) Banner (*b*) Buttons
(*c*) Website (*d*) E-mail
(*e*) None of these

89. Making payment through electronic media by using credit or debit cards for the products bought electronically is known as ....
(*a*) E-payment (*b*) E-mail
(*c*) E-marketing (*d*)
(*e*) None of these

90. .... includes debit cards, credit cards, smart cards etc.
(*a*) E-branding (*b*) E-cash
(*c*) E-mail (*d*)
(*e*) None of these

91. .... is a process that conceals meaning by changing messages into unintelligible messages.
(*a*) Encryption (*b*) Firewalls
(*c*) Backups (*d*)
(*e*) None of these

92. .... refers to marketing strategies under conditions of scarcity and during the period of shortage.
(*a*) E-commerce
(*b*) De-marketing
(*c*) Relationship marketing
(*d*)
(*e*) None of these

93. In response to threats from such companies as AOL, Amazon, Yahoo, eBay, E'TRADE, and dozens of others, established manufacturers and retailers became "brick-and-click" oriented by adding online services to their existing offerings. This process became known as ....

(*a*) Reintermediation
(*b*) Disintermediation
(*c*) E-commerce
(*d*) E-collaboration
(*e*) None of these

94. A banking product is an example for ....
(*a*) Tangible product
(*b*) Generic product
(*c*) Potential product
(*d*) Intangible product
(*e*) None of these

95. MPR stands for
(*a*) Managing public relations
(*b*) Measuring public relations
(*c*) Marketing public relations
(*d*) Monitories' public relations
(*e*) None of these

96. Which of the following is not a characteristic of service marketing
(*a*) Intangibility (*b*) Separability
(*c*) Heterogeneity (*d*) Perishability
(*e*) None of these

97. Medical treatment with ayurvedic massage is an example of
(*a*) Pure tangible (*b*) Hybrid
(*c*) Pure service (*d*) All of these
(*e*) None of these

98. Which of the following is not a service?
(*a*) Hospital (*b*) Banking
(*c*) Insurance (*d*) Marketing
(*e*) None of these

99. Which of the following is not an element of service marketing mix?
(*a*) People (*b*) Packaging
(*c*) Process (*d*) Physical evidence
(*e*) None of these

100. Being .... one cannot taste, touch, see, hear, smell or use services like physical products.
(*a*) Intangible (*b*) Tangible
(*c*) Perishable (*d*)
(*e*) None of these

101. In service marketing, apart from traditional four elements of marketing mix, there are three more elements, namely, people, process and ....
(*a*) Physical evidence (*b*) Publicity
(*c*) Packaging (*d*) All of the above
(*e*) None of these

102. .... reflects the perceived tangible and intangible benefits and costs to customers.
(*a*) Loyalty (*b*) Satisfaction
(*c*) Value (*d*) Expectations
(*e*) Comparison shopping

103. If a marketer decides to use warehouses, transportation companies, banks, and insurance companies to facilitate transactions with potential buyers, the marketer is using what is called a ....
(*a*) service channel
(*b*) distribution channel
(*c*) brand channel
(*d*) relationship channel
(*e*) intermediary channel

104. Companies are recognizing that much of their market value comes from ...., particularly their brands, customer base, employees, distributor and supplier relations, and intellectual capital.
(*a*) variable assets
(*b*) the value proposition
(*c*) intangible assets
(*d*) tangible assets
(*e*) customer preferences

105. Today, companies have to manage relation with their .... in order to ensure timely supplies and meet customer's requirements.
(*a*) Customers
(*b*) Government
(*c*) Suppliers
(*d*) International market
(*e*) None of these

ANSWERS

1	**2**	**3**	**4**	**5**	**6**	**7**	**8**	**9**	**10**
(*b*)	(*d*)	(*b*)	(*d*)	(*a*)	(*a*)	(*c*)	(*b*)	(*d*)	(*d*)
11	**12**	**13**	**14**	**15**	**16**	**17**	**18**	**19**	**20**
(*b*)	(*a*)	(*d*)	(*b*)	(*c*)	(*d*)	(*c*)	(*d*)	(*a*)	(*b*)
21	**22**	**23**	**24**	**25**	**26**	**27**	**28**	**29**	**30**
(*c*)	(*b*)	(*d*)	(*d*)	(*b*)	(*c*)	(*c*)	(*c*)	(*b*)	(*c*)
31	**32**	**33**	**34**	**35**	**36**	**37**	**38**	**39**	**40**
(*c*)	(*c*)	(*c*)	(*d*)	(*b*)	(*d*)	(*b*)	(*c*)	(*d*)	(*b*)
41	**42**	**43**	**44**	**45**	**46**	**47**	**48**	**49**	**50**
(*c*)	(*d*)	(*c*)	(*d*)	(*b*)	(*a*)	(*c*)	(*b*)	(*d*)	(*d*)
51	**52**	**53**	**54**	**55**	**56**	**57**	**58**	**59**	**60**
(*c*)	(*c*)	(*c*)	(*b*)	(*c*)	(*a*)	(*d*)	(*c*)	(*a*)	(*d*)
61	**62**	**63**	**64**	**65**	**66**	**67**	**68**	**69**	**70**
(*a*)	(*c*)	(*a*)	(*b*)	(*d*)	(*a*)	(*b*)	(*c*)	(*c*)	(*a*)
71	**72**	**73**	**74**	**75**	**76**	**77**	**78**	**79**	**80**
(*b*)	(*b*)	(*d*)	(*c*)	(*a*)	(*b*)	(*b*)	(*a*)	(*a*)	(*b*)
81	**82**	**83**	**84**	**85**	**86**	**87**	**88**	**89**	**90**
(*d*)	(*b*)	(*c*)	(*d*)	(*a*)	(*d*)	(*c*)	(*a*)	(*a*)	(*b*)
91	**92**	**93**	**94**	**95**	**96**	**97**	**98**	**99**	**100**
(*a*)	(*b*)	(*a*)	(*b*)	(*c*)	(*b*)	(*c*)	(*e*)	(*b*)	(*a*)
101	**102**	**103**	**104**	**105**					
(*a*)	(*c*)	(*a*)	(*c*)	(*c*)					

☞ CHAPTER-18

EVENT MARKETING

INTRODUCTION

An event can be described as a public assembly for the purpose of celebration, education, marketing or reunion. Events can be classified on the basis of their size, type and context. An event can be a social/lifecycle event like a birthday party, engagement, wedding, funeral etc. or an education and career event like an education fair, job fair, workshop, seminar, debate, contest, competition etc.

Event Management is the process of analysing, planning, marketing, producing and evaluating an event. It is a different way of promoting a product, service or idea. If an event is managed efficiently and effectively, it can be used as a very powerful promotional tool to launch or market a product or service. Events Management requires certain core values to be deployed to every element, process and decision to justify professional approach and achieve effective and efficient results.

Entertainment is available in society. Now people have an easy access to the modes of entertainment and thus they want to see something which is away from their common routine. An event needs to offer such entertainment, one cannot experience without participating the event. Such quality of entertainment offered needs to be better than the quality of entertainment one can experience at home. One needs to feel he/she is offered an experience that has value which cannot be received anywhere else. For people to be willing to leave home and attend an event, they should be gaining valuable experiences which are not possible to be experienced at home.

Excitement may seem intangible but it is real. It becomes a memorable moment for the event to be remembered in future. An event should create some kind of excitement for the attendees. The excitement should be promoted and successfully implemented. Excitement is different for different people, therefore the group of people invited (which is the target audience) to the event should be informed of the excitement they can experience and enjoy. The event organiser should remember to promise anticipation and then execute the promised enthusiasm.

For enterprise - Event Marketing is described as: "How to successfully promote events, festivals, conventions, and expositions" is a "readiness to take risks or try something untried; energy and initiative". By this is meant the importance of creating such an event which is able to lead the way to new level of event offering. In addition, a company should take risks in creating marketing for an event as in creating innovative fresh styles of event marketing. Creation of event marketing starts with analysing the event itself.

EVENT MARKETING MIX

A product should be identified as unique, valuable and beneficial for the attendees. History and continuation of an event add value as well as show reliability and increase willingness to join the event among the target audience as well as the sponsors. A long history of an event is not vital for success, but helps to execute the process. A successful marketer knows how to gather participants for a historical event, by defining the event as historical for the organisation as well as business in general. The uniqueness of an event is one of the key factors by which an event can have potential of becoming the top event to attend.

Pricing an event is determined by the main financial purpose of the event. If the purpose of the event is to profit, the incoming money has to be enough to pay the expenses yet be profitable. If the purpose is to create awareness, to create visibility, entertain customers etc. the incoming money is for paying the costs of the event, not necessarily creating monetary profit for the company. In addition, there are events which spend money without profiting.

These can be referred to as certain losses, as the company invests an amount of money on an event for charity or for creating goodwill, or maintaining a good image in the minds of the customer(s). It is vital for the marketer to know the main financial purpose of the event when starting the planning.

The three aspects of pricing are costs, value to the customer and competition within the market. Continuously expanding competition affects the pricing, as new events enter the market frequently. In addition to monetary costs, event consumer perceives other costs as well. These costs are time, physical effort, psychic costs as well as sensory costs. Visitors need to consume time to attend the event, physical effort to travel to the venue, psychic costs of being excited to attend the event and sensory costs which mean unpleasant experiences that might occur when attending an event.

Placing an event in correct location is important. The location in itself creates images in the customers' minds and the event can create negativity by being placed in a location which does not match the supposed image of the event. When the marketer is planning the location and the place for an event, it is very important for the marketer to value the purposes of the event. Issues of attractiveness or practicality of the location should support the decision of placing.

In event marketing, place does not only apply to the geographical location of the venue. It also implies the places from which a customer can purchase tickets for the event. This has to be limited in a way to serve the customers whether they wish to purchase over the internet or from a ticket-selling company or at the gates of the event venue.

Marketing without public relations is not effective. By marketing, the company releases images of itself and its events to customers determined by the company itself. What basic marketing fails to do with creating images in customers' minds, public relations can execute.

Public relations help in creating the right kinds of images in customers' minds. Public relations should be integrated as a continuing process within marketing to constantly influencing the customers with positive reminders of the company. Public relations can be executed with low costs, simply by sending news releases to newspapers which have readers from the company's target audience. To increase the participation rate for an event, the marketer needs to use all the available channels in communicating the right message which influences the target group. In order to be successful, all communications should be unified and it should increase the credibility of the company, event and everything related to these. When a marketer knows how to appeal to the public as a company which cares e.g. environmental issues the company communicates images of being compassionate, caring, people-oriented, (in other words, good, as importance is not only in money and profits,) resulting in valuable positive attitudes towards the company and events it hosts.

For the marketing plan to be good, positioning the event should be performed thoroughly and precisely as fulfilling the customers needs and bringing a unique experience to the attendees. The marketer should decide whether the event can create a niche, or if the event can be put in an existing niche. If so, the marketer has to determine whether the event can offer something different compared to what competitors offer, and whether their offering is better and more valuable for the target audience. Companies marketing their events should concentrate on solving the question of how the competitors' offerings can be exceeded.

The marketer should be aware of the different types of profits a company can receive from organising an event. The most beneficial for the company is to differentiate itself well from others, from competitors. Companies and advertising campaigns should always offer exactly what has been promised.

MARKETING ENVIRONMENT OF EVENTS

The marketing environment is divided into seven different sections separated from each other. All of these are dependent to the event organisation and its resources. Changes in society will affect the demand on different social events. Change in demand would directly increase or decrease certain type of events. To avoid a negative image, events should not harm the physical environment, but should be environmental-friendly.

Within technological environment, companies vary from organising events with high technological equipment and obtaining visibility on the internet, while there are companies which are questioning whether to create web pages or not. Many companies are placed between these two types of technological environments.

Some are fully electronic, while others have not developed their technological aspect. By technological environment is meant the technological competence and equipment the company acquires in everyday activities.

The physical environment matters a lot when an event is held outside. The physical environment should be in a perfect condition, to ensure the image of the company is not harmed. The weather, being part of the physical environment, affects the number of visitors when the event is organised outside.

The economic state of a country or region affects the economic environment as changes in the demand for expensive superficial events.

Legal regulations complicate the process of organising events. The event organiser should have a thorough knowledge regarding the legislations and rules concerning political and legal issues, e.g. sale of alcohol.

The event organiser should have examined the market of events and ensured by marketing research the number of visitors attending the event. In the leisure-event market, the number of offerings is broad, which affects directly the amount of possible customers. The competitive environment should be decided when the marketing plan is created.

The demographic environment consists of features of people; these are such as age, gender, income and interest. Changes in demographics are going to be in the near future significant, and as that will influence everything else, it affects the markets of events as well. The most significant change which affects all developed countries is the aging of the population. This creates either challenges or opportunities for companies organising events. It will be important to be able to appeal to the older group of people as well as maintaining interest within groups of younger people. The consumption of money spent on leisure activities will most likely increase within the aging population. Analysis of demographics helps the marketer to categorise the event consumer.

PLANNING OF EVENT

We follow 5 'Ws' (i.e. Why, What, When, Where, Who) and 1 'H' (i.e. How) principle to create an event plan.

Why

'Why' means, why you want to organise the event i.e. event objective. What do you want to get from the event? E.g. do you want to organise the event to enhance your company's brand image, to increase company's sales, to promote your client's products/ services or to promote a social cause etc. Defining event objectives at the very start of event planning is very important as it gives you the direction in which you should proceed to accomplish your objectives. Organising an event without clear objectives is a huge waste of both time and resources.

What

'What' means what you are going to do in the event i.e. name of the event? E.g. 'Auto Expo 2011'.

Food and Beverage Menu: It contains the list of food items and beverages you will serve during the event to guests and target audience. Always consult a caterer while deciding your food and beverage menu as he knows the best which wine is served with a particular course (i.e. meal).

Keep event theme, preferences and religion of target audience and guests in mind while deciding the menu. If majority of your target audience are vegetarian, then it is not a good idea to serve non-veg in the event. Similarly if majority of your guests are very health-conscious then there should also be some low calories food items in your menu. You don't want them to go back with an empty stomach.

Also keep climatic conditions into account. Don't serve out of season food items and beverages. Like serving ice cream/cold drink in winter, food (like spicy food) that provides warmth during summer or food that provides coolness during winter.

Event Profile: What the event is all about? E.g.: This event is an international exhibition on new models of cars and its accessories.

Guests Profile: Who will be your chief guest and other guests? Your guest list must include organisers, sponsors, partners, clients and specially media people. Use your imagination to create good titles to woo your guests. Like 'Guest of honor', star guest etc. Never give special treatment to one particular guest or guests' group.

Event Theme: Theme means subject. An event can be based on a particular theme like : Hollywood, retro, modern , balloon, clock, red, white etc. Theme based events are generally parties or wedding. Like, we can have party based on flowers theme. Such types of parties are known as theme parties. In a theme party, everything from dress code, decoration, games, music, gifts, flavours to food and beverages are based on a particular theme.

Service Providers: Who will be your service providers? Any professional providing any type of service in lieu of money is a service provider. E.g.: DJ, anchor, florist, videographer, photographer, make up artist, performers, decorator, models, technicians, etc.

Obligations: These are the compulsions on the guests like dress code or the knowledge of salsa dance.

Type of Entry: Decide how will be the entry. Entry will be by ticket, pass or through invitation only.

Favours: These are the gifts given to guests. We can give gifts to guests when they enter a party, when they win a game or when they leave the party.

Entry fees: What will be the entry fees? If you are going to charge entry fees, then be prepared to pay entertainment tax. Your entry fees should be according to your target audience's status. If you overcharge, you won't get any audience.

Event Highlights: These are those activities which you do to catch your target audience and media's attention. Like inauguration of your fashion show by Malaika Arora Khan, performance by some famous singer, dancer or display of the India's most expensive car etc.

Promotional Campaign: How you are going to promote your event, organisers, sponsors, partners and clients pre-event, at-event and post-event.

Programme Menu: It is the list of various activities that will occur as a part of the event. Sample Programme Menu of a Conference.

Event Budget: To determine your event budget' find out what will be the cost for producing and marketing the event. To determine production cost, create a list of logistics used in the event and then sum up there hiring/usage cost. You can determine marketing cost on the basis of historical data like past advertising expenditure for same or similar events. If you are a first timer, then take help from an ad agency. On the basis of production and marketing cost, determine your operating cost (i.e. cost to run the business). On the basis of operating cost, decide your own fees and the staff salary. If you are organising event for a client, then the client will bear the production and marketing cost of the event. If you are organising your own event then you will bear the production and marketing cost. As an event manager, you must be able to recover your production, marketing and operating costs plus you must be able to make considerable profit also. Developing event budget and managing cash flow pre-event, at-event and post-event is quite difficult and requires help from an experienced professional. Better leave this job to an Accountant if you are organising.

When

When you are going to organise the event (i.e. date and time)? Keep following things in mind while selecting date and time for the event:

1. Select date and time according to target audience convenience and availability. E.g.: don't organise events during work days, examination days or festival times. The best time to organise events is during weekends like Saturday or Sunday.
2. Make sure that your event's date and time, don't clash with other event's date and time specially bigger event's date and time. E.g.: it is not a good idea to organise your music concert on a day when there is some other major event or festival.
3. Keep climatic conditions into mind while selecting date and time for your event. It can be disastrous to organise event outdoor on a day when the weather is stormy or heavy rain is expected. Here you can take help of your own experience if you are familiar with the climatic conditions of the region where you intend to organise the event or you can take the help of the meteorological department for the weather forecast. Find out how the weather will be on the day of your event.

Where

Where you are going to organise the event (i.e. venue)? Check out the venue selection tips.

Who

Who will be your organisers, sponsors, partners, clients and target audience? How many target audience you are expecting to visit the event and why? You must have very good reason to this 'Why' as you will have to convince your prospective organisers and sponsors that why particular number of people will attend the event.

How

How exactly are you going to market and produce the event.

EVALUATION OF EVENT

Evaluation is an activity that seeks to understand and measure the extent to which an event has succeeded in achieving its purpose. The purpose of an event will differ with respect to the category and variation of event. However, to provide reach and interaction would be a generic purpose that events satisfy.

There can be two attitudes with which evaluation can be put in its proper perspective. The concept of evaluation stated above was a critical examination digging out what went wrong. A more constructive focus for evaluation is to make recommendations about how an event might be improved to achieve its aims more effectively. To carry out an evaluation and measurement exercise it is essential that the predefined objectives of the events have been properly understood. The brief should contain all the data to be communicated since if an event has been organised without a clearly defined purpose, any evaluation would be rather pointless.

The Basic Event Evaluation Process

In events, the basic evaluation process involves three steps:

- Establishing tangible objectives and incorporating sensitivity in evaluation
- Measuring the performance before, during and after the event
- Correcting deviations from plans

These steps are discussed below:

1. Establishing Tangible Objectives and Sensitivity in Evaluation

Setting objectives for an event is easier said than done. It is more difficult to set standards and declaring an event successful after it meets them. To provide tangibility to the problem, the best approach is to begin with definition of the target audience for whom the event has been organised. In the case of commercial events, the audience could be end users who use the company's products. An event might be conceptualised to achieve different things for different audience. Once the audience has been defined, the next step is to identify and put on paper what each of the audience is expected to think, feel and do having been to the event, that it did not think, feel or do beforehand. This adds an element of tangibility to the evaluation and measurement proceedings.

The number of mega-events has increased dramatically in the past few years and the costs of organising events have also increased exponentially. The costs of production in major events can be enormous and therefore, in the near future one can expect companies to start asking questions about the effectiveness of their events to see whether their money is being spent prudently.

Creativity is derived from the Greek word 'enthousiasm' which literally translates into 'God, within'. Setting out to evaluate such an effort that is considered to be the work of Gods themselves demands a certain amount of sensitivity during evaluation. Objective evaluation should also take into consideration the nature of the concept and the process of execution of the event in their entirety. However professional the evaluation, there is scope for error and misjudegment if sensitivity is not adhered to. This is because it takes a creative and sensitive mind to spot wrong questions or situations where asking questions might be the wrong method and observation might be more appropriate. One of the ways of nurturing and encouraging this sensitivity is to place evaluation within the context of a team approach all the way from conceptualisation to carrying out of the event.

From experience, it is known that people involved in an event are more openminded and less committed to any particular course of action before the event occurs. Yet another learning is that, if things are shown to be wrong after a decision has been taken, the majority of people involved in the decision-making process may try to wash their hands of the fault. Thus, adding sensitivity to the evaluation process is very important.

2. Measuring Performance

The measurement of performance against the objectives should ideally be done on a forward looking basis so that deviations may be detected in advance of their occurrence and avoided by appropriate actions. The concept research is used to anticipate the viability of a concept during the conceptualisation process. Formative and objective evaluations are carried out during the customisation phase of an event. Summative evaluation can be carried out to measure performance during the event.

- **Concept Research**: At the conceptualisation stage, if a concept team does not have a sound basis upon which to make a choice between various options, a commissioning of audience research to help in defining the strategic approach to be adopted in the event is appropriate. It essentially involves presenting the various options to a representative sample of the target audience in a story form and inviting their reactions. This provides enough material for understanding the pros and cons of the various available alternatives. The downside to this method is that it is speculative in nature since it deals with plans that nobody has as yet tried to implement. This method is called concept research.
- **Formative Evaluation:** Evaluation at this stage focuses on things that are actually happening. After the conceptualisation team makes an attempt to customise and implement an agreed strategy, steps can be taken to evaluate the success with which customisation is proceeding. These evaluations are aimed at shaping the form

of the final event. Mock-up displays and presentations of the event are used to carry out research to check whether they are achieving the desired reactions from the audience. These evaluations are conducted among small sample representative of the target audience in an open-ended and qualitative fashion since the main emphasis is on discovering how the concept might be better represented. The outcome of these formative evaluations lead to a discussion among the team in which proposals for rectifying any weak points in the communications can be put forward. A point, which should be safeguarded against whilst using this technique, is to interpret consumer reactions with considerable sensitivity to stimulate the creative process further and also to ensure that good ideas are not killed simply because they were not properly presented in mock-up form.

- **Objective Evaluation:** This is the stage when approval from the client is sought before starting the execution related activities of an event. The evaluation team has to provide the objective evidence that has been collected which justifies the proposed concept solutions. The team also provides reassurance on how and why the particular event will work among its intended audience. Since taking the client into confidence requires certain amount of objectivity and professionalism, this technique is called objective evaluation.
- **Summative Evaluation:** After the event has started, the evaluation team should be concerned with measuring the impact of the event upon its audience. Among other things, they should establish the extent to which the objectives or aims of the event have been met and whether the event can be improved in any way and if so, how this will not apply for short-term events though. A major purpose of evaluating an event after it has opened to the public is that it provides the team with the opportunity of learning from their mistakes. The team should assimilate the information thus collected so that they can avoid making similar mistakes in the future.

3. Correcting Deviations

The fundamental reason why event evaluation is carried out is to navigate the event so as to ensure that the event objectives are achieved in total. And since deviations may occur during any stage in the event designing phase, it is important that measurement is carried out at all possible stages.

- **Critical Evaluation Points:** Events can be evaluated based on the critical success factors listed below; from both the clients' and event organiser's viewpoints.
- **Critical Evaluation Points from Event Organiser's Point of View:** There are multiple criteria for evaluating the success of an event from the event organiser's point of view. These are over and above ensuring perfect reach and interaction for the client by networking on-time and at lowest cost. The client event-target audience fit should match the clients' brand/product/company image and personality perfectly, keeping the target audience as the focal point. This is a very critical evaluation point. Ensuring the profitability of an event such that there is maximum profitability with minimum mark ups is another critical evaluation point. Since resources are also a major constraint for event organisers, the resource management efficiency i.e., resources committed and span of time for which it stays committed – financial, human, equipment and infrastructure should be a minimum. The number of staff and volunteers involved should be appropriate to offer quality service.

  Logistics and efficiency of event execution for ensuring smooth proceedings without unnecessary delays and damages is another critical success factor. Creating avenues for lead generation and its proper management during the event is a critical factor. Each and every completed event should generate more inquiries and these should be responded to immediately. Opportunities for explanation of available synergies and expansion of services offered to client to keep strategic integration and diversification options open is also an important factor. Since an event is essentially a one-off affair and any last moment problem can convert an exceptionally well-planned event into a disaster, all care needs to be taken during the event execution. Yet, another important critical success factor is the degree of localisation or customisation accommodated in the concept to suit the demographic and other variables of various places where the event is to be carried out.

- **Critical Evaluation Points from Clients' Point of View:** We have discussed earlier that the impact an event has on its target audience is equivalent to the measure of reach and interaction that occur during the event. Whereas reach is tangible, interaction to a certain extent is intangible as well as not always quantifiable. Immediate and long-term benefits that accrue from an event are important when evaluating an event from the clients' point of view. A cost-benefit analysis concerning the effectiveness of reach and interaction is a must as a pre-event activity. Post-event stock taking activity should be done to confirm whether the event has occurred as per plans. This analysis should consider the actual cost of the event that includes the non-budgeted expenditure as well as the actual benefits that accrued to the client from the event. The accrual of benefits can be judged by measuring the tangible parts of the objectives that have been achieved.
- **Measuring Reach:** Reach is of two types – external and actual event reach. Since events require massive external publicity-press, radio, television and other media are needed to ensure that the event is noticed and the benefit of reach is provided to the client. Measurement of external reach is possible by using the circulation figures of newspapers and promotions on television and the radio. The DART and TRP ratings that rate the popularity of programmes on air and around which the promotion is slotted, is a very tangible though approximate method for measuring the external reach of a promotion campaign on television. Measurement of external reach should be tempered with the timing of the promotions as effectiveness of recall and action initiated amongst the target audience is highly dependent on this important variable. For example, releasing ads and promos one month ill advance should be considered more as an awareness exercise for propagating.

  The event concept, time, date and venue of these owe to the audience. The entry criteria – free, invited or ticketed show should be clearly mentioned here. The measurement of the actual reach of an event is relatively simple. The capacity of the venue is a figure that provides the upper limit for the actual reach. Ticket sales or numbers of invitees are also direct measurement tools. Registration of participants and requests for filling in questionnaires are also common methods of measuring the actual reach of an event.
- **Concept of event quality and measuring quality of event:** Exactly on the lines of the evaluation of effectiveness of an event comes the concept of event quality. In essence, quality of an event exists in the clients' perspective and thus varies from client to client. By aiming for quality by maintaining standards, preventing mistakes, never cutting corners and using only top quality infrastructure is looking at quality from a skewed angle.

  Unless the target audience and the clients perceive the quality of the job in the same way as the event organisers, the big picture of quality is not complete. Therefore, it is critical to match the clients' expectations and experiences by including even the minutest details to arrive at the perceived quality of event. In matters of dispute, it is value to the client that finally matters. For the client, quality of an event is a bundle of attributes. A few of these critical attributes are quality and reliability of equipment used, aesthetic appeal, appropriate cost and timely completion of the project.

  Each client will care more about some attribute than others. Thus, it is important to find out how clients would define quality event service.

Competence in project management from conceptualisation to carryout, reliability and integrity as in the past performances of events that have been executed by the event organiser is a very important quality criterion. Responsiveness to the clients' requirements i.e., empathy, mutual confidence and trust are also the criteria used by clients to size up the quality of event organisers. Every client expects the event to provide the ideal audience to associate with; impress and entice. Thus, the quality of an event can also be defined in terms of the audience quality. Clients should focus on three major statistics that define audience quality:

- **Net buying influences** which can be defined as the ratio of the number of audience that can recommend, specify or approve purchase to the total population at the event.
- **Total buying plans** imply the percentage of the audience planning to buy a product/service from the sponsors' stables within the next 12 months after the show.
- **Average audience interest** is the percentage of audience that shows an interest in the sponsors' products or services during the event itself and immediately after. This may be measured by keeping track of the number of visitors to the sponsors' stall or exhibit area during the event.

MULTIPLE CHOICE QUESTIONS

1. Re-marketing is related with creating demand for ....
(*a*) Fresh products
(*b*) Non-usable product
(*c*) Low quality products
(*d*) Renewed use of products
(*e*) None of these

2. .... is a strategy designed to cultivate customer loyalty, interaction and long term association with the company.
(*a*) Virtual Marketing
(*b*) Relationship Marketing
(*c*) Social Marketing
(*d*) De-Marketing
(*e*) None of these

3. .... is aimed at encouraging renewed use of a product in which market interest has declined.
(*a*) De-marketing (*b*) Re-marketing
(*c*) Synched (*d*) Tele-marketing
(*e*) None of these

4. The process of finding or creating new uses or users or satisfaction for an existing product is known as ....
(*a*) Niche-marketing (*b*) Re-marketing
(*c*) Social marketing (*d*)
(*e*) None of these

5. The word positioning was coined by
(*a*) All Ryes and Jack Trout
(*b*) Philip Kotler
(*c*) Peter Ducker
(*d*) Jack Trout
(*e*) None of these

6. Which of the following is against marketing concepts?
(*a*) Social marketing (*b*) De-marketing
(*c*) Niche marketing (*d*) Virtual marketing
(*e*) None of these

7. Which of the following involves targeting bulk purchasers and offering them special benefits and privileges.
(*a*) Frequency marketing
(*b*) Event marketing
(*c*) Viral marketing
(*d*) Relationship marketing
(*e*) None of these

8. Green marketing is a part of ....
(*a*) Re-marketing (*b*) Event marketing
(*c*) Social marketing (*d*) Mega marketing
(*e*) None of these

9. Which of the following is known as market aggregation?
(*a*) Social marketing (*b*) De-marketing

(*c*) Niche marketing (*d*) Mass marketing
(*e*) None of these

10. Which of the following is not responsible for the emergence of relationship marketing?
(*a*) Growth of service economy
(*b*) Rapid technological advancement
(*c*) Changing role of woman
(*d*) Changing role of society
(*e*) None of these

11. .... marketing means serving a small market not served by competitors.
(*a*) Relationship (*b*) Niche
(*c*) Re-marketing (*d*) Mass
(*e*) None of these

12. Social marketing is used as an instrument to achieve the goals of ....
(*a*) Marketer (*b*) Seller
(*c*) Society (*d*) All of these
(*e*) None of these

13. Green marketing is defined as developing eco-friendly products and their packages to control the negative effects on ....
(*a*) Environment (*b*) Organisation
(*c*) Products (*d*) Marketing
(*e*) None of these

14. .... marketing is based on interaction and dialogues.
(*a*) De-marketing (*b*) Viral marketing
(*c*) E-commerce (*d*) Relationships
(*e*) None of these

15. The aim of relationship marketing is .... delight.
(*a*) Product (*b*) Price
(*c*) Customer (*d*) Quality
(*e*) None of these

16. .... marketing means serving a small market not served by competitors.
(*a*) Niche (*b*) Mega
(*c*) Meta (*d*) De-marketing
(*e*) None of these

17. .... can be seen as the development, design, and implementation of marketing programs, processes, and activities that recognizes the breadth and interdependencies of their effects.
(*a*) Niche marketing
(*b*) Holistic marketing
(*c*) Relationship marketing
(*d*) Supply-chain marketing
(*e*) None of these

18. .... marketing has the aim of building mutually satisfying long-term relations with key parties such as customers, suppliers, distributors, and other marketing partners in order to earn and retain their business.
(*a*) Holistic (*b*) Demand-based
(*c*) Direct (*d*) Relationship
(*e*) None of these

19. Holistic marketing incorporates ...., ensuring that everyone in the organization embraces appropriate marketing principles, especially senior management.
(*a*) profit objectives (*b*) share of customer
(*c*) internal marketing (*d*) the marketing mix
(*e*) None of these

20. Holistic marketing incorporates .... and understanding broader concerns and the ethical, environmental, legal, and social context of marketing activities and programs.
(*a*) safe product design
(*b*) cultural marketing
(*c*) social responsibility marketing
(*d*) cross-functional teams
(*e*) None of these

21. The .... holds that the organization's task is to determine the needs, wants, and interests of target markets and to deliver the desired satisfactions more effectively and efficiently than competitors in a way that preserves or enhances the consumer's and the society's well-being.
(*a*) customer-centered business
(*b*) focused business model
(*c*) societal marketing concept
(*d*) ethically responsible marketing manager
(*e*) None of these

ANSWERS

1	2	3	4	5	6	7	8	9	10
(*d*)	(*b*)	(*b*)	(*b*)	(*a*)	(*b*)	(*a*)	(*c*)	(*d*)	(*c*)
11	**12**	**13**	**14**	**15**	**16**	**17**	**18**	**19**	**20**
(*b*)	(*c*)	(*a*)	(*d*)	(*c*)	(*a*)	(*b*)	(*d*)	(*c*)	(*c*)
21									
(*c*)									

☞ CHAPTER-19

ETHICS AND MARKETING

INTRODUCTION

While it may have been acceptable in the past for businesses to pursue profits single-mindedly with little or no consideration for the wider social and environmental impact of their activities, this is not the case today. The consumer movement and the environmental lobby are now firmly established as vigilant and powerful watchdogs, and have successfully brought about changes in business practice and in the laws which govern how businesses must operate. This is not to say that businesses have not responded to the criticisms levelled against them. Many have voluntarily changed their ways of operating to take these wider concerns into account. For example, in marketing, the 'marketing concept' has become synonymous with having a consumer orientation, and the more recent 'societal marketing concept' extols the need for marketers to consider the wants and long-run needs of both society and consumers. At first glance it would appear that marketers at least are facing up to their responsibilities to the world at large.

ETHICAL ISSUES CONCERNING PRODUCTS

There are three major ethical issues connected with products and services: product safety, planned obsolescence and deceptive packaging. Now you have to look at each of these in turn.

Product Safety

Recently, one of the major concerns about product safety has been that of the safety of genetically modified (GM) products. Vociferous pressure groups such as Green peace (www.greenpeace.org) have spoken out about the dangers of genetic modification. Such concerns, and the attendant publicity, have led one of the pioneers of genetic modification, Monsanto (www.monsanto.com), to lack away from further development of GM foods, and supermarket chains to ban such produce from their shelves. Supporters state that many new, products are introduced with a certain degree of risk being acceptable. For example, a new pharmaceutical product may harm a tiny percentage of users but the utilitarianist principle of the greatest good for the greatest number' would support its launch. It is the reality of modern day business that new products such as cars, pharmaceuticals and foods undergo extensive safety testing before launch. Anything less would violate the consumer's 'right to safety'.

Planned Obsolescence

Many of the products on the market have not been designed to last for a long time. From the producers' point of view this is sensible as it creates a repeat purchase situation. Hence, cars rust, computer software is quickly outdated and fashion items are replaced by the latest styles. Consumers accept that nothing lasts forever, but the main thrust of this issue concerns what is an acceptable length of time before replacement is necessary. One driving force is competition. To control the Japanese invasion, car manufacturers such as Ford (www.ford.com) and Volkswagen (www.vw.com) have made the body shells of their cars much more rust-resistant than they were before. Furthermore, it has to be recognised that many consumers welcome the chance to buy new clothes, new appliances with the latest features and the latest model of cars.

Critics argue that planned obsolescence reduces consumers' right to choose since some consumers may be quite content to drive an old car so long as its body shell is free from rust and the car functions well. As we have noted, the forces of competition may act to deter the excesses of planned obsolescence.

Deceptive Packaging

This is something that can happen when, say, a product is presented in an oversized package, giving the impression that the consumer is getting more than is actually the case. This is known as 'slack packaging' and has the potential to deceive when packaging is difficult. Products such as soap powders and breakfast cereals have the potential to suffer from 'slack packaging'. A second area where packaging may be deceptive is through misleading labelling. This may take the form of the 'sin of omission', for example the failure of a package to state that a product contains GM soya. This relates consumer's 'right to be informed', and can include the stating of ingredients (including flavorings colorants), nutritional contents and 'country of origin on labels. Nevertheless, labelling can still be misleading. For example, in the UK, the country of origin is only the last country where the product was 'significantly changed'. So oil pressed, Greek olives in France can be labelled 'French' and foreign imports that are packed in the UK can be labelled 'produce of the UK'. Consumers should be cautious of loose terminology. For example, smoked bacon may well have received its 'smoked flavour' from a synthetic liquid solution, 'farm fresh eggs' are likely to be eggs of indeterminate age (with no date mark) laid by battery hens, and 'farmhouse cheese may not come from farmhouses but from industrial factories.

ETHICAL ISSUES IN PRICING STRATEGY

Some key ethical issues relating to pricing include price fixing, predatory pricing, deceptive pricing, price discrimination and product dumping.

Price Fixing

Competition is one of the driving forces towards lower prices. Therefore, it can be in the interests of producers to agree among themselves not to compete on price. This is known as the 'act of collusion' and is banned in many countries and regions, including the EU. Article 83 of the Treaty of Rome is designed to ban practices preventing, restricting or distorting competition, except where these contribute to efficiency without inhibiting consumers' fair share of the benefit. Groups of companies that planned are said to be acting as a cartel, and these are by no means easy to uncover. One of the European Commission's most famous success stories is the uncovering of an illicit cartel among 23 of Europe's top chemical companies from the UK, France, Germany, Belgium, Italy, Spain, The Netherlands, Finland, Norway and Austria. Through collusion they were able to sustain levels of profitability for low density polyethylene and PVC in the face of severe overcapacity. Quotas were set to limit companies' attempts to gain market share through price competition, and prices were fixed to harmonise the differences between countries in order to discourage customers from shopping around for the cheapest deals. Opponents of price fixing claim that it is unethical because it restrains the consumer's freedom of choice and interferes with each firm's interest in offering high-quality products at the best price. Its proponents argue that, under harsh economic conditions, price fixing is necessary to ensure a fair profit for the industry and to avoid price wars that might lead to bankruptcies and unemployment.

Predatory Pricing

Predatory pricing refers to a situation that occurs when a firm reduces its prices with the aim of driving out the competition. The firm is content to incur losses with the intent that high profits will be generated through higher prices once the competition has been eliminated. Budget airline easyJet (www.easyjet.com) has accused British Airways of predatory pricing through its no-frills subsidiary Go; easyJet claims that the low prices charged by Go are being subsidised by the profits made by BA's other operations.

Deceptive Pricing

Deceptive pricing occurs when consumers are misled by the price deals offered by companies. Two examples are misleading price comparisons and 'bait and switch'. Misleading price comparisons occur when a store sets artificially high prices for a short time so that much lower 'sale' prices can be claimed later. The purpose is to deceive the customer into believing they are being offered bargains. Some countries, such as the UK and Germany, have laws that state the minimum period over which the regular price should have been charged before it can be used as a reference price in a sale. Bait and switch is the practice of advertising a very low price on a product (the bait) to attract customers to a retail outlet. Once in the store the salesperson persuades the customer to buy a higher-priced product (the switch). The customer may be told that the lower priced product is no longer in stock or that it is of inferior quality.

Price Discrimination

Price discrimination occurs when a supplier offers a better price for the same product to a buyer, resulting in that buyer gaining an unfair competitive advantage. Price discrimination can be justified when the costs of supplying different customers vary, where the price differences reflect differences in the level of competition, and where different volumes are purchased. Price discrimination can be a particular issue in international marketing where price levels vary across borders and parallel importing ensues. This is where importers buy products from distributors in one country to sell them to distributors in another country who are not part of the manufacturer's normal distribution channel. A recent contentious case has been that between Tesco (www.tesco.com) and Levi Strauss (www.levis.com), which has been before the European court. Tesco claimed to be within its rights when it bought cheap, though genuine, Levi's products from countries outside the European Union for sale in its stores. Levi's countered that, as it is owner of the trademark, this practice amounted to breaking the law.

Product Dumping

Product dumping involves products being exported at a much lower price than that charged in the domestic market, sometimes below the cost of production. Products are 'dumped' for a variety of reasons. First, unsold stocks may be exported at a low price rather than risk lowering prices in the home market. Second, products may be manufactured for sale overseas at low prices to fill otherwise unused production capacity. Finally, products that are regarded as unsafe at home may be dumped in countries that do not have such stringent safety rules. For example, the US Consumer Product Safety Commission ruled that three-wheeled cycles were dangerous. Many companies responded by selling their inventories at low prices in other countries.

ETHICAL ISSUES IN PROMOTION

The wide range of promotional techniques that we have discussed in this chapter gives rise to several ethical questions. These are discussed below.

Misleading Advertising

This can take the form of exaggerated claims and concealed facts. For example, it would be unethical to claim that a car achieved 50 miles to the gallon when in reality it was only 30 miles. Nevertheless, most countries accept a certain amount of puffery, recognising that consumers are intelligent and interpret the claims in such a way that they are not deceptive. In the UK, the advertising slogan 'Carlsberg-Probably the Best Lager in the World' is acceptable because of this. Advertising can also deceive by omitting important facts from its message. Such concealed facts may give a misleading impression to the audience. Many industrialised countries have their own codes of practice that protect the consumer from deceptive advertising. For example, in the UK the Advertising Standards Authority (www.asa.org.uk) administers the British Code of Advertising Practice, which insists that advertising should be 'legal, decent, honest and truthful'. Shock advertising such as that pursued by companies like Benetton and FCUK are often the subjects of many complaints to the Advertising Standards Authority.

Advertising to Children

One particularly controversial issue is that of advertising to children. Critics argue that children are especially susceptible to persuasion and that they therefore need special protection from advertising. Others counter by claiming that the children of today are remarkably 'streetwise' and can look after themselves. They are also protected by parents who can, to some extent, counteract advertising influence. Many European countries have regulations that control advertising to children. For example, in Germany, advertising specific types of toy is banned, and in the UK alcohol advertising is controlled. An example of self-regulation at work was the dropping of an advertisement for a soft drink that featured a gang of gingerhaired, middle-aged men taunting a fat youth. The advertisement was withdrawn after numerous complaints were received contending that it encouraged bullying in schools.

The Intrusiveness of Direct Marketing

Direct marketing is criticised for being intrusive and for invading people's privacy. Receiving unsolicited calls from telemarketing companies can be annoying, while many consumers fear that every time they subscribe to a club, society or magazine their names, addresses and other information will be entered on to a database, and that this will guarantee a flood of mail from the supplier. Poorly targeted mail, usually called junk mail, also irritates many people. The direct marketing industry is responding to these concerns and is becoming increasingly sophisticated in how it targets prospects. Many consumers are registering with suppression files indicating that they do not want to be recipients of direct marketing activities.

Use of Trade Inducements

To encourage their sales-people to push the manufacturers' products, retailers sometimes accept inducements from manufacturers. This often takes the form of bonus payments to salespeople. The result is that there is an incentive for salespeople, when talking to customers, to pay special attention to those product lines that are linked to such bonuses. Customers may, therefore, be subjected to pressure to buy products that do not best meet their needs.

Third-party Endorsements

The use of third-party endorsements to publicise a product is another subject for ethical debate. In such cases, a person gives a written, verbal and/or visual recommendation of a product. A well-known, well-respected person is usually chosen, but given that payment often accompanies the endorsement the question arises as to its credibility. Supporters of endorsements argue that consumers know that endorsers are usually paid, and are capable of making their own judgments regarding their credibility.

Deception by Salespeople

A dilemma that, sooner or later, is likely to face most salespeople is the choice of telling the customer the whole truth and risk losing a sale, or misleading the customer in order to wrap up a sale. Such deception may take the form of exaggeration, lying or withholding important information that significantly reduces the appeal of a product. Such actions can be avoided by influencing the behaviour of salespeople through training, by sales management that encourages ethical behaviour, which is demonstrated through salespeople's own actions and words, and by establishing codes of conduct for salespeople. Nevertheless, from time to time evidence of malpractice in selling reaches the media. For example, in the UK it was alleged that some financial services salespeople mis-sold pensions by exaggerating the expected returns. This scandal cost the companies involved millions of pounds in compensation.

The Hard Sale

The use of high-pressure sales tactics to close a sale is another criticism levelled at personal selling. Some car dealerships have been deemed unethical due to their use of hard-sell tactics to pressurise customers into making a fast decision on a complicated purchase that may involve expensive credit facilities. Such tactics encouraged Daewoo (www.daewoocars.co.uk) to approach the task of selling cars in a fundamentally different way by replacing salespeople with computer stations where consumers could gather product and price information.

Bribery

Bribery is the act of giving payment, gifts or other inducements in order to secure a sale. Bribes are considered unethical because they violate the principle of fairness in commercial negotiations. A major problem is that, in some countries, bribes are an accepted part of business life: bribes are an essential part of competing. When an organisation succumbs, it is usually castigated in its home country if the bribe becomes public knowledge. Yet, without the bribe, it may have been operating a major commercial disadvantage. Companies need to decide whether they are going to market those countries where bribes are commonplace. Taking an ethical stance may cause difficulties in the short term but in the long run the positive publicity that can follow may be of greater benefit.

ETHICAL ISSUES IN DISTRIBUTION

Five key ethical issues in distribution are the use of slotting allowances, grey markets, exclusive dealing, restrictions on supply and fair dealing.

Slotting Allowances

In the packaged consumer goods industry, the power shift from manufacturers to retailers has meant that slotting allowances are often demanded before products are taken. A slotting allowance is a fee paid to a retailer in exchange for an agreement to place a product on the retailer's shelves. Critics argue that these represent an abuse of power and work against small manufacturers who cannot afford to pay such fees. Retailers argue that they are simply charging rent for a valuable scarce commodity: shelf space.

Grey Markets

Nothing to do with the age-related 'grey market' (i.e. the burgeoning number of older people that make up the consumer population), this type of grey market occurs when a product is sold through an unauthorised distribution channel. When this occurs in international marketing the practice is called 'parallel importing'. Usually a distributor buys goods in one country (where prices are low) and sells them in another (where prices are high) at below the going market price. This causes anger among members of the authorised distribution channel who see their prices being undercut. Furthermore, the products may well be sold in down market outlets that discredit the image of the product, which has been built up by high advertising expenditures. Levi's recently won a court order against Tesco preventing it from sourcing cheaper products outside the European Union.

Exclusive Dealing

This restrictive arrangement involves a manufacturer prohibiting the distributors that market its products from selling the products of competing suppliers. This action may restrict competition and hamper the entry of new competitors and products into a market. It may be found where a large supplier can exercise power over weaker distributors. The supplier may be genuinely concerned that anything less than an exclusive agreement will mean that insufficient effort will be made to sell its products by a distributor and that, unless such an agreement is reached, it may be uneconomic to supply the distributor.

Restrictions in Supply

A particular concern of small suppliers is that the power of large manufacturers and retailers will lead to their being squeezed out of the supply chain altogether. In the UK, farmers and small grocery suppliers have joined forces to demand better treatment from large supermarket chains, which are forging exclusive deals with major manufacturers. They claim the problem is made worse by the growth of category management, where retailers appoint 'category captains' from their suppliers who act to improve the standing of the whole product category, such as breakfast cereals or confectionery. The small suppliers believe this forces them out of the category altogether as category captains look after their own interests. They would like to see a system similar to that is used in France where about 10 per cent of shelf space is given to small suppliers by law.

Fair Trading

One problem that arises from free market forces is that, when small commodity producers are faced with large powerful buyers, the result can be very low prices. This can bring severe economic hardship to the producers who may be situated in developing countries. In the face of a collapse in world coffee prices a fair trading brand, Café direct (www.cafedirect.co.uk), was launched. The company was founded on three principles: to influence positively producers' income security; to act as an example and catalyst for change; and to improve consumer understanding of fair trade values. It pays suppliers a minimum price for coffee beans pegged above market fluctuations, and provides tailor-made business support and development programmes. There are now more than 50 fair trade products on sale in the UK including Ridgeway's tea and Divine chocolate, and sales are rising.

ETHICAL ISSUES IN INTERNET AND ONLINE MARKETING

Although the growth of Internet and online marketing has had many beneficial effects—such as increasing customer choice and convenience, and allowing smaller companies access to global markets, there are also concerns about intrusions on privacy and social exclusion.

Intrusions on Privacy

Some of those people using the Internet are extremely wary of online shopping because of the use of cookies, and the information they store and provide about consumers. Cookies are tiny computer files that a marketer can download on to the computer of online shoppers who visit a company's website so that details of these visits may be recorded. Cookies serve many useful functions: they remember users' passwords so they do not have to log on each time they revisit a site; they remember users' preferences so they can be provided with the right pages or data; and they remember the contents of consumers' shopping baskets from one visit to the next. However, because they can provide a record of users' movements around the web, cookies can also give a very detailed picture of people's interests and circumstances. For example, cookies contain information provided by visitors such as product preferences, personal data and financial information, including credit card details. From a marketer's point of view, cookies allow customised and personalised content for online shoppers. However, most Internet users probably do not know this information is being collected and would object if they knew. (Incidentally, online users can check if their drive contains cookies by opening any file named 'cookies'.) Some people fear that companies will use this information to build psychographic profiles that will enable them to influence customer behaviour; others simply object to information about them being held without their express permission. Although users are identified by a code number rather than a name and address (and this, therefore, does not violate ED data protection regulations), the fear is that direct marketing databases will be combined with information on online shopping behaviour to create a vast new way of peering into people's private lives.

Social Exclusion

Another ethical consideration is the fear that the growing use of the Internet will exclude the poorest members of society from partaking of the benefits of online shopping since they can afford neither a computer nor the associated charges. For example, Prudential, the financial services company, has faced strong criticism for the way Egg (www.egg.com), its high-interest savings bank, cut itself off from mainstream customers by offering Internet-only access, thereby creating a system which ensures that it attracts only its wealthiest customers. In addition, some utility companies may be discriminating against low income groups by offering cut-price energy only over the Internet. However, as computer prices fall, and more and more service providers offer free access and low telephone charges, this situation may improve.

METHODS OF DEALING WITH ETHICAL ISSUES

There are following methods, which are responsible for ethical issues in society:

Denial of Responsibility

One option for people faced with a moral dilemma is to deny responsibility and one way of doing this is to claim 'moral sanctuary'. That is, the person essentially argues that the normal rules and constraints of ethics and morality do not apply in that situation. Adopting this approach, some have argued that there is no such thing as business ethics. Supporters of this argument either claim that business is like a game, and therefore the normal rules of society do not apply, or that "one cannot survive in business if one is too ethical". Neither of these arguments is convincing. In response to the first, it can be pointed out that, since games are governed by rules that specify not only how, but where and under what conditions a game is played, even games require ethical conduct. Furthermore, unlike games, where players can choose to participate and therefore voluntarily 'suspend' normal ethical considerations, no one has this option in business. Insofar as a person must make a living or purchase goods, he or she is of necessity a participant in the game. The second argument also falls down, on two counts. First, by claiming a right to survive, claimants are in fact accepting that there is such a thing as business ethics. Second, the assertion is simply not true; it is possible to be ethical and survive in business.

Neutralisation

A second option available to people faced with a moral dilemma is to transgress, then justify the transgression. Vitell and Grove refer this process as 'neutralization', and write: "Those who employ techniques of neutralisation do not feel that the norms they may be violating should be replaced, only that they do not or should not apply in these particular instances... These techniques of neutralisation......are essentially a learned vocabulary of motives for misconduct used to protect one from self-blame. By employing verbal symbols and rationalisations shared by society at large, the techniques allow one to make use of widely pursued and accepted, but publicly un-verbalised values, such as revenge, as a means of diminishing one's culpability for a socially disapproved act ..." .

Examples of neutralisation techniques, identified over thirty years ago, include:

1. **Denial of responsibility:** Individuals argue that they are not personally accountable for their actions because factors beyond their control are operating, e.g., "I couldn't help myself, and I was desperate."
2. **Denial of injury:** Individuals contend that their norm violating behaviour is not really serious, since no party directly suffers because of it, e.g., "What's the big deal? No one was hurt."
3. **Denial of victim:** Individuals counter any blame for their actions by arguing that the violated party deserved whatever happened, e.g., "If they're foolish enough to believe that, it's their own fault they were taken advantage of."
4. **Condemning the condemners:** Individuals deflect moral condemnation to those ridiculing them by pointing out that they engage in similar disapproved behaviour, e.g., "I was only doing what others do all the time."

5. **Appeal to higher loyalties:** Individuals argue that their norm violating behaviour is the by-product of their attempt to actualise a higher order ideal or value e.g., "I did it because it was better for all concerned."

Good Business is Good Ethics

A third approach, adopted by some people, accepts a need for ethical conduct, but never actually considers the question of ethics because proponents believe they behave ethically; that "good business is good ethics". The rationale for this approach is that the very requirements of profitable business constitute a morality, and leave managers with little choice but to "do well and avoid evil". Various groups have promoted this approach in New Zealand. However, organisations who adopt this philosophy put themselves seriously 'at risk' of unethical conduct, simply because they do not acknowledge the ethical consequences of their actions.

Good Ethics is Good Business

The view that "good business is good ethics" should not be confused with an alternative view that "good ethics is good business", expressed in books such as In Search of Excellence. Proponents of this argument suggest a corporation must have integrity in order to achieve long-term profitability; therefore good ethics is good business. While this appears an admirable sentiment, which would ensure ethical conduct, some writers take a far more cynical view, and argue that some corporations may be more concerned with public relations than action; "they want to **appear** good, not **be** good". On the other hand, this option does seem the most likely to lead to ethical behaviour, even if the hypothesised links between profitability and ethical behaviour are suspected.

FACTORS CONTRIBUTING TO UNETHICAL BEHAVIOUR IN BUSINESS

The following factors are responsible for unethical behaviour in marketing:

Business Objectives

Clearly, a variety of views about the role of ethics in business exist, and it would seem that most of these views actually put business people 'at risk' of unethical conduct. However, the problem extends even further than the arguments used to justify particular business and practices. To use marketing as an example, the objectives of marketing, the marketing concept, and even the language of marketing may also contribute to the problem. The ultimate goal in a commercial venture is some sort of profit achievement. As a consequence, the needs and wants of consumers and the wider concerns for the impact on society are only of concern to the marketer to the extent that they affect the objectives (e.g. profitability) of the operation. Marketers adopting this orientation may well remain oblivious to the likely consequences of their actions, unless there is a perceived threat to their operation. Furthermore, even if aware of possible consequences, business people faced with a moral dilemma will be predisposed to act in a way that has the least detrimental impact on profitability, even if this means adopting an unethical course of action.

The Language of Business

The language of business also presents problems. Two pervasive metaphors in marketing are those of 'war' and 'competition' ('strategy', 'tactics', 'competitors', 'heroes', 'targets'). This language emphasises the notions of power, control and dominance - the antithesis of concern, caring and cooperation, and scarcely consistent with the notion of moral or ethical behaviour. Paradoxically, even the 'marketing concept' and particularly the 'societal marketing concept' may add to the risk of unethical behaviour. Because these concepts appear to put the needs of consumers and society first, they may lead the public to believe marketers are behaving in an ethical manner, regardless of whether they are. Since the concepts embrace an ethical dimension, they may also lead marketers to believe their actions are ethical by definition. This may result in a situation where ethics are given little thought. This is not to suggest business and marketing practice is totally unethical. The point being made is that the language of business, the objectives of business, and the ways in which business people perceive their roles, put them 'at risk' of unethical conduct. The responsibility is therefore on business people to ensure that they are not unwittingly contributing to the problem.

Limitations

While these methods of analysis may offer some assistance, they are of only limited help to people faced with a moral dilemma. A common difficulty with a moral dilemma is that of identifying clearly what the issues are. It is relatively easy to identify violations of widely held norms or moral principles, thus the responsibilities of managers in such situations are well defined. Sometimes, however, the norms or moral principles themselves substantially conflict, and it, is not clear which option should be chosen. King observes that western moral philosophy offers no guidelines for dealing with what he calls "moral dilemmas of the second kind". His suggestion is that we must therefore begin to examine the types of social relationship that must exist for there to be agreement on what is right, good and just.

Re-examine the Moral Paradigm

King argues that mainstream philosophy accepts the ideal of the theorist as a detached observer, and operates according to what he calls the "ethics of justice", which emphasises objectivity and detachment. He suggests that this moral paradigm is also prevalent in business. The consequences of managers remaining detached, however, are that they can avoid accepting responsibility for the effects of their actions. A 'detached' manager is therefore at risk of acting in an unethical manner. Other authors, particularly with regard to accounting have made a similar point. The problem, according to King, is that mainstream philosophy, and business, ignores what he calls the "ethics of caring", with its connotations of compassion, empathy and relatedness. Drawing on the work of MacIntyre, King suggests that the ethics of caring is a necessary condition for any ethics of justice - that the ethics of caring is the moral paradigm and that the ethics of justice is subsumed under it. King suggests that human endeavour consists of empirical, interpretive and evaluative dimensions, but that while we have well developed empirical methodologies, we do not understand the methodologies of interpretation and evaluation. He argues that everything we know is necessarily interpretive in nature - that we do and must construct our social realities. Since narrow interpretation leads to limited or stupid behaviour, it is possible to construct realities in which evaluation becomes unintelligible. He concludes that caring is an essential part of the methodology of evaluation, and that this is the key to understanding the nature of "ethical encounters of the second kind".

The implications of what King is saying suggest radical changes to the way managers are educated. If we want managers to behave in an ethical manner, we must take into account the interpretive and evaluative, as well as the empirical dimensions of human endeavour. Since people construct their social reality and this affects evaluation, they must have a 'broad based' or 'general' education so they do not end up with a narrow interpretation of the world and construct a constricted or blinkered social reality. Furthermore, since caring is an important component of evaluation, education must encourage involvement in rather than detachment from issues and problems, and managers must be trained to understand others' point of view, to see the world through others' eyes.

Adopt Alternative Methods of Enquiry

The ideas presented so far suggest a different approach to ethics is required in marketing and in the training of marketing and business graduates. Hirschman, who argues that since marketing is a socially constructed enterprise, it requires different methods of enquiry developed specifically to address socially constructed phenomena, presents one possibility. In particular, he suggests that marketers should embrace humanistic methods of enquiry.

MULTIPLE CHOICE QUESTIONS

1. Corporate social responsibility can be defined as:
(*a*) a legal requirement to ensure companies take social responsibilities of their actions
(*b*) a commitment to improve community well-being through discretionary business practices and contributions of corporate resources
(*c*) an optional strategic approach to the creation of competitive global marketing strategies
(*d*) a responsibility that is undertaken by the public relation department of all business organizations
(*e*) None of these

2. Sustainable marketing (SM) involves principled marketing predicated on the tenets of the triple bottom lines, which cover:
(*a*) Social, environmental and economic responsibilities
(*b*) Social, legal and shareholder responsibilities
(*c*) Revenue, shareholder and ethical responsibilities
(*d*) Ethical, revenue and supplier responsibilities
(*e*) None of these

3. The following are the dangers of engaging in sustainable marketing except:
(*a*) Choosing the wrong social issue
(*b*) Too much 'bragging' about what you are doing
(*c*) Enhanced corporate image and clout
(*d*) Inadequate evaluation of the process
(*e*) None of these

4. Marketers are concerned about being ecologically responsible for the following reasons except:
(*a*) consumers are showing a propensity to spend their money in a way that shows least ecological harm
(*b*) there is a growing pressure on natural resources such as North Sea fish stocks and oil
(*c*) there is a growing problem of obesity in adults and children globally
(*d*) there is a growing concern in consumers of the impact of climate change and global warming
(*e*) None of these

5. Corporate codes of ethics are:
(*a*) always externally audited
(*b*) create guidelines for employees to work by
(*c*) always compliance based
(*d*) always integrity based
(*e*) None of these

6. Greenwashing refers to the practice of:
(*a*) Promoting sustainable development
(*b*) Engaging with environmental pressure groups
(*c*) The attempt to create a false impression of environmental friendliness
(*d*) Commitment to humanitarian causes
(*e*) None of these

7. Corruption can be defined as the abuse of public office for private gain and covers a wide range of local practices including:
(*a*) bribery, fraud, money laundering, extortion and embezzlement
(*b*) bribery, cheating, extortion and embezzlement
(*c*) stealing, fraud and embezzlement
(*d*) stealing, cheating, fraud and bribery
(*e*) None of these

8. Corruption may damage a country's future business potential by:
(*a*) reducing domestic companies' ability to bribe their own government for lucrative contracts
(*b*) directing scarce entrepreneurial talent away from the leading of growth and development activities into unproductive

activities of little benefit to the countries concerned

(*c*) attracting more talents to work in the corrupted public sectors while the private sectors are left with mediocre employees

(*d*) creating more productive and competitive industries as they need to cut costs in production in order to cover the cost of bribery

(*e*) None of these

9. Ethical investment:

(*a*) normally matches the performance of traditional investment

(*b*) normally underperforms against traditional investment

(*c*) is declining due to the high costs involved.

(*d*) is impossible to measure as it is difficult to quantified outcomes

(*e*) None of these

10. Socially responsible practice (SRP) is a major activity undertaken by a business organisation to:

(*a*) ensure compliance with legislation on corporate social responsibility

(*b*) to ward off negative publicity and potential consumer boycott

(*c*) support social causes and to fulfill commitments to corporate social responsibility

(*d*) invest in creating good public relations associated with a good cause in the local community

(*e*) None of these

ANSWERS

1	2	3	4	5	6	7	8	9	10
(*b*)	(*a*)	(*c*)	(*c*)	(*b*)	(*c*)	(*a*)	(*b*)	(*a*)	(*c*)

CHAPTER-20

GLOSSARY

5-Ws model of communication: A model of the communications process that contains five basic elements" who? (source), says what? (message), in what way? (channel), to whom? (receiver), and with what effect? (feedback).

Added value: Added value refers to the increase in worth of a product or service as a result of a particular activity. In the context of marketing, the added value is provided by features and benefits over and above those representing the "core product".

Advertising: Any paid form of non-personal communication, usually delivered through mass media by an identified sponsor.

Advertising budget: The total amount of money that a marketer allocates for advertising over a period of time.

Advocacy advertising: Advertising that is concerned with the propagation of ideas and elucidation of social issues of public importance in a manner that supports the position and interest of the sponsor.

Aerial advertising: A form of outdoor advertising where messages appear in the sky in the form of banners pulled by aeroplanes, skywriting, and on blimps.

After-sales service: The services received after the original goods or services have been paid for. Often this service is provided as part of a warranty or guarantee scheme.

AIDA model: A model that depicts the successive stages a buyer passes through in the personal selling process including: attention, interest, desire, and action.

Ambush marketing: A deliberate attempt by a business or brand to associate itself with an event (often a sporting event) in order to gain some of the benefits associated with being an official sponsor without incurring the costs of sponsorship. For example by advertising during television coverage of the event.

Ansoff matrix: A model used in strategic marketing planning. The Ansoff Product/Market matrix model links marketing strategy with the general strategic direction of a business. It maps four potential product-market strategies - e.g. market penetration, product development, market development and diversification - on a matrix showing new versus existing products along one axis and new versus existing markets along the other.

Attitude: A person's consistently favourable or unfavourable evaluations, feelings, and tendencies toward an object or idea.

Augmented product: A good, service, or idea enhanced by its accompanying benefits; synthesis of what the seller intends and the buyer perceives.

Backward integration: The approach by which the intermediaries acquire control over manufacturers.

Bait-and-switch promotion: A practice through which the retailer brings buyers to the store with advertising for a bargain price on a product which is not in adequate supply with the intent of switching the buyer to a higher priced product.

Behavioural segmentation: Dividing a market into groups based on consumer knowledge, attitude, use, or response to a product.

Belief: A descriptive thought that a person holds about something.

Benchmark measures: Measures of a target audience's status concerning response hierarchy variables such as awareness, knowledge, image, attitudes, preferences, intentions, or behaviour. These measures are taken at the beginning of an advertising or promotional campaign to determine the degree to which a target audience must be changed or moved by a promotional campaign.

Benchmarking: The process of comparing the products and services of a business against those of competitors in a market, or leading businesses in other markets, in order to find ways of improving quality and performance.

Boston Group Matrix: A means of analysing and categorizing the performance of business units in large diversified firms by reference to market share and growth rates. It was developed by the Boston Consultancy Group (BCG).

Brand: A name, term, symbol, or design or a combination of them that is intended to identify the goods or services of one seller or group of sellers and to differentiate them from products of competitors.

Brand building: Developing a brand's image and standing with a view to creating long term benefits for brand awareness and brand value.

Brand equity: Brand equity refers to the value of a brand. Brand equity is based on the extent to which the brand has high brand loyalty, name awareness, perceived quality and strong product associations. Brand equity also includes other "intangible" assets such as patents, trademarks and channel relationships.

Brand extension: Brand extension refers to the use of a successful brand name to launch a new or modified product in a new market. Virgin is perhaps the best example of how brand extension can be applied into quite diverse and distinct markets.

Brand extension strategy: The strategy of applying an existing brand name to a new product.

Brand image: Brand image refers to the set of beliefs that customers hold about a particular brand. These are important to develop well since a negative brand image can be very difficult to shake off.

Brand loyalty: Preferences by a consumer for a particular brand that results in continual purchase of it.

Breakeven point (BE): The point at which income generated from sales just equals the total costs incurred from those sales.

Build-up forecast: A sales forecast developed from data collected by the sales force or other employees with considerable customer interaction.

Cash Cows: A term used in the Boston Group Matrix. Cash cows are low-growth businesses or products with a relatively high market share. These are mature, successful businesses with relatively little need for investment. They need to be managed for continued profit - so that they continue to generate the strong cash flows that the company needs for its Stars.

Category development index (CDI): An index that is calculated by taking the percentage of a product category's total sales that occur in a given market area as compared to the percentage of the total population on the market.

Channel width: The number of intermediaries found at the same level in the channel.

Classified advertising: Advertising that runs in newspapers and magazines that generally contains text only and is arranged under subheadings according to the product, service, or offering. Employment, real estate, and automotive ads are the major forms of classified advertising.

Clients: The organisations with the products, services, or causes to be marketed and for which advertising agencies and other marketing promotional firms provide services.

Close: Obtaining the commitment of the prospect in a personal selling transaction.

Closing: The step in the selling process in which the salesperson asks the customer for an order.

Cognitive dissonance: Buyer discomfort caused by postpurchase conflict.

Collateral services: Companies that provide companies with specialised services such as package design, advertising production, and marketing research.

Commercialization: Introducing a new product into the market.

Compensatory decision rule: A type of decision rule for evaluating alternatives where consumers consider each brand with respect to how it performs on relevant or salient attributes and the importance of each attribute. This decision rule allows for a negative evaluation or performance on a particular attribute to be compensated for by a positive evaluation on another attribute.

Concept testing: A process involving the accumulation and evaluation of consumers' reactions to a new product idea before the product is actually developed.

Consumer behaviour: The acts of individuals that involve buying and using products, including the decision processes that precede and determine these acts.

Consumer buyer behaviour: The buying behaviour of final consumers-individuals and households who buy goods and services for personal consumption.

Consumer markets: The most visible markets, which consist of individual customers who buy products for their own use or for use by other members of their households.

Consumer oriented positioning: The strategy aimed at getting the consumer to perceive a product in some unique, personally related manner, regardless of the product's characteristics.

Consumer-oriented sales promotion: Sales promotion techniques that are targeted to the ultimate consumer such as coupons, samples, contests, rebates, sweepstakes, and premium offers.

Convenience products: Products that are widely available, usually inexpensive, and frequently purchased Consumer product that the customer usually buys frequently, immediately, and with a minimum of comparison and buying effort.

Convenience store: A small store, located near a residential area, that is open long hours seven days a week and carries a limited line of high-turnover convenience goods.

Core product: The set of problem-solving or need-meeting benefits that customers are buying when they purchase a product. Customers are rarely prepared to pay a premium for these elements of a product.

Cost leadership: A strategy of producing goods at a lower cost than the competition. This usually requires the business to enjoy higher economies of scale or have some kind of productivity advantage.

Coupon: Certificate that gives buyers a saving when they purchase a specified product.

Cross-selling: Using a customer's buying history to select them for related offers, e.g. a car alarm for new car buyers.

CTO pricing: A pricing method which encourages extra sales by reducing the price (while still covering variable costs) to generate additional contribution to profit (CTP).

Cultural environment: Institutions and other forces that affect society's basic value perceptions, preferences, and behaviours.

Customer loyalty: Feelings or attitudes that incline a customer either to return to a company, shop or outlet to purchase there again, or else to re-purchase a particular product, service or brand.

Customer profile: A written record of an account, including information such as type of business, buying influences, the product mix, buying policies and practices, environmental influences, purchase criteria, and competitor analysis.

DAGMAR: An acronym that stands for defining advertising goals for measured advertising results. An approach to setting goals and objectives developed by Russell Colley.

Decline stage: A stage in which total demand decreases, leading to a further dropout of competitors until only a few remain.

Delayed-action advertising: The advertisements which attempt to influence consumer attitudes and preferences, thus helping to set the stage for a purchase.

Delphi technique: The procedure of environmental forecasting by a group of experts who are solicited anonymously and asked to predict the likelihood and time of occurrence of significant events.

Demarketing: Marketing to reduce demand temporarily or permanently; the aim is not to destroy demand, but only to reduce or shift it.

Demography: The study of the changing characteristics of human populations-factors such as vital statistics, growth, size, density, and distribution.

Department stores: Stores characterised by wide and deep product mixes; individual departments within store; mid- to upper-level prices; and extensive services.

Derived demand: The demand based on expectations of upcoming demand for other industrial or consumer products.

Differentiation: making use of specific marketing mixes.

Direct marketing: (1) A form of non-store retailing in which a promotional message is delivered directly to potential customers, who respond directly to the company rather than through a traditional point of sale such as store. (2) Non-store sales to consumers and organisational buyers via mail and telephone. (3) Direct communications with carefully targeted individual consumers to obtain an immediate response, and cultivate lasting customer relationships.

Direct marketing channel: A marketing channel that has no intermediary levels.

Direct-mail marketing: Direct marketing through single mailings that include letters, ads, samples, foldouts, and other "salespeople with wings" sent to prospects on mailing lists.

Dissonance-reducing buying behaviour: Consumer buying behaviour in situations characterized by high involvement but few perceived differences among brands.

Distribution channel: A set of interdependent organizations involved in the process of making a product or service available for use or consumption by the consumer or business user.

Distribution channel: The network of organisations necessary to distribute goods or services from the manufacturers to the consumers; the distribution channel therefore potentially consists of manufacturers, distributors, wholesalers, and retailers.

District sales manager: A line executive who plans, directs, and controls the activities of field salespeople

Diversification: A strategy for company growth by starting up or acquiring businesses outside the company's current products and markets.

Divest: A strategy based on the Boston Matrix. Here the company can divest the SBU by phasing it out or selling it - in order to use the resources elsewhere (e.g. investing in the more promising "question marks").

Dogs: A term used in the Boston Group Matrix. Unsurprisingly, the term "dogs" refers to businesses or products that have low relative share in unattractive, low-growth markets. Dogs may generate enough cash to break-even, but they are rarely, if ever, worth investing in.

Dumping: Selling a product in a market other than a home market at prices below the cost of making and delivering them to that market.

Durable goods: The tangible items that can be expected to survive multiple use.

E-commerce: The use of technologies such as the Internet, electronic data exchange and industry extranets to streamline business transactions.

Economic environment: Factors that affect consumer buying power and spending patterns.

Electronic commerce (e-commerce): The general term for a buying and selling process that is supported by electronic means.

Electronic data interchange (EDI) systems: An information technology that allows business interactions between firms to take place electronically using a standard format.

Embargo: A ban on the import of a certain product.

Endorsement: The promotion of some kind of product recommendation or affirmation, usually from a celebrity, implying to the potential customer that a product is good.

Engel's Laws: Differences noted over a century ago by Ernst Engel in how people shift their spending across food, housing, transportation, health care, and other goods and services categories as family income rises.

Ethnic group: The social group determined by culturally transmitted, learned traits.

F.O.B. Pricing: F.O.B. stands for "free on board" and is followed by the designation "factory" or "destination" to indicate at what point the buyer assumes freight costs and title to the product.

Factory outlet: Off-price retailing operation that is owned and operated by a manufacturer and that normally carries the manufacturer's surplus, discontinued, or irregular goods.

Focus: Paying attention to a few market segments

Follow-up: The last step in the selling process in which the salesperson follows up after the sale to ensure customer satisfaction and repeat business.

Forecasting: The prediction of what buyers in a target market are likely to do under a given set of conditions, such as the prediction of how much of a product will be purchased by a particular market segment given a particular price of the product.

Forward integration: The approach in which the manufacturers acquire control over wholesalers and retailers.

Franchise: (1) A contractual association between a manufacturer, wholesaler, or service organization (a franchiser) and independent businesspeople (franchisees) who buy the right to own and operate one or more units in the franchise system. (2) The selling of a licence by the owner (franchisor) to a third party (franchisee) permitting the sale of a product or service for a specified period. In business format franchising the agreement will involve a common brand and marketing format. Many service businesses are operated under franchise include well-known brands such as Burger King, KFC and KwikPrint.

Full cost pricing: Full cost plus pricing seeks to set a price that takes into account all relevant costs of production.

Full-service wholesalers: Organisations which provide almost all the functions of intermediaries and generally are divided into three subgroups: general merchandise wholesalers, single-line wholesalers, and specialty wholesalers.

Gender segmentation: The segmentation of markets based on the sex of the customer. The cosmetic industry is a good example of widespread use of gender segmentation.

Generic products: Products which are not branded, are simply packed, and usually are priced well below both manufacturer's and private brands.

Geographic segmentation: Dividing a market into different geographical units such as nations, states, regions, counties, cities, or neighborhoods.

Global marketing: Refers to any marketing that involves two or more nations.

Growth stage: A stage in a product's life in which sales and profits grow rapidly, competitors are attracted to the growing market, and cash flow can still be negative because of firm's efforts to establish a strong market share ahead of competitors. The market is usually turbulent in this period.

Growth-share matrix: A matrix that explains how market share, market growth, and cash flows are related.

Habitual buying behaviour: Consumer buying behaviour in situations characterized by low consumer involvement and few significant perceived brand differences.

Historical and quantitative forecasts: A projection of future sales based on sales patterns and/or mathematical calculations.

Horizontal conflict: The conflict which arises between wholesalers and retailers of the same level and type in a channel.

Horizontal integration: The process which brings together a number of channel members at the same level and puts them under single ownership.

Horizontal marketing system: A channel arrangement in which two or more companies at one level join together to follow a new marketing opportunity.

Horizontal markets: Markets on which products are sold to a wide range of industries.

Hybrid marketing channel: Multichannel distribution system in which a single firm sets up two or more marketing channels to reach one or more customer segments.

Hypermarch: A very large store (80.000 square feet and up) that adds furniture, appliances, and clothing to the items found in superstores.

Impulse products: Those products which the consumer buys without having established intention to buy, often feature on racks arranged prominently and enticingly around checkout counters in supermarkets, drugstores, and variety stores.

Indirect marketing channel: Channel containing one or more intermediary levels.

Industrial markets: Markets made up of organisations which buy in order to produce goods.

Industrial products: Products purchased by an organisation for use either in other products or in its own operations.

Informative advertisements: Advertising for the purpose of creating knowledge of the product.

In-home retailing: Selling that usually takes the form of a small party given by a hostess or host to allow friends and neighbours to examine and order a product line.

Initiator: A person in a group buying situation (e.g. a family) who first suggests buying a particular product or service.

Innovators: Innovators are those who adopt new products first. They are usually relatively young, lively, intelligent, socially and geographically mobile. They are often of a high socioeconomic group ("AB's").

Integrated direct marketing: Direct-marketing campaigns that use multiple vehicles and multiple stages to improve response rates and profits.

Integrated marketing communications (IMC): The concept under which a company carefully integrates and coordinates its many communications channels to deliver a clear, consistent, and compelling message about the organization and its products.

Interactive marketing: Marketing by a service firm that recognizes that perceived service quality depends heavily on the quality of buyer–seller interaction.

Internal marketing: The process of eliciting support for a company and its activities among its own employees, in order to encourage them to promote its goals. This process can happen at a number of levels, from increasing awareness of individual products or marketing campaigns, to explaining overall business strategy.

Introduction stage: A product's first appearance in the marketplace, before any sales or profits have been made.

Introductory stage: A stage in a product's life in which an innovation is alone in the market.

Involvement: The level of interest, emotion and activity which the consumer is prepared to expend on a particular purchase.

Joint venturing: Entering foreign markets by joining with foreign companies to produce or market a product or service.

Judgement forecast: The prediction rely upon the opinions of informed participants or outside consultants.

Labelling: Packaging information that can be used for a variety of promotional, informational and legal purposes.

Laggards: Individuals, households, or organisations that resists or never adopt the new product.

Laggards: The group of consumers who are typically last to buy a new product.

Late majority: People who are quite sceptical about new products but eventually adopt them because of economic necessity or social pressure.

Licensing: A method of entering a foreign market in which the company enters into an agreement with a licensee in the foreign market, offering the right to use a manufacturing process, trademark, patent, trade secret, or other item of value for a fee or royalty.

Limited-service wholesalers: Wholesalers who perform only selected functions.

Line extension: Using a successful brand name to introduce additional items in a given product category under the same brand name, such as new flavours, forms, colours, added ingredients, or package sizes.

Logo: A graphic, usually consisting of a symbol and/or group of letters that identifies a company or brand.

Macro forecasting: Macro forecasting is concerned with forecasting markets in total. This is about determining the existing level of Market Demand and considering what will happen to market demand in the future.

Macro-environment: The larger societal forces that affect the microenvironment demographic, economic, natural, technological, political and cultural forces.

Market: The set of all actual and potential buyers of a product or service. A group of people or organisations that have similar needs and wants, the desire to satisfy those needs and wants, the means of exchange (money) to satisfy their needs and wants, and the ability and authority to make the exchange (purchase).

Market challenger: A runner-up firm in an industry that is fighting hard to increase its market share.

Market concentration: Market concentration is the proportion of market value that is owned by the leading brands or products/companies in the market. Where the market leaders own a large part of the overall market, the market is said to be highly concentrated. By contrast, where the market leader has a relatively small market share and there are many other competitors, a market is said to be "fragmented".

Market leader: The firm in an industry with the largest market share; it usually leads other firms in price changes, new product introductions, distribution coverage, and promotion spending.

Market modification: Turning non-users to users, entry on new segments, reaching customers of competitors, more frequent and heavier use of product.

Market nicher: A firm in an industry that serves small segments that other firms overlook or ignore.

Market penetration: A strategy for company growth by increasing sales of current products to current market segments without changing the product.

Market positioning: (1) Arranging for a product to occupy a clear, distinctive, and desirable place relative to competing products in the minds of target consumers. (2) A marketing strategy that will position a business' products and services against those of its competitors in the minds of consumers. To achieve positioning success it is suggested that there are four basic competitive strategies that a company can follow (based on work by Porter):

Market segmentation: (1) The division of large, dissimilar populations into smaller, more similar groups. (2) The process of subdividing large, heterogenous (dissimilar) whole markets into smaller, homogenous (similar) parts of submarkets Dividing a market into distinct groups of buyers on the basis of needs, characteristics, or behaviour who might require separate products or marketing mixes.

Market share analysis: An evaluation of the firm's performance in comparison to that of its competitors.

Market share: Market share can be defined as the percentage of all sales within a market that is held by one brand/product or company.

Marketing: A social and managerial process whereby individuals and groups obtain what they need and want through creating and exchanging products and value with others.

Marketing audit: A comprehensive, systematic, independent, and periodic examination of a company's environment, objectives, strategies, and activities to determine problem areas and opportunites and to recommend a plan of action to improve the company's marketing performance.

Marketing communications mix (promotion mix): The specific mix of advertising, personal selling, sales promotion, public relations, and direct-marketing tools a company uses to pursue its advertising and marketing objectives.

Marketing concept: The philosophy that business organisations achieve their profit and other goals by satisfying consumers. The marketing management philosophy that holds that achieving organizational goals depends on determining the needs and wants of target markets and delivering the desired satisfactions more effectively and efficiently than competitors do.

Marketing control: The process of measuring and evaluating the results of marketing strategies and plans and taking corrective action to ensure that marketing objectives are achieved The process of evaluating of achieved results against established standards, and of taking corrective action to exploit opportunities or solve problems.

Marketing environment: The actors and forces outside marketing that affect marketing management's ability to develop and maintain successful transactions with its target customers.

Marketing information system (MIS): The continuously interacting structure of people, machines, and procedures that produces information pertinent to marketing decisions.

Marketing intelligence: Everyday information about developments in the marketing environment that helps managers prepare and adjust marketing plans.

Marketing intermediaries: Firms that help the company to promote, sell, and distribute its goods to final buyers; they include resellers, physical distribution firms, marketing service agencies, and financial intermediaries.

Marketing management: The analysis, planning, implementation, and control of programs designed to create, build, and maintain beneficial exchanges with target buyers for the purpose of achieving organizational objectives.

Marketing mix: The set of controllable tactical marketing tools 'product, price, place, and promotion' that the firm blends to produce the response it wants in the target market Marketing programs including product conception (and development), pricing decisions, promotion of the product, and distribution to consumers.

Marketing plan: A detailed statement (usually prepared annually) of how a company's marketing mix will be used to achieve its market objectives. A marketing plan is usually prepared following a marketing audit.

Marketing process: The process of (1) analyzing marketing opportunites, (2) selecting target markets, (3) developing the marketing mix, and (4) managing the marketing effort.

Marketing research The systematic design, collection, analysis, and reporting of data relevent to a specific marketing situation facing an organization The systematic and objective research for and analysis of information relevant to the identification and solution of any problem in the field of marketing.

Marketing strategy: An overall statement of an organisation's goals in terms of markets (Who are our customers) and products (What are we selling) The marketing logic by which the business unit hopes to achieve its marketing objectives.

Maturity stage: A stage in which sales growth slows, the market becomes saturated, and profits are high but begin to decline as market leaders cut prices in order to gain share.

Micro-environment: The forces close to the company that affect its ability to serve customers' the company, suppliers, marketing channel firms, customer markets, competitors, and publics.

Micromarketing: The practice of tailoring products and marketing programs to suit the tastes of specific individuals and locations' includes *local marketing* and *individual marketing.*

Modified re-buy: The buying situation in which the buying organisation has some familiarity with the product but needs some assistance; it is buying behaviour between a strait re-buy and a new-task purchase.

Motivation: Persons' impulses to take action and the internal and external forces that energise, mobilise, and direct their behaviour toward goals.

Multi-channel marketing: When a business distributes its products through more than one distribution channel, this is known as multi-channel marketing. Retail chains, for example Argos, besides using the shops to distribute their products, quite often also use catalogue selling. The main purpose of multi-channel marketing is to more effectively reach different customer segments.

Multi-segment strategy: A strategy by which a business directs its marketing efforts towards two or more market segments by developing a marketing mix for each.

Need recognition: The first stage of the buyer decision process in which the consumer recognizes a problem or need.

New product development: The development of original products, product improvements, product modifications, and new brands through the firm's own R&D efforts.

New product: A new product can be defined as a good, service or idea that is "perceived" by some potential customers as new. It may have been available for some time, but many potential customers have not yet adopted the product nor decided to become a regular user of the product.

Niche marketing: Niche marketing refers to the exploitation of comparatively small market segments by businesses that decide to concentrate their efforts. Niche segments exist in nearly all markets – for example the self-build sports car segment of the motor industry.

Online ads: Ads that appear while subscribers are surfing online services or Web sites, including banners, pop-up windows, "tickers," and "roadblocks."

Online marketing: Marketing conducted through interactive online computer systems, which link consumers with sellers electronically.

Organisational marketing: All marketing efforts directed at buyers for formal institutions, including industrial, service, reseller, government, and not-for-profit groups.

Organisational markets: Business market Markets which include businesses, institutions, and governments that buy products or raw materials for their own use or to make other products that they, in turn, sell All organizations that buy goods and services for use in the production of other products and services that are sold, rented, or supplied to others.

Own-label brand: Own-label brands are created and owned by businesses that operate in the distribution channel – often referred to as "distributors". Often these distributors are retailers, but not exclusively. Sometimes the retailer's entire product range will be own-label. However, more often, the distributor will mix own-label and manufacturers brands.

Packaging: The activities of designing and producing the container or wrapper for a product.

Penetration: Marketers set low initial prices in an attempt to capture mass markets.

Penetration pricing: Penetration pricing involves the setting of lower, rather than higher prices in order to achieve a large, if not dominant market share.

Penetration strategy: A marketing strategy based on low prices and extensive advertising to increase a product's market share. For penetration strategy to be effective the market will have to be large enough for the seller to be able to sustain low profit margins.

Perception: Selective attention, distortion recall The process of becoming aware of phenomena, whether internal or external, tangible or intangible The process by which people select, organize, and interpret, information to form a meaningful picture of the world.

Peripheral values: Values that reflect, but are not as deeply embedded or as fundamental as, central values.

Personal selling: Personal presentation by the firm's sales force for the purpose of making sales and building customer relationships.

Pioneer advertisements: Advertisements that increase primary demand for the product that bring non-users into the users category.

Point-of-purchase (POP) promotion: Display and demonstration that takes place at the point of purchase or sale.

Political environment: Laws, government agencies and pressure groups that influence and limit various organizations and individuals in a given society.

Porter's Five Forces Model: An analytic model developed by Michael E. Porter. The five forces in terms of which the model analyses businesses and industries are: Buyers, Suppliers, Substitutes, New Entrants and Rivals.

Portfolio: A collection of businesses owned and managed by a parent corporation.

Portfolio planning: Portfolio planning is the process of managing groups of brands and product lines.

Positioning: Positioning is how a product appears in relation to other products in the market.

Presentation: The step in the selling process in which the salesperson tells the product "story" to the buyer, showing how the product will make or save money for the buyer.

Prestige pricing: Prestige pricing refers to the practice of setting a high price for an product, throughout its entire life cycle – as opposed to the short term 'opportunistic', high price of price 'skimming'. This is done in order to evoke perceptions of quality and prestige with the product or service.

Price discrimination: Price discrimination occurs when a firm charges a different price to different groups of consumers for an identical good or service, for reasons not associated with costs.

Price sensitivity: Price sensitivity is the effect a change in price will have on customers.

Price skimming: Price skimming involves charging a relatively high price for a short time where a new, innovative, or much-improved product is launched onto a market.

Problem/Need recognition: The first stage in the buying process where the potential customer recognises that a problem or a need can be met by buying a product or a service.

Product: (1) Anything and organisation or individual offers for exchange that may satisfy customers' or consumers' needs or the marketer's own needs. (2) Anything that can be offered to a market for attention, acquisition, use, or consumption that might satisfy a want or need. It includes physical objects, services, persons, places, organizations, and ideas.

Product adaptation: (1) A global marketing strategy whereby the product is adapted to foreign market needs, but the promotional program used in the domestic market is used in foreign markets. (2) Adapting a product to meet local conditions or wants in foreign markets.

Product class: All the brands of a good and service offered by all competitors to meet a basic consumer need.

Product concept: The idea that consumers will favour products that offer the most quality, performance, and features and that the organization should therefore devote its energy to making continuous product improvements. A detailed version of the new-product idea stated in meaningful consumer terms.

Product development: A strategy for company growth by offering modified or new products to current market segments. Developing the product concept into a physical product in order to ensure that the product idea can be turned into a workable product.

Product development process: The process comprising of series of steps involved in getting a product on the market: idea generation, screening, feasibility studies, prototype development, test marketing, and commercialisation.

Product elimination: Withdrawal of a product from the normal market place.

Product ladder: The concept that states that consumers perceive brands of a product to be arrayed from top to bottom in terms of their familiarity and preference.

Product life cycle: The product's stages of development, which consist of introductory, growth, maturity and decline stage.

Product line: A grouping of products managed and marketed as a unit because they have similar functions, are distributed in similar ways, or fall within the certain price range. Length, breadth, depth and continuum is distinguished.

Product line breadth: The number of product lines in the product mix of an organisation.

Product line depth: The number of individual items within each product line.

Product line pricing: Setting the price steps between various products in a product line based on cost differences between the products, customer evaluations of different features, and competitors' prices.

Product mix: A company's total offering of individual products.

Product mix: The set of all product lines and items that a particular business offers for sale to buyers.

Product modification: Improvement quality, features and style of product.

Product positioning: The process by which marketers create and image in buyers' minds and control buyers' perceptions of their product.

Product specification: The stage of the business buying process in which the buying organization decides on and specifies the best technical product characteristics for a needed item.

Product: A product is defined as anything that is capable of satisfying customer needs product.

Promotional mix: The promotional mix consists of a blend of five main kinds of promotional tools: advertising; direct marketing; personal selling; sales promotion and public relations.

Promotional pricing: Pricing that paves the way for a good old-fashioned sale; prices of selected items are lowered in an effort to attract customers.

Prospecting: The step in the selling process in which the salesperson identifies qualified potential customers.

Psychographic segmentation: Psychographic (or "lifestyle") segmentation seeks to classify people accordingly to their values, opinions, personality characteristics and interests.

Public relations: The planned and sustained effort to establish and maintain goodwill and mutual understanding between an organisation and its publics.

Publicity: A form of promotion composed of newsworthy messages sent through the media on a non-paid basis.

Publicity: Promotional activities designed to promote a business and its products by obtaining media coverage not paid for by the business.

Pull strategy: (1) A strategy through which marketers aim mass promotional efforts at consumers and customers with the intent to create demand which pulls the product through the channels A promotion strategy that calls for spending a lot on advertising and consumer promotion to build up consumer demand, which pulls the product through the channels. (2) A strategy through which personal selling and sales promotion are directed at channel members, who then promote product to consumers A promotion strategy that calls for using the sales force and trade promotion to push the product through channels.

Quota: A limit on the amount of goods that an importing country will accept in certain product categories.

Reinforcement advertisements: Advertise-ments that booster and enhance satisfaction with purchases already made.

Relationship marketing: The process of creating, maintaining, and enhancing strong, value-laden relationships with customers and other stakeholders

Relative market share: A firm's market share divided by the market share of its largest competitor.

Retailing: All activities involved in selling goods or services directly to final consumers for their personal, non-business use

Sales forecast: The sales forecast is the expected level of company sales based on a chosen marketing plan and an assumed marketing environment.

Sales promotion: Sales promotion refers to any activity designed to boost the sales of a product or service. It may include an advertising campaign, increased PR activity, a free-sample campaign, offering free gifts or trading stamps, arranging demonstrations or exhibitions, setting up competitions with attractive prizes, temporary price reductions, door-to-door calling, telephone-selling, personal letters on other methods.

Secular trends: The raising or falling patterns of sales over a period of years.

Segmented pricing: Selling a product or service at two or more prices, where the difference in prices is not based on differences in costs.

Selling concept: The idea that consumers will not buy enough of the organization's products unless the organization undertakes a large-scale selling and promotion effort.

Service: Any activity or benefit that one party can offer to another that is essentially intangible and does not result in the ownership of anything.

Service market: All organisations that buy in order to produce services.

Skimming: A strategy that is characterised by a high initial prices and promotional expenditures; the intent is to "skim the cream" from the market before anyone else can serve it.

Slice-of-life advertisements: Advertisements that show the product being used by 'ordinary people' in very common settings or engaged in everyday activities.

Social marketing: The design, implementation, and control of programs seeking to increase the acceptability of a social idea, cause, or practice among a target group.

Societal marketing orientation: An approach that adds a consideration to the marketing concept: the impact of a firm's activities on societal well-being, the very quality of life.

Sorting out: The process by which wholesalers and retailers separate quantities of products into sizes, colours, quality grades, and so on.

Specialty stores: Stores characterised by narrow product mixes with deep product lines, a high level of personal services, and relatively high prices.

Stakeholders: Those who use company's products or services, those who work for the firm, those who own it, and those who are affected by it.

Stars: A term used in the Boston Group Matrix. Stars are high growth businesses or products competing in markets where they are relatively strong compared with the competition. Often they need heavy investment to sustain their growth. Eventually their growth will slow and, assuming they maintain their relative market share, will become cash cows.

Strapline: A slogan often used in conjunction with a brand name, advertising and other promotional methods (e.g. "Guinness is good for you").

Strategic business unit (SBU): A SBU is a unit of the company that has a separate mission and objectives and that can be planned independently from the other businesses. An SBU can be a company division, a product line or even individual brands - it all depends on how the company is organised.

Supermarkets: Self-selection stores that sell a complete range of food and other items from various departments.

Sweepstakes: A promotional method in which consumers fill out a form to enter a random drawing for prizes.

Systems buying: Buying a packaged solution to a problem from a single seller.

Target costing: Pricing that starts with an ideal selling price, then targets costs that will ensure that the price is met.

Target market: A set of buyers sharing common needs or characteristics that the company decides to serve.

Target market: The group of potential customers sharing common needs and characteristics that a business decides to serve.

Tariff: A tax levied by a government against certain imported products. Tariffs are designed to raise revenue or to protect domestic firms.

Team selling: Using teams of people from sales, marketing, engineering, finance, technical support, and even upper management to service large, complex accounts.

Telemarketing: Telemarketing (sometimes also referred to as "telesales") is a method of direct marketing in which the telephone is used to contact potential customers in order to reduce the time spent in making personal visits. Traditionally, products such as double glazing and central heating have been marketed using this technique.

Telephone surveys: Surveys in which respondents' answers to a questionnaire are recorded by interviewers on the phone.

Test marketing: (1) The stage of new-product development in which the product and marketing program are tested in more realistic market settings The process in which the product is actually introduced into selected geographical markets where developers can observe how consumers and dealers react to the handling, use, and promotion of the product. (2) Test marketing occurs when a new product is tested with a sample of customers, or launched in a restricted geographical area, to judge customers' reactions. If the product is unsuccessful, the business will have minimised its costs and can either make changes before the main launch or decide to discontinue the product. Test marketing has a disadvantage in that competitors learn about the new product before its full launch.

Testimonial advertisements: Advertisements that attempt to get consumer to identify with someone who claims that he or she uses and likes the product.

Threats: Threats are any aspect of the external environment which cause problems and which may prevent achievement of objectives. Almost by definition, what presents a threat to one business offers an opportunity to other businesses.

Total quality management (TQM): Programs designed to constantly improve the quality of products, services, and marketing processes.

Trademark: (1) A brand or part of a brand that is given legal protection because it is capable of exclusive appropriation. (2) Legal designation indicating that the owner has exclusive use of a brand.

Transit time: The time from receipt of the order to delivery of the goods.

Urban shopping malls: Collections of shops and department stores located in or near central business districts.

Users: Members of the organization who will use the product or service; users often initiate the buying proposal and help define product specifications.

Value marketing: A principle of enlightened marketing that holds that a company should put most of its resources into value-building marketing investments.

Value-based pricing: Setting price based on buyers' perceptions of value rather than on the seller's cost.

Vertical conflict: The conflict which occurs between members above and below each other in the distribution channel-between the manufacturer and intermediaries, or between intermediaries such as wholesalers and retailers.

Vertical marketing system (VMS): (1) A distribution channel structure in which producers, wholesalers, and retailers act as a unified system. One channel member owns the others, has contracts with them, or has so much power that they all cooperate. (2) A system in which the functions of members at different levels in the distribution channel have been integrated under the ownership or influence of one member in order to set shared goals and to achieve effective performance.

Vertical markets: The markets on which products are tailored for specific industries.

Warehouse showrooms: Stores that are located on low-rent, suburban sites, and focus on medium-priced furniture and appliances.

Wholesaler: Organisations which buy products from producers or other wholesalers and resell them to retailers or organisational buyers, or to other wholesalers.

Word-of-mouth influence: Personal communication about a product between target buyers and neighbours, friends, family members, and associates.

REASONING ABILITY

1 Series

LETTER SERIES

In letter series, the letters follow a definite order. The given series of letters can be in natural order or in reverse order or combination of both. The letters may be skipped or repeated or consecutive. The given series may be single or may comprise two different series merged at alternate positions. While attempting questions on letter series one should note the pattern of alphabet series.

Alphabets in natural series

A B C D E F G H I J K L M N O P Q R S T U V W X Y Z
1st 5th 10th 15th 20th 25th

are:

Alphabets in reverse series

Z Y X W V U T S R Q P O N M L K J I H G F E D C B A
1st 5th 10th 15th 20th 25th

Note: On reaching Z, the series restarts from A and on reaching A, it restarts from Z.

Example

1. A Z B Y C ?

A. D
B. X
C. U
D. E

Ans.: (B) There are two alternate series.

Series I : A B C (Consecutive letters in natural series)

Series II : Z Y X (Consecutive letters in reverse series)

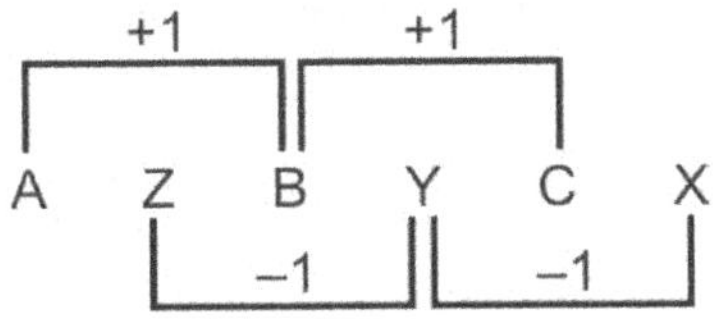

REPEAT SERIES

In this type of series small letters of the alphabet are used to make a set of letters which are repeated. The candidate has to find the set of letters which will fit the blanks left in the given series in such a manner that one section of the series is further repeated in the same manner.

Example

2. Which of the following groups of letters will complete the given series?

ba-b-aab-a-b

A. baab B. abba
C. abaa D. babb

Ans.: (B) The series is baab, baab, baab. Here the section 'baab' is repeated in the series. Solving steps : The candidate has to look for clues to solve such series pattern. 'aab' in the series indicates that 'b' in this series is preceded by two 'a' so, the first blank and the last blank will be filled by 'a'. Now the first set is formed, *i.e.*, 'baab' in the beginning. This set is repeated, so the second and third blanks will have 'b' filling them.

NUMBER SERIES

In this type of series, the set of given numbers in a series are related to one another in a particular pattern or manner. The relationship between the numbers may be (i) consecutive odd/even numbers; (ii) consecutive prime numbers; (iii) squares/cubes of some numbers with/without variation of addition or subtraction of some number; (iv) sum/product/difference of preceding numbers; (v) addition/subtraction/multiplication/division by some number; and (vi) many more combinations of the relationships given above.

Example

3. Complete the given series. 2, 14, 98, 686, ?

A. 1976 B. 2548

C. 980 D. 4802

Ans.: (D) The numbers are multiplied by 7 to obtain the next numbers.

2 14 98 686 4802

×7 ×7 ×7 ×7

The given series may also comprise of two alternate series merged as one.

MIXED SERIES

Mixed series comprises of the combinations of letters and numbers. In this type of series, the letters and numbers may have a common sequence pattern or may have separate sequence patterns.

Example

4. What should come in the place of question mark in the following letter-number combination?

F6, H8, J10, L12, ?

A. N15

B. O14

C. N14

D. O13

Ans.: (C) The letters are moved two steps forward and the number indicates the position of the letter in the alphabet series.

F6 H8 J10 L12 N14

+2 +2 +2 +2

EXERCISE

Directions (Qs. 1 to 8): *In each of the following series determine the order of the letters. Then from the given options select the one which will complete the given series.*

1. GH, JL, NQ, SW, YD, ?

A. EJ B. FJ

C. EL D. FL

2. AI, BJ, CK, ?

A. DL B. DM

C. GH D. LM

3. b e d f ? h j ? l

A. i m B. m i

C. i n D. j m

4. ADVENTURE, DVENTURE, DVENTUR, ?, VENTU

A. DVENT B. VENTURE

C. VENTUR D. DVENTU

E. None of these

5. PERPENDICULAR, ERPENDICULA, RPENDICUL, ?

A. PENDICUL B. PENDIC

C. ENDIC D. ENDICU

E. None of these

6. ATTRIBUTION, TTRIBUTIO, RIBUTIO, IBUTI, ?

A. IBU B. UT

C. UTI D. BUT

E. None of these

7. M, N, O, L, R, I, V, ?

A. A B. E

C. F D. H

E. Z

8. A, CD, GHI, ?, UVWXY

A. LMNO B. MNO

C. MNOP D. NOPQ

Directions (Qs. 9 to 15): *Which letter(s) in each of the following series is wrong or is misfit in the series?*

9. Z A W B X C

A. D B. C

C. X D. W

10. M L O N Q P T R

A. T B. O

C. Q D. L

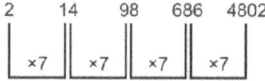

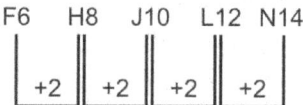

11. D K R Y F L
A. L B. D
C. R D. Y

12. L N Q T W Z C F
A. C B. Q
C. L D. F

13. XW, DC, CB, NM, PQ, QP
A. NM B. CB
C. PQ D. XW

14. B E I N S A I
A. A B. E
C. S D. I

15. Z T P K H F
A. Z B. P
C. T D. F

Directions (Qs. Nos. 16 to 20): *In each of the following letter series, some of the letters are missing which are given in that order as one of the alternatives below it. Choose the correct alternative.*

16. ba _ cb _ b _ bab _
A. acbb B. bacc
C. bcaa D. cabb

17. c _ bba _ cab _ ac _ ab _ ac
A. abebe B. acbcb
C. babec D. bcacb

18. ab _ _ baa _ _ ab _
A. aaaaa B. aabaa
C. aabab D. baabb

19. _ bc _ ca _ aba _ c _ ca
A. abcbb B. bbbec
C. bacba D. abbec

20. ab _ aa _ bbb _ aaa _ bbba
A. abba B. baab
C. aaab D. abab

Directions (Qs. 21 to 25): *Choose the correct alternative that will continue the same pattern and replace the question mark in the given series.*

21. 3, 9, 27, 81, 243, ?
A. 486 B. 729
C. 972 D. 359

22. 1, 6, 12, 19, 27 ?
A. 38 B. 35
C. 36 D. 54

23. 125, 80, 45, 20, ?
A. 5 B. 8
C. 10 D. 12

24. 120, 99, 80, 63, 48, ?
A. 35 B. 38
C. 39 D. 40

25. 589654237, 89654237, 8965423, 965423, ?
A. 58965 B. 65423
C. 89654 D. 96542

Directions (Qs. 26–33): *In each series given below, what would come in place of the question-mark?*

26. 2B, 4C, 8E, 14H, ?
A. 20L B. 22L
C. 21I D. 16K

27. C(1)L, F(4)O, I(9)R, L(16)U, ?
A. P(27)W B. N(24)Y
C. M(23)X D. O(25)X

28. 3F, 6G, 11I, 18L, ?
A. 27P B. 21O
C. 27Q D. 25N

29. W(1)A, X(4)Z, Y9Y, ?, A(25)W
A. X(11)Z B. Z(21)A
C. Z(16)X D. Z(14)X

30. 81Y, 27S, 9N, 3J, ?
A. 0H B. IG
C. 0F D. IE

31. E5, K11, Q17, ?
A. X20 B. Y24
C. V22 D. W25

32. D2, I3, N6, S18, ?
A. V72 B. W36
C. Y90 D. X108

33. 3J, 6M, 12L, ?, 48N
A. 24O B. 8M
C. 26M D. 22O

Directions (Qs. Nos. 34 and 35) : *Which of the following does not fit in the letter number series given below?*

34. G4T, J10R, M20P, P43N, S90L
A. J10R B. S90L
C. M20P D. G4T

35. B0R, G3U, E3P, J7S, H9N
A. E3P B. J7S
C. H9N D. G3U

ANSWERS

1	**2**	**3**	**4**	**5**	**6**	**7**	**8**	**9**	**10**
D	A	A	C	E	C	B	C	D	A
11	**12**	**13**	**14**	**15**	**16**	**17**	**18**	**19**	**20**
A	C	C	C	B	B	B	B	A	B
21	**22**	**23**	**24**	**25**	**26**	**27**	**28**	**29**	**30**
B	C	A	A	D	B	D	A	C	B
31	**32**	**33**	**34**	**35**					
C	D	A	A	B					

EXPLANATORY ANSWERS

1. 1st letter:

$G \xrightarrow{+3} J \xrightarrow{+4} N \xrightarrow{+5} S \xrightarrow{+6} Y \xrightarrow{+7} \textcircled{F}$

2nd letter:

$H \xrightarrow{+4} L \xrightarrow{+5} Q \xrightarrow{+6} W \xrightarrow{+7} D \xrightarrow{+8} \textcircled{L}$

2. 1st letter: $A \xrightarrow{+1} B \xrightarrow{+1} C \xrightarrow{+1} \textcircled{D}$

2nd letter: $I \xrightarrow{+1} J \xrightarrow{+1} K \xrightarrow{+1} \textcircled{L}$

3. The series may be divided into groups as shown: b e d / f ? h / j ? l
Clearly in the first group, the second and third letters are respectively three and two steps ahead of the first letter. A similar pattern would follow in the second and third groups.

4. One letter from the beginning and one from the end of a term are removed, one by one, in alternate steps.

5. Each term of the series is obtained by removing two letters from the preceding term one from the beginning and one from the end. So, the missing term is PENDICU.

6. In the first step, one letter from the beginning and one from the end of a term are removed to give the next term. In the second step, two letters from the beginning of a term are removed. These two steps are repeated alternately.

7. The given sequence is a combination of two series: I. M, O, R, V and II. N, L, I, ?

The pattern in I is: $M \xrightarrow{+2} O \xrightarrow{+3} R \xrightarrow{+4} V$

The pattern in II is: $N \xrightarrow{-2} L \xrightarrow{-3} I \xrightarrow{-4} \textcircled{E}$

8. Each term consists of consecutive letters in order. The number of letters in the terms goes on increasing by one at each step. Also, there is a gap of one letter between the last letter of the first term and the first letter of the second term; a gap of two letters between the last letter of the second term and the first letter of the third term; and so on. So, there should be a gap of three letters between the last letter of the third term and the first letter of the desired term.

9. There are two alternate series I. Z, Y, X and II. A, B, C

The pattern in I is : $Z \xrightarrow{-1} \textcircled{Y} \xrightarrow{-1} X$

The pattern in II is : $A \xrightarrow{+1} B \xrightarrow{+1} C$

10. Two consecutive letters are written backwards.

ML ON OP SR
← ← ← ←

S should be in place of T.

11. The pattern in this series is moving the letters seven steps forward.

D K R Y F (M)
+7 +7 +7 +7 +7

M should be in place of L.

12. The pattern in the series is +3

Ⓚ N Q T W Z C F
+3 +3 +3 +3 +3 +3 +3

K should be in place of L.

13. The series is made with any two consecutive letters written backwards.

XW DC CB NM QP
← ← ← ← ←

Q should come before P in the series.

14. The difference between the letters is increased by one at each step.

B E I N Ⓣ A I
+3 +4 +5 +6 +7 +8

T should be in place of S.

15. The difference between the letters is decreased by one at each step.

Z T O K H F
-6 -5 -4 -3 -2

O should be in place of P.

16. The series is babc/babc/babc. Thus, the pattern 'babc' is repeated.

17. The series is cabbac/cabbac/cabbac. Thus, the pattern 'cabbac' is repeated.

18. The series is aba/aba/aba/aba. Thus, the pattern 'aba' is repeated.

19. The series is abc/bca/cab/abc/bca. Thus, the letters change places in a cyclic order.

20. The series is abb/aaabbb/aaaabbbb/a. Thus, the letters are repeated twice, then thrice, then four times and so on.

21. The numbers in the series are multiplied by 3 to get the next numbers.

22. The difference between the numbers in the series increases by 1, after beginning from 5,

i.e., 1 6 12 19 27 36
+5 +6 +7 +8 +9

23. The pattern is –45, –35, –25, ...
So, missing term = 20 – 15 = 5.

24. The pattern is –21, –19, –17, –15,.....
So, missing term = 48 – 13 = 35.

25. The digits are removed one-by-one from the beginning and the end in order alternately, so as to obtain the subsequent terms of the series.

26. The sequence of numbers is +2, +4, +6, +8 and sequence of letters is +1, +2, +3, +4.

27. The corresponding letters are moved 3 steps forward and the sequence of numbers is +3, +5, +7, +9.

28. The sequence of numbers is +3, +5, +7, +9 and the letters are moved 1, 2, 3, 4 steps forward.

29. The letters on the left are in reverse series, the letters on the right are in natural series, and the numbers are squares of numbers in natural order starting from 1.

30. The numbers are divided by 3 at each step and the letters are moved 6, 5, 4, 3 steps backward.

31. The series comprises of random letters and numbers indicate the position of the letter in alphabet series.

32. The letters are moved five steps forward and every third number is the product of two preceding numbers.

33. Every number is double the previous number and the sequence of letters is +3, –1 (3 steps forward, 1 step backward) which is repeated.

34. The letters on the left are moved 3 steps forward, the letters on the right are moved 2 steps backward and the sequence of numbers is (4 × 2) +1, (9 × 2) +2, (20 × 2) +3, (43 × 2) +4. So, J9R should be in place of J10R.

35. The sequence of letters on the left is +5, –2 (5 steps forward, 2 steps backward) which is repeated, the sequence of letters on the right is +3, –5 (3 steps forward, 5 steps backward) which is repeated, and the numbers are the sum of two preceeding numbers. So, J6S should be in place of J7S.

❀ ❀ ❀

2 Coding-Decoding

Coding is a secretive language which is used to change the representation of the actual term/word/value. This coded language can be framed by

(*i*) moving the letters one or more steps forward or backward;

(*ii*) substituting numbers for letters and vice-versa;

(*iii*) writing the letters of the given word in reverse order in part or in whole; and

(*iv*) replacing the letters in their natural series by the same positioned letters in their reverse series.

Alphabet in natural series are :

A B C D E F G H I J K L M N O P Q R S T U V W X Y Z

1st 5th 10th 15th 20th 25th

Alphabet in reverse series are :

Z Y X W V U T S R Q P O N M L K J I H G F E D C B A

1st 5th 10th 15th 20th 25th

Note : On reaching Z, the series restarts from A and on reaching A, it restarts from Z

Example

1. If FACE is coded as GBDF, then BADE will be coded as :

A. CBEF B. CEBF

C. CFBE D. CBFE

Ans.: (A) The word is coded by moving the letters one step forward

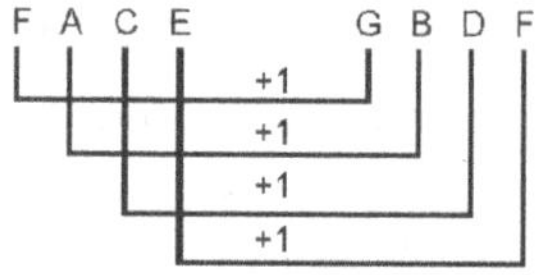

Similarly,

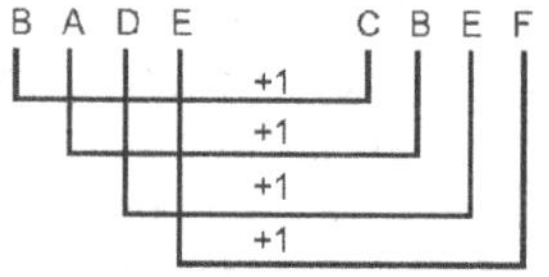

2. In a certain code 'ra mei ket' means 'he is rich'; 'rui pha jeu' means 'run for money'; and 'pha rui ket' means 'money for rich'. Which of the following is the code for 'rich'?

A. ra B. pha

C. ket D. jeu

Ans.: (C) The given information is :

Code	*Sentence*
1. ra mei ket	he is rich
2. rui pha jeu	run for money
3. pha rui ket	money for rich

After comparing codes and sentences 1 and 3, it is clear that word 'rich' is common and so is the code 'ket'.

3. If 'banana' is called 'jelly', 'jelly' is called 'green', 'green' is called 'apple'. 'apple' is called 'mango', what is the colour of leaf?

A. green B. mango

C. apple D. banana

Ans.: (C) Leaf is green in colour and according to the codes in the question 'green' is called 'apple'.

In another form of coding, the Digits and its coded Letters or vice versa are already given. One has to find out the answers to the given questions just by tallying the given codes.

EXERCISE

Directions (Qs. Nos. 1 to 8): *In the following questions select the right option which indicates the correct code for the word or letter given in the question.*

1. If PHILOSOPHY is coded as HPLISOPOYH, ornamental will be coded as :
A. ROANEMNTLA B. ONRAMNEALT
C. ROANEMTNLA D. ROANEMNATL

2. If OPFGBCST stands for NEAR, in the same manner IJVWHI will stand for :
A. HAG B. HUG
C. HUT D. KEG

3. If m is coded as g, g as o, a as *i* and *i* as y, then 'imagination' will be written as :
A. ygagynatyin B. ygioynityog
C. ygioynityon D. ygioyintyon

4. If OUT is coded as 152120, IN will be coded as :
A. 1015 B. 819
C. 1813 D. 914

5. If BAD is coded as 7. HIS as 9, LOW will be coded as :
A. 50 B. 8
C. 23 D. 5

6. In a certain code ABCD is written as 2468 and EFGH as 1357. How will CAGE be written in that code?
A. 6453 B. 6251
C. 6521 D. 6215

7. If HARD is coded as 1357 and SOFT as 2468, what will 21448 stand for?
A. SHAFT B. SHORT
C. SHOOT D. SHART

8. If FACE is coded as 6135, BIG as 297, HAD as 814 and BADGE as 21475, then what is the code for 'A'?
A. 3 B. 1
C. 2 D. 4

Directions (Qs. 9 to 13): *In the following questions study the coded patterns and then select the right option from the given alternatives.*

9. In a certain language, A. 'FOR' stands for 'old is gold'; B. 'ROT' stands for 'gold is pure'; C. 'ROM' stands for 'gold is costly'. How will 'pure old gold is costly' be written?
A. TFROM B. FOTRM
C. FTORM D. TOMRF

10. In a certain code '643' means 'she is beautiful', '593' means 'he is handsome', and '567' means 'handsome meets beautiful'. What number will indicate the word 'meets'?
A. 5 B. 3
C. 7 D. 6

11. In a certain code language, A. 'pic vic nic' stands for 'winter is cold'; B. 'to nic re' for 'summer is hot'; C. 're pic boo' for 'winter and summer' and D. 'vic tho pa' for nights are cold'. Which of the following word is the code for 'summer'?
A. nic B. boo
C. to D. re

12. In a certain language 'mu mit es' means 'who is she' and 'elb mu es' means 'where is she'. What is the code for 'where' in this language?
A. es B. elb
C. mu D. mit

13. In a certain code language 'roi ja kyo twa' means ' Moody is writing letters', 'pok ju ja twa' means 'Woody is writing cards', 'trn kyo pos un' means 'they are writing letters', and 'koi rus pok' means 'gifts and cards'. What is the code word for 'Moody'?
A. ja B. twa
C. roi D. kyo

Directions (Qs. 14 to 18): *Read the given coded information and choose the correct answer from the given options.*

14. If 'red' is called 'air', 'air' is called 'black', 'black' is called 'sky', 'sky' is called 'blue', 'blue' is called 'wind' and 'wind' is called 'white', where to birds fly?
A. air B. sky
C. blue D. wind
E. black

15. If 'green' is called 'pink', 'pink' is called 'blue', 'blue' is called 'purple', 'purple' is called 'white', 'white' is called 'orange' and 'orange' is called 'peach', what is the colour of snow?

A. peach B. orange
C. purple D. blue
E. white

16. If 'colour' is called 'blue', 'blue' is called 'light', 'light' is called 'showy', 'showy' is called 'dark' and 'dark' is called 'colour', what is the colour of ink?

A. blue B. showy
C. dark D. colour
E. light

17. If 'yellow', is called 'pale', 'pale' is called 'blue', 'blue' is called 'orange', 'orange' is called 'dull', 'dull' is called 'green' and 'green' is called 'yellow' , what is the colour of grass in a lawn?

A. pale B. yellow
C. blue D. green
E. orange

18. If 'black' is called 'pink', 'pink' is called 'blue', 'blue' is called 'brown', 'brown' is called 'orange', 'orange' is called 'violet', 'violet' is called 'red' and 'red' is called 'black', what is the colour of blood?

A. black B. brown
C. pink D. orange
E. red

Directions (Qs 19 to 23)*: The following questions are based on the code pattern given below :*

Letters :	T	R	A	H	U	X	C	I	B	L
Numbers :	3	0	1	7	4	9	6	8	2	5

Which of the given options has the correct coded form of the given letters?

19. RACIXT

A. 016823 B. 016873
C. 016843 D. 016893

20. BUHLAI

A. 247018 B. 247508
C. 247538 D. 247518

21. LBIHAR

A. 528471 B. 528710
C. 528947 D. 528103

22. UBAXTC

A. 421736 B. 421956
C. 421936 D. 421906

23. HULBRT

A. 745203 B. 723045
C. 752340 D. 732145

ANSWERS

1	**2**	**3**	**4**	**5**	**6**	**7**	**8**	**9**	**10**
C	B	C	D	D	B	B	B	A	C
11	**12**	**13**	**14**	**15**	**16**	**17**	**18**	**19**	**20**
D	B	C	C	B	E	B	A	D	D
21	**22**	**23**							
B	C	A							

EXPLANATORY ANSWERS

1. The places of two consecutive letters in the word are interchanged to form the coded word.

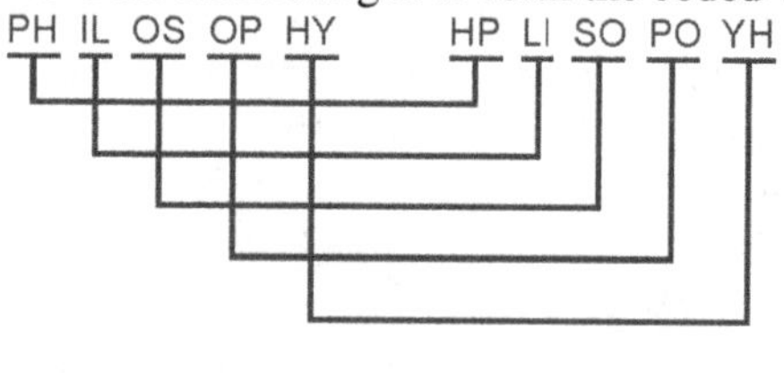

Similarly,

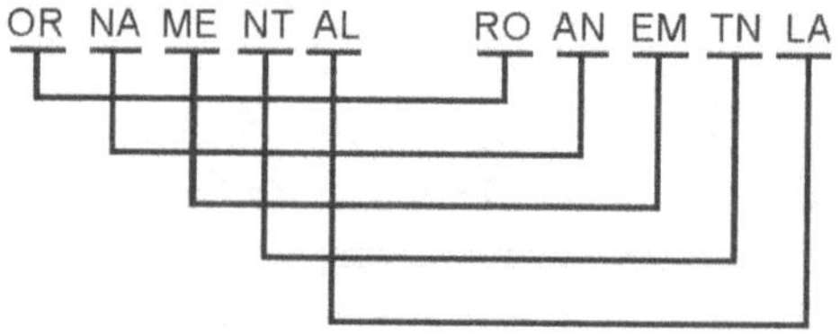

2. The manner of decoding is

↓ OP ↓ FG ↓ BC ↓ ST → codes

N E A R → given word

The letters preceeding two consecutive letters in the alphabetical series are picked to depict the words.

Similarly,

↓ IJ ↓ VW ↓ HI → given codes

H U G → answer word

3. Alphabet whose codes are given

m → g

g → o

a → i

i → y

All other alphabet will remain unchanged so, 'imagination' will be coded as :

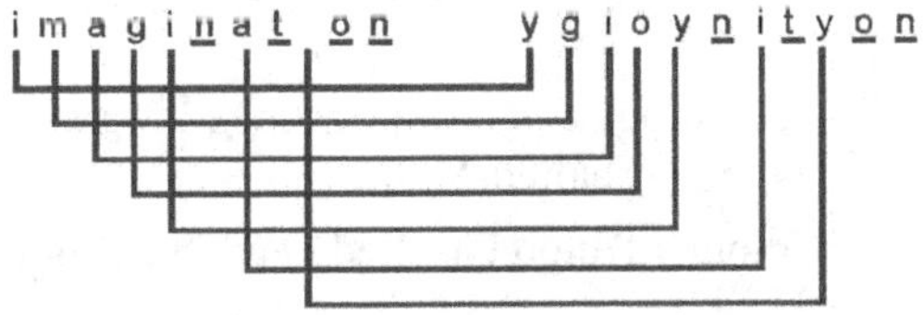

4. The coded number signifies the position of the alphabet in its natural alphabetical series (ABCD...)

O U T → OUT

15th 21st 20th→ 152120

Similarly,

I N → IN

9th 14th → 914

5. The coded number is the sum of number digits signifying the position of the alphabet in the natural order.

B A D

↓ ↓ ↓

2nd 1st 4th

i.e., 2 + 1 + 4 = 7

Similarly,

H I S

↓ ↓ ↓

8th 9th 19th

i.e., 8 + 9 + 19 = 36, further 3 + 6 = 9

Also,

L O W

↓ ↓ ↓

12th 15th 23rd

i.e., 12 + 15 + 23 = 50,

further, 5 + 0 = 5

6. The letters of the given groups are coded by numbers and the word CAGE is formed by letters from the given words. So, to find the answer, select the respective numbers.

A B C D E F G H → letters

2 4 6 8 1 3 5 7 → codes

So,

C A G E → letters

6 2 5 1 → answer codes

7. The numbers represent letters and to find the answer, select the respective letters.

1 3 5 7 2 4 6 8 → codes

H A R D S O F T → letters

So,

2 1 4 4 8 → codes

S H O O T → answer letters

8. The letter 'A' is present in three words and so is the number '1' in all the three words.

F<u>A</u>CE	H<u>A</u>D	B<u>A</u>DGE
6135	814	21475

9. ***Code*** ***Sentence***

1.

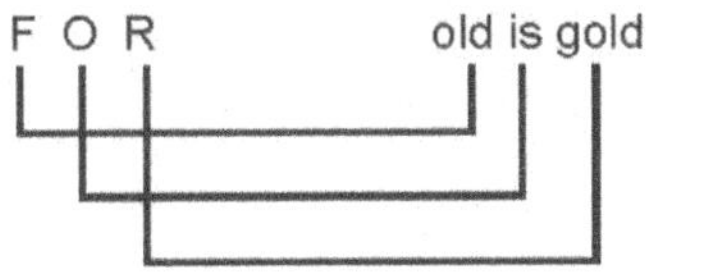

2.

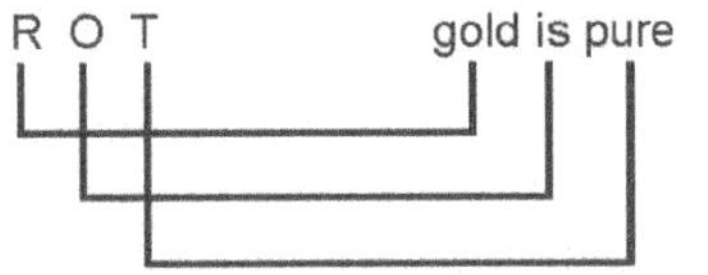

3.

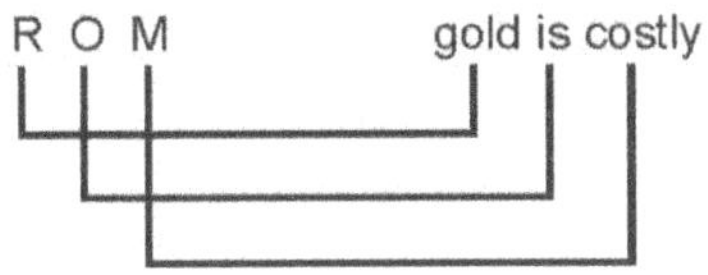

Therefore,

F	stands	for old
O	stands	for is
R	stands	for gold
T	stands	for pure
M	stands	for costly

So, 'pure old gold is costly' will be written as 'TFROM'.

10. ***Code*** ***Sentence***

Code	Sentence
1. 643	she is beautiful
2. 593	he is handsome
3. 567	handsome meets beautiful

From 3rd code and its sentence, neither number '7' nor the word 'meets' is repeated.

11. ***Code*** ***Sentence***

Code	Sentence
1. pic vic nic	winter is cold
2. to nic re	summer is hot
3. re pic boo	winter and summer
4. vic tho pa	nights are cold

The word 'summer' is common in 2nd and 3rd sentences and so is the code 're'

12. ***Code*** ***Sentence***

Code	Sentence
1. mu mite es	who is she
2. **elb** mu es	**where** is she

The code words 'mu' and 'es' are repeated in Ist sentence. The only code left is 'elb' which means 'where'

13. ***Code Sentence***

Code	Sentence
1. **roi** *ja kyo twa*	**Moody** is *writing letters*
2. pok ju *ja twa*	Woody is *writing* cards
3. trn *kyo* pos un	they are writing *letters*
4. koi rus pok	gifts and cards

'Moody' is in 1st sentence only. The code words 'ja' and 'twa' are repeated in 2nd sentence and 'kyo' in 3rd sentence. Only code 'roi' remains which stands for 'Moody'.

14. Birds fly in the 'sky' and 'sky' is called 'blue'.

15. Colour of snow is 'white' and 'white' is called 'orange'.

16. Colour of ink is 'blue' and 'blue' is called 'light'.

17. The colour of grass in a lawn is 'green' and 'green' is called 'yellow'.

18. Colour of blood is 'red' and 'red' is called 'black'.

❀ ❀ ❀

3 Symbol Substitution

Questions in these category are easy to attempt. Candidates must be quick in substituting symbols and calculations. The common pattern of questions asked are given below.

Example

1. If '+' stands for '×'; '×' stands for '÷'; '÷' stands for '–' and '–' stands for '+' then
$2 - 8 \times 2 + 6 \div 7 = ?$

A. 32 B. 19
C. 23 D. 9
E. 15

Ans. After substituting the symbols in the given expression the new expression will be :

$2 + 8 \div 2 \times 6 - 7$

The solving steps will be :

$2 + 4 \times 6 - 7$

$2 + 24 - 7$

$26 - 7 = 19$

2. If ▲ stands for '+'
■ stands for '–'
● stands for '÷'
✱ stands for '×' then

13 ▲ 5 ✱ 20 ● 10 ■ 9 = ?

A. 26 B. 37
C. 14 D. 55
E. 20

Ans. After substituting the symbols the new expression will be :

$13 + 5 \times 20 \div 10 - 9$

The solving steps will be :

$13 + 5 \times 2 - 9$

$13 + 10 - 9$

$23 - 9 = 14$

EXERCISE

1. If × stand for addition, ÷ stands for subtraction, + stands for multiplication and – stands for division, then $(20 \times 6 \div 6 \times 4)$ is equal to

A. 5 B. 24
C. 25 D. 80
E. None of these

2. If "+" means "×"; "÷" means "–"; "×"means "÷" and "–" means "+", what will be the value of the following expression?

$4 + 11 \div 5 - 50 = ?$

A. 79 B. – 11
C. 91 D. – 48.5
E. None of these

3. If P = 6, J = 4, L = 8, M = 24, then which of the given values can replace the question mark (?) in the following?

$M \times J \div L + J = ?$

A. 8 B. 36
C. 52 D. 0
E. 16

4. If A + B > C + D, B + E = 2 C and C + D > B + E, it necessarily follows that

A. A > C B. A + B > 2D
C. A + B > 2C D. A + B > 2E
E. D + B < 2C

5. If A + D > C + E, C + D = 2B and B + E > C + D, it necessarily follows that

A. A + D > B + E
B. A + D > B + C
C. A + B > 2D
D. B + D > C + E
E. A + D < B + C

6. What will be the correct mathematical signs that can be inserted in the following equation?
9 . . . 8 . . . 8 . . . 4 . . . 9 = 65
A. $- + \times \div$ B. $\div \times + -$
C. $\div + \times -$ D. $\times + \div -$
E. $+ \times \div -$

7. If "÷" means "+"; "–" means "÷"; "×" means "–" and "+" means "×", then
$32 \div 8 - 4 \times 12 + 4 = ?$
A. 40 B. 1/12
C. 16 D. 12
E. None of these

8. If "*x*" stands for "+"; "*y*" stands for "–"; "*z*" stands for "÷" and "*w*" stands for "×", then
10*w* 2*x* 5*y* 5 = ?
A. 15 B. 12
C. 20 D. 10
E. 25

9. If "–" stands for "×"; "×" stands for "+"; "+" stands for "÷" and "÷" stands for "–", then what will be the value of the following equation?
$8 - 4 + 16 \times 8 - 10 = ?$
A. 54 B. 82
C. 15 D. 10
E. 110

10. If Δ denotes =; + denotes >, – denotes <, □ denotes ≠, × denotes > and ÷ denotes < then a + b – c denotes
A. b Δ c □ a B. b □ a ÷ c
C. a ÷ b × c D. b – a + c
E. none of these

ANSWERS

1	2	3	4	5	6	7	8	9	10
B	E	E	C	B	D	E	C	B	D

EXPLANATORY ANSWERS

1. $20 + 6 - 6 + 4 = 24$

2. $4 \times 11 - 5 + 50$
$44 - 5 + 50 = 89$

3. $24 \times 4 \div 8 + 4$
$12 + 4 = 16$

4. A + B > C + D > B + E or 2 C
∴ A + B > 2C

5. 1. A + D > C + E
2. B + E > C + D or 2 B
Since, the relation between 1 and 2 is not clear it is however certain that A + D > B + C (combination with C is < A + D).

6. A. $9 - 8 + 8 \times 4 \div 9 = 65$
($8 \times 4 \div 9$ gives the result in fractions. So, there is no need for further calculation as the result 65 is a whole number.)

B. $9 \div 8 \times 8 + 4 - 9 = 65$
$9 + 4 - 9$ *ie* $4 = 65$

C. $9 \div 8 + 8 \times 4 - 9 = 65$
($9 \div 8$ gives the result in fraction)

D. $9 \times 8 + 8 \div 4 - 9 = 65$
$72 + 2 - 9$ *ie* $65 = 65$

E. $9 + 8 \times 8 \div 4 - 9$
$9 + 16 - 9$ *ie* $16 = 65$

7. $32 + 8 \div 4 - 12 \times 4$
$32 + 2 - 48 = - 14$

8. $10 \times 2 + 5 - 5$
$20 + 5 - 5 = 20$

9. $8 \times 4 \div 16 + 8 \times 10$
$2 + 80 = 82$

10. What is given is a > b < c
The equations are :
A. b = c ≠ a which is wrong
B. b ≠ a < c which is wrong
C. a < b > c which is wrong
D. b < a > c which is correct
Therefore, *'d'* is the answer.

❀ ❀ ❀

4 Blood Relation

Coded relationships problem involves interpreting a given relationship—string which is coded in a particular way and then matching it with the relationship mentioned in the questions. The process of decoding each and every relation and then interpreting from the given relationship—string the final relationship is a cumbersome process and doing it for all the choices makes it very time consuming. However systematic representation and some clever common sense observations may give a speedy solution.

BLOOD RELATIONSHIPS

While attempting questions on blood relations, one should be clear of all the relation patterns that can exist between any two individuals. Very well-known relations are:

Mother	Father	Son
Daughter	Brother	Sister
Niece	Nephew	Uncle
Aunt	Husband	Wife
Grandmother	Grandfather	Grandson
Granddaughter	Brother-in-law	Sister-in-law
Father-in-law	Mother-in-law	Son-in-law
Daughter-in-law	Cousin	

The patterns of some relationships which help in solving questions in these tests are :

Father's or Mother's Father	– Grandfather (Paternal or Maternal)
Father's or Mother's Mother	– Grandmother (Paternal or Maternal)
Father's or Mother's Son	– Brother
Father's or Mother's Daughter	– Sister
Father's Brother	– Paternal Uncle
Father's Sister	– Paternal Aunt
Mother's Brother	– Maternal Uncle
Mother's Sister	– Maternal Aunt
Uncle or Aunt's Son or Daughter	– Cousin
Son's Wife	– Daughter-in-law
Daughter's Husband	– Son-in-law
Husband's or Wife's Brother	– Brother-in-law
Husband's or Wife's Sister	– Sister-in-law
Brother's Wife	– Sister-in-law
Sister's Husband	– Brother-in-law
Brother's Son	– Nephew
Brother's Daughter	– Niece

Example

1. R is the daughter of Q. M is the sister of B, who is the son of Q. How is M related to R?

A. Cousin B. Niece
C. Sister D. Aunt
E. None of these

Ans. C. B is the son of Q and R is the daughter of Q. This means M is sister of B and R.

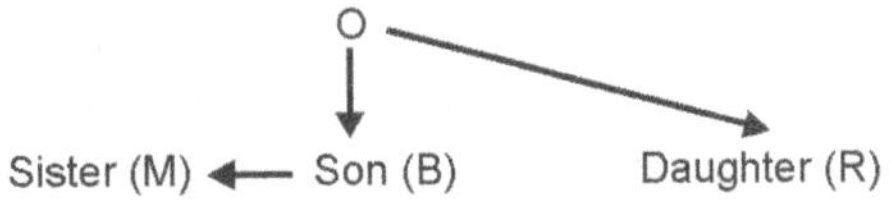

2. M is father of N. L is brother of M. P is mother of L. How is N related to P?

A. Grandson
B. Nephew
C. Granddaughter
D. Can't be determined
E. None of these

Ans. D. P is mother of L and M. N is child of M. Therefore, N is grandson or granddaughter of P.

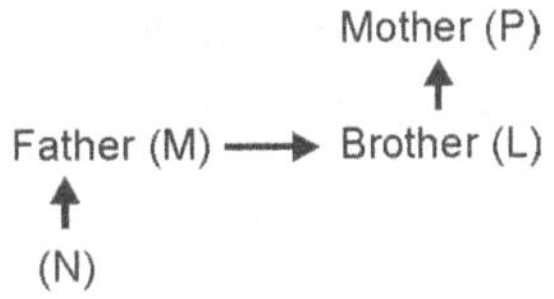

EXERCISE

1. Introducing a boy, a girl said, "He is the son of the daughter of the father of my uncle." How is the boy related to the girl?
   A. Brother B. Nephew
   C. Uncle D. Son-in-law
2. Pointing to a photograph of a boy Suresh said, "He is the son of the only son of my mother." How is Suresh related to that boy?
   A. Brother B. Uncle
   C. Cousin D. Father
3. If A + B means A is the brother of B; A – B means A is the sister of B and A × B means A is the father of B. Which of the following means that C is the son of M?
   A. M – N × C + F B. F – C + N × M
   C. N + M – F × C D. M × N – C + F
4. If A is the brother of B; B is the sister of C; and C is the father of D, how D is related to A?
   A. Brother
   B. Sister
   C. Nephew
   D. Cannot be determined
5. If A + B means A is the mother of B; A – B means A is the brother of B; A % B means A is the father of B and A × B means A is the sister of B, which of the following shows that P is the maternal uncle of Q?
   A. Q – N + M × P B. P + S × N – Q
   C. P – M + N × Q D. Q – S % P
6. Pointing to a photograph Lata says, "He is the son of the only son of my grandfather." How is the man in the photograph related to Lata?
   A. Brother B. Uncle
   C. Cousin D. Data is inadequate
7. If D is the brother of B, how B is related to C? To answer this question which of the statements is/are necessary?
   1. The son of D is the grandson of C.
   2. B is the sister of D.

   A. Only 1
   B. Only 2
   C. Either 1 or 2
   D. 1 and 2 both are required
8. Pointing to a photograph. Balram said, "He is the son of the only daughter of the father of my brother." How Balram is related to the man in the photograph?
   A. Nephew B. Brother
   C. Father D. Maternal Uncle
9. Pointing to a woman, Abhay said, "Her granddaughter is the only daughter of my brother." How is the woman related to Abhay?
   A. Sister B. Grandmother
   C. Mother-in-law D. Mother
10. If A + B means A is the sister of B; A × B means A is the wife of B, A % B means A is the father of B and A – B means A is the brother of B. Which of the following means T is the daughter of P?
    A. P × Q % R + S – T
    B. P × Q % R – T + S
    C. P × Q % R + T – S
    D. P × Q % R + S + T
11. Deepak said to Naresh, "That boy playing with the football is the younger of the two brothers of the daughter of my father's wife." How is the boy playing football related to Deepak?
    A. Son B. Brother
    C. Cousin D. Brother-in-law
12. Reena who is the sister-in-law of Ashok, is the daughter-in-law of Kalyani. Dheeraj is the father of Suresh who is the only brother of Ashok. How Kalyani is related to Ashok?
    A. Mother-in-law B. Aunt
    C. Wife D. None of these
13. A and B are children of M. Who is the father of A? To answer this question which of the statements 1 and 2 is necessary?
    1. C is the brother of A and the son of E.
    2. F is the mother B.

    A. Only 1 B. Only 2
    C. Either 1 or 2 D. 1 and 2 both

14. Anil said, "This girl is the wife of the grandson of my mother". How is Anil related to the girl?
A. Brother
B. Grandfather
C. Husband
D. Father-in-law

15. Pointing towards a man, a woman said, "His mother is the only daughter of my mother." How is the woman related to the man?
A. Mother B. Grandmother
C. Sister D. Daughter

16. If P $ Q means P is the brother of Q; P # Q means P is the mother of Q; P * Q means P is the daughter of Q in A # B $ C * D, who is the father?
A. D
B. B
C. C
D. Data is inadequate

17. Introducing Shalu, Aamir says, "She is the wife of only nephew of only brother of my mother." How Shalu is related to Aamir?
A. Wife
B. Sister
C. Sister-in-law
D. Data is inadequate

Directions (Qs. Nos. 18 and 19): *Read the following information to answer the questions:*
A + B means A is the father of B
A – B means A is the sister of B
A × B means A is the husband of B
A % B means A is the wife of B

18. Which of the following means 'T is the nephew of Q'?
A. Q × R – S + T
B. Q + R % S + T
C. Q – R % S + T
D. None of these

19. Which of the following means S is granddaughter of R?
A. R + P % Q + S
B. K % R + P × Q – L + S
C. K % R + P % Q + S – L
D. K % R + P % Q + S + L

20. If 'A + B' means 'A is brother of B', 'A – B' means 'A is sister of B', 'A × B' means 'A is wife of B' and 'A % B' means 'A is father of B', then which of the following indicates 'S is the son of P'?
A. P × Q % R + S – T
B. P × Q % S – R + T
C. P × Q % R – T + S
D. P × Q % R – S + T

ANSWERS

1	2	3	4	5	6	7	8	9	10
A	D	D	D	C	A	D	D	D	B
11	**12**	**13**	**14**	**15**	**16**	**17**	**18**	**19**	**20**
B	D	B	D	A	A	A	D	C	D

EXPLANATORY ANSWERS

1.
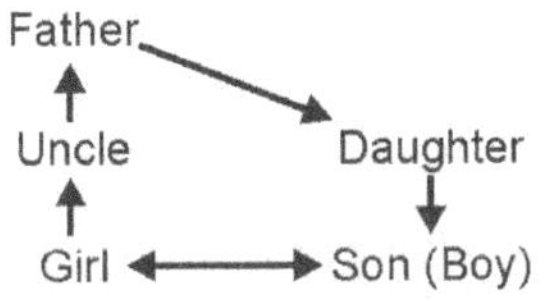

The father of the boy's uncle → the grandfather of the boy and daughter of the grandfather → sister of father.

2.
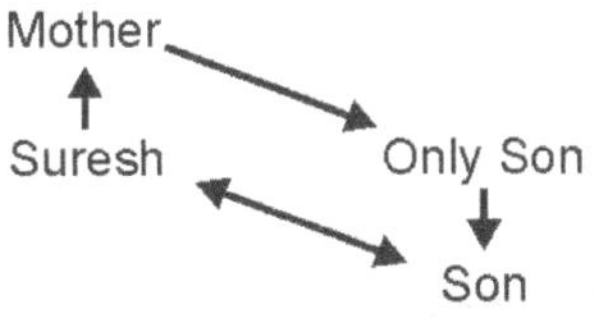

The boy in the photograph is the only son of the son of Suresh's mother *i.e.*, the son of Suresh. Hence, Suresh is the father of boy.

3. 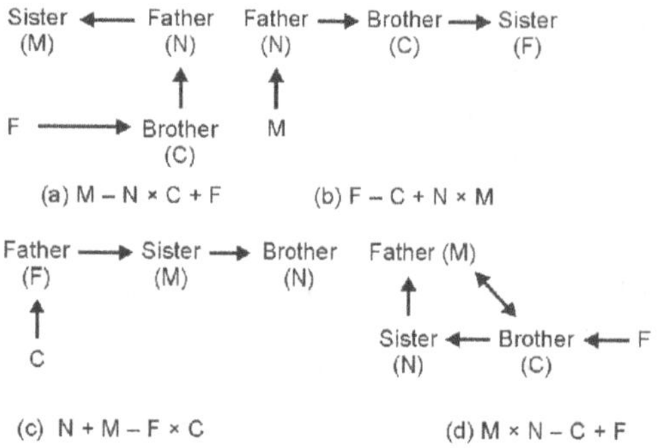

M × N → M is the father of N

N – C → N is the sister of C

and C + F → C is the brother of F.

Hence, M is the father of C or C is the son of M.

4. 

If D is Male, the answer is Nephew.

If D is Female, the answer is Niece.

As the sex of D is not known, hence, the relation between D and A cannot be determined.

Note: Niece - A daughter of one's brother or sister, or of one's brother-in-law or sister-in-law.

Nephew - A son of one's brother or sister, or of one's brother-in-law or sister-in-law.

5. 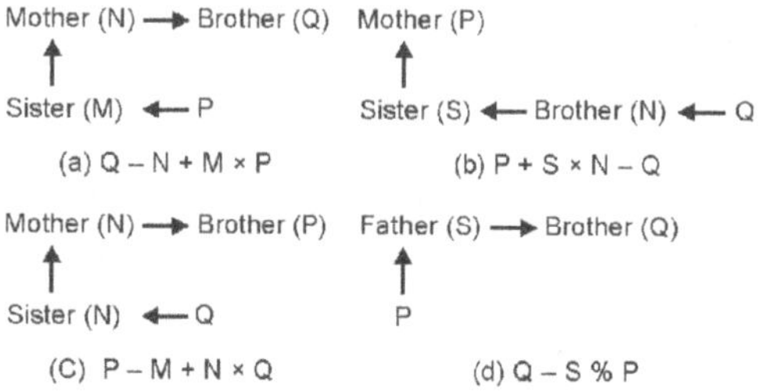

6. 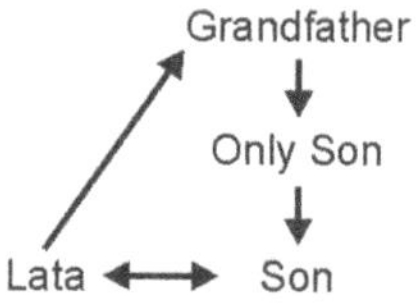

The man in the photograph is the son of the only son of Lata's grandfather *i.e.*, the man is the son of Lata's father. Hence, the man is the brother of Lata.

7. 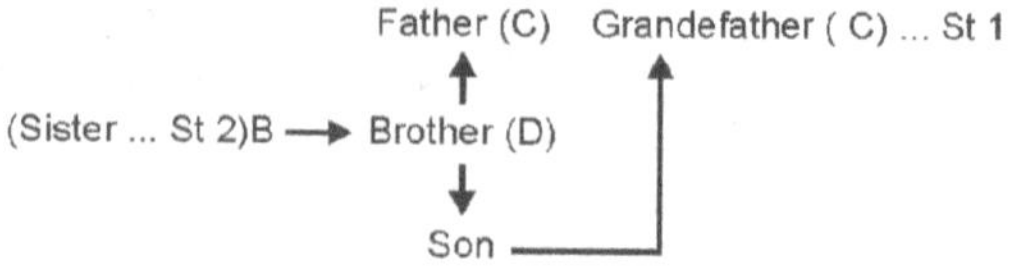

Given: D is the brother of B.

From statement 1, we can detect that D is son of C (son of D is the grandson of C).

From statement 2, we can detect that B is 'Female' (sister of D).

Therefore, B is daughter of C.

8. 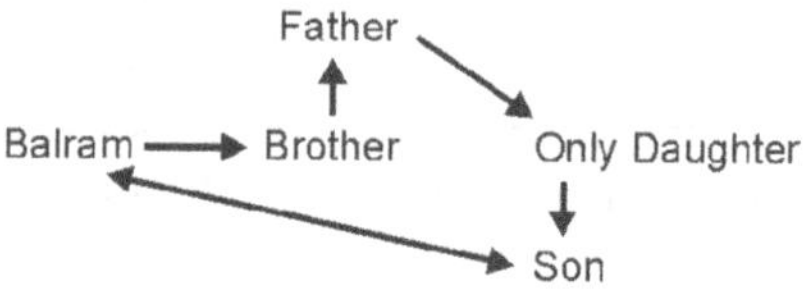

The man in the photograph is the son of the sister of Balram. Hence, Balram is the maternal uncle of the man in the photograph.

9. 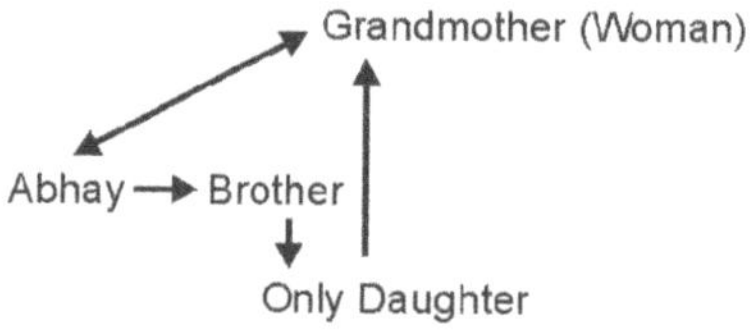

Daughter of Abhay's brother → niece of Abhay. Thus the granddaughter of the woman is Abhay's niece. Hence, the woman is the mother of Abhay.

10. We can note that sex of last person in each option will be unknown. Since T should be daughter of P so T will be definitely female in correct option. So options A and D are straightaway ruled out. Also in the correct option only '+' or '×' will follow T as T is definitely a female so option C is also ruled out.

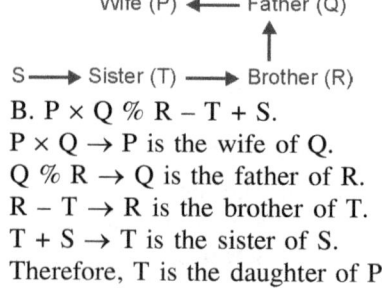

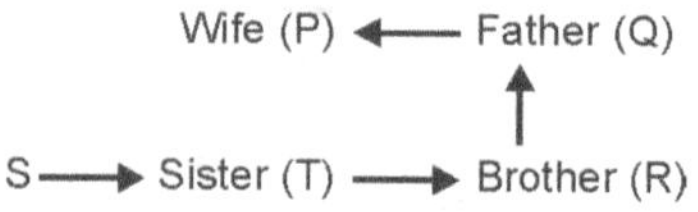

B. P × Q % R – T + S.

P × Q → P is the wife of Q.

Q % R → Q is the father of R.

R – T → R is the brother of T.

T + S → T is the sister of S.

Therefore, T is the daughter of P.

11. 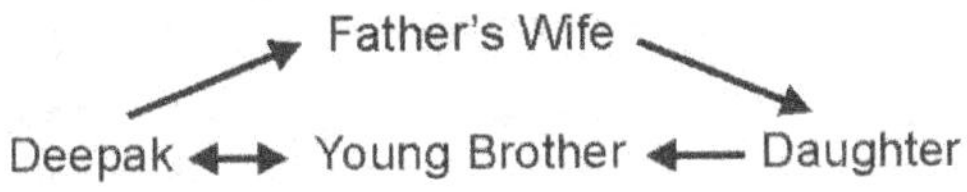

Father's wife → mother.
Hence, the daughter of the mother means sister and sister's younger brother means brother. Therefore, the boy is the brother of Deepak.

12. 

Ashok is the only brother of Suresh and Reena is the sister-in-law of Ashok. Hence, Reena is the wife of Suresh. Kalyani is the mother-in-law of Reena. Kalyani is the mother of Ashok.

13. 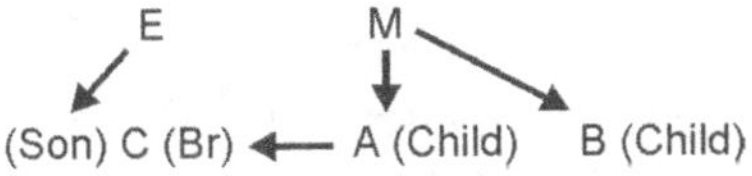

From main st. & st. 1

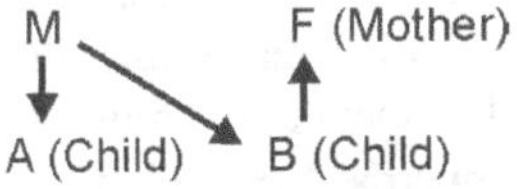

From main st. & st. 2
A and B are children of M. From 1, C is the brother B and son of E. Since, the sex of M and E are not known. Hence 1 is not sufficient to answer the question.
From 2. F is the mother of B. Hence, F is also the mother of A. Hence M is the father of A. Thus, 2 is sufficient to answer the question.

14. 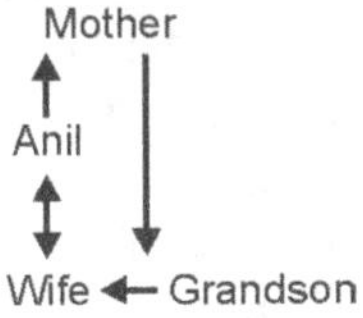

The girl is the wife of grandson of Anil's mother *i.e.*, the girl is the wife of son of Anil. Hence, Anil is the father-in-law of the girl.

15. 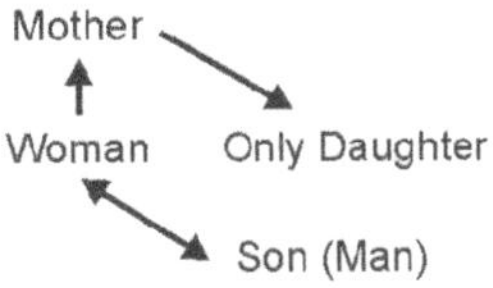

Only daughter of my mother → myself.
Hence, the woman is the mother of the man.

16. 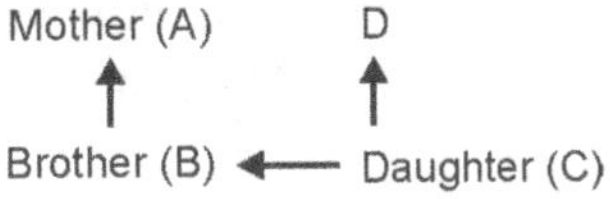

A is the mother of B, B is the brother of C and C is the daughter of D. Hence, D is the father.

17. 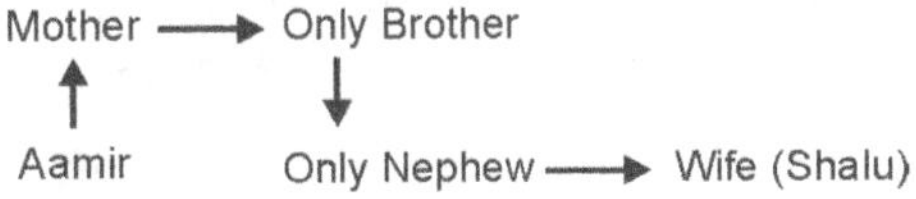

Brother of mother means maternal uncle. Hence only nephew of Aamir's maternal uncle means Aamir himself. Therefore Shalu is the wife of Aamir.

18. Since 'T is the nephew of Q' so 'T' must be a male but sex of 'T' cannot be established in any of the option.

19. Choice A, B is not correct as sex of S is not known. D is ruled out because S is a male here. Representation for choice C is as follows:

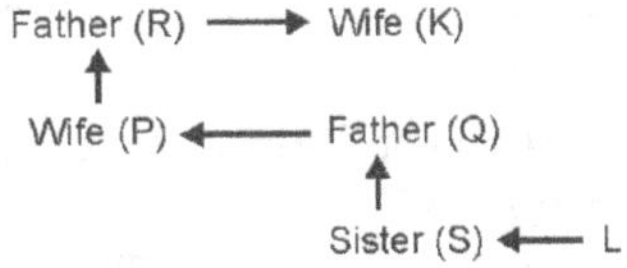

So, S is granddaughter of R is correct here.

20. As 'S' is female in option A and B, both are rejected directly. The sex of 'S' in option C is not known, hence it is also eliminated. Now, check option D.

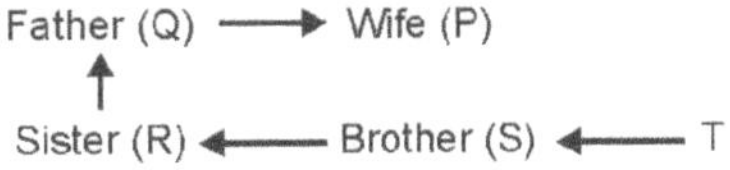

Clearly, S is son of P.

❀ ❀ ❀

5 Direction Sense

In these type of tests, the directions in questions needs to be perceived, Such questions are based on the direction chart.

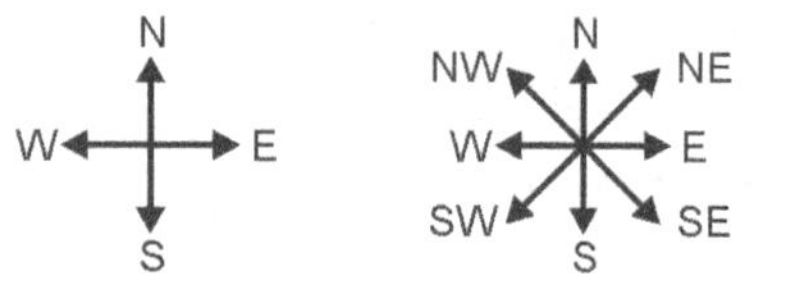

N = North, S = South, E = East, W = West

The sense of the different directions are guided by the left and righ turns or angular turns.

Example

1. Shobha was facing East. She walked 20 metres. Turning left she moved 15 metres and then turning right moved 25 metres. Finally, she turned right and moved 15 metres more. How far is she from her starting point?

(a) 25 metres
(b) 35 metres
(c) 50 metres
(d) 45 metres

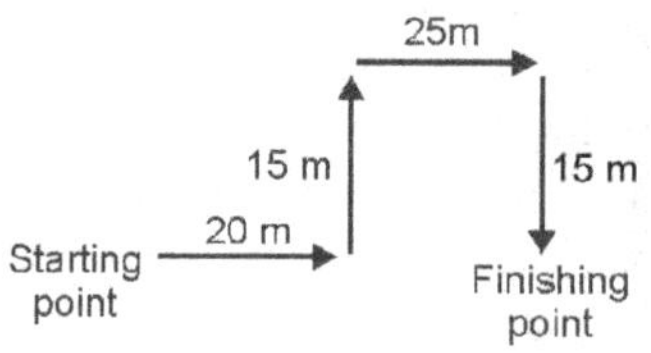

Ans.: Shobha turns left after walking 20 metres towards East. Now she walks 15 metres towards North. She turns right towards East again and walks 25 metres further. Finally turning right towards South, she walks 15 metres. The distance moved towards North and towards South is same, i.e., 15 metres. So, Shobha is 20 + 25 metres = 45 metres away from her starting point.

EXERCISE

1. One morning Urmilla and Vishal were talking to each other face to face at a crossing. If Vishal's shadow was exactly to the left of Urmilla, which direction was Urmilla facing?
A. East B. West
C. North D. South

2. If South-East becomes North, North-East becomes West and so on. What will West become?
A. North - East B. North - West
C. South - East D. South - West

3. Ravi put his timepiece on the table in such a way that at 6 P.M. hour hand points to North. In which direction the minute hand will point at 9.15 P.M. ?
A. South - East B. South
C. North D. West

4. Rakesh walked 20 m towards north. Then he turned right and walks 30 m. Then he turns right and walks 35 m. Then he turns left and walks 15 m. Finally he turns left and walks 15 m. In which direction and how many metres is he from the starting position?
A. 15 m West B. 30 m East
C. 30 m West D. 45 m East

5. Starting from the point X, John walked 15 m towards west. He turned left and walked 20 m. He then turned left and walked 15 m. After this he turned to his right and walked 12 m.

How far and in which directions is now John from X?

A. 32 m, South B. 47 m, East

C. 42 m, North D. 27 m, South

6. Suman is 40 metres South – West of Ashok, Prakash is 40 metres South – East of Ashok. Prakash is in which direction of Suman?

A. South B. West

C. East D. North – East

7. Vijayan started walking towards South. After walking 15 metres he turned to the left and walked 15 metres. He again turned to his left and walked 15 metres. How far is he from his original position and in which direction?

A. 15 metres, North

B. 15 metres, East

C. 30 metres, South

D. 15 metres, West

Directions (8 to 10): *Each of the following questions is based on the following information:*

1. P # Q means B is at 1 metre to the right of P.
2. P $ Q means B is at 1 metre to the North of P.
3. P * Q means B is at 1 metre to the left of P.
4. P @ Q means B is at 1 metre to the south of P.
5. In each question first person from the left is facing North.

8. According to X @ B * P, P is in which direction with respect to X?

A. North B. South

C. North - East D. South-West

9. According to M # N $ T, T is in which direction with respect to M?

A. North-West B. North-East

C. South-West D. South-East

10. According to P # R $ A * U, in which direction is U with respect to P?

A. East B. West

C. North D. South

Directions (Qs. 11 to 15): *P, Q, R and S are standing on four corners of a square piece of plot as shown in the given figure. They start moving, and the movements are explained in each of the questions. Read the question and select the right alternative.*

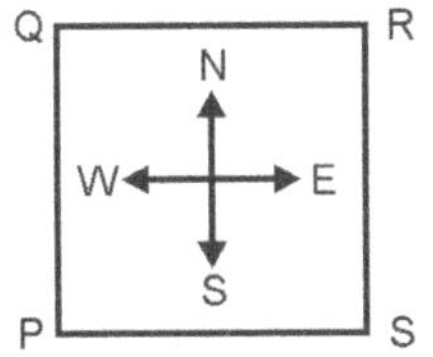

11. P, Q , R and S walk diagonally to opposite corners and from there Q and R walk one and a half sides anti-clockwise while P and S walk one side clockwise along the sides. Where is S now?

A. At the North – West corner

B. At the North -East

C. At the South – West corner

D. None of these

12. Q travelled straight to R, a distance of 10 m. He turned right and walked 7 m towards S, again he turned right and walked 8 m, and then finally turned right and walked 7m. How far is he from his original position?

A. 7 m B. 8 m

C. 2m D. 3m

13. From the original position, S starts crossing the field diagonally. After walking half the distance he turns right; walks some distance and turns left. Which direction is S facing now?

A. South - East B. North - West

C. South - West D. North

14. P and S walk one and a half length of the side clockwise and anti-clockwise respectively. Which one of the following statements is true?

A. P is at midpoint between Q and R and S at the corner originally occupied by P

B. P and S are both at the midpoint between R and S

C. P and S are both at the midpoint between Q and R.

D. S is at midpoint between Q and R and P is at the midpoint between original side of R and S

15. P, Q, R and S walk one and a half sides clockwise. Who is on the left of Q if he is facing West?

A. P B. R

C. S D. No one

ANSWERS

1	2	3	4	5	6	7	8	9	10
C	C	D	D	A	C	B	D	B	C
11	**12**	**13**	**14**	**15**					
B	C	B	C	B					

EXPLANATORY ANSWERS

1.

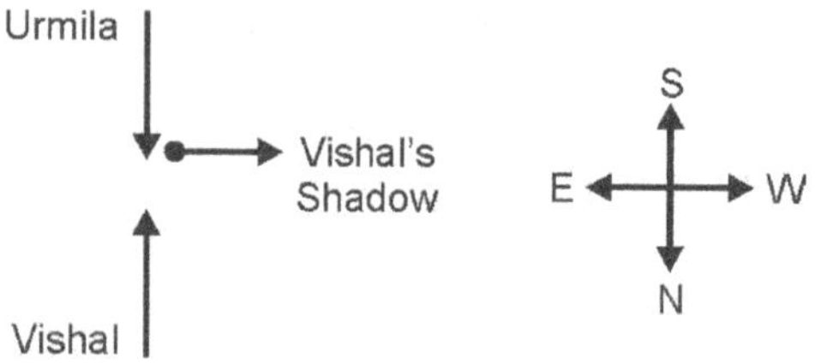

2.

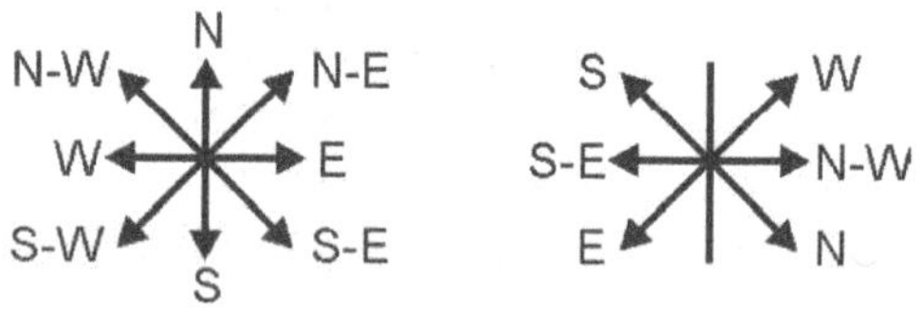

It is clear from the diagrams that new name of West will become South-East.

3.

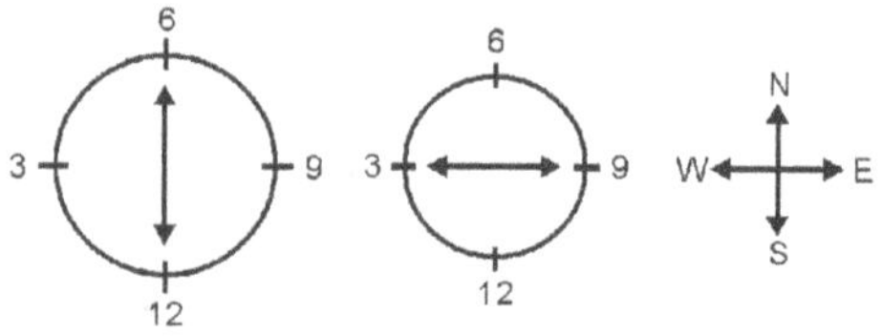

At 9.15 P.M., the minute hand will point towards west.

4.

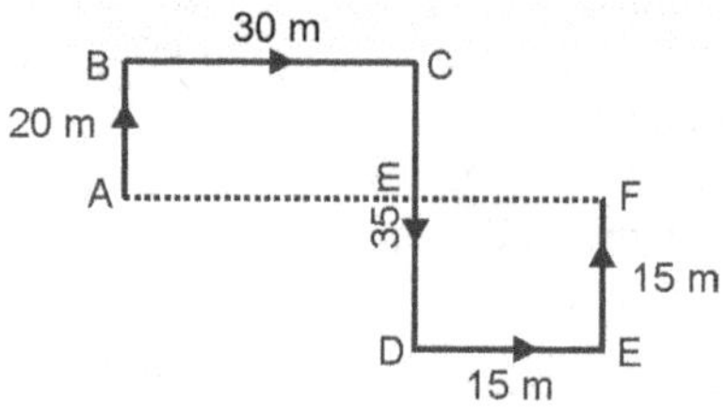

Required distance = AF = 30 + 15 = 45 m. From the above figure, F is in East direction from A. So the answer is '45 m East'.

5.

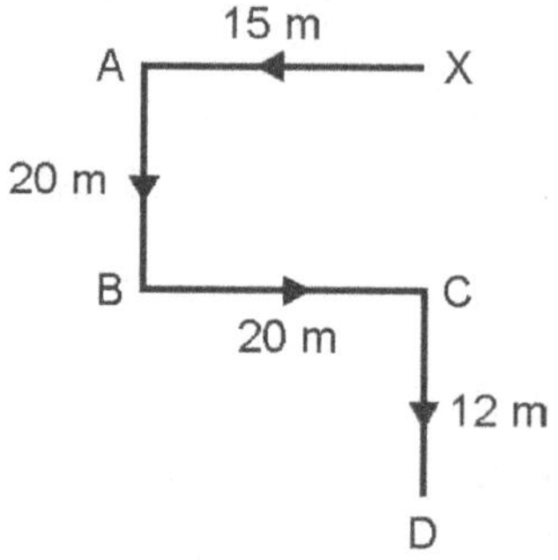

Required distance = 20 + 12 = 32 m South.

6.

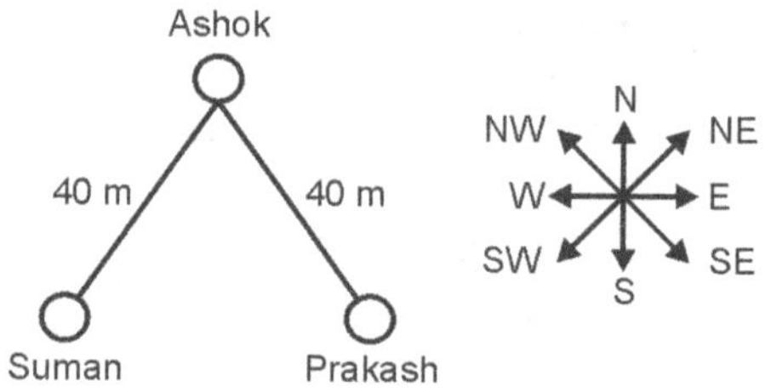

7.

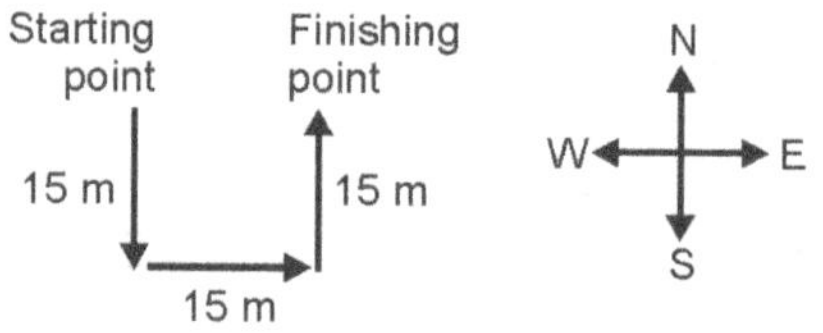

8. According to X @ B * Y

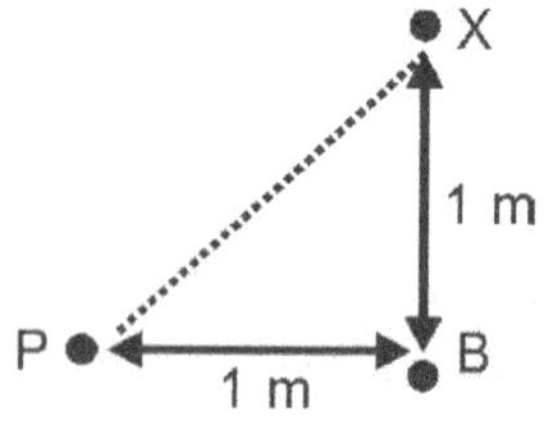

Hence, P is in South-West of X.

9. According to M # N $ T

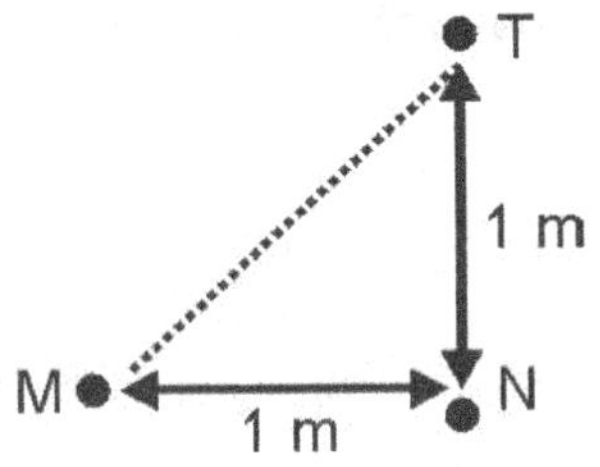

Hence, T is in the North-East of M.

10. According to P # R $ A * U

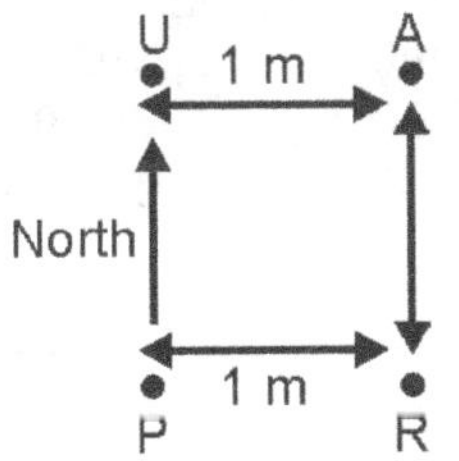

Hence, U is in North direction with respect to P.

11.

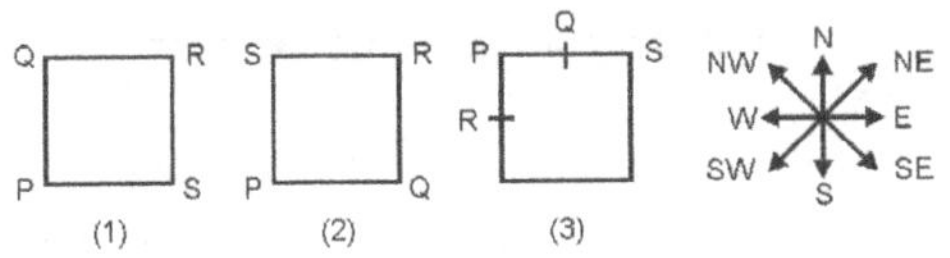

12. (10 m – 8 m = 2 m)

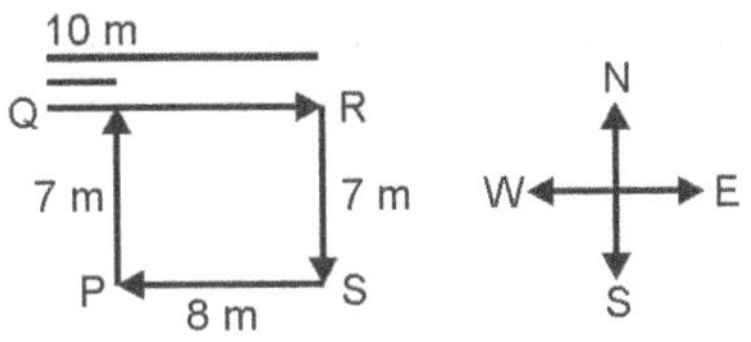

13.

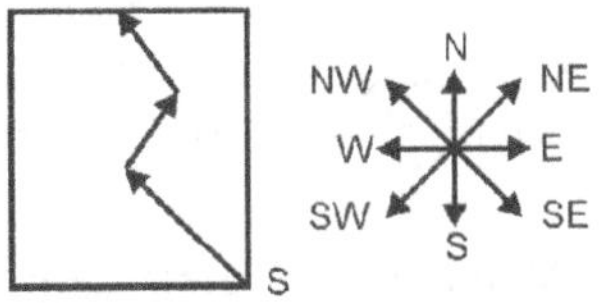

14. The movements are :

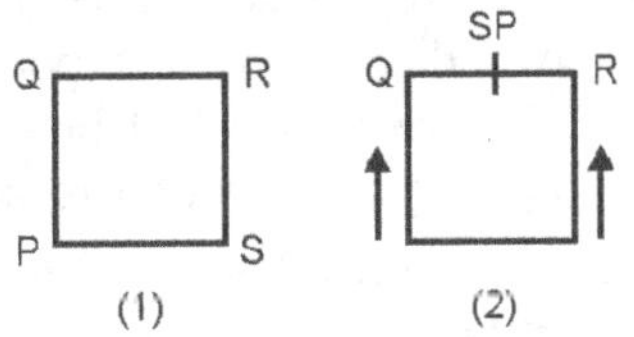

15.

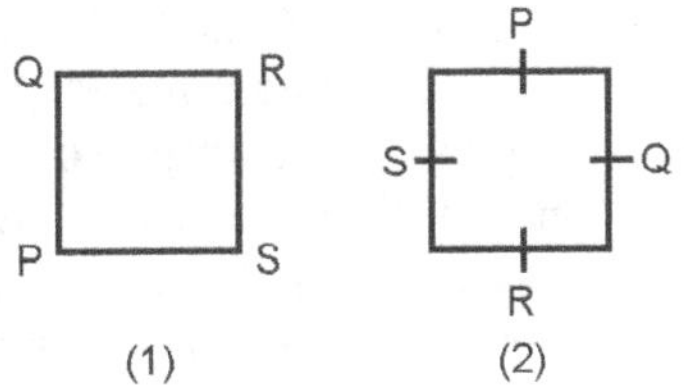

❀ ❀ ❀

6 Statement Analysis

In these questions, a series of interlinked information or data is given. Quantitatively analysis of given information or data provides certain conclusions.

In Statement Analysis (Problem Solving) questions, all given information has to be interpreted and arranged step-by-step. One should be careful that no given data is left incorporated. A brief glimpse to all questions asked on given data is helpful in preparing the solution format.

Directions: *Read the following information carefully and answer the questions given below:*

In a family of six persons—A, B, C, D, E and F—there are three males and three females. There are two married couples and two persons are unmarried. Each one of them reads different newspapers, viz. Times of India, Indian Express, Hindustan Times, Financial Times, Navbharat Times and Business Standard. E, who reads Indian Express, is mother-in-law of A, who is wife of C. D is the father of F and he does not read Times of India or Business Standard. B reads Navbharat Times and is the sister of F, who reads Hindustan Times. C does not read Business Standard.

1. Who among the following reads the Times of India?
A. C B. D
C. A D. Data inadequate
E. None of these

2. How is F related to E?
A. Daughter B. Brother
C. Son D. Data inadequate
E. None of these

3. Which of the following is one of the married couples?
A. D-B B. D-E
C. B-F D. E-F
E. None of these

4. Which of the following newspapers is read by 'A'?
A. Times of India B. Navbharat Times
C. Financial Times D. Data inadequate
E. None of these

5. How many sons does E have?
A. Four B. Three
C. Two D. One
E. None of these

Following is the detail presentation of mental approach for solution of the given problem. In practice these questions are solved briefly.

E, who reads Indian Express, is mother-in-law of A, who is the wife of C

Person	Newspaper read	Sex	Information/Reasons
A		Fe	A-C Couple
B			
C		M	A is the wife of C
D			
E	I.E	Fe	mother-in-law of A
F			

D is the father of F and he does not read TOI or B.S

Person	Newspaper read	Sex	Information/Reasons
A		Fe	A-C Couple
B			
C		M	A is the wife of C
D	H.T or F.T or N.T	M	father of F, (TOI, B.S,I.E- not)
E	I.E	Fe	mother-in-law of A

As there are two married couples. This implies that D and E are couples. B reads N.T and is the sister of F, who reads H.T. C does not read B.S

Person	Newspaper read	Sex	Information/Reasons
A	B.S	Fe	A-C Couple
B	N.T	Fe	Sister of F
C	TOI	M	B.S -no
D	F.T	M	father of F
E	I.E	Fe	D-E, Couple
F	H.T	M	There are 3 males- 3 females

E is mother in law of A and A is wife of C implies C is Son of E. D is father of F and D-E are couples implies F is Son of E.

1. A **2.** C **3.** B **4.** E **5.** C

EXERCISE

Directions (Qs. Nos. 1 to 4): *Read the following information carefully and answer the questions given below:*

1. There are five types of cards viz. A, B, C, D and E. There are three cards of each type. These are to be inserted in envelopes of three colours—red, yellow and brown. There are five envelopes of each colour.
2. B, D and E type cards are to be inserted in red envelopes; A, B and C type cards are to be inserted in yellow envelopes; and C, D and E type cards are to be inserted in brown envelopes.
3. Two cards each of B and D type are inserted in red envelopes.

1. How many cards of E type are inserted in brown envelopes?

A. Nil B. One
C. Two D. Three
E. Data inadequate

2. Which of the following combinations of the type of cards and the number of cards is **definitely correct** in respect of yellow-coloured envelopes?

A. A-2, B-1, C-2 B. B-1, C-2, D-2
C. A-2, E-1, D-2 D. A-3, B-1, C-1
E. None of these

3. Which of the following combinations of types of cards and the number of cards and colour of envelope is **definitely correct**?

A. C-2, D-1, E-2, Brown
B. C-1, D-2, E-2, Brown
C. B-2, D-2, A-1, Red
D. A-2, B-2, C-1, Yellow
E. None of these

4. Which of the following combinations of colour of the envelope and the number of cards is **definitely correct** in respect of E type cards?

A. Red-2, Brown-1
B. Red-1, Yellow-2
C. Red-2, Yellow-1
D. Yellow-1, Brown-2
E. None of these

Directions (Qs. Nos. 5 to 7): *Read the following information carefully and answer the questions given below:*

Six persons A, B, C, D, E and F took up a job with a firm in a week from Monday to Saturday. Each of them joined for different posts on different days. The posts were of–Clerk, Officer, Technician, Manager, Supervisor, and Sales Executive, though not respectively. F joined as a Manager on the first day. B joined as a Supervisor but neither on Wednesday nor Friday. D joined as a Technician on Thursday. Officer joined the firm on Wednesday. E joined as a clerk on Tuesday. A joined as a Sales Executive.

5. Who joined the firm on Wednesday?
A. B B. C
C. B or C D. Data inadequate
E. None of these

6. Who was the last person to join the firm?
A. E B. F
C. A D. B
E. None of these

7. On which of the following days did the Sales Executive join?
A. Tuesday B. Thursday
C. Saturday D. Wednesday
E. None of these

Directions (Qs. Nos. 8 to 11): *Read the following information carefully and answer the questions given below:*

(*a*) An examination board has organised examination for ten s ubjects viz. A, B, C, D, E, F, G, H, I and J on six days of the week with a holiday on Sunday, not having more than two papers on any of the days.
(*b*) Exam begins on Wednesday with subject F.
(*c*) D is accompained by some other subject but not on Thursday. A and G are on the same day immediately after holiday.
(*d*) There is only one paper on last day and Saturday. B is immediately followed by H, which is immediately followed by I.
(*e*) C is on Saturday. H is not on the same day as J.

8. Examination for which of the following pairs of subjects is on Thursday?
A. HE B. DB
C. FD D. Data inadequate
E. None of these

9. Examination for which of the following subjects is on the next day of D?
A. B (2) C
C. I D. H
E. None of these

10. Examination for which of the following subjects is on the last day?
A. B B. E
C. J D. Data inadequate
E. None of these

11. Examination for subject F is on the same day as which of the following subjects?
A. E (2) D
C. I D. B
E. None of these

Directions (Qs. Nos. 12 to 16): *Study the following information to answer the given questions:*

P, Q, R, S, T, V, W and Z are travelling to three destinations Delhi, Chennai and Hyderabad in three different vehicles Honda City, Swift D'Zire and Ford Ikon. There are three females among them one in each car. There are atleast two persons in each car. R is not travelling with Q and W. T , a male, is travelling with only Z and they are not travelling to Chennai. P is travelling in Honda City to Hyderabad. S is sister of P and travels by Ford Ikon. V and R travel together. W does not travel to Chennai.

12. Who is travelling with W?
A. Only Q
B. Only P
C. Both P and Q
D. Cannot be determined
E. None of these

13. Members in which of the following combinations are travelling in Honda City?

A. PRS B. PQW
C. PWS D. Data inadequate
E. None of these

14. In which car are four members travelling?

A. None
B. Honda City
C. Swift D'zire
D. Ford Ikon
E. Honda City or Ford Ikon

15. Which of the following combinations represents the three female members?

A. QSZ
B. WSZ
C. PSZ
D. Cannot be determined
E. None of these

16. Members in which car are travelling To Chennai?

A. Honda City
B. Swift D'Zire
C. Ford Ikon
D. Either Swift D'Zire or Ford Ikon
E. None of the above

Directions (Qs. 17-23): *Each problem consists of three statements. Based on the first two statements, the third statement may be true, false, or uncertain.*

17. (i) Tanya is older than Easha.
(ii) Celina is older than Tanya.
(iii) Easha is older than Celina.

If the first two statements are true, the third statement is

A. True B. False
C. Uncertain D. None of these

18. (i) Blueberries cost more than strawberries.
(ii) Blueberries cost less than raspberries.
(iii) Raspberries cost more than both strawberries and blueberries.

If the first two statements are true, the third statement is

A. True B. False
C. Uncertain D. None of these

19. (i) Maria runs faster than Gail.
(ii) Lily runs faster than Maria.
(iii) Gail runs faster than Lily.

If the first two statements are true, the third statement is

A. True B. False
C. Uncertain D. None of these

20. (i) A fruit basket contains more apples than mangoes.
(ii) There are more mangoes in the basket than there are oranges.
(iii) The basket contains more apples than oranges.

If the first two statements are true, the third statement is

A. True B. False
C. Uncertain D. None of these

21. (i) Jullie is younger than Katrina.
(ii) Maya was born after Jullie.
(iii) Katrina is older than Maya.

If the first two statements are true, the third statement is

A. True B. False
C. Uncertain D. None of these

22. (i) The temperature on Monday was lower than on Tuesday.
(ii) The temperature on Wednesday was lower than on Tuesday.
(iii) The temperature on Monday was higher than on Wednesday.

If the first two statements are true, the third statement is

A. True B. False
C. Uncertain D. None of these

23. (i) All Lamels are Signots with buttons.
(ii) No blue Signots have buttons.
(iii) No Lamels are blue.

If the first two statements are true, the third statement is

A. True
B. False
C. Uncertain
D. None of these

ANSWERS

1	**2**	**3**	**4**	**5**	**6**	**7**	**8**	**9**	**10**
C	D	A	E	B	D	E	A	B	C
11	**12**	**13**	**14**	**15**	**16**	**17**	**18**	**19**	**20**
D	C	B	A	D	C	B	A	B	C
21	**22**	**23**							
A	C	A							

EXPLANATORY ANSWERS

Solution (1-4): From (2), Out of fifteen cards nine cards will be inserted as following:

Red envelope	Yellow envelope	Brown envelope
B	A	C
D	B	D
E	C	E

From (3) and using the above table, we get

Red envelope	Yellow envelope	Brown envelope
B(2)	A	C
D(2)	B(1)	D(1)
E(1)	C	E(2)

The digits in brackets shows the no. of cards. Now, From (1), it is clear that each colour of envelope contains five cards, so there are two cards of C-type in brown envelope. Hence the remaining one card of C-type is in yellow envelope. Hence all the three A-type are in yellow envelope.

4. Brown-2, Red-1.

Solution (5-7): Summarising the given information in tabular form, we get

Person	Posts	Days
F	Manager	Monday
B	Supervisor	*Saturday*
D	Technician	Thursday
C	Officer	Wednesday
E	Clerk	Tuesday
A	Sales Executive	*Friday*

The places of italized letter/words is the last left one and can be filled easily by fulfilling all other given conditions.

Solution (8-11):

Wed	Thu	Fri	Sat	Sun	Mon	Tue
F, B	H, E	I, D	C	Hol	A, G	J

12-16: T(m) Z(f) Swift D'Zire Delhi
QWP Honda City Hyderabad
V(m)R(m)S(f) Ford Ikon Chennai.

17. Because the first two statements are true, Easha is the youngest of the three, so the third statement must be false.

18. Because the first two statements are true, raspberries are the most expensive of the three.

19. We know from the first two statements that Lily runs fastest. Therefore, the third statement must be false.

20. There are fewer oranges than either apples or mangoes, so the statement is true. (another approach)

1. A fruit basket contains more apples than mangoes = App > Mang.
2. There are more mangoes in the basket than there are oranges = Mang > Org
   Now, Combine the above two results: App > Mang > Org.
3. The basket contains more apples than oranges (App > ... > Org) = Yes.

Therefore, the given 3rd statement is true.

21. Jullie is younger than Katrina and older than Maya, so Maya must be younger than Katrina.

22. We know from the first two statements that Tuesday had the highest temperature, but we cannot know whether Monday's temperature was higher than Tuesday's.

23. We know that there are Signots with buttons, or Lamels, and that there are blue Signots, which have no buttons. Therefore, Lamels do not have buttons and cannot be blue.

❀ ❀ ❀

7 Sitting Arrangement

Sitting arrangement around circle: Nowadays in some competitive exams problems based on sitting arrangement around circle is frequently asked. These questions appear very simple but are not a cakewalk and are often solved wrongly. Main confusing point is deciding between left hand side and right hand side of a person when all persons are sitting around a circle facing centre. Because the left hand side of a person in lower semicircle is right hand side of a person in upper semicircle. This confusion is not met when these problems are solved by numbered line method. In numbered line method all members are first placed on a numbered line numbered up to total number of persons starting from one. For extreme end members line is assumed to be continued with other extreme member as immediate neighbour. Right hand side or left hand side confusion is by passed in this method. Following solved problems will make the method very clear.

Example

Directions (Qs. Nos. 1 to 6): *Study the following information carefully and answer the questions given below:*

P, Q, R, S, T, V, W and Z are sitting around a circle facing at the centre. R is fourth to the left of P who is second to the right of S. V is fourth to the right of S. Q is fourth to the left of W who is not an immediate neighbour of P or S. Z is not an immediate neighbour of R.

1. Who is to the immediate right of V?

A. R B. W
C. Z D. Data inadequate
E. None of these

2. Who is to the immediate right of R?

A. T B. S
C. W D. Data inadequate
E. None of these

3. Who is second to the left of Z?

A. Q B. V
C. S D. W
E. None of these

4. In which of the following pairs is the first person sitting to the immediate right of the second person?

A. VW B. RT
C. WR D. QP
E. ZP

5. Which of the following pairs are the immediate neighbours of Z?

A. WQ B. VQ
C. WP D. VP
E. None of these

6. Who is third to the right of R?

A. P B. S
C. Q D. Data inadequate
E. None of these

Solution (1-6):

(a) R is fourth to the left of P who is second to the right of S.
(b) V is fourth to the right of S.
(c) Q is fourh to the left of W who is not an immediate neighbour of P or S.
(d) Z is not an immediate neighbour of R.

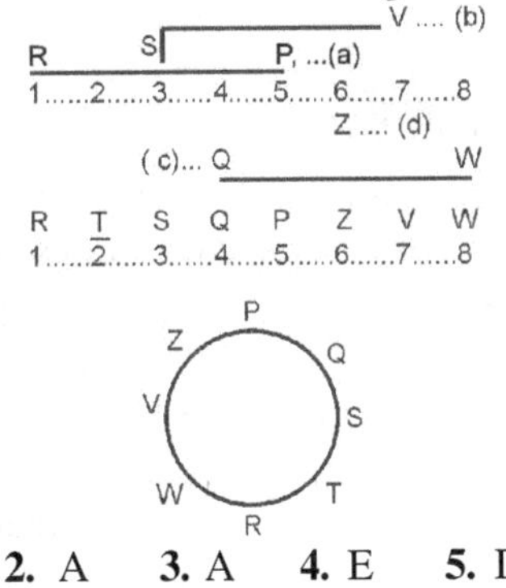

1. B **2.** A **3.** A **4.** E **5.** D **6.** C

EXERCISE

Directions (Qs. Nos. 1 to 5): *Study the following information carefully and answer the questions given below:*

M, P, J, B, R, T and F are sitting around a circle facing at the centre. B is third to the left of J who is second to the left of M. P is third to the left of B and second to the right of R. T is not an immediate neighbour of M.

1. Who is fourth to the right of M?
A. B
B. T
C. J
D. Data inadequate
E. None of these

2. Who is second to the left of T?
A. F
B. M
C. P
D. J
E. Data inadequate

3. In which of the following pairs the second person is sitting to the immediate right of the first person?
A. JR
B. PJ
C. TR
D. MP
E. None of these

4. What is F's position with respect to R?
A. Third to the left
B. Fourth to the right
C. Third to the right
D. Both A and B
E. None of these

5. Who is third to the right of B?
A. R
B. J
C. M
D. Data inadequate
E. None of these

Directions (Qs. Nos. 6 to 10): *Study the following information to answer the given questions:*

Representatives from eight different Banks viz. A, B, C, D, E, F, G and H are sitting around a circular table facing the centre but not necessarily in the same order. Each one of them is from a different Bank viz. UCO Bank, Oriental Bank of Commerce, Bank of Maharashtra, Canara Bank, Syndicate Bank, Punjab National Bank, Bank of India and Dena Bank. F sits second to right of the representative from Canara Bank. Representative from Bank of India is an immediate neighbour of the representative from Canara Bank. Two people sit between the representative of Bank of India and B. C and E are immediate neighbours of each other. Neither C nor E is an immediate neighbour of either B or the representative from Canara Bank. Representative from Bank of Maharashtra sits second to right of D. D is neither the representative of Canara Bank nor Bank of India. G and the representative from UCO Bank are immediate neighbours of each other. B is not the representative of UCO Bank. Only one person sits between C and the representative from Oriental Bank of Commerce. H sits third to left of the representative from Dena Bank. Representative from Punjab National Bank sits second to left of the representative from Syndicate Bank.

6. Who amongst the following sit exactly between B and the representative from Bank of India?
A. A and the representative from UCO Bank
B. F and G
C. H and the representative from Bank of Maharashtra
D. H and G
E. Representatives from Syndicate Bank and Oriental Bank of Commerce

7. Who amongst the following is the representative from Oriental Bank of Commerce?
A. A
B. C
C. H
D. G
E. D

8. Four of the following five are alike in a certain way based on the given arrangement and thus form a group. Which is the one that does not belong to that group?
A. H – UCO Bank
B. A – Canara Bank
C. D – Bank of Maharashtra
D. E – Syndicate Bank
E. F – Punjab National Bank

9. Who amongst the following sits second to left of B?
A. C
B. H
C. The representative from Canara Bank
D. The representative from Punjab National Bank
E. G

10. Which of the following is true with respect to the given sitting arrangement?
A. B is the representative from Bank of Maharashtra
B. C sits second to right of H
C. The representative from Dena Bank sits to the immediate left of the representative from UCO Bank
D. A sits second to right of the representative from Bank of India
E. The representatives from Bank of Maharashtra and Syndicate Bank are immediate neighbours of each other

Directions (Qs. Nos. 11 to 14): *Six friends P, Q, R, S, T and U are sitting around the hexagonal table each at one corner and are facing the centre of the hexagonal. P is second to the left of U. Q is neighbour of R and S. T is second to the left of S.*

11. Which one is sitting opposite to P?
A. R B. Q
C. T D. S

12. Who is the fourth person to the left of Q?
A. P
B. U
C. R
D. Data inadequate

13. Which of the following are the neighbours of P?
A. U and P
B. T and R
C. U and R
D. Data inadequate

14. Which one is sitting opposite to T?
A. R
B. Q
C. Cannot be determined
D. S

Direction (Qs. Nos. 15 and 16): *Five girls are sitting on a bench to be photographed. Seema is to the left of Rani and to the right of Bindu. Mary is to the right of Rani. Reeta is between Rani and Mary.*

15. Who is sitting immediate right to Reeta?
A. Bindu B. Rani
C. Mary D. Seema

16. Who is in the middle of the photograph?
A. Seema B. Rani
C. Reeta D. Seema

Directions (Qs. Nos. 17 to 20) : *In a class there are seven students (including boys and girls) A, B, C, D, E, F and G. They sit on three benches I, II and III. Such that at least two students on each bench and at least one girl on each bench. C who is a girl student, does not sit with A, E and D. F a boy student sits with only B. A boyfriend of D sits on the bench I with his best friends. G sits on the bench III. E is the brother of C.*

17. How many girls are there out of these 7 students?
A. 3 B. 3 or 4
C. 4 D. Data inadequate

18. Which of the following is the group of girls?
A. BAC B. BFC
C. BCD D. CDF

19. Who sits with C?
A. B B. D
C. G D. E

20. On which bench there are three students?
A. Bench I B. Bench II
C. Bench III D. Bench I or II

Directions (Qs. Nos. 21 to 25): *In an Exhibition seven cars of different companies—Tata, Ambassador, Fiat, Maruti, Mercedes, Bedford and Fargo are standing facing to east in the following order.*

I. Tata is next to right of Fargo.
II. Fargo is fourth to the right of Fiat.
III. Maruti car is between Ambassador and Bedford.
IV. Fiat which is third to the left of Ambassador, is at one end.

21. Which of the cars are on both the sides of Tata car?
A. Ambassador and Maruti
B. Maruti and Fiat
C. Fargo and Mercedes
D. Ambassador and Fargo

22. Which of the following statement is correct?
A. Maruti is next left of Ambassador.
B. Bedford is next left of Fiat.
C. Bedford is at one end.
D. Fiat is next second to the right of Maruti.

23. Which one of the following statements is correct?
A. Fargo car is in between Ambassador and Fiat.
B. Tata is next left to Mercedes car.
C. Fargo is next right of Tata.
D. Maruti is fourth right of Mercedes.

24. Which of the following groups of cars is to the right of Ambassador?
A. Tata, Fargo and Maruti
B. Mercedes, Tata and Fargo
C. Maruti, Bedford and Fiat
D. Bedford, Tata and Fargo

25. Which one of the following is the correct position of Mercedes?
A. Next to the left of Tata
B. Next to the left of Bedford
C. Fourth to the right of Maruti
D. Fourth to the right of Maruti

ANSWERS

1	**2**	**3**	**4**	**5**	**6**	**7**	**8**	**9**	**10**
E	A	C	D	B	C	E	B	D	E
11	**12**	**13**	**14**	**15**	**16**	**17**	**18**	**19**	**20**
D	A	B	B	C	B	A	C	C	A
21	**22**	**23**	**24**	**25**					
C	A	B	B	D					

EXPLANATORY ANSWERS

1-5: (a) B is third to the left of J who is second to the left of M.
(b) P is third to the left of B and second to the right of R.
(c) T is not an immediate neighbour of M.

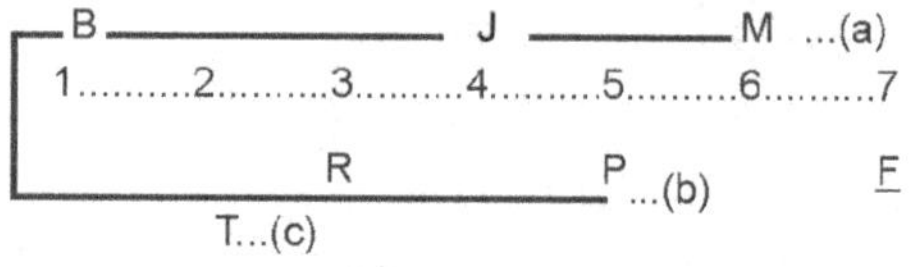

B T R J P M F
1..........2..........3..........4..........5..........6..........7

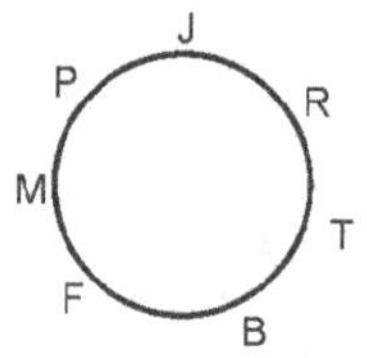

6-10:

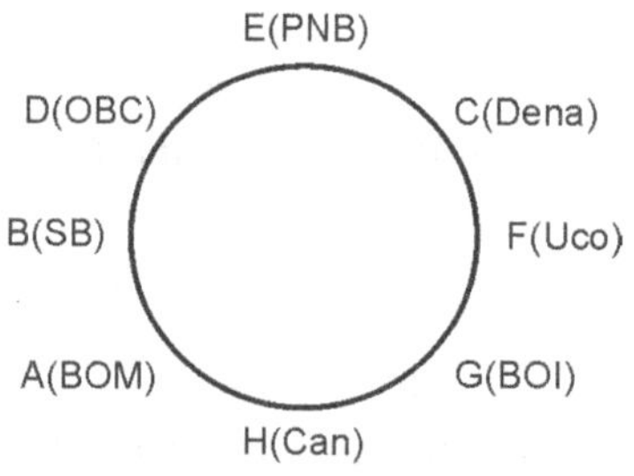

11-14:

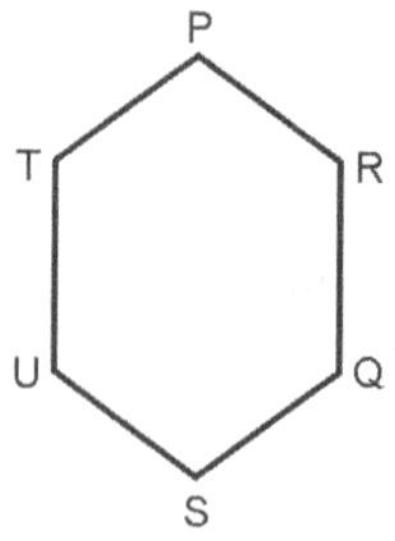

15-16:

Bindu Seema Rani Reeta Mary

17-20:

Bench I	A	E	Ⓓ
Bench II	F	Ⓑ	☐ Boy
Bench III	G	Ⓒ	◯ Girl

21-25:

→ Fiat

→ Bedford

→ Maruti

→ Ambassador W ← + → E

→ Fargo

→ Tata

→ Mercedes

N / S

❀ ❀ ❀

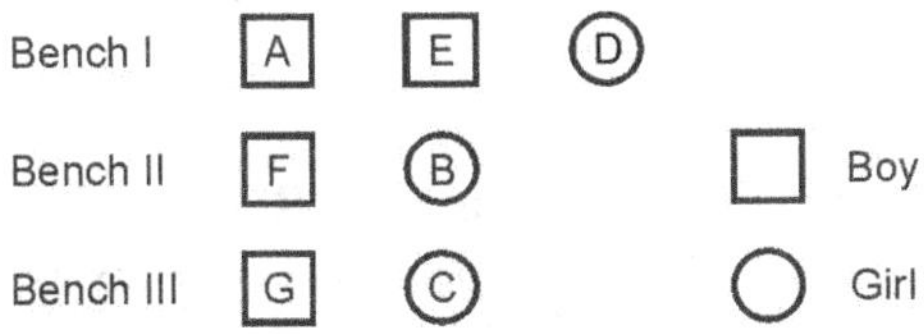

8 Data Sufficiency

In these questions, all one have to do is to analyse the given data and see if the answer to the problem can be given by all the data provided or by few of the data provided or cannot be answered with the data provided. Sometimes questions are qualitative in nature, wherein one has to apply his own value-judgement in order to reach a conclusion.

Example

Directions: *In the question below consists of a question and two or three statements given below it. You have to decide whether the data provided in the statements are sufficient to answer the question.*

2. Who is the North-East of R?

1. S is to the South-East of N, who is to the South-West of P, who is to the North of Q.
2. T is to the North-West of Q, who is to the South of P.
3. R, who is to the North of S, is midway between N and Q, N being to the West of R.

A. All 1, 2, 3 together are required
B. Only 1 and 3 together are sufficient
C. Only 2 and 3 together are sufficient
D. Either 1 and 3 together or 2 and 3 together are sufficient
E. None of these

Ans. D

EXERCISE

Directions (Qs. Nos. 1 to 30): *In each of the questions below consists of a question and two statements numbered I and II given below it. You have to decide whether the data provided in the statements are sufficient to answer the question. Read both the statements and* give answer:

A. If the data in statement I alone are sufficient to answer the question, while the data in statement II alone are not sufficient to answer the question.
B. If the data in statement II alone are sufficient to answer the question, while the data in statement I alone are not sufficient to answer the question.
C. If the data either in statement I alone or in statement II alone are sufficient to answer the question.
D. If the data given in both statements I and II together are not sufficient to answer the question and
E. If the data in both statements I and II together are necessary to answer the question.

1. The last Sunday of March, 2006 fell on which date?

Statements:

I. The first Sunday of that month fell on 5th.
II. The last day of that month was Friday.

2. In which year was Raju born?

Statements:

I. Raju at present is 25 years younger to his mother.
II. Raju's brother, who was born in 1964, is 35 years younger to his mother.

3. How many children does M have?

Statements:

I. H is the only daughter of X who is wife of M.
II. K and J are brothers of M.

4. How much was the total sale of the company?
Statements:
I. The company sold 8000 units of product A each costing ₹ 25.
II. This company has no other product line.

5. What will be the total weight of 10 rods, each of the same weight?
Statements:
I. One-fourth of the weight of each rod is 5 kg.
II. The total weight of three rods is 20 kilograms more than the total weight of two rods.

6. How is J related to Y?
Statements:
I. Y and Z are children of D who is wife of J.
II. R's sister J is married to Y's father.

7. How is T related to F?
Statements:
I. R's sister J has married T's brother L, who is the only son of his parents.
II. F is the only daughter of L and J.

8. What is the code for 'sky' in the code language?
Statements:
I. In the code language, 'sky is clear' is written as 'de ra fa'.
II. In the same code language, 'make it clear' is written as 'de ga jo'.

9. How is J related to P?
Statements:
I. M is brother of P and T is sister of P.
II. P's mother is married to J's husband who has one son and two daughters.

10. How many children are there between P and V in a row of children?
Statements:
I. P is fifteenth from the left in the row.
II. V is exactly in the middle and there are ten children towards his right.

11. B is the brother of A. How is A related to B?
Statements:
I. A is the sister of C.
II. E is the husband of A.

12. Who is to the immediate right of P among five persons P, Q, R, S and T facing North?
Statements:
I. R is third to the left of Q and P is second to the right of R.
II. Q is to the immediate left of T who is second to the right of P.

13. How is X related to Y?
Statements:
I. Y says, "I have only one brother".
II. X says, "I have only one sister".

14. How many children are there in the row of children facing North?
Statements:
I. Vibha who is fifth from the left end is eighth to the left of Ashish who is twelfth from the right end.
II. Rohit is fifth to the left of Nisha who is seventh from the right end and eighteenth from the left end.

15. How is Tannu related to the man in the photograph?
Statements:
I. Man in the photograph is the only son of Tannu's grandfather.
II. The man in the photograph has no brothers or sisters and his father is Tannu's grandfather.

16. On which day of the week was birthday of Salim?
Statements:
I. Salim celebrated his birthday the very next day on which Arun celebrated his birthday.
II. The sister of Salim was born on the third day of the week and two days after Salim was born.

17. How many doctors are practicing in this town?
Statements:
I. There is one doctor per seven hundred residents.
II. There are 16 wards with each ward having as many doctors as the number of wards.

18. How many pages of book C did Robert read on Sunday?
Statements:
I. The book has 300 pages out of which two-thirds were read by him before Sunday.
II. Robert read the last 40 pages of the book on the morning of Monday.

19. Among F, V, B, E and C, who is the third from the top when arranged in the descending order of their weights?
Statements:
I. B is heavier than F and C and is less heavier than V who is not the heaviest.
II. C is heavier than only F.

20. On a T.V. channel, four films A, B, C and D were screened, one on each day, on four consecutive days but not necessarily in that order. On which day was the film C screened?
Statements:
I. The first film was screened on 23rd, Tuesday and was followed by film D.
II. Film A was not screened on 25th and one serial was screened between films A and B.

21. Which word in the code language means 'flower'?
Statements:
I. 'de fu la pane' means 'rose flower is beautiful' and 'la quiz' means 'beautiful tree'.
II. 'de la chin' means 'red rose flower' and 'pa chin' means 'red tea'.

22. Who is C's partner in a game of cards involving four players A, B, C and D?
Statements:
I. D is sitting opposite to A.
II. B is sitting right of A and left of D.

23. How many students in a class play football?
Statements:
I. Only boys play football.
II. There are forty boys and thirty girls in the class.

24. Can Ramesh retire from office X in January 2020, with full pension benefits?
Statements:
I. Ramesh will complete 30 years of service in office X in April 2014 and desires to retire.
II. As per office X rules, an employee has to complete minimum 30 years of service and attain age of 60. Ramesh has 3 years to complete age of 60.

25. On which date in August was Kunal born?
Statements:
I. Kunal's mother remembers that Kunal was born before nineteenth but after fifteenth.
II. Kunal's brother remembers that Kunal was born before seventeenth but after twelfth.

26. Madan is elder than Kamal and Sharad is younger than Alok. Who among them is the youngest?
Statements:
I. Sharad is younger than Madan.
II. Alok is younger than Kamal.

27. What is the code for 'or' in the code language?
Statements:
I. 'nik sa te' means 'right or wrong', 'ro da nik' means 'he is right' and 'fe te ro' means 'that is wrong'.
II. 'pa nik la' means 'that right man', 'sa ne pa' means 'this or that' and 'ne ka re' means 'tell this there'.

28. What is Gagan's age?
Statements:
I. Gagan, Vimal and Kusum are all of the same age.
II. Total age of Vimal, Kusum and Anil is 32 years and Anil is as old as Vimal and Kusum together.

29. How much money do Vivek and Sunny have together?
Statements:
I. Sunny has 20 rupees less than what Tarun has.
II. Vivek has 30 rupees more than what Tarun has.

30. Who among P, Q, R, S and T is the lightest?
Statements:
I. R is heavier than Q and T but lighter than S.
II. S is not the heaviest.

ANSWERS

1	**2**	**3**	**4**	**5**	**6**	**7**	**8**	**9**	**10**
C	E	D	E	C	C	E	D	B	E
11	**12**	**13**	**14**	**15**	**16**	**17**	**18**	**19**	**20**
C	C	D	C	C	B	B	E	A	E
21	**22**	**23**	**24**	**25**	**26**	**27**	**28**	**29**	**30**
D	C	D	E	E	B	C	E	D	D

EXPLANATORY ANSWERS

1. From I, we conclude that 5th, 12th, 19th and 26th of March, 2006 were Sundays.
So, the last Sunday fell on 26th.
From II, we conclude that 31st March, 2006 was Friday. Thus, 26th March, 2006 was the last Sunday of the month.

2. From both I and II, we find that Raju is (35 – 25) = 10 years older than his brother, who was born in 1964. So, Raju was born in 1954.

3. From I, we conclude that H is the only daughter of M. But this does not indicate that M has no son. The information given in II is immaterial.

4. From I, total sale of product A = ₹ (8000 × 25) = ₹ 200000.

From II, we know that the company deals only in product A.

This implies that sale of product A is the total sale of the company, which is ₹ 200000.

5. From I, we conclude that weight of each rod $= (4 \times 5)$ kg = 20 kg.
So, total weight of 10 rods = (20×10) kg = 200 kg.

From II, we conclude that:
Weight of each rod = (weight of 3 rods) – (weight of 2 rods) = 20 kg.
So, total weight of 10 rods = (20×10) kg = 200 kg.

6. From I, we conclude that Y is the child of D who is wife of J i.e. J is Y's father.

From II, J is married to Y's father. This implies that J is Y's mother.

7. From I, we know that L is T's brother and J's husband. Since L is the only son of his parents, T is L's sister.

From II, we know that F is L's daughter. Thus, from I and II, we conclude that T is the sister of F's father i.e. T is F's aunt.

8. The only word common to I and II is 'clear' and as such, only the code for 'clear' can be ascertained from the given information.

9. From II, we know that P's mother is married to J's husband, which means that J is P's mother.

10. From II, V being in the middle, there are 10 children to his right as well as to his left. So, V is 11th from the left. From I, P is 15th from the left. Thus, from both I and II, we conclude that there are 3 children between P and V.

11. B is A's brother means A is either brother or sister of B. Now, each one of I and II individually indicates that A is a female, which means that A is B's sister.

12. From I, we have the order: R, –, P, Q.

From II, we have the order: P, Q, T. Clearly, each one of the above two orders indicates that Q is to the immediate right of P.

13. The statements in I and II do not provide any clue regarding relation between X and Y.

14. Since 8th to the left of 12th from the right is 20th from the right, so from I, we know that Vibha is 5th from left and 20th from right *i.e.* there are 4 children to the left and 19 to the right of Vibha.

So, there are (4 + 1 + 19) *i.e.* 24 children in the row.

From II, Nisha is 7th from right and 18th from left end of the row.

So, there are (6 + 1 + 17) = 24 children in the row.

15. From I, we conclude that the man is the only son of Tannu's grandfather *i.e.* he is Tannu's father or Tannu is the man's daughter.

From II, we conclude that the man's father is Tannu's grandfather. Since the man has no brothers or sisters, so he is Tannu's father or Tannu is the man's daughter.

16. I does not mention the day of the week on the birthday of either Arun or Salim. According to II, Salim's sister was born on Wednesday and Salim was born two days before Wednesday *i.e.* on Monday.

17. From I, total number of doctors in town = $(1/700 \times N)$, where N = total number of residents in town. But, the value of N is not known.

From II, total number of doctors in town

= (Number of wards in town) × (Number of doctors in each ward)

= $16 \times 16 = 256$.

18. From I and II, we find that Robert read $(300 \times 2/3)$ *i.e.* 200 pages before Sunday and the last 40 pages on Monday. This means that he read $[300 - (200 + 40)]$ *i.e.* 60 pages on Sunday.

19. From I, we have: $B > F$, $B > C$, $V > B$. Thus, V is heavier than each one of B, F and C. But V is not the heaviest. So, E is the heaviest.

Thus, we have the order:

$E > V > B > T > C$ or $E > V > B > C > F$.

Clearly, B is third from the top.

20. From I, we know that the films were screened on 23rd, 24th, 25th and 26th. Clearly, D was screened second *i.e.* on 24th, Wednesday.

From II, we know that one film was screened between A and B.

So, A and B were screened first and third, *i.e.* on 23rd and 25th. But, A was not screened on 25th.

So, A was screened on 23rd and B on 25th. Thus, C was screened on 26th, Friday.

21. From the given two statements in I, the code for the only common word 'beautiful' can be determined.

From the given two statements in II, the code for the only common word 'red' can be determined.

In I and II, the common words are 'rose and 'flower' and the common code words are 'de' and 'la'. So, the code for 'flower' is either 'de' or 'la'.

22. Clearly, each of the given statements shows that B is sitting opposite to C or B is the partner of C.

23. It is not mentioned whether all the boys or a proportion of them play football.

24. Clearly, the facts given in I and II contain two conditions to be fulfilled to get retirement and also indicate that Ramesh fulfils only one condition out of them.

25. From I, we conclude that Kunal was born on any one of the dates among 16th, 17th and 18th.

From II, we conclude that Kunal was born on any one of the dates among 13th, 14th, 15th and 16th.

Thus, from both I and II, we conclude that Kunal was born on 16th August.

26. As given, we have: $M > K$, $A > S$.

From II, $K > A$.

Thus, we have: $M > K > A > S$.

So, Sharad is the youngest. From I, $M > S$. Thus, we have: $M > K > A > S$ or $M > A > K > S$ or $M > A > S > K$.

27. I. In 'right or wrong' and 'he is right', the common word is 'right' and the common code word is 'nik'. So 'nik' means 'right'. In 'right or wrong' and 'that is wrong', the common word is 'wrong' and the common code word is 'te'. So, 'te' means 'wrong'. Thus, in 'right or wrong', 'sa' is the code for 'or'. II. In 'that right man' and 'this or that', the common word is 'that' and the common code word is 'pa'. So, 'pa' means 'that'. In 'this or that' and 'tell this there', the common word is 'this' and the common code word is 'ne'. So, 'ne' means 'this'. Thus, in 'this or that', 'sa' is the code for 'or'.

28. As given in I and II, we have: G = V = K, V + K + A = 32 and A = V + K.
Putting V + K = A in V + K + A = 32, we have: 2A = 32 or A = 16.
Thus, V + K = 16 and V = K. So, V = K = 8.
Thus, G = 8.

29. From I, we have: S = T – 20.

From II, we have: V = T + 30.

Thus, from both I and II, we have:

V + S = (T + 30) + (T – 20) = (2 T + 10).

So, to get the required amount, we need to know the amount that Tarun has.

30. From I, we have: R > Q, R > T, S > R *i.e.* S > R > Q > T or S > R > T > Q.
From II, S is not the heaviest. So, P is the heaviest.
Thus, we have: P > S > R > Q > T or P > S > R > T > Q.
Hence, either T or Q is the lightest.

❀ ❀ ❀

9 Coded Inequalities

To solve coded inequalities problem one's primarily task is to combine (visualise) two or more inequalities in to one combined notation.

Rule-Carry one directional lightest inequality to deduce conclusion from combined inequality Whenever inequalities are combined together in one combined notation writing common terms only once then conclusion will follow between any two terms if and only if all the inequalities between these two terms points in one same direction and conclusion will carry lightest ('<' is lighter than '≤' and '>'is lighter than '≥') inequality sign present between these two terms.

Basics of above rule

1. Two inequalities can be combined if and only if they have a common term.
2. Two inequalities can be combined (to give valid conclusion) if and only if the common term is greater than (or 'greater than or equal to') one and less than (or 'less than or equal to') the other.
3. The conclusion –inequality will have an '≥' sign (or a '≤' sign) if and only if both the signs in the combined inequality were '≥'(or '≤',as the case may be).

EXERCISE

Directions (Qs. Nos. 1 to 6): *In the following questions, the symbols @, ©, •, % and $ are used with the following meaning as illustrated below:*

'P © Q' means 'P is neither greater than nor smaller than Q'.

'P @ Q' means 'P is smaller than Q'.

'P $ Q' means 'P is greater than Q'.

'P • Q' means 'P is either smaller than or equal to Q'.

'P % Q' means 'P is either greater than or equal to Q'.

Now in each of the following questions assuming the given statements to be true, find which of the two conclusions I and II given below them is/are Definitely true?

Give answer :

A. if only conclusion I is true
B. if only conclusion II is true
C. if either conclusion I or II is true
D. if neither conclusion I nor II is true
E. if both conclusions I and II are true

1. **Statements:** J $ N, N % F, F • D
   Conclusions: I. F @ J II. D % N
2. **Statements:** J % N, N © D, D @ K
   Conclusions : I. D © J II. D @ J
3. **Statements:** R © M, M @ V, V $ F
   Conclusions: I. F @ M II. V $ R
4. **Statements:** N @ K, K • F, F $ W
   Conclusions: I. F % N II. W @ K
5. **Statements:** B •K, K $ R, R % E
   Conclusions: I. E @ K II. E @ B
6. **Statements:** M• T, T @ R, R © K
   Conclusions: I. K $ T II. R % M

Directions (Qs. Nos. 7 to 11): *In the following questions, the symbols @, ©, %, $ and β are used with the following meaning as illustrated below:*

'P © Q' means 'P is smaller than Q'.

'P @ Q' means 'P is either smaller than or equal to Q'.

'P % Q' means 'P is greater than Q'.

'P $ Q' means 'P is either greater than or equal to Q'.

'P β Q' means 'P is equal to Q'.

Now in each of the following questions

assuming the given statements to be true, find which of the two conclusions I and II given below them is/are Definitely true?

Give answer:

A. if only conclusion I is true
B. if only conclusion II is true
C. if either conclusion I or II is true
D. if neither conclusion I nor II is true
E. if both conclusions I and II are true

7. Statements: B © T, T β M, M % F
Conclusions: I. B © M II. B © F

8. Statements: M β R, R % T, T $ K
Conclusions: I. K @ M II. K © M

9. Statements: W © D, D @ H, H β N
Conclusions: I. N $ D II. W © N

10. Statements: W @ D, D $ R, R © K
Conclusions: I. R β W II. R % W

11. Statements : F $ J, J % V, V © N
Conclusions: I. N $ F II. N % J

Directions (Qs. Nos. 12 to 16): *In the following questions, certain symbols have been used to indicate relationships between elements as follows:*

A % B means A is neither smaller than nor greater than B.
A $ B means A is greater than B.
A & B means A is either greater than or equal to B.
A @ B means A is smaller than B.
A # B means A is either smaller than or equal to B.

In each question, three statements showing relationships have been given, which are followed by two conclusions I and II. Assuming that the given statements are true, find out which conclusion(s) is/are definitely true.

Mark answer :

A. if only conclusion I is true
B. if only conclusion II is true
C. if either conclusion I or II is true
D. if neither conclusion I nor II is true
E. if both conclusions I and II are true

12. Statements: P & Q, Q $ R, Q % S
Conclusions: I. P @ S II. R @ P

13. Statements: F & G, G % H, H $ K
Conclusions: I. H @ F II. F % H

14. Statements: T # V, V $ X, X & Y
Conclusions: I. V $ Y II. X # T

15. Statements: C % E, E # W, W @ Z
Conclusions: I. W & C II. C @ Z

16. Statements : L # M, M @ N, N $ P
Conclusions: I. L # N II. M & P

Directions (Qs. Nos. 17 to 22): *In the following questions, the symbols @, ©, %, $ and ? are used with the following meaning as illustrated below :*

'P © Q' means 'P is either smaller than or equal to Q.
'P Ω Q' means 'P is either greater than or equal to Q'.
'P % Q' means 'P is smaller than Q'.
'P $ Q' means 'P is greater than Q'.
'P @ Q' means 'P is equal to Q'

Now in each of the following questions assuming the given statements to be true, find which of the two conclusions I and II given below them is/are Definitely true?

Give answer:

A. if only conclusion I is true
B. if only conclusion II is true
C. if either conclusion I or II is true
D. if neither conclusion I nor II is true
E. if both conclusions I and II are true

17. Statements: M % T, T $ K, K © D
Conclusions: I. T $ D II. D $ M

18. Statements: F @ B, B % N, N $ H
Conclusions: I. N $ F II. H $ F

19. Statements: R Ω M, M @ K, K © J
Conclusions: I. J $ M II. J @ M

20. Statements: B $ N, N Ω R, R @ K
Conclusions: I. K © N II. B $ K

21. Statements: J © K, K $ N, N Ω D
Conclusions: I. J % N II. D % K

22. Statements: R @ D, D © M, M $ T
Conclusions: I. T % D II. M Ω R

Directions (Qs. Nos. 23 to 27): *In the following questions, the symbols $, •, %, Ω and @ are used with the following meaning as illustrated below :*

'P • Q' means ' P is neither greater than nor equal to Q'.
'P @ Q' means ' P is neither smaller than nor equal to Q,.
'P Ω Q' means ' P is not greater than Q'.
'P % Q' means 'P is not smaller than Q'.
'P $ Q' means 'P is neither greater than nor smaller than Q'.

Now in each of the following questions assuming the given statements to be true, find which of the two conclusions I and II given below them is/are Definitely true?

Give answer:

A. if only conclusion I is true
B. if only conclusion II is true
C. if either conclusion I or II is true
D. if neither conclusion I nor II is true
E. if both conclusions I and II are true

23. Statements: R % W, W @ F, F $ Z
Conclusions: I. F • R II. Z • W

24. Statements: B @ K, K % J, J • M
Conclusions: I. J • B II. M @ B

25. Statements: D $ T, T Ω H, H @ N
Conclusions: I. H $ D II. H @ D

26. Statements: H Ω N, N • K, K Ω D
Conclusions: I. D @ N II. H • K

27. Statements : W % E, E @ K, K $ J
Conclusions: I. J Ω E II. W % K

Directions (Qs. Nos. 28 to 30): *Read the information/statement given in each question carefully and answer the questions.*

28. Which of the following expressions will be true if the expression' $A > B \geq C < D$ is definitely true?
A. $A > D$ B. $C \leq A$
C. $D > B$ D. $D \geq A$
E. None is true

29. Which of the following expressions will not be true if the expression '$F \leq G = H < K$' is definitely true?
A. $K \geq F$ B. $H \geq F$
C. $G < K$ D. $F < K$
E. None of these

30. In which of the following expressions will the expression '$P < Q$' be definitely true?
A. $P \geq R > N = Q$ B. $Q < R \geq N > P$
C. $P < R \leq Q > N$ D. $P \geq N \geq M > Q$
E. None is true

ANSWERS

21	**22**	**23**	**24**	**25**	**26**	**27**	**28**	**29**	**30**
A	C	B	D	A	A	A	B	E	D
31	**32**	**33**	**34**	**35**	**36**	**37**	**38**	**39**	**40**
D	B	C	A	E	D	D	A	C	E
41	**42**	**43**	**44**	**45**	**46**	**47**	**48**	**49**	**50**
D	B	E	A	C	E	D	E	A	C

EXPLANATORY ANSWERS

(1-6): © → = • → ≤ @ → < $ → > % → ≥

1. J $ N → $J > N$, N % F → $N \geq F$,
F • D → $F \leq D$
Therefore, $J > N \geq F \leq D$
Conclusions:
I. F @ J → $F < J$: True
II. D % N → $D \geq N$: False

2. J % N → $J \geq N$, N © D → $N = D$,
D @ K → $D < K$
Therefore, $J \geq N = D < K$
Conclusions:
I. D © J → $D = J$: False
II. D @ J → $D < J$: False
Either I or II is true

3. R © M → $R = M$, M @ V → $M < V$,
V $ F → $V > F$
Therefore, $R = M < V > F$
Conclusions:
I. F @ M → $F < M$: False
II. V $ R → $V > R$: True

4. N @ K → $N < K$,
K • F → $K \leq F$,
F $ W → $F > W$
Therefore, $N < K \leq F > W$
Conclusions:
I. F % N → $F \geq N$: False
II. W @ K → $W < K$: False

5. B • K → B ≤ K,
K $ R → K > R,
R % E → R ≥ E
Therefore, B ≤ K > R ≥ E
Conclusions:
I. E @ K → E < K : True
II. E @ B → E < B : False

6. M • T → M ≤ T,
T @ R → T < R,
R © K → R = K
Therefore, M ≤ T < R = K
Conclusions:
I. K $ T → K > T : True
II. R % M → R ≥ M : False

(7- 11): © → < @ → ≤ % → > $ → ≥ β → =

7. B © T → B < T,
T β M → T = M,
M % F → M > F
Therefore, B < T = M > F
Conclusions:
I. B © M → B < M : True
II. B © F → B < F : False

8. M β R → M = R,
R % T → R > T,
T $ K → T ≥ K
Therefore, M = R > T ≥ K
Conclusions:
I. K @ M → K ≤ M : False
II. K © M → K < M : True

9. W © D → W < D,
D @ H → D ≤ H,
H β N → H = N
Therefore, W< D ≤ H = N
Conclusions:
I. N $ D → N ≥ D : True
II. W © N → W < N : True

10. W @ D → W ≤ D,
D $ R → D ≥ R,
R © K → R < K
Therefore, W ≤ D ≥ R < K
Conclusions:
I. R β W → R = W : False
II. R % W → R > W : False

11. F $ J → F ≥ J,
J % V → J > V,
V © N → V < N
Therefore, F ≥ J > V< N
Conclusions:
I. N $ F → N ≥ F : False
II. N % J → N > J : False

(12- 16): A % B → A = B, A $ B → A > B, A & B → A ≥ B, A @ B → A < B, A # B → A ≤ B

12. P & Q → P ≥ Q,
Q $ R → Q > R,
Q % S → Q = S
Therefore, P ≥ Q = S > R
Conclusions:
I. P @ S → P < S : False
II. R @ P → R < P : True

13. F & G → F ≥ G,
G % H → G = H,
H $ K → H > K
Therefore, F ≥ G = H > K
Conclusions:
I. H @ F → H < F : False
II. F % H → F = H : False
H is either smaller than or equal to F.

14. T # V → T ≤ V,
V $ X → V > X,
X & Y → X ≥ Y
Therefore, T ≤ V > X ≥ Y
Conclusions:
I. V $ Y → V > Y : True
II. X # T → X ≤ T : False

15. C % E → C = E,
E # W → E ≤ W,
W @ Z → W < Z
Therefore, C = E ≤ W < Z
Conclusions:
I. W & C → W ≥ C : True
II. C @ Z → C < Z : True

16. L # M → L ≤ M, M @ N → M < N,
N $ P → N > P
Therefore, L ≤ M < N > P
Conclusions:
I. L # N → L ≤ N : False
II. M & P → M ≥ P : False

(17-22): @ $\rightarrow$ =, © $\rightarrow$ $\leq$, % $\rightarrow$ <, \$ $\rightarrow$ >, Ω $\rightarrow$ $\geq$

17. M % T → M < T,
T \$ K → T > K,
K © D → K ≤ D
Therefore, M < T > K ≤ D
Conclusions:
I. T \$ D → T > D : False
II. D \$ M → D > M : False

18. F @ B → F = B,
B % N → B < N,
N \$ H → N > H
Therefore, F = B < N > H
Conclusions:
I. N \$ F → N > F : True
II. H \$ F → H > F : False

19. R Ω M → R ≥ M,
M @ K → M = K,
K © J → K ≤ J
Therefore, R ≥ M = K ≤ J
Conclusions:
I. J \$ M → J > M : False
II. J @ M → J = M : False
J is either greater than M or equal to M.

20. B \$ N → B > N,
N Ω R → N ≥ R,
R @ K → R = K
Therefore, B > N ≥ R = K
Conclusions:
I. K © N → K ≤ N : True
II. B \$ K → B > K : True

21. J © K → J ≤ K,
K \$ N → K > N,
N Ω D → N ≥ D
Therefore, J ≤ K > N ≥ D
Conclusions:
I. J % N → J < N : False
II. D % K → D < K: False

22. R @ D → R = D, D © M → D ≤ M,
M \$ T → M > T
Therefore, R = D ≤ M > T
Conclusions:
I. T % D → T < D : False
II. M Ω R → M ≥ R : True

(23 – 27): • → <, @ → >, Ω → ≤, % → ≥, \$ → =

23. Statements: R % W → R ≥ W,
W @ F → W > F,
F \$ Z → F = Z
Therefore, R ≥ W > F = Z
Conclusions:
I. F • R → F < R : True
II. Z • W → Z < W: True

24. Statements: B @ K → B > K,
K % J → K ≥ J,
J • M → J < M
Therefore, B > K ≥ J < M
Conclusions:
I. J • B → J < B : True
II. M @ B → M > B : False

25. Statements: D \$ T → D = T,
T Ω H → T ≤ H,
H @ N → H > N
Therefore, D = T ≤ H > N
Conclusions:
I. H \$ D → H = D : False
II. H @ D → H > D: False
H is greater than or equal to D.
So either I or II is true

26. Statements: H Ω N → H ≤ N,
N • K → N < K,
K Ω D → K ≤ D
Therefore, H ≤ N < K ≤ D
Conclusions:
I. D @ N → D > N : True
II. H • K → H < K : True

27. Statements: W % E → W ≥ E,
E @ K → E > K,
K \$ J → K = J
Therefore, W ≥ E > K = J
Conclusions:
I. J Ω E → J ≤ E : False
II. W % K → W ≥ K : False

28. A > B ≥ C < D None is true.

29. F ≤ G = H < K, we have K > F.
Therefore, K ≥ F is not true.

30. In P < R ≤ Q > N , P < Q is true.

❀ ❀ ❀

10 Input Interpretations

In input-output problems one is asked to imagine that there is some computer or a word-processing machine and it performs some operation on a given input. These operations are performed repeatedly as per a pre-fixed pattern and subsequently one has different output in different steps. One's primarily job is to deduce the rule followed by computer/ machine in arranging numbers and words. One should analyze final arranged step while deducing rule applied.

Example

Directions (Qs. Nos. 1 to 4): *Study the following information to answer the given questions:*
A word rearrangement machine when given an input line of words, rearranges them, following a particular rule, in each step. The following is an illustration of input and the steps of rearrangement.
Input: over you pat me crow easy to.
Steps: (I) pat over you crow easy to me
(II) crow pat over you to me easy
(III) over crow pat to me easy you
(IV) to over crow pat easy you me, and so on.

As per the rule followed in the above steps, find out the appropriate step for the given input in the following questions.

1. If step V of an input is 'put down col in as much sa', what would be the VIIIth step?
A. down in put much sa as col
B. in put down col much sa as
C. much in put down sa as col
D. col put down as much sa in
E. None of these

Ans. E. The steps followed are :
Step V : put down col in as much sa
Step VI : in put down col much sa as
Step VII : down in put much sa as col
Step VIII : much down in put as col sa

2. Input: but calm free are so not eat. Which of the following will be the IIIrd step for this input?
A. so free but calm eat are not
B. but calm are free not so eat
C. are but calm free not eat so
D. but so free eat are not calm
E. None of these

Ans. D. The step followed are :
Input : but calm free are so not eat
Step I : free but calm so not eat are
Step II : so free but calm eat are not
Step III : but so free eat are not calm

3. Input : rim bye eat klin fe to low. Which of the following steps would be 'fe low rim to bye klin eat'?
A. VIth
B. Vth
C. IVth
D. IIIrd
E. None of these

Ans. B. The step followed are :
Input : rim bye eat klin fe to low
Step I : eat rim bye fe to low klin
Step II : fe eat rim bye low klin to
Step III : rim fe eat low klin to bye
Step IV : low rim fe eat to bye klin
Step V : fe low rim to bye klin eat

4. If step II of an input is 'ge su he for game free but', what would be the step VI?
A. ge for but free he game su
B. for free ge game su he but
C. free ge for but game su he
D. he ge su but game free for
E. None of these

Ans. E. The step followed are :
Step II : ge su he for game free but
Step III : he ge su game free but for
Step IV : game he ge su but for free
Step V : ge game he but for free su
Step VI : but ge game he free su for

EXERCISE

Directions (Qs. Nos. 1 to 5): *Study the following information carefully and answer the questions given below:*

When an input line of words is given to a word arrangement machine, it rearranges them following a particular rule in each step.

Input: car some pour tie more tin bee goat
Step I : goat car some pour tie more tin bee
Step II : goat more car some pour tie tin bee
Step III : goat more pour car some tie tin bee
Step IV : goat more pour some car tie tin bee
Step V : goat more pour some bee car tie tin
and step V is the last output.

1. If the 3rd step of an input is:
bend take vide nut zeal pot car tin.
Which of the following will be the last step?
A. 6th B. 5th
C. 7th D. 4th
E. None of these

2. If the 2nd step of an input is:
coat some for die song kill bit son.
Which is certainly the input?
A. for come die song kill coat bit son
B. for die come song kill coat bit son
C. for die song come kill coat bit son
D. Can't be determined
E. None of these

3. Input : door site may for you mean now goal
Which of the following is the 3rd step of the above input?
A. door goal mean site for may now you
B. door goal mean site may for you now
C. door site goal mean may for you now
D. Can't be determined
E. None of these

4. Input: mute deal sit cut coat day long for
Which of the following will be the 4th step?
A. coat deal mute sit cut day long for
B. coat deal long mute sit cut day for
C. coat deal long mute cut sit day for
D. coat deal long mute cut day for sit
E. None of these

5. Input : ask not feel task opt sale dark den
Which of the following will be the last step?
A. 5th B. 6th
C. 4th D. 7th
E. None of these

Directions (Qs. Nos. 6 to 10): *Study the following information to answer the questions given below:*

A number arrangement machine when given an input of numbers, rearranges them following a particular rule in each step. The following is an illustration of input and steps of rearrangement.

Input:	48	245	182	26	99	542	378	297
Step I	542	48	245	182	26	99	378	297
Step II	542	26	48	245	182	99	378	297
Step III	542	26	378	48	245	182	99	297
Step IV	542	26	378	48	297	245	182	99
Step V	542	26	378	48	297	99	245	182

This is the final arrangement and step V is the last step for this input.

6. What will be the fourth step for an input whose second step is given below?
Step II: 765 42 183 289 542 65 110 350
A. 765 42 542 350 183 289 65 110
B. 765 42 542 65 110 183 289 350
C. 765 42 542 65 183 289 110 350
D. Cannot be determined
E. None of these

7. What should be the third step of the following input?
Input: 239 123 58 361 495 37
A. 495 37 361 123 239 58
B. 495 37 58 361 123 239
C. 495 37 58 123 361 239
D. 495 37 361 239 123 58
E. None of these

8. How many steps will be required to get the final output from the following input?
Input: 39 88 162 450 386 72 29
A. Two B. Three
C. Four D. Six
E. None of these

9. What should be the last step of the following input?
Input: 158 279 348 28 326 236
A. 348 28 326 158 279 236
B. 348 28 326 236 158 279
C. 348 28 236 158 279 326
D. 348 28 158 326 236 279
E. None of these

10. If the first step of an input is "785 198 32 426 373 96 49", then which of the following steps will be "785 32 426 49 198 373 96"?
A. Third
B. Fourth
C. Fifth
D. Second
E. None of these

Directions (Qs. Nos. 11 to 15): *A word-number arrangement machine, when given an input as a set of words and numbers, rearranges them following a particular rule and generates stepwise outputs till the rearrangement is complete following that rule.*

Followings is an illustration of input and steps of rearrangement till the last step.

Input: pour ask 57 dear 39 fight 17 28
Step I : ask pour 57 dear 39 fight 17 28
Step II : ask 57 pour dear 39 fight 17 28
Step III : ask 57 dear pour 39 fight 17 28
Step IV : ask 57 dear 39 pour fight 17 28
Step V : ask 57 dear 39 fight pour 17 28
Step VI : ask 57 dear 39 fight 28 pour 17
and Step VI is the last output.

As per the rule followed in the above steps find out the answer to each of the following questions:

11. If step II of an input is "cut 97 38 end for 29 46 down", which of the following will be the last step?
A. Fifth
B. Fourth
C. Sixth 4
D. Seventh
E. None of these

12. If the 4th step of an input is "ago 85 elite 79 exile fat 26 41", which of the following will definitely be the 2nd step of the input?
A. ago 85 79 elite fat 41 26 exile
B. ago 85 exile elite 41 26 fat 79
C. ago 85 26 exile 41 elite 79 fat
D. Cannot be determined
E. None of these

13. If the 1st step of an input is "car 17 vas tiger 92 87 like 52", which of the following will be the 4th step?
A. car 92 like 87 tiger 52 17 vas
B. car 92 like 87 17 vas tiger 52
C. car 92 like 87 tiger 17 vas 52
D. car 92 like 17 vas tiger 87 52
E. None of these

14. **Input:** zeal for 49 31 high 22 track 12
Which of the following will be the 3rd step?
A. for 49 high 31 track 22 zeal 12
B. for 49 high 31 zeal 22 track 12
C. for 49 high zeal 31 22 track 12
D. for 49 high 31 track zeal 22 12
E. None of these

15. **Input :** 19 feat 34 28 dog bag take 43
Which of the following steps would be "bag 43 dog 19 feat 34 28 take"?
A. Second
B. Fourth
C. First
D. Cannot be determined
E. None of these

Directions (Qs. Nos. 16 to 20): *A word-number arrangement machine, when given an input as a set of words and numbers, rearranges them following a particular rule and generates stepwise outputs till the rearrangement is complete following that rule.*

Followings is an illustration of input and steps of rearrangement till the last step.

Input: sine 88 71 cos theta 14 56 gamma delta 26
Step I: cos sine 71 theta 14 56 gamma delta 26 88
Step II: delta cos sine theta 14 56 gamma 26 88 71
Step III: gamma delta cos sine theta 14 26 88 71 56
Step IV: sine gamma delta cos theta 14 88 71 56 26
Step V: theta sine gamma delta cos 88 71 56 26 14

And Step V is the last Step of the arrangement of the above input as the intended arrangement is obtained.

As per the rules followed in the above steps, find out in each of the following questions the appropriate steps for the given input, Input for the questions

Input : for 52 all 96 25 jam road 15 hut 73 bus stop 38 46
(all numbers are in two digits)

16. Which word/number would be at the 6th position from the left in Step V?
A. 25 B. stop
C. jam D. all
E. road

17. Which of the following would be the Step III?
A. hut for bus all 25 jam road 15 stop 38 96 73 52 46
B. for us all 25 jam road 15 hut 38 stop 96 46 73 52
C. hut for bus all jam road 15 stop 38 96 73 52 46 25
D. for bus all 25 jam road 15 hut stop 38 46 96 73 52
E. None of the above

18. Which word/number would be at the 8th position from the right in Step IV?
A. 15 B. road
C. hut D. jam
E. stop

19. Which of the following would be Step VII?
A. stop road jam hut for bus all 15 96 73 52 46 38 25
B. road jam hut for bus all stop 15 25 38 46 52 73 96
C. stop road jam hut for bus all 96 73 52 46 38 25 15
D. jam hut for bus all 25 road stop 15 96 73 52 46 38
E. There will be no such step as the arrangement gets established at Step VI

20. Which step number would be the following output?
bus all for 52 25 jam road 15 hut stop 38 46 96 73
A. There will be no such step
B. III C. II
D. V E. VI

Directions (Qs 21 to 24.): *A word-number arrangement machine, when given an input as a set of words and numbers, rearranges them following a particular rule and generates stepwise outputs till the rearrangement is complete following that rule.*

Input : tall 48 13 rise alt 99 76 32 wise jar high 28 56 barn

Followings is an illustration of input and steps of rearrangement till the last step.

Input : tall 48 13 rise alt 99 76 32 wise jar high 28 56 barn

Step I: 13 tall 48 rise 99 76 32 wise jar high 28 56 barn alt

Step II: 28 13 tall 48 rise 99 76 32 wise jar high 56 alt barn

Step III: 32 28 13 tall 48 rise 99 76 wise jar 56 alt barn high

Step IV: 48 32 28 13 tall rise 99 76 wise 56 alt barn high jar

Step V: 56 48 32 28 13 tall 99 76 wise alt barn high jar rise

Step VI: 76 56 48 32 28 13 99 wise alt barn high jar rise tall

Step VII: 99 76 56 48 32 28 13 alt barn high jar rise tall wise

Step VII is the last step of the above input, as desired arrangement is obtained.

As per the rules followed in the above steps, find out in each of the following questions the appropriate steps for the given input.

Input: 84 why sit 14 32 not best ink feet 51 27 vain 68 92 (All the numbers are two digit numbers)

21. Which step number is the following output?
32 27 14 84 why sit not 51 vain 92 68 feet best ink
A. Step V B. Step VI
C. Step IV D. Step III
E. There is no such step

22. Which word/number would be at 5th position from the right in Step V?
A. 14 B. 92
C. feet D. best
E. why

23. How many elements (words or numbers) are there between 'feet' and '32' as they appear in the last step of the output?

A. One
B. Three
C. Four
D. Five
E. Seven

24. Which of the following represents the position of 'why' in the fourth step?
A. Eighth from the left
B. Fifth from the right
C. Sixth from the left
D. Fifth from the left
E. Seventh from the left

Directions (Qs. Nos. 25 to 30): *A word-number arrangement machine, when given an input as a set of words and numbers, rearranges them following a particular rule and generates stepwise outputs till the rearrangement is complete following that rule.*

Followings is an illustration of input and steps of rearrangement till the last step.

Input : rose girl 13 petal 16 go 35 ate 71 wild 22 87
Step I : go rose girl 13 petal 16 35 ate 71 wild 22 87
Step II : go 13 rose girl petal 16 35 ate 71 wild 22 87
Step III : go 13 ate rose girl petal 16 35 71 wild 22 87
Step IV : go 13 ate 16 rose girl petal 35 71 wild 22 87
Step V : go 13 ate 16 girl rose petal 35 71 wild 22 87
Step VI : go 13 ate 16 girl 22 rose petal 35 71 wild 87
Step VII: go 13 ate 16 girl 22 rose 35 petal 71 wild 87
Step VIII: go 13 ate 16 girl 22 rose 35 wild petal 71 87
Step IX : go 13 ate 16 girl 22 rose 35 wild 71 petal 87

and Step IX is the last step of the rearrangement.

25. Input: man 79 over 63 like 43 joy 15 never climbed 21 56
How many steps will be required to complete the arrangement?
A. Eight
B. Nine
C. Ten
D. Eleven
E. None of these

26. Step II of an input: to 13 world news 73 29 win 52.
How many more steps will be required to complete the arrangement?
A. Six
B. Four
C. Five
D. Two
E. None of these

27. Input : no 11 19 94 join for 81 style 37 matched.
Which of the following steps will be the last?
A. VI
B. VII
C. VIII
D. IX
E. None of these

28. Step III of an input is : we 12 you 19 meet 17 discuss 15 result 16.
Which of the following will be step II?
A. we 12 you 17 meet 19 discuss 15 result 16
B. we 12 17 you meet 19 discuss 15 result 16
C. we 12 you 15 17 meet 19 discuss result 16
D. Cannot be determined
E. None of these

29. Which of the following cannot be definitely Step V of an input?
A. be 13 did 27 eye 43 soon 34 39 wonder
B. be 13 did 27 eye 43 soon 39 34 wonder
C. be 13 did 27 soon 43 eye 39 wonder 34
D. Cannot be determined
E. None of these

30. If two given inputs gives identically same output, which of the following is definitely true?
A. Both require same number of steps for final arrangement.
B. Two inputs are identically same
C. Both contains same elements which may or may not be in same sequence
D. 2nd last step for both arrangements will be same
E. None of these

ANSWERS

1	**2**	**3**	**4**	**5**	**6**	**7**	**8**	**9**	**10**
B	D	E	C	A	C	D	E	A	B
11	**12**	**13**	**14**	**15**	**16**	**17**	**18**	**19**	**20**
A	D	B	C	E	A	D	B	C	A
21	**22**	**23**	**24**	**25**	**26**	**27**	**28**	**29**	**30**
E	D	B	C	C	B	A	D	C	C

EXPLANATORY ANSWERS

Solution (1 to 5): Following rule is followed here: Words are arranged according to their no. of letters. Words with largest no. of letters are arranged first. If two words have equal no. of letters then the word which comes first in English Dictionary is arranged first. In each step only one word is arranged and the rest shift one position rightwards. The process goes on until all the words are arranged.

1.

Step III: bend take vide nut zeal pot car tin
⑥ 4 ⑥ 5 ⑥

Step III : bend take vide nut zeal pot car tin
Step IV : bend take vide zeal nut pot car tin
Step V : bend take vide zeal car nut pot tin

2. Previous step can't be determined

3.

Input: door site may for you mean now goal
① ③ 3 2 1

Input : door site may for you mean now goal
Step I : door goal site may for you mean now
Step II : door goal mean site may for you now
Step III : door goal mean site for may you now

4.

Input: mute deal sit cut coat day long for
④ 2 4 1 3

Input: mute deal sit cut coat day long for
Step I: coat mute deal sit cut day long for
Step II: coat deal mute sit cut day long for
Step III: coat deal long mute sit cut day for
Step IV: coat deal long mute cut sit day for

5.

Input: ask not feel task opt sale dark den
⑤ ⑥ 2 4 ⑥ 3 4 5

Input : ask not feel task opt sale dark den
Step I : dark ask not feel task opt sale den
Step II : dark feel ask not task opt sale den
Step III : dark feel sale ask not task opt den
Step IV : dark feel sale task ask not opt den
Step V : dark feel sale task den ask not opt

Solution(6 to 10): On observing last step it is clear that there are two alternating series of numbers: one in descending order and the other in ascending order. When we reach step 1 through input, we find that the largest no. becomes the first and remaining numbers shift rightward. In the next step, the smallest no. becomes the second and the rest shift rightward. These two steps continue alternately until the two alternate series are formed.

6.

Step II: <u>765</u> <u>42</u> 183 289 542 65 110 350
3 4

Step II : 765 42 183 289 542 65 110 350
Step III : 765 42 542 183 289 65 110 350
Step IV : 765 42 542 65 183 289 110 350

7.

Input: 239 123 58 361 495 37
3 1 2

Input: 239 123 58 361 495 37
Step I : 495 239 123 58 361 37
Step II : 495 37 239 123 58 361
Step III : 495 37 361 239 123 58

8.

Input: 39 88 162 450 386 72 29
④ 4 1 3 5 2

Input: 39 88 162 450 386 72 29
Step I : 450 39 88 162 386 72 29

Step II : 450 29 39 88 162 386 72
Step III : 450 29 386 39 88 162 72
Step IV : 450 29 386 39 162 88 72
Step V : 450 29 386 39 162 72 88

9.

Input: 158 279 348 28 326 236
④ 4 1 2 3

Last step can be known directly.

10.

Step I : 785 198 32 426 373 96 49
1 2 3 4

Step I : 785 198 32 426 373 96 49
Step II : 785 32 198 426 373 96 49
Step III : 785 32 426 198 373 96 49
Step IV : 785 32 426 49 198 373 96

Solution (11 to 15): Following rule is followed here: Words are arranged in alphabetical order and nos. are arranged in decreasing order alternatcly. In output the word, which comes first in dictionary, comes to the first place and the rest shift one place rightwards. In the next step, the largest no. comes to the second place and the rest shift one place rightwards. These two steps occur alternately until the last step is obtained.

11.

Step II : <u>cut</u> <u>97</u> 38 end for 29 46 down
⑥ 5 ⑥ ⑥ 4 3

Step II : cut 97 38 end for 29 46 down
Step III : cut 97 down 38 end for 29 46
Step IV : cut 97 down 46 38 end for 29
Step V : cut 97 down 46 end 38 for 29

13.

Step I : <u>car</u> 17 vas tiger 92 87 like 52
2 4 3

Step I : car 17 vas tiger 92 87 like 52
Step II : car 92 17 vas tiger 87 like 52
Step III : car 92 like 17 vas tiger 87 52
Step IV : car 92 like 87 17 vas tiger 52

14.

Input: zeal for 49 31 high 22 track 12
1 2 3

Step I: for zeal 49 31 high 22 track 12
Step II: for 49 zeal 31 high 22 track 12
Step III: for 49 high zeal 31 22 track 12

15.

Input : 19 feat 34 28 dog bag take 43
3 1 2

Input : 19 feat 34 28 dog bag take 43
Step I : bag 19 feat 34 28 dog take 43
Step II : bag 43 19 feat 34 28 dog take
Step III : bag 43 dog 19 feat 34 28 take

Solution (16 to 20) : Here in Step I word which come first in dictionary takes first position from left and rest elements shifts one position rightwards and in the same step largest number takes first position from right and other elements shifts one step leftwards. In next step, same methodology is applied to only unarranged ones. Process continues until all words are arranged fzrom left to right in reverse dictionary order and numbers are arranged in increasing sequence from right to left.

Input: sine 88 71 cos theta 14 56 gamma delta 26
4 1B 2B 1 5 5B 3B 3 2 4B

Here, to get final arrangement sequence will be : 5 4 3 2 1 1B 2B 3B 4B 5B

(Note here first unnumbered from left or right will not be circled as no element could arrive at arranged position)

Input: for 52 all 96 25 jam road 15 hut73 bus stop 38 46
3 3B 1 1B 6B 5 6 7B 4 2B 2 7 5B 4B

Input : for 52 all 96 25 jam road 15 hut 73 bus stop 38 46

Step I : all for 52 25 jam road 15 hut 73 bus stop 38 46 96

Step II : bus all for 52 25 jam road 15 hut stop 38 46 96 73

Step III : for bus all 25 jam road 15 hut stop 38 46 96 73 52

Step IV : hut for bus all 25 jam road 15 stop 38 96 73 52 46

Step V : jam hut for bus all 25 road 15 stop 96 73 52 46 38

Step VI : road jam hut for bus all 15 stop 96 73 52 46 38 25

Step VII : stop road jam hut for bus all 96 73 52 46 38 25 15

Solution (21 to 24) : Here in Step I smallest number takes first position from left and rest elements shifts one position rightwards and in the same step word which comes first in dictionary takes first position from right and rest elements shifts one position leftwards. In next step, same methodology is applied to only unarranged ones. Process continues until all numbers are arranged in decreasing sequence from left to right and all words are arranged in reverse dictionary order from right to left.

Input: 84 why sit 14 32 not best ink feet 51 27vain 68 92
6 7B 5B 1 3 4B 1B 3B 2B 4 2 6B 5 7

Here, to get final arrangement sequence will be:

7 6 5 4 3 2 1 1B 2B 3B 4B 5B 6B 7B

(Note here first unnumbered from left or right will not be circled as no element could arrive at arranged position)

Input : 84 why sit 14 32 not best ink feet 51 27 vain 68 92

Step I : 14 84 why sit 32 not best ink feet 51 27 vain 68 92 best

Step II : 27 14 84 why sit 32 not ink 51 vain 68 92 best feet

Step III : 32 27 14 84 why sit not 51 vain 68 92 best feet ink

Step IV : 51 32 27 14 84 why sit vain 68 92 best feet ink not

Step V : 68 51 32 27 14 84 why vain 92 best feet ink not sit

Step VI : 84 68 51 32 27 14 why 92 best feet ink not sit vain

Step VII : 92 84 68 51 32 27 14 best feet ink not sit vain why

Solution (25 to 30) : Here numbers and words are arranged alternately. Numbers are arranged in increasing order while words are arranged in decreasing order of their dictionary placements. If a number or word is already arranged, then next member is arranged in the same step.

25.

Input :man 79 over63 like 43joy 15 never climbed21 56
③ 6 9 4 5 1 2 8 10 3 7

Input : man 79 over 63 like 43 joy 15 never climbed 21 56

Step I : joy man 79 over 63 like 43 15 never climbed 21 56

Step II : joy 15 man 79 over 63 like 43 never climbed 21 56

Step III : joy 15 man 21 79 over 63 like 43 never climbed 56

Step IV : joy 15 man 21 like 79 over 63 43 never climbed 56

Step V : joy 15 man 21 like 43 79 over 63 never climbed 56

Step VI : joy 15 man 21 like 43 over 79 63 never climbed 56

Step VII : joy 15 man 21 like 43 over 56 79 63 never climbed

Step VIII : joy 15 man 21 like 43 over 56 never 79 63 climbed

Step IX : joy 15 man 21 like 43 over 56 never 63 79 climbed

Step X : joy 15 man 21 like 43 over 56 never 63 climbed 79

26.

Step II: <u>to</u> <u>13</u> world news 73 29 win 52
⑦ 5 ⑦ 4 3 6

Step II: to 13 world news 73 29 win 52
Step III : to 13 win world news 73 29 52
Step IV : to 13 win 29 world news 73 52
Step V : to 13 win 29 news world 73 52
Step VI : to 13 win 29 news 52 world 73
This is the final arrangement.

27.

Input : no 11 19 94 joinfor 81 style 37matched
① ① ② ⑦ 2 1 5 4 3 6

Input : no 11 19 94 join for 81 style 37 matched
Step I : no 11 for 19 94 join 81 style 37 matched
Step II : no 11 for 19 join 94 81 style 37 matched
Step III : no 11 for 19 join 37 94 81 style matched
Step IV : no 11 for 19 join 37 style 94 81 matched
Step V : no 11 for 19 join 37 style 81 94 matched
Step VI : no 11 for 19 join 37 style 81 matched 94
This is the final arrangement.

28. Previous steps cannot be determined.

29. Step V of any input should have at least five elements arranged.

❀ ❀ ❀

11 Drawing Inference

In evaluating inferences problems a passage is followed by some inferences and the job is to decide whether a given inference follows or not in the context of the given passage. The most vital aspect of this question is intensity of probability of a particular inference. Some of the inferences can be easily and quickly judged because they are directly based on the facts given in the passage. But in some cases, an inference is indirect. Here the interference appears to be overlapping *i.e.* one may be confused between definitely true or probably true, probably truc or data inadcquate, data inadequate or probably false and probably false or data inadequate

The inference can

(1) directly follow from the passage

(2) be inferred from the passage

(3) be inferred with the help of some key words.

While evaluating inferences, first of all check whether it can be evaluated with the help of the passage directly. Check if the given inference is directly supported (or contradicted) by something in the passage. More or less direct inference is a restatement of something already stated in the passage.

EXERCISE

Directions (Qs. 1 to 20): *Below are given some passages followed by several possible inferences which can be drawn from the facts stated in the passage. You have to examine each inference separately in the context of the passage and decide upon its degree of truth or falsity.*

Mark answer

A. if the inference is definitely true, *i.e.* properly follows from the statement of facts given.

B. if the inference is probably true, though not 'definitely true' in the light of facts given.

C. if the data are inadequate, *i.e.* from the facts given you cannot say whether the inference is likely to be true or false.

D. if the inference is probably false, *i.e.* though not 'definitely false' in the light of the facts given.

E. if the inference is 'definitely false', *i.e.* it cannot possibly be drawn from the facts given or it contradicts the given facts.

PASSAGE 1

The immediate challenge is on the food front. Shortfalls in production have been allowed to affect supplies and hence prices. The government is planning to focus on investment in irrigation and strategy. It appears that the Green Revolution instruments to encourage farmers to invest are no longer effective. The Green Revolution strategy was based on the state taking out the risk of collapse in prices. Farmers were offered remunerative prices and a guaranteed procurement of their produce in case the open market could not absorb it. Farmers could then borrow from banks, acquire the Green Revolution Technology and produce as much as they could. The pressure on the food subsidy was manageable as long as there was a food shortage. Prices in the open market then tended to be above the procurement prices. But with the food surpluses the situation has changed. The situation was unsustainable not merely because of the magnitude of this subsidy. It was also inefficient. It meant farmers were being led to produce crops based just on the prices Government fixed and not in relation to any legal demand. In these circumstances, the Government was reluctant to keep increasing procurement prices at the pace that used to be the norm in earlier years.

1. The Government is planning to make crucial changes in the Green Revolution strategies.
2. The Government is no longer in a position to provide subsidy to farmers.
3. As the open market prices are lower, all the burden of procurement of crops is on the Government.
4. Demand is much higher than the quantity of crops produced by the farmers.
5. The farmers tend to produce the crops as per their convenience and not constant with the demand.

PASSAGE 2

Long term economic progress comes mainly from the invention and spread of improved technologies. The scientific revolution was made possible by the printing press, the industrial revolution by the steam engine and India's escape from famine by increased farm yields the so called 'Green Revolution'. Right now rich countries are changing the world's climate by emitting billions of tones of carbon dioxide each year from the use of coal, oil and natural gas. In future years, China and India will make massive contributions to increase carbon dioxide in the atmosphere. Yet no country rich or poor, is keen to cut its energy use, owing to concern that to do so would threaten jobs, incomes and economic growth. New technologies will provide a key part of the solution. Already, 'hybrid' automobiles, which combine gasoline and battery power, can roughly double fuel efficiency cutting carbon dioxide emission by half. Similarly, engineers have developed ways to capture the carbon dioxide that results from burning coal in power plants and store it safely underground. The new technology called "carbon capture and sequestration" can cut 80%, of the carbon dioxide emitted during the production of electricity.

6. It may not be practically possible to switch over to the new hybrid technologies from the present ones.
7. In the forthcoming years, India and China are going to be at the top of the list of world's developed countries.
8. The more developed is a country; less is the contribution to increase in air pollution.
9. The new technologies can control emission of carbon dioxide caused only during electricity generation.
10. The developing countries in the world are trying to evolve new technologies to reduce the emission of carbon dioxide.

PASSAGE 3

In the overall economy of India, agriculture is the largest sector of economic activity. It plays a crucial role in the country's economic development by providing food to its people and raw materials to industry. It accounts for the largest share to the national income. The share of the various agricultural commodities, animal husbandry and ancillary activities has been more than 40 per cent since independence. During the decade of the fifties, it actually contributed about half of the national output.

11. Agriculture is the mainstay of Indian economy.
12. The contribution of agricultural sector has decreased in recent years.
13. Agriculture is the only source of income in India.
14. The contribution of agriculture to Indian economy rose substantially after independence.
15. Agriculture contributes to national income more than all other activities put together.

PASSAGE 4

Gujarat has hardly 8.5 per cent of its total area under forest. Of this a considerable portion is covered by wild grass and marshes. Denuded of thick forests, fauna have disappeared from many places. Mandvi, for instance, had its share of panthers once. The state government has imposed a total ban on cutting of trees for five years from this year. The imminent destruction of over 40000 hectares of forest land by the Narmada project has led to nationwide strong protest.

16. People in Gujarat are quite conscious of the need of conservation of forests.

17. There is thick forest in 8.5 per cent of the total area of Gujarat.

18. Gujarat is the first state in India to impose a total ban on cutting of trees.

19. A dam on the Narmada river is planned.

20. Once there was thick forest in Mandvi.

ANSWERS

1	2	3	4	5	6	7	8	9	10
A	B	E	E	E	E	E	E	E	A
11	**12**	**13**	**14**	**15**	**16**	**17**	**18**	**19**	**20**
A	C	E	A	A	A	E	C	A	A

SOME SELECTED EXPLANATORY ANSWERS

6. A new technology is developed in view of its viability and acceptance. So, the inference is false.

7. A developed country does not emit huge quantity of carbon dioxide.

9. It is clear from the passage that the technologies are being developed to decrease the emission of carbon dioxide from automobiles as well as from the production of electricity.

❀ ❀ ❀

12 Syllogism

Syllogism was introduced by Aristotle (a reasoning consisting two premises and a conclusion). Aristotle gives the following definition of syllogism in his fundamental treatise Organon.

"A syllogism is discourse, in which, certain things being stated, something other than what is stated follows of necessity from their being so". Things that have stated are known as premises and the one that follows from the premises is known as the conclusion of the syllogism.

A categorical syllogism is a type of argument with two premises and one conclusion. Each of these three propositions is one of four forms of categorical proposition.

Type	Form	Example
A	All S are P	All monkeys are mammals
E	No S is P	No monkeys are birds
I	Some S are P	Some philosophers are logicians
O	Some S are not P	Some logicians are not philosophers

These four type of proposition are called A, E, I and O type propositions, the variables S and P are place-holders for terms which represent out a class or category of thing, hence the name "categorical" proposition.

Example

Directions (Qs. 1 to 3): *Below are given three or four statements followed by three or four conclusions. You have to take the given statements to be true even if they appear to be at variance with commonly known facts, and then decide which of the conclusions logically follow(s) from the given statements. For each question, mark out an appropriate answer choice that you think is correct.*

1. Statements: **Solution:**

(*a*) All locks are keys (*a*) LL – K

(*b*) All keys are bats (*b*) KK – B

(*c*) Some clocks are bats (*c*) C – B

Conclusions:

1. Some bats are locks. 1. B – L
2. Some clocks are keys. 2. C – K ×
3. All keys are locks. 3. KK – LL ×

A. Only 1 and 2 follow
B. Only 2 and 3 follow
C. Only 1 follows
D. Only 2 follows
E. 1, 2 and 3 follow

C. Only 1 follows

2. Statements: **Solution:**

(*a*) Some cups are pots (*a*) C – P

(*b*) All pots are tubes (*b*) PP – T

(*c*) All cups are bottles (*c*) CC – B

Conclusions:

1. Some bottles are tubes. 1. B – T
2. Some pots are bottles 2. P – B
3. Some tubes are cups 3. T – C

A. Only 1 and 2 follow
B. Only 2 and 3 follow
C. Only 1 and 3 follow
D. 1, 2 and 3 follow
E. None follows

D. 1, 2 and 3 follow

3. Statements: **Solution:**

(*a*) All papers are books. PP – B

(*b*) All bags are books. BaBa – B

(*c*) Some purses are bags Pu – Ba

Conclusions:

1. Some papers are bags. P – Ba ×
2. Some books are papers. B – P
3. Some books are purses. B – Pu

A. Only 1 follow
B. Only 2 and 3 follow
C. Only 1 and 3 follow
D. Only 1 and 2 follow
E. 1, 2 and 3 follow

D. Only 2 and 3 follow

EXERCISE

Directions (Qs. Nos. 1 to 10): *In each question below are given two statements followed by two conclusions numbered I and II. You have to take the given two statements to be true even if they seem to be at variance from commonly known facts. Read the conclusion and then decide which of the given conclusions logically follows from the two given statements, disregarding commonly known facts.*

Give answer:

A. If only conclusion I follows
B. If only conclusion II follows
C. If either I or II follows
D. If neither I nor II follows and
E. If both I and II follow.

1. Statements: I. All tables are chalks.
II. All chalks are chairs.
Conclusions: I. All chairs are tables.
II. All tables are chairs.

2. Statements: I. Some radios are stones.
II. All stones are rods.

3. Statements: I. Some birds are flowers.
II. Some flowers are books.
Conclusions: I. Some birds are books.
II. No book is a flower.

4. Statements: I. Some cows are jackals.
II. No fox is a cow.
Conclusions: I. Some jackals are foxes.
II. Some jackals are not foxes.

5. Statements: I. Only cats are animals.
II. No dog is an animal.
Conclusions: I. Some cats are not dogs.
II. Some dogs are cats.

6. Statements : I. All shoes are carpets.
II. No carpet is a pullover.
Conclusions: I. No shoes are pullovers.
II. All carpets are shoes.

7. Statements: I. No window is a wall.
II. No wall is a door.
Conclusions: I. No window is a door.
II. No door is a window.

8. Statements: I. All players are tall.
II. Johan is tall.
Conclusions: I. Johan is a player.
II. Johan is not a player.

9. Statements: I. All dogs are wolves.
II. Some wolves are tigers.
Conclusions: I. Some dogs are tigers.
II. Tigers which are wolves are not dogs.

10. Statements: I. All cars fly.
II. Some cycles fly.
Conclusions: I. All cars are cycles.
II. Some cycles do not fly.

Directions (Qs. Nos. 11 to 20): *In each question below are given three statements followed by two conclusions numbered I and II. You have to take the given two statements to be true even if they seem to be at variance from commonly known facts. Read the conclusion and then decide which of the given conclusions logically follows from the two given statements, disregarding commonly known facts.*

Give answer:

A. If only conclusion I follows
B. If only conclusion II follows
C. If either I or II follows
D. If neither I nor II follows and
E. If both I and II follow.

11. Statements: I. Some spoons are pots.
II. All pots are cups.
III. Some cups are cards.
Conclusions: I. Some cards are spoons.
II. Some cups are spoons.

12. Statements: I. Some keys are locks.
II. Some locks are doors.
III. Some doors are windows.
Conclusions: I. Some windows are locks.
II. Some doors are keys.

13. Statements: I. Some boys are flowers.
II. All flowers are jungles.
III. All jungles are houses

Conclusions: I. Some houses are flowers.
II. Some houses are boys.

14. Statements: I. All bottles are tanks.
II. All tanks are drums.
III. All drums are pipes.

Conclusions: I. Some pipes are tanks.
II. Some drums are bottles.

15. Statements: I. All sticks are brushes.
II. No brush is a fruit.
III. Some fruits are trees.

Conclusions: I. Some trees are sticks.
II. No tree is stick.

16. Statements: I. Some shirts are pants.
II. All pants are clothes.
III. Some clothes are napkins.

Conclusions: I. Some napkins are shirts.
II. Some clothes are shirts.

17. Statements: I. All packets are tents.
II. All tents are houses.
III. Some boxes are houses.

Conclusions: I. Some houses are packets.
II. Some boxes are tents.

18. Statements: I. Some nuts are bolts.
II. Some bolts are hammers.
III. Some hammers are nails.

Conclusions: I. Some nails are bolts.
II. No nail is a bolt.

19. Statements: I. All windows are doors.
II. No door is mountain.
III. Some mountains are roads.

Conclusions: I. Some roads are windows.
II. Some roads are doors.

20. Statements: I. Some phones are bangles.
II. Some bangles are rings.
III. All rings are sticks.

Conclusions: I. Some rings are phones.
II. Some sticks are bangles.

Directions (Qs. Nos. 21 to 25): *In each question below are given four statements followed by four conclusions numbered I, II, III and IV. You have to take the given two statements to be true even if they seem to be at variance from commonly known facts. Read the conclusion and then decide which of the given conclusions logically follows from the two given statements, disregarding commonly known facts.*

21. Statements: I. All silver are metals.
II. All metals are steel.
III. Some steel are stones.
IV. All stones are stands.

Conclusions: I. Some stands are metals.
II. Some stones are silver.
III. Some stands are steel.
IV. Some stones are steel.

A. Only conclusions III and IV follow
B. Only conclusion I follows
C. Only conclusion II follows
D. Only conclusion III follows
E. None of these

22. Statements: I. All chairs are tables.
II. All tables are songs.
III. Some songs are rhythms.
IV. Some rhythms are pillows.

Conclusions: I. Some tables are chairs.
II. All tables are rhythms.
III. All chairs are songs.
IV. Some pillows are songs.

A. Only conclusions I and III follow
B. Only conclusions I and IV follow
C. Only conclusion I follows
D. Only conclusion III follows
E. None of these

23. Statements: I. Some mobiles are pens.
II. Some pens are covers.
III. Some covers are plates.
IV. All plates are papers.

Conclusions: I. All mobiles are covers.
II. Some pens are papers.
III. All plates are pens.
IV. Some papers are mobiles.

A. Only conclusion I follows
B. Only conclusion II follows
C. Only conclusions I and IV follow
D. Only conclusions II and IV follow
E. None follows

24. Statements: I. All shoes are tables.
II. Some tables are lanes.
III. All caps are lanes.
IV. Some lanes are row.

Conclusions: I. Some tables are rows.
II. Some tables are shoes.
III. Some rows are caps.
IV. Some lanes are shoes.

A. Only conclusions I and II follow
B. Only conclusion II follows
C. Only conclusion III follows
D. Only conclusion I either or conclusion IV follows
E. None of these

25. Statements: I. Some symbols are numbers.
II. Some numbers are letters.
III. All alphabets are symbols.
IV. All pianos are letters.

Conclusions: I. Some symbols are letters.
II. Some numbers are pianos.
III. No letter is symbol.
IV. Some symbols are alphabets.

A. Only conclusion I follows
B. Only conclusion II follows
C. Only conclusions III and IV follow
D. Only conclusion IV follows
E. Only either I or III and IV follow

ANSWERS

1	**2**	**3**	**4**	**5**	**6**	**7**	**8**	**9**	**10**
B	E	D	B	A	A	D	C	D	D
11	**12**	**13**	**14**	**15**	**16**	**17**	**18**	**19**	**20**
B	D	E	E	C	B	A	C	D	B
21	**22**	**23**	**24**	**25**					
A	A	E	B	E					

EXPLANATORY ANSWERS

1. [A + A = A, All tables are chairs]
2. [I + A = I, Some radios are rods. Also, some radios are stones *conversion* Some stones are radios.]
3. [I + I = no conclusion]
4. [Change order of the statements to align. Now, No fox is a cow + Some cows are jackals = E + I = O*, Some jackals are not foxes.]
5. [Change order first. Now, No dog is an animal + Only cats are animals *implies* No dog is an animal + All animals are cats = E + A = O*, Some cats are not dogs.]
6. [A + E = E]
7. [E + E = no conclusion]
8. [Align: Johan is tall + Some tall are players = A + I = no conclusion. But, Johan should either be a player or a non-player. Hence either of the two choices follows.
9. [A + I = no conclusion]
10. [After alignment, All cars fly + Some fly are cycles = no conclusion]
11. [Some spoons are *pots,+ All pots* are cups. I + A = I type of conclusion "Some spoons are cups". Conclusion II is converse of it.]
12. [All the three premises are I type. No conclusion follows from two I premises.]
13. Some boys are *flowers. + All flowers* are jungles. I + A = I type conclusion, "Some boys are jungles". Some boys are flowers + *All jungles* are houses.

    I + A = I type conclusion, "Some boys are houses". Conclusion II is converse of it.

14. All bottles are tanks. + All tanks are drums. A + A = A – type of conclusion *i.e.* "all bottles are drums'. Conclusion II is converse of it. All tanks are drums + All drums are pipes A + A implies A-type of conclusion "All tanks are pipes". Conclusion I is converse of it.

15. All sticks are brushes + No brush is fruit. *i.e.* A + E = E type of conclusion. "No stick is fruit". No brush is fruit + Some fruits are trees. *i.e.* E + I = O*,"Some trees are not brushes". Conclusions I and II forms a complementary pair. Therefore, either I or II follows.

16. Some shirts are pants + All pants are clothes = Some shirts are clothes. Conclusion II is converse of it.

17. All packets are tents + All tents are houses = All packets are houses. Conclusion I is the converse of it.

18. All the three premises are particular affirmative. No conclusion can be reached from two particular premises (I type).

19. All windows are doors + No door is mountain = No window is mountain. No door is mountain + Some mountains are roads = Some roads are not doors.

20. Some bangles are rings + All rings are sticks = Some bangles are sticks. Conclusion II is converse of the third premise.

21. All silver are metals + All metals are steel = All silver are steel. Some steel are stones + All stones are stands = Some steel are stands conversion Conclusion III. Conclusion IV is converse of the third premise.

22. All chairs are tables + All tables are songs = All chairs are songs (Conclusion III) Conclusion I is converse of first premise.

23. Some covers are plates + All plates are papers = Some covers are papers.

24. All shoes are tables + Some tables are lanes = no conclusion.

Conclusion II is the converse of the first premise.

25. All alphabets are symbols + Some symbols are numbers = no conclusion.

Conclusion IV follows from the conversion of the third premise. Conclusion I and III form complementary pair.

❀ ❀ ❀

13 Cause & Effect

In these questions, the job is to determine whether a given event is the cause or the effect of some other event. Events do not just happen without any cause behind them. These causes are the conditions under which these events (or results or effects) happen. Cause is an event which leads to a said effect and this fact is either scientifically proven or logically expected. An immediate cause means a cause that immediately precedes the effect and a principal cause means a cause that immediately precedes the effect and a principal cause means a cause that was the most important reason behind the effect. Obviously cause must occur before the effect, we can merely look at the given two events first and by analyzing the time of occurrence, we can find which event can't be a cause.

Example

Directions (Qs. Nos. 1-4): *In each of the following questions, two statements numbered I and II are given. There may be cause and effect relationship between the two statements. These two statements may be the effect of the same cause or independent causes. These statements may be independent causes without having any relationship. Read both the statements in each question and mark your answer as*

A. If statement I is the cause and statement II is its effect;
B. If statement II is the cause and statement I is its effect;
C. If both the statements I and II are independent causes;
D. If both the statements I and II are effects of independent causes; and
E. If both the statements I and II are effects of some common cause.

1. **Statements:**
   I. Police had resorted to lathi-charge to disperse the unruly mob from the civic headquarters.
   II. The civic administration has recently hiked the property tax of the residential buildings by about 30 per cent.

Ans. D: Both the statements I and II are the effects of independent causes.

2. **Statements:**
   I. The government has allowed private airline companies in India to operate to overseas destinations.
   II. The national air carrier has increased its flights to overseas destinations.

Ans. A: Since the Government has allowed private airline companies in India to operate to overseas, so the national air carrier has increased its flights to overseas destinations.

3. **Statements:**
   I. Many people visited the religious place during the week-end.
   II. Few people visited the religious place during the week days.

Ans. E: Both the statements I and II are the effects of some common cause.

4. **Statements:**
   I. The performance of Indian sports persons in the recently held Olympics could not reach the level of expectation the country had on them.
   II. The performance of Indian sports person in the last Asian games was far better than any previous games.

Ans. E: Both the statements are effects of some common cause.

EXERCISE

Directions (Qs. Nos. 1 to 12): *In each of the following questions, two statements numbered I and II are given. There may be cause and effect relationship between the two statements. These two statements may be the effect of the same cause or independent causes. These statements may be independent causes without having any relationship. Read both the statements in each question and mark your answer as*

A. If statement I is the cause and statement II is its effect;
B. If statement II is the cause and statement I is its effect;
C. If both the statements I and II are independent causes;
D. If both the statements I and II are effects of independent causes; and
E. If both the statements I and II are effects of some common cause.

1. Statements:

I. The prices of petrol and diesel in the domestic market have remained unchanged for the past few months.

II. The crude oil prices in the international market have gone up substantially in the last few months.

2. Statements:

I. India has surpassed the value of tea exports this year over all the earlier years due to an increase in demand for quality tea in the European market.

II. There is an increase in demand of coffee in the domestic market during the last two years.

3. Statements:

I. The government has recently fixed the fees for professional courses offered by the unaided institutions which are much lower than the fees charged last year.

II. The parents of the aspiring students launched a severe agitation last year protesting against the high fees charged by the unaided institutions.

4. Statements:

I. The Reserve Bank of India has recently put restrictions on few small banks in the country.

II. The small banks in the private and co-operative sector in India are not in a position to withstand the competitions of the bigger in the public sector.

5. Statements:

I. All the schools in the area had to be kept closed for most part of the week.

II. Many parents have withdrawn their children from the local schools.

6. Statements:

I. There is unprecedented increase in the number of young unemployed in comparison to the previous year.

II. A large number of candidates submitted applications against an advertisement for the post of manager issued by a bank.

7. Statements:

I. The school authority has asked the X Std. students to attend special classes to be conducted on Sundays.

II. The parents of the X Std. students have withdrawn their wards from attending private tuitions conducted on Sundays.

8. Statements:

I. Majority of the students in the college expressed their opinion against the college authority's decision to break away from the university and become autonomous.

II. The university authorities have expressed their inability to provide grants to its constituent colleges.

9. Statements:

I. The police authority has recently caught a group of house breakers.

II. The citizens group in the locality have started night vigil in the area.

10. Statements:

I. The Government has imported large quantities of sugar as per trade agreement with other countries.

II. The prices of sugar in the domestic market have fallen sharply in the recent months.

11. Statements:

I. It is the aim of the city's civic authority to get the air pollution reduced by 20% in the next two months.

II. The number of asthma cases in the city is constantly increasing.

12. Statements:

I. The private medical colleges have increased the tuition fees in the current year by 200 per cent over the last year's fees to meet the expenses.

II. The Government medical colleges have not increased their fees in spite of price escalation.

ANSWERS

1	2	3	4	5	6	7	8	9	10
D	C	B	B	D	A	A	B	E	A
11	**12**								
B	C								

EXPLANATORY ANSWERS

1. The prices of petrol and diesel being stagnant in the domestic market and the increase in the same in the international market must be backed by independent causes.

2. The two statements discuss two separate statistical and generalised results.

3. The parents' protest against high fees being charged by the institutions led the government to interfere and fix the fees at a more affordable level.

4. The inability of the small banks to compete with the bigger ones shall not ensure security and good service to the customers, which is an essential concomitant that has to be looked into by the Reserve Bank. I seems to be a remedial step for the same.

5. Closing the schools for a week and the parents withdrawing their wards from the local schools are independent issues, which must have been triggered by different individual causes.

6. An increase in the number of unemployed youth is bound to draw in huge crowds for a single vacancy.

7. It seems quite evident that the parents have instructed their wards to abstain from private tuitions on Sundays and attend special classes organised by the school.

8. Clearly, the university's decision to refuse grant to the colleges must have triggered the college authority to become autonomous.

9. Both the statements are clearly backed by a common cause, which is clearly an increase in the number of thefts in the locality.

10. Since the Government has imported large quantities of sugar as per trade agreement with other countries, therefore, the prices of the sugar in the domestic market have fallen sharply in the recent months.

11. The increase in number of asthma cases must have alerted the authorities to take action to control air pollution that triggers the disease.

12. The increase in the fees of the private colleges and there being no increase in the same in Government colleges seem to be policy matters undertaken by the individual decisive boards at the two levels.

❀ ❀ ❀

14 Course of Action

In these questions, a situation is presented and some courses of action are suggested in the context of that situation. Job is to determine which of them should be followed. Such questions tests one's ability to judge a problem correctly, to determine the root cause of the problem and then to prescribe a suitable course of action.

Basically there are two broad types of patterns in such questions, it is a 'problem-solution' or 'fact-follow-up action' type.

To solve questions on 'course of action' first of all, determine whether it is a 'problem-solution' or 'fact-follow-up action' type.

Example

Directions (Qs. Nos. 1 and 2): *In each question given below a statement is followed by three courses of action denoted 1, 2 and 3. A course of action is a step or administrative decision to be taken for improvement, follow-up for further action in regard to the problem, policy etc. on the basis of the information given in the statement. You have to assume everything in the statement to be true, then decide which of the three given/suggested courses of action logically follows for pursuing and decide the answer.*

1. Statement: The chairman of the car company announced in the meeting that all trial of its first product of the new car model 'M' are over and company plans to launch its car in the market after six months.

Courses of action:

1. The network of dealers is to be finalised and all legal, financial and other matters in this connection will have to be finalised shortly.
2. The company will have to make plan for product other than car.
3. Material, managerial and other resources will have to be in fine tune to maintain production schedule.

A. 1 and 3 only B. Only 1
C. All the three D. Only 2
E. None of these

Ans. A: After trials, the best availability of material, managerial and other resources is necessary to maintain production schedule. Hence 3 follows. As stated 'model M is its first product', so it is necessary to finalise the network of dealers and all matters regarding the sale of the product. Hence 1 follows. 2 has no connection with the statement.

2. Statement: The Company 'X' has rejected first lot of valves supplied by company"Y' and has cancelled its entire huge order quoting use of inferior-quality material and poor crafts-manship.

Courses of action:

1. The Company 'Y' needs to investigate functioning of its purchase, production and quality control departments.
2. The Company 'Y' should inspect all the valves rejected by Company 'X'.
3. The Company 'Y' should inform Company 'X' that steps have been taken for improvement and renegotiate schedule of supply.

A. Only 1 and 2 B. Only 2
C. All 1, 2 and 3 D. 2 and either 1 or 3
E. None of these

Ans. 3: As stated 'rejection due to inferior-quality material and poor craftsmanship', since purchase deptt is responsible for purchasing the inferior quality material and for improper inspection. Hence investigation is compulsory for all the departments. Hence 1 follows. 2 follows because claim of company 'X' may not be true. 3 follows because relationships with a previous client should always be kept out.

EXERCISE

Directions (Qs. Nos. 1 to 15): *In each question below is given a statement followed by two courses of action numbered I and II. You have to assume everything in the statement to be true and on the basis of the information given in the statement, decide which of the suggested courses of action logically follow(s) for pursuing.*

A. If only I follows
B. If only II follows
C. If either I or II follows
D. If neither I nor II follows
E. If both I and II follow

1. **Statement:** Severe drought is reported to have set in several parts of the state.
   Courses of Action:
   I. Government should immediately make arrangement for providing financial assistance to those affected.
   II. Food, water and fodder should immediately be sent to all these areas to save the people and cattle.

2. **Statement:** A large number of people in ward J of the city are diagnosed to be suffering from a fatal dengue type fever.
   Courses of Action:
   I. The city municipal authority should take immediate steps to carry out extensive fumigation in ward J.
   II. The people in the area should be advised to take steps to avoid mosquito bites.

3. **Statement:** Since its launching in 2001, Kingfisher Airlines has so far accumulated losses amounting to ₹ 8000 crore.
   Courses of Action:
   I. Kingfisher Airlines should be directed to reduce wasteful expenditure and to increase passenger fare.
   II. An amount of about ₹ 300 crore should be provided to Kingfisher Airlines to make the airliner economically viable.

4. **Statement:** Exporters in the town are alleging that commercial banks are violating a Reserve Bank of India directive to operate a post shipment export credit denominated in foreign currency at international rates from March this year.
   Courses of Action:
   I. The officers concerned in the commercial banks are to be suspended.
   II. The RBI should be asked to stop giving such directives to commercial banks.

5. **Statement:** A large number of people suffer illness every year due to drinking polluted water during the rainy season.
   Courses of Action:
   I. The government should make adequate arrangements to provide safe drinking water to all its citizens.
   II. The people should be educated about the dangers of drinking polluted water.

6. **Statement:** Most of those who study in premier government engineering colleges in India migrate to developed nations for better prospects in their professional pursuits.
   Courses of Action:
   I. All the students joining these colleges should be asked to sign a bond at the time of admission to the effect that they will remain in India at least for ten years after they complete education.
   II. All those students who desire to settle in the developed nations should be asked to pay entire cost of their education which the government subsidies.

7. **Statement:** As stated in the last census report the female to male ratio is alarmingly low in most of the states.
   Courses of Action:
   I. The government should conduct another census to verify the results.
   II. The government should immediately issue orders to all the departments to encourage people to improve the ratio.

8. **Statement:** The retired Professors of the S Institute should also be invited to deliberate on restructuring of the organization, as their contribution may be beneficial to the Institute.
   Courses of Action:
   I. Management may seek opinion of the employees before calling retired professors.

II. Management should involve experienced people for the systematic restructuring of the organization.

9. Statement: Three districts in State F have been experiencing severe drought for the last four years resulting into exodus of people from these districts.

Courses of Action:

I. The government should immediately start food for work programme in these districts to put a halt to the exodus.

II. The government should make sincere efforts to provide drinking/potable water to these districts.

10. Statement: The sale of a particular product has gone down considerably causing great concern to the company.

Courses of Action:

I. The company should make a proper study of rival products in the market.

II. The price of the product should be reduced and quality improved.

11. Statement: A recent study revals that children below five die in the cities of the developing countries mainly from diarrhoea and parasitic intestinal worms.

Courses of Action:

I. Governments of the developing countries should take adequate measures to improve the hygienic conditions in the cities.

II. Children below five years in the cities of the developing countries need to be kept under periodic medical check-up.

12. Statement: A recent survey shows that the teachers are still not familiarised with the need, importance and meaning of population education in the higher education system. They are not even clearly aware about their role and responsibilities in the population education programme.

Courses of Action:

I. Population education programme should be included in the college curriculum.

II. Orientation programme should be conducted for teachers on population education.

13. Statement: STAR TV is concerned about the quality of its programmes particularly in view of stiff competition it is facing from SAB and other satellite TV channels and is contemplating various measures to attract talent for its programmes.

Courses of Action:

I. In an effort to attract talent, the STAR TV should revise its fee structure for the artists.

II. The fee structure should not be revised until other electronic media also revise it.

14. Statement: The Asian Development Bank has approved a $285 million loan to finance a project to construct coal ports by Coal India Limited in Kerala.

Courses of Action:

I. India should use financial assistance from other international financial organisations to develop such ports in other places.

II. India should not seek such financial assistance from the international financial agencies.

15. Statement: The Rabi crops have been affected by the insects for consecutive three years in the district and the farmers on average harvested less than fifty percent of produce during these years.

Courses of Action:

I. The farmers should seek measures to control the attack of insects to protect their crops next year.

II. The Government should increase the support price of Rabi crops considerably to protect the economic interests of farmers.

ANSWERS

1	2	3	4	5	6	7	8	9	10
B	E	A	D	E	B	B	B	E	A
11	**12**	**13**	**14**	**15**					
E	B	A	A	E					

EXPLANATORY ANSWERS

1. In the break-out of a natural calamity, the basic duty of the government becomes to provide the basic amenities essential to save the lives of people and cattle. Providing financial assistance to all would put undue burden on the country's resources. So, only II follows.
2. Clearly, prevention from mosquitoes and elimination of mosquitoes are two ways to prevent dengue. So, both the courses follow.
3. Clearly, for better economic gain, losses should be reduced and income increased. So, only course I follows.
4. The statement mentions that the commercial banks violate a directive issued by the RBI. The remedy is only to make the banks implement the Act. So, none of the courses follows.
5. The situation demands creating awareness among people about the dangers of drinking polluted water so that they themselves refrain from the same, and at the same time taking steps to provide safe drinking water. So, both the courses follow.
6. Clearly, no student can be bound to live and work in the country against his wish. So, I does not follow. However, it is quite right to recover the extra benefits awarded to students if they do not serve their own country. So, II follows.
7. A census is always conducted with the utmost precision, leaving negligible chances of differences. So, I does not follow. Further, the ratio can be improved by creating awareness among the masses and abolishing female foeticide. Thus, only course II follows.
8. The statement stresses that the contribution of retired Professors shall be beneficial. This means that these people's experience regarding working of the organisation is helpful. So, only course II follows.
9. The exodus can be checked by providing the people conditions conducive to living. So, both the courses follow.
10. Clearly, a study of rival products in the market will help assess the cause for the lowering down of sales and then a suitable action can be taken. Thus, I follows. The second course may not be implementable.
11. Clearly, the two diseases mentioned are caused by unhygienic conditions. So, improving the hygienic conditions will check the spread of disease. Also, periodic medical check-up will help timely detection of the disease and hence a proper treatment. So, both I and II follow.
12. The statement stresses on teachers' lack of awareness and knowledge in population education and as such the best remedy would be to guide them in this field through orientation programmes. So, only course II follows.
13. Revised its fee structure for artists will attract talent and enchance quality of STAR TV programmes. It cannot wait till other media take action. So, only course I follows.
14. Clearly, such projects will provide employment and shall be an asset and a source of income to the country later on. So, course I shall follows. Course II will slowdown country's economic growth.
15. Clearly, the problem demands taking extra care and adequate precautions to protect crops from insects and extending help to farmers to prevent them from incurring huge losses. Thus, both the courses follow.

❀ ❀ ❀

15 Distinguishing Argument

Arguments are the fundamentals unit of logic. An argument contains two explict constituents: supporting premises and conclusion. Some supporting premises make strong arguments while some make weak arguments. The question statement is (usually) in the form of a suggested course of action. Followed by the statement are two arguments, one argument advocates the suggested course of action by stating out the positive features or positive results of that action and the other argues against the suggested course of action by stating out the negative features or harmful results of that action.

To determine forcefulness of argument it should be preliminary screened first to reject an argument on the basis of preliminary observations. An argument can be rejected if it is ambiguous or if it is 'half-hearted' or if it is too simple to be acceptable or if it is in the form of a question. If a argument is not rejected in preliminary screening then argument is subjected to three steps to ascertain its strength.

Thus, solution consists of four stages: 1. Preliminary screening 2. Check, whether the result really follows or not 3. Check, whether the result really desirable or not (or harmful, in case of negative arguments)? 4. Check, whether the argument and the suggested course of action are properly related or not?

If an argument passes all the four checks, it is a strong argument, otherwise it is weak.

Example

Directions (Qs. Nos. 1 and 2): *In making decisions about important questions, it is desirable to be able to distinguish between "strong" arguments and "weak" arguments insofar as they relate to the question. "Strong" arguments are those which are both important and directly related to the question. "Weak" arguments are those which are of minor importance and also may not be directly related to the question or may be related to a trivial aspect of the question.*

Instructions: Each statement below is followed by two arguments denoted by I and II. you have to decide which of the arguments is a "strong" argument and which is a "weak" argument.

Give answer:

A. if only argument I is "strong".
B. if only argument II is "strong".
C. if either I or II is "strong".
D. if neither I nor II is "strong".
E. if both I and II are "strong".

1. **Statement:** Should one close relative of a retiring government employee be given a job in government services in India?

   Arguments:

   I. Yes, where else relative get a job like this?
   II. No, it will close doors of government service to competent and needy youth.

Ans. B: I is weak because that relative may not be suitable for the job. II is strong. As the seats will be filled by close relatives of retiring government employees, deserving and other needy youths won't get entry for government services.

2. **Statement:** Should purchase of gold by individuals be restricted in India to improve its foreign exchange position?

Arguments:

I. Yes, interference on customer's right and freedom is desirable.

II. No, business interest has to be guarded first.

Ans. D: I is weak because such interference is not desirable in a democracy. II is weak because it gives priority to business interest on foreign exchange position, which is undesirable.

EXERCISE

Directions (Qs. 1 to 10): *Each question given below consists of a statement, followed by two arguments numbered I and II. You have to decide which of the arguments is a 'strong' argument and which is a 'weak' argument.*

1. **Statement:** Should there be a restriction on the migration of people from one state to another state in India?
   Arguments:
   I. No. Any Indian citizen has a basic right to stay at any place of his/her choice and hence they cannot be stopped.
   II. Yes. This is the way to effect an equitable distribution of resources across the states in India.

2. **Statement:** Should there be a complete ban on use of all types of chemical pesticides in India?
   Arguments:
   I. No. The pests will destroy all the crops and the farmers will have nothing to harvest.
   II. Yes. The chemical pesticides used in agriculture pollute the water underground and this has become a serious health hazard.

3. **Statement:** Should officers accepting bribe be punished?
   Arguments:
   I. No. Certain circumstances may have compelled them to take bribe.
   II. Yes. They should do the job they are entrusted with, honestly.

4. **Statement:** Should cutting of trees be banned altogether?
   Arguments:
   I. Yes. It is very much necessary to do so to restore ecological balance.
   II. No. A total ban would harm timber based industries.

5. **Statement:** Should all refugees, who make unauthorized entry into a country, be forced to go back to their homeland?
   Arguments:
   I. Yes. They make their colonies and occupy a lot of land.
   II. No. They leave their homes because of hunger or some terror and on human grounds, should not be forced to go back.

6. **Statement:** Should all the practising doctors be brought under Government control so that they get salary from the Government and treat patients free of cost?
   Arguments:
   I. No. How can any country do such an undemocratic thing?
   II. Yes. Despite many problems, it will certainly help minimize, if not eradicate, unethical medical practices.

7. **Statement:** Should there be a ban on product advertising?
   Arguments:
   I. No. It is an age of advertising. Unless your advertisement is better than your other competitors, the product will not be sold.
   II. Yes. The money spent on advertising is very huge and it inflates the cost of the product.

8. **Statement:** Are nuclear families better than joint families?
   Arguments:
   I. No. Joint families ensure security and also reduce the burden of work.
   II. Yes. Nuclear families ensure greater freedom.

9. Statement: Should there be compulsory medical examination of both the man and the woman before they marry each other?

Arguments:

I. No. This is an intrusion to the privacy of an individual and hence cannot be tolerated.

II. Yes. This will substantially reduce the risk of giving birth to children with serious ailments.

10. Statement: Should government stop spending huge amounts of money on international sports?

Arguments:

I. Yes. This money can be utilized for upliftment of the poor.

II. No. Sports persons will be frustrated and will not get international exposure.

ANSWERS

1	2	3	4	5	6	7	8	9	10
A	E	B	E	B	B	E	E	B	B

EXPLANATORY ANSWERS

1. Clearly, argument I holds strong, while argument II is vague.

2. Obviously, pesticides are meant to prevent the crops from harmful pests. But at the same time, they get washed away with water and contaminate the groundwater. Thus, both the arguments hold strong.

3. Obviously, officers are paid duly for the jobs they do. So, they must do it honestly. Thus, argument II alone holds.

4. Definitely, trees play a vital role in maintaining ecological balance and so must be preserved. So, argument I holds. Also, trees form the basic source of timber and a complete ban on cutting of trees would harm timber based industries. So, only a controlled cutting of trees should be allowed and the loss replenished by planting more trees. So, argument II is also valid.

5. Obviously, refugees are people forced out of their homeland by some misery and need shelter desperately. So, argument II holds. Argument I against the statement is vague.

6. A doctor treating a patient individually can mislead the patient into wrong and unnecessary treatment for his personal gain. So, argument II holds strong. Also, a policy benefiting common people cannot be termed 'undemocratic'. So, I is vague.

7. Obviously, it is the advertisement which makes the customer aware of the qualities of the product and leads him to buy it. So, argument I is valid. But at the same time, advertising nowadays has become a costly affair and the expenses on it add to the price of the product. So, argument II also holds strong.

8. Obviously, with so many people around in a joint family, there is more security. Also, work is shared. So, argument I holds. In nuclear families, there are lesser number of people and so lesser responsibilities and more freedom. Thus, II also holds.

9. Definitely, such a step would help to prevent the growth of diseases like AIDS. So, only argument II is strong.

10. Obviously, spending money on sports should not be avoided merely because it can be spent on socio-economic problems. So, argument I does not hold. Also, if the expenses on sports are curtailed, the sports persons would face lack of facilities and training and our country will lag behind in the international sports competitions. So, II holds.

❀ ❀ ❀

16 Drawing Conclusions

In this reasoning pattern, a statement is given followed by two conclusions. The statement is to be taken as the fact. Then based on it one has to decide which of the conclusion(s) definitely follows or does not follow from the given statement.

Example

In the questions below the answer is given as:

A. If only conclusion I follows
B. If only conclusion II follows
C. If either I or II follows
D. If neither I nor II follows and
E. If both I and II follow.

1. **Statement:** It is said that teachers should not go on strike. Why should they not? Strike is an inherent right.

   Conclusions:

   I. Teachers cannot get justice unless they go on strike.
   II. Every teacher should go on strike.

Ans. A: Only conclusion I follows from the given statements, *i.e.*, as an inherent right the teachers can get justice in appropriate cases if they go on strike. Conclusion II does not follow.

2. **Statement:** The government of country 'X' has recently announced several concessions and offered attractive package tours for foreign visitors.

   Conclusions:

   I. Now, more numbers of foreign tourists will visit the country.
   II. The government of country 'X' seems to be serious in attracting foreign tourists.

Ans. E: Concessions and attractive package tours will encourage tourists and country 'X' has taken the step only because it seems to be serious about foreign visitors. So both conclusion I and conclusion II follow from the given statement.

EXERCISE

Directions (Qs. Nos. 1 to 10): *In each question below is given a statement followed by two conclusions numbered I and II. You have to assume everything in the statement to be true, then consider the two conclusions together and decide which of them logically follows beyond a reasonable doubt from the information given in the statement*

Give answer:

A. If only conclusion I follows
B. If only conclusion II follows
C. If either I or II follows
D. If neither I nor II follows and
E. If both I and II follow.

1. **Statement:** In a one day cricket match, the total runs made by a team were 200. Out of these 160 runs were made by spinners.

   Conclusions:

   I. 80% of the team consists of spinners.
   II. The opening batsmen were spinners.

2. **Statement:** The old order changed yielding place to new.

   Conclusions:

   I. Change is the law of nature.
   II. Discard old ideas because they are old.

3. **Statement:** Government has spoiled many top ranking financial institutions by appointing bureaucrats as Directors of these institutions.

Conclusions:

I. Government should appoint Directors of the financial institutes taking into consideration the expertise of the person in the area of finance.

II. The Director of the financial institute should have expertise commensurate with the financial work carried out by the institute.

4. **Statement:** Population increase coupled with depleting resources is going to be the scenario of many developing countries in days to come.

Conclusions:

I. The population of developing countries will not continue to increase in future.

II. It will be very difficult for the governments of developing countries to provide its people decent quality of life.

5. **Statement:** Prime age school-going children in urban India have now become avid as well as more regular viewers of television, even in households without a TV. As a result, there has been an alarming decline in the extent of readership of newspapers.

Conclusions:

I. Method of increasing the readership of newspapers should be devised.

II. A team of experts should be sent to other countries to study the impact of TV. On the readership of newspapers.

6. **Statement:** The Government run company had asked its employees to declare their income and assets but it has been strongly resisted by employees union and no employee is going to declare his income.

Conclusions:

I. The employees of this company do not seem to have any additional undisclosed income besides their salary.

II. The employees union wants all senior officers to declare their income first.

7. **Statement:** The distance of 900 km by road between Bombay and Jafra will be reduced to 280 km by sea. This will lead to a saving of ₹ 7.92 crores per annum on fuel.

Conclusions:

I. Transportation by sea is cheaper than that by road.

II. Fuel must be saved to the greatest extent.

8. **Statement:** The manager humiliated Sachin in the presence of his colleagues.

Conclusion:

I. The manager did not like Sachin.

II. Sachin was not popular with his colleagues.

9. **Statements:** Nation X faced growing international opposition for its decision to explode eight nuclear weapons at its test site.

Conclusions:

I. The citizens of the nation favoured the decision.

II. Some powerful countries do not want other nations to become as powerful as they are.

10. **Statement:** National Aluminium Company has moved India from a position of shortage to self-sufficiency in the metal.

Conclusions:

I. Previously, India had to import aluminium.

II. With this speed, it can soon become a foreign exchange earner.

ANSWERS

1	2	3	4	5	6	7	8	9	10
D	A	E	B	D	D	B	D	D	E

EXPLANATORY ANSWERS

1. According to the statement, 80% of the total runs were made by spinners. So, I does not follow. Nothing about the opening batsmen is mentioned in the statement. So, II also does not follow.

2. Clearly, I directly follows from the given statement. Also, it is mentioned that old ideas are replaced by new ones, as thinking changes with the progressing time. So, II does not follow.

3. According to the statement, Government has spoiled financial institutions by appointing bureaucrats as Directors. This means that only those persons should be appointed as Directors who are experts in finance and are acquainted with the financial work of the institute. So, both I and II follow.

4. The fact given in I is quite contrary to the given statement. So, I does not follow. II mentions the direct implications of the state discussed in the statement. Thus, II follows.

5. The statement concentrates on the increasing viewership of TV. and does not stress either on increasing the readership of newspapers or making studies regarding the same. So, neither I nor II follows.

6. Nothing about the details of the employees' income or the cause of their refusal to declare their income and assets, can be deduced from the given statement. So, neither I nor II follows.

7. According to the statement, sea transport is cheaper than road transport in the case of route from Bombay to Jafra, not in all the cases. So, conclusion I does not follow. The statement stresses on the saving of fuel. So, conclusion II follows.

8. The manager might have humiliated Sachin not because of his dislike but on account of certain negligence or mistake on his part. So, I does not follow. Also, nothing about Sachin's rapport with his colleagues can be deduced from the statement. So, II also does not follow.

9. Neither the citizens response to the decision nor the reason for opposition by other nations can be deduced from the statement. So, neither I nor II follows.

10. According to the statement, National Aluminium Company has moved India from a position of shortage in the past to self-sufficiency in the present. This means that previously, India had to import aluminium. So, I follows. Also, it can be deduced that if production increases at the same rate, India can export it in future. So, II also follows.

❀ ❀ ❀

17 Statement Assumptions

The mental recognition of cause-and-effect relationship is called reasoning. It may be the prediction of an event from an observed cause or the inference of a cause from an observed event. Logical reasoning is a process of passing from the known to the unknown. It is the process of deriving a logical inference from a hypothesis through reasoning.

Argumentation is fundamental to all logic. In logic, we advocate a certain point of view with the help of some evidences and certain assumptions. The whole thing is known as "argumentation". An argument contains two explict constituents: supporting premises and conclusion. There is also an implict (hidden) constituent called assumption. Conclusion is arrived at with the help of one or more than one statement, which may be called premise or proposition. In an argument, the number of premises can be more than one and it is not necessary that every argument have an assumption *i.e.* if an argument is complete in itself and does not have the hidden links, it will not have any assumptions. An assumption is something which is assumed, supposed and taken for granted.

Example

Directions: *In each question below is given a statement followed by two assumptions numbered 1 and 2. An assumption is something supposed or taken for granted. You have to consider the statement and the following assumptions and to decide which of the assumptions is implict in the statement.*

Give answer

A. if only assumption 1 is implict.
B. if only assumption 2 is implict.
C. if either 1 or 2 is implict.
D. if neither 1 nor 2 is implict.
E. if both 1 and 2 are implict.

1. Statement: The 'X' group of employees' association have opposed Voluntary Retirement Scheme to the employees of some organisations.

Assumptions:

1. Only those employees who are not efficient may opt for the scheme.
2. The response of the employees may be lukewarm towards the scheme and it may not the benefit the organisation to the desired level.

Ans. A: The employees association is generally concerned with the welfare of employees and not with benefit of the organisation, hence 2 is not implict. 1 is not related with the statement.

Alter: If assumptions 1 and 2 are considered wrong then too main statement is valid one so none of them follows.

2. Statement: In view of the statement on the ongoing strike of work by the employees, the government has agreed to work out an effective social security programme.

Assumptions:

1. The striking employees may not be satisfied with the announcement and continue the agitation.
2. The striking employees may withdraw their agitation with immediate effect and start working.

Ans. B: Assuming 2 only, the government has agreed to work out an effective social security programme.

Alter: If 1 is considered correct than the main statement is absurd so 1 does not follow. Main statement is meaningful only when 2 is considered correct, so 2 follows.

EXERCISE

Directions (Qs. Nos. 1-10): *In each question below is given a statement followed by two assumptions numbered I and II. You have to consider the statement and the following assumptions and decide which of the assumptions is implicit in the statement.*

Give answer

A. if only assumption I is implict.
B. if only assumption II is implict.
C. if either I or II is implict.
D. if neither I nor II is implict.
E. if both I and II are implict.

1. Statement: Many historians have done more harm than good by distorting truth.

Assumptions:

I. People believe what is reported by the historians.

II. Historians are seldom expected to depict the truth.

2. Statement: "As there is a great demand, every person seeking tickets of the programme will be given only five tickets."

Assumptions:

I. The organizers are not keen on selling the tickets.

II. No one is interested in getting more than five tickets.

3. Statement: "Computer education should start at schools itself."

Assumptions:

I. Learning computers is easy.

II. Computer educated is hardly unemployed.

4. Statement: "The programme will start at 6 p.m. but you can come there up to 7 p.m. or so and still there is no problem."

Assumptions:

I. The programme will continue even after 7 p.m.

II. The programme may not even start by that time.

5. Statement: The organization should promote employees on the basis of merit alone and not on the basis of length of service or seniority.

Assumptions:

I. Length of service or seniority do not alone reflect merit of an employee.

II. It is possible to determine and measure merit of an employee.

6. Statement: The higher echelons of any organization are expected to be models of observational learning and should not be considered as merely sources of reward and punishments.

Assumptions:

I. Employees are likely to be sensitive enough to learn by observing the behaviour of their bosses.

II. Normally bosses are considered as sources of reward and punishment.

7. Statement: "If you want to give any advertisement, give it in the newspaper X." — A tells B.

Assumptions:

I. B wants to publicise his products.

II. Newspaper X has a wide circulation.

8. Statement: Kundan left for Delhi on Tuesday by train to attend a function to be held on Friday at his uncle's house in Delhi.

Assumptions:

I. Kundan may reach Delhi on Wednesday.

II. Kundan may reach Delhi before Friday.

9. Statement: "Get rid of your past for future, get our new generation fridge at a discount in exchange of old".—An advertisement.

Assumptions:

I. The sales of the new fridge may increase in the coming months.

II. People prefer to exchange future with past.

10. Statement: "Ensure a good night's sleeps for your family with safe and effective X mosquito coil."—An advertisement.

Assumptions:

I. X mosquito coil is better than any other mosquito coil.

II. A good night's sleep is desirable.

ANSWERS

1	2	3	4	5	6	7	8	9	10
A	D	A	A	E	E	B	B	E	B

EXPLANATORY ANSWERS

1. The view that historians have done harm by distorting truth means that people believe what is reported by the historians. So, I is implicit. II does not follow from the statement and so is not implicit.

2. Clearly, the organizers are adopting this policy not to reduce the sale but to cope up with great demand so that maximum can get the ticket. So, I is not implicit. Also, due to great demand, the maximum number of tickets one person can get has been reduced to five. So, II is also not implicit.

3. Computer education can be started at the school level only if it is easy. So, I is implicit. Statement does not talk about the link between jobs and computer education. So, II is not implicit.

4. The statement tells that there is no problem if one comes up to 7 p.m. also. This means that the programme will continue even after 7 p.m. So, I is implicit. Also, it is clearly mentioned that the programme will start at 6 p.m. So, II is not implicit.

5. The statement advocates to award promotion to a person who has been displaying remarkable talent and performing extraordinarily for the organization rather than the one who has been working steadily for the organization since long. Thus, length of service does not alone prove a man worthy. His talent and his performance are the criteria to be considered. So, both I and II are implicit.

6. The statement advises people not to consider their bosses as mere 'instruments' to control and assess their acts, but as 'models' to imitate in their working. So, both I and II are implicit.

7. The statement speaks for any advertisement and it may not be restricted to promotion of products only. So I is not implicit. It is advised that advertisements be given in newspaper X. This means that X will help advertise better *i.e.*, it has wider circulation. So, II is implicit.

8. Clearly, it cannot be deduced as to which day Kundan would reach Delhi. But Kundan has left for Delhi to attend a function to be held on Friday. So, he must have planned his journey to reach Delhi before Friday. Thus, only II is implicit.

9. Obviously, the scheme is aimed to encourage those owning an old fridge to go for a new one at a reasonable price without the hassles of disposing off the old one. So, I is implicit. An advertisement highlights that which appeals to masses and which customers desire for. So, II is also implicit.

10. The statement mentions the good qualities of X coil but this does not necessitate it is the best. So, I is not implicit. Besides, an advertisement highlights the feature which is desirable by customers and can lure them. So, II is implicit.

❀ ❀ ❀

18 Cubes and Dice

The questions related to problems on cubes and dice are aimed to check the imaginative power of the candidate. The candidate must have the ability to visualise quickly in three-dimensional object for what is asked of it. To attempt such questions some basic facts should be kept in mind and the visualisation ability should be combined with fast and accurate calculations.

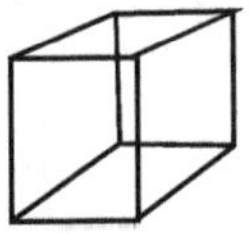

Cube

- Cube has six faces/sides and eight corners.
- Problems are based on the same or different coloured faces.
- Dice has six faces/sides.
- Problems are based only on the value occurring on the six faces.
- Problems are based on cutting the squares into specified number of smaller equal parts.

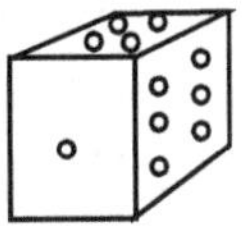

Dice

Diagrammatically, the explanation of a cube which is painted green on all sides can be understood easily taking one side of the cube.

a	b	a
b	c	b
a	b	a

This cube is divided into $3 \times 3 \times 3 = 27$ equal small cubes.

There are four corner pieces 'a', so 4×2, *i.e.*, 8 pieces will be painted on 3 sides.

There are four middle pieces 'b', so 4×3, *i.e.*, 12 pieces will be painted on 2 sides

There is one middle piece 'c', so 1×6, *i.e.*, 6 pieces will be painted only on 1 side.

There will be one piece right in the centre of this cube, *i.e.*, piece will not have paint at all.

So, this cube has $8 + 12 + 6 + 1$, *i.e.*, 27 smaller cubes.

EXERCISE

1. Two positions of a dice are shown below. When there are two circles at the bottom, the number of circles at the top will be :

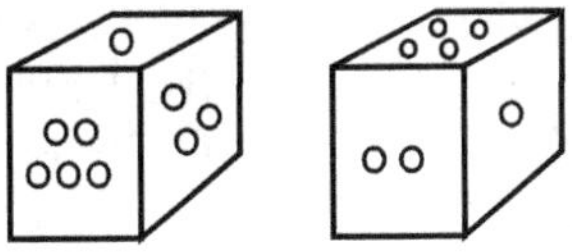

A. 5
B. 2
C. 3
D. 6
E. None of these

2. Two positions of a dice are shown below. When 4 is at the bottom, what number will be on the top?

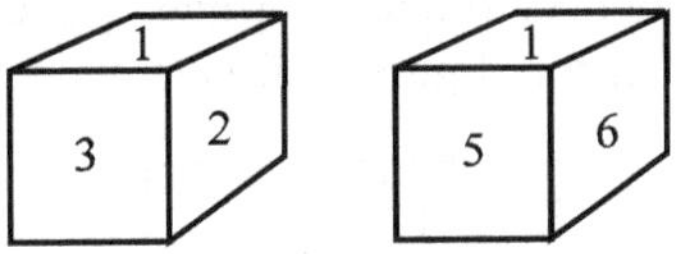

A. 1
B. 2
C. 5
D. 6
E. None of these

3. A cube is painted red on two adjacent faces and on one opposite face, yellow on two adjacent faces and green on the remaining face. It is then cut into 64 equal cubes. How many cubes have only one red and one green face?

A. 4 B. 8
C. 12 D. 16
E. None of these

4. A cube, on whose sides letters have been written, is shown below in different positions as can be seen from different directions. Find the missing letter?

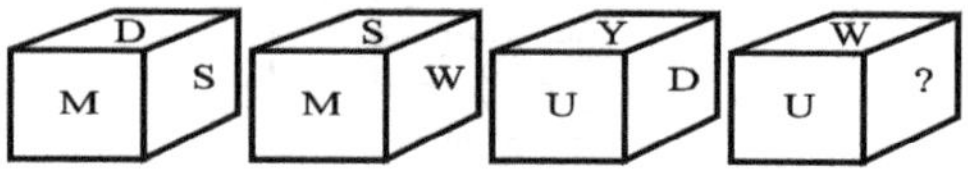

A. S B. D
C. Y D. W
E. None of these

5. In a dice a, b, c and d, are written on the adjacent faces, in a clockwise order and e and f at the top and bottom. When c is at the top, what will be at the bottom?

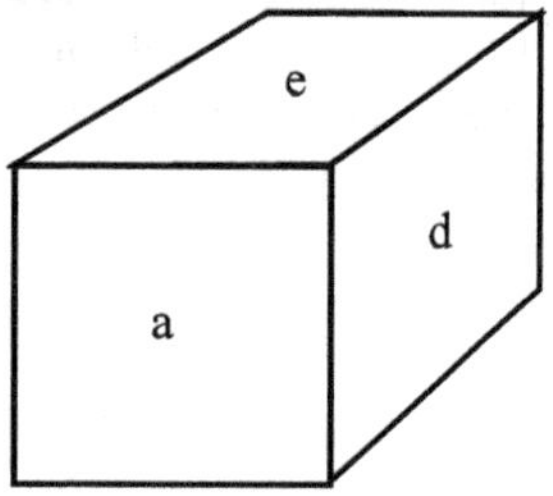

A. a B. c
C. e D. b
E. None of these

6. The number of cubes arranged one over the other in this figure will be :

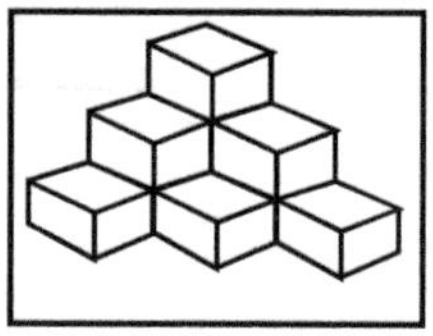

A. 8 B. 6
C. 5 D. 10
E. None of these

7. Two positions of a dice are shown below. When 2 is at the bottom, which number will be at the top?

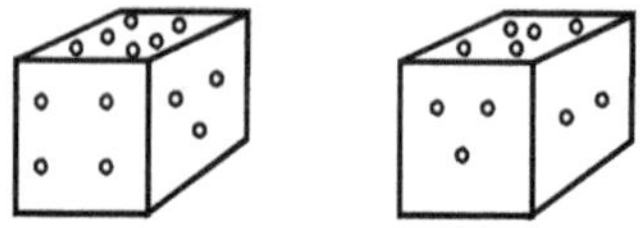

A. 1 B. 2
C. 3 D. 4
E. None of these

8. The sides of a cube are painted in different colours. Black side is opposite to red. White side is between black and red. Green side is adjacent to grey and blue side is adjacent to green. What colour will be on the side opposite to the white side of the cube?

A. Blue B. Green
C. Grey D. Data is insufficient
E. None of these

9. A cube is painted black on two adjacent faces and on one opposite face, red on two opposite faces and green on the remaining face. If it is cut into 64 equal cubes, then how many cubes will have only one black coloured face?

A. 32 B. 16
C. 12 D. 8
E. None of these

10. Six sides of a cube are coloured in the following manner

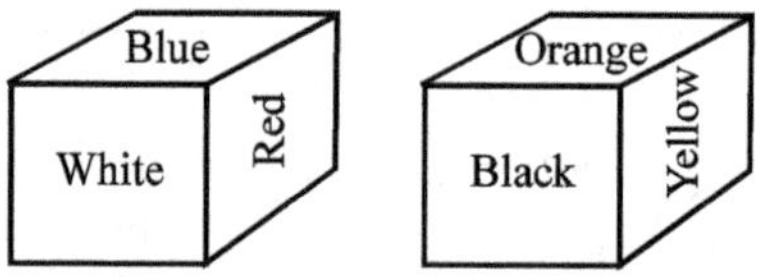

If blue and orange are opposite and red is on the top, which colour will be at the bottom?

A. Orange B. Purple
C. Black D. Yellow
E. None of these

11. A toy cube is painted orange on all sides. It is cut into 64 smaller cubes of equal size. How many smaller cubes are not painted at all?

A. 4 B. 8
C. 16 D. 20
E. None of these

Directions (Qs. 12-13) : *A die is thrown 4 times and its four different positions are given below :*

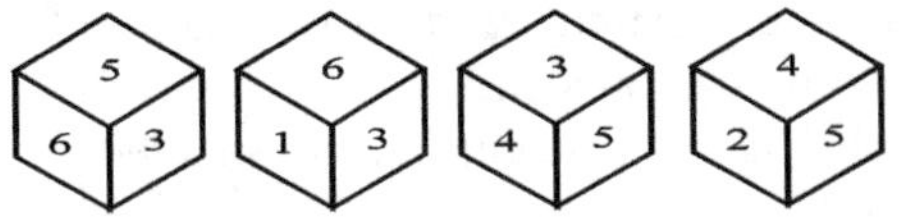

(i) (ii) (iii) (iv)

12. Find the number on the face opposite the face showing 3.

A. 2 B. 1
C. 5 D. 4
E. None of these

13. Find the number on the face opposite the face showing 6.

A. 5 B. 3
C. 4 D. 1
E. None of these

Directions (Qs. 14 to 16): *Study the information given below :*

The six faces of a cube are coloured black, brown, green, red, white and blue.

(i) Red is opposite of black
(ii) Green is between red and black
(iii) Blue is adjacent to white
(iv) Brown is adjacent to blue
(v) Red is at the bottom

14. Which colour is opposite of brown?

A. White B. Red
C. Green D. Blue
E. None of these

15. Which of the following can be deduced from (i) and (v)?

A. Black is on the top
B. Blue is on the top
C. Brown is on the top
D. Brown is opposite of black
E. None of these

16. The four adjacent colours are :

A. black, blue, brown, red
B. black, blue, brown, white
C. black, blue, red, white
D. black, blue, red, white
E. None of these

Directions (Qs. 17 to 19): *In each question below a dice has been marked with some letters or numerals and placed in three different positions. Answer the questions that follow :*

17. Which letter is opposite to Q?

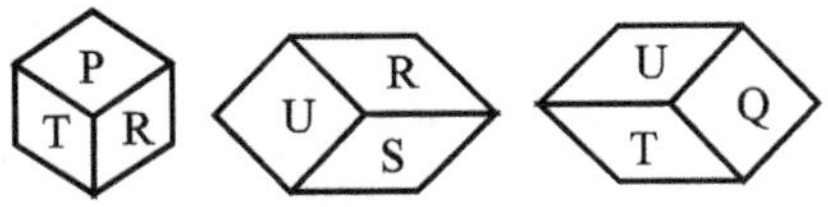

A. P B. R
C. S D. T
E. None of these

18. Which letter/numeral is opposite to 3?

A. 2 B. A
C. B D. C
E. None of these

19. If one of the 3 visible faces of the cube is hidden, which letter is opposite to O?

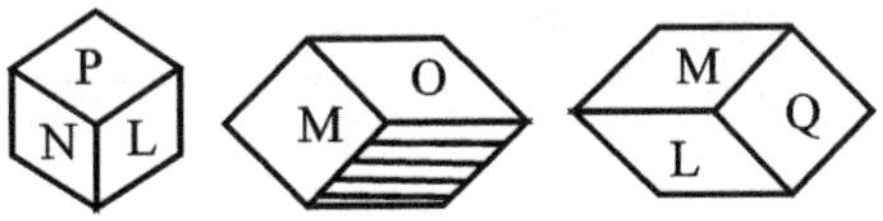

A. L B. N
C. P D. Q
E. None of these

Directions (Qs. 20 to 22): *Given below are the three positions of the same dice. Answer the questions that follow :*

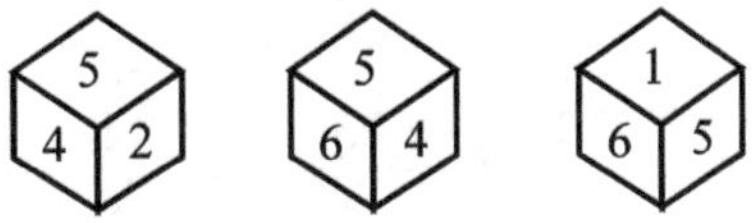

20. What is the number on the face opposite of face 2?

A. 1
B. 6
C. 5
D. Cannot be determined
E. None of these

21. In the third position of the dice which number lies on the face on the bottom?

A. 2 B. 3
C. 4 D. 5
E. None of these

22. When value 5 is on the face on the top, which value lies on the face on the bottom?
A. 3 B. 4
C. 1 D. 2
E. None of these

Directions (Qs. 23 to 25): *A solid cube with each side 3 cm has been painted red, blue and green on pairs of opposite faces. It is then cut into small cubes with each side 1 cm. Answer the questions that follow :*

23. How many cubes have one face painted red and one face painted green?
A. 12 B. 8
C. 6 D. 14
E. None of these

24. How many cubes have only one face painted?
A. 6 B. 4
C. 12 D. 9
E. None of these

25. How many cubes are painted blue on one face and either red or green on another face?
A. 4 B. 6
C. 8 D. 12
E. None of these

Directions (Qs. 26 to 29): *The questions are based on the following statement :*

A cube is painted red on two adjacent faces, yellow on two opposite faces and green on the remaining faces. It is cut into 64 smaller cubes of equal size.

26. How many cubes are painted on two faces only and that too with the same colour?
A. 0 B. 4
C. 8 D. 16
E. None of these

27. How many cubes have three faces painted?
A. 4 B. 8
C. 16 D. 32
E. None of these

28. How many cubes are painted on one face only and are yellow?
A. 32 B. 16
C. 8 D. 4
E. None of these

29. How many cubes are painted on all faces?
A. 0 B. 4
C. 8 D. 64
E. None of these

ANSWERS

1	**2**	**3**	**4**	**5**	**6**	**7**	**8**	**9**	**10**
A	A	B	C	A	D	D	B	C	D
11	**12**	**13**	**14**	**15**	**16**	**17**	**18**	**19**	**20**
B	A	C	A	A	D	B	D	A	B
21	**22**	**23**	**24**	**25**	**26**	**27**	**28**	**29**	
C	A	A	A	C	B	B	C	A	

SOME SELECTED EXPLANATORY ANSWERS

1. After observing the views of the same dice, the faces that can be clearly understood to be the opposites are :
2 – 5, 4 – 3 and 1 – 6.

3. 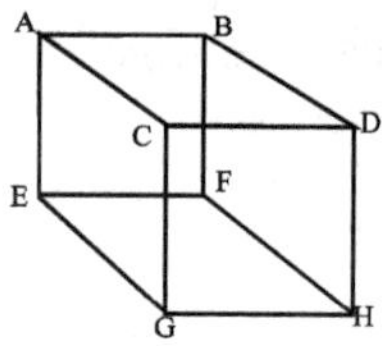

The red sides are EGAC, ABCD and BDFH.
The yellow sides are ABEF and EFGH
The green side is CDGH.

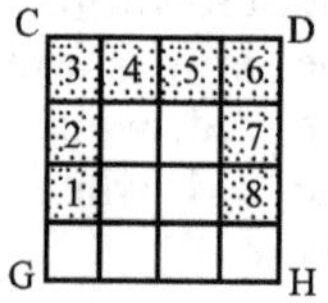

Sides GC, CD and DH are adjacent to red sides and side GH is adjacent to yellow side.

So, only 8 cubes will have one side red and one green.

4. The letters on the top and bottom sides are W and D respectively and the letters on the sides are U, Y, M and S clockwise.

5. The two positions of dice will be :

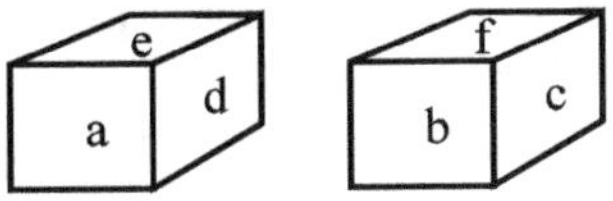

and the opposite sides will be a – c, b – d.

6.

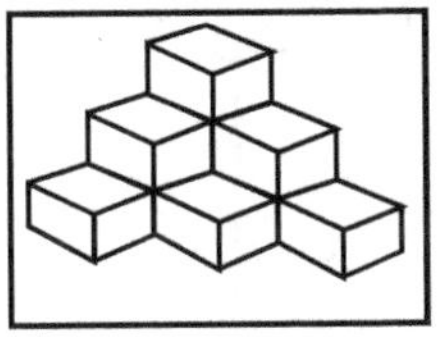

There are three columns containing 1 cube each. There are two columns containing 2 cubes each. There is one column containing 3 cubes. So, the total number of cubes is : (3 × 1) + (2 × 2) + (1 × 3), *i.e.*, 3 + 4 + 3 = 10.

9.

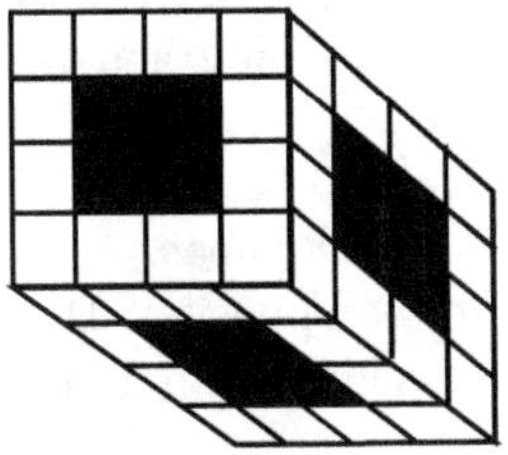

Three faces of the cube are painted black and the rest are in different colours. If this cube is cut into 64 equal cubes, then only the 4 cubes in centre of one face will come out with only one black coloured face. So, the total number of one black coloured face small cubes will be 4 × 3 = 12.

10.

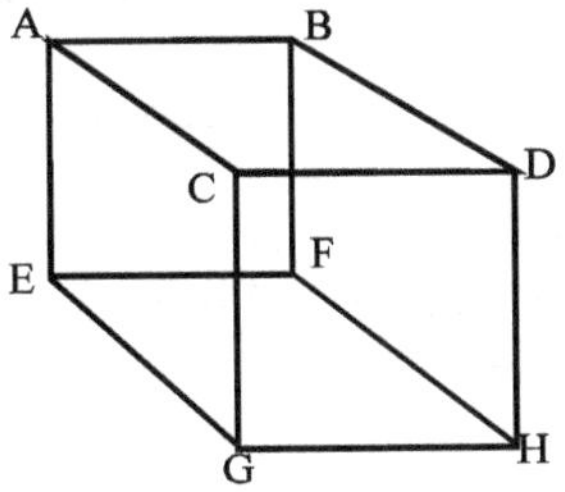

If side ABCD is red; then ABEF will be white; and ACEG will be blue. If side BDFH is orange (opposite to blue); then CDGH will be black; and EFGH will be yellow (opposite to red and at the bottom).

11. The smaller 64 pieces will be cut in the manner that :
1. 8 pieces will be painted on 3 sides,
2. 24 pieces on 2 sides.
3. 24 pieces on 1 side, and
4. 8 will not have paint at all.

Diagrammatically, the explanation taking one side of the cube will be :

a	b	b	a
b	c	c	b
b	c	c	b
a	b	b	a

1. 'a' are the corner pieces [4 × 2 = 8]
2. 'b' are the centre pieces of the cornered sides [8 × 3 = 24]
3. 'c' are the centre pieces [4 × 6 = 24]
4. Remaining interior pieces
= 64 – (8 + 24 + 24)
= 64 – 56 = 8.

12. From figures (*i*), (*ii*) and (*iii*) it is clear that the faces adjacent to 3 have numbers 6, 5, 1 and 4. So, the number on face opposite of face 3 will be 2.

13. From figures (*i*), (*iii*) and (*iv*) it is clear that the faces adjacent to 5 have numbers 6, 3, 4 and 2. So, the number on face opposite of face 5 is 1. In earlier question the face opposite 3 was 2. Now the opposite faces are 3 – 2, 5 – 1 and 4 – 6.

14. A, 15. A, 16. D :

According to the given information the two positions of the cube will be :

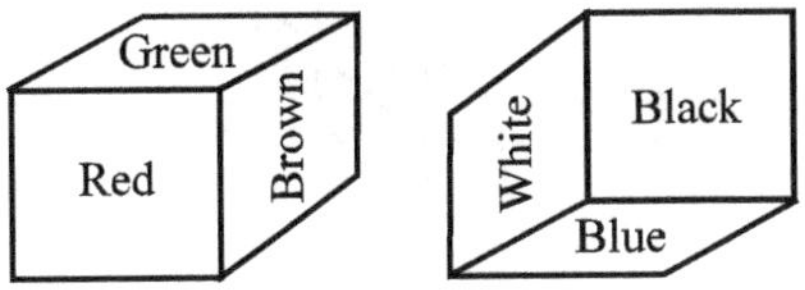

The whole cube will be :

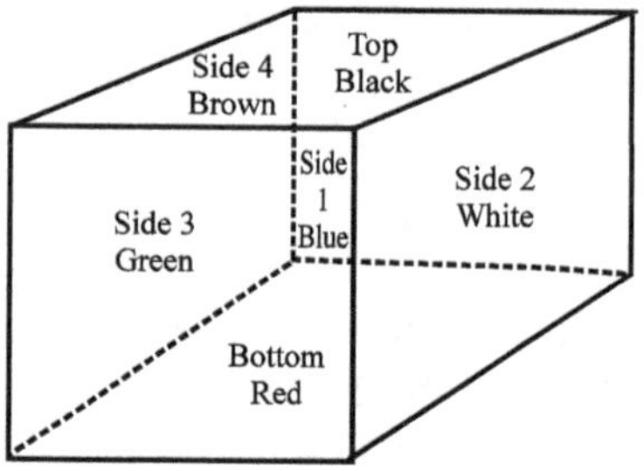

The colours on opposite faces will be : Red—Black, Green—Blue and Brown—White.

20. B, 21. C, 22. A,

The following observations can be made from the three positions of the same dice.

(*i*) Letters adjacent to 5 are 4, 2, 6 and 1. So, 3 is opposite 5.

(*ii*) Letters adjacent to 6 are 5, 4, 1 and necessarily 4. So, 2 is opposite 6.

(*iii*) When opposite numbers are 3–5 and 2–6 then 1 and 4 must be opposites.

23. A, 24. A, 25. C :

The whole cube is :

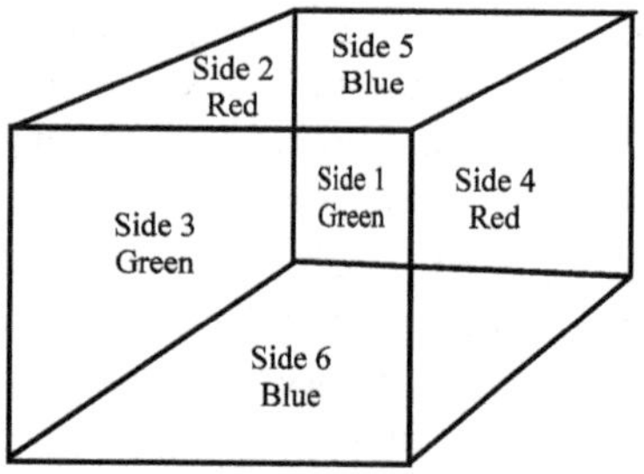

The divided cube is :

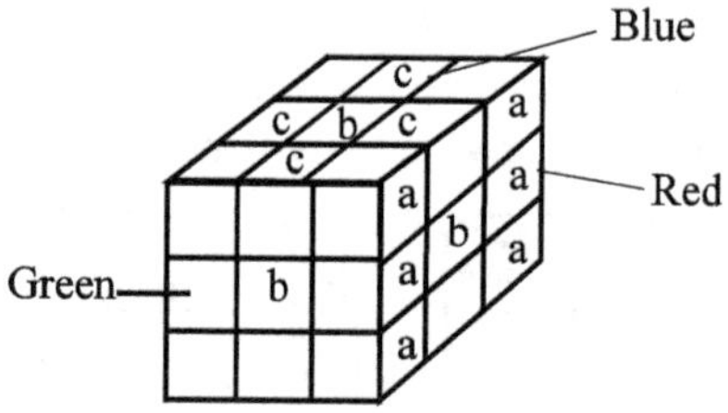

'a'— 12 cubes (6 each on opposite sides) have one face painted red and the other painted green.

'b'— 6 cubes (1 on each side) have only one face painted).

'c'— 8 cubes (4 each on opposite side) have one face painted blue and either red or green on the other.

26. B, 27. B, 28. C, 29. A :

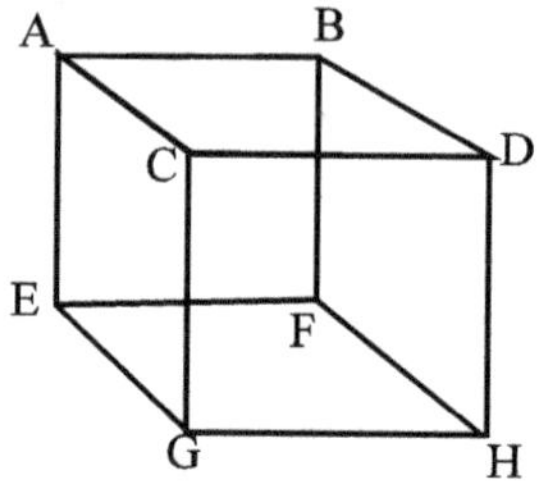

Red faces are ABCD and ABEF

Yellow faces are ACEG and BDFH

Green faces are EFGH and CDGH.

Note that Red and Green colours are on two adjacent faces. So, 2 corner cubical pieces of Red and 2 of Green (*i.e.*, total 4 cubes) will be painted on two faces only and that too with the same colour.

All the corners pieces of the cube will have three faces painted, *i.e.*, 8 cubes.

Yellow sides are on the opposites. Diagrammatically, the explanation taking one side will be :

a	b	b	a
b	c	c	b
b	c	c	b
a	b	b	a

'c' are the centered pieces and are painted on one face only in yellow. So, 4 × 2 (sides) *i.e.*, 8 cubes will have one side painted and in yellow.

Also, note that when a painted cube is cut into smaller cubes like this, not all pieces are coloured. The maximum number of sides painted in a small cube will be 3. No cube will be painted on all faces.

❀ ❀ ❀

19 Figure Series

In this form of non-verbal series, which are the most common, four or five consecutive problem figures form a definite sequence and one is required to select the one figure from the given set of Answer Figures that will continue the same sequence.

One has to try different set of moves, changes, replacements, rotations, repetitions and a lot more variations to arrive at the logical pattern making the series. Practising alone will sharpen one's skill of solving such sequences.

Example

1. Problem Figures

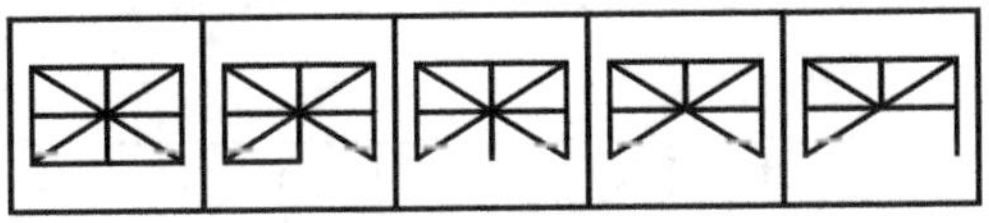

Answer Figures

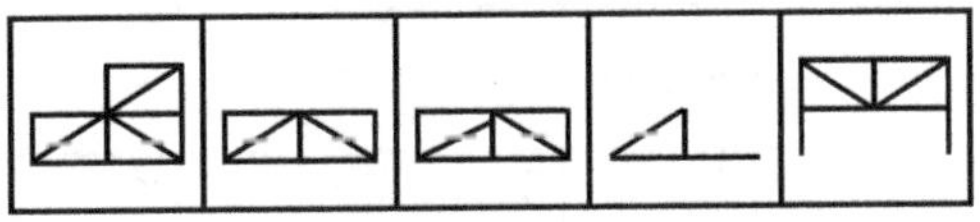

A B C D E

Answer E : Problem Figures consist of a rectangle divided into sections. At each step one of the lines is removed. First from the right, then left and then the centre. To continue this pattern, a right diagonal line is removed. In the answer figure a left diagonal line should be removed. Answer Figure 'E' continues the series.

EXERCISE

Directions : *Each of the following questions consist of problem figures followed by answer figures. Select a figure from amongst the answer figures which will continue the same series or pattern as established by the problem figures.*

1. Problem Figures

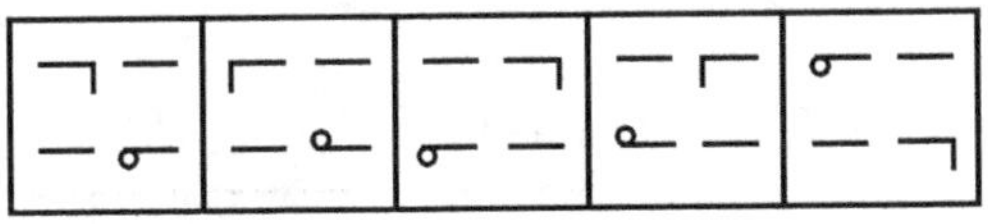

Answer Figures

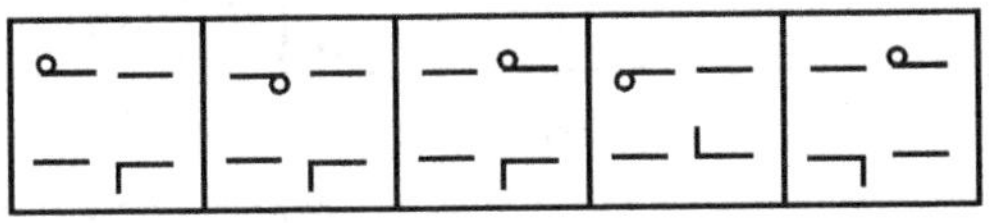

A B C D E

2. Problem Figures

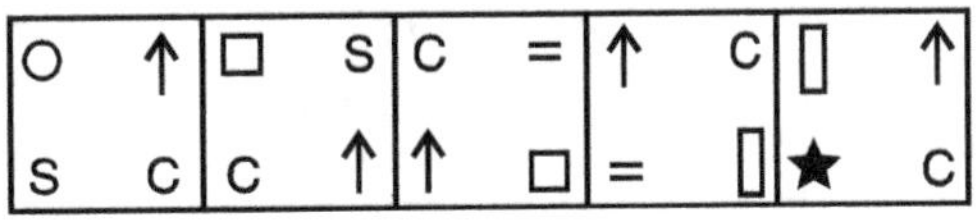

Answer Figures

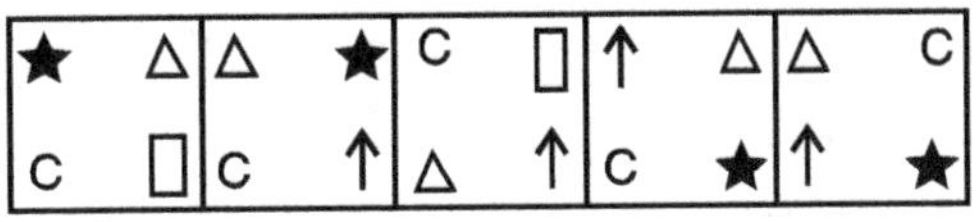

A B C D E

3. Problem Figures

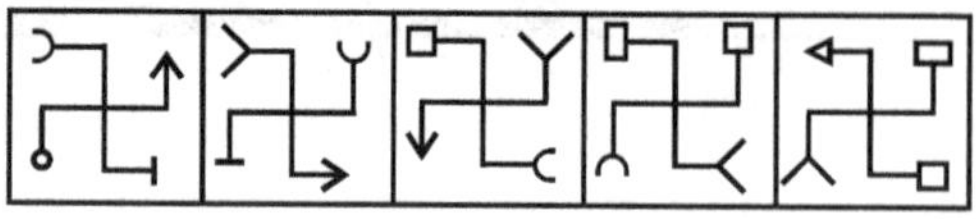

Answer Figures

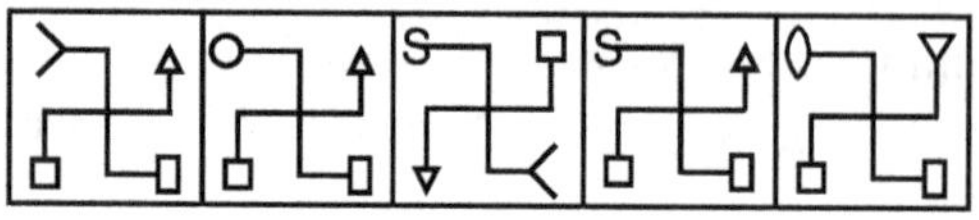

A B C D E

4. Problem Figures

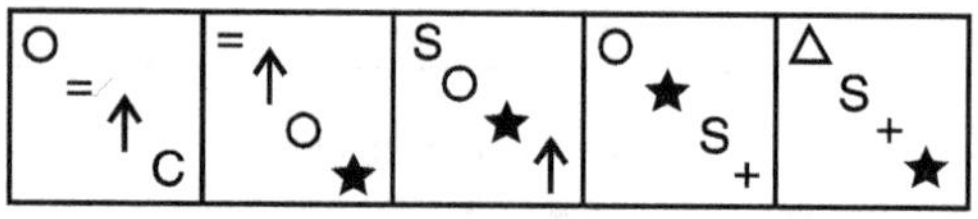

Answer Figures

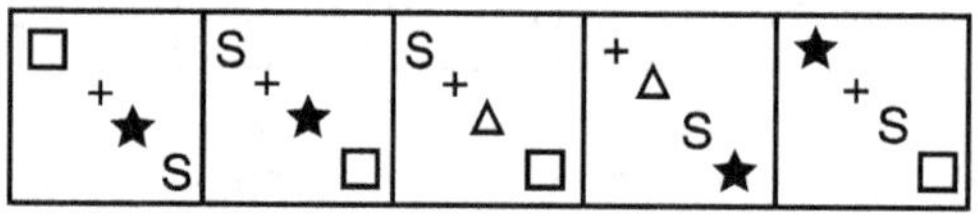

A B C D E

5. Problem Figures

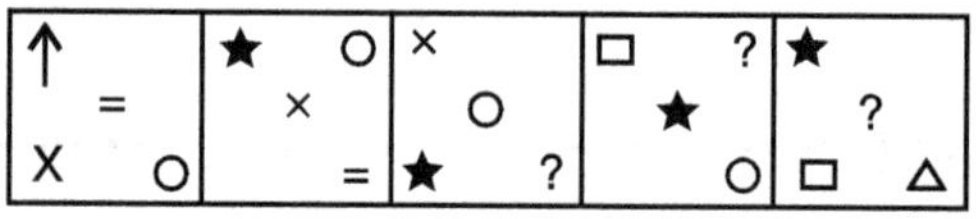

Answer Figures

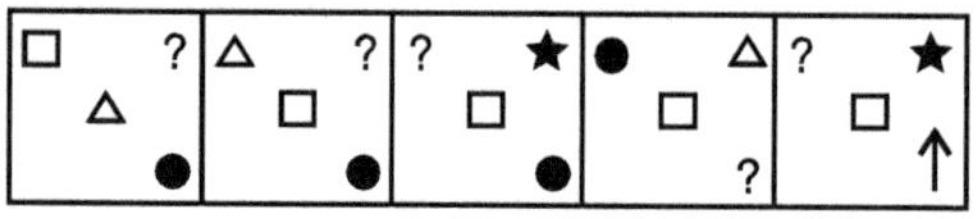

A B C D E

6. Problem Figures

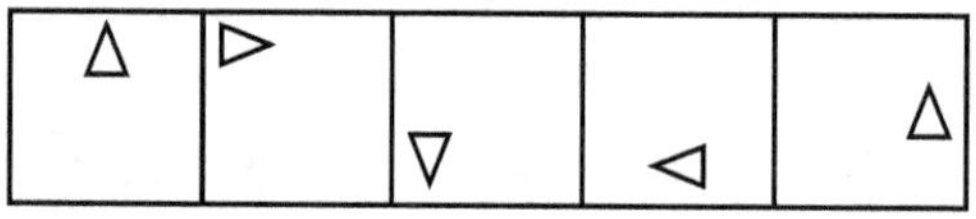

Answer Figures

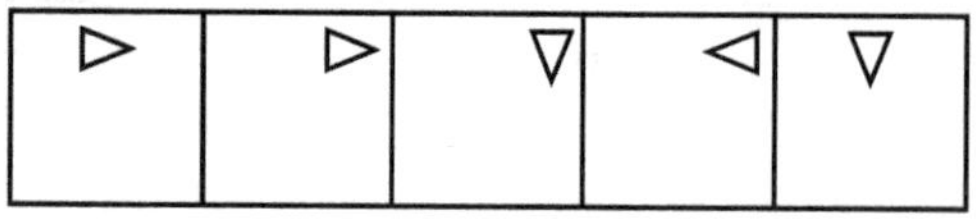

A B C D E

7. Problem Figures

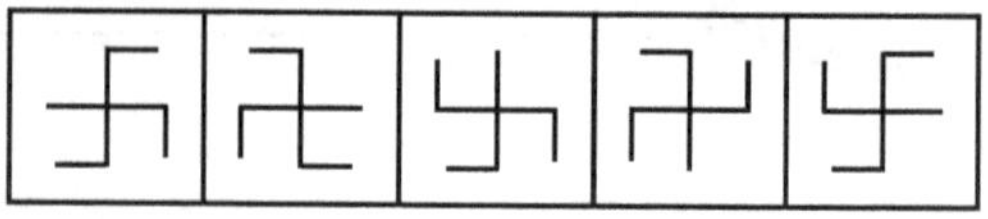

Answer Figures

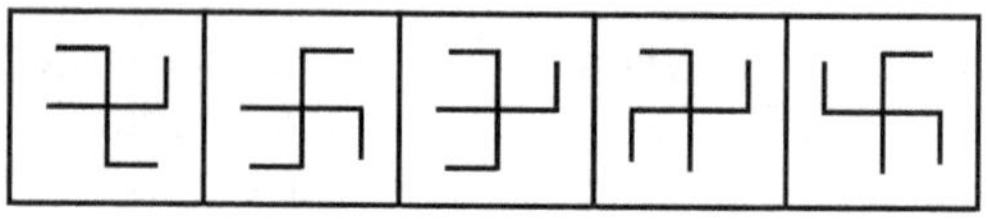

A B C D E

8. Problem Figures

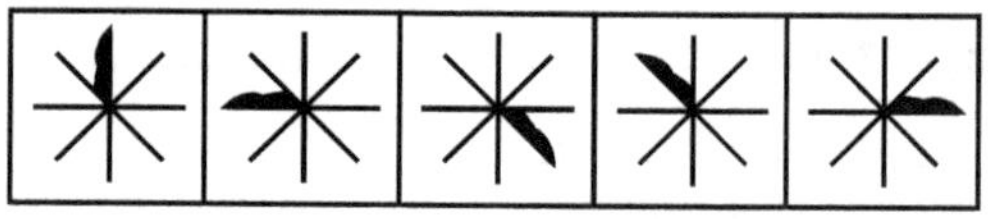

Answer Figures

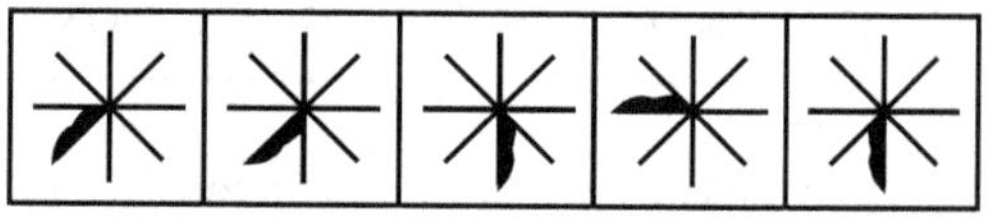

A B C D E

9. Problem Figures

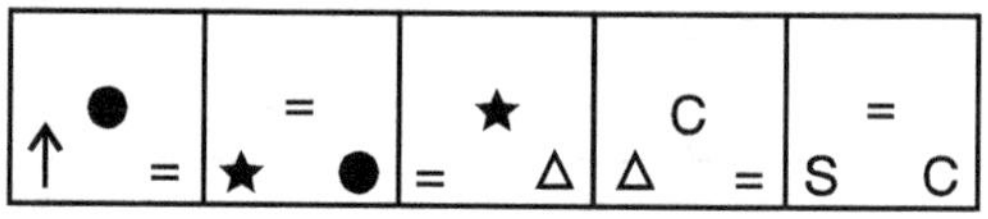

Answer Figures

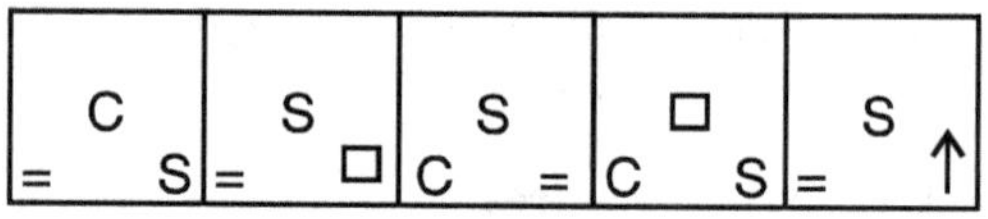

A B C D E

10. Problem Figures

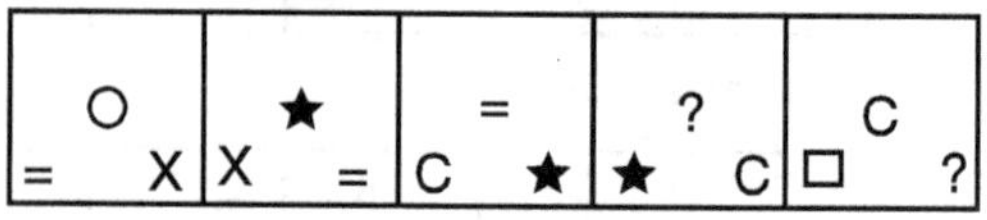

Answer Figures

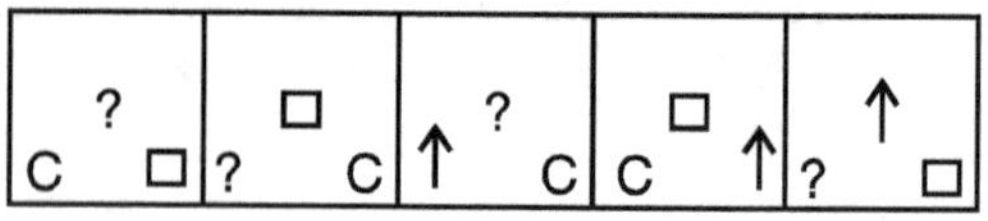

A B C D E

11. Problem Figures

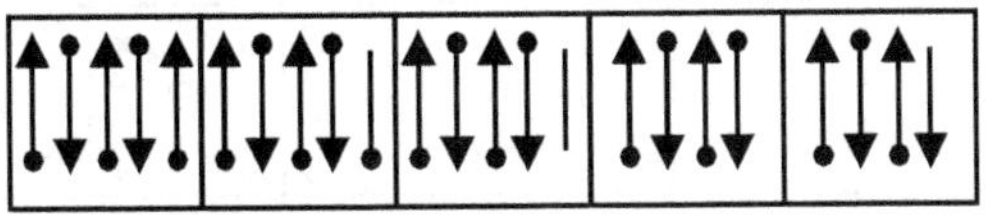

Answer Figures

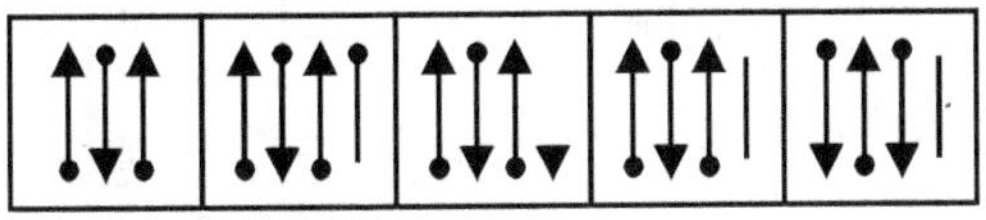

A B C D E

12. Problem Figures

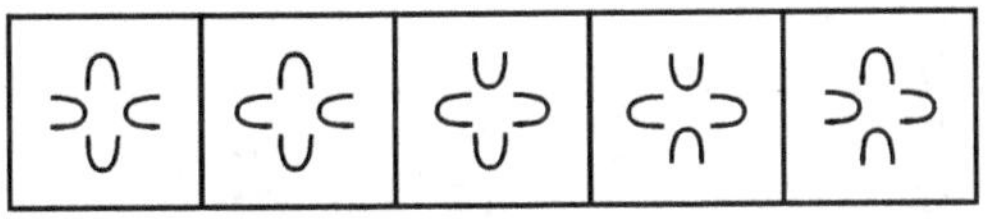

Answer Figures

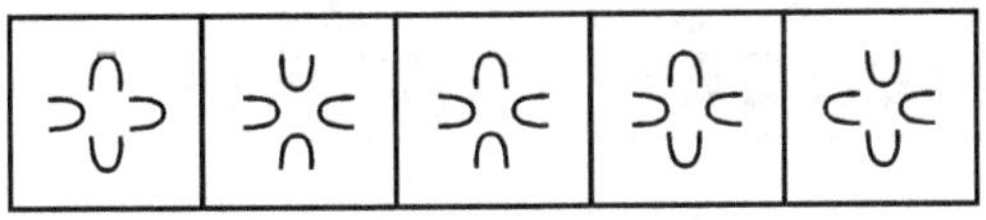

A B C D E

13. Problem Figures

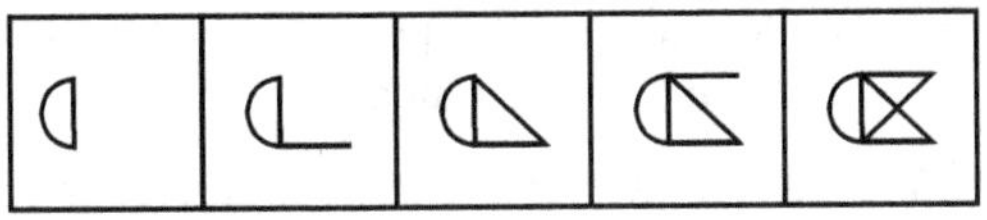

Answer Figures

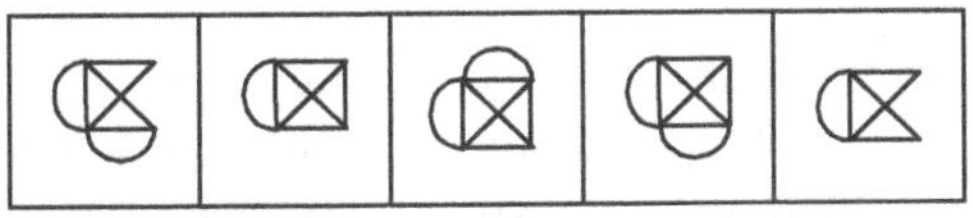

A B C D E

14. Problem Figures

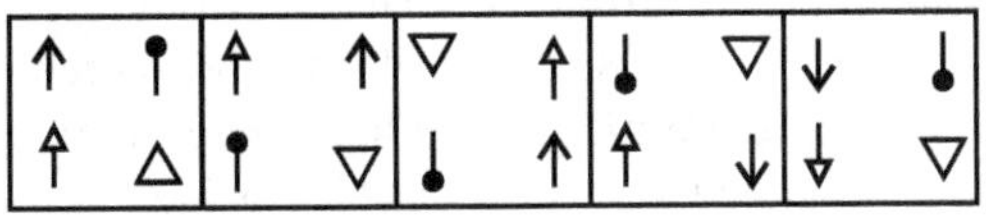

Answer Figures

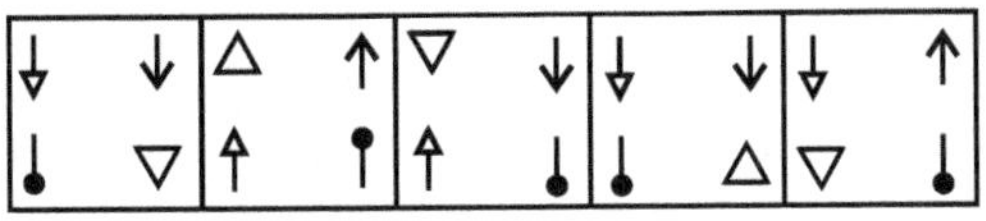

A B C D E

15. Problem Figures

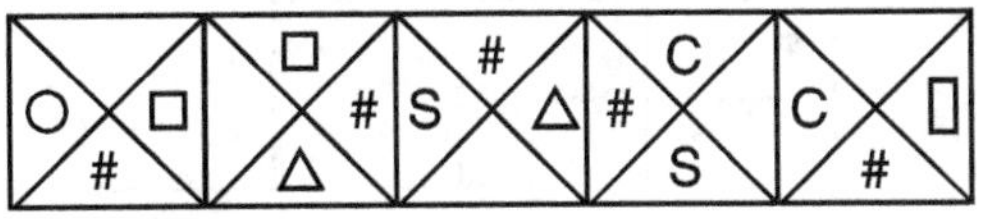

Answer Figures

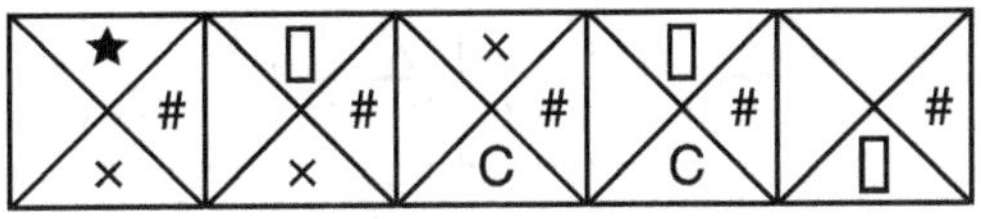

A B C D E

16. Problem Figures

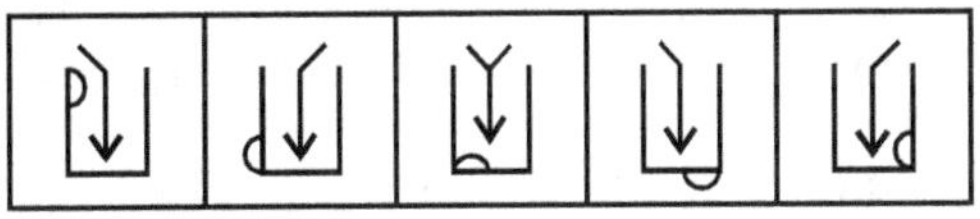

Answer Figures

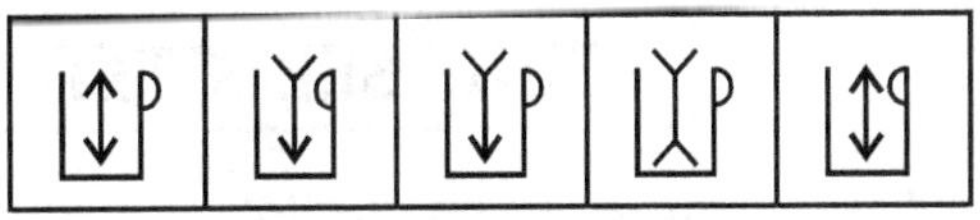

A B C D E

17. Problem Figures

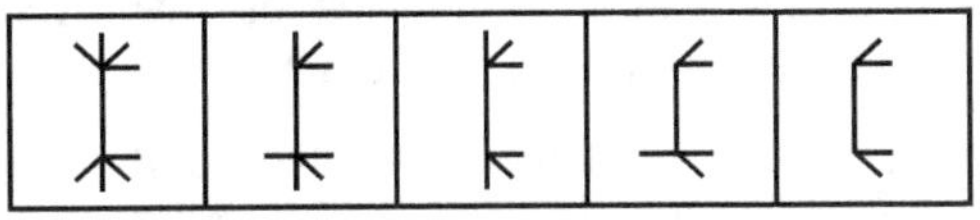

Answer Figures

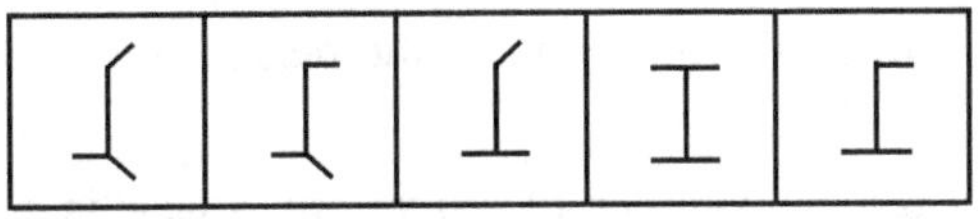

A B C D E

18. Problem Figures

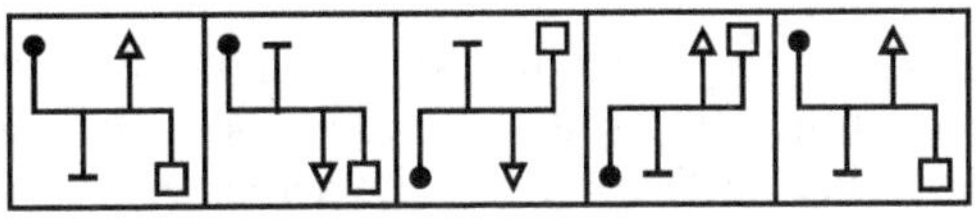

Answer Figures

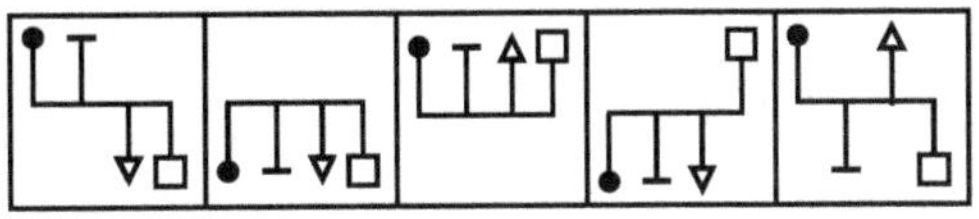

A B C D E

19. Problem Figures

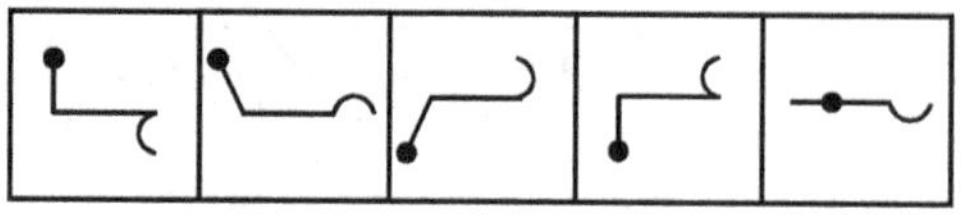

Answer Figures

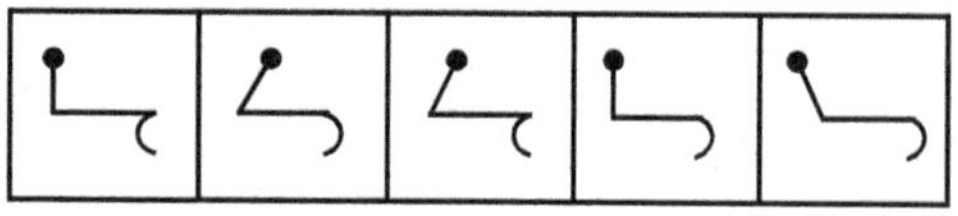

A B C D E

20. Problem Figures

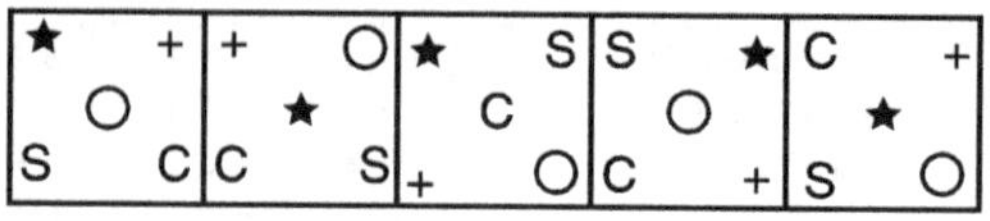

Answer Figures

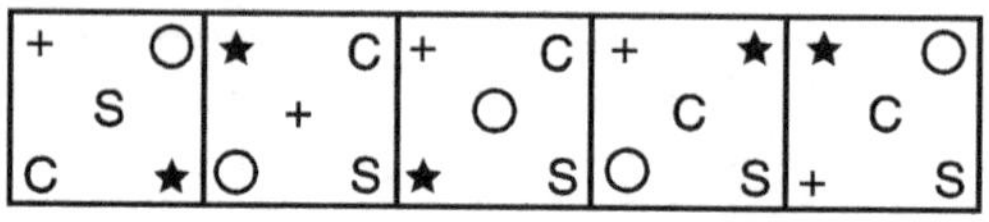

A B C D E

ANSWERS

1	2	3	4	5	6	7	8	9	10
A	B	D	C	D	B	A	E	B	E
11	**12**	**13**	**14**	**15**	**16**	**17**	**18**	**19**	**20**
D	C	A	D	B	C	E	A	B	D

SOME SELECTED EXPLANATORY ANSWERS

1. In alternate figures the four elements are moved clockwise.

3. The shape is turned 90° clockwise and the element attached to its top left side is replaced by an entirely new element.

6. The triangle is moved half and one steps anticlockwise alternately and turned 90° anticlockwise at each step.

7. In alternate figures the design is turned 90° clockwise.

8. The number of spikes the shade is moved anticlockwise, is increased by one at each step and the placement of the shade is same in alternate figures.

11. Starting from the extreme right element, at a time one part is removed in a set order. Answer Figure D continues the series.

12. Clockwise, starting from the left first one '*u*' shape and then two '*u*' shapes are turned by 180°. Option C fits the series.

13. Without lifting the pen one part is added to the figure at each step.

16. In alternate figures the semicircle is moved one step clockwise. The three stages of the arrow are repeated from the fourth figure.

18. First the two middle elements are turned to the other side of the horizontal line, then the two corner elements are turned. Also note, this series is repeated from the fifth figure.

20. Starting from the two bottom elements, anticlockwise, their places are interchanged, while the places of other three elements are changed one step anticlockwise.

❀ ❀ ❀

20 Analogies or Relationships

Analogy is a process of reasoning between two parallel cases. It relates to agreement or correspon-dence in certain respects between two things. It is a process whereby the underlying relationship that exists between two figures, designs or patterns is determined. Under the process, one has to discover the features common to the two figures or designs. This common feature is a model or base. The question seeks solution on the basis of this model or base.

EXERCISE

Directions : *The second figure in the first unit of the Problem Figures bears a certain relationship to the first figure. Similarly, one of the figures in the Answer Figures bears the same relationship to the first figure in the second unit of the Problem Figures. Locate the figure which would fit the question mark.*

1. Problem Figures

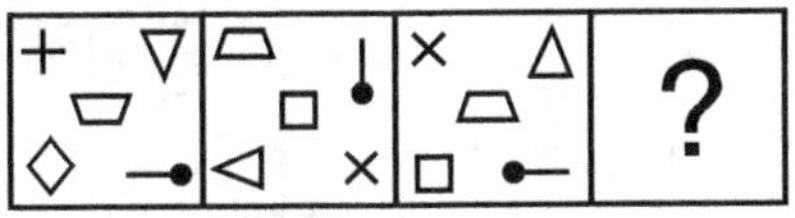

Answer Figures

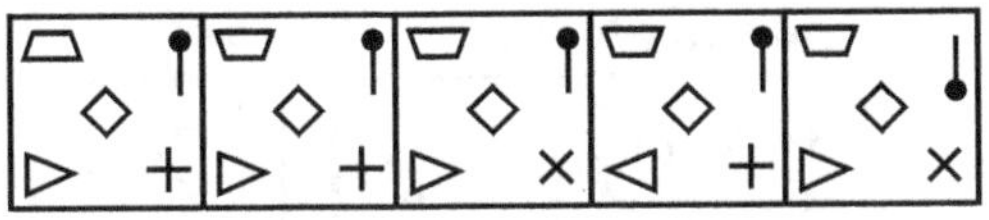

A B C D E

2. Problem Figures

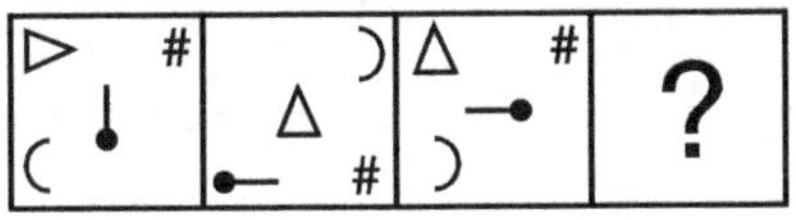

Answer Figures

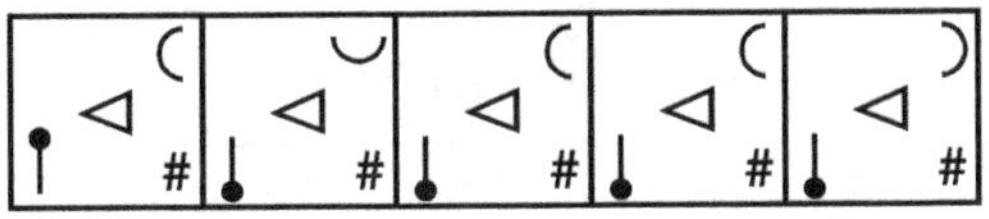

A B C D E

3. Problem Figures

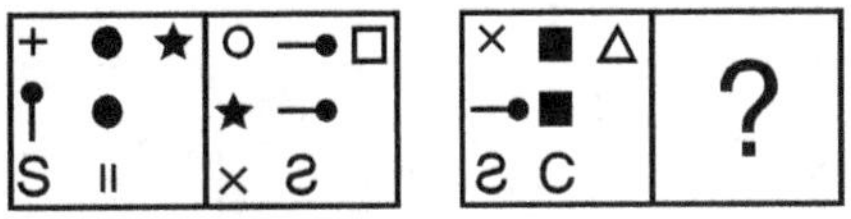

Answer Figures

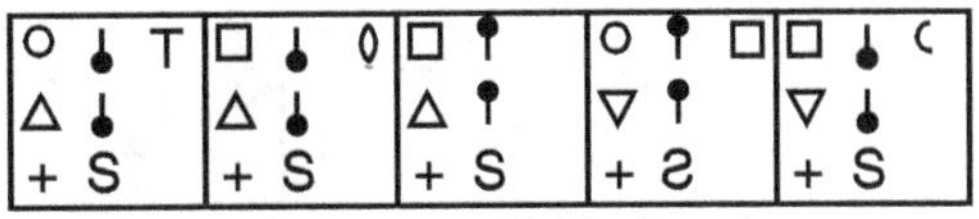

A B C D E

4. Problem Figures

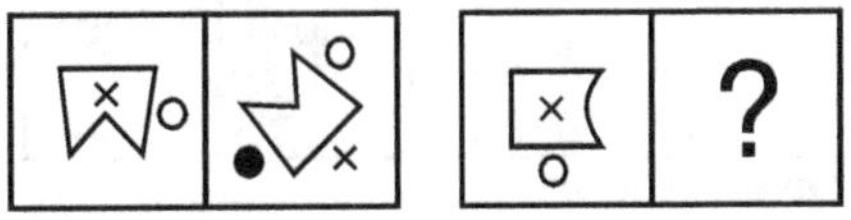

Answer Figures

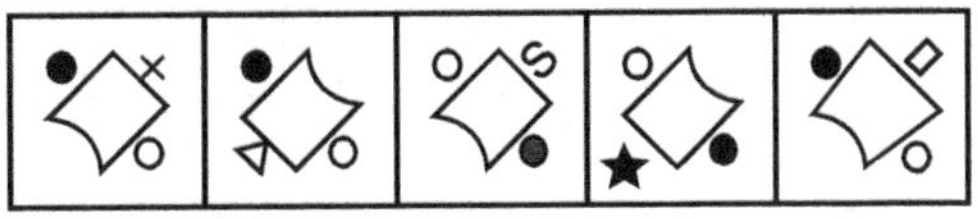

A B C D E

5. Problem Figures

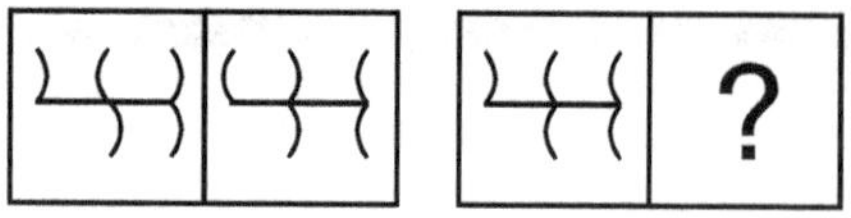

Answer Figures

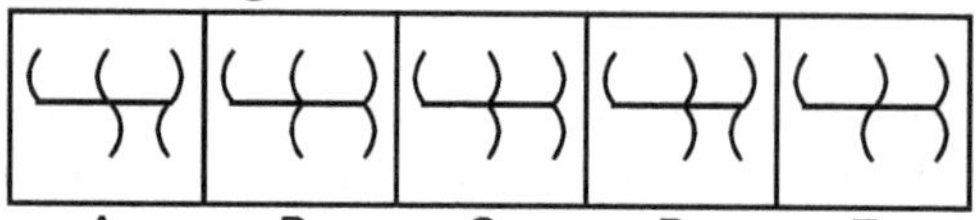

A B C D E

6. Problem Figures

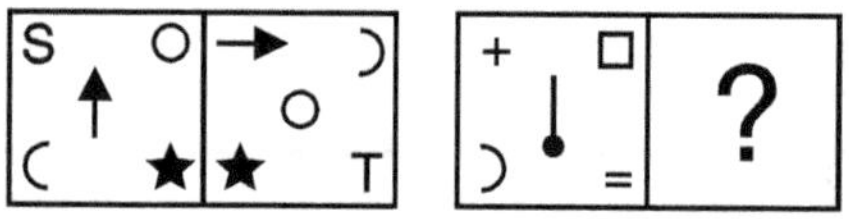

Answer Figures

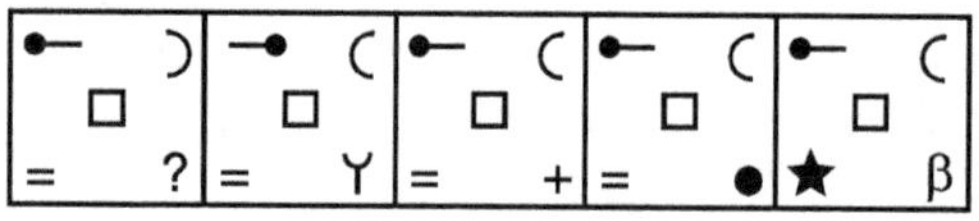

A B C D E

7. Problem Figures

Answer Figures

A B C D E

8. Problem Figures

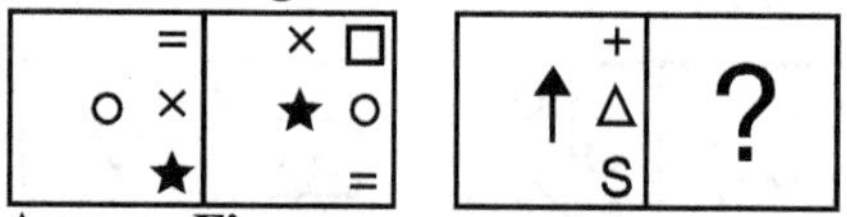

Answer Figures

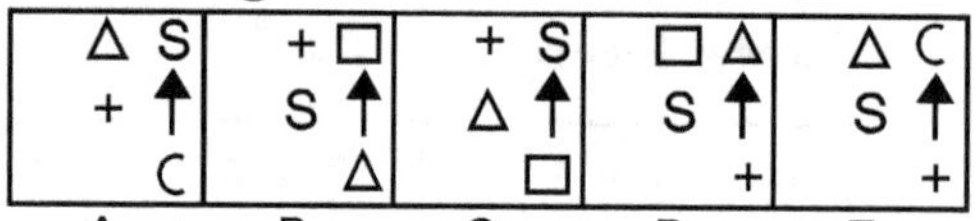

A B C D E

9. Problem Figures

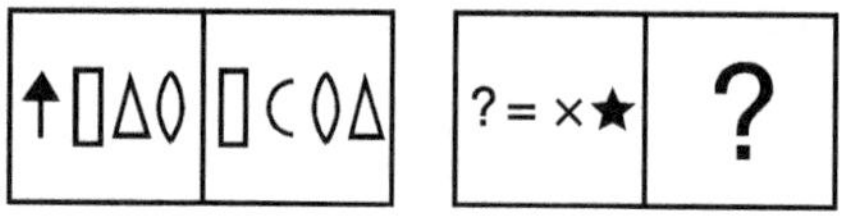

Answer Figures

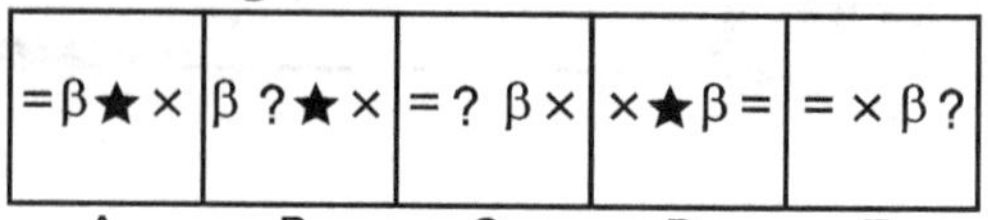

A B C D E

10. Problem Figures

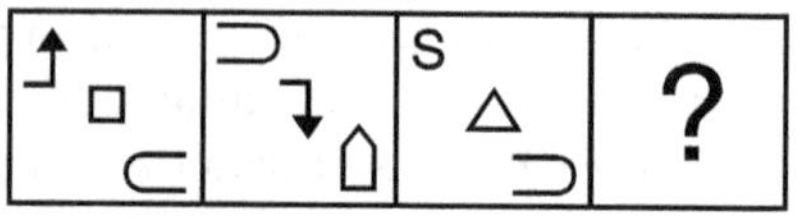

Answer Figures

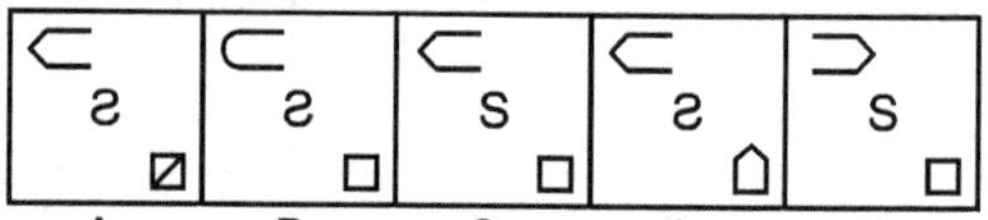

A B C D E

11. Problem Figures

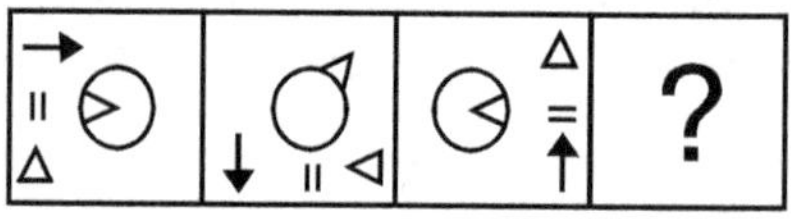

Answer Figures

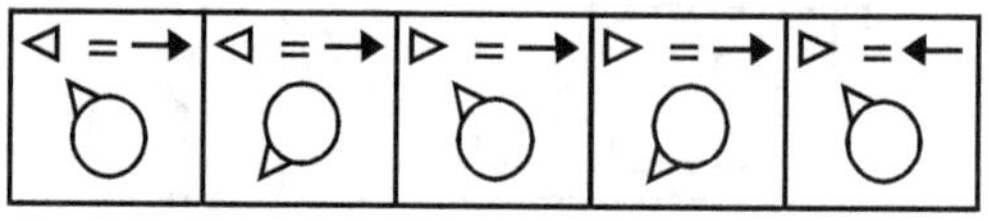

A B C D E

12. Problem Figures

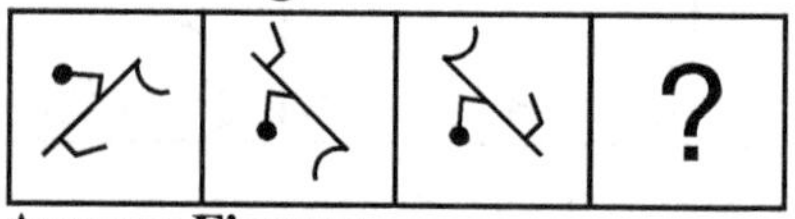

Answer Figures

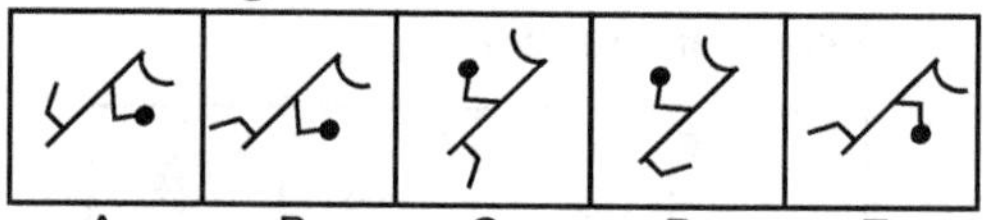

A B C D E

13. Problem Figures

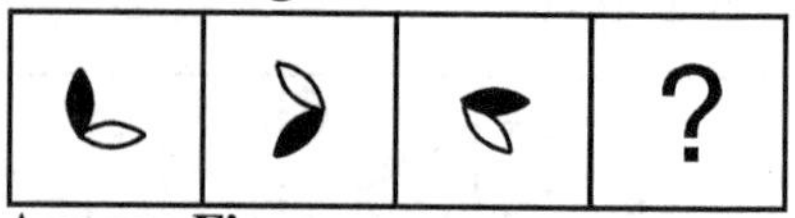

Answer Figures

A B C D E

14. Problem Figures

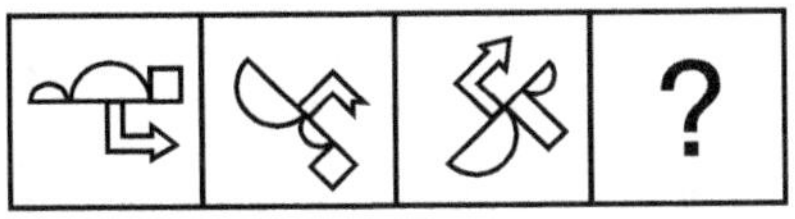

Answer Figures

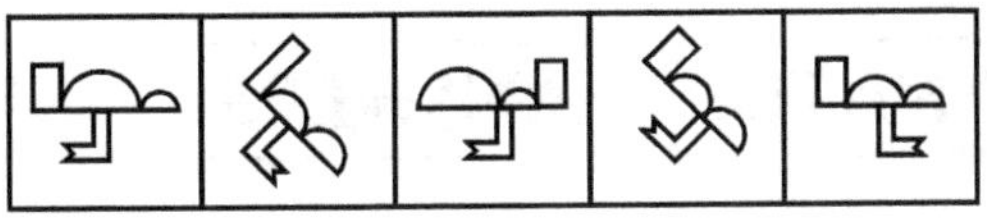

A B C D E

15. Problem Figures

Answer Figures

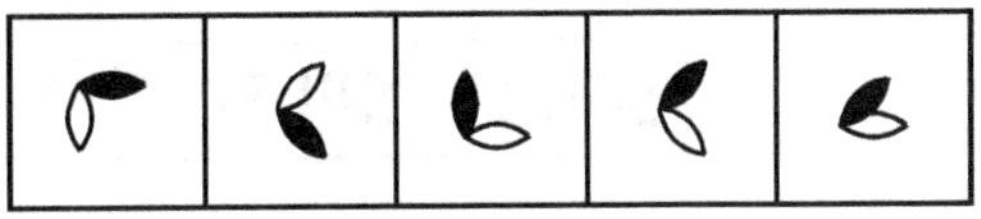

A B C D E

Directions (Q. 16–20): *In each of the following questions, a related pair of figures is followed by five numbered pairs of figures. Select the pair that has a relationship* **similar** *to that in the unnumbered pair.*

Problem Figure **Answer Figures**

16. 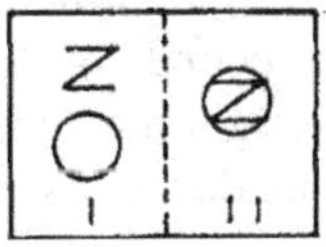 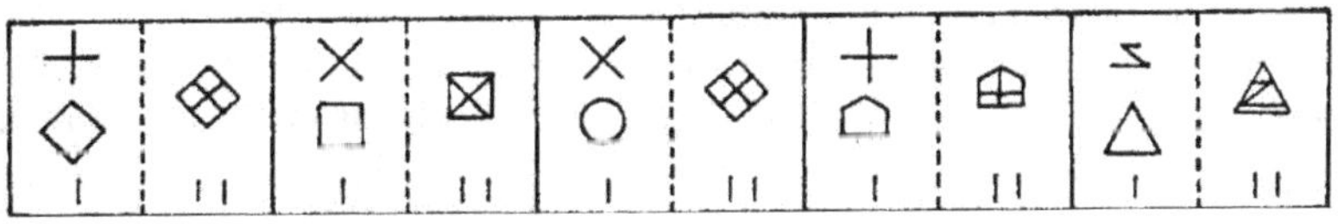

A B C D E

17. 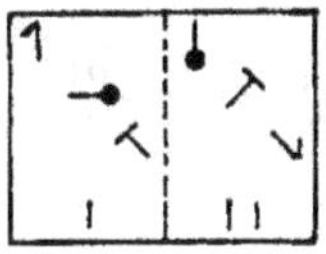 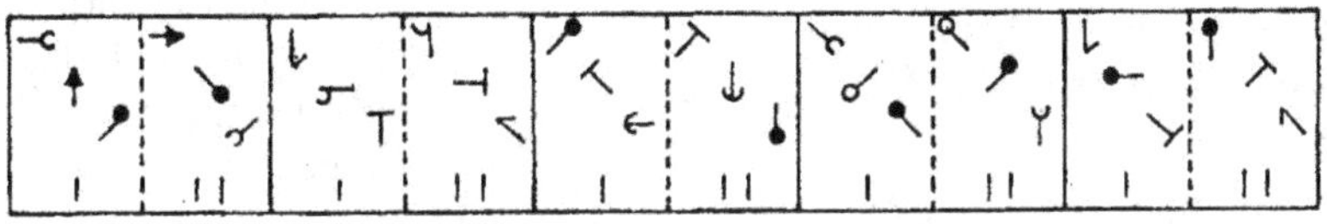

A B C D E

18. 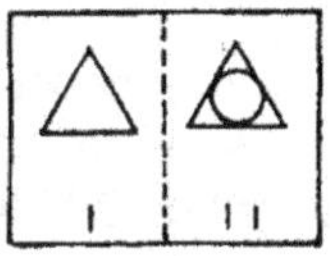 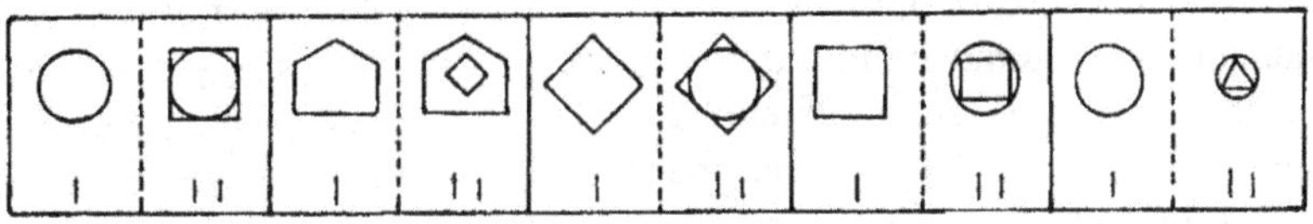

A B C D E

19. 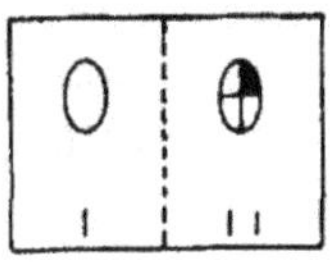 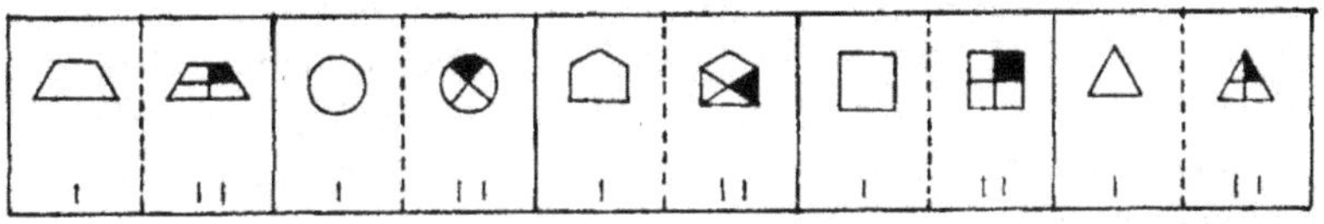

A B C D E

20. 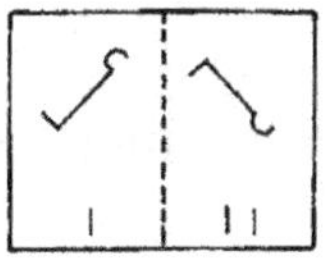 

A B C D E

ANSWERS

1	2	3	4	5	6	7	8	9	10
B	C	B	A	E	D	A	E	A	B
11	12	13	14	15	16	17	18	19	20
B	B	A	E	D	B	A	E	D	E

SOME SELECTED EXPLANATORY ANSWERS

2. The element in the top left corner is turned 90° anticlockwise and moved to the centre, the element in the centre is turned 90° clockwise and moved to the bottom left corner position, the element in the bottom left corner is laterally inverted and moved to the top right corner position, and the element in the top right corner is laterally inverted and moved to the bottom right corner position.

4. The first figure is turned 135° clockwise, the inner element is moved out towards the base, the blank circle is shaded and a circle is added on its opposite side to get the second figure.

5. All arcs in the first figure except the left are below the line segment are turned to the other side to get the second figure.

7. The human sketch is moved to the right side and its hands and legs are extended and shortened respectively in a particular manner. The other two elements are turned upside down, the smaller one is enclosed within the larger one and then the two together are moved to the left and rotated 45° anticlockwise.

9. The left most element is made new and then the two corner elements are moved inbetween the two middle elements.

11. The triangle inside the circle is moved one and a half steps clockwise and turned outside. The elements on the side arc moved one step anticlockwise, the arrow and the triangle are turned 90° clockwise, and 90° anticlockwise respectively.

12. The first figure is turned 90° anticlockwise, one arc is turned to the other side to be in front of the line with a dot to get the second figure.

13. The petals in first figure are turned 135° anticlockwise to get the second figure.

14. Of the three elements the right most element is moved to the left, the design is turned 135° anticlockwise, the arrow is turned to the other side and the lines making the arrowhead are turned inwards.

15. The blank and shaded petals in first figure are turned 90° and 135° anticlockwise respectively to get the second figure.

16. The uppermost design enters into innerside side of the lower design from Ist figure to the IInd figure.

17. In element I to II upper left design comes at lower right rotating 135° C.W. Middle design goes to upper left and rotates 90° CW. While lower right design goes to middle and it also rotates 90° C.W. The same changes occur in option A.

18. In element I to II and ellipse is put in the triangle. Similarly in option E a triangle is put in the ellipse.

19. From first figure to IInd figure, design is divided into four equal parts and right side of the upper portion becomes shaded.

20. From Ist figure to IInd figure, design is reversed after moving 90° anticlockwise direction.

❀ ❀ ❀

21 Classification or Odd-One Out

Classification means arranging the given content in groups or classes having qualities of same kind. In classification type questions, the figures or items are sorted out in groups on the basis of their similarities in qualities in shapes, size, pattern, structure, genus, order, species, grade, style, constituents and other specifications, and thus the answer is found out.

Example

Which one of the following figures is different from the rest. Spot the figure.

1. 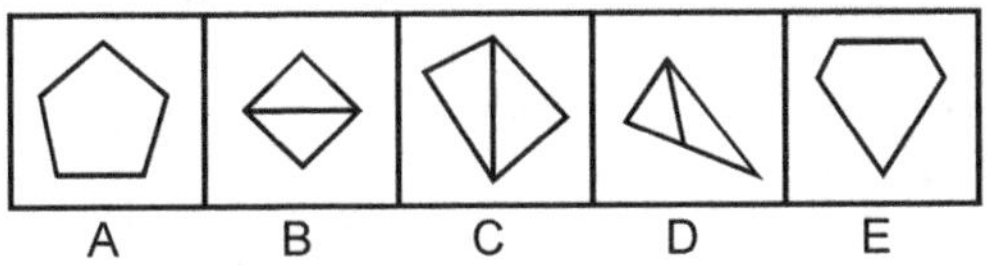

Answer D : Figures A, B, C and E are made of 5 straight lines, while D has only four straight lines. Thus A, B, C and E have a common characteristic (they have 5 straight lines each), but D does not have this characteristic. Therefore, D is different from the other four figures.

EXERCISE

Directions : *In each of the following questions one of the figures is different from the rest. Spot the figure.*

1. 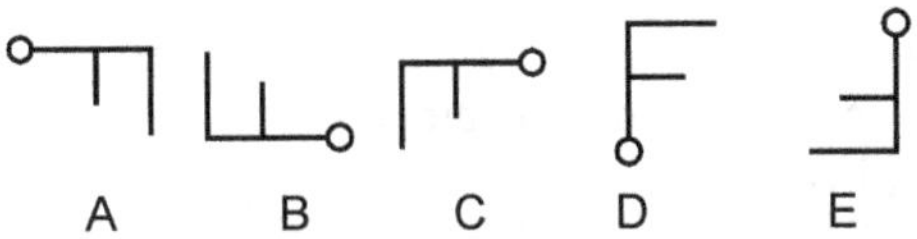

2. 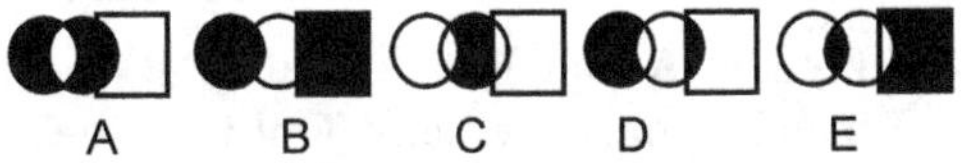

3. 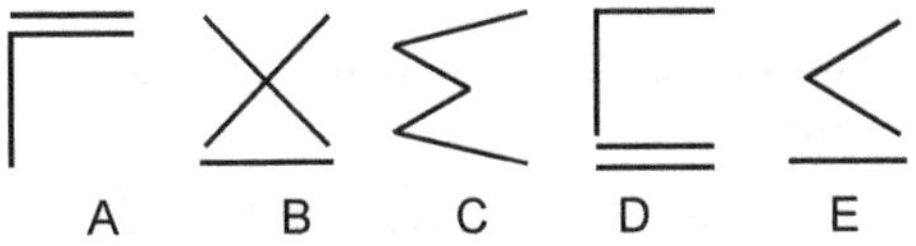

4. 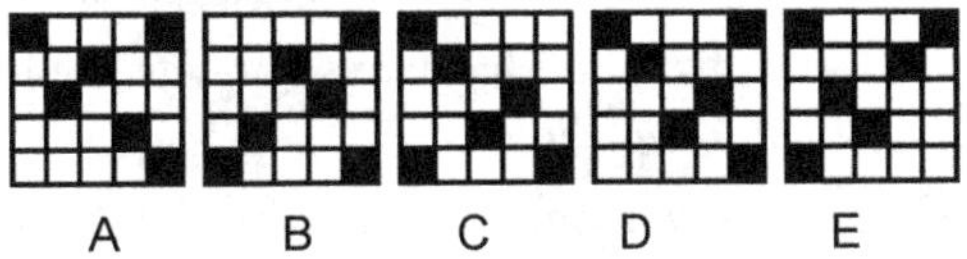

5. 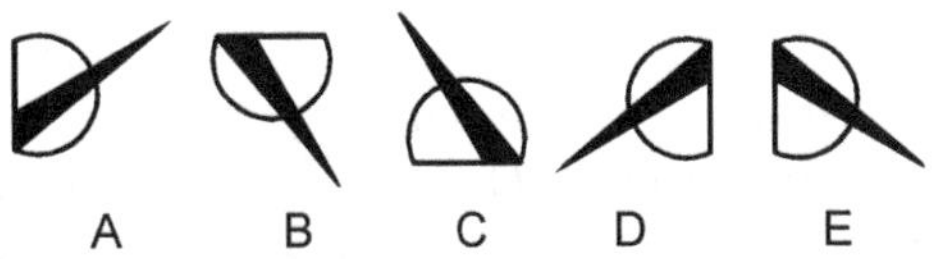

6. 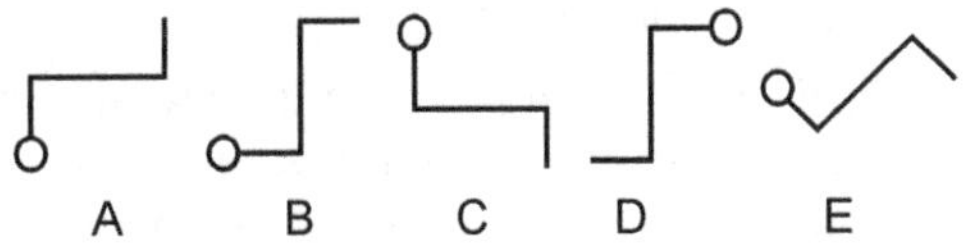

7. 

8. 

9. 

A B C D E

10. 

A B C D E

11. 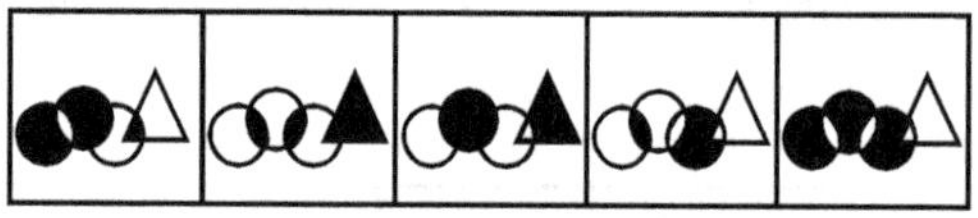

A B C D E

12. 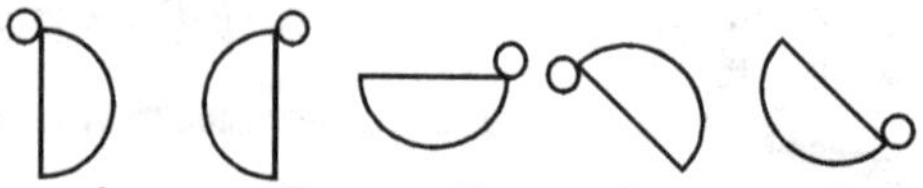

A B C D E

13. 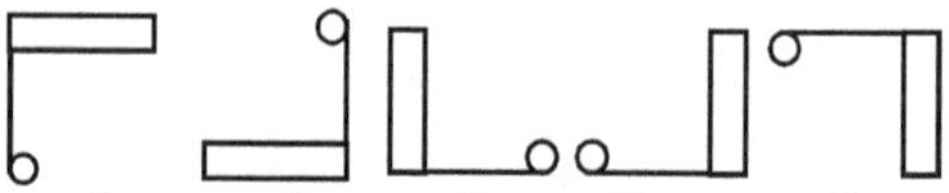

A B C D E

14. 

A B C D E

15. 

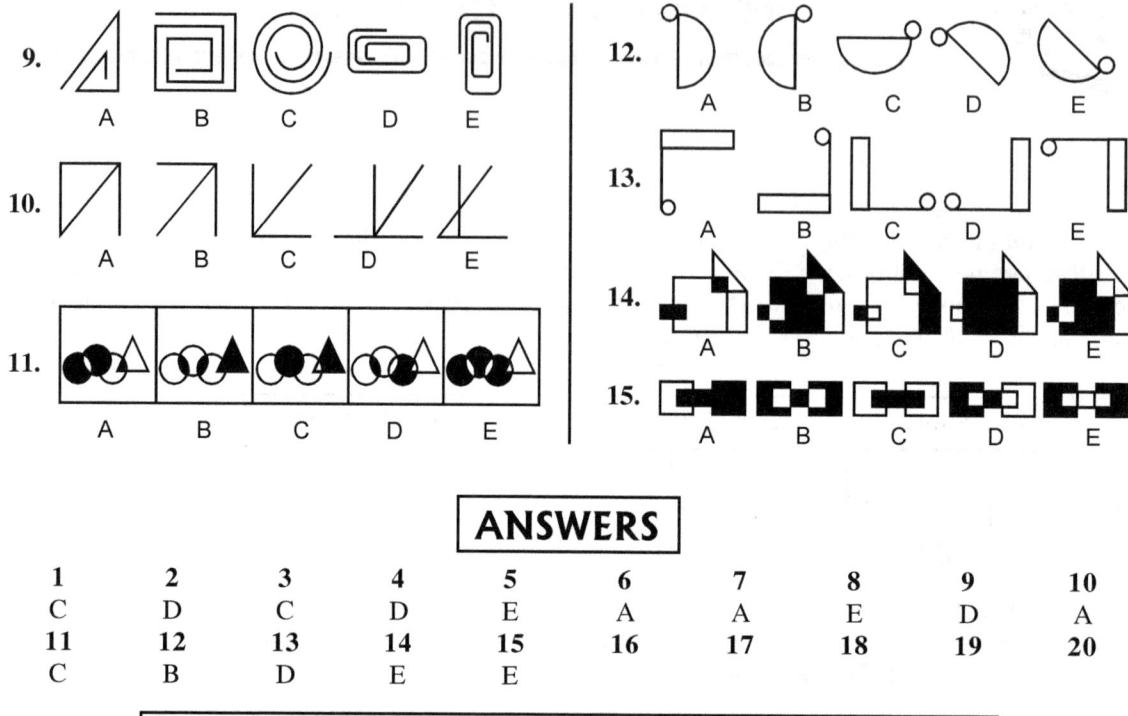

A B C D E

ANSWERS

1	**2**	**3**	**4**	**5**	**6**	**7**	**8**	**9**	**10**
C	D	C	D	E	A	A	E	D	A
11	**12**	**13**	**14**	**15**	**16**	**17**	**18**	**19**	**20**
C	B	D	E	E					

SOME SELECTED EXPLANATORY ANSWERS

1. All other figures are identical. The two line segments are to the left of the line with a circle in this option.

2. Figures A and E and figures B and C form opposite pairs. Only figure D is left single.

3. All other figures are Roman Numerals rotated 90° anticlockwise.

4. All other figures have identical squares shaded. In this option one shaded square is on the diagonally opposite corner.

5. All other figures are identical. In this option the shaded part is rising from the left of the base.

6. In all other figures the line segment with the circle is to the right of the straight line. In this option it is on the left side.

7. In all other figures only two sections are shaded.

8. All other figures are made of three straight lines.

9. In all other figures the line forming the pattern is drawn clockwise from outside to inside.

10. All other figures contain three straight lines.

11. Figures A and D and figures B and E are matched opposite pairs. Only figure C is left single.

12. All other figures can be rotated into each other.

13. In all other figures the line with the circle is to the right side at the rectangle base.

14. Only this figure has two segments shaded, all others have three.

15. This is the only figure with a white/blank middle square.

❀ ❀ ❀

General English

1

Comprehension Passages

Comprehension is a very important part of General English paper. The questions on comprehension lay particular stress on understanding a given passage. You are required to read a passage and answer a few questions based on it. Various comprehension questions are set solely with the objectives named below:

1. To test your ability to detect the central idea or the focal point in the given passage.
2. To test your ability to understand and interpret the given passage.
3. To judge your capability to pick out the various arguments put forward by the writer for or against something.
4. To test your accuracy and richness of vocabulary.
5. To test your academic ability to understand the implied and the clearly and fully expressed ideas of the writer of the passage.
6. To test, occasionally, your power of appreciating critically the views contained in the given passage.

While answering comprehension questions, you must comply with the following important points:

1. First, read the whole passage attentively, carefully and quickly.
2. Read it for the second time, slowly but steadily.
3. Work out the probable meaning of new words, from the context in which they have been used.
4. Underline and look for transitional words and phrases as an aid to comprehension.
5. The process of elimination should be used while selecting the correct answer.
6. Recheck your answers before marking in the answersheet.

Multiple Choice Questions

PASSAGE-1

Internet banking is the term used for new age banking system. Internet banking is also called as online banking and it is an outgrowth of PC banking. Internet banking uses the internet as the delivery channel by which to conduct banking activity, for example, transferring funds, paying bills, viewing checking and savings account balances, paying mortgages and purchasing financial instruments and certificates of deposits. Internet banking is a result of explored possibility to use internet application in one of the various domains of commerce. It is difficult to infer whether the internet tool has been applied for convenience of bankers or for the customers' convenience. But ultimately it contributes in increasing the efficiency of the banking operation as well providing more convenience to customers. Without even interacting with the bankers, customers *transact* from one corner of the country to another corner.

There are many advantages of online Banking. It is convenient, it isn't bound by operational timings, there are no geographical barriers and the services can be offered at a *minuscule* cost. Electronic banking has experienced explosive growth and has transformed traditional practices in banking.

Private Banks in India were the first to implement internet banking services in the banking industry. Private Banks, due to late entry into the industry, understood that the establishing network in remote corners of the country is a very difficult task. It was clear to them that the only way to stay connected to the customers at any place and at any time is through Internet applications. They took the Internet applications as a weapon of competitive advantage to corner the great *monoliths* like State Bank of India, Indian Bank etc. Private Banks are pioneer in India to explore the *versatility* of Internet applications in delivering services to customers.

Several studies have attempted to assess the relative importance of B2B and B2C business domains. There is wide difference in estimates of volume of business transacted over Internet and its components under B2C and B2B. However, most studies agree that volume of transactions in B2B domain far exceeds that in B2C. This is the expected result. There is also a growing opinion that the future of e-business lies in B2B domain, as compared to B2C. This has several reasons, like low penetration of PCs to households, low bandwidth availability etc., in a large part of the world. The success of B2C ventures depends to a large extent on the shopping habits of people in different parts of the world. A survey sponsored jointly by Confederation of Indian Industries and Infrastructure Leasing and Financial Services on e-commerce in India in 2010 the following observations. 62% of PC owners and 75% of PC non-owners but who have access to Internet would not buy through the net, as they were not sure of the product offered. The same study estimated the size of B2B business in India by the year 2011 to be varying between ₹ 1250 billion to ₹ 1500 billion. In a recent study done by Arthur Anderson, it has been estimated that 84% of total e-business revenue is generated from B2B segment and the growth prospects in this segment are substantial. It has estimated the revenues to be anywhere between US $ 8.1 trillion to over US $ 21 trillion within the next three years (2014).

1. Which bank(s) is/are pioneer in India to explore the versatility of Internet banking in serving customers?
A. State Bank of India
B. Indian Bank
C. Public Sector Banks
D. Private Banks
E. None of these

2. Which of the following is not an advantage of online banking?
A. It is convenient.
B. It is bound by operational timings.
C. The services can be offered at a minimum cost.
D. There is no geographical barrier.
E. None of these

3. What percentage of PC non-owners but who have access to Internet would not prefer to buy through the net, as they are not sure of the product offered?
A. 75% B. 62%
C. 84% D. 76%
E. None of these

4. Which type of activities are performed by Internet banking?
A. Paying bills
B. Transferring funds
C. Paying mortgages
D. Purchasing financial instruments and certificates of deposits
E. All of these

5. What estimate was made by Confederation of Indian Industries regarding the size of B2B business in India by the year 2011?
A. Between ₹ 250 billion to ₹ 500 billion
B. Between ₹ 1250 billion to ₹ 1500 billion
C. Between ₹ 850 billion to ₹ 1050 billion
D. Between $ 8.7 trillion to $ 21 trillion
E. None of these

Directions (Qs. 6 to 8) : *Choose the word which is MOST SIMILAR in meaning to the word printed in BOLD as used in the passage.*

6. VERSATILITY
A. multi-utility B. vesicle
C. dullness D. necessity
E. meanness

7. MONOLITHS
A. large blocks of stone
B. large organisations
C. monopoly
D. dwarfs
E. niche

8. TRANSACT
A. do business
B. tranquillize
C. transcend
D. exceed
E. transfer

Directions (Qs. 9 & 10) : *Choose the word which is MOST OPPOSITE in meaning to the word printed in BOLD as used in the passage.*

9. SUBSTANTIAL
A. meagre
B. considerable
C. large
D. submissive
E. sufficient

10. MINUSCULE
A. small
B. minimum
C. minute
D. large
E. maximum

PASSAGE-2

One could, in theory, conceive of a country "specialising" entirely in agriculture and obtaining all its industrial requirements from abroad. But it could never become a high income country simply because technologically developed agriculture could never absorb more than a fraction of the working population on the available land. Though in all underdeveloped countries the greater part of the working population is "occupied" in agriculture, most of this represents disguised unemployment; a rural community maintains all its members and expects everyone to share in the work. Much of the greater part of this labour could be withdrawn from agricultrue if alternative employment opportunities were available without any *adverse* effect, and probably with a beneficial effect, on total agricultural output. For the relief of the pressure of labour on the land is itself a most potent factor in *inducing* improvements in technology which raise yields per acre, as well as the yield per man. These improvements normally require an increase in the capital employed on the land; but the savings necessary for the increase in capital are themselves a by-product of reduced population pressure. The reduction in the agricultural population, and the increased use of capital in agriculture are thus different aspects of the same process. As there are fewer mouths to feed, the "agricultural surplus" rises (the excess of agricultural production over the self-consumption of the farming population). The rise in the "surplus" enables the farmers to plough back a higher proportion of their output—in the form of better tools, improved seeds, fertilisers, etc., and such improvements tend to both "labour saving" and "land saving"; they *diminish* the labour requirements at the same time as they increase the yield of the land.

1. According to the passage, it is theoretically possible to think of country
A. advanced both in agriculture and industry
B. specialised in industry but not in agriculture
C. backward both in agriculture and industry
D. specialised in agriculture but not in industry
E. borrowing all its requirements from abroad

2. What, according to the passage, will be the achievement of inducing improvement in technology?
A. Higher specialisation in agriculture
B. Better employment opportunities
C. Beneficial effects on quality of life of people
D. Relieving the pressure of employment in industry
E. None of these

3. What could be done, according to the passage, to induce improvement in agricultural technology?
A. Import of better agricultural technology
B. Providing better weather forecasts
C. To relieve pressure of labour on land
D. Providing irrigation facilities
E. None of these

4. According to the passage, in underdeveloped countries
A. agriculture is in a primitive stage
B. per acre yield is very high
C. land is available in plenty

D. alternative employment opportunities will have adverse effect on the lives of people
E. significant proportion of working population works in agriculture

5. Why, according to the passage, a country specialised in agriculture only cannot become a high income country?
A. It simply cannot borrow all its industrial requirements from abroad
B. It can absorb only a fraction of its working population
C. Agriculture needs huge investments and infrastructural facilities
D. Technological advancements in agriculture has limitations
E. None of these

6. Which of the following statements is TRUE in the context of the passage?
A. Underdeveloped countries are rapidly growing industrially
B. Technologically developed agriculture solves all the problems of unemployment
C. Relief of the pressure of labour on land raises yields per acre
D. Yield per acre and yield per man are unrelated
E. Surplus in agriculture is spent for domestic purposes

7. Which of the following statements is NOT TRUE in the context of the passage?
A. Theoretically there could be a country specialised entirely in agriculture
B. Capital is required to increase the per acre yield of the land
C. Agriculture surplus will rise if there are fewer mouths to feed
D. Technologically developed agriculture will absorb most of the working population on the available land
E. A rural community maintains all its members and expects everyone to share in the work

8. Which of the following is most OPPOSITE in meaning of the work ADVERSE as used in the passage?
A. Negative B. Facilitating
C. Supplementary D. Derogative
E. Decorative

9. Which of the following is most nearly the SAME in meaning as the word INDUCING as used in the passage?
A. Causing B. Augmenting
C. Reducing D. Developing
E. Increasing

10. Which of the following is most nearly the SAME in meaning as the word DIMINISH as used in the passage?
A. Reduce B, Shorten
C. Prohibit D. Increase
E. Worsen

PASSAGE-3

Morning and afternoon, all the young girls and maidens used to *gather* around the village well with their water pots. There they exchanged pleasantries, chatted and discussed. Lakshmi was the prettiest girl at the well. But, she was an orphan.

One day, a well-built man came to Lakshmi's house. He brought with him the richest clothes and jewels as presents for her, "I am your dead father's brother," he told the astonished girl. "You have not seen me before because I have been staying abroad. You must come and live with me now." Lakshmi believed his sweet words and in a short time, locked up her little house and set out with the man.

But a terrible surprise was in store for poor Lakshmi when she got to her new-found uncle's home. The man locked her in a room. "I am not your uncle, but a robber. And I am going to marry you," he told her. Lakshmi howled and wept when she heard this. Saying he would be back in a day or two after making arrangements for the wedding, the man went away. Lakshmi continued sobbing for a while and then stopped. "I must think of a plan to escape," she told herself. Lakshmi guessed that the robber would try to enter her room. So she kept near her bed a sharp knife which she could find in the room.

One night the robber did enter her room but Lakshmi did not make any sound. She just kept a tight hold of the knife and pretended to be sound asleep. When the robber was near her bed, she stood up suddenly, brandishing the knife. The robber was taken aback and with a loud cry, he ran out. Lakshmi *gave chase* and he climbed up the nearest tall tree. Lakshmi then gathered some dry figs and sticks around the foot of the tree and set them on fire. On seeing the rising flames, the robber gave a mighty yell and jumped down. But it was such a long way to the ground that he broke a couple of bones and was unable to move away from the place he fell.

In the mean time, the police was informed by someone about the robber. Very soon they reached the spot and arrested the robber. The people who had gathered at the spot were all praise for Lakshmi's courage and presence of mind,

1. The reason given by the man for his inability to meet Lakshmi was that
   A. he had not known earlier where she lived
   B. he was not friendly terms with her father
   C. he was living in a foreign country
   D. he was not sure whether she would recognise him
   E. he was staying in another village, far away from her place

2. Why did Lakshmi go with the man?
   A. She was convinced that the man was her uncle
   B. She wanted to accompany him and then get him arrested by the police
   C. She intended to teach him a good lesson
   D. She wanted the man to marry her
   E. She felt it necessary to verify his claim by accompanying him

3. Why did the robber run out of the room?
   A. He was stabbed by Lakshmi
   B. He got scared of the rising flames
   C. Lakshmi told him to go out as fast as possible
   D. He was afraid that Lakshmi would strike him with the knife
   E. He ran out to catch hold of Lakshmi and bring her back

4. How was the robber injured?
   A. Lakshmi stabbed him with the sharp knife
   B. He fell down accidently while climbing the tree
   C. He was beaten by Lakshmi and his bones were broken
   D. He jumped down from the tree to save his life
   E. He got burnt in the rising flames

5. "*But a terrible surprise was in store ..... uncle's home.*" What is the "terrible surprise" that is being referred to?
   A. The man told her that her father was dead
   B. The man refused to marry her
   C. The man took away her ornaments and locked her in a room
   D. The man told her that he was her real uncle
   E. The man turned out to be a robber interested in marrying her

6. Where did the robber apparently go after locking up Lakshmi?
   A. He went to her house to loot all the things
   B. He went out to bring a sharp knife
   C. He went away to bring clothes and jewels for her
   D. He went away to make preparations for his marriage
   E. He went out to bring the priest for performing the wedding ceremony

7. Which of the following is most nearly the SAME in meaning as the phrase, GAVE CHASE as used in the passage?
   A. escaped   B. continued
   C. followed   D. prevented
   E. raced

8. Which of the following is TRUE in the context of the passage?
   A. Lakshmi told the robber to climb up the tall tree
   B. At night, the robber entered Lakshmi's room with a knife
   C. Lakshmi had no near relatives and she stayed alone
   D. The robber started running after jumping from the tree
   E. The people who had gathered at the spot set fire to the tree

9. Which of the following is most OPPOSITE in meaning of the word GATHER as used in the passage?
A. Collect
B. Reduce
C. Distribute
D. Break
E. Disperse

10. Which of the following statements is NOT TRUE in the context of the passage?
A. The police was summoned by Lakshmi herself
B. The well-built man was not the real brother of Lakshmi's father
C. When the robber entered the room at night, Lakshmi was awake
D. Lakshmi used to go to the village well to collect water
E. Lakshmi's guess regarding the robber turned out to be correct

PASSAGE-4

Progress in life depends a good deal on crossing one threshold after another. Some time ago, a man watched his little nephew try to write his name. It was hardwork, very hardwork. The little boy had arrived at an effort threshold. Today he writes his name with comparative ease. No new threshold confronts him. This is the way with all of us. As soon as we cross one threshold, as soon as we conquer one difficulty, a new difficulty appears, or should appear. Some people make the mistake of steering clear of thresholds. Anything that requires genuine thinking and use of energy they avoid. They prefer to stay in a rut where thresholds are not met. Probably, they have been at their job a number of years. Things are easy for them. They make no effort to seek out new obstacles to overcome. Real progress stops under such circumstances.

Some middle-aged and elderly people greatly enrich their lives by continuing to cross thresholds. One man went into an entirely new business when he was past middle life and made success of it, De Morgan didn't start to write novels until he was past sixty. Psychologists have discovered that man can continue to learn throughout his life. And it is undoubtedly better to try and fail than not to try at all. There one can be placed in the category of the Swiss mountaineer of whom it was said, *"He died climbing"*. When a new difficulty arises to obstruct your path, do not complain. Accept the challenge. Determine to cross this threshold as you have crossed numerous other thresholds in your past. In the words of a poet, do not rest but strive *to pass from dream to grander dream.*

1. What obstructs real progress in life?
A. Remaining at one and the same post
B. Avoiding the thinking and energy
C. Shunning every work
D. Stopping education
E. Worrying about the future

2. What does progress in life depend upon?
A. Good habits
B. Hardwork
C. Overcoming one difficulty after another
D. Spirit of service and cooperation
E. None of these

3. What does '*He died climbing*' signify?
A. He died when he was climbing the hill
B. He died before getting at the top
C. He strove hard till the last moment of life
D. He climbed the hill and then died
E. He found it difficult to climb

4. What does '*to pass from dream to grander dream*' mean?
A. Always having greater and greater aspiration in life
B. Seeing one good dream and then greater aspiration in life
C. Making plan after plan
D. Seeing one dream after the other
E. None of these

5. What did the man entering a new business past middle life do of his business?
A. He miserably failed in it
B. He achieved partial success
C. He dropped the business after sometime
D. He achieved good success in it
E. He started writing novels

6. How can you accomplish the most difficult tasks?

A. By mobilizing all possible resources
B. By avoiding all obstacles
C. By sticking to hardwork
D. By getting other people to do your work for you
E. By doing it bit by bit and persisting in the effort

7. What does De Morgan's life teach?
A. That it is futile to learn many things
B. That one is never old in case he has vigour
C. That it is never too late to learn
D. That creative writing can be made even late in life
E. None of these

8. How do middle-aged and elderly people add brilliance to their lives?
A. By overcoming difficulty one after another
B. By getting sycophants to surround them
C. By making fine speeches
D. By acquiring resourcefulness
E. None of these

9. What should we do when a new difficulty obstructs our path?
A. Run away from it
B. Be bold and face it
C. Manoeuvre to get it removed
D. Enlist other people's help to get it over
E. None of these

10. When did De Morgan start to write novels?
A. When he was sixty years old
B. When he was below sixty
C. When he studied psychology
D. When he was a student
E. None of these

PASSAGE-5

In terms of the total energy consumed by different sectors, the largest consumer is understandably the industrial sector, which accounts for nearly half the total energy used in the country today. This is followed by the transport sector which consumes about 25%, the household sector (about 14%) and the agricultural sector (about 9%). This last sector has shown considerable increase in energy use over the last four decades. Among the primary fuels, the relative proportion of coal has dropped from nearly 80% to 40% and that of oil has gone up from 17% to 44% over the same period.

Total energy consumption in India today is equivalent to 291 million tons of oil of which 26% comes from wood. On a per capita basis it works out to about one litre of oil per day, which is extremely low by international standards. The future energy demand depends upon the level of development envisaged and also on the sections of people to be affected by it.

The energy disparity between the urban and the rural population is at present *as wide as* between nations on a *worldwide scale.* There is apparently a greater need to provide energy in the rural areas and to improve the efficiency of energy use than merely to increase the national figures for energy consumption limiting its use to those who are getting the bulk share already.

With the projected rate of population growth, improving upon the per capita energy consumption is a Herculean task as our coal reserves and the capacity to import oil cannot be increased beyond a point. *There is clearly no escape* from the utilisation of renewable energy sources in a big way if the gap between the desired levels of energy supply and available resources has to be kept at the minimum.

1. The author is laying greater emphasis on which of the following?
(*a*) Efficient use of energy
(*b*) Increasing national indices for energy consumption
(*c*) Controlling population growth
A. Only (*a*) B. Only (*b*)
C. Only (*c*) D. All the three
E. Both (*b*) and (*c*)

2. The author feels that increasing per capita use of energy is
A. rather difficult, but not impossible
B. not easy, but certainly achievable
C. not at all desirable
D. a matter of great difficulty
E. a routine matter

3. According to the passage, the energy requirement of the future will be decided on the basis of which of the following?
   (*a*) Total energy already consumed by us in the past
   (*b*) Level of development of oil industry
   (*c*) Profile of the affected people
   A. Only (*a*) B. Only (*b*)
   C. Only (*c*) D. Both (*a*) and (*b*)
   E. Both (*b*) and (*c*)

4. Which of the following shows correctly the different sectors consuming energy arranged in ascending order?
   A. Agriculture, transport, household, industrial
   B. Agriculture, household, transport, industrial
   C. Industrial, transport, household, agriculture
   D. Industrial, household, agriculture, transport
   E. None of these

5. Which of the following has been suggested by the author as the best possible solution to overcome energy crisis?
   A. Importing large quantities of coal
   B. Exploration of oil reserves
   C. Reducing share of bulk users
   D. Maximisation of renewable sources
   E. Reducing the energy disparity between urban and rural areas

6. Which of the following styles has been adopted by the author?
   A. Unsubstantiated arguments and views
   B. Data based, but coloured by socialism
   C. Highly subjective with bias for rural people
   D. Objective, descriptive, lacking clarity
   E. Data based, objective, positive, solution oriented

7. Which of the following has been mentioned as a major hurdle in enhancing per capita consumption of energy in India?
   A. Present level of development in India
   B. Increased use of energy in agriculture sector
   C. Disparity in use of energy in rural and urban areas
   D. International norm of 1 litre of oil per day per person
   E. None of these

8. Which of the following statements is TRUE in the context of the passage?
   A. The household sector has shown considerable increase in energy use
   B. Use of oil has increased from 40% to 80%
   C. Industrial sector uses 50% of total energy used in India
   D. Energy consumption in India is 26% of world consumption
   E. Import of oil to the extent required is quite possible

9. *The energy disparity ..... as wide as ..... worldwide scale*, the first sentence of third paragraph means
   A. disparity in urban and rural is observed in all nations
   B. in no other nation such disparity is observed
   C. developed countries consume more energy than developing countries
   D. worldwide scale is different for rural and urban areas
   E. None of these

10. *There is clearly no escape* ..... means.....
   A. there is a way out, but it is ambiguous
   B. there is a problem, but without solution
   C. there is also no solution to this
   D. there is hardly any alternative except
   E. there is more than one way

PASSAGE-6

Peace and order are necessary, not just in our own country but also at the international level, if we are to secure national progress and development. The different countries in the world are coming closer today due to faster means of transport and communication. Economically, they are becoming increasingly interdependent. If peace is disturbed in one part of the world, it has adverse effects in other parts of the world as well. Nuclear weapons have already threatened the world with nuclear war. If the conflicts between different nations are not settled in time, they might *culminate* in a nuclear war destroying the whole world. It is therefore, in our own interest that the world is free of conflicts. If at all there are any, they must be settled promptly and peace should be restored. That is why we have declared the establishment of international peace and understanding as an objective of our foreign policy.

We need the help and cooperation of other countries for our scientific, industrial and economic development, especially in those fields where we have yet to achieve self-sufficiency. We obtain the latest machinery, technology and financial aid from the developed countries. On our part we too offer help to the under-developed countries. We are keen on maintaining friendly relations with other countries. Such friendly relations *foster* international understanding.

We have always exerted ourselves to see that the disputes arising between the different nations are settled through peaceful negotiations. We play an active role in the United Nations, the South Asian Association for Regional Cooperation, the Commonwealth of Nations and other such international organisations. We make it a point to participate in the international conferences on issues like energy crisis, environmental imbalance, nuclear arms race etc. We always offer a helping hand to other nations affected by natural calamities such as famines, earthquakes, floods and so on. We strive to maintain peaceful and friendly relations with our neighbouring countries. *Why do we do all this!* We sincerely believe that conflicts in today's world should be minimised, making way for better cooperation among the nations. If this is achieved, human resources will no longer be wasted in things like war or aggression. There will be no destruction of wealth. We believe that, in a peaceful world, there will be greater scope for the economic and cultural development of countries.

1. According to the passage, maintaining friendly relations with other countries facilitate
   A. developing international understanding
   B. exchange of scientists and technologists
   C. strategic planning in defence matters
   D. import and export of several vital commodities
   E. None of these

2. If conflicts between nations do not cease
   A. international bodies will have to take up these issues
   B. international understanding will not be fostered
   C. nuclear war will destroy the whole world
   D. the means of transport and communication will be disrupted

3. Which of the following is obtained by us from the developed countries, according to the passage?
   A. Fertilisers
   B. Foodgrains
   C. Leather Products
   D. Technology
   E. Crude Oil

4. Which of the following according to the passage, is facilitating the process of different countries coming together?
   A. Emerging world order
   B. Asian Association for Regional Cooperation
   C. Our participation in international conferences
   D. Need for self-sufficiency
   E. Faster means of transport and communication

5. Minimising the conflicts and making way for better cooperation among the nations will result in
   A. useful and purposive utilisation of human resources
   B. better utilisation of means of transport and communication
   C. culmination of nuclear war destroying the world
   D. keenness on maintaining friendly relations with other countries
   E. preservation of our national unity and integrity

6. Which of the following statements is NOT TRUE in the context of the passage?
   A. International conflicts must be settled promptly
   B. We try to maintain friendly relations with our neighbours
   C. We participate in many international conferences
   D. Friendly relations with other countries foster international understanding

E. Each country can be considered isolated and insulated from the effects of other countries

7. Which of the following words is largely SIMILAR in meaning of the word CULMINATE as used in the passage?
A. Reach the highest point
B. Stretch to the maximum
C. Absolute standards
D. Total destruction
E. Coming of age

8. Which of the following words is MOST OPPOSITE in meaning of the word FOSTER as used in the passage?
A. Advocate
B. Hinder
C. Obviate
D. Facilitate
E. Jettison

9. The question "Why do we do all this" is asked in the passage in which of the following contexts?
A. We always offer a helping hand to other nations in improving their technology
B. We endeavour to maintain peaceful and friendly relations with our neighbours
C. We obtain the latest machinery, technology and financial aid from the developed countries
D. We have shaped our foreign policy in a balanced and purposeful manner
E. None of these

10. Does any of the following sentences contain any idea expressed in the passage?
A. We have to make conscious efforts to preserve our national unity
B. Our country is huge in size and population where many languages are spoken
C. We have adopted the objective of democracy in the interest of overall development of our country
D. Citizens must be well-informed about public issues in order to participate meaningfully in public
E. None of these statements contain any idea expressed in the passage

PASSAGE-7

There is a fairly universal sentiment that the use of nuclear weapon is clearly contrary to morality and that its production does not go far enough. These activities are not only opposed to morality but also to law and if the legal objection can be added to the moral, the argument against the use and the manufacture of these weapons will considerably be reinforced. Now the time is ripe to evaluate the responsibility of scientists who knowingly use their expertise for the construction of such weapons which has *deleterious* effect on mankind.

To this must be added the fact that more than 50 per cent of the skilled scientific manpower in the world is how engaged in the armaments industry. How appropriate it is that all this valuable skill should be *devoted* to the manufacture of weapons of death in a world of poverty is a question that must touch the scientific conscience.

A meeting of biologists on the Long-Term Worldwide Biological Consequences of Nuclear War added frightening dimensions to those forecasts. Its report suggested that the long biological effects resulting from climatic changes may at least be as serious as the immediate ones.

Subfreezing temperatures, low light levels and high dose of ionizing and ultraviolet radiation extending for many months, after a large-scale nuclear war, could destroy the biological support systems of civilization, at least in the Northern Hemisphere. Productivity in natural and agricultural ecosystems could be severely restricted for a year or more. Post-war survivors would face starvation as well as freezing conditions in the dark and be exposed to near-lethal dose of radiation. If, as now seems possible, the Southern Hemisphere were affected also, global disruption of the biosphere could ensue. In any event, there would be severe consequences, even in the areas not affected directly, because of the interdependence of the world economy. In either case the extinction of a large fraction of the earth's animals, plants, and microorganism seems possible. The population size of Homo Sapiens conceivably could be reduced to pre-historic levels or below and extinction of the human species itself cannot be excluded.

1. The author's most important objective of writing the above passage seems to
   A. highlight the use of nuclear weapons as an effective population control measure
   B. illustrate the devastating effects of use of nuclear weapons on mankind
   C. duly highlight the supremacy of the nations which possess nuclear weapons
   D. summarise the long biological effects of use of nuclear weapons
   E. explain scientifically the climatic changes resulting from use of nuclear weapons

2. The scientists possessing expertise in manufacturing destructive weapons are
   A. very few in number
   B. irresponsible and incompetent
   C. more than half of the total number
   D. engaged in the armaments industry against their desire
   E. not conscious of the repercussions of their actions

3. According to the passage, the argument against the use and manufacture of nuclear weapons
   A. does not stand the test of legality
   B. possess legal strength although it does not have moral standing
   C. is acceptable only on moral grounds
   D. becomes stronger if legal and moral considerations are combined
   E. None of these

4. Which of the following is one of the consequences of Nuclear War?
   A. Fertility of land will last only for a year or so
   B. Post-war survivors being very few will have abundant food
   C. Lights would be cooler and more comfortable
   D. Southern hemisphere would remain quite safe in the post-war period
   E. None of these

5. Choose the word which is MOST OPPOSITE in meaning of the word DELETERIOUS as used in the passage.
   A. Beneficial B. Harmful
   C. Irreparable D. Non-cognizable
   E. Revolutionary

6. The author of the passage seems to be of the view that
   A. utilization of scientific skills in manufacture of weapons is appropriate
   B. the evaluation of the scientists' expertise show their incompetence
   C. manufacture of weapons of death would help eradication of poverty
   D. spending money on manufacture of weapons may be justifiable subject to the availability of funds
   E. utilization of valuable knowledge for manufacture of lethal weapons is inhuman

7. Which of the following BEST EXPLAINS the word DEVOTED as used in the passage?
   A. dedicated for a good cause
   B. utilized for betterment
   C. abused for destruction
   D. underutilized
   E. overutilized

8. It appears from the passage that the use of nuclear weapons is considered against morality by
   A. only such of those nations who cannot afford to manufacture weapons
   B. almost all the nations of the world
   C. only the superpowers who can afford to manufacture and sell weapons
   D. a minority group of scientists who have the necessary skill and competence
   E. most of the scientists who devote their valuable skills to manufacture nuclear weapons

9. Which of the following statement(s) *(a)*, *(b)* and/ or *(c)* is/are definitely true in the context of the passage?
   (a) Living organisms in the areas which are not directly affected by the consequences of nuclear war would also suffer
   (b) There is a likelihood of extinction of the human species as a consequence of nuclear war

(*c*) The post-war survivors would be exposed to the risk of near-lethal radiation

A. Only (*a*)
B. Only (*b*)
C. Only (*c*)
D. Only (*a*) and (*b*)
E. All the three

10. The biological consequences of nuclear war as given in the passage include all the following except

A. fall in temperature below zero degree celsius
B. ultraviolet radiation
C. high dose of ionizing
D. low light levels
E. None of these

PASSAGE-8

Mahatma Gandhi has repeatedly called himself a truthseeker and has learned, in the course of his search, that truth is a condition of being, not a quality outside of oneself or a moral acquisition, that it is of the very essence of the divine in man. Though he saw deceit and falsehood all around him and knew that it was accepted as the standard of life by people occupying positions of authority and influence, he was never afterwards tempted to *yield to* it even when to have done so would have brought advantage and no condemnation.

For healing he always had a great love and some aptitude and when at the age of seventeen *his family in conclave* suggested his going to England to study law, he *begged* to be allowed to study medicine instead. This, however, was not permitted and law was chosen for him. But, the love of healing remained, and though he could not study in the *orthodox* schools of medicine, he *gratified* his desire by studying various forms of nature-cure treatment and by experimenting with these on his person and on his friends and relatives. Some of these experiments produced remarkable results possibly not only due to the treatment but also to his devoted and instinctive nursing.

1. On whom did Gandhiji practice nature-cure?

A. On sick patients in hospitals
B. On people occupying positions of authority and influence
C. Those who were in great need of the treatment
D. Those who were not cured by other medicines
E. None of these

2. Gandhiji studied law mainly because

A. he wanted to be an eminent lawyer
B. he wanted to go to England
C. his family thrust upon him the study of law
D. he knew he can make a good career in legal profession
E. he wanted to serve people by solving their legal problems

3. What was Gandhiji's idea of truth?

A. It should be assimilated as a personal quality
B. It should be observed with a healing touch
C. It should not be followed with an idea of sacrifice
D. It should be searched in the world around you
E. None of these

4. Mahatma Gandhi described himself as a man:

A. in search of divine qualities
B. who would like to serve people
C. who would like to set standard of life
D. who would not compromise on his principles
E. None of these

5. Choose the word that is MOST OPPOSITE in meaning of the word BEGGED as used in the passage.

A. Demanded
B. Appealed
C. Suggested
D. Requested
E. Protested

6. Choose the word which is MOST OPPOSITE in meaning of the word ORTHODOX as used in the passage.

A. Backward
B. Non-conventional
C. Unpopular
D. Modern
E. Customary

7. What temptation did Gandhiji always resist?

A. Getting attracted towards wordly comforts
B. Ignoring the dictates of elderly people
C. Healing the wound of other
D. Following deceit and falsehood
E. None of these

8. What was probably the real cause of Gandhiji's success in nature-cure?
A. His detailed study of various medicinal systems
B. His confidence and desire to help people
C. His skills and aptitude in nursing
D. His experiments in search of truth
E. None of these

9. What did Mahatma Gandhi learn in the course of his search?
A. Being truthful is a divine blessing
B. Truth is synonymous with one's existence
C. People are full of deceit and falsehood
D. Truth is a quality outside of oneself
E. None of these

10. What did Gandhiji see around him?
A. Sick and unhealthy people
B. People accepting proper standard of life
C. People suffering from poverty and disease
D. People not having love and aptitude for healing
E. Dishonesty and untruthfulness

11. Explain the meaning of expression '*his family in conclave*' as used in the passage.
A. Members of the family and relatives
B. Figurehead of the family
C. Private meeting of the family
D. Family meeting for celebrating Gandhiji's seventeenth birthday
E. None of these

12. Choose the word that is most nearly the SAME in meaning as the word GRATIFIED as used in the passage.
A. Purified B. Satisfied
C. Nurtured D. Glorified
E. Projected

13. Choose the word which is most nearly the SAME in meaning as the word YIELD as used in the passage.
A. Surrender B. Provoke
C. Confine D. Adapt
E. Adhere

14. Which of the following statements is NOT TRUE in the context of the passage?
A. Gandhiji did many experiments in the area of nature-cure
B. Gandhiji did not study medicine in the orthodox school
C. Studying law was Gandhiji's first love
D. Truthfulness is the condition of being
E. Gandhiji was always a truthseeker

15. Which of the following statement(s) is/are true in the context of the passage?
(a) Gandhiji had a love and aptitude for nursing
(b) Gandhiji experimented nature-cure on himself
(c) Gandhiji encouraged deceit and psychofancy
A. Only *(a)* B. *(a)* and *(c)*
C. Only *(c)* D. *(a)* and *(b)*
E. Only *(b)*

PASSAGE-9

Believe it or not, once a wonderful plate made of gold fell from heaven into the court of a temple at Banares. On the plate these words were inscribed: "A gift from Heaven to him who loves best." The priest at once made a proclamation that everyday, all those who would like to claim the plate should *assemble* at the temple to have their kind deeds *judged.*

Everyday for a whole year all kinds of holy men, hermits, scholars and nobles came and related to the priests their deeds of charity. The priests heard their claims. At last they decided that the one who seemed to be the greatest lover of mankind was a rich man who had every year given all his wealth to the-poor. So they gave him the plate of gold. But when he took it in his hand, it *turned* to worthless lead. When he dropped it in his amazement on to the floor, it became gold again.

For another year claimants came and the priests presented the heavenly gift three times. But the same thing happened, showing that Heaven did not consider these men *worthy* of the gift.

Meanwhile a large number of beggars came and lay about the temple gate, hoping that the claimants who came would give them alms to prove they were worthy of the golden plate. It was a good thing for the beggars because the pilgrims gave them money but showed no sympathy, nor even a look of pity.

At last a peasant who had heard nothing about the plate of gold came near the temple. He was so *touched* by the sight of the miserable beggars that he wept. When he saw a poor blind and maimed wretch at the temple gate, he knelt at his side and *comforted* him with kind words. When this peasant went inside the temple, he was shocked to find it full of men boasting of their kind deeds and quarrelling with the priests. The priest who held the golden plate in his hand saw the peasant standing there and beckoned to him to know what he wanted. The peasant went near the priest and knowing nothing about the plate, accidentally touched it. At once it shone out with three times its former splendour and the priest said: "Son, the gift is yours, for you are the one who loves best."

1. The gift from Heaven was meant for those who
A. were scholars
B. were highly religious and loved God best
C. gave money to the poor
D. loved others in the best way
E. were poor peasants

2. What did the peasant see inside the temple?
A. Miserable beggars and blind men
B. Priests quarrelling among themselves
C. People speaking high of their kind deeds and fighting with the priests
D. The golden plate being converted to worthless lead
E. None of these

3. For which of the following was the proclamation made by the priest?
A. To find the richest person in the town
B. To find the rightful owner of the plate
C. To judge the worth of the golden plate
D. To judge his own deeds with the help of the people

4. What happened to the plate when it was touched by the peasant?
A. It started glowing with greater splendour
B. It changed from gold to lead
C. It became heavier and fell on the ground
D. It turned into gold
E. Not mentioned in the passage

5. The rich man dropped the golden plate to the floor as he was
A. not intersted in possessing it
B. afraid of holding it
C. curious to know about its purity
D. surprised to see it turning to lead
E. the rightful owner of the plate

6. Why did the beggars stay near the temple gate? They
A. wanted to prove their claim on the golden plate
B. had come to pray in the temple
C. knew that the visitors would give them alms
D. wanted to seek the sympathy of the peasant
E. wanted to have a glimpse of the golden plate

7. The priests could decide on the rightful owner of the plate when the peasant
A. met with an accident
B. entered the temple and stood there
C. put forward his claim on the heavenly gift
D. touched the plate unknowingly
E. comforted the poor blind man with kind words

8. Which of the following statements is TRUE in the context of the passage?
A. The rich man did not turn out to be the greatest lover of humanity
B. The peasant touched the plate to know whether he was its rightful owner
C. The priest told the peasant to narrate his kind deeds
D. The plate shone out in splendour when the peasant dropped it on the floor
E. The peasant went near the priest to ask for the golden plate

9. What made the peasant weep?
A. The quarrel between the priests and some people

B. The greediness of the rich people
C. The boastful crowd inside the temple
D. The pitiable condition of the beggars
E. None of the above

Directions (Qs. 10 to 12): *Choose the word which is most nearly the SAME in meaning as the word given in BOLD as used in the passage.*

10. TURNED
A. bent B. moved
C. changed D. revolved
E. fell

11. WORTHY
A. useful B. promising
C. successful D. necessary
E. deserving

12. JUDGED
A. ordered B. justified
C. announced D. explainded
E. assessed

Directions (Qs. 13 to 15): *Choose the word which is most OPPOSITE in meaning of the word given in BOLD as used in the passage.*

13. COMFORTED
A. consoled B. ignored
C. advised D. scolded
E. controlled

14. ASSEMBLE
A. distribute B. gather
C. partition D. disperse
E. dismantle

15. TOUCHED
A. moved B. indifferent
C. disconnected D. excited
E. arrogant

PASSAGE-10

A struggle for power began with Bimbisara and Ajatshatru of the Kingdom of Magadha. In the 4th century BC, the Nandas came to power, with their capital at Pataliputra. The latter were replaced by the Mauryas at the close of the same century. This came about partly as a result of Alexander's invasion and the decline of Iranian strength in India. Chandragupta Maurya took advantage of the unsettled conditions and with the help of his adviser Kautilya, built the first great empire in India. Under him and his two great successors, Bindusara and Ashoka, almost the whole of India, with the exception of the farthest south, was unified into one empire.

Many important developments took place in the social, economic and cultural life of the Indian people in this period—322 to 184 BC. Particularly important was the spread of Buddhism, which had been introduced earlier.

The decline of the Mauryan Empire after the rule of Ashoka was followed by a long period of new invasions and the formation of small states. Of the foreign invasions, the first was that of the Greeks who were the rulers of Bactria. They conquered the Punjab and parts of Sind and their contact had a lasting influence on the culture of India. Gandhara style of art emerged and flourished. The greatest Greek ruler in India was Menander (Milinda) in the 2nd century BC, who became a Buddhist.

The Greek invasion was followed by that of the Sakas. The Sakas displaced the Greek in Bactria and spread their power in Western India. One of the Saka kings was Rudradaman who, as the name suggests, was a devotee of Siva. He was responsible for important irrigation works in Saurashtra. The Sakas, like other invaders, became a part of Indian life and played an important role in the development of Indian Culture. Another group of invaders from Central Asia was that of the Kushanas early in the first century AD. The greatest of the Kushana rulers was Kanishka who, according to some historians, started the Saka Era in AD 78. Kanishka ruled his vast empire in India and Central Asia from Purushapura (modern Peshwar) for 40 years. Kanishka's empire brought to India the cultural tradition of Iran, Greece and Rome. It also provided a stimulus to trade between India and other parts of the world Kanishka patronised the Mahayan form of Buddhism. It spread to Central Asia during this period and from there to China, Korea and Japan. The Kushana Empire declined in the third century AD.

1. A suitable title for the above passage is
A. Alexander's invasion of India
B. Kanishka, the great Kushana ruler
C. Development of India's Culture
D. India—the Period of Empires
E. None of these

2. The Kingdom of Magadha was ruled by the Nandas about
A. 2000 years ago
B. 2400 years ago
C. 2800 years ago
D. over 3000 years ago
E. None of these

3. The successors of the Nandas, whose capital was at Pataliputra, were the
A. Greeks B. Iranians
C. Mauryas D. Sakas
E. None of these

4. The cultural traditions of Iran, Greece and Rome came to India during the rule of
A. Ashoka B. Kanishka
C. Menander D. Rudradaman
E. None of these

5. Who, amongst the following, had their capital at Purushapura (modern Peshawar)?
A. The Mauryans B. The Nandas
C. The Kushanas D. The Sakas
E. None of these

6. The Saka Era is believed to have been established by
A. the Kushanas
B. Milinda, the Greek ruler
C. the Nandas
D. The Sakas
E. None of these

7. All of the following were foreign invaders of India, except
A. the Greeks B. the Kushanas
C. the Mauryas D. the Sakas
E. None of these

8. The greatest Greek ruler in India was
A. Ajatshatru B. Bimbisara
C. Bindusara D. Milinda
E. None of these

9. Who were the founders of the first great unified empire in India?
A. The Mauryans B. The Nandas
C. The Kushanas D. The Sakas
E. None of these

10. Which particularly important development took place in India between 322 to 184 BC?
A. The rulers of Bactria invaded India
B. Buddhism spread far and wide
C. The Sakas displaced the Greeks
D. Gandhara style of art attained its zenith
E. None of these

ANSWERS

PASSAGE-1

1	2	3	4	5	6	7	8	9	10
D	B	A	E	B	A	B	A	A	D

PASSAGE-2

1	2	3	4	5	6	7	8	9	10
D	E	C	E	B	C	D	B	B	A

PASSAGE-3

1	2	3	4	5	6	7	8	9	10
C	A	D	D	E	D	C	C	E	A

PASSAGE-4

1	2	3	4	5	6	7	8	9	10
A	C	C	A	D	E	B	A	B	E

PASSAGE-5

1	2	3	4	5	6	7	8	9	10
A	D	E	B	D	E	E	C	C	D

PASSAGE-6

1	2	3	4	5	6	7	8	9	10
A	C	D	E	A	E	A	B	B	E

PASSAGE-7

1	2	3	4	5	6	7	8	9	10
B	C	D	A	A	E	C	B	E	E

PASSAGE-8

1	2	3	4	5	6	7	8	9	10
E	C	A	A	E	B	D	C	B	E
11	**12**	**13**	**14**	**15**					
C	B	A	C	D					

PASSAGE-9

1	2	3	4	5	6	7	8	9	10
D	C	B	A	D	C	D	A	D	C
11	**12**	**13**	**14**	**15**					
E	E	D	D	B					

PASSAGE-10

1	2	3	4	5	6	7	8	9	10
C	D	C	B	C	A	C	D	A	B

2

Synonyms & Antonyms

There are thousands of words in English language. No one can remember their meanings easily but with regular practice one can memorise most of them. A number of words with their Synonyms and Antonyms are compiled here. Try to learn as many as you can and answer the questions thereafter.

Words	*Synonyms*	*Antonyms*
Abandon	Cease, Forsake	Continue
Abhor	Hate, Loathe, Detest	Like, Love
Abiding	Enduring, Durable	Fleeting
Able	Proficient, Competent	Incompetent, Unfit
Ability	Skill, Power	Disability, Inability
Abortive	Fruitless, Futile	Fruitful, Successful
Abolish	Destroy, Undo	Restore, Revive
Abridge	Shorten, Curtail	Lengthen, Expand
Absolve	Forgive, Pardon, Excuse	Condemn
Accelerate	Hasten	Retard
Accord	Agreement, Harmony	Discord, Disagreement
Accumulate	Collect, Store, Amass	Distribute, Scatter
Adamant	Hard, Inflexible	Flexible
Adversity	Misfortune, Distress	Prosperity
Adept	Expert, Skillful	Inexpert, Unskillful
Aggravate	Heighten, Intensify	Quell, Suppress
Agile	Nimble	Clumsy, Undeft
Alert	Vigilant	Heedless
Allay	Calm, Soothe, Assuage	Arouse
Ameliorate	Improve, Advance, Amend	Worsen, Deteriorate
Ambiguous	Vague, Unclear	Clear
Amiable	Lovable, Agreeable	Disagreeable
Annihilate	Destroy	Create
Arduous	Hard, Strenuous	Easy

Words	*Synonyms*	*Antonyms*
Attacks	Assault	Defend
Audacity	Boldness	Cowardice
Auspicious	Favourable, Propitious, Lucky	Ominous, Inauspicious, Unlucky
Austere	Harsh, Severe, Rigorous	Easy-going
Authentic	True, Genuine	Spurious, False
Avarice	Greed	Generosity
Averse	Unwilling, Loath, Disinclined	Willing, Inclined
Aversion	Hostility, Hatred	Affinity, Liking
Base	Low, Mean, Ignoble	Noble, Exalted
Boisterous	Noisy, Stormy	Calm, Quiet
Brave	Courageous, Daring, Bold, Plucky	Cowardly, Dastardly, Timid
Brief	Short, Concise, Laconic	Lengthy, Diffuse
Bright	Vivid, Radiant	Dull, Dark
Brutal	Savage, Cruel	Humane, Kindly
Callous	Hard, Cruel, Indifferent	Soft, Tender, Concerned
Cautious	Careful, Wary	Rash, Reckless, Foolhardy
Censure (*n*)	Blame, Condemnation	Praise
Censure (*vb*)	Blame, Condemn	Praise, Commend
Circumscribed	Restricted, Confined, Limited	Unconfined, Unrestricted
Civil	Polite, Courteous, Gracious, Urbane	Rude, Uncivil, Impolite, Ungracious
Coerce	Compel, Force	Volunteer
Compassionate	Pitiful, Sympathetic, Merciful	Unsympathetic, Merciless, Cruel
Compress	Condense, Abbreviate	Expand, Lengthen
Conspicuous	Noticeable, Manifest	Inconspicuous
Constant	Steady, Steadfast, Uniform	Inconstant, Variable
Cordial	Friendly, Warm, Hearty	Cold, Unfriendly
Covert	Hidden, Secret	Overt, Open
Cruel	Savage, Ruthless, Vicious	Kind, Gentle, Benevolent
Cursory	Rapid, Superficial	Thorough, Exhaustive, Intensive
Credible	Believable, Probable, Plausible	Incredible, Unbelievable, Fantastic
Crafty	Cunning, Sly	Artless, Simple, Ingenuous
Costly	Expensive, Dear	Cheap, Inexpensive
Confidence	Trust, Reliance	Distrust, Doubt
Death	Decease, Demise	Existence, Life
Dearth	Scarcity, Lack, Want, Paucity, Shortage	Plenty, Abundance
Decay	Dissolution, Decline, Decomposition, Disintegration	Regeneration

Words	*Synonyms*	*Antonyms*
Deference	Respect, Reverence	Disrespect, Irreverence
Deficient	Lacking, Inadequate	Complete, Sufficient
Desolate	Lonely, Deserted	Crowded, Occupied
Destitute	Wanting, Needy	Rich, Affluent
Diligence	Industry, Perseverance	Idleness
Disgrace	Dishonour, Discredit	Honour, Credit
Dwindle	Decrease, Shrink	Grow, Increase
Earthly	Terrestrial, Mundane	Celestial, Heavenly, Unearthly
Eligible	Qualified, Suitable	Ineligible, Unsuitable
Emancipate	Liberate, Free	Enslave
Excited	Impassioned, Stimulated	Composed, Cool, Impassive
Extraordinary	Uncommon, Remarkable, Marvellous	Commonplace, Ordinary
Extravagant	Lavish, Prodigal, Wastrel, Spendthrift	Thrifty, Economical, Frugal
Fabricate	Construct, Make	Destroy
Fabulous	Fictitious, Mythical	Actual, Real
False	Untrue, Mendacious	True, Genuine
Famous	Well-known, Renowned	Obscure, Unknown
Fantastic	Fanciful, Imaginative, Visionary	Practical, Down to earth
Fearful	Nervous, Anxious, Afraid, Scared	Fearless, Dauntless
Felicity	Happiness	Sorrow
Gaiety	Joyousness, Hilarity	Mourning, Dullness
Garrulous	Talkative, Loquacious	Taciturn, Silent, Reserved
Generous	Liberal, Magnanimous	Stingy, Miserly
Gigantic	Huge, Colossal	Minute, Small
Graphic	Vivid, Pictorial, Meaningful	Vague
Guest	Visitor	Host
Guile	Fraud, Trickery	Artlessness, Ingenuousness
Gratitude	Gratefulness	Ingratitude, Ungratefulness
Gratuitous	Voluntary, Spontaneous, Unwarranted	Involuntary, Forced
Hamper	Hinder, Obstruct	Facilitate, Ease
Haughty	Arrogant, Proud	Humble, Modest
Hazardous	Dangerous, Perilous	Safe, Secure Protected
Headstrong	Obstinate, Stubborn	Weak-willed, Flexible

Words	*Synonyms*	*Antonyms*
Hope	Belief, Conviction, Expectation	Despair, Hopelessness
Improvident	Prodigal, Carelessness	Provident, Economical
Incessant	Unceasing, Continuous	Discontinuous
Indolent	Slothful, Lethargic	Active, Energetic
Joy	Delight, Pleasure	Sadness, Gloom
Jolly	Jovial, Merry	Gloomy, Sad
Judicious	Discreet, Prudent	Indiscreet, Injudicious
Knowledge	Enlightenment, Learning	Ignorance, Stupidity
Laborious	Industrious, Assiduous	Slothful, Lazy
Laxity	Slackness, Looseness	Firmness
Lenient	Mild, Forbearing	Strict, Stern
Lethal	Deadly, Fatal, Mortal	Life-giving, Vital, Vivifying
Liberal	Generous, Tolerant	Intolerant, Illiberal
Liberty	Freedom, Independence	Slavery, Bondage
Lively	Animated, Activc	Dull, Listless
Loyal	Faithful, Devoted	Treacherous, Disloyal, Unfaithful
Lucky	Fortunate	Unlucky, Unfortunate
Lucrative	Profitable	Unprofitable
Magnanimous	Generous, Largehearted	Ungenerous, Stingy
Malady	Illness, Ailment	Health
Manifest	Noticeable, Obvious	Obscure, Puzzling
Meagre	Small	Plentiful, Large
Mean	Low, Abject	Noble, Exalted
Mendacious	False, Untruthful	Truthful
Misery	Sorrow, Distress	Happiness, Joy
Morbid	Sick, Diseased	Healthy
Mournful	Sorrowful, Sad	Joyful, Happy
Negligent	Careless, Heedless	Careful
Notorious	Infamous, Disreputable	Reputable
Obedient	Submissive, Compliant, Docile	Disobedient, Recalcitrant, Wayward
Obsolete	Antiquated, Out-of-Date	Current, Modern
Opportune	Timely, Seasonable	Inopportune
Opulence	Wealth, Riches	Penury, Poverty
Onerous	Heavy, Burdensome	Light, Easy
Palatable	Tasty, Delicious	Unpalatable
Pathetic	Touching	Joyous, Cheery
Persuade	Urge, Induce	Dissuade
Praise (*vb*)	Applaud, Eulogise	Condemn

Words	*Synonyms*	*Antonyms*
Praise (*n*)	Applause, Eulogy	Condemnation
Precarious	Risky, Uncertain	Safe, Certain
Pretence	Pretext, Excuse	Candour, Frankness
Propagate	Breed, Circulate	Terminate, Restrict
Quaint	Odd, Singular	Usual, Ordinary
Quell	Suppress, Subdue	Agitate, Arouse
Rare	Uncommon, Scarce	Common, Ordinary
Refined	Polished, Elegant	Crude, Coarse
Remote	Distant	Near, Close
Renown	Fame, Reputation	Infamy, Notoriety
Rigid	Stiff, Unyielding	Flexible, Yielding
Remorseful	Regretful, Repentant	Unrepentant
Rebellion	Revolt, Mutiny, Insurgency	Loyalty
Scared	Holy, Consecrated	Profane, Unholy
Sane	Sensible, Sound	Insane
Scold	Chide, Rebuke	Praise
Serious	Grave, Earnest	Frivolous
Shy	Bashful	Bold, Impudent
Simple	Plain, Artless	Complex, Cunning, Shrewd
Solitary	Single, Lonely, Secluded	Numerous, Multitude
Shallow	Superficial	Deep
Solace	Comfort, Relief	Discomfort, Grief
Spurious	Sham, False	Genuine, Authentic
Stagnant	Still, Motionless	Moving
Surplus	Excess	Deficit, Shortage
Tame	Gentle, Mild, Domesticated	Savage, Wild
Teacher	Instructor, Educator	Student, Pupil
Tedious	Wearisome, Monotonous	Agreeable, Lively
Temporal	Worldly, Secular	Spiritual
Temperate	Moderate	Immoderate, Intemperate
Tortuous	Winding, Circuitous	Straight, Direct
Tough	Hard, Strong	Tender, Soft, Flexible
Transient	Temporary, Fleeting	Lasting, Durable, Permanent
Trusworthy	Reliable	Unreliable, Untrustworthy
Tranquil	Calm	Agitated
Ugly	Unsightly, Repulsive	Beautiful, Attractive
Useful	Advantageous, Serviceable	Useless
Vehemence	Passion, Force	Apathy, Indifference

Words	*Synonyms*	*Antonyms*
Vindictive	Revengeful	Forgiving
Wholesome	Healthy	Unwholesome, Morbid, Unhealthy, Diseased
Wicked	Evil, Impious	Pious, Good
Wise	Sagacious, Erudite	Foolish, Stupid
Wrath	Anger, Fury, Rage	Love, Peace, Calm
Wreck	Ruin, Destroy	Create, Construct
Yield	Surrender, Submit	Resist, Revolt
Yielding	Submissive, Supple	Inflexible, Intractable
Yoke	Oppression, Bondage	Freedom
Zeal	Passion, Fervour	Apathy, Indifference
Zest	Relish, Enthusiasm	Distaste, Disrelish

Multiple Choice Questions

Directions (Qs. 1 to 100): *In the following questions choose the words which best expresses the MEANING of the given words.*

1. INDICT
A. Condemn B. Reprimand
C. Accuse D. Allege
E. Trap

2. SCINTILLATING
A. Smouldering B. Glittering
C. Touching D. Warming
E. Glowing

3. REFECTORY
A. Restaurant B. Parlour
C. Living Room D. Dining Room
E. Factory

4. DISTINCTION
A. Diffusion B. Disagreement
C. Difference D. Degree
E. Honour

5. IMPROVEMENT
A. Advancement B. Betterment
C. Promotion D. Preference
E. Enhance

6. ADVERSITY
A. Failure B. Helplessness
C. Misfortune D. Crisis
E. Negativity

7. TURN UP
A. Land up B. Show up
C. Crop up D. Come up
E. Rotate

8. DEIFY
A. Flatter B. Challenge
C. Worship D. Face
E. Obstruct

9. ERROR
A. Misadventure B. Misgiving
C. Ambiguity D. Blunder
E. Flaw

10. SHALLOW
A. Artificial B. Superficial
C. Foolish D. Worthless
E. Deep

11. MASSACRE
A. Murder B. Stab
C. Assassinate D. Slaughter
E. Shoot

12. COMBAT
A. Conflict B. Quarrel
C. Feud D. Fight
E. Jostle

13. VORACIOUS
A. Wild B. Hungry
C. Angry D. Quick
E. Beautiful

14. IMPROMPTU
A. Offhand B. Unimportant
C. Unreal D. Effective
E. Punctual

15. RABBLE
A. Mob B. Noise
C. Roar D. Rubbish
E. Erase

16. TEPID
A. Hot B. Warm
C. Cold D. Boiling
E. Sticky

17. MAYHEM
A. Jubilation B. Havoc
C. Excitement D. Defeat
E. Movement

18. TIMID
A. Fast B. Slow
C. Medium D. Shy
E. Rapid

19. CANTANKEROUS
A. Quarrelsome B. Rash
C. Disrepectful D. Noisy
E. Obese

20. PRECARIOUS
A. Cautious B. Critical
C. Perilous D. Brittle
E. Sharp

21. TACITURNITY
A. Dumbness B. Changeableness
C. Hesitation D. Reserveness
E. Preserve

22. INEBRIATED
A. Dreamy B. Stupefied
C. Unsteady D. Drunken
E. Broken

23. HARBINGER
A. Massenger B. Steward
C. Forerunner D. Pilot
E. Performer

24. INTIMIDATE
A. To hint B. Frighten
C. Bluff D. Harass
E. Inform

25. IRONIC
A. Inflexible
B. Bitter
C. Good-natured
D. Disguisedly sarcastic
E. Hard

26. STRINGENT
A. Tense
B. Stringy
C. Strict
D. Causing to shrink
E. Liberal

27. ECSTATIC
A. Animated B. Bewildered
C. Enraptured D. Erratic
E. Gloomy

28. COMMENSURATE
A. Measurable B. Proportionate
C. Beginning D. Appropriate
E. Finish

29. DESTITUTION
A. Humility B. Moderation
C. Poverty D. Beggary
E. Orphanage

30. ASCEND
A. Leap B. Grow
C. Deviate D. Mount
E. Invite

31. UNCOUTH
A. Ungraceful B. Rough
C. Slovenly D. Dirty
E. Gracious

32. LYNCH
A. Hang B. Madden
C. Kill D. Shoot
E. Start

33. LAUD
A. Lord B. Eulogy
C. Praise D. Extort
E. Clap

34. CORRESPONDENCE
A. Agreements B. Contracts
C. Documents D. Letters
E. News

35. VENUE
A. Place B. Agenda
C. Time D. Duration
E. Ceremony

36. STERILE
A. Barren B. Arid
C. Childless D. Dry
E. Fertile

37. SYNOPSIS
A. Index B. Mixture
C. Summary D. Puzzle
E. End

38. GERMANE
A. Responsible B. Logical
C. Possible D. Relevant
E. Foreigner

39. PONDER
A. Think B. Evaluate
C. Anticipate D. Increase
E. Sprinkle

40. CANNY
A. Obstinate B. Handsome
C. Clever D. Stout
E. Container

41. ABUNDANT
A. Ripe B. Cheap
C. Plenty D. Absent
E. Closed

42. CONSEQUENCES
A. Results B. Conclusions
C. Difficulties D. Applications
E. Series

43. SHIVER
A. Shake B. Rock
C. Tremble D. Move
E. Cry

44. DILIGENT
A. Progressive B. Brilliant
C. Inventive D. Hard-working
E. Masculine

45. DISTANT
A. Far B. Removed
C. Reserved D. Separate
E. Unreachable

46. FORAY
A. Excursion B. Contest
C. Ranger D. Intuition
E. Light

47. FRUGALITY
A. Foolishness B. Extremity
C. Enthusiasm D. Economy
E. Weakness

48. GARNISH
A. Paint B. Garner
C. Adorn D. Abuse
E. Attract

49. VIGOUR
A. Strength B. Boldness
C. Warmth D. Enthusiasm
E. Vitality

50. CANDID
A. Apparent B. Explicit
C. Frank D. Bright
E. Sweet

51. BRIEF
A. Limited B. Small
C. Little D. Short
E. Compress

52. GARRULITY
A. Credulity B. Senility
C. Loquaciousness D. Speciousness
E. Misery

53. FURORE
A. Excitement B. Worry
C. Flux D. Anteroom
E. Noise

54. NEUTRAL
A. Unbiased B. Non-aligned
C. Undecided D. Indifferent
E. Unmoved

55. LAMENT
A. Regret B. Comment
C. Condone D. Console
E. Sadden

56. MASTERLY
A. Crafty B. Skillful
C. Meaningful D. Cruel
E. Rightfully

57. MOROSE
A. Annoyed B. Gloomy
C. Moody D. Displeased
E. Happy

58. BARE
A. Uncovered B. Tolerate
C. Clear D. Neat
E. Least

59. FEEBLE
A. Weak B. Vain
C. Arrogant D. Sick
E. Sleek

60. PRESTIGE
A. Influence B. Quality
C. Name D. Wealth
E. Strength

61. WARRIOR
A. Soldier B. Sailor
C. Pirate D. Spy
E. Juggler

62. ENTIRE
A. Part B. Quarter
C. Whole D. Half
E. Tiring

63. RESCUE
A. Command B. Help
C. Defence D. Safety
E. Problem

64. INFREQUENT
A. Never B. Usual
C. Rare D. Sometimes
E. Often

65. WRETCHED
A. Poor B. Foolish
C. Insane D. Strained
E. Broken

66. DIVERSION
A. Amusement B. Distortion
C. Deviation D. Bylane
E. Subway

67. AWAKENED
A. Enlightened B. Realised
C. Shook D. Waken
E. Walking

68. HESITATED
A. Stopped B. Paused
C. Slowed D. Postponed
E. Obstructed

69. PIOUS
A. Pure B. Pretentious
C. Clean D. Devout
E. Thirsty

70. TORTURE
A. Torment B. Chastisement
C. Harassment D. Terror
E. Beat

71. ATTEMPT
A. Serve B. Explore
C. Try D. Explain
E. Chance

72. RESTRAINT
A. Hindrance B. Repression
C. Obstacle D. Restriction
E. Tolerance

73. CHASTE
A. Honest B. Dignified
C. Virtuous D. Noble
E. Truthful

74. INSOMNIA
A. Lethargy B. Sleeplessness
C. Drunkenness D. Unconsciousness
E. Blindness

75. TRANSIENT
A. Transparent B. Fleeting
C. Feeble D. Fanciful
E. Flowing

76. MANDACIOUS
A. Full of confidence B. False
C. Encouraging D. Provocative
E. Thinkable

77. VORACIOUS
A. Truthful B. Gluttonous
C. Funny D. Venturous
E. Fearful

78. CONNOISSEUR
A. Ignorant B. Lover of art
C. Interpreter D. Delinquent
E. Officer

79. REPERCUSSION
A. Clever reply B. Recollection
C. Remuneration D. Reaction
E. Discussion

80. REPEAL
A. Sanction B. Perpetuate
C. Pass D. Cancel
E. Appeal

81. INFAMY
A. Dishonour B. Glory
C. Integrity D. Reputation
E. Beauty

82. FAKE
A. Original B. Imitation
C. Trustworthy D. Loyal
E. Lie

83. DEBACLE
A. Collapse B. Decline
C. Defeat D. Disgrace
E. Mistake

84. ADMONISH
A. Punish B. Curse
C. Dismiss D. Reprimand
E. Admit

85. EMBEZZLE
A. Misappropriate B. Balance
C. Remunerate D. Clear
E. Mix

86. CORPULENT
A. Lean B. Gaunt
C. Emaciated D. Obese
E. Corrupt

87. AUGUST
A. Common B. Ridiculous
C. Dignified D. Petty
E. Month

88. STRINGENT
A. Dry B. Strained
C. Rigorous D. Shrill
E. Thready

89. INSOLVENT
A. Poor B. Bankrupt
C. Penniless D. Broke
E. Unsoluble

90. EXTRICATE
A. Pull B. Free
C. Tie D. Complicate
E. Expel

91. INEXPLICABLE
A. Confusing
B. Unaccountable
C. Chaotic
D. Unconnected
E. Undesired

92. GRATIFY
A. Appreciate B. Frank
C. Indulge D. Pacify
E. Regard

93. ALERT
A. Energetic B. Observant
C. Intelligent D. Watchful
E. Smart

94. UNTIE
A. Unfold B. Unchain
C. Undo D. Unhinge
E. Free

95. OBJECT
A. Challenge B. Disapprove
C. Deny D. Disobey
E. Refuse

96. BROWSE
A. Heal B. Deceive
C. Examine D. Strike
E. Vision

97. SALACITY
A. Bliss B. Depression
C. Indecency D. Recession
E. Urban

98. ZANY
A. Clown B. Pet
C. Thief D. Magician
E. Virtuous

99. WARY
A. Sad
B. Vigilant
C. Distorted
D. Tired
E. Different

100. RECKLESS
A. Courageous
B. Rash
C. Bold
D. Daring
E. Disorganised

Directions (Qs. 101 to 200): *In the following questions choose the word which is the exact OPPOSITE of the given words.*

101. DEAR
A. Priceless
B. Free
C. Worthless
D. Cheap
E. Expensive

102. FLAGITIOUS
A. Innocent
B. Vapid
C. Ignorant
D. Frivolous
E. Stupid

103. LIABILITY
A. Property
B. Assets
C. Debt
D. Treasure
E. Responsibilty

104. VIRTUOUS
A. Wicked
B. Corrupt
C. Vicious
D. Scandalous
E. Dishonest

105. ENCOURAGE
A. Dampen
B. Disapprove
C. Discourage
D. Warn
E. Land

106. MORTAL
A. Divine
B. Immortal
C. Spiritual
D. Eternal
E. Strong

107. LEND
A. Borrow
B. Cheat
C. Pawn
D. Hire
E. Ask

108. COMIC
A. Emotional
B. Tragic
C. Fearful
D. Painful
E. Adult

109. ADDITION
A. Division
B. Enumeration
C. Subtraction
D. Multiplication
E. Minus

110. MINOR
A. Big
B. Major
C. Tall
D. Heavy
E. Adult

111. REPEL
A. Attend
B. Concentrate
C. Continue
D. Attract
E. Expel

112. ARTIFICIAL
A. Red
B. Natural
C. Truthful
D. Solid
E. Superficial

113. CAPACIOUS
A. Limited
B. Caring
C. Foolish
D. Changeable
E. Spacious

114. PROVOCATION
A. Vocation
B. Pacification
C. Peace
D. Destruction
E. Convocation

115. METICULOUS
A. Mutual
B. Shaggy
C. Meretricious
D. Slovenly
E. Ridiculous

116. ABLE
A. Disable
B. Inable
C. Unable
D. Misable
E. Probable

117. COMFORT
A. Uncomfort
B. Miscomfort
C. Discomfort
D. Uneasy
E. Luxury

118. GAIN
A. Loose
B. Fall
C. Lost
D. Lose
E. Again

119. SYNTHETIC
A. Affable
B. Natural
C. Plastic
D. Cosmetic
E. Pathetic

120. ACQUITTED
A. Freed B. Burdened
C. Convicted D. Entrusted
E. Predicted

121. STRINGENT
A. General B. Vehement
C. Lenient D. Magnanimous
E. Astringent

122. FLIMSY
A. Frail B. Filthy
C. Firm D. Flippant
E. Fat

123. BUSY
A. Occupied B. Engrossed
C. Relaxed D. Engaged
E. Free

124. ADAPTABLE
A. Adoptable B. Flexible
C. Yielding D. Rigid
E. Solid

125. LOVE
A. Villainy B. Hatred
C. Compulsion D. Force
E. Fight

126. BALANCE
A. Disbalance B. Misbalance
C. Debalance D. Imbalance
E. Unbalance

127. RELINQUISH
A. Abdicate B. Renounce
C. Possess D. Deny
E. Occupy

128. MOUNTAIN
A. Plain B. Plateau
C. Precipice D. Valley
E. Ocean

129. FICKLE
A. Courageous B. Sincere
C. Steadfast D. Humble
E. Strong

130. PERENNIAL
A. Frequent B. Regular
C. Lasting D. Rare
E. Often

131. RARELY
A. Hardly B. Definitely
C. Frequently D. Periodically
E. Barely

132. STARTLED
A. Amused B. Relaxed
C. Endless D. Astonished
E. Finished

133. ADHERENT
A. Detractor B. Enemy
C. Alien D. Rival
E. Follower

134. QUIESCENT
A. Indifferent B. Troublesome
C. Weak D. Unconcerned
E. Silent

135. CONDENSE
A. Expand B. Distribute
C. Interpret D. Lengthen
E. Lighten

136. BENIGN
A. Malevolent B. Soft
C. Friendly D. Unwise
E. Kind

137. OBSCURE
A. Implicit B. Obnoxious
C. Explicit D. Pedantic
E. Incurable

138. HYPOCRITICAL
A. Gentle B. Sincere
C. Amiable D. Dependable
E. Critical

139. EVASIVE
A. Free B. Honest
C. Liberal D. Frank
E. Invasive

140. INDUSTRIOUS
A. Indifferent B. Indolent
C. Casual D. Passive
E. Serving

141. EXTRICATE
A. Manifest B. Palpable
C. Release D. Entangle
E. Intricate

142. LUCID
A. Glory B. Noisy
C. Obscure D. Distinct
E. Clear

143. INSIPID
A. Tasty B. Stupid
C. Discreet D. Feast
E. Flavoured

144. OBEYING
A. Ordering B. Following
C. Refusing D. Contradicting
E. Insulting

145. VICTORIOUS
A. Defeated B. Annexed
C. Destroyed D. Vanquished
E. Triumphant

146. COMMISSIONED
A. Started B. Closed
C. Finished D. Terminated
E. Salaried

147. VANITY
A. Pride B. Humility
C. Conceit D. Ostentious
E. Grace

148. ZENITH
A. Acme B. Top
C. Nadir D. Pinnacle
E. Core

149. TANGIBLE
A. Ethereal B. Concrete
C. Actual D. Solid
E. Delicious

150. REPRESS
A. Inhibit B. Liberate
C. Curb D. Quell
E. Suppress

151. EPILOGUE
A. Dialogue B. Prelude
C. Post script D. Epigram
E. Monologue

152. FRAUDULENT
A. Candid B. Direct
C. Forthright D. Genuine
E. Real

153. LOQUACIOUS
A. Reticent B. Talkative
C. Garrulous D. Verbose
E. Verbatim

154. NIGGARDLY
A. Frugal B. Thrifty
C. Stingy D. Generous
E. Mean

155. PERTINENT
A. Irrational B. Irregular
C. Insistent D. Irrelevant
E. Inconsistent

156. FAINT-HEARTED
A. Warm-hearted B. Full-blooded
C. Hot-blooded D. Stout-hearted
E. Kind-hearted

157. VIOLENT
A. Humble B. Harmless
C. Gentle D. Tame
E. Pet

158. STATIONARY
A. Active B. Mobile
C. Rapid D. Busy
E. Unfixed

159. HONORARY
A. Dishonourable B. Reputed
C. Paid D. Official
E. Obligatory

160. COMMON
A. Rare B. Small
C. Petty D. Poor
E. General

161. FRUGAL
A. Copious B. Extravagant
C. Generous D. Ostentatious
E. Thrifty

162. MALICIOUS
A. Kind B. Boastful
C. Generous D. Indifferent
E. Harmful

163. FAMILIAR
A. Unpleasant B. Dangerous
C. Friendly D. Strange
E. Known

164. PRELIMINARY
A. Final B. First
C. Secondary D. Initial
E. Main

165. DOUBTFUL
A. Famous B. Certain
C. Fixed D. Important
E. Vague

166. REMISS
A. Forgetful B. Watchful
C. Dutiful D. Harmful
E. Break

167. INDISCREET
A. Reliable B. Honest
C. Prudent D. Stupid
E. Credible

168. FRESH
A. Faulty B. Sluggish
C. Disgraceful D. Stale
E. Old

169. ANNOY
A. Praise B. Rejoice
C. Please D. Reward
E. Happy

170. TRANSPARENT
A. Semi-transparent B. Muddy
C. Opaque D. Dark
E. Clear

171. REVEALED
A. Denied B. Concealed
C. Ignored D. Overlooked
E. Appealed

172. EXTRAVAGANCE
A. Luxury B. Poverty
C. Economy D. Cheapness
E. Vengeance

173. CROWDED
A. Busy B. Congested
C. Quiet D. Deserted
E. Empty

174. SHRINK
A. Contract B. Spoil
C. Expand D. Stretch
E. Droop

175. ENMITY
A. Important B. Unnecessary
C. Friendship D. Likeness
E. Infamy

176. EXODUS
A. Influx B. Home-coming
C. Return D. Restoration
E. Entry

177. CULPABLE
A. Defendable B. Blameless
C. Careless D. Irresponsible
E. Bailable

178. SUBSERVIENT
A. Aggressive B. Straightforward
C. Dignified D. Supercilious
E. Submissive

179. AWARE
A. Uncertain B. Ignorant
C. Sure D. Doubtful
E. Beware

180. GRACEFUL
A. Rough B. Expert
C. Miserable D. Awkward
E. Beautiful

181. AUTONOMY
A. Slavery B. Subordination
C. Dependence D. Submissiveness
E. Democracy

182. NADIR
A. Modernity B. Zenith
C. Liberty D. Progress
E. Horizon

183. CONCEDE
A. Object B. Refuse
C. Grant D. Accede
E. Exceed

184. SUPPRESS
A. Encourage B. Grow
C. Praise D. Permit
E. Swell

185. FAMOUS
A. Disgraced B. Notorious
C. Evil D. Popular
E. Ugly

186. EXPAND
A. Contract B. Condense
C. Congest D. Conclude
E. Compact

187. ARROGANT
A. Polite B. Cowardly
C. Meek D. Gentlemanly
E. Vibrant

188. ENORMOUS
A. Soft B. Average
C. Tiny D. Weak
E. Gigantic

189. URBANE
A. Illiterate B. Backward
C. Discourteous D. Orthodox
E. Villager

190. HOSTILITY
A. Courtesy B. Hospitality
C. Relationship D. Friendliness
E. Casualty

191. BELITTLE
A. Praise B. Flatter
C. Exaggerate D. Adore
E. Decry

192. HAPLESS
A. Cheerful B. Consistent
C. Fortunate D. Shapely
E. Hopeful

193. HAPHAZARD
A. Fortuitous B. Indifferent
C. Deliberate D. Accidental
E. Random

194. GREGARIOUS
A. Antisocial B. Glorious
C. Horrendous D. Similar
E. Affable

195. VALUABLE
A. Invaluable B. Worthless
C. Inferior D. Lowly
E. Worthy

196. ABSOLUTE
A. Deficient B. Faulty
C. Limited D. Scarce
E. Whole

197. CONFESS
A. Deny B. Refuse
C. Contest D. Contend
E. Profess

198. GULLIBLE
A. Incredulous B. Fickle
C. Easy D. Stylish
E. Credulous

199. HIRSUTE
A. Scaly B. Bald
C. Erudite D. Quiet
E. Hairy

200. HINDRANCE
A. Aid B. Persuasion
C. Cooperation D. Agreement
E. Encumbrance

ANSWERS

1	**2**	**3**	**4**	**5**	**6**	**7**	**8**	**9**	**10**
C	B	D	C	B	C	B	C	D	B
11	**12**	**13**	**14**	**15**	**16**	**17**	**18**	**19**	**20**
D	D	B	A	A	B	B	D	A	B
21	**22**	**23**	**24**	**25**	**26**	**27**	**28**	**29**	**30**
D	D	C	B	D	C	C	B	C	D
31	**32**	**33**	**34**	**35**	**36**	**37**	**38**	**39**	**40**
A	C	C	D	A	A	C	D	A	C
41	**42**	**43**	**44**	**45**	**46**	**47**	**48**	**49**	**50**
C	A	C	D	A	A	D	C	A	C
51	**52**	**53**	**54**	**55**	**56**	**57**	**58**	**59**	**60**
D	C	A	A	A	B	B	A	A	C

61	**62**	**63**	**64**	**65**	**66**	**67**	**68**	**69**	**70**
A	C	B	D	A	C	D	B	A	A
71	**72**	**73**	**74**	**75**	**76**	**77**	**78**	**79**	**80**
C	D	C	B	B	B	B	B	D	D
81	**82**	**83**	**84**	**85**	**86**	**87**	**88**	**89**	**90**
A	B	A	D	A	D	C	C	B	B
91	**92**	**93**	**94**	**95**	**96**	**97**	**98**	**99**	**100**
B	D	D	C	B	C	C	A	B	B
101	**102**	**103**	**104**	**105**	**106**	**107**	**108**	**109**	**110**
D	A	B	C	C	B	A	B	C	B
111	**112**	**113**	**114**	**115**	**116**	**17**	**18**	**19**	**20**
D	B	A	B	D	C	C	D	B	C
121	**122**	**123**	**124**	**125**	**126**	**127**	**128**	**129**	**130**
C	C	C	D	B	D	C	D	C	D
131	**132**	**133**	**134**	**135**	**136**	**137**	**138**	**139**	**140**
D	B	B	A	C	A	C	B	B	B
141	**142**	**143**	**144**	**145**	**146**	**147**	**148**	**149**	**150**
D	C	A	A	A	D	B	C	A	B
151	**152**	**153**	**154**	**155**	**156**	**157**	**158**	**159**	**160**
B	D	A	D	D	D	C	B	C	A
161	**162**	**163**	**164**	**165**	**166**	**167**	**168**	**169**	**170**
B	C	D	A	B	C	C	D	C	C
171	**172**	**173**	**174**	**175**	**176**	**177**	**178**	**179**	**180**
B	C	D	D	C	A	A	C	B	D
181	**182**	**183**	**184**	**185**	**186**	**187**	**188**	**189**	**190**
C	B	B	B	B	B	A	C	C	D
191	**192**	**193**	**194**	**195**	**196**	**197**	**198**	**199**	**200**
C	C	C	A	B	C	A	A	B	A

3

Fill in the Blanks

Fill in the blanks is such an exercise that starts with the primary education and continues at the highest level of examinations. One must practise it regularly to score well in competitive exams.

Multiple Choice Questions

Directions: *Pick out the most effective word(s) from the given words to fill in the blanks to make the sentence meaningfully complete.*

1. Leadership defines what the future should look like and ..... people with that vision.
A. aligns B. develops
C. trains D. encourages
E. transforms

2. We upset ourselves by responding in an ..... manner to someone else's actions.
A. unabashed B. irrational
C. arduous D. arguable
E. invalid

3. Nothing probably has more contributed to ..... the poverty and backwardness of India than the want of good roads.
A. alleviate B. circumvent
C. perpetuate D. accelerate
E. accentuate

4. The main objective of this dedicated institution is to ..... poverty.
A. enhance B. magnify
C. manifest D. entertain
E. alleviate

5. He feels that the ..... of his achievements goes to his father.
A. reward B. compensation
C. attribute D. credit
E. gist

6. Both the brothers are equally handsome but the elder ..... the two is more intelligent.
A. among B. than
C. of D. in
E. between

7. ..... being a handicapped person, he is very co-operative and self-reliant.
A. Because B. Although
C. Since D. Basically
E. Despite

8. The employees were unhappy because their salary was not increased .....
A. marginally B. abruptly
C. substantially D. superfluously
E. negligibly

9. No sooner did the bell ring, ... the actor started singing.
A. when B. than
C. after D. before
E. through

10. Unfavourable weather conditions can ..... illness.
A. cure B. detect
C. treat D. enhance
E. diagnose

11. They demanded a lot of things, but he cannot ..... to grant them for want of funds.
A. afford B. decide
C. permit D. buy
E. expect

12. The little child was so excited that he could not ..... the burning candle.
A. threw B. thrown
C. drift D. lights
E. throw

13. Though the brothers are twins, they look .....
A. alike B. handsome
C. indifferent D. identical
E. different

14. If I ..... realized it, I would not have acted on his advice.
A. was B. had
C. were D. have
E. being

15. Why don't you ..... your work in advance before commencing it.
A. start B. complete
C. finish D. plan
E. execute

16. The manager is to help his subordinates ..... their potential in their present as well as in their future assignment.
A. respect B. train
C. delegate D. judge
E. realise

17. All the employees in the company are entitled ..... reimbursement of medical expenses.
A. of B. for
C. on D. to
E. with

18. It is ..... in pursuit of these very objectives that our Government has made some basic changes in our economic policies.
A. greatly B. constantly
C. clearly D. largely
E. precisely

19. The Management of so many projects and of different nature ..... no common capacity and vigour.
A. demands B. require
C. permits D. urge
E. offers

20. He could ..... a lot of money in such a short time by using his intelligence and working hard.
A. spend B. spoil
C. exchange D. accumulate
E. pay

21. With his ..... income, he finds it difficult to live a comfortable life.
A. brief B. sufficient
C. meagre D. huge
E. adequate

22. The child broke ..... from his mother and ran towards the painting.
A. away B. after
C. down D. with
E. heavily

23. His interest in the study of human behaviour is indeed very .....
A. broad B. strong
C. vast D. large
E. deep

24. Finally, the thief ..... that he had stolen the ornaments.
A. argued B. decided
C. appealed D. admitted
E. obeyed

25. Since there was no evidence to prove him ..... he was acquitted.
A. innocent B. offence
C. guilty D. honest
E. accused

26. Marketing is one area in which our country has been particularly ..... and new strategies need to be evolved to strengthen it.
A. efficient B. deficient
C. strongest D. overemphasised
E. powerful

27. There is no doubt that one has to keep ..... with the changing times.
A. himself B. tuning
C. pace D. oneself
E. aside

28. The poor ones continue to ..... out a living inspite of economic liberalisation in that country.
A. eke B. go
C. manage D. bring
E. find

29. ..... eye witnesses, the news reporter gave a graphic description of how the fire broke.
A. Reporting B. Seeing
C. Examining D. Quoting
E. Observing

30. Before getting elected, he was ..... to the welfare of the people.
A. devoted B. attended
C. focussed D. neglected
E. concentrated

31. The union leader was very critical ..... the attitude of the management.
A. for B. at
C. on D. against
E. of

32. The passengers and crew members of the aeroplane had a ..... escape when it was taking off from the runway.
A. little B. narrow
C. brief D. large
E. better

33. Eight scientists have ..... the national awards for outstanding contribution and dedication to the profession.
A. picked B. conferred
C. bagged D. discovered
E. bestowed

34. There has been a ..... lack of efficiency in all the crucial areas of the working of Public Sector Undertakings.
A. conspicuous B. stimulative
C. insignificant D. surprising
E. positive

35. Rohan is too ..... as far as his food habits are concerned.
A. curious B. enjoyable
C. interesting D. involved
E. fastidious

36. Some people ..... themselves into believing that they are indispensable to the organisation they work for.
A. force B. delude
C. denigrate D. fool
E. keep

37. Arpan had to drop his plan of going to picnic as he had certain ..... to take of during that period.
A. transactions B. preparations
C. commitments D. urgencies
E. observations

38. No country can ..... to practise a constant, rigid foreign policy in view of the world power dynamics.
A. envisage B. anticipate
C. afford D. visualise
E. obliviate

39. After a recent mild paralytic attack his movements are ..... restricted; otherwise he is still very active.
A. not B. entirely
C. slightly D. nowhere
E. frequently

40. ..... he woke up, he saw that his bag was stolen.
A. If B. When
C. Where D. So
E. Neither

41. I am going to Bhopal today and plan to ..... by tomorrow evening.
A. returning B. returned
C. have returned D. be returning
E. return

42. Since the priest did not arrive in time, the ceremony was ..... late.
A. begins B. begun
C. began D. beginning
E. begin

43. He succeeded in getting possession ..... his land after a long court case.
A. to B. against
C. of D. with
E. for

44. The villagers have not ..... over the shock of losing everything in the earthquake.
A. got B. made
C. forgotten D. freed
E. felt

45. Ajay is the ..... head of the family and commands a lot of respect from the family members.
A. solely B. strongest
C. undisputed D. full
E. controversial

46. The blood donation camp was organised ..... the Naval Youth Club.
A. to B. by
C. from D. with
E. along

47. Last year the performance of this production unit was ..... .
A. tall B. staggered
C. fantastic D. below
E. upwards

48. We all must ..... that people are the most important assets of any organisation.
A. find B. look
C. realise D. involve
E. dispel

49. Since Vivek stays far away from our place, we do not meet each other ..... .
A. rarely B. shortly
C. timely D. frequently
E. momentarily

50. The lights ..... just as we sat down to watch the movie on television.
A. went off B. shut out
C. put out D. blew down
E. gave off

51. To ..... yourself from ..... wear warm clothes.
A. save, heat B. suffer, cold
C. prevent, ice D. protect, cold
E. prohibit, heat

52. He is ..... to ..... any kind of work with due sincerity.
A. determined, undertake
B. found, perform
C. eager, avoid
D. willing, ignore
E. reluctant, entrust

53. They wanted to ..... all these books, but they could not find ..... time to do so.
A. buy, some B. read, sufficient
C. dispose, some D. pursue, necessary
E. cover, almost

54. They started their ..... branch in this city today; their other ..... branches are in the next by-lane.
A. first, new B. first, old
C. second, old D. third, two
E. new, several

55. Due to ..... rainfall this year, there will be ..... cut in water supply.
A. meagre, least
B. abundant, considerable
C. enough, substantial
D. surplus, abundant
E. sufficient, no

56. The judge ..... him because he was found ..... on the basis of the evidence.
A. acquitted, criminal
B. punished, guilty
C. sentenced, innocent
D. suspended, involved
E. pardoned, innocent

57. The speaker's ..... over his subject was seen through his ..... discourse.
A. mastery, fluent
B. efficiency, thorough
C. lethargy, dull
D. grip, boring
E. skill, pleasant

58. Workers in earlier days were ..... because of which the industries ..... a lot.
A. honest, lost
B. rich, flourished
C. autocrats, developed
D. inefficient, suffered
E. idle, prospered

59. A close ..... of the bill shows that the provisions are ..... and there is a need to add certain crucial elements to them.

A. examination, sufficient
B. observation, helpful
C. scrutiny, inadequate
D. file, numerous
E. account, excellent

60. His ..... speech has seriously ..... the young minds.
A. audacious, delighted
B. maiden, flattered
C. humorous, damaged
D. irresponsible, misled
E. eccentric, questioned

61. On ..... of the enquiry, if it is found that the ..... are true, the enquiry officer will report the matter to the higher authority.
A. demand, findings
B. completion, allegations
C. instituting, charges
D. withdrawal, inferences
E. establishment, results

62. After the present tax holiday period ....., the power cost to users may become ..... .
A. starts, unreasonable
B. sets, perishable
C. ends, less
D. enhances, negligible
E. ends, intolerable

63. A good teacher-student relationship helps create a ..... and peaceful atmosphere where there is no room for any ..... of educational activity.
A. harmonious, interruption
B. congenial, development
C. quiet, confusion
D. cordial, education
E. delightful, exaggeration

64. No self-made person would ever like to ..... to any ..... .
A. take, task
B. yield, cause
C. submit, dimension
D. surrender, proposal
E. succumb, pressure

65. Though I had behaved with him very ....., he was ....., enough to forgive me.
A. nicely, unkind
B. rudely, indecent
C. nastily, reluctant
D. impolitely, kind
E. politely, generous

66. We cannot ..... up with your requirements for want of ..... facilities.
A. put, urgent
B. take, expert
C. cope, infrastructural
D. end, ancillary
E. give, deployable

67. He is too ..... to tolerate ..... .
A. humble, lethargy
B. impatient, delay
C. fast, speed
D. wicked, vices
E. lazy, sluggishness

68. The flood ..... in the State ..... to 261 with four more deaths reported today.
A. water, rose
B. level, aroused
C. toll, mounted
D. destruction, spread
E. catchment, increased

69. Right from the earliest ages, India's ..... developed a sense of unity and ..... among its people.
A. people, diversity
B. rulers, commitment
C. culture, commonness
D. population, diversification
E. heritage, disparity

70. ....., there is a widespread ..... among the educated youth which makes them increasingly alienated.
A. Luckily, dedication
B. Co-incidentally, feeling
C. Obviously, enthusiasm
D. Unfortunately, frustration
E. Nevertheless, optimism

71. The problem of ..... another war has assumed great urgency because of the ..... of nuclear weapons.
A. fighting, destruction
B. preventing, invention
C. precipitating, disarmament
D. stopping, need
E. winning, growth

72. In many countries, ... development arising out of fast technological ..... has led to some problems.
A. meagre, inventions
B. cultural, practices
C. agricultural, development
D. optimum, intervention
E. excessive, progress

73. Shyness is ..... through abnormal behaviour in various ..... .
A. manifested, ways
B. removed, people
C. shown, kinds
D. developed, things
E. enhanced, aspects

74. In that country, bureaucracy is ..... as a group of men and women that had arrogated to itself power ..... responsibility.
A. perceived, without
B. believed, within
C. held, into
D. known, unto
E. allowed, for

75. The employees of the factory owing ..... to the workers union have ..... of an agitation from next week in support of their demands.
A. allegiance, warned
B. respect, called
C. shelter, started
D. pressure, proposal
E. assurance, sought

76. Yesterday, around 400 huts were ..... in a major fire which ..... the slum area.
A. burn. hit B. gutted, engulfed
C. fired, took D. burning, blazed
E. demolished, entered

77. As a ..... of Chetan's rude behaviour he was ..... a memo by his boss.
A. sequel, issued
B. part, delivered
C. consequence, given
D. punishment, rewarded
E. reaction, presented

78. Deepak has ..... some unfinished work to ..... up before he can go home.
A. yet, get B. since, come
C. still, clear D. let, take
E. set, give

79. After careful ..... the thief ..... that he has committed the crime.
A. investigation, refused
B. questioning, divulged
C. consideration, felt
D. action, agreed
E. finding, insisted

80. The mining activity comes under the ..... of the forest conservation act and we must ..... that the law is followed strictly.
A. debate, see B. course, observe
C. control, insist D. purview, ensure
E. limits, stipulate

81. All the teachers ..... that Arpita would stand at the top in the examination, she ..... short of their expectation.
A. thought, fell B. expected, ran
C. presumed, failed D. dreamt, achieved
E. started, reached

82. In a ..... decision the government has announced that elementary education for children in the age group of six to fourteen would be ..... a fundamental right.
A. historical, obtained
B. landmark, deplore
C. clear, absolved
D. significant, made
E. rush, given

83. The researcher ..... information about the number of villages in each state which are ..... as problem villages to be covered by National Drinking Water Mission.
A. invested, found
B. got, designed
C. collected, identified
D. investigated, imagined
E. knows, gathered

84. The rules of the institute ..... that employees should not undertake any outside ..... work without seeking written permission of the institute.
A. conclude, devoted
B. strengthen, assignment
C. allow, important
D. stipulate, remunerative
E. direct, extra

85. The television boom might not ..... newspaper readership but magazines which are not leaders in their segment might ..... .
A. link, close
B. effect, prosper
C. reduce, encourage
D. attract, continue
E. affect, suffer

86. The other servants had to ..... since Appu alone ..... all the food.
A. leave, prepared B. eat, cooked
C. wait, spoiled D. cook, wasted
E. starve, consumed

87. If you do not ..... all your monthly expenses would ..... your income.
A. spend, gain B. save, outwit
C. economise, exceed D. think, swallow
E. realise, enhance

88. Ankur ..... me coming to his table, he smiled and ..... me a chair.
A. looked, gave B. welcomed, took
C. saw, offered D. found, signalled
E. met, sat

89. The counter clerk was very busy and ..... not pay any ..... to my request.
A. did, attention B. had, cash
C. could, respect D. can, help
E. certainly, acceptance

90. The speech ..... with subtle threats has resulted in ..... tension in the sensitive areas of the city.
A. full, escalating
B. started, reduced
C. followed, continuous
D. replete, increased
E. forced, dissolving

91. The State Government employees ..... threatened to launch an indefinite strike from next month to ..... their demands.
A. have, press B. did, get
C. were, meet D. nearly, fulfil
E. has, press

92. Virat ..... another feather ..... his cap by his wonderful preformance in the one day match.
A. created, by B. took, in
C. captured from D. kept, in
E. added, to

93. We are ..... to have him ..... here to make this function a great success.
A. happy, arrive B. wonderful, again
C. sure, come D. pleased, over
E. proud, leave

94. The charges made in the system were so ..... that they didn't require any ..... .
A. marginal, expenses
B. big, time
C. obvious, modifications
D. certain, expertise
E. genuine, intelligence

95. The police ..... any attempt of arson by ..... at the trouble spot quite in time.
A. predisposed, visiting
B. preempted, arriving
C. made, encircling
D. thwarted, presenting
E. squashed, surrounding

96. It is ..... for every tax-payer to ..... the tax returns to the Income Tax Department.
A. binding, pay B. possible, remit
C. worthwhile, evade D. obligatory, submit
E. necessary, lodge

97. ..... by long queues and bad weather the voters ..... their way to polling stations any way they could.
A. Undaunted, made
B. Worried, lost
C. Encouraged, prepared
D. Going, dropped
E. Satisfied, turned

98. The Chief Minister ..... the House that ..... action would be taken against all those found involved in corruption.
A. instructed, preventive
B. called, strict
C. assured, stringent
D. reiterated, strictly
E. informed, constructive

99. In his ..... he followed the ..... course.
A. ignorance, wrong
B. bewilderment, appropriate
C. hurry, diversified
D. agony, funny
E. predicament, proper

100. He is usually ..... but today he appears rather ..... .
A. tense, restless
B. quiet, calm
C. happy, humorous
D. strict, unwell
E. calm, distrubed

ANSWERS

1	**2**	**3**	**4**	**5**	**6**	**7**	**8**	**9**	**10**
D	B	D	E	D	C	E	C	B	D
11	**12**	**13**	**14**	**15**	**16**	**17**	**18**	**19**	**20**
A	E	E	B	D	E	D	E	A	D
21	**22**	**23**	**24**	**25**	**26**	**27**	**28**	**29**	**30**
C	A	E	D	C	B	C	A	D	A
31	**32**	**33**	**34**	**35**	**36**	**37**	**38**	**39**	**40**
E	B	C	A	E	B	C	C	C	B
41	**42**	**43**	**44**	**45**	**46**	**47**	**48**	**49**	**50**
E	B	C	A	C	B	C	C	D	A
51	**52**	**53**	**54**	**55**	**56**	**57**	**58**	**59**	**60**
D	A	B	D	E	B	A	D	C	D
61	**62**	**63**	**64**	**65**	**66**	**67**	**68**	**69**	**70**
B	E	A	E	D	C	B	C	C	D
71	**72**	**73**	**74**	**75**	**76**	**77**	**78**	**79**	**80**
B	E	B	A	A	B	A	C	B	D
81	**82**	**83**	**84**	**85**	**86**	**87**	**88**	**89**	**90**
A	D	C	D	E	E	C	C	A	D
91	**92**	**93**	**94**	**95**	**96**	**97**	**98**	**99**	**100**
A	E	D	C	B	D	A	C	A	E

4

Spotting Errors

The most common errors in English are of spellings, grammar and usage of words. By regular practice, the errors can be easily spotted and minimised. Read the following sentences and learn to spot the errors. Test your learning in the exercise that follows.

Common Errors with Nouns and Noun-Phrases

Incorrect	Correct
1. I have bought new *furnitures.*	I have bought new *furniture.*
2. The wages of sin *are* death.	The wages of sin *is* death.
3. She told these *news* to her mother.	She told her mother this *news.*
4. He took *troubles* to do his work.	He took *trouble* (or pains) over his work.
5. The *cattles* were grazing.	The *cattle* were grazing.
6. He showered *many abuses* on me.	He showered *much abuse* on me.
7. I spent the holidays with my *family members.*	I spent the holidays with my *family.*
8. There is no *place* in this compartment.	There is no *room* in this compartment.
9. Write this new *poetry* in your *copy.*	Write this new *poem* in your *note-book.*
10. He took *insult* at this.	He took *offence* at this.
11. Put your *sign* here.	Put your *signatures* here.
12. She is my *cousin sister.*	She is my *cousin.*
13. *Sunil's* my *neighbour's* house was burgled.	*Sunil* my *neighbour's* house was burgled.
14. I lost a *ten-rupees* note.	I lost *a ten-rupee* note.
15. Road closed for *repair.*	Road closed for *repairs.*
16. His house is out of *repairs.*	His house is out of *repair.*
17. What is the *reason* of an earthquake?	What is the *cause* of an earthquake?
18. This building is made of *stones.*	This building is made of *stone.*
19. I disapprove of *these kinds* of games.	I disapprove of *this kind* of games.
20. Veena's and Sheela's father is ill.	Veena and Sheela's father is ill.
21. His *son-in-laws* are doctors.	His *sons-in-law* are doctors.
22. *Alms* is given to the *poor.*	*Alms* are given to the poor.
23. He always keeps his words.	He always keeps his *word.*
24. I carried the *luggages.*	I carried the *luggage.*
25. *Two-third* of the work is left.	*Two-thirds* of the work is left.

Common Errors with Pronouns

Incorrect	Correct
1. Both did not go.	Neither went.
2. We all did not go.	None of us went.
3. Each of these boys play.	Each of these boys plays.
4. Whoever does best he will get a prize.	Whoever does best will get a prize.
5. One should not waste his time.	A man should not waste his time.
6. I and she are sisters.	She and I are sisters.
7. He is wiser than me.	He is wiser than I.
8. Between you and I, Anil is not to be trusted.	Between you and me, Anil is not to be trusted.
9. Nobody was there but I.	Nobody was there but me.
10. Who is there ? It is me.	Who is there ? It is I.
11. Only he and me can use this card.	Only he and I can use this card.
12. Let you and I go now.	Let you and me go now.
13. Everyone got one's pay.	Everyone got his pay.
14. Everyone is frightened when they see a tiger.	Everyone is frightened when he sees a tiger.
15. These two friends are fond of one another.	These two friends are fond of each other.
16. I did not like him coming at that hour.	I did not like his coming at that hour.
17. Who do you think I met?	Whom do you think I met?
18. You should avail this opportunity.	You should avail yourself this opportunity.
19. When you have read these books, please return the same to me.	When you have read the books, please return them to me.
20. They that are humble need fear no fall.	Those that are humble need fear no fall.

Common Errors with Adjectives

Incorrect	Correct
1. These all oranges are good.	All these oranges are good.
2. He held the book in the both hands.	He held the book in both hands.
3. Both men have not come.	Neither man has come.
4. That man should do some or other work.	That man should do some work or other.
5. He is elder than I.	He is older than I.
6. Shakespeare is greater than any other poets.	Shakespeare is greater than any other poet.
7. He is a coward man.	He is a cowardly man.
8. Many villagers cannot write his own name.	Many villagers cannot write their own name.
9. Each of us loves our home.	Each of us loves his home.
10. Much efforts bring their reward.	Much effort brings its reward.
11. He found hundred rupees.	He found a hundred rupees.
12. He had leave of four days.	He had four days leave.

Incorrect	Correct
13. This is a worth seeing sight.	This is a sight worth seeing.
14. He will spend his future life here.	He will spend the rest of his life here.
15. There is a best teacher in that class.	There is a very good teacher in that class.
16. Of the two plans this is the best.	Of the two plans this is the better.
17. He is becoming strong every day.	He is becoming stronger every day.
18. He is worst than I.	He is worse than I.
19. Jaipur is hot than Delhi.	Jaipur is hotter than Delhi.
20. In our library the number of books is less.	In our library the number of books is small.

Common Errors with Verbs

Incorrect	Correct
1. He asked had we taken our luggage.	He asked if we had taken our luggage.
2. She asked what are you doing.	She asked what we were doing.
3. Rama asked to Anil why he is angry.	Rama asked Anil why he was angry.
4. He does not care for his money.	He does not take care of his money.
5. He does not care for his work.	He takes no care over his work.
6. No one cared for him after his mother died.	No one took care of him after his mother died.
7. He got angry before I said a word.	He got angry before I had said a word.
8. I met a man who was my tutor 20 years ago.	I met a man who had been my tutor twenty years ago.
9. I had been for walking yesterday.	I went for a walk yesterday.
10. If I shall do this I shall be wrong.	If I do this I shall be wrong.
11. I have left trekking.	I have given up trekking.
12. I came to know as to how he did this.	I learnt how he did this.
13. I came to know why he was sad.	I found out why he was sad.
14. He knows to swim.	He knows how to swim.
15. The criminal's head was cut.	The criminal's head was cut off.
16. I said to him to go.	I told him to go.
17. I told the teacher to excuse me.	I asked the teacher to excuse me.
18. He is troubling me.	He is giving me trouble.
19. I have got a hurt on my leg.	I have hurt my leg.
20. She gave a speech.	She made a speech.

Common Errors in Subject-Verb Agreement

Incorrect	Correct
1. The owners of this factory *is* very rich.	The owners of this factory *are* very rich.
2. The pleasures of nature that one can experience at Shimla *is* beyond description.	The pleasures of nature that one can experience at Shimla *are* beyond description.

Incorrect	*Correct*
3. There *is* no street lights in our colony.	There *are* no street lights in our colony.
4. He and I *am* entrusted with the job.	He and I *are* entrusted with the job.
5. Rice and curry *are* his favourite dish.	Rice and curry *is* his favourite dish.
6. The honour and glory of our country *are* at stake.	The honour and glory of our country *is* at stake.
7. Time and tide *waits* for none.	Time and tide *wait* for none.
8. All the passengers with the driver *was* killed.	All the passengers, with the driver, *were* killed.
9. The teacher, with her students, *were* going out.	The teacher, with her students, *was* going out.
10. I as well as they *am* tired.	I as well as they *are* tired.
11. Not only the soldiers but their captain also *were* captured.	Not only the soldiers but their captain also *was* captured.
12. Neither you nor I *were* selected.	Neither you nor I *was* selected.
13. Either of these two applicants *are* fit for the job but neither want to accept it.	Either of these two applicants *is* fit for the job but neither wants to accept it.
14. One of these students are sure to stand first.	One of these students *is* sure to stand first.
15. Everyone of these workers want a raise.	Everyone of these workers wants a raise.
16. None of these letters has been answered so far.	None of these letters *have* been answered so far.
17. None of the girls were present at the party.	None of the girls *was* present at the party.
18. Many a battle were fought on Indian soil.	Many a battle *was* fought on Indian soil.
19. A lot of work remain to be done.	A lot of work *remains* to be done.
20. The majority of these girls likes music.	The majority of these girls *like* music.

Common Errors in the Use of Modals/Auxiliary Verbs

Incorrect	*Correct*
1. When I shall see him I shall tell him this.	When I *see* him, I shall tell him this.
2. If I should do wrong, he would punish me.	If I *did* wrong, he would punish me.
3. Until he will have confessed his fault, he will be kept in prison.	Until he *has* confessed his fault, he will be kept in prison.
4. She will obey me.	She *shall* obey me.
5. You would work hard.	You *should* work hard.
6. You shall find him in the garden.	You *will* find him in the garden.
7. He must have died of exposure, but we cannot be certain.	He *might* have died of exposure, but we cannot be certain.
8. You might not show disrespect to your elders.	You *must* not show disrespect to your elders.
9. You may take exercise in order to maintain good health.	You *must* take exercise in order to maintain good health.
10. He must be a crook for all we know.	He *may* be a crook for all we know.

Common Errors in the Use of Adverbs

	Incorrect	*Correct*
1.	He is very much angry.	He is *very* angry.
2.	She was very good enough to help me.	She was *good enough* to help me.
3.	She runs much fast.	She runs *very* fast.
4.	She runs very faster than Seema.	She runs *much* faster than Seema.
5.	It is bitter cold today.	It is *bitterly* cold today.
6.	He is a much learned man.	He is a very learned man.
7.	She is thinking very hardly.	She is thinking very hard.
8.	To tell in brief the film was boring.	*In short* the film was boring.
9.	He told the story in details.	He told the story *in detail.*
10.	I did it anyhow.	I *managed to do* it somehow.
11.	Aeroplanes reach Europe soon.	Aeroplanes reach Europe quickly.
12.	Before long there were dinosaurs on the earth.	*Long ago,* there were dinosaurs on the earth.
13.	This book is too interesting.	This book is *very* interesting.
14.	He lives miserly.	He lives in *a miserly* way.
15.	Just I had gone when she came.	I had just gone when she came.
16.	He sings good.	He sings *well.*
17.	He sings good than I.	He sings *better* than I.
18.	Really speaking it is cold.	*As a matter of fact* it is cold.
19.	He is enough tall to reach the ceiling.	He is *tall enough* to reach the ceiling.
20.	He went directly to his college.	He went *direct* to his college.

Common Errors in the Use of Conjunctions

	Incorrect	*Correct*
1.	As he is fat so he runs slowly.	As he is fat *he* runs slowly.
2.	If he is fat then he will run slowly.	If he is fat, he will run slowly.
3.	Though he is fat still he runs fast.	Though he is fat, *he runs* fast.
4.	*As* I pulled the trigger at the sametime he shook my arm.	As I pulled the trigger, he shook my arm.
5.	No sooner I had spoken than he left.	No sooner *had* I spoken than he left.
6.	Not only he will go, but also he will stay there.	Not only *will he* go, but he *will also* stay there.
7.	Neither he comes nor he writes.	Neither *does he* come nor *does he* write.
8.	Scarcely he entered the room than the telephone rang.	Scarcely *had* he entered the room *when the* telephone rang.
9.	Hardly she had left the house than it began to rain.	Hardly *had she* left the house *when* it began to rain.
10.	He is the fastest runner and he comes last.	He is the fastest runner *but* he comes last.
11.	She is as innocent as if she looks.	She is as innocent as she looks.
12.	Until he does not try he must be punished.	He must be punished unless he tries.
13.	I want to know as to why you are late.	I want to know why you are late.

Incorrect	*Correct*
14. I am fond of Chinese food as for example sweet and sour prawns.	I am fond of Chinese food, for example, sweet and sour prawns.
15. He was angry therefore I ran away.	He was angry so I ran away.
16. I was trying to work, at that time he was disturbing me.	While I was trying to work, he was disturbing me.
17. Supposing if he is late, what will happen?	Supposing he is late (or if he is late) what will happen?
18. He asked me that why I was late.	He asked me why I was late.
19. Let us catch a taxi lest we should not get late.	Let us catch a taxi lest we should get late.
20. She dresses herself like the teacher does.	She dresses herself as the teacher does.
21. Wait while I come.	Wait *until* (or *till)* I come.
22. Until, there is corruption in India, there can be little progress.	*As long* as there is corruption in India there can be little progress.
23. I have never told a lie nor cheated anybody.	I have never told a lie *nor have I* cheated anybody.
24. Both Mohan as well as Arun are responsible for this action.	Both Mohan *and* Arun are responsible for this action.
25. Hindus and Muslims both are to blame for the riots.	*Both Hindus* and Muslims are to blame for the riots.

Common Errors in the Use of Prepositions

Incorrect	*Correct*
1. I will not listen him.	I will not listen *to* him.
2. Copy this word by word.	Copy this word *for* word.
3. He enquired from her where she lived.	He enquired *of* her where she lived.
4. Sign here with ink.	Sign here *in* ink.
5. Has she come in train or by foot?	Has she come *by* train or *on* foot?
6. She said this at his face.	She said this *to* his face.
7. Open the book on page one.	Open the book *at* page one.
8. I was invited for lunch.	I was *invited to* lunch.
9. I am ill since three months.	I have been *ill for* three months.
10. This paper is inferior than that.	This paper is inferior *to* that.
11. This resembles to that.	This *resembles* that.
12. My brother is superior than you in strength.	My brother is superior *to* you in strength.
13. He wrote me.	He wrote *to* me.
14. I shall explain them this.	I shall explain this *to* them.
15. Send this letter on my address.	Send this letter *to* my address.
16. He suggested me this.	He suggested this *to* me.
17. He goes *on his* work.	He goes *to his* work.
18. He *reached to* Nagpur.	He *reached* Nagpur.
19. He told *to me* to go.	He told *me* to go.
20. The term begins *from* July 1st.	The term begins *on* July 1st.

Miscellaneous Errors

	Incorrect	*Correct*
1.	Many *homes* are lying vacant.	Many *houses* are lying vacant.
2.	It is cool in the *shadow* of the tree.	It is cool in the *shade* of the tree.
3.	She *keeps* good health.	She *enjoys* good health.
4.	My leg is *paining*.	*I am feeling pain* in my leg.
5.	*See* this word in the dictionary.	*Look up* this word in the dictionary.
6.	The train will arrive *just now.*	The train will arrive *shortly.*
7.	They are *pulling* on well.	They are *getting* on well.
8.	The river has *over flown* its bank.	The river has *over flown* its banks.
9.	He was appointed *on* the post.	He was appointed *to* the post.
10.	Last but not *the least,* we have to discuss the problem of over population.	Last but not *least,* we have to discuss the problem of over population.
11.	*Cities* after *cities* fell.	*City* after *city* fell.
12.	What is the use Munir going there?	What is the use of Munir going there?
13.	He *did many mischief.*	He *made much mischief.*
14.	It is exact five *in* my watch.	It is exact five *by* my watch.
15.	I will dine with them on *next Sunday.*	I will dine with them *Sunday next.*
16.	Misfortunes when faced bravely and *manly* become less troublesome.	Misfortunes when faced bravely and *manfully* become less troublesome.
17.	I am *laid down* with fever.	I am *laid up* with fever.
18.	He is habituated to smoking.	He is *addicted* to smoking.
19.	*According to my opinion* he is right.	*In my opinion* (or according *to me)* he is right.
20.	Could you please *open* this knot?	Could you please *untie* this knot?

Multiple Choice Questions

Directions: *In each question below, a sentence is broken into four parts which are marked as (A), (B), (C) and (D). One of them may be grammatically or structurally wrong in the context of the sentence. The letter of that word is the answer. If there is no error, your answer will be (E), i.e., 'No error'. (Ignore the errors of punctuation, if any).*

1. (A) There is just not enough/(B) timing in my job to sit around/(C) talking about how we feel/(D) about each other./(E) No error.

2. (A) Reasonable ambition, if supported/(B) at persistent efforts,/(C) is likely to yield/(D) the desired results./(E) No error.

3. (A) Even after worked in the office/(B) for as many as fifteen years,/(C) he still does not understand/(D) the basic objectives of the work./(E) No error.

4. (A) Why some people don't get/(B) what they deserve/(C) and why others get what they don't deserve/(D) is a matter decided by luck./(E) No error.

5. (A) the five-member committee were/(B) of the view that the present service conditions/(C) of the employees of this company/(D) are quite good./(E) No error.

6. (A) If you would have/(B) gone to his house/(C) before 10 a.m., you would have/(D) got his autograph./(E) No error.

7. (A) His speech was/(B) judged by many/(C) as one of the most important speech/(D) given in the function./(E) No error.

8. (A) I am contacting you/(B) sometime in next week/(C) to explain to you/(D) my problem in detail./(E) No error.

9. (A) Whatever he was/(B) today is only because/(C) of his mother who/(D) was a renowned scientist./(E) No error.

10. (A) The Head of the Department along with his colleagues/(B) are coming to attend/(C) the conference which is/(D) scheduled this afternoon./(E) No error.

11. (A) One of the most effective/(B) solutions is that/(C) she should work on Sunday/(D) and complete the assignment./(E) No error.

12. (A) He had to/(B) seek legal help in/(C) order for settling/(D) the dispute./(E) No error.

13. (A) Since I had been gone/(B) through the book/(C) long back, I could/(D) not remember the contents./(E) No error.

14. (A) We have to take/(B)him to the hospital yesterday/(C) because he was/(D) suffering from fever./(E) No error.

15. (A) The interviewer asked the actress/(B) how could she/(C) manage to attain fame/(D) in a short period./(E) No error.

16. (A) The Head of the Department/(B) advised all the staff/(C) to not to/(D) indulge in gossip./(E) No error.

17. (A) I shall be able/(B) to complete the work in/(C) stipulated time provide/(D) you do not disturb me./(E) No error.

18. (A) Having learn my lessons/(B) I was very careful/(C) in dealing with him/(D) in front of his room-mate./(E) No error.

19. (A) In spite of his/(B) being a Quiz Master/(C) show was/(D) a big flop./(E) No error.

20. (A) No sooner the/(B) clock strike six than/(C) all the employees/(D) rushed out of office./(E) No error.

21. (A) He could not/(B) decide as to which/(C) course he should do/(D) after obtaining his Degree./(E) No error.

22. (A) One of the objective/(B) of the meeting which/(C) was held today was to/(D) elect new office-bearers./(E) No error.

23. (A) She would have/(B) surely got the job/(C) if she would have/(D) attended the interview./(E) No error.

24. (A) When the national/(B) anthem was being/(C) sung, everyone were/(D) standing in silence./(E) No error.

25. (A) She herself wash/(B) all the clothes and/(C) never gives them/(D) to the laundry./(E) No error.

26. (A) But for your/(B) kind help this/(C) task could not/(D) have been completed./(E) No error.

27. (A) Since it was a memory test/(B) the students were instructed/(C) to learn the/(D) passage with heart./(E) No error.

28. (A) So longer as/(B) you are honest/(C) and forthright I will/(D) support you in this task./(E) No error.

29. (A) The customer scarcely had/(B) enough money to pay/(C) to the cashier/(D) at the cash counter./(E) No error.

30. (A) Neither the earthquake/(B) nor the subsequent fire/(C) was able to dampen/(D) the spirit of the residents./(E) No error.

31. (A) Not one of the children/(B) has ever sang/(C) on any occasion/(D) in public before./(E) No error.

32. (A) If the by-stander had not been/(B) familiar with first-aid techniques,/(C) the driver which had met/(D) with the accident would have died./(E) No error.

33. (A) Even after requesting/(B) him, he did not/(C) tell us that how/(D) he solved the problem/(E) No error.

34. (A) We never thought/(B) that he is/(C) oldest than the other/(D) players in the team./(E) No error.

35. (A) No sooner did he/(B) got up from bed/(C) than he was sent/(D) to the dairy./(E) No error.

36. (A) By arresting the local criminals/(B) and encouraging good people/(C) we can end/(D) hostilities of that area./(E) No error.

37. (A) The apparently obvious solutions/(B) to most of his problems/(C) were overlook by/(D) many of his friends./(E) No error.

38. (A) In spite of the difficulties/(B) on the way,/ (C) they enjoyed their/(D) trip to Gangotri./(E) No error.

39. (A) We decided not tell to/(B) the patient about/ (C) the disease he was/(D) suffering from./(E) No error.

40. (A) The principals of equal justice/(B) for all is one of/(C) the cornerstones of our/(D) democratic way of life./(E) No error.

41. (A) The Trust has succeeded/(B) admirably in raising/(C) money for/(D) its future programmes./(E) No error.

42. (A) Honesty, integrity and being intelligent/ (B) are the qualities which/(C) we look for when/(D) we interview applicants./(E) No error.

43. (A) In order to save petrol,/(B) motorists must have to/(C) be very cautious/(D) while driving along the highways./(E) No error.

44. (A) The committee is thankful to you/(B) for preparing not only the main report/(C) but also for preparing/(D) the agenda notes and minutes./(E) No error.

45. (A) All of you will agree with me/(B) that no problem faced by our society/(C) is as grave and intractable/(D) as this problem is/(E) No error.

46. (A) I would have lost/(B) my luggage and other belongings/(C) if I would have left the compartment/(D) and gone out to fetch drinking water./(E) No error.

47. (A) He did not like/(B) leaving his old parents alone in the house/(C) but he had no alternative/(D) as he has to go out to work./(E) No error.

48. (A) I was being astonished/(B) when I heard that/(C) he had left the country/(D) without informing anyone of us./(E) No error.

49. (A) According to one survey/(B) only those forests which were/(C) not under village management/(D) succumbed from fires recently./(E) No error.

50. (A) We can not handle/(B) this complicated case today/(C) unless full details are not given/ (D) to us by now./(E) No error.

51. (A) We will pack not only/(B) the material properly/(C) but will also deliver it/(D) to your valued customers./(E) No error.

52. (A) While he was away/(B) on a long official tour/(C) his office receive an important letter/ (D) which was marked 'Urgent'./(E) No error.

53. (A) We now look forward for/(B) some great achievements/(C) which to some extent/(D) can restore the country's prestige once again./(E) No error.

54. (A) Mahatma Gandhi did not solve/(B) all the problems of the future/(C) but he did solve/(D) problems of his own age./(E) No error.

55. (A) No country can long endure/(B) if its foundations/(C) were not laid deep/(D) in the material prosperity./(E) No error.

56. (A) Though he suffered of fever,/(B) he attended office/(C) and completed all the pending/(D) work by sitting late./(E) No error.

57. (A) As always have been said,/(B) parents should not/(C) impose their desires/(D) on their wards./(E) No error.

58. (A) Being a very fast worker,/(B) he is always liking/(C) by all his colleagues./(D) and superiors too./(E) No error.

59. (A) We fail to understand/(B) why do most educated people/(C) lose their temper even/(D) without any apparent reason./(E) No error.

60. (A) You may not always/(B) get whatever you deserve/(C) but that does not belittle/(D) the importance for your work./(E) No error.

61. (A) On resuming his duty,/(B) he asked his superiors/(C) that whether he would be/(D) permitted to leave early./(E) No error.

62. (A) We don't deny/(B) your right to know/(C) whatever happened while/(D) you were not in the office./(E) No error.

63. (A) He loved his mentor immensely/(B) and gave him fullest loyalty,/(C) yet he had his own/(D) independent way of thinking./(E) No error.

64. (A) We have done everything/(B) that could be done/(C) to avert the storm/(D) which is now coming on./(E) No error.

65. (A) Our school is making/(B) every possible effort/(C) to provide best facilities/(D) and personal attention for each child./(E) No error.

66. (A) They have been/(B) struggling with the management/(C) from the past five years/(D) but their demands are not considered./(E) No error.

67. (A) When I stood up spontaneously/(B) and questioned the speaker;/(C) someone commented that/(D) it was a boldly step./(E) No error.

68. (A) Their only demand/(B) for additional wages were/(C) considered sympathetically/(D) by the progressive management./(E) No error.

69. (A) He has been undergoing/(B) the special training course/(C) which each of the employees/(D) is required to./(E) No error.

70. (A) You must had/(B) a kind and gentle heart/(C) if you want/(D) to be a successful doctor./(E) No error.

71. (A) If you cannot/(B) sympathy with the poor,/(C) how will you be/(D) able to do social work?/(E) No error.

72. (A) He loosened his temper/(B) whenever he knows/(C) things do not take place/(D) as per his planning./(E) No error.

73. (A) They wanted money/(B) to purchase certain things/(C) for themselves and/(D) for donated to their colleagues./(E) No error.

74. (A) As the ticket was/(B) firm affixed/(C) on the envelope, he/(D) could not remove it./(E) No error.

75. (A) I asked him/(B) whom he thought/(C) would be able to/(D) get the first prize./(E) No error.

76. (A) He was too/(B) irritated to/(C) concentrate on his work/(D) for a long time./(E) No error.

77. (A) Both the brothers are/(B) so good-natured that/(C) they look at their/(D) old and aged parents very well./(E) No error.

78. (A) The observers felt that/(B) the stronger team had to face/(C) defeat because the players/(D) didn't play wholehearted./(E) No error.

79. (A) Every animal in the zoo/(B) is fed regularly/(C) and attended to/(D) very promptly./(E) No error.

80. (A) How you eat/(B) is as important/(C) as what/(D) you eat./(E) No error.

81. (A) All his relatives/(B) expect his daughter/(C) have gone on/(D) a month's vacation tour./(E) No error.

82. (A) All renew licences/(B) may be collected from/(C) the cashier's counter after/(D) paying the fees./(E) No error.

83. (A) We are happy/(B) to know that/(C) the project completed/(D) strictly as per the schedule./(E) No crror.

84. (A) They would not/(B) have able to plan/(C) the details of the job,/(D) if you had no cooperated./(E) No error.

85. (A) Very few employees./(B) in our company are/(C) so dedicated as/(D) he will./(E) No error.

86. (A) He won the case as/(B) he argued very forcefully and/(C) in such the intelligent way/(D) that the judge changed his opinion./(E) No error.

87. (A) The basket of apples/(B) sent by the gardener/(C) contained a number of/(D) green mangoes also./(E) No error.

88. (A) In the absence of/(B) clear instructions/(C) one cannot be expected/(D) to be functioned effectively./(E) No error.

89. (A) They could have/(B) helped him/(C) had they approached by him./(D) for help well in advance./(E) No error.

90. (A) He has in/(B) his possession a/(C) price collection of very old coins,/(D) and some ancient paintings./(E) No error.

91. (A) Everyone is/(B) impress by/(C) his zeal/(D) and enthusiasm./(E) No error.

92. (A) The patient recover/(B) so fast that/(C) the expert doctors/(D) also were surprised/(E) No error.

93. (A) His father told me/(B) that though his son had/(C) worked very hard,/(D) but he had failed to make any mark in the examination./(E) No error.

94. (A) We must go/(B) and congratulate him for/ (C) his brilliant/(D) performance./(E) No error.

95. (A) He deserted the path of honour/(B) in order to/(C) satisfy his ambition/(D) and then went down his doom very quickly./(E) No error.

96. (A) At last the rain ceased/(B) and the sky was/ (C) cleared by clouds/(D) and lightening./(E) No error.

97. (A) He said that/(B) he had a difference/(C) with/(D) the chairman at his statement./(E) No error.

98. (A) The future is/(B) yet to come/(C) but you have a/(D) right to shape it./(E) No error.

99. (A) We have keep/(B) our promise and/(C) you can expect/(D) a lot from us in future./(E) No error.

100. (A) He has collected/(B) all the necessary documents/(C) and have written a good paper/ (D) for this conference./(E) No error.

ANSWERS

1	**2**	**3**	**4**	**5**	**6**	**7**	**8**	**9**	**10**
B	B	A	A	A	A	C	B	A	B
11	**12**	**13**	**14**	**15**	**16**	**17**	**18**	**19**	**20**
E	C	A	A	B	C	C	A	C	A
21	**22**	**23**	**24**	**25**	**26**	**27**	**28**	**29**	**30**
E	A	C	C	A	E	D	A	A	C
31	**32**	**33**	**34**	**35**	**36**	**37**	**38**	**39**	**40**
B	C	C	C	B	C	C	E	A	A
41	**42**	**43**	**44**	**45**	**46**	**47**	**48**	**49**	**50**
E	A	B	C	B	C	D	A	D	C
51	**52**	**53**	**54**	**55**	**56**	**57**	**58**	**59**	**60**
A	C	A	B	C	A	A	B	B	D
61	**62**	**63**	**64**	**65**	**66**	**67**	**68**	**69**	**70**
C	E	D	A	D	C	D	B	D	A
71	**72**	**73**	**74**	**75**	**76**	**77**	**78**	**79**	**80**
B	A	D	B	B	E	C	D	C	E
81	**82**	**83**	**84**	**85**	**86**	**87**	**88**	**89**	**90**
C	A	C	B	D	C	E	D	C	C
91	**92**	**93**	**94**	**95**	**96**	**97**	**98**	**99**	**100**
B	A	D	B	D	C	D	A	A	C

5

Sentence Correction

A sentence will convey its true meaning and make the right impact if it is written in a grammatically correct way. One must learn the general rules of grammar and practise well to improve one's English regularly. Try your skills in this exercise.

Multiple Choice Questions

Directions: *Which of the phrases given below each sentence should replace the phrase printed in* **bold** *type to make the sentence grammatically correct? If the sentence is correct as it is, mark 'E' as the answer.*

1. The research study is an eye-opener and **attempts to acquaint** us with the problems of the poor nations.
   A. attempted to acquaint
   B. attempts at acquainting
   C. attempt to acquaint
   D. attempting to acquaint
   E. No correction required
2. The man who has committed such a serious crime must **get the mostly severe** punishment.
   A. be getting the mostly severely
   B. get the most severe
   C. have got the most severely
   D. have been getting the severemost
   E. No correction required
3. Acquisition of certain specific skills **can be facilitated from** general awareness, education and exposure to novel situations.
   A. can be facilitated by
   B. may facilitate through
   C. can be felicitated with
   D. may be felicitated with
   E. No correction required
4. He confidently asked the crowd if they thought he was right and the crowd shouted **that they did.**
   A. that he did
   B. that they had
   C. that he is
   D. that he didn't
   E. No correction required
5. If he has to spend five hours in the queue, it **was really a wastage.**
   A. is a really wastage
   B. is real a wastage
   C. has really a wastage
   D. is really a wastage
   E. No correction required
6. Why **did you not threw** the bag away?
   A. did you not throw
   B. had you not threw
   C. did you not thrown
   D. you did not thrown
   E. No correction required
7. They **are not beware of** all the facts
   A. are not aware for
   B. are not aware of
   C. are not to be aware
   D. must not to be aware for
   E. No correction required

8. **If I would have** realised the nature of the job earlier, I would not have accepted it.
A. If I have had
B. In case I would have
C. Had I been
D. Had I
E. No correction required

9. The moment they saw me, they **were delight**
A. had delighted
B. were delighted
C. are delighted
D. have been delighted
E. No correction required

10. The small child does whatever his father **was done.**
A. has done
B. did
C. does
D. had done
E. No correction required

11. It was unanimously resolved that the parties **should unitedly undertook** launching of popular programmes.
A. should be united undertook
B. should be unitedly undertaken
C. should be unitedly undertake
D. should unitedly undertake
E. No correction required

12. One of my drawbacks is that **I do not have to** tolerance of ambiguity.
A. do not have
B. cannot have to
C. am not
D. did not have to
E. No correction required

13. They **should have calmly thought of** the advantages that would accrue to them.
A. should have been calm in thinking about
B. should be calmly thought of
C. shall have to calmly thought of
D. should have calmly think of
E. No correction required

14. Their earnings are such that they find it difficult **to make both ends to meet**.
A. to making both ends meet
B. to make both ends for meeting
C. to make both ends meet
D. for making both ends to meet
E. No correction required

15. They **were all shocked at** his failure in the competition.
A. were shocked at all
B. had all shocked at
C. had all shocked by
D. had been all shocked on
E. No correction required

16. He is too impatient **for tolerating** any delay.
A. to tolerate
B. to tolerating
C. at tolerating
D. with tolerating
E. No correction required

17. Why **should the candidates be** afraid of English Language is not clear.
A. the candidates should be
B. do the candidates be
C. should be the candidates
D. are the candidates
E. No correction required

18. Rohan is **as tall if not,** taller than Arpan.
A. not as tall but
B. not so tall but as
C. as tall as, if not
D. as if not
E. No correction required

19. The easiest **of the thing to do** is to ask the address to the shopkeeper.
A. of the things to do
B. among the things did
C. of the thing to be done
D. of all the things done
E. No correction required

20. The player was asked **that why he had not** attended the prayer.
A. why had he not
B. that why had he not
C. why he was not
D. is hesitated to listen to
E. No correction required

21. He **hesitated to listen to** what his brother was saying.
A. listened to hesitate
B. hesitated listen to
C. hesitates to listening
D. is hesitated to listen to
E. No correction required

22. Hardly **does the sun rise** when the stars disappeared.
A. have the sun rose B. had the sun risen
C. did the sun rose D. the sun rose
E. No correction required

23. The police has **so far succeeded in recovering** only a part of the stolen property.
A. thus far succeeded for recovery
B. so far succeed in the recovery of
C. as far as succeeded in recovery of
D. so far succeed to recover
E. No correction required

24. **What happens to** all those travellers on the ship was not known?
A. What happened of
B. That is what happens to
C. What is that happens to
D. What happened to
E. No correction required

25. Because of his ill health, the doctor has advised him **not to refrain** from smoking.
A. to not refrain from
B. to resort to
C. to refrain from
D. to be refrained from
E. No correction required

26. The courts **are actively to safeguard** the interests and the rights of the poor.
A. are actively to safeguarding
B. have been actively safeguarding
C. have to active in safeguarding
D. are actively in safeguarding
E. No correction required

27. He is a singer of repute, but his **yesterday's performance was** quite disappointing.
A. performances for yesterday were
B. yesterday performance was
C. yesterday performances were
D. performances about yesterday were
E. No correction required

28. **Despite of their** differences on matters of principles, they all agree on the demand of hike in salary.
A. Despite their B. Despite of the
C. Despite for their D. Despite off their
E. No correction required

29. The orator **had been left** the auditorium before the audience stood up.
A. had been leaving B. was left
C. left D. would leave
E. No correction required

30. This is one of the most important **inventions of this century**.
A. invention of this century
B. invention of these centuries
C. inventions of centuries
D. inventions of the centuries
E. No correction required

31. Can you tell me **why did you not speak** the truth?
A. why did not you speak
B. that why did you not speak
C. why you did not speak
D. why did you not spoke
E. No correction required

32. The chemist **hadn't hardly any of those kind** of medicines.
A. had hardly any of those kinds
B. had hardly not any of those kind
C. had scarcely any of those kind
D. had hardly any of those kind
E. No correction required

33. She cooks, washes dishes, does her homework and **then relaxing.**
A. relaxing then B. then is relaxing
C. relaxing is then D. then relaxes
E. No correction required

34. Anyone interested in the use of computers can learn much if **you have access** to a personal computer.
A. they have access
B. access can be available
C. he or she has access
D. one of them have access
E. No correction required

35. **By such time** you finish that chapter, I will write a letter.
A. The time when B. By the time
C. By that time D. The time
E. No correction required

36. **Had I realised** how close I was to the edge of the valley, I would not have carried the bags there.
A. Had I been realised
B. If I would have realised
C. When I realised
D. Had I had realised
E. No correction required

37. Later he became unpopular because he tried **to lord it on** his followers.
A. to lord it for B. to lord over
C. to lord it over D. to lord it over on
E. No correction required

38. **The long or short of it** is that I do not want to deal with that new firm.
A. The long and short of it
B. The long and short for it
C. The long or short for it
D. The short and long of it
E. No correction required

39. The people generally try to **curry favour** with the corrupt but influential person.
A. cook favour B. seek favour
C. extract favour D. display favour
E. No correction required

40. My hair **stood off ends** when I saw the horrible sight.
A. stood at ends B. stood on ends
C. stood to ends D. stands on ends
E. No correction required

41. "Friends and comrades, the light has gone **away from** our lives and there is darkness everywhere."
A. off B. out of
C. out from D. out off
E. No correction required

42. We **can not always convey** ourselves in simple sentences.
A. cannot always convey
B. can not always express
C. cannot always express
D. can not always communicate
E. No correction required

43. **Shapes** of gods and goddesses are worshipped by people.
A. Images B. Reflections
C. Clay shapes D. Clay toys
E. No correction required

44. The crops are dying; **it must not had** rained.
A. must had not
B. must not be
C. must not have
D. must not have been
E. No correction required

45. It is always better to make people realise the importance of discipline than to **impose them on it.**
A. impose it with them
B. impose them with it
C. imposing them on it
D. impose it on them
E. No correction required

46. The performance of our players was rather **worst than I had expected.**
A. bad as I had expected
B. worse than I had expected
C. worse than expectation
D. worst than was expected
E. No correction required

47. For some days the new professor lectured **above the heads of** his pupils.
A. over the head of
B. over the heads of
C. on the heads of
D. through the heads of
E. No correction required

48. For many centuries in Indian history there was no city so famous **like** the city of Ujjain.
A. as B. such as
C. likewise D. so like
E. No correction required

49. Making friends is more rewarding than **to make enemies**.
A. to be unsociable B. to be sociable
C. being unsociable D. making enemies
E. No correction required

50. You need not come unless you want to.
A. You don't need to come unless you want to
B. You come only when you want to
C. You come unless you don't want to
D. You needn't come until you don't want to
E. No correction required

51. The drama had many scenes which were so humorous that it was **hardly possible to keep** a straight face.
A. hardly possible for keeping
B. hardly impossible keeping
C. hardly impossible to keep
D. hardly possible keeping
E. No correction required

52. The moment the manager came to know of the fradulent action of his assistant, he **order immediately dismissed him**.
A. immediately ordered his dismissed
B. ordered his immediate dismissal
C. immediately order dismissal of his
D. ordered for immediately dismissal him
E. No correction required

53. We met him immediately after the session in which he **had been given** a nice speech.
A. would be giving
B. has been given
C. will have given
D. had given
E. No correction required

54. The world has seen **small** real attempt at population and resource planning.
A. few B. little
C. less D. a few
E. No correction required

55. One of the most significant **phenomenons** of our time has been the development of the cinema.
A. phenomenon B. phenomena
C. character D. symptom
E. No correction required

56. It was until many years later that Gandhi became a rebel against authority.
A. It was not until many years
B. It was till many years
C. It was not many years
D. Until it was many years
E. No correction required

57. There are not many men who are so famous that they are frequently referred to by their **short names** only.
A. initials B. signatures
C. pictures D. middle names
E. No correction required

58. Though we **have kept in mind to try and maintain** most facilities, we would like to request you to kindly bear with us any inconvenience that may be caused.
A. must keep in mind to try and maintain
B. have kept in mind trying and maintain
C. would keep in mind to try and maintain
D. should have kept in mind to try and to maintain
E. No correction required

59. The tea-estate administration is **in such mess there** is no leader to set the things right.
A. in such a mess here
B. in a such mess that here
C. in such a mess that there
D. with such a mess that there
E. No correction required

60. My doctor knew that I would eventually recover and do the kind of work **I would be doing** before.
A. would have been doing
B. would have done
C. had been done
D. had been doing
E. No correction required

61. If you are thinking about investigation overseas, **isn't it makes** sense to find an experience guide?
A. it is not making
B. doesn't it make
C. does it make
D. is it making
E. No correction required

62. The **crime has growth rapidly** in Russia since the disintegration of the communist system.
A. rapid crime has grown
B. crime has grown rapid
C. crimes grow rapidly
D. crimes have been rapidly grown
E. No correction required

63. Technology **must use to feed** the forces of change.
A. must be used to feed
B. must have been using to feed
C. must use having fed
D. must be using to feed
E. No correction required

64. In addition **to enhanced their reputations** through strategic use of philanthropy, companies are sponsoring social initiatives to open new markets.
A. of enhancing their reputations
B. to having enhance their reputation
C. to enhancing their reputation
D. to have their reputation enhancing
E. No correction required

65. They failed **in their attempt to repair** the demolished portion of the building.
A. for their attempt to repair
B. in their attempting to repair
C. with their attempt to repair
D. in their attempt for repairs
E. No correction required

66. We don't know **how did the thief made** an escape.
A. how the thief did make
B. how the thief does make
C. how the thief made
D. how was the thief made
E. No correction required

67. They have a scheme of rewarding **the best of the performers** every year.
A. a best performer
B. the best among the performer
C. a best among performers
D. the best of the performer
E. No correction required

68. No sooner **do the bells ring** than the curtain rose.
A. did the bell ring
B. did the bells ring
C. had the bell rang
D. had the bell rung
E. No correction required

69. Most of the Indian workers are **as healthy as, if not healthier** than, the British workers.
A. as if healthy as and not healthier
B. healthier but not as healthy
C. as healthy, if not healthier
D. so healthy, if not healthier
E. No correction required

70. He admired the speed with which he completed the work and **appreciating the method adopted** by him.
A. appreciate the method being adopted
B. appreciated the method adopted
C. appreciate the method of adoption
D. appreciated the adopting method
E. No correction required

71. The population of Tokyo is **greater than that of any other** town in the world.
A. greatest among any other
B. greater than all other
C. greater than those of any other
D. greater than any other
E. No correction required

72. They examined both the samples very carefully but failed to detect **any difference** in them.
A. some difference in
B. some difference between
C. any difference between
D. any difference among
E. No correction required

73. Tax evaders **should heavily fined** as they do it intentionally.
A. should be heavy fined
B. should have heavily fined
C. shall have heavy fine
D. should be heavily fined
E. No correction required

74. He never **has and ever will take** such strong measures.
A. had taken nor will ever take
B. had taken and will ever take
C. has and never will take
D. had and ever will take
E. No correction required

75. The intruder stood quietly **for few moments**.
A. for few time
B. for the few moments
C. for moments
D. for a few moments
E. No correction required

76. He **should not had** done it.
A. had not
B. should had not
C. should not have
D. should have
E. No correction required

77. The meeting was **attended to by all** the invitees.
A. all attended to by
B. attended by all
C. fully attended to by
D. like attending to all
E. No correction required

78. I have got some tea, but I do not have **a** sugar.
A. some
B. got
C. more
D. any
E. No correction required

79. I need not offer any explanation regarding this incident—my behaviour **is speaking itself**.
A. will speak to itself
B. speaks for itself
C. has been speaking
D. speaks about itself
E. No correction required

80. Ankur has the guts **to rise from** the occasion and come out successfully.
A. in rising from
B. to raise with
C. to rise against
D. to rise to
E. No correction required

81. Mary unnecessarily **picked up** a quarrel with Rosy and left the party hurriedly.
A. has picked up
B. picked on
C. picked
D. picking up
E. No correction required

82. The train will leave at 8.30 p.m., we **have been** ready by 7.30 p.m. so that we can reach the station in time.
A. were
B. must be
C. are
D. should have
E. No correction required

83. He dislikes the word dislike, **isn't he**?
A. didn't he
B. doesn't he
C. hasn't he
D. does he
E. No correction required

84. The prosecution failed **in** establish in every case today.
A. to
B. on
C. as
D. upon
E. No correction required

85. We were still standing in the queue when the **film was beginning**.
A. film began
B. film had begun
C. beginning of the film was over
D. film begins
E. No correction required

86. I **earnestly believe that** you will visit our relatives during your forthcoming trip to Mumbai.
A. had hardly believe that
B. sincerely would believe
C. certainly believing that
D. could not believe
E. No correction required

87. We must **take it granted** that she will not come for today's function.
A. take it for granted
B. taking it granted
C. took it as granted
D. have it granted
E. No correction required

88. He has received no other message than an urgent telegram **asking him to rush his village** immediately.
A. asked him to rush his village
B. asking him to have rush his village
C. asking him to rush to his village
D. asking him rushing at his village
E. No correction required

89. They continued to work in the field **despite of the heavy rains**.
A. even though there is heavy rain
B. although heavily rains
C. in spite the heavy rains
D. even though it rained heavily
E. No correction required

90. **Had you been told** me about your problem, I would have helped you.
A. If you would have told
B. Had you have told
C. had you told
D. If you have told
E. No correction required

91. They felt humiliated because they realised that they **had cheated**.
A. have been cheated
B. had been cheated
C. had been cheating
D. were to be cheated
E. No correction required

92. He found the gold coin **as he cleans** the floor.
A. as he had cleaned
B. while he cleans
C. which he is cleaning
D. while cleaning
E. No correction required

93. Because of his mastery in this field, his suggestions **are wide accepted**.
A. are widely accepted
B. are wide acceptance
C. have widely accepted
D. have been wide accepted
E. No correction required

94. The man to **who I sold** my house was a cheat.
A. to whom I sell
B. to who I sell
C. who was sold to
D. to whom I sold
E. No correction required

95. **If I was you,** I would not have joined the party.
A. If I am you
B. If I be you
C. As you
D. Were I you
E. No correction required

96. You will be late if you **do not leave** now.
A. did not leave
B. left
C. will not leave
D. do not happen to leave
E. No correction required

97. All the allegations **levelled against** him were found to be baseless.
A. level against
B. level with
C. levelling with
D. levelled for
E. No correction required

98. What **does agonise me most** is not this criticism, but the trivial reason behind it.
A. most agonising me
B. agonises me most
C. agonising me most
D. I most agonised
E. No correction required

99. The accused now flatly denies **have admitted** his guilt in his first statement.
A. having admitted
B. had admitted
C. have been admitting
D. has admitting
E. No correction required

100. We demonstrated to them how we **were prepared** the artistic patterns.
A. are prepared
B. have prepared
C. are preparing
D. had prepared
E. No correction required

ANSWERS

1	**2**	**3**	**4**	**5**	**6**	**7**	**8**	**9**	**10**
B	B	A	E	D	A	B	D	B	C
11	**12**	**13**	**14**	**15**	**16**	**17**	**18**	**19**	**20**
D	A	E	C	E	A	A	C	A	D
21	**22**	**23**	**24**	**25**	**26**	**27**	**28**	**29**	**30**
E	B	E	D	C	B	E	A	C	E
31	**32**	**33**	**34**	**35**	**36**	**37**	**38**	**39**	**40**
C	A	D	C	B	E	C	A	E	B
41	**42**	**43**	**44**	**45**	**46**	**47**	**48**	**49**	**50**
B	C	A	C	D	B	B	A	D	A
51	**52**	**53**	**54**	**55**	**56**	**57**	**58**	**59**	**60**
E	B	D	B	B	A	A	E	C	D
61	**62**	**63**	**64**	**65**	**66**	**67**	**68**	**69**	**70**
B	B	A	C	E	C	E	B	E	B
71	**72**	**73**	**74**	**75**	**76**	**77**	**78**	**79**	**80**
E	C	D	A	D	C	B	D	B	D
81	**82**	**83**	**84**	**85**	**86**	**87**	**88**	**89**	**90**
C	B	B	A	B	E	A	C	D	C
91	**92**	**93**	**94**	**95**	**96**	**97**	**98**	**99**	**100**
B	D	A	D	D	E	E	B	A	D

6

Cloze Test

A cloze test is a procedure in which you are asked to supply words which have been removed from a passage. It is meant to test your ability to comprehend text. Try and practise it to master it in this exercise.

Multiple Choice Questions

Directions: *In the following passages there are some blanks, each of which has been numbered. These numbers are also printed below the passages and against each five words are suggested, one of which fits the blank appropriately. Find out the appropriate word in each case.*

PASSAGE-1

Mobile banking (M banking) involves the use of a mobile phone or any other mobile device to **...(1)...** financial transactions linked to a client's account. M banking is new in most countries and most mobile payment models even in developed countries, to date operate on a **...(2)...** scale. A mobile network offers a **...(3)...** available technology platform onto which other services can be provided at low cost with effective results. For example, M banking services which use **...(4)...** such as SMS can be carried at a cost of less than one US cent per message. The low cost of using existing infrastructure makes such services more **...(5)...** to use by customers with lower purchasing power and opens up access to services which did not reach them earlier due to **...(6)...** cost of service delivery. Although M banking is one aspect in the wider **...(7)...** of e-banking there are reasons to single it out for focus-especially because there are a lot more people with mobile phones than bank accounts in India.

M banking could provide a **...(8)...** solution to bring more "unbanked" people to the financial mainstream. Without traditional credit, individuals are **...(9)...** to exploitation by abusive lenders offering very high interest rates on short term loans. Also of considerable importance are public safety implications for the unbanked—they are often victims of crime because many operate on a cash only basis and end up carrying significant amounts of cash on their **...(10)...** or store cash in their homes.

1. A. Disburse B. Undertake C. Subscribe D. Lure E. Amass

2. A. Full B. Voluminous C. Substantial D. Limited E. Rapid

3. A. Readily B. Tangible C. Routinely D. Securely E. Unique

4. A. Process B. Waves C. Deliveries D. Connection E. Channels

5. A. Valuable B. Answerable C. Amenable D. Exposed E. Responsible

6. A. Waning B. Stable
C. Proportionate D. Marginal
E. High

7. A. Archive B. Domain
C. Purpose D. Component
E. Aspect

8. A. Law abiding B. Tried
C. Reassuring D. Cost effective
E. Stopgap

9. A. Inclined B. Immune
C. Vulnerable D. Surrendered
E. Pressured

10. A. Person B. Own
C. Relatives D. Purses
E. Self

PASSAGE-2

The world economy is in recession—the deepest and the most widespread ...**(1)**... the 1930s. There are ...**(2)**... of ...**(3)**... in the industrial countries, but most serious economic ...**(4)**... anticipate that rates of growth and levels of economic activity will remain low.

In all that has been written about world ...**(5)**..., the ...**(6)**... have been overwhelmingly and narrowly economic. Few have ...**(7)**... the human consequences in more than a superficial manner. Not a single international study has ...**(8)**... the recession's ...**(9)**... on the most vulnerable half of the world's population—the children.

The need for ...**(10)**... clearly the ...**(11)**... between world economic conditions and child welfare has thus become even more urgent in the last few years. The worldscale of current child distress also makes it artificial to restrict the analysis of causes to the ...**(12)**... level.

1. A. in B. for
C. by D. before
E. since

2. A. risks B. glimmers
C. studies D. tips
E. histories

3. A. development B. downfall
C. recovery D. slackness
E. impact

4. A. analysts B. journalists
C. surveys D. findings
E. students

5. A. development B. economy
C. wars D. recession
E. conflicts

6. A. emphasis B. aims
C. glimpses D. suppositions
E. preoccupations

7. A. delved B. taught
C. propagated D. investigated
E. manifested

8. A. understood B. analysed
C. highlighted D. prepared
E. planned

9. A. analysis B. undercurrents
C. impact D. overtures
E. study

10. A. chalking out B. curbing
C. bringing out D. implementing
E. propagating

11. A. linkages B. fallouts
C. dependence D. contrasts
E. similarities

12. A. international B. political
C. low D. national
E. highest

PASSAGE-3

Nowadays, under the ...**(1)**... system of education, however good it may be, when a young man comes out of the University, there seems to be this ...**(2)**... in him that the higher the standard of living rises, the less should a man work. Thus, mathematically higher the standard of living, according to this misconceived notion, the less the ...**(3)**... . Ultimately, what should be the highest standard of living then? ...**(4)**... work! This leads to an unhealthy ...**(5)**... among the workers. A typist who types over twenty letters a day asks his ...**(6)**... how many letters he had typed that day. The latter ...**(7)**... "fifteen". The former thinks, "Tomorrow I should type only fifteen or even ...**(8)**... . This tendency is quite ...**(9)**..., and may ultimately lead to ...(10)... . Even one's family life may be affected adversely due to such tendency.

1. A. developed B. extinct
C. outdated D. proposed
E. modern
2. A. anxiety B. misconception
C. realisation D. worry
E. apprehension
3. A. salary B. comfort
C. work D. energy
E. time
4. A. Minimum B. Maximum
C. Less D. No
E. Ample
5. A. competition B. dispute
C. delay D. jealousy
E. ambition
6. A. employee B. subordinate
C. boss D. client
E. colleague
7. A. suggests B. remembers
C. replies D. types
E. all
8. A. less B. all
C. more D. few
E. some
9. A. discouraging B. heartening
C. healthy D. unfortunate
E. unnatural
10. A. evil B. retardation
C. progress D. denial
E. complexity

PASSAGE-4

Four cases of burglary have been ...(1)... with the arrest of one ...(2)... criminal. The police have ...(3)... gold and silver jewellery from him. The police increased their public contacts with the residents of the area after following a spate of burglaries. They held corner meetings to ...(4)... the residents on steps to ...(5)... prevention. They were ...(6)... to inform their neighbours if they had to ...(7)... their houses unattended. Consequently, some ...(8)... of the locality observed one ...(9)... leaving an empty house. He was ...(10)... and a case was registered.

1. A. connected B. adjusted
C. solved D. deferred
E. dealt
2. A. notorious B. more
C. thief D. imprisoned
E. extremely
3. A. withdrawn B. amassed
C. sold D. recovered
E. stolen
4. A. harass B. arrest
C. probe D. threaten
E. educate
5. A. loss B. crime
C. its D. burglar
E. their
6. A. required B. forbidden
C. instructed D. entrusted
E. forced
7. A. paint B. sell
C. protect D. leave
E. build
8. A. criminals B. neighbours
C. burglars D. pedestrians
E. residents
9. A. stranger B. resident
C. neighbour D. entrant
E. alien
10. A. misled B. apprehended
C. neglected D. boycotted
E. informed

PASSAGE-5

...(1)... change is the ...(2)... of the day, a proper orientation to ...(3)... with the change becomes a natural necessity ...(4)... assured organisational stability. In this ...(5)... of organisational change and survival, the author brings in the concept of 'praxis', ...(6)... it as the dynamo of change and uses it for ...(7)... a conceptual and methodological ...(8)... for the identification of training needs. Training, ...(9)... perceived as only one of the many elements in the organisational reflection process, is believed to stand ...(10)... as the means for relevant learning.

1. A. Few B. Many
C. No D. If
E. Why

2. A. order B. scope
C. large D. direction
E. result

3. A. assist B. renew
C. become D. try
E. cope

4. A. in B. for
C. from D. which
E. but

5. A. end B. decision
C. context D. scope
E. focus

6. A. describes B. throws
C. rejects D. leaves
E. derives

7. A. neglecting B. developing
C. calculating D. experiencing
E. diluting

8. A. routine B. idea
C. book D. follow up
E. framework

9. A. be B. may
C. though D. gets
E. as

10. A. in B. against
C. through D. out
E. with

PASSAGE-6

Each year, middle class Indian children ...**(1)**... hundreds of crores of rupees in pocket money and ...**(2)**... a heavy burden on parental ...**(3)**... . Like adults, these kids have ...**(4)**... connected with budgeting and saving money. Unfortunately, basic money ...**(5)**... is ...**(6)**... taught in schools. At home, very few parents ...**(7)**... money matters with their children. Kids who ...**(8)**... about money ...**(9)**... have been found to be way ahead of their peers. Indeed, learning to ...**(10)**... with money properly fosters discipline, good work habits and self-respect.

1. A. spend B. steal
C. save D. give
E. invest

2. A. move B. take
C. risk D. put
E. lift

3. A. promises B. payments
C. demands D. attitudes
E. incomes

4. A. expenses B. experience
C. problems D. guidance
E. necessities

5. A. availability B. inflation
C. economics D. problem
E. management

6. A. carefully B. rarely
C. generally D. always
E. thoroughly

7. A. discuss B. understand
C. teach D. reveal
E. advise

8. A. quarrel B. ask
C. learn D. waste
E. spend

9. A. slowly B. early
C. timely D. lately
E. regularly

10. A. decide B. earn
C. control D. deal
E. pay

PASSAGE-7

Architecture is a unique ...**(1)**... of art and science that has ...**(2)**... out of man's primary need for shelter. It is concerned with the design and ...**(3)**... of buildings in their sociological, technological and environmental context. This field is not only ...**(4)**...but also provide the ...**(5)**... of designing and building pleasing and ...**(6)**... refined structures to serve various needs. ...**(7)**... the fairly large number of practising architects, the countrywide ...**(8)**... in building activity offers scope for more. And though the initial earnings in the field are relatively ...**(9)**... what you make thereafter will depend entirely on your ...**(10)**... .

1. A. procedure B. process
C. portion D. blend
E. subject

2. A. drifted B. fizzled
C. contrived D. earned
E. arisen

3. A. painting B. construction
C. decoration D. repairing
E. appearance

4. A. fatiguing B. strenuous
C. encouraging D. vast
E. rewarding

5. A. satisfaction B. facility
C. infrastructure D. amenities
E. decorum

6. A. practically B. ideologically
C. aesthetically D. principally
E. readily

7. A. Considering B. Having
C. Assuming D. Regarding
E. Despite

8. A. variation B. slack
C. lethargy D. spurt
E. deterioration

9. A. escalating B. modest
C. unpredictable D. negligible
E. exorbitant

10. A. ambition B. appearance
C. expectation D. experience
E. need

PASSAGE-8

Without science there is no future for any society. Even with science, ...**(1)**... it is controlled by some spiritual impulses, there is also no future. One great thing about science is that it does not accept anything on mere ...**(2)**... . Everything has to be ...**(3)**... beyond any doubt. All acceptance comes after experiement which has no room for any ...**(4)**... . This is the reason ...**(5)**... development of science and technology has revolutionised human life all over the world. There are very few spheres of human activity which have not experienced the ...**(6)**... of such development. However, despite its manifold ...**(7)**... science has not been ...**(8)**... to solve any of man's moral or spiritual problems. Society is still ...**(9)**... in the dark to find out what its future will be. The need, therefore, is to make science ...**(10)**... for the ultimate truth.

1. A. unless B. without
C. if D. before
E. because

2. A. principles B. conjecture
C. experiment D. research
E. experience

3. A. accepted B. demonstrated
C. proved D. performed
E. understood

4. A. precision B. exactness
C. confirmation D. speculation
E. apprehension

5. A. for B. how
C. that D. about
E. why

6. A. impact B. futility
C. causes D. problems
E. nature

7. A. limitations B. benefits
C. shortcomings D. researches
E. inventions

8. A. employed B. developed
C. able D. entrusted
E. taught

9. A. engulfed B. lost
C. enlightening D. investigating
E. groping

10. A. useful B. worthy
C. ready D. search
E. fit

PASSAGE-9

Faced with an ...**(1)**... number and variety of products on the market, managers are finding it more difficult to ...**(2)**... demand and plan production and order ...**(3)**... . As a result ...**(4)**... forecasts are increasing and, along with them, the costs of those errors. Many managers today, ...**(5)**... speed is the ...**(6)**..., have turned to one or another popular production scheduling system. But these tools tackle only part of the problem. ...**(7)**... really needed is a way to ...**(8)**... forecasts and simultaneously redesign planning processes to ...**(9)**... the impact of ...**(10)**... forecasts.

1. A. exact B. equal
C. optimum D. eccentric
E. unprecedented

2. A. meet B. predict
C. ignore D. accept
E. register

3. A. immediately B. quickly
C. accordingly D. positively
E. spontaneously

4. A. inaccurate B. buoyant
C. frequent D. inadequate
E. exorbitant

5. A. consider B. neglecting
C. visualising D. believing
E. notwithstanding

6. A. problem B. answer
C. source D. outcome
E. lacuna

7. A. What's B. That's
C. One D. Managers
E. Companies

8. A. ignore B. obtain
C. vitiate D. negate
E. improve

9. A. rationalise B. substantiate
C. minimise D. counter
E. tolerate

10. A. dangerous B. absolute
C. unpredicted D. erroneous
E. popular

PASSAGE-10

In view of the ...**(1)**... demand for personnel with commerce background, in the post-liberalisation period, courses in commerce have ...**(2)**... the attention of students and parents. There is growing ...**(3)**... for these courses not only in schools but also in colleges. But the ...**(4)**... of commerce education in schools leaves ...**(5)**... to be desired. Its popularity, importance and quality, to a large extent, depends much on the teaching methodology being ...**(6)**... in schools. Of course, the ...**(7)**... review and ...**(8)**... of syllabic also ...**(9)**.... But this aspect is ...**(10)**... taken care of suitably, by the concerned organisations.

1. A. exaggerated B. unreasonable
C. tremendous D. increasing
E. diminishing

2. A. distorted B. ameliorated
C. attracted D. weighed
E. encouraged

3. A. demand B. contempt
C. dissatisfaction D. commotion
E. urgency

4. A. awareness B. intricacy
C. status D. necessity
E. quality

5. A. scope B. much
C. short D. everything
E. nothing

6. A. abandoned B. practised
C. contemplated D. assimilated
E. taught

7. A. unscrupulous B. partial
C. expert D. general
E. periodical

8. A. discussions B. perusal
C. reduction D. updating
E. formulation

9. A. matters B. flourishes
C. desires D. encompasses
E. needs

10. A. duly B. seldom
C. being D. often
E. never

ANSWERS

PASSAGE-1

1	2	3	4	5	6	7	8	9	10
B	D	D	A	D	E	B	D	C	A

PASSAGE-2

1	2	3	4	5	6	7	8	9	10
E	A	D	A	B	B	A	B	C	C
11	**12**								
D	D								

PASSAGE-3

1	2	3	4	5	6	7	8	9	10
E	B	C	D	E	C	C	A	A	B

PASSAGE-4

1	2	3	4	5	6	7	8	9	10
C	A	D	E	B	A	D	E	A	B

PASSAGE-5

1	2	3	4	5	6	7	8	9	10
D	A	E	B	C	A	B	E	C	D

PASSAGE-6

1	2	3	4	5	6	7	8	9	10
A	D	E	C	E	B	A	C	C	D

PASSAGE-7

1	2	3	4	5	6	7	8	9	10
D	E	B	D	C	C	E	D	B	D

PASSAGE-8

1	2	3	4	5	6	7	8	9	10
A	B	C	D	E	A	B	C	E	E

PASSAGE-9

1	2	3	4	5	6	7	8	9	10
E	B	C	A	D	B	A	E	C	E

PASSAGE-10

1	2	3	4	5	6	7	8	9	10
D	C	A	E	B	B	E	D	A	A

7

Idioms & Phrases

An idiom is a group of words established by usage having a meaning different from individual words.
A phrase is a small group of words standing together as an idiomatic expression.
Learn and practise as may as you can and test your knowledge in the exercise that follows.

Idioms and Idiomatic Phrases

- **ABC** (basic principles)
  I do not know the ABC of photography.
- **At one's beck and call** (ready to obey)
  He had a dozen men at his beck and call.
- **At sixes and sevens** (in disorder)
  The drawing room articles were lying at sixes and sevens on the floor.
- **A wet blanket** (a discouraging person)
  Don't allow him to accompany you to the hunting trip, he is a wet blanket.
- **A big gun** (an important person)
  Mr Tata is a big gun in our city.
- **At a stone's throw** (at a short distance from)
  My school is at a stone's throw from my house.
- **A man of word** (a person who keeps his promise)
  Mr Modi is a man of word.
- **A man of a few words** (a remarkable person)
  Gandhiji was a man of a few words.
- **At arm's length** (to keep away)
  We should always keep bad boys at arm's length
- **A bolt from the blue** (a sudden and unexpected event)
  The news of my friend's death came to me like a bolt from the blue.
- **A man of letters** (a scholar)
  Radha Krishnan was a man of letters.
- **A hard nut to crack.** (a puzzling problem)
  To get a win over American basket ball team is a hard nut to crack for India.
- **A yeoman's service** (service which is beneficial to the human beings)
  He did yeoman's service through his life.
- **A snake in the grass** (a hidden foe)
  Beware of him because he seems to be a snake in the grass.
- **Acid test** (hard test)
  The election will be an acid test for the ruling party.
- **A wolf in sheep's clothing** (a hypocrite)
  You should not keep company with him because he is a wolf in sheep's clothing.
- **At the eleventh hour** (at the last moment)
  The war was about to start but fortunately at the eleventh hour a messenger came to the PM with a message of peace.
- **A great card** (an important person)
  Mr Rajan is a great card in the ministry of finance.
- **A fool of the first water** (one completely foolish)
  Being a fool of the first water he could not solve even the simplest sum.
- **A bone of contention** (to be the cause of quarrel)
  Kashmir is the bone of contention between India and Pakistan.
- **A green hand** (not very much experienced)
  We shall pay a little to a green hand.
- **All in all** (completely)
  Rajesh is all in all in this office.

✦ **A bed of roses** (a comfort)
Life is not a bed of roses.

✦ **An apple of discord** (to be the cause of)
Kashmir is an apple of discord between India and Pakistan.

✦ **A white elephant** (of no use)
This sort of glib talker always proves a white elephant in the end.

✦ **A red letter day** (an important day)
15th August is a red letter day for the Indians.

✦ **By hook or by crook** (by any means fair or foul)
You must complete this job by hook or by crook.

✦ **Black sheep** (a traitor)
Later on the person proved a black sheep.

✦ **By dint of** (by means of)
By dint of hard work, she earned a lot of money.

✦ **Break ones back** (to work hard to get something)
He broke his back to earn his livelihood.

✦ **Break the back of** (accomplish the hardest part of a certain job)
There is nothing to be worried about as we've already broken the back of the problem.

✦ **Beat about the bush** (to go on talking on some worthless topic)
Stop this beating about the bush, come to the main task.

✦ **Beyond one's means** (beyond one's budget)
He is living beyond his means, therefore, he is sure to get ruined.

✦ **Cut loose** (keep away)
India should cut loose from bad politics.

✦ **Chips of the same block** (having the same taste)
They are the chips of the same block.

✦ **Cut-throat competition** (a stiff competition)
There is a cut-throat competition among the publishers in the market.

✦ **Come what may** (no matter what happens)
I'll do it, come what may.

✦ **Drop someone a line** (send a letter, etc.)
Please drop me a line of your well-being.

✦ **Dull the edge of** (reduce the intensity of)
Take this pill and it will dull the edge of pain.

✦ **From hand to mouth** (without any saving)
The poor factory worker is living from hand to mouth.

✦ **Fair and square** (clean)
One must be fair and square in one's dealing.

✦ **Hard of hearing** (somewhat deaf)
She is a bit hard of hearing.

✦ **In the good books of** (be good in one's mind)
Jack is in the good books of his teachers.

✦ **In black and white** (in written)
Don't give him anything in black and white.

✦ **In cold blood** (mercilessly)
The old woman was murdered in cold blood.

✦ **In a crack** (all of a sudden or rapidly)
The thief left the place in a crack.

✦ **In full swing** (in full force)
The studies of the students are going on in full swing.

✦ **In the twinkling of an eye** (quickly)
The monkey ate up grams in the twinkling of an eye.

✦ **Keep the ball rolling** (to maintain the progress of some activity)
After the death of his father he had to take the charge of his office to keep the ball rolling.

✦ **Neck and neck** (even)
There is a neck and neck fight between the two boxers.

✦ **Once in a blue moon** (seldom)
She visits her brother once in a blue moon.

✦ **Slow and steady** (slowly but continually)
Slow and steady wins the race.

✦ **To cut a sorry figure** (present oneself in a bad way)
She cut a sorry figure on the stage.

✦ **To give a red carpet reception** (to give a warm welcome)
The PM was given a red carpet reception in America.

✦ **To dance one's tune** (to follow someone submissively)
He always dances to his brother's tune.

✦ **To turn a deaf ear to** (to disregard)
She turned a deaf ear to her parents' advice.

- **To call a spade a spade** (to speak the truth)
  Gandhiji always called a spade a spade.
- **To bring to book** (to scold)
  The naughty boy was brought to book by the teacher.
- **To cut short** (to reduce)
  Smoking will cut short your life.
- **To grease the palm of** (to bribe)
  Rohit greased the palm of the clerk and got the file moved.
- **Through thick and thin.** (under all circumstances)
  We'll stand by you through thick and thin.
- **To die by inches** (to die a painful death)
  The old man died by inches.
- **To eat one's words** (to retract one's statement)
  You'll have to eat your words because you have spoken without thinking.
- **To burn the midnight oil** (to work hard)
  You'll have to burn the midnight oil if you want to get good marks.
- **To poke one's nose into** (to meddle with)
  It is bad to poke your nose into others' affair.
- **To fall flat** (to have no effect)
  His father's advice fell flat on him.
- **To make a clean breast of** (to confess)
  He made a clean breast of his involvement in the bomb blast.
- **To get the better of** (overcome)
  Anger got the better of him.
- **To break somebody's back** (to give too much work to him to do)
  She broke his back by giving him so much hard work to do.
- **Throw cold water on** (to discourage)
  She tried to throw cold water on his plan but he was well-determined.
- **The long and short of** (in brief)
  The long and short of his lecture is that we should live like brothers.
- **To burn one's fingers** (to get oneself in trouble)
  You have burnt your fingers by speaking against him.
- **To turn over a new leaf** (to change the course of life)
  He has turned over a new leaf in his life.
- **To have one's own axe to grind** (to have vested interest)
  He has his own axe to grind in this matter.
- **To take to one's heels** (to run away)
  The thief took to his heels as soon as he saw the policeman.
- **To move heaven and earth** (to make too much effort)
  The young man moved heaven and earth to find a job.
- **To be caught red handed** (to be caught at the time of committing a crime)
  The clerk was caught red handed when he was accepting bribe from Mr ABC.
- **To receive with open arms** (to give a warm welcome)
  The new president of the club was received with open arms by the members.
- **To be born with a silver spoon in one's mouth** (to be born in a rich family)
  Mr. J. L. Nehru was born with a silver spoon in his mouth.
- **To come to light** (to be known)
  A new disease has recently come to light.
- **To be the apple of one's eye** (be very dear)
  He is the apple of his parent's eye.
- **To make fun of** (laugh at)
  The children made fun of the waiter in the hotel.
- **To let the cat out of the bag** (to divulge secret)
  It was I who let the cat out of the bag by telling the real matter.
- **To open a new chapter** (to start some habit, etc.)
  By quitting drinking, you've opened a new chapter in your life.
- **To make the flesh creep** (to terrify)
  The story made my flesh creep.
- **To lose ground** (to retreat)
  After fighting for some time the Pakistani army began to lose ground.

- **To bring to book** (to punish)
  The student was brought to book by the teacher.
- **To show a clean pair of heels** (to run away)
  The thief showed a clean pair of heels as soon as he saw the policeman approaching.
- **To gain ground** (to be established)
  He gained ground in India in a few years.
- **To get wind of** (to get information)
  I got wind of his secret plans.
- **Under a cloud** (be in trouble or in a state of disgrace or suspicion)
  His company seemed to be under a cloud as it had no funds to pay the wages to the workers.

Verbal Phrases

- **Act upon** (to follow)
  I acted upon my father's advice.
- **Act upto** (to perform within limits)
  He acted upto his conscience.
- **Act beyond** (to perform crossing limits)
  We should not act beyond our capacity.
- **Act for** (to perform in place of someone else)
  The vice principal acted for the principal.
- **Back up** (to make a queue)
  The vehicles began to back up.
- **Back down** (withdraw claim in the presence of opposition)
  The leader backed down from his previous statement.
- **Back off** (draw back some plan or action)
  They backed off from building a flyover.
- **Back out** (withdraw from a promise, etc.)
  The government backed out of its promise.
- **Break down** (stop working) My car broke down on the highway.
- **Break into** (enter in certain premises by breaking the door, etc.)
  Last night a thief broke into my neighbour's.
- **Break off** (to detach by breaking)
  The branch broke off from the tree.
- **Break out** (spread)
  Cholera has broken out in the town.
- **Break out of** (escape from)
  A prisoner broke out of the prison last night.
- **Break up** (disperse)
  The cloud of fog began to break up as the sun rose.
- **Break something up** (cause something to break into small pieces)
  She broke up the chocolate to distribute it among the children.
- **Break with** (cut off connection after quarrelling with someone)
  He has broken with his brother.
- **Call on** (pay a visit to somebody)
  I'll call on Mohan's today.
- **Call out** (to start)
  The workers have called out a strike.
- **Call off** (to stop the strike etc.)
  The workers have called off the strike.
- **Call at** (to visit someone's house)
  I called at his house yesterday.
- **Call in** (send for)
  Please call in the doctor.
- **Carry on** (continue)
  Please carry on your work.
- **Carry something out** (perform a task)
  Our company is carrying out a big deal with a foreign company.
- **Carry something over** (postpone)
  The fancy dress competition had to be carried over till Monday)
- **Carry someone off** (kill somebody)
  Cancer carried her off on the day of her 20th birthday.
- **Come of age** (get established)
  As our company has come of age, so, there is no problem in selling our goods.
- **Come of** (belong to)
  She comes of a royal family.
- **Come over** (surmount)
  We at last came over all our problems.
- **Come off** (to take place)
  The marriage of my brother comes off in the next month.

- **Come round** (agree)
  At last he came round to my views.
- **Come under** (fall in the category of)
  All these animals come under the same species.
- **Come down with** (suffer from)
  She came down with whopping cough.
- **Come from** (be the native of)
  She came from London.
- **Come about** (happen)
  The explosion came about when the worker struck the match to light a cigarette.
- **Cut off** (die)
  The cricketer is cut off in the prime of his life.
- **Cut down** (reduce)
  The prices of consumer goods should be cut down.
- **Cut someone out** (exclude someone)
  His father cut him out of his will.
- **Fall in**
  She fell in love with the prince.
- **Fall down** (fail)
  The deal fell down for lack of transparency.
- **Fall out** (quarrel)
  She fell out with his elder brother.
- **Fall through** (fail)
  The project fell through for lack of funds.
- **Get away** (escape)
  She got away with her life.
- **Get by** (to accomplish something with great difficulty)
  She is not rich. She has just enough to get by.
- **Get on** (perform)
  How are you getting on with your studies?
- **Get out** (become known)
  The news got out that the PM was paying a visit to Russia.
- **Get over** (overcome)
  At last I got over all obstacles.
- **Get up** (rise)
  When do you get up in the morning?
- **Give up** (stop)
  He gave up smoking.
- **Give out** (emit)
  Garlic gives out a pungent smell.
- **Give in** (collapse)
  The bridge gave in under the heavy load.
- **Give away** (distribute)
  The Principal gave away the prizes.
- **Give out** (announce)
  It was given out that the President of India would visit the place soon.
- **Go off** (explode)
  The gun went off suddenly.
- **Go on** (continue)
  She went on about how she flew the aeroplane.
- **Go through** (examine)
  I'll go through this book later on.
- **Go up** (be built)
  The construction of the house is going up.
- **Grind on** (continue for a long time in a tedious way)
  The discussion over political issues ground on.
- **Grind something out** (produce something a tedious way)
  She will grind some more short stories.
- **Look out** (be careful)
  Look out! there is a snake.
- **Look down upon** (hate)
  We should not look down upon the poor.
- **Look at** (watch)
  Look at the blackboard.
- **Look after** (take care of)
  We ought to look after our old parents.
- **Look into** (investigate)
  The new police inspector will look into the matter.
- **Look up** (rise)
  The prices of consumer goods are looking up.
- **Look back** (think of the past)
  It made her feel disolate when she looked back on things of the past.
- **Make up** (to fulfil)
  I'll make up my deficiency in Mathematics.

- **Make out** (understand)
  I could not make out what she said.
- **Make up one' mind** (to resolve)
  I have made up my mind to settle in the USA.
- **Make off** (leave hurriedly)
  She made off without informing anybody.
- **Make something over** (transfer)
  She should make her property over to her sons.
- **Make over** (hand over)
  He made over the charge of the file to Mr Robert.
- **Pull back** (retreat)
  The government has pulled back from its previous policy.
- **Pull something down** (demolish)
  The authorities concerned pulled down a few building which were illegally built on government land.
- **Pull out** (pluck)
  The child pulled out a few petals of the flower.
- **Pull through** (recover)
  The patient will pull through.
- **Push on** (continue a journey)
  It was getting darker but we pushed on.
- **Push at** (exert force)
  He pushed at the bell, but it did not ring.
- **Push for** (demand persistently)
  The workers have been pushing for the installation of new machines for five years.
- **Put out** (extinguish)
  She put out the light.
- **Put on** (wear)
  He put on an overcoat.
- **Put off** (postpone)
  The plan had to be put off.
- **Put by** (spare something for future)
  We must put by some money for future.
- **Put up with** (stay)
  Your aunt is out of town for a couple of days, you may put up with us till she comes.
- **Put something down** (record something)
  She put a new idea down on the paper.
- **Take after** (resemble)
  He takes after his father.
- **Take off** (remove)
  He took off his shoes.
- **Take something out** (obtain)
  You may take out some money from Rohit if you want to purchase this car.
- **Take to** (fall into the habit of)
  He took to gambling.
- **Turn something down** (reject something)
  The judge turned down his appeal.
- **Turn on** (attack)
  The thief turned on him with a knife.

Multiple Choice Questions

Directions: *Some idioms/phrases are given below with their probable meanings. Select the options with their correct meanings.*

1. Carry out

A. To take from one place to another
B. To continue
C. To obey
D. To make efforts
E. None of these

2. In the same boat

A. A worn out choice
B. Indifferent
C. In identical circumstances
D. Carry off
E. None of these

3. In one's good book

A. A costly book
B. A priceless treasure
C. In one's favour
D. An enchanting beauty
E. None of these

4. Keep a straight face

A. To do make up
B. To change clothes
C. Assume responsibility
D. To remain serious
E. None of these

5. To be above board
A. To have a good height
B. To be honest in any business deal
C. To have no debts
D. To try to be beautiful
E. None of these

6. On the face of it
A. To agree B. From an action
C. More than enough D. Apparently
E. None of these

7. Let the bygones be bygones
A. In one's favour B. To pretend
C. To forget the past D. Other choice
E. None of these

8. To split hairs
A. Major distinctions
B. Hair with two ends
C. To make minute distinction
D. Without distinction
E. None of these

9. Bread and butter
A. Both bread and butter
B. Something essential
C. Livelihood
D. Relevant things
E. None of these

10. To bell the cat
A. To catch a cat and tie a bell round its neck
B. To make an effort
C. To be quick
D. To face a risk
E. None of these

11. Hard and fast
A. Strict B. Solid
C. Fast moving D. Some hard surface
E. None of these

12. Part and parcel
A. The part of a parcel
B. An essential part
C. A missing parcel
D. Some part of a machine sent by parcel
E. None of these

13. Null and void
A. Something invalid
B. Something that can be avoided
C. Something that can be nullified
D. Something evil
E. None of these

14. To make clean breast of
A. To gain prominence
B. To praise oneself
C. To confess without reserve
D. To destroy before it blooms
E. None of these

15. Trump card
A. A powerful means of achieving an object
B. Resourcefulness
C. The best gamble to attain success
D. A travel card
E. None of these

16. Tall talk
A. A discussion continued for a long time
B. A high sounding talk
C. A meaningful talk
D. A useless talk
E. None of these

17. Small talk
A. Gossip
B. A discussion carried on for a long time
C. A brief discussion
D. A talk of small children
E. None of these

18. Throw out of gear
A. To replace B. Hinder, disturb
C. To decide D. Take up tune
E. None of these

19. To and fro
A. Back and forth B. Puzzled
C. Amazed D. Reprove
E. None of these

20. To bell the cat
A. To do an easy job
B. To be indifferent to
C. To undertake a difficult job
D. To clarify
E. None of these

21. To be under cloud
A. Puzzle
B. Enjoy the favour
C. Talk thoughtlessly
D. To be under suspicion
E. None of these

22. A labour of love
A. A tragic end
B. A funny thing
C. Not fruitful
D. Work done without payment
E. None of these

23. Follow suit
A. Follow an example B. Wear a new dress
C. Irrelevant D. A gay person
E. None of these

24. Foul play
A. Bad intentions
B. A play not well acted
C. A play not liked by the audience
D. A foul scored at play
E. None of these

25. To pick holes
A. To find some reason to quarrel
B. To destroy something
C. To criticise someone
D. To cut some part of an item
E. None of these

26. To smell a rat
A. To see signs of plague epidemic
B. To get bad smell of a dead rat
C. To suspect foul dealings
D. To be in a bad mood
E. None of these

27. To put a spoke in one's wheel
A. To encourage
B. Act without restraint
C. Risk something
D. To obstruct one's progress
E. None of these

28. To pull one's leg
A. To give up B. Take care of
C. To befool D. To know
E. None of these

29. To play with fire
A. Grasp the truth
B. To handle something dangerous
C. To ridicule
D. To flee away
E. None of these

30. To reckon with
A. Take up time
B. Make an inventory
C. To deal with
D. Submit to punishment
E. None of these

31. To run short
A. Talk until one is tired at
B. Apply to oneself
C. To get rid of
D. To have or be too little
E. None of these

32. A man of letters
A. A postman B. A learned man
C. A hypocrite D. An ignorant man
E. None of these

33. A maiden speech
A. A speech made in the parliament
B. A speech made before unmarried girls
C. A speech made by a political leader
D. A speech made for the first time
E. None of these

34. Order of the day
A. An order passed on a particular day
B. A current law
C. Something common or general
D. A major order of court
E. None of these

35. To end in smoke
A. To make completely understand
B. To ruin oneself
C. To excite great applause
D. To die smoking
E. None of these

36. To give vent to
A. To allow to flow forth
B. To prove a failure
C. To amass wealth
D. To evade
E. None of these

37. To eat humble pie
A. To apologise or confess
B. To order
C. To flatter
D. To get a small share
E. None of these

38. A black sheep
A. An unlucky person
B. A negro
C. An ugly person

D. A man in animal skin
E. None of these

39. To catch a tartar
A. To trap wanted criminal with great difficulty
B. To catch a dangerous person
C. To meet with disaster
D. To deal with a person who is more than one's watch
E. None of these

40. Sit on fence
A. To remain neutral
B. To show contempt
C. To enjoy the surroundings
D. To become fond of
E. None of these

41. Pay off old scores
A. To repay the debt
B. To have revenge
C. To invite
D. Secretly
E. None of these

42. Turn turtle
A. To cheat
B. To be lopsided
C. To frustrate
D. To dance to the tune
E. None of these

43. Wash one's hands of
A. To refuse
B. To assist
C. To abuse
D. To refuse to be
E. None of these

44. Under duress
A. Under compulsion
B. Willing
C. To elicit information
D. To demand
E. None of these

45. To turn the tables
A. To ruin someone
B. To turn the situation to one's own side
C. To reverse the situation
D. To move from one point to another
E. None of these

46. On the cards
A. Possibly
B. Probably
C. Openly
D. Likely

47. To leave someone in the lurch
A. To come to compromise with someone
B. Constant source of annoyance to someone
C. To put someone at ease
D. To desert someone in his difficulties
E. None of these

48. To play second fiddle
A. To be happy, cheerful and healthy
B. To reduce importance of one's senior
C. To support the role and view of another person
D. To do backseat driving
E. None of these

49. To yearn for
A. To weep for
B. To remember
C. To admire
D. To long for intensely
E. None of these

50. Call off
A. To finish
B. To withdraw
C. To postpone
D. To cry
E. None of these

ANSWERS

1	**2**	**3**	**4**	**5**	**6**	**7**	**8**	**9**	**10**
C	C	C	D	B	D	C	C	C	D
11	**12**	**13**	**14**	**15**	**16**	**17**	**18**	**19**	**20**
A	B	A	C	C	B	A	B	A	C
21	**22**	**23**	**24**	**25**	**26**	**27**	**28**	**29**	**30**
D	D	A	A	C	C	D	C	B	C
31	**32**	**33**	**34**	**35**	**36**	**37**	**38**	**39**	**40**
D	B	D	C	D	A	A	D	B	A
41	**42**	**43**	**44**	**45**	**46**	**47**	**48**	**49**	**50**
B	B	D	A	C	D	D	C	D	B

8

Reordering Sentences

A paragraph is formed from sentences, it will convey its true meaning and purpose only when the sentences are arranged in a proper manner. One must try and practise it regularly to score well. Test your skills in this exercise.

Multiple Choice Questions

Directions (Qs. 1 to 60): *Each of these questions sets has a group of sentences marked with numbers. Rearrange them in proper sequence to form a meaningful paragraph and answer the questions given below each set.*

SET-1

1. After examining him, the doctor smiled at him mischievously and took out a syringe.
2. Thinking that he was really sick, his father summoned the family doctor.
3. That day, Banku wanted to take a day off from school.
4. Immediately, Banku jumped up from his bed and swore that he was fine.
5. Therefore; he pretended to be sick and remained in bed.

1. Which sentence should come **fourth** in the pargaraph?
A. 1 B. 2
C. 3 D. 4
E. 5

2. Which sentence should come **last** in the paragraph?
A. 1 B. 2
C. 3 D. 4
E. 5

3. Which sentence should come **first** in the paragraph?
A. 1 B. 2
C. 3 D. 4
E. 5

4. Which sentence should come **third** in the paragraph?
A. 1 B. 2
C. 3 D. 4
E. 5

5. Which sentence should come **second** in the paragraph?
A. 1 B. 2
C. 3 D. 4
E. 5

SET-2

1. In his literary work he spoke of that province of human life which mere intellect does not speak.
2. He has also given innocent joy to many children by his stories like 'Kabuliwalah'.
3. Thsese songs are sung not only in Bengal but all over the country.
4. Rabindranath's great works sprang from intensity of vision and feelings.
5. He sang of beauty and heroism, nobility and charm.

6. Which sentence should come **third** in the sequence?
A. 1 B. 2
C. 3 D. 4
E. 5

7. Which sentence should come **fourth** in the sequence?
A. 1 B. 2
C. 3 D. 4
E. 5

8. Which sentence should come **second** in the sequence?
A. 1 B. 2
C. 3 D. 4
E. 5

9. Which sentence should come **first** in the sequence?
A. 1 B. 2
C. 3 D. 4
E. 5

10. Which sentence should come **fifth** in the sequence?
A. 1 B. 2
C. 3 D. 4
E. 5

SET-3

1. I reached office at 11 o'clock after sending the money.
2. Some money had to be sent to my parents.
3. After that, I spent almost an hour at the post office.
4. Therefore, I went to the bank to withdraw some money.
5. However, I had no money with me.

11. Which statement should come **first** in the paragraph?
A. 1 B. 2
C. 3 D. 4
E. 5

12. Which statement should come **second** in the paragraph?
A. 1 B. 2
C. 3 D. 4
E. 5

13. Which statement should come **third** in the paragraph?
A. 1 B. 2
C. 3 D. 4
E. 5

14. Which statement should come **fourth** in the paragraph?
A. 1 B. 2
C. 3 D. 4
E. 5

15. Which statement should come **fifth** in the paragraph?
A. 1 B. 2
C. 3 D. 4
E. 5

SET-4

1. In fact, it prevents us from helping children to analyse conflict, to learn to cope with it and counter it.
2. Children have always known that there is conflict in the adult world.
3. However, the make-believe world that nineteenth century rationally imposed on childhood in Europe and which we impose in an institutionalised manner through our modern education system can hardly be described as related in this regard.
4. We may therefore conclude that conflict in an institutionalised manner is not a matter of faith in children's capacities, rather, it is a lack of faith in ourselves as adults.
5. Further, psychologists tell us and story tellers have always known that the child's desire to search for order and coherence gathers strength from the knowledge of conflict.

16. Which of the following should be the **last** sentence in the paragraph?
A. 1 B. 2
C. 3 D. 4
E. 5

17. Which of the following should be the **first** sentence in the paragraph?
A. 1 B. 2
C. 3 D. 4
E. 5

18. Which of the following should be the **fourth** sentence in the paragraph?

A. 1 B. 2
C. 3 D. 4
E. 5

19. Which of the following should be the **third** sentence in the paragraph?

A. 1 B. 2
C. 3 D. 4
E. 5

20. Which of the following should be the **second** sentence in the paragraph?

A. 1 B. 2
C. 3 D. 4
E. 5

SET-5

1. A case in point is the programme involving the Sardar Sarovar Dam which would displace about 2,00,000 people.
2. Critics decry the fact that a major development institution appears to absorb more capital than it distributes to borrowers.
3. For all its faults critics however, concede that the bank remains a relatively efficient instrument for distribution of development-aid money.
4. One of the key complaints focuses on this non-profit bank's recent "profitability".
5. Although the lives of millions of people around the globe have been improved by the bank's activities, it is now under fire.
6. The bank is also being blamed for large-scale involuntary resettlement to make way for dams and other construction projects.

21. Which sentence should come **third** in the paragraph?

A. 2 B. 5
C. 1 D. 4
E. 6

22. Which sentence should come **fourth** in the paragraph?

A. 6 B. 3
C. 5 D. 2
E. 1

23. Which sentence should come **first** in the paragraph?

A. 4 B. 6
C. 3 D. 2
E. 5

24. Which sentence should come **second** in the paragraph?

A. 3 B. 1
C. 4 D. 6
E. 5

25. Which sentence should come **last** (*i.e.* **sixth**) in the paragraph?

A. 5 B. 4
C. 2 D. 1
E. 3

SET-6

1. Akash was shocked when he realised that the leg had lost sensation.
2. When he tried to get up, he felt his left leg was very heavy.
3. He had to lie down hopelessly, till he saw a flashlight.
4. It was an odd night time and hence nobody heard his voice.
5. Due to sudden sprain Akash fell down.
6. Nervous with this realisation, he called out for help.

26. Which of the following should be the **third** sentence?

A. 1 B. 2
C. 3 D. 4
E. 5

27. Which of the following should be the **sixth (last)** sentence?

A. 6 B. 5
C. 4 D. 3
E. 2

28. Which of the following should be the **first** sentence?

A. 1 B. 2
C. 3 D. 4
E. 5

29. Which of the following should be the **second** sentence?

A. 1 B. 2
C. 3 D. 4
E. 5

30. Which of the following should be the **fourth** sentence?
A. 1 B. 2
C. 6 D. 4
E. 5

SET-7

1. The history of mankind is full of such fightings between communities, nation and people.
2. From the primitive weapons of warfare, man has advanced to the modern nuclear weapons.
3. Ever since the dawn of civilisation man has been fighting with man.
4. A modern war is scientific in character, but the effect is the same wiping human existence out of this earth.
5. The only difference now seems to be in the efficiency of the instruments used for killing each other.

31. Which of the following should be the **fifth (last)** sentence?
A. 1 B. 2
C. 3 D. 4
E. 5

32. Which of the following should be the **fourth** sentence?
A. 1 B. 2
C. 3 D. 4
E. 5

33. Which of the following should be the **first** sentence?
A. 1 B. 2
C. 3 D. 4
E. 5

34. Which of the following should be the **second** sentence?
A. 1 B. 2
C. 3 D. 4
E. 5

35. Which of the following should be the **third** sentence?
A. 1 B. 2
C. 3 D. 4
E. 5

SET-8

1. Its current was very powerful and could take away big tree trunks.
2. There were some children, playing on the bank of the waterway.
3. In the forest of Bharatpur, there is a big lake.
4. The excess water started flowing forcefully through the waterway.
5. Once there was a very heavy rain because of which the lake started overflowing.
6. A poor man noticed it and rushed to save them.

36. Which of the following should be the **first** sentence?
A. 6 B. 5
C. 4 D. 3
E. 2

37. Which of the following should be the **third** sentence?
A. 6 B. 5
C. 4 D. 3
E. 2

38. Which of the following should be the **sixth (last)** sentence?
A. 6 B. 5
C. 4 D. 3
E. 2

39. Which of the following should be the **fourth** sentence?
A. 5 B. 4
C. 3 D. 2
E. 1

40. Which of the following should be the **second** sentence?
A. 6 B. 5
C. 4 D. 3
E. 2

SET-9

1. The means and methods they employ to deal with public pressures are also different.
2. They will make no move unless the gallery is packed.
3. The poorest are over-hesitant, evasive and preoccupied with their relationships with others.

4. Enormous difference is generally observed in the ways in which various public officials respond to public pressures.
5. The best possess understanding of the forces that must be taken into account, determination not to be swerved from the path of public interest.
6. They confront all embarrasments with a stale general formula.

41. Which of the following should be the **third** sentence?
A. 1 B. 2
C. 3 D. 4
E. 5

42. Which of the following should be the **sixth (last)** sentence?
A. 2 B. 3
C. 4 D. 5
E. 6

43. Which of the following should be the **first** sentence?
A. 6 B. 5
C. 4 D. 3
E. 2

44. Which of the following should be the **second** sentence?
A. 1 B. 2
C. 3 D. 4
E. 5

45. Which of the following should be the **fourth** sentence?
A. 2 B. 3
C. 4 D. 5
E. 6

SET-10

1. A taxi was summoned and Raju was taken to Lifeline Hospital.
2. While hurrying home from school.
3. Since they did not succeed, they decided to take him to a hospital.
4. When Raju opened his eyes, he found himself surrounded by doctors and nurses.
5. Some people rushed towards him and tried to bring him to his senses.
6. He was thrown a couple of feet away and lost consciousness.

46. Which sentence should come **third** in the paragraph?
A. 6 B. 2
C. 5 D. 1
E. 4

47. Which sentence should come **fourth** in the paragraph?
A. 3 B. 5
C. 6 D. 2
E. 1

48. Which sentence should come **first** in the paragraph?
A. 4 B. 6
C. 2 D. 5
E. 3

49. Which sentence should come **last** (*i.e.*, **sixth**) in the paragraph?
A. 2 B. 3
C. 1 D. 4
E. 5

50. Which sentence should come **second** in the paragraph?
A. 5 B. 1
C. 4 D. 3
E. 6

SET-11

1. But by then it was too late to correct things.
2. It is impossible to steer such a large project to success without planning.
3. He had to stand by and watch helplessly.
4. The whole scheme was destined, to fail from the beginning.
5. Bhaskar started realising this only towards the end.

51. Which sentence should come **first** in the paragraph
A. 1 B. 2
C. 3 D. 4
E. 5

52. Which sentence should come **third** in the paragraph?
A. 1 B. 2
C. 3 D. 4
E. 5

53. Which sentence should come **last** in the paragraph?
A. 1 B. 2
C. 3 D. 4
E. 5

54. Which sentence should come **second** in the paragraph?
A. 1 B. 2
C. 3 D. 4
E. 5

55. Which sentence should come **fourth** in the paragraph?
A. 1 B. 2
C. 3 D. 4
E. 5

SET-12

1. John did not have the money to buy the beautiful clip.
2. After a while, Jane explained to John that she had sold her hair to buy a gold chain for his watch.
3. As it was Christmas, John wanted to give Jane a surprise present.
4. When Jane saw it, she felt like crying.
5. He decided to present her a clip made of ivory for her long flowing hair.
6. He, therefore, sold off his watch and brought home the present.

56. Which of the sentences should come **last** in the paragraph?
A. 5 B. 4
C. 1 D. 3
E. 2

57. Which of the sentences should come **first** in the paragraph?
A. 3 B. 6
C. 2 D. 5
E. 4

58. Which of the sentences should come **second** in the paragraph?
A. 6 B. 1
C. 5 D. 4
E. 3

59. Which of the sentences should come **third** in the paragraph?
A. 4 B. 5
C. 6 D. 2
E. 1

60. Which of the sentences should come **fourth** in the paragraph?
A. 1 B. 2
C. 3 D. 6
E. 5

ANSWERS

1	**2**	**3**	**4**	**5**	**6**	**7**	**8**	**9**	**10**
A	D	C	B	E	B	E	A	D	C
11	**12**	**13**	**14**	**15**	**16**	**17**	**18**	**19**	**20**
B	E	D	C	A	D	B	C	A	E
21	**22**	**23**	**24**	**25**	**26**	**27**	**28**	**29**	**30**
B	A	D	C	E	A	D	E	B	C
31	**32**	**33**	**34**	**35**	**36**	**37**	**38**	**39**	**40**
E	D	C	A	B	D	C	A	D	B
41	**42**	**43**	**44**	**45**	**46**	**47**	**48**	**49**	**50**
C	E	C	A	D	C	A	C	D	E
51	**52**	**53**	**54**	**55**	**56**	**57**	**58**	**59**	**60**
D	E	C	B	A	E	A	C	E	D

9

Spelling Errors

The most common errors in English are of spellings of words. Even the most learned men are sometimes confused about the correct spellings of some words. One must keep and use a dictionary religiously. Never ignore and let pass a new word casually.

A number of question to test your knowledge of spellings are compiled here. Try to solve as many as you can.

Multiple Choice Questions

Directions: *Find the correctly spelt word out of the four options in each question. If none of the words is correctly spelt, mark 'E' as your answer.*

1. A. Accompalish B. Ackmplesh
C. Acomplush D. Accomplish
E. None of these

2. A. Acommodation B. Acomodation
C. Accomodation D. Accommodation
E. None of these

3. A. Astonished B. Astronished
C. Astoneshed D. Asstonished
E. None of these

4. A. Benefeted B. Benefitted
C. Benifited D. Benefited
E. None of these

5. A. Belligerent B. Beligirent
C. Belligarant D. Belligerrent
E. None of these

6. A. Chancelery B. Chancellery
C. Chancellary D. Chancelary
E. None of these

7. A. Discriminate B. Discremineta
C. Discrimenate D. Discriminat
E. None of these

8. A. Damage B. Dammage
C. Damaige D. Dammege
E. None of these

9. A. Efficiant B. Effecient
C. Efficient D. Eficient
E. None of these

10. A. Extravagant B. Extreragent
C. Extreregant D. Extravegent
E. None of these

11. A. Efflorascence B. Eflorescene
C. Effllorescence D. Efflorescence
E. None of these

12. A. Equinimity B. Equanimmity
C. Equannimity D. Equanimity
E. None of these

13. A. Farmament B. Farmement
C. Fermament D. Fremament
E. None of these

14. A. Grieff B. Grief
C. Grieef D. Grrief
E. None of these

15. A. Guarantee B. Garuntee
C. Guaruntee D. Gaurantee
E. None of these

16. A. Hypocritical B. Hypocretical
C. Hypocriticel D. Hypocirticel
E. None of these

17. A. Humurous B. Humorous
C. Humoreus D. Humorrous
E. None of these

18. A. Itenerary B. Itinarery
C. Itinarary D. Itinerary
E. None of these

19. A. Indipenseble B. Indispansible
C. Indispensable D. Indipensable
E. None of these

20. A. Imprecticability B. Impracticebility
C. Impracticibility D. Impracticability
E. None of these

21. A. Incradulous B. Incredulous
C. Incridulous D. Incredalous
E. None of these

22. A. Juddicious B. Judiceous
C. Judicious D. Judiceus
E. None of these

23. A. Kleptomonia B. Kleptemonia
C. Kleptomania D. Klaptomania
E. None of these

24. A. Lackdaisical B. Lackadaisical
C. Lckadaisicle D. Lackadisical
E. None of these

25. A. Licentious B. Licontious
C. Licenttious D. Licientious
E. None of these

26. A. Meddicine B. Medicine
C. Medicene D. Medicinne
E. None of these

27. A. Meritricious B. Merefrecious
C. Meretricious D. Merritricious
E. None of these

28. A. Missunderstood B. Miesunderstood
C. Misunderstood D. Misunderstod
E. None of these

29. A. Occurad B. Occurred
C. Ocurred D. Occured
E. None of these

30. A. Osttentatious B. Ostentetious
C. Ostentatious D. Ostenttatious
E. None of these

31. A. Obnosious B. Obnoxeous
C. Obnoxious D. Obnoseous
E. None of these

32. A. Omenous B. Ominous
C. Ommineous D. Omineous
E. None of these

33. A. Pecification B. Pacification
C. Pecifacation D. Pecefication
E. None of these

34. A. Prograssive B. Progressive
C. Progresive D. Prograsive
E. None of these

35. A. Pasiveness B. Passiveness
C. Passeveniss D. Passivines
E. None of these

36. A. Polyendry B. Poliendry
C. Pollyendry D. Polyandry
E. None of these

37. A. Puerille B. Puerrile
C. Puerile D. Purrile
E. None of these

38. A. Pesanger B. Passenger
C. Pessenger D. Pasanger
E. None of these

39. A. Querrelsome B. Quarrelsame
C. Quarrelsome D. Querralsome
E. None of these

40. A. Rigourous B. Rigerous
C. Rigorous D. Regerous
E. None of these

41. A. Survellance B. Surveilance
C. Surveillance D. Survaillance
E. None of these

42. A. Schedule B. Schdule
C. Schedale D. Schedeule
E. None of these

43. A. Sepalchrle B. Sepalchral
C. Sepulchrle D. Sepulchral
E. None of these

44. A. Sympathetic B. Smypathetic
C. Sympothetic D. Sympethetic
E. None of these

45. A. Sincerely B. Sencerely
C. Sincerelly D. Sincerrely
E. None of these

46. A. Satellite B. Sattellite
C. Satelite D. Sattelite
E. None of these

47. A. Teracherous B. Treacherous
C. Treacheraus D. Treachereans
E. None of these

48. A. Uncivilized B. Uncevilized
C. Uncivillized D. Uncevelized
E. None of these

49. A. Vainglorious B. Vaniglorious
C. Vaniglerious D. Vaingloreus
E. None of these

50. A. Vulnarable B. Valnerable
C. Velnerable D. Vulnerable
E. None of these

51. A. Valuptuous B. Volluptous
C. Voluptuous D. Volupttuous
E. None of these

52. A. Veneration B. Venration
C. Venneration D. Venerration
E. None of these

53. A. Tacciturnity B. Taciturnity
C. Taciturrnity D. Tacitturnity
E. None of these

54. A. Tranquilitty B. Tranquility
C. Trenquility D. Tranquillity
E. None of these

55. A. Tranquil B. Trenquil
C. Tranquel D. Trinquil
E. None of these

56. A. Neggardly B. Nigardly
C. Niggerdly D. Niggardly
E. None of these

57. A. Quadruplets B. Quedruplets
C. Quadroplets D. Quadruplats
E. None of these

58. A. Schezophrenia B. Schizaphrenia
C. Schizophrenia D. Schizophrania
E. None of these

59. A. Transperency B. Transparency
C. Transpirency D. Tranporency
E. None of these

60. A. Superanuation B. Superennuation
C. Superannuation D. Superannuetion
E. None of these

ANSWERS

1	**2**	**3**	**4**	**5**	**6**	**7**	**8**	**9**	**10**
D	D	A	B	A	C	A	A	C	A
11	**12**	**13**	**14**	**15**	**16**	**17**	**18**	**19**	**20**
D	D	C	B	A	A	B	D	C	D
21	**22**	**23**	**24**	**25**	**26**	**27**	**28**	**29**	**30**
B	C	C	B	A	B	C	C	B	C
31	**32**	**33**	**34**	**35**	**36**	**37**	**38**	**39**	**40**
C	B	B	B	B	D	C	B	C	C
41	**42**	**43**	**44**	**45**	**46**	**47**	**48**	**49**	**50**
C	A	D	A	A	A	B	A	A	D
51	**52**	**53**	**54**	**55**	**56**	**57**	**58**	**59**	**60**
C	A	B	B	A	D	A	C	B	C

ARITHMETIC

1. NUMBERS

The development of the number system started with natural numbers. These are generally known as counting numbers.

Natural Numbers

Numbers which start from 1 are known as natural numbers. It is denoted by N. The smallest natural number is 1. It is written as,

$$N = \{1, 2, 3, ..., \infty\}$$

Whole Numbers

A number which starts from zero (0) is known as whole number. It is denoted by W. It is written as,

$$W = \{0, 1, 2, 3, ..., \infty\}$$

Integers

Natural numbers along with 0 and their negatives are known as integers. It is denoted by I. It is written as,

$$I = \{..., -4, -3, -2, -1, 0, 1, 2, 3, 4, ...\}$$

Even Numbers

A number which is divisible by 2 is known as even numbers.

Such as, 2, 4, 6, 10, 12, 128, 432 etc.

Odd Numbers

A number which is not divisible by 2 is known as odd numbers:

Such as, 1, 3, 5, 7, 9, 11, 13, 21, 29, 123 etc.

Prime Numbers

A number which is divided by itself is known as prime numbers. The smallest prime number is 2.

Such as, 2, 3, 5, 7, 11, 13, 17, 19, 23, ... etc.

Composite Numbers

A number which is divided by itself and others also is known as composite numbers. The smallest composite number is 4.

Such as, 4, 6, 8, 9, 10, 12, 14, 15, 16, 18, ... etc.

There are 25 prime numbers between 1 to 100.

Such as, 2, 3, 5, 7, 11, 13, 17, 19, 23, 29, 31, 37, 41, 43, 47, 53, 59, 61, 67, 71, 73, 79, 83, 89, 97.

Test, whether a given number is prime or composite: If we want to test any number more than 100, whether it is prime or not, take an integer larger than the approximate square root of that number. Let it be x. Test the divisibility of the given number by every prime number less than x. If it is not divisible by any of them, then it is prime; otherwise it is composite number.

EXAMPLE: Which of the following numbers are prime numbers?

(*i*) 421 (*ii*) 671

SOLUTION:

(*i*) The square root of 421 is nearly 21.
Prime numbers less than 21 are 2, 3, 5, 7, 11, 13, 17, 19. Clearly, 421 is not divisible by any of them. So, 421 is a prime number.

(*ii*) The square root of 671 is nearly 26.
Prime numbers less than 26 are 2, 3, 5, 7, 11, 13, 17, 19, 23. Out of these, 671 is divisible by 11. So, 671 is not a prime number. Hence it is composite number.

The formulae given below are quite useful for quick multiplication:

(*i*) $(a + b)^2 = a^2 + 2ab + b^2$

(*ii*) $(a - b)^2 = a^2 - 2ab + b^2$

(*iii*) $a^2 - b^2 = (a + b)(a - b)$

(*iv*) $a^2 + b^2 = (a + b)^2 - 2ab$

(*v*) $(a + b)^3 = a^3 + b^3 + 3ab(a + b)$

(*vi*) $(a - b)^3 = a^3 - b^3 - 3ab(a - b)$

(*vii*) $a^3 + b^3 = (a + b)(a^2 - ab + b^2)$

(*viii*) $a^3 - b^3 = (a - b)(a^2 + ab + b^2)$

EXAMPLE: Simplify the following.

(*i*) $\dfrac{348 \times 348 \times 348 + 252 \times 252 \times 252}{348 \times 348 - 348 \times 252 + 252 \times 252}$

(*ii*) $\dfrac{261 \times 261 \times 261 - 77 \times 77 \times 77}{261 \times 261 + 261 \times 77 + 77 \times 77}$

SOLUTION:

(*i*) $\dfrac{348 \times 348 \times 348 + 252 \times 252 \times 252}{348 \times 348 - 348 \times 252 + 252 \times 252}$

Let $348 = a$

and $252 = b$

$\therefore$ Given expression is written as

$$\frac{a \times a \times a + b \times b \times b}{a \times a - a \times b + b \times b} = \frac{a^3 + b^3}{a^2 - ab + b^2}$$

$$= \frac{(a+b)(a^2 - ab + b^2)}{(a^2 - ab + b^2)} = a + b$$

$= 348 + 252 = 600.$

(*ii*) $\dfrac{261 \times 261 \times 261 - 77 \times 77 \times 77}{261 \times 261 + 261 \times 77 + 77 \times 77}$

Let $261 = a$

and $77 = b$

$$\therefore \quad \frac{a^3 - b^3}{a^2 + ab + b^2} = \frac{(a-b)(a^2 + ab + b^2)}{(a^2 + ab + b^2)} = a - b$$

$\therefore \quad 261 - 77 = 184.$

If we divide a given number by another number, then

Dividend = (Divisor × Quotient) + Remainder

EXAMPLE: On dividing 18254 by a certain number, the quotient is 289 and the remainder is 47. Find the divisor.

SOLUTION: Here, Dividend = 18254

quotient = 289

remainder = 47

$$\therefore \quad \text{Divisor} = \frac{\text{Dividend} - \text{Remainder}}{\text{Quotient}}$$

$$= \frac{18254 - 47}{289} = \frac{18207}{289} = 63$$

Hence, divisor = 63.

EXAMPLE: What least number must be subtracted from 862 to get a number exactly divisible by 31?

SOLUTION: On dividing 862 by 31, the remainder obtained is 25.

Hence, the required number = 25.

MULTIPLE CHOICE QUESTIONS

1. The face value of 8 in the numeral 458926 is:

A. 8000 B. 8

C. 1000 D. 458000

2. $106 \times 106 + 94 \times 94 = x$, the value of x is:

A. 21032 B. 20032

C. 23032 D. 20072

3. If $m \times 48 = 173 \times 240$ then the value of m is:

A. 545 B. 685

C. 865 D. 495

4. $\left(1 - \dfrac{1}{3}\right)\left(1 - \dfrac{1}{4}\right)\left(1 - \dfrac{1}{5}\right)\ldots\left(1 - \dfrac{1}{n}\right) = x$

then the value of x is:

A. $\dfrac{1}{n}$ B. $\dfrac{2}{n}$

C. $\dfrac{2(n-1)}{n}$ D. $\dfrac{2}{n(n+1)}$

5. When simplified the product

$\left(2 - \dfrac{1}{3}\right)\left(2 - \dfrac{3}{5}\right)\left(2 - \dfrac{5}{7}\right)\ldots\left(2 - \dfrac{997}{999}\right)$ is

equal to:

A. $\dfrac{5}{999}$ B. $\dfrac{1001}{999}$

C. $\dfrac{1001}{3}$ D. None of these

6. Which number should replace both the asterisks in $\left(\frac{*}{21}\right) \times \left(\frac{*}{189}\right) = 1$?

A. 21 B. 63
C. 3969 D. 147

7. In a division sum, the divisor is 12 times the quotient and 5 times the remainder. If the remainder be 48, then the dividend is:

A. 240 B. 576
C. 4800 D. 4848

8. What least number must be subtracted from 1294 so that the remainder when divided by 9, 11, 13 will leave in each case the same remainder 6?

A. 0 B. 1
C. 2 D. 3

9. If $\sqrt{\left(1+\frac{27}{169}\right)} = \left(1+\frac{x}{13}\right)$, then the value of x is:

A. 1 B. 3
C. 5 D. 7

10. If $\frac{x}{y} = \frac{3}{4}$, then the value of $\left(\frac{6}{7}+\frac{y-x}{y+x}\right)$ equals:

A. $\frac{5}{7}$ B. $1\frac{1}{7}$
C. 1 D. 2

11. The largest natural number by which the product of three consecutive even natural numbers is always divisible, is:

A. 16 B. 24
C. 48 D. 96

12. The least number of five digits which is exactly divisible by 12, 15 and 18 is:

A. 10080 B. 10800
C. 18000 D. 81000

13. The least number which when divided by 8, 9, 12, 16 and 20 leaves the same remainder 1 in each case is:

A. 712 B. 271
C. 721 D. 720

14. The value of 0.8693 + 0.092 + 0.87 + 0.4 equals:

A. 2.3213 B. 2.2331
C. 3.2313 D. 2.2313

15. The prime numbers between 1 to 50 are:

A. 8 B. 12
C. 15 D. 10

ANSWERS

1	2	3	4	5	6	7	8	9	10
B	D	C	B	C	B	D	B	A	C
11	**12**	**13**	**14**	**15**					
C	A	C	D	C					

EXPLANATORY ANSWERS

1. The face value of 8 in the numeral 458926 is 8.

2. $106 \times 106 + 94 \times 94 = x$

$\Rightarrow \quad (106)^2 + (94)^2 = x$

$\Rightarrow \quad (100+6)^2 + (100-6)^2 = x$

$\Rightarrow \quad 10000 + 1200 + 36 + 10000 - 1200 + 36 = x$

$\Rightarrow \quad 20072 = x$

$\Rightarrow \quad x = 20072.$

3. $\because \ m = \frac{173 \times 240}{48} = 865.$

4. $\left(1-\frac{1}{3}\right)\left(1-\frac{1}{4}\right)\left(1-\frac{1}{5}\right)...\left(1-\frac{1}{n}\right) = x$

$\because \quad 1-\frac{1}{3} = \frac{3-1}{3} = \frac{2}{3}$

$$1-\frac{1}{4}=\frac{4-1}{4}=\frac{3}{4}$$

$$1-\frac{1}{5}=\frac{5-1}{5}=\frac{4}{5}$$

$$\vdots$$

$$1-\frac{1}{n}=\frac{n-1}{n}$$

$$\therefore \frac{2}{3}\times\frac{3}{4}\times\frac{4}{5}\times\ldots\times\frac{n-2}{n-1}\times\frac{n-1}{n}=\frac{2}{n}$$

5. $\left(2-\frac{1}{3}\right)\left(2-\frac{3}{5}\right)\left(2-\frac{5}{7}\right)\ldots\left(2-\frac{997}{999}\right)$

$$2-\frac{1}{3}=\frac{6-1}{3}=\frac{5}{3}$$

$$2-\frac{3}{5}=\frac{10-3}{5}=\frac{7}{5}$$

$$2-\frac{5}{7}=\frac{14-5}{7}=\frac{9}{7}$$

$$2-\frac{997}{999}=\frac{1998-997}{999}=\frac{1001}{999}$$

$$\therefore \frac{5}{3}\times\frac{7}{5}\times\frac{9}{7}\times\ldots\times\frac{999}{997}\times\frac{1001}{999}=\frac{1001}{3}$$

6. $\frac{*}{21}\times\frac{*}{189}=1$

$$\frac{x^2}{21\times189}=1$$

$\Rightarrow$ $x^2 = 21\times189 = 21\times21\times9$

$\Rightarrow$ $x^2 = 21\times21\times3\times3$

$\Rightarrow$ $x = 21\times3 = 63$

7. Let quotient = Q and remainder = R

Then, divisor = 12Q = 5R

Now, R = 48

$\Rightarrow$ 12Q = 5 × 48 $\Rightarrow$ Q = 20

$\therefore$ Dividend = (20 × 240 + 48) = 4848

8. The number when divided by 9, 11, 13 leaving remainder 6 = (LCM of 9, 11, 13) + 6 = 1293

$\therefore$ Required number = (1294 – 1293) = 1

9. $\sqrt{\left(1+\frac{27}{169}\right)}=\left(1+\frac{x}{13}\right)$

$\Rightarrow$ $\sqrt{\frac{169+27}{169}}=\frac{13+x}{13}$

$\Rightarrow$ $\sqrt{\frac{196}{169}}=\frac{x+13}{13}$

$\Rightarrow$ $\frac{14}{13}=\frac{x+13}{13}$

$\Rightarrow$ $x+13=14$

$\Rightarrow$ $x=1$

10. $\because \frac{x}{y}=\frac{3}{4}$ then,

$$\frac{6}{7}+\frac{y-x}{y+x}=\frac{6}{7}+\frac{\frac{y}{y}-\frac{x}{y}}{\frac{y}{y}+\frac{x}{y}}$$

[Divide numerator and denominator by y.]

$$=\frac{6}{7}+\frac{1-\frac{3}{4}}{1+\frac{3}{4}}=\frac{6}{7}+\frac{\frac{1}{4}}{\frac{7}{4}}=\frac{6}{7}+\frac{1}{7}=\frac{7}{7}=1$$

11. It is 2 × 4 × 6 = 48

12. Least number of 5 digits is 10000.

LCM of 12, 15, 18 is 180.

On dividing 10000 by 180, the remainder is 100.

$\therefore$ The least number = 10000 + (180 – 100) = 10080.

13. Least number = (LCM of 8, 9, 12, 16, 20) + 1

2	8,	9,	12,	16,	20
2	4,	9,	6,	8,	10
2	2,	9,	3,	4,	5
3	1,	9,	3,	2,	5
	1,	3,	1,	2,	5

$\therefore$ LCM = $2^4\times3^2\times5$ = 720

Hence, least number = (720 + 1) = 721.

14.

```
  0.8693
  0.092
  0.87
+ 0.4
  2.2313
```

$\therefore$ The value of 0.8693 + 0.092 + 0.87 + 0.4 = 2.2313.

15. The prime numbers between 1 to 50 are 2, 3, 5, 7, 11, 13, 17, 19, 23, 29, 31, 37, 41, 43, 47.

Hence, there are 15 prime numbers between 1 to 50.

2. HCF AND LCM

FACTORS

The numbers are said to be factors of a given number when they exactly divide that number.

Example: Factors of 15 are 1, 3, 5 and 15 because each of these completely divides 15.

Highest Common Factor

The HCF of two or more than two numbers is the greatest number that divides each of them exactly. The highest common factor is also known as Greatest Common Divisor or Greatest Common Measure.

EXAMPLE: Let us consider two numbers 24 and 36. All possible factors of 24 are 1, 2, 3, 4, 6, 8, 12 and 24. All possible factors of 36 are 1, 2, 3, 4, 6, 9, 12, 18 and 36. The common factors of 24 and 36 are 1, 2, 3, 4, 6, 12. The greatest factor among these common factors is 12.

Hence, 12 is the HCF of 24 and 36.

EXAMPLE: Let us consider two numbers 18 and 30.

Now, $18 = 2 \times 3 \times 3$

and $30 = 2 \times 3 \times 5$

The factors common to the two numbers are 2 and 3. Hence the required HCF $= 2 \times 3 = 6$.

There are two methods of determining the HCF of two or more numbers.

(*i*) HCF by Factorization method

(*ii*) HCF by Division method.

HCF by Factorization Method

Express each one of the given number as the product of prime factors. Now choose common factors and take the product of these factors to obtain the required HCF.

EXAMPLE: Find the HCF of 126, 396 and 5400.

SOLUTION: $126 = 2 \times 3 \times 3 \times 7$

$396 = 2 \times 2 \times 3 \times 3 \times 11$

$5400 = 2 \times 2 \times 2 \times 3 \times 3 \times 3 \times 5 \times 5$

Common factors are 2, 3 and 3.

Hence, the HCF $= 2 \times 3 \times 3 = 18$.

EXAMPLE: Find the HCF of 1056, 1584 and 2178.

SOLUTION: $1056 = 2^5 \times 3 \times 11$

$1584 = 2^4 \times 3^2 \times 11$

and $2178 = 2 \times 3^2 \times 11^2$

Hence, HCF $= (2 \times 3 \times 11) = 66$.

HCF by Division Method

Suppose we have to find the HCF of two given numbers. Divide the larger number by the smaller one. Now, divide the divisor by the remainder. Repeat the process of dividing the preceding divisor by the remainder last obtained till zero is obtained as remainder. The last divisor is the required HCF.

Suppose we have to find the HCF of three numbers. Then HCF of [(HCF of any two numbers) and (the third number)] gives the HCF of three given numbers. Similarly, the HCF of more than three numbers may be obtained.

EXAMPLE: Find the HCF of 48, 168 and 324.

SOLUTION: Firstly, we find the HCF of 48 and 168.

```
48) 1 6 8 (3
  - 1 4 4
    -------
     2 4) 4 8 (2
          4 8
          ---
           0
          ---
```

Thus, HCF of 48 and 168 = 24.

Now, we find the HCF of 24 and 324.

```
24) 3 2 4 (13
  − 2 4
    8 4
  − 7 2
    1 2) 2 4 (2
         2 4
          0
```

Thus, the HCF of 48, 168 and 324 is 12.

Lowest Common Multiple

The LCM of two or more numbers is the lowest or least number which is exactly divisible by each of them. In other words, it is the lowest number which contains each of them as a factor.

LCM by Factorization

Resolve each one of the given numbers into a product of prime factors. Then LCM is the product of highest powers of all the factors.

Example: Find the LCM of 72, 189 and 1026.

Solution: $72 = 2^3 \times 3^2$

$189 = 3^3 \times 7$

and $1026 = 2 \times 3^3 \times 19$

$\therefore$ $\text{LCM} = 2^3 \times 3^3 \times 7 \times 19$

$= 8 \times 27 \times 7 \times 19 = 28728$

Example: Find the LCM of 12, 15, 20 and 54 by short cut method.

Solution:

2	12,	15,	20,	54
2	6,	15,	10,	27
3	3,	15,	5,	27
5	1,	5,	5,	9
	1,	1,	1,	9

$\therefore$ LCM $= 2 \times 2 \times 3 \times 5 \times 9 = 540$

FORMULA

Product of two numbers = HCF × LCM.

$$\text{LCM} = \frac{\text{Product of numbers}}{\text{HCF}}$$

$$\text{HCF} = \frac{\text{Product of numbers}}{\text{LCM}}$$

$$\text{First number} = \frac{\text{LCM} \times \text{HCF}}{\text{2nd number}}$$

$$\text{2nd number} = \frac{\text{LCM} \times \text{HCF}}{\text{First number}}$$

HCF and LCM of Fractions

(*i*) $\text{HCF} = \dfrac{\text{HCF of numerators}}{\text{LCM of denominators}}$

(*ii*) $\text{LCM} = \dfrac{\text{LCM of numerators}}{\text{HCF of denominators}}$

Example: Find the HCF and LCM of $\frac{3}{4}, \frac{6}{8}, \frac{15}{64}$ and $\frac{12}{32}$.

Solution: $\text{HCF} = \dfrac{\text{HCF of 3, 6, 15, 12}}{\text{LCM of 4, 8, 64, 32}} = \dfrac{3}{64}$

$\text{LCM} = \dfrac{\text{LCM of 3, 6, 15, 12}}{\text{HCF of 4, 8, 64, 32}} = \dfrac{60}{4}.$

MULTIPLE CHOICE QUESTIONS

1. HCF of 1485 and 4356 is:
A. 189 B. 89
C. 99 D. 83

2. LCM of 18, 24, 42, 63 is:
A. 302 B. 604
C. 504 D. 404

3. Which of the following fractions is the greatest of all?

$$\frac{7}{8}, \frac{6}{7}, \frac{4}{5}, \frac{5}{6}$$

A. $\frac{6}{7}$ B. $\frac{4}{5}$
C. $\frac{5}{6}$ D. $\frac{7}{8}$

4. Which of the following is in ascending order?
A. $\frac{5}{7}, \frac{7}{8}, \frac{9}{11}$ B. $\frac{5}{7}, \frac{9}{11}, \frac{7}{8}$
C. $\frac{7}{8}, \frac{5}{7}, \frac{9}{11}$ D. $\frac{9}{11}, \frac{7}{8}, \frac{5}{7}$

5. HCF of three numbers is 12. If they be in the ratio 1 : 2 : 3, the numbers are:
A. 12, 24, 36 B. 10, 20, 30
C. 5, 10, 15 D. 4, 8, 12

6. The largest natural number which exactly divides the product of any four consecutive natural numbers is:
A. 6 B. 12
C. 24 D. 120

7. The traffic lights at three different road crossings change after every 48 seconds, 72 seconds and 108 seconds respectively. If they all change simultaneously at 8 : 20 : 00 hrs; then they will again change simultaneously at:
A. 8 : 27 : 12 hrs B. 8 : 27 : 24 hrs
C. 8 : 27 : 36 hrs D. 8 : 27 : 48 hrs

8. The HCF of two numbers is 16 and their LCM is 160. If one of the number is 32, then the other number is:
A. 48 B. 80
C. 96 D. 112

9. The HCF of two numbers is 12 and their difference is also 12. The numbers are:
A. 66, 78 B. 70, 82
C. 94, 106 D. 84, 96

10. The largest number which exactly divides 210, 315, 147 and 161 is:
A. 3 B. 7
C. 21 D. 4410

11. The least perfect square number which is divisible by 3, 4, 5, 6 and 8 is:
A. 900 B. 1200
C. 2500 D. 3600

12. The smallest number which is divisible by 12, 15, 20 and is a perfect square, is:
A. 400 B. 900
C. 1600 D. 3600

13. The sum of two numbers is 216 and their HCF is 27. The numbers are:
A. 54, 162 B. 108, 108
C. 27, 189 D. None of these

14. The HCF and LCM of two numbers are 44 and 264 respectively. If the first number is divided by 2, the quotient is 44. The other number is:
A. 33 B. 66
C. 132 D. 264

15. The number of prime factors in $2^{222} \times 3^{333} \times 5^{555}$ is:
A. 3 B. 1107
C. 1110 D. 1272

16. The number of prime factors in the expression $(6)^{10} \times (7)^{17} \times (11)^{27}$ is:
A. 54 B. 64
C. 71 D. 81

17. Three measuring rods are 64 cm, 80 cm and 96 cm in length. The least length of cloth that can be measured exact number of times using any one of the above rod is:
A. 0.96 m B. 19.20 m
C. 9.60 m D. 96.00 m

18. The product of two numbers is 1600 and their HCF is 5. The LCM of the numbers is:
A. 320 B. 1605
C. 1595 D. 8000

19. About the number of pairs which have 16 as their HCF and 136 as their LCM, we can definitely say that:
A. Only one such pair exists
B. Only two such pairs exist
C. Many such pairs exist
D. No such pair exist

20. The total number of prime factors of the product $(8)^{20} \times (15)^{24} \times (7)^{15}$ is:
A. 59 B. 98
C. 123 D. 138

ANSWERS

1	2	3	4	5	6	7	8	9	10
C	C	D	B	A	C	A	B	D	B
11	**12**	**13**	**14**	**15**	**16**	**17**	**18**	**19**	**20**
D	D	C	C	C	B	C	A	D	C

EXPLANATORY ANSWERS

1.
```
1485) 4 3 5 6 (2
      2 9 7 0
      1 3 8 6) 1 4 8 5 (1
               1 3 8 6
                  9 9) 1 3 8 6 (14
                         9 9
                         3 9 6
                         3 9 6
                           0
```
∴ HCF of 1485 and 4356 is 99.

2.

2	18, 24, 42, 63
3	9, 12, 21, 63
3	3, 4, 7, 21
7	1, 4, 7, 7
	1, 4, 1, 1

LCM of 18, 24, 42, 63 = $2 \times 3^2 \times 7 \times 4 = 504$.

3. $\frac{7}{8} = 0.875$, $\frac{6}{7} = 0.857$, $\frac{4}{5} = 0.8$

$\frac{5}{6} = 0.833$

Clearly, 0.875 is the greatest of all.

Hence, $\frac{7}{8}$ is the greatest of all.

4. $\frac{5}{7} = 0.714$, $\frac{7}{8} = 0.875$, $\frac{9}{11} = 0.818$

Now, $0.714 < 0.818 < 0.875$

Hence, $\frac{5}{7} < \frac{9}{11} < \frac{7}{8}$.

5. Let the numbers be x, $2x$ and $3x$.
Then, their HCF = x
According to the question, $x = 12$
∴ The numbers are 12, 24, 36.

6. $1 \times 2 \times 3 \times 4 = 24$
∴ Required number = 24.

7. LCM of 48, 72, 108 = 432
432 seconds = 7 min 12 seconds.
So, the next simultaneous change will take place at 8 : 27 : 12 hrs.

8. Other number = $\frac{\text{LCM} \times \text{HCF}}{\text{One number}} = \frac{160 \times 16}{32} = 80$
Hence, other number = 80.

9. 12 is not the HCF of given options A, B and C.
Hence, D is correct answer.
In 84, 96, 12 is HCF of 84 and 96
Difference of 96 – 84 = 12
So, required numbers are 84 and 96.

10. HCF of 210, 315, 147 and 161 = 7
Hence, the required number = 7.

11.

2	3, 4, 5, 6, 8
2	3, 2, 5, 3, 4
3	3, 1, 5, 3, 2
	1, 1, 5, 1, 2

LCM of 3, 4, 5, 6, 8 = $2 \times 2 \times 3 \times 5 \times 2$
Required number
$= (2 \times 2 \times 3 \times 3 \times 5 \times 5 \times 2 \times 2) = 3600$

12. LCM of 12, 15 and 20 = 60
Hence, required number = $60 \times 60 = 3600$.

13. HCF of 54, 162 = 54
HCF of 108, 108 = 108
HCF of 27, 189 = 27
Hence, required numbers are 27 and 189.

14. According to the question,
First number = $2 \times 44 = 88$
Other number
$= \frac{\text{LCM} \times \text{HCF}}{\text{First number}} = \frac{264 \times 44}{88} = 132$

15. The number of prime factors in the given product = (222 + 333 + 555) = 1110

16. 2, 3, 7, 11 are prime numbers in the given expression. The number of prime factors in the given expression (10 + 10 + 17 + 27) = 64

17. Required length = (LCM of 64, 80, 96) cm
= 960 cm = 9.60 m.

18. LCM = $\frac{\text{Product of numbers}}{\text{HCF}} = \frac{1600}{5} = 320$

19. HCF is always a factor of LCM. So no two numbers exist with HCF = 16 and LCM = 136.

20. Since 2, 3, 5, 7 are prime numbers and the given expression is $(2^3)^{20} \times (3 \times 5)^{24} \times (7)^{15}$ *i.e.* $2^{60} \times 3^{24} \times 5^{24} \times 7^{15}$, so the number of prime factors in the given expression
= (60 + 24 + 24 + 15) = 123

3. SIMPLIFICATION

Simplification means expressing in a simpler form. In order to simplify an expression we use the operations in the following order which is easily remembered as "BODMAS".

(*i*) Bracket (*ii*) Of (*iii*) Division (*iv*) Multiplication (*v*) Addition (*vi*) Subtraction.

'Of' means multiplication but it is operated even before division.

While removing brackets, first of all bar bracket '—' and after that small bracket '( )' is removed. Thereafter curley bracket '{ }' and at last square bracket '[ ]' is removed.

EXAMPLE: Simplify: $100 \div 25 \times 6 + 16 - 32$

SOLUTION: $100 \div 25 \times 6 + 16 - 32$

$= 4 \times 6 + 16 - 32$

$= 24 + 16 - 32$

$= 40 - 32 = 8$

EXAMPLE: Simplify: $54 + 24 \div 4 - 8 \times 5 + 4 \times 3$

SOLUTION: $54 + 24 \div 4 - 8 \times 5 + 4 \times 3$

$= 54 + 6 - 40 + 12$

$= 72 - 40 = 32$

EXAMPLE: Simplify: $10 - \left[6 - \left\{7 - \left(6 - \overline{8-5}\right)\right\}\right]$

SOLUTION: $10 - \left[6 - \left\{7 - \left(6 - 3\right)\right\}\right]$

$= 10 - [6 - \{7 - 3\}]$

$= 10 - [6 - 4] = 10 - 2 = 8.$

EXAMPLE: Simplify: $\dfrac{12 \times 12 \times 12 - 1 \times 1 \times 1}{12 \times 12 + 12 \times 1 + 1 \times 1}$

SOLUTION: Let $a = 12$ and $b = 1$

$$\therefore \quad \frac{a \times a \times a - b \times b \times b}{a \times a + a \times b + b \times b} = \frac{a^3 - b^3}{a^2 + ab + b^2}$$

$$= \frac{(a-b)(a^2 + ab + b^2)}{(a^2 + ab + b^2)}$$

$$= a - b = 12 - 1 = 11$$

EXAMPLE: Simplify:

$$\frac{2.33 \times 2.33 \times 2.33 + 7.67 \times 7.67 \times 7.67}{2.33 \times 2.33 - 2.33 \times 7.67 + 7.67 \times 7.67}$$

SOLUTION: Let $a = 2.33$ and $b = 7.67$

$$\frac{a^3 + b^3}{a^2 - ab + b^2} = \frac{(a+b)(a^2 - ab + b^2)}{(a^2 - ab + b^2)} = (a+b)$$

$$= 2.33 + 7.67 = 10$$

MULTIPLE CHOICE QUESTIONS

1. $\dfrac{48 - 12 \times 3 + 9}{12 - 9 \div 3}$ equals:

A. 3
B. 21
C. $\dfrac{7}{3}$
D. $\dfrac{1}{3}$

2. $\dfrac{69 - 14 \times 3 + 2}{9 \times 5 - (5)^2}$ equals:

A. 1.45
B. 2.75
C. 26.5
D. 265

3. If $\dfrac{17.28 \div x}{3.6 \times 0.2} = 2$ then, the value of x is:

A. 120 B. 1.20
C. 12 D. 0.12

4. $171 \div 19 \times 9$ equals:

A. 0 B. 1
C. 18 D. 81

5. $3120 \div 26 + 13 \times 30$ equals:

A. 2400 B. 3900
C. 536 D. None of these

6. $\dfrac{31}{10} \times \dfrac{3}{10} + \dfrac{7}{5} \div 20$ equals:

A. 0 B. 1
C. 100 D. $\dfrac{107}{200}$

7. The simplification of $1 + \dfrac{1}{2 + \dfrac{1}{1 - \dfrac{1}{3}}}$ yields the result:

A. $\dfrac{2}{7}$ B. $\dfrac{7}{9}$
C. $\dfrac{9}{7}$ D. $\dfrac{13}{7}$

8. The value of $1 + \dfrac{1}{4 \times 3} + \dfrac{1}{4 \times 3^2} + \dfrac{1}{4 \times 3^3}$ up to four places of decimals is:

A. 1.1202 B. 1.1203
C. 1.1204 D. None of these

9. $\dfrac{\dfrac{1}{2} \div 4 + 20}{\dfrac{1}{2} \times 4 + 20}$ equals:

A. $\dfrac{81}{88}$ B. $2\dfrac{3}{11}$
C. $\dfrac{161}{176}$ D. 1

10. $3 \div \left[(8 - 5) \div \left\{(4 - 2) \div \left(2 + \dfrac{8}{13}\right)\right\}\right]$ equals:

A. $\dfrac{13}{17}$ B. $\dfrac{68}{13}$
C. $\dfrac{17}{13}$ D. $\dfrac{13}{68}$

11. $10 - [9 - \{8 - (7 - 6)\}] - 5$ is equal to:

A. –5 B. 1
C. 3 D. 9

12. $\dfrac{\dfrac{1}{5} \div \dfrac{1}{5} \text{ of } \dfrac{1}{5}}{\dfrac{1}{5} \text{ of } \dfrac{1}{5} \div \dfrac{1}{5}}$ is equal to:

A. 1 B. 5
C. $\dfrac{1}{5}$ D. 25

13. The value of $1 + \dfrac{1}{1 + \dfrac{1}{1 + \dfrac{1}{9}}}$ is:

A. $\dfrac{29}{19}$ B. $\dfrac{10}{19}$
C. $\dfrac{29}{10}$ D. $\dfrac{10}{9}$

14. $\dfrac{3}{48}$ is what part of $\dfrac{1}{12}$?

A. $\dfrac{3}{7}$ B. $\dfrac{1}{12}$
C. $\dfrac{4}{3}$ D. None of these

15. How many $\dfrac{1}{8}$ s are there in $37\dfrac{1}{2}$?

A. 300 B. 400
C. 500 D. None of these

ANSWERS

1	2	3	4	5	6	7	8	9	10
C	A	C	D	D	B	C	B	C	A
11	**12**	**13**	**14**	**15**					
C	D	A	D	A					

EXPLANATORY ANSWERS

1. $\dfrac{48-12\times3+9}{12-9\div3} = \dfrac{48-36+9}{12-3}$

$= \dfrac{57-36}{9} = \dfrac{21}{9} = \dfrac{7}{3}.$

2. $\dfrac{69-14\times3+2}{9\times5-5^2} = \dfrac{69-42+2}{45-25}$

$= \dfrac{71-42}{20} = \dfrac{29}{20} = 1.45.$

3. $17.28 \div x = 2\times3.6\times0.2$

$\Rightarrow \dfrac{17.28}{x} = 1.44 \Rightarrow 1.44\,x = 17.28$

$\Rightarrow \quad x = \dfrac{17.28}{1.44} = \dfrac{1728}{144} = 12.$

4. $171 \div 19\times9 = 9\times9 = 81.$

5. $3120 \div 26 + 13\times30 = 120 + 390 = 510.$

6. $\dfrac{31}{10}\times\dfrac{3}{10}+\dfrac{7}{5}\div20 = \dfrac{31}{10}\times\dfrac{3}{10}+\dfrac{7}{5}\times\dfrac{1}{20}$

$= \dfrac{93}{100}+\dfrac{7}{100} = \dfrac{93+7}{100} = \dfrac{100}{100} = 1$

7. $1+\cfrac{1}{2+\cfrac{1}{1-\cfrac{1}{3}}} = 1+\cfrac{1}{2+\cfrac{1}{\cfrac{3-1}{3}}}$

$=1+\cfrac{1}{2+\cfrac{1}{\cfrac{2}{3}}} = 1+\cfrac{1}{2+\cfrac{3}{2}} = 1+\cfrac{1}{\cfrac{7}{2}} = 1+\dfrac{2}{7} = \dfrac{9}{7}$

8. $1+\dfrac{1}{4\times3}+\dfrac{1}{4\times3^2}+\dfrac{1}{4\times3^3}$

$= 1+\dfrac{1}{12}+\dfrac{1}{36}+\dfrac{1}{108} = \dfrac{108+9+3+1}{108}$

$= \dfrac{121}{108} = 1.1203$

9. $\dfrac{\frac{1}{2}\div4+20}{\frac{1}{2}\times4+20} = \dfrac{\frac{1}{8}+20}{2+20} = \dfrac{\frac{1+160}{8}}{22}$

$= \dfrac{161}{8\times22} = \dfrac{161}{176}$

10. $3\div\left[(8-5)\div\left\{(4-2)\div\left(2+\dfrac{8}{13}\right)\right\}\right]$

$= 3\div\left[3\div\left\{2\div\dfrac{34}{13}\right\}\right]$

$= 3\div\left[3\div\left\{2\times\dfrac{13}{34}\right\}\right] = 3\div\left[3\div\dfrac{13}{17}\right]$

$= 3\div\left[3\times\dfrac{17}{13}\right] = 3\div\dfrac{51}{13} = 3\times\dfrac{13}{51} = \dfrac{13}{17}$

11. $10-[9-\{8-(7-6)\}]-5$

$= 10-[9-\{8-1\}]-5$

$= 10-[9-7]-5 = 10-2-5 = 10-7 = 3$

12. $\dfrac{\frac{1}{5}\div\frac{1}{5}\text{of}\frac{1}{5}}{\frac{1}{5}\text{of}\frac{1}{5}\div\frac{1}{5}} = \dfrac{\frac{1}{5}\div\frac{1}{25}}{\frac{1}{25}\div\frac{1}{5}} = \dfrac{\frac{1}{5}\times\frac{25}{1}}{\frac{1}{25}\times\frac{5}{1}} = \dfrac{\frac{5}{1}}{\frac{1}{5}}$

$= \dfrac{5}{1}\times\dfrac{5}{1} = 25$

13. $1+\cfrac{1}{1+\cfrac{1}{1+\cfrac{1}{9}}} = 1+\cfrac{1}{1+\cfrac{1}{\cfrac{10}{9}}} = 1+\cfrac{1}{1+\cfrac{9}{10}}$

$= 1+\cfrac{1}{\cfrac{19}{10}} = 1+\dfrac{10}{19} = \dfrac{29}{19}$

14. Let x of $\dfrac{1}{12} = \dfrac{3}{48}$

$\Rightarrow \quad \dfrac{x}{12} = \dfrac{3}{48} \Rightarrow 48x = 36$

$\Rightarrow \quad x = \dfrac{36}{48} = \dfrac{3}{4}.$

15. Let n times $\dfrac{1}{8} = 37\dfrac{1}{2}$

$\Rightarrow \quad \dfrac{n}{8} = \dfrac{75}{2} \Rightarrow 2n = 8\times75$

$\Rightarrow \quad n = \dfrac{8\times75}{2} = 4\times75 = 300.$

4. SURDS AND INDICES

SURDS

If 'a' is a rational number and n is a positive integer such that nth root of 'a', *i.e.*, $a^{1/n}$ or $\sqrt[n]{a}$ is an irrational number, then $a^{1/n}$ is called a surd or radical.

In other words, an irrational root of a rational number is called a surd. The symbol '$\sqrt{}$' is known as surd sign or radical.

For example, $\sqrt{2} = 2^{1/2}$ = Square root of 2

$\sqrt[3]{5} = 5^{1/3}$ = Cube root of 5

Pure and Mixed Surds

Pure Surd: A surd which has unity only as rational factor, the other factor being irrational, is called a pure surd.

For example, $\sqrt{2}$, $\sqrt[3]{3}$, $\sqrt[5]{3}$ are pure surds.

Mixed Surd: A surd which has a rational factor other than unity, the other factor being irrational, is called a mixed surds.

For example, $2\sqrt{5}$ $3\sqrt[4]{7}$, $5\sqrt[3]{11}$ are mixed surds.

Rationalising Factor: When the product of two surds is a rational number, then each of them is called the rationalising factor (R.F.) of the other.

For example, $3\sqrt{5} \times \sqrt{5} = 3 \times 5 = 15$

$\therefore$ $\sqrt{5}$ is a rationalising factor of $3\sqrt{5}$.

Important Formulae Based on Surds

$\sqrt[n]{a} = a^{1/n}$ and it is called a surd of order n.

(*i*) $\sqrt[n]{a^n} = a$

(*ii*) $\sqrt[n]{ab} = \sqrt[n]{a}\,\sqrt[n]{b}$

(*iii*) $\sqrt{a} \times \sqrt{a} = a$

(*iv*) $\sqrt{a} \times \sqrt{b} = \sqrt{ab}$

(*v*) $\sqrt{a^2 b} = a\sqrt{b}$

(*vi*) $\left(\sqrt{a} + \sqrt{b}\right)^2 = a + b + 2\sqrt{ab}$

(*vii*) $\left(\sqrt{a} - \sqrt{b}\right)^2 = a + b - 2\sqrt{ab}$

(*viii*) $\left(\sqrt{a} + \sqrt{b}\right)\left(\sqrt{a} - \sqrt{b}\right) = a - b$ where a and b are positive rational numbers.

INDICES

Let n be a positive integer and 'a' be a real number. The continued product of n factors each equal to a *e.g.*, $a \times a \times a \times \ldots \times n$ times is written as a^n and is called "n^{th} power of a" or "a raised to the power n".

The expression a^n is termed as power function or simply power, a is called the base and n is called index or exponent of the power a^n.

For example, 2^2 = square of 2, 2^3 = cube of 2, etc.

Laws of Indices

(*i*) $a^m \times a^n = a^{m+n}$

(*ii*) $a^m \times a^n \times a^p \times \ldots = a^{m+n+p+\ldots}$

(*iii*) $\dfrac{a^m}{a^n} = a^{m-n}$, if $m > n$

(*iv*) $\dfrac{a^m}{a^n} = \dfrac{1}{a^{n-m}}$, if $m < n$

(*v*) $(a^m)^n = a^{mn}$

(*vi*) $(ab)^n = a^n b^n$

(*vii*) $a^0 = 1$

(*viii*) If $a^m = a^n$ then $m = n$

(*ix*) If $a^m = b^m$ then $a = b$

(*x*) $\dfrac{a^m}{a^m} = a^{m-m} = a^0 = 1$

MULTIPLE CHOICE QUESTIONS

1. If the infinite series is $x = \sqrt{6+\sqrt{6+\sqrt{6+...}}}$ then the value of x is:

A. 2.5 B. 3
C. 6 D. 8

2. If $\dfrac{9^n \cdot 3^2 \cdot 3^n - (27)^n}{3^{3m} \cdot 2^3} = \dfrac{1}{27}$, then the value of $(m-n)$ is:

A. 1 B. 2
C. $\sqrt{3}$ D. $\sqrt{\dfrac{2}{3}}$

3. If $x = \dfrac{\sqrt{5}+\sqrt{3}}{\sqrt{5}-\sqrt{3}}$ and $y = \dfrac{\sqrt{5}-\sqrt{3}}{\sqrt{5}+\sqrt{3}}$, then $(x+y)$ is equal to:

A. 8 B. 6
C. $2\sqrt{15}$ D. $2\left(\sqrt{5}+\sqrt{3}\right)$

4. $2^{x+1} + 2^{x+3} = 2560$, then x is equal to:

A. 12 B. 11
C. 8 D. 6

5. If $\dfrac{5+2\sqrt{3}}{7+4\sqrt{3}} = a + b\sqrt{3}$, then b is equal to:

A. –6 B. 6
C. –11 D. 11

6. If $\dfrac{(21)^{5.36}}{(21)^{3.47}} = (21)^x$, then the value of x is:

A. 8.88 B. 1.54
C. 9.32 D. 1.89

7. $\sqrt{24}+\sqrt{12}$ equal to:

A. $\sqrt{36}$ B. $2\sqrt{6}+2\sqrt{3}$
C. $6\sqrt{2}$ D. $\sqrt{288}$

8. If $a^b = 64$, where a and b are positive integers then $(a-b)^{a+b-4}$ is:

A. 0 B. 1
C. 2 D. $\dfrac{1}{2}$

9. The value of $\dfrac{5^{10+n} \cdot 25^{3n-4}}{5^{7n}}$ is:

A. 5 B. 8
C. 25 D. 16

10. $3^x - 3^{x-1} = 18$, then the value of x^x is:

A. 3 B. 8
C. 27 D. 216

11. If $x = \sqrt{10+\sqrt{25+\sqrt{121}}}$, then x is equal to:

A. –2 only B. 2 only
C. ±4 D. 4 only

12. If $a^x = b^y = c^z$ and $b^2 = ac$, then y is equal to:

A. $\dfrac{xz}{x+z}$ B. $\dfrac{xz}{2(x-z)}$
C. $\dfrac{xz}{2(z-x)}$ D. $\dfrac{2xz}{x+z}$

13. $\dfrac{5^{n+3} - 6 \times 5^{n+1}}{9 \times 5^n - 5^n \times 2^2}$ is equal to:

A. 5 B. 19
C. 25 D. 95

14. The value of $\left(\dfrac{x^a}{x^b}\right)^{(a+b)} \times \left(\dfrac{x^b}{x^c}\right)^{(b+c)} \times \left(\dfrac{x^c}{x^a}\right)^{(c+a)}$ is equal to:

A. 0 B. 2
C. 1 D. 3

15. If $\sqrt{3^n} = 729$, then the value of n is:

A. 12 B. 8
C. 10 D. 6

ANSWERS

1	2	3	4	5	6	7	8	9	10
B	A	A	C	A	D	B	B	C	C
11	**12**	**13**	**14**	**15**					
D	D	B	C	A					

EXPLANATORY ANSWERS

1. $x = \sqrt{6+x}$

Squaring both sides

$$x^2 = 6 + x$$

$$\Rightarrow \quad x^2 - x - 6 = 0$$

$$\Rightarrow \quad x^2 - 3x + 2x - 6 = 0$$

$$\Rightarrow \quad x(x-3) + 2(x-3) = 0$$

$$\Rightarrow \quad (x-3)(x+2) = 0$$

$$\Rightarrow \quad x = 3 \text{ or } x = -2$$

But x cannot be -2.

Hence, the required value of x is 3.

2.
$$\frac{9^n \cdot 3^2 \cdot 3^n - (27)^n}{3^{3m} \cdot 2^3} = \frac{1}{27}$$

$$\Rightarrow \quad \frac{3^{2n} \times 9 \times 3^n - 3^{3n}}{8 \times 3^{3m}} = \frac{1}{3^3}$$

$$\Rightarrow \quad \frac{3^{3n}(9-1)}{8\ 3^{3m}} = 3^{-3}$$

$$\Rightarrow \quad 3^{3n-3m} = (3)^{-3}$$

$$\Rightarrow \quad 3m - 3n = 3$$

$$\Rightarrow \quad 3(m-n) = 3$$

$$\Rightarrow \quad m - n = \frac{3}{3} = 1$$

3.
$$x = \frac{\sqrt{5}+\sqrt{3}}{\sqrt{5}-\sqrt{3}} \times \frac{\sqrt{5}+\sqrt{3}}{\sqrt{5}+\sqrt{3}} = \frac{\left(\sqrt{5}+\sqrt{3}\right)^2}{5-3}$$

$$\Rightarrow x = \frac{5+3+2\sqrt{15}}{2} = \frac{8+2\sqrt{15}}{2} = \frac{2\left(4+\sqrt{15}\right)}{2}$$

$$\therefore \quad x = 4 + \sqrt{15}$$

Again, $$y = \frac{\sqrt{5}-\sqrt{3}}{\sqrt{5}+\sqrt{3}} \times \frac{\sqrt{5}-\sqrt{3}}{\sqrt{5}-\sqrt{3}}$$

$$= \frac{\left(\sqrt{5}-\sqrt{3}\right)^2}{5-3}$$

$$\Rightarrow \quad y = \frac{5+3-2\sqrt{15}}{2}$$

$$= \frac{8-2\sqrt{15}}{2} = \frac{2\left(4-\sqrt{15}\right)}{2}$$

$$\Rightarrow \quad y = 4 - \sqrt{15}$$

$$\therefore \quad x + y = 4 + \sqrt{15} + 4 - \sqrt{15} = 8$$

4.
$$2^{x+1} + 2^{x+3} = 2560$$

$$\Rightarrow \quad 2^x \times 2 + 2^x \times 2^3 = 2560$$

$$\Rightarrow \quad 2 \times 2^x + 8 \times 2^x = 2560$$

$$\Rightarrow \quad 2^x(2+8) = 2560$$

$$\Rightarrow \quad 2^x = 256 = 2^8$$

$$\Rightarrow \quad x = 8$$

5.
$$\because \quad \frac{5+2\sqrt{3}}{7+4\sqrt{3}} = a + b\sqrt{3}$$

$$\frac{5+2\sqrt{3}}{7+4\sqrt{3}} \times \frac{7-4\sqrt{3}}{7-4\sqrt{3}} = \frac{35-20\sqrt{3}+14\sqrt{3}-24}{49-48}$$

$$= \frac{11-6\sqrt{3}}{1}$$

Comparing then we get,

$a = 11, b = -6$

Hence, $b = -6$.

6.
$$\frac{(21)^{5.36}}{(21)^{3.47}} = (21)^x$$

$$\Rightarrow \quad (21)^{5.36-3.47} = (21)^x$$

$$\Rightarrow \quad x = 1.89$$

7. $\sqrt{24} + \sqrt{12} = 2\sqrt{6} + 2\sqrt{3}$

8. $a^b = 64 = (4)^3 \Rightarrow a = 4, b = 3$

$\therefore (a-b)^{a+b-4} = (4-3)^{4+3-4} = (1)^3 = 1$

9.
$$\frac{5^{10+n} \cdot 25^{3n-4}}{5^{7n}} = \frac{5^{10} \times 5^n \times (5^2)^{3n-4}}{5^{7n}}$$

$$= \frac{5^{10} \times 5^n \times 5^{6n} \times 5^{-8}}{5^{7n}}$$

$$= \frac{5^{10-8} \times 5^{7n}}{5^{7n}} = 5^2 \times 5^{7n-7n}$$

$$= 25 \times 5^0 = 25 \times 1 = 25$$

10.
$$3^x - 3^{x-1} = 18$$

$$\Rightarrow \quad 3^x - 3^x \times 3^{-1} = 18$$

$$\Rightarrow \quad 3^x\left(1 - \frac{1}{3}\right) = 18$$

$$\Rightarrow \quad 3^x\left(\frac{2}{3}\right) = 18$$

$\Rightarrow \quad 3^x = \dfrac{18 \times 3}{2} = 27$

$\Rightarrow \quad 3^x = (3)^3 \Rightarrow x = 3$

$\therefore \quad x^x = (3)^3 = 27$

11. $x = \sqrt{10 + \sqrt{25 + \sqrt{121}}}$

$\Rightarrow \quad x = \sqrt{10 + \sqrt{25 + 11}}$

$\Rightarrow \quad x = \sqrt{10 + \sqrt{36}}$

$\Rightarrow \quad x = \sqrt{10 + 6} = \sqrt{16}$

$\Rightarrow \quad x = 4$

12. Let $a^x = b^y = c^z = k$

then $a = k^{\frac{1}{x}}$, $b = k^{\frac{1}{y}}$, $c = k^{\frac{1}{z}}$

Now, $b^2 = ac$

$\Rightarrow \quad \left(k^{\frac{1}{y}}\right)^2 = k^{\frac{1}{x}} \cdot k^{\frac{1}{z}}$

$\Rightarrow \quad k^{\frac{2}{y}} = k^{\frac{1}{x}+\frac{1}{z}}$

$\Rightarrow \quad \dfrac{2}{y} = \dfrac{z + x}{xz}$

$\Rightarrow \quad 2xz = y(x + z)$

$\Rightarrow \quad y = \dfrac{2xz}{x + z}$

13. $\dfrac{5^{n+3} - 6 \times 5^{n+1}}{9 \times 5^n - 5^n \times 2^2} = \dfrac{5^n \times 5^3 - 6 \times 5^n \times 5}{9 \times 5^n - 4 \times 5^n}$

$= \dfrac{5^n(125 - 30)}{5^n(9 - 4)} = 5^0 \times \dfrac{95}{5}$

$= 1 \times 19 = 19.$

14. $\left(\dfrac{x^a}{x^b}\right)^{(a+b)} \times \left(\dfrac{x^b}{x^c}\right)^{(b+c)} \times \left(\dfrac{x^c}{x^a}\right)^{(c+a)}$

$= \left(x^{a-b}\right)^{(a+b)} \times \left(x^{b-c}\right)^{(b+c)} \times \left(x^{c-a}\right)^{c+a}$

$= x^{a^2-b^2} \times x^{b^2-c^2} \times x^{c^2-a^2}$

$= x^{a^2-b^2+b^2-c^2+c^2-a^2}$

$= x^0 = 1$

15. $\sqrt{3^n} = 729 \Rightarrow 3^{n/2} = 3^6$

$\Rightarrow \quad \dfrac{n}{2} = 6$

$\Rightarrow \quad n = 12.$

5. RATIO AND PROPORTION

RATIO

When comparison is made by dividing one quantity by another of the same kind, the result is called ratio. If a and b are two numbers, ratio of a to b is denoted by $a : b$ or $\frac{a}{b}$. Here a is called first term and b is called the second term. The first term is also called antecedent and the second term is also called consequent.

EXAMPLE: The ratio 3 : 10 represents $\frac{3}{10}$ with antecedent 3 and consequent 10.

The multiplication or division of each term of a ratio by a same non-zero number does not effect the ratio.

PROPORTION

Equality of two ratios is called proportion. If $a : b = c : d$, then a, b, c, d are called in proportion. In a proportion $a : b : : c : d$, then a and d are called extremes and b and c are called means.

Product of extremes = Product of means

Comparison of Ratio: Suppose $\frac{a}{b} > \frac{c}{d}$ then we say that $a : b > c : d$.

Compounded Ratio: The compound ratio of the ratios $a : b$, $c : d$ and $e : f$ is $ace : bdf$.

Duplicate Ratio: The duplicate ratio of $a : b$ is $a^2 : b^2$.

Triplicate Ratio: The triplicate ratio of $a : b$ is $a^3 : b^3$.

Sub-duplicate and Sub-triplicate ratios

The sub-duplicate and Sub-triplicate ratios of ratio $a : b$ are $a^{1/2} : b^{1/2}$ and $a^{1/3} : b^{1/3}$ respectively.

Mean Proportional: Mean proportional between a and b is $\sqrt{ab}$.

Third Proportional: The third proportional to a, b is the fourth proportional to a, b, b.

Fourth Proportional: If $a : b : : c : d$ is a proportion, then d is called the fourth proportional to a, b, c.

EXAMPLE: If A : B = 3 : 4 and B : C = 8 : 9 then find A : C.

SOLUTION: $A : B = 3 : 4 \Rightarrow \frac{A}{B} = \frac{3}{4}$

$B : C = 8 : 9 \Rightarrow \frac{B}{C} = \frac{8}{9}$

$$\frac{A}{C} = \frac{A}{B} \times \frac{B}{C} = \frac{3}{4} \times \frac{8}{9} = \frac{2}{3}$$

$\Rightarrow \quad A : C = 2 : 3$

EXAMPLE: If 15% of A is the same as 20% of B, then find A : B.

SOLUTION: Given : 15% of A = 20% of B

$\Rightarrow \quad \frac{15}{100} \times A = \frac{20}{100} \times B$

$\Rightarrow \quad 3A = 4B$

$\Rightarrow \quad \frac{A}{B} = \frac{4}{3}$

$\Rightarrow \quad A : B = 4 : 3$

EXAMPLE: A stick 1.4 m long casts a shadow 1.3 m long at the same time when a pole casts a shadow 5.2 m long. Find the length of the pole.

SOLUTION: Clearly, more is the length of shadow, more is the length of the object.

Let the length of the pole be x metres.

Then, $1.3 : 5.2 :: 1.4 : x$

$$\Rightarrow \quad \frac{1.3}{5.2} = \frac{1.4}{x}$$

$$\Rightarrow \quad \frac{1}{4} = \frac{1.4}{x}$$

$$\Rightarrow \quad x = 1.4 \times 4 = 5.6$$

Hence, the length of the pole is 5.6 m.

MULTIPLE CHOICE QUESTIONS

1. If A : B = 2 : 3 and B : C = 4 : 5, then C : A is equal to:

A. 15 : 8 B. 12 : 10
C. 8 : 5 D. 8 : 15

2. If 10% of x is the same as 20% of y, then $x : y$ is equal to:

A. 1 : 2 B. 2 : 1
C. 5 : 1 D. 10 : 1

3. The mean proportional to $6+\sqrt{27}$ and $6-\sqrt{27}$ is:

A. 3 B. 9
C. 10 D. $\sqrt{10}$

4. If $x : y = 9 : 11$, the value of $\frac{5x+3y}{3x+5y}$ is:

A. 45 : 55 B. 18 : 22
C. 37 : 41 D. 39 : 41

5. If $a+b : b+c : c+a = 6 : 7 : 8$ and $a + b + c = 14$, then the value of c is:

A. 14 B. 7
C. 8 D. 6

6. Two numbers are in the ratio 2 : 3. If 5 is added to each number, the ratio becomes 5 : 7. The bigger number is:

A. 30 B. 40
C. 60 D. 20

7. What should be added to each of the numbers 12, 30, 40 and 86, so that they are in proportion?

A. 6 B. 4
C. –6 D. –4

8. The ratio of males and females of a village is 5 : 3. If there are 800 males in the village, females are:

A. 240 B. 480
C. 840 D. 488

9. In a mixture of 60 litres, the ratio of ethanol to ether is 4 : 1. How much ether must be added to the mixture to make this ratio 2 : 1?

A. 10 litres B. 12 litres
C. 18 litres D. 24 litres

10. The proportion of zinc and copper in a brass piece is 4 : 5. How much zinc will be there in 180 kg of such a piece?

A. 40 kg B. 80 kg
C. 100 kg D. 120 kg

11. The prices of a scooter and a television set are in the ratio 3 : 2. If a scooter costs ₹ 6000 more than the television set, the price of the television set is:

A. ₹ 18000 B. ₹ 12000
C. ₹ 10000 D. ₹ 6000

12. The weight of a 13 metres long iron rod be 23.4 kg. The weight of 6 metres long of such rod will be:

A. 7.2 kg B. 12.4 kg
C. 10.8 kg D. 18 kg

13. The ratio between the ages of Gayatri and Savitri is 6 : 5 and the sum of their ages is 44 years. The ratio of their ages after 8 years will be:

A. 5 : 6 B. 7 : 8
C. 8 : 7 D. 14 : 13

14. Two numbers are such that the ratio between them is 3 : 5 but if each is increased by 10, the ratio between them becomes 5 : 7. The numbers are:

A. 3, 5 B. 7, 9
C. 13, 22 D. 15, 25

15. In a factory the ratio of male workers to female workers was 5 : 3. If the number of female workers was less by 40, the total number of workers in the factory was:

A. 100
B. 500
C. 160
D. 200

ANSWERS

1	2	3	4	5	6	7	8	9	10
A	B	A	D	D	A	A	B	B	B
11	**12**	**13**	**14**	**15**					
B	C	C	D	C					

EXPLANATORY ANSWERS

1. $\frac{A}{B} = \frac{2}{3}$ and $\frac{B}{C} = \frac{4}{5}$

$\Rightarrow \quad \frac{A}{B} \times \frac{B}{C} = \frac{2}{3} \times \frac{4}{5} \Rightarrow \frac{A}{C} = \frac{8}{15}$

$\Rightarrow \quad \frac{C}{A} = \frac{15}{8}$

Hence, $C : A = 15 : 8$.

2. 10% of x = 20% of y

$\Rightarrow \quad \frac{10}{100}x = \frac{20}{100}y \quad \Rightarrow \quad \frac{x}{10} = \frac{y}{5}$

$\Rightarrow \quad \frac{x}{y} = \frac{10}{5} \quad \Rightarrow \quad x : y = 2 : 1$

3. Mean proportional $= \sqrt{(6+\sqrt{27})(6-\sqrt{27})}$

$= \sqrt{36-27} = \sqrt{9} = 3$

4. $\because \quad \frac{x}{y} = \frac{9}{11}$

$$\frac{5x+3y}{3x+5y} = \frac{\frac{5x}{y}+\frac{3y}{y}}{\frac{3x}{y}+\frac{5y}{y}} = \frac{5\left(\frac{x}{y}\right)+3}{3\left(\frac{x}{y}\right)+5}$$

$$= \frac{5\times\frac{9}{11}+3}{3\times\frac{9}{11}+5} = \frac{\frac{45+33}{11}}{\frac{27+55}{11}} = \frac{78}{82} = \frac{39}{41}$$

Hence, the value of $\frac{5x+3y}{3x+5y} = \frac{39}{41}$.

5. Given : $a + b = 6x,\ b + c = 7x$

and $\quad c + a = 8x$ ...(*i*)

and $\quad a + b + c = 14$ ...(*ii*)

Adding Eq. (*i*)

$a + b + b + c + c + a = 6x + 7x + 8x$

$\Rightarrow \quad 2(a + b + c) = 21x$

$\Rightarrow \quad 2 \times 14 = 21x \quad$ [from Eq. (*ii*)]

$\Rightarrow \quad x = \frac{28}{21} = \frac{4}{3}$

$\therefore \quad a + b = 6x = 6 \times \frac{4}{3} = 8$

$\because \quad a + b + c = 14 \Rightarrow c = 14 - 8 = 6$

6. Let the two numbers are a and b

According to the question,

$\frac{a}{b} = \frac{2}{3} \Rightarrow 3a = 2b \Rightarrow b = \frac{3a}{2}$

Now, $\quad \frac{a+5}{b+5} = \frac{5}{7} \Rightarrow 7a + 35 = 5b + 25$

$\Rightarrow \quad 7a - 5b = -10$

$\Rightarrow \quad 7a - 5\left(\frac{3a}{2}\right) = -10$

$\Rightarrow \quad 14a - 15a = -20 \Rightarrow -a = -20$

$\Rightarrow \quad a = 20, b = 3 \times \frac{20}{2} = 30$

Hence, the bigger number is 30.

7. Let x be added to each of the numbers.

Then, $(12 + x) : (30 + x) :: (40 + x) : (86 + x)$

$\Rightarrow \quad \frac{12+x}{30+x} = \frac{40+x}{86+x}$

$\Rightarrow (12 + x)(86 + x) = (30 + x)(40 + x)$

$\Rightarrow 12 \times 86 + 12x + 86x + x^2$

$= 30 \times 40 + 30x + 40x + x^2$

$\Rightarrow \quad 1032 + 98x = 1200 + 70x$

$\Rightarrow \quad 28x = 168 \Rightarrow x = 6$

8. Ratio of Males : Females = 5 : 3

$\Rightarrow \quad \frac{800}{x} = \frac{5}{3} \Rightarrow 5x = 3 \times 800$

$\Rightarrow \quad x = \frac{3 \times 800}{5} = 3 \times 160 = 480$

Hence, number of females = 480.

9. Let ethanol = $4x$ and ether = $1x$

$4x + 1x = 60 \Rightarrow 5x = 60 \Rightarrow x = 12$

Quantity of ethanol = $12 \times 4 = 48$ litres

Quantity of ether = $1 \times 12 = 12$ litres

Let m litres of ether be added to mixture to get the desired ratio. Then,

$$\frac{48}{12+m} = \frac{2}{1} \Rightarrow 24 + 2m = 48$$

$$\Rightarrow 2m = 24 \Rightarrow m = 12$$

Hence, 12 litres of ether is to be added.

10. In 9 kg of brass, zinc = 4 kg

$\therefore$ In 180 kg of brass, zinc = $\frac{4}{9} \times 180 = 80$ kg.

11. Let the prices of a scooter and a television be ₹ $3x$ and $2x$ respectively.

According to the question,

$3x - 2x = 6000 \Rightarrow x = 6000$

$\therefore$ Price of a television = 2×6000 = ₹ 12000.

12. Weight of 13 m long iron rod = 23.4 kg

Weight of 6 m long iron rod

$= \frac{23.4}{13} \times 6$ kg $= 1.8 \times 6 = 10.8$ kg.

13. Let present age of Gayatri = $6x$ years and present age of Savitri = $5x$ years.

According to the question,

$$6x + 5x = 44 \Rightarrow 11x = 44 \Rightarrow x = 4$$

Gayatri's age = $6 \times 4 = 24$ years

Savitri's age = $5 \times 4 = 20$ years

After 8 years their ages will be 32 years and 28 years.

Ratio of their ages after 8 years = $\frac{32}{28} = 8 : 7$.

14. Let numbers are x and y

$$\frac{x}{y} = \frac{3}{5}$$

$$\Rightarrow 5x = 3y \Rightarrow x = \frac{3y}{5}$$

According to the question,

$$\frac{x+10}{y+10} = \frac{5}{7} \Rightarrow 7x + 70 = 5y + 50$$

$$\Rightarrow 7x - 5y = -20$$

$$\Rightarrow 7\left(\frac{3y}{5}\right) - 5y = -20$$

$$\Rightarrow 21y - 25y = -100$$

$$\Rightarrow 4y = 100 \Rightarrow y = 25$$

$$\therefore x = \frac{3 \times 25}{5} = 15$$

Hence, numbers are 15 and 25.

15. Let the number of male and female workers be $5x$ and $3x$ respectively.

According to the question,

$5x - 3x = 40 \Rightarrow 2x = 40 \Rightarrow x = 20$

$\therefore$ Number of male = $5 \times 20 = 100$

and number of female = $3 \times 20 = 60$

Hence, total number of workers = $100 + 60 = 160$.

6. PARTNERSHIP

Partnership is a form of association of two or more persons who contribute resources like money together in order to carry on a business. It may be of simple or compound type.

Simple partnership is one in which the capitals of the partners are invested for the same time. The profits or losses are divided among the partners in the ratio of their investments.

Compound partnership is one in which the capitals of the partners are invested for different periods. In such cases, equivalent capitals are calculated for each partner by multiplying their capital contributions with time. The profits or losses are then divided in the ratio of these equivalent capitals. Thus, the ratio of profits is directly proportional to both capital invested as well as time.

The partner who invests the money in the business as well as takes part in its management, is known as **Working partner**.

The partner who only invests the money in the business and does not work, is known as **Sleeping partner**.

A working partner gets either monthly payment or a share in the profit for his contribution in the management of the business. This payment is deducted from the total profit before its distribution.

EXAMPLE: A, B and C invest ₹ 15000, ₹ 20000 and ₹ 25000 respectively in a business. The profit earned is ₹ 1200. Find the share of each in the profit.

SOLUTION: This is a case of simple partnership

Ratio of investments, A : B : C

= 15000 : 20000 : 25000

= 3 : 4 : 5

Sum of the ratios = 3 + 4 + 5 = 12

Share in the profit

$$\text{For A} = \frac{3}{12} \times 1200 = ₹\,300$$

$$\text{For B} = \frac{4}{12} \times 1200 = ₹\,400$$

$$\text{For C} = \frac{5}{12} \times 1200 = ₹\,500$$

EXAMPLE: A and B are partners in a firm. A invests ₹ 15000 and B ₹ 25000. A is the working partner and gets 20% of the profit for his contribution in the management of the firm. B is the sleeping partner. If the profit is ₹ 475, find the share of each.

SOLUTION: First we have to deduct the payment to be made to A from the total profit for his contribution in the management of the firm.

20% of ₹ 475 = ₹ 95

Balance profit = 475 – 95 = ₹ 380

This has to be divided between A and B in the ratio of their investments *i.e.*, ₹ 15000 : ₹ 25000 = 3 : 5

$$\text{A's share} = ₹\,380 \times \frac{3}{8} = ₹\,142.5$$

$$\text{B's share} = ₹\,380 \times \frac{5}{8} = ₹\,237.5$$

Finally, A gets a total of (95 + 142.5) = ₹ 237.5 and B gets = ₹ 237.5

EXAMPLE: In a business A and B gained some amount in a certain ratio. B and C received the profit in the ratio as that of A and B. If B received ₹ 6400 and C received ₹ 10,000 then find the amount invested by B.

SOLUTION: Let the ratio of A's and B's profit be $\frac{a}{b}$.

Hence, the ratio of B's and C's profit = $\frac{a}{b}$

Thus, $A : B : C = a : b : \frac{b^2}{a}$

when A's profit, a = ₹ 6400

and C's profit, $\frac{b^2}{a}$ = ₹ 10,000

$\Rightarrow \quad b^2 = 10,000 \times 6400 = 100 \times 100 \times 80 \times 80$

$\Rightarrow \quad b = 100 \times 80 = 8000$

Hence, the amount invested by B = ₹ 8000.

MULTIPLE CHOICE QUESTIONS

1. A, B and C share the profit in the ratio of 3 : 5 : 7. If the gain is ₹ 2040, then C's share is:

A. ₹ 360 B. ₹ 600
C. ₹ 952 D. ₹ 120

2. A, B and C started a business with ₹ 47000. A puts in ₹ 5000 more than B and B ₹ 3000 more than C. The share of A out of the profit of ₹ 14100 will be:

A. ₹ 3600 B. ₹ 4500
C. ₹ 6000 D. ₹ 6300

3. A starts a business with ₹ 5000. After 4 months B joins him with a sum of ₹ 4000. In the end of the year there is a profit of ₹ 8970. The share of A in the profit will be:

A. ₹ 3120 B. ₹ 4020
C. ₹ 5850 D. ₹ 6360

4. A, B, C are three partners in a business. The profit share of A is $\frac{3}{16}$ of the profit and B's share is $\frac{1}{4}$ of the profit. If C receives ₹ 243, then the amount received by B will be:

A. ₹ 90 B. ₹ 96
C. ₹ 108 D. ₹ 120

5. A, B and C share the profit in the ratio 2 : 3 : 7. If the average gain is ₹ 8000, then B's share is:

A. ₹ 2000 B. ₹ 1000
C. ₹ 1500 D. ₹ 3000

6. Ashok started a business investing ₹ 90,000. After 3 months Shabir joined him with a capital of ₹ 1,20,000. If at the end of one year the total profit made by them was ₹ 96,000, what will be the difference between their shares?

A. ₹ 24000 B. ₹ 8000
C. ₹ 20000 D. None of these

7. Mahesh received ₹ 6000 as his share out of the total profit of ₹ 9000 which he and Ram entered at the end of one year. If Mahesh invested ₹ 20,000 for 6 months, whereas Ram invested his amount for the whole year, what was the amount invested by Ram?

A. ₹ 4000 B. ₹ 5000
C. ₹ 3000 D. ₹ 6000

8. A and B started a business jointly. A's investment was thrice the investment of B and the period of his investment was two times the period of investment of B. If B received ₹ 40,000 as profit, then their total profit is:

A. ₹ 2,40,000 B. ₹ 28000
C. ₹ 24000 D. ₹ 2,80,000

9. Anil started a business investing ₹ 70,000. After 8 months Vimal joined him with a capital of ₹ 1,80,000. In what ratio should Anil and Vimal share the profit after two years?

A. 8 : 7 B. 7 : 5
C. 7 : 6 D. None of these

10. A, B and C starts a business. A invests ₹ 3,20,000 for four months. B invests ₹ 5,10,000 for three months and C invests ₹ 2,70,000 for five months. If at the end of year there is a profit of ₹ 1,24,800, then share of B is:

A. ₹ 79000 B. ₹ 49200
C. ₹ 50000 D. ₹ 45900

11. A, B and C contract a work for ₹ 550. Together A and B are to do $\frac{7}{11}$ of the work. The share of C should be:

A. ₹ 400 B. ₹ 300
C. ₹ 200 D. ₹ $183\frac{1}{3}$

12. Jagmohan, Rooplal and Pankaj rented a video cassette for one week at a rent of ₹ 350. If they use it for 6 hrs, 10 hrs and 12 hrs respectively, the rent to be paid by Pankaj is:

A. ₹ 75 B. ₹ 125
C. ₹ 35 D. ₹ 150

13. Manoj got ₹ 6000 as his share out of the total profit of ₹ 9000 which he and Ramesh earned at the end of one year. If Manoj invested ₹ 20,000 for 6 months, whereas Ramesh invested his amount for the whole year, the amount invested by Ramesh was:

A. ₹ 60,000 B. ₹ 10,000
C. ₹ 4000 D. ₹ 5000

14. A, B and C invest ₹ 2000, ₹ 3000 and ₹ 4000 in a business. After one year A removed his money, B and C continued the business for one more year. If the net profit after 2 years be ₹ 3200, then A's share in the profit is:

A. ₹ 1000 B. ₹ 600
C. ₹ 800 D. ₹ 400

15. A and B enter into partnership investing ₹ 12000 and ₹ 16000 respectively. After 8 months, C also joins the business with a capital of ₹ 15000. The share of C in a profit of ₹ 46500 after 2 years will be:

A. ₹ 12000 B. ₹ 14400
C. ₹ 19200 D. ₹ 21200

ANSWERS

1	2	3	4	5	6	7	8	9	10
C	C	C	C	A	D	B	D	D	D
11	**12**	**13**	**14**	**15**					
C	D	D	D	A					

EXPLANATORY ANSWERS

1. C's share $= \frac{7}{15} \times 2040 = ₹ 952.$

2. Let C's capital be ₹ x

Then B's capital = ₹ $(x + 3000)$

and A's capital = ₹ $(x + 3000 + 5000) = x + 8000$

$\Rightarrow \quad x + (x + 3000) + (x + 8000) = 47000$

$\Rightarrow \quad 3x + 11000 = 47000$

$\Rightarrow \quad 3x = 47000 - 11000$

$= 36000$

$\Rightarrow \quad x = 12000$

Thus, capital of A, B and C are ₹ 20000, ₹ 15000 and ₹ 12000 respectively.

∴ Profit sharing ratio = 20 : 15 : 12

∴ Profit of A $= \frac{20}{47} \times 14100 = ₹ 6000$

3. ₹ 5000 × 12 = ₹ 60,000 for A

₹ 4000 × (12 – 4) = 4000 × 8 = ₹ 32000 for B

Ratio of profit sharing = 60000 : 32000

= 60 : 32 = 15 : 8

∴ Share of A in the profit $= \frac{15}{23} \times 8970$

$= 15 \times 390 = ₹ 5850$

4. Let the profit be ₹ 1. Then,

$$A : B : C = \frac{3}{16} : \frac{1}{4} : \left[1 - \left(\frac{3}{16} + \frac{1}{4}\right)\right]$$

$$= \frac{3}{16} : \frac{1}{4} : \frac{9}{16}$$

$$= \frac{3}{16} : \frac{4}{16} : \frac{9}{16} \quad i.e., 3 : 4 : 9$$

when C's share is ₹ 9, then B's share = ₹ 4

when C's share is ₹ 243, then B's share

$$= \frac{4 \times 243}{9} = ₹ 108$$

5. B's share $= \frac{3}{2 + 3 + 7} \times 8000$

$= \frac{3 \times 8000}{12} = ₹ 2000$

6. The ratio of their investment

$= 12 \times 90000 : (12 - 3) \times 120000$

$= 12 \times 9 : 9 \times 12 = 1 : 1$

Ashok's share $= \frac{1}{1+1} \times 96000 = ₹ 48000$

Shabir's share $= \frac{1}{1+1} \times 96000 = ₹ 48000$

Difference between their shares

$= ₹\,48000 - ₹\,48000 = 0.$

7. The ratio of their profit

$= ₹\,6000 : ₹\,(9000 - 6000)$

$= ₹\,6000 : ₹\,3000 = 2 : 1$

Let ₹ x be the amount invested by Ram.

The ratio of their profit = The ratio of their investment

$\Rightarrow \quad 2 : 1 = 6 \times 20000 : 12 \times x$

$$\Rightarrow \quad \frac{2}{1} = \frac{6 \times 20000}{12 \times x} \Rightarrow 2x = 10000$$

$\Rightarrow \quad x = 5000$

$\therefore$ The investment of Ram is ₹ 5000.

8. Let ₹ x be the investment of B and n years be the period of investment of B.

Given : A's investment $= 3 \times ₹\,x = ₹\,3x$

and period of investment of A $= 2n$ years

$\therefore$ The ratio of investment of A and B

$= 2n \times 3x : n \times x$

$= 6nx : nx = 6 : 1$

Let the total profit be ₹ y

Given B's share in profit = ₹ 40,000

$$\Rightarrow \frac{1}{6+1} \times y = ₹\,40{,}000 \Rightarrow y = ₹\,2{,}80{,}000$$

$\therefore$ Total profit is ₹ 2,80,000.

9. The ratio of Anil's and Vimal's share in the profit

= Ratio of their investments

$= 24 \times 70000 : 16 \times 180000$

$= 24 \times 7 : 16 \times 18 = 7 : 12$

10. The ratio of investments of A, B and C

$= 4 \times 320000 : 3 \times 510000 : 5 \times 270000$

$= 4 \times 32 : 3 \times 51 : 5 \times 27$

$= 128 : 153 : 135$

Total profit after 1 year = ₹ 124800

$$\text{Share of B} = ₹\, \frac{153}{128 + 153 + 135} \times 124800$$

$$= ₹\, \frac{153}{416} \times 124800 = ₹\,45900$$

11. $$\text{C's share} = ₹\left(550 \times \frac{4}{11}\right) = ₹\,200$$

12. Ratio of rents $= 6 : 10 : 12 = 3 : 5 : 6$

$$\therefore \text{Pankaj's share of rent} = ₹\left(350 \times \frac{6}{14}\right) = ₹\,150$$

13. Let amount invested by Ramesh be ₹ x

$\therefore\ 20000 \times 6 : 12x = 6000 : 3000$

$$i.e., \quad \frac{12x}{120000} = \frac{3000}{6000} \quad \text{or } x = ₹\,5000$$

14. Ratio of investments

$= (2000 \times 1) : (3000 \times 2) : (4000 \times 2)$

$= 1 : 3 : 4$

$$\therefore \text{A's share} = ₹\left(3200 \times \frac{1}{8}\right) = ₹\,400.$$

15. Ratio of investments

$= (12000 \times 24) : (16000 \times 24) : (15000 \times 16)$

$= 6 : 8 : 5$

$$\text{C's share of profit} = ₹\left(45600 \times \frac{5}{19}\right) = ₹\,12000$$

7. AVERAGE

The sum of all the quantities of same kind divided by their number is called average (or mean) of those quantities.

FORMULAE

1. $\text{Average} = \left(\dfrac{\text{Sum of observations}}{\text{Number of observations}}\right)$
2. Sum of the first n natural numbers

   $= 1 + 2 + 3 + ... + n = \dfrac{n(n+1)}{2}$
3. Sum of the squares of the first n natural numbers

   $= 1^2 + 2^2 + ... + n^2 = \dfrac{n(n+1)(2n+1)}{6}$
4. Sum of the cubes of the first n natural numbers

   $= 1^3 + 2^3 + ... + n^3 = \left\{\dfrac{n(n+1)}{2}\right\}^2$
5. Sum of the first n odd numbers

   $= 1 + 3 + 5 + ... + (2n-1) = n^2$
6. Distance between two stations P and Q is x km. A person covers the journey from P to Q at 'a' km/hr and returns back to P with a uniform speed of 'b' km/hr. Then the average speed of the person during the whole journey

   $= \dfrac{2ab}{a+b}$ km/hr.

Different kinds of mean or average:

(*a*) Arithmetic mean

(*b*) Geometric mean

(*c*) Harmonic mean

(*a*) **Arithmetic Mean:** It is most popularly used of all the averages. For example, average income, average profit, average mileage etc. As defined earlier, it is the sum total of all values of items divided by the total number of items. For detailed discussion we will confine ourselves to Arithmetic Mean only because this is the most relevant of all the average for us.

Let $x_1, x_2, x_3, ..., x_n$ be the n values of x.

Their average is denoted by $\bar{x}$ and given by

$$\bar{x} = \frac{\text{Sum of observations}}{\text{Total number of observations}}$$

or $$\bar{x} = \frac{x_1 + x_2 + x_3 + ... + x_n}{n}$$

(*b*) **Geometric Mean :** For observations $x_1, x_2, x_3, ..., x_n$ the geometric mean denoted by G.M. is defined as:

$$\text{G.M.} = (x_1 \cdot x_2 \cdot x_3 \ldots x_n)^{1/n}$$

It is useful in calculating averages of ratios such as average population, growth rate, average percentage increase etc.

(*c*) **Harmonic Mean:** It is defined as

$$\text{H.M.} = \frac{n}{\frac{1}{x_1} + \frac{1}{x_2} + ... + \frac{1}{x_n}}.$$

EXAMPLE: Find the average of first ten prime numbers.

SOLUTION: First ten prime numbers are 2, 3, 5, 7, 11, 13, 17, 19, 23 and 29.

$$\therefore \text{Average} = \frac{2+3+5+7+11+13+17+19+23+29}{10}$$

$$= \frac{129}{10} = 12.9$$

EXAMPLE: If x_1, x_2, x_3, x_4, x_5 are five consecutive odd numbers then find the average of these numbers.

SOLUTION: Since x_1 is the first odd number.

$$\therefore \quad x_2 = x_1 + 2$$
$$x_3 = x_2 + 2 = x_1 + 4$$
$$x_4 = x_3 + 2 = x_1 + 6$$
$$x_5 = x_4 + 2 = x_1 + 8$$

$$\therefore \text{ Average} = \frac{x_1 + x_1 + 2 + x_1 + 4 + x_1 + 6 + x_1 + 8}{5}$$

$$= \frac{5x_1 + 20}{5} = \frac{5(x_1 + 4)}{5} = x_1 + 4$$

EXAMPLE: If the average of four consecutive even numbers is 27, then find the largest of these numbers.

SOLUTION: Let x be the first even number in the series of four consecutive even numbers.

$\therefore$ 2nd even number $= x + 2$

3rd even number $= x + 4$

4th even number $= x + 6$

$$\text{Average} = \frac{x + x + 2 + x + 4 + x + 6}{4}$$

$$\Rightarrow \quad 27 = \frac{4x + 12}{4}$$

$$\Rightarrow \quad 4x + 12 = 27 \times 4 = 108$$

$$\Rightarrow \quad 4x = 96$$

$$\Rightarrow \quad x = 24$$

Largest number in this series is $x + 6$

i.e., $24 + 6 = 30$

EXAMPLE: The average of eight numbers is 14. The average of six of these numbers is 16. What is the average of the remaining two numbers?

SOLUTION: Sum of the eight numbers $= 14 \times 8 = 112$

Sum of six of these eight numbers $= 16 \times 6 = 96$

$\therefore$ Sum of the remaining two numbers $= 112 - 96 = 16$

$\therefore$ Average of the remaining two numbers $= \frac{16}{2} = 8$

EXAMPLE: What is the average of first 30 multiples of 7?

SOLUTION: Required Average

$$= \frac{7 + 14 + 21 + ... + 210}{30}$$

$$= \frac{7(1 + 2 + 3 + ... + 30)}{30}$$

$$= \frac{7 \times 30(30 + 1)}{2 \times 30}$$

$$= \frac{7 \times 31}{2} = \frac{217}{2} = 108.5$$

EXAMPLE: The average of 11 results is 50. If the average of first six results is 49 and that of last six is 52, find the sixth result.

SOLUTION: Sum of 11 results $= 11 \times 50 = 550$

Sum of first 6 results $6 \times 49 = 294$

Sum of last 6 results $= 6 \times 52 = 312$

$\therefore$ 6th result $= 294 + 312 - 550$

$= 56$

EXAMPLE: The average age of three boys is 15 years. If their ages are in the ratio 3 : 5 : 7. What is the age of the youngest boy?

SOLUTION: Let the ages of the three boys be $3x$, $5x$ and $7x$.

$$\text{Average age} = \frac{3x + 5x + 7x}{3} = 5x$$

and $5x = 15 \Rightarrow x = 3$

The age of the youngest boy $= 3x = 3 \times 3 = 9$ years.

EXAMPLE: The average of 100 observations is 45. It was later found that two observations 19 and 31 were incorrectly recorded as 91 and 13. Find the correct average.

SOLUTION: Sum of 100 observations

$= 100 \times 45 = 4500$

New sum of 100 observations

$= 4500 + (19 + 31) - (91 + 13)$

$= 4500 + 50 - 104 = 4446$

$$\text{Correct average} = \frac{4446}{100} = 44.46$$

MULTIPLE CHOICE QUESTIONS

1. The average of first five multiples of 3 is:
A. 3 B. 9
C. 12 D. 15

2. The average of 25 results is 18, that of first 12 is 14 and of the last 12 is 17. Thirteenth result is:
A. 78 B. 85
C. 28 D. 72

3. Out of three numbers, the first is twice the second and is half of the third. If the average of the three numbers is 56, the three numbers in order are:
A. 48, 96, 24 B. 48, 24, 96
C. 96, 24, 48 D. 96, 48, 24

4. The sum of three numbers is 98. If the ratio between first and second be 2 : 3 and that between second and third be 5 : 8, then the second number is:
A. 30 B. 20
C. 58 D. 48

5. The average age of a committee of seven trustees is the same as it was 5 years ago; a young man having been substituted for one of them. The new man compared to the replaced old man, is younger in age by:
A. 5 years B. 7 years
C. 12 years D. 35 years

6. The average expenditure of a man for the first five months is ₹ 120 and for the next seven months is ₹ 130. His monthly average income if he saves ₹ 290 in that year, is:
A. ₹ 160 B. ₹ 170
C. ₹ 150 D. ₹ 140

7. The average salary of 20 workers in an office is ₹ 1900 per month. If the manager's salary is added, the average becomes ₹ 2000 per month. The manager's salary is:
A. ₹ 24000 B. ₹ 25200
C. ₹ 45600 D. None of these

8. The average temperature of first 3 days is 27°C and of the next 3 days is 29°C. If the average of the whole week is 28.5°C, the temperature of the last day is:
A. 31.5°C B. 10.5°C
C. 21°C D. 42°C

9. A cricketer scored 180 runs in the first test and 258 runs in the second. How many runs should he score in the third test so that his average score in the three tests would be 230 runs?
A. 219 B. 242
C. 334 D. None of these

10. The average of first five prime numbers is:
A. 5.0 B. 5.2
C. 5.6 D. 6.0

11. The average weight of 3 men A, B and C is 84 kg. Another man D joins the group and the average now becomes 80 kg. If another man E, whose weight is 3 kg more than that of D, replaces A, then average weight of B, C, D and E becomes 79 kg. The weight of A is:
A. 70 kg B. 72 kg
C. 75 kg D. 80 kg

12. The average age of A, B, C, D 5 years ago was 45 years. By including x, the present average of all the five is 49 years. The present age of x is:
A. 64 years B. 48 years
C. 45 years D. 40 years

13. The average height of 30 boys, out of a class of 50, is 160 cm. If the average height of the remaining boys is 165 cm, the average height of the whole class (in cm) is:
A. 161 B. 162
C. 163 D. 164

14. The average age of an adult class is 40 years. 12 new students with an average age of 32 years join the class, thereby decreasing the average of the class by 4 years. The original strength of the class was:
A. 10 B. 11
C. 12 D. 15

15. If a, b, c, d, e are five consecutive odd numbers, their average is:
A. $5(a+4)$ B. $\frac{abcde}{5}$
C. $5(a+b+c+d+e)$ D. None of these

16. Of the three numbers, second is twice the first and is also thrice the third. If the average of the three numbers is 44, the largest number is:
A. 24 B. 36
C. 72 D. 108

17. The average of 50 numbers is 38. If two numbers namely, 45 and 55 are discarded, the average of remaining number is:

A. 36.50 B. 37.00
C. 37.50 D. 37.52

18. The average height of 30 girls out of a class of 40 is 160 cm and that of the remaining girls is 156 cm. The average height of the whole class is:

A. 158 cm B. 158.5 cm
C. 159 cm D. 159.5 cm

19. The average of n numbers is x. If 36 is subtracted from any two numbers each, then new average is $(x - 8)$. The value of n is:

A. 6 B. 8
C. 9 D. 72

20. The average salary of male employees in a firm is ₹ 520 and that of female employees is ₹ 420. The mean salary of all the employees is ₹ 500. The percentage of female employees is:

A. 40% B. 30%
C. 25% D. 20%

ANSWERS

1	**2**	**3**	**4**	**5**	**6**	**7**	**8**	**9**	**10**
B	A	B	A	D	C	D	A	D	C
11	**12**	**13**	**14**	**15**	**16**	**17**	**18**	**19**	**20**
C	C	B	C	D	C	C	C	C	D

EXPLANATORY ANSWERS

1. Average $= \frac{3(1+2+3+4+5)}{5} = \frac{(3 \times 15)}{5} = 9$

2. Thirteenth result
$= [(25 \times 18) - (12 \times 14 + 12 \times 17)]$
$= [450 - (168 + 204)]$
$= 450 - 372 = 78.$

3. Let the numbers be $2x$, x and $4x$.

$$\text{Average} = \frac{2x + x + 4x}{3} = \frac{7x}{3}$$

According to the question,

$$\frac{7x}{3} = 56$$

$\Rightarrow$ $7x = 3 \times 56$

$\Rightarrow$ $x = \frac{3 \times 56}{7} = 24$

Hence, the numbers in order are 48, 24 and 96.

4. Let the numbers be x, y, z, then

$x + y + z = 98$

$$\frac{x}{y} = \frac{2}{3} \quad \text{and} \quad \frac{y}{z} = \frac{5}{8}$$

$\therefore$ $x = \frac{2y}{3}$ and $z = \frac{8y}{5}$

So, $\frac{2y}{3} + y + \frac{8y}{5} = 98$

$\Rightarrow$ $\frac{10y + 15y + 24y}{15} = 98$

$\Rightarrow$ $49y = 15 \times 98$

$\Rightarrow$ $y = \frac{15 \times 98}{49} = 30$

5. During these five years, the total age would have increased by $(7 \times 5) = 35$ years.
But, it remains the same as it was 5 years ago.
$\therefore$ The new man is younger than the replaced old man by 35 years.

6. Total income for 12 months
= ₹ $(120 \times 5 + 130 \times 7 + 290)$
= ₹ 1800

Average monthly income = ₹$\frac{1800}{12}$ = ₹150

7. Total salary of 20 workers
$= 20 \times 1900$ = ₹ 38000

Total salary of 20 workers and manager
$= 21 \times 2000$ = ₹ 42000

Monthly salary of the manager
$= 42000 - 38000$ = ₹ 4000.

8. Total temperature of first 3 days
$= 27 \times 3 = 81°C$

Total temperature of next 3 days
$= 29 \times 3 = 87°C$

Total temperature of 7 days

$= 28.5 \times 7 = 199.5°C$

Temperature of the last day

$= 199.5 - (81 + 87)$

$= 199.5 - 168 = 31.5°C$

9. Let runs he should score in third test be x :

Then, $\frac{180+258+x}{3} = 230$

$\Rightarrow \quad x = 690 - 438 = 252.$

10. Average $= \frac{2+3+5+7+11}{5} = \frac{28}{5} = 5.6.$

11. Weight of D = $(80 \times 4 - 84 \times 3)$ kg = 68 kg

Weight of E = $(68 + 3)$ kg = 71 kg

(B + C + D + E)'s weight = (79×4) kg = 316 kg

∴ (B + C)'s weight

$= [316 - (68 + 71)]$ kg = 177 kg

Hence, A's weight

$= [(84 \times 3) - 177]$kg = 75 kg

12. Total age of A, B, C and D 5 years ago

$= (45 \times 4)$ years = 180 years.

Total present age of A, B, C, D and x

$= (49 \times 5)$ years = 245 years.

Present age of A, B, C and D

$= (180 + 5 \times 4)$ years = 200 years.

∴ Present age of x = 45 years.

13. Total height of 30 boys = $30 \times 160 = 4800$

Total height of 20 boys = $20 \times 165 = 3300$

Total height of 50 boys = 8100

Average height of 50 boys = $\frac{8100}{50} = 162.$

14.
$$40x + 12 \times 32 = (12 + x) \times 36$$
$$\Rightarrow \quad 40x + 384 = 432 + 36x$$
$$\Rightarrow \quad 4x = 432 - 384 = 48$$
$$\Rightarrow \quad x = \frac{48}{4} = 12$$

Hence, the original strength of the class was 12.

15. Average $= \frac{a+a+2+a+4+a+6+a+8}{5}$

$$= \frac{5a+20}{5} = \frac{5(a+4)}{5} = a+4$$

16. Let the numbers be x, $2x$ and $\frac{2x}{3}$.

$$\text{Average} = \frac{x+2x+\frac{2x}{3}}{3}$$

$$\Rightarrow \quad \frac{11x}{9} = 44$$

$$\Rightarrow \quad x = \frac{44 \times 9}{11} = 36$$

So, the numbers are 36, 72 and 24.

Hence, the largest one is 72.

17. Total of 50 numbers = $50 \times 38 = 1900$

$$\text{Average of 48 numbers} = \frac{1900-(45+55)}{48}$$

$$= \frac{1800}{48} = 37.50$$

18. The average of the whole class

$$= \frac{(30 \times 160 + 10 \times 156)}{40} = \frac{4800+1560}{40}$$

$$= \frac{6360}{40} = 159 \text{ cm}$$

19.
$$\frac{nx-36-36}{n} = x - 8$$
$$\Rightarrow \quad nx - 72 = nx - 8n$$
$$\Rightarrow \quad 8n = 72$$
$$\Rightarrow \quad n = 9$$

20. Let the total employees be 100.

n_1 = number of females = x

n_2 = number of males = $100 - x$

$$\bar{x} = \frac{n_1\bar{x}_1 + n_2\bar{x}_2}{n_1 + n_2}$$

$$\Rightarrow \quad 500 = \frac{x \times 420 + (100-x) \times 520}{100}$$

$$\Rightarrow \quad 500 = \frac{42x + 5200 - 52x}{10}$$

$$\Rightarrow \quad 5000 = 5200 - 10x$$

$$\Rightarrow \quad 10x = 200$$

$\Rightarrow \quad x = 20$ *i.e.*, 20%.

8. PROFIT AND LOSS

Cost Price (CP)

The price at which an article is purchased is called the cost price of the article.

Selling Price (SP)

The price at which an article is sold is called the selling price of the article.

Profit or Gain

If SP is greater than the CP, the seller is said to have a profit or gain.

Clearly, $\text{Gain} = \text{SP} - \text{CP}$

Loss

If SP is less than CP, the seller is said to have a loss.

Clearly, $\text{Loss} = \text{CP} - \text{SP}$

Profit or loss per cent is calculated on cost price.

$$\text{Profit \%} = \frac{\text{Profit}}{\text{CP}} \times 100$$

$$\text{Loss \%} = \frac{\text{Loss}}{\text{CP}} \times 100$$

$$\text{SP} = \frac{\text{CP} \times (100 + \text{Profit\%})}{100}, \text{ if there is gain}$$

$$\text{SP} = \frac{\text{CP} \times (100 - \text{Loss\%})}{100}, \text{ if there is loss}$$

$$\text{CP} = \text{SP} \times \left(\frac{100}{100 + \text{Profit\%}}\right), \text{ if there is gain}$$

$$\text{CP} = \text{SP} \times \left(\frac{100}{100 - \text{Loss\%}}\right), \text{ if there is loss}$$

If an article is sold at a gain of 20%,

then, $\text{SP} = (120\% \text{ of CP})$

If an article is sold at a loss of 20%,

then, $\text{SP} = (80\% \text{ of CP})$

Overheads

The expenses incurred on transportation, rent, personnel salary, maintenance, packaging, advertisements and the like are included under the general heading of overheads. These overhead and the profit when added to the cost price determine the selling price. If the overheads are not separately mentioned in the problem, we assume it to be zero or else these have been included in the cost price itself.

Discount

It is an offer made by the seller to the buyer for reduction in price to be paid. There are several cases where discounts are allowed. For instance, to dispose off old goods, to increase its market share when the customer is ready to pay the whole amount in cash instead of instalment and so on. It is subtracted from the original price and is usually expressed as per cent or a fraction of the marked price. The price obtained after deducting the discount from the original price is the selling price which the customer has to pay.

Example: If an article is purchased for ₹ 570 and sold for ₹ 518.70, find the lost per cent.

Solution: CP = ₹ 570

SP = ₹ 518.70

∴ Loss = CP − SP

= 570 − 518.70 = ₹ 51.30

$$\text{Loss \%} = \frac{\text{Loss}}{\text{CP}} \times 100 = \frac{51.30}{570} \times 100$$

$$= \frac{5130}{570} = \frac{513}{57} = 9\%$$

EXAMPLE: A man buys a TV for ₹ 16,000. After two years he sells it for ₹ 12800. Find his loss per cent.

SOLUTION:
$$\text{Loss }\% = \frac{\text{Loss}}{\text{CP}} \times 100$$
$$= \frac{16000 - 12800}{16000} \times 100$$
$$= \frac{3200}{16000} \times 100 = 20\%$$

EXAMPLE: Mohan sells his watch at a loss of ₹ 500 for ₹ 1000. Find the cost price and loss per cent.

SOLUTION:
$$\text{CP} = \text{SP} + \text{Loss}$$
$$= 1000 + 500 = ₹\ 1500$$
$$\text{Loss }\% = \frac{\text{Loss}}{\text{CP}} \times 100 = \frac{500}{1500} \times 100$$
$$= \frac{100}{3} = 33\frac{1}{3}\%$$

EXAMPLE: Ravi buys an article for ₹ 5000 and sells it at 20% gain. Find it selling price.

SOLUTION:
$$\text{Profit} = 20\% \text{ of CP} = \frac{20}{100} \times 5000$$
$$\Rightarrow \quad \text{Profit} = ₹\ 1000$$
$$\text{SP} = \text{CP} + \text{Profit}$$
$$= 5000 + 1000$$
$$= ₹\ 6000$$

EXAMPLE: A man sells an article at 20% gain for ₹ 3600. Find its cost price.

SOLUTION: Let CP = ₹ 100

then SP = 100 + 20 = ₹ 120

When SP ₹ 120 then CP = ₹ 100

When SP ₹ 3600 then CP = $\frac{100}{120} \times 3600$

Hence CP = ₹ 3000

EXAMPLE: The cost price of 6 pens is equal to the selling price of 4 pens. Find the profit per cent.

SOLUTION: SP of 4 pens = CP of 6 pens

$$\text{SP of 2 pens} = \text{CP of } \frac{6}{4} \times 2 = 3 \text{ pens}$$
$$\text{Profit} = \text{CP of 3 pens}$$
$$\text{investment} = \text{CP of 6 pens}$$
$$\text{Profit }\% = \frac{3}{6} \times 100 = 50\%$$

Alternatively:

Let the CP of 1 pen be ₹ x.

$\therefore$ CP of 6 pens = ₹ $6x$

Also, SP of 4 pens = ₹ $6x$

$\therefore$ SP of 6 pens = $\frac{6x}{4} \times 6 = ₹\ 9x$

$$\text{Profit} = \text{SP} - \text{CP} = 9x - 6x = 3x$$
$$\text{Profit }\% = \frac{3x}{6x} \times 100 = 50\%$$

EXAMPLE: If CP of 20 tables is equal to the SP of 25 tables. Find the loss percent.

SOLUTION: Let the CP of 1 table be ₹ x.

$\therefore$ CP of 20 tables = ₹ $20x$

Also, SP of 25 tables = ₹ $20x$

$\therefore$ SP of 20 tables = ₹ $\frac{20x}{25} \times 20 = ₹\ 16x$

$$\text{Loss} = 20x - 16x = 4x$$
$$\text{Loss }\% = \frac{\text{Loss}}{\text{CP}} \times 100$$
$$= \frac{4x}{20x} \times 100 = 20\%$$

EXAMPLE: Ram sold a book at a profit of 6%. Had he sold it for ₹ 2 more he would have gained 10%. Find the cost price of the book.

SOLUTION: (10% – 6%) of CP = 4% of CP = ₹ 2

$$\Rightarrow \quad \frac{4}{100} \times \text{CP} = 2$$
$$\Rightarrow \quad \text{CP} = \frac{200}{4} = ₹\ 50$$

EXAMPLE: An article is sold for ₹ 4600 at a gain of 15%. What would be the profit or loss per cent if it is sold for ₹ 3600?

SOLUTION:
$$\text{CP} = 4600 \times \frac{100}{115} = ₹\ 4000$$
$$\text{Loss }\% = \frac{4000 - 3600}{4000} \times 100 = 10\%$$

MULTIPLE CHOICE QUESTIONS

1. A loss of 5% was suffered by selling a plot for ₹ 4085. The cost price of the plot was:
   A. ₹ 4350 B. ₹ 4259.25
   C. ₹ 4200 D. ₹ 4300
2. On selling an article for ₹ 240, a trader loses 4%. In order to gain 10%, he must sell that article for:
   A. ₹ 264.00 B. ₹ 273.20
   C. ₹ 275.00 D. ₹ 280.00
3. A man purchased a watch for ₹ 400 and sold it at a gain of 20% of the selling price. The selling price of the watch is:
   A. ₹ 300 B. ₹ 320
   C. ₹ 440 D. ₹ 500
4. If 5% more is gained by selling an article for ₹ 350 than by selling it for ₹ 340, the cost of the article is:
   A. ₹ 50 B. ₹ 160
   C. ₹ 200 D. ₹ 225
5. Profit after selling a commodity for ₹ 425 is same as loss after selling it for ₹ 355. The cost of the commodity is:
   A. ₹ 385 B. ₹ 390
   C. ₹ 395 D. ₹ 400
6. The cost price of an article, which on being sold at a gain of 12% yields ₹ 6 more than when it is sold at a loss of 12%, is:
   A. ₹ 30 B. ₹ 25
   C. ₹ 20 D. ₹ 24
7. The CP of an article which is sold at a loss of 25% for ₹150, is:
   A. ₹ 125 B. ₹ 175
   C. ₹ 200 D. ₹ 225
8. When the price of pressure cooker was increased by 15%, its sale fell down by 15%. The effect on the money receipt was:
   A. no effect B. 15% decrease
   C. 7.5% increase D. 2.25% decrease
9. A man sells 320 mangoes at the cost price of 400 mangoes. His gain per cent is:
   A. 10% B. 25%
   C. 15% D. 20%
10. By selling 12 oranges for one rupee a man loses 20%. How many for a rupee should he sell to get a gain of 20%?
    A. 5 B. 8
    C. 10 D. 15
11. A man sells a car to his friend at 10% loss. If the friend sells it for ₹ 54000 and gains 20%, the original CP of the car was:
    A. ₹ 25000 B. ₹ 37500
    C. ₹ 50000 D. ₹ 60000
12. The loss incurred on selling an article for ₹ 270 is as much as the profit made after selling it at 10% profit. The CP of the article is:
    A. ₹ 90 B. ₹ 110
    C. ₹ 363 D. ₹ 300
13. An item costing ₹ 200 is being sold at 10% loss. If the price is further reduced by 5%, the selling price will be:
    A. ₹ 179 B. ₹ 175
    C. ₹ 171 D. ₹ 170
14. A trader lists his articles 20% above CP and allows a discount of 10% on cash payment. His gain per cent is:
    A. 10% B. 6%
    C. 8% D. 5%
15. A discount series of 10%, 20% and 40% is equal to a single discount of:
    A. 50% B. 56.80%
    C. 70% D. 70.28%

ANSWERS

1	2	3	4	5	6	7	8	9	10
D	C	D	C	B	B	C	D	B	B
11	**12**	**13**	**14**	**15**					
C	D	C	C	B					

EXPLANATORY ANSWERS

1. Loss = 5%, SP = ₹ 4085

Let CP = ₹ 100

∴ SP = ₹ 100 – 5 = ₹ 95

When SP ₹ 95 then CP = ₹ 100

When SP ₹ 4085 then CP = $\frac{100}{95} \times 4085$

= 4300

Hence, the cost price of the plot was ₹ 4300.

2. Loss = 4%, SP = ₹ 240

Let CP = ₹ 100

∴ SP = 100 – 4 = 96

When SP ₹ 96 then CP = ₹ 100

When SP ₹ 240 then CP = $\frac{100}{96} \times 240$ = ₹ 250

Again 100 + 10 = 110

When CP 100 then SP = ₹ 110

When CP 250 then SP = $\frac{110}{100} \times 250$ = ₹ 275

3. Let SP = ₹ x

then, profit = $\frac{20}{100} \times x$ = ₹ $\frac{x}{5}$

CP = SP – profit = $x - \frac{x}{5}$ = ₹ $\frac{4x}{5}$

According to the question,

$$\frac{4x}{5} = 400 \Rightarrow 4x = 2000$$

$\Rightarrow$ $x = 500$

Hence, selling price of the watch = ₹ 500.

4. Let CP = ₹ x

Then, if SP = ₹350

Profit = SP – CP = ₹ $(350 - x)$

if SP = ₹ 340 then, profit = ₹ $(340 - x)$

$\therefore (350 - x) - (340 - x) = \frac{5}{100}x$

$\Rightarrow 10 = \frac{5}{100}x \quad \Rightarrow x = 200$

Hence, the cost of the article = ₹ 200.

5. Let CP = ₹ x,

then, $425 - x = x - 355 \Rightarrow 2x = 780$

$\Rightarrow x = 390$

Hence, the cost of commodity is ₹ 390.

6. Let CP of the article = ₹ x

Then, SP when profit is 12%

$$= \left(\frac{12x}{100} + x\right) = \frac{112x}{100}$$

$\therefore \quad \frac{112x}{100} - \frac{88x}{100} = 6$

$\Rightarrow \quad 24x = 600$

$\Rightarrow \quad x = \frac{600}{24} = 25$

∴ CP of the article is ₹ 25.

7. 100 – 25 = 75

When SP 75 then CP = ₹ 100

When SP 150 then CP = ₹ $\frac{100}{75} \times 150$ = ₹ 200

8. Let the original cost of each cooker be ₹ 1 and let the number sold originally be 100.

Total sale proceed = ₹ (100 × 1) = ₹ 100

New rate = (115% of ₹ 1) = ₹ 1.15

Number sold now = 85

∴ Sale proceed now = ₹(1.15 × 85) = ₹ 97.75

So, there is a decrease of 2.25% in the money receipt.

9. Let CP of each mango be ₹ 1.

Then, CP of 400 mangoes = ₹ 400

∴ CP of 320 mangoes = ₹ 320

SP of 320 mangoes = ₹ 400

Profit = 400 – 320 = ₹ 80

$$\text{Profit\%} = \frac{80}{320} \times 100 = 25\%$$

10. SP = ₹ 1, Loss = 20%

$\Rightarrow$ CP = $\left(\frac{100}{80} \times 1\right) \Rightarrow$ CP = ₹ $\frac{5}{4}$

Now, CP = ₹ $\frac{5}{4}$, gain, 20%

$\Rightarrow$ SP = $\frac{120}{100} \times \frac{5}{4}$ = ₹ $\frac{3}{2}$

For ₹$\frac{3}{2}$, he must sell 12 oranges

For ₹ 1, he must sell $\left(12 \times \frac{2}{3}\right)$ = 8 oranges.

11. SP = ₹ 54000 and gain earned = 20%

CP = ₹$\left(\frac{100}{120} \times 54000\right)$ = ₹ 45000

Now, SP = ₹ 45000 and Loss = 10%

∴ CP = ₹$\left(\frac{100}{90} \times 45000\right)$ = ₹ 50000

12. Let CP be ₹ x. Then,

$$x - 270 = 10\% \text{ of } x = \frac{x}{10}$$

$$\Rightarrow \quad x - \frac{x}{10} = 270$$

$$\Rightarrow \quad 9x = 10 \times 270$$

$$\Rightarrow \quad x = \frac{10 \times 270}{9}$$

$$\Rightarrow \quad x = 300$$

∴ CP of the article is ₹ 300.

13. SP = 90% of ₹ 200 = ₹ 180

Further, SP = (95% of ₹180) = ₹ 171

14. Let CP = ₹ 100. Then, MP = ₹ 120.

SP = 90% of ₹ 120 = $\frac{90}{100} \times 120$ = ₹ 108

Profit = SP – CP = 108 – 100 = ₹ 8

Profit % = $\frac{\text{Profit}}{\text{CP}} \times 100 = \frac{8}{100} \times 100 = 8\%$

15. Let original price = ₹ 100

Price after 1st discount = ₹ 90

Price after 2nd discount

= ₹$\left(\frac{80}{100} \times 90\right)$ = ₹ 72

Price after 3rd discount

= ₹$\left(\frac{60}{100} \times 72\right)$ = ₹ 43.20

∴ Single discount = 100 – 43.20 = 56.8%.

9. SIMPLE AND COMPOUND INTEREST

In any money transaction there is a **lender** who gives money, and a **borrower** who receives money. The amount of loan borrowed, is called the principal (P). The borrower pays a certain amount for the use of this money. This is called **Interest (I)**. Interest is always calculated on the principal borrowed. The borrowing is for a specified **Time (t)** and on specified terms. The specified term is expressed as per cent of the principal and is called rate of interest.

The sum of the principal and the interest is called the **Amount (A)**. In general, the rate of interest may be yearly, half yearly, quarterly or monthly as mutually agreed upon by both parties at the time of transaction. Depending upon the period of rate of interest, time is expressed in multiples of this period.

Interest is of two kinds—**Simple Interest and compound Interest**. If the interest is calculated only, on a certain sum borrowed it is called Simple Interest.

The simple interest (SI) on a principal P at R% per annum for T years is given by:

$$SI = \frac{P \times R \times T}{100}$$

$$\therefore \quad P = \frac{SI \times 100}{R \times T}$$

$$\therefore \quad R = \frac{SI \times 100}{P \times T}$$

$$\therefore \quad T = \frac{SI \times 100}{P \times R}$$

Compound Interest differs from Simple Interest that in CI the interest for the future period is calculated not only on the principal but also on the interest earned until the previous period. Thus, the total interest earned in case of CI is not uniformly distributed over time units whereas in Simple Interest it is uniformly distributed. The interest due at the end of the first unit of time is added to the principal and the amount so obtained becomes the principal for the second unit. Similarly, the amount after the 2nd unit of time becomes the principal for the third unit of time and continues till the last unit of time.

The difference between the final amount (A) obtained at the last unit of time and the original principal is called the **Compound Interest**.

Important Relations

Principal = ₹ P (in rupees)

Rate = R % (in per cent per annum)

Time period = T years (in years)

Amount = ₹ A (in rupees)

I. When interest is compounded annually,

$$A = P\left[1 + \frac{R}{100}\right]^T$$

II. When interest is compounded half-yearly,

$$A = P\left[1 + \frac{R/2}{100}\right]^{2T} = P\left[1 + \frac{R}{200}\right]^{2T}$$

[R is divided by 2 and T is multiplied by 2.]

III. When interest is compounded quarterly,

$$A = P\left[1+\frac{R/4}{100}\right]^{4T} = P\left[1+\frac{R}{400}\right]^{4T}$$

[R is divided by 4 and T is multiplied by 4.]

IV. When interest is $R_1\%$ for first year, $R_2\%$ for 2nd year and $R_3\%$ for third year;

$$A = P\left[1+\frac{R_1}{100}\right]\left[1+\frac{R_2}{100}\right]\left[1+\frac{R_3}{100}\right]$$

V. CI = A – P

EXAMPLE: Find the simple interest on ₹ 1000 for 3 years at 10% p.a.

SOLUTION: $SI = \frac{P \times R \times T}{100} = \frac{1000 \times 10 \times 3}{100} = ₹\ 300$

EXAMPLE: Find the amount of ₹ 600 in 4 years at 3% p.a.

SOLUTION: $SI = \frac{P \times R \times T}{100} = \frac{600 \times 3 \times 4}{100} = ₹\ 72$

$\therefore$ Amount = P + SI = 600 + 72 = ₹ 672

EXAMPLE: In what time will ₹ 7000 give ₹ 3675 as interest at the rate of 7% p.a. simple interest?

SOLUTION: $T = \frac{SI \times 100}{P \times R} = \frac{3675 \times 100}{7000 \times 7}$

$= \frac{15}{2} = 7\frac{1}{2}$ years.

EXAMPLE: At what rate per annum will a sum of ₹ 5000 amount to ₹ 6000 in 4 years?

SOLUTION: SI = A – P = 6000 – 5000 = ₹ 1000

$R = \frac{SI \times 100}{P \times T} = \frac{1000 \times 100}{5000 \times 4} = 5\%$

EXAMPLE: In how many years will a sum of money double itself at 5% rate of interest?

SOLUTION: A sum doubles itself when amount of interest becomes equal to the principal

SI = P, R = 5%

$\therefore \quad T = \frac{100 \times P}{P \times 5} = 20$ years

EXAMPLE: A certain sum amounts to ₹ 115200 in 2 years and to ₹ 165888 in 4 years. Find the sum and rate per cent.

SOLUTION: Here, amount on ₹ 115200 for 2 years at CI is ₹ 165888

$$\therefore \quad 115200\left(1+\frac{R}{100}\right)^2 = 165888$$

$$\left(1+\frac{R}{100}\right)^2 = \frac{165888}{115200} = 1.44$$

$$\therefore \quad 1+\frac{R}{100} = 1.2$$

$$\frac{R}{100} = 1.2 - 1 = 0.2$$

$$\Rightarrow \quad R = 0.2 \times 100 = 20\%$$

Amount after 2 years is ₹ 115200

$$\therefore \quad P\left(1+\frac{20}{100}\right)^2 = 115200$$

$$\Rightarrow \quad P = \frac{115200}{\left(1+\frac{20}{100}\right)^2} = \frac{115200}{1.44} = 80000$$

$\therefore$ Principal = ₹ 80000

EXAMPLE: A sum of money doubles itself at CI in 15 years. In how many years will it become eight times?

SOLUTION: $P\left(1+\frac{R}{100}\right)^{15} = 2P$

$$\Rightarrow \quad \left(1+\frac{R}{100}\right)^{15} = 2$$

Let T be the required number of years that makes the principal 8 times of it.

$$\therefore \quad P\left(1+\frac{R}{100}\right)^{T} = 8P$$

$$\Rightarrow \quad \left(1+\frac{R}{100}\right)^{T} = 8 = (2)^3$$

$$\Rightarrow \quad \left(1+\frac{R}{100}\right)^{T} = \left[\left(1+\frac{R}{100}\right)^{15}\right]^3$$

$$\Rightarrow \quad \left(1+\frac{R}{100}\right)^{T} = \left(1+\frac{R}{100}\right)^{45}$$

$$\Rightarrow \quad T = 45 \text{ years}$$

Hence, required number of years is 45 years.

EXAMPLE: The difference between simple and compound interest on a sum of money at 5% p.a. for 2 years is ₹ 25. Find the sum.

SOLUTION: Let P = ₹ 100

$$SI = \frac{P \times R \times T}{100} = \frac{100 \times 5 \times 2}{100} = ₹\ 10$$

$$A = P\left(1+\frac{R}{100}\right)^T = 100\left(1+\frac{5}{100}\right)^2$$

$$= \frac{100 \times 21 \times 21}{400} = ₹\frac{441}{4}$$

$$CI = A - P = \frac{441}{4} - 100 = ₹\frac{41}{4}$$

$$CI - SI = \frac{41}{4} - 10 = \frac{41-40}{4} = ₹\frac{1}{4}$$

When difference ₹$\frac{1}{4}$ then P = ₹ 100

When difference ₹ 25 then P = $100 \times 4 \times 25$

= ₹ 10000

Hence, sum = ₹ 10000.

MULTIPLE CHOICE QUESTIONS

1. The simple interest on ₹ 500 for 6 years at 5% p.a. is:

A. ₹ 250 B. ₹ 150
C. ₹ 140 D. ₹ 120

2. A certain sum of money at SI amounts to ₹ 1012 in $2\frac{1}{2}$ years and to ₹ 1067.20 in 4 years. The rate of interest per annum is:

A. 2.5% B. 3%
C. 4% D. 5%

3. ₹ 1200 amounts to ₹ 1632 in 4 years at a certain rate of simple interest. If the rate of interest is increased by 1%, it would amount to how much?

A. ₹ 1635 B. ₹ 1644
C. ₹ 1670 D. ₹ 1680

4. A man will get ₹ 87 as simple interest on ₹ 725 at 4% per annum in:

A. 3 years B. 3½ years
C. 4 years D. 5 years

5. At simple interest, a sum doubles after 20 years. The rate of interest per annum is:

A. 5% B. 10%
C. 20% D. Data inadequate

6. A lent ₹ 600 to B for 2 years and ₹ 150 to C for 4 years and received altogether from both ₹ 90 as simple interest. The rate of interest is:

A. 12% B. 10%
C. 5% D. 4%

7. Interest on a certain sum of money for $2\frac{1}{3}$ years at $3\frac{3}{4}\%$ per annum is ₹ 210. The sum is:

A. ₹ 2800 B. ₹ 1580
C. ₹ 2400 D. None of these

8. A certain sum of money at simple interest amounts to ₹ 1260 in 2 years and to ₹ 1350 in 5 years. The rate per cent per annum is:

A. 2.5% B. 3.75%
C. 5% D. 7.5%

9. A sum of money doubles itself in 5 years. It will become 4 times itself in:

A. 10 years B. 12 years
C. 15 years D. 20 years

10. The simple interest on a sum of money will be ₹ 600 after 10 years. If the principal is trebled after 5 years, the total interest at the end of 10 years will be:

A. ₹ 600 B. ₹ 900
C. ₹ 1200 D. Data inadequate

11. ₹ 800 amounts to ₹ 920 in 3 years at simple interest. If the interest rate is increased by 3%, it would amount to how much?

A. ₹ 1056 B. ₹ 1112
C. ₹ 1182 D. ₹ 992

12. A sum of money at simple interest amounts to ₹ 2240 in 2 years and ₹ 2600 in 5 years. The sum is:

A. ₹ 1880 B. ₹ 2000
C. ₹ 2120 D. Data inadequate

13. If ₹ 7500 are borrowed at CI at the rate of 4% per annum, then after 2 years the amount to be paid is:
A. ₹ 8082 B. ₹ 7800
C. ₹ 8100 D. ₹ 8112

14. Simple interest on a sum at 4% per annum is ₹ 80 in 2 years. The compound interest on the same sum for the same period is:
A. ₹ 81.60 B. ₹ 160
C. ₹ 1081.60 D. None of these

15. ₹ 800 at 5% per annum compound interest will amount to ₹ 882 in:
A. 1 year B. 2 years
C. 3 years D. 4 years

ANSWERS

1	2	3	4	5	6	7	8	9	10
B	C	D	A	A	C	C	A	C	C
11	**12**	**13**	**14**	**15**					
D	B	D	A	B					

EXPLANATORY ANSWERS

1. $SI = \frac{P \times R \times T}{100} = \frac{500 \times 5 \times 6}{100} = ₹\,150$

2. SI for $1\frac{1}{2}$ years $= 1067.20 - 1012 = ₹\,55.20$

SI for $2\frac{1}{2}$ years $= 55.20 \times \frac{2}{3} \times \frac{5}{2} = ₹\,92$

$\therefore$ Principal $= ₹\,(1012 - 92) = ₹\,920$

$R = \frac{SI \times 100}{P \times T} = \frac{92 \times 100 \times 2}{920 \times 5} = 4\%$

3. $R = \frac{SI \times 100}{P \times T} = \frac{432 \times 100}{1200 \times 4} = 9\%$

New rate $= (9 + 1)\% = 10\%$

$SI = \frac{P \times R \times T}{100} = \frac{1200 \times 10 \times 4}{100} = ₹\,480$

Amount $= P + SI = 1200 + 480 = ₹\,1680$

4. $T = \frac{SI \times 100}{P \times R} = \frac{87 \times 100}{725 \times 4} = 3$ years

5. Let P be ₹ x then A = ₹ $2x$

$SI = A - P = 2x - x = ₹\,x$

$R = \frac{SI \times 100}{P \times T} = \frac{x \times 100}{x \times 20} = 5\%$

6. $SI = \frac{P \times R \times T}{100} = \frac{600 \times R \times 2}{100} = 12R$

Again $SI = \frac{P \times R \times T}{100} = \frac{150 \times R \times 4}{100} = 6R$

Total SI = 12R + 6R = 18R

According to the question,

$18R = 90 \Rightarrow R = \frac{90}{18} = 5\%$

7. $T = 2\frac{1}{3} = \frac{7}{3}$ years,

$R = 3\frac{3}{4}\% = \frac{15}{4}\%$

$P = \frac{SI \times 100}{P \times T} = \frac{210 \times 100}{\frac{15}{4} \times \frac{7}{3}}$

$= \frac{210 \times 100 \times 4 \times 3}{15 \times 7} = ₹\,2400$

8. SI for 3 years $= ₹\,1350 - ₹\,1260 = ₹\,90$

SI for 1 year $= \frac{90}{3} = ₹\,30$

SI for 2 years $= ₹\,30 \times 2 = ₹\,60$

$P = A - SI = 1260 - 60 = ₹\,1200$

$R = \frac{SI \times 100}{P \times T} = \frac{60 \times 100}{1200 \times 2} = \frac{5}{2} = 2.5\%$

9. Let P be ₹ x, A = ₹ $2x$,
SI = $2x - x$ = ₹ x

$$R = \frac{SI \times 100}{P \times T} = \frac{x \times 100}{x \times 5} = 20\%$$

Again, P = ₹ x, A = $4x$,
SI = $4x - x = 3x$

$$T = \frac{SI \times 100}{P \times R} = \frac{3x \times 100}{x \times 20} = 15 \text{ years}$$

10. Let P be ₹ x
SI = ₹ 600, T = 10 years.

$$R = \frac{SI \times 100}{P \times T} = \frac{600 \times 100}{x \times 10} = \frac{6000}{x}\%$$

$$\text{SI for first 5 years} = \frac{x \times 5 \times 6000}{100 \times x} = ₹\, 300$$

$$\text{SI for last 5 years} = \frac{3x \times 5 \times 6000}{100 \times x} = ₹\, 900$$

Total interest at the end of 10 years
= 900 + 300 = ₹ 1200.

11. P = ₹ 800, SI = 920 – 800 = ₹ 120
T = 3 years

$$R = \frac{SI \times 100}{P \times T} = \frac{120 \times 100}{800 \times 3} = 5\%$$

New rate = 8% (increase 3%)

$$SI = \frac{P \times R \times T}{100} = \frac{800 \times 8 \times 3}{100} = ₹\, 192$$

∴ A = P + SI = 800 + 192 = ₹ 992.

12. SI for 3 years = 2600 – 2240 = ₹ 360

$$\text{SI for 2 years} = \frac{360}{3} \times 2 = ₹\, 240$$

∴ Sum = 2240 – 240 = ₹ 2000

13. $$A = P\left(1 + \frac{R}{100}\right)^T = 7500\left(1 + \frac{4}{100}\right)^2$$

$$= 7500 \times \frac{26}{25} \times \frac{26}{25} = ₹\, 8112$$

14. $$P = \frac{SI \times 100}{T \times R} = \frac{80 \times 100}{4 \times 2} = ₹\, 1000$$

$$A = P\left(1 + \frac{R}{100}\right)^T = 1000\left(1 + \frac{4}{100}\right)^2$$

$$= 1000 \times \frac{26}{25} \times \frac{26}{25} = 1081.60$$

CI = A – P = 1081.60 – 1000 = ₹ 81.60

15. Let time = x years

$$A = P\left(1 + \frac{R}{100}\right)^T$$

$$882 = 800\left(1 + \frac{5}{100}\right)^x$$

$$\Rightarrow \frac{882}{800} = \left(\frac{21}{20}\right)^x$$

$$\Rightarrow \left(\frac{21}{20}\right)^2 = \left(\frac{21}{20}\right)^x \Rightarrow x = 2$$

∴ Time = 2 years

10. TIME AND WORK

Performing or doing work of any amount involves efforts of person (S) over a period of time. Therefore, the number of persons (P), the quantity of work (W) and the period of time (T) are important variables in problems related to "Time and Work". Moreover time (T) taken to do a work depends not only on how many persons are employed to do it but also on how efficient they are. Efficiency here means rate of doing same work. This aspect comes into picture when the problem involves comparison of work done by different categories of persons. For instance, efficiencies of man, woman, boy, girl in general are different. Even efficiency of one man may not be same as that of other; but unless otherwise specifically stated in the problem, all men or women working in a group are assumed to do work with equal efficiency.

The problems on Time and Work can be solved by following two methods:

(*i*) Ratio and proportion method

(*ii*) Unitary method

(*i*) **Ratio and Proportion Method:** Since problems concerning to Time and Work have proportional relation, these can be solved by this method. We have tried to solve questions based on Time and Work in the chapter mentioned.

(*ii*) **Unitary Method:** This is a very simple and useful method. The term 'Unitary' is self-evident. In this method, we first proceed to reduce the problem to either work done by one person or work done in 1 day and so on as per the requirement of the problem. Let us try to understand it.

(*a*) If a man can do a piece of work in 10 days he will do $\frac{1}{10}$ of the work in 1 day. Conversely, if a man can do $\frac{1}{10}$ of the work in 1 day, he will do the work in 10 days.

(*b*) If the number of men engaged to do a piece of work be changed in the ratio 5 : 4, the time required for the work will be changed in the ratio 4 : 5.

(*c*) If A is x times as good a workman as B, then A will take $\frac{1}{x}$ of the time that B takes to do a certain work.

All the above points can be summarised into one and can be written in the following form:

If M_1 persons can do W_1 works in D_1 days and M_2 persons can do W_2 works in D_2 days then we have a very general formula in the relationship of

$$M_1 D_1 W_2 = M_2 D_2 W_1$$

The above relationship can be taken as a very basic and all-in-one formula we also derive:

(*i*) More men less days and conversely more days less men.

(*ii*) More men more work and conversely more work more men.

(*iii*) More days more work and conversely more work more days.

$$M_1 D_1 T_1 W_2 = M_2 D_2 T_2 W_1$$

EXAMPLE: 5 men can prepare 10 toys in 6 days working 6 hrs a day. How many days can 12 men prepare 16 toys working 8 hrs a day?

SOLUTION: $M_1 D_1 T_1 W_2 = M_2 D_2 T_2 W_1$

$$5 \times 6 \times 6 \times 16 = 12 \times D_2 \times 8 \times 10$$

$$D_2 = \frac{5 \times 6 \times 6 \times 16}{12 \times 8 \times 10} = 3 \text{ days.}$$

EXAMPLE: A can reap a field in 8 days, which B alone can reap in 12 days. In how many days, both together, can reap this field?

SOLUTION: A's 1 day's work $= \frac{1}{8}$

B's 1 day's work $= \frac{1}{12}$

(A + B)'s 1 day's work $= \left(\frac{1}{8}+\frac{1}{12}\right)$

$$= \frac{3+2}{24} = \frac{5}{24}$$

$\therefore$ Both together can reap the field in $\frac{24}{5}$ days

$$= 4\frac{4}{5} \text{ days.}$$

EXAMPLE: A and B together can do a piece of work in 12 days, B alone can finish it in 30 days. In how many days can A alone finish the work?

SOLUTION: (A + B)'s 1 day's work $= \frac{1}{12}$

B's 1 day's work $= \frac{1}{30}$

$\therefore$ A's 1 day's work $= \frac{1}{12} - \frac{1}{30}$

$$= \frac{5-2}{60} = \frac{3}{60} = \frac{1}{20}$$

Hence, A alone can finish the work in 20 days.

EXAMPLE: A and B can do a piece of work in 12 days, C and A in 20 days and B and C in 15 days. In how many days will they finish it together and separately?

SOLUTION: (A + B)'s 1 day's work $= \frac{1}{12}$

(B + C)'s 1 day's work $= \frac{1}{15}$

(C + A)'s 1 day's work $= \frac{1}{20}$

Adding, 2(A + B + C)'s 1 day's work

$$= \left(\frac{1}{12}+\frac{1}{15}+\frac{1}{20}\right) = \frac{5+4+3}{60}$$

$$= \frac{12}{60} = \frac{1}{5}$$

or (A + B + C)'s 1 day's work $= \frac{1}{10}$

$\therefore$ A, B, C together can finish the work in 10 days.

Now, C's 1 day's work $= \frac{1}{10} - \frac{1}{12} = \frac{1}{60}$

$\therefore$ C alone can finish the work in 60 days.

Similarly B's 1 day's work $= \frac{1}{10} - \frac{1}{20} = \frac{1}{20}$

$\therefore$ B alone can finish the work in 20 days.

A's 1 day's work $= \frac{1}{10} - \frac{1}{15} = \frac{1}{30}$

$\therefore$ A alone can finish the work in 30 days.

EXAMPLE: A can do a piece of work in 25 days and B can finish it in 20 days. They work together for 5 days and then A goes away. In how many days will B finish the work?

SOLUTION: (A + B)'s 5 days work $= 5\left(\frac{1}{25}+\frac{1}{20}\right) = \frac{9}{20}$

Remaining work $= 1 - \frac{9}{20} = \frac{11}{20}$

Now, $\frac{1}{20}$ work is finished by B in 1 day

$\therefore$ $\frac{11}{20}$ work will be finished by B in $\left(\frac{20 \times 11}{20}\right)$ = 11 days.

EXAMPLE: A is thrice as good a workman as B and is therefore able to finish a piece of work in 60 days less than B. Find the time in which they can do it, working together.

SOLUTION: Ratio of work done by A and B in the same time = 3 : 1

Ratio of time taken by A and B = 1 : 3

Suppose B takes x days to finish a work

then, A takes $(x - 60)$ days

$$\therefore \frac{x-60}{x} = \frac{1}{3} \text{ or } 3(x-60) = x \Rightarrow x = 90$$

$\therefore$ B can finish the work in 90 days.

A can finish the work in (90 – 60) = 30 days

Both finish the work $= \left[\frac{1}{30}+\frac{1}{90} = \frac{2}{45}\right]$

$$= \frac{45}{2} = 22\frac{1}{2} \text{ days.}$$

EXAMPLE: A certain number of men complete a piece of work in 60 days. If there were 8 men more, the work could be finished in 10 days less. How many men were originally there?

SOLUTION: Let the original number of men be x.
Now, x men can finish the work in 60 days
and $(x + 8)$ men can finish it in $(60 - 10)$ *i.e.*, 50 days.

$$\therefore \quad x + 8 : x :: 60 : 50$$

$$\Rightarrow \quad \frac{x+8}{x} = \frac{60}{50} = \frac{6}{5}$$

$$\Rightarrow \quad 6x = 5x + 40 \Rightarrow x = 40$$

Hence, the original number of men = 40.

EXAMPLE: If 4 men or 6 boys can finish a piece of work in 20 days, in how many days can 6 men and 11 boys finish it?

SOLUTION: 4 men = 6 boys

$$\therefore \quad 6 \text{ men} = \frac{6}{4} \times 6 = \frac{36}{4} = 9 \text{ boys}$$

6 men + 11 boys = 9 + 11 = 20 boys

Now, 6 boys can finish a work in 20 days.
1 boy can finish the same work in 6×20 days.

20 boys can finish the same work in $\frac{6 \times 20}{20}$

= 6 days.

EXAMPLE: If 12 men can build a wall 360 m long in 54 days, how many days will it take to build a similar wall 160 m long, if 16 men working on it?

SOLUTION: 12 men can build 360 m long wall in 54 days.

1 man can build 360 m long wall in 54×12 days.

1 man can build 1 m long wall in $\frac{54 \times 12}{360}$ days

16 men can build 1 m long wall in $\frac{54 \times 12}{360 \times 16}$ days

16 men can build 160 m long wall in $\frac{54 \times 12 \times 160}{360 \times 16}$ days

= 18 days.

EXAMPLE: If 3 persons weave 168 carpets in 7 days, how many carpets will 8 persons weave in 5 days?

SOLUTION: 3 persons can weave in 7 days 168 carpets

1 person can weave in 7 days = $\frac{168}{3}$ carpets

1 person can weave in 1 day = $\frac{168}{3 \times 7}$ carpets

8 persons can weave in 1 day = $\frac{168 \times 8}{3 \times 7}$ carpets

8 persons can weave in 5 days = $\frac{168 \times 8 \times 5}{3 \times 7}$ carpets

= 320 carpets

EXAMPLE: Mukesh can do a job in 12 days while Manoj can do the same job in 15 days. They undertake to complete the job for ₹ 5400. What will be the share of each in the income?

SOLUTION: Mukesh's 1 day's work = $\frac{1}{12}$

Manoj's 1 day's work = $\frac{1}{15}$

Ratio of their 1 day's work = $\frac{1}{12} : \frac{1}{15} = 5 : 4$

$\therefore$ Mukesh's share = ₹ $\frac{5}{9} \times 5400$ = ₹ 3000

Manoj's share = ₹ $\frac{4}{9} \times 5400$ = ₹ 2400

MULTIPLE CHOICE QUESTIONS

1. A and B can together do a piece of work in 15 days. B alone can do it in 20 days. In how many days can A alone do it?

A. 30 days B. 40 days
C. 45 days D. 60 days

2. A can do a piece of work in 30 days while B can do it in 40 days. A and B working together can do it in:

A. 70 days B. $42\frac{3}{4}$ days
C. $27\frac{1}{7}$ days D. $17\frac{1}{7}$ days

3. A can do $\frac{1}{3}$ of the work in 5 days and B can do $\frac{2}{5}$ of the work in 10 days. In how many days both A and B together can do the work?

A. $7\frac{3}{4}$ days B. $8\frac{4}{5}$ days

C. $9\frac{3}{8}$ days D. 10 days

4. A, B and C can do a piece of work in 6, 12 and 24 days respectively. They altogether will complete the work in:

A. $3\frac{3}{7}$ days B. $\frac{7}{24}$ days

C. $4\frac{4}{5}$ days D. $\frac{5}{24}$ days

5. A, B and C contract a work for ₹ 550. Together A and B are to do $\frac{7}{11}$ of the work. The share of C should be:

A. ₹ $183\frac{1}{3}$ B. ₹ 200

C. ₹ 300 D. ₹ 400

6. A and B finish a job in 12 days while A, B and C can finish it in 8 days. C alone will finish the job in:

A. 20 days B. 14 days

C. 24 days D. 16 days

7. 12 men can complete a work in 8 days. Three days after they started the work, 3 more men joined them. In how many days will all of them together complete the remaining work?

A. 2 B. 4

C. 5 D. 6

8. Mahesh and Umesh can complete a work in 10 and 15 days respectively. Umesh starts the work and after 5 days Mahesh joins him. In all, the work would be completed in:

A. 9 days B. 7 days

C. 11 days D. None of these

9. Sunil completes a work in 4 days whereas Dinesh completes the work in 6 days. Ramesh works $1\frac{1}{2}$ times as fast as Sunil. How many days it will take for the three together to complete the work?

A. $\frac{7}{12}$ B. $1\frac{5}{12}$

C. $1\frac{5}{7}$ D. None of these

10. A can complete a work in 6 days and B in 5 days. They work together, finish the job and receive ₹ 220 as wages. B's share should be:

A. ₹ 120 B. ₹ 110

C. ₹ 100 D. ₹ 90

11. 12 men and 8 children can finish a piece of work in 9 days. If each child takes twice the time taken by a man to finish the work, in how many days will 12 men finish the same work?

A. 8 days B. 15 days

C. 9 days D. 12 days

12. A, B and C together earn ₹ 150 per day while A and C together earn ₹ 94 and B and C together earn ₹ 76. The daily earning of C is:

A. ₹ 75 B. ₹ 56

C. ₹ 34 D. ₹ 20

13. If 5 men or 9 women can finish a piece of work in 19 days, 3 men and 6 women will do the same work in:

A. 10 days B. 12 days

C. 13 days D. 15 days

14. A can do a piece of work in 12 days. B is 60% more efficient than A. The number of days, it takes B to do the same piece of work, is:

A. $7\frac{1}{2}$ days B. $6\frac{1}{4}$ days

C. 8 days D. 6 days

15. A and B can do a piece of work in 45 and 40 days respectively. They began the work together, but A leaves after some days and B finished the remaining work in 23 days. After how many days did A leave?

A. 6 days B. 8 days

C. 9 days D. 12 days

ANSWERS

1	2	3	4	5	6	7	8	9	10
D	D	C	A	B	C	B	A	D	A
11	**12**	**13**	**14**	**15**					
D	D	D	A	C					

EXPLANATORY ANSWERS

1. (A + B)'s 1 day's work = $\frac{1}{15}$

B's 1 day's work = $\frac{1}{20}$

A's 1 day's work = $\frac{1}{15} - \frac{1}{20} = \frac{4-3}{60} = \frac{1}{60}$

∴ A can do this work alone in 60 days.

2. A's 1 day's work = $\frac{1}{30}$

B's 1 day's work = $\frac{1}{40}$

(A + B)'s 1 day's work

$= \frac{1}{30} + \frac{1}{40} = \frac{4+3}{120} = \frac{7}{120}$

∴ Both together will finish the work in $\frac{120}{7}$

$= 17\frac{1}{7}$ days.

3. $\frac{1}{3}$ of the work is done by A in 5 days.

∴ Whole work will be done by A in 3 × 5

= 15 days

$\frac{2}{5}$ of the work is done by B in 10 days.

Whole work will be done by B in $\left(10 \times \frac{5}{2}\right)$

= 25 days

(A + B)'s 1 day's work = $\frac{1}{15} + \frac{1}{25} = \frac{5+3}{75} = \frac{8}{75}$

∴ Both together can finish it in $\frac{75}{8} = 9\frac{3}{8}$ days.

4. A's 1 day's work = $\frac{1}{6}$

B's 1 day's work = $\frac{1}{12}$

C's 1 day's work = $\frac{1}{24}$

(A + B + C)'s 1 day's work = $\frac{1}{6} + \frac{1}{12} + \frac{1}{24}$

$= \frac{4+2+1}{24} = \frac{7}{24}$

∴ They all together will complete the work in

$\frac{24}{7}$ days = $3\frac{3}{7}$ days

5. Work to be done by C = $\left(1 - \frac{7}{11}\right) = \frac{4}{11}$

∴ (A + B) : C = $\frac{7}{11} : \frac{4}{11} = 7 : 4$

∴ C's share = ₹$\frac{4}{11} \times 550$ = ₹200

6. (A + B)'s 1 day's work = $\frac{1}{12}$

(A + B + C)'s 1 day's work = $\frac{1}{8}$

C's 1 day's work = $\frac{1}{8} - \frac{1}{12} = \frac{3-2}{24} = \frac{1}{24}$

Hence, C will complete the work in 24 days.

7. 1 man's 1 day's work = $\frac{1}{96}$

12 men's 3 day's work = $\frac{12}{96} \times 3 = \frac{3}{8}$

Remaining work = $\left(1-\frac{3}{8}\right) = \frac{5}{8}$

15 men's 1 day's work = $\frac{15}{96}$

Now, $\frac{15}{96}$ work is done by them in 1 day

$\therefore$ $\frac{5}{8}$ work will be done by them in $\frac{96}{15} \times \frac{5}{8}$

= 4 days

8. Umesh's 5 day's work = $\frac{5}{15} = \frac{1}{3}$

Remaining work = $\left(1-\frac{1}{3}\right) = \frac{2}{3}$

Now, $\left(\frac{1}{10}+\frac{1}{15}\right)$ work is done by A and B in 1 day.

$\therefore$ $\frac{2}{3}$ work will be done by A and B in $6 \times \frac{2}{3}$

= 4 days.

So, the work would be completed in (5 + 4)

= 9 days.

9. Time taken by Ramesh alone = $\frac{2}{3} \times 4 = \frac{8}{3}$ days

$\therefore$ Their 1 day's work = $\left(\frac{1}{4}+\frac{1}{6}+\frac{3}{8}\right)$

$= \frac{6+4+9}{24} = \frac{19}{24}$

So, together they can finish the work in $\frac{24}{19}$ days

$= 1\frac{5}{19}$ days.

10. Ratio of time taken by A and B = 6 : 5

Ratio of work done in same time = 5 : 6

So, the money is to be divided among A and B in the ratio 5 : 6.

$\therefore$ B's share = ₹ $\frac{6}{11} \times 220$ = ₹ 120

11. 2 children = 1 man

$\therefore$ 8 children + 12 men = 4 + 12 = 16 men

Now, less men, more days

$12 : 16 :: 9 : x \Rightarrow \frac{12}{16} = \frac{9}{x} \Rightarrow x = 12$ days

12. B's daily earning = ₹ (150 – 94) = ₹ 56

A's daily earning = ₹ (150 – 76) = ₹ 74

C's daily earning = ₹ [150 – (56 + 74)] = ₹ 20

13. 5 men = 9 women $\Rightarrow$ 1 man = $\frac{9}{5}$ women

$\therefore$ 3 men + 6 women = $\left(3 \times \frac{9}{5} + 6\right) = \frac{57}{5}$ women

Now, 9 women can do the work in 19 days

$\therefore$ $\frac{57}{5}$ women can do it in $\frac{9 \times 19 \times 5}{57}$ = 15 days

14. A's 1 day's work = $\frac{1}{12}$

B's 1 day's work = $\frac{1}{12}$ + 60% of $\frac{1}{12} = \frac{2}{15}$

Hence, B can do the whole work in $\frac{15}{2}$

$= 7\frac{1}{2}$ days.

15. B's 23 day's work = $\frac{23}{40}$

Remaining work = $\left(1-\frac{23}{40}\right) = \frac{17}{40}$

Now, (A + B)'s 1 day's work = $\left(\frac{1}{45}+\frac{1}{40}\right) = \frac{17}{360}$

$\frac{17}{360}$ work is done by A and B in 1 day

$\frac{17}{40}$ work is done by A and B in $\frac{360}{17} \times \frac{17}{40}$

= 9 days.

Hence, A left after 9 days.

11. AREA AND PERIMETER

The area of any figure is the amount of surface enclosed within its boundary lines. It is measured by the number of square metres or square centimetres or square inches (or some other units of square measure) it contains.

Perimeter

Perimeter of a geometrical figure is the total length of the sides enclosing the figure.

Triangle

A triangle is a plane figure bounded by three sides. It includes three angles. It is denoted by the symbol Δ. The sum of angles of a triangle is 180°.

(*i*) **Equilateral Triangle:** A triangle in which all sides are equal is called an equilateral triangle.

(*ii*) **Isosceles Triangle:** A triangle in which two sides are equal is called an isosceles triangle.

(*iii*) **Scalene Triangle:** A triangle in which all sides are different or unequal is called scalene triangle.

(*iv*) **Right Angled Triangle:** A triangle having one of the angles equal to 90° is called a right angled triangle. The side opposite to the right angle of a triangle is called its hypotenuse.

Quadrilateral

A plane figure bounded by four straight lines is called a quadrilateral.

Various Types of Quadrilaterals:

(*i*) **Rectangle:** A quadrilateral whose opposite sides are equal and all angles are at right angles. The diagonals of a rectangle are equal.

(*ii*) **Square:** A rectangle having all sides are equal is called a square.

(*iii*) **Parallelogram:** A quadrilateral whose opposite sides are equal and parallel is called parallelogram.

(*iv*) **Rhombus:** A parallelogram having all the sides equal is called a rhombus. Diagonals of a rhombus are not equal and they bisect each other at right angles.

(*v*) **Trapezium:** A quadrilateral having one pair of opposite sides parallel, is called a trapezium.

Circle

The path traced by a point which moves in such a way that its distance from a fixed point is always same, is called a circle. The fixed point is called its centre and fixed distance is called its radius. The length of the whole path of a circle is called its circumference.

(*i*) **Arc:** Any part of the circumference of a circle is called an arc.

(*ii*) **Chord:** The straight line joining the ends of an arc of a circle is called a chord.

(*iii*) **Diameter:** The chord passing through the centre of a circle is called its diameter.

The diameter of a circle divides the circle into two equal parts, each one of which is called a semi-circle.

(*iv*) **Segment:** The area enclosed by an arc and a chord is called a segment.

(*v*) **Sector:** The area bounded by an arc and two radii is called a sector.

Formulae for Area of Various Figures:

(*i*) **Rectangle:**

Area of rectangle = $l \times b$

Perimeter of rectangle = $2(l + b)$.

(*ii*) **Square:**

Area of square = $(\text{side})^2$

Perimeter of square = $4 \times \text{side}$

Area of room = $l \times b$

Area of 4 walls of a room = $2(l + b) \times h$

(*iii*) **Parallelogram:**

Area of $11^{gm} = b \times h$

Area of rhombus = $\frac{1}{2} \times d_1 \times d_2$.

(*iv*) **Trapezium:**

Area of trapezium = $\frac{1}{2}$(sum of parallel sides) × (distance between them)

(*v*) **Triangle:**

(*a*) Area of right triangle = $\frac{1}{2} \times b \times h$

(*b*) Area of equilateral triangle = $\frac{\sqrt{3}}{4} \times (\text{side})^2$

(*c*) Area of scalene triangle

$$= \sqrt{s(s-a)(s-b)(s-c)}$$

where, $s = \frac{a+b+c}{2}$

(*vi*) **Circle:**

(*a*) Area of circle = πr^2

(*b*) Circumference of a circle = $2\pi r$

(*c*) Length of arc = $\frac{\theta}{360} \times 2\pi r$

(*d*) Area of sector = $\frac{\theta}{360} \times \pi r^2$

Polygon

A polygon is plane figure bounded by multiple number of sides. Normally, it is used for figures enclosed by more than four sides: *e.g.*, pentagon, hexagon, octagon etc.

Regular Polygon

It is a polygon whose all sides are equal.

For a regular polygon of n equal sides, its vertex angle θ is given by

$$\theta = \left(\frac{n-2}{n}\right) \times 180°$$

Example: Find the area and perimeter of a rectangle whose length is 25 m and breadth is 15 m.

Solution: Area of rectangle $= l \times b$

$$= 25 \times 15 = 375 \text{ m}^2$$

Perimeter of rectangle $= 2(l + b)$

$$= 2(25 + 15) = 80 \text{ m}$$

Example: Find the area of a rectangle whose one side is 6 m and the diagonal is 10 m.

Solution: Another side of rectangle = $\sqrt{(10)^2 - (6)^2}$

$$= \sqrt{100 - 36} = \sqrt{64} = 8 \text{ m}$$

Area of rectangle = $l \times b = 8 \times 6 = 48 \text{ m}^2$

Example: Find area and perimeter of a square whose each side is 12 cm.

Solution: Area of square = $(\text{side})^2 = (12)^2 = 144 \text{ cm}^2$

Perimeter of square = $4 \times \text{side} = 4 \times 12 = 48$ cm

Example: Find the area of a parallelogram whose base is 35 m and altitude 18 m.

Solution: Area of parallelogram = $b \times h$

$$= 35 \times 18 = 630 \text{ m}^2$$

Example: Find the area of a rhombus one side of which measures 20 cm and one diagonal 24 cm.

Solution: Since the diagonals of a rhombus bisect at right angles, so one side and half of each of the diagonals form a right angled triangle. In this right angled triangle,

One side = 20 cm, another side = $\frac{24}{2} = 12$ cm

$$\text{Third side} = \sqrt{(20)^2 - (12)^2} = \sqrt{400 - 144}$$

$$= \sqrt{256} = 16 \text{ cm}$$

Hence other diagonal = $16 \times 2 = 32$ cm

$$\text{Area of rhombus} = \frac{1}{2} \times d_1 \times d_2$$

$$= \frac{1}{2} \times 24 \times 32 = 12 \times 32$$

$$= 384 \text{ cm}^2$$

Example: Find the area of an equilateral triangle each of whose sides measures 12 cm.

Solution: Area of equilateral triangle

$$= \frac{\sqrt{3}}{4} (\text{side})^2 = \frac{\sqrt{3}}{4} \times (12)^2$$

$= \frac{\sqrt{3}}{4} \times 144 = 36\sqrt{3}\ \text{cm}^2$

$= 36 \times 1.73 = 62.28\ \text{cm}^2$

EXAMPLE: Find the area of a triangle whose sides are 40 cm, 41 cm and 9 cm respectively.

SOLUTION: $s = \frac{a+b+c}{2} = \frac{9+40+41}{2}$

$= \frac{90}{2} = 45$ cm

Area of triangle $= \sqrt{s(s-a)(s-b)(s-c)}$

$= \sqrt{45(45-9)(45-40)(45-41)}$

$= \sqrt{45 \times 36 \times 5 \times 4}$

$= \sqrt{225 \times 144}$

$= 15 \times 12 = 180\ \text{cm}^2$

EXAMPLE: Find the circumference and the area of a circle of radius 3.5 cm.

SOLUTION: Circumference $= 2\pi r$

$= 2 \times \frac{22}{7} \times 3.5 = 22$ cm

Area of circle $= \pi r^2 = \frac{22}{7} \times 3.5 \times 3.5$

$= 38.5\ \text{cm}^2$

EXAMPLE: In a circle of radius 35 cm, an arc subtends an angle of 72° at the centre. Find the length of the arc and the area of the sector.

SOLUTION: Length of arc $= \frac{\theta}{360} \times 2\pi r$

$= \frac{72}{360} \times 2 \times \frac{22}{7} \times 35$

$= 44$ cm

Area of the sector $= \frac{\theta}{360} \times \pi r^2$

$= \frac{72}{360} \times \frac{22}{7} \times 35 \times 35$

$= 770\ \text{cm}^2$

EXAMPLE: Find the area of a trapezium whose parallel sides are 77 cm, 60 cm and the other sides are 25 cm and 26 cm.

SOLUTION:

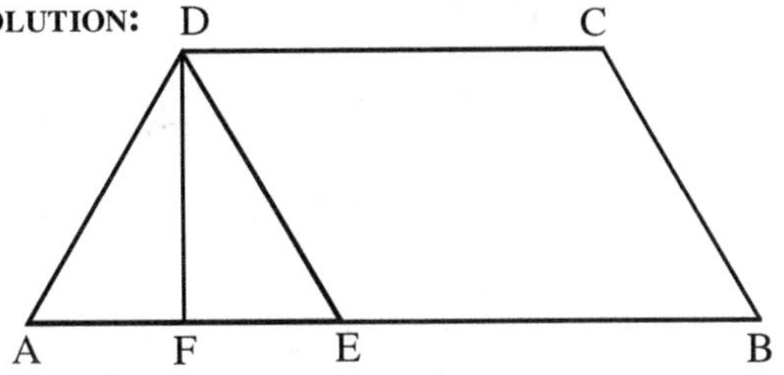

Let ABCD be the given trapezium in which AB = 77 cm, CD = 60 cm, BC = 25 cm, AD = 26 cm.

Draw DE ∥ BC and DF ⊥ AB

Now, DE = BC = 25 cm

AE = AB – EB = AB – CD

= 77 – 60 = 17 cm

In ΔDAE, $s = \frac{17+25+26}{2} = \frac{68}{2} = 34$ cm

Area of $\Delta DAE = \sqrt{34(34-17)(34-25)(34-26)}$

$= \sqrt{34 \times 17 \times 9 \times 8} = 204\ \text{cm}^2$

Again area of $\Delta DAE = \frac{1}{2} \times AE \times DF$

$204 = \frac{1}{2} \times 17 \times DF$

$\Rightarrow$ $DF = \frac{2 \times 204}{17} = 24$ cm

$\therefore$ Area of trapezium ABCD $= \frac{1}{2}(AB + CD) \times DF$

$= \frac{1}{2}(77 + 60) \times 24$

$= \frac{1}{2} \times 137 \times 24$

$= 1644\ \text{cm}^2$

EXAMPLE: A copper wire when bent in the form of a square, encloses an area of 484 cm². If the same wire is bent in the form of circle, find the area enclosed by it.

SOLUTION: Area of the square = 484 cm²

Side $= \sqrt{484} = 22$ cm

Length of wire = Perimeter of square

= 4 × side = 4 × 22

= 88 cm

Let r be the radius of the circle.

∴ Circumference of circle = Perimeter of square

$$\therefore \quad 2\pi r = 88 \Rightarrow r = \frac{88}{2\pi}$$

$$= \frac{88 \times 7}{2 \times 22} = 14 \text{ cm}$$

$$\text{Area of circle} = \pi r^2 = \frac{22}{7} \times 14 \times 14$$

$$= 616 \text{ cm}^2$$

EXAMPLE: A bicycle wheel makes 5000 revolutions in moving 11 km. Find the diameter of the wheel.

SOLUTION: Distance covered by the wheel in 1 revolution

$$= \frac{\text{Distance covered}}{\text{Number of revolutions}} = \frac{11}{5000} \text{ km}$$

$$= \frac{11 \times 1000 \times 100}{5000} \text{ cm} = 220 \text{ cm}$$

∴ Circumference of the wheel = 220 cm

$$2\pi r = 220 \Rightarrow 2 \times \frac{22}{7} \times r = 220$$

$$\Rightarrow \quad r = \frac{220 \times 7}{44} = 35 \text{ cm}$$

Hence, diameter of the wheel = 35 × 2 = 70 cm

EXAMPLE: The perimeter of a square is 44 cm and circumference of a circle is 44 cm. Which area is greater and by how much?

SOLUTION: Side of square $= \frac{44}{4} = 11$ cm

$$\text{Area of square} = (11)^2 = 121 \text{ cm}^2$$

Circumference of a circle $= 2\pi r$

$$\Rightarrow \quad 44 = 2 \times \frac{22}{7} \times r$$

$$\Rightarrow \quad r = \frac{44 \times 7}{44} = 7 \text{ cm}$$

$$\text{Area of circle} = \pi r^2$$

$$= \frac{22}{7} \times 7 \times 7 = 154 \text{ cm}^2$$

Clearly, area of circle > area of square

Difference = 154 – 121 = 33 cm^2.

EXAMPLE: A sheet of paper is in the form of a rectangle ABCD in which AB = 40 cm and AD = 28 cm. A semi-circular portion with BC as diameter is cut off. Find the area of the remaining paper.

SOLUTION:

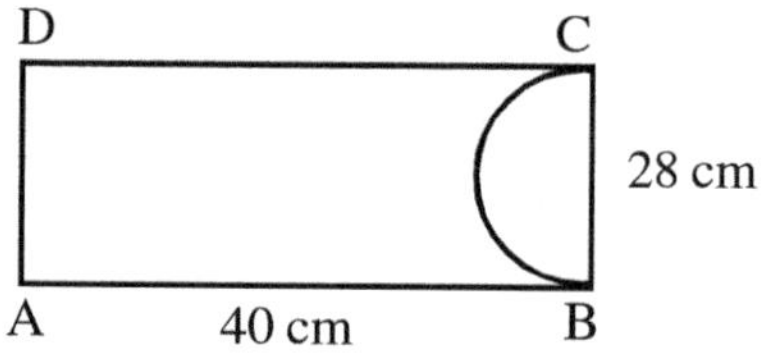

$$\text{Area of ABCD} = 40 \times 28 = 1120 \text{ cm}^2$$

$$\text{Area of semicircle} = \frac{1}{2}\pi r^2$$

$$= \frac{1}{2} \times \frac{22}{7} \times 14 \times 14$$

$$= 22 \times 14 = 308 \text{ cm}^2$$

Area of the remaining paper = 1120 – 308 = 812 cm^2

MULTIPLE CHOICE QUESTIONS

1. The length of a plot is four times its breadth. A playground measuring 1200 square metres occupies a third of the total area of the plot. What is the length of the plot, in metres?

A. 20 B. 30
C. 60 D. None of these

2. The width of a rectangular hall is $\frac{3}{4}$ of its length. If the area of the hall is 300 m^2, then the difference between its length and width is:

A. 3 m B. 4 m
C. 5 m D. 15 m

3. The length and breadth of a rectangular piece of land are in ratio of 5 : 3. The owner spent ₹ 3000 for surrounding it from all the sides at ₹ 7.50 per metre. The difference between its length and breadth is:

A. 50 m
B. 100 m
C. 150 m
D. 200 m

4. A room 8 m × 6 m is to be carpeted by a carpet 2 m wide. The length of carpet required is:
   A. 12 m B. 36 m
   C. 24 m D. 48 m
5. The length of a rectangle is increased by 60%. By what per cent would the width have to be decreased to maintain the same area?
   A. $37\frac{1}{2}\%$ B. 60%
   C. 75% D. 120%
6. A man walked 20 m to cross a rectangular field diagonally. If the length of the field is 16 m, the breadth of the rectangle is:
   A. 4 m
   B. 16 m
   C. 12 m
   D. Cannot be determined
7. If the ratio of the areas of two squares is 9 : 1, the ratio of their perimeters is:
   A. 9 : 1 B. 3 : 1
   C. 3 : 4 D. 1 : 3
8. The perimeter of both, a square and a rectangle are each equal to 48 m and the difference between their areas is 4 m^2. The breadth of the rectangle is:
   A. 10 m B. 12 m
   C. 14 m D. None of these
9. Area of a square with side x is equal to the area of a triangle with base x. The altitude of the triangle is:
   A. $\frac{x}{2}$ B. x
   C. $2x$ D. $4x$
10. If only the length of the rectangular plot is reduced to $\frac{2}{3}$rd of its original length, the ratio of original area to reduced area is:
    A. 2 : 3 B. 3 : 2
    C. 1 : 2 D. None of these
11. If the radius of a circle be reduced by 50%, its area is reduced by:
    A. 25% B. 50%
    C. 75% D. 100%
12. The perimeter of a rhombus is 52 m while its longer diagonal is 24 m. Its other diagonal is:
    A. 5 m B. 10 m
    C. 20 m D. 28 m
13. The circumference of a circle is 352 m, then its area in m^2 is:
    A. 9856 B. 8956
    C. 6589 D. 5986

ANSWERS

1	2	3	4	5	6	7	8	9	10
D	C	A	C	A	C	B	A	C	B
11	**12**	**13**							
C	B	A							

EXPLANATORY ANSWERS

1. Area of the plot = 3 × 1200 = 3600 m^2
   Let breadth be x m. Then length = $4x$ m
   According to the question,
   $4x \times x = 3600 \Rightarrow x^2 = 900 \Rightarrow x = 30$
   Hence, length of the plot = 4 × 30 = 120 m.
2. Let length be x m, then breadth = $\frac{3x}{4}$ m
   Area of the hall = $x \times \frac{3x}{4} = \frac{3x^2}{4}$
   According to the question,
   $\frac{3x^2}{4} = 300 \Rightarrow x^2 = 400 \Rightarrow x = 20$
   Length = 20 m and breadth = $\frac{3}{4} \times 20 = 15$ m
   Difference = 20 – 15 = 5 m
3. Let length = $5x$ m and breadth = $3x$ m
   Perimeter of rectangle = $2(5x + 3x) = 16x$ m
   But perimeter = $\frac{\text{Total cost}}{\text{Rate}} = \frac{3000}{7.50} = 400$ m

Now, $16x = 400 \Rightarrow x = 25$

length $= 5x = 5 \times 25 = 125$ m

breadth $= 3x = 25 \times 3 = 75$ m

Difference $= 125 - 75 = 50$ m

4. Length of the carpet $= \dfrac{8 \times 6}{2} = 24$ m.

5. Initially, let length $= x$ and breadth $= y$

Let new breadth $= z$.

Then new length $= \dfrac{160x}{100} = \dfrac{8x}{5}$

$\therefore \quad \dfrac{8x}{5} \times z = xy \Rightarrow z = \dfrac{5y}{8}$

Decrease in breadth $= \left(y - \dfrac{5y}{8}\right) = \dfrac{3y}{8}$

$\therefore$ Decrease per cent $= \dfrac{3y}{8} \times \dfrac{1}{y} \times 100$

$= \dfrac{75}{2} = 37.5\% =$

6. Breadth $= \sqrt{(20)^2 - (16)^2}$

$= \sqrt{400 - 256} = \sqrt{144} = 12$ m.

7. Let the areas of the squares be $(9x^2)$ m^2 and (x^2) m^2

Then, their sides are $3x$ m and x m respectively

Ratio of their perimeters $= \dfrac{12x}{4x} = 3 : 1$

8. Let length of rectangle $= x$ m

and breadth of rectangle $= y$ m

Also, let the side of the square be z m

According to the question,

$2(x + y) = 4z = 48$

$x + y = 24$ and $z = 12$

Also, $z^2 - xy = 4$

$\Rightarrow \quad (12)^2 - 4 = xy$

$\Rightarrow \quad xy = 140$

$\because \quad x + y = 24$ and $xy = 140$

$(x - y)^2 = (x + y)^2 - 4xy$

$\Rightarrow \quad (x - y)^2 = (24)^2 - 4(140)$

$\Rightarrow \quad (x - y)^2 = 576 - 560 = 16$

$\Rightarrow \quad x - y = 4$

Now, $x + y = 24$

$x - y = 4$

Solving and get $x = 14$, $y = 10$

Hence, breadth of rectangle $= 10$ m.

9. According to the question,

$x^2 = \dfrac{1}{2} \times x \times h$

$\Rightarrow \quad h = \dfrac{2x^2}{x} = 2x$

10. Let length $= x$ and breadth $= y$

New length $= \dfrac{2}{3}x$

$\therefore \quad \dfrac{\text{Original area}}{\text{Reduced area}} = \dfrac{xy}{\frac{2}{3}xy} = \dfrac{3}{2} = 3 : 2$

11. Original area $= \pi r^2$, New area $= \pi\left(\dfrac{r}{2}\right)^2 = \dfrac{\pi r^2}{4}$

Reduction in area $= \pi r^2 - \dfrac{\pi r^2}{4} = \dfrac{3\pi r^2}{4}$

Reduction per cent $= \dfrac{3\pi r^2}{4} \times \dfrac{1}{\pi r^2} \times 100 = 75\%$

12. Side of rhombus $= \dfrac{52}{4} = 13$ m

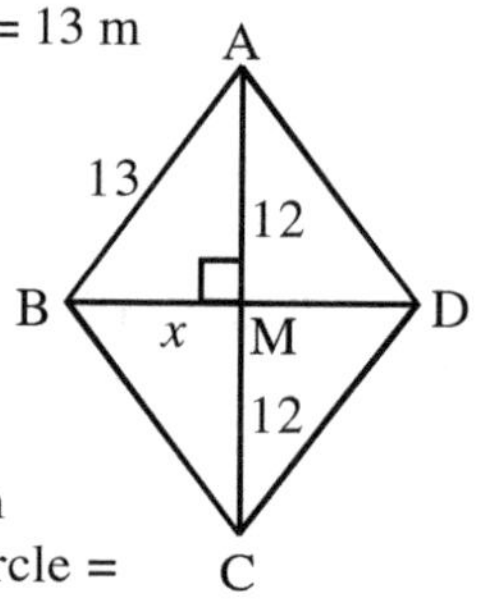

In ΔABM,

$x^2 = (13)^2 - (12)^2$

$x^2 = 169 - 144$

$x^2 = 25$

$\Rightarrow \quad x = 5$ m

$\therefore$ Another diagonal

$= 2 \times 5 = 10$ m

13. Circumference of a circle $= 2\pi r$

$\Rightarrow \quad 352 = 2 \times \dfrac{22}{7} \times r$

$\Rightarrow \quad r = \dfrac{352 \times 7}{44} = 56$ m

Area of circle $= \pi r^2 = \dfrac{22}{7} \times 56 \times 56$

$= 9856$ m^2

12. VOLUME AND SURFACE AREA

We know that every real object occupies some space. It is usually specified by its three dimensions—length, breadth and depth (or height or thickness). It may be a solid or a hollow object. In case of circular, cylindrical and spherical object the specifying dimensions may change to radius, angle etc. The amount of space occupied by the object is called its volume. Its unit of measurement is m^3, cm^3, $(\text{inches})^3$ etc. The area of the surfaces (plane/curved) of the object is called its surface area.

A Cuboid and A Cube

The solid like wooden boxes, tea containers, match box etc. which have six faces, each of which is a rectangle, are called cuboids. It has 12 edges.

A cuboid in which every face is a square is called a cube. Length of each face of a cube is called its edge.

Prism

A right prism is a solid in which the two ends are congruent parallel figures and the side faces are rectangles. The total area of side faces of a prism is called the lateral surface of the prism.

Cylinder

The solid generated by the revolution of a rectangle about one of its sides as axis is called a cylinder.

Pyramid

A solid whose base is a plane rectilinear figure having the side faces as triangles meeting at a common vertex is called a pyramid. When the base of a pyramid is a triangle, the pyramid is called a tetrahedron.

Cone

The solid generated by the revolution of a right angled triangle about one of the sides containing the right angle as the axis is called a right circular cone.

The perpendicular distance from the vertex to the base is called the height of the cone and the length of slant face from vertex to the base is called the slant height of the cone.

Frustum

If a cone is cut by a plane parallel to the base so as to divide the cone into two parts, then the lower part is called the frustum of the cone.

Sphere

When a semicircle moves about its diameter, the solid generated is called a sphere.

Formulae

Cuboid:

$$\text{Volume of cuboid} = l \times b \times h \text{ cubic units}$$

$$\text{Whole surface area} = 2(lb + bh + hl) \text{ square units}$$

$$\text{Diagonal of cuboid} = \sqrt{l^2 + b^2 + h^2} \text{ units}$$

$$\text{Area of 4 walls of a room} = 2(l + b) \times h \text{ square units}$$

Cube:

$$\text{Volume of cube} = a^3 \text{ cubic units}$$

$$\text{Side of cube} = \sqrt[3]{\text{Volume}}$$

$$\text{Lateral surface area} = 4a^2 \text{ square units}$$

$$\text{Total surface area} = 6a^2 \text{ square units}$$

$$\text{Diagonal of the cube} = \left(\sqrt{3}\, a\right) \text{ units}$$

Cylinder:

Volume of cylinder = $\pi r^2 h$ cubic units

Lateral surface area = $2\pi rh$ square units

Total surface area = $2\pi r(h + r)$ square units

Cone:

Volume of cone = $\frac{1}{3}\pi r^2 h$ cubic units

Lateral surface area = πrl square units

Total surface area = $\pi r(l + r)$ square units

Slant height (l) = $\sqrt{r^2 + h^2}$

Sphere:

Volume of sphere = $\frac{4}{3}\pi r^3$ cubic units

Surface area = $4\pi r^2$ square units

Hemisphere:

Volume = $\frac{2}{3}\pi r^3$ cubic units

Lateral surface area = $2\pi r^2$ square units

Total surface area = $3\pi r^2$ square units

Frustum:

Volume = $\frac{1}{3}\pi h(r_1^2 + r_1 r_2 + r_2^2)$ cubic units

Curved surface area = $\pi(r_1 + r_2) \times l$ square units

Total surface area = $\pi\left[r_1^2 + r_2^2 + (r_1 + r_2)l\right]$ square units

Pyramid:

Volume = $\frac{1}{2} \times$ (area of base) $\times$ height cubic units

EXAMPLE: The dimensions of a metallic cuboid are 100 cm × 80 cm × 64 cm. It is melted and recast into cube. Find the total surface area of the cube.

SOLUTION: Volume of cuboid = $l \times b \times h$

$$= 100 \times 80 \times 64$$

$$= 512000 \text{ cm}^3$$

Volume of cube = a^3

According to the question,

$$a^3 = 512000$$

$$\Rightarrow \quad a^3 = 8 \times 8 \times 8 \times 10 \times 10 \times 10$$

$$\Rightarrow \quad a = 8 \times 10 = 80 \text{ cm}$$

Total surface area of cube = $6a^2 = 6 \times 80 \times 80 = 38400$

Hence, total surface area of cube is 38400 cm^2.

EXAMPLE: Three cubes whose edges measure 3 cm, 4 cm and 5 cm respectively form a single cube. Find the total surface area of the new cube.

SOLUTION: Let the edge of new cube = x cm

$$x^3 = 3^3 + 4^3 + 5^3$$

$$= 27 + 64 + 125 = 216 \text{ cm}^3$$

$$\Rightarrow \quad x^3 = 6 \times 6 \times 6 \Rightarrow x = 6 \text{ cm}$$

Total surface area of cube = $6(x)^2 = 6 \times 6 \times 6 = 216$ cm^2

Hence, total surface area of new cube = 216 cm^2.

EXAMPLE: The capacity of a cylindrical tank is 6160 m^3. If the radius of its base is 14 m, find the depth of the tank.

SOLUTION: Volume of cylinder = $\pi r^2 h$

$$\pi r^2 h = 6160$$

$$\Rightarrow \quad \frac{22}{7} \times 14 \times 14 \times h = 6160$$

$$\Rightarrow \quad h = \frac{6160}{44 \times 14} = 10 \text{ m}$$

Hence, depth of the tank is 10 m.

EXAMPLE: How many bullets can be made out of a lead cylinder 28 cm high and 6 cm radius, each bullet being 1.5 cm in diameter?

SOLUTION: Number of bullets

$$= \frac{\text{Volume of cylinder}}{\text{Volume of 1 bullet}}$$

$$= \frac{\pi \times 6 \times 6 \times 28}{\frac{4}{3} \times \pi \times 0.75 \times 0.75 \times 0.75}$$

$$= \frac{6 \times 6 \times 28 \times 3}{4 \times \frac{3}{4} \times \frac{3}{4} \times \frac{3}{4}} = \frac{6 \times 6 \times 28 \times 4 \times 4 \times 3}{3 \times 3 \times 3}$$

$$= 1792$$

EXAMPLE: A metal sphere of diameter 42 cm is dropped into a cylindrical vessel, which is partly filled with water. The diameter of the vessel is 1.68 metres. If the sphere is completely submerged, find by how much the surface of water will rise.

SOLUTION: Radius of the sphere = 21 cm

$$\text{Volume of sphere} = \frac{4}{3}\pi r^3$$

$$= \frac{4}{3} \times \frac{22}{7} \times 21 \times 21 \times 21$$

$$= 38808 \text{ cm}^3$$

Volume of water displaced by sphere = 38808 cm^3
Let water rise by h cm.

Volume of cylinder $= \pi r^2 h$

$$\frac{22}{7} \times 84 \times 84 \times h = 38808$$

$$\Rightarrow \quad h = \frac{38808 \times 7}{22 \times 84 \times 84} = \frac{7}{4} = 1.75 \text{ cm}$$

EXAMPLE: A tent is in the form of a right circular cylinder surmounted by a cone. The diameter of cylinder is 24 m. The height of the cylindrical portion is 11 m while the vertex of the cone is 16 m above the ground. Find the area of the canvas required for the tent.

SOLUTION: Lateral surface area of cylinder $= 2\pi rh$

$$= 2 \times \frac{22}{7} \times 12 \times 11 = \frac{5808}{7} \text{ m}^2$$

Height of cone = 16 – 11 = 5 m

Radius of cone = 12 m

$$\text{Slant height } l = \sqrt{r^2 + h^2} = \sqrt{12^2 + 5^2}$$

$$= \sqrt{169} = 13 \text{ m}$$

Lateral surface area of cone $= \pi rl$

$$= \frac{22}{7} \times 12 \times 13 = \frac{3432}{7} \text{ m}^2$$

$$\text{Area of canvas} = \frac{5808}{7} + \frac{3432}{7}$$

$$= \frac{9240}{7} = 1320 \text{ m}^2$$

EXAMPLE: The slant height of the frustum of a cone is 20 cm and the height of the frustum is 16 cm. The radius of the smaller circle is 8 cm. Find the volume and total surface area of the frustum.

SOLUTION: $l = \sqrt{h^2 + (R - r)^2} = \sqrt{16^2 + (R - 8)^2}$

$$\Rightarrow \quad 20 = \sqrt{256 + R^2 - 16R + 64}$$

$$= \sqrt{R^2 - 16R + 320}$$

$\Rightarrow R^2 - 16R + 320 = 400$

$\Rightarrow R^2 - 16R - 80 = 0 \Rightarrow R = 20$ cm

$$\text{Volume of frustum} = \frac{1}{3}\pi h(R^2 + r^2 + Rr)$$

$$= \frac{1}{3} \times \frac{22}{7} \times 16(400 + 64 + 160)$$

$$= \frac{73216}{7} \text{ cm}^3$$

$$\text{Total surface area} = \pi(R^2 + r^2 + Rl + rl)$$

$$= \frac{22}{7}(400 + 64 + 400 + 160)$$

$$= \frac{22}{7} \times 1024 = \frac{22528}{7}$$

$$= 3218.28 \text{ cm}^2$$

EXAMPLE: The length of a garden roller is 2 m and diameter is 1.4 m. How much area will it cover in 10 revolutions?

SOLUTION: Area covered

= Curved surface × no. of revolutions

$= 2\pi rh \times 10$

$$= 2 \times \frac{22}{7} \times 0.7 \times 2 \times 10 = 88 \text{ m}^2$$

EXAMPLE: A cylinder is made by lead whose radius is 4 cm and height is 10 cm. By melting it how many spheres of radius 2 cm can be made?

SOLUTION: Given, radius of the cylinder = 4 cm

and height of the cylinder = 10 cm

$\therefore$ Volume of the cylinder $= \pi r^2 h = \pi(4)^2 \times 10$

$= 160\pi$ cm^3

$$\text{Volume of sphere} = \frac{4}{3}\pi r^3 = \frac{4}{3}\pi(2)^3$$

$$= \frac{32}{3}\pi \text{ cm}^3$$

$$\therefore \quad \text{Number of spheres} = \frac{\text{Volume of cylinder}}{\text{Volume of one sphere}}$$

$$= \frac{160\pi}{\frac{32}{3}\pi} = \frac{160 \times 3}{32} = 15$$

Hence, number of spheres that can be made are 15.

MULTIPLE CHOICE QUESTIONS

1. The surface area of a cube is 726 m^2. The volume of cube is:
A. 1300 m^3 B. 1331 m^3
C. 1452 m^3 D. 1542 m^3

2. Sum of the length, width and depth of a cuboid is s and its diagonal is d. Its surface area is:
A. s^2 B. d^2
C. $s^2 - d^2$ D. $s^2 + d^2$

3. A wooden box of dimensions 8 m × 7 m × 6 m is to carry rectangular boxes of dimensions 8 cm × 7 cm × 6 cm. The maximum number of boxes that can be carried in 1 wooden box is:
A. 1200000 B. 1000000
C. 9800000 D. 7500000

4. The length of the longest rod that can be placed in a room 30 m long, 24 m broad and 18 m high is:
A. 30 m B. $15\sqrt{2}$ m
C. 60 m D. $30\sqrt{2}$ m

5. If the volume of two cubes are in the ratio 8 : 1, the ratio of their edges is:
A. 8 : 1 B. $2\sqrt{2} : 1$
C. 2 : 1 D. None of these

6. A metal sheet 27 cm long 8 cm broad and 1 cm thick is melted into a cube. The difference between the surface areas of two solids will be:
A. 284 cm^2 B. 296 cm^2
C. 286 cm^2 D. 300 cm^2

7. If each edge of a cube is increased by 50%, the percentage increase in surface area is:
A. 50% B. 75%
C. 100% D. 125%

8. If a right circular cone of vertical height 24 cm has a volume of 1232 cm^3, then the area of its curved surface in cm^2 is:
A. 1254 B. 704
C. 550 D. 154

9. Two cubes have volumes in the ratio 1 : 27. The ratio of their surface areas is:
A. 1 : 3 B. 1 : 8
C. 1 : 9 D. 1 : 18

10. If the volumes of two cones are in the ratio 1 : 4 and their diameters are in the ratio 4 : 5, then the ratio of their heights is:
A. 1 : 5 B. 5 : 4
C. 5 : 16 D. 25 : 64

11. The radius of a wire is decreased to one-third. If volumes remains the same, length will increase:
A. 1 time B. 3 times
C. 6 times D. 9 times

12. A cylindrical piece of metal of radius 2 cm and height 6 cm is shaped into a cone of same radius. The height of cone is:
A. 18 cm B. 14 cm
C. 12 cm D. 8 cm

13. If 1 cubic cm of cast iron weight 21 g then the weight of a cast iron pipe of length 1 m with a bore of 3 cm and in which the thickness of the metal is 1 cm, is:
A. 21 kg B. 24.2 kg
C. 26.4 kg D. 18.6 kg

14. The number of solid spheres, each of diameter 6 cm, that could be moulded to form a solid metal cylinder of height 45 cm and diameter 4 cms, is:
A. 3 B. 4
C. 5 D. 6

15. A right cylinder and a right circular cone have the same radius and the same volume. The ratio of the height of the cylinder to that of the cone is:
A. 3 : 5 B. 2 : 5
C. 3 : 1 D. 1 : 3

ANSWERS

1	**2**	**3**	**4**	**5**	**6**	**7**	**8**	**9**	**10**
B	C	B	D	C	C	D	C	C	D
11	**12**	**13**	**14**	**15**					
D	A	C	C	D					

EXPLANATORY ANSWERS

1. Surface area of cube = $6a^2$

$$6a^2 = 726 \Rightarrow a^2 = \frac{726}{6} = 121 \Rightarrow a = 11 \text{ m}$$

Volume of cube = $a^3 = 11 \times 11 \times 11 = 1331 \text{ m}^3$

2. $l + b + h = s$

and $\sqrt{l^2 + b^2 + h^2} = d \Rightarrow l^2 + b^2 + h^2 = d^2$

$(l + b + h)^2 = s^2$

$\Rightarrow l^2 + b^2 + h^2 + 2(lb + bh + hl) = s^2$

$\Rightarrow d^2 + 2(lb + bh + hl) = s^2$

$\Rightarrow 2(lb + bh + hl) = s^2 - d^2$

$\therefore$ Surface area $= (s^2 - d^2)$.

3. Number of boxes $= \dfrac{800 \times 700 \times 600}{8 \times 7 \times 6} = 1000000$

4. Diagonal of cuboid $= \sqrt{l^2 + b^2 + h^2}$

$\therefore$ Length of longest rod $= \sqrt{30^2 + 24^2 + 18^2}$

$= \sqrt{900 + 576 + 324} = \sqrt{1800}$

$= \sqrt{30 \times 30 \times 2} = 30\sqrt{2}$ m

5. Let their volumes be $8x^3$ and x^3.
Then, their sides are $2x$ and x
$\therefore$ Ratio of their edges = 2 : 1

6. Volume of sheet $= 27 \times 8 \times 1 = 216 \text{ cm}^3$
Volume of cube formed $= 216 \text{ cm}^3$

Side of cube $= \sqrt[3]{216} = 6$ cm
Surface area of cuboid $= 2(lb + bh + hl)$
$= 2(27 \times 8 + 8 \times 1 + 1 \times 27) = 502 \text{ cm}^2$
Surface area of cube $= 6(\text{side})^2 = 6 \times 36 = 216 \text{ cm}^2$
Difference in areas $= 502 - 216 = 286 \text{ cm}^2$

7. Let original length of cube = x
then, its surface area = $6x^2$

$$\text{New edge} = \left(\frac{150}{100}x\right) = \frac{3}{2}x$$

$$\text{New surface area} = 6 \times \left(\frac{3}{2}x\right)^2$$

$$= 6 \times \frac{9}{4}x^2 = \frac{27}{2}x^2$$

$$\text{Increase in surface area} = \left(\frac{27}{2} - 6\right)x^2 = \frac{15}{2}x^2$$

$$\therefore \quad \text{Increase \%} = \frac{15x^2/2}{6x^2} \times 100$$

$$= \frac{15x^2}{12x^2} \times 100 = 125\%$$

8. Volume of cone = 1232

$$\Rightarrow \frac{1}{3}\pi r^2 h = 1232$$

$$\Rightarrow \frac{1}{3} \times \frac{22}{7} \times r^2 \times 24 = 1232$$

$$\Rightarrow r^2 = \frac{3 \times 7 \times 1232}{22 \times 24} = 49 \Rightarrow r = 7 \text{ cm}$$

$$\Rightarrow l = \sqrt{r^2 + h^2} = \sqrt{7^2 + 24^2} = \sqrt{625} = 25 \text{ cm}$$

Lateral surface area of cone = πrl

$$= \frac{22}{7} \times 7 \times 25 = 22 \times 25 = 550 \text{ cm}^2$$

9. Let their volumes are x^3 and $27x^3$.
Then, their sides are x and $3x$.

$$\text{Ratio of their surface areas} = \frac{6x^2}{6(3x)^2} = \frac{x^2}{9x^2}$$

$$= 1 : 9$$

10. Let the diameters of the bases of the cones be $4r$ and $5r$. Let their heights be h and H.

$$\text{then,} \quad \frac{\frac{1}{3}\pi \times \left(\frac{4r}{2}\right)^2 \times h}{\frac{1}{3}\pi\left(\frac{5r}{2}\right)^2 \times H} = \frac{1}{4}$$

$$\Rightarrow \frac{16}{25} \times \frac{h}{H} = \frac{1}{4}$$

$$\Rightarrow \frac{h}{H} = \frac{25}{64}$$

11. Let original radius = r

and original length = h

$$\text{New radius} = \frac{1}{3}r$$

Let new length = H

then, $$\pi r^2 h = \pi\left(\frac{1}{3}r\right)^2 \times H = \frac{\pi r^2 H}{9}$$

$\therefore$ $$H = 9h$$

Thus length becomes 9 times.

12. Volume of cone = Volume of cylinder

$$\frac{1}{3}\pi r^2 h = \pi r^2 h$$

$$\Rightarrow \quad \frac{1}{3} \times \frac{22}{7} \times 2 \times 2 \times h = \frac{22}{7} \times 2 \times 2 \times 6$$

$$\Rightarrow \quad \frac{h}{3} = 6 \Rightarrow h = 18 \text{ cm}$$

$\therefore$ Height of cone = 18 cm

13. Diameter = 3 cm, $h = 1$ m = 100 cm

$$\therefore \text{Radius} = \frac{3}{2} \text{cm} = 1.5 \text{ cm}$$

thickness = 1 cm

$\therefore$ R = 1.5 + 1 = 2.5 cm

r = 1.5 cm

$$\begin{aligned}\text{Volume of metal} &= \pi(R^2 - r^2) \times h \\ &= \pi[(2.5)^2 - (1.5)^2] \times 100 \\ &= \pi[4] \times 100 = \pi \times 400 \text{ cm}^3\end{aligned}$$

$\because$ $1 \text{ cm}^3 = 21$ g

$\therefore$ $\pi \times 400 \text{ cm}^3 = 21 \times \pi \times 400$ g

$$= 21 \times \frac{22}{7} \times \frac{400}{1000} \text{kg}$$

$$= 26.4 \text{ kg}$$

14. $$\text{Number of spheres} = \frac{\text{Volume of cylinder}}{\text{Volume of sphere}}$$

$$= \frac{\pi \times 2 \times 2 \times 45}{\frac{4}{3}\pi \times (3)^3} = \frac{4 \times 45 \times 3}{4 \times 27} = 5$$

15. Volume of cylinder = Volume of cone

$$\pi r^2 h = \frac{1}{3}\pi r^2 H$$

$$\Rightarrow \quad 3h = H \Rightarrow \frac{h}{H} = \frac{1}{3}$$

13. DATA INTERPRETATION

The collection of figures and facts in every field is called the statistical data. There are three types of statistical data.

(*a*) **Primary data:** The data collected by the investigator or the statistician to be used or integrated himself are called primary data. It is more reliable and relevant because it is collected by the investigator himself for the first time for his study.

(*b*) **Secondary data:** The data which are collected originally by someone else and used and interpreted by others for statistical analysis are called secondary data.

(*c*) **Grouped data:** When primary data is arranged in classes or groups to bring out certain sailent feature of the data is called grouped data.

Graphical Representation of Data

A graph is a visual form for presentation of data, highlighting their basic facts and relationship.

The word graph, chart and diagram are used interchangeably for the pictorial representation of data. However, the visual form made by using rectangular coordinate system is called a graph. In general, the other pictorial representation in which the coordinate system is not used are called diagrams or charts.

Variate: The quantity that we measure from observation-to-observation is called a variate.

Class-Interval: Every data is generally divided into small group using some interval is said to be in class-interval, *e.g.*, 0–5, 5–10, 10–15 etc.

Class-Size: The difference between the true upper limit and true lower limit of a class gives the size of a class-interval, *e.g.*, class-size of the class-interval 0–5 is 5.

Mid Value: The variable value which is mid-way between the lower and upper limit of a class is called its mid-value, *e.g.*, mid-value of class-interval 0–5 is $\frac{0+5}{2} = 2.5$.

Frequency: The number of observations corresponding to particular class is said to be the frequency of that class, *e.g.*, frequency of the interval 5–10 is 6. It means 6 persons have got 5 or more articles but less than 10.

Cumulative Frequency: The sum of the preceding frequencies is called cumulative frequency. Last frequency of cumulative frequency column is equal to the sum of the frequencies.

Class Limit: Every interval has two limits. Lower number of the interval is called lower limit while upper number of the interval is called upper limit, *e.g.*, in class-interval 0–5, 0 is lower limit while 5 is the upper limit.

Histogram

A statistical graph that represents by the height of a rectangular column the number of times that each class of result occurs in a sample or experiment, *e.g.*, the following table represents the number of matured persons in age group (15–20) in a city.

Age Group	Number of persons
15–20	200
20–25	350
25–30	475
30–35	600
35–40	750
40–45	900
45–50	100

Then the histogram of the data is given below:

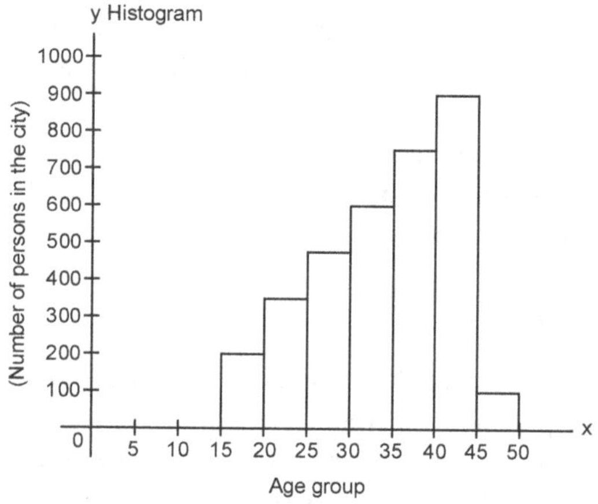

Bar Chart

A graph consisting of bars whose lengths are proportional to quantities in a set of data. It can be used when one axis cannot have a numerical scale, *e.g.*, to show how many different columns of flowers grow from a packet of mixed seeds, *e.g.*,

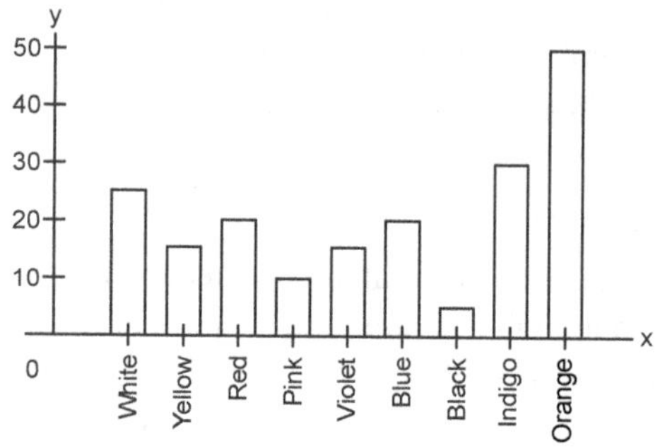

Pie Chart

A diagram in which proportions are illustrated as sectors of a circle. The relative area of the sectors representing the different proportions, *e.g.*, if out of 100 military personnels 25 personnels use tank, 30 personnels use warship, 40 personnels use aircraft and rest of them use rifles. Then pie-chart of the above data is

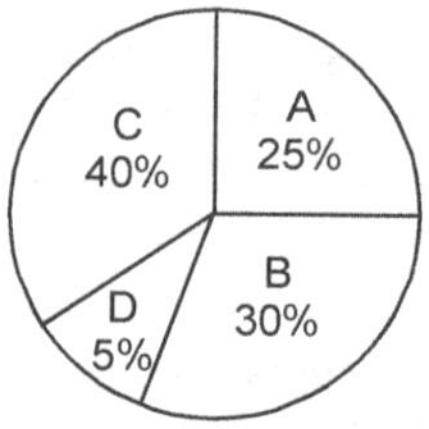

$$\text{A uses tank} = \frac{25}{100} \times 360 = 90°$$

$$\text{B uses warship} = \frac{30}{100} \times 360 = 108°$$

$$\text{C uses aircraft} = \frac{40}{100} \times 360 = 144°$$

$$\text{D uses rifles} = \frac{5}{100} \times 360 = 18°$$

EXAMPLE: Find out the marks obtained in different subjects from the following pie-diagram, if the total marks be 540.

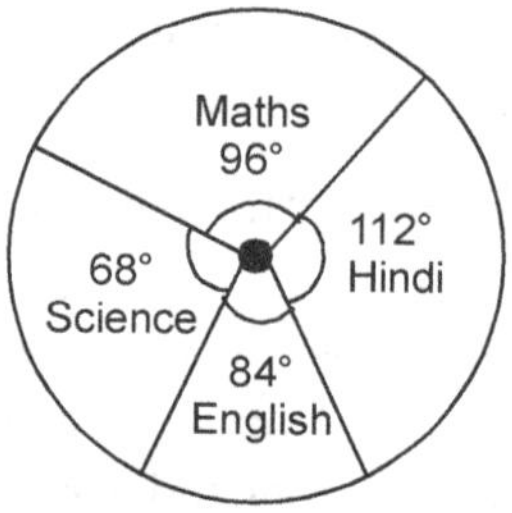

SOLUTION: Sum of the angles at the centre of circle = 360°

Total marks = 540

$$\therefore \text{ Marks obtained in Hindi} = \frac{112}{360} \times 540 = 168$$

$$\text{Marks obtained in English} = \frac{84}{360} \times 540 = 126$$

$$\text{Marks obtained in Science} = \frac{68}{360} \times 540 = 102$$

$$\text{Marks obtained in Maths} = \frac{96}{360} \times 540 = 144$$

MULTIPLE CHOICE QUESTIONS

Directions (Qs. 1 to 5): *Answers the questions on the basis of the following table:*

Assume all colleges sent equal number of candidates in all subjects for the examination.

Percentage of results for Subjects

College	Maths	Physics	Chemistry	Zoology	Botany
A	52	65	62	47	40
B	47	62	52	35	38
C	53	70	46	54	39
D	35	72	58	62	57

1. Taking all the colleges into account which subject has shown highest percentage result?
A. Chemistry
B. Maths
C. Zoology
D. Physics

2. Taking the performance in all the subjects into account which college has shown highest level of percentage results?
A. D B. A
C. B D. C

3. Seeing the performance of all the four colleges together which combination of groups has shown lowest level of percentage results?
A. Zoology and Botany
B. Physics and Chemistry
C. Maths and Physics
D. Chemistry and Botany

4. Taking all the colleges into account which subject has shown lowest percentage result?
A. Maths
B. Physics
C. Chemistry
D. Botany

5. Taking the performance in all subjects into account which college has shown lowest level?
A. A B. B
C. C D. D

Directions (Qs. 6 to 10): *These questions refer to the following circle graph showing the expenditure distribution of a certain family. The family spends ₹6500 per month.*

Expenditure Distribution of a Certain Family

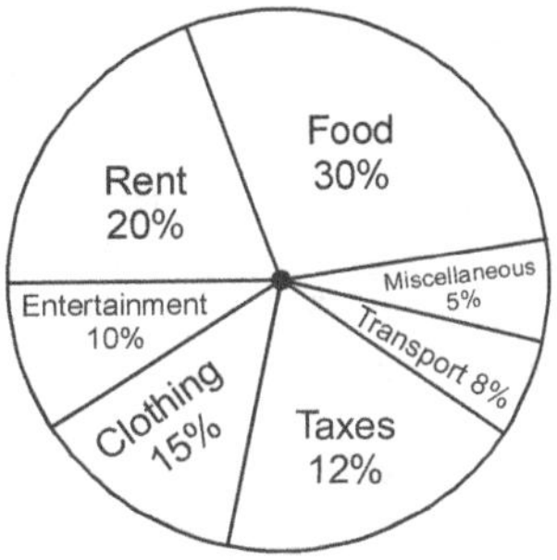

6. How much it spends on food per month?
A. ₹ 1950
B. ₹ 2950
C. ₹ 4850
D. ₹ 850

7. How much are its annual taxes?
A. ₹ 6500 B. ₹ 9360
C. ₹ 8900 D. ₹ 9500

8. How many degrees should there be in the central angle showing clothing, taxes and transportation combined?
A. 100 B. 115
C. 118 D. 126

9. How much more money per month is spent by the family on food as compared to the rent?
A. ₹ 650 B. ₹ 750
C. ₹ 550 D. ₹ 850

10. If the expenditure budget of the family is raised to ₹ 8000 per month and distribution on various items remain the same, then the monthly expenses on both, the entertainment and the transport, will be:
A. ₹ 1700
B. ₹ 1650
C. ₹ 1440
D. ₹ 1320

Directions (Qs. 11 to 15): *Study the following graph carefully and answer the following questions.*

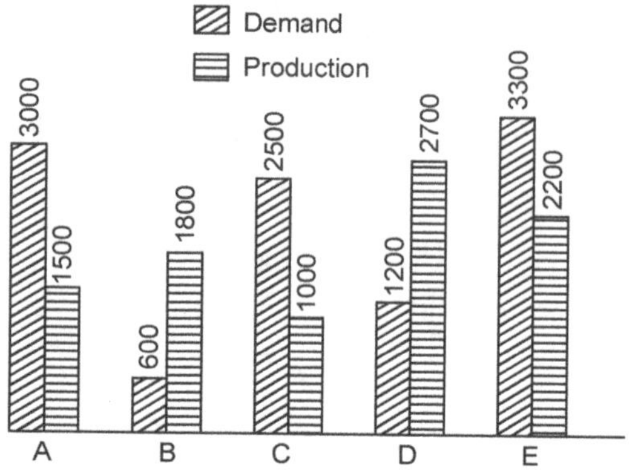

11. What is the ratio of companies having more demand than production of those having more production than demand?

A. 2 : 3 B. 4 : 1
C. 2 : 2 D. 3 : 2

12. What is the difference between average demand and average production of the five companies taken together?

A. 1400 B. 400
C. 280 D. 138

13. The production of Company 'D' is approximately how many times that of the production of the Company A?

A. 1.8 B. 4.5
C. 2.5 D. 4.9

14. The demand for Company 'B' is approximately what per cent of the demand for Company 'C'?

A. 4% B. 24%
C. 20% D. 60%

15. If Company A desires to meet the demand by purchasing surplus TV sets from a single company, which one of the following companies can meet the need adequately?

A. B B. C
C. D D. None of these

Directions (Qs. 16 to 20): *Study the following graph to answer the given questions.*

Per cent profit earned by two companies over the given years

$$\% \text{ Profit} = \frac{\text{Income} - \text{Expenditure}}{\text{Expenditure}} \times 100$$

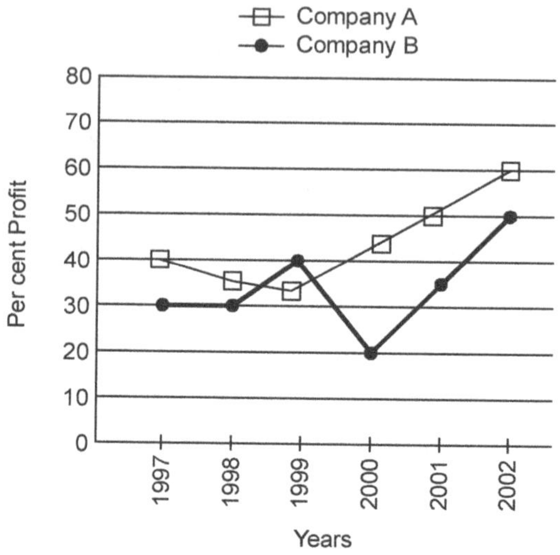

16. If the expenditure of Company B in 2000 was ₹ 200 crores, what was its income?

A. ₹ 240 crores B. ₹ 220 crores
C. ₹ 160 crores D. ₹ 180 crores

17. If the income of Company A in 2002 was ₹ 600 crores, what was its expenditure?

A. ₹ 360 crores B. ₹ 480 crores
C. ₹ 375 crores D. ₹ 320 crores

18. If the income of Company B in 1998 was ₹ 200 crores, what was its profit in 1999?

A. ₹ 21.5 crores
B. ₹ 153 crores
C. ₹ 46.15 crores
D. Cannot be determined

19. If the incomes of the two companies in 1998 were equal, what was the ratio of their expenditure?

A. 1 : 2 B. 26 : 27
C. 4 : 5 D. 100 : 67

20. What is the per cent increase in per cent profit for Company B from year 2000 to 2001?

A. 75 B. 175
C. 160 D. 150

ANSWERS

1	2	3	4	5	6	7	8	9	10
D	A	A	D	B	A	B	D	A	C
11	**12**	**13**	**14**	**15**	**16**	**17**	**18**	**19**	**20**
D	C	A	B	C	A	C	D	B	A

EXPLANATORY ANSWERS

1. Maths : $52 + 47 + 53 + 35 = 187$
Physics : $65 + 62 + 70 + 72 = 269$
Chemistry : $62 + 52 + 46 + 58 = 218$
Zoology : $47 + 35 + 54 + 62 = 198$
Botany : $40 + 38 + 39 + 57 = 174$
Clearly, Physics has shown highest percentage result.

2. $A : 52 + 65 + 62 + 47 + 40 = 266$
$B : 47 + 62 + 52 + 35 + 38 = 234$
$C : 53 + 70 + 46 + 54 + 39 = 262$
$D : 35 + 72 + 58 + 62 + 57 = 284$
Clearly, college D has shown highest level of percentage result.

3. Zoology and Botany of groups has shown lowest level of percentage result.

4. Total marks of Botany = 174 which shows lowest percentage result.

5. College B has shown lowest level because its total percentage result in all five subjects is 234 which is lowest.

6. Food 30% of ₹ 6500 = $\frac{30}{100} \times 6500$ = ₹ 1950

7. Taxes = 12% of ₹ 6500

= $\frac{12}{100} \times 6500$ = ₹ 780/month

= ₹ 780 × 12 = ₹ 9360/year

∴ Annual taxes = ₹ 9360

8. Clothing, taxes and transportation combined are 35%.

Now, $100\% = 360°$

$$35\% = \frac{360°}{100} \times 35 = 126°$$

9. 10% of ₹ 6500 = $\frac{10}{100} \times 6500$ = ₹ 650/month

10. 18% of ₹ 8000 = $\frac{18}{100} \times 8000$ = ₹ 1440

11. The companies having more demand than production are A, C and E *i.e.* their number is 3. The companies having more production than demand are B and D *i.e.* their number is 2.
So, the required ratio is 3 : 2.

12. Average demand

$$= \frac{1}{5}(3000 + 600 + 2500 + 1200 + 3300)$$

$$= \frac{10600}{5} = 2120$$

Average production

$$= \frac{1500 + 1800 + 1000 + 2700 + 2200}{5}$$

$$= \frac{9200}{5} = 1840$$

∴ Difference between average demand and average production = 2120 – 1840 = 280

13. Let $K(1500) = 2700$

$$\Rightarrow \quad K = \frac{2700}{1500} = \frac{9}{5} = 1.8.$$

14. Let x% of (demand for C) = (demand for B)

$$\Rightarrow \quad \frac{x}{100} \times 2500 = 600$$

$$\Rightarrow \quad x = \frac{600 \times 100}{2500} = 24\%$$

15. Since Company D produces highest number of TV sets and Company A desires to meet the demand by purchasing surplus TV sets from a single Company.
Clearly, D can meet the demand of A.
∴ Correct answer is C.

16. Let the income be ₹ x crores

$$\therefore \quad 20 = \frac{x - 200}{200} \times 100$$

$$\Rightarrow \quad 40 = x - 200$$

$$\Rightarrow \quad x = 240$$

$\therefore$ Income = ₹ 240 crores

17. The income of Company A in 2002 = ₹ 600 crores

% Profit = 60

Let the expenditure be ₹ x crores.

$$\therefore \quad 60 = \frac{600 - x}{x} \times 100$$

$$\Rightarrow \quad x = \frac{600 - x}{60} \times 100$$

$$\Rightarrow \quad x = \frac{(600 - x)5}{3}$$

$$\Rightarrow \quad 3x = 3000 - 5x$$

$$\Rightarrow \quad 8x = 3000$$

$$\Rightarrow \quad x = \frac{3000}{8} = 375$$

Hence, expenditure = ₹ 375 crores.

18. It cannot be determined as Income and Expenditure of respective year is not known.

19. Let their equal incomes be ₹ 1 crore. Also, let expenditure of Company A be ₹ E_1 crores and that of Company B be ₹ E_2 crores.

Now, $$35 = \frac{1 - E_1}{E_1} \times 100$$

$$35 E_1 = 100 - 100 E_1$$

$$135 E_1 = 100 \quad ...(i)$$

Similarly $$30 = \frac{1 - E_2}{E_2} \times 100$$

$$130 E_2 = 100 \quad ...(ii)$$

From (*i*) and (*ii*)

$$135 E_1 = 130 E_2$$

$$\Rightarrow \quad \frac{E_1}{E_2} = \frac{130}{135} = \frac{26}{27}$$

$$\therefore \quad E_1 : E_2 = 26 : 27$$

20. Required percentage $= \frac{35 - 20}{20} \times 100$

$$= \frac{15}{20} \times 100 = 75.$$

CPSIA information can be obtained
at www.ICGtesting.com
Printed in the USA
LVHW051913291120
672964LV00028B/1139

9 789386 845788